CURRICULUM DEVELOPMENT

CURRICULUM DEVELOPMENT
Theory into Practice

THIRD EDITION

Daniel Tanner
Rutgers University

Laurel Tanner
University of Houston
Temple University

Merrill, an imprint of
Prentice Hall
Englewood Cliffs, New Jersey   Columbus, Ohio

Library of Congress Cataloging-in-Publication Data

Tanner, Daniel.
      Curriculum development : theory into practice / Daniel Tanner, Laurel Tanner. — 3rd ed.
          p.   cm.
      Includes bibliographical references and index.
      ISBN 0-02-418931-6
      1. Education—United States—Curricula—History.   2. Curriculum planning—United
States.   I. Tanner, Laurel N.   II. Title.
    LB1570.T23   1995   94-18285
    375'.001—dc20   CIP

Editor: Debra A. Stollenwerk
Production Editor: Christine M. Harrington
Text/Cover Designer: Cathleen Carbery
Production Buyer: Deidra M. Schwartz
Electronic Text Management: Marilyn Wilson Phelps, Matthew Williams, Jane Lopez, Karen L.
   Bretz
Illustrations: Steve Botts

This book was set in Garamond ITC by Prentice Hall and was printed and bound by Courier
Corp. The cover was printed by Phoenix Color Corp.

© 1995 by Prentice-Hall, Inc.
A Simon & Schuster Company
Englewood Cliffs, New Jersey 07632

Earlier editions, © 1975, 1980 by Macmillan Publishing Co., Inc.

Printed in the United States of America

10 9 8 7 6 5 4 3 2 1

ISBN: 0-02-418931-6

Prentice-Hall International (UK) Limited, *London*
Prentice-Hall of Australia Pty. Limited, *Sydney*
Prentice-Hall of Canada, Inc., *Toronto*
Prentice-Hall Hispanoamericana, S. A., *Mexico*
Prentice-Hall of India Private Limited, *New Delhi*
Prentice-Hall of Japan, Inc., *Tokyo*
Simon & Schuster Asia Pte. Ltd., *Singapore*
Editora Prentice-Hall do Brasil, Ltda., *Rio de Janeiro*

To our students,
past and present,
whose friendship
is inspiration

FOREWORD TO THE THIRD EDITION

Writing a text is not an easy task. Texts seldom are readable for more than the assigned pages, are bland in texture, and often lack a point of view. Writing a text about curriculum in a comprehensive, readable, and engaging manner is even more difficult because of the stubborn disarray that marks the academic field of curriculum. Most academics who take on such a challenge often lack clarity of prose and fall short because of omissions in content and an absence of a viewpoint.

In this third edition of their text, the Tanners have substantially revised the earlier edition and produced a text on curriculum that students will read for assignments and keep on their bookshelves long after graduation. This is an encompassing treatment of the dominant curricular ideas and a useful source of historical information about key figures whose actions shaped the field. Although I believe that the field of curriculum continues to be in conceptual disarray, in this edition the Tanners have made a determined, sensible, and ultimately, noble effort to bring coherence to it.

Unlike the second edition, Daniel Tanner and Laurel Tanner begin with the history of public education, the formation of different curricula, and the fundamental curricular ideas that have continually appeared and reappeared in the century and a half of public education. They point out in early chapters and throughout the book the timelessness of certain ideas and how innovations keep returning. Their implicit message is: know the history of curriculum ideas and earlier reforms because the past keeps turning up in the present. To be ignorant of these repeat performances in different setttings can leave one gullible at best, and, at worst, lacking credible judgment.

Themes from earlier editions appear again but they are updated with events and vignettes from the last decade that give resonance and timelessness to the account. The authors' strong focus on the teacher as a key player in the curriculum game, for example, continues in this edition—as does the recognition of the fundamental interdependency between curriculum and instruction. The Tanners' commitment to the ideas of John Dewey, of course, give the text its backbone. Translated and amplified, Dewey's ideas are central to the Tanners' point of view. Dewey, Harold Rugg,

Ralph Tyler, and other progressive educators, past and present, emerge as powerful figures whose theories have had lasting effects on thinking about curriculum and form an important part of the hertiage of the field. Whether one agrees or disagrees with their position is of less importance than the simple fact that their perspective gives both texture and direction to the text.

The influence of the larger society upon curriculum-making and deliberations also emerges as a constant in this edition. In earlier editions, the Tanners documented that social reform movements spilled over onto schools and affected what occurred there. In discussing the last decade and a half of school reform efforts, they document the potent drive for national goals, testing, and nationalizing influences on the curriculum—under conditions of increasing social fragmentation in the larger culture. This movement, they point out, emerges far more strongly than earlier impulses toward a general or liberal education in schools and universities. The virtue of the rich historical detail in this text makes clear the following point that the Tanners stress in this edition: In making sense of current proposals and innovations, know what the major curricular thinkers had to say about the constantly changing social terrain and what they proposed and did.

Finally, the implicit aim of this revised edition, with its rich display of what professionals in curriculum have said and done over time, is to have this generation of students not only appreciate and understand the base of knowledge that is available to them, but also use that knowledge as practitioners and academics in their work in schools and universities. For those already engaged in curriculum work or considering it, this book is a marvelous resource.

Larry Cuban
Stanford University

FOREWORD TO THE
SECOND EDITION

The comments by Professor Foshay in his foreword to the first edition of *Curriculum Development* apply as well to this revised edition. However, some additional points should be made.

Often revisions of books simply bring developments in the field treated up-to-date in a rather superficial manner. This revision is far more fundamental than that.

The authors have carefully incorporated into this revision the refinements in their thinking on the curriculum achieved over the past five years, revising substantial sections of the book to achieve this purpose. Much significant new material is added that makes the work even more comprehensive. The first edition evidenced a broad acquaintance with relevant materials in the various fields of knowledge. This edition goes even further in drawing on the thinking and experience of leaders in such fields as the social and physical sciences and philosophy. A breadth of background is demonstrated that is all too rare in professional books on education.

A distinctive characteristic of the revision is the reasonable interpretation of points of view held by others on curriculum issues, usually followed by a presentation of the authors' position. All too often when this approach is used writers present caricatures of the positions with which they do not agree so that these positions may be more easily demolished. This book is singularly free from such presentations.

The treatment consistently drives back to the fundamental considerations underlying the many diverse practices that have been followed at one time or another in curriculum development. It is a wide-ranging book that should prove especially useful to serious, rigorous students who wish help in formulating their own thoughtful conception of the curriculum field with its many problems and issues and a theory that seems to them to provide a consistent approach to the varied tasks of curriculum development. It will also be found helpful by mature scholars in reviewing and reappraising the theories they accept.

To one who was directly involved in the curriculum movement for more than twenty years, this extensive and careful treatment makes apparent the need for further research to increase the available knowledge about many aspects of the movement. The leadership of Laurel Tanner, co-author of this book, in establishing the Society for the Study of Curriculum History is to be commended as a significant contribution to meeting this need.

Hollis L. Caswell
Marshall Field Jr. Professor Emeritus
and President Emeritus
Teachers College, Columbia University

FOREWORD TO THE
FIRST EDITION

The Tanners have written a thoroughly researched, strong book on the curriculum; they know the field in depth. In a time of educational ahistoricism, they have grounded their account of the field and their opinions about it in its most basic documents, each carefully summarized. The book will serve, along with Smith, Stanley, and Shores' *Fundamentals of Curriculum Development* of twenty years ago and Taba's curriculum book of ten years ago, as a principal statement of a field only slightly understood by the broad educational public.

The curriculum field was driven into disarray with the collapse of progressive education during the fifties; it was disheartening to observe the new generation of curriculum developers, who knew no better, make the same mistakes and suffer many of the same consequences that had been accurately described in many places by 1950. If the current generation will only take heed, the generalizations of an earlier day need not be rediscovered at the cost of public confidence in the process of rational curriculum making, as seems now to be happening in a number of cases. It is for this reason that the Tanners' book is timely as well as qualitatively up to its task.

To say this is not to agree with every judgment contained in the book. Like others in this field, the Tanners have opinions that they set forth and defend here. The virtue of their work is that their judgments can be argued, in large measure by using the very resources they offer here so richly. The book is, for all these reasons, a resource both for those who need a comprehensive introduction to the field and for those who are already identified with it.

Arthur W. Foshay
Teachers College, Columbia University

PREFACE

The ushering of a new century evokes renewed stirrings of the imagination and visions of great things to come. Indeed the word *millennium* conveys an imagined golden age. The history of progress reveals that neither fantasy nor utopianism has been a very fruitful harbinger of what is to come, simply because the created visions have few, if any, roots in the present—roots that take hold from progress in attacking the pervading problems of the here and now. The closest we can come to knowing and shaping the future is by knowing and shaping the present, and in giving thought to the present as the outgrowth of the past. It was only when humanity became conscious of a long past, as Robert Nisbet reminded us, "that a consciousness of progressive movement from past to present became possible, a consciousness easily extrapolated to the future."[1] The great stirrings of the imagination that come from anticipation of a new century and millennium nevertheless reflect a renewed optimism through which old limitations are cast aside by new possibilities. Without the spell of optimism, progress would not be possible.

Many of our colleagues have told us that the third edition of *Curriculum Development* is long overdue. During the intervening years, we witnessed a seemingly unrelenting retreat "back-to-basics" and the eventual and inevitable realization that a return to basics had failed—inevitable because all efforts to return to a simple past have reflected a position of retrenchment rather than renewal for school and society. Many of the current efforts at curriculum renewal and education reform are treated as entirely new inventions. The failure to recognize the knowledge base of the curriculum field upon which renewal measures need to be built raises the danger that these measures will be treated segmentally and in isolation with disappointing consequences.

In recent years, education reform has become a veritable slogan from the White House down to the statehouse and schoolhouse. We prefer the term *renewal* because *reform* carries a negative connotation that invites misguided actions only to be followed by counterreactions and counterreforms. At the same time reforms tend to be undertaken without due attention to their isolated character and without

[1]Robert Nisbet, *History of the Idea of Progress.* New York: Basic Books, 1980, p. 323.

addressing the extant contradictions that work against substantive renewal. For example, the call for higher-order thinking in the curriculum is long overdue, but such a call is reduced to a mere slogan when teaching and testing are more error-oriented than idea-oriented. The renewed emphasis on writing across the curriculum is to be applauded, but needs to be undertaken in the matrix of a fully articulated curriculum and not as another segmental program that is canceled out by the higher political stakes of teaching the (multiple-choice) test. The call for multiculturalism in the curriculum has attracted many adherents without giving needed recognition to the growing problems of cultural fragmentation and conflict that reflect self-interests as opposed to common or *intercultural* interests that mark a democratic society. The renewed search for a common curriculum core needs to be built upon a sense of unity through diversity in a multicultural society. All of these concerns and efforts for curriculum renewal and educational renewal—and many more—have a powerful knowledge base of precedent and promise.

Throughout this text we have sought to connect the deepest and most promising efforts for curriculum renewal in contemporary times to the knowledge base of the field with a view toward providing fresh insights. As with the earlier editions, we have sought to provide the student with a comprehensive treatment of the curriculum field in the expectation that it will be useful not only as a textbook but also as a source of ideas for professional practice and educational research. The book is carefully documented. The problems for study and discussion following each chapter are intended to extend the reader's insights into main ideas and issues, and to stimulate continued inquiry.

Part I is aimed at providing the student with a perspective of the curriculum field—the accomplishments, setbacks, and prospects for progress. One of the great legacies of visionary educators in their struggle for universal education—a legacy that has been of paramount significance throughout the twentieth century—is that a universal curriculum core is necessary for advancing the democratic prospect. At the same time they recognized that the schools and colleges must provide the diversified studies required of a society with diverse talents and interests.

Part II focuses on curriculum development as a professional field. As in the case of virtually all of the social sciences, the curriculum field is marked by significant ideological differences and disputations. Nevertheless, as documented in Part II, our forebears left us with a powerful conceptual and methodological knowledge base that has given curriculum universal recognition as a professional field of research and practice. Their struggle to develop a sense of community through fullness of communication and synthesis of achievement has provided contemporary practitioners with the means for revealing problem solutions for progress in the field. One of the lessons of this legacy is that any movement for education reform or curriculum reform or renewal cannot succeed if it is antagonistic to the nature of the learner and to the ideals of a free society. Many movements have failed because the nature of the learner had been ignored or distorted, or because shortsighted nationalistic interests or narrow vested interests were allowed to subvert the democratic-humanitarian-cosmopolitan interest.

There is a fundamental principle in the biological sciences that structure determines function, or the equivalent principle in architecture that form follows function. Part III is devoted to the various ways of designing the curriculum so as to provide for more effective articulation—balance, scope, and sequence. Many faculty in school and college seem unaware of or insufficiently concerned with the problems of curriculum isolation. Subject matter ("content") is treated as though it were properly self-contained and isolated from other subjects or disciplines. The consequence is a dysfunctional curriculum—with subject matter painfully put by the student to the task and to the test, only to be painlessly forgotten almost immediately after the test. In Part III, alternative ways of organizing and structuring the curriculum are explored systematically in relation to the functions of general education (as contrasted against mere basic education), specialized education, exploratory education, enrichment education, and special-interest education., These five functions might be likened to the five fingers of the hand which, in turn, represents the whole of education.

Part IV opens with a chapter on evaluation for curriculum improvement. This leads to the theme of Part IV—curriculum improvement and school renewal. The processes of curriculum development are examined and characterized according to different levels of sophistication and effectiveness—from the rudimentary level of *imitative-maintenance* to the *generative-creative* level. In reaction to the increasing nationalizing and statewide influences on the curriculum and the pressures to teach the test, many teachers, supervisors, and school administrators have tended to look upon the curriculum as a policy matter ordained at a higher political level. They fail to recognize that despite the external influences on the curriculum, the key person in shaping and interpreting the curriculum is the classroom teacher—the one who is closest to the learner. How to overcome the problem of teacher isolation is examined in Part IV along with that of curriculum isolation.

Finally, most curriculum texts treat the concept of the hidden curriculum in an entirely negative way. We have attempted to show how the hidden curriculum becomes a misnomer when it is revealed as a positive force for collateral learning— the kind of learning that is likely to endure as a result of the cultivation of interests, attitudes, and appreciations that generate the desire to go on learning.

To those who are no longer with us, but whose ideas and suggestions were invaluable in connection with the earlier editions and have carried to the third edition of *Curriculum Development,* we owe a special note of appreciation—namely, Hollis L. Caswell, Lawrence A. Cremin, and Ralph W. Tyler. We are indebted to Arthur W. Foshay and Gordon N. Mackenzie for their constructive ideas for the earlier editions, which are also reflected in this third edition.

During the course of this project we have benefited from insights and suggestions from Frank D. Adams, Robin Barrow, Myra D. Baughman, Frances S. Bolin, Joseph J. Chambliss, Ora L. Hill Cooks, Alice Denham, Kieran Egan, Lucille Freeman, Nathalie Gehrke, Bob Jickling, Craig Kridel, Michael Knoll, George F. Madaus, John E. Merryman, Martin Mülder, Esther P. Railton Rice, and Thomas Rusk Vickery. We owe special thanks to William D. Georgiades, who provided continuous interest and support throughout the development of the third edition.

We are especially grateful to Lloyd C. Chilton, our editor at Macmillan, who shepherded this project through the first two editions, and to Debbie Stollenwerk, our present editor at Prentice Hall, who gave full encouragement and support with the third edition.

Finally, we extend our appreciation to Marion Ann Keller, who prepared the final copy of the manuscript for the publisher.

D. T.
L. T.

TABLE OF CONTENTS

PART 3
Curriculum Design, Development, and Evaluation   347

CHAPTER 10
The Search for a Core Curriculum—Design for Synthesis   349

CHAPTER 11
Curriculum Fragmentation and Synthesis: Problems, Proposals, Prospects   409

PART 1 〜

PERSPECTIVES AND PROSPECTS

The skies do not change when a century is ushered in,
or the thunders roll when it passes out.
Imagination gives to the century an objective reality,
and feeling welds our thought to it.
We do well to resign ourselves to the spell of these creations
and learn to know our centuries.

—Nicholas Murray Butler, 1900

CHAPTER 1

EARLY PERSPECTIVES OF THE CURRICULUM

The beginning of a new century is a kind of turning point, and it is common to look for new ways of dealing with old and continuing problems. As early as 1989 a principal in New York State said that in the twenty-first century "we need kids who are problem solvers and critical thinkers. We have new technologies to help them add and subtract, but they need to know how to apply mathematics, both at home and on the job."[1]

The principal was describing a new mathematics curriculum at the high school. The new curriculum stressed broad problem-solving models and real-world applications over rote memorization and narrow formulas that are applicable only in the math class. The curriculum was featured in a newspaper report as the "math of tomorrow."[2]

These ideas are not new. They harken back to the greatest of American educational philosophers, John Dewey, who worked them out in his Laboratory School at the turn of the last century. Unfortunately, Dewey and his daughter, Evelyn, are no longer here to remind us that their *Schools of Tomorrow,* published in 1915, described public and private schools that were applying "some of the more widely recognized and accepted views of educational reformers."[3] One of these views was that schools must teach problem-solving in real life. One of the photographs in the Deweys' book is a picture of a classroom in the Francis Parker School in Chicago; it is captioned: "Solving problems in school as they would have to be met out of school."[4] It is revealing that the "curriculum of tomorrow" as conceived by the Deweys in *Schools of Tomorrow* remains valid to this day. The contemporary scene is marked by a vision of the future in which the curriculum is focused on problem solving and critical thinking as applied to living situations.

This is not the first, nor will it be the last, instance of treating an old educational model as new. Reinventing the wheel is a serious problem in education. But the more administrators, supervisors, and teachers know about curriculum history, the more likely they will be to build on the rich knowledge base that is the American heritage. Curriculum history is the memory of the curriculum field. Like a person would be lost without memory, those responsible for improving the curriculum of schooling are lost without the collective experience of the curriculum field. As the late historian Barbara Tuchman pointed out, applying past experience empowers us to "avoid past mistakes and to manage better in similar circumstances next time."[5]

There is much to learn from failed as well as successful efforts in the past. For example, the idea that the curriculum should consist almost entirely of a series of projects as an alternative to the traditional subject curriculum was tried and failed in the 1920s. But in the late 1980s and early 1990s a major curriculum development project offered a "new" teaching approach that would eliminate regular subjects. Instead, the curriculum from kindergarten to high school graduation would consist mainly of projects.[6] Those developing the plan neglected to turn to history to see what failed in the past and what succeeded. Our predecessors worked out some very effective ways to teach students to deal with real-life problems, without sacrificing logically organized subject matter.

History can be useful to contemporary curriculum developers—teachers, supervisors, and administrators. It helps us build on successes and avoid repeating failures. By remembering and acknowledging those who have gone before us, we are provided professional identity. We can experience their achievements and their failures. We are the curriculum pioneers. The first three chapters of this book are concerned with collective curriculum memory.

THE BATTLE TO IMPROVE AND EXPAND THE CURRICULUM

"The principles of instruction," wrote James G. Carter in 1824, "are well guarded against all innovation, even if it should be an improvement. Every change," he continued, "especially when fundamental principles are called into question, must force its way against fearful odds."[7] Carter was speaking from experience. He was at the center of the fight in Massachusetts for one of the most remarkable American educational achievements to this day—our public school system. There were a number of others who were involved in forging the great state school systems that developed during the period from 1779 to 1865; Henry Barnard in Connecticut and John Swett in California, for instance, were profoundly influential in bringing about educational reform in their states.

The story of James G. Carter, a Massachusetts educator, is particularly interesting because the problems he faced were fundamentally the same as those we encounter in curriculum work today. And the stakes are just as high. Take, for example, the problem of educational quality. If the quality of public education is poor, the public schools are abandoned by those who can afford private schools.

Indifference to public education puts self-governing society in peril. "Above all things," wrote Thomas Jefferson to James Madison in 1787, "I hope the education of the common people will be attended to; convinced that on their good sense we may rely with the most security for the preservation of a due degree of liberty."[8] In the United States, it was Jefferson who first forged the link between education and representative government. The state's obligation was to support a system of education that would equalize educational opportunity. For only if each individual was given the chance to develop to the fullest would responsible leadership be assured along with the freedom of the people.

Public education has had a long tradition in New England. In the early colonial period, Massachusetts had been an educational model for the other New England colonies in establishing free schools. But school legislation enacted in 1789 changed all that. Under the provisions of the law, towns had the power to create school districts, and under this decentralized system, local opposition to taxation for education, combined with public apathy, gradually led to a decline in the quality of the public schools. When Carter began his reform campaign through publications in support of public education, the point had been reached where, as Butts and Cremin noted, the public schools were "often deserted by almost everyone who could afford private education. With little state control, local districts managed schools in the interests of local economy, and in doing so, they often ignored even the barest standards of instruction."[9]

In the 1820s many things were wrong with Massachusetts' public schools. Individually and collectively the problems were restricting access to knowledge, which happened at a time when there was a new interest in science coupled with demands for a broader curriculum.

IMPROVING ACCESS TO KNOWLEDGE

As Carter pointed out in his calls to action, the Latin grammar (secondary) schools, to which the people had at one time felt a strong attachment, were disappearing, albeit for good reason in that they held to a classical curriculum unsuited to the practical needs of the changing times. However, there were no publicly supported secondary schools to take their place. Academies with modern curricular offerings were available to those who could afford the tuition, books, and board, but their advantages were far beyond the reach of most people.

"What would our ancestors have thought of their posterity?" asked Carter,[10] with reference to those who, nearly two hundred years before, despite their concern with the sheer need of staying alive in a new settlement, provided by law for the support of secondary schools in all towns of one hundred families. The people still needed secondary schools in order to realize the promise of their children's talents.

The Primary School

Primary education was not much better off. The primary schools, attended by children aged four to ten, were staffed by untrained teachers who, with some exceptions, viewed their employment as temporary. They were paid meager salaries, and schools were maintained for only a few months annually. In Carter's words,

> The whole business of instruction, with very few exceptions has hitherto been performed by those, who have felt little interest in the subject, beyond the immediate

pecuniary compensation for their services. And even that has been too inconsiderable, to render a want of success in the employment, a matter of much regret.[11]

LONG-INHERITED PROCEDURES.   Having nothing else to fall back on, the incompetent teachers taught just as they had been taught—rote and recitation, supported by the rod. The method of teaching by question and answer made it possible for pupils to *seem* to have learned a great many important facts, but the fact was that the pupils did not understand the memorized facts. They had connected the question and its answer with some outside association, and they were able to parrot passages with verbal accuracy—thus impressing and delighting those to whom the words had a correct meaning. But a more thorough examination showed their meaning for the pupil to be as much a mystery as the hocus pocus of a magician.

Carter provides as an illustration a child who was being examined on his knowledge of geography. "After answering all the questions, and giving an accurate account of the statistics of Turkey, on being asked where Turkey was, a question not in the book, the child replied, '"in the yard with the chickens."'"[12]

The relation of teacher to text was much the same as child to text. "Indeed, so superficial has the education of most instructors of common schools been," wrote Carter, "that a book is to them a new subject. The particular form and words, in which the principles of any branch of learning have been expressed, and the principles themselves, are with them identical; and if the words are varied, the principles are not recognized."[13] Teachers had much influence in the selection of textbooks and as might be expected, they preferred the same books they were taught as pupils.

But there had been enormous achievements in science, which resulted in new educational methods. The old books did not reflect the method of inductive science as a way of learning. The old methods would not help children develop knowledge from observation and experience. Granted that the books had been revised to keep pace with scientific discoveries, but they were still written to conform to traditional methods. And most primary school teachers tended to confine the curriculum to mechanical skills associated with reading, writing, and arithmetic.

Ultimately, it was the methods used by the teacher that so limited the teacher's effectiveness. One problem is of particular interest because it continues to stand in the way of access to knowledge: the failure of the classroom teacher to work with the "teacher in the text"—the author of the book. In *The District School as It Was* (1833), Warren Burton described his experience as a schoolboy in District No. 5 in Massachusetts. The approach to teaching grammar was parsing: pupils recited the parts of speech in each line of prose or poetry. Wrote Burton,

> The fact is neither we nor the teacher entered into the writer's meaning. . . . [T]he particular sense of the passages was not examined. We could not do it perhaps, from the want of maturity of mind; the teacher did not, because he had never been accustomed to anything of the kind in his own education. And it never occurred to him that he could deviate from the track, or improve upon the methods of those who taught him.[14]

To this day it is important for teachers and other educators to know how the writer of a poem or a novel teaches us. Authors are the classroom teacher's silent partners. It is enormously helpful for the teacher to know what and how the silent partner in the book is trying to teach.[15]

TEACHERS AND TEXTS TODAY.   Experts in teaching literature today have become increasingly concerned with how the classroom teacher can develop a curriculum that helps students construct "the meanings of the texts for themselves."[16] We have come a long way from the time when pupils displayed their knowledge by parsing a poem on which they had been drilled again and again "so as to become as familiar with the parts of speech, as we are with the buttons and button-holes of our jackets."[17]

Nevertheless, recent studies reveal that the standard pattern of instruction in literature continues to be mechanical. Students supply lower-order responses to error-oriented worksheet questions about the literary texts, yet curricula that help students to learn to deal with sophisticated meanings have been available for decades. Curricula rich in ideas are necessary if students are to develop higher-order thinking abilities and enrich their lives through literature and other studies.[18] An idea-oriented curriculum extends the learner's access to knowledge far beyond what is obvious and routine. It is the key to generative learning.

Secondary Education

THE LATIN SCHOOLS.   Returning to the 1820s: As Carter well knew, there was a reason for the decline of interest in the public secondary schools—the curriculum. The free schools were Latin grammar schools, an institution brought over from England. The curriculum was comprised of the classics—Latin and Greek—as well as religious principles. Only boys were welcome in the Latin schools.

The schools had remained stationary while society continued to change. To say that the classical curriculum of the colonial secondary school had failed to meet the needs of a society undergoing rapid economic and social change is a gross understatement. There was a growing demand for bookkeepers, mechanics, carpenters, agriculturalists, surveyors, navigators, and other skilled workers. But one could not learn a skill or a trade at a Latin grammar school, nor could one learn it at home. The demand for a utilitarian education generated the academy movement.

THE ACADEMY: TOLL ROAD TO THE MODERN CURRICULUM.   Academies were the immediate ancestors of American high schools but they were not free of charge. Those who wanted to build academies received endowments from state legislatures; the free schools received almost no legislative attention. The tuition academy began to make its appearance in the colonies around 1780, and by 1820 it had all but replaced the tax-supported grammar school, thus effectively denying most youth access to knowledge. (In his plea for public high schools, Carter argued that 95 percent of the population in Massachusetts was unable to pay the tuition.)

This question arises: Granted that many parents justifiably had come to see no utility in a Latin schooling for their children, why was there no attempt to reform the Latin grammar school? A possible answer is that it was less trouble to build new schools that fit the practical needs of the new nation than to reform an institution rooted in the classical tradition of the Old World. The academies often combined a practical education and the classical subject matter of the Latin schools, which was required for college entrance, in the same institution. Eventually the classical function became dominant in many academies. Nevertheless, the academies paved the way to a broader and more modern secondary school curriculum. As Butts and Cremin pointed out, "the academy brought into the secondary school curriculum some attention to English grammar, composition, literature and rhetoric, mathematics, the social studies, the modern languages, the sciences, the arts and music, and the practical career-oriented studies—none of which were being developed by the Latin schools."[19] Girls as well as boys could attend academies, usually in separate classes.

There may be yet another reason why the Latin school was allowed to disappear rather than being reformed. The earliest settlers who favored both education and equality for all, and were, themselves, well educated, had long since gone to their graves. In his *History of Education in Pennsylvania* (1886), James P. Wickersham, who was one of Pennsylvania's first superintendents of education, wrote:

> Life in the new world had proved unfavorable to the transmission of intellectual tastes, and the scholars were more numerous among the fathers than among their sons. The mass of people were too poor, too busy in earning a livelihood, too severely pressed by the hardships they were compelled to endure in an American wilderness . . . to make the necessary effort to provide means adequate for the education of their children.[20]

Wickersham clearly pointed out that although William Penn and his immediate successors had strongly supported education, and Penn's Frame of Government of 1682 gave the colonial governors and assembly power to "erect and order all public schools," for more than fifty years before the Revolution, "the subject was almost totally neglected by the public authorities."[21]

After the Revolution, there was much educational activity in Pennsylvania. New colleges were chartered. Sixty thousand acres were set aside for the support of public schools, but Wickersham reports that the public schools "never received any benefit from the land set apart in their behalf; it was probably given subsequently to the county academies."[22]

The fight for a public school system was not won in Pennsylvania until 1834. Prior to that time the legislature provided only for the education of poor children at public expense. Wickersham writes that parents who were unable to pay for their children's schooling were compelled to "make a public record of their poverty, to pauperize themselves, and to send their children to school with this invidious mark upon them."[23] The problem was not peculiar to Pennsylvania. In New Jersey, Maryland, Virginia, and Georgia, the use of public money for schools was confined "to the education of the children of the poor." As Jackson observed, there was a time when the school "was not close to the hearts of the American people," and the leaders of the Common School Revival (as the struggle to secure the public elementary school was called) "had to fight a real battle, against both the privileged and the underprivileged."[24] As we have noted, Carter was one of these leaders.

The curriculum of the Latin school consisted of Latin and, to a lesser extent, Greek, because it was a college preparatory school. College-bound boys in eighteenth-century America had to learn their Latin because college and university courses were based on Latin books. When the books for courses of study in the colleges and universities were no longer written in Latin and colleges changed their entrance requirements, the Latin schools died out. English was the language used in academies, which also forced the colleges to revise their entrance requirements to meet changing times. This began happening in the latter half of the eighteenth century—although Latin was to prevail over modern foreign languages as a college preparatory subject well into the twentieth century. It is of interest that the name Latin school has not been entirely abandoned in Boston. The Boston Latin School and Boston Academy are both public schools, but like the Latin schools that disappeared in the face of more useful knowledge, they operate like private schools in that they serve an academically elite population. These schools offer Greek and students are required to take Latin. Admission is by standardized tests and academic records. The effect on the students who do not get in recalls the unequal access to knowledge so decried by Carter in 1824. According to one contemporary observer, elite public schools are not necessarily a mark of excellence for a city's school system, but may instead reflect on the disparity between the rich resources devoted to an elite, and the lack of resources for those who are least able and in greatest need.[25]

In the early years after the founding of the republic, access to the curriculum was often limited to those children whose parents were able (and willing) to pay the tuition. Moreover, access was denied to slaves and American Indians, and often denied to girls as well. There has been much progress in improving access to schooling. Although the United States was the first nation to champion the cause of universal secondary education, this came about only after a long and hard struggle. As recently as 1940, almost 80 percent of adults over 25 years of age had less than twelve years of schooling. Today, some 60 percent have at least twelve years of schooling.[26]

ACCESS—AN UNFINISHED TASK.   Access to a public school does not guarantee access to knowledge. There are still wide variations in such access. It is noteworthy that some of the most critical problems of American education today are inherited from the colonial period. Access to the curriculum is one. Times have changed, but we are not really through with the Old World. The relationship between classical scholarship and social status remains with us along with other obsolete educational models that work against practical knowledge and equality of educational opportunity. Improving access to knowledge is an unfinished task.

MONITORIAL INSTRUCTION: THE PURSUIT OF EFFICIENCY

I can confidently recommend it as an invaluable improvement, which, by a wonderful combination of economy in expense, and rapidity of instruction, has created a new era in education. The system operates with the same efficacy in education as labor-saving machinery does in the useful arts.[27]

The speaker was Governor DeWitt Clinton of New York and the year 1818. The new method was the Lancaster plan for educating poor children. For a short time (1815–1830) it was the vogue—operating in the cities before the fight for state-supported schools open to the children of the rich and poor alike was won.

The Lancasterian method originated in London. At the age of twenty, Joseph Lancaster, a member of the Society of Friends, had opened a school for poor children. Because most of the children were unable to pay for their instruction and Lancaster himself could not afford to hire assistants, he devised a plan of appointing some pupils to teach others. Eventually more than a thousand children were in attendance, and the huge school literally taught itself under the general supervision of one master. The plan excited wide interest and schools were established throughout England. The excitement quickly passed to visitors. In 1805, the school in London was visited by a member of the New York Free School Society, who hastened to have the system adopted in the Society's schools.

The system worked this way: Bright pupils were selected as monitors. They were each assigned a row of pupils (usually ten in number) to instruct and to supervise. The teacher taught each lesson to the monitors who then took their "stations" by the wall and taught their charges what they had just learned. The Lancasterian school was organized, military fashion, down to the last detail, and teachers were required to follow every detail.

Limitations of Monitorial Instruction

Joseph Lancaster had a limited and very mechanical view of education: drill. This is clear from Lancaster's own explanation of what he perceived to be his method's advantages. "Each boy can spell one hundred words in a morning. If one hundred scholars can do that two hundred mornings yearly, the following will be the total of their efforts at improvement."[28] He then declared that this would result in an annual achievement of two million words spelled. He approached arithmetic from the same perspective—the number of sums done in a given period of time, not the computational skills learned through application. The point is that the monitorial system was not genuine instruction but mechanistic. Lancaster seems to have been ignorant of the psychologically based teaching method of reformers in Europe at the time. Pestalozzi, for example, sought to instruct children by experience and observation. Pestalozzi's perspective was radically different from that of Lancaster—although the aim of both was human welfare. (Pestalozzi's contributions to the curriculum are discussed shortly.)

It is just as true today as it was in Lancaster's time that attempts to teach large classes as cheaply as possible are bound to result in mechanical instruction. This is as true at the university level as it is in elementary, junior high, and high school. When classes are small, university teachers are more likely to help their students develop methods of observation and thinking than when the class is a very large lecture section. Under the latter condition, assessment of students' achievement is likely to take the form of multiple-choice tests rather than asking students to write a paper on a consequential problem or issue. The principle is clear: Class size controls the nature of instruction and form of assessment.

Dewey made the point very clearly in a paper given in 1902 when he was at the University of Chicago. It was there that he founded an elementary school in 1896 to serve as a testing ground for his theories. Dewey stood for the idea of education as the effort to provide a situation conducive to the child's complete development. Classes were large in the public schools at the time, especially in the big cities, and ran from thirty-five to sixty children in a room. But said Dewey, it was in "the face-to-face contact of teacher and child . . . that the real course of study, whatever be laid down on paper, is actually found." A large class, in Dewey's words

> can hardly be said to be an ideal condition, even from the standpoint of uniform progress in reading, writing, and arithmetic, and the symbols of geography and history; but it certainly is better adapted to securing these results than that of the symmetrical and complete development of all the powers, physical, mental, moral, aesthetic of each individual child. . . . How do we have the face to continue to speak at all of the complete development of the individual as the supreme end of educational effort? Excepting here and there with the genius who seems to rise above all conditions, the school environment and machinery (school organization and administration) almost compel the more mechanical features of school-work to lord it over the more vital aims.[29]

 Although we no longer have monitorial instruction, and classes of fifty are uncommon in the public schools, we still have what Dewey called "machinery constructed for turning out another kind of goods,"[30] a scheme for administration and teaching that lends itself to a curriculum based on rote and recitation and a limited contact between child and child and child with teacher. Class size is only one of the conditions that determine whether the teacher's work is mechanical or thoughtful. Others include how the curriculum is developed and how teachers are prepared and supervised.

Achievements of Monitorial Instruction

One might argue that monitorial instruction created a tradition of mechanical instruction in the large cities and that since that time, the emphasis in urban education has been on keeping large numbers of pupils under surveillance and on task. Indeed, this was the method of "direct instruction," a concept introduced in the 1970s and 1980s for working with educationally disadvantaged pupils in large group settings. The emphasis of direct instruction was on back-to-basics through drill and recitation, which meant children's ability to answer questions at a low cognitive level. It would seem that where schooling for poor children is concerned, we are always looking at the cheapest way out of difficulties, although we keep rediscovering that "good education can be neither mechanized nor made cheap."[31] (This was the conclusion from an analysis of the rise and fall of the monitorial system by the first professor of education at the University of Michigan back in 1898.) Proponents of cheap education for other people's children want the best education for their own children. This perpetuates inequalities with regard to cognitive skills and social development, and may be traced to the monitorial movement.

Yet a careful regard for history shows that public education in large cities underwent a great transformation in the late nineteenth and early twentieth centuries, based on the need to reduce inequalities with regard to knowledge. In the 1930s, for example, the most progressive developments in American education were found in American cities—New York and Houston are illustrations. Houston's integrated curriculum was based on the Deweyan principle that intelligence must guide action and reflect a clear conception of the role of education in the development of the democratic process. "A public school system," wrote Edison Ellsworth Oberholtzer, a curriculum expert in Houston, "must be concerned primarily with the general good. The curriculum development staff," he wrote, "aimed to develop this integrated curriculum in such a way that it would be of greatest service to the entire school interests of the city."[32]

The key words here are *public school system.* From its inception, the public school system was regarded as a system of "common schools," that is, free schools for *all* children, not just for poor children. Reformers stressed that these would have to be good schools or the pauper taint would remain. This would mean a more up-to-date curriculum with better methods of instruction than that offered by the private schools. There was no alternative if the public school system was not to be doomed before it even got started.

The monitorial system helped the development of the public school system. Indeed, in its way it performed a quite remarkable service for American education. In the early nineteenth century, American cities began to grow rapidly, and with the growth came an absolute increase and concentration in poverty, ignorance, and crime. Illiteracy was virtually universal among the children of the poor. When Americans suddenly saw the need for public education, legislators embraced the monitorial schools as the most economical way out of the problem. The provision they made for the Lancasterian schools gradually paved the way to the increases in taxation and expenditures required for the development of a common school system for all children. But before the middle of the nineteenth century, the monitorial system had met this function and monitorial methods were seen for what they were: sufficient only to meet an enormous educational emergency in the United States, but mechanical and without a psychological basis. The monitorial system was gravely inadequate for meeting the developmental needs of children and youth and the requirements for an intelligent citizenry for a democratic society.

There were two other contributions of the monitorial system to American education: the concept of a well-organized and administered system of schools and the beginnings of systematic teacher training. The schools were virtually remade by means of Lancaster's carefully planned management and well-prepared teachers. Training institutions for Lancasterian schools were the first formal teacher training institutions in the United States.

EMERGENCE OF A NEW SYSTEM OF CURRICULUM THOUGHT AND PRACTICE

If there were a single word to describe proposals concerning the curriculum in the years between 1830 and the Civil War it would probably be *expansion*. Providing the people with minimum knowledge, centered largely on the basics of reading, writing, and arithmetic, was still regarded by many, if not most, as the main job of the new common (public) schools. But increasingly there were demands for other subjects. Democratic ideals were, of course, closely linked with demands for the inclusion of new subjects in the curriculum. One finds demands for history, geography, and government as "preparation for citizenship." The growing interest in science during this period led to demands for natural science and natural history as well.

However, as Cremin noted, there were enormous differences among the various sections of the nation. In New England and in the cities, new subjects were gradually incorporated in the required curriculum. In areas where opponents of tax-supported public schools still reigned supreme, the curriculum reflected their victory. As Cremin put it, "the curriculum tended to remain even more rigidly within the confines of the older R's."[33]

The Textbook and Curriculum Expansion

The expansion of the curriculum was represented by an enormous increase in the number and kinds of textbooks available. In 1832 the list of available textbooks included thirty-nine kinds of geography books, thirty-five of history, ten of geometry, eleven of astronomy, six of botany, seven of algebra, three of government, and five of chemistry. There were also ten kinds of dictionaries available. In comparing the number of available textbooks in the years 1804 and 1832, a writer observed that "a number of works have been published in branches of study which were then [1804] unknown in our schools."[34]

Going Beyond the Minimum—A Principle from Yesterday for Today

With the leadership of Horace Mann, secretary of the Massachusetts Board of Education, Massachusetts had by 1850 developed a progressive system of public schools—an example before the eyes of other states. The list of required school subjects in Massachusetts included reading, writing, arithmetic, orthography, English grammar, and geography. However, as Mann pointed out to the board, these requirements were "the *minimum* but not the maximum. Any town may enlarge the course of studies to be pursued in its schools as much as it may choose."[35] Accordingly, the curriculum in some towns included subjects such as history and bookkeeping, and vocal music was offered in Boston.

Curriculum expansion had not yet occurred in many other areas, however. For example, until 1849, Ohio required only that reading, writing, and arithmetic be taught. In that year, English grammar and geography were added.[36]

As indicated, curriculum expansion depends no small way on the availability of textbooks and other materials on the new subject. A problem confronted by pioneer schools in the West in that period was that textbooks were not widely available, as they were published mainly in the East.

Turning to the present time, the principle of minimum curriculum requirements is still followed by the various states. One result is that students in poorer school districts do not have the same full range of educational opportunities offered in other schools. In 1990 New Jersey revised its school-financing formula in order to provide broader curricular offerings for students in the state's poorest urban districts.[37] However, the point that Horace Mann made so long ago still applies: Minimums should not be regarded as maximums, and all districts should continually seek to provide wider access to knowledge for all children. In effect, the effort must be directed at optimizing educational opportunity rather than setting minimum standards.

Ideas as Instruments of Curriculum Change

Conceptions of learning and intelligence generally parallel trends of thought regarding humankind, nature, and the world. And so it was with the new voice of science that in the seventeenth and eighteenth centuries led to dissatisfaction with the view of human nature as innately sinful. The new world view held that people were what they were for natural and discoverable reasons. Human nature had great possibilities. The groundwork was being laid for educational theories based on environmentalism. John Locke (1632–1704), the English philosopher who also had a background in medicine, argued that human nature is in part, at least, the outcome of the influence of the environment on the child. Locke believed that knowledge was attained empirically, through the method of inductive science, and he was a great promoter of the empirical approach to learning. According to Locke, the individual learned through perceptions of the world provided by the senses. But the individual gave form to his or her key perceptions through a process of reflection. And according to Locke, children learned through play.

ENVIRONMENTALISM, EMPIRICISM, AND METHOD.   Environmentalism and empiricism were two profoundly important influences on method. One learns through one's senses: sight, touch, hearing, smell, and taste. Was it not obvious, then, that this would be the most fruitful approach to classroom learning? Even before Locke, Francis Bacon (1561–1626) advanced the idea that learning would be most effective if the teacher started with careful observation of nature and developed the powers of induction rather than mere rote and recitation. It was precisely this idea that Colonel Francis W. Parker would apply in the Quincy, Massachusetts, public schools two and a half centuries later. The Quincy system was regarded as revolutionary even then (1875).

REALISM IN EDUCATION.   Even before Locke, the educational reformer and Moravian bishop Cominius (1592–1670) systematized the idea of developing the powers of induction into a method. The teacher should begin with the observation of simple phenomena, leading to the complex. Moreover (and this *was* revolutionary) learning aids should be used—pictures and actual objects—for developing children's sense experience.

In Germany, realism in education became a reality when educators established schools (Realschulen) where emphasis was put on the use of actual objects and excursions to acquire firsthand knowledge of life. In Switzerland, Rousseau (1712–1728) popularized interest in the idea of sense realism when he argued for the free expression of children's natural impulses and the substitution of play and observation of nature for books and the classical (linguistic) studies. In England, a number of proposals for educational reform were made, based on sense realism. Of these, the infant school was the most famous and successful.

Achievements as Instruments of Curriculum Change

Just as achievements in science led to new conceptions of human nature and new methods of inquiry, so they led to stunning practical achievements. Within a year of the Declaration of Independence, James Watt's steam engine made its appearance. A new technological age had begun. The practical accomplishments made possible by applying science to the development of new tools and machines were nothing less than spectacular. They pointed to the potential of secular knowledge for improving the conditions of living and for controlling the power of nature for human welfare.

Little wonder, then, that there were demands for a more practical education. New schools appeared (academies) and proposals were made for reforming the curriculum along the lines of sense realism. One of the most interesting of these proposals, and a portent for secondary education, was Benjamin Franklin's plan for the academy.

FRANKLIN'S ACADEMY.   Franklin envisioned a new kind of school—the academy—that would provide a useful education. In his *Proposals Relating to the Education of Youth in Pennsylvania* (1749), Franklin supported his arguments for an education that was secular and practical rather than religious and classical by citing the European empiricists and sense realists. His proposal called for a uniquely modern secondary school in sharp contradiction to the tradition-bound Latin grammar school brought over from Europe. Franklin knew well that a secular education, with the study of English rather than Latin, would meet with opposition from the classicists and religionists. Ultimately this is what happened and led eventually to the school's demise.

Throughout Franklin's curriculum proposal, practical educational experiences were stressed. The use of the English language was a primary goal. Art also was included as an aid to creative expression. Practical mathematics (particularly accounting) was another core study in the proposal. Franklin devoted special attention to the social studies, which included modern history, geography, social history, political history, religious and moral history, and political science. French, German, and Spanish were offered for prospective merchants and Latin and Greek for those preparing for the ministry.

In Franklin's proposal, actual experience with machines was important in developing insights into the contributions of science to commerce, manufacture, and civilization itself. Similarly, practical experiences in agriculture were an important part of the study of natural history. In line with the realist view of the importance of concrete teaching aids, Franklin envisioned a plentiful supply of maps, globes, and scientific apparatus.

It was Franklin's hope to develop an education for practical living that was as respectable as an education grounded in religion and the classics and, indeed, more valuable. But Franklin was one hundred years ahead of his time. Because of the heavy hand of the Latinists in the academy, the English school was neglected in favor of the Latin school. (Indeed the Latin teachers plotted the demise of the English school in the academy.) In 1789, Franklin demanded that the English school be separated from the Latin school and the corporation be dissolved. He had enough years of experience with the institution to pronounce a failure the first attempt to combine the values of a classical and a modern education. The classicists had won the first battle but they had not won the war. Gradually they lost ground. (To this day, however, they have not admitted defeat.) Franklin's academy was not a failure, for it gave impetus to the academy movement and a modern curriculum that ultimately led to the universalization of secondary education through the emergence of the public high school.

In sum, when such influential theorists as John Locke and Jean Jacques Rousseau began to insist that human nature is the function of the influences that saturate an individual's environment, for good or for evil, environmentalism was born. This idea not only came to have a profound effect on the curriculum, but also gave support to what was to become a passionate American belief in the educability of the people. Thus there were new opportunities for women who sought higher education. An illustration of this development in Pennsylvania was reported by Wickersham:

> Nothing is more remarkable in the educational policy inaugurated in 1838 than the place accorded to female education. From all the State had done for higher education previously, it could hardly be learned that such beings as women or girls were to be found within the borders of the state. . . . It seems to have been generally unknown either that girls could be educated beyond the simple arts of Reading, Writing or Arithmetic, or that they were entitled to any higher education. The credit of the discovery that girls should have an equal place with boys in a system of public instruction, higher as well as lower, belongs to the Legislature of 1838. It was a great discovery.[38]

Thus, environmentalism had begun to deeply effect educational policy. Environmentalism and learning from experience and observation were two main beliefs in what would over the course of a century become the basis for promoting educational opportunity, and for modernizing the curriculum in tune with the nature of the learner and with the democratic prospect.

The Vision of Human Development

To look back upon the years following the Civil War is to see the power of a tremendously influential idea on American education: evolution. The idea that the species of life (including the human) are not changeless, but had evolved and developed as the result of environmental changes and adaptive changes, had to be faced by professional philosophers and either rejected outright or worked into their philosophies. (It should be noted that teachers of philosophy were almost always clergymen.)

IDEALISM AND THE CHILD'S SELF.   The philosophy of idealism, of which there were many forms, was a response to the theory of evolution. The basic idea was that the real nature of the universe was spiritual, not material, and exists because of a universal mind: God's. Likewise, the most important thing about the human is the spiritual self or personality, not the physical being. Just as the universe is undergoing an evolutionary process of growth and development, so the individual's personality and spiritual nature is going through a similar process of growth and change. Thus it is important to respect the child's self and personality and provide the best conditions possible so that the child's (spiritual) nature can develop and unfold.

THE SOCIAL NATURE OF KNOWLEDGE.   Some idealists began to develop a social outlook, arguing that knowledge is the outcome not of an individual mind but a community of minds. They stressed the growth and development of human experience and the fact that the individual cannot exist in isolation from society. Idealism was probably the most influential philosophy taught in colleges and universities in the late nineteenth century. John Dewey drew very selectively from these views for their emphasis on child growth and the social nature of learning, discarding such dualisms as mind versus matter, ideas versus experience, and the individual versus society. He was also sharply critical of the notion that the child's personality could ever unfold of itself.[39] Dewey was to go on to forge a very different philosophy by orchestrating the American pragmatic spirit and the method of intelligence wrought by science with the democratic prospect.

EUROPEAN INFLUENCES ON THE ELEMENTARY SCHOOL

The phrase *the method* has been used from time to time by educators, its meaning depending on the teaching approach then in fashion. In the early nineteenth century in Europe, "the method" meant Pestalozzi's object-lesson approach. In 1861 object teaching was adopted in the schools in Oswego, New York, and a city normal school was created to train teachers in the new method. In the 1890s, a wave of pedagogical excitement was created in the United States by Herbart's formula for classroom instruction. "The method" meant the teaching steps developed by Herbart's followers and brought to the United States by Americans who had studied in Germany.

Pestalozzi (1746–1827), Herbart (1776–1841), and Froebel (1782–1852) had a great influence on nineteenth century education in America, but it was their practical ideas that attracted teachers. The principles behind the practices were not always well understood by teachers, with the result that "the method" often bore little resemblance to its original form. What was practical found its way first into American classrooms. Ideas that seemed unworkable or out of tune with the functions of public schooling were discarded by reformers. For example, Pestalozzi's naturalistic idea that the purpose of education was to free the child and at the same time shape him seemed somewhat conflicting to Horace Mann.[40] But Mann was strongly attracted to the Pestalozzian principle that children should be treated kindly and with respect, which Mann believed was essential for teaching self-discipline and for creating a good society.

In 1900 Dewey wrote that his laboratory school was attempting "to carry into effect certain principles which Froebel was perhaps the first to consciously set forth."[41] Among these principles was children's play (activity) as an educational method. But Dewey rejected the idea of Froebel's disciples that the materials used in the activity should be artificial and symbolic. Dewey contended that the materials and the activities "must be as 'real,' as direct and straightforward, as opportunity permits."[42] In the kindergarten of Dewey's school, the work centered on learnings related to home and neighborhood life.

Pestalozzi's Influence on the Curriculum

The nineteenth century was a decisive period in American curriculum development, and the ideas and practices of the Swiss educator Johann Pestalozzi deserved much credit. As we approach the twenty-first century, Pestalozzian ideas continue to influence American education through their further development by others, particularly Dewey. An illustration is the Pestalozzian conception of education as a developmental process, starting from the familiar and plain and moving toward the understanding and application of abstract ideas. This seems to anticipate Dewey's pedagogical principles as he worked them out in his laboratory school at the University of Chicago (1896–1904). At the time Dewey wrote: "The first pedagogical question is, How, out of the crude native experience which the child already has, the complete and systematic knowledge of the adult consciousness is gradually and systematically worked out."[43] For Dewey, as for Pestalozzi before him, the answer was by building on the child's real experiences; experience was the starting point of the curriculum.

OBJECT TEACHING.   For Pestalozzi the sense impressions obtained from the object lessons were the experiences. Object teaching required, first of all, an object—a flower, fruit, toy, tool, or animal (or a model or picture of the object). Through the use of the senses, the child gained ideas about the object. Through sense perception, the child would be able to develop concepts and basic ideas and translate them into appropriate words. The objectives of object teaching were to develop alertness, accuracy of perception, concepts and generalizations, and vocabulary. Although object teaching had serious limitations, such as the failure to reveal the interrelatedness of objects in the activity, these goals fit in strikingly well with the objectives of elementary education today. Unfortunately, however, teachers in the nineteenth century described the goals of object teaching in terms of faculty psychology (to cultivate the faculty of reasoning, as though reasoning is a separate and mechanistic function, for example) rather than for the development of a scientific frame of mind. This was because faculty psychology was the generally accepted pedagogical psychology of the times.

CRITICISMS OF OBJECT TEACHING.   As it became formalized into a method, a growing number of criticisms were associated with object teaching. In too many instances, lessons were unrelated because there was no overall plan. Also, what began as a lesson on fruit or flowers might end up as a lesson on religion instead of science. Another unfortunate ending could be (and often was) a senseless vocabulary lesson. Finally, some teachers would insist that appropriate responses were wrong when they were not couched in the teacher's terminology. Obviously, for the most part these problems were not implicit in the method itself; they were abuses of the method and, hence, problems of teacher education.

IMPACT ON EDUCATIONAL THINKING.   Despite the abuses, criticisms, and limitations, object teaching was a tremendously important reform. It revolutionized teaching. The prevailing educational method had been hearing individual recitations, but now the teacher had to stand before a class, ask the right questions, and get children to use their senses and their minds. It broadened and improved the curriculum. Oral language work entered the primary grades, and in the upper elementary grades, oral and written language work replaced somewhat the narrow emphasis on English grammar. Object teaching did much to introduce science as a school subject. Arithmetic also underwent changes—from words about numbers to concrete number ideas. Yet, as pointed out, an inherent limitation of object teaching was its focus on objects as finished products. The most profound revolution in teaching was to find its expression in Dewey's laboratory school, where the materials under study were subjected to the test of life experience. Hence, geography was revolutionized. The new "home geography" began with the study of local terrain. This required observation outdoors. The concept of learning as inquiry, the uses of visual aids, and the field trip were all here to stay.

Herbart's Influence on the Curriculum

Toward the end of the nineteenth century object teaching—which had become a fad—began to give way to a new method: five instructional steps to be followed in order. The instructional procedure grew out of the theories of the eminent German psychologist Johann Friedrich Herbart.

THE FORMAL STEPS OF INSTRUCTION.   Herbart was the first educational writer to put an emphasis on instruction as a process. According to Herbart, the teacher must present new ideas in a way that associates them with ideas that are already part of the pupil's experience. This meant, of course, that the teacher had to know of the child's previous knowledge and interest. In keeping this psychology in mind, the teacher would follow what became known as the *five formal steps of teaching and learning.* The steps were as follows:

1. *Preparation,* in which the previous learning experiences are called to the pupil's attention

2. *Presentation,* in which the new information is given out

3. *Association,* or showing the relationship between the new facts and the old

4. *Generalization,* or making up rules or general principles that express the meaning of the lesson

5. *Application,* or giving the general principles meaning by using them in practical situations or applying them to specific examples

For a period of some fifteen years, spanning into the early years of the twentieth century, more and more teachers organized their lessons along the five steps. "Without question," wrote Elsbree, "these five simply stated steps exercised more influence on teaching practice between 1890 and 1905 than all other psychological and philosophical creations combined."[44]

And there is no question that the method made it possible for teachers to provide instruction that was much more meaningful to their students. Yet most teachers rigidly followed the steps in organizing their lessons rather than using the method creatively. Needless to say, many of them used the method mechanically, without understanding its psychological principles. Perhaps the most serious limitation inherent in Herbartian theory, aside from its uniformity in all subjects for all pupils, was its emphasis on established and predictable learning to the neglect of learning interactions relating to the emergent or flexible situations.

ENTER: THE LESSON PLAN.   The formal lesson plan began with the five formal steps of Herbart. The steps were, of course, intended for teachers but the simple and systematic sequence of steps provided a handy tool for supervisors who evaluated teachers on their adherence to the steps in their lesson plans and in conducting the lesson itself.

"DOING MADELINE HUNTER": AN ECHO FROM THE PAST.   In the 1980s and early 1990s, another model for lesson design spread rapidly: the Hunter model. Developed by Madeline Hunter, a faculty member at the University of California at Los Angeles, the steps in the Hunter lesson were strikingly similar to Herbart's. Madeline Hunter owed much to Herbart. For example, her first step was called *anticipatory set,* and its purpose was to remind pupils of what they already know concerning the topic. It was Herbart who first advanced the theory of associationism—imparting knowledge by utilizing previous learning—and the importance of this has been stressed ever since. As Slavin observes, "these elements of lesson design are hardly unique to Madeline Hunter. Many theorists call for a comparable sequence of activities."[45]

The difficulty is that many state and local districts required teachers to use the model, although research does not support its effects on student learning. Then how can one explain the enthusiastic acceptance of Hunter's rigid pattern for teaching? One reason is surely political. In the 1980s the Reagan administration made education reform a key political issue, leaving much responsibility to the states, a policy continued by succeeding administrations. Under this pressure local school districts and state legislatures took a regulatory approach to school reform. According to two observers: "By linking a neatly designed teaching model to supervisory procedures, Hunter gave administrators the vehicle they needed to respond to political pressures generated by calls for school reform."[46]

A second factor associated with the Hunter phenomenon is the tendency of educational principles to become obscured when being translated into a stripped-down formula that then takes on a life of its own. This also happened with Herbart's psychology of associationism.

Yet the Herbartians' and Hunter's concern with the problem of method was a good thing for teaching. The ideas of Herbart on the unity of knowledge also drew educators' attention to the need for curriculum synthesis before the turn of the century.

Froebel's Influence on the Curriculum

As indicated, Dewey adopted (and adapted) Froebel's idea that play is the method of development and learning in his experimental school. Mention must be made of two other Froebelian principles that Dewey and his faculty tried to carry out in the curriculum. The first was Froebel's idea of group activity as a means of developing in children a sense of community and mutual interdependence or, put more simply, good social relations. The second idea was to use the activities to reproduce on the child's level the occupations of the mature society. Dewey wove this idea into the civilization theme on which his curriculum was based. But Dewey took Froebel's ideas much further in seeing learning as developmental: the evolution of human occupations and society and the increasing control of nature for human purposes. Thus, although the idea of occupations was Froebel's, Dewey went on to develop it in a quite different fashion. Whereas Froebel saw education as a kind of unfolding from within, Dewey viewed growth as stemming from the interaction of the organism with the environment.

Of course, Froebel is most famous for his concept of a less formal school environment where children could learn through play. He called the school the *kindergarten*, a garden where children could grow. His emphasis on manipulating objects, exploration, and self-expression led to a realization of the importance of activity in learning.

The first successful experiment with public school kindergartens was in St. Louis in 1873. The class was taught by Susan Blow, who had taken a course in kindergarten methods. The experiment was so successful that she organized a training school to educate co-workers. As graduates were produced the kindergartens grew in St. Louis. The movement quickly took root, and by the end of World War I the kindergarten had been accepted as the first rung of the American educational ladder. Nevertheless, a whole century later, a number of states still did not require school systems to offer kindergarten.

The Conservative Response

There is no question that the thought and writings of Pestalozzi, Froebel, and Herbart influenced the public school curriculum in the latter years of the nineteenth century. As one might quite properly expect, the influence on practice varied from one locale to another. But where it was adopted, the new education met with opposition, the critics calling for a return to an education that had gone out of existence years before. Such was the case in Detroit in the 1890s. The reforms resulting from the application of the principles of Herbart and Froebel were criticized by various groups who wanted to return to the fundamental curriculum of the three R's, a curriculum that had long since disappeared. Two attacks against the progressive principles will illustrate the nature of this opposition.

The first attack was on a change in the subject matter of arithmetic. The critics objected to the practical problems, because the great value of arithmetic was, according to them, in the mental discipline it afforded.

The second attack was leveled against a proposal by the assistant superintendent to use the daily newspaper for teaching reading, history, and geography. The principal supported her proposal on the grounds that the life of the surrounding adult community must be taken into account more directly in the curriculum. She interested the *Detroit Evening News* in her idea with the result that the paper submitted a proposal to the school board to supply a newspaper that was reduced in size, with editorial comment omitted for use in the schools. The board charged that this was a fad and vetoed the idea. They also restored the old kind of arithmetic.

In the 1896–97 school year, Detroit Superintendent William E. Robinson delivered a speech before the board in which he responded to the criticisms. Educational methods are always in a state of transition, he said, because educators are continually searching for better methods. Detroit, like every other city that had improved its methods to keep up with the requirements of the times, had been accused of introducing fads, but Detroit seemed not to realize that the changes were no longer considered radical and indeed had been incorporated into the curriculum for some time. Robinson noted that it was difficult to respond to the criticisms because the critics never defined what was meant by "fads and frills." Robinson stated the outlook of the "new education" as clearly as it could be put:

If by "fads" they mean drawing, music, physical culture and elementary science, then I say that these subjects have been a part of the course of study in Detroit for the past twenty-five years, and it seems rather late in the day to defend their introduction. If they mean that intelligent teaching of those subjects is a fad, then I confess that the schools are afflicted with this "fad" disease. A teacher who is able to teach reading so that a child can pick up any reading matter within his vocabulary and read it intelligently, instead of pronouncing mechanically the words on the page of the reader, is without doubt a "faddist." If they mean that it is better to recite in concert the various capes and bays and gulfs of North America than to have a knowledge of the construction of the continent of North America and give an intelligent expression of the effect of this construction on the occupations of the inhabitants with the commercial results, and from this knowledge of mathematics to estimate its size and distances, and to this add what he has learned of its history, then I will have to admit that much time is spent on fruitless ornamentation. . . .

If it is better to cram the mind with a lot of facts that are absolutely worthless when the child is thrown upon his own resources, than to lead him step by step to think for himself, to find out for himself that all subjects are dependent and related, and to become self-reliant, then the children of our schools are to be pitied for their visionary training. . . .

Parents have a right to demand accurate training in the common branches, and I believe reading, writing and arithmetic are taught better than ever before, but these are the means to an end, and the child is entitled to a glimpse of the vast resources in literature and history that they place at his disposal.[47]

Robinson retired in 1897, but his eleven-year administration was marked by continuous curriculum extension and expansion, the introduction of the kindergarten, and provision for the deaf and blind. As one writer noted, "the encouragement of the 'new education,' resulting from the stimulating influence of Herbart and Froebel, had taken root in the east and worked west rapidly."[48]

By 1900 the eight-year elementary school curriculum in Detroit included seventeen subjects: reading, writing, composition, literature, grammar, arithmetic, geography, history, spelling, government, drawing, music, physical culture, natural science, domestic science, domestic art and manual training. The growth of the curriculum from the ungraded school of the three R's in the 1840s was, in little more than a half-century, nothing short of remarkable.

FUNCTION DETERMINES FORM: THE HIGH SCHOOL

It has often been observed that form determines function. Actually, the reverse is just as true. A distinctively American invention, the public high school, originally did the work of the old academy—preparing the few for college—but very soon began to broaden its scope to provide equal opportunity to all and, in so doing, adjusted its organization and offerings.

An example of how this change took place is the high school in Galesburg, Illinois. In 1885, the Galesburg High School had a program that consisted mainly of the classics and foreign languages and was designed for college-preparatory students. William Steele, the Galesburg superintendent, noted that its function was so narrow that "its very existence was at times threatened."[49] In 1885, Galesburg High School recognized its responsibility to the many and added a more practical program for students who expected to complete their education in the high school. The subjects that were substituted for the Latin (classical) program were physiology, bookkeeping, English history, Constitution of the United States, chemistry, history of literature, and political economy. The instruction was organized into departments: Latin, mathematics, English, and science. In 1895, the curriculum was revised again and Galesburg High School offered three programs: the *Latin,* for college-preparatory youngsters, the *commercial,* for those wanting to prepare themselves for business, and the *scientific,* for those who did not plan to enter college but wanted a broader education than the elementary school provided. What was later to become known as a *comprehensive* high school was taking shape.

And in 1895 the Galesburg High School took a radical step indeed. All subjects were made elective. On entering the high school, the student, with the advice of the parents and eighth-grade teacher, chose the subjects he or she wanted to study for a semester. The value of each subject was first explained to the youngster.

The purpose of the Galesburg policy was to reduce the dropout rate. Forty percent of entering ninth-graders were dropping out in their first year. More than half of these were leaving school because they were failing their work in some subject. They knew that failure in any subject meant that they would never graduate from the school. As Steele recounted,

> This did not seem to be a sufficient reason for discouraging a youngster in his effort to get an education. A wise parent would not treat his own child in that way. He would make all the more effort to find some line of work that the child could follow advantageously. A school should treat its pupils as a wise parent does his child. . . .
>
> It was thought by the Board that nothing could be more absurd than to think of education as consisting of a knowledge of certain subjects. . . . It was certainly a recognition of this absurdity when the high schools first divided their curriculum into two or more courses (programs) of study.[50]

The diploma, however, was not deceptive. A certain number of credits was assigned to each subject, and when a required number had been made, the student was awarded a diploma on which was listed each subject that had been completed and the number of credits assigned. "The door to honorable graduation was never closed on the student by the school."[51] Within two years after the elective policy was adopted, the school building had to be more than doubled in capacity to accommodate the youngsters applying for admission. (In that period, there was almost no increase in the enrollment in the elementary school.)

From 1885 to 1911, the high school in Galesburg grew by more than 500 percent, increasing at nearly ten times the rate of either the elementary school or the population. The broadened curriculum—including public speaking, vocational subjects, and student activities such as clubs, literary contests, and musical organizations—were all factors in the growth. But according to Steele the critical factor was the school's objective: "to make it a place where every one, no matter what type of mind he might have, would find something that appealed to him and into which he could throw his energies and thus discover what kind of person he was."[52]

It would be misleading to imply that all high schools followed the radical policy of the Galesburg High School in offering a more comprehensive curriculum. Nevertheless, most large high schools had begun to adapt their programs to the needs of changing student populations. (Small high schools had one curriculum, geared to the college-bound.) High schools increased enormously during this period as did the number of youngsters who availed themselves of the opportunities. No sooner were high school buildings erected than they were deemed inadequate to accommodate the throngs. As indicated, one reason was that the principle of curricular uniformity (a single program for those preparing for college) had given way in many high schools to curricular flexibility. Another was the rapid development of cities and towns and the development of railroads (later, "electric roads," or "inter-urbans"), which helped to bring people together and to stimulate a desire for greater educational advantages. But yet another factor was the influence of the great state universities of the West, particularly with regard to coeducation.

IMPACT OF UNIVERSITIES. In the great universities of the West, opportunities for women to obtain a college or university education, at state expense, were pushed with great vigor. Every state university west of the Mississippi admitted women on equal terms with men from the time they opened (e.g., University of Iowa in 1855). In 1870, the Board of Regents of the University of Michigan voted to admit women on an equal footing with men. There seems little doubt that this decision had an enormous impact on Michigan high schools as was the case in Iowa and other western states. According to Davis,

> not only did many girls now remain for graduation from the local high school, and then enter the university, but the newly acquired college privileges stimulated high-school life and high-school attendance in general. . . . Not that all who came remained to graduate, or that all who graduated went on to college, or that all who went on to college entered the University of Michigan. The point is that the privilege granted by the university fired the imagination and the ambitions of more youths, stimulated an interest in the high schools, and thus vastly augmented the movement that was already so well under way—the movement fostering and developing public secondary education, open and available for all.[53]

The state colleges and universities had an enormous influence on high schools in another way—by admitting the graduates of selected high schools without examination. In Michigan, after 1870, all that the high school graduate had to do to be admitted to the University was to present his certificate of graduation from an approved secondary school. The foundation was being laid for an accreditation plan. By the end of the nineteenth century, several major associations of colleges and secondary schools had been founded in the United States. The advantages accruing to high school students were tremendous.

As one might expect, colleges and universities also began to play an increasingly significant role in the development of high school curriculums. This influence was advantageous, but also created problems. College pressures on high schools became organized. In the East in particular, courses were spelled out in detail that high schools ought to offer (including bibliographies). The Madison, New Jersey, superintendent commented that "the colleges had deliberately entered into a conspiracy to force a young man to secure a liberal education before entering college so that he may have the full four years to devote to football and baseball."[54]

THE PIED-PIPER CURRICULUM. On the positive side, colleges and universities were broadening their own curriculum. Davis noted that this expansion was "a particularly potent influence upon the high school."[55] In 1853, equal recognition was given to science in the curriculum at the University of Michigan when a scientific course was instituted. Up until that time, like most colleges, the University of Michigan had only one narrowly prescribed classical course of study. High school graduates could be admitted to the scientific course without having studied the ancient languages in high school.

Keeping step with the university, the high schools established a scientific course. As might be expected, in high school as in college, the restructuring of the curriculum did not stop with two parallel courses. "New changes were made, one after another, and always in the direction of greater freedom for individual choice."[56]

The trouble was, however, that the high school had not worked out its curriculum on its own account—to meet the needs of all of its students. As Davis described the situation: "Wherever the university led, the high schools readily and willingly followed."[57]

The college influenced the high school in yet another way that was more subtle but just as perverse. As some school officials complained, "too many high school teachers imitated their college professors' methods of classroom teaching."[58] Certainly one of the most perplexing problems facing the high school was the question of method. What was sought was a method "carefully differentiated from the elementary school, on the one hand, and from the college method, on the other."[59] In a very real sense, this problem is still facing the high school in the 1990s.

Many high schools found themselves being violently pulled in opposite directions simultaneously. The growing demand for more popular and practical subjects met with the restatement of the allegedly practical values of classical subjects. The college preparatory function of secondary education remained dominant although the overwhelming proportion of students was not college-bound. Nevertheless it was the comprehensive high school, a school with two or more programs, that had become the most popular form of secondary education by 1900. Yet the problem of developing a curriculum suitable for diverse groups and individuals in one public school and finding a common ground for a core curriculum had not been solved. It had merely been sharpened.

PERSPECTIVE

The availability of textbooks in subjects previously unknown and the expansion of minimum curriculum requirements are evidence of the vast enlargement of knowledge and the curriculum in the nineteenth century. But these hardly begin to tell the tale. For equally (and, perhaps, even more) important were changes in the outlook and content of the subjects themselves. In the early nineteenth century, the concept that individuals acquire their ideas through experience began to appear in American curriculum thought. In the thirty years following the Civil War, the new educational ideas that emphasized experience and understanding were popularized. The theories of Pestalozzi and Froebel were reflected in such methods as engaging children in the expression of their observations and experiences in writing. (Both reading and writing were taught this way in progressive public school classrooms.) In some schools children were encouraged to be helpful to each other. In his visits to schools in thirty-six cities in the 1892–93 school year, Joseph Mayer Rice found children in the schools of LaPorte, Indiana, who were "working together in groups, assisting each other in making and recording observations of plants and animals, of the wind and weather, and they frequently subdivide tasks."[60] Such practices were far from universal or even general. They did exist. Pestalozzian principles found their way into some classrooms via school magazines that were issued by nearly every state after 1850. The aim was to bring to teachers in a usable form the ideas that were uppermost in the thoughts of educational leaders. And they found their way through the work of administrators and supervisors who observed and critiqued lessons and gave model lessons.

Anachronistically, one of the earliest educational reforms was a mechanical method of teaching. The monitorial system (1815–1830) made the instruction of large numbers of children possible because it was cheap and it therefore overcame one of the earliest obstacles to the development of public education. When the plan was applied to more than the rudiments of reading, writing, and arithmetic, it showed its limitations and was abandoned. The new Pestalozzian (and later, Froebelian) ideas stressed pupil interest and conceived of education as a process of growth through the enrichment of experience by means of activities. There was a profound difference in the Lancasterian and Pestalozzian conception of education. The instructional method of the former was memorization and simultaneous (concert) recitation, under the control of monitors. It was military organization and discipline in a school setting. Pestalozzian principles stressed the development of independence of judgment that was the essence of democracy.

Object teaching, a Pestalozzian idea that enormously influenced the curriculum, did much to introduce science as a school subject and oral language work as a new primary grade subject. And it influenced the effort in all fields to publish textbooks that were interesting as well as comprehensible to youngsters. In arithmetic textbooks, for example, there was a growing emphasis on principles and practical problems.

Nevertheless, as the nineteenth century closed, one could still find many spellers consisting only of lists of words and geographies and histories with lengthy lists of questions involving names, dates, and questions, not to mention readers with discussion of things completely out of the child's experience. Be that as it may, the new education had begun. In coming decades it would play a far more influential role in the development of the curriculum.

John Dewey drew on the progressive views of Froebel and Pestalozzi in a selective way, going on to develop a concept of the curriculum and philosophy of education that were uniquely American.

The curriculum development over the century was truly remarkable. At the beginning we saw a system of privilege on the European model and at the end, a curriculum ladder for all, extending from elementary school to the university. All state universities west of the Mississippi admitted women on an equal footing with men from the start. The high school developed a close relationship with the university from the start. Affiliation with the university (being on the approved list for admission without examination) was considered a great honor by the local high school and guaranteed the university large freshman classes. High schools in the third quarter of the nineteenth century regarded themselves as "peoples" colleges. High school teachers emulated their professors' methods of teaching, with the result that many high school pupils dropped out in their first year. High schools were criticized for the great "mortality" of students. Instead of examining their own methods and subject matter, high schools proceeded to blame the teaching in the elementary grades.

Criticism of the curriculum as the reason why so many students were dropping out led to the making of new programs of study. Some schools offered students as many as a dozen different curriculum tracks. The multiplicity of choices was confusing, and once a student selected a program the student's fate was sealed; deviation was strictly forbidden in many schools. The only way a student could remedy a wrong choice was to begin all over again. The result was often the complete abandonment of school—with nothing to show for two or three years of work. How the situation (which had become ridiculous as well as tragic) was dealt with is discussed in the next chapter.

The history of American curriculum helps us to see the consequences of some of the steps that were taken in the past. It provides us with insights about possibly important factors to be considered in making intelligent decisions about present practices and proposals for the future.

PROBLEMS FOR STUDY AND DISCUSSION

1. In the 1980s and 1990s teachers were hearing much about cooperative learning and it had become an educational trend. In this connection, Robert Slavin wrote:

> The future of cooperative learning is difficult to predict. My hope is that even when cooperative learning is no longer the "hot" new method, schools and teachers will continue to use it as a routine part of instruction. My fear is that cooperative learning will largely disappear as a result of the faddism so common in American education. [Robert E. Slavin, "Here to Stay—Or Gone Tomorrow?" *Educational Leadership,* 47 (December 1989/January 1990), p. 4.]

As discussed in this chapter, cooperative learning was one of the newer educational ideas in practice in public schools regarded as excellent in the 1890s. Do you think that this is important for contemporary educators to know? Why or why not?

2. In 1821, Warren Colburn published his *First Lessons in Arithmetic on the Plan of Pestalozzi.* Its purpose was to do away with incomprehensible abstractions by teaching children in their first lessons that all numbers are numbers of things. In the last decades of the twentieth century, Colburn's objective still had not been achieved. Publishers were criticized for producing mathematics textbooks that failed to engage students in applying their mathematical knowledge in problem-solving situations. The books "are still not really as good as they have to be," said California's then–State Superintendent Bill Honig, "but now at least there's a lot of ferment in the publishing community." [Ron Brandt, "On Curriculum in California: A Conversation with Bill Honig," *Educational Leadership,* 47 (November 1989), p. 11.]

In your opinion, what can teachers and principals do to help in the achievement of the objective for which Colburn struggled?

3. The Latin grammar school died because its curriculum remained the same while the educational needs of society changed. In what ways does the curriculum of today fail to meet the needs of society? In what ways does it do so? Where does the solution lie?

4. In describing Joseph Lancaster's monitorial method, Sidney Smith, a contemporary of Lancaster wrote:

The beauty of Mr. Lancaster's system is that nothing is trusted to the boy himself; he does not only *repeat* the lesson before a superior, but he *learns* it before a superior. When he listens to the dictating process in arithmetic, and adds up as he is commanded, he does that, under the eye and command of a master, which in other schools he would be trusted to do by himself. In short, in these troops the appointed officer sees that the soldier shoulders his musket twenty times a day, who by doing it often cannot avoid doing it well. In other troops, the officer tells the soldiers how it is to be done, and leaves them to practice by themselves—which they do, of course, very unwillingly and very imperfectly, if they do it at all. [Cited in Paul Monroe, *Founding of the American Public School System* (New York: Macmillan, 1940), p. 369.)

What were the limitations of the method that became apparent when history, geography, and the natural sciences were introduced into the curriculum of Lancasterian schools?

5. As we have discussed in this chapter, in the nineteenth century remarkable progress was made in providing access to the curriculum for previously excluded groups (girls and women as well as the overwhelming proportion of youngsters whose parents could not afford the private academies). In your opinion, is unequal access to the curriculum still a problem in American education? Explain.

6. As discussed in this chapter, in the 1890s, educators attempting to deal with the dropout problem found that most youngsters who left school did so because they were failing in some subject. Is this still true today? In your opinion, do the policies of the Galesburg (Illinois) School Board that were adopted in 1895 for dealing with the dropout problem suggest ideas for contemporary educators who want to reduce dropouts? Why or why not?

7. As discussed in this chapter, a widely promoted instructional approach during the back-to-basics movement of the late 1970s was "direct instruction," a method that mainly found its application in inner-city classrooms. A noted researcher described the features of direct instruction as follows: "large groups, decision making by the teacher, limited choice of materials and activities by students, orderliness, factual questions, limited exploration of ideas, drill, and high percentages of correct answers" [Barak V. Rosenshine, "Content, Time and Direct Instruction," in Penelope L. Peterson and Herbert J. Walberg (eds.), *Research on Teaching* (Berkeley, CA: McCutchan, 1979), p. 47.] Compare the features of direct instruction with the Lancasterian organization and procedures of the early nineteenth century. What similarities do you find? In your view, what remnants of Lancaster's system and methods (if any) are still in evidence in inner-city schools today?

8. According to a revisionist historian, those who fought for the public elementary—or common—school were motivated by the belief "that the common school was the best means of controlling crime, social unrest, and political disruptions." [Joel Spring, *The American School 1642–1990* (New York: Longman, 1990), p. 111.]

Do you think that this is a fair assessment of the motives of such leaders as James G. Carter and Horace Mann in Massachusetts? Explain.

9. To what do you attribute the remarkable expansion of the curriculum in the course of the nineteenth century? Which of these forces continue to influence curriculum development today?

10. It has been observed that "there appears to be a perennial 'back to the basics' movement in American education; it coexists with constant pressures for a wide range of new subject matter." [Stanley M. Elam, Lowell C. Rose, and Alex M. Gallup, "The 25th Annual Phi Delta Kappa Gallup Poll of the Public's Attitudes toward the Public Schools," *Phi Delta Kappan,* 75 (October 1993), p. 144.] What evidence, if any, do you see today of a back to the basics movement in curriculum planning?

NOTES

1. "The Math of Tomorrow in a Classroom Today," *The New York Times* (March 22, 1989), p. 21.
2. Ibid.
3. John Dewey and Evelyn Dewey, *Schools of Tomorrow* (New York: E. P. Dutton, 1962). (Originally published in 1915). Preface.
4. Ibid., p. 117.
5. Barbara Tuchman, *Practicing History* (New York: Alfred A. Knopf, 1981), p. 249.
6. *Chicago Sun-Times* (February 25, 1989), p. 9.
7. James G. Carter, *Letters to the Hon. William Prescott, L.L.D. on the Free Schools of New England, With Remarks upon the Principles of Instruction* (Boston: Cummings Hilliard, 1824), p. 62.
8. Letter to James Madison, in Gordon C. Lee (ed.), *Crusade against Ignorance: Thomas Jefferson on Education* (New York: Teachers College Press, 1961), p. 38.
9. R. Freeman Butts and Lawrence A. Cremin, *A History of Education in American Culture* (New York: Holt, Rinehart and Winston, 1953), p. 246.
10. Carter, op. cit., p. 8.
11. Ibid., p. 56.
12. Ibid., p. 61.
13. Ibid., p. 63.
14. Warren Burton, *The District School as It Was* (Boston: Carter, Hendee, 1833), p. 41.
15. Laurel N. Tanner, "Presentation of NSSE Yearbook," Annual Conference of the Association for Supervision and Curriculum Development, Orlando, Florida, March 12, 1989.
16. George Hillocks, Jr., "Literacy Texts in Classrooms," Chapter 7 in *From Socrates to Software: The Teacher as Text and the Text as Teacher,* Eighty-eighth Yearbook of the National Society for the Study of Education, Part I (Chicago: University of Chicago Press, 1989), p. 149.
17. Burton, op. cit., p. 148.
18. Hillocks, op. cit., pp. 156–157.
19. Butts and Cremin, op. cit., p. 127.
20. James P. Wickersham, *A History of Education in Pennsylvania* (Lancaster, PA: Inquirer, 1886), p. 255.
21. Ibid.
22. Ibid., p. 257.
23. Ibid., p. 266.
24. Sidney L. Jackson, *America's Struggle for Free Schools* (New York: Russell and Russell, 1965), p. 1.
25. Anne Wheelock, "Boston's Last Hope: The Exam Schools," *National Center on Effective Secondary Schools Newsletter,* 3 (Fall 1988), p. 7.
26. National Center for Education Statistics. *Digest of Education Statistics 1993* (Washington, DC: U.S. Department of Education, 1993), p. 9.
27. Cited in Wickersham, op. cit., p. 283.
28. Cited in Frank P. Graves, *A History of Education in Modern Times* (New York: Macmillan, 1914), p. 57.
29. John Dewey, "As Concerns the Elementary School," in *The Educational Situation* (Chicago: University of Chicago Press, 1902), pp. 24–25.
30. Ibid., p. 24.
31. Burke A. Hinsdale, *Horace Mann and the Common School Revival* (New York: Scribner's, 1898), p. 60.
32. Edison Ellsworth Oberholtzer, *An Integrated Curriculum in Practice* (New York: Bureau of Publications, Teachers College, 1937), p. 5.
33. Lawrence A. Cremin, *The American Common School* (New York: Teachers College Press, 1951), p. 188.
34. Cited in Cremin, op. cit., p. 188.
35. Horace Mann, *Eleventh Annual Report of the Board of Education, Together with the Eleventh Annual Report of the Secretary of the Board* (Boston: Dutton and Wentworth, 1848), p. 89.
36. Cremin, op. cit., p. 190.
37. *The New York Times* (June 23, 1990), p. 30.
38. Wickersham, op. cit., pp. 389–390.
39. John Dewey, *The Child and the Curriculum* (Chicago: University of Chicago Press, 1902).
40. Lawrence A. Cremin, *The Transformation of the School* (New York: Alfred A. Knopf, 1961), p. 12.
41. John Dewey, "Froebel's Educational Principles," *Elementary School Record,* a series of nine monographs (June 1900), p. 143.
42. Ibid., p. 147.
43. John Dewey, "The Psychological Aspect of the School Curriculum," *Educational Review,* 13 (April 1897), p. 364.

44. Willard S. Elsbree, *The American Teacher* (New York: American Book, 1938), p. 407.

45. Robert Slavin, "The Hunterization of America's Schools," *Instructor,* 96 (April 1987), p. 57.

46. Noreen B. Garman and Helen M. Hazi, "Teachers Ask: Is There Life after Madeline Hunter?" *Phi Delta Kappan,* 69 (May 1988), p. 672.

47. Cited in Arthur B. Moehlman, *Public Education in Detroit* (Bloomington, IL: Public School Publishing, 1925), pp. 148–150.

48. Ibid., p. 152.

49. William L. Steele, *Galesburg Public Schools: 1861–1911* (Galesburg, IL: Cadmus Press, 1911), p. 184.

50. Ibid., p. 203.

51. Ibid., p. 204.

52. Ibid., p. 201.

53. Calvin O. Davis, *Public Secondary Education* (New York: Rand McNally, 1917), pp. 201–202.

54. Cited in Robert D. Bole and Laurence B. Johnson, *The New Jersey High School: A History* (Princeton, NJ: D. Van Nostrand, 1964), p. 86.

55. Davis, op. cit., p. 202.

56. Ibid., p. 203.

57. Ibid., p. 206.

58. Ibid., p. 87.

59. Frank Webster Smith, *The High School* (New York: Sturgis and Walton, 1916), p. 354.

60. Joseph Mayer Rice, *The Public School System of the United States* (New York: Century, 1893), p. 207.

SELECTED REFERENCES

Burton, Warren. *The District School as It Was.* New York: Arno Press and *The New York Times,* 1969; originally published in 1833 by Carter, Hendee.

Cremin, Lawrence A. *The American Common School.* New York: Teachers College Press, 1951.

Cremin, Lawrence A. *American Education: The Colonial Experience, 1607–1783.* New York: Harper and Row, 1970.

Cremin, Lawrence A. *The Transformation of the School.* New York: Alfred A. Knopf, 1961.

Davis, Calvin O. *Public Secondary Education.* New York: Rand McNally, 1917.

DeGarmo, Charles. *Herbart and the Herbartians.* New York: Scribner's, 1912.

Dewey, John. *The Child and the Curriculum.* Chicago: University of Chicago Press, 1902.

Dewey, John. *The Educational Situation.* Chicago: University of Chicago Press, 1902.

Dewey, John, and Evelyn Dewey. Preface. *Schools of Tomorrow.* New York: E. P. Dutton, 1962. (Originally published in 1915.)

Hinsdale, Burke A. *Horace Mann and the Common School Revival.* New York: Scribner's, 1898.

Kaestle, Carl F. *Joseph Lancaster and the Monitorial School Movement.* New York: Teachers College Press, 1973.

Moehlman, Arthur B. *Public Education in Detroit.* Bloomington, IL: Public School Publishing, 1925.

Monroe, Will S. *History of the Pestalozzian Movement in the United States.* Syracuse, NY: C. W. Bardeen, 1907.

National Society for the Study of Education. *Critical Issues in Curriculum.* Eighty-seventh Yearbook, Part I. Chicago: University of Chicago Press, 1988.

National Society for the Study of Education. *From Socrates to Software: The Teacher as Text and the Text as Teacher.* Eighty-eighth Yearbook, Part I. Chicago: University of Chicago Press, 1989.

Pestalozzi, Johann Heinrich. *How Gertrude Teaches Her Children.* London: George Allen Unwin, 1894.

Rice, Joseph Mayer. *The Public School System of the United States.* New York: Century, 1893.

Steele, William L. *Galesburg Public Schools: 1861–1911.* Galesburg, IL: Cadmus Press, 1911.

Swett, John. *History of the Public School System in California.* San Francisco: A. L. Bancroft, 1876.

Tanner, Daniel, and Laurel Tanner. *History of the School Curriculum.* New York: Macmillan, 1990.

Vandewalker, Nina C. *The Kindergarten in American Education.* New York: Macmillan, 1917.

Wickersham, James P. *A History of Education in Pennsylvania.* New York: Arno Press and *The New York Times,* 1969; originally published by Inquirer in 1886.

CRITICAL TURNING POINTS

In the nineteenth century certain events occurred that proved to be turning points in the development of the curriculum and in thought about the curriculum. Dewey's laboratory school at Chicago was one such event and so was Spencer's raising the entire question of the purpose of education. The purpose of the Dewey school was in Dewey's own words "to discover in administration, selection of subject-matter, methods of learning, teaching, and discipline, how a school could become a cooperative community while developing in individuals their own capacities and satisfying their own needs."[1] Dewey's school produced results of continuing value and significance.

 The essay by the English philosopher Herbert Spencer (1820–1903) *What Knowledge Is of Most Worth?* (1859) had considerable influence on curriculum thinking (and on the curriculum as well). Since its publication, we have never stopped asking Spencerian questions.

The work of Francis Parker in Quincy, Massachusetts, in the 1870s proved to be a turning point in the course of curricular events. Parker achieved something constructive and of continuing usefulness to those who seek to improve the curriculum for children. Yet not all of the turning points in the curriculum signalled progress. Some, such as the report of the Committee of Ten on Secondary School Studies (1893) and the report of the Committee of Fifteen on Elementary Education (1895) are generally considered as conservative and perhaps regressive in their impact. The history of the curriculum has had its ups and downs.

This chapter considers the great events and the great ideas of the nineteenth century that proved to be very influential in the evolution of the curriculum. Among the turning points examined are Spencer's ideas on education, Parker's work in the Quincy schools, the work of the National Education Association's Committee of Ten and Committee of Fifteen, the Laboratory School at the University of Chicago and, finally, the founding of standardizing or accreditation associations to establish criteria for college entrance.

WHAT KNOWLEDGE IS OF MOST WORTH?

Occasionally a field takes an amazingly new course after the appearance of a single publication. An example with which most people are familiar is Darwin's *Origin of Species,* which marked a titanic turning point in the development of science, and had a resounding impact on social science, philosophy, and theology. Although not as well celebrated and, indeed, probably unknown to most people outside the field of education, the curriculum took just as startling a new course following the publication of Spencer's essay *What Knowledge Is of Most Worth?*[2] His essay was published in the United States in 1860. Spencer insisted that because of the importance of the knowledge of natural sciences to human welfare and social progress, the sciences should be included in the curriculum. He was but one of many English and American writers who argued that a curriculum confined to study of the classics was not adequate preparation for living.

Breaking Up the Classical Monopoly

It will be remembered that the methods of science led to changes in the methods of education. The idea that children should be taught to corroborate what they learn from their own investigation was a Pestalozzian method and strikingly parallels the scientific method. Pestalozzi and his followers opposed the prevailing education on the ground that it was not the way people acquired knowledge of the world and was, therefore, unpsychological. The moment that dissatisfaction arose with a closed approach to natural phenomena the die was cast: Science would enter the curriculum. The conflict between the classicists, who thought that the mind was formed through mastery of subjects such as grammar and logic—which were believed to state the actual rules of mental operation—and the progressives, who urged that science should be brought into the schools, continued until the middle of the nineteenth century. Although science was to gain a prominent place in the curriculum, the conflict between the humanities or classics on one side, and science on the other, continued to rage throughout the twentieth century.

In the nineteenth century, prominent scientists wrote treatises on education, methodically pointing out the reasons for giving science due recognition in the curriculum. Recommending science to curriculum makers in England (the home of the Industrial Revolution) occupied the attention of Thomas Henry Huxley, a champion of Darwin's theory of evolution. Huxley pointed out that it was a highly improvident policy for a great country like England with enormous commercial interests to fail to offer instruction in chemistry and physics, on which its industrial greatness and world leadership depended. The growing industrial competition in international trade during this period eventually caused England to accede to this view. Knowing about this episode helps us to understand our own time. As the twentieth century draws to a close, the place of science in American schools continues to gain significance for strikingly similar reasons.

It was Herbert Spencer who made the representative argument for science in the curriculum. In his famous essay he stated that the purpose of education was "to prepare for complete living," and that the only way of determining the worth of an educational program was first to classify, in order of importance, the leading activities of life, and then to evaluate the educational program on the basis of the extent to which it offered this preparation. Spencer's classification of life activities, in order of their importance, was as follows:

1. Those ministering directly to self-preservation
2. Those securing the necessities of life (ministering indirectly to self-preservation)
3. Those that aid in the rearing and discipline of offspring
4. Those involved in maintaining one's political and social relations
5. Those that occupy the leisure part of life, gratifying tastes and feelings[3]

In applying his own test, Spencer found that science was the knowledge of most worth in educating for self-preservation, yet it received the least attention in the curriculum. Spencer was one of the most respected and admired—even revered—philosophers of his time and had a large following in America. "I believe there is no other man whose thoughts are so valuable for our needs as yours are," wrote Edward L. Youmans, editor of *Popular Science Monthly,* to Spencer in 1863.[4] As a result of the publication of Spencer's essay and the discussion that followed, the study of science gained a new stature and was more rapidly introduced into all levels of the curriculum.

The Decision of "Most Worth"

Spencer's influence on the curriculum would have been profound simply on the basis of his advocacy of science. This was the immediate effect of his essay. But the larger and probably more important effect has been on curriculum theory. Spencer's question paved the way to theory development. What knowledge is of most worth? We know that schools cannot teach everything, and somehow the society and school faculty must determine "worth." The problem of worth is both practical and philosophical. Ralph Tyler dealt with the problem in his famous rationale for planning a program of instruction (1949).[5] Tyler's guide for determining the greatest worth would be the school's objectives.

MAKING VALUE JUDGMENTS.   But Tyler was well aware that the objectives, themselves, "are matters of choice, and they must be therefore the considered value judgments of those responsible for the school."[6] Tyler quickly got down to business in his rationale. The faculty must have a philosophy for guidance in the making of judgments. Data must also be available to decision makers if judgments about objectives are to be wise. Neither philosophy nor information stands by itself as a sufficient basis for arriving at objectives. When Tyler spoke of "*considered* value judgments" he was saying that the value (worth) assigned to a topic or subject should be determined by knowledge and information (about important problems of the day, for example) as well as the school's philosophy (emphasis added).

NO PERMANENT ANSWER.   Equally important in curriculum development is the need to ask Spencer's question continually. "When Spencer asked, 'What knowledge is of most worth?' he posed a question which must always be considered and reconsidered," observes Oliver, who goes on to point out that what might have been of great worth at one time has given way to a new worth with the advancement of knowledge.[7] Indeed, virtually every national report on school reform throughout the twentieth century has addressed this question implicitly if not explicitly. A chief problem has been that in periods of perceived crisis, the schools find themselves vulnerable to narrow sociopolitical demands for shifting curriculum priorities, giving emphasis to one side of the curriculum at the expense of an equally worthy side.[8]

ARRIVING AT CONSENSUS.   It is one thing to theorize that "most worth" should be determined on the basis of philosophy and the best available evidence. It is quite another, however, for the theory to be put into practice. Curriculum is the responsibility of various groups, often with conflicting ideas and ideals. A guiding principle offered by Richard Clark is genuine participation. Faculty members, parents, and students should not be asked condescendingly for input. They should be "mobilized to participate actively in the developmental processes and decision making of the school. Not only do they participate eagerly, but their participation is authentic."[9]

Clark offers as an example the development of a high school core curriculum. A study committee of parents, teachers, and district curriculum persons spent a year developing recommendations under the leadership of a school principal. Local community groups conducted hearings, and each faculty member worked intensively to develop recommendations. The developmental process involved task forces of teachers representing all areas of the curriculum working with district curriculum specialists. The point of importance is that the process took time (actually, three years) and required interactions among the individuals who participated in the development of the curriculum as well as in decision making on related concerns. Conflicts became secondary to the goal. Moreover, as Clark points out, the participants did not regard the work as something to be finished, but viewed the outcomes as requiring follow-up. All participants are seen as members of an "active" school.[10] Clark speaks from his experience as an educational leader.

Researchers have shown considerable interest in the concept of curriculum deliberation, the process by which persons representing groups with differing ideals arrive at consensus about the curriculum. Needless to say, deliberation can take place in many settings and under many institutional arrangements. It has been found that the curriculum conference is a particularly useful way of arriving at consensus.[11] A curriculum conference is a well-planned and prepared deliberation situation in which participants meet to work on matters of common concern with regard to the curriculum and to determine and approve the curriculum. Clearly this is different from a standing curriculum committee meeting or special workshop. The curriculum conference requires a great deal of planning or "prestructuring," in which "a preliminary study takes place to write a report that contains information from multiple datasources about . . . subject matter, learners and teachers. But existing curricula are also analyzed."[12] The report highlights the best available evidence as well as differences in viewpoints. (Here the material may be useful in sorting evidence from opinion.) The report reflects on the tentative conclusions about the curriculum's design. At this point the report becomes what is, willy nilly, a proposal. Participants are expected to read the material before the conference.

In a study about curriculum conferences as means of arriving at consensus, Mulder and Thijsen found that participants who had large differences of opinion prior to the conference approached high levels of agreement during the conference. But the same participants held different opinions several weeks after the conference, compared with the decisions reached by the group during the conference.[13] Thus one is forced to raise the possibility that the agreement was superficial and a matter of expediency, or the effects of subtle social pressure. The report that the participants read in advance of the conference was probably well intended. It was assumed that they came new to the curriculum issue and they needed material that would make it easier to grasp. Nevertheless, there is a price to be paid from the press of time and when the decision-making process does not involve participants in the preliminary study. When participants meet only once, and many have glanced at papers while someone else is talking, their initial presumptions are likely to remain unchanged.

The insight to be gained from this study is that consensus should not be a curriculum group's greatest concern; the paramount concern is building a sound basis for decisions, and this requires full and open communication.

Until Spencer's essay, most educators did not even think in terms of "most worth." Making choices is more difficult than anyone seems to admit. Curriculum development and decision making should be seen as part of a problem-solving process.[14]

FRANCIS PARKER'S "QUINCY SYSTEM"

Like many young educators of his day, Francis W. Parker (1831–1902) studied pedagogy in Germany. He was greatly impressed by Pestalozzi's emphasis on study of the physical world and Herbart's principle of curriculum correlation. Parker was also inspired by the educational ideas of Froebel, in particular, the importance of the pupil's activity and the social aspect of education. Particularly attractive to Parker was Froebel's principle of learning through social participation rather than as an isolated individual. Thanks to Parker, these ideas landed, spread out, and altered the American educational landscape. In his elementary school work, Parker extended these ideas to include a whole language approach in the curriculum. Interestingly, Froebel's ideas were suppressed in Germany. German educational tradition stressed passive obedience to authority. Froebel found fertile soil in democratic United States.

What is the turning point with which we are concerned? Here it was the application of progressive methods of instruction in Quincy, Massachusetts. For if progressive education had a beginning it was surely with Parker's work in Quincy. Indeed, Dewey (who made the most creative contribution to American education) called Parker the father of progressive education.

The Problem in Quincy

The educational moment that proved to be a turning point in the curriculum began in 1875 when Parker was named superintendent of schools in Quincy. His charge was to examine and improve education in Quincy. Two years before, on public examination day, the Quincy School Committee had made an appalling discovery. The graduates of the grammar schools were unable to spell, write, or speak effectively. When asked by the committee members to read from an unfamiliar book, they were bewildered and lost. They had been trained only for examination and could not read with fluency or comprehension. Furthermore, questions about their studies revealed that the children had no understanding of the thinking process. All they could do was parrot memorized responses to memorized questions prepared in advance by their teacher.

Buttressed with his study of elementary-school methods in Germany, Parker had his opportunity to apply them as superintendent. Unlike many superintendents of today, he carried out curriculum development responsibilities personally. Parker understood his charge clearly: to help the children of Quincy to develop the power of expression.

Parker's Pedagogy

Because Parker believed that methods of teaching should be patterned on the child's natural way of learning, he adopted the word method of teaching reading. This, after all, was the way children learned to speak the language. Grammar was thrown out of the school and talking and writing were put in.

Conversation, which was one of the innovations in Quincy schools, was cultivated as an art. "What did you do last evening?" or "What did you see on your way to school this morning?" were questions being answered by children who previously had been mouthing words by rote, without understanding the ideas they represented. All writing was related to children's activities, experiences, and feelings. Spelling was taught through this meaningful kind of writing.

Parker was opposed to teaching geography via the disconnected morass of facts and statistics in geography textbooks. Instead, the children took field trips around Quincy and made mud models and sketches of the landscape. These methods were indeed revolutionary at a time when in most schools pupils were expected to remain in the same position throughout the day without turning their heads.

The novel approaches of the "Quincy system," as it came to be known, attracted national attention. Children were learning to read, write, spell, and think simultaneously and holistically. As Parker said, they were learning to "talk" with their pens, as they had learned to talk with their tongues—by using them.[15]

The reaction to these methods was mixed. There were those who called Parker a charlatan, as they would have called anyone who tried to teach children how to think before they had thoroughly memorized the implements (facts) for thinking. In the main, however, his methods were widely acclaimed in both the general press and professional literature. Typical was the statement of B. G. Northrup, secretary of the Connecticut State Board of Education: "In Quincy, the children write better *throughout all the schools of the town* than is the case in *all* the schools of any other town within my knowledge in our country."[16]

A London journal, however, was unimpressed, finding the developments in Quincy to be nothing more than Froebel's theories put into action.[17] A comment frequently heard in educational circles was that Parker's ideas were not original. This was true; they had been tried in various places in this country and abroad, and Parker was the first to say so. But he had brought them together as a set of ideas and given them flesh and blood in one New England town. Moreover, Parker was the first to attempt to systematize and adopt the "new education" on a district-wide basis.

Parker viewed the developments in Quincy more as a "spirit of study," a *search* for the natural methods of teaching, than as a system or a method. Quincy was an educational breakthrough, Parker said, because of its rejection of traditional education and its penetration into the "very thick crust of conservatism and conceit."[18]

Parker's Ideas Today

Parker's work in Quincy opened the way for classroom learning environments in which children's uses of reading and writing are inseparable. By the 1960s, most elementary teachers had abandoned the old traditional credo that reading and writing must be taught separately. Language experience approaches where children learned to read from the stories that they dictated about their experiences (oral language transposed to experience charts) were often the main part of reading instruction.

Even so, the traditional fractured curriculum was a stubborn foe. In the 1970s and 1980s legislative mandates seriously undermined both functional learning and curriculum synthesis. Policymakers became enamored of minimum competency testing as a means of supervising instruction from afar (as from some state capital). As Jensen and Roser observed, reading and writing were reduced "to collections of separate skills that, even when mastered, do not add up to literacy."[19] Who could have believed that one hundred years after Parker's work in Quincy, reading would revert once again to a mindless activity—in this case, blank-filling on worksheets?

Then in the 1990s, Parker's principle was literally reinvented. "Learning to read and write are interrelated processes that develop in concert with oral language," wrote one reading expert.[20] The whole language approach of the late 1980s and 1990s was markedly similar to the language experience approach of the 1960s. Nevertheless, there were differences. In comparing them, Stahl and Miller noted, for example, that whole language approaches place more emphasis on children's own writing rather than on children's dictation.[21] They point out that the objective of both approaches is "natural" learning. Parker would have applauded the use of the word.

The importance of Parker's idea where we are concerned is this: Once it entered the literature, it never left. Many theorists continued to emphasize that the "art of language" is a unity, created out of our own lives and the lives of others in our experience.

THE REPORT OF THE COMMITTEE OF TEN

The high school has always been close to the hearts of Americans, for from its birth it reflected the new age of equal opportunity. It was open to all of the children of all of the people and it would provide all of the advantages of the academy for progressing up the socioeconomic ladder. One point is of central importance in our discussion of the report of the Committee of Ten (1893) of the National Education Association (NEA). When the high school idea was born in the 1820s, it was not intended to be a college preparatory institution. The Boston School Committee had been pressured by the public to establish a school that would "furnish the young men who are not intended for a collegiate course of studies, and who have enjoyed the usual advantages of the public schools, with the means of completing a good English education, and of fitting themselves for all the departments of commercial life."[22]

The school for young men opened in 1821, and a high school for girls five years later. But secondary education was not completely democratic until it took on the college preparatory function of the academy as well as preparing terminal students. The high school chose very early to take on both functions. This almost could have been predicted, particularly in frontier states such as Ohio and Indiana, where people were just too egalitarian to like the idea of a dual school system and where elementary and secondary education were distinguished from one another on the basis of social status.

But egalitarianism was also evident in the state of Massachusetts, which in 1827 passed the first general legislation under which high schools could be established. People liked the high school because it offered a curriculum for "life"; that is, it provided students with the foundation for careers in commercial and mechanical fields and education beyond the 3 R's to meet people's thirst for learning. The first high school in Boston, for example, included work in geometry, trigonometry, philosophy, and history, in addition to surveying, bookkeeping, and navigation. Because there was usually only one high school in most towns and because it was felt to be more democratic, the American high school also took on the college preparatory function.

The Secondary Curriculum in Conflict

As the nineteenth century progressed, the college preparatory function took on increasing importance. The variety of purposes that the high school tried to serve seemed inevitably to conflict. Some saw the high school as a college preparatory institution and others as a place where noncollege-bound students could prepare for life in the American community. When only a small percentage of the population even attended high school, these conflicts were not urgent. But when secondary education began to expand enormously in the last decades of the nineteenth century, these problems became pressing. Although some were demanding a more practical education, others were continuing to argue for mental discipline and a curriculum with heavy emphasis on the classics. What was happening is well expressed by Butts and Cremin: "The lines of battle were being formed that were to last for a hundred years to the present."[23]

THE PROBLEM OF ARTICULATION.   Efforts by colleges to spell out the secondary curriculum in detail have already been mentioned in Chapter 1. No doubt that high schools were uneven in the variety and quality of their courses, but the high school had not been originally intended to be a college preparatory institution. Nevertheless, the growing interest in high schools focused on the articulation of high school and college. From 1870 until the report of the Committee of Ten in 1893, this issue overshadowed other problems of secondary education. According to Wesley, the college-preparatory function of the high school "gained almost a monopoly of the thought and attention devoted to high schools" at conventions of the National Education Association during this period.[24] From 1888 to 1890, only 14.4 percent of those enrolled in high school were preparing for college.[25] Thus the curriculum for more than 85 percent of the students was being ignored in favor of discussing the program for less than 15 percent.

PRESIDENT ELIOT'S CONCERN.   The appointment of the Committee of Ten probably began with the concerns of President Charles W. Eliot of Harvard, a powerful figure in the NEA. Eliot was concerned about the rising age of entering freshman at Harvard, a problem also being experienced by other American colleges. As he saw it, the problem lay in both the organization and the curricula of elementary and secondary education.

The ten-year elementary curriculum was long and narrow and was followed by an enormously crowded secondary program, usually of four years. In 1888, Eliot gave a speech entitled "Can School Programs Be Shortened and Enriched?" before the NEA's Department of Superintendence.[26] Eliot, who had an extensive acquaintance with the curriculum problems of the schools, believed that the answer to the question was yes.

Eliot was especially concerned with arithmetic, particularly the undue amount of time devoted to reviews in the upper elementary grades. He proposed that the number of grades in the elementary school be reduced from ten to eight. He suggested that the program in arithmetic, which was taking up to one sixth of the school time for ten years, be contracted to six years, thus making room for algebra and geometry in the seventh and eighth grades. He held that the amount of time devoted to the study of grammar was too long and should be limited by culling out the memorization of rules and precepts and, instead, teaching the use of English through practice. Eliot suggested that beginning in the primary grades children be taught natural science by means of demonstrations and laboratory experiences rather than only from books. Elementary physics, also taught by laboratory methods, would be introduced in the upper-elementary grades.

Eliot argued that the idea that democratic theory implied an identical curriculum for every child and uniform tests for promotion was "fallacious and ruinous. Democratic theory," he said,

> does not undertake to fly in the face of nature by asserting that all children . . . are alike and should be treated alike. Everybody knows that children are infinitely diverse. . . . Every child is a unique personality. . . . Hence, in the public schools of a democracy the aim should be to give the utmost possible amount of individual instruction, to grade according to capacity . . . and to promote not by battalions, but in the most irregular way possible.[27]

Eliot's speech stimulated much discussion over the next few years and calls for education reform. The result was the appointment by the NEA of three committees:

the Committee of Ten on Secondary School Studies, the Committee of Fifteen on Elementary Education, and the Committee on College Entrance Requirements. Of these, the Committee of Ten was the most influential.

COMPOSITION OF THE COMMITTEE OF TEN.   College professors predominated the composition of the committees; indeed, the Committee of Ten included five college presidents. It is obvious from the major recommendations of the committee that the report was dominated by the more conservative beliefs and ideas of the colleges and universities of the 1890s. For example, the report reflected a belief in the value of the classical subjects for mental training.

Determining the Course of Secondary Education

The report of the Committee of Ten was enormously influential on the secondary curriculum for a generation after its publication in 1893. Interestingly, one of the ways in which it was influential concerns the rise of national committees for guidance on curriculum problems. The procedure has continued to operate to this day. Since the Committee of Ten, the recommendations of groups of eminent persons have influenced educational policy. The 1980s and 1990s witnessed a veritable foray of such reports on educational reform. The most notorious of these documents, *A Nation at Risk,* was issued in 1983 by the National Commission on Excellence in Education, appointed by the U.S. Secretary of Education.[28]

The procedure usually operates in this fashion: National task forces or committees are appointed and meet to deliberate on the problems assigned to them, for example, the decline of U.S. preeminence in global industrial markets. Following the discussions, one or two committee members write up the agreements, and the report is circulated among the other committee members for their verification. By the time the recommendations are implemented, the group of experts has scattered to the four winds. Eminent persons who decide what to include or remove from the curriculum are seldom around to take responsibility for the outcomes.[29]

A PARADOXICAL REPORT.   The report of the Committee of Ten cast the mold for secondary education for years to come, but the report itself was strikingly paradoxical. Two paradoxes are particularly noteworthy. The report states without equivocation that "secondary schools do not exist for the purpose of preparing boys and girls for colleges."[30] Yet despite this recognition, the report proceeds to recommend curricular offerings geared almost entirely toward college preparation. The second paradox concerned whether subjects should be taught differently to students going to college. The committee decided that every subject should be taught in the same way and in the same depth to every student, no matter what the student's probable destination, and despite the fact that the high school was a terminal educational institution for the overwhelming proportion of the students.

What actually was behind this recommendation? Was it the spirit of democracy or a conservative spirit? Did the Committee sincerely believe that the traditional college preparatory subjects were best for those who sought from the high school some kind of vocational preparation? These questions have been endlessly debated by students of curriculum. We know that some of the people on the committee believed that study of the classics (such as Latin) developed mental power and was therefore eminently practical. The committee based its curriculum recommendations on the doctrine of mental discipline. Concluding its recommendations on the regrouping of subjects, the report contended: "[E]very youth who entered college would have spent four years in studying a few subjects thoroughly; and, on the theory that all the subjects are to be considered equivalent in educational rank for the purposes of admission to college, it would make no difference which subjects he had chosen from the programme—he would have had four years of strong and effective mental training."[31]

Students could elect a curriculum from one of four programs: Classical, Latin Scientific, Modern Languages, or English. (See Figure 2–1.) Election from a variety of subjects, however, was not recognized.

Following the recommendations of the Committee of Ten led to problems. According to Brubacher, "Insistence on this kind of curriculum resulted in a high dropout rate among high school students."[32] In some sense, at least, the report was unremittingly conservative. Although it was a response to calls for reform, it both reaffirmed and restored the traditional doctrine of mental discipline. Similarly, ninety years later, the writers of *A Nation at Risk* harkened back to the alleged benefits of a failed curriculum of university-based academic disciplines that had been implemented in the schools during the years of the Cold War and space race. "The writers of *A Nation at Risk* are, one feels, not far removed in spirit from the members of the Committee of Ten," noted one observer.[33]

Yet for all of its conservative recommendations, the report of the Committee of Ten was devoted to the concept of a common curriculum for all youth. When the report was attacked for this stand, Eliot defended the committee's position, arguing that the European system of classifying children into "future peasants, mechanics, trades-people, merchants, and professional people" was unacceptable in a democratic society.[34]

The affirmation of this principle by a group of experts was of critical importance for high school students in a democracy. This college-professor–dominated group might well have arrived at a very different conclusion—such as calling for separate academic high schools for the college bound and vocational schools for the others.

Actually, as Brubacher pointed out, the Committee of Ten "looked forward to the day when colleges would be accessible to all secondary school students who had creditably accomplished their work no matter what group of subjects they had studied."[35] Certainly the committee tried to equate the value of subjects. The report stated that "all the subjects between which choice is allowed should be approximately equivalent to each other in seriousness, dignity, and efficacy."[36] This included science. As Cremin commented, Spencer's unqualified endorsement of science as the most important learning "was obviously influential in the formulations of the NEA's Committee of Ten (1893), which gave parity to the sciences in the secondary school program."[37]

Figure 2–1. Range of Curricular Offerings (High School) as Proposed by the Committee of Ten on Secondary School Studies, 1893.

1st Secondary School Year	2nd Secondary School Year

Latin ·················· 5 p.
English Literature, 2 p.⎫
English Composition, 2 p.⎬ ·········· 4 p.
German [or French] ·········· 5 p.
Algebra ·················· 4 p.
History of Italy, Spain, and France ·· 3 p.
Applied Geography (European
  political—continental and
  oceanic flora and fauna) ·········· 4 p.
 	
  25 p.
	Latin ·················· 4 p.
	Greek ·················· 5 p.
	English Literature, 2 p.⎫
	English Composition, 2 p.⎬ ·········· 4 p.
	German, continued ·········· 4 p.
	French, begun ·········· 5 p.
	Algebra,* 2 p.⎫
	Geometry, 2 p.⎬ ·········· 4 p.
	Botany or Zoology ·········· 4 p.
	English History to 1688 ·········· 3 p.
	
	  33 p.
	
	*Option of bookkeeping and commercial
	  arithmetic.

3rd Secondary School Year	**4th Secondary School Year**

Latin ·················· 4 p.
Greek ·················· 4 p.
English Literature, 2 p.⎫
English Composition, 1 p.⎬ ·········· 4 p.
Rhetoric, 1 p.⎭
German ·················· 4 p.
French ·················· 4 p.
Algebra,* 2 p.⎫
Geometry, 2 p.⎬ ·········· 4 p.
Physics ·················· 4 p.
History, English and American ·········· 3 p.
Astronomy, 3 p. 1st 1/2 yr.⎫
Meterology, 3 p. 2nd 1/2 yr.⎬ ·········· 3 p.
  34 p.
 	
*Option of bookkeeping and commercial
  arithmetic.
	Latin ·················· 4 p.
	Greek ·················· 4 p.
	English Literature, 2 p.⎫
	English Composition, 1 p.⎬ ·········· 4 p.
	English Grammar, 1 p.⎭
	German ·················· 4 p.
	French ·················· 4 p.
	Trigonometry,⎫
	Higher Algebra,⎬ ·········· 2 p.
	Chemistry ·················· 4 p.
	History, (intensive) and Civil
	  Government ·········· 3 p.
	Geology or Physiography,⎫
	  4 p. 1st 1/2 yr.
	Anatomy, Physiology, and⎬ ·········· 4 p.
	  Hygiene, 4 p. 2nd 1/2 yr.⎭
	  33 p.

Source: Committee of Ten. *Report of the Committee of Ten on Secondary School Studies* (Washington, DC: National Education Association, 1893), p. 4.

The Legacy of the Committee of Ten

The committee's hope that the high school curriculum ought to permit any student to go to college came to be increasingly realized through the course of the twentieth century. The tendency in a growing number of states was to provide the opportunity for all high school graduates to attend college, even those who did not follow a pre-scribed college preparatory course. Access to higher education also increased for students with a graduate equivalency diploma (GED), and for those without a diploma who had reached the age of eighteen. In California, for example, every eighteen-year-old is guaranteed admission to a state-supported community college.

Unfortunately, however, the national emphasis has been on open-access higher education rather than on a modern reconstruction of the secondary school curriculum.

As the nineteenth century came to a close, the college was also experiencing a remarkable development. Its curriculum was being adapted more and more to preparation for various vocations along with the traditional classical courses. In 1904 Dewey observed that "things seem to be taking their own course" where the question of preparation for college versus preparation for community life was concerned. He wrote prophetically that when

> the high school has worked out on its own account the broadening of its own curriculum, I believe we shall find that the high school and the college have arrived at a common point. The college course will be so broad and varied that it will be entirely feasible to take any judicious group of studies from any well organized and well managed high school, and accept them as preparation for college. It has been the narrowness of the traditional college curriculum on the one side and the inadequacy of the content of high school work on the other, which have caused a large part of our mutual embarrassments.[38]

THE PREDOMINANT FUNCTION. Generally speaking, Dewey's prophecy has arrived. The college curriculum has undergone a vast revolution. Indeed, colleges and universities today are vocational institutions. Adolescents, even late bloomers, can go to college and study from among a very wide range of offerings. What Dewey could not foresee a mere decade after the report of the Committee of Ten was that the report would reinforce the trend toward college domination of the high school curriculum. Thus the high school, which was not originally intended to become a college preparatory institution, was transformed into one—at least in the eyes of the committee and many school faculties. It became increasingly difficult for the high school to work out effective programs for noncollege preparatory students. The report of the Committee of Ten was a turning point: reactionary in some ways, progressive in others.

THE REPORT OF THE COMMITTEE OF FIFTEEN

Agitators for educational reform do not always achieve what they hope for once they have set the reform machinery in motion. In fact, the final result may well be the opposite of what they had hoped for. A case in point was the report of the Committee of Fifteen. As noted, Eliot was opposed to dealing with children en masse and promoting them in flocks. He also favored the teaching of science by means of laboratory experiences instead of merely from books. Eliot knew full well that science is far more than a body of knowledge. It is also a way of thinking. It asks us to allow the facts in even when they may not conform to preconceptions. It advises us to formulate alternative hypotheses and see which are best supported by the evidence. Eliot knew that this kind of thinking is a necessary tool for a democracy.

However, the Committee of Fifteen (1895) protested strongly against the scientific method in elementary science teaching.

> It is important not to hasten the use of a strictly scientific method on the part of the child. . . . He is rather in the imitation stage of mind than in that of criticism. He will not reach the comparative or critical method until the era of higher education.[39]

In light of this conclusion, one hour of "oral lessons" in natural science (which included hygiene) was recommended.

The committee's approach to the development of the child was mechanical. School work was distributed into eight separate years, each with its own definite subjects to be covered. The committee was cool to the concept of curriculum synthesis. "Rigid isolation of the elements of each branch" was considered essential in elementary learning.[40] The committee's outlook almost compelled the teacher of a given grade to take an isolated view of her work rather than being guided by the ideal of the child's whole development. The number of children in a room, which in the graded schools of the time often ran as high as sixty, was an added condition that, in Dewey's words, "compel them to be led in flocks, if not in hordes."[41]

Class size was not dealt with by the Committee of Fifteen. But as every teacher knows, the curriculum is profoundly influenced by school conditions. Large classes make it less likely for teachers to plan lessons that stress individual inquiry and judgment and provide for the individual child's needs. As it happened, the committee emphasized a curriculum broken up into isolated parts that did not require individual inquiry. Had the committee included observation and experimentation in science instruction and treating each child as unique, there would have been conflict with at least two existing conditions: a large number of children in a room that limited the contact of teacher with child, and of child with child, and the teacher's outlook, which was confined to one year of the child's development. But the committee's report merely reinforced existing conditions.

Solidifying the Status Quo

Eliot had proposed that the number of elementary grades be reduced from ten to eight. This recommendation was endorsed in the report of the Committee of Fifteen, as was his plan to substitute the study of algebra for arithmetic in the seventh and eighth grade. (See Figure 2–2.) At the outset of the report the committee stated that grammar, literature, arithmetic, geography, and history are the subjects in the elementary school with the greatest value for training the mind. This was the philosophy of William T. Harris, who authored most of the report and was the most well-known educational philosopher of the time.[42] Throughout the report, the committee held the line against the newer subjects, allotting them relatively little time in the school program.

There were some vigorous expressions of dissent by committee members on such points as "oral lessons" in science (telling by the teacher) and the failure to include observation and experimentation in science instruction. But Harris and

Figure 2–2. The Elementary School Curriculum as Proposed by the Committee of Fifteen, 1895.

Branches	1st year	2nd year	3rd year	4th year	5th year	6th year	7th year	8th year
Reading	10 lessons a week	5 lessons a week						
Writing	10 lessons a week	5 lessons a week	3 lessons a week					
Spelling lists			4 lessons a week					
English Grammar	Oral, with composition lessons					5 lessons a week with text-book		
Latin								5 lessons
Arithmetic	Oral, sixty minutes a week		5 lessons a week with text-book					
Algebra							5 lessons a week	
Geography	Oral, sixty minutes a week			*5 lessons a week with text-book			3 lessons a week	
National Science and Hygiene	Sixty minutes a week							
U.S. History							5 lessons a week	
U.S. Constitution								*5 les.
General History	Oral, 60 minutes a week							
Physical Culture	Sixty minutes a week							
Vocal Music	Sixty minutes a week divided into 4 lessons							
Drawing	Sixty minutes a week							
Manual Train, or Sewing and Cookery							One-half day each	
No. of Lessons	20 + 7 daily exer.	20 + 7 daily exer.	20 + 5 daily exer.	24 + 7 daily exer.	27 + 5 daily exer.	27 + 5 daily exer.	23 + 6 daily exer.	23 + 6 daily exer.
Total Hours of Recitations	12	12	11	13	16¼	16¼	17½	17½
Length of Recitations	15 min.	15 min.	20 min.	20 min.	25 min.	25 min.	30 min.	30 min.

*Begins in second half year.

Source: Committee of Fifteen. "Report of the Sub-Committee on the Correlation of Studies in Elementary Education." *Educational Review,* 9 (March 1895), p. 284.

other conservatives won out, despite the mounting evidence on the need for hands-on experience in children's mental and social development.

The Final Result

In the paper he presented at the 1893 NEA meeting, Eliot had suggested a reduction in the time devoted to grammar and arithmetic so that the elementary-school program could be diversified and enriched. But the end result of the committee's deliberations was to give these subjects even higher priority than they had before. Indeed, grammar now topped what had become the official list of the common branches. It may be said that the effect of the report of the Committee of Fifteen on the elementary curriculum was to further entrench and intensify the problems that Eliot had sought to solve.

On the matter of curriculum synthesis, the report of the Committee of Fifteen was a turning point for the worse. The problem of curriculum segmentation and isolation continues to this day.

DEWEY'S LABORATORY SCHOOL AT CHICAGO

On the occasion of Dewey's ninetieth birthday, the British Ambassador to the United States wrote:

> For fifty years Dr. Dewey has urged us to relate the school to life and above all to the life of the child. Wherever British children today are active, purposeful, and happy in school there is little doubt that they owe something to the active, purposeful, and long life of a great American philosopher.[43]

The tribute was one of many from leaders in education, government, and the arts from all over the world. In *The New Leader* magazine, which had run many of Dewey's articles, Dewey was honored for his contributions to the fields of education, psychology, ethics, art, and political science. Although Dewey wrote on a range of problems, it was education that had, as *The New Leader* noted, virtually been revolutionized by his ideas. And not only in the United States, but abroad as well.[44]

If that revolution had a beginning, it was surely in the experimental school founded by Dewey at the University of Chicago in 1896. Like any laboratory, the purpose of the school was to test theoretical ideas and advance the body of knowledge in a field—in this case, education. The ideas to be tested were Dewey's philosophical and psychological principles, or as Dewey put it, his "philosophical interpretation of psychology."[45] Dewey believed that thinking (and knowledge) developed as children attempted to solve problems that originated in active situations. For Dewey, this (or any) theoretical principle is of little value unless tested.

The Curriculum Problem—What Dewey Hoped to Discover

With regard to the curriculum, Dewey and the teachers in the Laboratory School hoped to identify the direct, present experiences of children from which more organized and technical knowledge would grow as the children progressed through school.[46]

The solution of this curriculum problem was, in Dewey's words, "extremely difficult," and he wrote many years later that "we did not reach it; it has not yet been reached and in its fullness will never be reached."[47]

But the problem was posed and that in itself was a lasting contribution. And the records, notes, and plans of the school indicate that Dewey and the Laboratory School teachers probably went a greater distance toward its solution than Dewey recognized.[48] Indeed, Dewey's comments may have been intended to indicate that the development of knowledge is never ending. In a sense the journey of education should make for turning points in the lives of learners, rather than mere endpoints.

DIFFERENCES WITH HARRIS. The Laboratory School was founded a year after the Report of the Committee of Fifteen and was a striking study in contrast. For Harris, the conservative leader in education who authored the report, a school subject is an entity unto itself, external to the pupil and mastered through effort rather than interest. It was up to the teacher to take the systematic knowledge of adult consciousness, which had been hammered out through centuries, and do the best he or she could with it. The child must enter on the "fruits of civilization" in their mature form.[49] Dewey took issue with this view. As he pointed out in an article entitled "The Psychological Aspect of the School Curriculum" (1897), a school subject is both a logical whole (a system of facts and principles), and a form of living personal experience.

"Geography," said Dewey, "is not only a set of facts and principles, which may be classified and discussed by themselves; it is also a way in which some individual feels and thinks the world. It must be the latter before it can be the former."[50]

Dewey was to elaborate on this principle a few years later in *The Child and the Curriculum* (1902).

In his article published in 1897, Dewey went on to state that

> [w]ith the child, instruction must take the standpoint not of accomplished results, but of the crude beginnings. We must discover what there is lying within the child's present sphere of experience (or within the scope of experiences which he can easily get) which deserves to be called geographical. It is not a question of *how* to teach the child geography, but first of all the question of *what* geography is for the child.[51]

Dewey then emphasized his substantial disagreement "with the view taken by Dr. Harris in the Report of the Committee of Fifteen regarding the comparative worthlessness of the psychological basis."[52] Dewey argued that "the primary point of concern in education is beyond question with the subject as a special mode of personal experience, rather than with the subject as a body of wrought-out facts and scientifically tested principles."[53]

Harris's view of instruction was the opposite, and it had become educational policy through the report of the Committee of Fifteen. Dewey found this view dangerously deficient. "The crying evil in instruction today," he wrote, "is that the subject-matter of the curriculum, both as a whole and in its various stages, is selected and determined on the objective or logical basis instead of upon the psychological.[54]

SUBJECT MATTER AS EXPERIENCE.   At the heart of Dewey's approach to curriculum development was his theory of knowledge. Learning and education are social in nature because there is always human interaction involved—the influence of some people on others. The sets of facts, concepts, and generalizations that we label geography, mathematics, science, and so on are nothing more or less than selections from past social life and "represent the answers found for social needs."[55]

It is all too easy to regard these sets of facts, concepts, and generalizations as external to the learner, to be mastered by encouragement and devices by the teacher. But Dewey believed that the maximum benefit for the child was when systematic knowledge grows out of the experiences and interests that he or she already has. The instructional problem is how to bring about this growth. The first thing to be determined is the kind of experience appropriate for the child at a given time— what kind of experiences get a hold on the youngster, what he is capable of doing and can do to the greatest advantage and with the least waste of time. These interests and experiences offer a key to the selection of subject matter.

SUBJECT MATTER AS PURPOSE.   What a ridiculous thing to insist that there is a fixed body of knowledge that is forever set off and labeled physics, geography, or history, said Dewey. "Exactly the same objective reality will be one or the other or none of these three, according to the interest and intellectual standpoint from which it is viewed."[56] For example, a square mile of territory, when viewed from one interest, would be labeled trigonometry, from another standpoint we would label the facts regarding it geography, and from still another interest, it would become historical knowledge. "There is absolutely nothing in the fact, as an objective fact, which places it under one head," pointed out Dewey. "Only as we ask what purpose or end some individual has in view do we find a basis for selecting and arranging the facts under the label of any particular study."[57]

Dewey and the Laboratory School teachers hoped to determine how, out of the child's interest and purpose, a subject as a form of experience gradually differentiated itself from other experiences and developed into the systematic knowledge of the adult.

The Three-Dimensional Curriculum

The curriculum in the school conducted by Dewey had three dimensions: the child's side (activities), the teacher's side (logically organized bodies of subject matter: chemistry, physics, biology, mathematics, history, language, literature, music, and physical culture), and the side of democratic social life and purpose.

REASONS FOR ACTIVITIES.   Behind the activities was Dewey's conception of the psychological nature of the child. Dewey argued that children are inherently active with strong impulses to investigate, to share with others what they have found out, to construct practical things, and to create. Dewey developed this psychological concept into a curriculum principle: The child's impulses are an enormously important educational resource, and opportunities should be provided to children to develop them through engagement in activities.

Dewey also saw activities as a means of achieving curriculum synthesis. A constructive activity (cooking, carpentry, or sewing) provides the opportunity for learning about materials and processes. "Animal, vegetable life, soil, climate, etc. are studied not as mere *objects* (a psychological unreality) but as factors in action," wrote Dewey in his plan for the school.[58]

The activities, then, had three important functions:

1. They led to the sets of useful facts and principles known as science, history, literature—bodies of systematized knowledge.
2. They were the means of curriculum synthesis and revealing the social significance of knowledge.
3. They were means of utilizing and developing the child's inherent impulses so as to enhance the growth of the child.

INTERRELATING THE DIMENSIONS. The development of the curriculum depended on teachers keeping the dimensions clearly in mind. In order to do this, they organized their plans by subheadings, "From the Child's Standpoint" and "From the Teacher's Standpoint." The teachers' plans were published every Friday in the *University [of Chicago] Record*. In reading the plans, one notes that the teacher's standpoint is first. Ideas and concepts are classified by subject, followed by the child's standpoint—the activities in which children engage in learning the concepts and how social life developed.

What is of importance is that teachers began with the subject field and planned the activities that called for progressively more complex understandings. They did *not* begin with the activities and try to extrapolate ideas from the subject field.

GENERALISTS AND SPECIALISTS. So weighty was the intellectual load on the teacher that Dewey dropped the idea of having one teacher teach the children in all studies. Instead the school assumed a recognized role for teacher specialists as well as generalists. Dewey's reason is worth quoting:

> One of the reasons for this modification of the original plan was the difficulty of getting scientific facts presented that were facts and truths. It has been assumed that any phenomenon that interested a child was good enough, and that if he were aroused and made alert that was all that could be expected. It is, however, just as necessary that what he gets should be truth and should not be subordinated to anything else. . . . The difficulty of getting scientific work presented except by those who were specialists has led to the change in regard to other subjects as well.[59]

Although one person was responsible for coordinating each child's program, the children learned to take their questions to the teachers who were specialists in whatever area a problem belonged.

CURRICULUM COHERENCE. Dewey found that specialization need not lead to compartmentalization. "The undue separation which often follows teaching by specialists," he wrote, "is not inherent in the method, but is the result of lack of supervision, cooperation and control by a unified plan."[60] The Laboratory School had such a plan: a civilizational theme. Beginning with activities familiar to four- and five-year-olds because they were activities of the home, the developing curriculum led to the study of related occupations in early civilization. Following the way of social evolution, it traced human progress through discovery and invention to the occupations and organization of contemporary society.

The study of occupations provided opportunities for and required the child's increasing ability to abstract, that is, to bring out a special idea. For instance, farming as studied by six-year-olds simply showed what some people do and how they serve others. Seven-year-olds reviewed this material, but the emphasis was on the evolving needs in human history that required this occupation and the way it has affected present social life.

Dewey and his Laboratory School faculty, and members of the university faculty in pedagogy, chose occupations as an organizing theme, although there are other possible organizing themes, noted Dewey. What is of critical importance, Dewey found, is that teachers confer constantly to achieve a coherent curriculum. The Laboratory School appears to have pioneered in collaborative decision making and teacher reflection. Dewey recounted that "fellows and members of the faculty of the pedagogical department, graduate-student assistants, and the regular teaching staff of the school all met weekly with the directors to discuss the reports of the school in relation to theoretical principles and to revise future plans accordingly."[61]

The Laboratory School experimented with and discarded many different activities in subject matter fields, which was its purpose. The teachers' work proceeded in accord with a clearly defined framework—the occupations that make for society, and Dewey's concept of progression from activities to formal studies. As Wirth points out in his discussion of the Laboratory School, there was a well-considered curriculum design.[62]

One can see readily from the records of the Laboratory School, the photographs of student activities, and the examples of student work that remain, that the curriculum was based on psychological knowledge about children and on logically organized and useful facts, concepts, ideas, and generalizations and principles from the major fields of knowledge. It appears to have been a curriculum of high quality in which the youngsters engaged in knowledge applications on a daily basis.

The Dewey School, as it became known, served to introduce educators and parents to the possibilities of what a curriculum can be. As Dewey reminds us, the three-dimensional curriculum is always in the making, it is never made.[63]

ACCREDITATION OF SECONDARY SCHOOLS

In the years following the Civil War, school and college people became increasingly concerned with a fundamental question: What are the best criteria for determining admission to college? The concern stemmed from a chaotic situation. Procedures were inadequately defined and carelessly applied. Sometimes they depended on the relationship between a certain college and a certain teacher. The variety of acceptable high school programs and the diversity of college entrance requirements led educators to become interested in the problem of high school accreditation for college admissions. Setting up an accreditation plan called for common action that would be beneficial to both schools and colleges, not to mention students. The effort to formalize the cooperation and establish it on a permanent basis led to the establishment of regional accrediting associations before the turn of the century. These have been of enduring value.

Standards and Accreditation

Accreditation began in the American west, where the state university was considered part (the third level) of the public school system. And so it was that in 1869–1870, the University of Michigan admitted graduates from selected high schools without examination, on the principal's recommendation and on the submission of a certificate of courses and grades. Committees of university faculty visited the schools to evaluate them and, thus, determine whether their graduates would be eligible for acceptance into the university.

What did the school visitors look at? The visiting committees emphasized such criteria as the number of qualified faculty, the size of classes, and the facilities and resources in judging the academic fitness of the high schools. But of particular importance here is that they also evaluated the curriculum. For example, Krug tells of a report on a rejected high school that recommended changes in the course of study and textbooks.[64] However, for the most part, the procedure served to impel the colleges to eliminate their highly specified and widely differing entrance requirements and examinations.

In examining the reports, Krug found frequent criticisms of the attitudes of school boards. Some school people "appreciated this as a help in getting what they wanted." As one superintendent told Michigan's president, James B. Angell, the accreditation system "had strengthened the high schools of the state by providing support against lukewarm board members."[65] The accreditation system also served to work against the not uncommon practice of faculty and administrative appointment by political influence.

Other state universities established similar admissions policies. The University of Indiana's accrediting plan, adopted in 1873, provided for accreditation of high schools by the state board of education. The practice was well regarded and was soon found in other parts of the country.

REGIONAL ASSOCIATIONS OF COLLEGES AND SECONDARY SCHOOLS. Bringing the state systems together on a regional and permanent basis was the next logical step. In 1895, the North Central Association of Colleges and Secondary Schools was established. In 1902, this association worked out standards to be applied in judging the fitness of secondary schools for accreditation. Using the term *unit* to represent a year of secondary-school study in a subject, the North Central Association defined acceptable high schools as those requiring fifteen units for graduation. Detailed requirements were specified for subjects that were acceptable to colleges in terms of entrance units.

In addition to the North Central Association, five other regional associations were formed. In order of their founding, they are: The New England Association (1885), the Middle States Association (1887), the Southern Association (1895), the Northwest Association (1917), and the Western Association (1924).

THE COLLEGE ENTRANCE EXAMINATION BOARD.   In 1900 another institution of continuing influence came into being. The College Entrance Examination Board was founded for the purpose of constructing and administering examinations for high school students applying for admission to college. Once again, the purpose was standardization and the solution of a very practical problem: Teachers and principals no longer had to prepare different students "going to different colleges in different amounts and different books of Latin, Greek and other subjects."[66] This had not been as much of a problem when only a tiny proportion of the age group attended college.

The College Entrance Examination Board was an East Coast invention. The founding college members were Barnard, Bryn Mawr, Columbia, Cornell, Johns Hopkins, New York University, Rutgers, Swarthmore, Union, Pennsylvania, and Vassar. (Harvard joined later.) One reason for the board's founding was that as public high schools grew in number, the link between high school preparation and college requirements lessened. Students far from the East Coast could not sit for the college's own examinations, and admissions officers lacked enough information to evaluate unknown applicants from unknown schools. The member Eastern colleges allowed applicants to take the College Board examinations in place of their own examinations. Most colleges continued to rely on high school accreditation in admitting applicants.

The time came, however, when the number of qualified high school graduates increased to the point where colleges had more qualified applicants than they could admit. The Scholastic Aptitude Test, intended to provide colleges with a way to evaluate an applicant's ability to learn, was administered by the College Board beginning in 1926 with a limited population. Renamed the Scholastic Assessment Test in 1993 in belated but masked recognition of the limited validity of the test as a measure of aptitude, the SAT has grown enormously over the years and has come to garner great media attention, especially when declining scores can be cited.

From Regulation to Service

The creation of the College Entrance Examination Board allowed the newly established regional accrediting associations to work toward the improvement of secondary schools generally, rather than focusing mainly on standards thought to be most applicable for college preparation. But for many years the accreditation standards tended to be defined along quantitative lines, having tenuous relationship to the actual quality of the school.

Then in 1932 the six regional associations embarked on an effort to form and test new criteria along such dimensions as the school's philosophy, student population, curriculum, community, faculty, guidance services, student activities program, instructional resources and facilities, and other educational factors. As a result of these efforts, principles were established in recognition that schools must, within broadly defined limits, vary their programs according to the particular needs of their own communities and student populations. Criteria were developed for identifying characteristics and functions of "good" secondary schools. These criteria were stated in manuals that have been continually revised over the years.[67]

Local school staffs are required to complete a comprehensive self-appraisal of the educational program, followed by an evaluation conducted by a visiting committee of educators from other schools and colleges. The local school then receives a report concerning its strengths and areas of needed improvement in connection with the accreditation status.

Of enormous importance here is the approach of the National Study of School Evaluation, which places emphasis on continuous growth and improvement rather than on the meeting of minimum quantitative standards. Self-appraisal, outside expert judgment, objective evidence, and practices in comparable schools with successful programs are identified as important aspects of accreditation.

Representatives of the six voluntary regional accrediting associations comprising the National Study of School Evaluation have attempted to influence a change "from maintaining minimum standards to the striving for excellence in all aspects of a school's work."[68] It has been an uphill battle. Today state mandates and nationalizing influences have weakened the effects of regional accrediting organizations. Since the report of the National Commission on Excellence in Education (1983), legislatures and state departments of education have taken a regulatory approach to improving the quality of schools. The number of academic courses required for graduation from high school have been increased; schools think that they have to have three years of this course and two of that. The regulatory changes have not dealt with fundamental school problems such as those concerning the quality of the curriculum, the availability of modern and rich learning resources and facilities, and teacher morale.

Since the end of World War II, colleges and universities have increasingly assumed the responsibility of remediation for poorly prepared students. Today, however, some colleges are attempting to shift remedial responsibilities to the high schools. Moreover, differences among high school curriculums have become a source of increasing frustration to university administrators, who believe that students would be better prepared if they all took the same courses. For example, in 1991, the City University of New York (CUNY) proposed that high school students be required to take a set of traditional academic courses geared to the Regents' examinations of the State of New York.[69]

This is a striking change in policy from the 1960s when the City University of New York sought to extend educational opportunities to the disadvantaged. In 1969, a CUNY administrator summed up the policy this way: "Standards ought to refer to what a university does for its students, rather than to their opening handicap."[70]

The Eight-Year Study, which was conducted in the 1930s, examined thirty schools and nearly 3,000 students enrolled in 300 colleges to determine the effect of traditional academic subject admission requirements on the success of college students. The study found that what was needed was a good high school with a well-integrated curriculum, and students would succeed in college.[71] The approach to accreditation of the National Study of School Evaluation is supported by this study. The Eight-Year Study is discussed in Chapter 3 and other sections of this text.

The diversity of American postsecondary education is enormous. Differences in mission among institutions of higher education mean that there is no single "best method" of admission, and that there is a college suited more or less for almost anyone who is motivated for further education.

PERSPECTIVE

The effects of the nineteenth century turning points for education are all around us. Blue-ribbon panels continue to ask Spencer's question: What knowledge is of most worth? (Spencer's answer was science.) School teachers and curriculum personnel need to learn to ask Spencer's question themselves. The question has no final answer. The curriculum is necessarily unfinished and unfinishable. Like education itself, curriculum development is a continuing journey for progressive improvement. Consensus should not be a curriculum committee's main concern; a sound basis for decisions should be the main concern.

Reading specialists and early childhood educators continue to rediscover (indeed, reinvent) Francis Parker's "Quincy system." Parker demonstrated in a public school system (Quincy, Massachusetts) before the turn of the twentieth century that children can have a more meaningful educational experience if reading, writing, and oral language are taught holistically. Indeed, an independent study by an inspector from the Massachusetts State Board of Education found that the children in Quincy excelled in reading, writing, and spelling. This is not to imply that Parker's principle was without opposition. There were always critics. In the 1970s and 1980s reading was once again reduced to an assortment of isolated skills as the result of the curriculum retrenchment of back to basics. Nevertheless, the idea that learning to read and write are interrelated processes was here to stay. Recently, Parker's method was reinvented under a new label: the whole language approach.

Parker's emphasis throughout the curriculum in Quincy (and later, at the Cook County Normal School in Chicago) was on observing, describing, and understanding phenomena appropriate to the child's experience. When these abilities had begun to develop, conventional school subjects were introduced. Little wonder that Dewey referred to Parker as "the father of progressive education." Dewey himself built on Parker's developmental concept in working out the curriculum in his own school.

To this day, educators continue to try to integrate the traditional subject curriculum. This curriculum became fully entrenched by the reports of the Committee of Ten on Secondary School Studies and the Committee of Fifteen on Elementary School Studies issued toward the close of the nineteenth century. The Committee of Ten was created in response to demands for uniform college entrance requirements. The high school was not originally intended to be a college preparatory institution. Although most students did not go to college, the larger effect of the committee's recommendations was to turn the high school into a college preparatory institution.

(This was not surprising because the committee included five college presidents.) The only subjects discussed by the committee were those required for college entrance. The subjects were to be taught the same way whether or not a student was college-bound.

At the close of the nineteenth century, the high school curriculum ignored the needs of adolescents. Many students dropped out, pointing to the need for a more useful curriculum. The report of the Committee of Ten was a big setback in this regard. Was the document simply an expression of conservative caution and self-interest? It is all too easy to dismiss it as such. But we know that the ideal of equality—of both status and opportunity—has shaped institutions including public schools. The idea of a dual educational system, such as that found in European countries, was repugnant to committee members, particularly Charles W. Eliot, president of Harvard University. The committee called for a common curriculum because they believed that all high school students should have an opportunity to go to college.

Yet the committee's report was based on the premise that there is only one right answer to the question of "most worth." There are many "most worths" depending on the needs of students and society. This fact has been clearly recognized by the regional accrediting associations that were established just before the turn of the century. In the 1930s, the six regional associations formed a national committee that established principles that recognized the need for schools to vary their programs according to the particular needs of their communities and student populations. The National Study of School Evaluation has continued to publish *Evaluative Criteria,* intended to serve the needs of various types of high schools and programs. In 1900 the College Entrance Examination Board was established, and it continues to be the leading agency in college admission testing and has served its purpose well. However, there is the continuing problem of the high school curriculum being driven by the external influences of the colleges and college admissions testing. It is a more direct shortcut to showing educational results, and much cheaper as well, to teach the test than to improve the school learning environment and the qualities of the learning experiences. This makes standardized testing very appealing to public officials, and fast results also make ready copy for the mass media. As a result, the testing industry has undergone enormous growth during the second half of the twentieth century.

The regional accrediting associations are institutions of great value in recognizing the need for appropriate resources and facilities to support a full and rich curriculum. The diversification of American life has served to promote the comprehensiveness of the curriculum in schools and colleges. What Dewey predicted has come to pass, despite the pressures for standardization and uniformity.

One of the great turning points for American education was the establishment of the Dewey school at the University of Chicago in 1896. It was demonstrated that the nature of the learner, the structure and function of knowledge, and the ideals of a free society can be wrought harmoniously in the life and program of the school. Dewey and the teachers attempted to build up the child's experience so that it would eventually grow to encompass systematized knowledge. Dewey found that curriculum coherence can be achieved by basing instructional strategies on an organizational framework.

The nineteenth century was a time of new beginnings in education, of great optimism for a better future. The idea of progress in education and society continued to prevail with the challenges of the twentieth century.

Problems for Study and Discussion

1. In discussing Ralph Tyler's basic work in curriculum development, John Goodlad notes: "The question of what knowledge is of most worth becomes an integral part of curriculum planning." [John I. Goodlad, *What Schools Are For* (Bloomington, IN: Phi Delta Kappa Educational Foundation, 1979), p. 43.] From your own experience, do teachers and administrators ask Spencer's question? Explain. Do you think that it is important for them to do so? Why or why not?

2. How would you answer Spencer's question today?

3. What illustrations can you give of Parker's reforms in the curriculum today?

4. According to two staff development specialists, "Busy people typically do not engage in reflection. They rarely treat themselves to reflective experiences, unless they are given some time, some structure, and the expectations to do so." [Joellen P. Killion and Guy R. Todnem, "A Process for Personal Theory Building," *Educational Leadership,* 48 (March 1991), p. 14.] Were these conditions for reflection all present in Dewey's Laboratory School? Explain.

5. Why was Dewey's three-dimensional curriculum a critical turning point in curriculum thought and educational improvement?

6. Dewey and the teachers in his school attempted to establish their school as a form of community life. They believed that schools could only prepare children for social living if the school was a small cooperative society. "The idea involved a radical departure from the notion that the school is just a place in which to learn lessons and acquire certain forms of skill," recounted Dewey years later. "It assimilated study and learning within the school to the education which takes place when out-of-school living goes on in a rich and significant social medium." [John Dewey, "The Chicago Experiment," in Katherine Camp Mayhew and Anna Camp Edwards, *The Dewey School* (New York: Appleton-Century, 1936), p. 466.] Do the curriculum and school organization today reflect the concept that the school is just a place to acquire skills or the school is a small cooperative community? Give examples.

7. Do you believe that Dewey's idea in question 6 was a positive contribution? Why or why not?

8. The *Evaluative Criteria* for secondary schools states the following expectations for faculty involvement in curriculum development:

   The faculty, under the leadership of the building administrator, is actively involved in curriculum development procedures; curriculum evaluation and revision procedures; the selection of instructional materials; and the resolution of curriculum/instruction-related problems. [National Study of School Evaluation, *Evaluative Criteria,* 6th ed. (National Study: Falls Church, VA: 1987), p. 59.]

   Evaluate your own school on the above expectations, indicating the extent to which each expectation is being met.

9. Do you believe that a high school subject should be taught the same way to all students whether or not they are college-bound?

10. What is your appraisal of the proposal of the Committee of Fifteen as a curriculum for today's schools?

11. Compare the Report of the Committee of Ten with a more recent report for educational reform in terms of (a) the problems addressed, (b) the evidence cited, and (c) the remedies proposed. In your opinion were these reports well grounded in their diagnoses and prescriptions? Explain.

NOTES

1. John Dewey, "Introduction," in Katherine Camp Mayhew and Anna Camp Edwards, *The Dewey School* (New York: D. Appleton-Century, 1936), p. xvi.

2. Herbert Spencer, "What Knowledge Is of Most Worth?" Chapter 1 in *Education* (New York: Appleton, 1860), pp. 21–97.

3. Ibid., p. 32.

4. Cited in Lawrence A. Cremin, *The Transformation of the School* (New York: Knopf, 1961), p. 91.

5. Ralph W. Tyler, *Basic Principles of Curriculum and Instruction* (Chicago: University of Chicago, 1949).

6. Ibid., p. 4.

7. Albert I. Oliver, *Curriculum Improvement: A Guide to Problems, Principles and Procedures* (New York: Dodd, Mead, 1969), p. 250.

8. Daniel Tanner, "Are Reforms Like Swinging Pendulums?" Chapter 2 in Herbert J. Walberg and James W. Keefe (eds.), *Rethinking Reform* (Reston, VA: National Association of Secondary School Principals, 1986).

9. Richard W. Clark, "Who Decides? The Basic Policy Issue," Chapter 8 in *Critical Issues in Curriculum,* Eighty-seventh Yearbook, Part I, National Society for the Study of Education (Chicago: University of Chicago Press, 1988), pp. 191–192.

10. Ibid., p. 193.

11. Karl Frey, *Curriculum Conference: An Approach for Curriculum Development in Groups* (Kiel, Germany: Institute for Science Education, 1982).

12. Martin Mulder and Anke Thijsen, "Decision Making in Curriculum Conferences: A Study of Convergence of Opinion," *Journal of Curriculum Studies,* 22 (July–August 1990), p. 346.

13. Ibid.

14. Daniel Tanner and Laurel Tanner, *Supervision in Education* (New York: Macmillan, 1987), pp. 340–347.

15. Jack K. Campbell, *Colonel Parker: The Children's Crusader* (New York: Teachers College Press, 1967), p. 82.

16. B. G. Northrup, "The Quincy Methods," *Education,* 1 (November 1880), p. 131.

17. Campbell, op. cit., p. 88.

18. Ibid.

19. Julie M. Jensen and Nancy L. Roser, "Are There Really Three R's?" *Educational Leadership,* 47 (March 1990), p. 10.

20. Dorothy S. Strickland, "Emergent Literacy: How Young Children Learn to Read and Write," *Educational Leadership,* 47 (March 1990), p. 19.

21. Steven A. Stahl and Patricia D. Miller, "Whole Language and Language Experience Approaches for Beginning Reading: A Quantitative Research Synthesis," *Review of Educational Research,* 59 (Spring 1989), p. 88.

22. Emit D. Grizzell, *Origin and Development of the High School in New England before 1865* (New York: Macmillan, 1923), p. 42.

23. R. Freeman Butts and Lawrence A. Cremin, *A History of Education in American Culture* (New York: Holt, Rinehart and Winston, 1953), p. 184.

24. Edgar B. Wesley, *NEA: The First Hundred Years* (New York: Harper, 1957), p. 67.

25. Commissioner of Education, *Report for the Year 1889–90* (Washington, DC: Bureau of Education, 1893), Vol. 2, pp. 1388–1389.

26. Charles W. Eliot, "Can School Programs Be Shortened and Enriched?" National Education Association *Proceedings* (Washington, DC: National Education Association, 1893), pp. 617–625.

27. Ibid.

28. National Commission on Excellence in Education, *A Nation at Risk: The Imperative for Educational Reform* (Washington, DC: U.S. Department of Education, 1983), see also Daniel Tanner, "A Nation 'Truly' at Risk," *Phi Delta Kappan,* 75 (December 1993). pp. 288–297.

29. Fred M. Hechinger, "Critical Commission Is Criticized," *The New York Times* (February 28, 1984), p. 6.

30. National Education Association, *Report of the Committee of Ten on Secondary School Studies* (New York: American Book, 1894), p. 51.

31. Ibid., p. 53.

32. John S. Brubacher, *A History of the Problems of Education,* 2nd ed. (New York: McGraw-Hill, 1966), p. 422.

33. William A. Reid, "The Technological Society and the Concept of General Education," Chapter 7 in *Cultural Literacy and the Idea of General Edu-*

cation, Eighty-seventh Yearbook, Part II, National Society for the Study of Education, Part II (Chicago: University of Chicago Press, 1988), p. 127.

34. "The Fundamental Assumptions in the Report of the Committee of Ten," *Educational Review,* 30 (November 1905), p. 330.

35. Ibid., p. 414.

36. National Education Association, *Report of the Committee of Ten on Secondary School Studies,* op. cit., p. 43.

37. Cremin, op. cit., pp. 92–93.

38. John Dewey, *The Educational Situation* (Chicago: University of Chicago Press, 1904), pp. 65–66.

39. National Education Association, "Report of the Committee of Fifteen," *Educational Review,* 9 (March 1895), p. 270.

40. Ibid., p. 275.

41. Dewey, *The Educational Situation,* op. cit., p. 26.

42. William T. Harris, "My Pedagogical Creed," in Ossian H. Lang (ed.), *Educational Creeds of the Century* (New York: E. L. Kellogg, 1898), pp. 36–46.

43. Oliver Franks, cited in "Highlights of Dewey's Life," *The New Leader,* October 22, 1949, S-2.

44. "Salute to John Dewey," *The New Leader,* October 22, 1949, p. S-1.

45. John Dewey, "The Theory of the Chicago Experiment," in Mayhew and Edwards, op. cit., p. 464.

46. Ibid., p. 468.

47. Ibid.

48. Laurel N. Tanner, "The Meaning of Curriculum in Dewey's Laboratory School," *Journal of Curriculum Studies,* 23 (March–April 1991), pp. 101–117.

49. Harris, op. cit., p. 36.

50. John Dewey, "The Psychological Aspect of the Curriculum," *Educational Review,* 13 (April 1897), p. 361.

51. Ibid.

52. Ibid., p. 357.

53. Ibid., p. 361.

54. Ibid., p. 363.

55. John Dewey, "The Psychology of the Elementary Curriculum," *The Elementary School Record* (A Series of Nine Monographs), February 1990, pp. 223–224.

56. Dewey, "The Psychological Aspect of the School Curriculum," op. cit., p. 362.

57. Ibid.

58. John Dewey, "Plan of Organization of the University Primary School," privately printed, 1895, p. 10.

59. Mayhew and Edwards, op. cit., pp. 35–36.

60. John Dewey, "The University Elementary School," *University [of Chicago] Record,* 2 (May 21, 1897), p. 75.

61. Mayhew and Edwards, op. cit., p. 370.

62. Arthur G. Wirth, *John Dewey as Educator: His Design for Work in Education 1894–1904* (New York: Wiley, 1966), p. 198.

63. Dewey, "The Theory of the Chicago Experiment," op. cit., p. 464.

64. Edward A. Krug, *The Shaping of the American High School* (New York: Harper, 1964), pp. 151–152.

65. Ibid., p. 152.

66. Ibid., p. 150.

67. National Study of School Evaluation, *Evaluative Criteria for the Evaluation of Secondary Schools,* 6th ed. (Falls Church, VA: Author, 1987).

68. Ibid., p. 9.

69. Heather Lewis, "CUNY's High School Plan Looks Backward," *The New York Times,* February 16, 1991, p. 18.

70. Timothy S. Healy, "Will Everyman Destroy the University?" *Saturday Review of Literature* (December 20, 1969), p. 55.

71. Wilford M. Aikin. *The Story of the Eight-Year Study* (New York: Harper, 1942).

SELECTED REFERENCES

Cremin, Lawrence A. *The Transformation of the School.* New York: Alfred A. Knopf, 1961.

Dewey, John. *The Child and the Curriculum.* Chicago: University of Chicago Press, 1902.

Dewey, John. *The Educational Situation.* Chicago: University of Chicago Press, 1904.

Dewey, John. *The School and Society.* Chicago: University of Chicago Press, 1899.

Grizzell, Emit D. *Origin and Development of the High School in New England before 1865.* New York: Macmillan, 1923.

Krug, Edward A. *The Shaping of the American High School.* New York: Harper and Row, 1964.

Mayhew, Katherine Camp, and Anna Camp Edwards. *The Dewey School.* New York: D. Appleton-Century, 1936.

National Education Association. *Report of the Committee of Fifteen.* New York: Arno Press and *The New York Times,* 1969; originally published in 1895 by the New England Publishing Company.

National Education Association. *Report of the Committee of Ten on Secondary School Studies.* New York: Arno Press and *The New York Times,* 1969; originally published in 1893 by the U.S. Government Printing Office.

National Study of School Evaluation. *Evaluative Criteria,* 6th ed. Falls Church, VA: Author, 1987.

Parker, Francis W. *Talks on Pedagogics.* New York: E. L. Kellogg, 1894.

Payne, Bruce Ryburn. *Public Elementary School Curricula.* New York: Silver, Burdett, 1905.

Spencer, Herbert. *Education.* New York: D. Appleton-Century, 1894.

Stout, John Elbert. *The Development of High-School Curricula in the North Central States from 1860 to 1918.* Chicago: University of Chicago Press, 1921.

Tanner, Daniel, and Laurel Tanner. *History of the School Curriculum.* New York: Macmillan, 1990.

Tyler, Ralph W. *Basic Principles of Curriculum and Instruction.* Chicago: University of Chicago Press, 1949.

CHAPTER 3

THE CENTURY OF THE CURRICULUM

A century is an utterly arbitrary division of time. In 1900, the National Education Association (NEA) was eloquently reminded of this by Nicholas Murray Butler, president of Columbia University. "The skies do not change when a century is ushered in, or the thunders roll when it passes out," he said in a speech before NEA's Department of Superintendence. "Imagination, however, gives to the century an objective reality and feeling welds our thoughts to it. We do well to resign ourselves to the spell of these creations and learn to know our centuries."[1]

Butler looked back at curricular accomplishments of the nineteenth century and found them indeed remarkable: development of diverse kinds of schools, higher and lower, with many new subjects to meet diverse needs and interests and "yet with a common fund of basic knowledge which they all impart." Educators talked enthusiastically about developing the talents of individuals and the realization of their talents in the life and interests of a free society. Particularly noteworthy was "the marked emphasis now laid upon the social aspect of education, and also upon the school as a social institution and a social center."[2]

The crowning accomplishment of the nineteenth century was the establishment of a public school system. Because this had already been done, what was there left to do in the twentieth century? "The glory of founding educational systems cannot be ours," Butler told the superintendents, "but the effort for improvement, by building wise practice upon sound theory is within the reach of each of us."[3]

Curriculum improvement was the charge of the twentieth century, or as Butler put it: "Our proper business is improvement."[4]

Butler was right, of course, for our business was (and is) improvement. The nineteenth century was a time of founding institutions that were of permanent value. The modern university (which Butler did not specifically mention) had been created by the end of the nineteenth century. But granted the achievements, the nineteenth century left puzzling and serious problems in its wake. Charles W. Eliot, who was a discussant at Butler's speech, described the industrial changes in the last half of the nineteenth century that profoundly affected the public provision of education. The population had been rushing into cities. "This rush into urban life has had a very ill effect on schools," said Eliot.

> It has tended to make schools large machines. The grading of classes in a large school had to be inflexible and the product had to be uniform like that of a flour mill. That meant that the quick children were held back and the slow driven forward, to the great disadvantage of both. It meant marking time. It meant bad air and crowded rooms with fifty or seventy pupils to a teacher. These are impossible conditions for good teaching.[5]

Crowding was a problem both in school and out, introducing new risks to children's health. Eliot said that some of the conditions in the schools had been improved by the turn of the century. More attention had been given to good air, proper heat and light, and more flexibility had been given to programs and curriculum choice. But, he said, much more remained to be done to solve the problems in urban education.

Today, the problems of "disadvantaged" children or children "at risk" still plague the nation despite the great progress made in promoting child welfare during the twentieth century. Since the War on Poverty programs of the 1960s, we have learned much about how to help children growing up under conditions that negatively shape their lives. An integrated program of interventions including curriculum improvement, safe housing, access to health care, and ties to the world of work can "break the cycle of disadvantage, but a concerted attack remains to be undertaken."[6]

In a very real sense, the twentieth century closes like the nineteenth—with attempts to solve social problems and open the door to America's mainstream through the curriculum. But there is one striking difference: We know a great deal more. Research and experience have taught us much since 1900 and the problem now is to use and build on what we have learned.

The trouble is that the body of research and conceptualization in the field is often forgotten. A new education fad comes along occupying educators' attention as well as space in educational journals. Examples in the early 1990s were cooperative learning and "whole language"—the integration of reading and writing. Both were sound ideas but were carried to extremes (particularly cooperative learning) that threatened to destroy their value. According to MacGinitie, one reason why educational ideas become fads is that:

> [t]he chance of being published is greatly increased if you write about the latest trend. If you were a professor wanting to get published in *The Reading Teacher,* what would you write about? Transfer of learning? No. Thirty years ago you might have written about transfer. . . . Although teachers could profit more from a good article on transfer than from one more article on whole language, what gets published is that article on whole language.[7]

As we have noted previously in this book, the practice of cooperative-collaborative learning was given its theoretical formulation by Dewey at the University of Chicago before the turn of the century. Parker introduced the integration of reading and writing in Quincy, Massachusetts, in 1875. Yet, as MacGinitie points out, both ideas were treated as new in the 1990s.[8] Treating old ideas as new cuts them off from their theoretical underpinnings and impedes curriculum improvement. The graveyard of education fads is crowded. They were often based on sound concepts but were misunderstood and misapplied and therefore abandoned in disappointment by teachers and administrators. The newest approach is often labeled a *reform,* a counterreaction intended to undo the excesses of the previous reform. If we are to have real curriculum improvement, curriculum development must be directed at problem solutions through the use of the best available evidence consistent with research findings and past experience in education.

The twentieth century is the century of the curriculum. It is the century of Thorndike and of Dewey, of Newlon and of Rugg, of Bobbitt and of Charters, of Flexner and of Hutchins, of Tyler and of Taba, of Caswell and of Schwab, of Goodlad and many others. More ideas about curriculum improvement appeared during the twentieth century than in all previous centuries. (In fact, the study of curriculum as an academic specialization began in the 1920s.) We turn now to a discussion of these ideas and the problems they were meant to solve.

TRANSFER OF LEARNING

A basic problem in curriculum development is the purposes of schooling: what we want students to learn. Everyone agrees that what is learned should transfer to new situations, both in and out of school. But when interested citizens and educators talk about what should be included in the school curriculum there is strong disagreement about the probability of transfer. It has long been argued that the study of the traditional academic disciplines and classical languages is the best kind of education and will provide for mental discipline and transfer of learning. When the evidence fails to reveal these claimed benefits, instead of seeking ways of integrating these studies and relating them to the life of the learner and to social reality, there is the tendency to look to extreme learner-centered approaches and to negate systematically organized knowledge. These viewpoints are not merely extremes, they are dangerous dualisms—the kind that Dewey sought to eliminate in his Laboratory School. Most curriculum workers reject them. They believe that transfer frequently fails to occur but that transfer can be accomplished.[9] They seek to improve the curriculum so as to optimize the transfer effects.

Certainly conventional education affords some transfer. Even through conventional methods, youngsters learn to read and most are able to bring their reading skills to bear in ordinary situations. As adults, they are able to apply their arithmetic skills to ordinary situations. This type of transfer is taken for granted. Educators are concerned with the kind of transfer that involves reflective thought in applying what has been learned in one situation to other contexts—the learning of other things and the solution of unanticipated problems. An example of the former (skill transfer) would be for high school students to utilize the process skills from mathematics in solving chemistry problems as a matter of course. Students in chemistry classes typically have difficulties with basic mathematical procedures, much less higher mathematics.[10] An example of the latter—namely, reflective transfer—might be students' ability to use concepts from chemistry in considering ecological problems.

Research and experience over the past century have taught us that we are more likely to achieve transfer when the curriculum is deliberately planned to foster transfer.[11] Yet every curriculum worker is sure to encounter the older, discredited theories on transfer, and must know why they should be rejected. Moreover, this knowledge can help in considering curriculum alternatives as well as judging current curricula and methods. Many current practices in the schools were adopted under the influence of the long-discredited theory that certain studies improve the mind and improve one's ability to master other subjects.

Thorndike's Research

One of the most portentous pieces of research for the curriculum field was conducted by Edward L. Thorndike in the early 1920s. In a huge study involving some 8,564 pupils, Thorndike sought to measure the relative disciplinary value of various high school subjects by assessing gains in "general intelligence" that could be attributed to the study of one subject or group of subjects instead of another. For instance, he compared the gains in intelligence test scores of pupils who studied English, history, geometry, and *Latin* with those who studied English, history, geometry, and *shopwork*. Thus, he was trying to measure the relative disciplinary value of Latin and shopwork. Thorndike found that no one study (be it Latin or anything else) is more likely than any other study to result in a general improvement of the mind. Thorndike concluded:

> By any reasonable interpretation of the results, the intellectual values of studies should be determined largely by the special information, habits, interests, attitudes, and ideals which they demonstrably produce. The expectation of any large difference in general improvement of the mind from one study rather than another seems doomed to disappointment. The chief reason why good thinkers seem superficially to have been made such by having taken certain school studies is that good thinkers have taken such studies, becoming better by the inherent tendency of the good to gain more than the poor from any study. When the good thinkers studied Greek and Latin, these studies seemed to make good thinking. Now that the good thinkers study Physics and Trigonometry, these seem to make good thinkers. If the abler pupils should all study Physical Education and Dramatic Art, these subjects would seem to make good thinkers. These were, indeed, a large fraction of the program of studies for the best thinkers the world has produced, the Athenian Greeks.[12]

What Thorndike was saying was that those who had the most to start with gained the most regardless of the particular studies they pursued, and that there is no hierarchy of subjects for mental discipline. He also argued that learning is specific rather than a matter of mental discipline.

The Demolition of Mental Discipline

Actually, Thorndike's research was part of a chain of events that demolished the theory of mental discipline as a basis for curriculum development. It will be recalled from our discussion in Chapter 1 that educational theorists enthusiastically picked up Herbartian educational psychology, which stressed that new subject matter must be related in the pupil's mind to his or her previous learning. Thus, the "psychology" of mental discipline was abandoned in favor of Herbartian psychology. This happened in the United States by 1885. (In Europe, Herbartian psychology had taken hold some twenty years earlier.) Another early link in the chain was William James of Harvard, who proposed in his book *Principles of Psychology,* published in 1890, that psychology is a natural science. This left many in the intellectual world thunderstruck because the study of the mind had always been the domain of philosophers. James said that the study of the mind must be based on the study of behavior, that it was fallacious to conceive of the mind as composed of separate faculties as did the faculty psychologists.

James was the founder of the school of objective psychology. His ideas were pursued, developed, and applied by Edward Thorndike of Teachers College. Other erosive influences on the notion of the inherent disciplinary value of the classical studies were the application of the evolutionary idea to society, child interests, the need for practical knowledge, and the necessity of the secondary school to meet the needs of an increasingly heterogeneous population.

Research on Transfer

Thorndike began challenging the doctrine of transfer shortly after the turn of the century. His first frontal attack was a study conducted with Woodworth in 1901, which showed that improvement in one mental function seldom brings about commensurate improvement in another function, regardless of similarity.[13] Transfer could occur but not because of the disciplinary value of any classical study; it would occur only if the old and new activities had common or related content or methods of study.[14]

Curriculum developers could (and did) conclude from Thorndike's research that the best way to prepare a student for a given activity or goal was to have the student take a direct route: the study of the subject or the practice of the activity itself.

A host of studies conducted during the 1920s, 1930s, and 1940s confirmed Thorndike's findings that demolished the disciplinary doctrine. Thorndike's study was repeated in 1927. Broyler, Thorndike, and Woodward reported that the findings of their study concurred with the earlier study; both studies "agree in disagreeing with the traditional doctrine that Latin, algebra and geometry are the prime disciplinary subjects of high school."[15] Thorndike's study was repeated again in 1945 by Wesman, whose investigation "failed to reveal superior transfer to intelligence for any one of the achievement areas or subjects measured (Latin, German, French, mathematics, natural science, social studies, contemporary affairs) and indicated the desirability of direct training in mental processes rather than dependence on transfer from school subjects."[16]

But probably the most stunning attack (aside from Thorndike's 1924 study) on the idea that certain subjects have superior transfer to intelligence was delivered by the Progressive Education Association's Eight-Year Study (1933–1941). As is shown in the discussion on the Eight-Year Study in Chapter 4, the study proved that success in college is not dependent on credits earned in high school in prescribed academic subjects.

Effects of Thorndike's Studies

Thorndike's findings on transfer had an enormous effect on education. The findings were cited as justification for eliminating classical studies such as Latin and ancient history from the curriculum. Thorndike's findings on transfer produced two other striking effects. First, because Spencerian questions could no longer be answered on the basis of the alleged disciplinary value of given subjects, there had to be other means of determining the relative values of studies. Concern over finding such means was an important factor in the appointment by the NEA in 1911 of a Committee on Economy of Time in Education, charged with identifying the "minimum essentials" of the curriculum. There can be little doubt that Thorndike's emphasis on teaching specific knowledge and skills influenced the committee's decision to pursue a mechanistic approach to curriculum development. Second, Thorndike's work lent justification to the inclusion of modern, practical, and technical studies in the curriculum taught as nearly as possible in the context in which they were to be used. Nevertheless, the effort to bring the modern and career-oriented studies into an honorable place in the school curriculum has been a continuing struggle. In the early 1970s, some educational policymakers—most notably the U.S. Commissioner of Education—reasserted the "equal status" of vocational and academic subjects.[17] But in the 1980s and early 1990s, governors and state legislatures were enacting programs for "excellence in education," which in several states involved reducing the number of units that high school students were permitted to take in elective courses and programs, including vocational education, and instituting new requirements in science and mathematics for graduation. These programs were based on the policy of reform in science and mathematics education established by President Reagan and continued by succeeding administrations (of Bush and Clinton), promoting a system of national examinations in the name of academic excellence to meet "world-class standards." The policy was established following the publication of the Report of the National Commission on Excellence in Education (1983).[18]

Inquiry-Discovery and Transfer

During the national curriculum reform movement of the 1950s and 1960s, in the wake of the Cold War and space race, there was renewed interest in general transfer.

Although educational theorists looked again to wide transfer, their theoretical basis was *not* that of mental discipline. It was, rather, that inquiry-discovery and learning how to learn (ways of learning) as taught via the disciplines could be applied by students in new situations. According to Bruner, it was "indeed a fact that massive general transfer can be achieved by appropriate learning, even to the degree that learning properly under optimum conditions leads one to 'learn how to learn.'"[19] Bruner was clearly not calling for a return to the doctrine of mental discipline. Yet he held that each academic discipline is undergirded by a structure of abstract knowledge, and by revealing this structure, massive learning transfer would occur.

STRUCTURE AND TRANSFER. During the 1950s and 1960s, educators enthusiastically picked up on the idea of the structure of the disciplines as the key for maximizing transfer. Bruner argued that understanding structures and fundamental principles "appears to be the main road to adequate 'transfer of training.'"[20] The emphasis during this period was on improving learning efficiency, but again, within individual disciplines. However, the idea of the structure of knowledge failed to effect the promised transfer of learning. First, most subjects had nothing resembling a single structure or organizing principle. Even in fields such as physics and mathematics, there was little if any agreement among university scholars on a single structure. Organizing principles change in accordance with one's purpose in studying a given subject. Thus, the idea of structure was a fiction. Second, the notion of holding abstract knowledge above and apart from practical knowledge worked against the possible transfer of learning. Third, if each discipline has its own independent structure, then each must be treated as a separate cocoon in the curriculum.

BRUNER AND DEWEY. Initially, educational theorists were struck by apparent similarities between Bruner's ideas and those of Dewey. Learning how to learn and inquiry-discovery stem in no small way from Dewey's reflective thinking. Yet there are important differences. On the one hand, Bruner was addressing himself to ways of learning *within individual disciplines* such as physics and mathematics. He insisted that these would transfer to other kinds of problems faced by the student. Dewey, on the other hand, was referring to interdisciplinary and applied knowledge for social problem solving as a task for which the school must prepare the rising generation. Here Dewey's idea was similar to that of Thorndike, who suggested that the best way to learn something was by the most direct route possible: to practice the process itself. Dewey went much further. Whereas Thorndike held that we must match learning situations specifically for transfer, Dewey held that knowledge must be made generalizable for transfer.

Enhancing Transfer

As Prawat points out, promoting knowledge, transfer, and skill in students "is a major—many would say *the* major—goal of education."[21] And as Taba emphasized, "Since no program, no matter how thorough, can teach everything, the task of all education is to cause a maximum amount of transfer."[22] In summarizing the recent research on transfer, Prawat concluded that in order to facilitate transfer, "teachers need a firm grasp of the most important ideas in each of the subject matter areas they teach," and further, "[t]hey should have at their command detailed information about the developmental course of children's thinking in those content areas."[23] Concerning key ideas, as Bruner stated in 1960, "[t]he basic ideas that lie at the heart of all science and mathematics and the basic themes that give form to life and literature are as simple as they are powerful."[24] More recently, learning theorists have come to recognize that key ideas or understandings "allow for a rich set of connections," and "serve as anchors for the cognitive structure."[25] It is the connections, of course, that we want students to make. Our understanding of transfer supports the view that broad generalizations or big (key) ideas and practical applications of these ideas increase the possibility of transfer as opposed to unrelated fragments of subject matter. This means that a curriculum based on innumerable minute objectives or abstractions is not addressed to transfer. Transfer is also enhanced when pupils understand why they are engaging in a given activity or a learning task. In this regard, research shows that transfer increases when pupils are deliberately made aware that what they are learning might be useful in other situations.[26]

Unfortunately, Thorndike chose to interpret his findings to buttress the theory of stimulus-response (S-R) psychology rather than seeing it as evidence of the need for subject matter that is designed to be highly generalized for applicability or transfer to a wide range of situations. The consequence was a doctrine of narrow specificity that was manifested in the scientism of Franklin Bobbitt and found its legacy in present-day behavioristic objectives. According to Cronbach, developmental objectives, when the teacher states how he or she would like the learner to function after instruction, are more generalized and more concerned with transfer than are narrow behavioristic objectives.[27] Developing social problem-solving skills has a similar transfer objective. As Cornbleth has noted, there is no way to list all the occasions for transfer.[28] Social problems are emergent situations. Nevertheless, suitable levels of accomplishment can be specified as Tyler and his staff did in the Eight-Year Study.

Attitudes are one kind of learning that transfers widely. Here we are referring to attitudes toward one's self and other people and institutions—the school, society, and the curriculum. Attitudes may or may not be in the teacher's plan but they are learned nevertheless. As discussed in detail in Chapter 5, this is commonly referred to as the hidden curriculum, or what Dewey called the collateral curriculum or collateral learning. To Dewey, the most important attitude is the desire to go on learning.[29] This most important objective of all must be kept in mind or we miss opportunities for providing students with the truly generative powers of an education.

SCIENTISM IN CURRICULUM MAKING

Thorndike argued that there must be elements in situations outside of school that are identical with the elements taught in school if students are to apply school learning to these out-of-school situations. Thorndike's studies had an immediate effect on curriculum development. Those developing public school curricula began looking at the quantitative problems encountered by adults in order to select arithmetic topics.

They also examined the newspapers and other reading materials read by adults in order to develop reading and spelling objectives and the materials used in the teaching of reading and spelling. Tyler writes:

> Shortly after Thorndike developed the idea of identical elements, curriculum objectives were broken down into tiny specific things to be learned. In Thorndike's psychology of arithmetic, more than 2000 objectives for elementary school arithmetic were listed in such detail that $1 + 2 = 3$ is a separate learning objective from $2 + 1 = 3$. Fortunately this practice was discontinued when Charles Judd and his students showed that students could learn to use general principles to guide them and could learn a few dozen general principles in a subject which they could adapt to the hundreds of specific matters they encountered.[30]

 As Tyler points out, after 1925, curriculum developers formulated generalized educational objectives. However, in the 1960s and 1970s the practice of breaking down curriculum objectives into minute things to be learned was revived in the so-called behavioral (behavioristic) objectives movement.

can be measured

Scientific Management and Education

In the second decade of the twentieth century there was great national excitement over a new system of industrial control known as scientific management. Franklin Bobbitt, a member of the faculty in educational administration at the University of Chicago, argued that school systems could operate more efficiently and economically if they would borrow the principles of scientific management. The principles of management being applied in business and industry were particularly applicable to a "backward" institution such as education, held Bobbitt. The analogy between the two institutions, education and industry, was obvious; "education is a shaping process as much as the manufacture of steel rails," said Bobbitt.[31] Bobbitt's theme was that education must follow the example of industry and focus on the product. Standards for that product must be established and scales of measurement utilized to see "whether the product rises to standard." Educators now realized that

> it is possible to set up definite standards for the various educational products. The ability to add at a speed of 65 combinations per minute, with an accuracy of 94 per cent is as definite a specification as can be set up for any aspect of the work of the steel plant.[32]

Educators as Mechanics

Bobbitt's argument for the need for educational standards elicited no appreciable objections from the nation's educational leaders. But his proposal for establishing these standards was to become a matter of continuing controversy as standards for educational products or outcomes were to be set by the business and industrial world. It was the role of men of practical affairs to decide what they wanted and the role of educators to determine how it could be produced and to produce it without question. Thus, educators would no longer be concerned with the what of the curriculum but only the how. As Callahan commented in his classic study of the influence of industry on public-school administration: "Doubtless many educators who had devoted years of study and thought to the aims and purposes of education were surprised to learn that they had misunderstood their function. They were to be mechanics, not philosophers."[33]

How would the needs and desires of practical people become known? The kinds of educational products they needed would be determined via the survey method. But the surveys would not be conducted by school people; scientific educational management as efficient as that found in the business world required that the surveys be conducted by those in business. In this way, education would be turned to the needs of business. With scientifically determined job specifications, scales of measurement, and standards of attainment, said Bobbitt, "we shall have [for] the first time a scientific curriculum for education worthy of our age of science."[34] A few years later, when his attention turned from school administration to curriculum making, Bobbitt himself used the survey method for defining curricular aims and content.

BUSINESS LEADERSHIP.   At the time Bobbitt published his ideas on the role of business people in determining educational objectives, people of influence were advancing a theory of business leadership for the society as a whole. Among them was Arthur Twining Hadley, president of Yale University, who, in his book *Standards of Morality* (1907), proposed that business people assume a larger role in the solution of contemporary social problems in return for protection of their vested interests. Thus, Bobbitt's argument that business people should set educational standards was a not unexpected outcome of the theory of business leadership.

Although easily explainable, the importance of Bobbitt's advocacy of a business-led education system should not be underestimated. Two policies were set that appear to stem directly from this advocacy and continue to operate to this day: First, business values and procedures are the model for educational administration with the result that educational decisions tend to be made on economic rather than educational grounds. Second, education (and government) has turned to business and industry for the solution of pedagogical problems. An illustration of this from the 1960s is performance contracting, in which some school districts turned to industry for learning systems to improve pupil performance in reading and arithmetic as measured by standardized achievement tests. Performance contracting not only failed to produce the results that were promised, but the practices also proved to be counterproductive. This was disappointing yet hardly unexpected. What remains a puzzle is why educators continue to believe that business can do everything better—including education.[35]

In the early 1990s the chancellor of the New York City Schools proposed that complete control of some of the new schools to be built in New York City be turned over to private, for-profit companies.[36] The proposal was rejected by the Board of Education. Some cities such as Baltimore have entered into such contracts. However, the targeted schools have been those serving the most disadvantaged pupil populations.

THE INEFFICIENT CURRICULUM.   Not the least of the effects of the national infatua-
tion with efficiency in Bobbitt's day was a barrage of criticism directed at the public-
school curriculum. The curriculum was characterized by some critics as impractical
and ineffective (failing to prepare for a living) and therefore a waste of the taxpayers'
money. It was characterized by others as failing to prepare pupils in academic work
and moral training. Still a third group criticized the school for its failure to hold
pupils; this problem was regarded as a direct reflection of the curriculum and a
source of educational waste. A fourth criticism was more of an ultimatum; some
reform economists demanded that either the schools show measured results of their
outcomes in terms of social betterment or have their budgets reduced. In short,
what was being called for by the critics was a more efficient curriculum, although
what this meant certainly varied with the interests of the critics. Nevertheless, almost
all the critics were in agreement about one thing: The schools were extravagant with
public funds. Curriculum efficiency hence meant economy. This could be achieved
by having pupils study *only* what they needed (the basics), and nothing more. This
way of thinking formed the backdrop for the operations of the Committee on Economy of Time created in 1911 by the NEA's Department of Superintendence.

The Committee on Economy of Time

Let us examine the reasons for the committee's charge to define the minimum
essentials of the curriculum. First, research had exploded the myth that certain subjects had value for mental discipline so there was urgent need for a new answer to
Spencer's question, "What knowledge is of most worth?" This would require new
approaches to curriculum development. Second, friends of education as well as ene-
mies were demanding that the selection of curriculum content be based on quantitative evidence instead of opinion. The quantitative method was being applied to the
solution of all educational problems including the definition of the standard units in
a course of study. Last but not least was a growing body of research that seemed to
show that the amount of time spent on a given subject had little influence on the
results. The pioneering study (which was ignored by educators when first reported)
had been conducted in 1897 by Rice, who concluded that more than fifteen minutes
per day for spelling was utterly wasteful.[37]

The temper of the times was clear, as expressed in a speech by Leonard Ayres of
the Russell Sage Foundation to the Harvard Teachers Association in 1912. "'How
much?' and 'how many?' and 'with what result?' are going to displace guess-work,
imagination, and oratory as criteria for shaping educational policies," said Ayres.[38]

CURRICULUM MAKING BY COMMON DENOMINATOR.   The first phase of the committee's work was to find out what was being taught (and where achievement data were
available, what was being learned) in representative school districts and make recommendations based on the findings. The result was curriculum making by common
denominator. To illustrate, in his report on arithmetic, Walter Jessup of Iowa State
College noted that there was wide variation among the cities in the amount of time
given to arithmetic. He recommended that the time devoted to arithmetic in the var-

ious grades not exceed the median time expenditure throughout the country. The first grade, for example, should not exceed seventy-five minutes per week as that was the median time expended in first grades.[39]

There was absolutely no theoretical basis for the idea that the median time spent on a given subject should become the standard. Yet this was what the committee found desirable for spelling, arithmetic, and handwriting.

This is not to imply that the committee's four major reports (published as the yearbooks of the National Society for the Study of Education in 1915, 1917, 1918, and 1919) contributed nothing of value to educators. This would be manifestly unfair and misleading. What was being taught in other school systems was of intense interest to superintendents, and the surveys reported in the NSSE yearbooks were widely circulated and discussed. However, prevailing practice was hardly a sound basis for curriculum improvement.

Determining Curriculum Content.   The second phase of the committee's work was to make recommendations concerning the content of the curriculum. All of the recommendations were based on the principle of social utility. The approach used for determining what should be taught was to find out what people who are living and working successfully need to be able to do and just what information and skills they need in order to live and work successfully. The committee relied heavily on the method of collective judgment or consensus. Library books, for instance, were recommended on the basis of the number of times each book appeared on supplementary reading lists in fifty American cities. History content was selected by analyzing books, encyclopedias, newspapers, and periodicals to see which persons, places, and dates were most frequently mentioned.

A Conservative Response.   Nevertheless, it was the committee's initial decision to derive a curriculum from current practice, rather than the committee's inadequate methodology, that was to plague the curriculum maker in succeeding years. For as Cremin put it,

> the Committee had ended by defining the goals of education in terms of life as it was, and hence by proposing a curriculum that would accommodate youngsters to existing conditions with little emphasis on improving them. This was hardly the progressive or Deweyan ideal, however much it was construed as such in some circles.[40]

The Doctrine of Specific Objectives

The principal method for curriculum construction embraced by the Committee on Economy of Time had the appearance of being scientific, and educators were striving for the academic respectability associated with the new age of science. Therefore, one would expect that this method would attract adherents. This is exactly what happened. As with the movement for scientific management in industry at the time, many educators proceeded to confuse measurement with science. Franklin Bobbitt, W. W. Charters, Charles C. Peters, and David Snedden, all professors of education, trod in the steps of the committee.

THE METHOD OF JOB ANALYSIS.　"Let us discover what the activities are which make up man's life and we have the objectives of education," wrote Bobbitt in *The Elementary School Journal* in 1924.[41] It was Bobbitt's theory that the curriculum that prepared the learner for these specific activities was the curriculum that prepared the learner for life. Because educational objectives were activities and activities were learned through performance, activity analysis discovered both the objectives of the curriculum and the curriculum itself. The method of activity analysis is also known as job analysis. As implied by the name, the method concerns the analysis of the specific activities in the performance of a given job, such as operating a machine. Bobbitt and Charters applied this method to curriculum construction, the implication being that whatever the schools taught could be reduced to twenty or thirty thousand specific mechanical skills or behaviors.

JOB ANALYSIS AND BEHAVIORISM.　In addition to appearing businesslike and efficient, the new method was also highly compatible with the mechanistic psychology, behaviorism, which described human behavior in connectionist terms of S-R (stimulus-response) bonds. Habit formation and uniformity of response are the predominant concepts in both doctrines. Significantly, Charters wrote of the desirability of automatic responses on the part of the learner "when given situations recur frequently."[42] Indeed, behaviorism provided a theoretical basis for job analysis as a curriculum-making technique. Many educators, even Kilpatrick, a student of Dewey's, who emphasized that activity must be at one with the child's goals, began describing education in connectionist terms.[43] Peters actually defined education as "the acquisition of a large aggregate of 'hair-trigger sets' for responding to the particular problems that will confront the educand in the future."[44]

　　Needless to say, the ideal of humans behaving like automatons was the antithesis of the Deweyan ideal. Dewey, like Lester Ward before him, saw the improvement of individual and social welfare through the expanding power of human intelligence. But as another famous educational philosopher, Boyd Bode, observed, behaviorism is "a psychology that explains intelligence by explaining it away."[45] Behaviorism also contributed to the divorce of education theory from the goal of social reform.

A DANGEROUS DEFICIENCY.　Obviously, not all educational objectives concern repetitive tasks. Far from it. In our society, many of the most important objectives, such as the ability to make adequate decisions in public policy matters, involve varying and unforeseeable conditions. Curriculum objectives such as these involve the transfer of learning rather than the repetition of identical operations. This points to a dangerous deficiency in activity or job analysis as a means for curriculum development; it is fixed on the lowest level of objectives—those requiring mechanical responses. Objectives that require higher-level thinking processes are avoided because they do not fit in a theory that trains people to act mechanically. Activity or job analysis simply cannot be made to cover the entire gamut of curriculum objectives.

EDUCATIONAL ENGINEERING　In his book *How to Make a Curriculum,* published in 1924, Bobbitt developed the committee's basic premise and methodology into a well-organized curriculum theory. Bobbitt compared the curriculum maker to an engineer.

It was the task of the educational engineer to use his or her educational surveying instruments to locate the specific objectives in the various subject fields. Education, said Bobbitt, should "prepare for the fifty years of adulthood, not for the twenty years of childhood and youth."[46] It was the task of the curriculum maker to define the major fields of adult experience and analyze them into smaller and smaller units until he or she found the specific activities to be performed. The specific activities, similar to job specifications in industry, comprised the content of the various subjects.

Significantly, curriculum making by activity or job analysis in no way conflicted with the traditional subject organization of the curriculum. The "scientific" curriculum was the old subject curriculum with a new authority.

DEVISING CURRICULUM OBJECTIVES.   Although Bobbitt and Charters were of one mind concerning the nature of subject matter, their ideas on the source for curriculum objectives differed. Whereas Bobbitt's scheme was to "discover" curriculum objectives by scientific analysis, Charters held that the philosopher sets up the aim and the analyst provides only the technique for working the aim down "into the terms of a curriculum."[47]

This difference is very significant. Bobbitt maintained that we can determine what people *should* do by identifying the things they *do* do. Charters warned against this and saw activity analysis as a means for implementing previously selected objectives. It was Bobbitt's scheme that prevailed. The idea that curriculum objectives can be discovered by scientific means, much as one discovers oil, was basic to the new notion of curriculum making.

Peters and Snedden were educational sociologists who walked in Bobbitt's footsteps, endorsing the idea without question that the curriculum should consist of thousands of minute objectives to be obtained by consensus. Snedden's "sociological determination of objectives in education" divided educational objectives into two categories, production and consumption (the ability to do and the ability to appreciate). The result was to further compartmentalize vocation and culture.[48] This again was the antithesis of the Deweyan goal, which was to demolish the barriers between the social classes and between vocational education and education for leisure.

Clearly the effect of job analysis was to atomize subject matter in the mind of both teacher and learner. This doctrine was diametrically opposed to the movement to humanize subject matter through curricular synthesis. The curriculum field was to be characterized by such conflicting currents and movements throughout the twentieth century.

BEHAVIORISTIC OBJECTIVES: THE SECOND TIME AROUND.   During the 1960s interest in specific (behavioristic) objectives was revived. The same approach—analyzing subject matter into atomistic performance objectives—was used in the contemporary movement. Ironically, both movements were reactions against the discipline-centered curriculum that was patterned on the demands of the academic specialist rather than needed human abilities. Present at the same time in both cases was a contravening movement toward curriculum synthesis. And, in both instances, behaviorism was the educational psychology of the day. Finally, there was at both times a dominant faith among educators that technology would solve all educational problems, including those in the realm of curriculum and method. This faith was intensified in the late 1970s when the popular press reduced the outcomes of education to the mechanics of basic skills.

Nevertheless, there is an important difference between these two movements that occurred a half century apart. Bobbitt's doctrine was reformist in spirit; it was based on the theory of utilitarianism. Although the curriculum produced by Bobbitt's method turned out to be the traditional curriculum with a new authority (that of "science"), his objective, nonetheless, was to make a curriculum that would prepare the learner to perform real-life activities.[49] The behavioristic objectives movement of the 1960s and early 1970s did not subject the curriculum to a reappraisal. The assumption was that content would not be changed, only divided into minute behaviors. These were, in most instances, not behaviors at all in the sense of changes in relation to one's environment but verbalisms at a mechanical level. The following "behavioral" objective is illustrative: "Given a diagram of the human body illustrating one or more human body systems (including skeletal, muscular, digestive, circulatory, and respiratory systems), [the student will] be able to name the body systems shown."[50]

The result of both activity analysis as a method for curriculum making and its reinvention in the late 1960s and 1970s was a narrow-minded curriculum focused on lower cognitive processes. Both movements were static as far as the curriculum was concerned in that they viewed the curriculum as the means for adapting the learner to existing conditions. Breaking down the curriculum into minute particles has another damaging result: It leads away from an understanding of the unity of all knowledge. Obviously, also a disintegrated curriculum and reductionist conception of the learner are not likely to lead to transfer of learning.

Scientism, Technology, and the Curriculum

The scientism of Bobbitt and Charters was essentially rooted in technology. (It will be recalled that Bobbitt compared the curriculum maker to an engineer.) As has been shown, efficiency, an aim in industry where the process is mechanical, was adopted as a goal for all aspects of education including curriculum making. The job analysis approach to curriculum development was the factory system imposed on the curriculum. It was nonphilosophical, treating curriculum making as mainly a technological problem. The difference between this group who labeled its curriculum theories "scientific," and those who argued that education decisions should be based on carefully tested hypotheses, open to continuous verification and correction, is fundamental. Included in the latter group were Dewey, Bode, and Rugg.

CHILD DEVELOPMENT AND THE CURRICULUM

One of the signal movements in twentieth-century curriculum theory was (and continues to be) the gathering of knowledge about children's development. We realized that curriculum alternatives must take into consideration children's developmental levels, and at the same time assure that they foster further development. Actually, child development as a field began in the 1890s, in a movement with great pedagogical popularity: child study. Although labeled a fad by some and steeped in sentimentality by others, the child-study movement gained academic respectability after 1900 when it became associated with experimental psychology. But even in its early stages, child study had an impact on curriculum and method, particularly in the kindergarten. Early studies conducted by Hall, Bryan, and Hancock, for example, revealed that movement involving the large muscles should be free in young children. For this reason, and because of possible danger to the children's eyesight, the handwork in kindergarten that required delicate coordination and precision was dropped from the curriculum.

It is important to note that leaders in the child-study movement saw it as an instrument for education reform as well as a means for gaining new knowledge about children. As G. Stanley Hall, who started the movement, said, the method and curriculum of the school would have to change if practice was to be in accordance with the new knowledge.

In its infancy, child study was closely tied to the school. Not only did teachers gather the data for those engaged in research but teachers themselves became deeply involved in the process of child watching. What they themselves learned as they observed the children, questioned them, collected and compiled miscellaneous facts about them, wrote their biographies, checked their sight and hearing, and weighed and measured them for science was that each child was indeed unique. Whether this new insight was translated into action in the form of new ways of working with children was another question.

CLASSROOM APPLICATION.   Child study was both systematic and unsystematic, and much worthless as well as worthwhile information was accumulated. Quality of research, however, was not the primary problem for those trying to reform the schools. There was, after all, plenty of good research on which there was a consensus. The question was how could the findings be applied in the classroom? Their concern was well borne out by what happened (or failed to happen) to the findings of child study. An excellent illustration is the method of freely chosen activities that was confirmed by child study in the early years of the movement. The idea that the child should choose his or her own activities had been promoted by Parker and he was delighted when it was sanctioned by research. But it was not until well into the second decade of the twentieth century that the idea worked its way into the elementary classroom (via, of course, the kindergarten).

As child study gained academic status in the university, it lost its identification with educational concerns. The questions being asked by researchers were less often the questions asked by educators. When they happened to be the same, by coincidence, the answers took longer to have an impact on school practice because child study and education had become parallel developments. This continues to pose problems for today's teachers and children. Nearly all teacher education programs, at least at the elementary-school level, require courses in child development. But knowing the principles of child development does not automatically result in the selection of instructional methods most likely to have a positive effect on learning.

With child development and teaching methods assigned to separate departments administratively and conceptually, knowledge of the principles of child development has not been linked sufficiently to teaching so as to effect a significant transformation of the methods of teaching.

Child study, or child development, as it is now generally known, has continued to influence educational practice, but the delay in implementing findings continues to be a matter for genuine concern. The findings of child study do not, of course, answer the paramount curriculum question; although researchers have, on the whole, determined what children are able to learn at various ages, they cannot provide answers to what children should learn. The fact that it can be demonstrated that children can learn certain things or that their learning of certain things can be accelerated appreciably does not solve the problem of curriculum choices and priorities.

PROGRESSIVE EDUCATION AND G. STANLEY HALL.   Hall's ideas both advanced and slowed down the progressive movement in education. A social Darwinian, Hall believed that social change was to come via the slow-paced process of evolutionary development. He did not believe that education was a remedy for societal ills because, given the process of evolution, education could not reverse or speed up the changes in human nature. What education could do was to identify the gifted, the "best blood," and give them better educational opportunities.[51] In this connection, Hall believed that heredity, not environment, was the governing factor in producing the fit and the unfit.

Hall advanced the radical thesis that the curriculum and methods of teaching be determined by the needs of the child as revealed through child study; the content of the curriculum was to be based on data from child development as determined by questionnaire and inventory. Hall wanted the curriculum to be individualized from the moment the child entered the school. To this end, he stressed the importance of ascertaining what children actually knew on entering school and developing the child's program in accordance with this knowledge.[52]

In very real sense, Hall's work provided the capstone for the works of Rousseau, Pestalozzi, and, to some extent, Parker, because it supplied a "scientific" basis for child-centeredness. Unlike Hall, however, Parker saw the public school as a great force for the improvement of society.

Insofar as Hall's theory of curriculum development had authoritative underpinnings (experimental psychology), it was a radical-progressive idea. Oddly, however, his rationale for the individualization of education was conservative: It was in support of the doctrine of *laissez faire,* for the purpose of individualization was to identify the gifted child, give him or her encouragement, and expend less energy on the dull child. Wrote Curti about Hall's influence:

> Although Hall opened up new fields and emphasized new aspects of human life his influence was largely directed to the support of individualism and *laissez-faire.* This was the effect of the cult of child study, which tended to make the curriculum child-centered, and to single out for particular attention the gifted child.[53]

Child-Centeredness and Laissez Faire.   The point Curti was making was that a child-centered curriculum is a *laissez faire* curriculum; it does not direct itself to social needs and concerns. This was actually a contrapositive force in the progressive movement, both in the very early stages of the movement and in the 1920s. As Dewey stressed, education reform cannot be conceived apart from social reform; the two are deeply interwoven. As Fass points out, our experience with school reform over the century has "linked the reform of the schools directly to the reform of the society as John Dewey had intended."[54]

When carried to its ultimate extreme, a child-centered *laissez faire* curriculum is no organized curriculum at all. In the 1920s, the child-centered curriculum was built, in some places, entirely on the momentary interests of children. By stressing individual values at the expense of social values, and by discounting the role of the school in social change, Hall cast the die for the progressive education of the 1920s, a mold that some progressive educators regarded as disastrous and tried their utmost to break.

✳ In developing his own curriculum theory based on *laissez faire,* Hall literally turned his back on the mounting and often frightening problems being faced by a rapidly changing society. When the progressive movement in education finally gathered momentum it did so, in the words of Cremin, "as part of a vast humanitarian effort to apply the promise of American life—the ideal of government by, of, and for the people—to the puzzling new urban-industrial civilization that came into being during the latter half of the nineteenth century."[55]

EDUCATIONAL OPPORTUNITY AND SOCIAL PROGRESS: THE BIOLOGICAL CONNECTION

Despite the social philosophies of Hall and William T. Harris, *laissez faire* was on the decline. (Harris, whom we met in the first and second chapters, believed that it was the purpose of education to serve existing social and economic conditions. He also thought that the idea of pupil self-discipline was antithetical to the social purpose of the school, which was to train the child to accept authority.)

A new curricular age was dawning. "The recognition of the shortcomings of our individualistic social philosophy has made many people look at our schools from an entirely new point of view," wrote William D. Lewis, principal of Philadelphia's William Penn High School in 1914.[56] "If they emerge from the high school with an indifferent, selfish, *laissez faire* philosophy, they will become either the unthinking victims or the plunderers of our devil-take-the hindmost social order."[57]

American progressivists attributed many of the pervading social ills to a long-standing condition of "rugged individualism" or *laissez faire,* and sought to attack these social ills through enlightened social action. The new progressive social philosophy was to generate a veritable revolution in the role and function of the high school.

The Concept of Planned Change

The outlook of the education progressivists toward evolutionary improvement was that progress is possible but certainly not inevitable. Progress is most likely to occur when humans *plan* for what they consider to be a better human condition and focus their energies on achieving these goals.

THE IDEAS OF LESTER WARD.   The new point of view had been in the making since 1883 when Lester F. Ward, in his now classic *Dynamic Sociology,* attacked the weaknesses of *laissez faire* and proposed instead a planned society. In other words, progress is not controlled by the laws of evolution but, rather, by the human's control of nature. Education has a leading role in making a better life.

THE FORGOTTEN GIANT.   Curiously, Ward is almost forgotten. But Ward was the creator of some of our most fundamental conceptions about the curriculum—ideas that were further developed by Dewey. Ward was a founder of the field of sociology but spent most of his life as a government paleontologist. At the age of sixty-five he became a professor of sociology at Brown University. What makes Ward so fascinating (and important) was that he applied his biological knowledge to the problem of social reform.

The measure of progress as defined in the field of biology—control over the environment—is found in Ward's book, *Dynamic Sociology.* In our own time, Francisco Ayala, the evolutionary biologist, tells us that *Homo sapiens* is marked off from other animals by "extreme advance in the ability to perceive and react to the environment . . . complex social organization, control over the environment, *the ability to envision future states and to work toward them,* and values and ethics are developments made possible by the human's greatly developed capacity to obtain and process information about the state of the environment."[58]

Ward's ideas are not only still useful but can be found in contemporary ideas. In effect, Ward had anticipated the emergence of the field of sociobiology by almost a century.

EDUCATION: AN ENVIRONMENTAL QUALITY.   In *Dynamic Sociology,* Ward's emphasis is on humans' ability to deliberately plan alterations in their environment. Ward explained the basic difference between biological, unconscious evolution (genesis) and deliberate, conscious evolution (telesis). Late on the evolutionary scale the capacity for telic progress had come out of the meandering processes of biological evolution. Although the human capacity for thought evolved genetically, it is up to humans to take advantage of the opportunities it offers to improve their lives. Telic progress is a planned, conscious process that requires the development and application of intelligence. The means is education, which is a "quality of the environment" and it is in government's interest to make it as widely available as possible.[59]

The ability to consciously change the natural and social environment—the criterion of progress in evolutionary biology today—is that of Ward's telesis, conceived by him more than one hundred years ago. As the present authors have noted,

> [i]n Ward's writings we find the biological basis for educational opportunity, and for the development of intelligence as the most important purpose of the curriculum: The human, unlike other organisms, has knowingly adapted its social environment

and with reflective intelligence will effect social progress. This will be done through education, which develops the ability to study situations and work out solutions. . . . That there *is* a scientific basis for educational opportunity is often forgotten, probably because Ward has been forgotten. Educational opportunity is usually supported by its advocates on ideological grounds rather than on biological grounds. It has both. It is the science—the telic conception—that makes Ward's argument different from earlier arguments.[60]

As Henry Steele Commager pointed out about Ward's place in history, "No earlier American educator—neither Jefferson nor Horace Mann nor Henry Barnard—had based his educational program so firmly on scientific foundations or had faced so clearly its logical implications or consequences."[61]

With clarity unlike others in his time, Ward saw the influence of environment on talent and intellectual ability. "Like plants and animals," he wrote, humans have "latent capacities which for their development simply require opportunity."[62]

Progress and the Curriculum

The curriculum was vital to telic progress and Ward gave it a great deal of thought. He knew that unless the curriculum fostered the development of intelligence, education could not be a means of social reform. As it was, education tended to be superficial and disconnected from the natural world. What was needed was a curriculum "which continually knits the physical being to his environment and does not ultimately depend upon memory or upon tradition."[63]

Ward's ideas about the curriculum were sound, but they needed to be transformed instrumentally into ways to guide teachers. How does one teach children to apply their intelligence and how is intelligence developed? Dewey provided the approach: a problem-solving method for the school that corresponded to the scientific method.[64] Dewey's problem-solving method or method of intelligence made Ward's more general concepts about the curriculum operational. The connection between Ward's idea that human progress is achieved by applied human intelligence and Dewey's problem-solving method or method of intelligence is direct. If progress is to be achieved by applied human intelligence instead of by waiting for nature's slow processes, there has to be a way, and Dewey supplied it. For Dewey, thinking is problem solving and his paradigm has come to be called variously *problem solving, critical thinking, reflective thinking, functional thinking, scientific thinking,* the *complete act of thought,* and the *method of intelligence.*

 EQUALLY AVAILABLE KNOWLEDGE.   Dewey built on a second feature of Ward's philosophy: the idea that knowledge should be equally available to all members of society. Ward argued for this passionately because he was so certain that unless knowledge was democratized, the possibilities for social progress and democracy were nil. Ward believed that the huge gap between the ignorant and the intelligent was caused by the "unequal distribution" of knowledge.[65]

But how, then, is knowledge distributed? Dewey viewed the problem this way: Educational opportunity is shared knowledge and concerns, and progress is achieved through breaking the class barriers to sharing. Thus, the problem was one of learning together as well as what is to be learned. Today, as in Dewey's time and that of Ward who preceded him, to conduct education programs so that students cannot learn together, not only betrays the democratic dream but reduces the possibilities for telic progress.

CONTEMPORARY FORMS OF WARD'S ARGUMENT.   Ward's own argument that knowledge must be equally available still stands on its own. More important, perhaps, it is still found in contemporary forms. The principle of equal educational opportunity involves more than the right to go to school; it is deeply concerned with the curriculum—with what Goodlad calls "access to knowledge."[66] Goodlad's study of schools found large differences from school to school in children's opportunities for knowledge. In arguments well supported both by his own research and by principles from the curriculum literature, Goodlad argued for change and improvement.

Similarly, those who are fighting against the censorship of curriculum materials are embracing the principle of access to knowledge so that students have the opportunity to investigate significant social ideas and problems. Such opportunities are essential for developing the critical thinking skills required for participation in telic progress. Those engaged in dropout-prevention programs in schools today are following Ward's advice that opportunities must be "actively thrust" on individuals.[67]

Unlike advocates of eugenics (improving intelligence through controlled mating and parentage), Ward believed "that the human brain is adequate today—and always has been adequate—for any purposes which it may be called upon to perform."[68] The great need, argued Ward, was not to increase humankind's hereditary genius, but to develop human intelligence through education.

In looking at our history it is very clear that Ward's environmentalism won out in the end. Developments in curriculum and educational policy throughout the twentieth century reveal that environmentalism became the dominant influence in American education. As we have stated elsewhere:

> Environmentalism was not a mere abstract idea. American educators took their cues from a society that clearly believed (since the Revolution) that environment shapes human destiny, and they proceeded to expand educational programs and opportunities on a scale unprecedented anywhere else in the world. They were relentless in their efforts as environmentalism, rather than eugenics or hereditary social privilege, became the great twentieth-century credo for American education.[69]

DEMOCRACY AND EDUCATION

In establishing a new relationship between school and society, Ward irrevocably linked democracy and education, for at the heart of dynamic democracy lay the ability to make intelligent decisions, and this required training in citizenship as well as a certain atmosphere or way of life in the school itself. It was unrealistic, for instance, to suppose that pupils could learn to think independently in a situation that required unthinking obedience. Thus, it was quite naturally concluded that in order to produce good citizenship, the schools themselves would have to become laboratories for citizenship where school problems were being solved.

A decade after Ward's book was published, Francis Parker pointed to the common school as the key to human progress and fused the philosophies and fortunes of democracy and education. In a chapter in *Talks on Pedagogics* (1894) entitled "Democracy and Education," Parker wrote that the democratic principle of mutual responsibility—the idea that each member of society contributes to the good of all—must be translated into educational goals that reflect the enormous responsibility of citizenship. But more important even than the formalized curriculum was the social power of the school to break down the clannishness and prejudices of people from all parts of the world who were learning together in the school. "The common school," wrote Parker, "is the embryonic democracy."[70]

Dewey Forges the Link

In 1916, Dewey's *Democracy and Education* was published. This remarkable work forged the definitive link between democracy as a social process for achieving people's highest goals and education as the democratic way of preparing people to make intelligent decisions about social change. Like Parker, Dewey saw the school as a democracy in microcosm. And like Parker, Dewey viewed education as a social process and a social function. But, cautioned Dewey, "the conception of education as a social process and function has no definite meaning until we define the kind of society we have in mind."[71]

Thus unless our ideal of society is clear, the definition of education as a social function would fit as appropriately in a dictatorship as in a democracy. And even in a democracy, the social aim of education could become perverted into a narrow nationalistic aim. This happened twice in the second half of the twentieth century: In the late 1950s and early 1960s the science and mathematics curricula were given priority to meet the nationalistic goal of supremacy in the Cold War and space race, and from the 1980s into the 1990s when graduation requirements for high school students were increased in these fields in order to regain leadership and dominance in global industrial markets. In both instances, the public schools were held scapegoat for shortcomings in our political, industrial, and military sectors.

To Dewey, the democratic ideal of education was "a freeing of individual capacity in a progressive growth directed to social aims."[72] Education was growth but it had a distinctly social as well as individual purpose.

Could not the desire for social change produced by education result in civil disorder, if not revolution? It could not, according to Dewey's definition of democracy. Dewey anticipated that question (which he must have felt would trouble educators as well as the lay public). He answered it this way:

> A society which makes provision for participation in its good of all its members on equal terms and which secures flexible readjustments of its institutions through interaction of the different forms of associated life is in so far democratic. Such a society must have a type of education which gives individuals a personal interest in

social relationships and control, and the habits of mind which secure social changes without introducing disorder.[73]

Although Dewey made the definitive statement on democracy and education that formed the bedrock of progressive educational theory, the connection between an enlightened citizenry, social change, and the school was being made by education practitioners and theorists well in advance of 1916. Indeed, Dewey himself advanced the educational goal of the development of social consciousness and conceptualized the school as "an embryonic society" (using almost the same words as Parker) in 1899 in three lectures to parents that he delivered at the University of Chicago. These lectures were published as *The School and Society*.[74]

UNITY THROUGH DIVERSITY.   In 1909, historian Ellwood P. Cubberley pointed out that well before 1900 the school had experienced a shift in purpose and direction. Said Cubberley: "The task is thrown more and more upon the school of instilling into all a social and political consciousness that will lead to unity amid diversity, and to united action for the preservation and betterment of our democratic institutions."[75] Our forebearers saw clearly that every nation must have a common culture in order to thrive and survive. Our uniqueness resided in the strength to be drawn from a polyglot populace sharing the ideals of American democracy.

DIVERSITY VERSUS UNITY.   To see unity and diversity as conflicting forces was to raise ominous problems for school and society to this very day. In the 1990s, a battle over the social studies curriculum broke out that, as one observer put it, was "fundamentally a battle over the idea of America."[76] The curriculum debate was essentially over the principle that the curriculum should emphasize themes that unite Americans. In a number of cities and states, educators reviewing history and social studies curricula were recommending that far greater emphasis be put on the roles of non-white cultures in American society. In the 1990s, many educators were wrestling with the question of how to impart a greater sense of America's cultural diversity without misconstruing the Western intellectual roots of our founding fathers and the major roles played by the European immigrants who laid the foundation for government and other institutions in America.

Many teachers began to put more emphasis on the contributions of non-European immigrant groups to America, such as the role of Chinese-American laborers in developing the American West. And more students were studying varying interpretations of such themes in America's history, such as the question of who "discovered" America. Some educators expressed concern, however, over emphasizing "ethnic and racial themes at the expense of the unifying ideals that precariously hold our highly differentiated society together."[77]

The issues in the battle concerned multicultural education—one of the most emotional curriculum issues confronted by education in the 1990s.

DEWEY'S CONCEPTION OF DEMOCRACY.   In *Democracy and Education,* Dewey orchestrated the theory of American democracy into a philosophy of education. No less important is Dewey's definition of democracy as a social process, as an *experience* rather than simply as a form of government. In a very real sense, democracy and education were part of the same process of growth. That is why education could not be genuinely democratic unless democratic values pervaded the entire school.

THE REVOLUTION IN SECONDARY EDUCATION

In 1991, a study conducted for the U.S. Congress on the status of vocational education found that far more students take considerable coursework in vocational education than most people believe. The study found that

> [o]f all the vocational education courses taken by students, nearly 29 per cent are taken by students who plan to go to a four year college; 20 per cent by students who plan to go to a community college; and 27 per cent by students who plan to go to a postsecondary vocational/technical school. The remaining 24 per cent are taken by students who plan to go to work full-time after high school.[78]

All of the conclusions of this important study cannot be reported here, but two seem particularly important for our discussion. First, the study's findings from analyzing national samples contradict the conventional view that the American high school has rigid tracks and that the vocational track enrolls the least-able students academically. The study revealed that students planning on college took "a substantial number" of vocational education courses. Second, by providing students with more opportunities than they now have to use knowledge for practical purposes, vocational education can contribute to the goal of improving education for all students.[79]

A Comprehensive Structure

Let us examine the story implicit, and explicit, in this study. The student transcripts were found to reflect a curriculum that is more diversified than in the common perception of the American public high school. Tracking still exists but a more accurate portrayal of the high school indicates that it includes one track for about 29 percent of higher ability students who are college bound and another track for the other 71 percent of students who are "taking a variety of courses for a variety of purposes."[80] But the main point of importance is that whatever their plans after high school, students devote a not insignificant amount of time to vocational studies. Thus they are able to pursue their interests—whether vocational or avocational. This diversification is only possible because of the continued existence of a flexible school structure—the comprehensive high school—despite efforts to reduce the high school to a traditional academic curriculum. This is not to say that high schools have a fully diversified curriculum without tracking, but that a peculiarly American invention—the comprehensive high school—is friendly to the breadth of student participation in programs that interest them. This flexibility was the intention of its creators with the opening of the twentieth century.

Moving Ahead into the Past

The reader will recall from the first chapter that educators learned long ago that the curriculum, and its requirements, had to meet the needs and values of adolescents if they were to stay in school. It had to do this for an increasingly diversified population of young people. During the 1980s and 1990s, most states increased graduation requirements in academic subjects as a means of improving education. The industrial and studio arts courses were taken off youngsters' programs of study. A number of school districts actually reduced their offerings in the studio arts, industrial arts, and vocational programs. One industrial arts teacher recounted, "After my school district closed the power technology/metal shop in the high school, several students said to me, 'Now there's nothing at school that I'm good at.'"[81]

Not only have such schools experienced an increasing dropout rate but as the teacher pointed out, academically talented students are also deprived of the opportunity to develop practical problem-solving skills and collaborative learning experiences through hands-on projects. The teacher predicted that educators and policymakers will recognize once again that all children need to develop "three-dimensional problem-solving and practical skills," and, "the cycle of education will be complete as we move ahead into the past."[82] However that may be, there is a great cost to students and society when education policies are developed without examining our vast experience with educational reform. Such experience points to the great value of work in the studio arts, industrial arts, and vocational areas.

Educational Theory and the Adolescent

The theoretical basis for curriculum change in the first two decades of the century had two main strands. The first strand was social reformism. In 1899 in *The School and Society,* Dewey described the school as an "embryonic community" that would improve the society by making it "worthy, lovely and harmonious."[83] As Cremin wrote, "what was new in Dewey's analysis is his social reformism. The school is recalled from isolation to the center of the struggle for a better life."[84] In 1916, Dewey defined democracy in educational terms in *Democracy and Education.* By then, he had become widely recognized as the leading spokesman for progressive education. According to Cremin, the work "orchestrated the many diverse strands of pedagogical progressivism into a single inclusive theory and gave them unity and direction. Its very existence lent new vigor to the drive for educational reform."[85]

The second major strand was child developmentalism, which turned the spotlight of teaching on the student. According to psychologist G. Stanley Hall, effective education must consider the student's needs, nature, and development. In this regard, Hall's work, *Adolescence,* which appeared in 1904, was a milestone.[86] It put the pedagogical spotlight on adolescence as a period of mental and physical development and stimulated inquiries into the psychological significance of adolescence. These studies had a profound effect on school organization, educational aims, subject matter, and methods in secondary education.

Operationally, under the principles of the new educational theory, subjects should be included in the curriculum only if they have immediate value for the present needs and growth of the student. To build the curriculum on the basis of mere tradition or deferred values was to invite the failure of the student and the failure of the school. These principles also provided a basis for revising or dropping existing subjects. In connection with the latter, the new societal emphasis on efficiency and economy had a buttressing effect. Those subjects that were dropped usually were the least popular and therefore the most expensive to offer. Greek was dropped from the curriculum in many high schools for this reason.

The flexibility in the American high school curriculum, though not complete, is a far cry from the report of the Committee of Ten, which ignored the needs of adolescents. Granted that the report predated the publication of Hall's *Adolescence* by several years, educators and school board members had already recognized the need to take into account the child's nature, needs, and interests in keeping him or her in school, coupled with the expanding social need for a better educated populace.

The Junior High School

The junior high school was foreshadowed by the recommendations of the Committee of Ten to introduce secondary school subjects in the seventh and eighth grades. It was also a response to a substantially different problem: Compulsory education laws generally prescribed school attendance only until the child was fourteen years of age. With the 8–4 plan of school organization, the break between the eight-year elementary and high school came at the wrong time. It was easier for many pupils, particularly those of uncertain purpose, to terminate their education with graduation from elementary school than to enter a distant and unfamiliar building and take new and strange subjects under several new and strange teachers. A three-year junior high school extending from grades seven through nine, particularly if the program provided the opportunity for election of courses in accordance with pupils' interests and aptitudes, would retain many pupils through the period when most dropping out took place.

It was also argued by its proponents that the junior high school was supported by the findings of G. Stanley Hall and others and that early adolescence is a period of changing and developing interests. A varied curriculum was needed that was exploratory in purpose. Those who objected to the junior high school argued that curriculum reform could be accomplished within the present organizational framework. Although administrative changes, per se, are no guarantee of an improved program, it can be said with certainty that junior high schools showed more activity in curriculum reform than did conventional schools. Junior high schools *could* be more experimental because they were not a part of the high school (which had its requirements dictated by the colleges). Hence, by shifting the ninth grade to the junior high school, the college dominance over the ninth-grade curriculum would be diminished. At the same time, the problem of holding budding adolescents together with young children in the eight-year elementary school would be solved by reducing the elementary school to six years.

In addition to beginning secondary education earlier, and starting each pupil on studies leading to a suitable goal, junior high schools were to provide training for those who would soon enter the world of work. The first junior high schools (originally called intermediate schools) were established in Berkeley, California, and Columbus, Ohio, in 1909, and in Los Angeles in 1910. The fact that by 1930 there were approximately 4,000 junior high schools attests to the remarkable popularity of the new school. The 6–3–3 plan was well on its way toward replacing the old 8–4 system.[87]

THE CURRICULUM. The curriculum principle of variety characterized junior high schools. In the more progressive schools pupils changed curricula and dropped courses freely. This created a concern on the part of many teachers and principals that the curriculum for some, at least, was disjointed. A related question was how long a course was to run to be worthwhile. The curriculum was frankly exploratory but it was uncertain if the material could be reorganized into courses as short as two months or even two weeks with promise of satisfactory results. The values of some studies could be realized only if courses continued longer than most students were likely to remain in school. Yet continuity was needed if education was to have an integrating rather than a disintegrating effect. Thus, curriculum development was also based on a second principle, that of continuity in learning.

Most educators subscribed to the principle that the junior high school program should become increasingly differentiated as the pupil continued in school. At the beginning there would be common learnings or general education consisting of what all citizens should know. The time devoted to common learnings would gradually decrease as pupils pursued options into differentiated curricula in accordance with their different interests and goals.

This reopened the question of what is a common, integrating education. It also posed the question of whether it was not undemocratic to differentiate pupils on the basis of future vocations at the age of twelve or thirteen. It was also feared that those pupils who should have extended education would be attracted into trade courses by short-term goals. According to Thomas H. Briggs, who was instrumental in the development of the junior high school and who had served on the Commission on the Reorganization of Secondary Education (1918), there was small chance that irrevocable errors of choice would be made at this early stage, as long as mistakes were rectified through a flexible curriculum when pupils changed their life aims.[88]

Still, it was difficult in some schools to transfer into a new program under the practice of curriculum tracking. And democracy demanded an open-ended educational system that permitted all individuals to proceed with their education as far as their capabilities, interests, and ambitions carried them. This was most likely to happen when education was of a broad nature for as long as possible. Even when "academic," "industrial," and "commercial" curricula were housed in the same junior high school, pupils were not likely to be exposed in any significant degree to knowledge that ought to be common to all.

EXPLORATORY COURSES. Although there was astonishing variation in practice, many junior high schools offered general exploratory courses in major fields of learning. The basic idea behind courses in general science, general mathematics, general history, general social studies and language arts was to reveal to each pupil the possibilities of a general field of knowledge and aid in the intelligent election of those subjects attracting his or her interest. In line with educational theory, exploratory courses were to be life-related through the elimination of artificial barriers among the various specializations within each field and through the application of broad principles to everyday experience.

The general exploratory courses were also regarded as an essential part of a general education. But the unique feature of exploratory courses was their "guidance" function; this was a way of discovering each pupil's interests and aptitudes so that he or she could be given intelligent guidance.

In practice, however, the general courses proved, on the whole, to be disappointing and invited much criticism. In retrospect, this appears to be a consequence of the failure to translate general aims into a more integrated curriculum and into specific teaching practices rather than a failure of the concept of exploratory learning, per se. Put another way, the idea of revealing to pupils the basic principles of the major fields of learning through unified courses had never been tested.

CRITICISM OF JUNIOR HIGH SCHOOLS.   In the 1960s there was a rising chorus of criticism aimed at the junior high school by persons advocating a different plan of organization and a different curriculum for young adolescents. One criticism was that the junior high school had not lived up to its commitment to provide a program attuned to the nature and needs of young adolescents. As Kindred and his associates pointed out in 1968, nationalizing influences since the late 1950s had brought a disturbing change: "the thrust downward of the senior high school program with its emphasis upon subject matter specialization."[89]

Supporters of the middle school plan of school organization argued that the junior high school had a conventional subject matter curriculum; that is, its curriculum was organized virtually by subject areas and did not provide for horizontal articulation. This kind of curriculum was unsuitable for ten- to fourteen-year-olds. Supporters stressed that the middle school was an opportunity to develop interdisciplinary block-time programs. These were especially appropriate for easing youngsters' transition from a self-contained to a departmentalized program. Different ways could be found to organize the curriculum to meet personal-social needs. This could be done unhampered by the stresses inherent in a school that was continually made aware that the ninth grade is part of the high school program (and record).

Yet according to Kindred and his associates, the real reason for adoption of the middle school was that it was a simple solution to the problem of overcrowded buildings. Space could be freed in elementary and high schools; two grades could be taken from each unit and put in the middle school. "This reason . . . and a desire for better racial balance, has been responsible for its adoption rather than the educational program to be conducted in the middle school."[90]

In 1968, there were 7,437 American public junior high schools, including grades seven and eight or grades seven through nine. Data were not available for middle schools. By 1990, there were 8,272 middle schools, with grade spans beginning with four, five, or six and ending with grade six, seven, or eight. There were only 4,512 junior high schools.[91] Whatever their motives, middle school advocates had clearly been successful in changing the grades and ages included in the unit of schooling for young adolescents.

WHAT COUNTS.   More recently, among the many questions asked in Goodlad's study of elementary and secondary education was whether the junior high school met its transition purpose. In a book growing out of the Goodlad study, Tye put the question this way: "Did the junior highs in our sample provide for a gradual transition for early adolescents from the self-contained, more child-centered elementary program to the departmentalized, subject-centered high school program?"[92]

The answer to the question was that they did not, according to Tye. "What they did do in the name of articulation," wrote Tye, "was to reinforce many of the practices of schooling which growth and development literature tells us are not good for early adolescents."[93] The junior highs were departmentalized and the students were tracked. The study found little evidence of block-time or core classes as a transition step from elementary school to high school. Pupils' experiences in the junior high schools were much like those in the high schools except that classes were larger and not as well-equipped.

"Neither does it matter if schools are called 'middle' schools," said Tye. "In our sample, student experiences were about the same at middle schools and junior highs except that they were begun earlier (grade 6) in the middle schools."[94]

Clearly, changing a school's grade span does not, in itself, lead to program reform. As Epstein concluded in her study of middle-grade schools,

> what happens in a school or classroom is more important than the name on the school door. . . . The hard work of developing excellent programs is not accomplished merely by changing grade spans or constructing smaller buildings, but by attending to practices that are responsive to the needs of early adolescents.[95]

What really counts, then, in middle-grade schools is whether they follow recommended practices for young adolescents such as exploratory education, that is, giving students opportunities to explore a range of fields. Another recommendation is block-of-time programs that afford the opportunity to build the needed coherence and units for meaningful learning. In this connection, it should be noted that an integrated curriculum plan does more than attempt to establish some sort of contact between different subject fields. As Leonard pointed out many years ago, it "endeavors to establish new threads of relationships by cutting across subject lines."[96] These are the "big ideas" that were discussed earlier in this chapter on transfer of learning.

According to Epstein, also recommended are interdisciplinary teams of teachers and common planning time for the teams.[97] Nevertheless, team teaching is not a curriculum design. It is only an organizational tactic designed to improve what teachers are already doing. Some middle school teams emphasize the pupil guidance function. The teachers on the team represent individual subjects such as mathematics, science, English, and social studies—and teams are organized by grade level. The teams themselves may be interdisciplinary but the curriculum is apt to be the conventional subject curriculum.

Curriculum correlation is fostered by regular planning meetings. This is a problem in many schools. Indeed, a national study of middle-grade practices by researchers at Johns Hopkins University found that only about a third of the schools that utilize interdisciplinary teams give the teams at least two hours of scheduled common planning time weekly. The study concluded that "the majority of teams do not have the common planning time they need to become truly effective."[98]

It gives us pause for thought that earlier in the century, many of the advantages now being claimed for middle schools were given for the junior high school. Junior high schools, it was said, offered more opportunities than the self-contained elementary classroom and the departmentalized high school for exploratory education, pupil guidance, interdisciplinary teaching, and horizontal plans of curriculum articulation. By the 1960s, it was felt by critics of junior high schools that they had not met these opportunities.

A Rose by Any Other Name.   According to a national study reported by Becker, only 30 percent of middle-grade students had an exploratory course in the seventh and eighth grades. Moreover, a narrow curriculum and the tendency toward drill, memorization, and the use of worksheets persist in many middle schools. Regarding differences in the curriculum and teaching practice between middle schools and junior highs, the study found that there were far greater differences between individual schools of a given kind than the differences between kinds.[99]

Yet the curriculum in some middle-grade schools does seek to develop skills in reading and communication through activities and projects and broadly integrative concepts. Becker reported that schools giving attention to higher-order thinking tend to be those serving upper-middle-class families. This is the case for junior and senior high schools as well. Such schools are providing more students with more electives, and more academic opportunities and "an intellectually richer academic life."[100] It is crucial to create such opportunities for all children and youth.

The junior high school was an early twentieth century development. As the century comes to a close it is clear that the attainment of the reformers' ideal has been wanting in many aspects. Despite the criticisms leveled at this institution, it did serve to open the gates to secondary education at a time when so many were ending their formal schooling with the eight-year elementary school. At the same time, it gave recognition to early adolescence as a crucial period of development. It provided for a more diversified curriculum and also served as an experimental base for block-time core classes. Unfortunately, the junior high was diverted from its mission as the raising of standardized test scores became a primary concern. Designing a curriculum to meet the needs of early adolescents has been put on the back burner and the curriculum has been frozen in its separate-subject state in the process. Yet in the 1990s it had become increasingly important in our society to help students meet such developmental tasks as desiring and acquiring social responsibility and independence of thought. These are crossdisciplinary and interdisciplinary in nature. Interdisciplinary teams of teachers are a step in the right direction, but only a step. There is much work to be done on the curriculum, and a number of schools and school districts have initiated experimental programs.

The Problems of Secondary Education

The first two decades of the twentieth century were given over by secondary educators to the urgent business of reshaping the curriculum along the lines of a new and utterly different educational and social philosophy. In so doing they were faced with enormous problems, both theoretical and practical—some seeming to defy solution.

In pushing secondary education down to the seventh grade, the school had put twelve-year-olds in a forked-road situation; they would have to choose a specialization. Those entering vocational programs in junior high schools were unlikely to change their programs; they were cut off from associations with pupils pursuing different aims and life goals. In a very real sense this was predestination—the antithesis of the educational opportunity that educators had been trying to improve by increasing the holding power of the school. (As mentioned, the latter was the *raison d'être* of the junior high school as stressed in the Cardinal Principles report of 1918.)

This problem was far more common in the high school. Curriculum tracking had led, in many cases, to social isolation, even where the various curricula were offered under the same roof. In such instances, students were unlikely to be aroused by new interests and unlikely to revise their ambitions. Equally important was the loss of opportunity to identify and acquire common interests and common ideals.

THEORETICAL ISSUES. The basic problem with which educators wrestled was how to provide a distinct curriculum for each individual that would meet personal goals and also meet broad social needs. This raised several theoretical issues: Which were the courses that were most likely to meet democratic social objectives, or should all courses be revised to this end? Which courses should be required of all students? How should the problem of what appeared to be an innate dualism between vocational and so-called cultural courses with its unfortunate social concomitants be resolved? Even within the same subject there were various, apparently opposing, aspects. Science, for example, had both applied and theoretical sides.

Related to the foregoing, should subjects be taught differently according to pupils' needs? The Committee of Ten (1893) had answered this question with a resounding "no." The committee had viewed preparation for college as the best preparation for life. Thinking on this question had undergone radical change. Indeed, many had swung to the opposite extreme, holding that preparation for "life"—industrial efficiency and public service—was the best preparation for college.[101] Some educators believed that this was equally epigrammatic but just as baseless as the dictum of the Committee of Ten.

DEWEY POINTS THE WAY. In 1901, Dewey addressed a conference of secondary educators in Chicago on these problems. It was time, he said, for separate vocational high schools to become integral parts of the city high school.[102] As for the conflict in studies, this could be approached in two ways: (1) by viewing the curriculum in the context of the needs of the individual and (2) by viewing what appear to be opposing elements as complementary and essential parts of a whole. Training in a vocation, unless that training were moored in its cultural context, was narrowing. "Just as in life the technological pursuits reach out and affect society on all sides, so in the school corresponding studies need to be imbedded in a broad and deep matrix," said Dewey. The converse was also true; those studies regarded as preparing for college were "relatively dead and meaningless unless surrounded with a context of obvious meanings"—such as studies in industrial arts, for instance.[103] In other words, their applications to human activities should be made apparent.

Dewey also spoke of another concern of secondary educators—fragmentation in the curriculum because of increasing specialization. Isolation was needed for the unhindered development of a specialization, he said. But the time came when it was necessary to pull the connecting elements of the various specializations together into a meaningful whole. That time had come. "The sole object of the separation is to serve as a means to the end of more effective interaction," he pointed out.[104] What subjects should be required of all students? Here Dewey stressed the importance of those subjects that "deal directly with the problems of health, citizenship, and the means of communication through the vernacular."[105] The principle to follow in curriculum reorganization, Dewey said, was to view all the school studies in light of their place in human activities. Expansion of the curriculum should also follow this principle.

Dewey's criteria for curriculum development provided a theoretical vehicle for educators to use in their attempted escape from college domination. Educational reformers also followed Dewey's lead in developing specific principles for reorganizing the secondary school curriculum. A succession of books based on Dewey's view followed. Thus, according to Albert Yocum, professor of education at the University of Pennsylvania, preparation for a vocation was being confused with preparation for life. This had produced "two almost equally unhappy extremes: a professional specialization which ignores general training and culture and an academic specialization which refuses to relate itself to life." This, he said, was a crisis that could only be resolved by "the paralleling of general education and specialization, and the relating of each as fully as possible to life."[106]

Yocum pointed out that in their anxiety to individualize education, school people were inadvertently encouraging premature specialization. They were also excluding from the curriculum "much that all students should possess in common, whether as part of a common culture or as a means to the direct preparation for a common life from which a common culture can result."[107]

The Commission on the Reorganization of Secondary Education

These ideas had gained currency in 1913 when the National Education Association appointed a committee to develop fundamental principles for the reorganization of secondary education. The report of the Commission on the Reorganization of Secondary Education was five years in the making. Its impact on educational policy has yet to be equalled.

BASES FOR CURRICULUM DEVELOPMENT.   "Secondary education should be determined by the needs of the society to be served, the character of the individuals to be educated, and the knowledge of educational theory and practice available," wrote the commission, thereby indicating the bases for curriculum development.[108] All three—the society, the nature of the secondary school population, and educational theory—had undergone changes requiring extensive modification of secondary education.

But the overriding objective of the secondary school was to give flesh and blood reality to the ideal of democracy, declared the commission. Democratic education "should develop in each individual the knowledge, interests, ideals, habits, and powers whereby he will find his place and use that place to shape both himself and society toward ever nobler ends."[109] This was the dominant theme of the report and, by no mere coincidence, the theme of Dewey's *Democracy and Education* published two years earlier.[110]

CARDINAL PRINCIPLES OF SECONDARY EDUCATION.   The commission named seven principal objectives—"Cardinal Principles"—of education: health, command of fundamental processes (reading, writing, arithmetic, and oral and written expression), worthy home membership, vocation, citizenship, worthy use of leisure, and ethical character. These objectives could best be met in a unified organization embracing all curricula—the comprehensive high school, a school with no counterpart anywhere in the world.

Far from being isolated, the objectives were actually closely interrelated; their interrelation must be reflected in the curriculum throughout the period of secondary education if the student were to be prepared for effective functioning in a democratic society. An illustration was the relation between vocational and citizenship education (social studies). Favored in the report was "the infusion of vocation with the spirit of service" and "the vitalization of culture by the world's work."[111]

The report addressed itself squarely to the formidable problems of secondary education, finding every subject in need of reorganization so that it could contribute more effectively to the seven Cardinal Principles. Indeed, the place of each subject in the curriculum was dependent on the value of its contribution.

SPECIALIZATION AND UNIFICATION.   "With increasing specialization in any society comes a corresponding necessity for unification. So in the secondary school, increased attention to specialization calls for more purposeful plans for unification," stated the report, paraphrasing Dewey's words of nearly two decades earlier.[112] Unification would be accomplished mainly through *constants,* those courses required of all students. These were to be determined by the objectives of health, command of fundamental processes, worthy home membership, citizenship, and ethical character.

Unification was, of course, a fundamental purpose of education in a democracy. In addition to the comprehensive organization of the school itself and the curriculum in general education, unification could be attained through the mingling of students from all walks of life as they participated in social activities, school government, and athletics.

In addition to *constants,* the secondary school should provide *curriculum variables* (specialized courses determined by the student's goals) and *free electives* to be taken in accordance with interests, generally to meet the objective of the worthy use of leisure (although electives could also be taken in accordance with vocational needs or interests other than avocational).

The commission advanced two important principles in connection with specialization and unification: (1) the more time for curriculum variables, the more purposefully should be the time spent on constants as a vehicle for unification and (2) the more differentiated the curriculum, the more important is the students' social mingling.

CONTINUOUS PROGRESS.   The idea that individual development is a continuous process was being emphasized in educational theory. An abrupt break between elementary and secondary education was therefore undesirable. On this basis, the commission endorsed the division of secondary education into junior and senior periods, each ordinarily three years in length and each with discrete purposes. The junior high school should offer the pupil an opportunity to follow his or her interests, to explore his or her abilities and aptitudes. Seventh-graders should not be required to select a specialization but, rather, should have some experience with a variety of vocations—agricultural, commercial, and industrial—plus homemaking for girls and, for some pupils, some work in a foreign language. The foregoing should be organized into short units so that every pupil could take several units. The commission stressed, however, that the work "should be of real educational value, in addition to its exploratory value."[113]

Both junior and senior high schools should be of the comprehensive type to provide students with a sound basis for a wise curriculum choice in addition to serving as organs of unification.

CURRICULUM DIFFERENTIATION AND COURSE CONTENT.   On the one hand, the commission endorsed the idea of teaching subjects differently in accordance with the needs and interests of pupils. On the other hand, curriculum differentiation did not mean that the content of every course should be determined by the dominant element in the curriculum. Such a practice, warned the report, "would ignore other objectives of education just as important as that of vocational efficiency."[114]

IMMEDIATE VERSUS DEFERRED VALUES.   As a reaction against formalism, some educators advocated that pupils study only that which was of immediate interest or value to them. Here the commission drew the line; "This extreme," they declared, "is neither necessary nor desirable. They [the pupils] should be helped to acquire the habits, insights, and ideals that will enable them to meet the duties and responsibilities of later life."[115] However, they should be encouraged to respond to present duties and responsibilities as well, as a foundation for future behavior.

OVERAGE ELEMENTARY PUPILS.   In a section of the report dealing with the articulation of secondary education with elementary education, it was recommended that overage pupils who are retained in the elementary school when they can no longer benefit from it be admitted to the secondary school. "Experience has shown," argued the commission, "that the secondary school can provide special instruction for over-age pupils more successfully than the elementary school can."[116] Experience continues to support the wisdom of this recommendation made so many years ago. The wisest promotion policies give attention to social and emotional factors as well as achievement levels.

A VISION OF DAYS TO COME.   It can be said in retrospect that the authors of the Cardinal Principles had not only an accurate grasp of the pedagogic present but also a remarkable sense of days to come. They, in no small way, determined the shape of the secondary school. They had a vision of secondary education for all youth. That vision was fulfilled in this century.

Prophetically, the report declared that in the interests of democracy higher education could no longer be the province of the privileged.[117] Just as secondary schools should admit those who can no longer be served adequately by the elementary school, so should institutions of higher learning admit those whose needs are no longer met by the secondary school, maintained the commission. This reform did not begin to emerge in any significant way until after midcentury when public junior and community colleges in some states began enrolling persons over age eighteen who had not graduated from high school. Another nontraditional path to postsecondary education has been the high school equivalency credential. Today, hundreds of thousands take the GED tests and are awarded high school equivalency certificates.[118] Thousands of these persons prepare for the tests independently.

The Cardinal Principles were more than a declaration of independence by the high school from college domination. As Arthur Wirth has pointed out, the report's insistent message was that the high school should meet the needs of all youth "rather than cater to the minority that was college bound."[119] The commission members had in mind a design to adjust the curriculum to changing times and a movement toward social democracy. But probably even they failed to realize the magnitude of their contribution to the field of curriculum development. Since its publication, the report has provided the framework for the continual development of the secondary school curriculum.

This is not to say that the comprehensive high school has been free of criticism. Far from it. Let us examine some of the leading criticisms. Almost immediately, the commission's report was vigorously assailed in David Snedden's book *Vocational Education* (1920). Snedden, a vocational educator, opposed the proposal to include vocational education in a comprehensive high school. He argued that it was only possible to provide effective training for vocations in specialized schools. Snedden minced no words about his view of the commission. It was "confused" and its proposals, "vague, if not mystical."[120] Study about vocations had been confused with true vocational education, held Snedden, who contended that the comprehensive high school idea reflected an academic snobbishness. "Toward all current problems, intricate and baffling, of vocational education the committee maintains a serene scholastic aloofness, possibly the same slightly contemptuous indifference which characterized the attitude of our scholastic forebears toward manual labor in general."[121]

Snedden's criticism is fascinating indeed, in view of recent interpretations of the report by revisionist historians who portray the comprehensive high school proposal as an elitist plot to isolate vocational students from mainstream secondary schooling and maintain the appearance of equality.[122] There is no denying that outcomes in many urban high schools have differed from the commission's stated intentions. As Goodlad, Oakes, Tyler, and countless others have pointed out, rigid tracking is the practice in many high schools, and where it exists it makes equal access to the curriculum impossible.[123]

The commission expressed its downright opposition to segregated vocational programs that at that time were under serious consideration. In Illinois, for example, a proposal was put before the legislature that would have split the entire school system in two for youngsters over age fourteen. Dewey attacked the proposal as undemocratic. The separation of general education from vocational education would be used "to mark off to the interests of employers a separate class of laborers," and was "the greatest evil now threatening democracy in education."[124]

Dewey's proposal and subsequent influence on the comprehensive high school idea were discussed extensively and acrimoniously by Snedden in his book on vocational education.[125]

So Dewey won out, but the point of importance here is that a comprehensive plan was radical indeed, just at a time when many bankers and industrialists were supporting a measure that would have established a system of schools completely separate from the regular schools and with a completely different curriculum.

In the 1940s and 1950s, James B. Conant, whose writings were highly influential, recommended the continuation of comprehensive secondary education as the best assurance of a "classless" and free society.[126]

Conant recognized that the challenges of providing high quality academic and vocational programs for all students in a comprehensive setting were enormous, but believed that it can and must be done. Since the turn of the century, access to knowledge has improved, albeit grudgingly in some quarters, for previously excluded groups. Indeed, it has improved since Conant's day. Since Goodlad's study of schooling in 1984, more schools have adopted a diversified curriculum without tracking.

PERSPECTIVE

Founding a public school system was the great nineteenth century accomplishment and the effort to improve it, the charge of the twentieth. This is not to say that the twentieth century can be cut cleanly from the nineteenth any more than the twentieth from the twenty-first. The problems carried over from the nineteenth century are the persistent problems that continue to confront us and in some cases grow ever more urgent. Conditions in some urban schools today recall those described by Charles Eliot as we entered the twentieth century. They have poor equipment and inadequate resources for learning and are unattractive, if not unsafe, places. Some teachers have no desks, files, or classrooms of their own. It is harder to develop in students the desire to go on learning that according to Dewey is the most important objective of all. As Eliot recognized, curriculum improvement is crucial in creating opportunities for children in poverty. Today we know it is also crucial for battling the dropout rate.

Curriculum improvement is what we have been about, and the principle enunciated by Nicholas Murray Butler—basing "wise practice on sound theory"—still holds and is within the reach of each curriculum worker.

Early in the century, Thorndike's research refuted the accepted doctrines for offering certain subjects in the school curriculum, thereby setting into action a chain of events that has continued to influence the curriculum (not always in wise ways). For centuries, certain classical subjects were included in the curriculum because they were believed to develop the mind and disciplined habits of thinking. One outcome of Thorndike's studies was that such subjects could no longer be justified on the basis that they developed the mind. Another was that educators had to find other ways of determining the relative value of subjects. This led to the appointment of NEA's Committee on Economy of Time in Education, which followed a mechanistic approach to curriculum development in identifying the "minimum essentials" of the curriculum. Thorndike had interpreted his research to mean that elements in the school curriculum should be identical with opportunities for their use by learners (or adults) outside of school. This idea was applied in strikingly different ways. It led to the reductionist activity-analysis approach to curriculum making of Bobbitt and Charters but also to such more holistic learning activities as students defining a local community problem and generating actual solutions. This is a practice followed in some schools today in helping young people learn to participate intelligently in a democratic society.

All educators want to improve the probability of transfer of learning, both to school learning and life outside the school. The curriculum must be deliberately planned to foster transfer. We know that a fractured and fragmented curriculum decreases the likelihood of transfer and that broad generalizations and knowledge applications that transcend disciplines increase the possibility of transfer. Following Bruner, basic ideas from science and mathematics and the themes underlying life and literature are simple and powerful. They increase the probability of transfer. Although many schools for middle-grade children have interdisciplinary teams, the teams tend to serve a pupil guidance function and the curriculum often is laid out in separate subjects. Whether called middle schools or junior high schools, schools for middle-grade children have not lived up to their opportunity and responsibility for providing a coherent curriculum along with exploratory studies for older children and young adolescents. Minicourses are not synonymous with exploratory education. The values of some subjects cannot be realized in courses of very short duration.

Progressive educators believed in evolution but not the creeping kind. Progress was possible but not inevitable. In view of our present situation, Lester Ward's ideas concerning education and human progress have been lasting and significant. Only humans have the capacity for telic progress, which is deliberate conscious progress requiring the development and application of intelligence. According to Ward, this is the most important purpose of the curriculum and it is in the interest of government to provide the educational opportunity that will ultimately effect social progress. To this end, government must thrust educational opportunities on individuals. Intellectual ability is the outcome of opportunity, not of native capacity. The curriculum should link the individual with the environment—the real world—and not depend on either memory or empty traditions. The application of the learner's intelligence can speed up the slow processes of human progress.

Dewey's problem-solving method or method of intelligence built on Ward's more general ideas about the curriculum and made them operational. Dewey also built on a second feature of Ward's philosophy—the principle that knowledge should be equally available. According to Dewey, educational opportunity means shared knowledge and concerns; the problem is one of learning together as well as what is learned. Learning together in a school that fosters the development of individual interests and talents as well as a sense of social responsibility and the means for its realization were ideas behind the comprehensive high school proposal in the second decade of the twentieth century. They were straight from Dewey. The contemporary emphasis on multiculturalism places even greater demands on the unifying functions of democratic education.

Outcomes do not always equal intentions and some schools became rigidly tracked. The result was what Dewey feared and Ward before him. Students, all too often, are denied equal access to knowledge. (This includes college-bound students who also need opportunities to use practical knowledge.) Today school restructuring proposals are looking once more to the early twentieth century ideal of integrating academic and vocational education. As one educator pointed out in the 1990s, "In integrating academic and vocational education we would promote greater intermingling of students."[127] Dewey and the authors of the Cardinal Principles report would have applauded. In new times, educators continue to look for new ideas and initiatives for meeting the old ideal of unification. The search is unending. This is what Ralph Tyler called an "unfinished task" in education.

PROBLEMS FOR STUDY AND DISCUSSION

1. You are a curriculum supervisor. How would you respond to the argument that Latin should be included in the curriculum because it trains the mind and facilitates the development of disciplined habits of thinking?

2. Is the principle that citizenship tasks taught by the school should be genuine and involve practice supported by research? Explain. To what extent is citizenship education made genuine or real to students in your school?

3. What is your assessment of the following method of developing an interdisciplinary curriculum as described by the school's principal: "Fourteen hundred goals and objectives for the primary grades have been 'compacted' into 200 themes and concepts." [Cited in "Curriculum Integration: Modest Efforts to Link Disciplines Gain Support," *ASCD Update,* 32 (January, 1990), p. 2.]

4. In connection with the preceding question, although knowing nothing about this individual school, might its fragmentation into so many minute objectives reflect the influence of a previous reform movement? Explain.

5. The Commission on the Reorganization of Secondary Education viewed the social studies and the humanities as studies contributing to social solidarity; they should, therefore, be taken by all students. What is the implication of this principle for grouping? A growing number of high schools today are permitting students to elect courses in

these fields rather than requiring the same courses to be taken by all students. Does this weaken the social unification function of the curriculum? Why or why not?

6. In your view is social unification still a valid function for today's curriculum or should ethnicity be emphasized above any shared heritage? Explain.

7. As described in this chapter, some urban school superintendents have proposed that the management of certain schools be turned over to private, for-profit companies. Are such proposals supported by research and past experience? Justify your answer.

8. What are the implications of Ward's and Dewey's conceptions of educational opportunity for curriculum development?

9. Examine the curriculum guides of several high schools, junior high schools, and middle schools. What evidence do you find of efforts to develop interdisciplinary curriculums?

10. In connection with the preceding question, visit one or more of the schools. What evidence do you find of interdisciplinary teaching and integrated learning (where interdisciplinary teams, for example, are helping students make links between concepts in various subject areas)?

11. In this chapter it was pointed out that early in the century Dewey spoke bluntly about the need to integrate academic and vocational education, yet only recently have some schools begun to move in this direction. How do you account for the lack of attention given to Dewey's proposal over the greater part of a century? For the urgency of some of the recent proposals?

12. As discussed in this chapter, in 1920 Snedden described Dewey's proposals for vocational education as vague and impractical. Snedden strongly implied that Dewey had vocational education confused with education about vocations. Examine Dewey's chapter on vocational education in *Democracy and Education* (1916). Do you think that Snedden's criticism was justifiable? Support your response.

13. What principles and supporting examples can you give teachers to help them develop in children the desire to go on learning?

14. Do you agree with the statement that "[s]tudents should have a range of curriculum experiences that reflects both a discipline-field and an interdisciplinary orientation"? [Heidi H. Jacobs, "The Growing need for Interdisciplinary Curriculum Content," Chapter 1 in Heidi H. Jacobs (ed.), *Interdisciplinary Curriculum: Design and Implementation* (Alexandria, VA: Association for Supervision and Curriculum Development, 1989), p. 9.] Why or why not?

NOTES

1. Nicholas Murray Butler, "Status of Education at the Close of the Century," National Education Association *Proceedings* (Chicago: University of Chicago Press, 1900), p. 188.

2. Ibid., p. 194.

3. Ibid., p. 196.

4. Ibid.

5. Charles W. Eliot, "Discussion," National Education Association *Proceedings* (Chicago: University of Chicago Press, 1900), pp. 197–198.

6. Lisbeth B. Schorr, *Within Our Reach: Breaking the Cycle of Disadvantage* (New York: Anchor Books, 1989).

7. Walter H. MacGinitie, "Reading Instruction: Plus Ca Change.—," *Educational Leadership,* 48 (March 1991), p. 56.

8. Ibid., pp. 55–58.

9. D. N. Perkins and Gabriel Salomon, "Teaching for Transfer," *Educational Leadership,* 46 (September 1988), pp. 22–31.

10. Joseph Menis, "Students' Ability to Transfer Basic Mathematical Concepts from Mathematics to Chemistry," *Studies in Educational Evaluation,* 13 (1987), pp. 105–109.

11. Perkins and Salomon, op. cit., p. 28.

12. Edward L. Thorndike, "Mental Discipline in High School Studies," *Journal of Educational Psychology,* 15 (January 1924), pp. 1–22; (February 1924), p. 98.

13. E. L. Thorndike and R. S. Woodworth, "The Influence of Improvement in One Mental Function upon Efficiency of Other Functions," *Psychological Review,* 8 (May, July, November, 1901), pp. 247–261, 384–395, 553–564.

14. Edward L. Thorndike, *The Principles of Teaching* (New York: Seiler, 1906), p. 244.

15. C. R. Broyler, E. L. Thorndike, and Ella Woodward, "A Second Study of Mental Discipline in High School Studies," *Journal of Educational Psychology,* 18 (September 1927), p. 382.

16. Alexander Wesman, "A Study of Transfer of Training from High School Subjects to Intelligence," *Teachers College Record,* 46 (March 1945), pp. 391–393.

17. Sidney P. Marland, Jr., "Career Education Now," Address delivered at the 1971 convention of the National Association of Secondary School Principals, Houston, Texas (January 25, 1971).

18. National Commission on Excellence in Education, *A Nation at Risk: The Imperative for Educational Reform* (Washington, DC: U.S. Government Printing Office, April 1983); U.S. Department of Education, *America 2000: An Education Strategy* (Washington, DC: Author, 1991).

19. Jerome S. Bruner, *The Process of Education* (Cambridge, MA: Harvard University Press, 1960), p. 6.

20. Ibid., p. 23.

21. Richard S. Prawat, "Promoting Access to Knowledge, Strategy, and Disposition in Students: A Research Synthesis," *Review of Educational Research,* 59 (Spring 1989), p. 1.

22. Hilda Taba, *Curriculum Development: Theory and Practice* (New York: Harcourt, 1962), p. 21.

23. Prawat, op. cit., p. 34.

24. Bruner, op. cit., p. 12.

25. Prawat, op. cit., p. 6.

26. Ibid., p. 15; Perkins and Salomon, op. cit., p. 30.

27. Lee J. Cronbach, *Educational Psychology,* 3rd ed. (New York: Harcourt, 1977), p. 65.

28. Catherine Cornbleth, "Critical Thinking and Cognitive Process," in *Review of Research in Social Studies Education,* William B. Stanley (ed.) (Boulder, CO: Social Science Education Consortium), pp. 11–55.

29. John Dewey, *Experience and Education* (New York: Macmillan, 1938), p. 49.

30. Ralph W. Tyler, "Progress in Dealing with Curriculum Problems," Chapter 12 in *Critical Issues in Curriculum,* Eighty-seventh Yearbook of the National Society for the Study of Education, Part I (Chicago: University of Chicago Press, 1988), p. 271.

31. Franklin Bobbitt, *The Supervision of City Schools: Some General Principles of Management Applied to the Problems of City-School Systems,* Twelfth Yearbook of the National Society for the Study of Education, Part I (Bloomington, IL: Public School Publishing, 1913), p. 11.

32. Ibid., p. 15.

33. Raymond E. Callahan, *Education and the Cult of Efficiency* (Chicago: University of Chicago Press, 1962), p. 84.

34. Bobbitt, *The Supervision of City Schools,* op. cit., p. 49.

35. See Daniel Tanner, "Performance Contracting: Contrivance of the Industrial-Governmental-Education Complex," *Intellect,* 101 (March 1973), pp. 361–365.

36. Chris Pipho, "Tents and Pushy Camels," *Phi Delta Kappan,* 72 (March 1991), p. 494.

37. Joseph M. Rice, "Futility of the Spelling Grind," *The Forum,* 23 (April 1897), pp. 163–172.

38. Leonard P. Ayres, "Measuring Educational Processes through Educational Results," *The School Review,* 20 (May 1912), p. 309.

39. Walter A. Jessup, "Current Practices and Standards in Arithmetic," Chapter 8 in *Minimum Essentials in Elementary-School Subjects—Standards and Current Practices,* Fourteenth Yearbook of the National Society for the Study of Education, op. cit., p. 129.

40. Lawrence A. Cremin, *The Transformation of the School* (New York: Alfred A. Knopf, 1961), p. 196.

41. Franklin Bobbitt, "The New Technique of Curriculum Making," *The Elementary School Journal,* 25 (September 1924), p. 49.

42. W. W. Charters, *Teaching of Ideals* (New York: Macmillan, 1927), p. 24.

43. William H. Kilpatrick, "The Project Method," *Teachers College Record,* 19 (September 1918), pp. 319–335.

44. Charles C. Peters, *Foundations of Educational Sociology* (New York: Macmillan, 1930), p. 33.

45. Boyd H. Bode, *Modern Educational Theories* (New York: Macmillan, 1927), p. 191.

46. Franklin Bobbitt, *How to Make a Curriculum* (Boston: Houghton Mifflin, 1924), p. 4.

47. W. W. Charters, "Functional Analysis as the Basis for Curriculum Construction," *Journal of Educational Research,* 10 (October 1924), pp. 214–221.

48. David Snedden, *Sociological Determination of Objectives in Education* (Philadelphia: Lippincott, 1921).

49. See Herbert M. Kliebard, "Fads, Fashions and Rituals: The Instability of Curriculum Change," Chapter 2 in *Critical Issues in Curriculum,* op. cit., pp. 18–20.

50. Caroline M. Dillman and Harold F. Rahmlow, *Writing Instructional Objectives* (Belmont, CA: Fearon, 1972), p. 51.

51. G. Stanley Hall, "Education: A Life-Long Development," *Chautauquan,* 47 (July 1907), p. 155.

52. G. Stanley Hall, "The Contents of Children's Minds on Entering School," *Pedagogical Seminary,* 1 (1891), pp. 139–173.

53. Merle Curti, *The Social Ideas of American Educators* (New York: Scribner, 1935), pp. 426–427.

54. Paula S. Fass, *Outside In: Minorities and the Transformation of American Education* (New York: Oxford University Press, 1989), p. 14.

55. Cremin, op. cit., p. viii.

56. William D. Lewis, *Democracy's High School* (Boston: Houghton Mifflin, 1914), p. 4.

57. Ibid., p. 6.

58. Francisco J. Ayala, "The Evolutionary Concept of Biology," in *Progress and Its Discontents,* Gabriel A. Almond, Marvin Chodorow, and Roy Harvey Pearce (eds.) (Berkeley: University of California Press, 1982), p. 122. Emphasis in original.

59. Lester F. Ward, *Dynamic Sociology* (New York: D. Appleton, 1883), p. 631.

60. Laurel N. Tanner and Daniel Tanner, "Environmentalism in American Pedagogy: The Legacy of Lester Ward," *Teachers College Record,* 88 (Summer 1987), pp. 540–541.

61. Henry Steele Commager, *Lester Ward and the Welfare State* (Indianapolis: Bobbs-Merrill, 1967), pp. xxxvi–xxxvii.

62. Lester F. Ward, "Broadening the Way to Success," *The Forum,* 12 (December 1886), p. 349.

63. Ward, *Dynamic Sociology,* op. cit., p. 602.

64. John Dewey, *Democracy and Education* (New York: Macmillan, 1916), pp. 179–192; *How We Think,* 2nd ed. (Lexington, MA: D. C. Heath, 1933). (Originally published in 1910.)

65. Ward, *Dynamic Sociology,* op. cit., p. 602.

66. John I. Goodlad, *A Place Called School* (New York: McGraw-Hill, 1984), pp. 130–166.

67. Ward, "Broadening the Way to Success," op. cit., p. 345.

68. Lester F. Ward, "Education and Progress," *The "Plebs" Magazine,* 1 (November 1909), p. 221.

69. Tanner and Tanner, op. cit., p. 539.

70. Francis W. Parker, *Talks on Pedagogics* (New York: E. L. Kellogg, 1894), p. 423.

71. John Dewey, *Democracy and Education* (New York: Macmillan, 1916), p. 112.

72. Ibid., p. 115.

73. Ibid.

74. John Dewey, *The School and Society* (Chicago: University of Chicago Press, rev. ed., 1915), pp. 16–18. (Originally published in 1899.)

75. Ellwood P. Cubberley, *Changing Conceptions of Education* (Boston: Houghton Mifflin, 1909), p. 55.

76. Joseph Berger, "Arguing about America," *The New York Times,* June 21, 1991, p. 1.

77. See, for example, Arthur M. Schlesinger, Jr., cited in Sam H. Verhovek, "A New York Panel Urges Emphasizing Minority Cultures," *The New York Times,* June 20, 1991, p. A14.

78. John G. Wirt, "A New Federal Law on Vocational Education: Will Reform Follow?," *Phi Delta Kappan,* 72 (February 1991), p. 427.

79. Ibid.

80. Ibid.

81. Lynn Rannels, "The Place of Industrial Art in the Academic Community," *Phi Delta Kappan,* 72 (February 1991), p. 457.

82. Ibid.

83. Dewey, *The School and Society,* op. cit., p. 44.

84. Cremin, op. cit., p. 119.

85. Ibid., p. 121.

86. G. Stanley Hall, *Adolescence* (New York: Arno Press and *The New York Times,* 1969; originally published by Appleton in 1904).

87. Ellwood P. Cubberley, *Public Education in the United States,* rev. ed. (Boston: Houghton Mifflin, 1947), pp. 554–555.

88. Thomas H. Briggs, *The Junior High School* (Boston: Houghton Mifflin, 1920), p. 39.

89. Leslie W. Kindred (ed.), *The Intermediate Schools* (Englewood Cliffs, NJ: Prentice Hall, 1968), p. 29.

90. Ibid., p. 35.

91. National Center for Education Statistics, *Digest of Education Statistics, 1991* (Washington, DC: U.S. Government Printing Office, 1991), p. 101.

92. Kenneth A. Tye, *The Junior High: School in Search of a Mission* (Landam, MD: University Press of America, 1985), p. 276.

93. Ibid.

94. Ibid., pp. 276–277.

95. Joyce L. Epstein, "What Matters in the Middle Grades–Grade Span or Practices?," *Phi Delta Kappan,* 71 (February 1990), p. 444.

96. J. Paul Leonard, *Developing the Secondary School Curriculum* (New York: Holt, Rinehart and Winston, 1947), p. 293.

97. Epstein, op. cit., pp. 436–444.

98. Douglas J. MacIver, "Meeting the Needs of Young Adolescents: Advisory Groups, Interdisciplinary Teaching Teams, and School Transition Programs," *Phi Delta Kappan,* 71 (February 1990), p. 460.

99. Henry Jay Becker, "Curriculum and Instruction in Middle-Grade Schools," *Phi Delta Kappan,* 71 (February 1990), pp. 450–456.

100. Ibid., p. 457.

101. Albert D. Yocum, *Culture, Discipline and Democracy* (Philadelphia: Sower, 1913), p. 19.

102. John Dewey, "Current Problems in Secondary Education," *The School Review,* 10 (January 1902), p. 21.

103. Ibid., p. 25.

104. Ibid., p. 16.

105. Ibid., p. 8.

106. Yocum, op. cit., p. 25.

107. Ibid., p. 28.

108. Commission on Reorganization of Secondary Education, *Cardinal Principles of Secondary Education* (Washington, DC: U.S. Government Printing Office, 1918), p. 7.

109. Ibid., p. 9.

110. See R. Freeman Butts, *Public Education in the United States: From Revolution To Reform* (New York: Holt, 1978), p. 220.

111. Commission on Reorganization of Secondary Education, op. cit., p. 16.

112. Ibid., p. 23.

113. Ibid., p. 24.

114. Ibid., p. 22.

115. Ibid., p. 17.

116. Ibid., p. 19.

117. Ibid., p. 20.

118. National Center for Education Statistics, op. cit., p. 107.

119. Arthur G. Wirth, *Education in the Technological Society* (Scranton, PA: Intext, 1972), p. 125.

120. David S. Snedden, *Vocational Education* (New York: Macmillan, 1920), pp. 96, 103.

121. Ibid., p. 104.

122. See, for example, Marvin Lazerson and W. Norton Grubb (eds.), *American Education and Vocationalism* (New York: Teachers College Press, 1974), p. 39.

123. John I. Goodlad, op. cit.; Jeannie Oakes, *Keeping Track* (New Haven, CT: Yale University Press, 1985); Ralph W. Tyler, op. cit., pp. 267–276; The Carnegie Foundation for the Advancement of Teaching, *An Imperiled Generation: Saving Urban Schools* (Princeton, NJ: Author, 1990).

124. John Dewey, "An Undemocratic Proposal," *Vocational Education,* 2 (1913), p. 374.

125. Snedden, op. cit., pp. 397–410.

126. James B. Conant and Francis Spaulding, *Education for a Classless Society* (Cambridge, MA: Harvard University Press, 1940); James B. Conant, *Education and Liberty: The Role of Schools in a Modern Democracy* (Cambridge, MA: Harvard University Press, 1953).

127. Kenneth Gray, "Vocational Education in High School," *Phi Delta Kappan,* 72 (February 1991), p. 443.

SELECTED REFERENCES

Bobbitt, Franklin. *How to Make a Curriculum.* Boston: Houghton Mifflin, 1924.

Bode, Boyd H. *Modern Educational Theories.* New York: Macmillan, 1927.

Briggs, Thomas H. *The Junior High School.* Boston: Houghton Mifflin, 1920.

Bruner, Jerome S. *The Process of Education.* Cambridge, MA: Harvard University Press, 1960.

Callahan, Raymond E. *Education and the Cult of Efficiency.* Chicago: University of Chicago Press, 1962.

Conant, James B., and Francis Spaulding. *Education*

for a Classless Society. Cambridge, MA: Harvard University Press, 1940.

Cremin, Lawrence A. *Popular Education and Its Discontents.* New York: Harper, 1990.

Cremin, Lawrence A. *The Transformation of the School.* New York: Alfred A. Knopf, 1961.

Cuban, Larry. *How Teachers Taught: Constancy and Change in American Classrooms, 1890–1980.* New York: Longman, 1984.

Cubberley, Elwood P. *Changing Conceptions of Education.* Boston: Houghton Mifflin, 1909.

Dewey, John. *Democracy and Education.* New York: Macmillan, 1916.

Dewey, John. *Experience and Education.* New York: Macmillan, 1938.

Fass, Paula S. *Outside In: Minorities and the Transformation of American Education.* New York: Oxford University Press, 1989.

Goodlad, John. *A Place Called School.* New York: McGraw-Hill, 1984.

Jacobs, Heidi H. *Interdisciplinary Curriculum: Design and Implementation.* Alexandria, VA: Association for Supervision and Curriculum Development, 1989.

Lipsitz, Joan. *Successful Schools for Young Adolescents.* New Brunswick, NJ: Transaction Books, 1984.

Lounsbury, John H., and Gordon F. Vars. *A Curriculum for the Middle School Years.* New York: Harper, 1978.

Oakes, Jeannie. *Keeping Track.* New Haven, CT: Yale University Press, 1985.

Schorr, Lisbeth B. *Within Our Reach: Breaking the Cycle of Disadvantage.* New York: Anchor Books, 1989.

Snedden, David S. *Vocational Education.* New York: Macmillan, 1920.

Taba, Hilda. *Curriculum Development: Theory and Practice.* New York: Harcourt Brace Jovanovich, 1962.

Tanner, Daniel. *Secondary Curriculum: Theory and Development.* New York: Macmillan, 1971.

Tanner, Daniel. *Secondary Education: Perspectives and Prospects.* New York: Macmillan, 1972.

Tanner, Laurel N. (ed.). *Critical Issues in Curriculum,* Eighty-seventh Yearbook of the National Society for the Study of Education, Part I. Chicago: University of Chicago Press, 1988.

Thorndike, Edward L. *The Principles of Teaching.* New York: Seiler, 1906.

Tye, Kenneth A. *The Junior High: School in Search of a Mission.* Lanham, MD: University Press of America, 1985.

Ward, Lester F. *Dynamic Sociology.* New York: D. Appleton, 1883.

Wright, Grace S. *Block-Time Classes and the Core Program in the Junior High School.* Washington, DC: U.S. Office of Education, 1958.

Zilversmit, Arthur. *Changing Schools: Progressive Education Theory and Practice 1930–1960.* Chicago: University of Chicago Press, 1993.

CHAPTER 4

EVOLUTION OF THE MODERN CURRICULUM

The fall of mental discipline as a curriculum theory had left a great void. That nature abhors a vacuum was certainly true of education. Into the vacuum came activity analysis, child centeredness, ways of investigating learning, studies of children and adolescents, and last but not least, efforts to use our democratic principles in identifying curriculum objectives. The void was filled but not with a unified theory; instead, various curriculum reform efforts were undertaken, based on incomplete and often conflicting criteria for determining what knowledge is of most worth. For the interested reader, the reform efforts have been catalogued and described in their own time.[1] A few examples are described in this chapter.

The diversity of reform efforts might have made consensus seem impossible. But rather than decrying the confusion and conflict that characterized curriculum making, our forbearers decided to do something about it. The ultimate result was a theoretically based system for curriculum development that has continued to guide educators to this day. Of course this did not happen overnight, but rather, over decades, by succeeding generations of educational theorists. We also have learned a great deal over the twentieth century about who should be involved in curriculum development and how. This chapter is concerned with principles that are still basic to curriculum development work and how a curriculum comes alive.

CONSENSUS ON CURRICULUM MAKING

If there was a hero in the curriculum making movement, it was Harold Rugg, whose idea it was to bring together the varying and opposing viewpoints and, as much as possible, unify them. As in other professions, the services of the curriculum specialist must rest on the mastery of a common body of knowledge and skills. Rugg, a professor at Columbia's Teachers College, saw this clearly, and it lay at the heart of his deep concern for the reconciliation of opposing viewpoints.

The Twenty-sixth Yearbook

In 1924 Rugg and a group of curriculum professors associated with the National Society for the Study of Education (NSSE) received a grant to prepare a yearbook for the society on the theme of curriculum making. Thus began the monumental work of NSSE's Committee on Curriculum Making, chaired by Rugg. For two years the committee of twelve reviewed trends, studied outcomes, and endeavored, in Rugg's own words, "to map out new paths."[2] They met regularly in what were described by Rugg as "prolonged round-table conferences over similarities and divergences in educational theory."[3] Their report was published in 1927 in two volumes as NSSE's Twenty-sixth Yearbook. The Twenty-sixth Yearbook is regarded today as a landmark in the evolution of curriculum theory.

ADMINISTRATION VERSUS ANALYSIS.   The Committee on Curriculum Making sent a questionnaire to selected American school systems to determine their involvement in curriculum development. Based on the returns, it seemed clear that curriculum revision was widespread in the 1920s and that a nationwide movement for curriculum revision was under way. In elementary and secondary schools and even in colleges, dissatisfaction with the existing program was growing. Hundreds of school systems were engaged in the curriculum revision. The problem was, as Counts pointed out in his chapter on high schools, change was not being "directed intelligently." It was just happening.[4] Courses were dropped from and added to the curriculum in the dark, so to speak—without evaluation and an overall design.

The problem of design was compounded by the problem of theory. Theory had been largely neglected. According to Rugg, the development of educational theory required

> the vigorous impact of opposed schools of thought upon each other. The development of education theory has been much hampered in our day by the lack of intellectual controversy. School men have been more concerned with educational practice, with administration, than with hard thinking concerning the direction in which education is moving and ought to move. Administration is ousting analysis.[5]

LISTENING ORGANIZATIONS.   Rugg recounted that many years earlier the National Herbart Society had served as a way for people to come together and exchange views. The meetings of the Herbartians were genuine open forums. Much of contemporary educational theory, he said, was the result of their early meetings and publications. This was evident from the first few yearbooks of the Herbart Society. For example, members presented their theoretical positions on how to integrate the curriculum.[6] But with the phenomenal multiplication of teacher associations and other educational associations and institutions, said Rugg, "our national societies have become 'listening' organizations. Discussion has waned. Intellectual resistance has dwindled."[7]

Rugg was wrestling with the kind of questions that beset us today. Indeed this very problem—the importance of organizational unity in countering poorly conceived curriculum changes—is the subject of a chapter in a recent yearbook of the National Society for the Study of Education.[8] (The National Herbart Society was the ancestor of the National Society for the Study of Education.)

APPROACH TO CURRICULUM MAKING.   The Committee on Curriculum Making found that curriculum development was being approached by methods that were lamentably inadequate. In the words of Rugg and Counts,

> [t]he responsibility for curriculum making is commonly borne by committees composed of teachers and administrators who are already overburdened with work. As a consequence, the existing program is always taken as the point of departure, and attention is centered on the addition of new materials or the subtraction of old materials from the established school subjects.[9]

In effect, there was virtually no movement toward fundamental reconstruction of the school curriculum.

Having described the situation regarding curriculum development in most schools, the committee proceeded to make recommendations based on practices and past experience in the more progressive cities. These practices—or steps to be taken—had been observed by committee members. First in importance in the committee's view was the development of a "thoroughly professional and research attitude" toward the problem of curriculum improvement on the part of those in charge—the superintendent, supervisory staff, board of education, and teachers.[10] Effective curriculum development was impossible without recognition of the professional nature of the task.

Second, funds must be provided for a continuous and comprehensive program of curriculum development. Its effectiveness was contingent on the establishment of a central and autonomous department of curriculum. The heart of the instructional work, which the committee noted usually constitutes the major portion of school administration, would be the department of the curriculum.

The third suggestion was the appointment of professionally prepared curriculum development specialists, whose responsibilities would be carried out under the leadership of an assistant superintendent or curriculum director. The committee's survey had found that in most districts there was no individual with expertise in curriculum development who was responsible for the total program of curriculum development.

Fourth, the administrator in charge of curriculum improvement should be provided with adequate facilities and resources for the development of her or his work. The department should be located in a central building with the other administrators and a professional library was of the essence.

The fifth suggestion or step concerned the actual work of curriculum making. Most of the work of preparing courses of study would be done by committees of principals and teachers. The fifth step was to organize the committees. Here the committee interjected a word of advice based on the experience of Denver, Winnetka, and other systems: Funds must be appropriated to release those doing the work of curriculum making from all classroom responsibilities. This was an absolutely essential condition, argued Rugg and Counts, for doing the "laborious work of assembling and organizing materials, preparing, criticizing and revising outlines, selecting books, phrasing objectives and illustrating methods of teaching," and to assure that it was done professionally, teachers who are released from the classroom "should be chosen for professional rather than for political reasons."[11]

Finally, the number of committees should be small. There should be a coordinating committee, including the curriculum director or assistant superintendent, who can see the curriculum whole and not as disjointed, independent subject specializations and domains. Another critically important suggestion was to merge the separate subject committees to form broad fields of interrelated subjects—for example, a committee on the social studies rather than on history, civics, geography, economics, and so on.

Curriculum continuity, the committee maintained, could be achieved by having a single committee for each broad curriculum field, which would consider the entire program from the first through the twelfth grade. "Individuals responsible for visualizing the whole scheme must constantly be integrating the work of these smaller groups. By no other method," concluded Rugg and Counts, "can we secure the unification of related activities and materials and the continuity and development which our current school system so sadly lacks."[12] This need remains paramount to this very day in connection with the curriculum at all levels—from the elementary school through the college.

THEORY DEVELOPMENT: UNIFYING OPPOSING POSITIONS.   The Committee on Curriculum Making was able to achieve unexpected consensus on questions involving philosophical differences. Much of the debate revolved around the issue of child growth versus social needs as the starting point for curriculum construction. The group finally agreed that both views were important and both were incorporated in the final statement.[13] The committee, under the leadership of Harold Rugg, had made a clear beginning in the search for a curriculum paradigm, as discussed in detail in Chapter 7.

The committee stressed that the key to curriculum making lay in the application of scientific principles. Looking at the process itself, there were essentially three tasks: to determine the objectives of education, the modes and materials of instruction, and the organization (appropriate grade placement) of learning experiences. The goals of education and the content of the curriculum would emerge from studies of American society and individual development. But above all, "care should be exercised to validate proposal changes experimentally."[14]

According to Tyler, the curriculum development process as outlined by Rugg and Counts presented some limitations "from the failure to recognize that preparing lists of activities and materials is only part of the task which also includes developing interest in using them on the part of teachers and overcoming the passive attitudes of pupils toward school work."[15] Tyler went on to explain that unless a teacher actually discovers and believes that the instructional program is grievously lacking, he or she will not invest time and energy to make effective use of a different one. Those engaged in the leading curriculum improvement projects of the 1930s learned this lesson and found ways of devising and evaluating alternative curriculum designs and learning outcomes.

In looking back on the contributions of the NSSE Committee on Curriculum Making, Walker pointed out that the "Twenty-sixth Yearbook is an admirable piece of work, deserving of more attention and appreciation than it receives," and, unlike most recent work, it "kept everyone's eye pretty much on the ball of curricula and curriculum making."[16] It was indeed admirable; it focused on the problem, and it was more: It established principles of curriculum development for a newly emerging field of university study and systematic professional practice.

The Society for Curriculum Study

The Society for Curriculum Study grew out of the efforts of pioneer Henry Harap in the field of curriculum. It started in 1928 with Harap's efforts to find a means of exchanging ideas on curriculum making. By 1932 the group had become known as the Society for Curriculum Study.[17] As the decade progressed instructional supervision came to be recognized as an integral part of curriculum improvement. In 1941 the Society merged with the NEA's Department of Supervision and Directors of Instruction to become the Association for Supervision and Curriculum Development, and the relationship between supervision and curriculum development was signalized.

In a very real sense, the Society for Curriculum Study viewed its function as continuing the work of the Rugg committee. In 1936, the Society embarked on a joint project with the Department of Supervision and Directors of Instruction to produce a summary of then-current curriculum thought and practice. Such a book, they believed, might be useful to school officials and teachers. Like the Rugg committee, the Harap committee put forward a point of view and proposed an approach to curriculum development.

The Harap committee took the position that "it is the function of the school to improve living in a democratic society."[18] What this meant was that school life, and particularly the curriculum, must have a social focus. "Problems of our common life, suitable to the experience and maturity of each group, should make up the major portion of the curriculum," said the committee.[19] The curriculum would be evaluated in terms of students' ability and desire to react with increasing intelligence to lifelike problem situations. The good society was never static but encouraged human achievements and was evidenced by a society undergoing progressive change. The good life was social—what seemed promising for the society as a whole was paramount. "As a consequence," concluded the committee, "the school should be society centered rather than child centered."[20]

To be sure this was a theoretical step, but unfortunately the Harap committee seemed to have fallen into the trap of either-or thinking by setting democratic social aims against learner centeredness, rather than seeing the two as interdependent. In the light of world and national events in the 1930s, however, it is not difficult to see why the Harap committee took the position that the curriculum should emphasize activities that would prepare children to be involved in sharing the responsibility and power that was the heart of democracy. These goals were, of course, not new.

DEMOCRACY, DESPOTISM, AND THE CURRICULUM.   Four major totalitarian dictatorships had come to power—in Germany, Italy, the Soviet Union, and Spain. All were based on the idea that it is the leader's job to regiment the people and lead them for the good of the state. The promises and political preachings of the dictators captured the imaginations of disenchanted Europeans who paid the price of having their political liberties completely suppressed. The horror of the Holocaust in which millions of Jews and other minority scapegoats and political dissidents lost their lives still continues to shock the world, but the fact that it happened in Germany—one of the world's leading centers of university scholarship—made American educators uneasy. Americans began to feel that their democracy was being threatened. Added to this, America was experiencing the worst economic depression in modern times. These problems were uppermost in the minds of the Harap committee members.

DICTATORSHIP VERSUS DEMOCRACY IN THE CLASSROOM.   One does not have to live in a dictatorship to be a dictator. As the committee pointed out, a teacher can either function as a leader or "be a little dictator in the classroom."[21] Teaching children the skills of democratic living required that neither they nor their teachers feel that they work in a dictatorship. "Where does dictatorship leave off and leadership begin, and how can the distinction be reflected by the curriculum and methods of learning?"[22] This question was destined to be asked by educators again and again in succeeding decades. As Tyler pointed out, educating for democratic citizenship is "the most generally accepted goal of American education," and, further, the question of "what young people should learn in order to participate intelligently in this changing society must be faced anew by each new generation."[23]

UNITS OF WORK.   The Harap committee proposed that the curriculum be composed of a series of learning units. The term *unit,* as the committee pointed out, had gained acceptance since Kilpatrick had popularized the project two decades earlier. According to Harap, the concept of the learning unit could be traced to Kilpatrick's attempt to unify the traditional curriculum, which was broken up into small unrelated pieces.[24] As we have pointed out, however, the idea of giving unity to the curriculum through the learner's experience was advanced by Dewey much earlier and was applied in his Laboratory School.

According to the Harap committee, a learning unit—also known as a unit of work—was based on a real situation. These situations gave the learning units coherence. Units were not kept within the confines of a single subject field. Take, for example, the learner's question of how his or her family obtains food. As Harap argued, "To keep a child's inquiry concerning his food supply within the limits of geography is manifestly absurd. Even if one set out deliberately to do so, it could not be accomplished."[25] Many units drew on all school subjects. For instance, the study of water supply originating in the social studies involved map study, graphic representation, science, mathematics, government, and history. Today such a problem might originate in the broad field of ecology.

Units of work were viewed by the Harap committee as the smallest subdivision of the curriculum. The committee selected eight "areas of living" or groups of related activities for learning units: living in the home, leisure, citizenship, organized group life, consumption, production, communication, and transportation.

The conventional subjects were viewed as merely accessory in a "functional curriculum."[26] In other words, concepts from fields of knowledge were used as needed in the study of areas of living. However, remedial classes in reading and arithmetic could be offered to treat deficiencies in these areas, and separate subjects could be studied as electives.

Even though the Harap committee called its proposal society-centered, it was based on the recognition that children go through stages of development. Educational programs must be geared to these levels. The activities for a given class depended on their maturity. Moreover, "the choice of the pupils themselves will determine exactly what enterprises should be undertaken in any grade."[27] There is no doubt that the Harap proposal drew on knowledge about the child, realizing that interests must be considered if children are to learn. The Harap committee's conception of the appropriate curriculum encompassed the psychological as well as the social point of view.

CHARACTERISTICS OF A PROGRAM OF CURRICULUM DEVELOPMENT. The Harap committee identified concepts on which modern curriculum development is based. The individual events may be different for each of us as we seek to improve the curriculum, but we still should proceed on the following:

1. No professional staff has to start from scratch. For more than a century researchers and practitioners have studied curriculum problems and reported their findings. An enormous number of studies is to be found. Even better, summaries of findings on major curriculum problems (transfer of learning, for example) are readily available in the search for the best available evidence.

2. Curriculum development is a continuous process. Change is the most constant characteristic of our society and the rising generation must be able to understand and deal intelligently with the issues of a changing society. The world of knowledge is undergoing continuous change; the advancement of knowledge requires that curriculum development be continuous.

3. Curriculum development activities should result in resources that are adaptable to the special needs of particular groups of students. Teachers should be encouraged to adapt the materials they have developed collaboratively to their own students and to utilize other resources and lessons of their own.

4. A major change in curriculum requires broad-based involvement and support. No one group—be it teachers or administrators—should carry out the work independently. Teachers, principals, supervisors, parents, and other community members should be involved in making major decisions concerning basic principles, objectives, scope, and organization.

5. A constantly improving education to meet the needs of students and a democratic society requires the personal commitment of the teacher. Teachers must believe that a curriculum problem is serious, not just hear that it is. This is most likely to happen if they identify the problem.

6. Planning for curriculum improvement requires adequate resources—financial and material, time, and expertise. Every school district can (and should) have a curriculum development program, but its nature depends greatly on the commitment of resources. Financial limitations must be faced, but what the Harap committee counseled long ago is still true: "more money can usually be secured if the public is convinced that the proposal will materially improve the prospect of pupil growth."[28] It also should be remembered that much can be accomplished with a knowledgeable and committed existing staff.

7. Proposed solutions to problems should be based on the best available evidence rather than popular trends. Proposed solutions to curriculum problems should be tried out for a time. (The professional staff should not impose their answer.) The curriculum should be evaluated continuously in terms of its effects on students, teachers, and the community. (Curriculum evaluation is often, and wrongly, equated with testing.)

8. A good curriculum development program is characterized by enthusiasm and commitment. "No great accomplishment," the Harap committee observed, "comes in any field without people who *care*, without leaders who have faith in their principles and who have a certain fervor in seeing that these principles have a fair trial."[29]

Modern curriculum development owes much to the Society for Curriculum Study but perhaps even more to Rugg and his committee, who sought to unify opposing views and contributed to the development of a curriculum paradigm.

THE LANDMARK SCHOOLS

The lives of students today continue to be touched by the contributions of curriculum pioneers in days gone by. As Cremin pointed out, there were many diverse strands of progressive education, and each represented at first an idea in one person's mind.[30] Some of these strands became woven into the modern curriculum. Two program strands in particular deserve to be discussed here because the ideas behind them became principles on which modern curriculum development is based. One was developed in the experimental private school, the Lincoln School of Teacher College, and the other in a suburban public school system, the Winnetka, Illinois, schools.

The Lincoln School

The Lincoln School was the creation of a curriculum reformer par excellence, Abraham Flexner, whose name is generally associated with reform in medical education.

The origins of the school can be traced to Flexner's brilliant and monumental essay entitled "The Modern School" (1916) in which Flexner wrote that the purpose of education was to develop in children "the power to handle themselves in our own world."[31] This power was dependent on an understanding of the physical and social world. The former required the ability to observe and interpret phenomena; the latter required an understanding of contemporary industry, science, and politics.

Flexner believed that "useless" subjects should be eliminated from the curriculum.[32] Claims for a place in the curriculum because of their historical or cultural value alone were not sufficient for including traditional subjects. The curriculum should include purposeful subjects. The objective of the modern school was intellectual power that, Flexner believed, would most likely be developed by realistic education.

The curriculum of the modern school would be organized around activities in four basic fields: science, industry, aesthetics, and civics, but science would be the central field. Flexner also stressed the importance of making cross-connections among the four fundamental fields.

Flexner saw the modern school as a center for scientific curriculum making, a laboratory school. The teachers would develop and test educational materials and methods as they proceeded with curriculum reconstruction in accord with Flexner's principles. Their findings would serve as guidelines for curriculum development in other schools.

Things moved quickly where Flexner was concerned. In 1917 his Modern School opened as the Lincoln School of Teachers College, Columbia University. The school was founded by the General Education Board (which had been created by John D. Rockefeller in 1902 as an instrument of educational philanthropy and to promote the idea and practice of general education). Flexner had been a member of the board since 1913. The purpose of Lincoln was to bring about curriculum reform. The General Education Board was not set up for administering a school, so they decided that a highly regarded institution should supervise what appeared to be a radical project. It selected Teachers College. A study at Teachers College found that this decision resulted in critical problems for Lincoln.[33] They are discussed shortly.

Lincoln was established as a laboratory school, just as Dewey's school had been two decades earlier, but in this case, the venture was supported by Rockefeller funds. According to Buttenwieser, Lincoln's purpose was to change the character of American education just as Johns Hopkins had changed the nature of medical studies.[34]

At Lincoln, attention was to be directed particularly to the problem of curriculum synthesis within and between the major fields of knowledge. As Gehrke observes, this is still an enormous practical problem today.[35]

UNITS OF WORK.   The curriculum of the elementary division of the Lincoln School was organized around the unit of work. Operationally, however, the separate subject was still omnipotent. This was evident in the evaluation process; the final step of the unit was a summary of subject areas covered, and reporting to parents was by subjects.

Hypothetically, at least, the idea for a unit originated with the children. The child-centered school of thought held that nothing should be learned that does not arise from the child's interests or "felt needs." But in reality, units often were teacher initiated or chosen "cooperatively" by teacher and class. When pupils showed little inclination to hunt for a worthwhile problem, the teacher had to compensate and assign one (theory notwithstanding). Details for the units—even teacher-assigned ones—were generally not planned in advance.

The new education held that subject matter and skills were most effectively learned when there was a real need for them. Theoretically, there was no place in the new curriculum for isolated subject matter and drill. Did Lincoln teachers dispense with subject matter and skill development except as the need arose? Put another way, were all skills—reading, for instance—taught via the unit of work? This decision, like all curriculum decisions at Lincoln, was individual. Some teachers relied completely on the unit as both the vehicle and the criterion for worthwhile learning. Thus, which arithmetical operations they taught depended on the children's need to use these processes to solve a problem about which they had become curious. Other teachers scheduled separate periods for instruction and practice in skill development. Second-grade teachers Katharine Keelor and Pauline Miner, for example, set aside thirty-five minutes per day for formal reading instruction (including an individualized silent reading program for able readers).[36]

On completion, units of work were broken down into subject-matter components to determine what kinds of content had grown out of the various activities. This was an essential part of summarizing and assessing the educational effectiveness of the unit. As an example, one teacher's summary of a fourth-grade unit on foods indicates that the pupils had done work in the following subjects of study: reading, composition, geography, history, science and household arts, fine arts, and arithmetic. The specific topics covered were listed under each subject; in history, for example, students had studied primitive ways of getting food. In composition, they had written original poems on orchards, farms, and gardens and a book on the jelly business. In geography, they had studied the effects of climate, altitude, and latitude on fruit growing.[37]

Significantly, reporting to parents was based on pupil progress in the traditional subjects, although the report card also had a section dealing with habits and attitudes. The latter included specific behaviors under the headings of appreciations, initiative, cooperation, responsibility, work habits, consideration of others, honesty and trustworthiness, personal habits, and health habits.

It will be recalled from our discussion in Chapter 2 that the program in Dewey's Laboratory School was based on his theory of curriculum. Dewey wrote about the child: "He goes to school and various studies divide and fractionalize the world for him."[38] But Dewey did not advocate that the subjects be discontinued. In children's activities and trips were the sources of the major fields of knowledge. In Dewey's curriculum theory the subjects were given an experiential nature that served to integrate the child's world. As Mayhew and Edwards, who taught in Dewey's school, wrote, when the children reached adolescence, the faculty found that their perspective slowly changed "from the psychological approach of the learner or mere observer of facts to the logical one of the adult, who observes to an end and classifies what he has observed with the purpose of its further use."[39]

But Lincoln was not guided by a coherent curriculum theory. According to Buttenwieser, one reason was that Teachers College was unable to provide effective leadership.[40] The Teachers College faculty represented widely divergent outlooks.

Nevertheless, during the first decade of Lincoln's existence, excellent curriculums were accomplished. Harold Rugg developed an entire social studies curriculum, focusing on social problems and the interrelationships of several subject fields. A new approach to mathematics that focused on everyday, useful problems was developed by two Lincoln teachers. Another Lincoln contribution, as previously discussed and as reported by Buttenwieser, was the "unit of work" concept. Indeed, Buttenwieser's study reported that the Elementary Division at Lincoln invented the learning unit.[41] Nevertheless, the unit idea—an effort to provide the child with a coherent learning experience, concerned with a real problem and having a purpose accepted by the child as his or her own—is an outgrowth of the cooperative problem-solving activities that Dewey and his colleagues initiated in the Laboratory School at Chicago.

Invention or not, the units and other curriculums produced at Lincoln were widely disseminated, and probably served as models for organizing the curriculum in many of the nation's public schools. The units are still useful models of a way of organizing the curriculum, and collections are available in leading libraries for teacher education today.[42]

CURRICULUM INTEGRATION IN THE HIGH SCHOOL.   One of the purposes for establishing Lincoln School was to develop models for curriculum integration. The Rugg social studies materials, developed in the 1920s at the junior high school level, helped to realize this promise. Curriculum synthesis was achieved through problem-focused study of American social, political, and economic institutions. The impact of Rugg's social studies series of texts was national (he was the first to integrate the social sciences into the social studies). But more importantly, it was the very breadth of Rugg's conception of the social studies that provided the foundation for curriculum reorganization at Lincoln. As Nelson writes, "Not only the social sciences, but English, the physical and biological sciences, even mathematics, would be restructured under the broad umbrella of social studies, the central vehicle of curriculum essentials."[43] In 1927, plans were made at Lincoln to develop integrated courses at the secondary school level.

THE GENERAL COURSE.   The model for curriculum synthesis that evolved was the block-time core or "general course," an effort to integrate social studies, English, and the fine arts (except in the ninth grade where the core was social studies and science). By 1935, about half of student time was spent in the core course for general education, the balance being allocated to required and elective courses in mathematics, science, modern foreign languages, music, physical education, home economics, and the fine and industrial arts. Ultimately, the core courses that developed were as follows:

1. Seventh grade—Man and His Environment
2. Eighth grade—Early American Life

3. Ninth grade—Living in a Machine Age

4. Tenth and eleventh grade—Ancient and Modern Cultures (a two-year sequence)

5. Twelfth grade—Youth in America Today (vocations, the individual, family, citizen)

The integrated program had two major objectives: the development of the individual to full capacity and participation of the school in the progressive improvement of an industrial democracy. Here the influence of Harold Rugg and George Counts is evident: The secondary school was to participate in the process of social reconstruction.

SOCIOECONOMIC REALITIES.   Problems and projects served as organizing centers for the curriculum in the core courses. The high school staff at Lincoln attempted to include socioeconomic realities in the curriculum, particularly during the Great Depression of the 1930s. It was felt that firsthand experience with the problems of our society would be the best way to generate interest and concern on the part of youth and, not incidentally, to lay the groundwork for imaginative solutions when youth reached adulthood.

It was further believed that an intimate acquaintance with the problems of democracy was essential for personal development. Youth would find a purpose in life. Moreover, youth would discover that personal satisfactions harmonize with societal needs. Without purpose an integrated personality was an impossibility. A major goal of child-centered schools was personality integration; the term *integration* as used by educational philosophers during the 1920s and 1930s referred to personality. It was contended that a curriculum integrated through units or projects was the best, indeed, the *only,* path to the larger goal of personality integration.

FIELD-STUDY EXPERIENCES.   It is every social studies teacher's dream to provide students with extensive travel-study opportunities. At the Lincoln School the dream became a reality in 1937. A sizable grant from the Alfred P. Sloan Foundation made it possible to take large groups of students on trips to study the socioeconomic realities of American life as part of the core curriculum. As preparation for Living in a Machine Age, fifty ninth-graders lived for eight days in the homes of rural New England farmers to study a less mechanized society than their own. As part of their study of "economic and social planning in a democracy," fifty twelfth-graders toured the Tennessee Valley Authority and various other federal reconstruction projects and cooperative enterprises in Georgia and Maryland undertaken in the wake of the Great Depression. Fifteen eleventh-graders were selected to go to Pennsylvania and West Virginia to do a field study about the poverty-stricken communities that were then being affected by the massive technological unemployment in the coal and steel industries.

An attempt was made to evaluate the educational outcomes of the eleventh-grade field-study experience. The investigation, conducted with the assistance of the Progressive Education Association's evaluation staff, found "evidence of an astounding development on the part of fifteen boys and girls in a relatively short time."[44] The group that went on the trip made significantly greater academic gains than the group that remained at home and, not surprisingly, they revealed greater sensitivity toward the social issues involved.[45]

CURRICULUM RESEARCH.   Development of the core concept in a laboratory school was an unparalleled opportunity to gain theoretical knowledge in the curriculum field. Although it was believed that the core course was a more effective approach to learning than were the traditional subject courses, no one was really certain of this.

Mention should be made here of the kinds of curriculum studies conducted at Lincoln. In 1926, Otis W. Caldwell, director of the school, described three types of curriculum studies in progress: a retrospective-descriptive study of a third-grade unit on boats, a study to determine what map facts were used by adults as a basis for curriculum construction in the social studies, and a similar study in biology.[46]

Obviously, these investigations were not part of a systematic attempt to test the theoretical bases of the new education. Nor were they efforts to test the effectiveness of the unit of work as a model for curriculum integration. Typically, curriculum making in the units of work (and later the core courses) was based on a combination of intuition, educational philosophy, and chance occurrences (spontaneous events). This process was labeled *experimentation,* yet those so engaged tended to shun the idea of putting on paper a curriculum that could be tested.

One must not get the idea that the Lincoln staff and its mother institution were unmindful of the need for studies that would produce an objective account of results. Although there was not a consensus that such studies were needed or even possible, curriculum evaluation was a persistent concern for Rugg, Shumaker, Bonser, and undoubtedly other members of the Teachers College faculty.[47]

THE PROBLEM OF CURRICULUM EVALUATION.   In 1934, in an appraisal of student achievement, L. Thomas Hopkins, Lincoln's curriculum specialist, and James E. Mendenhall, a professor of social studies at Teachers College, reported that there was a need for a new type of achievement test to determine the results of the new curriculum of the school.[48] Like most laboratory schools, Lincoln had demonstrated clearly that its students did not suffer in terms of achievement, as measured by standardized tests. But studies were needed to measure the additional kinds of learnings and benefits purportedly afforded students by the new curriculum.

Teachers College had a long-abiding faith that evidence supporting the school's program would ultimately be produced. Although the Lincoln staff did not undertake such research, the systematic research on the idea and practice of correlation and synthesis through the core curriculum was to be conducted on a massive scale nationally in the Eight-year Study (1933–1941) in which the Lincoln School participated.

MISSION UNACCOMPLISHED.   The year 1941 marked the beginning of the end for the Lincoln School. Teachers College decided to merge it with the Horace Mann School, a subject-centered demonstration school also connected with the college. In 1947, a New York State Supreme Court decision dealt the final blow to the Lincoln

School, upholding a decision by Teachers College to close the school and transfer the funds from the sale of land and buildings to the Horace Mann-Lincoln Institute. The decision of college trustees to close the Lincoln School was couched in these words: It "had not functioned to the fullest extent of its potentialities for experimentation."[49] The credibility gap had become too wide for even the most faithful. However, the ordeals of the Great Depression found Teachers College under great pressures to consolidate its resources and draw on the Lincoln School endowment. Hence, the merger and eventual closing of the Lincoln School became part of the picture despite the protests of the Lincoln School staff, alumni, and parents.

CURRICULUM THEORY AND DESIGN.   Why did the Lincoln School staff generally neglect to undertake systematic and continuous curriculum research? From the outset, the inability of the staff to agree on the need for a curriculum design was a hindrance to productive experimentation. There was no paper curriculum to test. This is indeed regrettable, especially in view of the observation of Hollis L. Caswell that the Lincoln School curriculum "possessed substantial unity and rested upon a reasonably easily perceived theoretical base." (In 1938 Caswell established and chaired at Teachers College the first Department of Curriculum and Teaching in the United States.) Moreover, in the words of Caswell, "Rugg's search for a 'new synthesis of knowledge' was a definite, clear-cut approach to curriculum reorganization based on a well-defined theory."[50]

But if the staff met the prior condition for a curriculum design, namely a clearly explicated curriculum theory, they were nevertheless remiss in neglecting to formulate and test the overall design based on that theory. What are some possible reasons?

In the late 1920s, the heyday of child-centered schools, the staffs of such schools "displayed very little interest in either of these two matters" (theory and design).[51] This was to be the pattern of such schools in years to come.

AGAINST SCOPE AND SEQUENCE.   A curriculum planned in advance was simply contrary to the philosophy of many progressivists, not to mention the holder of the chair of philosophy at Teachers College, William Kilpatrick. Throughout the 1930s there was an aversion by many on the Lincoln staff to any plan that would state in advance the concepts and generalizations to be taught—the ends of instruction. It was believed that any plan would hamper, indeed stultify, curriculum building by teacher and student. Little wonder, then, that there was no agreement on the need for a curriculum design.

Would educational leadership on the part of the overseeing institution, Teachers College, have made a difference? Might Lincoln have functioned more effectively as a laboratory? In his study, Buttenwieser indicates that the fate of Lincoln was really sealed at the beginning when the General Education Board chose Teachers College to administer the school. Teachers College appeared primarily interested in psychological experimentation and testing, whereas Flexner and the board were concerned only with curriculum reform. Interestingly, both Flexner and Caldwell (the school's first director) predicted that one day the college would undercut Lincoln's purpose by transferring Lincoln's endowment resources into its own purposes.

Generally speaking, the objective of curriculum makers in the 1920s was to reorganize subject matter in accord with the findings of child development. There was little questioning of the conventional school subjects by education leaders; rather, the emphasis was on curriculum adaptation, that is, using the principles of child development as a guide for the organization and placement of subject matter.

In Winnetka, Illinois, Superintendent Carleton Washburne and his staff conducted grade-placement investigations to determine when children could most effectively learn to read. They conducted similar studies on arithmetical operations, spelling words, and basic facts in history and geography. Following this approach to its logical conclusion, the Winnetka system attempted to adapt its curriculum to the needs of individual children. The method used—the forerunner of programmed instruction and mastery learning—is examined in the paragraphs that follow.

 THE TWO-PART CURRICULUM.   In 1926, Carleton Washburne wrote: "Our observation has been that schools which attempt to develop all their knowledge-and-skill subjects from childlike activities often do a 'sloppy' job in giving the children mastery of the tool subjects and sometimes distort the so-called 'childlike' activities in an attempt to bring in knowledge and skills."[52] Washburne also was seeking a scheme for answering any criticisms that the basic skills would be neglected in an integrated curriculum. The Winnetka curriculum was divided into two distinct parts: the *tool subjects,* also called *common essentials,* and activities. The tool subjects—arithmetic, reading, the language arts, and, at first, the social studies—were subdivided into units of achievement. (Ultimately, the social studies were placed in the activities curriculum.)

INDIVIDUAL INSTRUCTION.   Children were allowed to work on an achievement-skills unit as long as needed for "mastery." They worked independently, using self-instructive, self-corrective materials developed by the Winnetka staff. After each self-test, the child was given a check test by the teacher. Class assignments and recitations were abolished. All elementary grades in Winnetka were organized on this basis.

 What came to be known as the Winnetka Plan was the first systemwide attempt to individualize the subject curriculum. It was based on the idea that the best way to improve the curriculum was to reorganize it so that each child could master it at his or her own individual rate. Pupil assignments were based on curriculum studies conducted by Washburne and his staff who wrote teaching materials for reading, arithmetic, spelling, history, geography, and science. The idea was based on a plan for individual instruction developed in 1913 by Frederic L. Burk at the San Francisco State Teachers College laboratory school.

CURRICULUM INVESTIGATIONS.   A major point of interest is that when Washburne began his work at Winnetka in 1919, textbooks and the school curriculum (which tended to follow textbooks) were arbitrarily graded. In arithmetic, for example, some schools in the United States taught long division in the third grade whereas others introduced it in the fourth or fifth grade. Washburne and his associates conducted investigations involving more than five hundred cities to determine at what mental age children could most effectively learn the various arithmetical operations. They found that the mental age necessary for each arithmetical operation was considerably higher than the age at which it was usually taught in school.

The findings from this study formed the basis for arithmetic assignments made to individual pupils in the Winnetka elementary schools and influenced the content of textbooks throughout North America; there was, for the first time, an attempt to gear the order of arithmetic topics to the developmental abilities of the child. Ultimately, however, Washburne was to be disappointed in the application of research findings to the teaching of arithmetic. Textbooks, after all, were still written in terms of the mental age of the average child, although research indicated it was the mental age of the individual that was the key to his or her learning effectively. Wrote Washburne in 1963: "Tradition and inertia (and lack of knowledge as to how to individualize instruction) have made practice lag behind scientific findings in this (as in all fields)."[53]

THEORETICAL ISSUES.   There were two grave theoretical problems with Washburne's scheme that continue to concern modern educators. The first is whether the "common essentials" were really nothing more or less than a convenience system. At the time, William Kilpatrick pointed out that there was no agreement among educators on what constituted *the* common essentials." "Not 'the common essentials' but 'some common essentials' that lend themselves to self-teaching assignment—these constitute the content of the first part of the Winnetka scheme," he contended.[54] This issue is as critical today as it was when Kilpatrick raised it in 1924.

The second issue concerns individualized instruction as programmed instruction. Often we hear the terms *individualized instruction, programmed instruction, self-paced instruction,* and *computer-assisted instruction* used interchangeably. Many proponents of programmed instruction believe erroneously that to use self-paced programs is automatically to individualize instruction. In actuality, the only factor individualized is the rate of correct items completed. The really provocative issue, as Kilpatrick had pointed out, was that the subjects identified as "essential" were those that were most easily subjected to itemized programming and testing. Certain operations—like calculation in mathematics, for example—may lend themselves to mechanical teaching more than do other subjects, such as social studies. Even the skills involved in calculation are only mechanical tasks until they become operational tools in the processes of critical thinking for problem solving.

If we follow Dewey, critical thinking is motivated by a problem. It must be a real problem—the pupil's own problem. Neither a simulated problem nor a practice problem intended to help pupils perform well on reasoning items on tests would qualify, for as Dewey noted, such problems "are his *only* as a pupil, not as a human being."[55] For Dewey, things happen as a result of inquiry. The course of events has been influenced.

The following illustrates Dewey's view of thinking as a developing process that involves seeing a real problem through:

> Children in one third grade class were uneasy about the number of sledding accidents in their town involving children and cars. A survey of community recreation facilities revealed that there was no safe place for children to use their sleds, causing

many sledding accidents each winter. The class planned and made a snow slide on the side of a hill and developed rules and regulations for its safe use.[56]

The only way that children will learn to solve real problems is by using firsthand experience. The point of importance, however, is that there are many desirable educational experiences and outcomes that do not lend themselves to a system of self-paced instruction. This was shown in the Winnetka Plan.

CURRICULUM ADAPTATION.   The Winnetka Plan was a notable example of curriculum adaptation, the idea that the school could best be improved by rearranging the existing curriculum in accord with the findings of child development. In this connection, nothing conveys the interest of educators in curriculum adaptation more clearly than the title of the Twenty-fourth Yearbook of the National Society for the Study of Education, published in 1925: *Adapting the Schools to Individual Differences.*

Curriculum adaptation continues to be the most common approach to curriculum development. That the curriculum will be encapsulated in separate subjects is still generally accepted as a given. What have become known as *mastery learning, outcome-based education,* and *second-chance systems*[57] are essentially variations on the Winnetka Plan, with all of the same problems of Washburne's system of individual instruction—and more. They are based on the concept of "equality of outcomes" as a goal of education rather than optimization of opportunity.

In modern times, Washburne's approach has been given its theoretical formulation by Benjamin Bloom. According to Bloom and other psychologists, virtually all children can learn what schools have to teach through a rich and stimulating learning environment, well-designed instruction, remedial help when needed, and the time they need to "master" the material.[58]

Bloom's idea is sound and constructive, but easily misapplied. The difficulty comes in putting Bloom's idea into practice. The focus in many districts is on learner outcomes and assessing the outcomes, rather than on skilled teaching and providing remedial help as needed. Time is often viewed as a fully expendable and limitless resource. "What matters is not *when* the student achieves the outcome but, rather, *whether* the student eventually achieves success."[59] This statement by an assistant superintendent for instruction in a high school district may appear on the surface to be sensible, but what happens to a student who is locked into an unproductive curriculum and learning environment? Will more time solve the problem, or will the student, in frustration, give up in failure or drop out?

In the foregoing school district, exit outcomes were defined in each subject area. As in Washburne's time, school subjects continue to provide the framework for curriculum development in most school systems. The focus is on modifying instructional strategies rather than changing the design and function of the curriculum.

CURRICULUM RESEARCH

The word *profession* comes from the Latin, meaning "a public declaration or vow." One of the hallmarks of a profession concerns research: Professionals have a responsibility to base decisions on the best available knowledge. But educators receive surprisingly little information about their obligation to look to research for help in making decisions. The assumption is that they learn about this professional responsibility as they complete teacher or administrator certification requirements. But the assumption is not always correct, and the responsibility must be made more explicit. Ralph Tyler called on those preparing teachers and administrators to address this need systematically. "I believe the student should early in the study of education understand the effect of relevant research findings in limiting the consideration of curriculum alternatives to those that are consistent with what is known about learning and other relevant factors in education," declared Tyler.[60]

This tradition of research-based practice is part of the evolution of the modern curriculum. The tradition is not always followed. Educational leaders frequently find that it is difficult to change beliefs with mere facts.

According to Tyler, "The purpose of research is to get a more generalized understanding of a phenomenon," and the responsibility of policy makers and school personnel is "to seek to get an understanding of research" in attempting to meet the needs of particular schools.[61] Tyler's point is that it is the school's responsibility to use research in addressing local problems. Researchers should not use their general findings to impose programs on particular schools. It is not their responsibility. "While researchers and school personnel have common interests, they do not have common responsibilities."[62] We consider the relation between researchers and school persons in this section.

Research from Relevant Fields

Research in fields other than curriculum development, such as educational psychology, child development, and sociology, do not answer the ultimate curriculum questions, such as "What knowledge is of most worth?" but may be useful in making decisions about what should be taught and how it is taught. A good illustration is Thorndike's research on transfer of learning, which was discussed in Chapter 3. Thorndike was not a curriculum specialist; in fact, curriculum as a formal field of study had not yet emerged when he conducted his monumental studies. But Thorndike's findings influenced curriculum thought and provided justification for opening the classroom doors to fields such as the vocational-technical studies, social studies, laboratory sciences, and studio arts.

Similarly, Bloom's research has greatly increased our understanding of the relationship between teacher behavior and student learning. Bloom views the classroom as an ecological system consisting of factors or variables that directly influence students' achievement in school. As Bloom points out, by focusing on alterable variables (such as styles of interactions with students), teachers can improve student learning greatly.[63]

According to Bloom, "When these interactions of teachers with their students are altered, there are significant improvements in student learning."[64] For example, one variable is the quality of teachers' explanations; students who have difficulty in learning do better when teachers provide strong explanations and directions. Supervisors have used the variables in providing teachers with feedback about what they are (or are not) doing and what they can do to change. Moreover, and more important perhaps, the variables provide ways of analyzing teachers' classroom problems. As we have pointed out, Bloom's view that all children can learn also has influenced the curriculum, although his challenge most often has been applied to the curriculum in mechanistic ways.[65]

Bloom and his associates developed a classification of cognitive processes in a hierarchical order. Higher-level cognitive outcomes of the curriculum are defined as those involving the development of thinking processes rather than simply recall.[66] The cognitive taxonomy has been used by many teachers as a means for designing instructional activities encompassing a wider range of cognitive learnings.

Much of modern curriculum thought rests on the Deweyan view that children play an active role in their own intellectual development and its outcomes. Sociologist James Coleman's landmark study, *Equality of Opportunity* (1966) described this feeling of self-responsibility as fate control. Coleman found that the achievement of children who perceive a causal relationship between what happens to them and their own behavior was significantly higher than those who perceive that what happens to them is the result of luck or other forces outside themselves or beyond their control. This finding attracted great educational interest and influenced the curriculum by revealing the potential benefits of heterogeneous classes and the deleterious effects of social isolation of economically disadvantaged children.

The point of this section can be summed up in these words by Dewey: "The scientific content of education consists of whatever subject-matter, selected from other fields, enables the educator, whether administrator or teacher, to see and think more clearly and deeply about whatever he is doing."[67]

Vocabulary Research

One of the most influential kinds of research on practice has been vocabulary research—efforts to determine children's word knowledge for the purpose of grading textbooks. Washburne's work on this problem at Winnetka has already been mentioned. Washburne was deeply concerned and worked hard to base curriculum material on scientific research. As Clifford points out, much of the education research conducted in the first decades of the twentieth century was directed at vocabulary and readability studies.[68]

Hundreds of such studies were conducted. Edward L. Thorndike was an early leader in vocabulary investigation; his publications on language in particular from 1908 to 1949 numbered about 75.[69]

According to Clifford, vocabulary research supported the curriculum reforms of the progressives who sought to make classroom experiences more meaningful. It was thought that teachers with more information about vocabulary and readability would be better equipped to develop units of study engaging students in the use of a wider variety of printed materials.

Vocabulary research was a battering ram against the irrational in education. But it was more: "[I]t was part of a much larger campaign against a false psychology of mental discipline, against the scholar's arrogances and the teacher's self-deceptions, and on behalf of a clear specification of the social utilities of schooling and a determination to fit teaching procedures more precisely to these objectives."[70] Nevertheless, in their penchant for quantification, there was the tendency for researchers to overlook the most powerful factor in readability and vocabulary building—interesting ideas. In effect, readability formulas, word counts, and vocabulary lists mean little if the material is devoid of interesting ideas.

Obviously, studies concerned with factors bearing on curriculum development are far too numerous to permit adequate discussion in the space available, but some of the major studies in the twentieth century will be considered.

The Eight-Year Study

The most important and comprehensive curriculum experiment ever carried on in the United States was the Eight-Year Study sponsored by the Progressive Education Association (PEA) in the 1930s. The study grew out of the realization of secondary school educators that they would never be able to establish an experimental basis for curriculum revision unless they were granted the freedom to do so by the colleges. College entrance requirements determined the major part of the secondary curriculum; these requirements had frozen the curriculum into sixteen Carnegie units.

Thus, in 1930 the PEA took the first step by establishing a commission to deal with the problem of the relation between school and college. In 1931, after a year's study, the commission issued a report on the shortcomings of the secondary school. Most of these shortcomings could be attributed at least indirectly to the unsatisfactory relation between school and college that made fundamental reconstruction an impossibility. The curriculum was unrelated to the real concerns of youth. It had neither the purpose nor the direction needed for unity and continuity. Schools did not know their students and failed to be concerned about what happened to them after graduation (or dropping out). The content and organization of the curriculum prevented the student from developing his or her own educational power. Nearly always the curriculum was laid out in isolated fragments as work for the students to do. They passed through the curriculum with neither an awareness nor an understanding of the forces shaping human destiny and were left unprepared for community life. Anthropologically speaking, the schools were failing as inductors of the young into society.

The commission doubted whether success in college was dependent on the study of certain subjects for a prescribed length of time. The time had come to test this assumption and plan a better education for secondary schoolers.

The Experiment.   The Commission gained the cooperation of more than three hundred colleges and universities in 1932, and a plan was developed that released a small number of secondary schools (to be chosen by the commission's directing committee) from the restrictions of college entrance requirements. The waiver from the usual subject and unit requirements would be for a five-year period beginning with the class entering college in 1936. The colleges were assured by the commission that "only schools of the highest character and established reputation would be selected." This was not the primary concern of the commission, however, in selecting the schools. It was, rather, that the schools chosen had to be willing to experiment in a "progressive" direction.

Apparently, not all of the selected schools actually lived up to these expectations. Twenty-one years later, Wilford Aikin, director of the study, said that were he to do it again, any school "failing to carry on significant curriculum developments" would "be dropped early in the study."[71]

THE THIRTY SCHOOLS. The committee chose thirty schools that seemed both willing and able to conduct exploratory studies and make creative changes in the secondary school curriculum. Schools began to change their curriculums in the fall of 1933. The commission did not prescribe a curriculum to be tested. Each school determined what changes should be made in the curriculum in view of the special needs of its students and the community. The schools were both public and private (half and half), located from Los Angeles to Boston and Madison, Wisconsin, to Tulsa, Oklahoma. However, most of the students in the study were from the public schools. The schools ranged from large city high schools with large groups of minority students to small private schools. Six of the participating schools were laboratory schools connected with universities.

FUNCTIONS OF EVALUATION. Evaluation was an ongoing process from the beginning of the experiment. It had to be. To begin with, data concerning the progress of the college-bound students had to be obtained for the colleges. And then there were the new programs; the participating schools needed to be able to identify the strengths and weaknesses of the programs to make improvements on the basis of evidence. Last, but not least, the clarification of objectives demanded by a program of evaluation was needed to give direction to curriculum change. A number of the schools had vague and fuzzy objectives that had to be clarified to serve as guides for curriculum development and the construction of evaluation instruments.

One of the most monumental tasks of the evaluation committee, headed by Ralph W. Tyler of the University of Chicago, was to help the participating schools develop instruments to evaluate student progress in terms of objectives that dealt with thinking processes. The only tests available were for measuring achievement in the traditional subject curriculum. Interschool evaluation committees were formed for the objectives that were most commonly stressed by the thirty schools, such as the development of effective ways of thinking, increased sensitivity to social problems, and effective work habits and skills. Each committee's task was to define an objective in terms of the behaviors sought and to identify ways of obtaining evidence about these kinds of behavior. These methods—tests, questionnaires, interviews, and the like—became the basis for evaluative instruments developed by Tyler's staff. The instruments were used in appraising student progress.

COLLEGE FOLLOW-UP STUDY. The second phase of the evaluation program took place in the colleges under the direction of college staff. Each graduate of the thirty schools was matched with another student in the same college who had graduated from a school not in the Eight-Year Study and, thus, had met the usual college entrance requirements. The students were matched on the basis of age, sex, race, scholastic aptitude scores, home and community background, and interests. The matching was done by the colleges. Through personal interviews and information from college records and college personnel, the college staff of the Eight-Year Study became well acquainted with each student. A total of 1,475 matched pairs of students were studied.

The Findings.   Established beyond question by the study was the fact that the graduates of the thirty schools were not handicapped in college by their experimental high school programs. In fact, graduates of the thirty schools had higher grade point averages, received more academic honors, and were found to be more precise, systematic, and objective thinkers and more intellectually curious than their matchees. Furthermore, they were more actively concerned about what was happening in the world, earned more nonacademic honors each year in college, and were more resourceful in meeting new situations.

Interestingly enough, those students graduating from the six schools judged to be the most experimental (departed most from tradition)

> were strikingly more successful than their matchees. Differences in their favor were much greater than the differences between the total Thirty Schools and their comparison group. Conversely, there were no large or consistent differences between the least experimental graduates and their comparison group.[72]

It was thus clear that, at least as far as the thirty schools were concerned, the more experimental the school, the greater was the success of students in college. It was also evident that success in college does not depend on the study of a prescribed sequence of subjects in high school.

Curriculum Development in the Thirty Schools.   "My teachers and I do not know what to do with this freedom. It challenges and frightens us. I fear that we have come to love our chains."[73] This remark made by one principal a short time after the thirty schools were selected probably reflected the feelings of many in the experiment. Here, in a very real sense, was the predicament of progressivism in the 1930s. As Dewey had warned, it was time to stop being a movement of protest and to start the search for a new curriculum. Thus, it was one thing to sit back and blame the problems of the high-school curriculum on the stranglehold of the colleges. It was quite another thing to build something better when that stranglehold was removed. This was progressivism's moment of truth, and the Eight-Year Study more than met the challenge.

Curriculum Consultants.   The thirty schools were guided in their efforts to make significant curriculum changes by specialists in the field of curriculum. As indicated earlier, the policy of the directing committee was to encourage and assist each school in developing its own plans rather than deciding what curriculum changes should be made.

As mentioned previously, the Commission on the Relation of School and College issued a report indicating areas needing improvement by secondary schools. These suggestions provided a starting point for many of the schools, but this was hardly enough to help the schools find a sense of direction. Those that asked for help were provided curriculum consultants. Years later, Aikin (who served as a curriculum consultant as well as director of the study) said that "many of the Thirty Schools were ready for such assistance long before it was available to them. Had that been done earlier and in greater abundance, the contribution of the Eight-Year Study to secondary education would have been greater than it was."[74]

The curriculum staff of the Eight-Year Study attempted to keep each school informed of developments in the other schools, made class visits, taught demonstration lessons, and conducted workshops or curriculum clinics. Each member of the staff visited each school once for the purpose of getting mutually acquainted. After that visits were made only by invitation. According to Aikin, those schools that took the most advantage of staff assistance made the most significant curriculum changes.[75]

ENTER: THE WORKSHOP.   One of the most important approaches for helping teachers deal with their curriculum problems is the workshop. The workshop is actually a contribution of the Eight-Year Study.[76] The first workshop was organized in the summer of 1936 by Ralph W. Tyler, director of evaluation for the Eight-Year Study, in response to demands by teachers from the thirty schools. The teachers were feeling confused about how to approach the task of developing a curriculum. They came to the Tyler-led six-week institute at The Ohio State University with definite problems on which they wished to work. The term *workshop* was then coined. The participants received assistance from various faculty members and the results were so useful that more workshops were organized. There can be little doubt that the workshops contributed to the experiment's outcomes. As time passed, workshops became a common inservice education approach. Within a generation or two, however, supervisors had lost sight of the key factor in the success of the original workshop: The teachers themselves had identified the problems they wanted to work on, and on which they needed assistance.

CURRICULUM SYNTHESIS.   Although each school went its own way in making changes in the curriculum, there were three goals sought by all schools:

1. To identify ways of breaking down the barriers between subjects so that the real meaning of fields of knowledge could be made apparent to the student
2. To encourage student self-direction
3. To provide individual guidance

Schools in the study attempted to bring the curriculum closer to the real concerns of youth by designing correlated and fusion courses, broad-fields courses, culture-epoch courses, career-centered courses, and problem-focused core curricula. (In some schools, the problems of job training and employment were studied in core curricula based on adolescent needs.) As Vars points out, "The evolving concept of core curriculum was tested in the famous Eight-Year Study of the Progressive Education Association."[77]

Giles, McCutchen, and Zechiel reported that schools experimenting with fusion courses such as mathematics-science found that the scope of a course was determined by the logical organization of one of the fields. Consequently, in some cases one field tended to dominate the other, thereby mitigating the principle of unification.[78]

Forced to find organizing centers other than systematized bodies of knowledge, teachers and curriculum consultants turned to problem-centered core curriculums. Subject matter from various fields was brought in as needed for the understanding and solution of problems.

The culture-epoch approach, where subject matter was controlled by broad themes, was used by the Horace Mann School of Teachers College, Columbia University, to unify the curriculum. This was a very broad approach to unification, far broader than fused studies such as mathematics-science or English-social studies because a culture-epoch could be dealt with in terms of its literature, science, technology, art, music, economic system, social system, or political system. A criticism frequently associated with this approach to curriculum synthesis was that although the senior year was usually devoted to a study of contemporary American problems, the entire first three years (grades nine through eleven) were devoted to a study of the past.

The core curriculum is discussed in considerable detail in Chapter 10. However, mention should be made here of the fact that in 1950, just eight years after the study, only one of the schools in the experiment had continued to develop a problem-focused core curriculum.[79] One might well ponder the reasons why this was so when the results of the study so strikingly favored the continued development of this approach to curriculum reorganization. One answer could be the Cold War and McCarthyism, which began in the late 1940s and led to the censorship of virtually any aspect of the curriculum adjudged to be controversial. Problem-centered core curricula required the free and open examination of the issues that marked our economic and political life. This was not easy in an era of censorship of ideas and guilt by association. Even the NEA's Educational Policies Commission took the position in 1949 that members of the Communist Party should not be employed as teachers. Little wonder, then, that many teachers were unwilling to subject our economic system to scrutiny for fear of being labeled *red*. The social forces of the day exerted a far stronger influence on the curriculum than the findings of the Eight-Year Study.

As discussed in detail in Chapter 11, a second and related factor was the drive for the discipline-centered curriculum through the national curriculum projects in the wake of the Cold War and space race, with priority given to the sciences and mathematics. This nationalistic drive served to put the idea and practice of the integrated core curriculum and general education into a virtual eclipse for decades. A number of studies have since buttressed the Eight-Year Study's findings,[80] and, as discussed in

Chapter 10, the 1990s witnessed the rediscovery of the need for an integrated core curriculum.

IMPACT OF THE STUDY.   The Eight-Year Study was not a continuing force after the experiment. Clearly, the study was also a casualty of World War II; the findings were released in 1942 when war headlines blotted out such matters as curriculum experimentation. After the war the criticism of progressive education that began in the late 1930s gained in intensity. This, combined with the Cold War, strengthened education conservatism. The international situation caused a return to more authoritarian and traditional programs. Discipline-centered reforms were viewed as the answer to the crisis in national security. Interdisciplinary curricula became a casualty of that crisis.[81]

However, as noted, the concept of interdisciplinarity never died and the need for curriculum articulation and synthesis through problem-focused studies is resurgent in a free society. The times today are different, of course, but as in the 1930s the timing of curriculum integration efforts with critical societal problems is more than coincidental. In the 1990s American society is faced with the need to deal with poverty, ethnic conflict, public health, youth unemployment, economic dislocations, social disaffection, drugs and narcotics, child welfare, the homeless, violent crime, and environmental protection—not to mention the related problems on a global scale along with war and peace.

To study real-life problems is, inevitably, to break down the barriers between and among the academic disciplines. And some schools and colleges are rediscovering the problem-focused core course.

Despite the fact that there was a smothering wave of conservatism in the years immediately following the Eight-Year Study, the study is alive and well today in the education literature. Even during the era of discipline-centered curriculum reforms, the study was never really out of the literature. Its fascination remains, leading one to ponder why, with our modern statistical techniques, we do not undertake comparable comprehensive and large-scale experimentation in American education.

The Activity Curriculum

As noted, elementary-school curriculum research during the 1920s was slanted toward curriculum adaptation. In Winnetka, for example, studies were conducted to determine the optimum time for beginning instruction in reading and fundamental arithmetic processes. These investigations were mainly concerned with fitting the conventional subjects to the child rather than with evaluating new forms of curriculum organization. Undeniably, making the traditional curriculum serve the child better was a revolution in and of itself (and one that passed many schools by).

THE ACTIVITY MOVEMENT.   The idea of the child's doing—learning through activity—is part of our curriculum legacy. Beginning in the 1920s, this idea assumed the proportions of a movement. The activity movement in the progressive education era was a reaction to the formal school where all learning was to be conducted in utter silence and the learner was to remain motionless unless given permission to move.

This clearly worked against the nature of the growing, developing child. Hence, it was understandable that activity was defined in terms of gross, overt movement. Overlooked was the idea that learning in itself is an active process; it can (and often does) go on without overt signs.

Activity programs were, on the whole, expressions of child-centered education; most proponents of activity conceived of education as a process that transcended codified knowledge. The objective was child growth through experiences, active experience that was visible to the naked eye. For many, however, activity was an end, rather than a means. Indeed, some even ascribed magical properties to child activity.

By 1930, the terms *activity movement, activity program,* and *activity curriculum* had become the commonplace in pedagogical parlance. Used freely and sometimes interchangeably with these terms were *units, unit of work, central theme,* and *center of interest.*

As might be expected, some schools tried to build the curriculum entirely around child activity. Most of these efforts were to be found in the primary grades. In the Francis W. Parker School, for example, there were no subjects in either the first or second grade; the curriculum at these levels was based on centers of interest, which were never the same two years consecutively.

Where public school enthusiasts jumped abruptly from a subject-matter format to a total program of activities, they tended to resume the traditional pattern for teaching the three R's; activities generally were continued in social studies and the creative arts. Although a curriculum organized in toto on the basis of activities seemed well-suited to the gifted and the above-average, it did not appear (as revealed by achievement test scores) to provide sufficient opportunity for the mastery of basic skills for the less able. On this basis, the time allocated for activities was reduced, and reading, spelling, and arithmetic were taught again as separate subjects.[82]

By the 1930s, the activity movement had moved away from activity for its own sake and was beginning to include the objectives of individual, social, and intellectual development through purposeful activity, as expressed in the writings of John Dewey.

There was a need to test the relative worth of activity and subject matter curriculum organization. Obviously, in order to evaluate the outcomes of activity programs, there had to be agreement on what an activity program was. In a recent reminiscence, Ralph Tyler, who was involved in evaluating activity programs in the 1930s and 1940s, described the problems of defining an activity program.[83]

RESEARCH ON THE ACTIVITY CURRICULUM.   The education literature of the 1930s contains scores of studies designed to assess the relative value of activity and subject-centered curricula. A number of school systems conducted experimental studies of their own programs. The overwhelming majority of studies used standardized achievement tests that were developed in terms of subject-centered curricula. Some studies did attempt to evaluate gains in terms of both subject matter and activity goals. Unfortunately, these were in the decided minority. In most studies, investigators concluded that the activity curriculums led to little or no loss in the mastery of basic skills and subject-matter knowledge and substantial gains over a subject organization in goals involving thought processes and responsible independence.

THE NEW YORK CITY EXPERIMENT.   The most comprehensive and well designed of these investigations was a New York City experiment involving some 75,000 children and 2,500 teachers over a six-year period. In 1935, the Board of Education of New York City launched an experimental program with progressive educational methods. Typical schools were designated as activity schools, and were encouraged to develop curriculums based on units and projects originating from pupil interest rather than traditional textbook learning. Although seventy schools initiated experimental programs, it was not feasible to conduct a careful evaluation on such a large scale. Most of the research involved eight activity schools, each matched with a control school. The schools were matched for neighborhood, average intelligence, and socioeconomic status of pupils.

The research program was aimed at measuring growth in a wide variety of educational outcomes, both tangible and intangible. Tests of study skills, social attitudes, "work spirit," and individual adjustment were developed by J. Wayne Wrightstone, then a research associate at Teachers College. Evaluation procedures included both tests and classroom observations.

Activity children surpassed control children in growth in critical thinking, initiative, leadership, and other objectives of activity curriculums. Control pupils gained somewhat more in some academic subjects (notably arithmetic) although the differences were small and statistically insignificant. Unquestionably, the objectives of the activity program had been achieved. In their final report on the experiment, Jersild, Thorndike, and Goldman concluded:

> While the control children seem to have a slight but statistically unreliable advantage as far as achievement in academic subject matter is concerned, the activity children surpass the controls in the frequency with which they exercise such presumably wholesome activities as leadership, experimentation, self-initiated enterprises, participation in oral discussion, and the like. The activity children have more experiences and show more tangible accomplishments in the field of arts and crafts. The activity children, as already noted, tend to be superior in tests that call for intellectual operations. [These were the Wrightstone tests of working skills, explaining facts applying generalizations, critical thinking, and current events.][84]

DISCIPLINE AND CURRICULUM ORGANIZATION.   Of great interest is the fact that children in the activity program also tended to surpass the control children in discipline. This is contrary to the opinion held by many teachers (and parents) that children in traditional programs show better discipline and "respect for school authority." In the first three of the five semesters in which the children were observed, the control children exhibited fewer behavioral problems whereas the activity children showed better discipline than the controls in the last two semesters. As Jersild, Thorndike, and Goldman emphasized:

> The greater degree of freedom and self-direction afforded by the activity program has not been a signal for poor discipline and disorder on the part of the pupils. Rather, according to the findings in connection with the "work spirit" category, as well as according to the independent testimony of observers who have visited many

classes and have gone into the same classes day after day, the pupils have risen to the occasion in a highly satisfactory way.[85]

Wrightstone's Study.   Wrightstone conducted an important study in which he focused on outcomes that were emphasized by progressive educators, such as being able to interpret facts, apply generalizations, work independently, and organize materials. Using matched pairs of elementary and secondary pupils from three pairs of public school situations, he found that in no case (other than the quantity of recitation in classrooms) did the subject-centered schools show a statistically significant superiority over the experimental schools.[86] Schools with various kinds of reorganized curricula demonstrated a significant superiority in recall of physics and chemistry facts, literature acquaintance, and working-skills ability. In reporting the results of his study, Wrightstone concluded that his findings were "tentative proof of the validity of the educational theory and principles upon which the newer-type practices in the selected schools are established."[87]

Decline of Interest in Activity Organization.   Despite these encouraging findings, interest in the activity organization of the elementary curriculum, as revealed by the educational literature, had faded by the mid-1940s. This is a striking parallel with the core curriculum. In both cases, research findings were highly encouraging but the interest of educators dropped off nonetheless. Research findings were not used as a basis for curriculum decision making. Nevertheless, purposeful activity requiring freedom of movement and discussion is today deemed essential for the development of cooperation, critical thinking, and otherwise expanding intellectual horizons and productive social behavior.

The Decline of Curriculum Experimentation

"What we sorely need," wrote John Goodlad in 1966, "is a rejuvenation of the experimental quest."[88] Goodlad was questioning the discipline-centered curriculum reform projects of the late 1950s and 1960s. The major goal of the projects was to have students develop the modes of inquiry in a discipline so as to think like scholar-specialists. These goals and the means for reaching them were established in advance by university scholar-specialists. The discipline-centered projects were federally supported in a nationalistic effort in response to the Cold War and space race. The materials were trial-taught and refined, but as Goodlad pointed out at the time, "[r]arely, if at all, are two sets of means contrasted with each other and compared as to their effectiveness in achieving a given objective."[89] In effect, the scientists and mathematicians leading these projects had avoided the scientific method(s) and resorted to promotional tactics and claims.

Actually, application of the scientific method(s) to curriculum problems had begun to decline much earlier. In 1950, Caswell pointed out that most of the references cited in recent reviews of curriculum research were general discussions. Very few presented rigorous studies of well-defined problems.[90] He contrasted this against the 1930s when hundreds of studies using methods of scientific inquiry were conducted.

DEMONSTRATIONS VERSUS EXPERIMENTS.   Goodlad was not to have his wish. Whereas the purpose of experimental testing of new programs is to determine the effects, tests of social and educational programs over subsequent years—extending through 1970s and 1980s—were usually intended to provide accountability data concerning the supplying of services. They were demonstration projects, not experiments. Demonstration of a program implies that its value has been established. This, however, was rarely the case. As Stake points out, "Evaluation is invoked for many purposes, many of them with little concern about the production of information. Evaluation studies are prescribed to legitimize authority and to protect program operations from criticism."[91]

Be that as it may, a field test of a program can and should address both the program's effects and implementation issues such as the question, "What is going on?" If evaluation policies are to be sound, including those of the U.S. Department of Education, systematic consideration must be given to the above."[92]

THE ONE-SIZE-FITS-ALL REFORM CURRICULUM.   In the 1960s, evaluation specialists, like others involved in the War on Poverty, were enthused and energized by the charge to improve educational opportunities for the disadvantaged. Attempting to find which practices work best, some evaluation specialists sought a universally accepted or one-best set of instructional procedures and a single-reform curriculum. Others cautioned against sweeping generalization and standard curriculum design. Recognizing that local circumstances and programs differ, they urged that evaluators turn their attention to assisting practitioners to experiment and adapt evaluations from the large studies to their own situations.[93] This did not happen.

Educational opinion in the late 1960s and early 1970s was "do your own thing." Radical romantic reformers were mainly concerned with "freeing" children to learn. Lawrence Cremin described the open classroom movement as "ahistorical and atheoretical."[94] It did not, he said "pose educational problems with the profundity of the earlier progressive movement and it did not advance constructive suggestions for reform."[95]

Radical reformers showed little or no interest in testing their ideas. Their impact on schools was mainly in the sector of alternative schools, which were not used for experimentation. Although the curriculum in these schools differed little from the curriculum in conventional schools, calls began to be heard for an authoritarian pedagogy.

The schools were criticized for not doing their job, which prompted reactions for a return to the "basics." Educators, under the iron hand of their state legislators, defined sets of narrow objectives for which teachers and administrators were to be held accountable through statewide minimum-competency testing.

Recounting the story, Stake points out that

> under the pressure for accountability, much of the appetite for understanding was overwhelmed by a craving for protection. Educators implored measurement specialists to develop a methodology that pointed to the shortcomings of students. By 1980, student assessment rather than program evaluation was the major player in the school improvement movement.[96]

THE ENDURANCE OF CURIOSITY.   But local schools could not remain inattentive to their own curriculum and morale problems. Indeed, as Stake continues, "Within some schools, classrooms, and networks of educators, curiosity endured. What additional knowledge might improve things? Pretty clearly there was a confidence in local knowledge, situational knowledge and teacher based knowledge."[97] What Stake was describing, of course, was the democratic-participative approach to problem solving based on use of the scientific method. In the 1990s, there was renewed interest in collaborative action research, which focuses on teachers' practical problems. Actually, action research is not a new idea, but in its most recent form involves teachers and university researchers "who work together to solve school and classroom problems."[98]

Action research was initially criticized for its lack of attention to the scientific method. Individual teachers were expected to improve the curriculum through investigations into their classroom problems. Very often the research was conducted without the help of consultants and statisticians. What we learned from our early experiences with action research is that along with the commitment to teacher participation in curriculum research must go a commitment to giving teachers the kind of help required to do the job.

Using Approved Practices: Goodlad's Study of Schooling

What is all too easy to forget is that we have a heritage of research and evaluation on which we can draw—benchmarks on which to evaluate our curriculum. This is another kind of curriculum research, one used by Goodlad in his national study of schooling. Goodlad looked at U.S. schools in terms of the approved practices that have emanated over the years in the research literature, for example, the importance of discussion and other activities requiring student participation in preparing students for effective citizenship. The Goodlad study found too much "teacher-talk."[99] Goodlad also looked at the problem of ability grouping in terms of the literature, which finds that teachers of homogeneously grouped low-achievers do not expect students to succeed and transmit their low expectations to the students.[100] Goodlad's report sharply criticizes the practice of grouping students into fast- and slow-ability groups in core subjects.

Goodlad's study was a landmark because it told us what was going on in the schools in comparison with what should be going on. The point is that the professional staff of a school can do what Goodlad did, on a much smaller scale, of course. Dependable criteria exist in the literature for evaluating a school and developing an agenda for curriculum improvement.

The Mythical Average School

Recently, reports have been published that begin by accepting the proposition that schools *in general* are worse than they used to be. They imply a judgment about individual schools based on studies of the "current condition of American education."[101] Beside the fact that there is no evidence to support the generalization about a systemwide crisis, such studies may actually prevent individual schools from addressing their own genuine problems. There are problems in every school, but they may not be the problems identified in national reports on the condition of education.[102]

There is no such thing as a typical school; schools, like persons, are individuals. "It is possible to make valid judgments about American secondary education but only *school by school*," wrote James B. Conant in 1959."[103] Many years have elapsed since the publication of Conant's famous report, *The American High School Today*, but his point remains valid. In Conant's time, like our own, there was a rising chorus of criticism about the quality of American education, but he remained firm in his insistence that the typical high school simply does not exist. Therefore, he insisted, it is unscientific to pass judgment on secondary schooling as a whole.

Large-scale studies, such as the National Assessment of Educational Progress and reports of the National Center for Educational Statistics on the conditions of education, can point to large-scale national problems, but it is up to the local district and school to determine whether a given problem exists in their own school. If it does, they can face it openly, rather than shoving it under the rug, knowing that other schools also have the problem. If it does not, there is nothing worse in terms of staff morale and wasted resources than working on a nonexistent problem. (One school, for example, had a dropout rate that was almost nonexistent. Yet the mandate from the central office was to devote staff development sessions to dealing with the problems of potential dropouts.)

The Future of Curriculum Research

We have traveled far since the first use of research results in the curriculum-improvement process. The idea of improving the curriculum through research at one time led every major school system to have as part of its central office staff some kind of research unit. Small school systems can seek the help of schools of education in universities, which all have research responsibilities (some of which are written into the institution's legislative charter). A cooperative, ongoing school/university program should be in operation for this purpose.

In this and the previous chapters we have presented some of the most important examples of curriculum research in the twentieth century. Yet it is just a sampling of the research in various areas of the curriculum and teaching. The research division of the National Education Association, and the work of such organizations as the John Dewey Society, the Society for Curriculum Study, and the National Society for the Study of Education all were early leaders in conducting curriculum research. In recent years, the American Federation of Teachers has devoted special attention to the study of curriculum problems. If the future is built on the best work already done, the impact of research on practice will be more marked.

But the "if" is a big one. A better and brighter future depends on whether educational policies and practices are based on the best available evidence. In recent years national education policies have had a crisis orientation. They have often been politically motivated rather than based on convincing proof. But lest we forget, each teacher and administrator also makes the policies that he or she follows in their own work. They can advance the impact of research by basing practice on the best that is known.

PERSPECTIVE

In curriculum development we need not start from scratch. It is our great and good fortune that our forbearers laid down a set of principles for us to follow. These ideas and steps to be taken were based on practices and past experience in the more progressive cities and have stood the test of time. Curriculum development is a professional task and its effectiveness depends on the establishment of a central department of curriculum and the appointment of an individual (assistant superintendent or curriculum director) with expertise in curriculum development who has responsibility for the total program of curriculum development. Most of the work of preparing materials and activities is done by teachers and principals who are organized into a small number of committees, coordinated by the curriculum director who can see the curriculum whole. Curriculum continuity is achieved by having committees that consider not only entire fields from first through the twelfth grade, but the interrelationships of the fields in creating a totally integrated plan. As Dewey found in his laboratory school, a coherent curriculum is no accident; it is achieved through careful design, continuous evaluation, supervision, cooperation, and basing instruction on a unified plan. Teachers involved in curriculum work should be released from classroom duties and should be chosen for professional rather than political reasons.

Tyler added another evolutionary dimension to curriculum work: the understanding that developing materials and activities is only part of the work of curriculum development. Teachers must develop an interest in using them and students' passive or negative attitudes toward school work must be overcome.

Both the learner's development and society's needs are considerations in curriculum development. We owe much to the Committee on Curriculum Making under Harold Rugg's leadership, for they were able to merge conflicting perspectives into a new perspective. Over the course of the twentieth century it would develop into an instrumentation for curriculum development that is used in one form or another today.[104]

No less of an achievement was the set of principles developed by the Society for Curriculum Study, which built on the work of the Rugg committee. Curriculum development is a continuous process because the world of knowledge is undergoing continuous change and the rising generation must be able to understand and deal intelligently with the issues of a changing society. Curriculum development should result in materials that are adaptable to the needs of particular groups of students. A major change in curriculum requires broad-based involvement; no single group, be it teachers or supervisors, should carry out the work independently. An improved curriculum to meet the needs of children and a democratic society requires the teacher's personal commitment. Teachers must believe that a curriculum problem is serious, and this is most apt to happen when the teachers identify the problem. The nature of the school district's curriculum development program depends greatly on the financial resources available, but more money can usually be obtained if the public is convinced that the proposal will make children's lives better and richer. The solution to a curriculum problem should be evaluated over time; the school staff should never be sure they have the answer. The curriculum should be evaluated in terms of its effects on students, teachers, and the community. Learning units that are truly unitary give the curriculum coherence because they are not confined to a single subject field. A good curriculum development program is characterized by enthusiasm—there can be no real accomplishment in any field without people who care.

All of the foregoing principles, ideas, and practices had evolved well before mid-century.

The units of work developed in elementary classrooms at the Lincoln School remain exemplary models of curriculum integration. They may still be located in leading education libraries. At the secondary school level the model that developed was the core course. Its major purposes were individual and democratic social development. Nelson Rockefeller, who became the governor of New York and later vice president of the United States, was a graduate of the Lincoln School. In a television interview many years later he said that his education at Lincoln fostered in him the spirit of social consciousness and public service. From Lincoln we learn that the key to a coherent learning experience links ideas to reality. The curriculum choices we make should be guided by and be consistent with what is known about learning. *Should* is the key word here, for the principle is not always followed in practice. In landmark curriculum studies—such as the Eight-Year Study—some of the most sophisticated evaluation instruments were developed. The researchers did not depend on existing tests designed to evaluate conventional curriculums. Indeed, much can be learned today from the evaluation instruments developed in the Eight-Year Study. Unfortunately, we have not drawn from these instruments as schools are pressured to make good showings on standardized tests of limited predictive validity. At the same time we have allowed the tests to drive the curriculum rather than using tests and comprehensive evaluation techniques to serve the cause of curriculum improvement. Dependable criteria exist in the literature for evaluating a school and developing a program of curriculum improvement. There is no such thing as an average school.

PROBLEMS FOR STUDY AND DISCUSSION

1. In discussing the conditions required for curriculum improvement, an educator states: "It will require all of those in your school who want change and are expected to implement it to work beyond the regular hours of the classroom and school day." [Frances M. Klein, *Curriculum Reform in the Elementary School: Creating Your Own Agenda* (New York: Teachers College Press, 1989), pp. 4–5.] Do you agree? Why or why not?

2. In this chapter it was pointed out that Harold Rugg was able to get the curriculum leaders of his time to agree that adequate curriculum design should give attention to both child growth and the needs of society. Examine the

curriculum of a school. Give examples of ways that the curriculum reflects the consensus achieved by the Committee on Curriculum Making.

3. What are the implications of your analysis in problem 2 for improving the curriculum?

4. As discussed in this chapter, the Committee on Curriculum Making was concerned with the problem of achieving curriculum continuity and synthesis. Examine the curriculum in your own school district and identify any efforts to improve the continuity and integration of the curriculum. Is there a single committee for each curriculum area that considers the entire program from the first through the twelfth grade? What roles are played by administrators and supervisors to promote the articulation and continuity about which Rugg and Counts were so concerned in the 1920s?

5. Some veteran teachers serving on curriculum improvement teams or projects can remember earlier projects in which they participated. Often these projects had similar purposes, for example, the development of interdisciplinary thematic approaches to teaching the humanities. And often these teachers have strong feelings about what was most and least worthwhile. Do you believe that these teachers can provide the team with curriculum lessons from the past about the pitfalls and potentialities of local curriculum development efforts? Explain. Should a deliberate effort be made to include as participants in local curriculum development efforts teachers who well remember previous efforts? Why?

6. According to Heidi Hayes Jacobs, "[t]o develop an inter-disciplinary curriculum, a district needs an action plan." [Heidi Hayes Jacobs, "Planning for Curriculum Integration," *Educational Leadership,* 49 (October 1991), p. 27.] The plan she proposes is the interdisciplinary unit of work. Trace the history of unit teaching as described in this chapter. In your view, are the objectives of modern educators who attempt to develop interdisciplinary units fundamentally the same as those of curriculum pioneers in the 1920s and 1930s? Explain.

7. What are the consequences of basing instruction on the concept of equality of outcomes rather than optimization of opportunity?

8. During the progressive era public school reformers attempted to find means to improve the curriculum that would leave it in some form of subject organization. Draw up a list of contemporary reforms that accepts the subject form of organization as a given.

9. Do you believe that the three curriculum goals sought by schools involved in the Eight-Year Study have validity for today's schools? Explain.

10. According to Edmund C. Short,

> While the people dealing with curriculum practice may know what they need more knowledge about, the researchers capable of generating the knowledge often do not hear the practitioners' questions and are removed enough from practice that they do not generate similar questions on their own. [Edmund C. Short, "Setting Priorities in Curriculum Research," *Journal of Curriculum and Supervision,* 6 (Summer 1991), pp. 363–364.]

Two possible solutions to this dilemma are offered by Short: (1) teachers and supervisors could conduct research into real curriculum problems and (2) the two groups—university researchers and school practitioners—be brought more closely together. What real curriculum problems would you like to see investigated?

11. Does curriculum research today deal with entire curriculum patterns or segments of the curriculum? Give examples.

12. The following statement was made by John Goodlad, concerning Bloom's mastery approach to learning:

> One of the problems in programs geared to individual differences in learning rates is that the slower children become bored or discouraged when called upon to persevere for long periods of time. This problem can be significantly reduced if teachers employ a variety of approaches to the same concepts or skills; that is, the activities vary from dance, to field trips, to reading, to writing, to drawing, even though the body of knowledge or skills to be learned remains unchanged. Instruction

appears to me to be too much oriented to covering material in textbooks and workbooks. [John I. Goodlad, *What Schools Are For* (Bloomington, IN: Phi Delta Kappan, 1979), p. 93.]

Do you agree with Goodlad? Why or why not?

13. In connection with problem 12, how has teaching been affected by state-mandated testing programs?

14. Ralph Tyler pointed out that some curriculum leaders have "been able to translate external pressures into constructive responses." [Ralph W. Tyler, "What the Curriculum Field Needs to Learn From Its History," *Journal of Thought,* 21 (Spring 1986), p. 78.] He went on to mention that we know very little about such persons. Identify curriculum leaders (either teachers or supervisors) in your school or school district who have translated such pressures into insightful forces for improvement. Describe what they have done.

NOTES

1. See, for example, National Society for the Study of Education, *Curriculum Making: Past and Present,* Twenty-sixth Yearbook, Part I (Bloomington, IL: Public School Publishing, 1927); Henry Harap et al., *The Changing Curriculum* (New York: D. Appleton-Century, 1937).

2. Foreword, *Curriculum Making: Past and Present,* op. cit., p. x.

3. Ibid., p. xii.

4. George S. Counts, "Current Practices in Curriculum Making in Public High Schools," Chapter 7 in *Curriculum Making: Past and Present,* op. cit., p. 161.

5. Harold Rugg, "Introduction," *The Foundations of Curriculum-Making,* Twenty-sixth Yearbook, National Society for the Study of Education, Part II (Bloomington, IN: Public School Publishing, 1927) p. 1.

6. See National Society for the Study of Education, *The National Herbart Society Yearbooks,* 1–5, 1895–1899 (New York: Arno Press and *The New York Times,* 1969).

7. Rugg, "Introduction," *The Foundations of Curriculum Making,* op. cit., p. 1.

8. Robert H. Anderson, "Political Pressures on Supervisors," Chapter 4 in National Society for the Study of Education, *Critical Issues in Curriculum,* Eighty-seventh Yearbook, Part I (Chicago: University of Chicago Press, 1988), pp. 60–82.

9. Harold Rugg and George S. Counts, "A Critical Appraisal of Current Methods of Curriculum Making," Chapter 30 in *Curriculum Making: Past and Present,* op. cit., p. 427.

10. Ibid., p. 439.

11. Rugg and Counts, op. cit., pp. 441–442.

12. Ibid., pp. 442–443.

13. Committee on Curriculum Making, *The Foundations of Curriculum Making,* op. cit., pp. 11–18.

14. Ibid., p. 23.

15. Ralph W. Tyler, "Curriculum Development in the Twenties and Thirties," Chapter 2 in National Society for the Study of Education, *The Curriculum: Retrospect and Prospect,* Seventieth Yearbook, Part I (Chicago: University of Chicago Press, 1971), p. 36.

16. Decker Walker, "The Curriculum Field in Formation," *Curriculum Theory Network,* 4 (1975), p. 279.

17. Daniel Tanner, *Crusade for Democracy: Progressive Education at the Crossroads* (Albany: State University of New York Press, 1991), p. 44.

18. Henry Harap, Preface, *The Changing Curriculum,* op. cit., p. vii.

19. Ibid., p. 49.

20. Ibid., p. 54.

21. Ibid., p. 28.

22. Ibid.

23. Ralph W. Tyler, "Progress in Dealing with Curriculum Problems," Chapter 12 in *Critical Issues in Curriculum,* op. cit., p. 268.

24. Henry Harap, "The Organization of the Curriculum," in *The Changing Curriculum,* op. cit., pp. 76–77.

25. Ibid., p. 78.

26. Ibid., p. 97.

27. Ibid., p. 110.

28. Ibid., p. 116.

29. Ibid., p. 117.

30. Lawrence A. Cremin, *The Transformation of the School* (New York: Alfred A. Knopf, 1961), pp. 281, 291.

31. Abraham Flexner, *A Modern College and a Modern School* (New York: Doubleday, 1923), p. 98. (Originally published in 1916 in *American Review of Reviews*, 8, pp. 465–474.)

32. Ibid.

33. Peter L. Buttenwieser, "The Lincoln School and Its Times" (unpublished doctoral dissertation, New York, Columbia University, 1969).

34. Ibid.

35. Nathalie J. Gehrke, "Explorations of Teachers' Development of Integrative Curriculums," *Journal of Curriculum and Supervision*, 6 (Winter 1991), p. 107.

36. An experiment to determine the comparative effectiveness of formal reading instruction and "individualized" silent reading was conducted in the early 1920s by teachers Keelor and Miner with the assistance of Laura Zirbes. See Laura Zirbes, *Practice Exercises and Checks on Silent Reading in the Primary Grades* (New York: Lincoln School of Teachers College, 1925).

37. James S. Tippett et al., *Curriculum Making in an Elementary School* (Lexington, MA: Ginn, 1927), pp. 167—168.

38. John Dewey, *The Child and the Curriculum* (Chicago: University of Chicago, 1902), p. 6.

39. Katherine Camp Mayhew and Anna Camp Edwards, *The Dewey School* (New York: D. Appleton-Century, 1936), p. 223.

40. Buttenwieser, op. cit.

41. Ibid.

42. The theory of the units and a bibliography are found in Tippett, op. cit. See also Cremin, op. cit., pp. 283–287.

43. Murray R. Nelson, "Rugg on Rugg: His Theories and His Curriculum," *Curriculum Inquiry*, 8 (Summer 1978), p. 122.

44. G. Derwood Baker, "An Eleventh-Grade Field Study: The Coal Industry," *Educational Research Bulletin*, 17 (October 19, 1938), p. 174.

45. Louis Raths, "Some Evaluations of the Trip," *Educational Research Bulletin*, 17 (October 19, 1938), p. 207.

46. Otis W. Caldwell, "The Lincoln Experimental School," Chapter 16 in *Curriculum Making: Past and Present*, op. cit., pp. 280–289.

47. Frederick G. Bonser, "Curriculum Making in Laboratory or Experimental Schools," Chapter 26 in *Curriculum Making: Past and Present*, op. cit., pp. 353–362.

48. L. Thomas Hopkins and James E. Mendelhall, *Achievement at the Lincoln School* (New York: Teachers College Press, 1934).

49. "Court Upholds Closing of Horace Mann-Lincoln School," *Teachers College Record*, 48 (May 1947), p. 533.

50. Hollis L. Caswell, in a letter to the authors of this text, May 29, 1976.

51. Harold Rugg and Ann Shumaker, *The Child-Centered School* (New York: Arno Press and *The New York Times*, 1969), p. 15. (Originally published by World Book in 1928.)

52. Carleton W. Washburne, "The Philosophy of the Winnetka Curriculum," Chapter 11 in *Curriculum Making: Past and Present*, op cit., p. 227.

53. Carleton W. Washburne and Sidney P. Marland, Jr., *Winnetka: The History and Significance of an Educational Experiment* (Englewood Cliffs, NJ: Prentice Hall, 1963), p. 38.

54. William H. Kilpatrick, "An Effort at Appraisal," Chapter 6 in National Society for the Study of Education, *Adapting the Schools to Individual Differences*, Twenty-fourth Yearbook, Part II (Bloomington, IL: Public School Publishing, 1925), p. 281.

55. John Dewey, *Democracy and Education* (New York: Macmillan, 1916), p. 183.

56. Laurel N. Tanner, "The Path Not Taken: Dewey's Model of Inquiry," *Curriculum Inquiry*, 18 (Winter 1988), p. 472.

57. Kathleen A. Fitzpatrick, "Restructuring to Achieve Outcomes of Significance for All Students," *Educational Leadership*, 48 (May 1991), pp. 18–22.

58. Benjamin S. Bloom, *Human Characteristics and School Learning* (New York: McGraw-Hill, 1976), p. 4.

59. Fitzpatrick, op. cit., p. 21.

60. Ralph W. Tyler, "Book Reviews," *Teachers College Record*, 88 (Summer 1987), p. 604.

61. Jean Evangelof, "Education Reform Seen Hinging on Truce between Researchers, School Officials," *The Chronicle of Higher Education* (April 19, 1989), p. A18.

62. Ibid.

63. Benjamin S. Bloom, "The New Direction in Educational Research: Alterable Variables," *Phi Delta Kappan,* 61 (February 1980), p. 382.

64. Ibid.

65. Ibid., p. 384.

66. Benjamin S. Bloom (ed.), *Taxonomy of Educational Objectives, Handbook I: Cognitive Domain* (New York: McKay, 1956).

67. John Dewey, *The Sources of a Science of Education* (New York: Liveright, 1929), p. 75.

68. Geraldine Joncich Clifford, "Words for the Schools: The Applications in Education of the Vocabulary Researches of Edward L. Thorndike," Chapter 2 in Patrick Suppes (ed.), *Impact of Research on Education: Some Case Studies* (Washington, DC: National Academy of Education, 1978), pp. 107–198.

69. Ibid., p. 108.

70. Ibid., p. 183.

71. Wilford M. Aikin, "The Eight-Year Study: If We Were to Do It Again," *Progressive Education,* 31 (October 1953), p. 11.

72. Dean Chamberlin, Enid S. Chamberlin, Neal E. Drought, and William E. Scott, *Did They Succeed in College?* (New York: Harper, 1942), p. 209.

73. Wilford M. Aikin, *The Story of the Eight-Year Study,* (New York: Harper, 1942).

74. Aikin, "The Eight-Year Study: If We Were to Do It Again," op. cit., p. 14.

75. Ibid., p. 12.

76. Laurel N. Tanner, "Contributions of the Eight-Year Study," *Journal of Thought,* 21 (Spring 1986), pp. 33–35.

77. Gordon F. Vars, "Integrated Curriculum in Historical Perspective," *Educational Leadership,* 49 (October 1991), pp. 14–15.

78. H. H. Giles, S. P. McCutchen, and A. N. Zechiel, *Exploring the Curriculum* (New York: Harper, 1942), p. 35.

79. Frederick L. Redefer, "The Eight-Year Study . . . After Eight Years," *Progressive Education,* 28 (November 1950), p. 34.

80. See Daniel Tanner and Laurel N. Tanner, *History of the School Curriculum* (New York: Macmillan, 1990), pp. 233–234.

81. Jerome S. Bruner, *The Process of Education* (Cambridge, MA: Harvard University Press, 1960).

82. See "Comments and Criticisms by Some Educational Leaders in the Field," Chapter 6 in National Society for the Study of Education, *The Activity Movement,* Thirty-third Yearbook, Part II (Bloomington, IL: Public School Publishing, 1934).

83. Ralph W. Tyler, "General Statement on Program Evaluation," Chapter 1 in National Society for the Study of Education, *Evaluation and Education: At Quarter Century,* Nineteenth Yearbook, Part II (Chicago: University of Chicago Press, 1991), pp. 4–5.

84. Arthur T. Jersild, Robert L. Thorndike, and Bernard Goldman, "A Further Comparison of Pupils in 'Activity' and 'Non-activity' Schools," *Journal of Experimental Education,* 9 (June 1941), p. 308.

85. Arthur T. Jersild, Robert L. Thorndike, and Bernard Goldman, "An Evaluation of Aspects of the Activity Program in the New York City Elementary Schools," *Journal of Experimental Education,* 8 (December 1939), p. 206.

86. J. Wayne Wrightstone, *Appraisal of Newer Practices in Selected Public Schools* (New York: Teachers College Press, 1935).

87. Ibid., p. 116.

88. John Goodlad, *The Changing School Curriculum* (New York: The Fund for the Advancement of Education, 1966), p. 110.

89. Ibid., p. 108.

90. Hollis L. Caswell, "Research in the Curriculum," *Educational Leadership,* 7 (April 1950), p. 439.

91. Robert E. Stake, "Retrospective on 'The Countenance of Educational Evaluation,'" Chapter 3 in National Society for the Study of Education, *Evaluation and Education: At Quarter Century,* Nineteenth Yearbook, Part II (Chicago: University of Chicago, 1991), p. 80.

92. Robert F. Boruch, "The President's Mandate: Discovering What Works and What Works Better," Chapter 6 in *Evaluation and Education: At Quarter Century,* op. cit., p. 153.

93. Stake, op. cit., pp. 67–68.

94. Lawrence A. Cremin, "The Free School Movement: A Perspective," *Notes on Education* (October 1973), p. 5.

95. Kevin Ryan et al., "An Interview with Lawrence A. Cremin," *Phi Delta Kappan,* 60 (October 1978), p. 113.

96. Stake, op. cit., pp. 74–75.

97. Ibid., p. 75.

98. Renee Clift, Mary Lou Veal, Marlene Johnson, and Patricia Holland, "Strengths and Limitations of Collaborative Action Research: Implications for Teachers' Learning," Paper presented at the Conference of the Canadian Association of Teacher Education, Laval University, Montreal, June 1–2, 1989), p. 2.

99. John I. Goodlad, *A Place Called School* (New York: McGraw-Hill, 1984), pp. 230–232.

100. Ibid., pp. 153–157.

101. Laurel N. Tanner, "Despite Weaknesses, New Carnegie Report Offers Valuable Support for School Improvement," *Phi Delta Kappan,* 65

(January 1984), p. 369; Daniel Tanner, "A Nation 'Truly' at Risk," *Phi Delta Kappan,* 75 (December, 1993), pp. 288–297.

102. Prudence S. Posner, "Data, Crises, and a Controversial Report," *Education Week,* 11 (October 9, 1992), p. 25.

103. James B. Conant, *The American High School Today* (New York: McGraw-Hill, 1959), p. 16.

104. Karen Zumwalt, "Beginning Professional Teachers: The Need for a Curricular Vision of Teaching," in Maynard C. Reynolds (ed.), *Knowledge Base for the Beginning Teacher* (Oxford: Pergamon Press, 1989), p. 176.

SELECTED REFERENCES

Aikin, Wilford M. *The Story of the Eight-Year Study.* New York: Harper, 1942.

Aikin, Wilford M. *Thirty Schools Tell Their Story.* New York: Harper and Row, 1942.

Bloom, Benjamin S. (ed.). *Taxonomy of Educational Objectives, Handbook I: Cognitive Domain.* New York: David McKay, 1956.

Bloom, Benjamin S., Hastings, J. Thomas, and Madaus, George F. *Handbook on Summative and Formative Evaluation of Student Learning.* New York: McGraw-Hill, 1971.

Bruner, Jerome S. *The Process of Education.* Cambridge, MA: Harvard University Press, 1960.

Buttenwieser, Peter L. "The Lincoln School and Its Times" (unpublished doctoral dissertation, Columbia University, New York, 1969).

Chamberlin, Dean, Chamberlin, Enid S., Drought, Neal E., and Scott, William E. *Did They Succeed in College?* New York: Harper, 1942.

Conant, James B. *The American High School Today.* New York: McGraw-Hill, 1959.

Cremin, Lawrence A. *The Transformation of the School.* New York: Alfred A. Knopf, 1961.

Dewey, John. *Democracy and Education.* New York: Macmillan, 1916.

Dewey, John. *The School and Society.* Chicago: University of Chicago Press, 1915. (Originally published in 1899.)

Dewey, John. *The Sources of a Science of Education.* New York: Liveright, 1929.

Giles, H. H., McCutchen, S. P., and Zechiel, A. N.

Exploring the Curriculum. New York: Harper, 1942.

Goodlad, John I. *A Place Called School.* New York: McGraw-Hill, 1984.

Goodlad, John I. *What Schools Are For.* Bloomington, IN: Phi Delta Kappa, 1979.

Harap, Henry (ed.). *The Changing Curriculum.* New York: D. Appleton-Century, 1937.

Jacobs, Heidi Hayes (ed.). *Interdisciplinary Curriculum: Design and Implementation.* Alexandria, VA: Association for Supervision and Curriculum Development, 1989.

National Society for the Study of Education. *The Activity Movement.* Thirty-third Yearbook, Part II. Bloomington, IL: Public School Publishing, 1934.

National Society for the Study of Education. *Adapting the Schools to Individual Differences.* Twenty-fourth Yearbook, Part II. Bloomington, IL: Public School Publishing, 1925.

National Society for the Study of Education. *Bloom's Taxonomy: A Forty-Year Retrospective.* Ninety-third Yearbook, Part II. Chicago: University of Chicago Press, 1994.

National Society for the Study of Education. *Child Development and the Curriculum.* Thirty-eighth Yearbook, Part I. Chicago: University of Chicago Press, 1939.

National Society for the Study of Education. *Critical Issues in Curriculum.* Eighty-seventh Yearbook, Part I. Chicago: University of Chicago Press, 1988.

National Society for the Study of Education. *Curricu-*

lum Making: Past and Present. Twenty-sixth Yearbook, Part I. Bloomington, IL: Public School Publishing, 1927.

National Society for the Study of Education. *The Curriculum: Retrospect and Prospect*. Seventieth Yearbook, Part I. Chicago: University of Chicago Press, 1971.

National Society for the Study of Education. *Evaluation and Education: At Quarter Century*. Nineteenth Yearbook, Part II. Chicago: University of Chicago Press, 1991.

National Society for the Study of Education. *The Foundations of Curriculum making*. Twenty-sixth Yearbook, Part II. Bloomington, IL: Public School Publishing, 1927.

Seguel, Mary Louise. *The Curriculum Field: Its Formative Years*. New York: Teachers College Press, 1966.

Short, Edmund C. (ed.). *Forms of Curriculum Inquiry*. Albany: State University of New York Press, 1991.

Tanner, Daniel. *Crusade for Democracy: Progressive Education at the Crossroads*. Albany: State University of New York Press, 1991.

Tanner, Daniel, and Tanner, Laurel. *History of the School Curriculum*. New York: Macmillan, 1990.

Tippett, James S., et al. *Curriculum Making in an Elementary School*. Lexington, MA: Ginn, 1927.

Washburne, Carleton W., and Marland, Sidney P., Jr. *Winnetka: The History and Significance of an Educational Experiment*. Englewood Cliffs, NJ: Prentice Hall, 1963.

PART 2 ≋

THE EMERGENT CURRICULUM FIELD

I had the feeling that, like the Austro-Hungarian Empire of the nineteenth century, if John Dewey hadn't existed he would have had to be invented.

—James B. Conant

CHAPTER 5

CHANGING CONCEPTIONS
OF CURRICULUM

Mark Van Doren observed that "the curriculum is not something which it is fashionable to ponder; and as for being rational about it, few oddities are more suspect."[1] In making this observation, Van Doren was reiterating an identical concern voiced by Herbert Spencer a century earlier.

In his essay, "What Knowledge Is of Most Worth?" (1859), Spencer proposed that this was "the question of questions" in education. "Before there can be a rational *curriculum*," held Spencer, "we must settle which things it most concerns us to know."[2]

That *curriculum* as a systematic field of study is of recent development may seem to be outlandish when one considers that there is no such institution as a school, college, or university without a curriculum. Yet in the eyes of the student, the process of formal education is viewed merely as subjects or courses to be taken. And although teachers and professors tend to devote considerable attention to the adoption and revision of subject matter as encapsulated in courses or subjects, they give relatively little attention to the necessary interaction and interdependence of the various elements that comprise the concept that has come to be called *curriculum*.

The rise of virtually all civilized societies has been accompanied by educational prescriptions and programs for the acculturation of successive generations. The concept of curriculum is implicit even in the earliest educational prescriptions and programs of civilized societies. Aristotle was concerned with curriculum when he wrote, "As things are . . . mankind are by no means agreed about the things to be taught. . . . Again about the means there is no agreement. . . ."[3] Yet the actual term *curriculum* is a relatively modern term, dating from the nineteenth century, according to *The Oxford English Dictionary*, whereas the term *pedagogy* dates back to the early seventeenth century.

It can be contended that virtually every institution of society has a curriculum—the family, church, business, industry, library, museum, newspaper, and radio and television stations (including the commercials that teach people to want what they do not need). Aside from the miseducative functions of some of these institutions, and aside from the fact that most such institutions do not ordinarily utilize the concept *curriculum* to denote the nature of their operations, the school (and the college and university) performs a constellation of educative functions that is not matched by any other institution. Chief among these is the systematic organization and interpretation of the knowledge and skills of a culture needed for the growth of the rising generation.

When the term *educational institution* is used, one immediately thinks of the school, college, or university—although other institutions do indeed perform educational functions. The school, college, and university contain libraries of their own, and they may also make use of other kinds of libraries. But the library does not contain the school, college, or university. The library is charged with the storage, retrieval, and dissemination of codified scholarship and other material and media, but only the school, college, and university are concertedly responsible for the systematic reconstruction of the necessary knowledge paradigms and skills. This orchestral function of the school encompasses a program of systematic instruction and evaluation unmatched by any other institution.

The question of whether institutions other than the school, college, or university do indeed have a curriculum becomes irrelevant when the unique educative and curricular functions of the school, college, and university are recognized. It is possible to develop literacy in individuals and small populations without the curriculum of schooling; but no society has attained literacy without the curriculum of schooling. It is not by accident that the term *curriculum* has come to be so closely identified with the school, college, and university—and not with any other institution of society. It is therefore puzzling that contemporary curricularists have tended to define curriculum as though it were independent of the knowledge paradigms of the cumulative cultural experience. We shall meet this problem again.

According to Cremin, sustained concern with curriculum emerged in this country during the early decades of the progressive period of the twentieth century and "with the rapid growth of professional training for educators during the progressive period, the burgeoning literature of curriculum-making became the substance of a distinct field of study. . . ."[4] Hence it can be said that curriculum has a long past but a short history.

A MATTER OF DEFINITION

As in the case of most newly emerging distinct fields of study, considerable effort is directed at finding curriculum's appropriate definition, ascertaining its parameters, and seeking a measure of recognition commensurate with its bordering fields of scholarship. Newly emerging fields are also characterized by sharply conflicting schools of thought, which reflect the dramatic conceptual changes of the field.

The concept *curriculum* has undergone marked changes during the twentieth century without any consensus having been reached on an appropriate definition.

Today, most textbooks on curriculum and many works on educational theory offer some definition of curriculum. Many contemporary curricularists regard the matter of definition as highly significant, even crucial, for conceptual and operational progress. Whether the matter of definition holds such great significance is examined in the concluding section of this chapter. But regardless of this issue, an analysis of differing definitions of curriculum reveals to the student the profound changes that have occurred during the twentieth century concerning the role of the school in our society, conceptions of the learner, and the nature of knowledge.

Moreover, these factors in the educative process (namely, the nature of knowledge, the nature of the learner, and the wider social conditions) are conceived differently, and often on conflicting terms, by educators holding differing educational ideologies or philosophies. A traditionalist, then, would be at odds with a progressivist on the definition and function of the curriculum. In this chapter, an examination is made of the conflicting conceptions and functions of the curriculum as reflected in conflicting educational ideologies or philosophies. The issues raised in this chapter are developed in greater detail throughout Part II of this text and especially in Chapter 8.

TRADITIONALIST CONCEPTIONS AND FUNCTIONS OF CURRICULUM

Curriculum as the Cumulative Tradition of Organized Knowledge

During the early years of the twentieth century, most educators held to the traditional concept of curriculum as the body of subjects or subject matters set out by teachers for students to cover. Many traditionalists found such a definition far too broad, for it allowed room for any new subject to be added and any established subject to be deleted from the curriculum. Holding that there are permanent or essential subjects or bodies of knowledge, these traditionalists contended that any conception of curriculum must embrace these particular studies. In their view, any concept of curriculum that does not reveal what the body of subjects or subject matters should consist of is meaningless. Adding to the confusion, such terms as *course of study* and *syllabus* were also being used synonymously with curriculum.

PERENNIALIST CONCEPTIONS OF CURRICULUM. The perennialist position, as explicated by Robert M. Hutchins, holds that the curriculum should consist principally of the "permanent studies"—the rules of grammar, reading, rhetoric and logic, and mathematics (for the elementary and secondary levels of schooling), and the greatest books of the Western world (beginning at the secondary level of schooling). "If our hope has been to frame a curriculum which educes the elements of our common human nature," declared Hutchins, "this program should realize our hope."[5]

In effect, the curriculum exemplar for the truly educated individual is identified in the liberal arts. "The liberal arts are the maturing rituals of our civilized tribe," declared Mark Van Doren in his best-selling book, *Liberal Education* (1943), while "the three R's rightly recognize and state the studies which are proper in elementary education because they require no special knowledge or experience for their comprehension."[6]

Aside from suffering from archaic notions of mind and experience, the perennialist (or classical humanist) devalues the dynamic nature of knowledge, the modern scientific studies, and the practical applications of knowledge. The fundamental premise is that the best exemplars of the past, the so-called permanent studies, are valid for the present and for all time. "Knowledge is truth. The truth is everywhere the same. Hence education should be everywhere the same," declared Hutchins.[7]

Another problem with perennialism is its fundamental premise that the sole purpose of education should be the cultivation of the intellect, and that only certain studies have this power. According to Hutchins, "Grammar disciplines the mind and develops the logical faculty. . . . Correctness in thinking may be more directly and impressively taught through mathematics than in any other way," and the permanent studies "cultivate the intellectual virtues."[8] The perennialist position embraces the long-refuted doctrine of mental discipline (faculty psychology) and rejects any consideration of the interests and needs of the learner, or the treatment of contemporary problems in the curriculum, on the ground that such concerns are temporal and only detract from the school's mission of cultivating the mind.

The emerging demands for social reform during the early decades of the twentieth century—coupled with developments in psychiatry, medicine, and the various behavioral sciences—led to a more integrated conception of human nature. Progressive educators, buttressed by research findings on the transfer of learning, demolished the old conception of mind as a separate entity and challenged the notion that certain studies possess uniquely inherent powers for the cultivation of the intellect (mental discipline).

As discussed later, the advances in our knowledge of human behavior and the learning process, coupled with the growing recognition of the need for modern studies in the curriculum and the need for the vast extension of educational opportunity in and for a free society, all augured for a modern conception of curriculum. Nevertheless, the reader would be remiss in concluding that the perennialist conceptions of education and curriculum are artifacts of a bygone age that might better be relegated to a museum, for perennialist expositions on the curriculum have garnered considerable attention to this day. Because the perennialist shares with the essentialist the premise that the school curriculum must be properly delimited to basic education on which the traditional academic studies are built, as opposed to elective options (vocational, exploratory, enrichment studies), perennialism shares in any resurgence gained by essentialism. The late 1970s and the 1980s witnessed a sweeping retrenchment of curriculum in the schools under the slogan "Back to Basics." For the first time in American history, the chief federal official for education was a perennialist (William J. Bennett), appointed U.S. Secretary of Education by President Reagan in 1984. In that office, Bennett was an outspoken advocate of basic education and the study of the literary classics from the elementary school through the undergraduate curriculum. A best-selling book, written by a University of Chicago classicist under the title, *The Closing of the American Mind* (1987), and bearing the subtitle, *How Higher Education Has Failed Democracy and Impoverished the Souls of Today's Students,* attacked the colleges for having abandoned the perennialist cause in the curriculum.[9] In 1982, under the chairmanship of Mortimer

Adler and with a grant from the MacArthur Foundation, a perennialist prescription for the school curriculum was published under the title, *The Paideia Proposal: An Educational Manifesto.* This small book called for a course of study over twelve years entirely delimited to "basic schooling."[10] Adler had been a disciple of Robert M. Hutchins during Hutchins's long tenure as president of the University of Chicago, and later went on to publish and promote the one hundred great books of the Western World as the true canons of Western Civilization.

Although the colleges had no difficulty in warding off perennialist criticisms, the schools were completely vulnerable. In an era of social retrenchment, essentialism became the ruling curriculum doctrine over a period spanning from the late 1970s through the 1980s.

ESSENTIALIST CONCEPTIONS OF CURRICULUM. Perhaps the most comprehensive case for essentialism was developed by the historian Arthur Bestor in *The Restoration of Learning* (1956). To Bestor, the mission of the school is "intellectual training," and this is to be accomplished through a curriculum concentrated on "the fundamental intellectual disciplines . . . disciplined study in five great areas: (1) command of the mother tongue and the systematic study of grammar, literature, and writing; (2) mathematics; (3) sciences; (4) history; and (5) foreign language."[11] To the essentialist, certain so-called academic areas of systematized knowledge best represent the race experience that is to be transmitted to children and youth.

In 1907, the essentialist William C. Bagley wrote that the curriculum and the work of the teacher "must represent a storehouse of organized race experience, conserved against the time when knowledge shall be needed in the constructive solution of new and untried problems."[12] Although, as discussed later, many progressives also recognize the importance of the codified experience of the human race, their conception of such experience extends far beyond that of the essentialist, who delimits it primarily to certain organized bodies of academic knowledge. Moreover, where the essentialist tends to see such knowledge largely as something to be acquired and stored for some future use, the progressive is concerned with the significance of such knowledge in the immediate life of the learner.

Essentialism shares with perennialism the position that the curriculum must be centered on intellective training and that the path to intellective power is to be found only in certain academic studies. Although the essentialist, unlike the perennialist, recognizes the place of the modern laboratory sciences in the curriculum, the essentialist places the modern social sciences, vocational education, physical education, art, music, and other "nonacademic" studies at the lowest priority levels in the curriculum. "The first duty of the school, if it values its own educational integrity," declares Bestor, "is to provide a standard program of intellectual training in the fundamental disciplines."[13] Pupil interests and needs are of limited concern as a basis for determining the curriculum. According to Bestor, "To such an extreme have many educationalists gone that they seem anxious to satisfy all imaginable needs except those of the mind."[14]

Despite the fact that the essentialist notion of mental discipline was refuted by the findings of educational psychology during the early decades of the twentieth century,[15] and despite the narrow conception of curriculum promulgated by the essentialists, essentialism was able to capitalize on the era of the Cold War. The essentialist cry for academic excellence and concerted emphasis on mathematics, science, and modern foreign language was in tune with the needs of the Cold War arsenal. "If we take education seriously," wrote Bestor, "we can no more afford to gamble our safety upon inferior intellectual training in our schools than upon inferior weapons in our armory."[16] However, as discussed later, the essentialist thunder came to be superseded by the neo-essentialist disciplines doctrine of the Cold War and space race. *essential for now.*

As noted earlier, essentialism, with its economical curriculum of basic education, is revivified during periods of economic and social retrenchment. Also, periodic sweeps of educational (curriculum) reform tend to occur by successive reactions and counterreactions, given the influence on public education from the wider sociopolitical forces and the mass media. Consequently, the back-to-basics retrenchment of the latter 1970s came as a counterreaction to the laissez-faire excesses of the late 1960s in the curriculum from the elementary school through the college. This retrenchment proved to be long-lasting, extending into the early 1990s. In fact, the new curriculum fundamentalism became so pervasive that the Council for Basic Education, founded in 1956 by Arthur Bestor and other leading essentialists to promote a return to basics, was impelled to shift to a relatively moderate position. Hence the council began calling for a more balanced curriculum diet and made allowance for the place of some of the so-called nonacademic studies in the curriculum, such as the studio arts.[17]

In issuing his program in early 1991 to "revolutionize" the nation's public schools, as outlined in the federal document, *America 2000: An Education Strategy,* President George Bush called for the development of American achievement tests "in the five core (academic) subjects"—virtually the identical curriculum prescription that was promoted by Bestor back in the fifties.[18]

CULTURAL LITERACY: THE NEW ESSENTIALIST CATCHWORD.   One of the national best-sellers of 1987 was *Cultural Literacy: What Every American Needs to Know,* which contained a clever marketing gimmick in the form of nearly 5,000 items in the back of the book that "every American needs to know."[19] The items, obviously drawn up arbitrarily and giving rather short shrift to the sciences, were promoted by the author as defining the cultural knowledge base for the schools and the nation. To the unwary public, the items offered as "knowledge" were nothing less than information in the form of isolated facts. The use of the term *literacy* was soon seized on by virtually every special-interest group for each subject area of the curriculum in promoting prescriptions for their own brand of literacy—mathematical literacy, scientific literacy, technological literacy, computer literacy, economic literacy, political literacy, artistic literacy, and so on.[20] In embracing the term, the essentialists had forgotten the humble historic origins of literacy that had emerged early in the twentieth century to mark a rudimentary capability in English for the waves of immigrants reaching our shores.

To Hirsch and many essentialists, a fact-based curriculum is fundamental to any further learning. It seemed that Dickens's Mr. Gradgrind in *Hard Times* had come back to life in the curriculum hard times during the educational retrenchment of the 1980s.

A work very similar to *Cultural Literacy,* also published in 1987, was *What Do Our 17-Year-Olds Know?* by Diane Ravitch and Chester Finn. (Finn was serving under William Bennett as Associate Secretary for Research in the U.S. Department of Education, and was to be succeeded by Ravitch in the Bush administration.) Drawing from the test results of the National Assessment of Educational Progress, Finn and Ravitch focused their work not on "What Do Our 17-Year-Olds Know?" but on what they didn't know as revealed by their wrong answers to multiple-choice test items predominantly geared to the recall of factual information.[21]

Needless to say, these books provided the mass media with a field day for the bashing of the public schools, and gave renewed impetus to the curriculum fundamentalism in an extended era of education retrenchment.

Neo-essentialism

STRUCTURE OF THE DISCIPLINE.   In reaction to the Cold War and space race, hundreds of millions of dollars were allocated by the National Science Foundation to university scholars for the development of new courses of study in the sciences and mathematics at the elementary and secondary levels. The specialized nature of university scholarship resulted in a like model imposed on the schools. University scholars held that the school curriculum should be formulated according to the "structures of the disciplines." This notion soon became a doctrine that dominated the curriculum field from the late 1950s through much of the 1960s. Specialists in the social studies, the visual and performing arts, and the language arts sought to emulate the physical sciences and mathematics in the elusive search for disciplinary structure. Leading curriculum theorists, such as Joseph Schwab, seized on *disciplinarity,* to coin a term, as the ruling doctrine for curriculum development at all levels.[22] Some scholars went even further than Schwab in arguing the case for the disciplines as the sole source of the curriculum. Phenix declared that "[t]he curriculum should consist entirely of knowledge which comes from the disciplines."[23]

The disciplinary doctrine resulted in a multiplicity of disciplines vying for a distinct place in the curriculum at the elementary and secondary levels. Moreover, there was disagreement, even among scholars in the same areas of specialized knowledge, as to the elements that constitute the structure of the discipline.

Although disciplinarity is a valuable mode for organizing certain specialized areas of knowledge in order to facilitate scholarly communication and, at the university level, to advance such knowledge, its appropriateness as *the* ruling principle for curriculum development came into question. Other modes of organizing knowledge for the curriculum can be justified in terms of life relevance, the nature of the learner, and the demands of society.

The advocate of disciplinarity may share with the perennialist and the essentialist the conception of curriculum as the cumulative tradition of organized knowledge and the devaluation of practical knowledge, but here is where the cause for common ground ends. Unlike the perennialist view, the disciplinary conception regards knowledge as dynamic and places the methods of science as central to the development of new knowledge. Whereas the perennialist and essentialist regard the mind as a vessel to be filled or a muscle to be exercised, the advocate of disciplinarity regards disciplinary inquiry as the key to intellective development. Whereas the essentialist view is focused strongly on the fundamental skills, particularly at the elementary and intermediate phases of schooling, the disciplinary advocate regards such skills as merely instrumental to the wider and deeper organizing concepts and principles of each discipline and to the process of disciplinary inquiry. Finally, whereas the essentialist deprecates contemporary studies and rejects the social sciences in favor of history, the proponent of disciplinarity regards the various social sciences as having a legitimate place in the curriculum.

Although the disciplines doctrine rejects the traditional conception of knowledge as fixed or permanent, and regards knowledge as the product of a process known as disciplined inquiry, it confines such inquiry to the boundaries of the established disciplines. The fact that many problems transcend the individual disciplines and call for interdisciplinary approaches is virtually ignored or rejected by proponents of the disciplines doctrine.

What about the nature, needs, and interests of the learner? Concern for the nature of the learner is dismissed as the learner is to be viewed ideally as a miniature version of the university scholar on the forefront of his or her discipline. According to Phenix, "There is no place in the curriculum for ideas which are regarded as suitable for teaching because of the supposed nature, needs, and interests of the learner, but which do not belong within the regular structure of the disciplines."[24]

Although the disciplines doctrine was to collapse by the late 1960s as a result of neglecting the practical needs of society, ignoring the nature of the learner and practical knowledge in the life of the learner, and producing myriad competing disciplinary domains for a place in the school curriculum, the disciplines doctrine remained alive and well in the university culture of specialized knowledge production.

Curriculum as an Instructional Plan or Course of Study

One of the most longstanding conceptions of curriculum is that of an instructional plan or, synonymously, a course of study. The most systematic application of this concept of curriculum was made through the disciplinary curriculum reforms during the height of the Cold War and space race. Although the method claimed for the implementation of the discipline-centered curriculum was to be that of inquiry learning, the method of inquiry (or discovery) became little more than a slogan, especially when many of those responsible for creating the disciplinary curriculum packages sought to make them "teacher proof"—a contradiction in terms, to say the least.[25] Furthermore, the "inquiry" was directed at specialized knowledge to the deliberate exclusion of practical knowledge geared to the learner's development and life experience, and to the wider social situation.

In 1964, Jerrold Zacharias of M.I.T., who had led the way eight years earlier in the establishment of the archetype project for the discipline-centered curriculum reforms (Physical Science Study Committee), proposed that curriculum revision encompass four distinct components: (1) determining the precise boundaries of the educational unit, (2) identifying the subject matter within the unit, (3) embodying the subject matter in material form (textbook, laboratory and classroom materials, and other learning aids), and (4) preparing teachers in the subject matter and use of materials.[26] In effect, the curriculum was seen by Zacharias as synonymous with the course of study.

Paul Woodring noted that, to some extent, the disciplinary movement represented a return to the older tradition that dominated the schools before the progressive revolution in that it conceived of curriculum as subject matter organized as separate academic disciplines.[27] As discussed earlier, the disciplinary movement departed from the older tradition in many significant ways, but the conception of curriculum embraced by this movement was nonetheless a return to the notion of curriculum as a course of study.

Taba rejected the progressive concept of curriculum (e.g., "the life and program of the school") for being so broad as to be nonfunctional, and proposed in 1962 that "[a] curriculum is a plan for learning."[28] Beauchamp proffered a similar definition in successive editions of *Curriculum Theory,* namely that "a curriculum is a written document."[29] Standing by itself, Beauchamp's definition fails to distinguish curriculum from any other kind of written document—whether a business contract, a marriage license, or a store coupon. But Beauchamp goes on to point out that a curriculum includes at least one of the following four elements: (1) an outline of the culture content to be taught, (2) a statement of goals and/or specific objectives, (3) a statement of the purposes for the creation of the curriculum and ways in which the curriculum is to be used, and, more rarely, (4) an appraisal scheme.[30]

PROBLEM OF DUALISM.   One of the difficulties with the definitions offered by Taba and Beauchamp is that they do not distinguish between a curriculum and a lesson plan or unit plan—mere instruments of a curriculum. More significantly, these definitions do not distinguish a curriculum from a syllabus—the latter having been used synonymously with the term *curriculum* before the progressive period, as we have noted. But perhaps the most significant issue is that such definitions imply that the *processes* by which such plans are put into action are outside the curriculum. As discussed later, many contemporary curriculum writers maintain that instruction is indeed separate from curriculum. This notion of separation is reflected in Macdonald's definition of curriculum as "those planning endeavors which take place prior to instruction."[31]

The problem of dualism between curriculum and instruction arises in all definitions where curriculum is regarded as a plan. Hirst defines curriculum as "a plan of activities deliberately organized so that pupils will attain, by learning, certain educational ends or objectives."[32] Although Hirst sees a curriculum arising only in a teaching situation, his definition is that of a *plan* for teaching and learning activities and not of the experience itself. An almost identical definition, which raises the same difficulties, is offered by Saylor and Alexander: "[W]e define curriculum as a plan for providing sets of learning opportunities to achieve broad goals and related specific objectives for an identifiable population served by a single school center."[33]

A definition by Eisner is virtually identical to that of Hirst, in that the curriculum is to be seen "as a series of planned events that are intended to have educational consequences for one or more students."[34] Such definitions also fail to account for what Dewey referred to as "collateral learning"[35] or the collateral curriculum, which is commonly called the hidden curriculum. The collateral curriculum or hidden curriculum may often be far more powerful than the intended curriculum. For example, after completing their geography lessons with wall maps, young children may point to the ceiling when asked the direction of North, and to the floor when asked the direction of South. And they may be unable to transfer their map work in geography to conceptualizing the geography of their locale and to the practical uses of simple maps. Under such circumstances, the intended curriculum is dysfunctional and miseducative. It is also not uncommon for the collateral (hidden) curriculum to have effects that are far more powerful in a positive direction than the intended curriculum. The significance of the collateral or hidden curriculum is discussed later in this chapter.

Similar to Eisner's definition is that offered by Oliva, who sees curriculum as "a plan or program for all experiences which the learner encounters [sic] under the direction of the school."[36] As discussed later, such definitions do not account for what commonly happens to the best-laid plans or programs when they are implemented. An incidental but educationally significant question might be raised concerning Oliva's choice of the word *encounter* in defining the curriculum, for encounter is commonly defined and used as a meeting or engagement in conflict. This may accurately portray the all-too-common relationship between the student and the curriculum as oppositional. But as Dewey stated in a lecture to parents—in traditional education, instead of productive interaction—"[w]e get the case of the child vs. the curriculum."[37]

Curriculum as Measured Instructional Outcomes (Products)— A Technological Production Model

The new instructional technology and the growing trend toward standardized-achievement testing have given impetus to conceiving of the curriculum in terms of test results. With schools and teachers being evaluated according to student scores on standardized tests, there has been an increasing tendency for teachers to teach to the test. Hence the test not only provides the quantitative data on the outcomes of instruction, but also exerts a powerful influence on instructional processes and very largely determines the curriculum. In effect the curriculum is seen as the quantitatively measured outcomes of instruction. Such a conception of curriculum reduces the schooling process to a technological system of production.

The origin of the notion of curriculum as a production system can be traced to the efforts in education during the early decades of the twentieth century to apply industrial "scientific management" to education.[38] These efforts were exemplified in the method of job analysis. In recent years, the notion of curriculum as a production system has been embodied in the doctrine of specific "behavioral" objectives, behaviorism and the theory of operant conditioning, developments in instructional technology (including systems analysis), performance contracting, and accountability.

ACTIVITY ANALYSIS.   Although activity analysis incorporated the progressive idea of
linking the curriculum to life experience, it departed from the progressive rationale
by reducing curriculum to an analysis of adult activity and thereby overlooked the
authentic life of the learner. The operation of job analysis or activity analysis was
designed to secure educational objectives in an efficient way, corresponding to the
analysis of activities involved in the performance of jobs in the world of industry and
business. Because education is concerned with processes that extend beyond job
performance, the term *activity analysis* came to be more popular among curriculum developers during the early decades of this century.

Developed by Franklin Bobbitt and W. W. Charters, the method of activity analysis
came to be cloaked as the scientific way to build a curriculum. According to Bobbitt,
life consists of the performance of specific activities. If education is preparation for life
then it must prepare for these specific activities. These activities, however numerous,
are definite and particularized, and can be taught; therefore, these activities will be
the objectives of the curriculum. "The curriculum will then be that series of experience which children and youth must have by way of attaining these objectives," reasoned Bobbitt, who proceeded to define curriculum as *"that series of things which
children and youth must do and experience* by way of developing abilities to do the
things well that make up the affairs of adult life; and to be in all respects what adults
should be."[39] The school, according to Bobbitt, simply deals with those objectives that
are not sufficiently attained through undirected experience.

Aside from certain problems inherent in activity analysis—such as its static orientation toward society, the virtually unlimited number of objectives possible, its
notion of the child as merely an adult in the making, its misuse of the term *scientific,*
and so on—this method was derived by Bobbitt and Charters from analyses of the
production models of business and industry. To Bobbitt, curriculum making is the
job of the "educational engineer,"[40] and to Charters, "[i]n its simplest forms it
involves the analysis of definite operations, to which the term job analysis is applied,
as in the analysis of the operations involved in running a machine."[41] This mechanistic model shows its legacy in various education doctrines and proposals in contemporary education, such as behavioristic objectives and accountability.

CURRICULUM AS ENDS.   The conception of curriculum as a plan is extended considerably further by Popham and Baker, who define curriculum as "all planned learning
outcomes for which the school is responsible," and who maintain that "curriculum
refers to the desired *consequences* of instruction." They go on to contend that "The
distinction between ends and means is not difficult to make, and can help the
teacher greatly in his instructional planning."[42] This view is highly mechanistic, for
the focal point is the ends and the assessment of end products; only those end products that can be measured quantitatively as behavioral (behavioristic) objectives are
considered legitimate. Curriculum is reduced to ends, and instruction is reduced to
means.

A similar dualistic view is held by Johnson, who argues that the generally
accepted definition of curriculum as "planned learning experiences" is unsatisfactory
because it fails to distinguish curriculum from instruction. He proceeds to define

curriculum as "a structured series of intended learning outcomes."[43] It is possible to interpret such a definition in terms of outcomes that are far more comprehensive than behavioristic objectives. In such a case, the concept of curriculum as ends would not fall into the instructional technology camp. But the dominant view of curriculum as ends resides with the proponents of behavioristic objectives as the controlling curriculum mode.

The process-product dualism is most explicitly set forth in efforts to base course content on behavioristic objectives. According to Popham, "*Curriculum* questions revolve around consideration of *ends,* that is, the objectives an educational system hopes its learners will achieve," and he declares that "[a] properly stated behavioral objective must describe *without ambiguity* the nature of learner behavior or product to be measured," and, as mentioned earlier, that "the terms *curriculum* and *instruction* should be contrasted as entirely separate 'components.' The distinction is one of ends and means."[44] Thus, the curriculum is seen as one component, and instruction as another component, in a production process that leads to a measurable product called terminal behavior.

Popham advocates that we "divert some of our national resources into constructing lists of potential objectives in precise form from which the teachers can choose. In this way teachers don't have to go to the work of generating their own goals, they need only to select them."[45] Thus, the teacher is regarded as a sort of mechanic whose job it is to see to it that the curriculum and other components of the technological process of production yield the sufficient quantity of products under the necessary quality controls. Curriculum is reduced to lists of behavioral objectives, or, more accurately, behavioristic objectives.

Popham's behavioristic dogmatics were widely shared in education during the 1970s when the back-to-basics reductionism and statewide minimum-competency testing were spreading throughout the nation. Twenty years later, with the rediscovery of the need for higher-order thinking, writing across the curriculum, and other approaches to curriculum synthesis, behaviorism went into retreat and cognitive-developmental psychology seemed to be rising to the occasion. Popham confesses to making a retreat following an encounter with curriculum reality in a developing nation where practical needs are paramount.[46] Nevertheless, as long as teachers continue to use worksheets and gear their lessons and tests to rote learning, behaviorism will prevail and learning will remain largely convergent rather than emergent.

Although those curriculum writers who see curriculum as ends are in sharp conflict with those who regard curriculum as instructional content, each group shares the notion of a dualism between curriculum and instruction, between ends and means. However logical such a distinction may appear in theory, it leads to serious conceptual and practical difficulties. To separate curriculum from instruction, or to separate subject matter from method, is to make the same error as in separating knowledge from that which renders our actions intelligent. Thus, to see the curriculum merely as ends is like conceiving of getting to a destination without having to take the trip.

The behaviorist B. F. Skinner, who developed the rationale for operant conditioning, sees the curriculum being formulated according to behavioristic objectives or terminal behaviors. He describes the teacher's role as mechanical, for, according to Skinner, the teacher merely is one "who arranges the contingencies of reinforcement" under which the pupils are automatically conditioned toward specified terminal behaviors.[47] Method, then, is conceived as the schedule of reinforcement contingencies established by the programmer. An automatic model of the learner is assumed. The learner is reduced to a response system; instruction becomes a stimulus system; curriculum is conceived as the planned learning outcomes as represented by lists of quantifiable behavioristic or terminal objectives.

Skinner and other behaviorists not only view the curriculum as a component of a technological production process but they also see the pupil as a kind of mechanical learning unit in the production process. According to Gagné, "curriculum is a sequence of content units arranged in such a way that the learning of each unit may be accomplished as a single act, provided the capabilities described by specified prior units (in the sequence) have already been mastered by the learner."[48] Gagné defines a unit of content as a specific description of a single student capability or, essentially, a behavioristic objective. The definition of curriculum offered by Gagné assumes that learning is mechanical and linear, and that the learner is a mere mechanism to be conditioned toward making the right automatic responses.

Like activity analysis, behavioristic objectives are limitless in number. Because modern-day proponents of behavioristic objectives insist that such objectives be quantifiably assessed as terminal products, the curriculum becomes necessarily narrow and mechanical. Advocates of behavioral specification of objectives share with proponents of behavior modification the doctrine that all behavior is controlled. According to Bandura, "the operation of psychological laws cannot be suspended by romantic conceptions of human behavior, any more than indignant rejection of the law of gravity as antihumanistic can stop people from falling."[49] However, the so-called laws of psychology are not the same as the laws of physics. Moreover, behaviorism is only one of several schools of psychology. The doctrine of behavioristic objectives appears to be based on the notion that the broken egg can be put back together again. All it takes, after the proper analysis, is the reassemblage of the constituent parts.

With regard to the behaviorist's doctrine that all behavior is inevitably controlled, we might well heed the wry admonition of the late Nobel laureate Isaac Beshevis Singer, who stated in a TV interview shortly before his death in 1991 that "[w]e must believe in free will; we have no choice."

The foregoing discussion of behavioristic objectives reveals how some educators regard the curriculum as a mere component of a technological production process. According to Skinner,

> Technology clarifies the variables the teacher is manipulating, as well as their effects . . . a technology of teaching helps most by increasing the teacher's productivity. It simply permits him to teach more—more of a given subject, in more subjects, and to more students.[50]

Thus technological approaches tend to reduce the significance of curriculum to a kind of plug-in parameter. An example of this is the conception of curriculum offered by Bush and Allen in their technological proposal for redesigning the high school: "The entire curriculum can be thought of as an *area* to be scheduled. The horizontal dimension represents the number of students, the vertical dimension represents the length of time in the schedule module."[51] Regardless of whatever merits their proposal has, their technological orientation reduces curriculum to a rectangular box in which the variables are (1) the number of pupils to be processed and (2) the time available for their processing in order to produce the expected outcomes. Unfortunately, all too many secondary school principals act as though they have settled the main curriculum problem when they have settled on the schedule of classes.

Accountability and Performance Contracting.   The conception of curriculum as a technological system of production is also embodied in performance contracting. The late 1960s and early 1970s witnessed a revival of the conception of the school as a production system not unlike an industrial plant. Under the banner of accountability, the schools were pressured to adopt the techniques of industrial plant management in assessing their efficiency through quantitative input-output measures. Addressing school principals, an officer of The Ford Foundation stated:

> Similar to the plant manager in a large industrial corporation, the principal is the key person responsible for the productivity of the organization. The school, like the industrial plant, represents a process. Raw material goes in and a product comes out. The change that occurs between input, that is the entering pupil, and output, the departing pupil, . . . measures the school.[52]

A former U.S. associate commissioner of education argued that the schools be made accountable through performance contracting: "In the same way that planning . . . and performance warranties determine industrial production and its worth to consumers, so should we be able to engineer, organize, refine, and manage the educational system to prepare students to contribute to the most complex and exciting country on earth."[53] Under such accountability and performance contracting, curriculum is reduced to a component of a production process called educational engineering, and the efficiency of the process is assessed in terms of quantifiable performance specifications, warranties, and outcomes.

Evaluations have revealed some perverse effects of performance contracting on the curriculum.[54] Contractors tended to exclude those areas of the curriculum that are not amenable to quantifiable specifications and output measurements. Yet, despite the narrow curricular focus of these projects, the evaluations revealed that they were no more successful in academic achievement, and often less successful, than control classes as measured by the performance-contracting criteria. The industrial model has not been valid for the world of education because education is concerned not with the production of inanimate objects but with growing, developing human beings who must be capable of dealing competently not merely with fixed problems but with emergent problems as well.

Educational and curricular problems are not the same as engineering and production problems of a factory. This does not mean that curricular processes and learning outcomes cannot be assessed but rather that the ways and means of such assessment cannot be likened to the quality controls and efficiency measurement specifications of the industrial plant. The human equation is infinitely more complex in an institution, the school, that is concerned with the rising generation—the generation that is our society's own future.

Nevertheless, educators continue to be pressured into adopting the relatively simplistic paradigms of business, industry, and the military. Although performance contracting for accountability collapsed during the early seventies for reasons noted previously, coupled with questionable techniques in teaching to the test, such contracting with the private sector received an incredible resurrection from President George Bush's "Education Strategy" unveiled in early 1991 under the title *America 2000*. Many educators were astonished when the President of Yale University, with the endorsement of President Bush, announced in May 1992 that he was resigning to become the chief executive officer of the Edison Project—a plan to build a national chain of schools for profit through funds that otherwise would be allocated to the public schools. The chain of schools would be designed to operate with optimum efficiency through the uses of educational technology, thereby reducing the costs of people power and building facilities. Although President Bush strongly endorsed the Edison Project and other efforts for engaging the private sector in the enterprise of public education under the banner of "schools of choice," his successor, President Bill Clinton, announced his opposition to such schemes. However, the early 1990s witnessed a resurgence of performance-contracting arrangements with the public schools. In 1992 the Baltimore City Public Schools contracted with a private educational management company to oversee the day-to-day operation of eight elementary schools and one middle school—all in the inner city. The company had also completed similar contractual arrangements with public schools in other parts of the nation. Clearly, the goal of such contracting, or of the Edison Project chain of schools, is cost effectiveness as measured by the relationship of inputs to outputs (scores on standardized achievement tests). In *America 2000,* President Bush called for a national system of examinations through American achievement tests in the five (academic) core areas that, obviously, define the school curriculum, or the curriculum that really "counts."

SYSTEMS ANALYSIS.   An orchestral outgrowth of technology is systems analysis. Popularized through its use in the Defense Department and its rapid spread through the industrial-commercial arena, systems analysis has been promoted by some educators as a promising technique for solving pervasive educational problems. Oettinger offers this view of systems analysis:

> There is today a widely held point of view from which most anything, and education in particular, can be described as a collection or system of interdependent parts belonging to a hierarchy in which a system may have subsystems of its own while acting as a mere part of a suprasystem. The process of analyzing or synthesizing such systems, called "systems analysis" for short, is touted as one of the shiniest of new technologies.[55]

Although systems analysis can be an invaluable technique for dealing with complex organizational and productivity problems, and in seeing such problems wholly as well as in detail, the trouble begins when attempts are made to apply systems analysis to problems that are not strictly quantitative. Even in the realm of the Defense Department, where the variables in connection with contracts for the production of weapons are known and quantifiable, it is common to find that cost overruns are upwards of 200 and 300 percent of the contractual specifications. Because education is largely an emergent sphere with all kinds of changing, value-laden, qualitative influences—and not merely an established sphere with fixed, quantitative components—systems analysis has severe limitations in education.

A systems definition of curriculum has been offered by Westbury and Steimer:

> We hold that curriculum is a methodological inquiry exploring the range of ways in which the subject matter elements of teacher, student, subject, and milieu can be seen. . . . The study of curriculum as *means* should become an inquiry into the devices and modes for actualizing the interactions of the commonplace curricular elements: subject, student, milieu, and teacher.[56]

This definition conceives of curriculum as a production process concerned with the manipulation of means and components and includes the idea that "ends can be located in some way that makes it possible to measure the effectiveness of different uses of means."[57] Thus, this definition not only conceives of the learner as simply one of the components to be manipulated to produce specified outcomes, but it also follows an ends-means dualism.

When applied to education, systems analysis reduces curriculum to a mere technological component containing many subcomponents. Dissected from its ecological conditions, the concept of curriculum becomes mechanistic and artificial, and has little bearing on actual curricular problems. An illustration of what happens to the concept of curriculum when treated by systems analysis is this statement from the final report of a $1.5 million Ford Foundation project in the School of Engineering at the University of California, Los Angeles:

> The professional curriculum is a highly complex, information transmitting system. It acts upon inputs from the high schools to convert this raw material into a semi-finished product to be shipped out into practice. Viewed in this sense, the educational design problem is comparable to any other large-scale system problem.[58]

The results of this effort, as in the case of other efforts to apply systems analysis to curriculum development, failed to yield what was promised, despite twelve years of work. Unable to derive meaningful empirical data from the systems analysis, the project fell back on a set of recommendations based on conventional wisdom—such as the need for professional schools to foster research that is relevant to the professions.

In contrast, a curriculum-study project undertaken by a faculty-student commission at M.I.T. deliberately avoided systems analysis. Utilizing a variety of methods—

including case history, surveys, and review of pertinent literature—and dra
knowledgeable consultants through task forces, symposia, conferences, and se
nars, the commission addressed several molar problems of curriculum. Among these
were the fragmentation of the curriculum and the emergence of the warehouse or
supermarket model of curriculum as a result of the knowledge explosion, the growing specialization of knowledge, and the vested departmentalized interests in the
university. Through such a focus, the commission was able to reject "mechanical curricular tinkering" and come to grips with the problem of how to reconstruct the curriculum for the integration of knowledge from the various disciplines so that knowledge could be related effectively to human action.[59] This called for a restructuring of
the university. Of course, other evaluative methods might have guided such a study,
including experimental research, but in any case, when curriculum is studied in its
broadest conceptual sense and in its natural ecological setting, the outcomes are
more likely to be realistic, meaningful, and practical. And the findings are more likely
to be transformed into practice.

Although the recommendations of the M.I.T. curriculum study of 1970 were not
implemented in the face of the mounting forces for specialism and specialized
research, the problems and issues addressed in the 1970 report were being attacked
systematically at M.I.T. during the early 1990s, and in various national reports on the
undergraduate curriculum.[60]

One of the most successful efforts at comprehensive curriculum reconstruction
was undertaken at Western Reserve University's School of Medicine during the
1950s. Avoiding a systems approach, the total effort was directed at developing an
integrated curriculum. Traditional departmental barriers were broken down and
replaced by interdisciplinary faculty committees, and the traditional separate subjects were synthesized into broad functional areas. Departmental laboratories were
transformed into multidisciplinary laboratories, and clinical experiences were interrelated with the coursework throughout the entire program beginning with the
freshman year. Concerted efforts were made to develop more positive and professional attitudes toward learning. The entire effort was subjected to systematic formative and summative evaluation.[61] The successes at Western Reserve, now Case Western Reserve, exerted a significant influence on curriculum improvement in major
medical schools throughout the United States.

Curriculum as Cultural Reproduction

Growing out of the college-student protest movement of the sixties and early seventies, and its countercultural rhetoric, the new academic left gained a strong presence
in education faculties in colleges and universities during the eighties. Functioning as
a kind of academic federation of critical theorists, revisionists, neo-Marxists, anarchists, and radical reconstructionists, the new academic left portrayed the school
curriculum as cultural reproduction—a selection of studies or subject matters
designed to maintain the existing social order. As the historian Freeman Butts
observed, the new academic left, or neo-radicals, were portraying the public schools
as mere instruments of oppression by American capitalism on behalf of the privi-

Ɑes.[62] And the teacher was portrayed largely as an unwitting accomplice to ⱯⱯve social inequities and oppression perpetuated by the social system. The ⱭⱭdemic left proceeded to hold the school as a powerless or, at best, a marⱭ ∩stitution for effecting social change—leading one to question why those idenⱯ. with the new academic left were devoting their careers to heaving polemical ⱭⱭades at the public schools.[63] To the new academic left, the best that the schools Ɑould do is focus on the fundamental skills and standard academic studies. In Ɛffect, the proper role of the public school as advocated by the new academic left closely resembled that of the conservative.

However, whereas the perennialist sees the function of curriculum as preservation and transmission of the cultural heritage in terms of the great exemplars of Western civilization, and whereas the perennialist sees this as constituting a powerful curriculum, the new academic left, in couching curriculum as cultural reproduction, is negating the power of the school curriculum. This negation appears to stem from the negation implicit in the term counterculture and in the counterculture literature of the late sixties and early seventies, which sounded its trumpet call as the "great refusal."[64]

PROGRESSIVIST CONCEPTIONS AND FUNCTIONS OF CURRICULUM

The influence of progressive education during the first half of the twentieth century brought about a profound change in the conception of curriculum. The need for a radically new conception of curriculum was the inevitable result of a number of forces—changes in the conceptions of knowledge, particularly scientific knowledge; changes in the knowledge of the learning process as a result of the child-study movement; and the need to link formal school studies with the life of the learner and the changing demands of the larger social scene. Nevertheless, in the process of rejecting traditional conceptions of curriculum, progressive educators were far from universal agreement as to how curriculum should be defined. Moreover, traditional conceptions of curriculum have remained influential to this day.

To the progressivists, a body of school subjects, subject matters, syllabi, course of study, list of courses, or documented program of studies are inert and do not a curriculum make until the material becomes actualized by the learner. Hence curriculum is far more than a representation of the cumulative tradition of knowledge. To some progressivists, curriculum was seen as the embodiment of the best elements of the experience of culture in the process of acculturation. For other progressivists, buttressed by advances in educational psychology and the movement for democratic social reform, curriculum was to be conceived as more dynamically experiential.

Curriculum as Knowledge Selection/Organization from the Experience of the Culture

Although the conception of curriculum as the cumulative tradition of knowledge, as exemplified by perennialist and essentialist educators, is an essential part of the human race experience, it is only a limited part of such experience. Such experience embodies not only the cumulative tradition of knowledge but also the total culture of a society, the common elements that make a society more than a mere aggregation of individuals. Dewey's mandate for recognizing the vital importance of transferring and reconstructing the cultural experience through the curriculum is reflected in the definition of curriculum offered by Smith, Stanley, and Shores. After pointing out that in all literate societies the institution known as the school is charged with the specialized function of teaching certain things, Smith, Stanley, and Shores offer this definition of curriculum: "A sequence of potential experiences is set up in the school for the purpose of disciplining children and youth in group ways of thinking and acting. This set of experiences is referred to as the *curriculum*."[65]

Despite the apparent legitimacy of such an anthropological definition, its exclusive focus on acculturation treats schooling "as if the education of the immature which fills them with the spirit of the social group to which they belong, were a sort of catching up of the child with the aptitudes and resources of the adult group." Progressive communities "endeavor to shape the experiences of the young so that instead of reproducing current habits, better habits shall be formed, and thus the future adult society be an improvement on their own."[66] Thus, to Dewey, by virtue of educating the rising generation, the school is serving to develop the potentials of the future society. Although Dewey recognized the importance of encompassing in curriculum the codified experience of the culture, to Dewey such experience is not an end point but a turning point in the continuous reconstruction of knowledge and society.

In their anthropological definition, Smith, Stanley, and Shores stressed that in a democratic society curriculum is far more than *cultural reproduction* (a favorite term used by the radical left in attacking the public schools). A democratic society values independent thinking in the context of the widest sense of social responsibility.

In the same vein, Lawton, a British educator, views curriculum as "*a selection from the culture of society*." Lawton goes on to state that "[c]ertain aspects of our way of life, certain kinds of knowledge, certain attitudes and values are regarded as so important that their transmission to the next generation is not left to chance," and so society entrusts the *selection* to professional educators in institutions known as schools.[67] Although this definition is far more comprehensive than the traditional conception of curriculum as the established bodies of knowledge or the courses of study, it raises the question of whether the curriculum represents merely a *selection* from the culture, or, more provocatively, a *reconstruction* of knowledge and experience for the improvement of the culture. There is indeed a vast difference between curriculum as conceived merely for cultural transmission to the next generation or for cultural improvement.

Clearly stressing the significance of the role of the school in a democratic society, Lawton is not characterizing curriculum as merely cultural reproduction, although his definition might be so construed by a critical theorist.

As the universities were begetting more knowledge at what seemed to be an incessantly accelerated pace, these institutions and the lower schools were faced with the dilemma of how this knowledge should be assimilated into the curriculum. The immediate response was the accretion of subjects in the existing curriculum, the revision of course content, and, to a somewhat lesser extent, the displacement of some studies. Paradoxically, the specialization of knowledge was both a cause of and a response to the knowledge explosion.

The increasing specialization of knowledge made the curriculum more remote from pervading personal and social needs and problems. During the early decades of the twentieth century, emerging social reforms and the new demands for education reforms called for a closer relationship between the curriculum and life. Newer and wider conceptions of curriculum were the inevitable result.

Curriculum as Modes of Thought

In *How We Think* (1910, 1933), Dewey noted how the traditional concept of curriculum as a collection of different subject matters or disciplines, each logically organized as to "content" within its own boundaries, tended to impose a misconception of logical method on the teacher, while fragmenting knowledge and isolating it from the life of the learner. Dewey saw reflective thinking as the unifying process in curriculum—the mode of thought so vital to productive citizenship in a free society. Dewey clearly stressed that this was not to be confused with disciplinary inquiry, which is abstract, specialized, and remote from practical applications in the affairs of living.[68] Yet proponents of the disciplines doctrine were to identify disciplinary inquiry as Deweyan.

DISCIPLINARY INQUIRY. With the doctrine of disciplinarity contending that the intellectual activity of the child is not qualitatively different from that of the scholar-specialist, some education theorists proceeded to formulate definitions of education and curriculum based on disciplinary inquiry—the modes of inquiry developed by specialized scholars in the various disciplines. "Education should be conceived as a *guided recapitulation of the processes of inquiry which gave rise to the fruitful bodies of organized knowledge comprising the established disciplines,*" declared Phenix.[69]

According to Belth, "the curriculum is considered to be the increasingly wide range of possible modes of thinking about men's experiences—not the conclusions, but the models from which conclusions derive, and in context of which these conclusions, these so-called truths, are grounded and validated."[70] Belth's rationale clearly is that embraced by the disciplinary doctrine. However, if the broader view of curriculum as modes of thought is taken, then a major difficulty is overcome. The modes of thinking, as far as crossdisciplinary and interdisciplinary problems are concerned, now become relevant to the curriculum. If this definition is allowed to stand by itself, "modes of thinking" might be interpreted as extending beyond the confines of the established disciplines, thereby extending curriculum significantly beyond Phenix's conception. But Belth sees education and curriculum as "a matter of developing the power to use the models of a variety of disciplines," and the necessary condition "is the ability to sort out the many concepts about the methods of inquiry indigenous to each of the separate disciplines."[71]

170

Unaccountably, a number of leading educators
between disciplinary inquiry and Dewey's concer
Glass, a leading figure in the discipline-centered
nary inquiry as stemming from the ideas of D
discovery method as explicated by Jerome F
nary inquiry, with Dewey's ideas on the relatic
inquiry-discovery embraced in the discipline-centc
blow at the traditional notion of separation between cc.
traditional pedagogical methodology of memorization-regu.
unity between content and process, or subject matter and methc
expounded by Dewey. To Dewey, learning is learning to think, but the
thinking is qualitatively different from that of the adult scholar. Dewey a.
that the "so-called disciplinary studies" raise the "danger of the isolation of t.
tual activity from the ordinary affairs of life."[74]

REFLECTIVE THINKING. Although Dewey did not confine his conception of curriculum to modes of thought, he saw reflective thinking as the means through which curriculum elements are unified. To Dewey, reflection is not merely confined within specialized domains of knowledge but is extended to social problem solving. Thought is not divorced from action but is tested by application. Dewey identified the following as essentials of reflection:

> They are first that the pupil have a genuine situation of experience—that there be a continuous activity in which he is interested for its own sake; secondly, that a genuine problem develop within this situation as a stimulus to thought; third, that he possess the information and make the observations needed to deal with it; fourth, that suggested solutions occur to him which he shall be responsible for developing in an orderly way; fifth, that he may have the opportunity and occasion to test his ideas by application, to make their meaning clear and to discover for himself their validity.[75]

Unfortunately, many educators have misinterpreted Dewey by alleging that his essentials of reflection were intended as hard and fast—as the actual step-by-step means, and the only means, by which problems are solved scientifically—as *the* scientific method. But Dewey's opening statement in *How We Think* says: "No one can tell another person in any definite way how he *should* think any more than how he ought to breathe or to have his blood circulate."[76] Dewey went on to stress that the different ways of thinking can be described in their general features and that some ways of thinking are better than others; he then explained why reflective thinking is the better way. But Dewey was careful to point out that the phases or steps in reflective thinking are not rigid or uniform. "No set rules can be laid down on such matters," he wrote.[77]

Dewey attacked the separation between thought and action and between thinking and doing. Explicit in his rationale for reflective thinking is the testing of conclusions through application. Some definitions of curriculum as modes of thought treat these modes as thought severed from action in the pupil's own life situation. This is particularly characteristic of the disciplines doctrine, which imposes the mature scholar-specialist's mode of thought on the immature learner and ignores modes of thought that are relevant to social problem solving from the vantage point of the pupil. Thus, Dewey viewed curriculum as more than the transmission of established modes of thought and the validating of so-called truths within disciplinary boundaries.

Curriculum as Experience

Although the progressivists were united in criticizing the discontinuity between traditional subject matter and the learner, and the divorce of the school studies from the realities and demands of life, they were divided as to the conception and function of curriculum. "The scheme of a curriculum must take account of the adaptation of studies to the needs of existing community life; it must select with the intention of improving the life we live in common so that the future shall be better than the past," wrote Dewey.[78]

CHILD-CENTERED VERSUS SUBJECT-CENTERED RATIONALES.   In their battle to make the curriculum more relevant to the life experience of the learner, some romantic progressivists went so far as to advocate that virtually all school learning activities be centered around the felt needs and interests of the child. As early as 1902, Dewey pointed to the fallacies assumed by two warring sects—the subject or discipline-centered proponents who regard the learner as a ductile and docile recipient of established subject matter, and those who regard the child as "the starting-point, the center, and the end" of school activity. Dewey stressed the need to develop and conceive of the various studies as exemplifying the reflectively formulated human experience. "They embody the cumulative outcome of the efforts, the strivings, and the successes of the human race generation after generation," declared Dewey. Similarly, the child is to be conceived of as "fluent, embryonic, vital," with the curriculum serving to develop the child's present experience to a richer maturity. "Abandon the notion of subject-matter as something fixed and ready-made in itself, outside the child's experience; cease thinking of the child's experience as something hard and fast . . . and we realize that the child and the curriculum are simply two limits which define a single process. Just as two points define a straight line," wrote Dewey.[79]

Eventually the Cold War and space age gave impetus to the disciplines rationale with the center of curriculum gravity moving decisively toward specialized knowledge. The late 1960s and early 1970s witnessed resurgent demands by romantic progressives for learner-centered education, accompanied by new attacks on the public schools and efforts to establish alternative schools.

In his educational best-seller, *The Lives of Children,* Dennison described how he scrapped the idea of a preplanned formal curriculum in his own First Street School, where virtually all learning activities were centered on the children's felt needs and interests as related to their immediate experiences. "Here we come to one of the damaging myths of education," he declared, "namely, that learning is the result of teaching; that the progress of the child bears a direct relation to the methods of instruction and internal relationships of curriculum. Nothing can be further from the truth."[80] Dennison went on to relate how lesson plans and the formal curriculum were abolished in his school and how the school activities were guided through a kind of group therapy administered by teachers. Like many such schools, the First Street School was short-lived, having met its demise after only two years. Romantic naturalists, who see freedom and "doing your own thing" as the surest way of enabling the child to unfold in all of his or her natural goodness, eventually face a crisis of reality. Faith and well-meaning are insufficient to fill the vacuum created by the abandonment of a planned curriculum. In a literate, technological society, the child cannot be turned back on himself or herself as the sole source of the curriculum.

As Dewey observed, when personal fulfillment is severed from intellectual activity, "freedom of self-expression turns into something that might better be called 'self-exposure.'"[81]

CURRICULUM AS GUIDED LEARNING EXPERIENCE. Foshay observes that since the late 1930s the term *curriculum* came to be defined as "all the experiences a learner has under the guidance of the school" and, according to Foshay, "this definition had stood unchallenged for a generation."[82] Such definitions were being offered by an increasing number of curricularists as early as 1920. A definition by Bonser in 1920 regards the curriculum as "the experiences in which pupils are expected to engage in school, and the general order of sequence in which these experiences are to come."[83]

A definition offered by Caswell and Campbell in 1935 states that the curriculum is "composed of all the experiences children have under the guidance of teachers."[84] A report on the Eight-Year Study, published in 1942, concluded that "the curriculum is now seen as the total experience with which the school deals in educating young people."[85]

These emerging definitions were a sharp break from the traditional conception of curriculum. The recognition that what pupils learn is not limited to the formal course of study but is affected, directly and indirectly, by the total school environment, called for a broad definition of curriculum as guided school experience. The implication was that "everything that influences the learner must be considered during the process of curriculum making."[86]

But the very breadth of such definitions presents no clues as to the kinds of experiences that properly should be provided by the school and those that can be secured through other agencies and from the wider society. In fact, under such definitions, guided learning experience conceivably could exclude systematized knowledge, although the proponents of these broad definitions did not appear to have this in mind. Another problem with these definitions is that even under the guidance of the school and the teacher, learners encounter undesirable as well as desirable experiences. Thus, these definitions fail to make this important distinction. Furthermore, these broad definitions appear to treat learning experiences as objectives in themselves, with no mention being made of the needed outcomes of such experiences.

Nevertheless, curriculum writers continued to proffer similarly broad definitions. In 1946, Spears noted that "the concept of curriculum had broken loose from its academic moorings and moved on out into the total program of activities that was to serve the individual learner while under the guidance of the school." Although Spears went on to endorse this broad definition, he failed to acknowledge that its focus on the individual learner leaves each individual with his own curriculum. It is doubtful that Spears conceived of the definition in this way because he described general education as "that part of the student's complete program that is being experienced by the entire group."[87] Nevertheless, as is the case with many broad definitions offered by contemporary curriculum scholars (i.e., "all the experiences a learner has under the auspices of the school"), the implication is that because each learner's experiences are different, each learner has his or her own curriculum. Another problem with such broad definitions is that they do not differentiate between educative and other kinds of experience (noneducative and miseducative) that students have in the school setting. This problem is overcome in the definition offered by Tyler in 1956, which sees curriculum as "all of the learning of students which is planned by and directed by the school to attain its educational goals."[88] Tyler went on to point out that this inclusive definition encompasses educational objectives, all planned learning experiences (including extraclass and learning activities at home insofar as they are planned and directed by the school to attain its aims), and the appraisal of student learning. At the time, Tyler was addressing a national conference on testing problems, and so it seemed appropriate to include the assessment of student learning in his conception of curriculum. The inclusion of goals and learning outcomes implies continuity between ends and means. However, Tyler's definition, like the aforementioned definitions that see curriculum as planned learning experiences, gives no indication of how school learning experiences differ from those that are not under the purview of the school. The definition offered by Alberty and Alberty in 1962, which described curriculum as "all of the activities that are provided for students by the school," also fails to indicate the uniqueness of the learning experiences provided by the school although they pointed out that "[i]t is by means of these activities that the school hopes to bring about changes in the behavior of students in terms of its philosophy and goals."[89]

Changes in the conception of curriculum are reflected in three succeeding editions of the *Dictionary of Education*. The 1959 edition of the *Dictionary of Education* offered the following three definitions of curriculum:

> (1) a systematic group of courses or sequences of subjects required for graduation or certification in a major field of study, for example, *social studies curriculum, physical education curriculum*; (2) a general over-all plan of the content or specific materials of instruction that the school should offer the student by way of qualifying him for graduation or certification or for entrance into a professional or vocational field; (3) a group of courses and planned experiences which a student has under the guidance of the school or college.[90]

With the exception of the latter part of the third definition, which sees curriculum as "planned learning experiences," these definitions reflect the traditional conceptions of curriculum that were dominant until the 1930s. The last edition of the *Dictionary of Education* broadened the conception of curriculum significantly by adding to the earlier definitions the statement that curriculum "may refer to what is intended, as planned courses and other activities or intended opportunities or experiences, or to what was actualized for the learner, as in actual educational treatment or all experiences of the learner under the direction of the school."[91]

Although the latter definition may be criticized as too vague and broad, just as the other definitions in the *Dictionary of Education* may be criticized as too narrow and traditional, these different definitions reflect the conflicting and changing conceptions of curriculum during the twentieth century. The traditional conception of curriculum was no longer deemed appropriate for a progressive society.

Similar changes have occurred on the other side of the Atlantic. A British educator, for example, points out that over the long period of post-World War II reconstruction involving the expansion of educational opportunity, a new impetus in curriculum has emerged, bringing about changing conceptions of curriculum. Acknowledging that "[t]o this day, the common tendency is to equate the curriculum with the 'syllabus,' . . . 'a course of study,' or quite simply, 'subjects,'" Richmond notes that even a random selection of definitions from the *Journal of Curriculum Studies* (Britain) reveals the contemporary movement of ideas in that nation.[92] Among the various definitions cited by Richmond are the following, which conceive of the curriculum as guided learning activity:

> All learning which is planned or guided by the school, whether it is carried out in groups, or individually, inside or outside the school.
>
> A programme of activities designed so that pupils will attain, as far as possible, certain educational ends or objectives.
>
> The contrived activity and experience—organized, focused, systematic—that life, unaided, would not provide. . . . It is properly artificial, selecting, organizing, elaborating and speeding up the process of real life.[93]

Of these three definitions, the first two closely resemble those developed by American progressive educators before midcentury. The third definition may appear to depart somewhat from progressivist theory, which criticized the school for creating in the curriculum "detached and independent systems of knowledge that inertly overlay the ordinary systems of experience instead of reacting to enlarge and refine them."[94] However, this difficulty appears to be overcome when the curriculum is seen as a catalyzing process of making life experience more manageable and meaningful.

Most significantly, the concept of curriculum as guided learning experience conceives of the teaching-learning process as integral to curriculum. However, no explicit mention is made of *knowledge* in most definitions that regard curriculum as guided learning experience. The dominant view among contemporary curriculum theorists regards curriculum and instruction as separate and distinct realms. The implications of this dualistic view are discussed later in this chapter.

Over the years, certain education agencies have changed their definition of curriculum to conform to the dominant influences of the times. Moreover, not all of these changes have been in the direction of broadening the conception of curriculum. For example, in 1940 the Cooperative Study of Secondary School Standards (now known as the National Study of Secondary School Evaluation) defined curriculum as "all the experiences which pupils have while under the direction of the school," and defined courses of study as "that part of the curriculum which is organized for classroom use."[95] However, reflecting the discipline-centered curriculum reforms of the late 1950s and the 1960s, this agency in 1969 took the position that "[a]lthough the term 'curriculum' may be interpreted to include all constructive learning experiences provided under the direction of the school, it is used here to designate those activities, both formal and informal, carried on in relation to planned courses of instruction."[96] Whereas the earlier definition viewed the courses of study as a part of curriculum, the latter definition reduced curriculum to merely the courses of study. Thus, this change in definition represented a retrenchment toward a conception of curriculum that was dominant at the turn of the century.

Ironically, the unprecedented curriculum reforms of the late 1950s and 1960s, which sought to modernize the curriculum in terms of advanced scholarship in the disciplines, actually induced a reversion to the traditional subject-centered conception of curriculum. With curriculum reforms during this modern era being confined to each of the separate disciplines, the National Study of Secondary School Evaluation came to reject its broad definition in favor of a subject-centered definition that was more attuned to the curriculum-reform pressures of the times.

More recently, the National Study chose yet another narrow definition of curriculum as "the plan of learning for achieving the intended outcomes of the school."[97] Here again, the curriculum is seen as a plan, separated from the experience that brings the plan to life.

CURRICULUM AS GUIDED LIVING: THE PLANNED LEARNING ENVIRONMENT IN ACTION.   Another example of a broad definition, offered by Rugg in 1947, is that the curriculum is "[t]he life and program of the school . . . an enterprise in guided living . . . the curriculum becomes the very stream of dynamic activities that constitute the life of young people and their elders."[98]

Although Rugg's definition calls for continuity between school studies and life, it fails to differentiate between school functions and those of other social institutions. For example, the family might also be described as an "enterprise in guided living."

Nevertheless, the broadened conception of curriculum as guided living or as the planned learning environment was to have profound implications for what previously was regarded as extracurricular in the school and college. With a mounting body of research revealing that extracurricular activities, and even patterns of informal student association in school and college life (including college dormitory life), have powerful influences on educational growth, educators were impelled to see the educational institution as a uniquely comprehensive environment for linking codified knowledge to the life and growth of the learner.

EXTRACLASS ACTIVITIES.   The conception of curriculum as an all-school learning experience and as guided living necessitated a breakdown in the traditional, rigid separation between classroom course work and other school-sponsored learning activities. In fact, the growing acceptance of the broader conception of curriculum led to the rejection of the term *extracurriculum,* which had been used in reference to those school activities deemed outside the curriculum. Such terms as *cocurricular activities* and *allied activities* began to be used, but even these were unsatisfactory because they indicated that such activities were conjoint to rather than integral to the curriculum.

Nevertheless, the practice was not to allow extraclass activities to carry credits toward graduation. However, with the broadening of the curriculum, the lines between some of these activities and classroom course work became less distinct. Many schools began to organize such activities as band, orchestra, chorus, journalism, photography, filmmaking, drama, dance, and the like into formal courses carrying academic credits. A similar transformation occurred in our colleges and universities. (Today, some universities offer doctorates in filmmaking and drama, for example.)

Great impetus was given to student activity programs in progressive schools during the 1930s in growing recognition that such activities help children and youth to learn to live together and also contribute to so-called academic coursework. Field trips extended into field projects. Camping and outdoor education sponsored by the schools included not only nature study but conservation and community service activities. An entire issue of the *Phi Delta Kappan* in 1938 was devoted to camping and outdoor education. "In all probability," wrote one of the authors, "the educationist of the year 2000 A.D. will look back on us and wonder why we, the school people of 1938, failed to include the camp as an integral unit of our educational system."[99] Perhaps the most outstanding early school-camp and outdoor-education programs for elementary and secondary school students were developed in California in San Diego County. In its visionary scenario for American education for the post-World War II years, the NEA's Educational Policies Commission viewed community service as integral to the educative mission of the school.[100] Community-service activities were incorporated in the problem-focused, block-time, core curriculum in progressive secondary schools. Faunce and Bossing describe how students and the core teacher in a small community traced a health problem to the water supply and effectively enlisted the state department of health and the local government to undertake a water-system project to correct the problem.[101]

By the late 1950s, the curriculum retrenchment of essentialism, followed by the "pursuit of academic excellence" through the discipline-centered curriculum of the Cold War and space race, resulted in a sharp curtailment of extraclass activities and the elimination of most problem-focused core programs. To the essentialists and perennialists, extraclass activities were seen as trivial and beyond the school's purview of intellectual training. Community-service activities were caricatured by Bestor as "busywork in good causes," and the problem-focused, integrative core curriculum was seen by Bestor as producing nothing but "complete intellectual chaos."[102]

However, emerging empirical research was showing a positive relationship between participation in school activities and college aspiration and achievement. An investigation of two heterogeneous populations of high-school students yielded findings that led the researcher to the following conclusions:

> Specifically, distinctive patterns of extracurricular involvement were associated with high levels of aspiration and subsequent college attainment, controlling for various measures of family socioeconomic status, ability, grade performance (in high school), and peer status. Students whose extracurricular pursuits included both athletic and service-leadership roles had not only the highest level of aspirations but also the greatest chance of fulfilling those aspirations after graduating. . . . These findings seem to suggest that the experiences provided by participation in service and leadership activities helped the student develop resources and capacities which facilitated his adjustment to the greater academic and independence demands of college.[103]

From a recent analysis of the body of research on participation in extraclass activities in the secondary school, Berk concluded that the most involved participants score higher in academic performance and educational aspirations.[104] Obviously, such participation should effect an even more powerful influence in secondary school, during the formative years of adolescence, as compared with the college years. Yet the research literature on student activities in college tends to be even more unequivocally favorable than that pertaining to the secondary school. This may reflect the popular fashion of university researchers to engage in fault-finding and skepticism regarding the school experience, whereas they tend to look favorably at the college experience, which, after all, is reflective of the vineyard in which they labor.

At the college level, there is increasing recognition that informal student activities and interactions may have at least as powerful an influence on the lives of students as the formal course of study. Large-scale analyses of the research literature over a twenty-year period concerning the impact of college on students led to the conclusion that, "The educational impact of a college's faculty is enhanced when their contacts with students extend beyond the formal classroom to informal non-classroom settings." This influence went beyond the student background characteristic and was found to be linked with such positive outcomes as "perceptions of intellectual growth during college, increases in intellectual orientation, liberalization of social and political values, growth in autonomy and independence, increases in interpersonal skills, gains in general maturity and personal development, educational aspirations and attainment, orientation toward scholarly careers, and women's interest in and choice of sex-atypical (male-dominant) careers."[105] These outcomes were also evident from student peer interactions, revealing a strong influence on growth in intellectual development and orientation, academic and social self-concept, general maturity and personal development, and educational aspirations and attainment.

In another study of the research literature on the impact of the college experience on students, Astin reported similar findings revealing that the educational development of the undergraduate is strongly connected to the degree to which the student is actively engaged or involved in the extraclass college experience. General education outcomes are enhanced not only when students devote a lot of time to study, but also "when they socialize with diverse student peers, when they serve as tutors for each other, and when they engage each other in discussions of contemporary issues." Astin concluded that in view of the findings, it was clear that faculty need to rethink radically their approach to curriculum in that they focus excessively on course "content" in their identification with their own disciplines. Instead, there would be much greater payoffs in learning outcomes by placing more emphasis on pedagogy and the interpersonal and environmental context of college life.[106] In effect, Astin was alluding to the power of the hidden curriculum or what might be called the *collateral curriculum* in educational development. If the hidden curriculum or collateral curriculum exerts such a powerful influence on the college student's educational development, then it must surely be at least equally influential on the youngsters at the secondary and elementary levels. In effect, extraclass activities cannot be regarded as merely extracurricular because they have a pervasive bearing on educational development.

Significantly, in 1993 President Clinton chose Rutgers University to announce his program of national service for college students because Rutgers had in place the Civic Education and Community Service Program involving over 600 students in which students can choose nontraditional ways to obtain academic credit. Such programs are not new, although most do not involve academic credit. The Columbia College Citizenship Council at Columbia University has engaged undergraduates in organized community service since its founding in 1957. During the mid-1960s, students in the Citizenship Council worked with the City University of New York's pioneering College Discovery and Development Program—a citywide effort to discover and develop the college potential of at-risk youngsters beginning at the end of the ninth grade.[107] The City University program was a forerunner of the federal Upward Bound program. Today, the City University and Columbia projects are administered separately, but have been in continuous operation over a period spanning almost three decades.

The reader should recall that the report of the Educational Policies Commission dating back to 1944 had described how secondary schools can institute community service programs as integral to the curriculum. In *High School: A Report on Secondary Education in America* (1983), Ernest Boyer of the Carnegie Foundation recommended that every student be required to complete a community service activity.[108]

Recognizing the connection between participation in student activities in high school and college success, leading colleges have been regarding such participation as a key criterion for admission.

The inescapable connection between student activities and the formal coursework came to be recognized by the U.S. Supreme Court in a decision in 1988 in which students had protested the principal's excision of two pages from the school newspaper. The Court ruled that the work on the newspaper was indeed curricular in that it was under teacher supervision and carried academic credit. Consequently, reasoned the Court, the students were not entitled to full protection of the First Amendment.[109] Nevertheless, educators have come to recognize increasingly the powerful effects of participation in student activities on learning outcomes, cognitive as well as affective, regardless of whether such participation carries academic credit. Even though participation may not carry academic credit, it cannot be treated effectively as outside the real curriculum. Because the success of the formal course of study is not independent of student activities and the wider life of the school, effective curriculum planning requires that student activities be conceived and conducted as integral to curriculum and not as "extracurricular." In the case of the U.S. Supreme Court decision upholding the power of the school administration to censor the school newspaper, the collateral or hidden lesson for students is that Constitutional rights do not apply to them, and that such rights are merely abstractions from an abstract document. As discussed later in this chapter, it should not be surprising, then, when it is found that students develop antidemocratic attitudes from their experience in school and society.

The Curriculum-Instruction Dualism

The contention that curriculum and instruction are two separate realms has gained widespread acceptance among contemporary curriculum theorists. The emergence of this dualistic view, as mentioned earlier in this chapter, stems from several developments, not the least of which is the burgeoning body of research on instruction and the technology of instruction. Such research has become so specialized that much of it is focused on the analysis of teaching as severed from subject matter and from the learning that occurs as a result of teaching. Hence the behaviorists are not alone in ascribing to the curriculum-instruction dualism. Many curricularists argue this separation on logical grounds. Moreover, in the world of specialized university scholarship, it is a considerable convenience and advantage to conduct research when complex interaction contexts are reducible and divisible. For analytical purposes this is perfectly justifiable. But when the reducibles and divisibles are taken for the real world of the action-context, namely the classroom and the school, the outcome is likely to be artificial and mechanistic. Synthesis is sacrificed for analysis, as the specialized research pursuits divert curricularists from the substantive problems of the field. The curriculum-instruction dualism has emerged as a veritable doctrine for the curriculum field.

CURRICULUM AND INSTRUCTION.   "A specific failure or irresponsibility of curriculum developers," argued Macdonald, "is a failure to distinguish two distinct realms of relevant operation." According to Macdonald, "They are essentially two separate action contexts, one (curriculum) producing plans for further action; and, the other (instruction) putting plans into action." He went on to declare that "[u]ntil such time as there can be common agreement upon at least the basic phenomena we are labeling, there will be little chance of making conceptual progress."[110]

Does the doctrine of dualism give promise of enabling curriculum scholars to make conception progress? As indicated earlier in this chapter, Macdonald defined curriculum as "those planning endeavors which take place prior to instruction."[111] This definition of curriculum is so vague and narrow that it fails to provide any clue whatsoever as to the kinds of endeavors that are rightfully called curriculum. Furthermore, it fails to recognize that many planning endeavors are an outgrowth of the learning situation. Very often the learning situation is a problem situation from which existing plans are modified and new plans are conceived and tested.

According to Macdonald, instruction is defined as "the pupil-teacher interaction situation."[112] Again, this definition is not very revealing because it fails to distinguish this interaction situation from any other interaction situation, apart from the fact that a teacher and pupil(s) are interacting. Obviously, there can be pupil-teacher interaction independently of instruction. Moreover, this definition of instruction provides no insight into the concept of curriculum. It is difficult to see how such a definition and the notion of curriculum and instruction as two distinct realms will help curriculum workers make conceptual progress.

SEEKING SYNTHESIS.   Macdonald subsequently came to revise his position. Pointing to the narrow and mechanistic implications of behavioristic objectives and the failure of the behavioristic rationale to recognize the complex nature of learning and developmental processes, Macdonald, Wolfson, and Zaret offered this definition of curriculum: "'curriculum' is the cultural environment which has been purposely selected as a set of possibilities for facilitating educative transactions."[113] This definition fails to distinguish the kind of cultural environment provided by the school from that of any other educative agency, such as a museum. Allowed to stand by itself, this definition provides no clue as to what is meant by cultural environment or educative transactions (e.g., Skinnerian or Deweyan). Although Macdonald, Wolfson, and Zaret viewed these transactions in the existential terms of "transcendent" and "liberating," the definition, itself, allows for any interpretation. Nevertheless, it does appear to resolve the functional problems stemming from the curriculum-instruction dualism, for it recognizes instruction as integral to curriculum.

In a similar effort to find a workable definition, and thereby resolve this same dualism, Doll offers this definition: "The curriculum of a school is the formal and informal content and process by which learners gain knowledge and understanding, develop skills, and alter attitudes, appreciations, and values under the auspices of that school."[114] Doll's definition, again, fails to distinguish the school's content and process from the content and process of any other educative agency. And the expression "to alter attitudes, appreciations, and values" may raise considerable disagreement among those educators who see the school as providing for enlightenment and not "altering" the learner, because "altering" implies an externally controlled behavior—the kind of behavior associated with indoctrination or conditioning. Aside from these problems, which are considerable in themselves, Doll's definition regards instruction or "process" as integral to curriculum and, thereby, represents an effort toward synthesis.

Egan sees curriculum as such an inclusive concept that he offers this definition: "Curriculum is the study of any and all educational phenomena."[115] Although this definition resolves the curriculum-instruction dualism, it is so broad that it could encompass the reading of a newspaper at the breakfast table or the listening to a concert on the car radio. In short, it carries no special meaning for the school or college.

Content and Process.   The traditional notion of curriculum as content and instruction as process has been embraced by educators over many years. As held by Broudy, Smith, and Burnett, "curriculum consists primarily of certain content organized into categories of instruction . . . modes of teaching are not, strictly speaking, a part of curriculum.[116] In effect, curriculum is merely content or subject matter having an existence independent of the processes through which the knowledge is produced. Such dualistic conceptions of curriculum and instruction regard knowledge as independent of the processes through which the learner becomes knowledgeable. Yet knowledge is both a product of inquiry and, at the same time, the raw material for fueling, shaping, and controlling inquiry. To ascribe a separate existence to knowledge, an existence independent of the ways and means through which knowledge is developed and through which people become knowledgeable, is like separating the act of swimming from water.

The divorce between content and method is reflected to this day in the test-driven curriculum, the treatment of subject matter as ends rather than raw material, and the isolation of studies from life experience.

Skill and Meaning.   Virtually every teacher has observed children who are able to read aloud, but are unable to explain the meaning of what they have just finished reading. In effect their performance in the act of reading demonstrates that the *skill* of reading can be attained in the absence of meaning. Without meaning there can be no transformation of the skill and the material that is read into the working power of intelligence.

Curiously, the research literature on reading uses such terminology as "reading of content materials" and "content textbooks," and some of the leading textbooks on the teaching of reading bear such titles as *Content Area Reading,* indicating that reading is also taught as a skill apart from "content" or ideas.[117] Reading is a process of communication of ideas. As a thought process, it is inseparable from what it is that is being communicated. The material that is to be read remains inert until it becomes meaningfully actualized by the reader.

In the same vein, subject matter is just subject matter, and a plan for learning is just a plan for learning. The material is inert until it is put into operation and tested on the anvil of experience. This is why experimentalist-progressives rejected the traditional conceptions of curriculum and struggled to bring a fuller, richer, and more functional meaning to curriculum.

Ends-Means Dualism.   Although contemporary curriculum writers differ markedly in their definitions of curriculum, we have seen how an ends-means dualism is inherent in many of these definitions. A dualistic doctrine has come to be embraced that severs curriculum from instruction. Johnson argues that "curriculum prescribes the results of instruction. It does not prescribe the *means,* i.e, the activities, materials, or even the instructional content, to be used in achieving the results."[118]

Such distinctions lead to serious conceptual and practical difficulties. For example, if curriculum does not prescribe content or subject matter, then it could be said that curriculum exists independently of content or subject matter. In the practical context of curriculum development, organized knowledge (or "content" or "subject matter") is treated as inseparable from curriculum.

The doctrine of dualism violates Dewey's thesis of the intrinsic continuity of ends and means. According to Dewey, "an end which grows up within an activity as plan for its direction is always both ends and means . . . every divorce of end from means diminishes by that much the significance of the activity."[119]

To conceive of knowledge as merely results that are separate from the actions and events that produced the results robs any activity of its meaning. "An aim implies an orderly and ordered activity, one in which the order consists in the progressive completing of a process," wrote Dewey, and when one is shooting at a target, "not the target but *hitting* the target is the end in view."[120] To conceive of ends and means as separate or discontinuous is to separate artificially functions that are organically interdependent. There is no point in shooting without a target to shoot at, nor is there any sense in devising targets without conceiving of the act of hitting the targets.

In a similar vein, to separate science from its bodies of organized knowledge and its methods of inquiry would be destructive to science. Thus, to sever curriculum from instruction not only is of doubtful use and validity in the practical world of the school but also creates ruptures and stumbling blocks in curriculum research and development. For example, as plans were being made for the national curriculum-reform projects during the second half of the 1950s, it soon became apparent that curriculum reform required much more than course-content revision. The traditional notion of science as organized subject matter had to be rejected in view of the realization that science also is a way of thinking and involves certain systematic methods of inquiry. It thus became necessary to conceive of subject matter and method as inseparable.

Indeed scientific progress has required dramatic changes in the conceptions of science. As Einstein put the matter, "the realm of physics has so expanded that it seems to be limited only by the limitations of the method itself."[121] This observation should give curriculum theorists food for thought concerning the long-held dualism between content and method, or curriculum and instruction. Knowledge has come to be seen as a way of knowing and searching, and not as an end product or body of subject matter separate from the methods through which it was developed and through which it is made comprehensible and applicable.

When contemporary curriculum scholars dissect curriculum from instruction, they are embracing a dualism leading to educational discontinuity and isolation.

The classic philosophical systems embraced many dualisms, such as the separation of mind from activity. Dewey pointed out in 1899 that the then current question of separating subject matter and method "is a survival of the medieval philosophic dualism."[122] Contemporary educators who separate curriculum from instruction are, in a similar vein, separating knowledge from the activities known as teaching and learning. One of the consequences is that a considerable portion of the research on classroom instruction has been conducted with a focus on teacher-pupil verbal interaction without any connection whatsoever with the organized knowledge known as subject matter and resultant outcomes in pupil growth.

Research on Teaching

In separating instruction from curriculum, a growing number of educational researchers have developed a specialty of analyzing the act of teaching. Through these efforts, a considerable number of systems for analyzing teaching have been produced. Dunkin and Biddle observe that, "In spite of the sharp increase in studies of classroom events, most recent research has focused on the *activities* rather than the *effects* of teaching." In the same vein, much of the research on learning has been directed only at special kinds of learning and such research "does not meet the challenge provided by the sheer complexity of the classroom setting and of the learning tasks pursued there."[123]

An examination of the latest edition of the *Handbook of Research on Teaching* reveals a perpetuation of this problem and the acknowledgment that only a beginning has been made in linking teacher behavior to student achievement and to other outcomes. Moreover, much of this research on learning outcomes as related to teaching has been directed at basic skills at the primary level.[124] Researchers tend to focus on that which is most amenable to measurement, not necessarily that which is most significant in education. The need to study the effects of different classroom and school learning environments and resources remains an unmet challenge.

What is the point of studying teaching unless such study is related to student growth? Is such study undertaken merely to provide teachers with alternative and prescriptive models of teaching? After discussing some of the "evils in education that flow from the isolation of method from subject matter," Dewey observed that "[n]othing has brought pedagogical theory into greater disrepute than the belief that it is identified with the handing out to teachers recipes and models to be followed in teaching."[125]

The investigation of instruction apart from curriculum leads to somewhat bizarre conceptions of the teacher. For example, McNeil and Popham define the teacher as "a person engaged in interactive behavior with one or more students for the purpose of effecting a change in those students."[126] Such a definition fails to distinguish the work of a teacher from that of a group therapist or an animal trainer. (One only has to substitute the word *client* or *animal* for student, whichever the case may be.) Moreover, inasmuch as change can be effected by manipulation as opposed to the freeing of intelligence, this definition is unacceptable to educators who conceive of teaching and education as vitally connected with the freeing of intelligence.

Search for a Theory of Instruction.   In his book *Theory of Instruction,* Bruner reaches the following conclusion:

> Finally, a theory of instruction seeks to take account of the fact that a curriculum reflects not only the nature of knowledge itself but also the nature of the knower and the knowledge-getting process. It is an enterprise par excellence where the line between subject matter and method grows necessarily indistinct. . . . Knowledge is a process, not a product.[127]

If Bruner's thesis is valid, then a search for a theory of instruction apart from a theory of curriculum would seem fruitless. Although Bruner appears to recognize this, he proposes several elements or features for a so-called theory of instruction, which appear to be largely behavioristic (i.e., narrow sequencing of material, specifying and pacing rewards and punishments, and so on), without attempting to attack the problem of a theory of curriculum. This is not to fault Bruner for failing to produce a theory of curriculum but rather to point out the contradiction in seeking a theory of instruction apart from a theory of curriculum and, at the same time, vaingloriously declaring that instruction and curriculum are necessarily indistinct.

The terms *teaching* and *instruction* are generally used interchangeably. It is revealing that although Dewey did not directly ascribe different meanings to these terms, he tended to use the term *teaching* in a broader sense as a vitally shared experience in the art of communication. In contrast, he tended to use the term *instruction* in a narrower framework, such as in criticizing traditional education as proceeding "by instruction taken in a literal sense, a building into mind from without." In acknowledging the contributions of Herbart to teaching method, Dewey pointed out that Herbart's "philosophy is eloquent about the duty of the teacher in instructing pupils . . . it slurs over the fact that the environment involves a personal sharing in common experiences. . . . It takes, in brief, everything educational into account save its essence."[128]

THE COLLATERAL CURRICULUM OR HIDDEN CURRICULUM

In recent years the literature in education has given increasing attention to the hidden curriculum, or the discrepancy between what is intended and what is actually experienced.[129] The tendency has been to couch the hidden curriculum negatively, although its power may indeed be positive. The impact of college coursework is so interrelated with the college experience as a way of life that educators have come to recognize the vital significance of college as a designed environment for learning. Consequently, it appears to be more productive to use the term *collateral curriculum* rather than hidden curriculum if educators are to unleash its positive potential.

Critical theorists may hold that the hidden curriculum invokes deliberate concealment, but more likely it is manifested through a lack of awareness of conditions and effects, or in effects that are unanticipated.

COLLATERAL LEARNING. In focusing narrowly on the information and skills to be learned through the formal course of study, teachers tend to overlook the importance of collateral learning. Pupils may receive a grade of A in a literature course, but if they have learned to dislike good literature it is doubtful that they will be impelled to read such literature on their own. In this case the collateral learning will have a more powerful and enduring impact on the learner's present and future behavior than the target subject matter. Indeed, most of the factual information learned in school is readily forgotten soon after the examination, whereas collateral learning as connected with attitudes, appreciations, and values can be far more enduring. "Perhaps the greatest of all pedagogical fallacies is the notion that a person learns only the particular thing he is studying at the time," observed Dewey, who went on to stress how "collateral learning in the way of formation of enduring attitudes, of likes and dislikes, may be and often is much more important than the spelling lesson or lesson in geography or history that is learned." And, added Dewey, "The most important attitude that can be formed is that of desire to go on learning."[130] If the curriculum weakens this impetus, it will have failed to realize its most important meaning and mission.

Those involved in conducting the Eight-Year Study were well aware of the collateral curriculum in addressing the significance of learning outcomes as evidenced by growth in interests, attitudes, appreciations, and intellectual curiosity. Ingenious evaluation instruments were developed to assess these outcomes that, to this day, more than a half century later, are rarely treated in curriculum evaluation.[131] One of the lessons from the Eight-Year Study is that collateral learning must not be regarded as something outside the curriculum or as merely an incidental and accidental outcome of the curriculum. Desirable collateral learning is much more apt to occur if it is treated as integral to the planned and guided learning experiences that comprise the curriculum.

Similarly, extraclass activities should not be considered as outside the curriculum. As discussed earlier, such activities can exert powerful influences on the learner. If the curriculum is so conceived as to correlate such activities with those more directly connected with the formal course of study, the possibilities for realizing the desired learning outcomes of the curriculum are enhanced enormously.

As noted, the concept of hidden curriculum has been used by education critics to describe only unintended and negative outcomes from school settings, such as learning to dislike mathematics, or learning to be docile. It has also been used to describe intended and positive outcomes that are provided for implicitly rather than as an explicit part of the curriculum—such as those pertaining to socialization. The broadening of the conception of curriculum to encompass all of the learning experiences provided by the school attests to the recognition of the importance of what heretofore was treated as of peripheral significance or as nonexistent. One may learn about the social significance of cooperation or minority rights in the abstract in the social studies class, but whether such learning has become part of the developmental process of the learner is evidenced by actual behavior in the laboratory, shop, or playing field.

Dreeben has pointed out that in addition to the learnings that occur as a result of the formal course of study, students learn to accept certain social norms and to act in accordance with them. He observes that, ironically, some of the bureaucratic properties of school organization, which have been regarded negatively in some of the literature on schooling, such as those which call for the submergence of self-interest and the breakdown of certain parochial divisions, also have positive functions. According to Dreeben, ". . . it should also be remembered that the same norms seem to contribute also to a sense of tolerance, fairness, consideration, and trustfulness, and to the expectation among members of the populace that they possess a legitimate claim to participate in all areas of public life and that none shall be entitled to special treatment of whatever kind—expectations whose prevalence today underlie some of the more radical social changes that have taken place in American history."[132]

FURTHER ILLUSTRATIONS AND IMPLICATIONS. A few rather common examples will help illustrate the power of the collateral curriculum. When Shakespeare is studied as literature, many students learn to dislike Shakespeare. When Shakespeare is studied as theater and is *performed,* students are more likely to appreciate and even enjoy Shakespeare; and they also learn about Shakespeare's work authentically—in the medium for which the work was intended—from the stage, not the page.

As another example, when seventh-graders memorize the various formulas using π in solving problems on the dimensions of a circle, they make frequent errors in calculation. Several months later, when taking a multiple-choice achievement test, they proceed to calculate laboriously the answers to each item without realizing that calculation may not even be necessary. Under the time pressures of the test, they are more apt to make some absurd errors, such as coming up with a diameter that is, say, little more than half the circumference. And because they are taking so much time to do their calculations, they must rush through the other test items that may require calculation as well as cogitation to the extent that they suffer a penalty for lack of time. Many of the students learn that they dislike mathematics.

In contrast, when the students discover the meaning of π (and its significance in history) through the use of string, ruler, and all sorts of circular objects, and proceed to formulate "lawful" statements in their own words concerning the relationships between the various dimensions of the circular objects, they learn collaterally what a formula is and why formulas are so indispensable in solving mathematical and scientific problems. When taking an achievement test several months later, they are able to select the correct answers for the circumference, diameter, and radius of a circle without having to do calculations. (Or, if they should need to do some calculations, they are able to move ahead with the test more confidently.) But the most telling outcome is that mathematics is more meaningful and is more likely to be appreciated and even enjoyed when approached thoughtfully rather than mechanistically.

From the above, it can be seen that the collateral curriculum resides in learning to understand, appreciate, and even enjoy mathematics (or Shakespeare), or learning to dislike mathematics (or Shakespeare).

As another example, students are studying a unit on the Middle Ages and the event of bubonic plague. They then go on to study Chaucer, the Anglo-French wars, and so on. Chronology determines the topic. In a contrasting classroom and school, when students are studying the devastating effects of the bubonic plague on Europe, the curriculum is made truly unitary by studying science as well as politics in history and relating the Black Death of 1347 to twentieth-century epidemics, including influenza, tuberculosis (the "white plague"), and AIDS. In the former illustration, the curriculum is governed by a factual order of events and dates that are painstakingly memorized for the test and painlessly forgotten. And the curriculum is likely to be boring. In the latter case, the curriculum is governed by *ideas* that relate to the life of the learner in the widest social context. Capitalizing on students' interests, the teacher of history will work with the teacher of literature and science on an interrelated curriculum so that, for example, students may be reading biographies of scientists while studying history.

Virtually every state mandates the teaching of U.S. history and government or civics, including the Constitution and Bill of Rights, on the ground that it will foster good citizenship. During the late 1950s and early 1960s the Purdue Opinion Panel under H. H. Remmers found that although the U.S. Constitution and Bill of Rights were universally required to be studied in history and social studies, adolescents might have been learning the factual material for the test, but they were unable to relate the facts to their own lives and to the wider social issues. As a consequence, a very high proportion of the adolescents were found to be embracing antidemocratic and authoritarian attitudes in direct violation of the Constitution and Bill of Rights.

Replications of Remmers's studies a quarter of a century later revealed that the same conditions were still prevalent despite the fact that the Purdue research was conducted in an era of rank McCarthyism, whereas we like to think of our contemporary era as more enlightened.[133] Such findings reveal that it is not sufficient to mandate certain studies in the curriculum, but that the attitudes, understandings, and values that adolescents bring with them to school cannot be ignored or compartmentalized as outside the curriculum. The social life of the school may serve to enhance democratic attitudes, or to perpetuate antidemocratic attitudes, and the mandated study of the Bill of Rights, treated in splendid academic isolation, becomes "purely academic" or "merely academic." As such, it has no bearing on the life and times of adolescents.

Clearly, then, if educators recognize the significance of learning experience and outcomes, positively and negatively, then they will see the need to take the fullest possible account of them in curriculum development and evaluation. Hence they will not be working unwittingly with a hidden curriculum; instead, they will be taking into account the collateral learning that gives full measure to that thing we call curriculum.

As mentioned, the experimentalist-progressive educators who designed and evaluated the Eight-Year Study were well aware of the significance of the collateral curriculum, and so there was no need to mull over a hidden curriculum. For example, they investigated not only the learnings that grew out of the literary works in the syllabi, but also the nature and extent of voluntary, recreational reading in which students were engaged. Obviously, when students are encouraged to use the school library at all hours for recreational reading, browsing, and working on projects of their own making as well as on assignments, the school curriculum takes on a wider and richer meaning and function.

The experimentalist-progressives who sought a definition of curriculum as "the life and program of the school," or as "all the experiences a learner has under the auspices of the school," appear well justified in their efforts despite the problem of ambiguity and vulnerability to assault by the essentialists who viewed this as license to call "anything the cat dragged in" as having a legitimate place in the curriculum.

A UNITARY CONCEPTION OF CURRICULUM—A MODEST PROPOSAL

The emergence of the curriculum field as a distinct subject of study has given rise to many conflicting conceptions of curriculum. The reader may justifiably conclude that no single definition can satisfy all parties concerned, because, after all, the different definitions reflect the different schools of thought in the curriculum field—as well as changing conceptions of organized knowledge, the learner, the educative process, and the larger social situation. If this is the case, then, is agreement on definition so essential to conceptual progress, as many curricularists believe? Is it possible to have a general basis for consensus in a field without agreement on definition? In this concluding section, the foregoing questions are addressed in connection with the importance of consensus for conceptual progress in the curriculum field.

Codified Knowledge and Becoming Knowledge/able

Over the years curricularists have sought an adequate definition of curriculum. We have seen how the conception of curriculum has changed very dramatically over time, reflecting the advances in organized knowledge, advances in our understanding of the learner, and changing expectations concerning the reciprocal roles of school and society. How these factors are seen is dependent on the philosophy of the educator. Hence we have seen how a traditionalist defines curriculum differently than an experimentalist-progressive.

As shown in Table 5–1, curriculum has been variously defined as (1) the cumulative tradition of organized knowledge, (2) the instructional plan or course of study, (3) measured instructional outcomes (technological production system), (4) cultural reproduction, (5) knowledge selection/organization from the culture, (6) modes of thought, and (7) guided living/planned learning environment. As discussed throughout this chapter, each definition reflects a particular and often conflicting perspective—and fails to engender a full meaning of curriculum. Some definitions are so narrow that they convey a restricted and only partial meaning of curriculum—at least with regard to how the concept has been treated in the practical world of the educational institution. Other definitions are so broad that they fail to distinguish between the function of the school or university from that of any other agency having some sort of educative function, whether central or peripheral to its mission.

The meaning of curriculum has changed so significantly over the years and reflects so many conflicting schools of thought that it is highly unlikely that any universally accepted definition can be reached. Nevertheless, curricularists may utilize a definition to describe the orientation of their work in the field. The present authors contend that the school or university is unique in its organization and treatment of knowledge and experience in attempting to meet its educative function. No other institution of society compares with the school or university in the systematic reconstruction of knowledge and experience for educative purposes. Furthermore, the dynamic nature of knowledge and experience invalidates the notion of knowledge or learning as terminal achievements or ends. If knowledge and experience are dynamic, then education should have no end beyond itself. Obviously the concept of curriculum takes on a special meaning in a democratic society as opposed to a totalitarian society. Of course, all civilized societies regard curriculum as the medium through which codified knowledge is so treated as to enable the rising generation to become knowledge/able. In a democratic society, being knowledge/able puts the

Table 5–1. Conflicting Conceptions of Curriculum

Conception of Curriculum	Controlling Mode	Function
Traditionalist		
Cumulative tradition of organized knowledge	"Permanent" studies (classics) "Essential" studies/skills Established disciplines	Cultural inheritance Mental discipline Knowledge transmission
Modes of thought (as specialist)	Disciplinary inquiry	Specialized knowledge production
Instructional plan/course of study	Stated intentions for instruction	(Eclectic)
Measured instructional outcomes	Technological production (input/output measures) Behavioristic objectives	Efficiency Accountability Controlled behavior
Cultural reproduction	Cultural norms for thinking and acting	Cultural maintenance
Progressivist		
Knowledge selection/ organization from the culture	Cultural norms for individual and social growth	Cultural assimilation and improvement
Modes of thought (as citizen)	Reflective thinking Problem method	Personal-social growth
Guided experience/ planned learning environment	Community life Felt needs Reflective thinking Problem method	Effective living Self-realization
Reconstruction of knowledge and experience	Reflective thinking Cultural experience related to life experience Problem method	Personal control of knowledge and experience Personal-social growth

individual *in* control of experience as opposed to being put *under* control. This brings us to a more comprehensive and unified concept of curriculum.

A Proposed, Tentative Definition

The most profound and systematic analysis of the curriculum and its social significance was made by the American philosopher John Dewey (1859–1952). In his lectures to parents of children attending his laboratory school at the University of Chicago before the turn of the century (published in 1899 in *The School and Society*), Dewey called for a new conception, organization, and treatment of curriculum in accord with the dynamic nature of knowledge and the changing social conditions auguring for the democratic prospect. Consequently, the mission of the school and its curriculum must be seen in these terms: "All that society has accomplished for itself is put, through the agency of the school, at the disposal of its future members. All its better thoughts of itself it hopes to realize through the new possibilities thus open to its future self."[134]

In effect, the school curriculum is presumably designed not only to inculcate each member of the rising generation in the best elements of knowledge, systematically organized or codified since the dawn of civilization, but to enable each member of the rising generation to utilize that knowledge to improve the life of the individual and the life of society. (And all this through a system of universal public education spanning twelve short years.)

Although Dewey never explicitly defined the curriculum, his exhaustive writings on curriculum did provide definitive meaning to the concept. Indeed his definition of education renders such a definitive meaning. For Dewey viewed education as a *generative* process—that is, a process through which the learner extends and deepens the capability of exercising intelligent control over changing conditions of life. In his orchestral work, *Democracy and Education* (1916), Dewey not only forged a systematic theory of education in a free society, but devoted a series of chapters to the nature of knowledge and subject matter, and to the various areas of the curriculum and how they must be treated in their interdependence. He proceeded to offer a definition of education as "that reconstruction or reorganization of experience which adds to the meaning of experience, and which increases ability to direct the course of subsequent experience."[135]

From such a definition of education, the authors of this text offer the following definition of curriculum: *that reconstruction of knowledge and experience that enables the learner to grow in exercising intelligent control of subsequent knowledge and experience* (see Table 5–1). Through the medium of that thing we call curriculum, the learner is to grow in knowledge/ability—or in the social power and insight required of the good person leading the good life in the good society.

PERSPECTIVE

Educational institutions are constantly engaged in curriculum decisions without giving corresponding attention to curriculum as a subject of thought. As education begets new knowledge at a seemingly accelerated pace, the response has been to parcel such knowledge into increasingly separate and specialized domains. However, the specialization and segmentation of knowledge have made the curriculum more remote from life at a time of a rising demand to make the curriculum more responsive to emerging societal needs and problems.

During the early decades of the twentieth century, the long-standing conception of curriculum as the cumulative tradition of organized knowledge came to be challenged.

Traditionalists continued to see the curriculum as a distillation of the cumulative tradition of organized knowledge, or as synonymous with the course of study. Pressures to promote educational efficiency and accountability gave impetus to the test-driven curriculum, with curriculum seen in terms of instructional ends or measurable (test) results or products. Progressivists sought a more comprehensive and functional conception of curriculum as a planned learning environment or as the guided experiences provided under the auspices of the school. They were keenly aware that experiences in the wider life of the school often have a more powerful and lasting impact on what is learned than the formal course of study. In effect they began to recognize the power of collateral learning and the need to take deliberate account of such experience as integral to curriculum.

The great variety of conflicting definitions of curriculum emerging in the twentieth century reflected differences in the vantage points from which curriculum is studied, conflicting educational philosophies, changing societal influences and demands on education, and the enormous difficulty in seeking to define such a complex concept, which, like knowledge itself, is limited only by the boundaries and tools of thought.

Each of the types of definitions of curriculum enumerated presents serious difficulties. When curriculum is conceived as guided experience, we are left with no clues as to how such experience in school differs from guided experience provided by other societal institutions and processes. Although it can be argued that there should be no sharp lines of demarcation between school and life, the school would not exist if it did not provide unique and authentic learning experiences—experiences that could not be provided for adequately in any other way.

Most of the other types of definitions of curriculum raise the specter of dualism—between thought and action, between subject matter and instruction, between ends and means. It is as if to separate the act of talking from the language that is spoken. Knowledge is severed from the processes by which it is created, transmitted, and transformed. However theoretically derived, such separations are fictional constructs that cannot be taken as representing the real, practical world of curriculum and the school. In order to avoid drowning in a sea of complexities, humans create systems or ways of analyzing phenomena, but the trouble begins when they take their own fictional constructs and assume that these constructs are true in the larger ecological picture. In thinking about curriculum, various curriculum writers have sought to dissect it so that each specialist is given a piece of the action. Thus, for example, in separating curriculum from instruction, we have researchers who study instruction apart from whatever it is that is being taught and learned. Although such separations may enhance specialized scholarship, they tend to become self-serving exercises that cloud rather than illuminate curricular problems.

The conceptions of curriculum as used by experimentalist-progressives were more encompassing and functional in giving recognition to the wider nature of knowledge and the learning process, as well as the school as a specially designed environment for learning. Yet their proposed definitions remained somewhat vague in not being connected with the conception of knowledge as codified or systematized, and necessarily coupled with the processes through which one becomes knowledge/able. John Dewey defined education as "that reconstruction or reorganization of experience which adds to the meaning of experience, and which increases ability to direct the course of subsequent experience." Dewey's definition clearly sees education as an open process to transform experience into the working power of intelligence. Extending Dewey's definition of education, the authors of this text offer the following definition of curriculum: *that reconstruction of knowledge and experience that enables the learner to grow in exercising intelligent control of subsequent knowledge and experience.*

Educators have no way of knowing the exact nature of the subsequent experience of the learner in life. But if the process of education and that thing we call curriculum are successful here and now, the learner will be enabled to grow in social power and insight throughout life.

In the definition of curriculum proposed by the authors of this text, the curriculum is seen as a unity in which the reconstruction of knowledge is integrally related to the learner's ability to increase his or her control of knowledge and experience. If the school conceives of curriculum in this way, the curriculum will be unified rather than fragmented, and personal-social problems and needs will not be considered as intrusions on the work of the school.

PROBLEMS FOR STUDY AND DISCUSSION

1. How do you account for the wide differences among contemporary curriculum writers in defining curriculum?

2. What are your views on the issue concerning the dualism between curriculum and instruction, or between subject matter and method?

3. In searching for a theory of instruction, Bruner acknowledges that "a curriculum reflects not only the nature of knowledge itself but also the nature of the knower and the knowledge-getting process," and he concludes that "knowledge is a process, not a product." [Jerome S. Bruner, *Toward a Theory of Instruction* (Cambridge, MA: Harvard University Press, 1966), p. 72.]

   In view of Bruner's statement, does it makes sense to seek a theory of instruction apart from a theory of curriculum? Explain.

4. What significance for curriculum lies in Einstein's observation that "the realm of physics has so expanded that it seems to be limited only by the method itself"? [Albert Einstein, *Out of My Later Years* (New York: Philosophical Library, 1950), p. 98.]

5. What is your assessment of the definition of curriculum proposed by the authors of this text?

6. Would you say that the curriculum in your school is test-driven? Why or why not? What are the consequences of the test-driven curriculum?

7. What is the significance of collateral learning and the collateral curriculum? The authors of this text point out that if collateral learning and the collateral curriculum are taken into account, much of what lies in what has been called the hidden curriculum would be revealed. (It would no longer be hidden.) Do you agree? Explain.

8. As a high school student, did you participate in any school activities (collateral learning/collateral curriculum) outside the formal course of study that exerted a positive or negative influence on your attitudes, interests, appreciations, values, or academic achievement? As a college student? Explain.

9. In what ways is the concept of curriculum given special meaning and treatment in connection with the school or college as contrasted against other major social institutions?

10. During the early 1990s, the expression *curriculum delivery* came into common usage in the education literature. What does this expression signify for the role of the teacher? If the curriculum is to be "delivered," who makes the curriculum? What is implied by this expression for the concept of *knowledge* and the process through which the learner is to become *knowledge/able*?

11. The cover of a leading educational journal featured an article captioned, "The Content of Instruction" (*Phi Delta Kappan*, 74, February, 1993). What issues for curriculum are connected with the dual concepts in the caption? Explain.

NOTES

1. Mark Van Doren, *Liberal Education* (Boston: Beacon, 1959), p. 108.
2. Herbert Spencer, "What Knowledge Is of Most Worth?" (Originally published in 1859), in *Education: Intellectual, Moral, and Physical* (New York: Appleton, 1883), p. 29.
3. *The Works of Aristotle, Politica,* Book VIII, Ch. 2, trans. by Benjamin Jowett, Vol. X (Oxford, England: Clarendon, 1921), pp. 1, 338.
4. Lawrence A. Cremin, "Curriculum-Making in the United States," *Teachers College Record,* 73 (December 1971), pp. 207, 212.
5. Robert M. Hutchins, *The Higher Learning in America* (New Haven, CT: Yale University Press, 1936), pp. 82–85.
6. Van Doren, op. cit., pp. 75, 91.
7. Hutchins, op. cit., p. 66.
8. Ibid., pp. 62, 82, 84.
9. Allan Bloom, *The Closing of the American Mind* (New York: Simon and Schuster, 1987).
10. Mortimer J. Adler, *The Paideia Proposal* (New York: Macmillan, 1982).
11. Arthur Bestor, *The Restoration of Learning* (New York: Alfred A. Knopf, 1956), pp. 48–49.
12. William C. Bagley, *Classroom Management* (New York: Macmillan, 1907), p. 2.
13. Bestor, op. cit., p. 364.
14. Ibid., p. 120.
15. Edward L. Thorndike, "Mental Discipline in High School Studies," *Journal of Educational Psychology,* 15 (January–February, 1924), pp. 1–22, 83–98.
16. Bestor, op. cit., p. 20.
17. Jacques Barzun and Robert J. Saunders, *Art in Basic Education,* Occasional Paper 25 (Washington, DC: Council for Basic Education, 1979).
18. George H. S. Bush in U.S. Department of Education, *America 2000: An Education Strategy* (Washington, DC: Author, 1991), p. 53.
19. Edward D. Hirsch, Jr., *Cultural Literacy* (Boston: Houghton Mifflin, 1987).
20. Daniel Tanner, "A Brief Historical Perspective of the Struggle for an Integrative Curriculum," *Educational Horizons,* 68 (Fall, 1989), p. 10.
21. Diane Ravitch and Chester E. Finn, Jr., *What Do Our 17-Year-Olds Know?* (New York: Harper, 1987).
22. Joseph J. Schwab, "The Concept of the Structure of a Discipline," *The Educational Record,* 43 (July 1962), p. 197.
23. Philip H. Phenix, in A. Harry Passow (ed.), *Curriculum Crossroads* (New York: Teachers College Press, 1962), p. 64.
24. Ibid.
25. William D. Romey, "The Curriculum-Proof Teacher," *Phi Delta Kappan,* 54 (February, 1973), p. 407.
26. Jerrold R. Zacharias, "The Requirements for Major Curriculum Revision" in Robert W. Heath (ed.), *New Curricula* (New York: Harper, 1964), p. 69.
27. Paul Woodring in Robert W. Heath, ibid., p. 5.
28. Hilda Taba, *Curriculum Development: Theory and Practice* (New York: Harcourt, 1962), p. 11.
29. George A. Beauchamp, *Curriculum Theory,* 3rd ed. (Wilmette, IL: Kagg, 1975), p. 103.
30. Ibid., pp. 107–109.
31. James B. Macdonald, "Educational Models for Instruction," in James B. Macdonald and Robert R. Leeper (eds.), *Theories of Instruction* (Washington, DC: Association for Supervision and Curriculum Development, 1965), p. 6.
32. Paul H. Hirst, *Knowledge and the Curriculum* (London: Routledge, 1974), p. 132.
33. B. Galen Saylor and William M. Alexander, *Planning Curriculum for Schools* (New York: Holt, 1974), p. 6.
34. Elliot W. Eisner, *The Educational Imagination,* 3rd ed. (New York: Macmillan, 1994), p. 31.
35. John Dewey, *Experience and Education* (New York: Macmillan, 1935), p. 48.
36. Peter F. Oliva, *Developing the Curriculum* (Boston: Little, Brown, 1982), p. 10.
37. John Dewey, *The Child and the Curriculum* (Chicago: University of Chicago Press, 1902), p. 5.
38. Raymond E. Callahan, *Education and the Cult of Efficiency* (Chicago: University of Chicago Press, 1962).
39. Franklin Bobbitt, *The Curriculum* (Boston: Houghton, 1918), p. 42.
40. Franklin Bobbitt, *How to Make a Curriculum* (Boston: Houghton Mifflin, 1924), p. 2.
41. W. W. Charters, "Activity Analysis and Curricu-

lum Construction," *Journal of Educational Research,* 5 (May 1922), p. 359.

42. W. James Popham and Eva I. Baker, *Systematic Instruction* (Englewood Cliffs, NJ: Prentice Hall, 1970), p. 48.

43. Mauritz Johnson, Jr., "Definitions and Models in Curriculum Theory," *Educational Theory,* 17 (April 1967), p. 127.

44. W. James Popham in W. James Popham, Elliot W. Eisner, Howard J. Sullivan, and Louise L. Tyler, *Instructional Objectives* (Chicago: Rand McNally, 1969), pp. 34, 37.

45. Ibid., p. 60.

46. W. James Popham, *Educational Evaluation,* 3rd ed. (Boston: Allyn and Bacon, 1993), pp. 335–336.

47. B. F. Skinner, *The Technology of Teaching* (New York: Appleton, 1968), pp. 249, 256.

48. Robert M. Gagné, "Curriculum Research and the Promotion of Learning," in Ralph W. Tyler, Robert M. Gagné, and Michael Scriven, *Perspectives of Curriculum Evaluation* (Chicago: Rand McNally, 1967), p. 23.

49. Albert Bandura, *Principles of Behavior Modification* (New York: Holt, 1969), p. 85.

50. Skinner, op. cit., pp. 256, 258.

51. Robert N. Bush and Dwight W. Allen, *A New Design for High School Education* (New York: McGraw-Hill, 1964), p. 21.

52. Edward J. Meade, Jr., *Accountability and Governance in Public Education* (New York: The Ford Foundation, 1968), pp. 6–7.

53. Leon M. Lessinger, "Accountability for Results," in Leon M. Lessinger and Ralph W. Tyler (eds.), *Accountability in Education* (Worthington, OH: Jones, 1971), p. 14.

54. *The Office of Economic Opportunity Experiment in Educational Performance Contracting, Research Report* (Columbus, OH: Battelle Memorial Institute, 1972), p. 85.

55. Anthony G. Oettinger, *Run, Computer, Run* (Cambridge, MA: Harvard University Press, 1969), p. 53.

56. Ian Westbury and William Steimer, "Curriculum: A Discipline in Search of Its Problems," *School Review,* 79 (February 1971), pp. 251, 261.

57. Ibid, p. 262.

58. Allen B. Rosenstein, *A Study of a Profession and Professional Education* (Los Angeles: Uni-

versity of California, School of Engineering and Applied Science, December 1968), p. III–1.

59. Commission on MIT Education, *Creative Renewal in a Time of Crisis* (Cambridge, MA: M.I.T. Press, 1970).

60. Ernest L. Boyer, *College: A Report on Undergraduate Education in America* (New York: Harper, 1986); Lynne V. Cheney, *50 Hours* (Washington, DC: National Endowment for the Humanities, 1989).

61. Greer Williams, *Western Reserve's Experiment in Medical Education and Its Outcome* (New York: Oxford, 1980); Thomas Hale Ham, "The Approaches of the Faculty to Medical Education at Western Reserve University," *The Journal of Medical Education,* 34 (December 1959), p. 1163.

62. I. Freeman Butts, *Public Education in the United States* (New York: Holt, 1978), p. 372.

63. Henry A. Giroux, *Theory and Resistance in Education: A Pedagogy for the Opposition* (South Hadley, MA: Bergin, 1983).

64. Theodore Roszak, *The Making of a Counter Culture* (New York: Doubleday, 1969), p. 41.

65. B. Othanel Smith, William O. Stanley, and J. Harlan Shores, *Fundamentals of Curriculum Development,* rev. ed. (New York: Harcourt, 1957), p. 3.

66. John Dewey, *Democracy and Education* (New York: Macmillan, 1916), p. 92.

67. Denis Lawton, *Class, Culture and the Curriculum* (London: Routledge, 1975), pp. 6–7.

68. John Dewey, *How We Think,* rev. ed. (Lexington, MA: D. C. Heath, 1933), pp. 62, 81.

69. Philip H. Phenix, in *Curriculum Crossroads,* op. cit., p. 64.

70. Marc Belth, *Education as a Discipline* (Boston: Allyn and Bacon, 1965), p. 262.

71. Ibid., pp. 170, 174.

72. Bentley Glass, *The Timely and the Timeless* (New York: Basic Books, 1970), pp. 29–30.

73. Hilda Taba, *Curriculum Development: Theory and Practice* (New York: Harcourt, 1962), pp. 214–215.

74. John Dewey, *How We Think,* op. cit., p. 62.

75. John Dewey, *Democracy and Education* (New York: Macmillan, 1916), p. 102.

76. Dewey, *How We Think,* op. cit., p. 3.

77. Ibid., p. 116.

78. Dewey, *Democracy and Education,* op. cit., p. 125.

79. Dewey, *Child and Curriculum,* op. cit., pp. 8–9, 11, 12.

80. George Dennison, *The Lives of Children* (New York: Random, 1969), p. 73.

81. Dewey, *How We Think,* op. cit., p. 278.

82. Arthur W. Foshay, "Curriculum," in Robert L. Ebel (ed.), *Encyclopedia of Educational Research,* p. 275.

83. Frederick G. Bonser, *The Elementary Curriculum* (New York: Macmillan, 1920), p. 1.

84. Hollis L. Caswell and Doak S. Campbell, *Curriculum Development* (New York: American Book, 1935), p. 66.

85. H. H. Giles, S. P. McCutchen, and A. N. Zechiel, *Exploring the Curriculum* (New York: Harper, 1942), p. 293.

86. Caswell and Campbell, op. cit., p. 66.

87. Harold Spears, "The Changing Curriculum," Chapter 7 in Hollis L. Caswell (ed.), *The American High School: Its Responsibility and Opportunity,* Eighth Yearbook of the John Dewey Society (New York: Harper, 1946), p. 116, 117.

88. Ralph W. Tyler, "The Curriculum—Then and Now," in *Proceedings of the 1956 Invitational Conference on Testing Problems* (Princeton, NJ: Educational Testing Service, 1957), p. 79.

89. Harold B. Alberty and Elsie J. Alberty, *Reorganizing the High School Curriculum,* 3rd ed. (New York: Macmillan, 1962), p. 155.

90. Carter V. Good, *Dictionary of Education,* 2nd ed. (New York: McGraw-Hill, 1959), p. 149.

91. Carter V. Good, *Dictionary of Education,* 3rd ed. (New York: McGraw-Hill, 1973), p. 157.

92. W. Kenneth Richmond, *The School Curriculum* (London: Methuen, 1971), p. 11.

93. Ibid., p. 10.

94. Dewey, *How We Think,* op. cit., p. 259.

95. Cooperative Study of Secondary School Standards, *Evaluative Criteria* (Washington, DC: American Council on Education, 1940), p. 31.

96. National Study of Secondary School Evaluation, *Evaluative Criteria,* 4th ed. (Washington, DC: Author, 1969), p. 33.

97. National Study for School Evaluation, *Evaluative Criteria for the Evaluation of Secondary Schools,* 6th ed. (Falls Church, VA: Author: 1987), p. 59.

98. Harold Rugg, *Foundations for American Education* (New York: Harcourt, 1947), p. 650.

99. "Camping Education," *Phi Delta Kappan,* 21 (December 1938), p. 114.

100. Educational Policies Commission, *Education for ALL American Youth* (Washington, DC: NEA, 1944, 1952).

101. Roland C. Faunce and Nelson L. Bossing, *Developing the Core Curriculum,* 2nd ed. (Englewood Cliffs, NJ: Prentice Hall, 1958), p. 321.

102. Bestor. op. cit., pp. 59, 203.

103. William G. Spady, "Status, Achievement, and Motivation in the American High School," *School Review,* 79 (May 1971), pp. 384-385.

104. Laura E. Berk in Philip W. Jackson (ed.), *Handbook of Research on Curriculum* (New York: Macmillan, 1992), p. 1003.

105. Ernest T. Pascarella and Patrick T. Terenzini, *How College Affects Students* (San Francisco: Jossey-Bass, 1991), pp. 620–621.

106. Alexander W. Astin, *What Matters Most in College?* (San Francisco: Jossey-Bass, 1993), pp. 425–427.

107. Daniel Tanner and Genaro Lachica, *Discovering and Developing the College Potential of Disadvantaged High School Youth* (New York: Office of Research, The City University of New York, 1967).

108. Ernest L. Boyer, *High School* (New York: Harper, 1983), p. 209.

109. *Hazelwood School District v. Kuhlmeier,* U.S. 260 (1988).

110. James B. Macdonald in Elliot W. Eisner (ed.), *Confronting Curriculum Reform* (Boston: Little, Brown, 1971), p. 126; *Theories of Instruction,* op. cit., p. 5.

111. *Theories of Instruction,* ibid., p. 6.

112. Ibid.

113. James B. Macdonald, Bernice J. Wolfson, and Esther Zaret, *Reschooling Society: A Conceptual Model* (Washington, DC: Association for Supervision and Curriculum Development, 1973), p. 22.

114. Ronald C. Doll, *Curriculum Improvement: Decision Making and Process,* 8th ed. (Boston: Allyn and Bacon, 1992), p. 6.

115. Kieran Egan, "What Is Curriculum?" *Curriculum Inquiry,* 8 (Spring 1978), p. 71.

116. Harry S. Broudy, B. Othanel Smith, and Joe R. Burnett, *Democracy and Excellence in American Secondary Education* (Chicago: Rand McNally, 1964), p. 79.

117. Jeanne S. Chall and Sue S. Conrad, "Resources and Their Use for Reading Instruction," Chapter 8 in National Society for the Study of Education, Eighty-third Yearbook, Part I, *Becoming Readers in a Complex Society* (Chicago: University of Chicago Press, 1984), p. 214; Richard T. Vacca and Jo Anne L. Vacca, *Content Area Reading*, 4th ed. (New York: Harper, 1993).

118. Johnson, op. cit., p. 130.
119. Dewey, *Democracy and Education*, op. cit., p. 124.
120. Ibid., pp. 119, 123.
121. Albert Einstein, *Out of My Later Years* (New York: Philosophical Library, 1950), p. 98.
122. John Dewey in Reginald D. Archambault (ed.), *Lectures in the Philosophy of Education: 1899* (New York: Random, 1966), p. 132.
123. Michael J. Dunkin and Bruce J. Biddle, *The Study of Teaching* (New York: Holt, 1974), pp. 15–16, 22–23.
124. Jere Brophy and Thomas L. Good in Merlin C. Wittrock (ed.), *Handbook of Research on Teaching*, 3rd ed. (New York: Macmillan, 1986), pp. 360–367.
125. Dewey, *Democracy and Education*, op. cit., p. 199.
126. John D. McNeil and W. James Popham in Robert W. Travers (ed.), *Second Handbook of Research on Teaching* (New York: Macmillan, 1973), p. 219.
127. Jerome S. Bruner, *Toward a Theory of Instruction* (Cambridge, MA: Harvard University Press, 1966), p. 72.
128. Dewey, *Democracy and Education*, op. cit., pp. 81, 84.

129. Frederick Erickson and Jeffrey Shutz in Philip W. Jackson (ed.), *Handbook of Research on Curriculum*, op. cit., pp. 474–475.
130. Dewey, *Experience and Education*, op. cit., p. 48.
131. Eugene R. Smith, Ralph W. Tyler, and the Evaluation Staff, *Appraising and Recording Student Progress* (New York: Harper, 1942); Dean Chamberlin, Enid S. Chamberlin, Neal E. Drought, and William E. Scott, *Did They Succeed in College?* (New York: Harper, 1942).
132. Robert Dreeben, *On What Is Learned in School* (Reading, MA: Addison-Wesley, 1968), pp. 147–148.
133. H. H. Remmers (ed.), *Antidemocratic Attitudes in American Schools* (Evanston, IL: Northwestern University Press, 1963); Barry J. Galasso, *Attitudes of Youth toward Issues of Democracy*, unpublished doctoral dissertation (New Brunswick, NJ: Rutgers University, 1986); Virgil M. Johnson, *Antidemocratic Attitudes of High School Students*, unpublished doctoral dissertation (New Brunswick, NJ: Rutgers University, 1986). See also John H. Flathmann, *The General Education Function of the Curriculum for Democratic Citizenship*, unpublished doctoral dissertation (New Brunswick, NJ: Rutgers University, 1987).
134. Dewey, *The School and Society*, op. cit., p. 7.
135. Dewey, *Democracy and Education*, op. cit., pp. 89–90.

SELECTED REFERENCES

Adler, Mortimer J. *The Paideia Proposal: An Educational Manifesto.* New York: Macmillan, 1982.

Aikin, Wilford M. *The Story of the Eight-Year Study.* New York: Harper, 1942.

Alberty, Harold B., and Alberty, Elsie J. *Reorganizing the High School Curriculum,* 3rd ed. New York: Macmillan, 1962.

Astin, Alexander W. *What Matters Most in College?* San Francisco: Jossey-Bass, 1993.

Belth, Marc. *Education as a Discipline.* Boston: Allyn and Bacon, 1965.

Bernal, J. D. *Science in History,* Vol. I: *The Emergence of Science.* Cambridge, MA: M.I.T. Press, 1971.

Bestor, Arthur. *The Restoration of Learning.* New York: Alfred A. Knopf, 1956.

Bloom, Allan. *The Closing of the American Mind.* New York: Simon and Schuster, 1987.

Bobbitt, Franklin. *The Curriculum.* Boston: Houghton Mifflin, 1918.

Bobbitt, Franklin. *How to Make a Curriculum.* Boston: Houghton Mifflin, 1924.

Bode, Boyd H. *Modern Educational Theories.* New York: Macmillan, 1927.

Boyer, Ernest L. *College: A Report on Undergraduate Education in America.* New York: Harper and Row, 1986.

Boyer, Ernest L. *High School: A Report on Secondary Education in America.* New York: Harper and Row, 1983.

Bronowski, Jacob. *The Origins of Knowledge and the Imagination.* New Haven, CT: Yale University Press, 1978.

Bruner, Jerome S. *The Process of Education.* Cambridge, MA: Harvard University Press, 1960.

Bruner, Jerome S. *Toward a Theory of Instruction.* Cambridge, MA: Harvard University Press, 1966.

Callahan, Raymond E. *Education and the Cult of Efficiency.* Chicago: University of Chicago Press, 1962.

Caswell, Hollis L. (ed.). *The American High School: Its Responsibility and Opportunity.* Eighth Yearbook of the John Dewey Society. New York: American Book Company, 1935.

Cheney, Lynne V. *50 Hours.* Washington, DC: National Endowment for the Humanities, 1989.

Childs, John L. *Education and the Philosophy of Experimentalism.* New York: Appleton-Century-Crofts, 1931.

Cremin, Lawrence A. *Public Education.* New York: Basic Books, 1976.

Dewey, John. *The Child and the Curriculum.* Chicago: University of Chicago Press, 1902.

Dewey, John. *Democracy and Education.* New York: Macmillan, 1916.

Dewey, John. *Experience and Education.* New York: Macmillan, 1935.

Dewey, John. *How We Think,* rev. ed. Lexington, MA: D. C. Heath, 1933.

Dewey, John. *The School and Society and the Child and the Curriculum.* Chicago: University of Chicago Press, 1990 (Originally published separately, 1899, 1902).

Educational Policies Commission. *Education for ALL American Youth—A Further Look.* Washington, DC: NEA, 1952.

Giles, H. H., McCutchen, S. P., and Zechiel, A. N. *Exploring the Curriculum.* New York: Harper and Row, 1942.

Goodlad, John I. *A Place Called School.* New York: McGraw-Hill, 1984.

Harap, Henry, Chairman, Joint Committee on Curriculum. *The Changing Curriculum.* New York: D. Appleton-Century, 1937.

Hirsch, Edward D., Jr. *Cultural Literacy.* Boston: Houghton Mifflin, 1987.

Hutchins, Robert M. *The Higher Learning in America.* New Haven, CT: Yale University Press, 1936.

Jackson, Philip W. (ed.). *Handbook of Research on Curriculum.* New York: Macmillan, 1992.

Lawton, Denis. *Class, Culture and the Curriculum.* London: Routledge & Kegan Paul, 1975.

National Society for the Study of Education. *Critical Issues in Curriculum.* Eighty-seventh Yearbook, Part I. Chicago: University of Chicago Press, 1988.

National Society for the Study of Education. *Curriculum-Making: Past and Present.* Twenty-sixth Yearbook, Part I. Bloomington, IL: Public School Publishing, 1927.

National Society for the Study of Education. *The Curriculum: Retrospect and Prospect.* Seventieth Yearbook, Part I. Chicago: University of Chicago Press, 1971.

National Society for the Study of Education. *The Foundations of Curriculum-Making.* Twenty-sixth Yearbook, Part II. Bloomington, IL: Public School Publishing, 1927.

Oettinger, Anthony G. *Run, Computer, Run.* Cambridge, MA: Harvard University Press, 1969.

Pascarella, Ernest T., and Terenzini, Patrick T. *How College Affects Students.* San Francisco: Jossey-Bass, 1991.

Phenix, Philip H. *Realms of Meaning.* New York: McGraw-Hill, 1964.

Smith, B. Othanel, Stanley, William O., and Shores, J. Harlan. *Fundamentals of Curriculum Development,* rev. ed. New York: Harcourt Brace Jovanovich, 1957.

Smith, Eugene R., Tyler, Ralph W., and the Evaluation Staff. *Appraising and Recording Student Progress.* New York: Harper, 1942.

Stratemeyer, Florence B., et al. *Developing a Curriculum for Modern Living,* 2nd ed. New York: Teachers College Press, 1957.

Taba, Hilda. *Curriculum Development: Theory and Practice.* New York: Harcourt Brace Jovanovich, 1962.

Tanner, Daniel. *Secondary Curriculum: Theory and Development.* New York: Macmillan, 1971.

Tanner, Daniel, and Tanner, Laurel. *History of the School Curriculum.* New York: Macmillan, 1990.

Tyler, Ralph W. *Basic Principles of Curriculum and Instruction.* Chicago: University of Chicago Press, 1949.

U.S. Department of Education. *America 2000: An Education Strategy.* Washington, DC: Author, 1991.

Van Doren, Mark. *Liberal Education.* Boston: Beacon Press, 1943.

Weinberg, Alvin M. *Reflections on Big Science.* Cambridge, MA: M.I.T. Press, 1965.

Whitehead, Alfred North. *The Aims of Education.* New York: Macmillan, 1929.

Wittrock, Merlin C. (ed.). *Handbook of Research on Teaching,* 3rd ed. New York: Macmillan, 1986.

CHAPTER 6

CURRICULUM AS A FIELD FOR SYSTEMATIC STUDY

"What nutrition and reproduction are to physiological life, education is to social life," observed Dewey. Education not only is the means through which a culture is transmitted but also the means through which it is transformed. A primitive society is able to accomplish its educational functions without schools and formal curricula because the gap between what the rising generation needs to know and do in order to take over the tasks of the established generation can be bridged by direct shared experience. But in the modern, literate, technological society, the growing complexity of knowledge and life is such that society looks to the school and something that has come to be called the curriculum as necessary for enabling the rising generation to gain the needed insight and power to build a better society.

The changing nature of knowledge, changing conceptions of the learner, and changing demands of social life have called for a changing conception and function of curriculum. In this chapter, the relationship between knowledge and the curriculum is examined in the light of problems relating to the expansion of knowledge, the specialization of knowledge, and the search for synthesis.

KNOWLEDGE, EDUCATION, AND LIFE

Early in this century, the German philosopher Hans Vaihinger described how human beings have developed knowledge systems or thought edifices in order to keep from drowning in an ever-expanding sea of knowledge and information. Manifest in what has come to be called *curriculum,* these knowledge systems or thought edifices were developed to meet the practical need for making the world more comprehensible and also to serve to facilitate the development of new knowledge. But Vaihinger pointed out that these systematic representations are fictional constructs and, although they are necessary, scholars make the error of treating them as if the real world were organized in this fashion. The consequence is that these isolated, compartmentalized constructs are treated as accomplishments in themselves and thus undermine the very purpose for which they were conceived—to facilitate communication and action.[2]

Education and Life

Dewey noted that one of the weightiest problems of education is the isolation of the curriculum from life experience.[3] Alfred North Whitehead, the noted British philosopher and mathematician, also addressed this problem. Calling on educators "to eradicate the fatal disconnection of subjects which kills the vitality of our modern curriculum," Whitehead advocated the study of "[l]ife in all its manifestations" as the subject matter for education. After reviewing a list of isolated subjects that comprise the curriculum, Whitehead observed, "[t]he best that can be said of it is, that it is a rapid table of contents which a deity might run over in his mind while he was thinking of creating a world, and had not yet determined how to put it together."[4]

Dewey and Whitehead went to great lengths to show the need for curriculum synthesis and to show how the curriculum might be made relevant to life experience.

At various times during the twentieth century, radical critics were revivifying the romanticist ideas of Jean Jacques Rousseau, the French philosopher, as set forth in his iconoclastic *Emile* (1762). This revival of Rousseau's ideas became manifest most notably in the writings of radical critics, such as Paul Goodman and Ivan Illich, at the height of the college-student protest movement of the 1960s and extending into the early 1970s. In effect, they were advocating that the school be abolished entirely and replaced by informal, spontaneous arrangements where children and youth would learn directly from life.[5] Dewey went to some length in exposing the fallacies and shortcomings in Rousseau's theory, as well as in the radical-romanticist proposals and practices that emerged during Dewey's time.[6]

To assume that children and youth are capable of learning whatever may be necessary directly from life not only assumes a romantic perspective of the younger generation but also of the established society itself. Only primitive societies, where knowledge is static, have been able to function without schools. It would be equally absurd to advocate that our colleges and universities be abolished and that the education of physicists, physicians, architects, engineers, lawyers, and other professional workers be provided through apprenticeship.

Unique Functions of the School.   Of course, significant educational functions are performed by agencies other than the school and university—public libraries, museums, the mass media, the military, civic and professional organizations, business, industrial enterprises, and so on. The school and university are conceived by modern societies as laboratories for the testing of ideas in ways that are not otherwise possible. This requires the continual and systematic reconstruction of knowledge as represented in what has come to be called the *curriculum.* The school and university, unlike any other institution of society, are engaged in this systematic process. The university is conceived not merely for the preservation and transmission of knowledge, but for the development of new knowledge with the expectation that this will make for a better society. And because the school, more than any other social institution, is responsible for the formal education of the rising generation, the school is society's chief agency for shaping society's future. As special places to perform these unique functions, including the function of enlightened criticism of society, the free society creates special protections for the school and university, under the principle of academic freedom, to ensure the possibilities of its own improvement.

This is not an easy task, particularly for the school, which is always under pressure to confine itself to the narrowest and least controversial functions—namely skill development and knowledge transmission (the latter often being construed as information rather than knowledge). At the university level, the multiplicity of knowledge edifices and compartments of specialized knowledge often are taken as the spoils of inquiry rather than as the means of facilitating the solving of pervading life problems. Not only are the specialized knowledge compartments isolated from one another, but also when they are treated as self-serving domains they become remote from life experience. The problem of curriculum congestion, isolation, and remoteness has been a persistent one, and has become more acute with the incessant expansion and increasing specialization of knowledge.

As laboratories for the testing of ideas, the schools also are expected to enable educators to learn more about the learner and, hence, to continually improve the teaching-learning process. Although this function is not explicitly recognized in many schools, administrators and teachers in more successful schools are cognizant of the necessary role of the school in performing this function.

Knowledge and the Curriculum

The survival of society is predicated on its capacity to resolve practical problems—wide-ranging problems encompassing such varied concerns as water, food, energy, health, population growth and migration, ethnic relations, international relations, transportation, communication, housing, recreation, poverty, crime, employment, and so on. Thus society, of necessity, is mission oriented. Its survival and prosperity derive from its capability of applying its knowledge to the resolution of practical problems. A host of institutions are created to accomplish this mission. The most global of these institutions, other than government itself, is the educational institution—for it not only is concerned with the development of knowledge but also with making each rising generation more knowledgeable than its predecessor so as to make possible a better future society.

As mentioned earlier, the educational institution, in its effort to meet the practical need of making the world more comprehensible, has proceeded to organize knowledge (and the ways of dealing with knowledge) into thought edifices and categories, which comprise the curriculum. Although intended to serve this practical need, these edifices and compartments have come to represent myriad knowledge specializations, especially in the university. This has led to the fragmentation of knowledge and the further separation of knowledge from life problems. Pointing to the self-serving tendencies of specialized scholars working in separate knowledge domains, Weinberg has criticized the resulting knowledge fragmentation in our universities and has noted how this fragmentation has even invaded our elementary classroom.[7] Although in this connection Weinberg was referring to the impact of the discipline-centered curriculum reforms of the late 1950s and 1960s, the problem of curriculum fragmentation and remoteness from life experience remains a persistent one. Weinberg calls for a renewed effort to develop the relatedness of the knowledge domains so that knowledge will be made relevant to the mission of society in addressing its pervading problems. Obviously, this calls for the reconstruction and resynthesis of the curriculum if the educational institution is to meet its public purpose.

The back-to-basics retrenchment of the 1970s and 1980s not only treated the basic skills in isolation from one another, but also in isolation from life applications. Removed from ideas and practical application, it was no wonder then, that the curriculum fundamentalism of that era resulted in a decline in thinking ability and writing proficiency as worksheets and workbooks proliferated. During the early 1990s, in belated recognition of the deleterious effects of curriculum fundamentalism, renewed emphasis was being given to "writing across the curriculum" and "higher-order thinking" or critical thinking (key elements in the progressive curriculum reforms during the first half of the twentieth century). Nevertheless, unlike the earlier progressive reforms, the common practice was not to teach critical thinking as a unifying theme for the curriculum, but as a separate item of emphasis so as not to bring unsettling social ideas into the curriculum. At the same time, the relentless trend toward nationalized testing found teachers coming under increasing pressure to teach to the test. A study for the National Science Foundation reported in 1992 that the national standardized tests were giving emphasis to low-level thinking and knowledge recall, as well as exerting other undesirable influences on the curriculum.[8]

The Knowledge Explosion

Much has been made of the so-called knowledge explosion. "It can be affirmed unequivocally that the amount of scientific knowledge available at the end of one's life will be about one hundred times what it was when he was born," declared Bentley Glass in 1970. The exponential increase in scientific knowledge, argued Glass, meant that "education in rapidly developing fields of knowledge has become about equal in rate to the obsolescence of an automobile. In five to seven years it is due for a complete replacement."[9]

In advancing this thesis, noted educators such as Glass and Schwab[10] contended that the curriculum becomes totally obsolete and must be replaced every several years. Aside from the fact that the automobile requires replacement every several years, not because it becomes obsolete but because it is designed to wear out, the thesis advanced by Glass and others is open to question. There is little dispute that scientific knowledge has increased exponentially over the course of the past two or three centuries. But to assume that this explosion of knowledge can go on indefinitely is to ignore the fact that we live in a world of finite resources. Moreover, the most rapidly developing areas of knowledge, science and technology, have not become obsolescent every five to seven years. New knowledge is systematically assimilated as existing knowledge is systematically revised and reconstructed to accommodate the new knowledge. Unfortunately, like the cosmetic changes in the automobile, curriculum innovations often tend to be overblown, superficial, and trendy—while the substantive and persistent problems of curriculum balance, articulation, and coherence receive only scant and sporadic attention.

Eclosion and Synthesis—The Unfolding of Knowledge

In his study of the history of knowledge, the mathematician Salomon Bochner challenges the notion that we are living in an age of knowledge explosion. The development of systematic knowledge is seen by Bochner as the product of two contraposed though not necessarily oppositional forces—eclosion and synthesis.[11] Eclosion represents a bursting forth of new knowledge characterized by fluidity, penetration, and proliferation; synthesis is characterized as a reaction to eclosion in which areas of knowledge mature, become highly systematic and verifiable, and, therefore, less prone to being upset by new developments or disputations. Bochner terms the period of the half century around 1800 as the Age of Eclosion and sees the twentieth century as the Age of Synthesis.

The influence of Darwin's *Voyage of the Beagle* (1839) and *Origin of Species* (1859) exerted a revolutionary impact not only on the natural sciences, but also on philosophy, theology, and social science. Pasteur's unceasing work in advancing the germ theory of disease around 1865, despite enormous opposition from the medical profession, was indeed a revolution, laying the foundation of scientific medicine and creating the new field of bacteriology, as well as influencing the development of such fields as immunology, antisepsis, sanitation, and biochemistry. However revolutionary were the scientific breakthroughs of the twentieth century, the new knowledge did not produce the overthrow or require a veritable upheaval of existing systematized knowledge. For example, the revolutionary work of Einstein was accommodated into physics and philosophy. The revolutionary work of Freud was accommodated into medicine, psychology, and education (despite continuing disputations to this day).

During the Age of Eclosion, when the amount of systematic knowledge was relatively small, new knowledge of any significance was likely to exert fundamental changes and disputations and also give rise to the major organizational areas of knowledge. In the Age of Synthesis, the mature network of knowledge insights tends to accommodate new developments without major disruptions to the established areas of knowledge. Thus, despite the alleged knowledge explosion of the twentieth century, the mature domains of scholarship have managed to assimilate the new knowledge without having to undergo the severe reformulations that were characteristic of the Age of Eclosion.

A parallel of this revolutionary-evolutionary development of knowledge might be found in Hegel's renowned triad of thesis-antithesis-synthesis.[12] Dualisms, contradictions, and oppositions are not end points; they are steps toward progress as resolutions are found. Resolutions are not mere compromises, but represent a new and more holistic development of knowledge—a kind of ecological recognition of the necessary interdependence of knowledge. Thus synthesis makes possible new understandings and perspectives, and opens the possibilities for new breakthroughs.

Efforts toward the synthesis of knowledge are no less creative than the earlier developments characteristic of the Age of Eclosion. To resolve difficulties and dualisms, to harmonize oppositions, and to internalize contrarieties requires a profound creativity no less significant than the spectacular developments in knowledge breakthroughs characteristic of the Age of Eclosion. Although this can be demonstrated more clearly in the physical sciences than in the social sciences or humanities, even in the latter fields it is becoming increasingly evident that various systematic positions and frameworks are making valuable contributions.

KNOWLEDGE SPECIALIZATION AND FRAGMENTATION.   Nevertheless, the Age of Synthesis has been accompanied by an age of knowledge specialization that creates new problems of knowledge fragmentation. The knowledge specialization is not a product of the Age of Synthesis but rather a result of the growth of the knowledge industry and the sociology of its institutions. In the words of Glass,

> [i]t is well recognized that many, if not most, scientific breakthroughs come about when the techniques and concepts of quite different scientific fields are brought together in an original synthesis of insight and imagination. Yet it seems unavoidable that the increasing narrowness of specialization tends to reduce the possibility that this will happen.[13]

Glass went on to discuss how our university scholars seek to enhance their reputation by digging out minuscule facts and information, whereas a lower premium is given to publishing comprehensive books and reviews that reveal the needed interrelationships of knowledge and its domains. The Nobel laureate Eugene Wigner recounted how his own field has become so specialized that he could not understand half the reports in *Physical Review Abstracts*. "Perhaps it is partly the jargon—the technical expressions. It hurts me," stated Wigner, "and I'm afraid it will hurt physics."[14] Weinberg proposed that the university "accord the generalist of broad outlook the status and prestige it now confers upon the specialist of narrow outlook," and he proposed that "the university reestablish its relevance to the interdisciplinary real world."[15] Indeed we find that despite the obsession with specialization in the university, the need for synthesis is exemplified in the emergence of new cross-disciplinary and interdisciplinary fields such as biophysics, sociobiology, ecology, and integrated studies in the broad field of humanities.

The Search for Synthesis

Perhaps the major curriculum problem during the second half of the twentieth century stems more from a problems explosion than a knowledge explosion. Beginning in the late 1960s, the scientific establishment and the general public were impelled to become less concerned with the exponential rate of growth of knowledge than with the uses to which knowledge is put in the face of exploding societal problems. Only a decade earlier, the public had been led to believe that the age of space would usher in a future of unlimited knowledge frontiers to be conquered.

But instead of turning people outward, the age of space seemed to focus our concerns back to planet earth as we realized that the capability of going to the moon is in no way an escape from the problems on earth. Perhaps the most profound comment made by our astronauts on their first visit to the moon was how beautiful the earth is when viewed from this distant vantage point! Meanwhile, back on earth there was a growing realization that the quality of life on earth, indeed our very survival, was not so much dependent on coping with a knowledge explosion but on our capacity to deal with a problems explosion. A new awareness of our finite resources on earth gave us cause to consider the problems of environmental deterioration, overpopulation, energy utilization, food production, and so on—with the likelihood of economic and social stagnation unless we turn our intelligence to the wise use of these resources. A widely discussed report prepared by an M.I.T. project team warned that exponential growth cannot continue indefinitely in a situation of finite resources, and that mere faith in science and technology will only divert us from taking the action necessary for solving this problem by using the knowledge, tools, and resources already in our possession.[16]

The Problems Explosion

Reflecting a growing awareness of this problem of global ecology, and in response to the exploding social protest in our central cities and on our college campuses during the 1960s, the American Association for the Advancement of Science activated its Committee on Science to Improve Human Welfare. A report on the activities of this committee described a number of projects undertaken in such areas as health care and the energy crisis, and cited a committee proposal "that society develop multidisciplinary, problem-oriented institutions to deal with the growing complexity of today's problems."[17] The concern for such problems impelled the association to reassess the priorities of scientific inquiry, so that from the late 1970s and into the 1990s the annual meetings of the association turned from science per se to science as it affects society. New impetus was being given to interdisciplinary approaches to societal problems.

The university scholars who engaged in course-content improvement during the preceding two decades had been concerned with organizing the subject matter of their disciplines. In the face of a so-called knowledge explosion it now was becoming apparent that humanity faced serious limits to growth in view of the finite resources on earth. Perhaps these scholars had mistaken an information explosion for a knowledge explosion and, in so doing, had ignored the problems explosion in their efforts to reform the school curriculum.

Only a year after Glass had advanced his ideas regarding the knowledge explosion, he embraced a radically different perspective in the face of the problems explosion on earth. According to Glass, "[i]ndeed, so awesome is already the accelerating rate of our scientific and technological advance that simple extrapolation of the exponential curves shows unmistakably that we have at most a generation or two before progress must cease, whether because the world's population becomes insufferably dense, or because we exhaust the possible sources of physical energy or deplete some irreplaceable resource, or because, most likely of all, we pollute our environment to toxic, irremediable limits."[18]

Regardless of whether or not the picture portrayed by Glass is overly pessimistic, it is clear that our institutions of learning cannot ignore the wider problems of society. If the twentieth century is to be described as the Age of Synthesis, such a description will likely find its justification in mankind's ability to solve pervading social problems. This will require the building of new interrelationships between and among the established domains of knowledge in school and society. Renewed attention will have to be given to the macrocurriculum and not just the microcurriculum.

During the late 1980s, the American Association for the Advancement of Science launched a long-range program called Project 2061 (named for the year Comet Halley returns to visibility from Earth), designed to break down the traditional subject-matter categories and build connections in the K–12 curriculum (biological and health sciences, physical and information sciences and engineering, mathematics, technology, and the social and behavioral sciences). From the start the project embraced a comprehensive approach in seeking curriculum synthesis as opposed to the traditional curriculum of compartmentalized subjects, and in revealing the relationships between science and society. In this effort, it became clear from the outset that the traditional curriculum is overloaded with facts and information, and neglects the important concepts, ideas, and knowledge applications and relationships. In a similar vein, the National Science Teachers Association launched a program for the 1990s, funded by the National Science Foundation, for the full articulation of the school science curriculum.[19]

The Macrocurriculum and the Microcurriculum

The early decades of the twentieth century witnessed a growing awareness of problems created by course proliferation, knowledge fragmentation, and the isolation and remoteness of studies from life. Coupled with the development of new knowledge concerning the nature of the child and adolescent, the need for a reconstruction of the curriculum became apparent to progressive educators. They proceeded to develop new curricular frameworks and designs leading to correlation, fusion, broad fields, and integrated core approaches.

These efforts, which would appear to lend credence to Bochner's thesis regarding the twentieth century as the Age of Synthesis, represented an unprecedented concern for addressing macrocurricular problems and not merely microcurricular problems. The whole was seen as more than the sum of its parts. Curriculum development required attention to the interactions of the constituent subject matters and relevance of these subject matters to the life of the learner. Segmental approaches to curriculum development within each subject-matter area had resulted in the fragmentation and isolation of knowledge and learning.

Attention to macrocurricular problems resulted in efforts to develop vertical and horizontal curriculum articulation—the former referring to developing coherence *within* given fields of study over the various grade levels or years of schooling, the latter to developing the interrelationships *between* and *among* different fields of study at either a given level or over various levels of schooling. The segmental approach was no longer adequate to the task of curriculum development, contended progressive educators who sought an ecological approach. The concern for general education—or that part of the curriculum designed to provide for a common universe of discourse, understanding, and competence—during the first half of the twentieth century represented a macrocurricular concern and resulted in the creation of various new curricular designs and frameworks, ranging from correlational to interdisciplinary approaches. Nevertheless, the specialization of knowledge, the segmental organizational structure of the university and the secondary school, the influence of tax conservatives and essentialists, narrow national priorities concerned with military defense, and the difficult task of grappling with macrocurricular problems all served as countervailing influences to curriculum synthesis. The problem of synthesis remains a profound and persistent one to this day.

Curriculum as a Subject of Thought

If the entire realm of knowledge were limited only to the classics, there would be little disagreement and change in our conception of curriculum. Society, too, would be static and the task of the school would be the mere transference of a maximum quantity of past knowledge to each future generation. To regard the school as such an instrument is to treat knowledge as dead matter, whereas the school serves the living, noted Einstein.[20]

The incessant emergence of problems in our society requires new ways of dealing with knowledge and a constant quest for new knowledge for purposes of social problem solving. Thus, knowledge is not a mere end product of inquiry but a byproduct and resource for solving problems and producing intelligent action. Similarly, the curriculum of the school cannot be conceived of as a mere catalog of fixed subject matters if the rising generation is to develop the capacity for building a better life for itself. This does not mean that the curriculum should bend to whatever ill wind may be dominant at any given time, but rather that the school curriculum must be constantly evaluated and improved so as to ensure the fulfillment of its mission for the rising generation.

Although an essential characteristic of the collegiate community is to expose rational activity to rational scrutiny, or "to think about our thinking," Schwab points to the neglect of engaging in thought about the curriculum:

> Such thought about thinking is, however, notably uncommon and invisible in the one place which matters most to the collegiate community—its curriculum. As far as students are allowed to see, the curriculum is not a subject of thought; it merely is. In many cases, indeed, thought about curriculum is not merely invisible; it barely occurs.[21]

Whether at the level of the university or secondary school, little attention is given to the wider functions of the curriculum that transcend the separate subject fields. Insufficient attention is given to examining the scope and sequence of the curriculum or to improving the vertical and horizontal articulation of the curriculum. This neglect is an outcome of the rewards of specialization in the university, the organizational structure of the educational institution, the influence of tradition, and the inertia that besets institutions that are based on tradition. When changes and innovations are implemented, they tend to be a response to fashions and trends rather than to the need for problem solving. Typically, the adoption of new administrative or managerial arrangements and labels is mistaken for curriculum development.

Specialization, Departmentalization, and Compartmentalization

The engagement of university scholars in the pursuit of specialized knowledge, within the departmentalized structure of the university, mitigates against thinking about the curriculum beyond compartmentalized and specialized domains. Curricular change tends to occur mainly within each domain by means of accretion, deletion, and certain modifications of courses and programs. The secondary school tends to imitate the college in its departmentalized structure. Departments add new courses to their offerings, modify old courses, and occasionally delete a course here and there. Rarely does the faculty of a high school or a college engage in comprehensive and systematic curriculum development and evaluation that transcends department lines. At the elementary level, although it has been contended that the self-contained classroom, with the teacher as curriculum generalist, provides greater opportunities for curricular synthesis, the curriculum typically is organized and treated as separate subjects.[22] The discipline-centered curriculum reforms of the late 1950s and 1960s serve to exacerbate such separations. A notable response to this problem was the resurgent interest in the open classroom during the 1970s, giving promise of bringing about new patterns for curricular synthesis. However, many different kinds of arrangements were lumped together under the label of open classroom. It was not unusual for open classrooms to be so organized as to have the differentiated activities occurring mainly along separate subject lines. Instead of implementing the open classroom for purposes of curriculum synthesis, it was adopted in many instances as a new administrative arrangement to economize on space and staff utilization. In some areas, school hallways were used for instructional activities to the extent that the term *open classroom* became synonymous with *open corridor*.[23] All too often the concern for managerial arrangements and efficiency in the deployment of personnel and resources is taken by school administrators as curriculum development. New labels and advertising slogans are adopted and discarded like changing clothing fashions without addressing the substantive problems of curriculum development.

The Collapse of the Disciplinary Doctrine

The discipline-centered curriculum reforms of the late 1950s and 1960s were based on the premise that all organized knowledge for curriculum construction should be derived from the disciplines. Phenix held that in curriculum development "[t]he first principle is that the content of instruction should be drawn entirely from the fields of disciplined inquiry" as developed by "organized communities of specialists."[24] Another leading proponent of the disciplinary doctrine, Joseph Schwab wrote, "[t]o identify the disciplines which constitute contemporary knowledge is to identify the various materials which constitute the resources of education and its obligations."[25]

In response to the student protest movement of the late 1960s, Phenix, Schwab, and other advocates of the disciplinary doctrine markedly altered their positions. Phenix acknowledged that strictly following the disciplinary approach to curriculum organization tends toward curriculum fragmentation and fails to address basic personal and social issues.[26] Schwab presented an extended analysis of the differing uses of subject matter for organizing the curriculum. After pointing to certain advantages of the disciplinary mode, he also discussed the weaknesses of this mode. According to Schwab,

> . . . of greatest importance to our purposes here, this mode precludes any systematic use of arts which aim to discover the relations which exist or which can be induced among various subject areas—the arts which make possible recognition and repair of divorces. . . .
>
> Pervasive specialism unexamined creates in students the illusion from which we all suffer to some degree—the illusion that subject matters as now distinguished are inevitable products of natural divisions.[27]

ECLECTIC PRESCRIPTION.   Schwab proceeded to offer an eclectic prescription for developing some sense of curriculum coherence through the accommodation of different curriculum modes and through the use of a wide range of curriculum resources. Acknowledging the limitations of seeking "invariant elements" for curriculum construction, Schwab pointed to the need to incorporate the practical mode as a guide for action under changing circumstances.[28] Here Schwab appeared to be recognizing Dewey's admonition concerning the emptiness of theory when divorced from practical considerations, along with the limitations of university scholar-specialists and their specialized disciplinary orientation to curriculum construction.[29] Schwab had come around to recognizing the consequences of what Weinberg had warned against—the divorce between the discipline-centered university and the mission-oriented society.

The recognition of the necessary function of the curriculum to facilitate communication and action, as expounded by Vaihinger early in this century, was being rediscovered in modern times. However, as discussed later in this chapter, the eclectic approach, such as the prescription offered by Schwab (and like all eclectic approaches), tends to be an admixture of elements rather than providing for the needed curriculum synthesis. As discussed later, a number of progressive educators during the first half of the twentieth century sought to identify areas of consensus in the curriculum field so as to develop a model or paradigm for the scientific and practical advancement of education. Whereas the eclectic construction is one of compromise, the function of a paradigm is one of synthesis.

PARADIGM AS KEY TO SYNTHESIS AND PROGRESS.   The notion of a paradigm for the curriculum field should not be seen as esoteric or particularly complex, but as serving as a practical model for gauging and directing our professional work so as to ensure progress. Although the curriculum paradigm is discussed in detail in the next chapter, a brief illustration is offered here regarding one of the determinants in curriculum development and its relationship with other determinants in the paradigm. That determinant is the nature of the learner. If the nature of the learner is ignored or distorted in the process of developing and implementing the curriculum, then the process will invariably go awry. Another determinant is the kind of society we stand for (and the social ideals embraced). Hence the nature of the learner will be conceived differently in a democratic society than in a totalitarian society. In a free society, there is the expectation that the curriculum will foster independent (critical) thinking in the context of democratic social responsibility (e.g., respecting the rights of others). In a totalitarian society, indoctrination is legitimized in the curriculum to ensure the subordination of the individual in service to the superior interests of the nationalistic state. Hence the very structure and function of the curriculum cannot be considered apart from these determinants and how these determinants interact (the learner, society, and the selection, organization, design, and function of the curriculum). Unfortunately, it has not been uncommon for the curriculum to be in conflict with the nature of the learner and with our democratic social ideals. We shall return to this problem throughout this text.

In short, the paradigm represents the knowledgeability of a field, in the form of models or exemplars, for revealing concrete problems and for solving these problems. The collapse of the disciplinary doctrine points to the inadequacy of any narrow approach to curriculum reform and reveals the need for a curriculum paradigm or set of paradigms rather than simply seeking compromise among incompatible elements. The paradigm enables the community of scholars and practitioners to put new prescriptions to the test of all that a field has accomplished. Thus it helps the members of the given community to anticipate problems and to avoid the temporal tides of vogue and shortsighted solutions.

UNANTICIPATED PROBLEMS.   The disciplinary doctrine, which had ruled the curriculum field for almost two decades after midcentury, eventually came to be questioned by even some of its most avid advocates who had failed to anticipate the serious problems arising from such a narrow doctrine for curriculum development. Some of the unanticipated problems were (1) an almost exclusive emphasis on puristic and abstract knowledge and a corresponding neglect of practical or applied knowledge; (2) an almost exclusive emphasis on specialized knowledge and a corresponding neglect of general education; (3) an overemphasis on isolated and compartmentalized knowledge categories and a corresponding neglect of interdisciplinary approaches in curriculum development; (4) the emergence of a curriculum hierarchy and a corresponding curriculum imbalance as those areas of knowledge most amenable to "disciplinarity" (i.e., mathematics and physics) were given priority; (5) the efforts on the part of scholars in other fields to imitate the sciences and mathematics in the search for "structure-of-the-discipline," with the result that emphasis was given to abstracting puristic concepts and neglecting personal-social problems in the social studies, literature, science (e.g., ecology, health), and performance in such areas as music and the visual arts; (6) the failure of scholars to reach agreement on the elements that constitute the structure of a discipline and their failure to demonstrate its validity as the guiding principle for curriculum development even in the university; (7) the questionable assumption that the immature learner is a miniature incarnation of the mature scholar-specialist on the forefront of his or her discipline, and the corresponding neglect of the qualitative differences in the cognitive or inquiry process that distinguish the child and adolescent from the adult; (8) the virtually exclusive emphasis on inquiry within the separate specialized domains of knowledge and the corresponding neglect of inquiry into personal-social problems; and (9) the neglect of the affective processes that are particularly significant in child and adolescent development.

The Knowledge Categories and General Education

Influenced by the doctrine of disciplinarity and the search for structure of the discipline, some educational theorists proceeded to devise schemes for classifying or categorizing areas of knowledge for general education. In so doing, it appeared that artificial and arbitrary divisions were made for the various areas of knowledge. For example, in his schema Phenix ascribed esthetics to the arts (music, the visual arts, literature, and dance) "in contrast to the sciences which are concerned with abstract cognitive understanding." Phenix proceeded to ascribe ethics to another separate realm of knowledge, while he classified the sciences under "empirics."[30] Here Phenix revealed his profound lack of understanding of how virtually all areas of knowledge, from machine tool design to physics, biology, architecture, and all fields of engineering embrace esthetics. Indeed esthetics played a role in the discovery of DNA when the researchers, working with spheroid models, hypothesized that nature seeks symmetry.[31]

The validity of knowledge categories as construed by Phenix and other curricularists cited previously must be questioned not only because nature knows no such departments of knowledge. (Indeed, some of our most profound modern scientific breakthroughs have been made through interdisciplinary inquiry.) The validity of such categories must be questioned because the paramount curriculum problem in general education has not been that of construing the separate boundaries of the disciplines, but of revealing the vital interdependence of knowledge for the improvement of the human condition. Consequently, we must ask: Are the social sciences, natural sciences, and literature logically separated from ethics? The Nobel laureate Jacques Monod pointed out that the very principle of objectivity in science serves to define a value, and one's adherence to this principle is a basic statement of an ethical principle[32]—for it rejects blind authority, superstition, or mere tradition. Are the arts and literature the exclusive or paramount realms of aesthetic experience? Are the sciences merely based on empirics? Creative acts in the sciences are not devoid of aesthetic and emotional experiences. Moreover, although the areas of choice in science are not the same as those of fictional literature, science involves dimensions of inquiry, in the words of Einstein, "which are no longer directly connected with sense experience."[33] To reduce science to a category of empirics is a caricature of the meaning of science. Moreover, to ascribe symbolics and empirics to separate realms appears to make for an artificial division not only because science makes intricate use of mathematics and symbolic language, but also because science utilizes concepts and language of a supernational character.[34]

Moreover, Phenix's notion that all subject matter be drawn from the disciplines raises a host of other problems. As modes of specialized knowledge, the disciplines appear to be more suited to specialized education than general education. There are so many specialized knowledge domains that lay claim to being disciplines that the task of putting the separate disciplines together for a coherent curriculum in general education becomes virtually insurmountable. Even in his espousal of the disciplinary doctrine, Phenix did not follow this to its logical conclusion. Instead of interpreting his "realms" in terms of the discrete disciplines, he interpreted them primarily in terms of broad fields—such as physical science, social science, visual arts, and so on.

By eventually retreating from the disciplinary doctrine, Phenix and Schwab had come to recognize the need for various modes or frameworks of curriculum organization—ranging from crossdisciplinary or correlational approaches, to interdisciplinary approaches—to make the curriculum relevant to life and to keep it from collapsing of its own weight.

A schema similar to that offered by Phenix was proposed by Broudy, Smith, and Burnett in which aesthetic experience is delimited to exemplars in art, music, drama, and literature. But we must ask, are there not exemplars in the sciences, architecture, and technology? Why are the modes of aesthetic experience limited to the four exemplars? Why are the basic sciences separated from what Broudy, Smith, and Burnett categorize as "developmental studies" ("evaluation of the cosmos")?

Why is there a separate category for the basic sciences and not one for the social sciences? Broudy, Smith, and Burnett acknowledge that their schema makes no specific provisions for performance in music, literature, drama, and the visual arts, and they justify this on the ground that performance in these areas has been provided in the elementary school.[35] Consequently, the exemplars are conceived for studying *about* various artistic works for purposes of aesthetic appreciation rather than for aesthetic creation. Justification for this separation between appreciating and creating smacks of the medieval dualism of mind and matter, thought and action—a dualism that runs counter to human development and experience. The category of molar problems or typical social problems, along with the category of developmental studies, appears to offer significant opportunities for curriculum synthesis. But when performance is deprecated in favor of appreciation, it is doubtful that adolescents will gain the level of appreciation expected, for they are denied the opportunity of concertedly engaging in the act of doing, or making, or creating. Such separation would appear to work against appreciation as a function of general education.

As noted, the penchant in academia for creating so many separations of knowledge into distinct categories and jurisdictions, as opposed to building on the interdependence of knowledge, appears to be a reflection of the departmentalized and specialized structure of the university. The aforementioned examples are not unusual but typical of the segmental mindset. At times, proposals for demarcating knowledge categories go to such extremes as if to set boundaries on all sorts of artificial turfs to be protected from intrusion. One recently proposed schema designates a special knowledge typology for radical leftist ideology, and makes no provision for scientific modes of inquiry. In effect, such radical ideology in academia is not to be tested in the light of the fullest available evidence, but is to be granted a special immunity on the grounds that it resides as a special type of knowledge, as opposed to "main-stream academic knowledge."[36] Under such circumstances there is the danger that what is passed for knowledge might be little more than dogma.

TO FACILITATE COMMUNICATION AND ACTION.   However logically the curriculum categories may be construed (and the aforementioned approaches raise serious questions as to their logicality), they need to be justified on psychological and practical grounds. Furthermore, the categories should be recognized as fictional constructs—designed to facilitate communication and action. The test of their validity lies in how effectively they do this. It appears that the preceding schemes for classifying areas of knowledge for the curriculum fall short on all of these grounds.

The traditional approach has been to conceive of general education as composed of the following three broad areas of knowledge: natural science, social science, and the humanities.[37] However, even those comprehensive divisions necessarily disappear under practical conditions. For example, the concern for the environment gives rise to the study of ecology—a study that bridges the natural sciences and social sciences. Only tradition separates the humanities from the natural sciences, for if the humanities exemplify the great human achievements and moral concerns, how can they exclude science and technology? Yet as Monod pointed out, modern societies have accepted the treasures and powers of science without accepting science as a source of truth that demands a thorough revision of ethical premises. "Armed with all the powers, enjoying all the riches they owe to science, our societies are still trying to live by and teach systems of values already blasted at the root by science itself."[38] The consequence has been a widening split or inner division in our culture—leading to two cultures in conflict.[39] Although the world of academia has contributed to this dualism, it is uniquely endowed to develop the needed synthesis; more than any other institution, its chief function is the reconstruction of knowledge for the improvement of society.[40]

The Macrocurriculum—Complementary Functions

In view of the virtually infinite number of knowledge categories that can be construed to comprise the curriculum, it may be more useful to see the curriculum in terms of five comprehensive and complementary functions: (1) general education, (2) specialized education, (3) exploratory education, (4) enrichment education, and (5) special-interest education. These paradigmatic functions are shown in Figure 6–1. Various approaches to organizing knowledge are developed in connection with the five functions. The approaches may be disciplinary, crossdisciplinary, multidisciplinary, interdisciplinary, or even directly experiential.

Figure 6–1. The Five Complementary Functions of the Macrocurriculum.

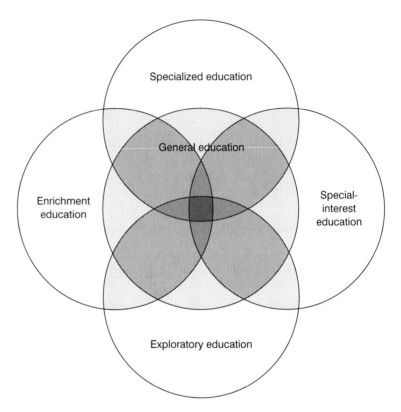

Source: Adapted from Daniel Tanner, *Secondary Education: Perspectives and Prospects.* New York: Macmillan, 1972, p. 319; and Daniel Tanner and Laurel Tanner, *Supervision in Education: Problems and Practices.* New York: Macmillan, 1987, p. 428.

General education may be regarded as that part of the curriculum designed to provide for a common universe of discourse, understanding, and competence. General education is ordinarily referred to as the *common core,* or that part of the curriculum in school or college that is required of all students.

Because disciplinary knowledge is a product of knowledge specialization, and because so many of the knowledge specialties lay claim to being disciplines, the disciplinary mode has been regarded by many educators as more suitable for specialized education than for general education. Specialized education is ordinarily regarded as representing the student's major field or his or her preprofessional, professional, prevocational, and vocational studies. Exploratory education is intended to enable the student to investigate and extend inquiry into areas that the student might consider as a possible field for specialization or career preparation.

Enrichment education is intended to supplement, broaden, and deepen the learner's educative experience. Exploratory, enrichment, and special-interest education may be provided through the free or controlled election of formal courses, as well as through participation in the student activities program.

The various curriculum functions are complementary or interdependent. General education should facilitate and illuminate all other curriculum functions. Exploratory and enrichment education often serve to influence a student's decisions regarding specialized education, and so on. Curriculum balance and coherence require that these functions be taken into account in ecological relationship. The lines between and among the five macrocurricular functions must be fluid and functional. This is the imperative of the macrocurriculum.

THE POWER OF PARADIGMS

In Chapter 5, it was shown how the differing definitions of curriculum reflect the great changes that have occurred in the twentieth century concerning the conception and function of curriculum. It was also noted in Chapter 5 that there is considerable debate among curricularists concerning the definition of curriculum. Some curricularists contend that there can be little conceptual progress in the field unless common agreement on definition is reached.

The question of definition has been a matter of concern in the various social sciences for some time. However, Thomas Kuhn has stressed that conceptual progress is not derived from agreement on definition, but from problem solving.[41] Kuhn contends that the concern for definition tends to conceal the truly profound questions as to why certain fields fail to progress as do other fields, and what changes in thought and method are needed to facilitate progress. The question of definition will be seen as irrelevant when the various conflicting and self-doubting schools of thought achieve consensus regarding their past and present accomplishments. Such consensus is the basis for a paradigm or set of paradigms essential for making a concerted attack on problem solutions, and thereby advancing knowledge in the field.

Conflicting Schools of Thought and Shifting Grounds

Kuhn's criticisms concerning the propensity of social scientists to be obsessed with matters such as the proper definition of their fields is not made in derision. Nor is he saying that there is no room for disputation if progress is to be made. His point is that the social sciences are beset by many conflicting schools and lack the paradigms needed to synthesize past achievements with present activity and to provide for further progress through ongoing concrete problem solutions. Hence social scientists either tend to hold allegiance to various schools that often behave like warring factions or, at the other extreme, they shift their ground all too easily in accordance with the dominant trends in the field or the demands of the wider social situation. The consequence is that old ground is constantly being exhumed or that novel tides and superficial fashions are taken for progress.

Thus Kuhn contends that progress in the social sciences is impeded by the tendency of social scientists to put more energy into factional disputation than into efforts toward synthesizing knowledge for the purpose of solving substantive problems, the tendency to ride the dominant tide of the times, and the tendency to shift their ground in research for the sake of expedience. Examples of such events are all too numerous. Myrdal has given this problem concerted attention in *Objectivity in Social Research*.[42] Some of our most eminent social scientists contribute to this problem. For example, the influence of the wider social situation on the interpretation of research is reflected in Coleman's shifts in interpreting the implications of his own research for school desegregation. At one point he strongly advocated reducing the social and racial homogeneity of the school, whereas only a few years later he contended that there was not sufficient evidence to preclude the possibility that the benefits derived from reducing this homogeneity might be obtained by other means.[43] Or take, for example, Bruner's influential pronouncement in one era that the chief educational problem stems from our neglect of the top quarter of our students (our future intellectual leaders), whereas in a subsequent era he fixed the chief problem on our neglect of children at the bottom. In one era, Bruner offered us the disciplinary curriculum prescription; in a subsequent era he discarded this prescription in favor of social relevance of the curriculum.[44] Where curricularists all too readily embraced disciplinarity as the ruling doctrine for curriculum development during the late 1950s and most of the 1960s, they readily abandoned this doctrine by the late 1960s in favor of curriculum relevance as a response to the rising social protest and disaffection. By the mid-1970s the tide of relevance had yielded to the demand for curriculum retrenchment by returning to the "fundamentals" or "essentials."

By the latter 1980s it was becoming increasingly evident that the narrow-minded curriculum fundamentalism had resulted in declines in thinking and writing proficiency, as well as neglecting the macrocurricular functions. Basic education could not fulfill the profound function of general education (that universe of discourse, understanding, and competence necessary for effective citizenship in a free society). Moreover, the macrocurricular functions of exploration, enrichment, special-interest, and specialization were treated as "nonessential," leaving the schools with a curriculum of poverty and much emphasis on "drill-skill-kill" through worksheets and workbooks. As discussed earlier, from the late 1980s and into the 1990s the call was for curriculum synthesis, higher-order thinking, and curriculum balance. Various professional associations were rediscovering much of what had been found out and advanced by earlier generations of experimentalist-progressive educators.[45] Unfortunately, instead of building on the rich body of knowledge in the curriculum field, the rediscovery was taking place in all too many instances as though the ideas and practices were derived from new discoveries.

Coupled with the tendency for curriculum shifts to reflect the dominant shifts in the sociopolitical tides are the disputations in the social sciences and education reflecting differences of specialization and sociopolitical/philosophical orientation. Taken together, these factors make conceptual progress and improved practice very difficult. Hence, for example, leading figures such as B. F. Skinner would not recognize that various systematic positions are making valuable contributions and that no one position, such as behaviorism, represents the totality of human nature.[46] Under such circumstances, the quest for some coherence in the foundations of the social sciences is thwarted and precludes the possibility of the emergence of paradigms for progress in theory and practice.

Contemporary behaviorists have sought to seek some accommodation with cognitive-developmental psychology, which had virtually eclipsed behaviorism since midcentury as a result of advancements in the study of human behavior. Nevertheless, many aspects of behaviorism are incompatible with the holistic cognitive-developmental psychology, so that eclectic combinations are often contradictory. Ironically, the schools remain mired in many respects in the mold of the drill-skill repertoires of behaviorism with the cheap pedagogical instruments of worksheets, workbooks, and mechanistic testing. The school continues to suffer this incompatibility.

The Development of Paradigms

Virtually every professional field is governed by systems of principles, exemplars, models, and procedural techniques that serve to advance the knowledge and practice of the field. Taken together, these systems of principles, exemplars, and techniques are referred to as paradigms. Professional fields also utilize these paradigms in the preparation of future practitioners.

Although Chapter 7 is devoted to tracing the professionalization of the curriculum field as related to the development of a curriculum paradigm by experimentalist-progressives during the first half of the twentieth century, some discussion of the paradigm concept is presented here because it is so vitally connected with key problems already addressed, such as those relating to knowledge eclosion and synthesis, the macrocurriculum (e.g., the relationship between general education and specialism), and the need to build on our professional body of knowledge and advancing that knowledge through problem solving.

Since the appearance of Thomas Kuhn's *Structure of Scientific Revolutions* (1962, 1970), there has been a growing body of literature on the significance of paradigms in scholarly inquiry. Unfortunately, some of the literature has treated the paradigm concept in esoteric and excessively complex ways. Kuhn and others have held that the social sciences still remain in a preparadigm stage, in contrast to the natural sciences and mathematics. This may indeed be the case, but it nevertheless does not diminish the significance of the efforts and accomplishments in seeking to develop problem-solving models to advance our knowledge in the social sciences, including the field of education and the curriculum.

With regard to the obsession with agreement on definitions in the social sciences, Kuhn contends that verbal definitions have little meaning by themselves, other than serving as pedagogic aids. The concepts to which they point gain full significance only in the context of the interactions of phenomena, methodology, and paradigm applications.[47]

In describing how those concerned with natural phenomena adopt the simplest conceptual scheme into which the complex elements of raw experience can be fitted and arranged, Conant endorsed the view that "it is meaningless to inquire into the absolute correctness of a conceptual scheme as a mirror of reality."[48] Conant went on to show how, even in the sciences, the same term will acquire radically different meanings according to the context in which it is used. Consequently, the lack of agreement on a definition is, in and of itself, not a fruitful issue because it diverts us from far more profound concerns, such as those connected with paradigms and paradigm applications.

Kuhn describes paradigms as the entire constellation of beliefs, values, and techniques shared by a given scientific community and employed by that community as models or exemplars for denoting concrete puzzle solutions that are the basis for the solution of other puzzles or problems. "The study of paradigms," notes Kuhn, "is what mainly prepares the student for membership in the particular scientific community with which he will later practice."[49] A paradigm or set of paradigms constitutes what members of scientific communities share in common in accounting for the relative fullness of their professional communication and the relative unanimity of their professional judgments. A paradigm is not a mere compromise or eclectic representation, but a consensual model or exemplar for problem solutions. It is a synthesis of modes of thought and methodology of a field that makes progress possible through substantive problem solving.

The preparadigm period in any community of scholars is marked by "deep debates over legitimate methods, problems, and standards of solution, though these serve rather to define schools than to produce agreement."[50] The conflicting schools vie with one another for allegiance and only disappear when paradigms are developed.

From Kuhn's analysis, it appears that the social sciences, including the curriculum field, are struggling to emerge from the preparadigm period. Bochner is more sanguine about this emergence. In a chapter called "Psychology and Pedagogy," he relates how the conflicting schools were largely outgrown by the third decade of the twentieth century as it became increasingly difficult not to recognize that different schools and systematic positions were all making significant contributions.[51] Although at times the void between the behaviorist and humanist schools is so great that the situation tends more toward opposition than accommodation, the key issue regarding behaviorism, for example, needs to be directed at questioning its viability as a comprehensive theory of human behavior rather than whether or not humans can be conditioned.

Paradigm-Based Fields and the Value of the Textbook

Kuhn goes to some lengths to discuss the importance of the textbook as a pedagogical tool in fields that are paradigm-based, such as the natural sciences. "These textbooks expound the body of accepted theory, illustrate many or all of its successful applications, and compare these applications with exemplary observations and experiments."[52] Not until the very last stages in the education of a scientist, observes Kuhn, is the textbook supplemented or replaced by the actual scientific literature on which the textbook has systematically organized the knowledge of the field. "Given the confidence in their paradigms, which makes the educational technique possible," continues Kuhn, "few scientists would wish to change it." Accordingly, "one cannot help but notice that in general it has been immensely effective," he concludes.[53] Kuhn is not contending that the textbook is the only proper pedagogical device or that it is immune from abuse. Instead he points to it as a key means of initiation to the systematic organization of knowledge and paradigms in mature fields of scholarship. Kuhn contrasts the role of the textbook in the natural sciences with other fields, including the social sciences, in which textbooks play a less decisive role. In the social sciences and education, most notably during the late 1960s and early 1970s when "relevance" was the ruling slogan, it was not uncommon for college professors to use popular literature on *au courant* topics as substitutes for textbooks and the systematic treatment of organized knowledge and practice in their fields. Best-sellers such as *Crisis in the Classroom,* written by the journalist Charles Silberman,[54] were being used with other popular readings in the place of textbooks in courses ranging from curriculum to educational administration and educational sociology, with the result that some college students were required to read identical material in different courses. (As a journalist, Silberman readily turned his interest to another topic, namely criminal violence and the justice system, when he was "finished" with education.)[55]

Although it is difficult to imagine a student of chemistry, physics, biological science, engineering, medicine, mathematics, or law without having the benefit of textbooks, it is not uncommon to this day to find some faculty in the social sciences actually boasting that they have discarded the use of textbooks. A sociology professor, for example, boasts that she has been teaching sociology to undergraduates for ten years without textbooks.[56]

There is no question that it is helpful and often necessary to supplement the textbook with current materials and primary source materials, but if there is a systematic knowledge base in a field, a good text should serve as a key vehicle for helping the student develop in understanding and competence through the systematic exposure to the knowledge base. The use of *au courant* materials to promote temporarily fashionable topics and practices, and neglecting to benefit from and build on the vast body of professional knowledge and practice, finds both neophytes and veteran practitioners repeatedly rediscovering the wheel and repeating errors of the past. Thus we find that the rediscovered practices of the early 1990s—such as writing across the curriculum, higher-order thinking, heterogeneous grouping or student inclusion, and curriculum articulation and synthesis—are being promoted without benefit of the vast and rich knowledge base of the curriculum field.[57]

GENERAL EDUCATION AND SPECIALIZED EDUCATION. It should be recognized that, even in the strongly paradigm-based field of physical science, the material encompassed in the textbook allows for different orientations depending, for example, on whether the textbook is designed to prepare the student as a physicist or to serve the function of general education. In the latter case, there is more of a tendency to include biographies and some illustrative material from the works of the great physicists and to treat some of the great disputations in the evolution of physics along with practical applications.[58] This is justified on the ground that, for most students, the general education course in physical science may be the only systematic encounter with the field, and hence such material cannot be postponed as in the case of the education of the future physicist. Of greater significance is the fact that the function of general education requires a qualitatively different treatment as well as organization of scope and sequence of subject matter. To study physical science for purposes of becoming a physicist is very different from studying it to become an enlightened member of society. The general education course not only should reveal the most significant relationships between the field under study and the wider society, but also be made relevant to the life of the learner. Such considerations have resulted in the development of broad-fields courses and textbooks in physical science and natural science, whereas the future physical scientist will be exposed to specialized courses in physics, chemistry, and so on. But this does not mean that the future physical scientist should not engage in study of his or her field from the vantage point of general education because that function is uniquely different from the specialization function. The former looks to the education of the student not as a future scientist, but as a citizen.

It is not by accident that the idea and practice of general education and the search for a common core have been advanced in the United States more than in any other nation. In an age of knowledge specialism and in a multicultural society committed to democratic ideals, the incessant forces for fragmentation and the conflicting special interests have affected the school and college curriculum. A free society not only requires specialism and the divisions of labor, but also the interdependence of specialties and a sense of mutual interest, respect, and common cause.

PERSPECTIVE

Educational institutions are constantly engaged in curriculum decisions without giving corresponding attention to curriculum as a subject of thought. The expansion of knowledge and the growing specialization of knowledge have given rise to various domains and divisions of knowledge for the purpose of making knowledge more comprehensible and useful, or to facilitate communication and action. But this purpose has often been lost in the seemingly endless multiplicity of subject matters and the compartmentalization of specialized knowledge. Relatively little thought has been given to the curriculum beyond the compartmentalized and specialized domains. The consequence has been curriculum fragmentation, imbalance, and incoherence. Within each knowledge compartment or organizational component, new courses are added, old courses are modified, and occasionally a course is actually deleted in favor of a new course. The process is one of accretion, modification, multiplication, and deletion rather than of curriculum development and reconstruction. The focus is on the microcurriculum to the neglect of the macrocurriculum. As a result, in the face of knowledge specialization, the need for knowledge synthesis has been neglected along with the need for using knowledge to address pervading life problems.

The competing, self-serving knowledge domains have created a two-culture split—a conflict between science and the humanities. The separation of science as a mode of thought from other affairs of life is manifested in the continuing and renewed fascination with superstition, mysticism, the occult, and other forms of escape. It has diverted the human race from fully utilizing science and the fruits of technology to improve the human condition. The repair of this divorce rests with the university and the school—those special institutions uniquely endowed to engage in the continual and systematic reconstruction of knowledge as represented in what has come to be called the *curriculum.*

In the absence of a paradigm or set of paradigms to synthesize past achievements with contemporary activity, and to provide the means for making progress through ongoing problem solutions, the curriculum field has been buffeted by shifting demands and trends. In one era the call is for disciplinarity. The reaction to the excesses of disciplinarity then gives rise to a call for relevance. The reaction to the excesses of relevance is succeeded by a call for back to the basics. Each successive call for reform is a reaction to the excesses of its preceding reform movement. The result is movement but not progress. Innovations are adopted, discarded, and reinvented like changing fashions. Rather than being conceived and implemented for substantive problem solving, they more often represent cosmetic changes or the inconsequential manipulation of managerial arrangements.

If the twentieth century is the Age of Synthesis, as some scholars maintain, curricularists will have to think less about the alleged knowledge explosion and more about the problems explosion. A concerted focus on substantive problems will require a movement toward synthesis in the curriculum field. Far more energy has been expended in the curriculum field for resurrecting old disputations and inventing new causes for disputation rather than for substantive problem solving. The curriculum field has a rich heritage of past achievements that can lend perspective to the contemporary educational situation and thereby serve as a basis for consensus and progress.

PROBLEMS FOR STUDY
AND DISCUSSION

1. It has been pointed out that many institutions other than schools and universities perform important educative functions. How do the school and the university differ from these other institutions in their treatment of knowledge and in the performance of educative functions?

2. It is contended that it is uncommon for the collegiate community to concertedly examine its thinking about the curriculum, although it is engaged in concerted thought within the different knowledge specializations. What is your assessment of this allegation in the light of your own experiences as a college student? To what extent do teachers and administrators engage in such thought? To what extent is such thought conveyed to students?

3. In connection with your response to the preceding problem, would you say that educators have devoted more attention to microcurricular con-

cerns than to macrocurricular concerns? If so, how do you account for this, and what implications has this had for curriculum development in the school and university? If not, explain your position.

4. A traditional educational position holds that actual performance, or doing, or constructing something is not as important as studying *about* the subject in question. Proponents of this position contend, for example, that the study of art appreciation is more educative than "doing" art. What are your views on this issue? Is this issue extant in the sciences as it is in the arts? Why or why not?

5. What are the implications of knowledge eclosion and synthesis for curriculum development?

6. A British educator observed in 1974 that "[e]ven a cursory glance at contemporary proposals for curriculum reform serves to show that ideas of cur-

riculum integration are immensely popular." [Paul H. Hirst, *Knowledge and the Curriculum* (London: Routledge, 1974), p. 132.] Would you say that this statement characterizes present-day proposals for curriculum reform in the United States? Explain.

7. In connection with the shifting tides of curriculum reform, it was noted in this chapter that this has led to much movement but little progress in solving pervading problems. What are your views on this analysis?

8. Do you agree with the position of the authors of this text that different functions of the curriculum require different modes or frameworks of curriculum organization (i.e., general education as contrasted with specialized education)? Explain.

9. At the height of the discipline-centered curriculum reforms, some educators contended that the criterion of disciplinarity is the only adequate criterion for determining the subject matters that comprise the curriculum. What is your assessment of this position?

NOTES

1. John Dewey, *Democracy and Education* (New York: Macmillan, 1916), p. 11.
2. Hans Vaihinger, *The Philosophy of "As If,"* 2nd ed. (London: Routledge, 1935), pp. 17, 170–172. (Originally published in Germany in 1911.)
3. Dewey, op. cit., p. 10.
4. Alfred North Whitehead, *The Aims of Education* (New York: Macmillan, 1929), pp. 10–11.
5. Ivan Illich, *Deschooling Society* (New York: Harper, 1971).
6. Dewey, op. cit., pp. 109, 131–138.
7. Alvin M. Weinberg, *Reflections on Big Science* (Cambridge, MA: M.I.T. Press, 1967), p. 117.
8. George F. Madaus and Mary M. West, *The Influence of Testing on Teaching Math and Science in Grades 4–12.* Chestnut Hill, MA: Center for the Study of Testing, 1992.
9. Bentley Glass. *The Timely and the Timeless* (New York: Basic Books, 1970), pp. 39, 44.
10. Joseph J. Schwab, "The Concept of the Structure of a Discipline," *The Educational Records,* 43 (July 1962), p. 200.
11. Salomon Bochner, *Eclosion and Synthesis: Perspectives on the History of Knowledge* (New York: W. A. Benjamin, 1969).
12. Ibid., p. 28.
13. Glass, op. cit., p. 72.
14. John Walsh, "A Conversation with Eugene Wigner," *Science,* 181 (August 10, 1973), p. 533.
15. Weinberg, op. cit., pp. 161, 163.
16. Donella H. Meadows, Dennis L. Meadows, Jørgen Randers, and William W. Beherns III, *The Limits of Growth* (New York: Universe, 1972), pp. 154, 156, 183–184.

17. "Committee on Science in the Promotion of Human Welfare." *AAAS Bulletin,* 18 (December–January, 1974), p. 2.
18. Bentley Glass, "Science: Endless Horizons or Golden Age?" *Science,* 171 (January 8, 1971), p. 26.
19. American Association for the Advancement of Science, *Science for ALL Americans* (Washington, DC: Author, 1989); National Science Teachers Association, *The Core Content* (Washington, DC: Author, 1992).
20. Albert Einstein, *Out of My Later Years* (New York: Philosophical Library, 1950), p. 32.
21. Joseph J. Schwab, *College Curriculum and Student Protest* (Chicago: University of Chicago Press, 1969), p. 246.
22. John I. Goodlad, *A Place Called School* (New York: McGraw-Hill, 1984), pp. 183–186.
23. Walter Schneir and Miriam Schneir, "The Joy of Learning—In the Open Corridor," *The New York Times Magazine* (April 4, 1971), pp. 30–31.
24. Philip H. Phenix, *Realms of Meaning* (New York: McGraw-Hill, 1964), p. 10.
25. Joseph J. Schwab, in Stanley Elam (ed.), *Education and the Structure of Knowledge* (Chicago: Rand McNally, 1964), p. 7.
26. Philip H. Phenix, "The Moral Imperative in Contemporary Education," *Perspectives on Education,* 2 (Winter 1969), p. 13.
27. Schwab, *College Curriculum,* op. cit., pp. 240–241.
28. Joseph J. Schwab, *The Practical: A Language for Curriculum* (Washington, DC: National Education Association, 1970), pp. 2–5, 19.

29. Dewey, op. cit., pp. 156–159.
30. Phenix, *Realms,* op. cit., pp. 7, 61.
31. James D. Watson, *The Double Helix* (New York: Atheneum Press, 1968).
32. Jacques Monod, *Chance and Necessity* (New York: Vintage, 1972), p. 176.
33. See Jacob Bronowski, *The Origins of Knowledge and Imagination* (New Haven, CT: Yale University Press, 1978).
34. Albert Einstein, op. cit., p. 72.
35. Harry S. Broudy, B. Othanel Smith, and Joe R. Burnett, *Democracy and Excellence in American Secondary Education* (Chicago: Rand McNally, 1964), pp. 247, 270.
36. James A. Banks, "The Canon Debate," *Educational Researcher,* 22 (June–July 1993), p. 7.
37. Report of the Harvard Committee, *General Education in a Free Society* (Cambridge, MA: Harvard University Press, 1945), pp. 56–59.
38. Monod, op. cit., pp. 170–171.
39. See John Dewey, *Human Nature and Conduct* (New York: Holt, 1922), pp. 11, 13; C. P. Snow, *The Two Cultures and the Scientific Revolution* (New York: Cambridge University Press, 1959).
40. Daniel Tanner, "Knowledge Divided against Itself." *Bulletin of the Atomic Scientists,* 39 (March 1983), pp. 34–38.
41. Thomas S. Kuhn, *The Structure of Scientific Revolutions,* 2nd ed. (Chicago: University of Chicago Press, 1970), pp. 160–161.
42. Gunnar Myrdal, *Objectivity in Social Research* (New York: Pantheon, 1969).
43. James S. Coleman, "Equal Schools or Equal Students?" *The Public Interest* (Summer 1966), p. 74; "Coleman on the Coleman Report," *Educational Researcher,* 1 (March 1972), p. 13.
44. Jerome S. Bruner, *The Process of Education* (Cambridge, MA: Harvard University Press, 1960), pp. 10, 17–32; "The Process of Education Revisited," *Phi Delta Kappan,* 53 (September 1971), pp. 18–21.
45. "Integrating the Curriculum," theme issue of *Educational Leadership,* 49 (October 1991).
46. B. F. Skinner, *Beyond Freedom and Dignity* (New York: Knopf, 1971).
47. Kuhn, op. cit., p. 142.
48. James B. Conant, *Two Modes of Thought* (New York: Trident, 1964), pp. 14–15.
49. Kuhn, op. cit., pp. 11, 175, 182.
50. Ibid., pp. 47–48.
51. Bochner, op. cit., p. 75.
52. Kuhn, op. cit., p. 10.
53. Ibid., p. 165.
54. Charles E. Silberman, *Crisis in the Classroom* (New York: Random House, 1970).
55. Charles E. Silberman, *Criminal Violence, Criminal Justice* (New York: Random House, 1978).
56. Mary F. Rogers, "Confessions of a Reformed Textbook Junkie," *Chronicle of Higher Education,* 33 (February 4, 1987), pp. 36–37.
57. Daniel Tanner, "A Brief Historical Perspective of the Struggle for an Integrative Curriculum," *Educational Horizons,* 68 (Fall 1989), pp. 6–11; Daniel Tanner, "The Curriculum Frontier," *Social Education,* 54 (April/May 1990), pp. 195–197.
58. Harvard Project Physics is an example, although it neglects practical applications.

SELECTED REFERENCES

American Association for the Advancement of Science. *Science for All Americans, Project 2061.* Washington, DC: Author, 1989.

Association of American Colleges. *Integrity in the College Curriculum.* Washington, DC: Author, 1985.

Belth, Marc. *Education as a Discipline.* Boston: Allyn and Bacon, 1965.

Bochner, Salomon. *Eclosion and Synthesis: Perspectives on the History of Knowledge.* New York: W. A. Benjamin, 1969.

Bode, Boyd H. *Modern Educational Theories.* New York: Macmillan, 1927.

Boyer, Ernest L. *High School: A Report on Secondary Education in America.* New York: Harper and Row, 1983.

Boyer, Ernest L., and Levine, Arthur. *A Quest for Common Learning: The Aims of General Education.* Washington, DC: Carnegie Foundation for the Advancement of Teaching, 1981.

Bronowski, Jacob. *The Origins of Knowledge and Imagination.* New Haven, CT: Yale University Press, 1978.

Broudy, Harry S., Smith, B. Othanel, and Burnett, Joe R. *Democracy and Excellence in American Secondary Education.* Chicago: Rand McNally, 1964.

Bruner, Jerome S. *The Process of Education.* Cambridge, MA: Harvard University Press, 1960.

Cohen, I. Bernard. *Revolution in Science.* Cambridge, MA: Harvard University Press, 1985.

Commission on the Reorganization of Secondary Education. *Cardinal Principles of Secondary Education.* Washington, DC: U.S. Bureau of Education, 1918.

Conant, James B. *Two Modes of Thought.* New York: Trident Press, 1964.

Cremin, Lawrence A. *Public Education.* New York: Basic Books, 1976.

Dewey, John. *Democracy and Education.* New York: Macmillan, 1916.

Dewey, John. *The School and Society/The Child and the Curriculum.* Chicago: University of Chicago, 1900, 1915/1902; combined edition, 1990.

Dewey, John. *The Sources of a Science Education.* New York: Liveright, 1929.

Giles, H. H., McCutchen, S. P., and Zechiel, A. N. *Exploring the Curriculum.* New York: Harper, 1942.

Glass, Bentley. *The Timely and the Timeless.* New York: Basic Books, 1970.

Grant, Gerald, and Riesman, David. *The Perpetual Dream: Reform and Experiment in the American College.* Chicago: University of Chicago Press, 1978.

Harap, Henry, Chairman, Joint Committee on Curriculum. *The Changing Curriculum.* New York: D. Appleton-Century, 1937.

Hirst, Paul H. *Knowledge and the Curriculum.* London: Routledge & Kegan Paul, 1974.

Inglis, Alexander. *Principles of Secondary Education.* Boston: Houghton Mifflin, 1918.

Jackson, Philip W. (ed.), *Handbook of Research on Curriculum.* New York: Macmillan, 1992.

King, Arthur R., Jr., and Brownell, John A. *The Curriculum and the Disciplines of Knowledge.* New York: John Wiley & Sons, 1966.

Kuhn, Thomas S. *The Structure of Scientific Revolutions,* 2nd ed. Chicago: University of Chicago Press, 1970.

Lakatos, Imre, and Musgrave, Alan (eds.). *Criticism and the Growth of Knowledge.* Cambridge, MA: Harvard University Press, 1970.

Myrdal, Gunnar. *Objectivity in Social Research.* New York: Pantheon, 1969.

National Society for the Study of Education. *Critical Issues in Curriculum.* Eighty-seventh Yearbook, Part I. Chicago: University of Chicago Press, 1988.

National Society for the Study of Education. *Curriculum Making: Past and Present.* Twenty-sixth Yearbook, Part I. Bloomington, IL: Public School Publishing, 1926.

National Society for the Study of Education. *The Foundations of Curriculum-Making.* Twenty-sixth Yearbook, Part II. Bloomington, IL: Public School Publishing, 1926.

Phenix, Philip H. *Realms of Meaning.* New York: McGraw-Hill, 1964.

Planck, Max. *Scientific Autobiography and Other Papers.* New York: Philosophical Library, 1949.

Report of the Harvard Committee. *General Education in a Free Society.* Cambridge, MA: Harvard University Press, 1945.

Schwab, Joseph J. *The College Curriculum and Student Protest.* Chicago: University of Chicago Press, 1969.

Schwab, Joseph J. *The Practical: A Language for Curriculum.* Washington, DC: National Education Association, 1970.

Skinner, B. F. *Beyond Freedom and Dignity.* New York: Alfred A. Knopf, 1971.

Smith, B. Othanel, Stanley, William O., and Shores, J. Harlan. *Fundamentals of Curriculum Development,* rev. ed. New York: Harcourt Brace Publishers, 1957.

Snow, C. P. *The Two Cultures and the Scientific Revolution.* New York: Cambridge University Press, 1959.

Taba, Hilda. *Curriculum Development: Theory and Practice.* New York: Harcourt Brace Publishers, 1962.

Tanner, Daniel. "Curriculum History," in Harold E. Mitzel (ed.), *Encyclopedia of Educational Research,* 5th ed. New York: The Free Press, 1982.

Tanner, Daniel, and Tanner, Laurel. *History of the School Curriculum.* New York: Macmillan, 1990.

Tyler, Ralph W. *Basic Principles of Curriculum and Instruction.* Chicago: University of Chicago Press, 1949.

Vaihinger, Hans. *The Philosophy of "As If."* 2nd ed., trans. by C. K. Ogden. London: Routledge & Kegan Paul, 1935.

Whitehead, Alfred North. *The Aims of Education.* New York: Macmillan, 1929.

Wittrock, Merlin C., ed. *Handbook of Research on Teaching,* 3rd ed. New York: Macmillan, 1986.

CHAPTER 7

A PARADIGM FOR THE CURRICULUM FIELD

The maturity of a field of scholarship is characterized by a struggle to find unity; the formative years are characterized by fragmentation and disputation. The struggle for unity is not aimed at building conformity or eliminating diversity, but at enhancing comprehensibility. In this effort, the specifics of analysis yield to the interrelations of synthesis. Specification yields to generalization. The practical world of experience becomes more comprehensible and manageable.

THE ROUTE TOWARD A PARADIGM FOR THE CURRICULUM FIELD

In the preceding chapters, some discussion was devoted to two theses: (1) Bochner's belief that in the various fields of inquiry, including education, eclosion of knowledge has given way to synthesis during the twentieth century;[1] and (2) Kuhn's belief that the sense of community for any group of practitioners derives from a paradigm or set of paradigms that governs their work by accounting for the relative fullness of their professional communication and consensus. The paradigm or set of paradigms denotes not only the entire constellation of beliefs, values, and techniques shared by the members of the community of practitioners but also the employment of concrete problem solutions as models for solving other problems.[2] The paradigm or set of paradigms does not eliminate debate or disagreement in a field but provides for a consensual basis of community and fullness so as to enhance communication and progress.

In this chapter, the efforts to develop a paradigm for the curriculum field are examined in connection with the practical world of curriculum development.

Systematic Curriculum Development

The rise of experimentalist thought during the early decades of the twentieth century called for the assessment of educational practices through more rigorous intellectual forms. Dewey pointed out that although traditional schools could set great store in standardized tests and measurements, progressive schools were faced with the more complex task of organizing and assessing qualitative processes and results that are not entirely amenable to quantitative measures. "If he [the educator] can organize his qualitative processes and results into some connected intellectual form," wrote Dewey in 1908, "he is really advancing scientific method much more than if, ignoring what is actually most important, he devotes his energies to such unimportant by-products as may now be measured."[3]

Dewey went on to stress that if we want schools to perpetuate the present order, then attempts to determine educational objectives and select subject matter through wide collections and accurate measurements of data may be perfectly appropriate. However, if the schools are to educate with social change in view, a quite different method and content are required for education science. Here it is necessary to employ trained and acute methods not only for ascertaining progress and failure in learning, and in assessing the appropriateness of the ways of organizing the curriculum, but also for detecting the causes of the observed effects. To Dewey, this requires a far more highly skilled kind of research than the mere notation of the results of mechanically applied tests.

Even in mathematics and physics, observed Dewey, quantitative data are secondary to qualitative ideas and, in the absence of guiding principles and rationale, what is taken for scholarly activity is really a kind of scrap collecting. Dewey also warned that many of the progressive schools of that day were so enmeshed with protest against traditional forms of education that their activities centered on deviation, innovation, and removal of restrictions with the consequence that they neglected their responsibility for building up the theoretical side of education.[4]

The Sources of a Science of Education

What is it that marks a field as scientific? In posing this question in 1929, Dewey pointed out that such a question leads to a shift away from the notion of uniform objective traits in subject matter and toward the *ways* or *methods* of dealing with subject matter or problems—the systematic methods of inquiry that enable us to understand and control knowledge more intelligently, less haphazardly. Such inquiry helps to solve problems, suggests new problems for solution, refines old procedures, and creates new and better ones. In posing the question as to the sources of a science of education, continued Dewey, we must ask,

(1) What are the ways by means of which the function of education in all its branches and phases—selection of material for the curriculum, methods of instruction and discipline, organization and administration of schools—can be conducted with systematic increase of intelligent control and understanding?

(2) What are the materials upon which we may—and should—draw in order that educational activities may become in a less degree products of routine, tradition, accident and transitory accidental influences?

(3) From what sources shall we draw so that there shall be steady and cumulative growth of intelligent, communicable insight and power of direction?[5]

EDUCATIONAL PRACTICE.   Dewey went on to stress that educational *practices* are the sole source of the ultimate problems to be investigated and are also the final test of value of research conclusions. "Concrete educational experience is the primary source of all inquiry and reflection because it sets the problems, and tests, modifies, confirms or refutes the conclusions of intellectual investigations," wrote Dewey.[6] This necessitates sympathetic contact between the researcher and the teacher. Education then screens the knowledge sources of the various human sciences (biology, psychology, sociology, and so on); but such knowledge does not become scientific, as far as education is concerned, until it serves educational purposes. This is accomplished when it enables us to solve problems that arise in education.

THE HUMAN SCIENCES AND SOCIAL CONDITIONS.   Regarding psychology and the social sciences as screens, Dewey warned against making a sharp distinction between *what* is learned and *how* we learn it. This concludes in the tendency to assign the determination of the process of learning to psychology and of subject matter to social science, with the result that we deal with segments rather than continuities of the learning process. "That a person can learn efficiently to read and yet not form a taste for reading good literature, or without having curiosities aroused that will lead him to apply his ability to read to explore fields outside of what is conventionally termed good reading matter, are sad facts of experience."[7] With regard to the relationship between the social sciences and social conditions, Dewey criticized the tendency to separate the psychological processes of skill acquisition from the social conditions and needs through which the skill is applied. He also criticized the dominant psychology of the times for being mechanistic and neglecting the most important factor in education, namely, the longitudinal or span-of-growth factor.

In connection with the study of social conditions as a source for determining the curriculum, Dewey leveled this criticism at the pseudoscience of activity analysis:

> The shortest cut to get something that looks scientific is to make a statistical study of existing practices and desires, with the supposition that their accurate determination will settle the subject matter to be taught, thus taking curriculum-forming out of the air, putting it on a solid factual basis. This signifies, in effect and in logic, that the kind of education which the social environment gives unconsciously and in connection with all its defects, perversions and distortions, is the kind of education the schools give consciously. Such an idea is almost enough to cause one to turn back to the theories of classicists who would confine the important subject matter of instruction to the best of the products of the past, in disregard of the present and prospective social conditions.[8]

PHILOSOPHY.   Turning to philosophy as a source, Dewey criticized the notion that philosophy is concerned with determining ends, whereas the science of education is concerned with determining means. According to Dewey, philosophy serves a regulative function and is significant to the extent to which it provides working hypotheses of comprehensive application. "But if a philosophy starts to reason out its conclusions without definite and constant regard to the concrete experiences that define the problem for thought," cautioned Dewey, "it becomes speculative in a way that justifies contempt."[9]

Unfortunately, this has been the case all too often. As discussed in Chapter 9, there has been a tendency in recent times for many educational philosophers to remove themselves from the practical concerns and problems of schooling and to become engaged in self-serving esoteric academicism. In the case of the critical theorists, neo-Marxists, and others of the new left in academia, the focus has been on negation—portraying the school as a tool of the existing power elite for cultural reproduction or maintenance of the existing social order.[10] Their professional work has been centered on attacking the public schools rather than on working constructively on ways to improve conditions and to test hypotheses for problem solutions. As related in Part I of this text, experimentalist-progressives throughout the twentieth century sought to forge a democratic vision for the American public schools and to address the practical problems of promoting educational opportunity, academic freedom, curriculum unity and diversity, curriculum modernization and enrichment, creation of a productive environment for learning, and linking school life with social needs. Such problems require continual attention in a free society. Democracy requires a shared vision and belief in the potentials of school and society, and as a philosophy serves as our compass. To remove educational philosophy from the practical problems of our schools is to surrender the educational cause and make philosophy irrelevant.

EDUCATIONAL OBJECTIVES.   Finally, Dewey emphasized that educational objectives must be determined from the educational function. Here he was careful to point out that this does not mean that only educators should determine objectives, but rather that the educative process is the means whereby truly educative objectives can be formulated, tested, and met. In activity analysis, nationalized testing, or any scheme where educational objectives are determined from outside the educational function or process, the educational cause is surrendered. In Dewey's words, "the *educative process* in its integrity and continuity should determine them. . . . For education is itself a process of discovering what values are worth while and are to be pursued as objectives."[11] The incessant external pressures on schools to censor certain materials, to avoid controversial issues, to indoctrinate for certain ends, or to minister to narrow and special interests—all are examples of forces that impinge on the educative process and serve to make it noneducative or miseducative. Such pressures stem from conditions that are outside the educative process and run counter to the concept of education as enlightenment.

Sources of Educational Objectives

In 1902 Dewey noted that the fundamental factors in the educative process are (1) the learner ("the immature, undeveloped being"); (2) society ("certain social aims;

meanings, values incarnate with the matured experience of the adult"); and (3) organized subject matter ("the specialization and divisions of the curriculum").[12] Dewey warned that the tendency is for these factors to be treated "in their separateness, to insist upon one at the expense of the other, to make antagonists of them" with the result that, instead of seeing them in organic interaction, each becomes the basis for a warring sect with its own set of independent truths.[13]

> When this happens a really serious practical problem—that of interaction—is transformed into an unreal, and hence insoluble, theoretical problem. Instead of seeing the educative process steadily and as a whole, we see conflicting terms. We get the case of the child versus the curriculum; of the individual nature versus social culture. Below all other divisions in pedagogic opinion lies this opposition.[14]

In modern times, many educators have switched their allegiance in succeeding periods from discipline-centered studies to learner-centered curricula; from curricula for social relevance to curricula for development of basic skills. Instead of seeking to determine how the various sources can contribute coherently to the task of education, each source is regarded as the basis for allegiance or opposition. Each source becomes a sect for its own doctrines. "The educative process is the due interaction of these forces," observed Dewey, and "such a conception of each in relation to the other as facilitates completest and freest interaction is the essence of educational theory."[15]

Dewey's rationale as explicated in *The Sources of a Science of Education* and in his other writings, and particularly his identification and analysis of the three sources of educational objectives, were subjected to considerable refinement and elaboration over the ensuing decades.

In 1931, referring to the prodigious amount of activity in curriculum change, ranging from miscellaneous tinkering to radical reconstruction, Bode observed that the ensuing welter of diverse and conflicting curricular aims stems from three sources or points of view: (1) the standpoint of the subject-matter specialist, (2) the standpoint of the practical man, and (3) the interests of the learner. Although Bode's second source may appear at first glance to be different from any of Dewey's sources, it actually corresponds to Dewey's second source, namely, "certain social aims; meanings, values incarnate with the matured experience of the adult."[16] Bode warned of the pitfalls inherent in these sources or determinants in the absence of consideration of what constitutes a good life in a good society. Education should be a means for acquiring an outlook on life rather than receiving a ready-made outlook, contended Bode. In tune with Dewey, Bode pointed out that the schools in a democracy cannot impose an official creed on the learner, but must enable the learner to develop a philosophy of life or social outlook through genuine educative participation.

SEARCH FOR CONSENSUS.   As we have pointed out, a field can be said to come of age when its practitioners share a sense of community as exemplified by a paradigm or set of paradigms that governs their work and accounts for the relative fullness of their professional communication and consensus of judgment. Recall from our discussion in Chapter 4 that the search for such consensus was vividly expressed in the monumental, two-volume, twenty-sixth yearbook of the National Society for the Study of Education, issued in 1927. This was the society's first yearbook devoted to curriculum. The second volume of the yearbook contained fifty-eight numbered paragraphs representing points of consensus in a composite statement. The first group of paragraphs was addressed to the resolution of the conflict between the nature and interests of the learner and the demands of adult life, and the selection and organization of subject matter—in essence, the three fundamental factors explicated by Dewey. Regarding the relationship between the first two factors, the report emphasized that there should be no conflict between proper education and preparation for later life. Reaffirming the experimentalist commitment, the report stated, "[t]he ultimate test (of either principle) is the effectiveness with which subsequent situations are met by the individual so educated."[17] In a supplementary statement as to whether education should be focused on the present life of the learner or the life of the adult, George S. Counts wrote, "The end of education is to be found in neither the one period nor the other, but rather in the growth of the power of the learner to cope with his environment."[18]

Addressing the matter of selection and organization of subject matter, the composite statement acknowledged the importance of thoroughly systematized, codified, and specialized knowledge "developed through a long social evolution," but concluded that the curriculum should be developed "from the starting point of the needs of the learner, irrespective of the content and boundaries of existing subjects."[19]

Although the twenty-sixth yearbook represented a search for consensus, the yearbook chairman, Harold Rugg, acknowledged differences in the schools of thought in the curriculum field, and he attributed some of these differences to the lack of a common professional vocabulary—obviously reflecting the immaturity of the field.[20] The curriculum field had not yet come of age; nevertheless the yearbook was testimony to the emergence of a notable group of professionals who were able to focus their concerns on the key factors of the curriculum field and the profound issues of the educational situation.

As noted by Cremin, the curriculum field was emerging as a specialized area of professional activity during the 1920s.[21] The sense of professional community in the curriculum field was to draw impetus with the establishment of the Society for Curriculum Study during the early years of the Great Depression (which was to merge in 1942 with the NEA's Department of Supervision and Directors of Instruction to become the Association for Supervision and Curriculum Development). Following the establishment of the first department of curriculum at Teachers College under Hollis Caswell in 1938, leading schools of education throughout North America and elsewhere were instituting similar departments. At the same time, a notable body of research literature was becoming evident about curriculum—a field that was coming of age.

THE CURRICULUM PARADIGM

The need for a scientific foundation for education was becoming clearly evident to Dewey and his fellow experimentalists in order to advance educational practice, as opposed to allowing the determining factors in education to be set by "tradition, imitative reproduction, and response to various external pressures wherein the strongest force wins out"—to use Dewey's own words.[22] In effect, a scientific basis for education would create teachers who would no longer seek simple recipes and whose success would be measured by examination results and regimental order in the classroom.

As mentioned, Dewey was very explicit in stressing that the scientific base was not to be confused with empiricism or quantitative measurement, but would serve to create and unleash richly conceptual and imaginative avenues for finding problem solutions through systematic inquiry. Although Dewey noted that there is a distinction between art and science, there should be no opposition between the two. As in medicine or architecture, professional practice is indeed an art that is scientifically grounded. So be it in education.

Paradigms are not concocted out of a hat, but from the world of practice. Dewey had formulated his three fundamental factors in the educative process from the work in his laboratory school at the University of Chicago. These, in turn, became the basis for the development of a paradigm for curriculum development in the Eight-Year Study (1932–1940), perhaps the largest-scale longitudinal study ever undertaken in education. As discussed in Chapter 4, the Eight-Year Study grew out of the need to free the secondary-school curriculum from college-preparatory dominance so that an experimental basis for curriculum development could be established.

Curriculum Development as Inquiry

If education is to advance in knowledge and practice, then it must employ the methods of scientific inquiry as opposed to tradition, imitation, dictate, narrow interests, and external political pressures, contended Dewey. Dewey variously referred to the methods of scientific inquiry as scientific method, reflective thinking, method of intelligence, hypothetical thinking, and the problem method. In explicating scientific method as phases in a chain of systematic inquiry, Dewey was careful to point out that the phases are not rigidly sequential or step-like.[23]

As shown in Table 7–1, Dewey's phases of scientific inquiry or reflective thinking for problem solving were to be restated by leading curricularists in their efforts to promote systematic approaches to curriculum development throughout the twentieth century. This was to be coupled with the systematic study of the fundamental factors in the educative process or sources of educational objectives—(1) the nature of the learner; (2) our highest and most inclusive social ideals, values, and needs; and (3) the selection and organization of knowledge in the creation of curriculum. Taken together, the problem method and the fundamental factors were to be fashioned as a paradigm to advance curriculum development as a professional field.

To guide the program of curriculum development and evaluation, the staff of the Eight-Year Study developed a paradigm, which was later published by Giles, McCutchen, and Zechiel in 1942 in their curriculum report after completion of the study.[24] The report, *Exploring the Curriculum,* described how curriculum develop-

Table 7–1. Educational Improvement (and Curriculum Development) as a Problem-Solving Process

Dewey, 1916	Dewey, 1933	Giles, McCutchen, and Zechiel, 1942	Taba, 1945, 1962	Tyler, 1949
Situation of significant experience	Suggestions stemming from a perplexing situation (pre-reflective)	Identifying objectives	Diagnosis of needs	What educational purposes should be sought?
Identification of problem(s) deriving from situation	Intellectualization of the difficulty into a problem to be solved	Selecting the means for attaining these objectives	Formulation of objectives	What educational experiences can be provided that are likely to attain these purposes?
Observations and information bearing on the problem(s)	Use of leading ideas/ *hypotheses* to initiate and guide investigation	Organizing these means	Selection of content	
Formulations of suggested solutions (hypotheses)	Mental elaboration of ideas, evidence, and possibilities	Evaluating the outcomes	Organization of content	How can these educational experiences be effectively organized?
Applications and validation of suggested solutions	Testing *hypotheses* by action		Selection of learning experiences	How can we determine whether these purposes are being attained?
	Deriving and implementing solutions, resulting in a cleared-up, unified situation and the advancement of knowledge and practice		Organization of learning experiences	
			Evaluation	

Source: Adapted from Daniel Tanner, "Curriculum History," in Harold E. Mitzel (ed.), *Encyclopedia of Educational Research*, 5th ed., Vol. 1 (New York: Macmillan/Free Press, 1982), p. 417.

ment and evaluation for the Eight-Year Study required attention to four fundamental questions pertaining to (1) identifying objectives, (2) selecting the means for attaining these objectives, (3) organizing these means, and (4) evaluating the outcomes. (These questions have a correspondence with Dewey's essentials of reflection or inquiry, as shown in Table 7–1.) In keeping with Dewey's conception of continuity and interdependence between aims and means, Giles, McCutchen, and Zechiel presented a model for curriculum development, shown in Figure 7–1, in which the four fundamental questions or problem areas are represented as interdependent determinants: objectives, subject matter, methods and organization, and evaluation. Recognizing that these determinants arise from an educational situation, and are necessarily interdependent, they avoided portraying them as linear steps.

There are many ways of illustrating how aims derive from existing situations. For example, a given school might find that a dramatic change in the ethnic makeup of its pupil population has been accompanied by various forms of overt conflict between and among the pupil reference groups. An examination of the existing curriculum may reveal that no provisions are made for the study of intergroup conflict. After diagnosing the situation, the faculty might decide to revise its program in social studies, or it may opt to make more substantive curricular changes. In the latter instance, a problem-focused unified studies curriculum might be developed in which history, the social studies, and literature are synthesized. Through the unified studies curriculum, students would investigate the causes, effects, and possible solutions of intergroup conflict in school and society, along with other pervading problems. Key

Figure 7–1. Interrelationship of Determinants in Curriculum Development.

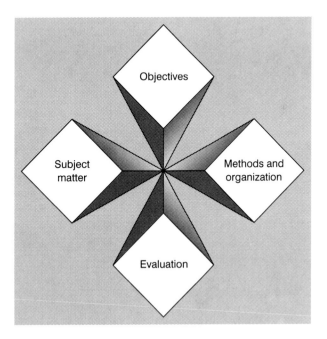

Source: Adapted from H. H. Giles, S. P. McCutchen, and A. N. Zechiel, *Exploring the Curriculum* (New York: Harper, 1942), p. 2.

educational aims derived from this situation might be to develop understandings, skills, and obligations for applying democratic ideals as a guide for everyday living, and to develop competencies in and commitment to reflective thinking as the means for solving social problems. Various behavioral objectives might be identified in connection with these larger educational aims (not to be construed in the narrow-minded behavioristic sense). In evaluating the outcomes of the curriculum, a variety of techniques and instruments might be employed, such as attitude scales, pupil questionnaires, classroom interaction studies, anecdotal records, and achievement tests. Thus, not only do the objectives derive from the educational situation but also changes in curricular content, methods of teaching, and organization of subject matter become necessary in attempting to deal with the situation effectively. Moreover, special techniques and instruments for evaluation may be required.

THREE FUNDAMENTAL APPROACHES TO SOURCES.   In connection with the Eight-Year Study, the following three approaches or sources were identified in the process of curricular organization and analysis: (1) the social-demands approach, (2) the adolescent-needs approach, and (3) the specialized subject-matter approach.[25] These approaches clearly correspond to Dewey's three sources, namely, the learner, society, and organized subject matter. In 1945, Taba elaborated on the significance of these three sources of data in curriculum planning: (1) studies of society, (2) studies of learners, and (3) studies of subject-matter content.[26]

Although the various elements of the curriculum paradigm for the Eight-Year Study were discussed rather extensively in *Exploring the Curriculum* (1942), it was to be orchestrated more fully as a paradigm by Ralph W. Tyler in 1949.

In his monumental text on secondary education, published posthumously in 1918, Alexander Inglis, a leading member of the Commission on the Reorganization of Secondary Education, offered three primary criteria for meeting the educative function: (1) "the psychological demands of the learning process as determined by the mental development and previous experiences of the pupils" (nature of the learner and the learning process), (2) "the demands and activities of life in which the students will utilize the various elements of their education," and (3) "the entire organization of (curricular) materials and methods."[27] Inglis went on to stress that the traditional curriculum as logically organized subjects will have to undergo radical reorganization in the light of the nature of the learner and the emerging conditions of modern life. In effect, the three fundamental determinants or sources for curriculum development identified by Inglis in 1918 corresponded to Dewey's three sources and to the factors or determinants identified by the Commission on the Reorganization of Secondary Education. As shown in Table 7–2, the same three sources were explicated by the Committee on Curriculum Making in 1927 (chaired by Harold Rugg), by Boyd Bode in 1931, in the Eight-Year Study (1932–1940), by Hilda Taba in 1945, and by Ralph Tyler in 1949.

Dewey's influence on the Commission on the Reorganization of Secondary Education is clearly indicated in the commission's report, *Cardinal Principles of Secondary Education* (1918). In its opening pages, the report identified the key factors or determinants for education as (1) the character and nature of the learners to be

Table 7–2. Fundamental Factors, Sources, or Determinants for Curriculum Development

Dewey, 1902	Commission on the Reorganization of Secondary Education, 1918	Inglis, 1918	Rugg (Ch.), Committee on Curriculum Making, 1927
Learner (developing, immature individual)	Learner (character of)	Learner (nature of) and learning process	Learner (nature and interests of)
Society (social aims, meanings, values from the matured experience of the adult)	Society (needs of)	Life (demands of)	Adult life (demands of)
Reflectively formulated, systematized, life-related knowledge (subject matter)	Subject matter and methods (knowledge applications to life activities)	Curriculum (selection and organization of materials and methods)	Curriculum (selection and organization of the)

Bode, 1931	Giles, McCutchen, Zechiel, Eight-Year Study, 1942	Taba, 1945	Tyler, 1949
Learner (interests of)	Adolescent needs	Learners (studies of)	Learners (studies of)
Practical man (standpoint of)	Social demands	Society (studies of)	Contemporary life outside the school (studies of)
Logical, systematized subject matter	Specialized subject matter	Subject matter (studies of)	Subject specialists (suggestions from or relevance of subject matter for the nonspecialist)

served, (2) the needs of society, and (3) the organization of subject matter and methods to reveal the applications of knowledge to life activities.

Table 7–2 reveals how leading scholars, throughout the first half of the twentieth century identified the identical three factors, sources, or determinants for curriculum development. As discussed earlier, Dewey had warned in 1902 that when there is failure to consider these fundamental factors, or when they are treated separately, or when one is advanced at the expense of the others, or when antagonists are made of them, the educational process goes awry as insoluble problems are piled one on another. From Tables 7–1 and 7–2 we see the consensual elements and structure for systematically advancing research and practice in the curriculum field. In effect the structural elements for the curriculum paradigm were clearly identified and utilized in the Eight-Year Study. The paradigm served as a compass for treating the fundamental factors in vital interaction, rather than in opposition. The paradigm clearly provided the elements for making wiser curriculum decisions based on the best available evidence and served to advance knowledge in the field derived through scientific inquiry or the problem method.

The Tyler Rationale

Based on Dewey's work, as explicated in *The Sources of a Science of Education,* and the work of Giles, McCutchen, and Zechiel on the Eight-Year Study, Tyler presented a full elaboration of the paradigm for curriculum development in *Basic Principles of Curriculum and Instruction,* published in 1949. Developed as a syllabus for a basic curriculum course at the University of Chicago, Tyler's handbook has been widely used in curriculum courses and widely discussed in the curriculum literature from midcentury to the present day. Although various modifications have been proposed, Tyler's explication of the curriculum paradigm has not been fundamentally changed.

The connection of Tyler's model with the work of Dewey and the model that guided the Eight-Year Study is unmistakable. Yet to this day Tyler's *Basic Principles* is commonly referred to as *the Tyler rationale* and as one man's version of how a curriculum should be developed.[28] Although there are many ways to derive a curriculum (e.g., from tradition, external influences, trial and error, authoritative dictate, imitation, etc.), the experimentalist curriculum paradigm stemming from the work of John Dewey, the Commission on the Reorganization of Secondary Education, Alexander Inglis, Harold Rugg et al., the Eight-Year Study, Ralph Tyler, Hilda Taba, and others has served to put the curriculum field on a more scientific and professional footing. Moreover, as discussed in various sections of this text, many of the reductionist curriculum reforms externally and politically imposed on the schools throughout the twentieth century might have been exposed as doomed to failure from the beginning had the reform proposals been tested against the paradigm. Many of these reforms violated the nature of the learner, conflicted with our democratic social ideals under the pressure of vested interests and narrow nationalistic interests (e.g., the Cold War and space race), created unsound priorities and hierarchies of subject matters that set one side of the curriculum against another (e.g., the sciences over the arts, the "essentials" over the "nonessentials"), and led to the fragmentation of the curriculum and its isolation from life experience.

The experimentalist curriculum paradigm not only has been used for school curriculum development, but also for curriculum development in higher education, particularly in professional schools such as social work, engineering, and medicine. For example, perhaps the most provocative, comprehensive, influential, and long-term program to reform medical education since midcentury was the one undertaken at Western Reserve University (now Case Western Reserve), which drew upon the curriculum paradigm.[29]

FOUR FUNDAMENTAL QUESTIONS. The rationale proposed by Tyler for analyzing and developing the curriculum begins with a mandate for seeking answers to the following four fundamental questions:

1. What educational purposes should the school seek to attain?
2. What educational experiences can be provided that are likely to attain these purposes?
3. How can these educational experiences be effectively organized?
4. How can we determine whether these purposes are being attained?[30]

In essence, Tyler's questions represent the four-step sequence of (1) identifying objectives, (2) selecting the means for the attainment of these objectives, (3) organizing these means, and (4) evaluating the outcomes. A striking feature of Tyler's questions is that they relate to Dewey's essentials of reflection. However, Dewey repeatedly emphasized that aims derive from existing situations—from the resources and difficulties of these situations—and he noted that theories about the proper ends of our activities often violate this principle by assuming that ends are established outside our activities, with the consequence that they limit intelligence because they are externally derived or imposed.[31]

INTERDEPENDENT FUNCTIONS. If we conceive of aims as properly deriving from the existing situation, rather than being externally derived or imposed, the function of identifying aims must be interdependent with other functions in curriculum development. Consequently, Tyler's linear sequence of questions appears to be faulty because it fails to show this necessary interdependence. A more satisfactory model was developed by Giles, McCutchen, and Zechiel in their curriculum report on the Eight-Year Study, published in 1942. After raising essentially the same four questions that appeared in the Tyler rationale several years later, Giles, McCutchen, and Zechiel presented a schematic representation for curriculum development, shown in Figure 7–1, in which four functions are represented as interdependent rather than as linear steps.

A number of curricularists have treated the four questions as linear steps. Taba further divided them into a seven-step sequence, as follows:

Step 1: Diagnosis of needs
Step 2: Formulation of objectives
Step 3: Selection of content
Step 4: Organization of content
Step 5: Selection of learning experiences
Step 6: Organization of learning experiences
Step 7: Determination of what to evaluate and of the ways and means of doing it[32]

However logical the preceding sequence may appear, there is an educational situation already in existence, operating with implicit if not explicit objectives, and other curriculum determinants. If there is any starting point, it derives from that situation and should be focused on a diagnosis of the problems arising from that situation. The diagnosis involves evaluation from the very start, and evaluation should be continuous and not merely a final step. In other words, a four-step or seven-step sequence may be suitably logical for analytical purposes, but in the real world of curriculum development, the processes must be treated in ecological relationship beginning with the situation itself and its attendant problems.

In essence, then, the four functions in curriculum development (identifying objectives, selecting the means for the attainment of these objectives, organizing these means, and evaluating the outcomes) are interdependent functions rather than rigidly sequential steps. Although Figure 7–1 shows these functions as interdependent, it does not indicate the bases on which decisions regarding these functions are made. Decisions on the selection of educational objectives, selection and organization of subject matter, organization of instructional methods and learning experiences, and utilization of systematic evaluation procedures should be philosophically based. As discussed earlier, Dewey had pointed to the regulative function of philosophy in curriculum development and its significance of providing working hypotheses of comprehensive application. Tyler was well aware of the use of philosophy and, in virtually the same words as Bode, noted that "philosophy attempts to define the nature of a good life and a good society."[33] However, Tyler viewed philosophy, along with psychology, as a mere screen for selecting objectives. Dewey considered philosophy as more of a compass, and he viewed all of the "human sciences" as screens through which knowledge can be drawn to serve educational purposes. It appears that Tyler's identification of the "psychology of learning" as a screen for educational objectives and his omission of other human sciences was an oversight. Otherwise, he would likely have made a case for the pertinence of psychology over the other human (behavioral) sciences.

SOURCES OF OBJECTIVES.   In answer to the question What educational purposes should the school seek to attain? Tyler identified the following three sources: (1) studies of the learners themselves, (2) studies of contemporary life outside the school, and (3) suggestions from subject specialists.[34] In the curriculum literature, Tyler is generally credited with having identified these key sources of educational objectives. However, as discussed earlier, these same sources had been formulated by Dewey in 1902 and had served as a basis for curriculum theory and development throughout the first half of the century. But Dewey had warned that these sources must be treated as interactive; otherwise, in their separateness they become the basis of warring sects—the learner versus subject matter, needs of the learner versus social demands, and so on. Kliebard has pointed out that where Dewey creatively reformulated these sources relative to the educative process, Tyler simply opted for an eclectic approach of laying them out side by side.[35] Although Tyler took the position that no single source provides an adequate basis for educational objectives and curriculum development, he tended to treat them separately rather than as interactive sources. According to Tyler, "Each of these sources has certain values to commend it. Each source should be given some consideration in planning any comprehensive curriculum program."[36] If these sources are treated as mere components rather than as organically interacting factors in curriculum development, their treatment often tends to become mechanical and the task of curriculum development tends to be regarded as merely technological, as evidenced by the earlier efforts in activity analysis and the more recent work on behavioristic objectives. Moreover, the so-called sources are not merely sources as such but also are influences that affect not only educational objectives but also the structure and content of the curriculum per se.

In connection with Tyler's third source, suggestions from subject specialists, Tyler cautions that the question to be directed at specialists should be, "What can your subject contribute to the education of young people who are not going to be specialists in your field?"[37] Tyler goes into considerable detail in differentiating between specialized education and general education and in discussing the advantages of devising organizing structures other than the traditional subject divisions or disciplines. Here he notes the value of broad fields and core approaches for integrating knowledge and making it more life-relevant. Yet such efforts for developing curriculum synthesis have been made by generalists rather than specialists. Indeed, the era of the discipline-centered curriculum reforms of the 1960s was marked by a war among the disciplines as each discipline vied for priority in the curriculum. Moreover, the specialists rejected the function of general education and opted instead for disciplinary courses designed as though each student were to become a scholar-specialist in each of the numerous disciplines.

How the pieces fit together is the key concern of the curricularist. In this sense, the curricularist is not merely a specialist in the field of curriculum theory and development but a generalist in that his or her concern goes beyond the separate specialized subject matters. The curricularist is concerned with interrelationships in the totality of curriculum. Oddly, Tyler only identified the subject specialist in his scheme, although his syllabus was obviously directed at the curricularist as generalist. Consequently, the concept of organized subject matter as one of the sources, as explicated by Dewey and others, appears to be more satisfactory when treated integratively rather than segmentally.

Interaction of Determinants and Sources

If we regard philosophy as performing a regulative function, then it appears appropriate to incorporate it in the model showing the interrelationship of the determinants in curriculum development. Similarly, if we heed Dewey's admonition that objectives and other determinants must be derived from and tested in the educative process, then the educative process should be incorporated in this model. Dewey regarded this as a crucial matter because, otherwise, sources external to the educational process tend to impinge on the curriculum with the result that the school becomes vulnerable to narrow and vested miseducative interests. This is commonly manifested in externally imposed and self-imposed censorship of the curriculum, the avoidance of controversial problems in the curriculum, the tendency toward indoctrination as a curricular function, and the delimitation of the curriculum to the safe function of skill development and the transmission of facts and information.

Figure 7–2 shows the interrelationships of determinants in curriculum development with philosophy as regulator in the context of the educative process. This schematic representation resolves the difficulties stemming from a linear conception of curriculum development. In a linear conception, one ordinarily assumes that objectives are always the starting point, but objectives always arise from a situation. In education, they should arise from the educative process and should be tested by that process. When objectives are regarded as the starting point, they tend to be derived from outside the educative process and are imposed on that process. Similarly, the selection and organization of subject matter, the methods of instruction, and the techniques and procedures of evaluation cannot be treated apart from objectives and as separate entities. They are organically interactive and interdependent. What one learns in history or science or literature is inseparable from how one learns the so-called subject matter. Evaluation is shortsighted and narrow-minded if it only deals with the retention of facts and information and not with the ways in which the learner is able to reconstruct knowledge in a variety of novel problem situations.

In a similar vein, the sources of curriculum objectives should be viewed as interactive. The three sources, namely the learner, society, and organized subject matter—identified by Dewey, utilized in the Eight-Year Study, and further explicated in the Tyler rationale—should also be regarded as curricular *influences*. For example, changes in society exert certain demands on the school, which need to be interpreted by educators in the light of the educative process. Otherwise, the externally imposed demands may undermine the educative process. We have already alluded to certain problems encountered by schools, such as externally imposed censorship, self-censorship in response to the general public climate, the elimination of controversial material in the curriculum, the constriction of the curriculum to skill development, the perversion of the educative process to one of indoctrination or to narrow nationalistic interests, and so on. Similarly, changes in the wider world of knowledge serve to influence the curriculum. But again, it is the responsibility of educators to interpret these changes in terms of appropriate subject matter and in consideration of the nature of the learner and democratic social ideals. All of these should be regulated by educational philosophy and tested by the educative process.

The curricular sources and influences are portrayed as interactive in Figure 7–3. Included is an added category that might be called the world of knowledge. It

Figure 7–2. Interrelationship of Determinants with Philosophy in Curriculum Development.

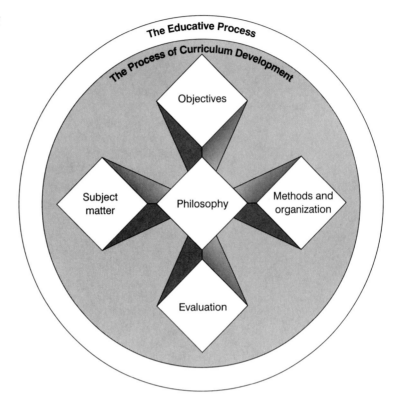

is from the larger world of knowledge that educational institutions create subject-matter divisions for teaching and learning. As discussed in Chapter 5, the creation of such divisions and specialization is convenient for organizing knowledge into subject matters for systematic instruction; but serious difficulties arise when the separate domains of specialized subject matter have to be resynthesized if they are to be useful in social problem solving and even in the development of new knowledge.

It is also seen in Figure 7–3 how the curriculum is developed through the various sources and forces in interaction. In building the curriculum, decisions must be made not only in the selection of subject matter but also in determining the context for the subject mater, including the structure or framework for the courses of study (i.e., discipline-centered or interdisciplinary studies), the modes of instruction, and the relationship of the courses of study to the life of the learner, the wider world of knowledge, and the larger society.

How these sources are drawn on and the nature and extent of their influence in building the curriculum should be determined by philosophy. In the absence of a guiding philosophy, the curriculum tends to be a product of ad hoc decisions—typically stemming from a combination of traditional practices and more immediate expediencies.

Figure 7–3. Curricular Sources and Influences.

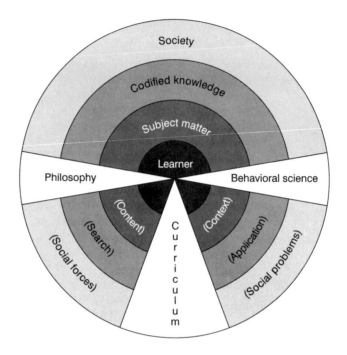

REASSESSMENT OF THE CURRICULUM PARADIGM

Thomas Kuhn has pointed out that on the matter of disagreement on values for theory choice, the differences cannot be resolved by empirical proof.

> What one must understand is the manner in which a particular set of shared values interacts with the particular experiences shared by a community of specialists to ensure that most members of the group will ultimately find one set of arguments rather than another decisive. That process is persuasion.[38]

Kuhn goes on to discuss how practice in a scientific field (and here we are using the term scientific in the Deweyan sense) depends on the ability, acquired from exemplars or models, to group situations into similarity sets. These similarity sets may well be rather crude, but they become a basis for persuasion and eventual consensus through which the field can make progress. "Counter-arguments are, in any case, always available, and no rules prescribe how the balance must be struck," states Kuhn, but nevertheless, "as argument piles on argument and as challenge after challenge is successfully met, only blind stubbornness can at the end account for continued resistance."[39]

As mentioned earlier, Tyler's reconstruction of the curriculum paradigm has been subjected to great debate to this day. Certain weaknesses in Tyler's model have been identified and modifications have been suggested by the authors of this text in an effort to refine the model and to clarify points of misunderstanding. Although different writers have criticized Tyler's version, their proposals, for the most part, have followed the same general model explicated by Tyler. Even those writers who have dismissed Tyler's version entirely have tended to follow this same general model in their own proposals. Thus it appears that the model is indeed a basis for consensus in the curriculum field and can be considered a paradigm for the field. In this section, some of the more recent criticisms and proposals of curricularists are examined in the light of a paradigm for the curriculum field.

Tyler's Version of the Curriculum Paradigm: Criticism and Modification

Perhaps the most common criticism leveled at Tyler's model is that it treats curriculum development as though it were a linear and almost a technological production process. This problem is easily overcome by treating the sources and determinants in curriculum development as organically interactive, as was done in the Eight-Year Study and as represented in Figures 7–2 and 7–3.

The paradigm refined by Tyler has been criticized by Kliebard as suitable "for those who conceive of the curriculum as a complex machinery for transforming the crude raw material that children bring with them to school into a finished and useful product."[40] Indeed, Tyler's model has been misused by the behaviorists in this fashion.[41] But virtually the same model was used by experimentalists in the Eight-Year Study. The point is that the paradigm is not inherently a mechanical production model, but a problem-solving model based upon the method of intelligence.

Throughout his syllabus, Tyler repeatedly cautions against any singular approach as universally valid. His discussion of learning experiences, particularly in the development of reflective thinking ability, can hardly be interpreted as a production process to transform raw materials into a finished product. Moreover, his conception of behavioral objectives is comprehensive and consistent with the experimentalist view of the learner as an autonomously thinking individual, and is at odds with the behaviorist description of the learner as a response system. Unfortunately, Tyler's conception of education as a "process of changing the behavior patterns of people" is indeed behavioristic.[42] However, his statement of rationale reveals a far more comprehensive and sophisticated conception of education.

It should be realized that the origins of behavioral objectives were not behavioristic, but stemmed from the ingenious efforts in the Eight-Year Study to evaluate student progress through evidence of learning outcomes that would be more comprehensive and enduring.[43] As director of evaluation for the study, Tyler's conception of behavior clearly was in this vein and was not rooted in behaviorism. This work on behavioral goals was extended significantly in the efforts to develop programs in general education in the secondary school and college after World War II. Will French and others undertook a systematic study of behavioral goals of general education in the high school and proceeded to identify illustrative behaviors for evaluation. For example, under the goal of intellectual self-realization, evidence is sought of the student's ability to work independently (e.g., planning and carrying out a research report or project), to seek evidence on all sides of problems, to evaluate evidence (e.g., distinguishing fact from opinion, recognizing bias), to formulate and test hypotheses in seeking problem solutions, and so on.[44] However, what was originally a progressive and holistic concept came to be seized on by the behaviorists who proceeded to whittle the concept of behavioral objectives down into a minutiae of mechanistic and disjointed responses suited to programmed instruction, workbooks, and worksheets. In an era of curricular reductionism and essentialism, behaviorism became enormously appealing in that it fitted the production-efficiency model of schooling (reduced inputs/high output specifications).

Many curricularists have faulted the logical linearity of the Tyler rationale. Such criticism may be well justified, but it does not invalidate the rationale as a viable model or paradigm. Indeed, in the final section of his syllabus, Tyler explains that his analysis is presented to provide the student with a rational picture of the field. But in the actual work of curriculum development in the school or college, no such sequence is to be followed. In Tyler's words,

> Another question arising in our attempt at curriculum revision by a school or part of a school is whether the sequence of steps to be followed should be the same as the order of presentation in this syllabus. The answer is clearly "No." The concern of the staff, the problems already identified, the available data are all factors to consider in deciding on the initial point of attack. . . . The program may be improved by attacks beginning at any point, providing the resulting modifications are followed through the related elements until eventually all aspects of the curriculum have been studied and revised.[45]

ALTERNATIVE PROPOSALS.   Schwab criticized the continuing restatement of the Tyler rationale in the curriculum literature; yet Schwab's analysis actually utilizes the various curricular sources and determinants explicated by Tyler.[46] It will be recalled that Schwab was one of the leading advocates of the disciplinary doctrine that governed the curriculum reforms of the late 1950s and 1960s. Toward the end of the 1960s, the disciplinary doctrine was in a state of collapse as a result of the student-protest movement and the demand for curricular relevance. It was at this point in time that Schwab described the curriculum field as being in a state of crisis. One cause of this crisis, acknowledged Schwab in a remarkable turnabout, was the domination by subject-matter specialists and the general absence of curricularists and other educationists in the discipline-centered reforms. Schwab stressed the need to take account of all sources for deliberation—teachers, supervisors, administrators, curricularists, philosophers, specialists in the subject-matter fields, and specialists in the various behavioral sciences.

Schwab then turned to the numerous and conflicting orientations to the curriculum. "One curriculum effort is grounded in concern only for the individual, another in concern only for groups, others in concern only for cultures, or communities, or societies, or minds, or the extant bodies of knowledge," observed Schwab. Each orientation, continued Schwab, concerns a different subject matter, and each orientation is grounded in a theory borrowed from one of the behavioral sciences. "No curriculum, grounded in but one of these subjects, can possibly be adequate or defensible," he maintained.[47] Schwab then pointed to the need to take account of all the human sciences in any defensible curriculum. (It will be recalled that Dewey had made this point in *The Sources of a Science of Education,* and that these knowledge sources must serve educational purposes.)

Schwab contended that the crisis in the curriculum field was a result of undue reliance on theory. A renascence of the field would come about only if energies are diverted from theoretic pursuits to three other modes of operation: the practical, the quasi-practical, and the eclectic. The practical mode is concerned with the diagnosis of problems or ills of the curriculum and leads to decisions for action. When the problem situation is more cloudy, or when gaps exist in our practical knowledge, then we would resort to quasi-practical modes for resolving difficulties. The eclectic mode recognizes the usefulness of theory, seeks to repair as much as possible any of the weaknesses of theory and to find some common ground even from conflicting theories to shed light on practical problems. However, "[t]he eclectic does not make it possible to combine the alternative theories into one coherent theory," acknowledged Schwab.[48]

Schwab then went to considerable length to show what can be gained from the practical mode. This mode is indeed appealing and sensible. Not many educators would hold that we need not address practical problems. However, the experimentalist, the perennialist, the essentialist, the reconstructionist, and the eclectic will each have a different view as to the nature of the practical problem and the means by which the problem is to be treated. Schwab's assumption that all orientations will yield readily to the power of the best available evidence appears to be naive. The very diagnosis of practical problems, the determination of the priorities among myriad practical problems to be attacked, the means for attacking these problems, the interpretation of the findings, and the application of the results will be influenced by theory. In the long run, human progress is determined by our practical decision making based on the *theoretical* criterion of the best available evidence. Except in the most obvious and routine matters, knowledge is never final but is treated as tentative. Practical decisions are made according to the best available evidence—pending the emergence of yet better evidence.

The Curriculum Paradigm: Further Assessment and Application

As discussed earlier, a significant number of curricularists have not recognized the continuity and impetus of ideas and practical applications that led to the emergence of the experimentalist paradigm for the curriculum field during the first half of the twentieth century. Drawing on Kuhn's thesis that the hard sciences are the true exemplars of paradigm-guided inquiry, Jickling has contended that scientific inquiry is an objectionable model for the curriculum field.[49] In reply to Kuhn's critique of the social sciences as sciences, Paul Samuelson, Nobel laureate in economics, quipped that economics is "neither astrology nor theology."[50] We might add that such is the case for the curriculum field and indeed for all fields of social science. Despite the differences in philosophy (e.g., liberalism or conservatism), there are sets of tools and parameters, models and exemplars, that define the field and guide inquiry by professionals.

This should not be construed to mean that the levels of predictability and understanding of social phenomena are to be compared with those attained in the physical sciences or even in the biological sciences. Social behavior, fortunately, will always be too complex for that. But this does not lessen the significance of the paradigms of scientific inquiry that guide the social sciences as scholarly communities.

In his contention that the curriculum field has no paradigm base for systematic inquiry, Jickling proceeded to cite the earlier writings of Robin Barrow. However, after reading the present authors' historical tracings concerning the emergence of a curriculum paradigm, Barrow took issue with Jickling and concluded that "the 'model' or 'paradigm' ought to be recognized as fundamental to curriculum."[51]

In her study of the national programs for school reform, past and present, Barbara Presseisen of the Regional Educational Laboratory on Research for Better Schools made use of the curriculum paradigm as presented in the 1980 edition of *Curriculum Development* by the authors of this text. In her study, appropriately titled *Unlearned Lessons,* Presseisen found that most of the reforms were largely misguided in failing to derive lessons from the past and in violating the fundamental factors in the paradigm.[52] A more detailed study by Peter Hlebowitsh, tracing the national educational reform efforts since midcentury, also found that failures were vividly connected with violations of the curriculum paradigm—such as ignoring or distorting the nature of the learner, bending the curriculum to narrow nationalistic purposes at the expense of the cosmopolitan democratic interest, avoiding systematic research for problem solutions, and neglecting to build on the vast body of research and approved practices in the curriculum field.[53]

The testing of the curriculum paradigm by Presseisen, Hlebowitsh, and others has served to reveal its practicality and validity. Surely it will be refined and modified as new knowledge emerges in the curriculum field. But educational reformers would do well to test their schemes against the paradigm and with the benefit of the great store of research and experience in curriculum development, past and present. Otherwise, we shall continue to witness successive periods of educational and curriculum reform by reaction and counterreaction at great loss to the rising generation and to our society.

The Practicality of Theory

Dewey stated the following: "Theory is in the end the most practical of all things, because this widening of the range of attention beyond nearby purpose and desire eventually results in the creation of wider and father-reaching purposes and enables us to use a much wider and deeper range of conditions and means than were expressed in the observation of primitive practical purposes."[54] Theory that is treated as an end in itself is not really theory because it cannot be tested in the world of experience. For Dewey, the working hypotheses provided by theory are tested by application to problems in the world of concrete experience. Otherwise, theory or philosophy becomes "fantastic in content and dogmatic in form."[55] As Einstein observed, "[t]he most satisfactory situation is evidently to be found in cases where the new fundamental hypotheses are suggested by the world of experience itself."[56]

Schwab's criticism of theory when it is treated apart from the reality of the practical world of curriculum is consistent with Dewey's view. In Schwab's analysis of the curriculum field and in his practical, quasi-practical, and eclectic modes for curriculum development, the various sources and determinants in the curriculum paradigm are inescapably treated. His criticisms and conclusions bear a striking resemblance to Dewey's analysis in *Sources of a Science of Education*. The paradigm stemming from Dewey's *Sources of Science of Education* and the Tyler rationale served Schwab well in the formulation of his proposals for the curriculum field.

The crisis in the curriculum field that Schwab addressed had resulted from the reliance on a *single* source, namely, the university scholar-specialists in curriculum reform. The discipline-centered reforms deliberately turned away from the practical applications of knowledge, the problems of society, and the nature of the learner. Had the paradigm stemming from Dewey's *Sources of a Science of Education,* the work of Alexander Inglis, the Eight-Year Study, and the Tyler version been followed, the curriculum reforms would not have been one-sided and the crisis would have been averted. The paradigm is immanently practical in that it shows how the sources and determinants must be treated in balance and in vital interrelationship. In the very opening comments to his syllabus, Tyler cautions that no single source is adequate to provide a basis for wise and comprehensive decisions. Schwab reaches the same conclusion.

Consequently, most of the criticisms leveled at the Tyler rationale can be resolved by modifying the paradigm to show the necessary interrelationship of determinants and sources in curriculum development. Other criticisms appear to stem from a misreading of the paradigm—for example, the allegation that it is mechanistic and suited mainly to behavioristic approaches. We have seen how the paradigm has been useful to curricularists representing virtually any discipline or professional field undergoing curriculum renewal. That the Tyler syllabus is simply one man's version of how a curriculum should be developed and that this version is a production model, is not borne out by the fact that the paradigm on which Tyler's syllabus was based has been used by curricularists in wide-ranging situations. Furthermore, we have seen how the paradigm is not simply one man's invention. It was developed as a distillation of the key sources and determinants in curriculum development from theory and practice spanning the first half of this century. Kliebard has sought to formulate the central question of curriculum and the problems attendant to that question, namely, what should be taught; this, in turn, leads to problems of curriculum differentiation, the modes and effects of teaching what has been selected, and how the various parts of the curriculum should be interrelated in order to create the whole. In his analysis, Kliebard draws from the heritage of the field since the turn of the century and particularly from the work of Dewey. Despite his criticisms of Tyler, Kliebard's question and the attendant problems are well within the paradigm explicated by Tyler.[57]

Tyler's orchestration of the paradigm has been criticized as an oversimplified conception of the complex process of curriculum development. Of course, curriculum development is a highly complex process. But the function of a model or paradigm is to make complex phenomena comprehensible and manageable. In seeking clarity, situations are grouped into similarity sets, which are represented in some kind of equilibrium. The effort toward clarity results in a simplification and rather crude representation of reality. Yet the very simplification makes it possible to test theory in practice, though the paradigm itself should not be treated or assessed as a literal representation of reality. Most of the criticisms leveled at the Tyler rationale have stemmed from such misreadings of the paradigm. This paradigm can be continually refined and modified. It is not an immutable monument, but simply a way of enhancing communication and enabling practitioners to test theory in the real world of curriculum development. Conversion to another model or paradigm awaits another revolution in the curriculum field. Until that revolution is forthcoming, the existing model or paradigm will remain in use and will be studied by serious students of curriculum.

PERSPECTIVE

Throughout the twentieth century, education opinion and practice have been sharply divided as to whether the dominant source and influence for curriculum development should be the body of organized scholarship (the specializations and divisions of academic knowledge), the learner (the immature, developing being), or society (contemporary adult life). Instead of seeing these sources and influences as organically interactive, each becomes a rallying point for a warring sect. Each era of societal crisis witnesses a clamor to make one source and influence dominant over the other. The result is that curriculum development becomes a piecemeal enterprise and the curriculum suffers from imbalance and fragmentation.

It has been shown how the curriculum becomes vulnerable to narrow and even miseducative interests when objectives are derived from sources that are external to the educative process. Objectives must be derived from and tested through the educative process. When theory is similarly treated, that is, when it is derived from and tested in the educative process, it serves to make immediate practice useful in a far wider range of contexts and under far deeper conditions. Theory then provides the hypotheses to be tested in efforts to solve practical problems. Practice in the absence of theory has limited applicability to wider and novel conditions. In this vein, theory is in the end the most practical of all things. But when theorizing is not tested in the educative process, it becomes self-serving and is not theory; instead, it becomes mere speculation or dogmatic assertion. One group asserts that the curriculum should be delimited to the established academic disciplines; another group sees it being properly concentrated on facts and skills; another group maintains that the curriculum should derive from the interests and needs of the learner; yet another group contends that it must be attuned to the demands of adult life. Nothing is resolved and nothing is solved. Each sect has its day as the schools shift from one extreme to another in response to shifting external crises and demands.

The curriculum field came to be identified as a distinct area of study by midcentury with the emergence of a model or paradigm intended to represent a consensual basis for systematic curriculum development. The model or paradigm serves to account for the various sources and determinants in curriculum development and is based on the reflective formulation and testing of alternatives for the solution of practical problems. Although commonly referred to as the Tyler rationale, its conceptual origins span the entire first half of the twentieth century. This model or paradigm has been subsequently modified and refined, though it continues to be a source of debate among leading contemporary curricularists. Alternative proposals have been made, but such proposals appear to be derived from factors that are accounted for in this extant model or paradigm. In this sense, the model or paradigm has served as a basis for communication in the curriculum field. It also has been followed to some extent in working on problem solutions in the curriculum field, such as those attacked in the Eight-Year Study. Because some have used the paradigm mechanically, it has been criticized as mechanistic. But the paradigm has also been used in an organically interactive way. Crises in the curriculum field have arisen when a single source of determinant is allowed to overpower all of the other sources and determinants. The paradigm helps practitioners to recognize the need to consider the necessary interrelationships of all sources and determinants if the curriculum is to be balanced and coherent, and if problem solutions are to be addressed.

It has been shown that the curriculum paradigm has been eminently useful in setting the criteria for evaluating the efficacy of educational reform proposals and in ascertaining the causes of failure of various reform efforts. If the curriculum is to be consonant with the ideals of American democracy, it must then be structured to meet the function of general education, and not merely basic education at one end of the educational ladder and specialized education at the other. This requires a synthesis of the curriculum so as to address our most pervasive social problems in a technological age. A free society requires an enlightened citizenry capable of higher-order thinking in solving personal-social problems in the context of social responsibility. Throughout the twentieth century, many of the national reform efforts for American education were doomed to failure from the start because they neglected or distorted the nature of the learner, subverted the democratic interest to narrow nationalistic or special interests, imposed aims on the schools that were outside the educational situation, and failed to develop an integrated curriculum structure to meet the unified and diversified functions required of a cosmopolitan society.

No model or paradigm rightly serves to eliminate debate or differences in theoretical orientation. Progress depends on such differences provided that they are tested reflectively in the field of practice. The model or paradigm provides a basis for such testing. It is not a literal representation of the world of curriculum development, but an economical and simplified scheme for dealing practicably with the complex process of curriculum development. It serves to synthesize past achievements with current practice. It cannot be dismissed lightly unless something that is more comprehensive and convincing can take its place.

PROBLEMS FOR STUDY AND DISCUSSION

1. According to Bode, "We believe that our curricula should be revised, but we do not know where or how to begin. Our susceptibility to educational fads has become notorious." [Boyd H. Bode, *Modern Educational Theories* (New York: Macmillan, 1927), p. 232.]

   Although Bode made this comment in 1927, would you say it is valid for the educational situation today? Explain.

2. With regard to curriculum development, what is the significance of the statement that "theory is in the end the most practical of all things"?

3. It has been observed that "*expertise* consists in such an analytic comprehension of a special realm of facts that the power to see that realm in the perspective of totality is lost." [Harold J. Laski, "The Limitations of the Expert," in U.S. Senate Committee on Government Operations, *Specialists and Generalists* (Washington, DC: U.S. Government Printing Office, 1968), p. 55. (Originally published in 1930.)]

   What is the significance of this statement concerning the roles of various persons other than the subject specialist in curriculum development?

4. "The user of the house," wrote Aristotle, "will even be a better judge than the builder." ["Specialization and the General Ability to Judge," from *Politica,* Book III, Chapter 11.] What role, if any, should the student have in curriculum development and evaluation?

5. Mark Van Doren observed that although the college (or school) is meaningless without a curriculum, the problem of what should be studied and how this should be interrelated and fitted together is not accepted as a real problem. "All other (educational) problems are solved when the problem of the curriculum is solved." [Mark Van Doren, *Liberal Education* (Boston: Beacon, 1959), p. 108.]

   From your own experience, do teachers and administrators devote adequate time to the interrelationships of studies and the problem of developing a balanced, coherent total curriculum for the school? Explain. Is the curriculum problem the most significant educational problem? Explain.

6. What is your assessment of the Tyler rationale? Do you see the need for modifying it in any way? Explain.

7. In the curriculum literature, considerable attention has been devoted to three fundamental factors in the educative process that have served as sources for educational objectives and other curricular decisions. These factors are (1) the learner, (2) society (social aims and conditions, and meanings and values from matured experience of adult life), and (3) organized subject matter.

   How do you account for the tendency of these factors to be treated as separate and even antagonistic to one another in connection with the curriculum? Give examples of how this has affected the curriculum.

8. What illustrations can you give of situations whereby noneducative and even miseducative influences are exerted on the curriculum from sources external to the school?

NOTES

1. Salomon Bochner, *Eclosion and Synthesis: Perspectives on the History of Knowledge* (New York: W. A. Benjamin, 1969).

2. Thomas S. Kuhn, *The Structure of Scientific Revolutions,* 2nd ed. (Chicago: University of Chicago Press, 1970), pp. 175–180.

3. John Dewey, "Progressive Education and the Science of Education," *Progressive Education,* 5 (July–September 1928), p. 200.

4. Ibid., pp. 199–200, 204.

5. John Dewey, *The Sources of a Science of Education* (New York: Liveright, 1929), pp. 9–10.

6. Ibid., p. 56.

7. Ibid., pp. 62–63.

8. Ibid., pp. 72–73.

9. Ibid., p. 56.

10. Samuel Bowles and Herbert Gintis, *Schooling in Capitalist America* (New York: Basic Books, 1976).

11. Dewey, *Sources of a Science,* op. cit., p. 74.

12. John Dewey, *The Child and the Curriculum*

(Chicago: University of Chicago Press, 1902), pp. 4–8.

13. Ibid., p. 4.
14. Ibid., pp. 4–5.
15. Ibid., p. 4.
16. Boyd H. Bode, "Education at the Crossroads," *Progressive Education,* 8 (November 1931), pp. 543–544.
17. National Society for the Study of Education, *The Foundations of Curriculum Making,* Twenty-sixth Yearbook, Part II (Bloomington, IL: Public School Publishing, 1927), p. 13.
18. Ibid., p. 74.
19. Ibid., p. 22.
20. Ibid., p. 3.
21. Lawrence A. Cremin, Curriculum Making in the United States. *Teachers College Record,* 73 (December 1971), pp. 207–220.
22. Dewey, *Sources of a Science,* op. cit., pp. 14–15.
23. Dewey, *How We Think,* rev. ed. (Lexington, MA: D. C. Heath, 1933), pp. 106–118.
24. H. H. Giles, S. P. McCutchen, and A. N. Zechiel, *Exploring the Curriculum* (New York: Harper, 1942).
25. Ibid., pp. 22–48.
26. Hilda Taba, "General Techniques of Curriculum Planning," Chapter 5 in *American Education in the Postwar Period: Curriculum Reconstruction,* Forty-fourth Yearbook, Part I, National Society for the Study of Education (Chicago: University of Chicago Press, 1945), pp. 85–92.
27. Alexander Inglis, *Principles of Secondary Education* (Cambridge, MA: Houghton Mifflin, 1918), pp. 712–713.
28. Herbert M. Kliebard, *The Struggle for the American Curriculum 1893–1958* (Boston: Routledge & Kegan Paul, 1986), p. 81.
29. Greer Williams, *Western Reserve's Experiment in Medical Education and Its Outcome* (New York: Oxford University Press, 1980).
30. Ralph W. Tyler, *Basic Principles of Curriculum and Instruction* (Chicago: University of Chicago Press, 1949), p. 1.
31. John Dewey, *Democracy and Education* (New York: Macmillan, 1916), pp. 121–122.
32. Hilda Taba, *Curriculum Development* (New York: Harcourt, 1962), p. 12.
33. Tyler, op, cit., p. 34.
34. Ibid., pp. 5–33.
35. Herbert M. Kliebard, "Reappraisal: The Tyler Rationale," *School Review,* 3 (Fall 1969), p. 260.

36. Tyler, op. cit., p. 5.
37. Ibid., p. 26.
38. Kuhn, op, cit., p. 200.
39. Ibid., p. 204.
40. Kliebard, op, cit., p. 81.
41. See W. James Popham and Eva L. Baker, *Systematic Instruction* (New York: Prentice Hall, 1970), pp. 48–61.
42. Tyler, op. cit., pp. 5–6.
43. Eugene R. Smith, Ralph W. Tyler, and the Evaluation Staff, *Apppraising and Recording Student Progress* (New York: Harper, 1942).
44. Will French and Associates, *Behavioral Goals of General Education in High School* (New York: Russell Sage, 1957), pp. 92–102. See also Paul L. Dressel and Lewis B. Mayhew, *General Education: Explorations in Evaluation* (Washington, DC: American Council on Education, 1954).
45. Tyler, op. cit., p. 128.
46. Joseph J. Schwab, *The Practical: A Language for Curriculum* (Washington, DC: National Education Association, 1970), pp. 20, 38.
47. Ibid., p. 23.
48. Ibid., p. 13.
49. Bob Jickling, "Paradigms in Curriculum Development: Critical Comments on the Work of Tanner and Tanner"; Daniel Tanner and Laurel Tanner, "The Emergence of a Paradigm in the Curriculum Field," *Interchange,* 19 (Summer 1988), pp. 41–48, 50–58.
50. Paul A. Samuelson, "Economics in a Golden Age," in Edgar C. Brown and Robert M. Solow (eds.), *Paul Samuelson and Modern Economic Theory* (New York: McGraw-Hill, 1983).
51. Robin Barrow, "Over the Top: A Misuse of Philosophical Techniques?" *Interchange,* 19 (Summer 1988), p. 62.
52. Barbara Z. Presseisen, *Unlearned Lessons: Current and Past Reforms for School Improvement* (Philadelphia: Falmer Press, 1985).
53. Peter S. Hlebowitsh, *Purpose and Change in American Educational Policymaking and Practice: The National Education Reports Since Mid-century.* Unpublished doctoral dissertation (New Brunswick, NJ: Rutgers University, 1987).
54. Dewey, *Sources of a Science,* op. cit., p. 17.
55. Ibid., p. 57.
56. Albert Einstein, *Out of My Later Years* (New York: Philosophical Library, 1950), p. 78.
57. Herbert M. Kliebard, "Curriculum Theory: Give Me a For Instance," *Curriculum Inquiry,* 6, 4 (1977), p. 202.

SELECTED REFERENCES

Aikin, Wilford M. *The Story of the Eight-Year Study.* New York: Harper, 1942.

Association for Supervision and Curriculum Development. *Challenges and Achievements of American Education.* 1993 Yearbook. Alexandria, VA: Author, 1993.

Bochner, Salomon. *Eclosion and Synthesis: Perspectives on the History of Knowledge.* New York: W. A. Benjamin, 1969.

Bode, Boyd H. *Modern Educational Theories.* New York: Macmillan, 1927.

Bronowski, Jacob. *The Origins of Knowledge and Imagination.* New Haven, CT: Yale University Press, 1978.

Bruner, Jerome S. *The Process of Education.* Cambridge, MA: Harvard University Press, 1960.

Conant, James B. *Two Modes of Thought.* New York: Trident Press, 1964.

Dewey, John. *The Child and the Curriculum.* Chicago: University of Chicago Press, 1902.

Dewey, John. *Democracy and Education.* New York: Macmillan, 1916.

Dewey, John. *How We Think,* rev. ed. Lexington, MA: D. C. Heath, 1933.

Dewey, John. *Philosophy of Education.* Totowa, NJ: Littlefield, Adams, 1958. (Originally published as *Problems of Men,* 1946.)

Dewey, John. *The Sources of a Science of Education.* New York: Liveright, 1929.

Giles, H. H., McCutchen, S. P., and Zechiel, A. N. *Exploring the Curriculum.* New York: Harper, 1942.

Inglis, Alexander. *Principles of Secondary Education.* Cambridge, MA: Houghton Mifflin, 1918.

Jackson, Philip W. (ed.). *Handbook of Research on Curriculum.* New York: Macmillan, 1992.

Kuhn, Thomas S. *The Structure of Scientific Revolutions,* 2nd ed. Chicago: University of Chicago Press, 1970.

Lewy, Arieh (ed.). *Handbook of Curriculum Evaluation.* New York: Longman, 1977.

Macdonald, James B., Wolfson, Bernice J., and Zaret, Esther. *Reschooling Society: A Conceptual Model.* Washington, DC: Association for Supervision and Curriculum Development, 1973.

National Society for the Study of Education. *Curriculum-Making: Past and Present,* Twenty-sixth Yearbook, Part I. Bloomington, IL: Public School Publishing, 1926.

National Society for the Study of Education. *The Foundations of Curriculum-Making.* Twenty-sixth Yearbook, Part II. Bloomington, Ill.: Public School Publishing, 1926.

Presseisen, Barbara Z. *Unlearned Lessons: Current and Past Reforms for School Improvement.* Philadelphia: Falmer Press, 1985.

Schon, Donald A. *Educating the Reflective Practitioner.* San Francisco: Jossey-Bass, 1987.

Schwab, Joseph J. *The Practical: A Language for Curriculum.* Washington, DC: National Education Association, 1970.

Skinner, B. F. *Beyond Freedom and Dignity.* New York: Alfred A. Knopf, 1971.

Taba, Hilda. *Curriculum Development.* New York: Harcourt Brace, 1962.

Tanner, Daniel, and Tanner, Laurel. *History of the School Curriculum.* New York: Macmillan, 1990.

Tyler, Ralph W. *Basic Principles of Curriculum and Instruction.* Chicago: University of Chicago Press, 1949.

Weinberg, Alvin M. *Reflections on Big Science.* Cambridge, MA: M.I.T. Press, 1967.

Whitehead, Alfred North. *The Aims of Education.* New York: Macmillan, 1929.

CHAPTER 8

SOURCES AND FORCES FOR CURRICULUM RENEWAL— SOCIETY, KNOWLEDGE, AND THE LEARNER

The modern history of curriculum reform, indeed education reform, reveals the repeated failure to recognize and treat the three fundamental factors in the educative process in vital interdependence—namely (1) the nature of the learner, (2) social conditions and ideals, and (3) the selection and organization of knowledge or subject matter in the development of the curriculum. Instead, at various times the fundamental factors have been treated independently of one another or even antagonistically. Thus we have the pupil-centered curriculum versus the society-relevant curriculum. We have witnessed how narrow nationalistic interests, from the "crisis" of the Cold War and space race to the "crisis" of the "Japanese challenge," have created priorities favoring certain subjects at the expense of a balanced and articulated curriculum (e.g., the sciences and mathematics over the humanities, the arts, and the practical studies). We have seen how, at various times, the college-bound population has been favored over all others. Then, during periods of economic and social retrenchment there is the predictable curriculum retrenchment of "back to basics."

It should be obvious that education reform efforts are destined to fail when the fundamental factors are treated separately or in opposition to one another. Moreover, when reforms are fueled by successive waves of reaction and counterreaction, special interests tend to be served at the expense of the wider social interest of democracy.

The need for recognizing the vital interdependence of the fundamental factors in the educative process has been neglected in the schools, especially at times of narrowly directed sociopolitical pressures and influences. But surprisingly, this neglect has been a common shortcoming among educational theorists despite the rich legacy handed down by experimentalist-progressive educators throughout the first half of the twentieth century.

Borrowing from the curriculum paradigm as presented in earlier editions of this text, Presseisen proceeded to analyze some of the major national reports as to whether they were (1) subject-centered ("academic excellence"), (2) society-driven (nationalistic), or (3) learner-centered.[1] Although Presseisen offered many constructive insights into the shortcomings of these reports, she did not give adequate attention to the most significant lesson to be learned as to why so many of the national reports for school reform inflict so much damage on the rising generation—namely that each report advances narrow priorities and prescriptions that set the fundamental factors in the educative process in opposition to one another. Denis Lawton, a British sociologist and curricularist, has wisely cautioned that the school curriculum cannot justifiably be developed on the basis of any one of the three determinants without creating insurmountable problems.[2] Recall from the preceding chapter that this warning was offered by Dewey back in 1902.

Authors of textbooks on curriculum unfortunately have chosen to treat the three fundamental factors in the educative process as three separate and oppositional theories—again without learning the lesson from the experimentalist paradigm.[3]

There has also been a tendency, even among those who have sought to build on the experimentalist legacy, to treat the three fundamental factors or determinants as *sources* of data for curriculum development and neglect to recognize and treat them also as *influences* on educational aims and the curriculum.

The focus of this chapter is on the needed recognition of the vital interdependence of society, the world of codified knowledge, and the learner as both *sources* and *influences* for curriculum design and development.

SOCIETY AS CURRICULAR SOURCE AND INFLUENCE

According to Tyler, the school must employ some system for analyzing and selecting from contemporary life learning objectives appropriate to the school's clientele.[4] Although this point may appear to be a common-sense principle, great controversy has raged over the system and criteria to be employed and the extent to which the curriculum should be based on contemporary life. Furthermore, any realistic and useful analysis of society as a *source* of data should include society as a powerful *influence* on the school's objectives and curriculum.

Contemporary Life Needs

When Herbert Spencer posed the question in 1860 "What knowledge is of most worth?" he answered his own question by pointing to science as the most important subject matter for preparing children and youth for complete living. According to Spencer, science is the key to complete living: for preservation of health, earning a living, effective parenthood, good citizenship, the highest production and enjoyment of the arts, and intellectual and moral discipline.[5]

Spencer's view that the function of the school should be focused on effective living, and that the knowledge key to successful life in society is science, came as a disturbing blow to the custodians of the classics who had enjoyed a long and unyielding grip on the school and college curriculum. Not only did Spencer attack the classical studies for being irrelevant to modern living but he also challenged the claim that such studies are best for disciplining the mind by contending that the sciences are far superior to this task. Dewey was to criticize Spencer more than half a century later for having failed to recognize that unless science as subject matter is methodologically transformed so as to be applied to life needs and problems, it may be treated in the curriculum as just another inert body of information.[6] Nevertheless, Spencer's thesis gave impetus to the idea that the aims and functions of education must be relevant to effective living in modern society rather than merely being designed to transmit the cultural heritage—an idea that was embraced by American progressive educators in their efforts to reform education during the early decades of the twentieth century.

However, the study of contemporary life as a basis for educational objectives and curriculum construction came to be undertaken in some quarters in a mechanistic and static way. The scientific management movement in industry during the early decades of the twentieth century influenced such educators as Bobbitt and Charters to adopt the technique of job analysis or activity analysis to curriculum construction. The fundamental assumption underlying this technique—namely, that each area of life activity is reducible to perfectly specifiable components and tasks—ignores the fact that many activities in American society require independence of judgment and the use of free intelligence under incessantly changing conditions. In a free society the school is expected to do more than prepare the rising generation to become acceptable cogs in society's machinery—no matter how satisfactory that machinery may be at a given time. The widespread use of narrowly conceived behavioristic objectives in fashioning the curriculum during the 1970s likewise ignored the fact that life activities are dynamic, not static, and require a high order of free intelligence for social insight and problem solving.

SOCIAL PROBLEM SOLVING.   The attempt to focus the curriculum on social problem solving gained considerable momentum through the efforts of progressive educators during the Great Depression. Reviewing the emerging curricula in the secondary schools during the 1930s, Mackenzie offered these observations:

> Current problems facing the American people, alternative solutions to social difficulties, and the viewing of future possibilities are common centers of attention. The immediate community is surveyed and studied. Community needs are analyzed and programs of action developed. . . . Students not only read about problems in these areas; they actually work out solutions. Parents are brought in frequently to participate and aid in the development of solutions to persistent problems of life outside the school. Situations more directly under the school are attacked by students and teachers. . . .
>
> Whether one views the recent curriculum developments in general education from the standpoint of stated purposes, course organization, scope of the required program, units of work, or actual learning experiences, there are unmistakable evi-

dences of a recognition of a social goal and responsibility as well as a concern for the full development of the individual for effective democratic living.[7]

Progressive schools of that era commonly designed their curricula so as to focus on such life-problem areas as personal and community health, conservation of natural resources, intercultural relations, world peace, consumer education, technology, housing, vocations and employment, economic relations, and so on. Although these efforts were countermanded at midcentury by Cold War pressures, the demand for curricular "relevance" during the late 1960s and early 1970s witnessed a re-emergence of efforts to open the curriculum to the treatment of pervading social problems. Where the earlier efforts were directed at total curricular reconstruction and synthesis, as exemplified by the core curriculum, the later response was to make allowance for these needs by adding new and specialized courses to the existing programs of studies and to increase the elective options through a kind of warehouse curriculum. The new fragmentation of the curriculum, noted a British theoretical physicist, is a reflection of the general condition of fragmentation in society.[8]

During the 1930s progressive educators sought to develop the notion of the community school, with the aim of building closer ties between the school and the community, by having the school serve the comprehensive educational needs of all residents of its area, whether children or adults, and by linking the curriculum to community needs. However, the late 1960s and early 1970s witnessed the use of the term *community school* in American major inner cities as a militant demand for control of the school by the dominant ethnic group in the immediate neighborhood served by the school. Ironically, where the earlier concept of community school sought greater unity among the diverse elements of the region served by the school, it more recently came to be associated with political conflict over the control of the local school by special-interest groups.

From the late 1980s into the 1990s, various professional associations were rediscovering the need for curriculum synthesis in order to relate the school curriculum to wider social conditions. For example, instead of focusing on the gifted and talented, the American Association for the Advancement of Science addressed the problem of identifying a common core of understandings, appreciations, and capabilities in science, mathematics, and technology to be developed by all members of a free society by the time they complete their schooling.[9] The National Council for the Social Studies joined with the American Historical Association as a commission to formulate guidelines for developing a coherent curriculum core for effective citizenship and a rich cultural life for the twenty-first century.[10] However, with the dearth of problem-focused curriculum materials in the social studies available to teachers and students in the 1990s, Ralph Nader's Center for Study of Responsive Law sought to help fill the vacuum by issuing in 1992 an action-oriented text or sourcebook, *Civics for Democracy: A Journey for Teachers and Students.*[11] Unfortunately, it seemed doubtful that the schools were ready for such a dynamic approach as offered in *Civics for Democracy.*

Educational and social conservatives have long been opposed to introducing unsettling ideas and issues into the school curriculum. Instead, they have held that the schools would do well to be concerned with the "essentials" or basic education for the masses.

Efforts to derive objectives and construct the curriculum through studies of contemporary life have been attacked over the years by traditionalists. In *The Restoration of Learning,* Arthur Bestor devoted an entire chapter to "The Menace of Excessive Contemporaneity," in which he contended that the study of contemporary problems detracts the school from its essential mission of developing intellectual discipline.[12] He went on to argue that when the school addresses contemporary problems and issues, it makes itself vulnerable to pressure groups and thereby waives its academic immunity. However, if the school avoids all treatment of contemporary problems and issues, it is abrogating the very principle of academic freedom that Bestor seeks to protect. Avoidance of a principle serves only to undermine, and not to protect, the principle. Furthermore, when the school divorces itself from contemporary problems and issues it is failing to meet its responsibility to students as citizens. Because the future has its roots in the present, and because the rising generation represents the future society, the school that holds itself oblivious to problems and issues in contemporary life is denying its students learning experiences that are essential to the building of a better society.

From the early 1980s and into the 1990s, some of the leading national reports on secondary education and higher education were calling for community service as a curriculum requirement or option.[13] Most significantly, within only a few months into his election, President Bill Clinton led the way toward the establishment of a program of social service on the part of college students which would apply toward the repayment of their tuition loans. In effect, it was being increasingly recognized that the rising generation in a free society has an obligation to be of service to society while also gaining educatively from such social service.

LIFE EXPERIENCE.   In response to the demand to make the curriculum relevant to life, many schools and colleges during the late 1960s and early 1970s began to offer academic credit for a wide range of social experience, such as community service and travel, in the belief that such experience is a desirable substitute for formal education. Heretofore, the common practice was to provide academic credit for such experience when it was organized and conducted under the direct supervision of the school or college. More recently, in response to the demand for curricular relevance, an increasing number of schools and colleges have allowed academic credit for work experience beyond their immediate purview. Addressing this trend and the tendency to misconceive Dewey's philosophy by drawing an equation between education and experience, Sidney Hook offered these criticisms:

> From this equation it is inferred that experience itself is educative, and that any series of experiences—the more direct and dynamic the better—can be substituted for formal schooling which is often disparaged as an artificial experience. . . . In short *having* an experience is identified with knowing it or understanding it.
>
> One hardly knows where to begin in exposing the absurdity of this equation. But one thing should be clear. It should not be fathered on Dewey. For Dewey makes

a central distinction between experiences that are "educative" and experiences that are "non-educative" or "miseducative." The first are those that result in increased power and growth, in informed conviction and sympathetic attitudes of understanding, in learning how to face and meet new experiences with some sense of mastery, without fear or panic or relying on the treadmill of blind routine. The second may give excitement but not genuine insight, may result in a mechanical training or conditioning that incapacitates individuals when the situations encountered in life change and must be met by intelligent improvisation.[14]

During the college-student protests of the 1960s, such radical educational critics as the late Paul Goodman, Edgar Z. Friedenberg, and Ivan Illich went so far as to advocate direct societal experience as a total substitution for formal schooling on the part of large segments of American youth population.[15] By the mid-1970s the schools were buffeted by a new economic retrenchment accompanied by the familiar call for the austerity curriculum of back to basics, the raising of academic and promotion standards, and the implementation of statewide competency-based testing programs. Once again, instead of examining the educational situation with a view toward diagnosing and solving pervasive problems, the schools were simply responding to external demands and pressures.

SCHOOL AND SOCIETY.   By the mid-1970s several commissions were advocating the cutting back of formal schooling in favor of schemes to induct adolescents into the work force at an earlier age. The so-called National Commission on the Reform of Secondary Education of the Kettering Foundation advocated the end of compulsory schooling at age fourteen; the Panel on Youth of the President's Science Advisory Committee advocated a variety of alternatives to full-time schooling, including work experience and instruction under the auspices of a work organization; the National Panel on High School and Adolescent Education, supported by the U.S. Office of Education, recommended that high-school attendance be reduced from all-day sessions to an "academic" day of from two to four hours—with the curriculum being concentrated on "the education of the intellect."[16]

These reports were followed by a marked increase in school dropouts or "pushouts" in the name of higher academic standards. The new retrenchment policies found New York City and other urban school districts instituting nonpromotion and other get-tough academic policies that only served to fuel the dropout epidemic. During the 1980s educators and political leaders were awakened once again to the dropout problem and the plight of unemployed and socially disaffected youth. A host of dropout-prevention programs was instituted to attack a problem that had been created in large measure by the misguided and segmental educational-reform policies adopted in the preceding era under the banner of raising "standards."

Aside from the inevitability that the implementation of the recommendations offered in the national education reform reports of the 1960s would apply only to disadvantaged youth, and would serve to perpetuate the existing social order, other serious social and educational questions must be raised. In making these recommendations, the commissions or panels conveniently overlooked the noneducative and miseducative influences of society and its industrial machinery. They also overlooked the special mission of the school to equip the rising generation with the skills and ideals for building a better society and not merely to preserve the status quo. This means that the schools have a responsibility to counter the perverse effects of society on youth and to ensure that work experience for in-school youth be monitored by the school to see to it that it is educative and not exploitative. Referring to the special mission of the school, Dewey wrote:

> Every society gets encumbered with what is trivial . . . with what is positively perverse. The school has the duty of omitting such things from the environment which it supplies, and thereby doing what it can to counteract their influence in the ordinary social environment. By selecting the best for its exclusive use, it strives to reinforce the power of this best. As a society becomes more enlightened, it realizes that it is responsible *not* to transmit and conserve the whole of its existing achievements, but only such as to make for a better future society. The school is its chief agency for the accomplishment of this end.[17]

Thus, society is both a source and an influence whereby the school develops its objectives and curriculum. In an enlightened society, the school is endowed with the mission of drawing from the social environment the best elements that give promise of enabling the rising generation to build a better society.

Societal Demands and Pressures

"No educational system can escape from the political community in which it operates," observed Robert Hutchins, who went on to declare that "[t]he system must reflect what the political community wants it to do. The system can set out formally to change the community only if the community includes change of this kind among its aims."[18]

Free societies look to the school as a key agency of social improvement and recognize the need to protect academic freedom. However, at times of national crisis, there is the tendency to regard the school more narrowly as an instrument of national purpose. Examples since midcentury are the censorship of instructional materials under the influence of McCarthyism during the early years of the Cold War, the narrow curricular focus of the National Defense Education Act of 1958 and of the projects sponsored by the National Science Foundation during the Cold War and post-Sputnik era, and the efforts to exploit for nationalistic purposes the most academically talented children and youth during this same era. Beginning with the mid-1960s, the United States drastically changed its education priorities by turning away from the academically talented and toward the disadvantaged children and youth. When in one era the schools were blamed for neglecting the academically talented, in a succeeding era the schools were blamed for having failed the disadvantaged. When education had been seen as the key instrument of national supremacy in the era of the Cold War and space race, it had come to be regarded in a succeeding era of social protest as a chief means for attacking poverty, racial isolation, and other social inequities. As discussed earlier, this in turn was followed by the curricular retrenchment brought on by the wave of tax conservatism during the latter half of the 1970s.

The 1980s witnessed yet another nationalistic assault on the schools reminiscent of the hysteria of the Cold War and space race. But this time the threat was "the Japanese challenge" in competition for world industrial markets. In *A Nation at Risk* (1983), issued by the U.S. Department of Education, the public schools were blamed for the nation's declining position in the global industrial marketplace, whereas no blame was leveled at the military-industrial complex and government for the misallocation of resources and misguided priorities. As was the case at the height of the space race, the call of the 1980s was for curriculum priority in the sciences and mathematics (to which was added computer literacy), national achievement testing, and special programs for the academically gifted and talented.

Despite the continuing influences in these directions during the 1990s, the need for a more balanced and coherent core curriculum in the schools and colleges, coupled with the need for educational and social equity and remediation, could not be denied in the face of the rising fragmentation and conflict among the multitude of cultures. The key question was whether cosmopolitanism would be served in the spirit of democracy, by fostering a sense of unity through diversity, or whether U.S. diversity will be the basis for cultural division and conflict. United States history reveals that no institution has been more pivotal than the public schools. United States history also reveals that the public tends to recoil against extreme measures and seeks a balanced and comprehensive role for American schools. As John Goodlad found in his Study of Schooling, "We want it all"[19]—to which might be added, "And why not?"

SOCIETY AS CURRICULAR SOURCE AND INFLUENCE— CHANGING FUNCTIONS OF SCHOOLING

The function of the school and the model of curriculum embraced at a particular time are reflections of the demands and expectations of the larger society. As discussed previously, changing sociopolitical forces have exerted changing demands and expectations on the school. In various eras, the tendency is for the school to respond to whatever pressures are most dominant. Although the school in a pluralistic society embracing democratic ideals is expected to be responsive to the demands and expectations of society, there is the tendency in eras of crisis to react with imbalanced prescriptions. Instead of viewing these functions as interactive and symbiotic, and seeking ways of developing them within a unified and coherent curriculum structure, they are viewed as incompatible alternatives. Should the curriculum focus on preserving and transmitting the cultural heritage or should its emphasis be on developing fundamental skills? Should the curriculum be geared to fostering personal growth or should its focus be on achieving social growth? Should the main emphasis of the curriculum be on promoting the disciplines of academic scholarship or should it be geared to social correction? These are some of the dichotomies raised when different functions of the school and its curriculum are seen as conflicting alternatives.

Although the ways of organizing the curriculum are discussed in detail in Part III, a brief review of several conceptions of the function of the school will serve to illustrate how these conceptions are set off against one another to reflect philosophical polarities and societal priorities.

Fundamental Skills

The late J. D. Bernal noted how the rising industrialism in England during the early nineteenth century made it necessary to provide instruction in the three R's for children of the working classes. According to Bernal,

> the new working class needed enough acquaintance with the three R's to do their jobs properly, and provision for teaching them was reluctantly provided on the cheapest possible basis. But there was all the more reason for seeing that the education of the masses did not go too far, and that it introduced no unsettling ideas.[20]

In the United States, the waves of immigrants during the first three decades of the twentieth century brought special focus to education for literacy. This educational function was broadened to include Americanization for these millions of new citizens. However, American progressive educators were concerned that the schools would yield to the Old World conservatism and to the demands of the corporate sector that education of children be limited to the three R's. Attempts by progressive educators to enrich the curriculum were attacked as "frills." For their own children, the privileged sought a rich and balanced curriculum. Criticizing these antidemocratic influences, Dewey wrote:

> He who is poorly acquainted with the history of the efforts to improve elementary education in our large cities does not know that the chief protest against progress is likely to come from successful business men. They have clamored for the three R's as the essential and exclusive material of primary education—knowing well enough that their own children would be able to get the things they protest against. Thus they have attacked as fads and frills every enrichment of the curriculum which did not lend itself to narrow economic ends. Let us stick to business, to the essentials, has been their plea, and by business they meant enough of the routine skills in letters and figures to make those leaving the elementary school at about the fifth or sixth grade useful in *their* business, irrespective of whether pupils left school with an equipment for advance and with the ambition to try to secure better social and economic conditions for their children than they themselves had enjoyed.[21]

Although American society and schools have long since passed the days of child labor and exploitation, back to basics has been a recurrent movement throughout the twentieth century. In examining the views of the de-schoolers and school blamers, along with the simplistic prescription of back to basics, one must wonder whether those who consciously portray the school as ineffectual are unconsciously fearful that a rich curriculum will convey too many unsettling ideas for the rising generation.

SKILL MASTERY AS PREPARATION.   Education conservatives embrace the fundamental-skills model of curriculum for the elementary level of schooling on the ground that the mastery of the three R's is essential for successful later learning in the academic disciplines. "On the elementary level," declares Mortimer Smith, "the task of the school is to provide those sets of symbols and sets of facts that are necessary preliminary to all later learning and understanding."[22] (Smith was co-founder, with Arthur Bestor, of the Council for Basic Education—a national organization to promote basic education.)

Mortimer Adler's widely read book, *The Paideia Proposal: An Educational Manifesto* (1982), called for twelve years of basic schooling for all, without any electives except for foreign languages. The curriculum would be composed of the basic academic subject and art appreciation.[23] (The word *paideia* was taken from ancient Greece, meaning "rearing the child.")

Although progressive educators recognize the importance of the fundamental skills, they see these skills not merely as preparatory for later learning but as relevant to the child's present life. Moreover, they do not regard the function of elementary schooling as being limited to mastery of the three R's but see the elementary-school curriculum fulfilling a wide range of functions—from cognitive development to socialization. In this connection, they recognize that the fundamental skills are not learned for their own sake but must be developed in a wide range of life contexts. Hence, they see these skills and understandings being developed through a comprehensive curriculum including learning activities in the social studies, sciences, the arts, industrial arts, health education, and so on.

RECURRENT EMPHASIS.   During the early 1970s, the fundamental-skills model received renewed emphasis in connection with the education of the disadvantaged through the National Right to Read program of the U.S. Office of Education and through the new wave of educational reform calling for accountability, as measured by standardized achievement tests. During this period, the schools utilized a considerable portion of their allocated federal funds for programmed instructional materials and hardware, along with workbooks and other skill-drill-oriented materials. No magic solutions were found. These devices, materials, and drill techniques simply were not substitutes for the kind of learning environment in the home, school, and larger social situation that provides rich stimulation for effective concept formation and cognitive development.

The fundamental-skills model of curriculum receives dominant emphasis periodically in American society in the ebb and flow of education criticism. For example, only several months before the launching of Sputnik I, the editors of *U.S. News & World Report* ran a cover story on the "new trend developing in education" in which "America's public schools now are heading back to the three R's." Three months after Sputnik I, the same publication featured a cover story on "What Went Wrong with U.S. Schools," which advocated that we emulate the stress on science and mathematics that was characteristic of the Soviet schools. A decade later, *U.S. News & World Report* carried an article that attributed American problems of crime, violence, and racial unrest to an education policy that neglected vocational education and favored the academic side of the curriculum. In 1973, this magazine turned once again to the question of whether American schools are placing sufficient emphasis on the academic side of the curriculum. By 1976, this same publication featured articles on the new trend of back to the three R's and education retrenchment though the elimination of frills, the elimination of social promotion, the tightening of discipline, and the dropping of ambitious social goals of education. In 1978, reviewing the trend toward competency-based testing programs, *U.S. News & World Report* observed that "[t]he impact of the competency movement is such that some educators foresee a day when entire curricula are competency-based."[24]

Virtually identical shifts for school reform by reaction and counterreaction were to be found in other leading business publications such as *Fortune* and *Forbes,* as well as in such general news magazines as *Time* and *Newsweek.* (No matter what the schools were doing, the schools were wrong according to the media.)

As mentioned in Chapter 5, although the concept of literacy originally was associated with the Americanization of immigrants during the first three decades of the twentieth century by learning the rudiments of reading and writing, *literacy* came to be used widely by essentialists during the late 1980s and the 1990s in their attacks on the schools for neglecting the essentials in the curriculum. The national best-seller by Edward D. Hirsch, *Cultural Literacy: What Every American Needs to Know* (1987), revivified the term *literacy* along with the notion that "mastery" of lists of factual information, as evidenced on multiple-choice tests, defined the educated person.[25] In a similar vein, Ravitch and Finn of the U.S. Department of Education drew on the periodic report cards on the nation's schools in the National Assessment of Educational Progress, administered by Educational Testing Service, to expose what seventeen-year olds do not know (in their book titled *What Do Our 17-Year Olds Know?* 1987).[26] Soon the term *literacy* was being attached to virtually each and every academic subject, resulting in a multitude of literacies (e.g., scientific literacy, mathematical literacy, economic literacy, cultural literacy, computer literacy, and so on). There appeared to be a general failure to recognize that such segmental uses of the term only served to exacerbate the fragmentation of the curriculum.

COMPETENCY-BASED TESTING AND THE CURRICULUM. Some of the most significant learning experiences cannot be evaluated through paper-and-pencil tests. Aside from the affective outcomes, there are experiences in the laboratory, shop, and studio that require other forms of evaluation. Oral communication, including the expression of dissenting ideas in a social studies or literature class, is another example of significant learning experience that cannot be assessed through such tests. To develop a total competency-based curriculum would result in the neglect of some of the most profound learnings. The curriculum would then be determined by the test, rather than the test being determined by the curriculum. The role of the teacher, supervisor, and curriculum coordinator in curriculum development would be reduced to the more routine, mechanical functions.

Nevertheless, the back-to-basics movement of the 1970s was accompanied by widespread efforts to base promotion in the elementary grades according to results on standardized achievement tests. By the end of the 1970s, most states had adopted competency-based testing programs at both the elementary and secondary levels.

Some states instituted special testing programs for the diploma. For example, as a reaction to the student unrest in the high schools during the 1960s, the California legislature authorized in 1971 an "early-out" examination for high-school students at age sixteen or seventeen. The program was justified on the assumption that many students did not want to be in school until the age of eighteen, as required by law. However, since 1975, when the examination was first administered, less than 2 percent of the eligible students have taken the examination, and an infinitesimal number has actually opted to leave school on passing. (The examination is mainly of the multiple-choice type, with items on reading, mathematics, and general knowledge, supplemented by writing exercises.) Apparently, the value of schooling has become so culturally ingrained that the examination alternative to the high-school diploma has not been attractive to in-school youth.

TESTING AS A NATIONALIZING INFLUENCE ON THE CURRICULUM.   Educational policymakers at the state and national levels have been using standardized tests increasingly to buttress their political agenda for school reform. In so doing, the test data are commonly misinterpreted and distorted. The media and the public have been led to believe that tests such as the SAT and the tests used in the International Study of Educational Achievement are valid national indicators of American academic achievement, when in fact they have severe limitations and have been widely misused.[27]

The key mechanism for assessing "excellence" in President Bush's *America 2000* (1991) was to be manifested in the American Achievement Tests to be made available nationally and to be used in ascertaining the progress toward achieving the national educational goals for the year 2000 (e.g., "U.S. students will be first in the world in science and mathematics achievement").[28] *America 2000* was the outgrowth of the 1989 Education Summit meeting of the nation's governors and President Bush, a meeting at which Bill Clinton played a key leadership role. On his election as President, Clinton endorsed the development of the American Achievement Tests.

As in the case with statewide assessment testing, and with the PSAT and SAT, it can be anticipated that teachers will come under pressure to teach to the test. (The National Association of Secondary School Principals has been marketing such a package to its membership in connection with the SAT over many years.) To the extent that teaching to the test is practiced, the test becomes the curriculum or, at least, serves to shape the curriculum.

Considering the powerful influence of testing on the curriculum, it is surprising that the *Handbook of Research on Curriculum* (1992) does not have more entries on testing. Writing in the handbook, Madaus and Kellaghan cite data showing that the space devoted to testing in the *Education Index* has exploded to such a proportion in recent years that it far exceeds the space devoted to curriculum. Madaus and Kellaghan also point out that although policymakers cannot mandate what goes on in the classroom, they have been using testing programs as an accountability device, coupled with important rewards or sanctions for school administrators and teachers, to the extent that the curriculum eventually conforms to the test.[29]

Cultural Heritage

As noted in Chapter 5, the perennialist sees the chief task of education as the preservation and transmission of the cultural heritage. The schism between cultural or liberal education and education for life in contemporary society stems from the centuries-old notion that the humanistic studies are the "treasuries of truth" to be protected by a "high priesthood" for the privileged classes.[30] Although many modern-day perennialists advocate the humanistic studies for all, the traditional social distinction attached to such studies has been reflected in a curriculum schism that holds the liberal studies above the practical in intellective worth. Indicative of the schisms in American society, as Dewey noted, is the "separation and mutual contempt of the 'practical' man and the man of theory and culture."[31] When culture is taken as merely an internal refinement of mind as opposed to social efficiency, and when the latter is interpreted narrowly as skills divorced from the spirit and meaning of social action, warned Dewey, two separate educational aims emerge that are "fatal to democracy."[32]

CULTURAL TRANSMISSION AND SOCIAL POWER.   Addressing the implications of this schism for general education at midcentury, Conant made this observation:

> Roughly speaking, the basic argument about general education turns on the degree to which the literary and philosophic traditions of the western world, as interpreted by scholars and connoisseurs before World War I, should be the basis of the education of *all* American youth. The watershed between two fundamentally opposed positions can be located by raising the question: For what purpose do we have a system of public education? If the answer is to develop effective citizens of a free democratic country, then we seem to be facing in one direction. If the answer is to develop the student's rational powers and immerse him in the stream of our cultural heritage, then we appear to be facing in the opposite direction. By and large, the first position represents the modern approach to education; the latter the more conventional view. Those who look down one valley regard conventional "book learning" as only one element in the landscape; those who look down the other believe that developing the "life of the mind" is the primary aim of civilization and this can be accomplished only by steeping youth in our literary and philosophical heritage.[33]

Conant went on to stress that we will have to discard the "cultural presuppositions" that undergirded education in an earlier era in view of the fact that "the social setting of maturing youths as well as grown men and women is vastly different in this country . . . from anything the world has ever seen before." Allies of the humanities must ruthlessly reexamine their premises and must make their studies "really relevant to the present scene," warned Conant.[34]

Nevertheless, the cultural presuppositions for traditional liberal education remain more than a museum piece. Despite the revolutionary transformation of the undergraduate curriculum in the twentieth century through the modern and practical studies, the failure to build a coherent core curriculum in general education in the face of knowledge specialism and fragmentation gives cause for perennialists to vent their timeworn call for a return to the "timeless" liberal arts. Moreover, old traditions die hard. The belief that liberal education marks a truly cultural education, as opposed to practical studies, continues to garner snob appeal on the part of so many liberal arts graduates (who must face the practical reality of going on to graduate and professional studies if they are to earn a living). The phenomenon of Allan Bloom's *Closing of the American Mind* holding the number one position over many weeks on national lists of best-sellers during 1987 revealed that a belligerent perennialist attack on the university for neglecting the traditional liberal arts was vastly appealing to American readers.[35]

Traditionalists see the school as well as the college as appropriately being concerned, predominantly if not solely, with the transmission of the cultural heritage, built on a foundation of facts and skills in the elementary grades. Mortimer Adler's *Paideia Proposal* (1982) exemplifies this view.

In an essay on education, Einstein observed that "[s]ometimes one sees in the school simply the instrument for transferring a certain maximum quantity of knowledge to the growing generation," and he proceeded to warn that such knowledge is dead. Accordingly, "the aim must be the training of independently acting and thinking individuals who," contended Einstein, "see in the service of the community their highest life problem."[36]

The dualism between cultural heritage and social power as educational aims, noted Dewey, is taken as intrinsic and absolute when it is actually historical and cultural. "The problem of education in a democratic society is to do away with the dualism," wrote Dewey.[37] This problem continues to haunt education to this day.

Knowledge Production—Disciplinarity

As we have noted, the era of the Cold War and space race was marked by an unprecedented curriculum-reform effort in the United States that sought to create a new generation of knowledge producers in emulation of the specialized university scholar. The pursuit of academic excellence embodied in the knowledge production-disciplinary model of curriculum was seen as serving nationalistic interests at a time when U.S. leaders feared Americans were in danger of falling behind the Soviets in scientific-technological-military developments. University scholars in the academic disciplines led the curriculum reforms during this era with the support of enormous federal funds.

These reforms were governed by a neo-essentialist doctrine of disciplinarity that saw curriculum content at the elementary and secondary levels being derived from and molded to the established academic disciplines of university scholarship. Although leading essentialists at first applauded these curriculum reforms, many of them began to have second thoughts regarding the priority given to the sciences and mathematics, and to the decline of history in favor of the contemporary social science disciplines in the curriculum.

During the late 1960s, the dominance of the knowledge production-disciplinary model came to be challenged as a result of the clamor for curriculum relevance on the part of high-school and college youth, rising social disaffection and protest, and a growing awareness that American quality of life was eroding and that education and knowledge must be geared to social problem solving if the American dream is to be fulfilled. The impact and consequences of the knowledge production-disciplinary model of curriculum are treated in detail in Chapter 11.

Individual-Social Growth

The function of education for individual and social growth is orchestrated in the writings of John Dewey. Although some of Dewey's educational and social theories have been discussed in earlier chapters, and are treated in detail in Chapter 9, along with their curricular implications, a brief mention of his theory of education as individual and social growth is presented here to contrast it with traditional conceptions of the function of education. According to Dewey,

> Education has been traditionally thought of as preparation: as learning, acquiring certain things because they will later be useful. The end is remote, and education is getting ready, is a preliminary to something more important to happen later on. Childhood is only a preparation for adult life, and adult life for another life. . . .
>
> If at whatever period we choose to take a person, he is still in the process of growth, then education is not, save as a by-product, a preparation for something coming later. . . . The best thing that can be said about any special process of education . . . is that it renders its subject capable of further education. . . . Acquisition of skill, possession of knowledge, attainment of culture are not ends: they are marks of growth and means to its continuing.[38]

DEMOCRACY AND SOCIAL PROGRESS.   The vital connection between individual growth to the social growth of a democracy is stressed by Dewey in describing the purpose of democratic social institutions.

> That purpose is to set free and to develop the capacities of human individuals without respect to race, sex, class or economic status. And this is all one with saying that the test of their value is the extent to which they educate every individual into the full stature of his possibility. Democracy has many meanings, but if it has a moral meaning, it is found in resolving that the supreme test of all political institutions and social arrangements shall be the contribution they make to the all-around growth of every member of society.[39]

Dewey saw the means to such growth as deriving from a curriculum model of personal-social problem solving through the method of intelligence. He warned of the dangers inherent in confining this method to scientific and technological advancement while neglecting the political-social-moral sphere. "Not only has the improvement in the method of knowing remained so far mainly limited to technical and economic matters, but this progress has brought with it serious new moral disturbances," wrote Dewey as he went on to state, "I need only cite the late war, the problem of capital and labor, the relation of economic classes, the fact that while the new science has achieved wonders . . . it has also produced and spread occasions for diseases and weaknesses."[40]

Ironically, Dewey's views were distorted by many of his attackers who caricatured his message as a call for "life adjustment."[41] It was Dewey who stated that "the social definition of education as getting adjusted to civilization, makes of it a forced and external process, and results in subordinating the freedom of the individual to a preconceived social and political status."[42] According to Dewey, "education is the fundamental method of social progress and reform," but he warned that the only sure method of social reconstruction is when individual activity has a responsible sharing of the social consciousness. "I believe that education is a regulation of the process of coming to share in the social consciousness," wrote Dewey.[43]

Although both the individual-social growth function and the knowledge production-disciplinary function focus on inquiry-discovery as educational method, the former tends to be geared to solving pervading social problems (ecology, racial conflict, poverty), whereas the latter is more concerned with the problems that are of significance to specialized scholars on the forefront of their disciplines.

As we entered the closing years of the twentieth century, efforts toward educational improvement appeared to take the form of peripatetic responses to the demands of special-interest groups in a social situation marked by fragmentation and conflict. The call for education as a regulation of the process of coming to share in the democratic social consciousness seemed to be drowned out by social confusion for the time being, at least.

SKILLS VERSUS GROWTH.   As discussed earlier, changing societal priorities and expectations have wrought marked shifts in the direction of education in recent decades. Because educational objectives are conceived at different levels (from the wider society to the local school system and to the individual classroom), and because they represent a broad spectrum of expectations (from the most general ideal to the most specific objective), it is useful to make some distinctions. Thus, when education is seen by the larger society as fostering democratic citizenship, ethical character, worthy use of leisure time, or mental health, such broad expectations of the school may be considered as *ideals*. At a more specific level, education may be seen as developing in pupils a command of the fundamental processes; the ability to purchase and use goods and services wisely; the appreciation of beauty in literature, art, music, and nature; the development of salable skills; and the ability to think critically—such expectations may be referred to as educational *aims*. Finally, at an even more specific point of reference, educators identify such measurable expectations as the ability to identify and define problems; to make relevant hypotheses; to select and analyze data pertinent to the solution of problems; and to formulate valid conclusions, solutions, and generalizations. Such specific expectations may be referred to as *behavioral objectives* (not to be confused with *behavioristic objectives*).

Tyler has noted that where behavioral objectives were conceived in evaluating the Eight-Year Study so as to assess such abilities of pupils as "applying principles to concrete situations" and "interpreting experimental data," in recent years behavioral objectives in education have been patterned after the industrial and military world of training and management by objectives—with the result that these objectives have been so narrowly specific as to lose sight of the wider nature of the human learner and the purposes of education. Referring to the tendency on the part of a number of education leaders to fashion behavioral objectives with excessive specificity and narrowness, Tyler observed that "they failed to distinguish between (1) the learning of highly specific skills for limited job performance and (2) the more generalized understanding, problem-solving skills and other kinds of behavior patterns that thoughtful teachers and educators seek to help students develop."[44] In this sense, they are not really behavioral objectives, but *behavioristic* objectives. Obviously, educators who see the function of the school as patterned properly according to the skills model, for example, will differ markedly in the formulation of educational ideals, aims, and behavioral objectives from those educators who opt for the growth model. Table 8–1 illustrates how these two contrasting models result in sharply different educational ideals, aims, and behavioral objectives.

Although the data in Table 8–1 are focused on cognitive abilities, it should be stressed that educational ideals, aims, and behavioral objectives may also encompass affective learning such as attitudes, appreciations, and values. Thus, for example, the

Table 8–1. Contrasting Functions of the School with Regard to Ideals, Aims, and Objectives

	Function	
Expectation	**Skills (behavioristic)**	**Growth (behavioral)**
Ideal	Skilled learner	Democratic (enlightened) citizen
Aim	Subject-matter mastery	Reflective thinking
Objective (examples)	Conjugates correctly at least 90 percent of any regular "ie" verb in Spanish Changes percents to decimals with accuracy to three decimal places Given a list of 35 chemical elements, recalls and writes the valences of at least 30 of them Calculates the area of a circle correctly	Recognizes existence of a problem Makes relevant hypotheses Selects pertinent data Applies data to solution(s) Forms tentative solution(s) Tests validity of solution(s) through application Reaches valid conclusion(s) Makes applications to new problem situations
Method	Coaching drills (error-oriented)	Problem solving/hypothetical thinking (idea-oriented)
Evaluative resource activity (example)	Worksheet exercises Workbooks Programmed instruction Standardized achievement tests Teaching to the test Recitation	Projects (individual/group) in school laboratories, studios, shops, and in the field Student portfolios Field trips Supervised field experience Critical-thinking tests (comprehensive)

ideal of democratic citizenship embraces the value of open-mindedness (as an educational aim), and may be evidenced (as a behavioral objective) in the learner's commitment to seeking and testing pertinent data representing all sides of an issue or problem.

As another illustration of how attitudes and appreciations may be encompassed in the growth model, let us assume that an educational aim calls for developing in the learner a love of good literature. A behavioral objective consonant with this aim is seeking to ascertain the extent to which the learner, as a result of curricular experiences, is impelled to read good literature for his or her own enjoyment.

Under the individual-social growth function, skills are recognized not as ends in themselves but as instrumental to the development of the ability to think reflectively. The ideal is the democratic (autonomously thinking, socially responsible) citizen. In connection with the skills function, the mastery of skills tends to be considered an adequate end in itself.

Significantly, the problem method, student school-community projects, and student portfolios (Table 8–1) were used with great success in the more experimental schools in the Eight-Year Study.[45] The portfolio idea was virtually forgotten until it was revived by Ernest Boyer in his report on the American high school (1983), in recognition that conventional testing instruments fail to represent and assess much of the most significant classroom learning experiences.[46] By the 1990s, Educational Testing Service (ETS) was seeking to co-opt the student portfolio among the "new forms of assessment" being developed.[47] Nevertheless, there was no danger that the ETS standardized achievement tests would be playing a diminished role in American education.

Returning to the individual-social growth function (Table 8–1), the students are engaged in addressing authentic problems in school and society—problems that are authentic to the life and growth of the learner. Unfortunately, opposition to the problem method arises because it often engages the learner with unsettled and unsettling ideas that may be unacceptable to special-interest groups. The easy way out is to focus the school years on facts and skills and relegate authentic problem solving to the college years as some educators have suggested.[48] A free society requires that all of its members have a common cause and shared concerns, and that problems be revealed rather than concealed for the enlightenment of the rising generation.

The problem method is inherently optimistic in opening up the possibilities for improved conditions and progress. Curiously, although acknowledging that cognitive and developmental psychologists universally recognize the great educative power in engaging students in authentic problem solving, Prawat has characterized problem solving as "defining the world in negative terms, as a series of obstacles to be overcome." He proposes that the focus be "less on problems and more on possibilities in a given situation" through what he terms "idea-based social constructivism."[49] However, Prawat not only has mischaracterized authentic or practical problem solving as pessimistic, while overlooking the fact that it is indeed idea based, but he has also created an artificial dualism between problems and possibilities. Authentic or practical problem solving is inherently rich in possibilities because it is an open system of inquiry and seeks solutions based on the best available evidence. The danger of focusing the curriculum on possibilities as opposed to problem solutions is that of indoctrination, for the possibilities are not put through the systematic test of problem solving.

The significance of personal-social problem solving in generating the powers of independent thinking in the context of democratic social responsibility gains renewed recognition at times of social disaffection and conflict. Paradoxically, when the growth function of the school should provide learning experiences to enhance intercultural understandings and cooperation, as opposed to multicultural separation and conflict, the curriculum emphasis in the social studies during the early 1990s has been on multicultural education.

The Panel on Youth of the President's Science Advisory Committee, under the chairmanship of James S. Coleman, pointed out that the schools have traditionally focused on narrow skills at the self-centered or individualistic level. The committee emphasized that it is also important for the schools to develop learning environments to enhance "mutually responsible and mutually rewarding involvement with others that constitutes social maturity."[50]

Any effort to conduct research on the effects of schooling, or to devise testing programs to assess learning outcomes, must take into account the various comprehensive functions of schooling and their interactions.

As discussed earlier, the public, education policymakers, and the media have embraced the notion that standardized achievement tests are the most valid indicators in assessing academic achievement of individuals and populations, along with measuring the effects of schooling. The political response, then, is for school administrators to have teachers align the curriculum to the tests so as to raise the test scores in their districts. Such tactics may well serve the political agenda, but do not serve as valid indicators of educational improvement.[51] Aside from the exceedingly low predictive validity of standardized tests in connection with academic achievement, and aside from the fact that such tests measure only a small fraction of the kinds of learning that actually occur in the school, teaching to the test, or "curriculum alignment," has deleterious effects on the teaching-learning process and the curriculum. Much can be done to improve these tests by gearing them to knowledge applications and critical-thinking processes. Standardized achievement tests have inherent limitations that must be recognized by the profession, policymakers, and the public.

THE WORLD OF KNOWLEDGE AS CURRICULAR SOURCE AND INFLUENCE

An extended discussion concerning the relationship between the world of knowledge and the curriculum is provided in Chapter 6. It shows how the search for and application of knowledge go on in the larger society in a wide range of contexts that transcend the subject-matter boundaries or disciplines of specialized scholarship. Emphasis is given to the vital mediative role played by the school in relating organized scholarship to life experience. In performing this mediative role, the school curriculum cannot be limited to disciplinary knowledge or specialized subject matter but must be concerned with the interrelationships and applications of knowledge in a wide variety of contexts.

Subject-Matter Specialists

Although the curriculum of the school and college must be influenced profoundly by the wider world of knowledge, Tyler viewed subject specialists as the key source of educational objectives as far as organized knowledge is concerned.[52] Disciplinary knowledge has been an outgrowth of specialized university scholarship and has served as a most effective means of generating problem solutions within the disciplines. However, efforts to make disciplinarity the single ruling theory for curriculum development, from the elementary school through the university, reached a crisis by the end of the 1960s when it was realized that knowledge applications for social problem solving required interdisciplinary and social-problems approaches in curriculum development. Disciplinary knowledge has a central and vital place in specialized education, but the school and even the college must also be concerned with general education and exploratory and enrichment education.

The influence of subject-matter specialists has been so pervasive that the curriculum often is conceived as merely a total list of separate subject matters with courses designed within the confines of each subject-matter domain. Curriculum revision thus becomes a matter of accretion and deletion of courses and course content within each of these separate domains. Whitehead addressed this problem when he urged educators "to eradicate the fatal disconnection of subjects which kills the vitality of our modern curriculum."[53]

Although Tyler recognized the problem of curriculum fragmentation as a result of knowledge specialization, and although he urged that knowledge specialists ask "What can this subject contribute to the education of young people who are not to specialize in it?" he assumed that this problem can be solved by the specialists themselves.[54] When knowledge specialists address this question, along with the question of how their knowledge can contribute to the solving of larger societal problems, they must be willing and able to pursue cross-disciplinary and interdisciplinary approaches. For example, ecological problems such as energy conservation are not confined to a single discipline but require a synthesis of many areas of knowledge—economics, politics, geography, chemistry, physics, engineering, biology, public health, and the like. The same situation applies to curriculum construction when the curriculum is to serve the need for the development of social power and insight for the rising generation, rather than for the training of specialists. In the absence of the perspective of the generalist, the specialist has little inclination to address these larger problems. This brings us to the necessary role of the generalist in school and society. (An extended discussion of the discipline-centered curriculum is presented in Chapter 11).

Curriculum Generalists

The problem of the specialist's and generalist's roles has been so pervasive in government, education, and society that a subcommittee of the U.S. Senate Committee on Government Operations published a selection of readings in 1968 entitled *Specialists and Generalists,* from which the following quote from an essay by Whitehead (1925) is extracted:

> Another great fact confronting the modern world is the discovery of the method of training professionals, who specialise in particular regions of thought and thereby progressively add to the sum of knowledge within their respective limitations of the subject. . . .
>
> This situation has its dangers. It produces minds in grooves. Each profession makes progress, but it is progress in its own groove. Now to be mentally in a groove is to live in contemplating a given set of abstractions. The groove prevents straying across country, and the abstraction abstracts from something to which no further attention is paid. But there is no groove of abstractions which is adequate for the comprehension of human life. Thus in the modern world, the celibacy of the medieval learned class has been replaced by a celibacy of the intellect which is divorced from the concrete contemplation of the complete facts. . . .
>
> The dangers arising from this aspect of professionalism are great, particularly in our democratic societies. The directive force of reason is weakened. The leading intellects lack balance. They see this set of circumstances, or that set; but not both sets together. . . . In short, the specialized functions of the community are performed better and more progressively, but the generalized direction lacks vision. The progressiveness in detail only adds to the danger produced by the feebleness of coordination.
>
> This criticism of modern life applies throughout, in whatever sense you construe the meaning of a community. It holds if you apply it to a nation, a city, a district, an institution, a family, or even to an individual. . . .
>
> Wisdom is the fruit of a balanced development. It is this balanced growth of individuality which it should be the aim of education to secure. . . .
>
> My own criticism of our traditional educational methods is that they are far too much occupied with intellectual analysis, and with the acquirement of formalised information. What I mean is, that we neglect to strengthen habits of concrete appreciation of the individual facts in their full interplay of emergent values, and that we merely emphasize abstract formulations which ignore this aspect of the interplay of diverse values.
>
> In every country the problem of the balance of the general and specialist education is under consideration. . . . I know that among practical educationalists, there is considerable dissatisfaction with the existing practice. Also, the adaptation of the whole system to the needs of a democratic community is very far from being solved. I do not think that the secret of the solution lies in terms of the antithesis between thoroughness in special knowledge and general knowledge of a slighter character. The make-weight which balances the thoroughness of the specialist intellectual training should be of a radically different kind from purely intellectual analytical knowledge.[55]

Whitehead's call for a radically different kind of make-weight for general knowledge in contrast to specialized knowledge has profound implications for curriculum development. In this task, general education—that is, the universe of discourse, understanding, and competence that enlightened citizens of a free society must share in common—cannot be construed as an amalgam of the existing disciplines of knowledge. A new structure for interdisciplinary studies that is focused on social-problem solving, and guided by some image of the good person leading the good life in the good society, becomes necessary. (A discussion of alternative ways of organizing subject matter and structuring the curriculum is presented in Chapter 10.)

MICRO- AND MACROCURRICULAR PROBLEMS.   When addressing problems of general education, educators are concerned with macrocurricular problems—problems that transcend the knowledge compartments of the specialized disciplines. In contrast, the subject-matter specialists tend to be concerned with microcurricular problems, or those kinds of questions that come within the province of their own disciplines. The problem of specialization that Whitehead addressed in 1925 has become even more acute as a result of the advances in specialized knowledge and the neglect of organizing and utilizing knowledge more broadly for solving pervading societal problems.

A number of contemporary educators, including knowledge specialists, have recognized the need for the generalist in attacking the problem of curriculum fragmentation and in developing a more coherent curriculum that is relevant to life problems. In pointing to the dangers of the discipline-centered curriculum reforms of the 1950s and 1960s—with their emphasis on purity, abstraction, and fragmentation—and their neglect of social problem solving, a nuclear physicist observes that "education at the elementary level of a field is too important to be left entirely to the professionals in that field, especially if the professionals are themselves too narrowly specialized in outlook." He concludes that "[s]pecialization is 'blessed' in the sense that only the specialist knows *what* he is talking about; yet, if only the specialist knows what he is talking about, only the generalist knows *why* he should talk at all."[56]

Caswell put the matter very directly in addressing the problem of curriculum articulation, stressing the role of curriculum generalists who are able to see across the subject divisions and boundaries with a view of the total educational offering of the school or college. In Caswell's words,

> They must be able to build a whole of educational experience that is larger than the sum of its parts because of the mutual support and interrelationship of the parts. Only general curriculum workers are in a position to discharge this responsibility. Others must of course contribute, but no one else has the freedom from vested interest to look impartially at the competing claims of various groups of specialists and to balance these interests in terms of the best service to students and society.[57]

What priorities should be given to the various studies? How should these studies interrelate with one another? How should these studies relate to the life of the learner and the problems of the larger society? How can the curriculum best be designed to serve the function of individual-social growth? These are only some of the questions that educators do not seek to answer unless they are oriented as generalists and are able to come to grips with some philosophical questions. As Cremin pointed out, someone must look at the curriculum whole and raise insistent questions of priority and relationship. Education is more than a succession of units, courses, and programs, however excellent; and to refuse to look at curricula in their entirety is to relegate to intraschool politics a series of decisions that ought to call into play the most fundamental philosophical principles.[58]

Such decisions call into play philosophical questions of no less import than those that undergird specialized subject matters and, therefore, cannot be thought of as matters to be dealt with by administrators alone through mere organizational arrangements of the curriculum.

Mediative Role of the School

In pointing to the educative influences of various societal institutions other than the school, some educators have advocated that the school curriculum be limited to the so-called academic studies. The National Panel on High School and Adolescent Education recommended that compulsory daily attendance be reduced from all-day sessions to an academic day of two to four hours concentrated on "education of the intellect" on the ground that the schools cannot possibly measure up to the influences exerted by television, for example. "By casting off all the extraneous activities and responsibilities that have accrued through the years, the Panel believes the resources of the high school can be concentrated in the areas of maturing intellectual competency," stated the report, as it went on to emphasize that the "essential skills" are most susceptible to "school training."[59] (The implication is that the child and adolescent are to come to school with only their intellect, and leave everything else at home.)

The schools of a free society are expected to play a mediative role in connection with the influences of other social institutions on the child and adolescent. Often such influences are miseducative and propagandistic, as in the case of television advertising—not to mention the obsession with crime, violence, and escapism through the video tube. The thought-provoking character of the curriculum derives from reflective consideration of experiences outside the school. The educative effectiveness of the school hinges on this mediative role of the school. Of course, other societal institutions, such as the museum, art gallery, and concert hall provide educative experiences for which there are no substitutes. The fact that a sizable proportion of children and adolescents have never visited a museum or art gallery, or attended a professional symphonic concert, cannot be ignored by the school. Even if all youngsters engaged in such experiences, the school can play an important mediative role in relating the knowledge sources outside the school to the school curriculum and vice versa. If the school is to be effective in its educative mission, it cannot ignore the way youngsters use their leisure time. For example, success in the teaching of reading is related to the learner's interest in reading for pleasure outside of school.

It is tempting to simplify the role of the school by confining its curriculum to the essentials or to the traditional academic disciplines. Learners also live outside the school, and they bring this life experience to the school. Whether learners bring their school experience to their life experience outside of school hinges on this mediative role of the school. To ignore this role is to ignore the essential mission of the school in a free society.

Behavioral Science

It will be recalled that Tyler viewed psychology as a screen for education objectives and curriculum development. Tyler pointed out that every teacher and curriculum developer must operate on some kind of theory of learning and that it is useful to have the learning theory formulated in concrete terms to assess its tenability for the curriculum.[60] But the problem is *which* theory of learning? The theory of learning that is most easily applied to curriculum objectives, sequencing of subject matter, and so on is behaviorism. Because it reduces human behavior to conditioned responses, everything can be laid out and accounted for in rather simple operational terms. Its mode of programmed instruction carries all of the operational conveniences of the old-fashioned workbook, and is also far more efficient in its repertoire of sequenced exercises and the feeding of correct answers. However, cognitive and developmental psychology present a far more complex view of the learner and, consequently, the applications to curriculum development are far more profound. It is not enough to select a learning theory because of its operational convenience, for it may run counter to one's conception of the learner and one's conception of the good life in the good society. Thus philosophy is the regulator. Because each school of psychology can marshal some evidence in its support, the evidence must be carefully evaluated in terms of its applicability to the function of schooling (e.g., whether a skill-based or growth function). If educators envision the school as performing a growth function, the selection of a mechanistic psychology will be contradictory to such a function.

As emphasized in Chapter 7, the educational process must be the source of the problems of inquiry. To use psychology as the source results in the distortion of the educational process in order to make it fit a schema of psychology. Many behaviorists, for example, would have the curriculum and educational objectives molded to behavioristic psychology. Such a reversal precludes the possibility of examining various alternatives for inquiry into problems deriving from the educational process that do not conform to the schema of behaviorism.

Although psychology is an important area of knowledge from which to draw in curriculum development, other behavioral sciences—such as sociology and anthropology—are also important. Social and biological knowledge provide a fuller conception of the human organism and the social environment—considerations that are pertinent to the educative process. Let us now turn to the learner as a curricular source and influence.

THE NATURE OF THE LEARNER AS CURRICULAR SOURCE AND INFLUENCE

According to Tyler, "[e]ducation is a process of changing the behavior patterns of people."[61] Such a narrow definition fails to distinguish the process of educating from that of propagandizing people. Moreover, it connotes a kind of mechanistic training function for education in which the learners are to be manipulated and shaped and in which their destiny is not of their own making.

Although Tyler was not a behaviorist and did not opt for a behavioristic model of humanity, and although he called for a broad conception of behavior, his definition of education is nevertheless so narrow that it is virtually identical to the behaviorist conception of education. According to Skinner, "[a] student is 'taught' in the sense that he is induced to engage in new forms of behavior and in specific forms upon specific occasions . . . teaching is simply the arrangement of contingencies of reinforcement."[62] In sharp opposition to this view is Dewey's definition of education as "that reconstruction or reorganization of experience which adds to the meaning of experience, and which increases ability to direct the course of subsequent experience."[63] Thus, Dewey sees the learner as having control of his or her destiny and not as an object to be manipulated and shaped by contingencies of reinforcement. Dewey's ideal of the learner as an autonomously thinking, socially responsible being is contiguous with the ideal of democratic citizenship.

Obviously, then, educators' conceptions of the nature of the learner, and their idealizations of the good person leading the good life in the good society, have a direct bearing on how they formulate educational objectives and the curriculum. The philosophy and ideals we have for education do not derive from the pieces of evidence obtained from psychology, but govern the direction and uses to which psychology is put. Moreover, personal philosophy and ideals govern the ways in which we view the learner as a source of educational objectives and as an influence on the curriculum.

Conflicting Conceptions of the Learner

Our discussion thus far points to two sharply conflicting conceptions of the learner: (1) the learner as an autonomously thinking, socially responsible individual who is capable of controlling his or her destiny and (2) the learner as an organism to be conditioned so as to respond in an externally controlled and predictable way. The first conception is based on organismic, gestalt, and field theories of learning, coupled with democratic social theory, whereas the second is derived from behaviorist theory. Behaviorist theory is derived from experimental work with lower organisms, namely, laboratory rats and pigeons. "In shaping the behavior of a pigeon, success depends on how the requirements for reinforcement are set," declared Skinner, and he went on to advise that "[i]n deciding what behavior to reinforce at any given time, the basic rule is 'Don't lose your pigeon.'"[64] When applied to human learning, behaviorist theory tends to be focused on the lower cognitive processes with motives being controlled through conditioning by rewards and punishments. The mechanistic model of the learner assumed by behaviorist theory leads to a curriculum that is programmed step by step in small units, focused on immediately observable and measurable learning products.

Dewey criticized those who seek scientific support for a theory of human learning based on the notion of fixity and certainty in the behavior of lower organisms as being victims of an outgrown psychology. "He is a victim of a popular zoology of the bird, bee, and beaver, which was largely framed to the greater glory of God," wrote Dewey, who then pointed out that such mechanical responses or "instincts in the animals are less infallible and definite than is supposed, and also that the human being differs from the lower animals in precisely the fact that his native activities lack the complex ready-made organization of the animals' original abilities."[65]

FREEDOM OF INTELLIGENCE.   Dewey contended that educational aims in a democracy must be governed and derived through learning activities that enable the learner to have foresight of results, rather than having such aims dictated by the teacher and met through a serial aggregate of imposed tasks.

> To talk about an educational aim when approximately each act of a pupil is dictated by the teacher, when the only order in the sequence of his acts is that which comes from the assignment of lessons and the giving of directions by another, is to talk nonsense. It is equally fatal to an aim to permit capricious or discontinuous action in the name of spontaneous self-expression . . . aim means foresight in advance of the end or possible termination. If bees anticipated the consequences of their activity, if they perceived their end in imaginative foresight, they would have the primary element in an aim. Hence it is nonsense to talk about the aim of education—or any other undertaking—where conditions do not permit of foresight of results. . . .[66]

Externally imposed aims limit intelligence, holds Dewey. "They limit intelligence because, given ready-made, they must be imposed by some authority external to intelligence, leaving to the latter nothing but a mechanical choice of means."[67]

In this connection, the behaviorist opts for a model of the learner, and the culture, as being derived from greater, not less, control. "What is needed is more control, not less, and this is itself an engineering problem of the first importance," contended Skinner.[68] Indicative of the influence of behaviorism in educational theory and practice is the growing use of the term *educational engineering,* along with attempts to shape the curriculum and the learner according to narrowly conceived and externally imposed behavioristic objectives.[69]

MENTAL DISCIPLINE.   Contrasted against the two conflicting conceptions of the learner discussed in the preceding pages is a third view, which sees the learner as a mind to be disciplined. This conception derives from the theory of mental discipline or faculty psychology, which has been virtually displaced as a psychological theory largely as a result of Thorndike's research early in this century.[70] Nevertheless, it continues to have its adherents, particularly among perennialists and essentialists, who see the mental faculties being strengthened through rigorous exercise. Traditionally, it was held that certain studies—Latin, classical literature, mathematics, and other classical liberal studies—are most suitable for training the mind and that such training is transferable to whatever mental tasks the learner may confront.

In attacking progressive education as "anti-intellectualist," Hofstadter argued that the experimental evidence has not refuted the notion of mental discipline and learning transfer, and he saw validity in Bruner's thesis that massive general transfer can be achieved under circumstances in which the learner learns how to learn.[71]

However, Bruner's thesis is based on a model of the learner who is capable of thinking by means of a process of inquiry-discovery. Although parallels have been drawn between this process of inquiry-discovery and Dewey's reflective thinking, Bruner confined such learning to the style of the mature scholar-specialist on the forefront of his or her academic discipline, whereas Dewey viewed reflective thinking as a process of individual-social problem solving that transcends subject matter boundaries. Moreover, where Bruner's thesis that "intellectual activity anywhere is the same" presupposes that the learner is to be regarded as a miniature adult scholar,[72] Dewey held that the child is a child, qualitatively different from the adult in cognitive style, interests, and needs.[73] Bruner's thesis, which served as a basis for the rationale that guided the discipline-centered curriculum reforms of the 1950s and 1960s, allowed the curriculum developers to ignore the nature of the learner as a source of educational objectives and as an influence on the curriculum, because the immature learner was to be created in the image of the university scholar-specialist.

Cognitive Processes

Considerable effort has been devoted to the study of cognitive processes for the purpose of assessing learning outcomes. One of the most systematic approaches has been developed by Bloom and his associates.[74] As shown in Table 8–2, the cognitive processes are classified in a hierarchical order, from simple to complex levels of thinking: (1) knowledge, (2) comprehension, (3) application, (4) analysis, (5) synthesis, (6) evaluation, (7) problem solving, and (8) creation. (Categories 7 and 8 have been added by the authors of this text.)

Although this schema is intended as a taxonomy, it cannot be considered as such in a truly scientific sense, for even Bloom and his associates acknowledge that the determination of the cognitive levels is somewhat arbitrary and that any number of approaches can be employed in identifying and classifying cognitive categories. Furthermore, although the taxonomy lists the cognitive processes in a hierarchical order, it is doubtful that the processes literally follow such an order in actual learning situations. For example, it is not uncommon for learners to engage in the application of knowledge before they proceed with an in-depth analysis of the knowledge. Thus, a youngster may build an electromagnet before he or she decides to analyze the principles of electromagnetism, or he or she may build a model steam-propelled boat before proceeding to analyze its working principles. In both instances, principles are being put into applications prior to analyzing the principles. As another example, the learner may engage in the cognitive process of synthesis, say in the use of language to communicate certain unique ideas (i.e., a poem), and afterward engage in an analysis of the structural elements and relationships of the communication.

Nevertheless, the cognitive taxonomy can serve as a valuable device for enabling teachers to design instructional activities encompassing a wider range of cognitive learnings. Classroom recitation, pupil assignments, and teacher-made tests typically focus mainly on the recall of specifics and the ways and means of dealing with specifics. As shown in Table 8–2, such learning is classified at the lowest cognitive level. One reason why teachers tend to place so much emphasis on teaching and

Table 8–2. Classification of Cognitive Categories

1.00	*Knowledge*
	1.10 Knowledge of specifics
	1.11 Knowledge of terminology
	1.12 Knowledge of specific acts
1.20	*Knowledge of Ways and Means of Dealing with Specifics*
	1.21 Knowledge of conventions
	1.22 Knowledge of trends and sequences
	1.23 Knowledge of classifications and categories
	1.24 Knowledge of criteria
	1.25 Knowledge of methodology
1.30	*Knowledge of Universals and Abstractions in a Field*
	1.31 Knowledge of principles and generalizations
	1.32 Knowledge of theories and structures
2.00	*Comprehension*
	2.10 Translation
	2.20 Interpretation
	2.30 Extrapolation
3.00	*Application*
4.00	*Analysis*
	4.10 Analysis of elements
	4.20 Analysis of relationships
	4.30 Analysis of organizational principles
5.00	*Synthesis*
	5.10 Production of a unique communication
	5.20 Production of a plan or proposed set of operations
	5.30 Derivation of a set of abstract relations
6.00	*Evaluation*
	6.10 Judgments in terms of internal evidence
	6.20 Judgments in terms of external criteria
*7.00	*Problem Solving*
	7.10 Defining the problem
	7.20 Formulating hypotheses
	7.30 Testing the hypotheses
*8.00	*Creation*
	8.10 Formulation of a unique idea, product, or process

Source: Condensed from Benjamin S. Bloom, J. Thomas Hastings, and George F. Madaus, *Handbook on Formative and Summative Evaluation of Student Learning* (New York: McGraw-Hill, 1971), pp. 271–273. * Categories not in the original; added by Tanner and Tanner.

testing for lower cognitive learning is that they find such material easiest to evaluate. The cognitive taxonomy can be useful in helping teachers to gauge instruction so as to encompass a fuller spectrum of cognitive learning styles.

KNOWLEDGE AND INFORMATION.   Although the cognitive taxonomy categorizes the retention of information as knowledge, students often find themselves memorizing and regurgitating such information without comprehending the material and without the ability to apply the information to different situations. All too often information is treated in education as an end product or commodity rather than being used as working power. The error of equating information with knowledge is pointed out by Dewey.

> Probably the most conspicuous connotation of the word knowledge for most persons today is just the body of facts and truths ascertained by others; the material found in the rows and rows of atlases, cyclopedias, histories, biographies, books of travel, scientific treatises, on the shelves of libraries.
>
> The imposing stupendous bulk of this material has unconsciously influenced men's notions of the nature of knowledge itself. The statements, the propositions, in which knowledge, the issue of active concern with problems, is deposited are taken to be themselves knowledge. The record of knowledge, independent of its place as an outcome of inquiry and a resource in further inquiry, is taken to *be* knowledge. The mind of man is taken captive by the spoils of its prior victories; the spoils, not the weapons and the acts of waging the battle against the unknown, are used to fix the meaning of knowledge, of fact, and truth.
>
> If this identification of knowledge with propositions stating information has fastened itself upon logicians and philosophers, it is not surprising that the same ideal has almost dominated instruction.[75]

PROBLEM SOLVING AND CREATIVITY.   Although the various elements in the cognitive taxonomy are essential to the act of problem solving through reflective thinking, the fact that the learner is engaged in certain activities that fit each category of the taxonomy does not necessarily mean that he or she is engaged in such problem solving. Thus, it would appear that a provision needs to be made in the taxonomy for the kind of problem solving that Dewey regarded as the complete act of thought.[76]

Finally, although the cognitive taxonomy provides no category for the act of creation, it is conceivable that certain attributes of creativity may become manifest as the learner engages in synthesis and evaluation—for example, when he or she develops unique ideas, plans, or products instead of converging on a singularly correct, established end. But because the act of creation is not happenstance (although relatively little is known about it), and because a growing body of literature on the subject is emerging in view of the fact that human progress is dependent on creativity,[77] it seems reasonable to hold that it should be included as a category in the cognitive taxonomy.

Thus, the case can be made for refining the cognitive taxonomy further by making a distinction between information and knowledge, and by adding the processes of problem solving and creation to the taxonomy. The major categories of the taxonomy might be reclassified as follows: (1) Information, (2) Comprehension, (3) Application, (4) Analysis, (5) Synthesis, (6) Evaluation, (7) Problem solving, and (8) Creation.

As discussed later, the cognitive processes are inseparable in life from the affective processes (interests, attitudes, appreciations, and values). Our treatment of these processes in terms of contrasting schema or classifications is done for analytical purposes only.

Affective Processes

In life, the affective processes—interests, attitudes, appreciations, and values—are inseparable from the cognitive processes. Yet some contemporary educators paint a stereotypic portrait of the research scientist as one who is engaged "in the cool neutrality of experimental inquiry."[78] Almost any account of the trials and tribulations of the scientist engaged in research on a significant problem reveals that the scientist's technical work is given force and direction through his or her imagination and motives.[79] Although the technical aspects of science differ significantly from the technical aspects of art, the dedicated scientist, no less than the dedicated artist, is passionately engaged in his or her work. On a more mundane level, whether the learner is approaching a social problem or a scientific problem, one cannot speak of being open to data on all sides of a problem or of being able to recognize bias on which data are formulated and selected, or of using one's intuition in developing a hypothesis and testing possible solutions—without having one's interests, attitudes, appreciations, and values engaged.

UNTENABLE DUALISM.   In short, how we think is virtually directed by an organic interaction of cognitive and affective processes. Yet some educators erroneously view these processes as though they were two virtually separate domains or functions. A former U.S. commissioner of education makes this highly questionable distinction:

> The cognitive function of instruction is directed to the achievement and communication of knowledge, both the factual knowledge of the sciences and the formal relationships of logic and mathematics—knowledge as both specific data and generalized structure. It is discipline in the ways of knowing, involving perception, the inductive, deductive, and intuitive processes, and the techniques of analysis and generalization. It involves both the immediate grasp of sensory objects and the abstractive processes by which the intellect constructs its ideas and fashions its ideals.
>
> The affective function of instruction pertains to the practical life—to the emotions, the passions, the dispositions, the motives, the moral and aesthetic sensibilities, the capacity for feeling, concern, attachment or detachment, sympathy, empathy, and appreciation.[80]

This statement is a schizoid portrayal of human nature. The learner is divided into two separate faculties for purposes of instruction. Modern behavioral science does not reveal such a separation. To assume that perception, intuition, and various systematic modes of thought are within the province of the cognitive domain and are independent of affective processes represents a mechanical conception of human nature not unlike that promulgated by the faculty psychologists of some generations past. Moreover, to hold that the affective function, not the cognitive function, pertains to the practical life leaves us with the notion that our practical life is governed independently of our ways of knowing. To face this kind of practical life would make human progress an impossibility. As Dewey pointed out, "[m]ethods that, in developing abstract intellectual abilities, weaken habits of practical or concrete thinking fall as much short of the educational ideal as do the methods that, in cultivating ability to plan, to invent, to arrange, to forecast, fail to secure some delight in thinking, irrespective of practical consequences."[81] Furthermore, the fact that one is knowledgeable about the different forms of thought is no guarantee that one will be a good thinker. Good thinking is dependent on the attitudes, values, and motivations that animate one's character.[82]

Critical thinking and problem solving require a penetrating curiosity, an openness to considering all pertinent data in seeking the best available evidence, and the use of the imagination in visualizing possible solutions to be put to the test of application. Obviously, these attributes do not accrue independently of attitudes, motivations, appreciations, and a value system.

The effective teacher knows that it is not enough for students to learn their lessons. However successful a teacher may be in developing the student's ability to make technical analyses of classical literary works or of scientific phenomena, the educational process cannot be considered successful if it leaves the pupil with a dislike for such material. Similarly, as a result of his or her learning experiences, a student may come to be committed to a value (e.g., women should receive equal pay for equal work), but if, in the commitment to such a value, the student deliberately avoids consideration of views alien to his or her own, then this commitment, however righteous, is dogmatically based rather than being a product of reason.

THE NECESSARY INTERDEPENDENCE OF COGNITIVE AND AFFECTIVE PROCESSES. As we have noted, as a reaction to what was regarded as a crisis in national security during the Cold War era, the pursuit of academic excellence became an overriding educational goal. The national, discipline-centered curriculum projects tended to focus on cognitive learning to the neglect of affective processes. One-sided reactions tend to be succeeded by counterreactions. The eventual counterreaction to the one-sided pursuit of academic excellence was an equally one-sided demand for curricular relevance and humanized schooling. Ironically, some elements of the very establishment that had promoted academic excellence turned their efforts toward developing proposals for humanistic curriculum building based on affective processes. An example is The Ford Foundation report *Toward Humanistic Education: A Curriculum of Affect,* which takes the view that the needed prescription is "to reverse the direction of the prevailing cognitive emphasis."[83] But such a simplistic solution calling for a reversal of focus ignores the need to redesign the curriculum so that cognitive and affective processes are organically interrelated. To focus the curriculum on the affective processes as an antidote to a narrowly cognitive-based curriculum suffers from the danger of creating a new imbalance to counter the old. The problem is not one of finding proper antidotes but rather of developing the interdependence between the cognitive and affective processes. Just as the traditional curriculum suffered from treating knowledge as though it were a kind of fixed and ready-made subject matter to be imposed upon the learner, a one-sided emphasis on affective processes deprives the learner of the working power that comes when knowledge is the material for reflective thinking.

Psychomotor Processes

Integrally related to the cognitive and affective processes are the psychomotor processes. Outside of the work undertaken by neurologists, physiologists, psychologists, and educators in connection with neuromuscular disorders, relatively little systematic investigation has been undertaken to ascertain how various educational programs can contribute to the effective development of psychomotor processes among normal children and youth. The most systematic work in this area has been conducted in the field of physical education, health, dance, and athletics, with the emergence of kinesiology or the study of human movement. In recent years, increasing attention has been given to psychomotor processes in the field of industrial education in connection with the learning of techniques involving complex manipulative skills.

As discussed later in this chapter, the work of Piaget points to the essential relationship between the experiences of the infant and young child in manipulating objects and the development of perception and intelligence. Although most psychomotor tasks are inherent in the human organism and are developed naturally under normal conditions, there is a need to build on this natural development various skills of a more complex nature for the effective performance of a wide variety of life tasks ranging from swimming to the development of manipulative skills in typing, playing a musical instrument, or operating a piece of industrial machinery. Other examples are perceptual abilities involving visual, auditory, tactile discrimination, and coordinated action; physical abilities; skilled movements; and expressive-interpretive movements.

The higher psychomotor processes do not operate independently of the cognitive and affective processes. For example, whether one is concerned with the learning of handwriting, learning to send and receive Morse Code, improving one's swimming style, learning a new art technique, performing an industrial operation requiring skilled manipulative technique, playing the piano, developing expressive and interpretive movement in modern dance, or learning a surgical technique, the cognitive and affective processes are interdependent with the psychomotor processes.

Stages of Intellectual Development

Traditional educational practice has been based largely on the notion that the child's mental structure is the same as that of the adult, and that the child merely lacks the adult's range and depth of knowledge and experience. Under this assumption, curriculum construction was regarded as properly the adult's logical formulation of organized subject matter to be imposed unilaterally on the child (as a miniature adult). As we have seen, a modern statement of this view is made by Bruner who, as chief theoretician for the discipline-centered curriculum reforms of the space-age era, proposed that the child's intellectual activity is essentially the same as that of the adult scholar and that any differences are a matter of degree, not of kind.[84]

QUALITATIVE DIFFERENCES.   The research of Piaget over several decades points to the identification of significant qualitative differences between the cognitive processes of the child and the adult. Piaget theorized that intellective capability undergoes qualitative developmental changes linked to the child's maturation. In this connection, Piaget identified four developmental stages: (1) the *sensory-motor* stage (first two years), when the child learns to control perception and motor responses in dealing with physical objects and language: (2) the *preoperational* or *representational* stage (to about age six or seven), in which the child learns to extract concepts from experience and later to make perceptual and intuitive judgments; (3) the stage of *concrete operations* (between ages seven and eleven), in which the child learns to solve physical problems by anticipating consequences perceptually; and (4) the stage of *formal operations* (late childhood or early adolescence), in which the youngster learns to think hypothetically and to theorize and experiment.[85]

According to Piaget, each developmental stage is a necessary condition for subsequent intellective development and these stages cannot be telescoped or accelerated appreciably, although there is some overlapping. The failure of traditional education, observed Piaget, lies in its treatment of the child "as a small adult, as a being who reasons and feels just as we do while merely lacking our knowledge and experience," and "since the child viewed in this way was no more than an ignorant adult, the educator's task was not so much as to form its mind as simply to furnish it; the subject matter provided from outside was thought to be exercise enough in itself."[86] When confronted with Bruner's thesis that "intellectual activity anywhere is the same," Piaget was quoted as saying, "I never understand Jerome Bruner and I don't think he ever understood me."[87]

As early as 1899, Dewey warned that the child is not capable of engaging in technical scientific inquiry. "There is no distinction between experimental science for little children and the work done in the carpenter shop," noted Dewey, and "such work as they can do in physics or chemistry is not for the purpose of making technical generalizations or even arriving at abstract truths. Children simply like to do things and watch to see what will happen."[88] Dewey later proposed three stages in intellectual development. The first stage, in earliest childhood, is manifested by a curiosity that leads the child into everything and to manipulate objects until they cease to reveal new properties, but this curiosity is not the same as reflective thinking. The second stage occurs through social interaction when the child learns that he or she can learn from others. At this second stage, the child's incessant "whys" are not demands for technical or scientific explanations but for more and bigger facts or ideas. Yet the child is seeking more than a mere heap of information or disconnected facts.[89] Dewey's third stage is manifest as the youngster's curiosity is no longer satisfied with immediate answers to spontaneous questions. Instead the learner seeks more remote relationships and, through reflective thinking, "[a] distant end controls a sequence of inquiries and observations and binds them together as a means to an end."[90]

EDUCATIONAL IMPLICATIONS OF DEVELOPMENTAL STAGES.   The educational implication of the theories of Dewey and Piaget is not that the child's intellective development will unfold of its own accord under any conditions but that appropriate environment conditions in the school and home must be provided in connection with each developmental stage. Differences in the school or home environment will produce differences in the quality of the child's performance at each developmental stage and subsequent stages.

To deny adolescents the stimulation of hypothetical thinking is no less an error than to impose this style of thinking on the young child. For the young child, a group project such as that involving the construction of objects can be an invaluable experience in developing the child's perceptions and impulses toward trying things out, and in developing his or her capabilities for social cooperation. The vital role of such cooperation in the intellectual development of the learner and in laying the groundwork for reflective thinking was noted by Piaget, who pointed out that "it is such cooperation that is most apt to encourage real exchange of thought and discussion, which is to say, all the forms of behavior capable of developing the critical attitude of mind, objectivity and discursive reflection." Moreover, instead of "submission to external constraint," the collaboration and self-discipline derived through such classroom activity is "morality in action, just as 'active' work is intelligence as act."[91] Obviously, it takes a highly skilled and sensitive teacher to design and organize appropriate learning environments and to select and arrange suitable curricular materials for children and youth at various developmental stages.

Erikson's Developmental Stage Theory

Erik Erikson, a disciple of Freud, extended Freud's psychodynamic theory so as to stress the significance of sociocultural factors in development. Although Erikson's early stages of development are very similar to Freud's, his later stages are less concerned with internal conflicts and are directed at the resolution of biosocial-psychological crises in human development. Clearly the school must play a vital role in Erikson's developmental stage theory, for the school is uniquely endowed with the mission of socializing the rising generation and engaging children and youth in a systematic learning environment so as to develop their fullest potentials. Obviously, failure in home life and school life will hinder the full and wholesome development of the individual.

Erikson's developmental stages are summarized as follows:

1. *Oral-sensory stage,* during which the infant is entirely dependent on the parents for nurturance and protection, through which the infant develops a basic sense of trust (or insecurity and mistrust)

2. *Muscular-anal stage,* during which the young child masters control of elimination and gains a rudimentary sense of autonomy

3. *Locomotor-genital stage,* during which the child learns to channel sexual urges into socially acceptable behavior and gains initiative

4. *Latency stage,* during which the child enters school and moves beyond the family into society, thereby developing a sense of industry and competence (as opposed to failure and inferiority)

5. *Pubescent/adolescent stage,* during which the adolescent must face an identity crisis ("Who am I?" "What are my life goals?"), must cope with problems of developing sexuality, and learns to control psychosocial impulses (identity versus role confusion)

6. *Young adulthood stage,* during which the individual must develop a clearer sense of identity, progress toward career goals, and develop meaningful relationships with members of the opposite sex as well as wider and more mature social relationships (intimacy versus isolation)

7. *Adulthood stage,* during which productive/generative working relationships are fully developed (as opposed to stagnation) in one's career and social life

8. *Maturity-stage,* during which the individual achieves a sense of ego integrity and wisdom, as opposed to despair and futility[92]

Needs and Developmental Tasks

There has been a great deal of confusion and debate over the uses of the term *needs* and the extent to which the curriculum should be based on pupil needs. "Needs" have been used in the education literature as curricular aims, such as the "ten imperative needs of youth" proposed by the Educational Policies Commission at midcentury,[93] as well as in selecting subject matter and learning experiences.

Over the years, educational psychologists have developed various statements of needs that generally fit into Maslow's categories of (1) physiological needs—such as physical health; (2) social needs—such as belonging, security, competence, and status; and (3) ego-integrative needs—such as self-esteem, enlightenment, autonomy, aesthetic-creative self-actualization, and overall personality integration.[94]

Havighurst attempted to orchestrate needs into biosocial-psychological tasks that he refered to as the developmental tasks of life. A developmental task is defined as "a task which arises at or about a certain period in the life of the individual, successful achievement of which leads to his happiness and to success with later tasks, while failure leads to unhappiness to the individual, disapproval by society, and difficulty with later tasks."[95] Table 8–3 presents a list of developmental tasks beyond those that occur in earliest childhood.

EDUCATIONAL IMPLICATIONS OF DEVELOPMENTAL TASKS.   The implications of developmental tasks for the school and curriculum should be apparent to educators. For example, the developmental tasks in early childhood of forming concepts and learning language to describe social and physical reality and getting ready to read are not provided for adequately in many disadvantaged homes, thereby raising special problems for the pupil and the teacher. At the adolescent level, the failure of the school to provide vocational curricula to prepare youngsters for gainful employment (along with the failure of society to find places for adolescents in the world of work) prevents them from meeting the developmental task of preparing for a career.

Little attention has been given to the necessary interaction and interdependence of developmental tasks. An adolescent who is denied the means of preparing for a

Table 8–3. Developmental Tasks of Childhood, Adolescence

Early Childhood
1. Forming concepts and learning language to describe social and physical reality
2. Getting ready to read
3. Learning to distinguish right and wrong and beginning to develop a conscience

Middle Childhood
1. Learning physical skills necessary for ordinary games
2. Building wholesome attitudes toward oneself as a growing organism
3. Learning to get along with age-mates
4. Learning an appropriate masculine or feminine social role
5. Developing fundamental skills in reading, writing, and calculating
6. Developing concepts necessary for everyday living
7. Developing conscience, morality, and a scale of values
8. Achieving personal independence
9. Developing attitudes (democratic) toward social groups and institutions

Adolescence
1. Achieving new and more mature relations with age-mates of both sexes
2. Achieving a masculine or feminine social role
3. Accepting one's physique and using the body effectively
4. Achieving emotional independence of parents and other adults
5. Preparing for marriage and family life
6. Preparing for an economic career
7. Acquiring a set of values and an ethical system as a guide to behavior
8. Desiring and achieving socially responsible behavior

Source: Condensed from Robert J. Havighurst, *Developmental Tasks and Education,* 3rd ed. (New York: McKay, 1972).

career and, as a result, cannot find gainful employment will encounter severe problems with other developmental tasks—such as achieving emotional independence of parents and other adults, achieving new and more mature relations with age-mates of both sexes, achieving a masculine or feminine social role, preparing for marriage and family life, acquiring a set of values and an ethical system as a guide to behavior, and desiring and achieving socially responsible behavior. Surveying the conditions in our major cities with regard to inadequate vocational curricula in the high schools and unemployment among the majority of boys who were school dropouts, Conant described the situation in 1961 as "social dynamite."[96] In 1968, after surveying the wreckage of the epidemic of urban riots, the National Commission on Civil Disorders reported that most of the rioters were older teenagers and young adults and recommended that vocational programs in the high schools, which were reaching only a small fraction of youth, be greatly expanded and strengthened.[97] Subsequent reports have reiterated the importance of the acculturation of the adolescent in society by relating education to the world of work through actual work experience.[98] However, these reports have given less attention to the need to ensure that such work experience is educative in the fullest sense. For example, how can the school enable adolescents to gain insight into the existing deficiencies and inequities in the world of work and the possibilities for effecting improvements and solutions?

When adolescents are denied the means of achieving socially responsible behavior, the result often is socially undesirable and irresponsible behavior. Increasing recognition is being given to the socializing and vocational-education function of the college in preparing college youth to meet the developmental tasks of life. However, a majority of our youth do not go on to college and, for them, the high school is the key social institution in laying the groundwork for these life tasks. More systematic efforts must be given to designing the high school curriculum to enable adolescents to meet the biosocial-psychological tasks that provide the basis for life success.

The failure to meet the biosocial-psychological needs of adolescents has been a chronic problem in the United States, as evidenced by the huge populations of unemployed youth who become engaged in antisocial activity. In a 1992 report issued by a commission of the U.S. Department of Labor, *Learning a Living,* the commission seemed to miss the mark by calling for the schools to develop a standardized system for the certification of fundamental academic skills and recommending the allocation of public funds for business and industry to provide apprenticeship-training programs for adolescents at age sixteen, as practiced in Germany.[99] No mention was made as to why the United States rejected the apprenticeship system after World War I and opted instead to incorporate vocational education in the comprehensive high school—a uniquely American institution.

Organic Interdependence of Tasks and Processes

Stressed repeatedly throughout this section of the chapter is the necessary interdependence of the various cognitive, affective, and biosocial developmental processes. Figure 8–1 presents a three-dimensional schema showing this interdependence. Represented on one plane are the various levels of cognitive development. On a second plane are the affective processes, needs, developmental tasks, and moral stages. The third plane represents the various developmental stages.

Each category on a given plane should be thought of as organically interactive not only with the other categories on the same plane but also with those on the other two planes. Thus, for example, the act of creation is actually a wedding of cognitive, affective, and the various other biosocial-psychological processes. Similarly, value systems not only are connected organically to moral development but if they are also founded on reason, rather than bias and impulses, such systems are developed and modified through the continuous evaluation of knowledge and experience. Consequently, the human organism is seen not as a set of mechanical responses but as a being capable of continuous growth through the reconstruction of experience.

The organic interdependence of affective and cognitive processes is supported by research that consistently shows a causal link between affect and achievement. Concludes Bloom, "[t]he relatively high relation between cognitive behaviors and

Figure 8–1. Interaction of Cognitive, Affective, and Biosocial Developmental Processes.

affective characteristics under most school conditions suggests that instruction must take these into consideration in determining what is necessary to develop both high cognitive learning outcomes as well as more positive affective characteristics."[100]

If the school ascribes to a growth function, the organic interdependence of the various tasks and processes (Figure 8–1) must be taken into account. If, for example, the older child and adolescent are denied experiences in the formal operations of hypothetical thinking on social problems, and the testing of ideas in action situations, then cognitive development and other aspects of affective-biosocial development will be hindered. To study ecology, literature, history, social studies, composition, or drama without examining moral questions is to rob education of its authentic mission in free society. The study of moral questions in the absence of reflectively formulated data is equally bankrupt. The fact that students are engaged in a heated debate is no indication of an enlightening learning experience.

Spectrum of Human Intelligences

"The notion that intelligence is a personal endowment or personal attainment is the great conceit of the intellectual class," commented Dewey, in holding that we were only beginning to tap the intelligence of the masses. Dewey went on to differentiate between the specialized intelligences that make for expertise in the sciences, arts, and other areas, and the wider social intelligence required of a democracy.[101]

Contemporary investigations into cognitive development have led to a view of intelligence as multifaceted—in recognition that people have different cognitive strengths and styles. Howard Gardner has identified seven types of intelligence: (1) linguistic, (2) logical-mathematical, (3) musical, (4) bodily-kinesthetic, (5) spatial, (6) interpersonal, and (7) intrapersonal.[102] Gardner's pluralistic concept of intelligence may not be as radical as he claims, that is if one realizes that we have long recognized the different talents of different people. Moreover, every advanced society requires that these talents be developed and made effective in a social matrix of interdependence. The especially dynamic quality of a free, diverse society requires the unleashing of the pluralistic talents and intelligence through a system of popular education that provides multiple opportunities for success.

One might argue that Gardner gives insufficient attention to the kind of hands-on, practical, inventive intelligence that has produced all sorts of mechanical and electronic devices and processes. One might argue that the visual arts require more than spatial intelligence. Indeed, one might proceed to modify or elaborate on Gardner's seven types of intelligence without taking issue with the thesis of multiple intelligence.

Gardner applies his theory of multiple intelligences to the school curriculum. In calling for a diversified curriculum to unleash the multiple latent talents of children, Gardner seems to be attuned to the reforms advocated by experimentalist-progressives throughout the twentieth century. However, whereas these progressivists also sought a core curriculum being focused on the common concerns, interests and capabilities that make for a productive and democratic citizenry, Gardner has dismissed the significance of the core as "the uniform view" for the "uniform school." He goes on to propose that school personnel include "assessment specialists" and a "curriculum broker" to "match students' profiles, goals, and interests to particular curricula and to particular styles of learning." Although Gardner acknowledges the problem of "premature billeting," he fails to give sufficient consideration to the problem of ghetto-izing the curriculum and to the fact that so many talents develop throughout the school years (and throughout life) to the extent that children and adolescents are constantly changing their career goals and avocational interests.[103] In view of his call for the early identification of these seven different intelligences in children, and the corresponding curriculum channeling, Gardner seems to imply that these intelligences are inherent or native. To Dewey,

> *effective* intelligence is not an original, innate endowment. No matter what the differences are in native intelligence (allowing for the moment that intelligence can be native), the actuality of mind is dependent upon the education which social conditions effect.[104]

The proposal that the secondary school curriculum be composed of *constants* (the core of studies shared by all) and *variables* (the diverse studies that provide for enrichment, exploratory, special interests, and specialized learning experiences) as embodied in the 1918 report of the Commission on the Reorganization of Secondary Education—and which gave impetus to the comprehensive high school—served to combine the concept of multiple interests and talents with multiple opportunities.[105] The comprehensive high school has its corresponding model in the land-grant university. The advocacy for creating schools of choice in recent years, with each school focused on a specialized area (such as the sciences and technology, the arts, and so on), beginning at the elementary level, raises ominous questions as to utilizing the schools for social separation and isolation of youngsters according to special interests.

Moral Education

A characteristic concern of traditional education has been to instill children and youth with the moral virtues through lists of moralistic homilies and commandments—ranging from obedience to constituted authority to honesty and fair play. Such verbal moralizing in terms of virtues and vices not only has been shown to have little effect on the moral character of the pupil but it also regards morals as something apart from knowledge and growth.

Many contemporary educators who reject the traditional precepts of moralistic education choose to see morality as something beyond intelligence. "*Why* aim for intelligence more than personal sensitivity or aesthetic awareness or openness to others or the growth of feeling?" asks Maxine Greene.[106] Such a question conceives of intelligence and morality too narrowly and creates a schism between the two. Is the truly intelligent individual not aesthetically aware? Is he or she closed-minded or insensitive to the ideas and feelings of others? If we conceive of intelligence merely as command of a high degree of technical knowledge or having a high I.Q., then a case can be made for viewing morality as something beyond intelligence. But if we conceive of intelligence and knowledge as organically connected with conduct, then such intelligence and knowledge bind individual growth to social growth. Morals that are not shaped and directed by intelligence tend to be reduced to mere lists of slogans or catechetical commandments. According to Dewey,

> [m]orals is [sic] often thought to be an affair with which ordinary knowledge has nothing to do. Moral knowledge is thought to be a thing apart, and conscience is thought of as something radically different from consciousness. . . . Moral education in school is practically hopeless when we set up the development of character as a supreme end, and at the same time treat the acquiring of knowledge and the development of understanding, which of necessity occupy the chief part of school time, as having nothing to do with character.[107]

Dewey pointed out that if the school studies are taken merely as knowledge acquisition, then they have only a narrow technical worth, but when they are engaged in "under conditions where their social significance is realized, they feed moral interests and develop moral insight." He also noted that "the great danger which threatens school work is the absence of conditions which make possible a permeating social spirit," and he held that "all education which develops power to share effectively in social life is moral."[108]

STAGES OF MORAL DEVELOPMENT.   A number of efforts have been made to examine systematically moral behavior as a developmental or growth process. A systematic scheme was developed by Kohlberg, who identified three levels and six stages of moral development. Kohlberg held that "[t]here is a general factor of maturity of moral judgment much like the general factor of intelligence in cognitive tasks."[109]

Thus, at the preconventional level, the child moves from the stage of obeying authority simply to avoid punishment or to gain rewards to the stage of acting mainly to satisfy himself or herself. At the conventional level, the individual moves from the stage of conforming in order to gain approval or to avoid disapproval, to a stage of "doing one's duty" in maintaining the existing social order for its own sake. Finally, at the postconventional level, the individual moves from an orientation of morality of contract, in which the rights of others are respected and honored, to an orientation of choice and conscience—based on universal ethical principles, such as those pertaining to justice, reciprocity and equality of human rights, and respect for the dignity of man.

Kohlberg reported that his experimental studies with youngsters in the junior high school demonstrated that when pupils who are at various moral stages are engaged by their teachers in an examination of moral conflict situations, a significant proportion of youngsters from the lower stages moved up at least one stage in his schema of moral development. However, Kohlberg acknowledged that such developmental progress is not a matter of special lessons but requires that the total school be imbued with justice as a living matter.

The decline of social controls, the emergence of the do-your-own-thing ethic, and the rising problems of social disorder and corruption have led to a resurgent interest in moral education. Unless moral education is connected to action and is governed by the principle of reason, it will be reduced to moralistic homilies, sentimentalism, or indoctrination. Traditionally, moral values have been associated with maintenance of a tranquil social order. From the educational standpoint, moral values acquire a far more profound meaning. If moral education is focused on democratic ideals of equality of opportunity, equality of human rights, and the dignity of humanity, then it must necessarily come to grips with existing social iniquities and inequities. The preservation of privilege at the expense of human deprivation and suffering becomes open to examination and question through education. Social ideals are tested on the anvil of social reality. This kind of moral education, contrasted against the traditional preachments for moral and "spiritual" values, is unsettling to the status quo. As long as the power of reason prevails, the likely outcome is social improvement. In a free society, the school is the chief agency for instilling the rising generation with the power of reason.

Group Dynamics and Cooperative Learning

From the late 1930s through the mid-1950s, the research on group dynamics from the field of social psychology attracted considerable interest among educators, including curricularists. The leading researcher in the study of group processes was Kurt Lewin (1890–1947), who also built the foundation for action research. Lewin, a leading Gestaltist at the University of Berlin, developed his field theory in the United States through the study of human behavior in the total or naturalistic social situation. As a refugee from Nazi Germany who worked out of "America's heartland" at the University of Iowa, Lewin had an abiding faith in the democratic prospect. He and his associates conducted ingenious experiments in holistic situations assessing group productivity comparing democratic against authoritarian and laissez-faire classroom conditions. The findings clearly supported Lewin's democratic faith. In a typical Lewinian action-research experiment, he attacked the problem of farm mothers failing to follow the prescribed instructions on the nutrition of their first child, despite one-to-one sessions with a nutritionist at the University hospital in Iowa City, and despite their being given printed materials on discharge from the hospital. Lewin set up an experiment comparing the individual treatment to having the farm mothers meet in small discussion groups with the nutritionist, for the purpose of reaching a consensual decision at the end of the group session. The findings revealed that the group-decision and longer-term method was far superior to the one-on-one instruction, both in immediate and longer-term effects, as well as being far more economical.[110]

From the work of Lewin and his associates, educators began giving systematic attention to group processes and cooperative learning in the classroom and to human relations on a broader level. Hilda Taba was one of the curriculum leaders in this work during the 1950s.[111] However, some educators tended to overlook the negative side of group process whereby conformity reigns, and there is little or no tolerance for divergent thinking.

The rediscovery of cooperative learning during the late 1980s has yielded positive findings and promising prospects for participative-group approaches, but the research and program implementation have been undertaken without building on the pioneering work of yesteryear, and without consideration of the lessons to be learned from the negative side of group process.[112]

Collateral Learning—The Hidden Curriculum

As discussed in Chapter 5, contemporary writers on curriculum have treated the concept of the hidden curriculum as a newly discovered phenomenon, whereas experimentalist-progressive educators have long given attention to the significance of the curriculum in effecting unanticipated learning outcomes. Whereas contemporary curricularists and school critics have tended to treat the hidden curriculum mainly as a detrimental influence, experimentalist-progressives recognized the enormous productive powers of what they have variously termed the *collateral curriculum,* the *informal curriculum,* and the *incidental curriculum.* As a consequence, they gave concerted attention to designing the classroom and school as a living learning environment so as to optimize the possibilities for stimulating pupils to develop enduring interests and appreciations that go beyond the formal curriculum and examinations. (They even went so far as to redesign the classroom furniture so as to stimulate student engagement in the curriculum.)

The excessive concern for specificity in setting educational objectives and assessing learning outcomes through worksheets, standardized achievement tests, and teacher-made tests focused on recall and narrow skills all reflect the undue emphasis given to the lower cognitive levels when education is seen as a production process as opposed to a growth process. Moreover, these practices are based on the questionable assumption that pupils learn only the particular thing that educators have targeted for them. Yet certain unanticipated collateral learnings may be far more significant to the pupil than the targeted material. In addressing this problem, Dewey noted that much of the knowledge and technical material that is supposed to be amassed in school, and on which the pupil is tested, eventually is forgotten and has to be learned over again in changed form, or actually has to be unlearned, if he or she is to make progress intellectually. But collateral learning—enduring attitudes toward what is learned and toward learning itself—may count for much more in one's future because such learning governs whether or not one will have the desire to go on learning.[113]

An exclusive emphasis on quantifiable objectives and outcomes delimits the possibilities for important qualitative outcomes. Teachers commonly find that pupils develop interests in pursuing ideas or probing into material in far greater depth and breadth than the particular lesson was intended to take them. Yet unless teachers make provisions for the further pursuit of such collateral learning, such as through individual and group projects, the impetus for self-impelled learning will be lost and the prescribed lessons will take on a mechanical character.

Another related educational problem connected with the obsession with narrowly specific objectives and quantitative measurements of outcomes is the failure to appreciate that in life some of the most significant learning occurs through fruitful mistakes. Too often mistakes in schoolwork are counted as penalties rather than treated as opportunities for effective learning. Correct answers memorized and regurgitated for the examination have little bearing on developing the pupil's desire and capability for continued learning, whereas the pupil who is investigating significant problems and is allowed to learn through mistakes will be better equipped to deal intelligently with future problems. The whole notion of hypothetical thinking is based on a recognition that the solutions to problems are not always self-evident and that solutions often are derived by pursuing divergent paths. Longer-term projects in the classroom, seminar, laboratory, shop, and studio environments—designed to stimulate pupils to think divergently in formulating and investigating problems—can provide opportunities for valuable kinds of collateral learnings and can serve to enhance the pupil's desire and capability for continued learning.

Such practices as teaching to the test ("curriculum alignment"), along with recitation and the employment of worksheets and tests for memorization-regurgitation, or "drill-skill-kill" exercises, reflect an error-oriented curriculum as opposed to an idea-oriented curriculum. The outcome of the error-oriented curriculum clearly tends to be manifested in boredom and negative attitudes toward learning. Exercises and assignments are to be "gotten over" as "chores" as painlessly as possible. The collateral or unintended learning outcomes understandably tend to be negative. In contrast, when learning experiences are idea-oriented so as to engage students in inquiry into substantive concerns, and into problems and issues that are of vital significance to them, and when adequate curriculum resources are available for such inquiry, then the learning becomes generative. The focus is shifted from specificity to possibility. Unforeseen and more enduring learning outcomes of a positive nature, then, are more likely to emerge from both the formal and collateral curriculum.

Collateral learning is not accidental learning. It derives from a planned curriculum that engages students in emergent learning situations, ensuring that the curriculum is not delimited to established-convergent experiences. In effect, the hidden curriculum could not really be hidden when human variability rather than predictability is valued.

PERSPECTIVE

A number of sources and influences whereby the school develops its objectives and curriculum were discussed in this chapter, namely, (1) society, (2) the world of knowledge, and (3) the nature of the learner. The vital interdependence of these sources and influences was examined. For example, the growing fragmentation of the school and college curriculum today reflects the general condition of fragmentation in society.

The function of the school and the model of curriculum followed tend to reflect the demands and expectations of the larger society. In different epochs there are shifting demands and expectations that have impelled the school to change its dominant function. Some of these major functions have been (1) the development of fundamental skills, (2) the transmission and preservation of the cultural heritage, (3) knowledge-production disciplinarity, and (4) individual-social growth. Not only do the larger sociopolitical forces exert a profound influence on the goals and functions of the school but they also influence the direction, interpretation, and application of educational research.

Specialization and fragmentation in the larger world of knowledge have had their concomitant effects on the curriculum of the school and college. The influence of the subject-matter specialist has been so pervasive that the curriculum tends to be conceived as a total list of separate subject matters. As a result, the dominant focus in curriculum development in recent years has been on microcurricular problems to the neglect of macrocurricular problems—the latter referring to those problems that transcend the knowledge compartments of the separate subject matters or disciplines. Insufficient attention has been given to the needed interrelationship of studies and the relevance of school studies to the life of the learner and the problems of the larger society. If the curriculum is to have relevance for social problem solving, a new synthesis will be required, and the role of the curriculum generalist will need greater recognition.

Education has been narrowly interpreted as a process of changing the behavior patterns of people. Such a narrow interpretation conceives of the learner as a mere cog in the machinery of the technological society. In contrast is the interpretation of education as that reconstruction or reorganization of experience that adds to the meaning of experience and that increases ability to direct the course of subsequent experience. This interpretation views the learner as an autonomously thinking, socially responsible individual who has control of his or her own destiny. The two radically different interpretations of education and conceptions of the learner vitally affect the uses educators make of psychology in the design and operation of the instructional program. The broader vision of education and the learner requires a broader vision of the curriculum and of the society. In this broader vision, cognitive goals cannot be considered apart from affective processes and moral principles, and such goals must be directed at competence in reflective thinking for the development of social power and insight.

Moral education can no longer be regarded as mere moralistic preachments to maintain the status quo of the social order. Democratic social ideals require that the rising generation be equipped with the power of reason in attacking social inequities and iniquities, and thereby to make possible a better society. The schools of a free society are the chief agency for developing in the rising generation the power of reason so as to bring about the needed social transformation.

The history of the curriculum reveals repetitive periods of reform and counter-reform reflecting the shifts in sociopolitical tides. Educators must be able to draw on the larger social situation for curriculum improvement. Concomitantly, they must examine external demands and pressures critically and constructively with a view toward solving problems stemming from the educational situation. Otherwise, the curriculum will be bent to whatever special interests are dominant at a particular time. Programs will be adopted that treat mere symptoms, only to be discarded in a succeeding epoch. It is the responsibility of educators to ensure that the schools serve the widest public interest so as to be true to the principles of democracy.

PROBLEMS FOR STUDY AND DISCUSSION

1. What illustrations can you give of how sociopolitical forces have influenced the curriculum? How have these forces influenced the kinds of educational research undertaken and the interpretation of this research?

2. Cremin contended that "someone must look at the curriculum whole and raise insistent questions of priority and relationship," and "to refuse to look at curricula in their entirety is to relegate to intraschool politics a series of decisions that ought to call into play the most fundamental philosophical principles." [Lawrence A. Cremin, *The Genius of American Education* (New York: Random House-Vintage, 1966), p. 58.]

Do you agree with Cremin? Why or why not? To what extent have curricular changes in your own school been guided by philosophical principles? Explain.

3. Tyler defined education as "a process of changing the behavior patterns of people." [Ralph W. Tyler, *Basic Principles of Curriculum and Instruction* (Chicago: University of Chicago Press, 1949), pp. 5–6.] In contrast, Dewey defined education as "that reconstruction or reorganization of experience which adds to the meaning of experience and which increases ability to direct the course of subsequent experience." [John Dewey, *Democracy and Education* (New York: Macmillan, 1916), pp. 89–90.]

How do these two definitions reflect different conceptions of the learner and the function of the curriculum? How would you define education?

4. Describe any collateral learning experiences on the part of yourself or your pupils that turned out to be far more significant educationally than the target subject matter.

5. Bruner has contended that "there is a continuity between what a scholar does on the forefront of his discipline and what a child does in approaching it for the first time." [Jerome S. Bruner, *The Process of Education* (Cambridge, MA: Harvard University Press, 1960), p. 28.]

How does this statement conflict with Piaget's theory of intellectual development? What are the implications of these two conflicting views for curriculum development?

6. What is the significance of developmental tasks for curriculum development? Moral stages?

7. Sidney Hook noted that "[w]e don't hear as much about democracy on the lower levels of instruction as about humanism which unfortunately gets translated too often as an attitude of extreme permissiveness with the teacher playing a largely passive part." [Sidney Hook, *Education & the Taming of Power* (LaSalle, IL: Open Court, 1973), p. 100.] Do you agree with Hook? Explain.

8. Examine some of the statements of educational goals and some of the major curriculum proposals prior to 1955 and compare these with statements and proposals from the 1970s to today with regard to the treatment of "democracy." [e.g., Educational Policies Commission, *Education for ALL American Youth—A Further Look* (Washington, DC: National Education Association, 1952); National Commission on the Reform of Secondary Education, *The Reform of Secondary Education* (New York: McGraw-Hill, 1973); and National Panel on High School and Adolescent Education, *The Education of Adolescents* (Washington, DC: U.S. Office of Education, 1976); National Commission on Excellence in Education, *A Nation at Risk* (Washington, DC:

U.S. Department of Education, 1983); and *America 2000* (Washington, DC: U.S. Department of Education, 1991). What differences do you find? How do you account for these differences?

9. In consideration of the changing functions of schooling discussed in this chapter, which function do you believe to be most appropriate for the schools of our society? Explain.

10. Using the cognitive categories in Table 8–2, examine some teacher-made tests in terms of the proportion of items devoted to the various categories. To what extent do the items require comprehension, application, synthesis, and evaluation—as compared to recall of information and specific-skill operations? What implications do such considerations have for the curriculum?

NOTES

1. Barbara Z. Presseisen, *Unlearned Lessons* (Philadelphia: Falmer Press, 1985), pp. 60, 64.
2. Denis Lawton, "Why Curriculum Studies?" Introduction in Denis Lawton (ed.), *Theory and Practice of Curriculum Studies* (London: Routledge, 1978), pp. 2–6.
3. Allan A. Glatthorn, *Curriculum Leadership* (Glenview, IL: Scott, Foresman, 1987), pp. 106–113; Wilma Longstreet and Harold G. Shane, *Curriculum for a New Millennium* (Boston: Allyn and Bacon, 1993).
4. Ralph W. Tyler, *Basic Principles of Curriculum and Instruction* (Chicago: University of Chicago Press, 1949), pp. 16–25.
5. Herbert Spencer, *Education: Intellectual, Moral, and Physical* (New York: Appleton, 1860), pp. 32–70.
6. John Dewey, *Democracy and Education* (New York: Macmillan, 1916), pp. 258–259.
7. Gordon N. Mackenzie, "Emerging Curriculums," Chapter 3 in General Education Committee of the North Central Association of Colleges and Secondary Schools, *General Education in the High School* (Glenview, IL: Scott, Foresman, 1942), pp. 85–86.
8. David Bohm, "Fragmentation," *The Science Teacher,* 38 (January 1971), p. 10.
9. American Association for the Advancement of

Science, *Science for ALL Americans* (Washington, DC: Author, 1989), p. 19.
10. National Commission on the Social Studies, *Charting a Course: Social Studies for the 21st Century* (Washington, DC: Author, 1989).
11. Katherine Isaac, *Civics for Democracy: A Journey for Teachers and Students* (Washington, DC: Essential Books, 1992).
12. Arthur Bestor, *The Restoration of Learning* (New York: Alfred A. Knopf, 1956), pp. 125–138.
13. Ernest L. Boyer, *High School* (New York: Harper, 1983) and *College: The Undergraduate Experience in America* (New York: Harper, 1988).
14. Sidney Hook, *Education and the Taming of Power* (LaSalle, IL: Open Court, 1973), pp. 92–93.
15. Paul Goodman, *Compulsory Mis-education* (New York: Horizon Press, 1964); Edgar Z. Friedenberg, *Coming of Age in America* (New York: Vintage, 1967), Ivan Illich, *Deschooling Society* (New York: Harper, 1971).
16. National Commission on the Reform of Secondary Education, *The Reform of Secondary Education* (New York: McGraw-Hill, 1973), p. 21; Panel on Youth of the President's Science Advisory Committee, *Youth: Transition to Adulthood* (Chicago: University of Chicago

Press, 1974), pp. 160–161; National Panel on High School and Adolescent Education, *The Education of Adolescents* (Washington, DC: U.S. Office of Education, 1976), p. 13.

17. Dewey, *Democracy and Education,* op. cit., p. 24.

18. Robert M. Hutchins, *The Learning Society* (New York: Praeger, 1968), p. ix.

19. John I. Goodlad, *A Place Called School* (New York: McGraw- Hill, 1984).

20. J. D. Bernal, *Science in History,* 4 (Cambridge, MA: M.I.T. Press, 1971), p. 1149.

21. John Dewey, "Learning to Earn," *School and Society,* 5 (March 24, 1917), p. 332.

22. Mortimer Smith, "Divergent Paths to Educational Change," in *Papers on Educational Reform* (LaSalle, IL: Open Court, 1970), p. 443.

23. Mortimer J. Adler, *The Paideia Proposal: An Educational Manifesto* (New York: Macmillan, 1982).

24. *U.S. News & World Report,* 43 (March 15, 1957), pp. 38–44; *U.S. News & World Report,* 44 (January 24, 1958), pp. 68–77; *U.S. News & World Report,* 67 (October 13, 1969), pp. 45–46; *U.S. News & World Report,* 75 (December 31, 1973), p. 39; *U.S. News & World Report,* 81 (September 6, 1976), "'Three R's' in Schools Now: Retrenchment, Results, Realism," pp. 50–51; *U.S. News & World Report,* "Competency Tests: New Furor in Schools," 84 (February 6, 1978), p. 49.

25. Edward D. Hirsch, Jr., *Cultural Literacy: What Every American Needs to Know* (Boston: Houghton Mifflin, 1987).

26. Diane Ravitch and Chester E. Finn, Jr., *What Do Our 17-Year-Olds Know?* (New York: Harper, 1987).

27. George F. Madaus, *The Influence of Testing on Teaching Math and Science in Grades 4–12* (Chestnut Hill, MA: Center for the Study of Testing, 1992); Charles C. Carson, Robert M. Huelskamp, and Thomas D. Woodall, "Perspectives on Education in America," *Journal of Educational Research,* 86 (May/June 1993), pp. 259–310.

28. U.S. Department of Education, *America 2000* (Washington, DC: Author, 1991). See also National Education Goals Panel, *Building a Nation of Learners* (Washington, DC: Superintendent of Documents, 1992).

29. George F. Madaus and Thomas Kellaghan, "Curriculum Evaluation and Assessment" in Philip W. Jackson (ed.), *Handbook of Research on Curriculum* (New York: Macmillan, 1992), pp. 126, 137.

30. John Dewey, *The School and Society* (Chicago: University of Chicago Press, 1915), p. 25.

31. Dewey, *Democracy and Education,* op. cit., p. 159.

32. Ibid., pp. 142–143.

33. James B. Conant, *Education in a Divided World* (Cambridge, MA: Harvard University Press, 1949), pp. 74–75.

34. Ibid., pp. 79, 83, 92.

35. Allan Bloom, *The Closing of the American Mind* (New York: Simon and Schuster, 1987).

36. Albert Einstein, *Out of My Later Years* (New York: Philosophical Library, 1950), p. 32.

37. Dewey, *Democracy and Education,* op. cit., p. 305.

38. John Dewey, *Reconstruction in Philosophy* (Boston: Beacon, 1957), pp. 184–185. (Originally published in 1920 by Holt.)

39. Ibid., p. 186.

40. Ibid., p. 125.

41. See H. G. Rickover, *Education and Freedom* (New York: Dutton, 1960), p. 136.

42. John Dewey, "My Pedagogic Creed," in Reginald D. Archambault (ed.), *John Dewey on Education* (New York: The Modern Library, 1964), p. 429. (Originally published by E. L. Kellogg, 1897.)

43. Ibid., p. 437.

44. Ralph W. Tyler, "The Father of Behavioral Objectives Criticizes Them: An Interview," *Phi Delta Kappan,* 55 (September 1973), p. 57.

45. Wilford M. Aikin, *The Story of the Eight-Year Study* (New York: Harper, 1942).

46. Boyer, op. cit., p. 135.

47. Educational Testing Service, *1992 Annual Report,* p. 12.

48. Daniel Bell, *The Reforming of General Education* (New York: Doubleday/Anchor, 1968), p. 181.

49. Richard S. Prawat, "The Value of Ideas: Problems versus Possibilities in Learning," *Educational Researcher,* 22 (August–September 1993), pp. 5–14.

50. Panel on Youth, op. cit., p. 3.

51. John Hollifield, "Improved Test Scores Don't Mean Higher Achievement," *R&D Preview,* 5 (December 1990), pp. 2–3.

52. Tyler, *Basic Principles of Curriculum and Instruction,* op. cit., pp. 25–33.

53. Alfred North Whitehead. *The Aims of Education* (New York: Macmillan, 1929), p. 10.

54. Tyler, op. cit., pp. 27–33.

55. Alfred North Whitehead, "Dangers of Specialization," in U.S. Senate Committee on Government Operations, *Specialists and Generalists* (Washington, DC: U.S. Government Printing Office, 1968), pp. 47–48 (New York: Free Press, 1925). (Originally published in *Science and the Modern World.*)

56. Alvin M. Weinberg, *Reflections on Big Science* (Cambridge, MA: M.I.T. Press, 1967), pp. 154–155, 161.

57. Hollis L. Caswell, "Emergence of the Curriculum as a Field of Professional Work and Study," in Helen F. Robison (ed.), *Precedents and Promises in the Curriculum Field* (New York: Teachers College Press, 1966), p. 8.

58. Lawrence A. Cremin, *The Genius of American Education* (New York: Random House-Vintage, 1966), p. 58.

59. National Panel on High School and Adolescent Education, op. cit., pp. 13–14. *NAEP Newsletter,* 11 (June 1978), pp. 1–2.

60. Tyler, op. cit., pp. 41–42.

61. Ibid., pp. 5–6.

62. B. F. Skinner, *The Technology of Teaching* (New York: Appleton, 1968), pp. 5, 33.

63. Dewey, *Democracy and Education,* op. cit., pp. 89–90.

64. Skinner, *The Technology of Teaching,* op. cit., p. 158.

65. John Dewey, *Human Nature and Conduct* (New York: Holt, 1922), p. 107.

66. Dewey, *Democracy and Education,* op. cit., pp. 118–119.

67. Ibid., p. 122.

68. B. F. Skinner, *Beyond Freedom and Dignity* (New York: Alfred A. Knopf, 1971), p. 177.

69. Theodore R. Sizer, "High School Reform: The Need for Engineering," *Phi Delta Kappan,* 64 (June 1983), pp. 679–683.

70. E. L. Thorndike, "Mental Discipline in High School Subjects," *Journal of Educational Psychology,* 15 (January–February 1924), pp. 1–22, 83–98.

71. Richard Hofstadter, *Anti-intellectualism in American Life* (New York: Alfred A. Knopf, 1963), p. 350.

72. Jerome S. Bruner, *The Process of Education* (Cambridge, MA: Harvard University Press, 1960), p. 14.

73. John Dewey, *The Child and the Curriculum* (Chicago: University of Chicago Press, 1902), pp. 5–6.

74. Benjamin S. Bloom (ed.), *Taxonomy of Educational Objectives, Handbook I: Cognitive Domain* (New York: McKay, 1956).

75. Dewey, *Democracy and Education,* op. cit., p. 220.

76. Ibid., p. 192.

77. See Jacob Bronowski, *The Origins of Knowledge and Imagination* (New Haven, CT: Yale University Press), 1978.

78. Maxine Greene, *Teacher as Stranger* (Belmont, CA: Wadsworth, 1973), p. 137.

79. See James D. Watson, *The Double Helix* (New York: Atheneum, 1969).

80. Sterling M. McMurrin, "What Tasks for Schools?" *Saturday Review,* 49 (January 14, 1967), p. 41.

81. John Dewey, *How We Think,* rev. ed. (Lexington, MA: D. C. Heath, 1933), pp. 228.

82. Ibid., p. 29.

83. Gerald Weinstein and Mario D. Fantini (eds.), *Toward Humanistic Education: A Curriculum of Affect* (New York: Praeger, 1970), p. 31.

84. Bruner, op. cit., p. 14.

85. Jean Piaget, *The Psychology of Intelligence* (New York: Harcourt, 1950), pp. 87–158.

86. Jean Piaget, *Science of Education and the Psychology of the Child* (New York: Orion, 1970), pp. 159–160.

87. *The New York Times* (October 19, 1972), p. 49.

88. Dewey, *The School and Society,* op. cit., p. 44.

89. Dewey, *How We Think* (Lexington, MA: D. C. Heath, 1910), pp. 31–32.

90. Dewey, *How We Think,* rev. ed., op. cit., p. 39.

91. Piaget, *Science of Education,* op, cit., p. 180.

92. Erik H. Erikson, *Childhood and Society,* 2nd ed. (New York: W. W. Norton, 1950).

93. Educational Policies Commission, *Education for ALL American Youth—A Further Look*

(Washington, DC: National Education Association, 1952), p. 216.

94. Abraham Maslow, *Motivation and Personality,* 2nd ed. (New York: Harper, 1970), pp. 35–51.

95. Robert J. Havighurst, *Developmental Tasks and Education,* 3rd ed. (New York: McKay, 1972), p. 2.

96. James B. Conant, *Slums and Suburbs* (New York: McGraw-Hill, 1961), p. 2.

97. *Report of the National Commission on Civil Disorders* (Washington, DC: U.S. Government Printing Office, 1968), p. 74.

98. Report of the Panel on Youth, op. cit.; National Panel on High School and Adolescent Education, op. cit.

99. U.S. Department of Labor, *Learning a Living* (Washington, DC: Author, 1992).

100. Benjamin S. Bloom, *Human Characteristics and School Learning* (New York: McGraw-Hill, 1976), p. 106.

101. John Dewey, *The Public and Its Problems* (Chicago: Swallow Press, 1927), pp. 209, 211.

102. Howard Gardner, "Developing the Spectrum of Human Intelligence," *Harvard Educational Review,* 57 (May 1987), pp. 187–193.

103. Ibid., pp. 190–192.

104. Dewey, *The Public,* op. cit., p. 209.

105. Commission on the Reorganization of Secondary Education, *Cardinal Principles of Secondary Education* (Washington, DC: U.S. Bureau of Education, 1918).

106. Greene, op. cit., p. 182.

107. Dewey, *Democracy and Education,* op. cit., p. 411.

108. Ibid., p. 414–416, 418.

109. See Lawrence Kohlberg, "Education for Justice," in *Moral Education* (Cambridge, MA: Harvard University Press, 1970), pp. 71–72.

110. Kurt Lewin, "Group Decision and Social Change," in Guy E. Swanson, Theodore M. Newcomb, and Eugene L. Hartley (eds.), *Readings in Social Psychology,* rev. ed. (New York: Holt, 1952), pp. 467–473.

111. Hilda Taba, *With Perspective on Human Relations* (Washington, DC: American Council on Education, 1955).

112. Jane A. Stallings and Deborah Stipek, "Research on Early Childhood and Elementary School Teaching," in Merlin C. Wittrock (ed.), *Handbook of Research on Teaching,* 3rd ed. (New York: Macmillan, 1986), pp. 746–749.

113. John Dewey, *Experience and Education* (New York: Macmillan, 1938), p. 48.

SELECTED REFERENCES

Adler, Mortimer J. *The Paideia Proposal: An Educational Manifesto.* New York: Macmillan, 1982.

Aikin, Wilford M. *The Story of the Eight-Year Study.* New York: Harper, 1942.

American Association for the Advancement of Science. *Science for All Americans.* Washington, DC: Author, 1989.

Bernal, J. D. *Science in History,* 4. Cambridge, MA: M.I.T. Press, 1971.

Bloom, Allan. *The Closing of the American Mind.* New York: Simon and Schuster, 1987.

Bloom, Benjamin S. *Stability and Change in Human Characteristics.* New York: John Wiley & Sons, 1964.

Bloom, Benjamin S., Hastings, J. Thomas, and Madaus, George F. *Handbook on Formative and Summative Evaluation of Student Learning.* New York: McGraw-Hill, 1971.

Bode, Boyd H. *Modern Educational Theories.* New York: Macmillan, 1927.

Bower, Gordon N., and Hilgard, Ernest R. *Theories of Learning,* 5th ed. New York: Prentice Hall, 1981.

Boyer, Ernest L. *College: The Undergraduate Experience in America.* New York: Harper, 1988.

Boyer, Ernest L. *High School: A Report on Secondary Education in America.* New York: Harper, 1983.

Bronowski, Jacob. *The Origins of Knowledge and Imagination.* New Haven, CT: Yale University Press, 1978.

Bruner, Jerome S. *The Process of Education.* Cambridge, MA: Harvard University Press, 1960.

Chaplin, James P., and Krawiec, T. S. *Systems and Theories of Psychology,* 4th ed. New York: Holt, Rinehart and Winston, 1979.

Commission on the Relation of School and College. *Thirty Schools Tell Their Story.* New York: Harper, 1943.

Commission on the Reorganization of Secondary Education. *Cardinal Principles of Secondary Education.* Washington, DC: U.S. Bureau of Education, 1918.

Conant, James B. *Education in a Divided World.* Cambridge, MA: Harvard University Press, 1949.

Conant, James B. *Slums and Suburbs.* New York: McGraw-Hill, 1961.

Cremin, Lawrence A. *The Genius of American Education.* New York: Random House/Vintage, 1966.

Cremin, Lawrence A. *The Transformation of the School.* New York: Alfred A. Knopf, 1961.

Dewey, John. *Democracy and Education.* New York: Macmillan, 1916.

Dewey, John. *Experience and Education.* New York: Macmillan, 1938.

Dewey, John. *How We Think,* rev. ed. Lexington, MA: D. C. Heath, 1933.

Dewey, John. *Human Nature and Conduct.* New York: Henry Holt, 1922.

Dewey, John. *The School and Society/The Child and the Curriculum.* Chicago: University of Chicago Press, 1900, 1902; combined edition, 1990.

Dewey, John. *The Sources of a Science of Education.* New York: Liveright, 1929.

Erikson, Erik H. *Childhood and Society,* 2nd ed. New York: W. W. Norton, 1963.

Erikson, Erik H. *Identity: Youth in Crisis.* New York: W. W. Norton, 1968.

Gardner, Howard. *Frames of Mind: The Theory of Multiple Intelligences.* New York: Basic Books, 1983.

Giles, H. W., McCutchen, S. P., and Zechiel, A. N. *Exploring the Curriculum.* New York: Harper, 1942.

Goodlad, John I. *A Place Called School.* New York: McGraw-Hill, 1984.

Havighurst, Robert J. *Developmental Tasks and Education,* 3rd ed. New York: David McKay, 1972.

Hirsch, Edward D., Jr. *Cultural Literacy: What Every American Needs to Know.* Boston: Houghton Mifflin, 1987.

Isaac, Katherine. *Civics for Democracy: A Journey for Teachers and Students.* Washington, DC: Essential Books, 1992.

Jackson, Philip W. (ed.). *Handbook of Research on Curriculum.* New York: Macmillan, 1992.

Kitcher, Philip. *How to Think About Science.* New York: Oxford University Press, 1993.

Malone, John C. *Theories of Learning: A Historical Approach.* Belmont, CA: Wadsworth, 1991.

Maslow, Abraham. *Motivation and Personality,* 2nd ed. New York: Harper and Row, 1970.

National Commission on Excellence in Education. *A Nation at Risk.* Washington, DC: U.S. Department of Education, 1983.

National Commission on Social Studies. *Charting a Course: Social Studies for the 21st Century,* 1989.

National Education Goals Panel. *Building a Nation of Learners.* Washington, DC: Superintendent of Documents, 1992.

National Society for the Study of Education. *Critical Issues in Curriculum.* Eighty-seventh Yearbook, Part I. Chicago: University of Chicago Press, 1988.

National Society for the Study of Education. *Education in School and Nonschool Settings.* Eighty-fourth Yearbook, Part I. Chicago: University of Chicago Press, 1985.

Panel on Youth of the President's Science Advisory Committee. *Youth: Transition to Adulthood.* Chicago: University of Chicago Press, 1974.

Piaget, Jean. *Science of Education and Psychology of the Child.* New York: Orion Press, 1970.

Skinner, B. F. *Beyond Freedom and Dignity.* New York: Alfred A. Knopf, 1971.

Skinner, B. F. *The Technology of Teaching.* New York: Appleton-Century-Crofts, 1968.

Tanner, Daniel. "Curriculum History," in Harold E. Mitzell (ed.), *Encyclopedia of Educational Research,* 5th ed., Vol. 1. New York: Macmillan and Free Press, 1982, pp. 412–420.

Tanner, Daniel, and Tanner, Laurel. *History of the School Curriculum.* New York: Macmillan, 1990.

Tyler, Ralph W. *Basic Principles of Curriculum and Instruction.* Chicago: University of Chicago Press, 1949.

U.S. Department of Education. *America 2000: An Education Strategy.* Washington, DC: Author, 1991.

U.S. Department of Labor. *Learning a Living.* Washington, DC: Author, 1992.

Weinberg, Alvin M. *Reflections on Big Science.* Cambridge, MA: M.I.T. Press, 1967.

Whitehead, Alfred N. *Adventures of Ideas.* New York: Macmillan, 1933.

Whitehead, Alfred N. *The Aims of Education.* New York: Macmillan, 1929.

CHAPTER 9

CURRICULAR SOURCES AND INFLUENCES—CONFLICTING EDUCATIONAL THEORIES

"If we are willing to conceive education as the process of forming fundamental dispositions, intellectual and emotional, toward nature and fellow men," wrote Dewey, "philosophy may even be defined as *the general theory of education.*" And, accordingly, "the business of schooling tends to become a routine empirical affair unless its aims and methods are animated by such a broad and sympathetic survey of its place in contemporary life as it is the business of philosophy to provide."[1]

One cannot penetrate very deeply into any significant curricular problem or issue without encountering philosophical considerations. The term *philosophy* is often used by teachers and administrators to convey their common-sense outlook on educational and curriculum matters. However, educational philosophy emerges from concrete and systematic consideration of the uncertainties and most significant aspects of the educational condition. It serves not only to animate and assess aims, values, and means, but also to provide generalized meaning for the widest range of conditions. Educational philosophy is not the external imposition of prefabricated ideas on a given situation that have radically different origins; rather, it is a formulation of theoretical ideas derived from systematic consideration of the educational condition, whereas "[e]ducation is the laboratory in which philosophic distinctions become concrete and are tested."[2]

In most treatments concerning the conflicting schools of educational philosophy or theory, curriculum is subordinated to a host of other considerations. In this chapter the various schools of thought are examined in terms of curriculum as the focal point.

NEED FOR A GUIDING PHILOSOPHY

In Tyler's conceptual scheme, philosophy is employed chiefly "to screen the heterogeneous collection of objectives thus far obtained so as to eliminate the unimportant and the contradictory ones."[3] Tyler's conception of philosophy as a mere "screen" for selecting educational objectives appears to make its function mainly mechanical and somewhat external to the educative process.

Bode recognized the function of philosophy as a source of illuminating educational aims and practice when he wrote, "if the younger generation is to achieve 'participation' in our social life the emphasis in curriculum construction and in teaching must be placed on social outlook, on reflective consideration of what constitutes a good life in the social order."[4] In the absence of reflective consideration of what constitutes the good person leading the good life in the good society, the curriculum tends to be regarded as a mechanical means of developing the necessary skills of young people in conformance with the pervading demands of the larger social scene. Under such circumstances, the school does not need to bring into question the existing social situation, nor does it need to enable pupils to examine through reflective thinking possible alternative solutions to social problems. Instead, the school merely is expected to do the bidding of whatever powers and forces are most dominant in the larger society at any given time. A vivid example of this condition was the era of discipline-centered curriculum reforms, extended from the mid-1950s to the late 1960s, in which the curriculum was retooled to serve the nation's Cold War interests while the problems of poverty and social disaffection were largely ignored.

Philosophy and Objectives

It is a common practice for the school to have a formal statement of philosophy and objectives developed by its faculty and administration for circulation to parents, students, and the general public. At the secondary level, such a statement may appear in the student handbook. Accreditation procedures commonly require each secondary school to develop a statement of philosophy and objectives, and it typically includes a number of items holding to the fostering of democratic values, the recognition of individual differences, the school's commitment to community needs, and other general statements. Obviously, such statements are meaningless if they are inconsistent with or contradictory to actual educational practice.

EDUCATIONAL PRACTICE MAY CONTRADICT STATED PHILOSOPHY.   Unfortunately, it is the exceptional school faculty and administration that seek to test the curriculum and administrative practices against the school's statement of philosophy. It is not at all unusual to find faculties that have developed elaborate lists of objectives for the curriculum when these objectives have little or no connection with, or actually may be contradictory to, the overall statement of philosophy established for the school. For example, a school's statement of philosophy might include an aim upholding democratic principles and fostering democratic values. Unless the school is able to translate such ideals into effective practice, the ideals are nonfunctional and the school actually may be working against its own professed ideals. Thus, a school's statement of philosophy and aims might include the development of reflective thinking skills in pupils, whereas the actual curriculum is geared to pupil indoctrination, or to narrow-minded behavioristic objectives, and significant problems of controversy are ignored or avoided in the curriculum. In contrast, another school's faculty might decide that one of the ways of fostering democratic values is to develop students' abilities in reflective thinking as applied to social problems and issues. Examples of behavioral objectives that might be identified and assessed in connection with this goal are that students are able to recognize the existence of a problem or issue, are committed to examining all sides of an issue and to seeking pertinent data from different sides, are able to distinguish fact from opinion, are able to recognize bias in determining the pertinence of data to the solution of the problem, are able to formulate workable hypotheses for the solution of the problem, are able to test these hypotheses through appropriate methods and procedures, are able to verify the conclusions or solutions reached by testing them in a variety of situations pertinent to their own lives, and so on.

NO SUBSTITUTE FOR THEORY.   The point to be made is that objectives and educational practices must be governed by a theory of what the school seeks to achieve. Objectives are not a substitute for such a theory. Moreover, in the absence of a theory of what the school seeks to achieve, or when mere lip service is given to the school's statement of philosophy and goals, the school becomes vulnerable to all sorts of whims and doctrines. And objectives are employed chiefly for training in facts and narrow skills, and in the fitting of the learner as a mere cog in the mechanism of school and society. As Bode pointed out, "[t]he purpose of education is not to fit the individual for a place in society, but to enable him to make his own place. . . . We put shoes on a child to protect his health and not to bind his feet."[5]

Throughout the 1980s and into the 1990s, the nationalistic pressures on the schools shifted to mobilization to meet the Japanese technoindustrial "threat." Although mounting evidence was to emerge exposing the false and misleading allegations made against American public education during the era of the Cold War and during the current era of technoindustrial mobilization,[6] many reforms were instituted with the result that the schools were left with problems of misguided curriculum priorities, curriculum imbalance, and insufficient consideration of the need to articulate the curriculum with the nature of the learner and with the democratic social outlook. Without a guiding philosophy that is put to the test of everyday practice, the school is without a compass or without a rudder, and school administrators and faculty are without a vision of the democratic prospect.

Conflicting Educational Philosophies

The foregoing discussion has pointed out how the school needs a philosophy to guide its ends and means. Philosophy serves as both a source and an influence for educational objectives and curriculum development. However, there are many diverse and conflicting philosophies of education that may be classified according to various degrees of conservative and progressive polarity.

Theodore Brameld (1950) is often credited with having developed a system of categorizing educational philosophies or theories—namely essentialism, perennialism, progressivism, and reconstructionism.[7] However, these terms were widely used long before Brameld's categorization. For example, Dewey's powerful case for experimentalist theory and the experimental method in *Democracy and Education* (1916) found many progressive educators eventually referring to themselves as experimentalists. In 1931 John L. Childs of Teachers College, Columbia, authored a book, *Education and the Philosophy of Experimentalism,* in which he systematically stated the case for experimentalism. The first major figure to lead the cause for essentialism and who referred to himself as an essentialist early in the twentieth century was William C. Bagley, also of Teachers College. In *Foundations of American Education* (1947), Harold Rugg, who had been Bagley's first Ph.D. student at the University of Illinois, describes Bagley's essentialism, which was far more moderate in tone and substance than the essentialism that was to follow after mid-twentieth century.[8] In the same work, Rugg uses the term *perennialism* in noting that Mortimer Adler, a leading exponent of that philosophy, had indicated his preference for the term over *scholasticism,* derived from the Church schoolmen of the Middle Ages and premised on the ideas of St. Thomas Aquinas (1225–1247). Adler's preference can be understood in the recognition that scholasticism is ecclesiastical in origin, whereas perennialism is secular.

Nevertheless, Brameld did examine the various philosophies systematically. The authors of this text have chosen to use these classificatory terms and have added certain categories and subcategories to help clarify some of the emerging differences and points of confusion. The categories used are clearly descriptive in delineating the fundamental differences concerning the nature of knowledge, the structure and function of the curriculum, and the nature of the learner.

Table 9–1 presents a synoptic view of several major conflicting philosophies of education representing a wide range of conflicting educational pathways and destinies. The purpose here is not to present a systematic and exhaustive treatment of each of these philosophies but rather to illustrate briefly how they serve as sources and influences for contemporary educational aims and curricular decisions.

Teachers are so caught up with the need to develop effective classroom practices that they understandably look on educational theory as a field of esoteric specialization removed from the practical concerns of the school. Although theory will not provide simplistic answers to such questions as "What do I do on Monday?" it does provide a basis for ascertaining whether one's practices are consonant with one's beliefs and for understanding the implications of alternative educational pathways and destinies. As "the endeavor to attain as unified, consistent, and complete an outlook upon experience as possible,"[9] philosophy gives meaning and direction to our actions. In the absence of philosophy, the teacher is vulnerable to externally imposed prescriptions, often mechanically treated, and to whatever schemes are dominant and fashionable at any given time. This does not mean that philosophy is a shield against change. "Any person who is open-minded and sensitive to new perceptions, and who has concentration and responsibility in connecting them has, in so far, a philosophic disposition," noted Dewey.[10]

Table 9–1. Synoptic View of Conflicting Educational Philosophies

Philosophy	Controlling Aim	Curriculum	Method	Ideal of Learner
Perennialism *(truly centered)* ✳	Cultivation of the rational powers: academic excellence	Basic educational/liberal arts; Great Books of the Western World	Mental discipline; drill teaching; literary discussion/Socratic questioning	Rational being guided by first principles; mind elevated above biological universe
Essentialism	Academic excellence; cultivation of the intellect	Basic education/fundamental academic disciplines	Mental discipline; mastery of academic subject matter; drill/coaching; disciplinary inquiry	Rational being in command of essential facts and skills that undergird the intellective disciplines
Experimentalism	Reflective thinking for social problem solving; democratic citizenship; growth	Comprehensive, unified, problem-focused studies, in democratic classroom/school setting	Social problem solving through reflective thinking (scientific method) and democratic processes	Autonomously thinking, socially responsible democratic citizen; organism in biological continuity with nature
Reconstructionism	Building an ideal democratic social order (a practical Utopia)	Social problems, corrective programs scientifically determined for collective action	Critical analysis of societal flaws and programmatic needs for corrective action	Rebel committed to and involved in constructive social redirection and renewal
Romantic Naturalism	Individual freedom to develop one's potentials	Learning activities based on child's felt needs	Laissez faire; free learning environment for artistic self-expression; spontaneous activity	Unfolding flower
Existentialism	Inner search for meaning of one's own existence	Themes on the human condition; learning activities, free of rational constraints, designed to free the individual to find one's own being	Introspection (examining one's own feelings, impulses, thoughts) in a free learning environment	Flower in search of the meaning of its own existence

THE CONSERVATIVE VISION

The conservative sees the curriculum as being properly concentrated on the cultural inheritance—the tried, the tested, and the true studies. The chief task of education is to conserve the best of our past and, in this way, the present will be adequately dealt with. The traditional studies are seen as the best means of cultivating the intellect, and it is the power of the intellect that enables humanity to cope successfully with the present. Efforts to build or reconstruct the curriculum to make it relevant to contemporary problems or to the interests of the learner are misguided and detract education from its only truly legitimate mission—cultivation of the intellect.

Conservatives differ significantly in their curricular prescriptions. For example, the perennialist sees the best thinking of the past exemplified in the great literary works of the ages. The essentialist sees it exemplified in the traditional "intellective" or academic disciplines. Both see such studies being properly built on a solid foundation in the three R's provided in the elementary grades. Both view mind as an entity to be developed and strengthened through exercise and, for this purpose, abstract studies are valued over direct experience. Retrospection is valued over action.

That the overwhelming evidence from cognitive and developmental psychology has discredited such a notion of mind is of no matter to the perennialist or essentialist. Mind is mind and it is the paramount province of the educational institution to be engaged in developing the intellect through the intellectual studies.

Perennialism

The perennialist believes that because people are uniquely endowed with the rational faculty, education must be aimed exclusively at the cultivation of the intellectual virtues. In contrast to the experimentalist who recognizes the continuity between the human being and the biological universe, the perennialist sees mind as transcending biological nature. Education must pursue the perennial truths and not be misdirected toward meeting contemporary needs that are only temporal. According to the late Robert M. Hutchins, education must "draw out the elements of our common human nature [that] are the same in any time or place," and any notion of educating a person to live in any particular time or place is "foreign to the true concept of education."[11]

PERMANENT STUDIES.   For the perennialist, the cultivation of the intellectual virtues is accomplished only through the "permanent" studies that constitute our intellectual inheritance. These virtues are embodied in the Great Books of the Western world that "cover every department of knowledge," wrote Hutchins, who saw the foundation for the Great Books as consisting of grammar, which "disciplines the mind and develops the logical faculty, . . . the rules of reading, rhetoric and logic," and mathematics, which provides for "correctness in thinking."[12] The perennialist's conception of the ideal education is presented succinctly in this statement by Hutchins:

The ideal education is not an *ad hoc* education, not an education directed to immediate needs; it is not a specialized education, or a preprofessional education; it is not a utilitarian education. It is an education calculated to develop the mind.

I have old-fashioned prejudices in favor of the three R's and the liberal arts, in favor of trying to understand the greatest works that the human race has produced. I believe that these are the permanent necessities, the intellectual tools that are needed to understand the ideas and the ideals of our world.[13]

An identical curricular prescription is offered by Adler, who sees education as properly delimited to the basics at the elementary level. It is then to be realized in the college by means of the cultivation of the rational powers through the liberal arts, capped by the Great Books of ancient, medieval, and modern times, which "are a repository of knowledge and wisdom, a tradition of culture which must initiate each new generation."[14] The Great Books are timeless because they deal with the permanent ideas and problems of humanity, argues the perennialist. Some perennialists would add the classical languages and perhaps a modern language such as French to this list. Vocational or practical studies have no place in the school curriculum because such studies are temporal and do not cultivate the intellectual virtues. The same is said for physical education and the study of contemporary affairs. "Our erroneous notion of progress has thrown the classics and the liberal arts out of the curriculum, over-emphasized the empirical sciences, and made education the servant of any contemporary movements in society," argued Hutchins.[15]

Because the perennialist is concerned with "perennial truths" or "immutable values" that can only be derived through "pure reason," the perennialist categorically dismisses any empirical data from the behavioral sciences that reveal, for example, that the so-called perennial studies are not more effective than other studies in disciplining the intellect. Similarly, the perennialist dismisses the research findings on the importance of affective influences in learning. As far as student interests are concerned, they are irrelevant to the determination of the curriculum because students are immature and unable to judge what is best for themselves. Whether the students dislike the permanent studies also is irrelevant.[16] "The primary aim of the educational system in a democratic country is to draw out the common humanity of those committed to its charge. This requires careful avoidance of that attractive trap, the *ad hoc,* that which may be immediately interesting, but which is transitory, or that which is thought to have some practical value under the circumstances of the time. . . ,"[17] wrote Hutchins.

OPPOSITION TO ELECTIVES.   In the quest for curricular relevance, many secondary schools and colleges have resorted to ad hoc changes in course offerings and the expansion of elective options without undertaking a fundamental assessment and redesign of the total curriculum. The perennialist is not calling for such assessment and redesign from the standpoint of the pervading problems and needs of the learner and society; instead, a return to the permanent studies is the answer, on the ground that such studies are never transitory but are of value in any time or place. Although the perennialist maintains that the vocational studies are valueless not only on the grounds that they are not intellective but also because such studies readily become obsolescent as a result of technological change, it is the skilled technical graduate, and not the liberal arts graduate, whose services are in greatest demand in the technological society.

Perennialist prescriptions for education, particularly for the lower levels of schooling, portray the mind as a kind of vessel to be filled with facts and truths, or muscle to be strengthened by memoriter exercise. "Elementary education can do nothing better for a child than store his memory with things deserving to be there," declared Mark Van Doren, and, "[h]e will be grateful for them when he grows up, even if he kicks now."[18]

TRADITIONAL DUALISMS.   Inherent in perennialist thinking are the traditional dualisms of mind versus body, cultural studies versus vocational studies, permanent studies versus contemporary studies, intellect versus emotion, knowledge versus experience, and so on. Anchored in perennialist thought is the metaphysical notion, developed by Plato and Aristotle, that rational knowledge is derived from a higher source than experience. The advent of experimental science demolished this notion. Yet, as Dewey noted, we are left with a curriculum that clings to the artifacts of the old education—a curriculum that is an inorganic composite of inconsistent, dualistic, and antagonistic tenets.

> Certain studies and methods are retained on the supposition that they have the sanction of peculiar liberality, the chief content of the term liberal being uselessness for practical ends. . . . The result is a system in which both "cultural" and "utilitarian" subjects exist in an inorganic composite where the former are not by dominant purpose socially serviceable and the latter not liberative of imagination of thinking power.
>
> Only superstition makes us believe that the two are necessarily hostile so that a subject is illiberal because it is useful and cultural because it is useless.[19]

RECURRENT EFFORTS TO REGAIN INFLUENCE.   Although perennialism has long lost the place of dominance it once held in higher education, its leading proponents have been persistently visible and opportunistic. When Robert M. Hutchins (1899–1977) became president and chancellor of the University of Chicago in 1929 he sought to establish an undergraduate core curriculum based on the Great Books of the Western World. However, the faculty opted for a broad-fields curriculum in general education that provided for the natural sciences, social sciences, and humanities—each as integrative areas. Under Hutchins's administration, many progressive innovations were instituted for general education. The undergraduate college was established to spearhead the curriculum in general education. A nucleus of experimentalist-progressives who had been working on the evaluation of educational outcomes in general education at The Ohio State University were recruited to Chicago to develop a system of comprehensive examinations and an independent board of examiners so as to evaluate longer-term learning outcomes through the curriculum in general education. Under the influence of Hutchins, the university dropped intercollegiate football and other varsity sports, along with its Big Ten membership.

Although Hutchins envisioned the undergraduate college as a four-year program combining the last two years of high school with the freshman and sophomore undergraduate years, with the curriculum devoted entirely to general education, the plan proved unworkable despite the claims made for its viability.[20] Nevertheless, the Chicago program in general education gained wide attention and exerted considerable influence in American higher education. One of the great ironies of Hutchins's tenure at Chicago was that, unbeknown to Hutchins, the world's first self-sustaining nuclear chain reaction was achieved by a University of Chicago team conducting their experimental work under the stands of the university's football stadium during World War II, proving that such a reaction was possible for the creation of a nuclear bomb.

Following his tenure at Chicago (1929–1951), Hutchins devoted himself to the cause of academic freedom at a time of the Cold War and the rise of McCarthyism. In his later years, he was impelled to change his perspective and became a defender of America's public schools.

Ironically, although the perennialists have long been severe critics of many features of American education and have opposed Dewey's progressive education, the rise of the radical romanticists during the late 1960s and early 1970s found some of the leading perennialists defending our system of education and reappraising Dewey's theories in a far more favorable light and defending him from misrepresentation.[21] The extremist nature of the criticisms leveled at the schools by the radical romanticists during this period led some leading perennialists to stand up in defense of American public education. Noting that for the first time in American history the value of universal, free, compulsory education was being questioned, Hutchins observed that "nobody has a kind word for the public school, the institution that only the other day was looked upon as the foundation of our freedom, the guaranty of our future, the cause of our prosperity and power, the bastion of our security, and the source of our enlightenment."[22] Hutchins went on to point out that radical criticism of public education had reached the stage of overkill with its call for abolishing compulsory education, eliminating the formal curriculum and catering to the evanescent whims of children, using public funds to establish alternative school systems, and even for abolishing the public schools altogether. To Hutchins, such decisions would only promote social segregation and the kind of individualism that is a danger to democracy.

Although perennialism has long lost the place of dominance it once held in education, student activism, the demand for curriculum relevance, and the situation ethic of doing your own thing left some education critics nostalgically yearning for a return to education as the contemplation of immutable values. As one critic opined,

> Sensation now has priority over sense, reason has become the first casualty of revolution.
>
> The young turn to movies rather than books. . . . The blissful hedonism of illiteracy—a boon to those of little talent and no control—now reigns. . . .
>
> Standards were a set of measurements designed to determine what was Good and what was Bad . . . evolved through the centuries by superior minds in the con-

> templation of immutable values—that is, those values not susceptible to the climate of fashion or what is now called "relevancy." . . .
>
> Now happily, due to a mass education designed to produce illiterates, these values have been discarded. . . .[23]

Many perennialists view higher education as properly the province of an academically elite class and look on mass higher education as a kind of education inflation that has lessened the value of education by replacing the intellective literacy studies with all sorts of "relevant" contemporary studies. However, in the emergent age of science and technology, it was not possible for the traditional literary studies to retain their exalted reign over the curriculum in higher education.

At the same time, the fragmented and competing special interests of the undergraduate student population have found college students and faculty challenging the sanctity of the Great Books or canons of Western Civilization as the appropriate core for liberal or general education. From the 1960s through much of the 1980s, college faculties had yielded to the demands for relevance in the undergraduate curriculum to the extent that any semblance to a core curriculum in general education was replaced by distribution electives involving hundreds of courses. In effect, each student could pursue one's own pattern of coursework to meet one's special interests. College faculties were more concerned with knowledge specialism and their departmentalized knowledge bases, so they readily acceded to the student demands for relevance, through electives. At the same time, the specialization requirements (for the student's major field) remained largely intact.

Nevertheless, it is one thing to call for a return to a classical literary curriculum and quite another to design an interdisciplinary core of studies revealing the interdependence of knowledge and addressing the common and pervasive problems of a free society in a scientific/technological age. During an extended period from the late 1970s into the 1990s, leading colleges and universities were grappling with the problem of curriculum fragmentation and were rediscovering the need to develop a common core for general education. Although it was clear that there would be no return to the perennialist curriculum of liberal education, it was not clear that the colleges were ready to drop their competing interests and act progressively to develop an articulated curriculum for general education.

Resurgent Controversy.   The perennialist-essentialist cause was given considerable impetus during the tenure of William J. Bennett as chair of the National Endowment for the Humanities followed by his position as U.S. Secretary of Education (1985–1988) in the Reagan administration at the height of the back-to-basics retrenchment. From the time when a chief federal officer for education was first appointed (Henry Barnard, 1867), virtually every person in that office was a progressive educator, or at least became a progressivist during their tenure—with one notable exception—William Bennett. Bennett's tenure was marked by repeated attacks on the schools for allegedly neglecting the basics. His proposals for reforming the curriculum of the elementary school and high school were centered on a core of basics giving emphasis to literary works of Western civilization.[24] As long as

Bennett focused his attacks on the public schools, he seemed to be on safe ground, but when he proceeded to attack the undergraduate college curriculum at some of our prominent universities, he found himself a target of powerful counterattacks by influential university leaders. The situation became so rancorous that it impelled the presidents of Harvard and Stanford to make a joint appearance in May 1987 to denounce Bennett's charges.[25] As a consequence, with an election year impending, President Reagan reassigned Bennett to head the federal program for drug control where his efforts, understandably, were seen as less successful. Bennett's successor at the National Endowment for the Humanities, Lynne V. Cheney, continued in the same vein as Bennett in extolling *McGuffey's Readers* and the work of the Committee of Ten (1892), and in attacking the schools for neglecting the traditional humanities.[26]

During 1987 and 1988 a book by Allan Bloom of the University of Chicago, *The Closing of the American Mind,* became a national best-seller and a text for conservative attacks on higher education for having acquiesced to student demands for relevance, and for having abandoned the traditional reliance on the Great Books of Western culture as the bedrock of the liberal arts curriculum. Although Bloom's criticisms, leveled against the fragmentation of the curriculum as a result of the competing disciplines seemed well grounded, his sweeping diatribes against mass education appeared ill considered. For example, he could title a chapter, "Our Ignorance," and declare in his concluding chapter that "[a]ll that is human, all that is of concern to us, lies outside natural science."[27] Here Bloom appeared to be hallowing his own ignorance of how science has contributed not only to our understanding and control of the material world, but also to the democratic prospect in revealing the unrealized potentials of humanity.

The dynamic conditions of modern industrial societies require a dynamic and not a static curriculum. It is easy to put the onus on mass education. However, the notion that the curriculum should be limited to the so-called estate of timeless knowledge came to be shattered by the inevitable force of changing knowledge.

That many of our college students have turned to sensation over reason cannot be explained away as simply the result of mass education or the demise of the perennial curriculum. These students also reject the method of intelligence wrought by science and choose to blame science and technology for the evil uses to which so-called rational knowledge is put. They mistakenly place the blame on the rational methods of science rather than on the political forces that have turned the products of science and technology to ill use.

PERENNIALISM POPULARIZED.   Perhaps the most successful and surely the most durable popularizer of perennialism has been Mortimer J. Adler, a disciple of Hutchins at the University of Chicago, who went on to serve as associate editor of the anointed One Hundred Great Books of the Western World for almost half a century. Facetiously called "the Lawrence Welk of philosophy," Adler's Socratic dialogues in conducting seminar discussions of the "Great Ideas" from the Great Books were shown on public television during the late 1980s. The limitations of the Socratic method may well have been apparent to discerning viewers in that it inevitably leads to convergence on the "master's" established conclusions. (This contrasts sharply against Dewey's reflective thinking.)

The back-to-basics retrenchment of the 1970s and 1980s proved opportune for Adler to endorse the essentialist school-reform menu of basics with drill and coaching exercises, leading up to perennialist literary study and Socratic questioning on ideas rooted in the classics, as presented in his *Paideia Proposal: An Educational Manifesto* (1982). Adler dedicated his book to Horace Mann, John Dewey, and Robert Hutchins. Yet throughout Adler's career he was a leading critic of Dewey. Indeed Dewey's writings clearly run counter to Adler's perennialist prescriptions, as embodied in *The Paideia,* along with Adler's conception of mind as a vessel or muscle, and Adler's doctrine that the One Hundred Great Books are the true repositories of permanent knowledge. To Adler, "[y]outh itself is the most serious impediment—in fact, youth is an insuperable obstacle to being an educated person."[28] To Dewey, childhood and youth are not obstacles, but genuine phases of growth and development, for, in Dewey's words, "immaturity designates a positive force or ability—the *power* to grow."[29]

The popular stereotype of the truly educated individual steeped in the traditional literary classics of Western civilization and in possession of an encyclopedic mind was promoted as never before on the leading network TV quiz show of the latter 1950s. It so happened that the indomitable winner week after week was an ordinary-looking young man from New York who did have an encyclopedic mind. However, when a young instructor of literature at Columbia was chosen as challenger and was found to be enormously more appealing to the national audience, the reigning winner was induced by the TV producers to give the wrong answer and yield to the more attractive opponent. The opponent was Charles Van Doren, the son of the distinguished Columbia literary scholar, Mark Van Doren. Week after week, the young Van Doren came up with the correct answer. In a guest appearance on another show for his network, Van Doren topped the "Ed Sullivan Show" in audience ratings—a feat accomplished only once before, by Elvis Presley. With his appearance on the quiz show, Van Doren was threatening to topple the shows of the two rival networks. Van Doren's portrait appeared on the cover of *Time.* Thousands of marriage proposals to the young bachelor poured into the network offices each week. After four months of successfully defending his title, Van Doren finally lost to a challenger. Not only had he broken TV's record for quiz-show winnings, but he now had an agent to handle the avalanche of TV offers.

Newspaper and magazine articles were extolling the virtues of a classical education as epitomized by Van Doren's demonstrated mnemonic powers. As a graduate of St. John's College, Annapolis, Maryland, the media pointed to Van Doren as a beneficiary of a purely classical curriculum—devoted entirely to the canons of Western civilization: The One Hundred Great Books. *Time* chronicled the Van Doren family's intellectual literary heritage. As the son of Mark and nephew of Carl, both of whom had made their mark as literary scholars of first rank, young Charles was following "a family tradition of literary excellence based on forthright thinking." As quoted in *Time,* "[t]he Van Dorens represent a tradition of people that is almost dead now, like Thoreau and Emerson. They have their roots in the 19th century. They are content and confident in themselves." The *Time* chronicle took note that, "[t]he Van Doren tradition of self-reliance crossed the Atlantic in the 1650s when Pieter van Doren arrived in Peter Stuyvesant's Manhattan from Gravezand, Holland."[30]

However, the bubble was to burst with a thud when it was revealed that Charles Van Doren's initial steps to TV success had been staged. When it was also discovered that Van Doren had been fed the clues to the correct answers prior to each show, the ensuing scandal led to Congressional hearings and investigations of fraud and deceit on the part of the TV networks. Not until three decades later did network quiz shows begin to reappear, but they never regained the mass audience appeal they once commanded. Charles Van Doren, who had been heralded as "Columbia's most cherished hero since Sid Luckman was tossing passes [football] at Baker Field," left Columbia to join Mortimer Adler's Institute for Philosophic Research, and subsequently worked on Adler's operations on the Great Books for Encyclopaedia Britannica and as a member of the Paideia Group, which produced *The Paideia Proposal.* To this day, many people identify the highly educated person as one who is in possession of encyclopedic knowledge.

Essentialism

Where the perennialist views the liberal arts and Great Books as embodying the timeless intellectual virtues and perpetuating the cultural heritage, the essentialist sees this heritage being directed at modern needs through the fundamental academic disciplines of English (grammar, literature, and composition), mathematics, science, history, and modern foreign languages. These subjects, logically organized, are essential to the development of our mental capacities. The performing arts, industrial arts, vocational studies, physical education, and other areas of the curriculum are regarded as frills.

TRAINING OF THE INTELLECT.   Essentialists contend that the school's "full-time task lies" in "equipping students with intellectual powers," and that the "concern with the personal problems of adolescents has grown so excessive as to push into the background what should be the school's central concern, the intellectual development of its students."[31] The school is seen as being side-tracked from its central task of intellectual training when it ministers to personal-social needs of youth by embracing such tasks as developing saleable skills, health and physical fitness, democratic citizenship, consumer competence, and worthy use of leisure time.[32]

Essentialists regard efforts to integrate or synthesize the studies below the college level as misguided. They hold that integration or synthesis arrives only after the student "has marshalled the array of separate intellectual powers" derived from each of the fundamental academic disciplines. Thus, the task of the school is to distinguish the elements that make up these disciplines and, "[t]hese various elements having been distinguished, the secondary school has as its primary task the systematic exploration of them, through study of the separate organized disciplines."[33]

The essentialist shares the same views as the perennialist with regard to the school's focus on mental discipline and the irrelevance of pupil interests. According to Admiral Rickover, a leading essentialist during the Cold War era:

For all children, the educational process must be one of collecting factual knowledge to the limit of their absorptive capacity. Recreation, manual or clerical training, etiquette, and similar know-how have little effect on the mind itself and it is with the mind that the school must solely concern itself. The poorer a child's natural endowments, the more does he need to have his mind trained. . . . To acquire such knowledge, fact upon fact, takes time and effort. Nothing can really make it "fun."[34]

Here the essentialist shares with the perennialist Aristotle's notion that "youths are not to be instructed with a view to their amusement, for learning is no amusement, but is accompanied with pain."[35]

Like the perennialist, the essentialist conceives of the mind as a vessel or container. Individual differences are marked off according to mental capacities, and education is simply a matter of filling and stretching each mind with the same curricular brew to the utmost of each mind's capacity. "After thirty years or more in the business," writes an educator, "I think I know something about individual differences. There are jugs of different capacity, and there are powers of different capacity, too. What I am talking about here is the nature of the wine and its availability to all."[36] However, where the perennialist sees the proper curricular brew as consisting of the liberal arts and Great Books, which embody the timeless intellectual virtues and perpetuate the cultural heritage, the essentialist holds that intellectual excellence is exemplified by the logically organized, fundamental academic disciplines. Both the perennialist and the essentialist see the role of the elementary school as concentrated simply on providing mastery of the basic skills and facts that are necessary preliminary to subsequent learning.

EDUCATIONAL MERITOCRACY.   Many essentialists advocate the establishment of high academic standards through a system of uniform and rigorous examinations. In calling for such examinations to be administered as pupils move from elementary to secondary school and at the completion of compulsory schooling, the historian Arthur Bestor sees the examinations being used to sort out pupils for "the standard program of disciplined intellectual training"—to "furnish part of the data upon which the school administrator can begin the delicate process of advising the square pegs not to head for the round holes"—and to dramatize that the continuance of educational opportunity is "a privilege bestowed upon the meritorious and the energetic."[37]

After stating the case for the standardized test as the chief instrument to be used in the search for talent, John Gardner, as president of the Carnegie Corporation, viewed the school as a stringent sorting-out process whereby the less able youngsters discover their limitations.

But as education becomes increasingly effective in pulling [sic] the bright youngsters to the top, it becomes an increasingly rugged sorting-out process for everyone concerned. This is true today and it will be very much more so in the future. The schools are the golden avenue of opportunity for able youngsters; but by the same token they are the arena in which less able youngsters discover their limitations. This thought rarely occurred to the generations of Americans who dreamed of universal education. They saw the beauty of a system in which every young person could go as far as his ability and ambition would take him, without obstacles of money, social standing, religion, or race. They didn't reflect on the pain involved for those who lacked the necessary ability. Yet pain there is and must be.[38]

In sharp contrast is Dewey's view that education must focus on the development of potentialities and not on the setting of limitations. The quantitative measurement of mind is a fiction, maintained Dewey, and, "[h]ow one person's abilities compare in quantity with those of another is none of the teacher's business. It is irrelevant to his work."[39]

The essentialist position—with its strong emphasis on basic education and academic excellence through science, mathematics, and modern foreign languages, and its call for developing our nation's intellective resources through ability grouping and rigorous scholarship standards—was in tune with the tenor of the Cold War era. During the early years of this period, essentialists exerted a considerable influence on the elementary and secondary school curriculum with great impetus being given to standardized testing. However, the federal support of national curriculum reform projects, led by university scholar-specialists, eventuated in the emergence of neo-essentialism, with the disciplines doctrine as the dominant influence on the curriculum during the late 1950s and 1960s. By the late 1960s, disciplinarity as the single ruling doctrine for curriculum reform was shattered by the demand for relevance. Essentialism appeared to be hopelessly out of date. The call was for humanizing the schools. Suddenly such themes as alternative education, values education, moral education, and death education were appearing in the educational literature and in the curriculum. At the elementary level, the open classroom was in vogue. At the secondary and collegiate levels, the concept of general education was all but forgotten. Instead of undertaking the difficult task of developing a balanced and coherent curriculum, the response of educators was a kind of default—simply allow for more free and distributed elective options and introduce more *au courant* courses.

Each excessive action inevitably eventuates in an equal and opposite excessive reaction. Essentialism was to have its place in the sun once again.

BACK TO BASICS.   By the mid-1970s, the old essentialism was in a state of renascence with the rallying cry of back to basics being heard once again throughout the land. The National Assessment of Educational Progress, which had been inaugurated a decade earlier, was now being followed by statewide programs of minimum-competence testing.

Essentialists see competency-based education as being concentrated on the fundamental skills. They are opposed to those who would employ it in terms of the meaning and importance of competency in life-role activities, such as in consumer education or political citizenship.

Many essentialists are opposed to the comprehensive secondary school. They not only see the high-school curriculum appropriately concentrated on the traditional academic subjects but they also favor separate academic high schools for those of higher scholastic ability. The American essentialist influence has had its counterpart in Britain, where it had been focused on opposing the government policy of developing comprehensive schools in place of the traditional tripartite and selective system. In response to a 1965 government "White Paper" calling for a policy of developing comprehensive schools in Britain, a group of essentialists began issuing a series of "Black Papers," which appeared almost annually from 1969 into the 1980s. In addition to opposing open education and the government-mandated development of comprehensive secondary schools, the Black Papers embraced a back-to-basics prescription and the use of tests for "the national monitoring of basic standards for all children at the ages of 7, 11, and 14 or 15."[40]

All kinds of sweeping allegations are found in the Black Papers, such as "[i]n mathematics, the obsession with the need for understanding before learning, usually citing poor Piaget as proof, is the major cause of low standards."[41] (The assumption being that understanding is not real learning or that one must learn before one can understand.) Like their American compeers, British essentialists rest much of the blame for allegedly lower standards on John Dewey. In response to a government report showing that standards have not fallen, the report was quickly dismissed and Dewey was blamed in these words: "During the past forty years, as the 'progressive' philosophy of education adumbrated by John Dewey has gained ground in British and American schools, the teaching of English has probably been more adversely affected than any branch of the curriculum."[42]

In the United States, the back-to-basics retrenchment was to extend throughout the 1970s and 1980s, buttressed by statewide minimum-competency testing and national standardized tests of academic achievement. Even the professional education associations seemed to join the tide backward to the essentials. For example, a publication issued by the National Association of Secondary School Principals entitled *Reducing the Curriculum* (1982) presented itself as a blueprint for cutbacks and recommended that priorities be established, with "essential" courses being given number one priority, and "desirable" courses be given number two priority. Soon the studio arts and industrial arts were being eliminated from the curriculum. The old adage, "Beware of what you want, for you might get it," seemed to hold true with respect to the Council for Basic Education, an organization founded by Arthur Bestor for the purpose of promoting basic education and eliminating the curriculum "frills." The curriculum fundamentalism had become so extreme that in 1975 the council added the arts to its canon of officially accredited basic subjects, and in 1979 actually issued papers defending the place of the arts in basic education.[43]

The popular appeal of essentialism was evidenced in the appearance of Edward D. Hirsch's *Cultural Literacy: What Every American Needs to Know* on the national best-seller lists of 1987. Hirsch proceeded to equate the ability to recall factual information as the mark of the educated individual. Hirsch revealed his essentialist-perennialist learnings by ascribing cultural literacy and scientific literacy to separate domains. It was clear that Hirsch was concerned with cultural literary as the true mark of the educated citizen.

By the early 1990s it was becoming increasingly evident that the fundamentalist curriculum retrenchment, along with the statewide minimum-competency testing and the national achievement testing programs, had resulted in lowering the achievement of our student populations.[44] Progressive ideas such as whole language, writing across the curriculum, teaching for higher-order thinking, teaching mathematics and science through hands-on experience, student projects and portfolios, and so on were being rediscovered as though they were new inventions. Nevertheless, certain reports on national education policy, such as the one issued by the U.S. Secretary of Labor's Commission on Achieving Necessary Skills (1992) proposed that beginning in middle school, a record be kept of every youngster's performance standard in qualifying for a "Certificate of Initial Mastery" in each performance competency so as to leave school with the essential skills sought by employers.[45] The endorsement of a new national testing program (American Achievement Tests) by both the Bush and Clinton administrations, stemming from the National Education Goals in *America 2000,* was testimony to the enduring appeal of curriculum reductionism as a simple solution to the complex problems of education.

Essentialism predictably is resurrected during periods of economic retrenchment and conservative social influence. Few educators would hold that the fundamental processes should not have a fundamental place in the curriculum. The progressivist sees the fundamental processes as tool processes and sees education as the means of improving the social condition rather than merely fitting individuals in the basic competencies required of the existing social machinery.

Eclecticism

Many teachers and administrators appear to function intuitively or expediently in response to whatever trends may be dominant. They do not base their choices or test their choices in terms of a systematic philosophy or theory of education. "We may fasten together many different beliefs, not fusing them into a harmonious pattern but keeping them as separate pieces, ready to shift about into different positions, checkerlike, as the need arises," states Brameld in describing the eclectic approach. He sees eclecticism in the curriculum as "smatterings of many things without purpose or design."[46]

Although this may well be an accurate portrayal of how many educators function, and an accurate description of the condition of the school and college curriculum, those who ascribe to the eclectic view contend that their choices are more deliberate. The eclectic borrows from various philosophies in the belief that each philosophy has something of value, and that no one philosophy is sufficiently complete or suited to varying conditions. But because eclecticism finds many elements from the traditional philosophies appropriate for contemporary times, its outlook tends to be conservative.

Selecting the "best" from each of all possible worlds is deceptively seductive. The best for one eclectic may be the worst for another. Because the different philosophies are conflicting, the eclectic selection involves compromise rather than resolution. For example, how does one resolve the conflict between the behaviorist's conception of the learner and the humanist's conception—not to mention the conflicting curricular prescriptions? On some such issues, even compromise is not practicable. Because eclectic representations differ so markedly from one another, eclecticism is not a philosophy per se, but a synthetic formulation compounded from differing systems. (Consequently, eclecticism is not represented in Table 9–1.)

Perhaps the most thoughtfully formulated eclectic statement on the curriculum is the Harvard Report, *General Education in a Free Society.* Its eclectic spirit is revealed in such statements as the following: "[e]ducation can therefore be wholly devoted neither to tradition or experiment. . . . It must uphold at the same time tradition and experiment . . . though common aims must bind together the whole educational system, there exists no one body of knowledge, no single system of instructional equally valid for every part of it."[47]

Another example of an eclectic curricular prescription that exerted a powerful influence on American education was the Conant report.[48] In this work, Conant embraced the democratizing function of the comprehensive secondary school, with its heterogeneous pupil population. At the same time he advocated the use of standardized tests for ability grouping, and special counseling and sorting of the academically talented, to meet nationalistic interests in the space race and in the Cold War battle for global leadership. (The experimentalist would regard the use of education for narrow nationalistic interests as inimical to democracy and as a contradiction of what education should be.)

Another example of an eclectic proposal for school reform, *High School: A Report on Secondary Education in America* by Ernest L. Boyer, was issued in 1983 under the auspices of the Carnegie Foundation for the Advancement of Teaching. Boyer's report, as in the case of Conant's report of a quarter of a century earlier, avoided the accusatory and condemnatory language characteristic of so many reports on school reform during the 1970s and 1980s. Although Boyer embraced a number of progressive ideas and practices, such as the need for curriculum integration through common learnings or general education and the abandonment of the Carnegie unit in inventorying academic credits, he proceeded to propose a standard list of courses and credits by academic units required for graduation—units virtually identical to Carnegie units. As did Conant, Boyer addressed the democratizing function of the American high school. But unlike Conant, Boyer failed to support the comprehensive high school. Although he touched on the problems of dropouts and youth unemployment, he focused on the weaknesses of existing programs of vocational education without showing how they might be strengthened. He seemed willing to scrap the comprehensive high school in favor of a general academic high school geared primarily to serving the precollege population. For the academic elite in the sciences and mathematics, Boyer proposed the establishment of a national network of federally supported residential academies.

The weakness of the eclectic approach lies in the inconsistencies and contradictions that are inevitable when conflicting philosophical elements are drawn together, or when the eclectic simply decides not to deal with such elements, however significant they may be. Omission or avoidance is not a substitute for resolution or even compromise.

THE PROGRESSIVE VISION

The progressive sees humanity in an evolving universe. Hence knowledge is not static or timeless but dynamic. Education must be viewed as a process of growth, and not merely a process of cultural transmission. Mind is viewed in biological continuity with nature, not a thing apart. The nature and interests of the learner and social conditions, as well as the race experience, must be considered in developing a balanced and coherent curriculum.

The natural sciences, which have brought about a revolution in our conception of ourselves and of the universe, are based on the method of intelligence. Applied to the human condition, the method of intelligence has enabled us to exercise greater control over our own destiny. It has served to free humanity from dogmatic authority, superstition, blind fear, and prejudice—thereby serving as the key tool of democracy. A society that aspires to democratic ideals must employ democratic means if such ideals are to become a reality. The curriculum must be based on the method of intelligence if an enlightened citizenry is to emerge. The method of intelligence is not something apart from attitudes, feelings, and emotions—but enables us to better understand and constructively direct our affective dispositions.

The progressive vision has been defracted into several widely differing and even conflicting images. The most systematic and consistent progressive educational theory is experimentalism. It is not by accident that experimentalist theory emerged from the democratic currents of American life and thought in the twentieth century. Virtually all other educational theories or philosophies in Western Civilization stem from European origins.

Some progressivists are impatient with the open-mindedness of the experimentalist vision. They think the school needs to play a more direct function in reconstructing society for a democratic social order. In a sense their theory of reconstructionism may be more radical than progressive. Other progressives have avoided entirely the social message of the progressive vision by embracing only the humanitarian precepts of child-centeredness. In so doing, they have tended to romanticize the nature of the learner with the result that their vision is more romantic than progressive. As discussed later in this chapter, the romanticist view of the learner has also been embraced by many radical critics of American education.

✳Experimentalism

In a remarkable book, *Dynamic Sociology, or Applied Social Science,* published in 1883, Lester Ward systematically explicated the idea of progress and the belief in the educability of the people as essential to a progressive democratic society. Ward held that the dynamic evolutionary forces in the natural world require a dynamic conception of knowledge. But where evolution in nature is a meandering process, human progress requires the release of intelligence through popular education to improve the human condition.

Ward prophetically pointed out that this would require a dynamic and articulated curriculum—a curriculum that did not as yet exist. For Ward, the curriculum must meet the test of relative *generality* and relative *practicality.* Ward proceeded to propose three universal curricula. The first universal curriculum for the school should be aimed at general and practical knowledge. The second universal curriculum should provide for even greater generality and practicality and embrace many interdependent branches. The third universal curriculum should be directed at advanced studies, elected by the student with teacher guidance, for life pursuits (specialization). These ideas came to be expressed in a rudimentary way through the concept of curriculum constants and variables in the Cardinal Principles report of 1918. However, Ward's prophecy called for a macrocurricular design and function that was not to be given full and systematic attention for almost half a century when experimentalist educators directed their efforts to the idea and practice of general education as the keystone for specialized education, enrichment education, exploratory education, and special-interest education in the context of the cosmopolitan, comprehensive high school. (See the Venn diagram, Figure 6–1.)

To social reformers who contended that the solution to social inequity resides in the redistribution of wealth, Ward pointed out that "[t]hey are working at the roof instead of at the foundation of the structure which they desire to erect." The foundation, Ward held, rests with the diffusion of knowledge through universal education whereby intelligence would be released for individual and social improvement.[49] Ward's riposte of 1883 seemed just as apropos to the radical critics of contemporary times who have sought to portray the public schools as either a marginal institution or one that is designed to delimit social opportunity.[50] (For their own children, of course, they have great belief in the positive power of education.[51])

Ward's passionate belief in the power of the environment and his faith in the school as a planned environment for releasing intelligence for a progressive and democratic society was to find expression in Dewey's experimentalist philosophy. "He anticipated John Dewey," wrote Commager, "and supplied him with a scientific basis for much of his educational philosophy."[52] Unfortunately, Ward never gained the recognition he deserved during his lifetime, and even to this day.[53]

Dewey's experimentalist philosophy also took roots from the pragmatism of two contemporaries of Ward, mathematician Charles Peirce (1839–1914) and psychologist William James (1842–1910). As with Ward, they rejected the doctrine of absolute or *a priori* truths of the traditionalists and held that truth derives from the scientific investigation of ideas through the test of consequences. "Science is dynamic. Whatever it touches is transformed," observed Ward.[54]

As shown in Table 9–1, experimentalist views on the curriculum and on educational aims are in vivid contrast to the conservative theories of essentialism and perennialism, and to the radical theories of reconstructionism, romantic naturalism, and existentialism.

To the experimentalist, absolute philosophies, with their fixed truths, appeal to authority and privilege because they promote dogmas that are not to be tested by scientific inquiry. Hence the suffix *-ism* is inimical to experimentalist thinking, for *ism* implies a certain closed-minded belief. The experimentalist commitment is to the testing of ideas and the holding of beliefs as tentative pending verification through the method of intelligence. Dewey put the matter in these words in addressing the reconstructionists:

> . . . those who are looking ahead to a new movement in education adapted to the existing need for a new social order, should think in terms of Education itself rather

than in terms of some 'ism about education, even such an 'ism as "progressivism." For in spite of itself any movement that thinks and acts in terms of an 'ism becomes so involved in reaction against other 'isms that it is unwittingly controlled by them. For it then forms its principles by reaction against them instead of a comprehensive constructive survey of actual needs, problems, and possibilities.[55]

In this chapter, *ism* is used to denote the contrasting and conflicting theoretical systems. It is acknowledged that *ism* in the sense of a fixed doctrine does not apply to experimentalist theory.

SEARCH FOR UNITY AND THE DEMOCRATIC PROSPECT.   In pointing out how experimentalism, as orchestrated by John Dewey, was inescapably the expression of the uniquely American experience, James Conant wrote, "I had the feeling that, like the Austro-Hungarian Empire of the nineteenth century, if John Dewey hadn't existed he would have had to be invented."[56]

As orchestrator of experimentalist thought, Dewey held that a democracy requires a citizenry committed to and capable of reflective thinking in solving pervasive social problems. Dewey rejected the traditional philosophies and their dualistic, oppositional tenets: mind versus body, intellectual versus character development, knowing versus doing, intellect versus emotion, theoretical versus practical knowledge, logical versus psychological knowledge, scientific versus humanistic studies, mind versus matter, nature versus nurture, ends versus means. He pointed out the need to view the person as a whole being in continuity with the biological universe. Where Dewey rejected the traditional educational theories for their reliance on external imposition and authoritarian methods, he opposed the romantic progressivists for viewing the child as a naturally unfolding being whose fruition is best realized through spontaneous activity and self-fulfillment in an environment without social direction. "Freedom means essentially the part played by thinking—which is personal—in learning: it means intellectual initiative, independence in observation, judicious invention, foresight of consequences, and ingenuity of adaptation to them," wrote Dewey.[57]

Dewey contended that the curriculum should not be a mere conglomeration of divided and specialized subject matters but should be reflectively formulated, coherently designed, and meaningfully attuned to the improvement of existing community life. He observed that the traditional educational philosophies had failed to come to grips with "the deepest problems of common humanity," had overlooked the fact that the curriculum "is humanized in the degree in which it connects with the common interests of men as men," and had created conditions in the curriculum that "infect the education called liberal with illiberality." According to Dewey, "[a] curriculum which acknowledges the social responsibilities of education must present situations where problems are relevant to the problems of living together, and where observation and information are calculated to develop social insight and interest."[58]

REFLECTIVE THINKING.   Dewey held that the processes of instruction should be based on the processes of reflection. Traditional education, with its "method of imposition from the side of the teacher and reception, absorption, from the side of the pupil," observed Dewey, "may be compared to inscribing records upon a passive phonographic disc to result in giving back what has been inscribed when the proper button is pressed in recitation or examination."[59] He viewed traditional practices as inimical to the development of the enlightened democratic citizen.

As discussed earlier, Dewey deplored the mechanical and specialized treatment of science as something separate from social problems and moral direction. To Dewey, science should serve in the interests of humanity. Its methods in education have a clear moral purpose: to combat bias and ignorance, to act by reason rather than by authority or superstition, to free intelligence and to provide intellectual control over conduct, and to judge truly. Human progress is not served when scientific judgments are separated from moral judgments, believed Dewey. Witness the misuses of science to destroy rather than to improve civilization, or the harmful effects in our history when moral standards are established and imposed by unreasoning authority or through superstition.

Dewey criticized the old ideal that held that the pursuit of knowledge for its own sake is good in itself. To Dewey, intelligence and knowledge must be directed at foreseeing the consequences of existing social conditions and taking sides in behalf of the consequences that are preferred.[60] In 1964, the Nobel physicist Max Born put the matter in these words:

> In the operation of science and its ethics a change has taken place that makes it impossible to maintain the old ideal of the pursuit of knowledge for its own sake which my generation believed in. We were convinced that this could never lead to any evil since the search for truth was good in itself. That was a beautiful dream from which we were awakened by world events.[61]

Born was not expressing his disillusionment with science and rational intelligence, but was pointing to the need for science and rationality to be directed at the human condition. More than half a century earlier, Dewey had warned the scientists that because science was divorced from concern with the social and moral ideals for which it is used, its discoveries are used for aims that are "survivors of a pre-scientific age, that is, of barbarism."—to which he added, "[e]ven where science has received its most attentive recognition, it has remained a servant of ends imposed from alien traditions."[62]

QUANTIFICATION IN EDUCATION.   Dewey repeatedly took issue with those who sought to reduce education to quantifiable measurements as though such reductionism made education scientific. He noted that quantitative measures in education through IQ and standardized achievement testing, as well as in determining objectives, were being promoted on the grounds of educational efficiency; but such efficiency was conceived in terms of perpetuating the present order. For Dewey the function of education is to unleash human potentials, not to set limitations, so that the existing order can be transformed into a better one.[63] The outcome of scientific methods is not uniformity and standardization of procedure but the liberation of individuals by enabling them to see new problems, devise new procedures—thereby making for diversification rather than for set uniformity.[64]

Addressing the same problem, Bode took issue with those who view education as being properly reduced to the attainment and assessment of quantifiable skills as though such a function removed education from the wider social concerns and made education neutral. To Bode, such efforts limited education to fitting individuals as cogs in the existing social mechanism and thereby reflected the aristocratic tradition. "The irony of the situation is that these highly modern persons are a century or two behind the times," wrote Bode, and "[t]here is no such thing as being neutral."[65]

Ironically, Dewey has been attacked by essentialists for the excesses taken in humanizing the curriculum, whereas he has been attacked by humanists for the excesses taken in reducing the curriculum to that which is most amenable to quantifiable and standardized measures. Despite the clear stance taken by Dewey against simplistic and mechanistic approaches to complex education problems, contemporary humanists often rest the blame for such approaches on Dewey. For example, Eisner asked, "Why do the schools, so often, pursue simplistic, mechanical solutions to complex educational problems?" Eisner proceeded to fix the blame on Dewey and Thorndike. Not until the third edition of *The Educational Imagination* did Eisner excise his attack on Dewey in linking him with Thorndike in fixing the blame for the mechanistic state of the curriculum.[66] In earlier editions, Eisner concluded that Franklin Bobbitt's curriculum work in activity analysis stemmed from the tradition established by Dewey and Thorndike. How Dewey could be so linked with Thorndike and Bobbitt, when he clearly and repeatedly criticized the mechanistic approaches developed by these men, is indeed puzzling. But as we have seen, Dewey has been anathema for educators at opposite poles of the educational spectrum, whether perennialist or humanist. As discussed later, by the late 1980s many of those who had previously attacked Dewey came to see him as a true seer for education and the democratic prospect.

DEMOCRATIC IDEAL. Dewey's democratic educational theory also continues to be a subject of misinterpretation to this day. For example, Broudy caricatures Dewey's democratic ideal as an effort to restore our society to the spirit of the New England town meeting.[67] But it was Dewey who pointed out that

> [t]he old principles do not fit contemporary life as it is lived, however well they may have expressed the vital interests of the times in which they arose. . . . The older publics, in being local communities, largely homogeneous with one another, were also, as the phrase goes, static.[68]

Dewey emphasized repeatedly that if democracy is to come into its own, it will require a kind of knowledge and insight that does not yet exist. One of the necessary conditions relevant to our time is that the scientific attitude be adopted in human affairs so that science and technology are used as servants of a humane life and for an enlightened social order rather than being used for private power and profit and public intimidation.[69]

DEMAND FOR RELEVANCE.   Following a rash of riots in urban ghettos and violent protest on college campuses during the 1960s, college and high-school students began demanding curriculum relevance. The discipline-centered curriculum at the secondary level was now regarded as irrelevant to the social situation. However, the call was not to reconstruct the curriculum along the lines of experimentalist thinking but to pursue radical alternatives in education. Aside from the appearance of some alternative schools and the implementation of certain administrative innovations to humanize education, the response of most secondary schools and colleges was manifested in ad hoc changes, such as the expansion of elective options and the allowance of some academic credit for work experience. At the elementary level, open education came into vogue. But instead of being implemented as a means of curriculum reconstruction, open education was often adopted as an administrative rearrangement for teaching the fundamental skills under the theme of individualized instruction.

Yet the late 1960s and early 1970s witnessed an unprecedented interest in the attacks on schools leveled by the radical romanticists—attacks that were publicized widely in the mass media. In his essay, "John Dewey and His Betrayers," Sidney Hook noted that whereas in the past the severest criticisms of American public education came from the traditionalists who opposed the alleged inroads of progressive education on the curriculum, the new wave of attacks "comes from those who regard themselves as libertarians and humanists and who profess themselves inspired to a considerable degree by the thought of John Dewey."[70] Hook accused the radical romanticists of being intellectually irresponsible in disregarding and distorting Dewey's writings.

Where the radical romanticists advocated "incidental" education and even the elimination of the public school, Dewey had looked to public education as the key means of social insight and progress. To Dewey, freedom is not the lack of control and direction, or the right of everyone to do his or her own thing, but rather "the basic freedom is that of freedom of *mind* and of whatever degree of freedom of action and experience is necessary to produce freedom of intelligence."[71]

Reconstructionism

To many progressive educators, experimentalist ideas are too neutral and thereby do not provide the sweeping educational reforms that are needed. Those progressivists who sought a more direct ideology for correcting social ills and building a better society embraced reconstructionism.

EDUCATION FOR SOCIAL RECONSTRUCTION.   The reconstructionist views the school as a chief means for building a new social order. Although reconstructionist ideas are found in the historic stream of utopian writings, the Great Depression witnessed a call to harness the school for social reconstruction. In a series of addresses delivered in 1932 to various education associations, George S. Counts called for progressive educators to address the great crises of the times, fashion a new vision of human destiny based on social welfare, and challenge the schools to the task of giving the rising generation the means toward realizing such a vision.[72] Although Counts acknowledged that the school is but one of the many formative social agencies, he held that this should not deter progressive educators from channeling the powers of the school toward social reconstruction. Nor should educators fear that such a role of the school will result in ideological impositions on the learner, for any kind of powerful education is indeed a kind of imposition, contended Counts.

As noted, Dewey warned the reconstructionists that their cause in directing the curriculum at prescriptive social correction raised the danger of ideological imposition or indoctrination—anathema to democracy. At the 1934 NEA conference, Dewey pointed out that it would be revolution enough if educators were to recognize social changes and act on that recognition in the schools.[73]

Counts's reconstructionism was to take on a militant advocacy that went far beyond his vision and intent. During the Great Depression, educators with Marxist leanings, such as Theodore Brameld, called on teachers to "influence their students, subtly if necessary, frankly if possible, toward acceptance of . . . the collectivist ideal."[74] Years later, Brameld was to repeat his call for teachers "to strengthen control of the schools by and for the goal-seeking interests of the majority of mankind," which are "the fountainhead of utopian potentials."[75]

THE NEW ACADEMIC LEFT.   As might be expected, reconstructionism exerted virtually no impact on the schools. However, it came to be embraced by the radical academic left of the 1980s who grew out of the radical student-protest movement of the 1960s and early 1970s, and who had gained a presence on the faculties of colleges and universities. Turning to European sources for their ideologies, they proceeded to identify themselves as critical theorists, deconstructionists, revisionists, reconceptualists, and neo-Marxists. They proceeded to fault the schools for their impotence on the one hand and for exercising a powerful repressive role in maintaining the existing social order on the other hand. When not portraying the role of the school as inconsequential, they were portraying the teacher as an unwitting accomplice to a hidden scheme (in the hidden curriculum) for promoting "cultural reproduction" or "social control"—as opposed to "emancipation of the masses." With regard to Dewey, on the one hand they would attack him for his liberal ideology and for having provided the groundwork that led to the existing state of affairs in the public schools;[76] on the other hand, they would see the work of Dewey and his fellow experimentalists as having but little impact on the schools.[77] In making their case, they did not hesitate to revise the historic record so as to buttress their assault on the schools and on progressive educators who did not fit into the radical fold. For example, Bowles and Gintis contended that "[p]roponents of the use of tests for educational tracking found support in John Dewey's writings."[78] However, in *Democracy and Education* (1916), Dewey actually attacked the efforts to measure differences in mental abilities in these words: "How one person's abilities compare in quantity with those of another is none of the teacher's business. It is irrelevant to his work."[79] Jencks portrayed the public school as a "marginal institution," whereas Illich verified Spring's thesis that "the primary purpose of the school system is social control for a corporate state."[80] Spring ended his book with these words: "The only possible solution is ending the power of the school."[81]

Regardless of which position was taken on the power, importance, or impotence of the public school, the academic left shared a profound negativism toward the public schools, and even sought righteous justification in distancing themselves from the problems of school people. As Hlebowitsh points out, "radical commentators have written much about how schools fail . . . , but they have also left us with little in the way of solutions that might work within the social and political realities of our schools."[82] Those of the academic left in schools of education seemed to forget that the role of professional schools is to prepare professional practitioners and to advance professional practice. Instead, they patterned themselves after their compeers in the liberal arts who followed a long tradition of school blaming, as Conant had pointed out.[83]

Curiously, in their attacks on the comprehensive high school and their call for equity by reducing the curriculum to academic subjects, the academic left were in league with the essentialists. Instead of working to promote a common core for general education, within the context of diversified studies (without tracking) for a cosmopolitan pupil population, the academic left, like the essentialists, called for the return of the high school to a one-track academic curriculum.

By the late 1980s, the wider university community began to object to the ideological imposition of political correctness and the ethical problem of indoctrination in academe. The academic left were also facing problems with internal theoretical contradictions.[84] Their destructive stance of negation left them without any program for constructive practical action for the schools. At the same time, the academic left were beset by fractious multiculturalist elements within their ranks. The crisis was capped by the forced suppression of student protests in Beijing, China, in May 1989 and the collapse of the Soviet Union and Marxist ideology.

In the face of the growing ideological crisis on the American college campus, the academic left turned to Dewey. In doing so, they had to rehabilitate Dewey. Whereas they had once debased him as a liberal, he was now a radical liberal or reconstructionist. In 1985 Aronowitz and Giroux could attack Dewey's instrumentalism as having "resulted in a curriculum that, far from widening the base of the citizenry in the classical sense of the term, resulted in the educational complement to the specialization and degradation of the labor force in factories and offices." Only three years later, Giroux would write that "radicals and conservatives alike have ignored John Dewey's vision of public schools as democratic spheres, as places where the skills of democracy can be practiced, debated, and analyzed."[85]

Appropriating Dewey to their camp, the academic left turned to Richard Rorty's scholarship on Dewey and to Robert Westbrook's *John Dewey and American Democracy* (1991).[86]

PLURALISTIC AND CENTRIST CHARACTER OF AMERICAN SOCIETY. Unlike the new academic left, the reconstructionists of yesteryear did direct their efforts toward school problems including school improvement. However, their influence was tempered by the indoctrination issue and the pluralistic and centrist character of American society, which buffers any militant attempt toward doctrinal agreement for collective social reconstruction, just as it buffers or resists any extremist political platform.

Implementing experimentalist ideas in the curriculum would, in itself, constitute a revolutionary transformation; for it would defeat censorship and open the curriculum to the reflective examination of alternative ideologies, however controversial; and it would seek to develop autonomously thinking, socially responsible citizens.

The pluralistic character and centrist tendencies of American society need not be viewed pessimistically as barriers to social correction and improvement. As a foreign observer noted before midcentury, if an ordinary American faces a problem without having any specific clues for its solution, one of the recommendations he or she is likely to resort to is "education"—for "the belief in 'education' is a part of, or a principal conclusion from the American creed."[87] Americans look to education as a key institution for social improvement. Their tendency to lend an open ear to every attack on the schools that comes along during periods of social crisis stems from their great expectations of the role of the school in correcting social problems and not from their lack of faith in education. At the same time, the American public has resisted radical proposals for its schools, whether it be the abandonment of the comprehensive secondary school in favor of the dual European model or the use of the school for imposing reconstructionist ideology on children and youth. Radical educational reforms have been left to the alternative schools that are on the periphery of the mainstream of American education.

UTOPIAN VISIONS.   Although reconstructionism embraces democracy as the appropriate goal of education, experimentalists see the educational means of reconstructionism as inculcating prescribed beliefs in the learner. To the experimentalist this is indoctrination, and democratic ends cannot be attained by indoctrination. There is all the difference in the world between prescribing beliefs and in identifying problem areas for reflective consideration of issues and solutions on the part of the learner.[88]

History is replete with utopian schemes for education and society. However noble and admirable may be the utopian visions of reconstructionism, the history of utopian schemes, noted Mumford, reveals an unmistakable absolutism:

> Strangely, though the word *freedom* is sometimes included in the description of utopia—indeed, one nineteenth-century utopia was called Freeland—the pervasive character of all utopias is their totalitarian absolutism, the reduction of variety and choice, and the effort to escape from such natural conditions or historical traditions as would support variety and make choice possible. These uniformities and compulsions constitute utopia's inner tie to the megamachine.[89]

Whatever their techniques for realizing their ends, "almost all utopias emphasize regularity, uniformity, authoritarianism, isolation, and autocracy," contended Mumford, for the strategies for creating the coming world invariably are placed in the hands of a narrow elite who are the "accredited ministers of progress."[90] The prescriptions of reconstructionism are concerned with promoting the welfare of the masses in a democratically regulated utopian society. The reconstructionist prescriptions do not preclude indoctrination, and indoctrination is ideological imposition on the learner. As such it raises the question as to whether reconstructionism embraces a kind of political absolutism that Mumford was concerned about.

THE ROMANTIC VISION

Romantic Naturalism

As discussed in Chapter 1, the quest for progressive educational reforms during the early decades of this century witnessed the emergence of child-centered doctrines. In rejecting the traditional conception of child as a miniature adult, and in battling against the coercive, authoritarian methods of traditional education, the romantic progressivists embraced the notion of the child as a flower to unfold naturally into fruition. This unfoldment and fruition could best be realized by capitalizing on the natural propensities of the child. The pervasive idea of the child's natural development led to the notion that the school must be an environment in which the child's spontaneity, felt needs, and activity are seen as positive energies for effective learning.

SCIENCE AND SENTIMENT.   Ironically, whereas the child-study movement in education had begun as an effort to induce educational reform through the scientific study of the child, it came to be dominated by sentiment rather than by science. At the annual meeting of the National Education Association at the turn of the century, an officer of the Child-Study Division of the NEA carried the case for sentiment over science by declaring "[b]etter is it to know nothing of the plant's structure and functions, but to love in order to gain knowledge. Better still that love and knowledge should kiss each other."[91]

Undoubtedly, the efforts of the romantic progressivists to kindle in teachers more affectionate and empathic attitudes toward children were well justified in view of the authoritarian educational practices of the times. Their belief in the centrality of child life in the curriculum led them to regard child interests and spontaneous activity indulgently as achievements rather than as means toward intellective and social growth. Dewey repeatedly admonished the romantic progressivists for this failure. To Dewey, their view "fails to see that even the most pleasing and beautiful exhibitions are but signs, and that they begin to spoil and rot the moment they are treated as achievements." When such activities are continually initiated but do not arrive at a higher level, we have a situation as bad as the continual repression of initiative in conformity with authority, contended Dewey. "It is as if the child were forever tasting and never eating; always having his palate tickled upon the emotional side, but never getting the organic satisfaction that comes only with digestion of food and transformation of it into working power."[92]

RADICAL SCHOOL REFORM.   In their zeal for radical educational reform, many contemporary critics have embraced the tenets of romantic naturalism, although they rarely acknowledge that their ideas have an earlier record in modern history. The reaction against the pursuit of academic excellence beginning in the mid-1960s brought forth a rash of best-selling books exposing the schools for every conceivable failure and evil, and proposing a variety of formulas for freeing pupils to learn. It was a time when many college students were embracing activism and self-sensation and rejecting reflection and self-discipline. Doing your own thing—the situation ethic of the ghetto street—became fashionable on the college campus.

A. S. Neill's *Summerhill,* although published in 1960, became a best-seller in the United States several years later when the atmosphere was ripe for romantic educational ideas. Recounting the precepts on which his school has operated since the time of its founding in England in 1921, Neill revealed his romantic notion of the child's innate goodness and the need for the school to provide freedom for the child to flower forth.

> Well, we set out to make a school in which we should allow children to be themselves. In order to do this, we had to renounce all discipline, all direction, all suggestion, all moral training. . . . All it required was what we had—a complete belief in the child as a good, not an evil being. For almost forty years, this belief in the goodness of the child has never wavered; it rather has become a final faith.
>
> My view is that a child is innately wise and realistic. If left to himself without adult suggestions of any kind, he will develop as far as he is capable of developing.[93]

Although Neill denied the need for a formal curriculum, he explained that the offering of traditional academic subjects at Summerhill is a necessary concession to the university entrance examinations. "Books are the least important apparatus in a school," announced Neill, and "[m]ost of the school work that adolescents do is simply a waste of time, of energy, of patience. It robs youth of its right to play and play and play."[94]

Neill's *Summerhill* was read widely in the United States, but few of his readers and followers were aware that the Summerhill School failed to attract and serve a significant constituency in England. The total enrollment at Summerhill has ranged only from forty-five to sixty pupils, with the majority of the youngsters from American families residing temporarily in England.

Although Neill belonged to an earlier generation of romantic progressivists, the new wave of romanticists and romantic anarchists carried the same echo, telling the American public that the child's natural capacity for education is destroyed by the schools. "The purpose of elementary pedagogy, through age twelve, should be to delay socialization, to protect children's free growth," declared Paul Goodman as he went on to advocate that "[w]e must drastically cut back formal schooling because the present extended tutelage is against nature and arrests growth."[95]

The persistent indictment of middle-class values permeates much of the radical-reformist literature. The schools are often portrayed as socialization instruments for perpetuating all of the evils associated with the profit-making system. Kozol went so far as to link the atrocities in Vietnam with the learning inculcated by the schools as early as the elementary grades,[96] overlooking the fact that the colleges and high schools were a chief source of protest against the war. Kozol later turned to education in Castro's Cuba as an appropriate model. He portrayed education in Cuba as humanizing, whereas education for the poor in the United States is exploitative and debilitating. He went on to describe how 100,000 Cuban children, half of them below the age of fourteen, were sent to the fields and mountains to teach the nation to read and write.[97] The romantic portrayal of child as the parent of humanity is a common element in the literature on radical school reform. To a considerable extent the radical school reform effort of the 1960s was more of a literary movement than an educational movement. The literature on radical school reform was well represented on the nation's lists of best-sellers, and was widely discussed in the media and in teacher-education classes. Its impact on the schools was mainly in the sector of alternative schools and through some cosmetic adjustments of mainstream education. Ironically, where the rationale for alternative schooling during the 1960s was to provide child-centered approaches to education, the alternative schools of the late 1970s and 1980s were centered largely on academic achievement, with particular emphasis on the basics. More recently, alternative schools have been centered on serving the special-interest needs of special-interest groups, or concentrated on specialized academic functions, such as science and technology or the arts. In recent years, Kozol emerged as a passionate defender of American public schools and opponent of school vouchers and alternative schools. His concern for children at-risk remained unshaken, but now he looked to the potentials for school regeneration.[98]

CONCEPTION OF THE LEARNER.   Even at the college level, the innate goodness of youth is proclaimed. Theodore Roszak, theoretician for the counter culture of the 1960s and early 1970s, sees the student as a wildflower that must not be crushed by the world of scientific rationality.

> The young, miserably educated as they are, bring with them almost nothing but healthy instincts. The project of building a sophisticated framework of thought atop those instincts is like trying to graft an oak tree upon a wildflower. How to sustain the oak tree? More important, how to avoid crushing the wildflower? And yet such is the project that confronts those of us who are concerned with radical social change. For the young have become one of the very few social levers dissent has to work with. This is that "significant soil" in which the Great Refusal has begun to take root. If we reject it in frustration for the youthful follies that also sprout here, where then do we turn?[99]

In answering his own question, Roszak went beyond the romantic naturalist's simple prescription of allowing the learner to blossom into full flower by removing constraints and enriching the environment. Roszak's answer is that we must turn away from the rationality of science and toward nonintellective consciousness, as exemplified in the tranquil inner contemplativeness of the Eastern religions, in order to proclaim a new, vast, marvelous heaven and earth. In a later work, Roszak viewed the true source of spiritual regeneration in the transcendent "rhapsodic ideal" of the Romantic poets.[100] Like the existentialists and the radical critics of rationality and science, Roszak confused the scientific outlook and methods of science with the evil political uses to which science is put. They romanticized the magic of nonintellective consciousness and ignored the fact that antirationality and antiscience have their own tyrannies.

Turning again to the romanticist's view of the young child, we find it proclaimed that the schools and the adult world destroy the creative capacity of children.

Nobody starts off stupid. You only have to watch babies and infants, and think seriously about what all of them learn and do, to see that, except for the most grossly retarded, they show a style of life, and a desire and ability to learn that in an older person we might well call genius. Hardly an adult in a thousand, or ten thousand, could in any three years of his life learn as much, grow as much in his understanding of the world around him, as every infant learns and grows in his first three years. But what happens, as we get older, to this extraordinary capacity for learning and intellectual growth?

What happens is that it is destroyed, and more than by any other one thing, by the process that we misname education—a process that goes on in most homes and schools. We adults destroy most of the intellectual and creative capacity of children by the things we do to them or make them do.[101]

In portraying the child as good and the school as evil, romantic critics conveniently ignore the body of research on child development. To expect the individual to grow and develop cognitively throughout life at the same rate and in the same way as during the first three years of life would deny one the qualitative changes that are manifest as one progresses through the developmental stages. If we could envision such a fantastic phenomenon, we would see the child as simply developing into an even bigger and better child—a child monster.

Furthermore, the fact that the young child learns his or her native language so readily and "naturally" without a formal curriculum is not a valid basis for assuming that all learning can be realized in the same way if only educators allow the child's genius to find its own fruition. The development of oral language, although still a mystery, may be psychobiologically rooted, believes Chomsky, in a way essentially different from other forms of cognitive learning.[102] Thus, learning to speak one's native language does not require the systematic organization of knowledge and experience requisite for learning mathematics, chemistry, drafting, or carpentry. Language is the medium of social communication. It finds expression and growth in every dimension of meaning and purposeful action. In a rich and stimulating social environment, oral language learning becomes fluid and generative. This should give us pause to consider how in the traditional error-oriented classroom of rote and recitation, children will tend to avoid speaking in paragraphs and asking why and what-if questions for fear of revealing their ignorance.

ROUSSEAU.   The romantic portrayal of the child as innately good and the adult world as a conspiracy of evil parallels Rousseau's romantic vision of education as expressed in his iconoclastic *Émile,* published in 1762. "God makes all things good; man meddles with them and they become evil," wrote Rousseau. Other Rousseauian aphorisms are:[103]

We can do much, but the chief thing is to prevent anything being done.

Reverse the usual practice and you will almost always do right.

Young teacher, I am setting before you a difficult task, the art of controlling without precepts, and doing everything without doing anything at all.

Let the child do nothing because he is told; nothing is good for him but what he recognizes as good.

Yet Rousseau tempered his romantic view of child with a call for "well-regulated liberty," and he recognized that the child's cognitive capabilities undergo qualitative changes as he or she undergoes new developmental stages. Thus, curiosity must be "rightly directed" according to "the means of development for the age which we are dealing," Rousseau contended. Nor is the curriculum without focus and direction. "The real object of our study is man and his environment," wrote Rousseau. He emphasized that as the child approaches adolescence, "much skill and discretion are required to lead him toward theoretical studies." In teaching the pupil to observe the phenomena of nature, the teacher's responsibility is to "[p]ut the problems before him and let him solve them himself. . . . Let him not be taught science, let him discover it."[104]

CURRICULUM. Contemporary romanticists go so far as to deny the idea of curriculum on the grounds that knowledge is so subject to change it is senseless to plan in advance what it is that the child should be taught.

> The notion of a curriculum, as an essential body of knowledge, would be absurd even if children remembered everything we "taught" them. We don't and can't agree on what knowledge is essential. . . .
> The idea of the curriculum would not be valid even if we could agree what ought to be in it. For knowledge changes. Much of what a child learns in school will be found, or thought, before many years, to be untrue. . . . Since we can't know what knowledge will be most needed in the future, it is senseless to try to teach it in advance. . . .
> Learning is not everything, and certainly one piece of learning is as good as another.[105]

According to Paul Goodman, "The effort to channel the process of growing up according to a preconceived curriculum and method discourages and wastes many of the best human powers to learn and cope." What, then, should the teacher and the school provide in the absence of a curriculum? Goodman's answer is that "[i]ncidental education, taking part in the ongoing activities of society, must again be made the chief means of learning and teaching."[106] Goodman even went so far as to claim that "[v]ery many of our youth, both poor and middle class, might be better off if the system did not exist, even if they had no formal schooling at all."[107] However, he later qualified this view by acknowledging that academic schools should continue to serve the academically talented, "and such schools are better off unencumbered by the sullen uninterested bodies of the others."[108] Although romanticists typically profess egalitarian principles, and many have a penchant for claiming to find genius in the disadvantaged slow learner, Goodman revealed his educational elitism by advocating that secondary schooling be confined to the academically talented youth, and the others should be left to gain whatever "incidental education" that might be found in the ongoing activities of society. Oddly, Goodman saw the larger society as corrupt and repressive, and yet he somehow viewed it as providing a more meaningful education than formal schooling for most of our youth who only clog the schools with their "uninterested bodies." A similarly elitist view was propounded by Edgar Friedenberg, another radical romanticist.[109] Ivan Illich went so far as to advocate that all schools be abolished, and he romanticized the powers of society and the growing information technology as capable of fulfilling the educational needs of children and youth.[110]

In contrast, other romanticists advocate radical changes in the school by doing away with the notion of a preplanned curriculum and centering all learning activities on the child's present felt needs. They envision the school as a giant smorgasbord of learning activities with the child free to pick out whatever pursuits he or she wants.

> We cannot know, at any moment, what particular bit of knowledge or understanding a child needs most, will most strengthen and best fit his model of reality. Only he can do this. He may not do it very well, but he can do it a hundred times better than we can. The most we can do is try to help, by letting him know roughly what is available and when he can look for it. Choosing what he wants to learn and what he does not is something he must do for himself. . . . In short, the school should be a great smorgasbord of intellectual, artistic, creative, and athletic activities, from which each child could take whatever he wanted, and as much as he wanted, or as little.[111]

In attacking the dogmatisms of traditional education, the romanticists would impose a new set of dogmatisms on the teacher and the school. Do away with curriculum and allow the child to find fulfillment through his or her immediate interests, teachers are told. Recounting his own teaching experiences in a traditional school, even a more moderate romanticist writes, "I had little impact on the school and ultimately quit. Still I gradually found ways of teaching that were not based on compulsion but on participation; not on grades or tests or curriculum, but on pursuing what interested the children."[112]

The romantic radical finds no meeting ground with the organized knowledge of humanity. Curriculum planning is an imposition on the teacher and pupil. Presentism is the key doctrine of relevance. Free verbal interaction and overt activity in the classroom replace systematic reflection and are taken for freedom. The teacher's role is indirect, that of a guide and facilitator who must get out of the way of children. "What we need to do, and all we need to do," contends Holt, "is bring as much of the world as we can into the school and the classroom; give the children as much help and guidance as they need and ask for, listen respectfully when they feel like talking; and then get out of the way. We can trust them to do the rest."[113]

When put into operation through private alternative schools, romanticist ideology soon faces a crisis of reality. As in the case of other forms of protest schools, the very few that manage to survive wind up with curricula that are not substantively different from the curricula of conventional schools.[114] Consequently, alternative schools have not been useful for experimentation.[115]

As mentioned, to a considerable extent the radical romanticism of the 1960s was a literary movement with many of the books on educational reform directed at the general public and making national best-seller lists. When the tide shifted away from radical school reform, some of the authors left for more fertile fields, and others did a virtual about face by embracing the conservative backlash of back to basics. Jonathan Kozol turned to basic education or literacy.[116] Whereas Postman co-authored *Teaching as a Subversive Activity* in 1969, he authored *Teaching as a Conserving Activity* in 1979. As in professional sports, one could simply join the opposition team and change uniforms.

ROMANTIC NATURALISM AND EXPERIMENTALISM.   The contemporary educational romanticists almost invariably promote their ideas as though they were newly discovered. Only rarely is mention made of the rootings of their ideas. Sadly, when a romanticist acknowledges that these ideas have earlier rootings, the acknowledgment is given to Dewey: "Like Dewey, Neill stressed free animal expression, learning by doing, and very democratic community processes," propounded Goodman, revealing that he either never read or understood Dewey.[117] Time and again Dewey criticized the romantic progressivists who believed that pupils should not be exposed to a curriculum plan or suggestion from the teacher on the ground that it would be "an unwarranted trespass upon their sacred intellectual individuality." Dewey called such a position "really stupid . . . [because] it misconceives the conditions for independent thinking."[118] He went on to stress that spontaneous pupil activity only undermines freedom because it subjects immature children to uncontrolled, haphazard influences, with the result that learning activities are superficial and lacking in intelligently directed thought. "Direct immediate discharge or expression of an impulsive tendency is fatal to thinking," argued Dewey, for "[g]enuine freedom, in short, is intellectual, it rests in the trained *power of thought*. . . . To cultivate unhindered unreflective external activity is to foster enslavement, for it leaves the person at the mercy of appetite, sense, and circumstance."[119]

THE INNER VISION

 ## Existentialism

The search for the meaning of human existence in an indifferent universe, the quest for personal significance in an age of impersonal technology, and the need for individual awareness in an age of the mechanical masses led to the resurrection of existentialist thought during the second half of the twentieth century. Rooted in the works of the nineteenth-century Danish philosopher-theologian Søren Kierkegaard, existentialist ideas were extended greatly in the writings of such men as Nietzsche, Heidegger, Jaspers, Camus, Buber, and Sartre. Kierkegaard contended that humanity cannot find reality through the grand designs of rational thought, but can find it through the passion of faith. Faith and the meaning of existence are not things that can be imposed on the individual by some outside authority. Our highest interest is our own existence, held Kierkegaard, and our interest in our existence constitutes our reality.

The plight of the lonely individual in an uncaring universe became an overwhelming theme in literature during the years since midcentury. This concern and the search for authentic personal identity also became central in the writings of a number of theorists in the field of psychotherapy during this period. In an era of mechanical impersonalization and depersonalization, alienation, disappearance of religious control and influence, and disillusionment with science, the idea of finding meaning through subjective introspection rather than through objective rational thought became vastly appealing to certain segments of the college generation. Seeing themselves freed from rational constraints, they could challenge the repressions and inadequacies of our social institutions through a metaphysical revolt. Rather than losing oneself in the drug scene or in occultism, or even in the esoteric mysticism of Roszak's counter culture, one could find oneself in the private estheticism of existential thought.

Because the universe is indifferent to humanity, the individual must assign to himself or herself the meaning of one's own existence, believes the existentialist. Humanity cannot find such meaning in religious dogma, social philosophies, or science. People are absolutely worthless in the cosmos, so the individual must find his or her own absolute worth. By finding the meaning of one's own existence, one is free to choose what he or she is and becomes and one can find the authentic self through the full awakening of spontaneous human powers. The self-encounter rather than the group-encounter is stressed. If this appears to some to be excessively self-centered and individualistic, the existentialist argues that this condition applies to each of us and so it becomes reciprocal between individuals, or, in Buber's words, between "I" and "Thou." One's own need to be free must be reciprocal; it must recognize the need for another person to be free.

FREEDOM AND RATIONAL THOUGHT.   In setting limits on rational thought, in seeking to be free of the excess baggage of intelligence, the existentialist is acting to restrict rather than to free intelligence. Thus their quest for freedom is marred by the very limits existentialists set on rational thought, limits that serve the cause of anti-intellectualism. In Dewey's words,

> It is a curious state of mind which finds pleasure in setting forth the "limits of science." For the intrinsic limit of knowledge is simply ignorance; and the point in extolling ignorance is not clear except when expressed by those who profit by keeping others in ignorance. There is of course an extrinsic limit of science. But that limitation lies in the ineptitude of those who put it to use; its removal lies in rectification of its use, not in abuse of the thing used.[120]

To denigrate rational thought because the uses to which science is put are abusive of human beings is to misplace the blame, argued Dewey. "The eye sees many foul things and the arm and the hand do many cruel things. Yet the fanatic who would pluck out the eye and cut off the arm is recognized for what he is."[121]

In rejecting the rational mode of science, existentialists tend to caricature science as being coldly neutral, and they see scientific thought as being devoid of morality. In this connection they confuse scientific thought with the political misuses to which the products of science and technology are put. "The best available evidence has nothing to do with morality or human fulfillment," argues Maxine Greene as she points out that "[w]e need only recall the testing that led to the A-bomb and the H-bomb, to extermination camps, to nerve gas, to napalm." Political reasoning, not scientific reasoning, led to the uses of nuclear energy for bombs rather than for building a better humanity. When Greene alleges that science is not moral or beneficent, witness "the Nazis' final solution of 'the Jewish problem': the application of scientific knowledge to mass extermination,"[122] Greene confuses scientific thought with political decision making. The fact that an evil act can be planned and executed rationally does not mean that such an act is the logical outcome of rational thought. The problem of how to exterminate a people is not a problem of science any more than is the problem of how to assassinate a president. To pose such a problem in the first place is indicative of irrational forces at work. The conception of an evil act does not originate with the motives of science but derives from personal, social, or political motives. Moreover, the fact that an evil act can be planned and executed rationally fails to make a case in favor of irrationality or nonrational thought. What kind of case could be made to show that human history would have been better through irrational or nonrational thought rather than rational thought?[123] Human history has been a battle between irrational and rational thought. When Greene holds that "[t]he best available evidence has nothing to do with morality or human fulfillment," the implication is that we should not guide our thoughts and actions according to "the best available evidence." If one is thinking scientifically, one must know the *problem* to which the best available evidence is being put. If the problem is how to eliminate disease, starvation, environmental pollution, poverty, crime, and so on, is there a better prospect for solution or remediation than making use of the best available evidence? The persistence of these problems is not the result of rational thought but of people's failure to wage an attack on these problems through rational ends and means.

Greene contends that science is an inadequate model for the existentialist because "scientific thinking is concerned with objectification and excludes the intuitive awareness and self-encounters required of philosophy," and she goes on to declare that "[w]hen the existentialist speaks of knowing, he speaks of passionately engaging and of vouching for his ideas with his life. The cool neutrality of experimental inquiry is usually alien to such a man."[124] Here Greene confuses science with cold empiricism. To emasculate philosophy from science is to have no science. Science is philosophy. The key scientific ideas do not stem from empiricism. The record of history reveals that scientists, no less than any group, have vouched for their ideas with their lives. The historic record is not very kind to the leading existentialists in their relationship to totalitarianism.[125]

It is fallacious to assume that the existentialist thinker, the artist, and the poet are passionately engaged, whereas scientific inquiry is coldly neutral and devoid of passion. As Bronowski pointed out, creation—whether in art or in science—engages the whole being. "A gifted man cannot handle bacteria or equations without taking fire from what he does and having his emotions engaged."[126] Einstein discussed the profound faith with which scientists must be imbued in their aspiration toward truth and understanding. "I cannot conceive of a genuine scientist without such profound faith," he wrote, as he proceeded to liken the profound reverence for rationality to a spirit of religiosity:

> [W]hoever has undergone the intense experience of successful advances made in this domain [science], is moved by profound reverence for the rationality made manifest in existence. By way of the understanding he achieves a far-reaching emancipation from the shackles of personal hopes and desires, and thereby attains a humble attitude of mind towards the grandeur of reason incarnate in existence, and which in its profoundest depths, is inaccessible to man. This attitude, however, appears to me to be religious, in the highest sense of the word. . . .
>
> The further the spiritual evolution of mankind advances, the more certain it seems to me that the path to genuine religiosity does not lie through the fear of life, and the fear of death, and blind faith, but through striving after rational knowledge.[127]

The existentialist seeks to engage in introspection beyond reason because he or she cannot find through reason the answer to the ultimate question of the meaning of one's existence. "Whatever its ultimate meaning, the universe into which we have been thrown cannot satisfy our reason; let us have the courage to admit it once and for all," wrote Marcel.[128] If people turn away from reason, can they really be free, or will they merely become shackled by the illusions of their own creation? This is the pitfall in the existentialist dream. Turning again to Dewey,

> For the neglect of sciences that deal specifically with facts of the natural and social environment leads to a side-tracking of moral forces into an unreal privacy of an unreal self. . . . Each sign of disregard for the moral potentialities of science drafts the conscience of mankind away from concern with the interactions of man and nature which must be mastered if freedom is to be reality. It diverts intelligence to anxious preoccupation with the unrealities of a purely inner life.[129]

But to Greene, Dewey failed to deal with the existentialist "experience of nothingness" and ennui, "a pervasive boredom of which Dewey [in his healthy mindedness] seemed to know little."[130] It would appear, then, that the existentialists were offering educators a philosophy of futility and despair, masquerading as hyper-radicalism. Their profound negativism found them allied with the multicultural admixture of the academic left. But as far as the role of the school is concerned, their programmatic prescriptions took the form of radical romanticism. The healthy child and adolescent intuitively knows that there is nothing in the "experience of nothingness."

EXISTENTIALISM AND THE CURRICULUM.   To the existentialist, the route to knowledge is personal; education should help the individual find the meaning of one's own existence. Because the child is born into "a world of meaninglessness, that is, a world that does not have meaning already woven into and embedded in it," he or she can extract "possibilities without exacting reciprocal tribute of human compliance." The school, therefore, must be an environment in which "the full exercise of the spontaneous human self is the avenue to authenticity as a person." Educators must extricate the child from "the crushing overload of social controls," and "the school must direct its attention to the release of the human self, to the involvement of the child in personal decision and moral judgment to a far greater degree than he knows at present."[131]

To awaken the child existentially, the curriculum should provide considerable time for private introspection and the study of moral questions concerning humanity's predicament. Neither the standard curriculum of essential subject matters nor the experimentalist focus on the development of trained intelligence through social problem solving is adequate to the task of enabling the pupil to find oneself. This does not mean that all organized subject matter must be discarded, but rather that the pupil must be allowed the widest possible latitude in determining the portions of organized subject matter that are authentic to one's own being. Moreover, the subject matter should not be focused on objective or practical knowledge but on the individual predicament. The sciences and vocational studies are of least significance. The social studies should deal with the meaning of individual freedom rather than citizenship, social institutions, or codified knowledge. Obviously, literature, poetry, art, and music can be significant sources for enabling students to confront the human condition. The goal is self-development and self-fulfillment.

Knowledge is not transmitted but offered to the pupil, and the teacher engages in dialogue with the pupil to encourage thinking for oneself and to make knowledge personal. Some existentialists, such as Kneller, would abolish the school altogether, and have each youngster go to a teacher for an "I" and "Thou" dialogue.[132] Such an arrangement is reminiscent of Rousseau's *Émile* and of the proposals of some contemporary radical romanticists who see organized schooling as thwarting the child's powers for spontaneous self-realization.

When efforts are made to put existentialist ideas into practice in an actual school (invariably it is a small private school with a relatively homogeneous pupil population), the ideas and functions tend to resemble many features associated with romantic naturalism. For example, a description of one existential school calls for "the absence of authoritarian hierarchical structures, required courses, assigned groups, prescribed number of classroom hours, grades, evaluations"—with emphasis given to "learning through self-motivation and self-regulation . . . equal status of all pursuits . . . evaluation through self-criticism . . . teaching based on interest . . . spontaneous formation of learning groups, centered on common interests . . . teacher retention based on student demand."[133] As in A. S. Neill's Summerhill School, young children—four-year-olds—have an equal vote with faculty at the general school meetings, although it is admitted that they rarely attend these meetings. The descriptions of the school are pregnant with sentimental idealization of the child.

Existentialists may argue justifiably that such a school is not a valid representation of existential education, but the point is that whatever has been presented as an existential school in operation appears unwittingly to have succumbed to practices that the romantic naturalist would applaud. Aside from the enormous practical problems of existential schooling is the question of how it is possible for a child to find the meaning of his or her existence—to develop a philosophy of life—when education is focused on spontaneous self-realization. "It is certainly as futile to expect a child to evolve a universe out of his own mere mind as it is for a philosopher to attempt that task," observed Dewey.[134] This leads to the philosophical problem of how the personal measures for individual self-direction and self-fulfillment will become unselfishly directed toward the goal of remaking a civilization. Somehow this quest for self-fulfillment will become transformed to the social task of rebuilding a civilization, contends Kneller as he offers this quote of Camus: "There is a whole civilization to be remade."[135] The question is whether the existentialist's private vision can lead to the realization of the public promise.

PERSPECTIVE

"The most important educational problem today is the problem of direction," wrote Bode.[136] The problem of educational ends and means is of signal consideration in any philosophy or theory of education. Many teachers and administrators regard educational philosophizing as a kind of academic exercise remote from the real world of the school. This may indeed be the case when philosophical positions are derived from *outside* the educational situation and then imposed *on* the educational situation. When the educational situation is the source and testing ground of philosophical ideas, such ideas become crucial to the direction and means of education and to educational progress. For example, a school's statement of philosophy may be premised on democratic principles, but if these principles are not tested in practice they are meaningless.

Schools commonly have a statement of philosophy, formulated by the faculty and administration, although the statement is rarely systematically formulated from and tested against actual practice. Without such testing, the school curriculum is vulnerable to whatever external demands and pressures are most pervasive at any given time. Because the external demands and pressures are constantly being recycled, the school often tends to yield to them on a superficial level of adopting certain prepackaged programs and theories along with their labels and slogans. The up-to-date school is the trendy school, rather than the school that is engaged in curricular problem solving by testing alternative ideas in the light of practice. To say that a given practice works is not saying much. It may work in terms of maintaining the status quo or in terms of regressing to some ideal alien to democracy, such as indoctrination. Educational theories and practices must be tested against alternative theories and practices if progress is to be made.

Dewey regarded philosophy as the general theory of education, for he viewed education as the process of forming fundamental dispositions toward nature and fellow humans, and he saw education as the laboratory in which philosophic distinctions become concrete and are tested. However, educational decisions and practices often have been derived in the absence of a guiding philosophy. Insufficient attention has been given to basing such decisions on reflective consideration of the good person leading the good life in the good social order. Under these circumstances, the school becomes vulnerable to whatever influences are most pervasive at a particular time, and the response is a kind of mechanical tinkering with the curriculum.

Because few proponents of conflicting educational theories have sought to see education as the laboratory in which philosophical distinctions become concrete and are tested, each theory becomes a matter of theological allegiance, and curriculum change becomes a mechanical response to external imposition.

Hutchins observed that "[t]he failure of educational philosophy reflects the failure of our philosophy in general. It is not the schools that make their purposes, but the people that control them."[137] Yet, despite these shortcomings, no other society has made education so accessible to its people as the United States, and no other society has managed to provide within a unitary educational system such a diversified and comprehensive curriculum for such a pluralistic population. In this sense, education in the United States is indeed a laboratory in which philosophical distinctions become concrete and are tested. It was not by chance that the United States gave birth to experimentalist theory.

PROBLEMS FOR STUDY AND DISCUSSION

1. How do you account for the constant recycling of educational reform movements in which the same themes, such as back to basics, reappear at periodic intervals?

2. Make an approximation of the number of articles appearing under the topic of "democracy" in the latest annual edition of *Education Index*. Compare this with (1) any year between the end of World War II and midcentury and (2) any year during the 1970s. What conclusions can you draw regarding the concern with this topic in the contrasting eras?

3. Do you agree with the following statement? Why or why not?

It is necessary to bear in mind that education cannot be divorced from social theory, from a conception or standard of social organization. This proposition is not enjoying wide favor at present. There are many educators nowadays who have scant patience with what they call philosophizing. To them the problems of education are all problems to be worked out with a yardstick and statistical curves. . . . No account is taken of the fact that the individual must either be fitted to become a cog in the social mechanism, or else must be educated according to some notion of how this mechanism should be changed. To

suppose that the work of education can be carried on effectively without reference to the larger issue is plain self-deception. There is no such thing as being neutral. [Boyd H. Bode, *Modern Educational Theories* (New York: Macmillan, 1927), p. 234.]

4. According to Hutchins, "Knowledge is truth. The truth is everywhere the same." [Robert M. Hutchins, *The Higher Learning in America* (New Haven, CT: Yale University Press, 1936), p. 66.] According to Bruner, "intellectual activity anywhere is the same." [Jerome S. Bruner, *The Process of Education* (Cambridge, MA: Harvard University Press, 1960), p. 14.]

What are the implications of these statements for curriculum development?

5. Dewey identified these fundamental factors in the educative process: (1) the learner, (2) society, and (3) organized subject matter, and he noted that the tendency is to treat these factors "in their separateness, to insist upon one at the expense of the other, to make antagonists of them." [John Dewey, *The Child and the Curriculum* (Chicago: University of Chicago Press, 1902), pp. 4–8.]

How is this antagonism reflected in the views of the essentialist and the romantic naturalist? How do these views compare with your own?

6. The following are two contrasting statements on the curriculum. What are your reactions to these statements?

> For all children, the educational process must be one of collecting factual knowledge to the limit of their absorptive capacity. Recreation, manual or clerical training, etiquette, and similar know-how have little effect on the mind itself and it is with the mind that the school must solely concern itself. The poorer a child's natural endowments, the more does he need to have his mind trained. . . . To acquire such knowledge, fact upon fact, takes time and effort. Nothing can really make it "fun." [Hyman G. Rickover, "European vs. American Secondary Schools," *Phi Delta Kappan,* 40 (November, 1958), p. 61.]

> Learning is not everything, and certainly one piece of learning is as good as another. . . . In short, the school should be a great smorgasbord of intellectual, artistic, creative, and athletic activities, from which each child could take whatever he wanted, and as much as he wanted, or as little. [John Holt, *How Children Fail* (New York: Dell, 1964), pp. 177, 180.]

7. According to Dewey, "the basic freedom is that of freedom of mind and of whatever degree of freedom of action and experience is necessary to produce freedom of intelligence." [John Dewey, *Problems of Men* (New York: Philosophical Library, 1946), p. 61.]

How does Dewey's conception of freedom contrast with that of the romantic naturalist? What are the curricular implications of these contrasting views of freedom?

8. Does the following statement present a fair portrayal of scientific thinking? Explain.

> For the existentialist, science cannot serve as model or paradigm, largely because scientific thinking is concerned with objectification and excludes the intuitive awareness and the self-encounters required of philosophy. When the existentialist speaks of knowing, he speaks of passionately engaging and of vouching for his ideas with his life. The cool neutrality of experimental inquiry is usually alien to such a man. . . . [Maxine Greene, *Teacher as Stranger* (Belmont, CA: Wadsworth, 1973), p. 137.]

9. In a national best-seller, a humanities professor wrote: "All that is human, all that is of concern to us, lies outside natural science." [Allan Bloom, *The Closing of the American Mind* (New York: Simon and Schuster, 1987), p. 356.]

How does such a statement reflect on the two cultures or divorce between the humanities and sciences? Why was this divorce of such great concern to Dewey and later to C. P. Snow? [John Dewey, *Freedom and Culture* (New York: Putnam, 1939), p. 154; C. P. Snow, *The Two Cultures and the Scientific Revolution* (New York: Cambridge University Press, 1959).]

10. Does your school have a formal statement of philosophy? If so, does the life and curriculum of your school reflect the statement of philosophy in action? Why or why not? What changes would you like to see in the life and curriculum of your school?

NOTES

1. John Dewey, *Democracy and Education* (New York: Macmillan, 1916), pp. 383–384.
2. Ibid., p. 384.
3. Ralph W. Tyler, *Basic Principles of Curriculum and Instruction* (Chicago: University of Chicago Press, 1949), p. 33.
4. Boyd H. Bode, "Education at the Crossroads," *Progressive Education,* 8 (November 1931), p. 548.
5. Boyd H. Bode, *Modern Educational Theories* (New York: Macmillan, 1927), p. 237.
6. National Commission on Excellence in Education, *A Nation at Risk: The Imperative for Educational Reform* (Washington, DC: U.S. Department of Education, 1983).
7. Theodore Brameld, *Patterns of Educational Philosophy* (New York: Holt, Rinehart and Win-

ston, 1971; Tomás Englund, Chapter 7 in *Curriculum as a Political Problem* (Lund, Sweden: Studentlitteratur, 1986).

8. William C. Bagley, *Education and Emergent Man* (New York: Nelson, 1934).

9. Dewey, *Democracy and Education,* op. cit., p. 378.

10. Ibid., p. 380.

11. Robert M. Hutchins, *The Higher Learning in America* (New Haven, CT: Yale University Press, 1936), p. 66.

12. Ibid., pp. 81–84.

13. Robert M. Hutchins, *On Education* (Santa Barbara, CA: Center for the Study of Democratic Institutions, 1963), p. 18.

14. Mortimer J. Adler, "The Crisis in Contemporary Education," *The Social Frontier,* 5 (February 1939), pp. 62–63.

15. Hutchins, *The Higher Learning in America,* op. cit., p. 65.

16. Ibid., p. 86.

17. Robert M. Hutchins, "The Great Anti-School Campaign" in Robert M. Hutchins and Mortimer J. Adler (eds.), *The Great Ideas Today* (Chicago: Encyclopedia Britannica, 1972), p. 209.

18. Mark Van Doren, *Liberal Education* (Boston: Beacon, 1959), p. 94.

19. Dewey, *Democracy and Education,* op. cit., pp. 301–302.

20. Daniel Tanner, "An Educational Speedup Appropriate for Some," *The New York Times* (February 12, 1983), p. 21; Ford Foundation, *They Went to College Early* (New York: Author, 1957).

21. Jacques Barzun, "Where the Educational Nonsense Comes From," *Papers on Educational Reform,* Vol. II (LaSalle, IL: Open Court, 1971), pp. 1–8; Hutchins, *The Great Ideas Today,* op. cit., pp. 200, 226.

22. Robert M. Hutchins, "The Schools Must Stay," *The Center Magazine,* 6 (January–February 1973), pp. 12–13.

23. Marya Mannes, "A Manual for Survival," *The New York Times Book Review* (April 27, 1969), p. 2.

24. William J. Bennett, *James Madison Elementary School,* and *James Madison High School* (Washington, DC: U.S. Department of Education, 1988, 1987).

25. *Chronicle of Higher Education,* 32 (May 27, 1987), pp. 17, 21.

26. Lynne V. Cheney, *American Memory* (Washington, DC: National Endowment for the Humanities, n.d.), pp. 7, 15.

27. Allan Bloom, *The Closing of the American Mind* (New York: Simon and Schuster, 1987), p. 356.

28. Mortimer J. Adler, *The Paideia Proposal* (New York: Macmillan, 1982), p. 9.

29. Dewey, *Democracy and Education,* op. cit., p. 50.

30. "The Wizard of Quiz," *Time,* 69 (February 11, 1957), p. 46.

31. Arthur Bestor, *The Restoration of Learning* (New York: Alfred A. Knopf, 1955), p. 120.

32. Ibid., p. 118.

33. Ibid., pp. 60, 62–63.

34. Hyman G. Rickover, "European vs. American Secondary Schools," *Phi Delta Kappan,* 40 (November 1958), p. 61.

35. Aristotle, *Politics, Great Books of the Western World,* 9 (Chicago: Encyclopedia Britannica, 1952), p. 544.

36. William H. Cornog, *What Are the Priorities for the Public Schools in the 1960s?* Occasional Papers, 5 (Washington, DC: Council for Basic Education, 1963), p. 3.

37. Bestor, op. cit., p. 354.

38. John W. Gardner, *Excellence* (New York: Harper, 1962), p. 68.

39. Dewey, *Democracy and Education,* op. cit., p. 203.

40. C. B. Cox and Rhodes Boyson (eds.), *Black Paper 1977* (London: Temple Smith, 1977), p. 8.

41. Ibid., p. 24.

42. Ibid., p. 30.

43. Jacques Barzun and Robert J. Saunders, *Art in Basic Education* (Washington, DC: Council for Basic Education, 1979).

44. George F. Madaus, *The Influence of Testing on Teaching Math and Science in Grades 4–12* (Chestnut Hill, MA: Center for the Study of Testing, 1992).

45. Commission on Achieving Necessary Skills, *Learning a Living* (Washington, DC: U.S. Department of Labor, 1992).

46. Brameld, op. cit., pp. 59, 62.

47. Report of the Harvard Committee, *General Education in a Free Society* (Cambridge, MA: Harvard University Press, 1945), pp. 51, 79.

48. James B. Conant, *The American High School Today* (New York: McGraw-Hill, 1959).

49. Lester F. Ward, *Dynamic Sociology or Applied Social Science* (New York: D. Appleton, 1883), pp. 497, 597.

50. For a criticism of revisionist portrayals and distortions, see Diane Ravitch, *The Revisionists Revised* (New York: Basic Books, 1978).

51. John Dewey, *The School and Society* (Chicago: University of Chicago Press, 1951), p. 7. (Originally published in 1899.)

52. Henry Steele Commager, *The Search for a Usable Past* (New York: Alfred A. Knopf, 1967), p. 258.

53. Laurel Tanner and Daniel Tanner, "Environmentalism in American Pedagogy: The Legacy of Lester Ward," *Teachers College Record*, 88 (Summer 1987), pp. 537–547.

54. Ward, op. cit., p. 497.

55. John Dewey, *Experience and Education* (New York: Macmillan, 1938), pp. vi–vii.

56. James B. Conant, *The Child the Parent and the State* (Cambridge, MA: Harvard University Press, 1959), p. 94.

57. Dewey, *Democracy and Education,* op. cit., p. 352.

58. Ibid., pp. 225–226.

59. John Dewey, "Need for a Philosophy of Education," *The New Era in Home and School* (England), 15 (November 1934), p. 212.

60. John Dewey, *Individualism Old and New* (New York: Capricorn, 1962), p. 144. (Originally published in 1929.)

61. Max Born, "What Is Left to Hope For," *Bulletin of the Atomic Scientists,* 20 (April 1964), p. 2.

62. John Dewey, "Science as Subject-Matter and as Method," *Science,* 31 (January 1910), p. 127.

63. John Dewey, "Progressive Education and the Science of Education," *Progressive Education,* 5 (July–September 1928), p. 200.

64. John Dewey, *The Sources of a Science of Education* (New York: Liveright, 1929), p. 12.

65. Bode, *Modern Educational Theories,* op. cit., p. 234.

66. Elliot Eisner, *The Educational Imagination,* 2nd ed. (New York: Macmillan, 1985), pp. 8, 10. The attack on Dewey is excised from the third edition, 1994.

67. Harry S. Broudy, *The Real World of the Public Schools* (New York: Harcourt, 1972), p. 142.

68. John Dewey, *The Public and Its Problems* (Chicago: Swallow Press, 1927), pp. 135, 139.

69. Dewey, *Individualism Old and New,* op. cit., p. 155.

70. Sidney Hook, *Education and the Taming of Power* (LaSalle, IL: Open Court, 1973), p. 89.

71. John Dewey, *Problems of Men* (New York: Philosophical Library, 1946), p. 61.

72. George S. Counts, *Dare the School Build a New Social Order?* (New York: Day, 1932).

73. John Dewey, "Education for a Changing Social Order," *National Education Association Proceedings* (Washington, DC: National Education Association, 1934), p. 745.

74. Theodore Brameld, "Karl Marx and the American Teacher," *The Social Frontier,* 2 (November 1935), p. 55.

75. Brameld, *Patterns,* op. cit., p. 519.

76. Samuel Bowles and Herbert Gintis, *Schooling in Capitalist America* (New York: Basic Books, 1976).

77. Michael W. Apple, *Ideology and Curriculum,* 2nd ed. (New York: Routledge, 1990), p. 176.

78. Bowles and Gintis, op. cit., p. 197.

79. Dewey, *Democracy and Education,* op. cit., p. 172.

80. Christopher Jencks et al., *Inequality* (New York: Basic Books, 1972), p. 265; Ivan Illich, Foreword in Joel H. Spring, *Education and the Rise of the Corporate State* (Boston: Beacon, 1972), p. x.

81. Illich, op cit., p. 172.

82. Peter S. Hlebowitsh, *Radical Curriculum Theory Reconsidered* (New York: Teachers College, 1992), p. 46.

83. James B. Conant, *Education in a Divided World* (Cambridge, MA: Harvard University Press, 1949), p. 146.

84. Roger Kimball, *Tenured Radicals* (New York: Harper, 1990).

85. Stanley Aronowitz and Henry A. Giroux, *Education under Siege* (South Hadley, MA: Bergin and Garvey, 1983), p. 50; Henry A. Giroux, *Schooling and the Struggle for Public Life* (Minneapolis: University of Minnesota Press, 1988), p. 114.

86. Daniel Tanner, *Dewey Decimated, Dewey Rehabilitated,* Paper Presented at the 1993 Annual Meeting of the American Educational Research Association, Atlanta, GA.

87. Gunnar Myrdal, *An American Dilemma* (New York: Harper, 1962), p. 709. (Originally published in 1944.)

88. Boyd H. Bode, "Education and Social Reconstruction," *The Social Frontier,* I (January 1935), p. 22; John Dewey, "Educational and Social Change," *The Social Frontier,* 3 (May 1937), p. 235.

89. Lewis Mumford, *The Pentagon of Power: The Myth of the Machine* (New York: Harcourt, 1970), p. 210.

90. Ibid., pp. 210–211.

91. Thomas P. Bailey, "Some Difficulties of Child-Study, *National Education Association Proceedings* (Chicago: University of Chicago Press, 1900), p. 583.

92. John Dewey, *The Child and the Curriculum* (Chicago: University of Chicago Press, 1902), pp. 13–16.

93. A. S. Neill, *Summerhill* (New York: Hart, 1960), p. 4.

94. Ibid., p. 25.

95. Paul Goodman, *New Reformation* (New York: Random, 1970), p. 86.

96. See Jonathan Kozol, *The Night Is Dark and I Am Far from Home* (Boston: Houghton Mifflin, 1975).

97. Jonathan Kozol, *Children of the Revolution* (New York: Delacorte, 1978).

98. Jonathan Kozol, *Savage Inequalities* (New York: Crown, 1991).

99. Theodore Roszak, *The Making of a Counter Culture* (New York: Doubleday, 1969), p. 41.

100. Theodore Roszak, *Where the Wasteland Ends* (New York: Doubleday, 1972).

101. John Holt, *How Children Fail* (New York: Dell, 1964), p. 167.

102. See Noam Chomsky, *Language and Mind* (New York: Harcourt, 1968).

103. Jean Jacques Rousseau, *Émile* (London: Dent, 1911), p. 5.

104. Ibid., pp. 9, 56, 58, 84, 130, 141.

105. Holt, op. cit., pp. 175–177.

106. Goodman, op. cit., pp. 85–86.

107. Paul Goodman, *Compulsory Mis-education* (New York: Horizon, 1964), p. 39.

108. Goodman, *New Reformation,* op.cit., p. 88.

109. Edgar Z. Friedenberg, *Coming of Age in America* (New York: Vintage, 1967), pp. 250–251, 257.

110. Ivan Illich, *Deschooling Society* (New York: Harper, 1971).

111. John Holt, op. cit., pp. 179–180.

112. Herbert R. Kohl, *The Open Classroom* (New York: Random, 1969), p. 14.

113. John Holt, *How Children Learn* (New York: Pitman, 1967), p. 189.

114. Daniel L. Duke, *The Retransformation of the School* (Chicago: Nelson-Hall, 1978).

115. Panel on Youth of the President's Science Advisory Committee, *Youth: Transition to Adulthood* (Chicago: University of Chicago Press, 1974), p. 86.

116. Jonathan Kozol, *Illiterate America* (Garden City, NY: Anchor/Doubleday, 1985).

117. Goodman, *Compulsory Mis-education,* op. cit., p. 55.

118. John Dewey, "Individuality and Experience," in *Art and Education,* 2nd ed. (Merion, PA: The Barnes Foundation Press, 1946), pp. 37–38.

119. John Dewey, *How We Think* (Lexington, MA: D. C. Heath, 1933), pp. 87, 90.

120. John Dewey, *Individualism Old and New,* op. cit., p. 98.

121. Ibid., p. 97.

122. Maxine Greene, *Teacher as Stranger* (Belmont, CA: Wadsworth, 1973), pp. 103, 129.

123. Daniel Tanner, "Knowledge Divided against Itself," *Bulletin of the Atomic Scientists,* 39 (March 1983), pp. 34–38.

124. Maxine Greene, op. cit., p. 137.

125. Herbert R. Lottman, *The Left Bank* (Boston: Houghton Mifflin, 1982); Victor Farias, *Heidegger and Nazism* (Philadelphia: Temple University Press, 1990).

126. Jacob Bronowski, "The Creative Process," *Scientific American,* 199 (September 1958), p. 59.

127. Albert Einstein, *Out of My Later Years* (New York: Philosophical Library, 1950), pp. 29–30.

128. Gabriel Marcel, *The Philosophy of Existence,* trans. by Manya Harai (New York: Philosophical Library, 1949), p. 92.

129. John Dewey, *Human Nature and Conduct* (New York: Holt, 1922), pp. 10–11.

130. Greene, op. cit., p. 130.

131. Van Cleve Morris, "Existentialism and the Education of Twentieth-Century Man," in Stanley Dropkin, Harold Full, and Ernest Schwarcz

(eds.), *Contemporary American Education*, 2nd ed. (New York: Macmillan, 1970), pp. 258, 260.

132. George F. Kneller (ed.), *Foundations of Education*, 3rd ed. (New York: Wiley, 1971), p. 264.

133. Arnold J. Rosenberg, "Educational Existentialism and the Sudbury Valley School," *Educational Leadership*, 30 (February 1973), pp. 479–480.

134. Dewey, *The Child and the Curriculum*, op. cit., p. 18.

135. Kneller, op. cit., p. 264.

136. Bode, *Modern Educational Theories*, op. cit., p. 40.

137. Hutchins, "The Schools Must Stay," op. cit., p. 14.

SELECTED REFERENCES

Adler, Mortimer J. *The Paideia Proposal: An Educational Manifesto*. New York: Macmillan, 1982.

Bagley, William C. *Education and Emergent Man*. New York: Nelson, 1934.

Bestor, Arthur. *The Restoration of Learning*. New York: Alfred A. Knopf, 1955.

Bloom, Allan. *The Closing of the American Mind*. New York: Simon and Schuster, 1987.

Bode, Boyd H. *Modern Educational Theories*. New York: Macmillan, 1927.

Boyer, Ernest L. *High School*. New York: Harper and Row, 1983.

Brameld, Theodore. *Patterns of Educational Philosophy*. New York: Holt, Rinehart and Winston, 1971.

Carnochan, W. B. *The Battleground of the Curriculum: Liberal Education and American Experience*. Palo Alto, CA: Stanford University Press, 1993.

Commission on the Reorganization of Secondary Education. *Cardinal Principles of Secondary Education*. Washington, DC: U.S. Bureau of Education, 1918.

Conant, James B. *The Child the Parent and the State*. Cambridge, MA: Harvard University Press, 1959.

Conant, James B. *Education in a Divided World*. Cambridge, MA: Harvard University Press, 1949.

Counts, George S. *Dare the School Build a New Social Order?* New York: John Day, 1932.

Cremin, Lawrence, A. *The Transformation of the School*. New York: Alfred A. Knopf, 1961.

Dewey, John. *Democracy and Education*. New York: Macmillan, 1916.

Dewey, John. *Human Nature and Conduct*. New York: Holt, Rinehart and Winston, 1922.

Dewey, John. *Individualism Old and New*. New York: Capricorn Books, 1962. (Originally published in 1929.)

Dewey, John. *The School and Society/The Child and the Curriculum*. Chicago: University of Chicago Press, 1990. (Originally published 1899, 1902.)

Dewey, John. *The Sources of a Science of Education*. New York: Liveright, 1929.

Diggins, John P. *The Rise and Fall of the American Left*. New York: W. W. Norton, 1992.

Dzuback, Mary Ann. *Robert M. Hutchins*. Chicago: University of Chicago Press, 1991.

Engler, William H. *Radical School Reformers of the 1960s*. Unpublished doctoral dissertation. New Brunswick, NJ: Rutgers University, 1973.

Goodman, Paul. *Compulsory Mis-education*. New York: Horizon Press, 1964.

Goodman, Paul. *New Reformation*. New York: Random House, 1970.

Greene, Maxine. *Teacher as Stranger*. Belmont, CA: Wadsworth, 1973.

Harvard Committee on General Education. *General Education in a Free Society*. Cambridge, MA: Harvard University Press, 1945.

Hirsch, Edward D., Jr. *Cultural Literacy: What Every American Needs to Know*. Boston: Houghton Mifflin, 1987.

Hlebowitsch, Peter S. *Radical Curriculum Theory Reconsidered*. New York: Teachers College Press, 1993.

Holt, John. *How Children Fail*. New York: Dell, 1964.

Holt, John. *How Children Learn*. New York: Pitman, 1967.

Holt, John. *Instead of Education*. New York: E. P. Dutton, 1976.

Hutchins, Robert M. *The Higher Learning in America*. New Haven, CT: Yale University Press, 1936.

Hutchins, Robert M. "The Great Anti-School Campaign," in Robert M. Hutchins and Mortimer J.

Adler (eds.). *The Great Ideas Today.* Chicago: Encyclopedia Britannica, 1972.

Illich, Ivan. *Deschooling Society.* New York: Harper, 1971.

Kimball, Roger. *Tenured Radicals.* New York: Harper, 1990.

Kohl, Herbert R. *The Open Classroom.* New York: Random House, 1969.

McNeil, William. *Hutchins' University.* Chicago: University of Chicago Press, 1991.

Postman, Neil. *Teaching as Conserving Activity.* New York: Delacorte, 1979.

Postman, Neil, and Weingartner, Charles. *Teaching as a Subversive Activity.* New York: Delacorte, 1969.

Ravitch, Diane. *The Revisionists Revised.* New York: Basic Books, 1978.

Ravitch, Diane, and Finn, Chester E., Jr. *What Do Our 17-Year-Olds Know?* New York: Harper, 1987.

Rickover, Hyman G. *Education and Freedom.* New York: Doubleday, 1967.

Rorty, Richard. *Objectivity, Relativism, and Truth.* New York: Cambridge University Press, 1991.

Roszak, Theodore. *The Making of a Counter Culture.* New York: Doubleday, 1969.

Rousseau, Jean Jacques. *Émile.* Translated by Barbara Foxley. London: J. M. Dent & Sons Ltd, 1911.

Sizer, Theodore R. *Horace's Compromise.* Boston: Houghton Mifflin, 1984.

Tanner, Daniel. *Crusade for Democracy: Progressive Education at the Crossroads.* Albany: State University of New York Press, 1991.

Tanner, Daniel. *Secondary Education—Perspectives and Prospects.* New York: Macmillan, 1972, Chapters 2 and 3.

Tanner, Daniel, and Tanner, Laurel. *History of the School Curriculum.* New York: Macmillan, 1990.

Ward, Lester F. *Dynamic Sociology or Applied Social Science.* New York: D. Appleton, 1883.

Watson, James D. *The Double Helix.* New York: Atheneum Books, 1969.

Westbrook, Robert B. *John Dewey and American Democracy.* Ithaca, NY: Cornell University Press, 1991.

PART 3

CURRICULUM DESIGN, DEVELOPMENT, AND EVALUATION

In everything which has to do with the shaping
and expression of thought and feeling,
"the letter killeth; the spirit giveth life."
And if the models we put before them have no spirit
our student's progress must be slight.

—Harvard Committee on General Education in a Free Society

CHAPTER 10

THE SEARCH FOR A CORE CURRICULUM—DESIGN FOR SYNTHESIS

"In the nation, 'general education' is at last in vogue. Its principles bid fair to become the operative educational theory of the remainder of this century."[1] So wrote F. Champion Ward, dean of the College of the University of Chicago, in a 1950 faculty report on general education. Ward's optimism concerning the prospects for general education was widely shared by educators at midcentury. Instead of becoming "the operative educational theory of the remainder of this century," general education yielded to the forces of departmental specialism and special-interest constituencies in the undergraduate population. As far as the schools were concerned, the pressures of the Cold War and space race led to a neo-essentialism of federally funded discipline-centered curriculum reforms with priority given to the sciences and mathematics.

A quarter of a century after Ward's pronouncement, general education appeared to be in vogue once again in American colleges. The response to the campus turmoil of the 1960s had impelled faculties in colleges and secondary schools to reduce requirements, to multiply options, and to devise a host of special-interest electives. The curriculum had come to be referred to as a cafeteria or warehouse curriculum, and it was being described as in a state of anarchy. University scholars, concerned mainly with specialized knowledge, had been all too ready to abandon responsibility for developing a balanced and coherent core curriculum for general education. The struggle for rights seemed to give way to a battle for special interests on the part of competing groups, and the school and college curriculum began to reflect the growing fragmentation of society. In the curriculum literature the terms *general educa-*

tion and *democracy* received little discussion in contrast to the literature of midcentury.

In response to the student demand for relevance, a number of significant efforts had been made to develop interdisciplinary courses in the colleges and secondary schools during the 1960s and early 1970s. Again, these courses were mainly offered as electives among the myriad special-interest courses available. By the mid-1970s, it was becoming clear that the undergraduate curriculum required reconstruction for general education. During the latter part of the 1970s, the term *general education* was appearing once again not only in professional journals but in newspaper and magazine articles describing the latest efforts to reconstruct the undergraduate curriculum at leading colleges. On occasion, general education was even front-page news.[2] The words of Ward at midcentury seemed to be echoing in the halls of academia as we entered the last quarter of the century. An article in the *Saturday Review* on curriculum reforms at Harvard opined that if the reforms are successful, "they will exert a powerful influence on higher education for the balance of the century."[3] The reforms at the undergraduate level, calling for curriculum reconstruction for general education, contrasted sharply with the curriculum retrenchment in elementary and secondary schools under the back-to-basics and competency-based banners.

As we entered the 1990s, colleges were struggling to find some degree of consensus on a core curriculum for general education in the wake of pressures from the divided interests of the academic left and multiculturalism. At the same time, perennialists were renewing their case for a classical core of Western literary studies—all in the midst of an academic culture that values specialized knowledge production above all else. The typical but tentative solution was one of compromise, with the colleges proceeding to reduce the vast number of electives under the rubric of general education options and establishing criteria for elective courses designated as acceptable for general education. Although the numbers of such electives were sharply reduced, the practice of distribution requirements or controlled electives by designated categories (e.g., humanities, natural science, social sciences, gender studies, and so on) found students continuing to divide themselves according to their special interests. The need for a coherent core curriculum for general education for a free society remained ever urgent, especially in an era of social fragmentation and conflict.

As far as the school curriculum was concerned—despite unifying efforts such as whole language, writing across the curriculum, and higher-order thinking—the focus was on a multitude of separate literacies (cultural literacy, mathematics literacy, scientific literacy, technological literacy, aesthetic literacy, economic literacy, political literacy, computer literacy, and so on).

All but forgotten throughout the last half of the twentieth century was that the very idea and practice of general education grew out of the experimentalist-progressive efforts for universal secondary education and the democratization of the high school, along with a progressive parallel movement in higher education in recognition of the limits of traditional liberal education. The great divide between liberal education and general education, as James Conant pointed out, marked the difference between the old literary education, as interpreted by scholars and connoisseurs before World War I and the modern requirements of an enlightened citizenry in a free society. "The watershed between [the] two fundamentally opposed positions," Conant contended, "can be located by raising the question: For what purpose do we have a system of public education?"[4]

To this day, even those contemporary educators who are allies of general education in the college tend to look on the function of the secondary school curriculum principally as preparation for college. Obviously, this works against the development of an authentic curriculum of general education along with diversified studies for the adolescent population, and it reduces the curriculum function for the elementary school to basic education or literacies. Clearly, a larger vision of the curriculum was required of educators at all levels.

GENERAL EDUCATION FOR A FREE SOCIETY

At midcentury general education for a free society had been the dominant theme for curriculum reconstruction for *both* the secondary school and college. There were great expectations that general education would help create unity out of diversity. Education in the service of the democratic ideal was a main current of American thought.

The universalization of secondary education and the forces for open-access higher education led to a great and growing heterogeneity of the student population in school and college—a heterogeneity that mirrored the diversity of society at large. The accompanying diversification of the curriculum in school and college reflected not only the growth of knowledge and the changing conceptions of knowledge but also the heterogeneous character of the student populations as well.

The notion of liberal education as the province of a privileged class came to be recognized as untenable in modern democratic society. Liberal education bore an aristocratic invidium that was rooted historically in ancient Greece, where society was divided into freemen and slaves. The aristocratic and leisure class of freemen could pursue the cultural or liberal studies, whereas the utilitarian needs of the social order were carried out by slaves. The belief that liberal education is properly the exclusive province of the privileged class, along with the idea that it is superior to and should be divorced from the practical studies, had been perpetuated for centuries. Because the privileged were free to cultivate their intellect in contemplation of the good life, those studies that were above practical concerns, namely the liberal arts, were deemed to be most suitable for such cultivation.

Modern democratic society holds to the ideal that all individuals are free and that all have a share in the productive work of society. The traditional concept of the liberal arts not only suffered from a social exclusiveness but also from a knowledge exclusiveness favoring the literary studies. Science and technology not only helped destroy slavery and drudgery, but also required a broader conception of the knowledge that all citizens of a free society must share in common. Thus, the term *general education* emerged in place of liberal education. General education, then, is regarded as "that part of a student's whole education which looks first of all to his life as a responsible human being and citizen."[5] It is that part of the curriculum that is designed to provide for a common universe of discourse, understanding, and competence. In essence, general education is intended to develop autonomously thinking, socially responsible citizens of a free society. This requires a curriculum that is not concerned exclusively with the human heritage but also with the pervading problems of humanity. General education necessitates an outlook on knowledge that is essentially different from the knowledge world of specialized education. The difference in outlook on knowledge also requires a different organization and treatment of knowledge for general education as contrasted with specialized education.

This chapter explores some of the problems and issues of general education, in the light of various developments and proposals, with a focus on the patterns of organizing the curriculum.

GENERAL EDUCATION AND THE PHASES OF SCHOOLING

The Secondary School

Some of the most avid allies of general education at the college level are prone to disregard the importance of general education in the schools where they see education as being properly concentrated on facts and skills. For example, in stating the case for general education in the undergraduate years, Daniel Bell sees the college experience as "the testing years—the testing of oneself and one's values" with the college being an environment "of broad intellectual adventure, the place where one can resist, momentarily, the harness that society now seeks to impose at an earlier and earlier stage on its youth," whereas the function of the secondary school is that of "concentrating on facts and skills."[6] In choosing to see the secondary school as mere preparation for college, Bell ignores the fact that a majority of youth do not go on to college. For them the end of secondary schooling signals the end of their formal education. Are they to be denied the opportunity of general education and the testing of their values? Are they not expected to share fully the rights and responsibilities that accrue to all members of a free society? And for those who do go on to college, are the secondary-school years merely to be a tooling-up for the "broad intellectual adventure" of the college years?

Throughout the twentieth century the American secondary school has waged a struggle to develop its own authentic curriculum in general education. On the one hand, there are those college educators who have chosen to see the secondary-school curriculum as concentrated on facts and skills to tool-up pupils for college. Then there are those college educators who have sought to see the secondary-school curriculum as properly being limited to the academic disciplines that correspond to the liberal arts studies of the college.[7] Because the secondary school is concerned with the developing adolescent, and because its student population is so diverse, it cannot simply be limited to a precollege function. The struggle of the secondary school to develop its own authentic curriculum has been long and hard. The cosmopolitan character of its pupil population not only requires a curriculum that is diversified but also a curriculum that enables all of the youth of all of the people to share in a common universe of discourse, understanding, and competence—in short, to become independently thinking and socially responsible members of a free society. This is the purpose of general education.

THE COMPREHENSIVE HIGH SCHOOL.   The comprehensive high school has been rightly called "a peculiarly American phenomenon."[8] Early in this century the United States chose not to pattern its system of secondary education after the dualistic system of European nations whereby the terminal student and the student who is destined for the university attend separate schools. Such separations are marked not only by differences in ability and achievement but also by differences in social class. With the establishment of cooperative federal-state programs for vocational education in 1917, some educators and many industrialists advocated separate specialized vocational schools after the European pattern. When the dust was settled, the prevailing sentiment favored a unitary school that, in the words of the 1918 report of the NEA Commission on the Reorganization of Secondary Education, would serve as "the prototype of a democracy in which various groups must have a degree of self-consciousness as groups and yet be federated into a larger whole through the recognition of common interests and ideals."[9]

Thus evolved a unitary, multipurpose school—the comprehensive high school—that was designed to provide (1) a general education for all youth as citizens of a democratic society, (2) specialized programs for vocational proficiency for those youngsters planning to enter the world of work after high school, (3) the specialized program of academic preparation for college, (4) exploratory studies and experiences to enable adolescents to investigate new sources of learning, (5) enrichment studies and experiences to widen and deepen the sources of learning for all adolescents, and (6) special-interest studies to meet individual interests apart from specialized studies.

Although these functions often have been more of an ideal than a reality, over the years the idea of the comprehensive high school has prevailed in the face of constant criticism. The criticism has come from widely divergent sources. For example, during the height of the space race, Admiral Rickover had this to say:

> One cannot argue the issue of comprehensive schooling versus separate secondary education on a philosophical basis. But one can argue it on the basis whether the country really has a choice as between efficient education—that is, separate schools above the elementary levels—and pure "democratic" education which insists on the inefficient time-wasting comprehensive high school. In my opinion, we no longer have that choice. We must opt for efficiency.[10]

Although subsequent studies, discussed later in this chapter and in Chapter 12, failed to support Rickover's allegations regarding the superiority of the dual European system over the American comprehensive high school, Rickover's views attracted national attention and came to be shared by many college educators. Even some of the radical romanticists of the middle and late 1960s, whose attacks on American education appeared to be cloaked in an egalitarian humanism, went much further than Rickover. Such "egalitarians" as Paul Goodman and Edgar Friedenberg went so far as to advocate that the high school continue to serve the academically able youth whereas the other less able youth would be better off out of school.[11]

The ranks of educators supporting the comprehensive school and general education were growing thin under the new onslaught of education criticism, the new thrust for specialized vocational and academic high schools, and the nationalizing influences that had led to a new curriculum hierarchy under the banner of disciplinarity. Among the few national figures supporting the comprehensive ideal was the late James B. Conant. Despite his narrow prescriptions for gearing the high school to the exigencies of the Cold War, Conant's faith in the democratizing function of the comprehensive high school remained unshaken. As president of Harvard over a period of two decades—extending from the Great Depression to midcentury—he had presided over reforms that led to a cosmopolitan student population. During this transformation, Harvard students who came from the nation's comprehensive high schools were demolishing the myth that the best preparation for college is provided by the specialized academic high schools.

Citing a study on admissions policy by a Harvard faculty committee, Harvard psychologist Jerome Bruner pointed out that "Harvard students enrolled from public high schools carry away more honors than students of like aptitude enrolled from the great independent preparatory schools of the Eastern seaboard."[12] In his recognition of such findings at Harvard and at other leading universities, Conant became convinced that the comprehensive high school not only could meet the test of academic excellence but also was the key educational institution for advancing the democratic ideal of a unity based on diversity. Observing in 1970 that some of the more progressive European nations were adopting the comprehensive model, Conant expressed perplexity as to why Americans were not more fully supportive of the very institution that was their very own creation.

> I am an advocate of the comprehensive school, yet I must admit that the future of this institution is far from certain in the United States. It is strange that the enthusiasm for an American invention is so limited in this country just at the time when other nations are beginning to explore application of the basic idea. . . . Are the high schools of the United States to be so designed as to be effective means of forwarding the idea of a unity based on diversity in a democratic community, or is the comprehensive concept to be given at best only lip service? Far more than the nature of our schools is involved in the answer to this question. The entire structure of our nation may be at stake—possibly even its survival as an open society of free men.[13]

In his autobiography, *My Several Lives* (1970), Conant remarked, "[i]f someone had told me when I was a chemist that in my old age I would devote a considerable amount of time and energy to examining the public high schools of the United States, I should have branded him as demented."[14] In this same work, Conant selected only four of his many major addresses for inclusion in their entirety in an appendix, one of which was a 1952 speech, "Unity and Diversity in Secondary Education"—stating the case for the comprehensive high school and general education. As discussed in Chapter 11, the reports of various national committees on youth education during the 1970s expressed virtually no support for the comprehensive high school and made little mention of the theory and practice of general education.

Moreover, from the 1980s into the 1990s, various reports on educational reform were conceiving the high school as properly delimited to a general academic curriculum.[15] If the comprehensive high school was mentioned at all, it was dismissed or criticized as the vehicle for student tracking. At the same time, some education historians were lending credence to this notion by fixing the blame back to the *Cardinal Principles* report of 1918 when, in fact, the 1918 report of the Commission on the Reorganization of Secondary Education had clearly and repeatedly opposed tracking.[16] It envisioned a universal curriculum of constants (general education) coupled with curriculum variables selected to meet the exploratory and specialized needs (vocational and academic) of a cosmopolitan student population. The commission report of 1918 held that vocational studies should not be a barrier to higher education. The report pointed to the pitfalls of tracking and social segregation and predestination by means of specialized or special-type schools as opposed to the comprehensive high school.[17]

Curiously, critics of the comprehensive high school during the 1980s and 1990s were strangely silent or even favorably disposed toward special-type or alternative schools that were being promoted and established in various sections of the nation.[18] Under the banner of "choice," the Reagan and Bush administrations had promoted alternative schools and had engaged the U.S. Secretary of Education in that effort. The director of the federally funded National Center on Effective Secondary Schools questioned the primacy of the comprehensive high school and summarized the case being made for alternative or special-type schools to serve the "increased diversity in learning styles, career aspirations, and social values."[19] It seemed that the growing fragmentation of American society was to be mirrored by a splitting up of the school system to serve the special interests of different populations. Although the general public was not ready to split up the schools and abandon the comprehensive concept and function of the American high school, the events of the closing years of the twentieth century gave credence to Conant's concerns about the future of this uniquely American institution.

Conant was aware that if the comprehensive high school is to be the "effective means of forwarding the idea of a unity based on diversity in a democratic community," such a quest for unity must be reflected in the curriculum. The diversity of the pupil population in the comprehensive high school requires a diversified curriculum, but the ideal of unity based on diversity in a democracy also requires that the curriculum provide a common ground whereon the rising generation can examine problems that are shared by all members of society. This is the task of general education. Moreover, the very nature of the problems confronted by all members of a democratic society requires that attention be given to curriculum synthesis, because these problems do not fit into the established disciplines or the knowledge categories that comprise the subject curriculum. Before exploring the various approaches to reorganizing the curriculum for general education, a brief examination of the role of general education at the earlier phases of schooling is presented.

The Junior High School.   The task of general education in the comprehensive high school applies fully to the junior high school. Yet, because the needs, interests, and other characteristics of the young adolescent differ significantly from those of the older adolescent, and from the child, the junior high school should not be regarded as a miniature senior high school or as an extension of elementary schooling.

The phenomenal growth and widespread acceptance of the junior high school during the first half of the twentieth century served to remove the ninth grade from the college preparatory influence. Prior to the development of the junior high school, the colleges traditionally evaluated the four years of high school studies as a basis for college admission. By incorporating the ninth grade into the junior high school, opportunities were opened to redesign the curriculum at this level for the early adolescent, despite the fact that many colleges continued to view the ninth grade as part of the college preparatory program. During the 1930s, 1940s, and early 1950s, notable efforts were made to develop block-time and core classes for general education at the junior-high-school level.

Also, by incorporating grades seven and eight into its structure, the junior high school was able to provide youngsters at this level with a wider range of curricular experiences than was offered by the traditional eight-year elementary school, which tended to concentrate its curriculum on skill development in the fundamental processes. With young adolescents entering the stage of formal operations in their cognitive development, whereby they are developing their capabilities for hypothetical thinking and more sophisticated problem solving, the junior high school appeared to offer promising opportunities for designing a curriculum that was particularly suited to this age group. Moreover, the junior high school was equipped with special facilities and resources not ordinarily available in the elementary school, such as libraries, laboratories, shops, gymnasiums, art and music studios, and so on. It also served to attract more male teachers to grades seven and eight.

The pursuit of academic excellence during the 1950s and 1960s found many junior high schools moving to pattern their curricula after the senior high school, particularly with regard to the academic studies. Grouping pupils by ability in all academic subjects became a widespread practice. The priority given the academic studies was accompanied by a neglect of the general education function—not to mention the exploratory and enrichment functions. In many respects, the junior high school assumed a function of sifting and sorting youngsters in preparation for the senior high school. In accommodating itself to the pressures of the times, the junior high school curriculum was showing signs of losing the small but recognizable curriculum authenticity it had managed to gain throughout its formative years.

The call to humanize the schools during the second half of the 1960s and early 1970s witnessed increasing attacks on the junior high school. In his report for The Carnegie Corporation, Silberman attacked the junior high school along with the senior high school as being slow to reform and for being repressive and authoritarian. "And the junior high school, by almost unanimous agreement," declared Silberman, "is the wasteland—one is tempted to say cesspool—of American education."[20] Silberman, however, failed to identify the source of "almost unanimous agreement," and he made no specific recommendations for the junior high school.

Although the junior high school has received more than its share of criticism, its effort to develop curriculum authenticity is evidenced by the fact that through the decades of its development and expansion, the junior high school, more commonly than the senior high school, instituted block-time, core, and broad-fields approaches to curriculum organization for purposes of general education.[21] These approaches to curriculum organization are discussed later in this chapter.

The Middle School

From the 1960s through the 1980s, an increasing number of educators looked to the emerging middle school as being particularly well suited to the task of bridging the childhood phase of elementary schooling with the adolescent phase of secondary schooling. Advocates of the middle school contended that the junior high had become an imitation of the high school. They also held that because youngsters were reaching puberty about a year earlier than previous generations, ninth-graders now were capable of adjusting to the senior high school and, at the same time, the middle school would be more appropriately geared to the educational needs of youngsters as they mature from late childhood into early adolescence.

Surely the legitimacy of these assumptions and claims is well grounded. However, the middle-school revival gained impetus from the 1960s through the 1980s as a result of demographic changes in which the adolescent population was in a state of decline, whereas the childhood population was increasing. In effect, school boards were converting junior high school buildings to middle schools in order to take the pressure off the elementary schools.

Middle schools most commonly incorporate grades six through eight, thereby placing the ninth grade back into the high school where it had been during the early years of the twentieth century prior to the emergence of the junior high school. With more than four out of every ten secondary-school students going on to college, the re-establishment of the four-year high school has served to place added emphasis on the ninth grade as being integral to the college preparatory program. This places additional constraints on the curriculum in the ninth grade, although it also can be argued that the pursuit of academic excellence during the 1950s and 1960s had already impelled the junior high school to imitate the senior high school in concentrating its reforms on the academic side of the curriculum. Nevertheless, the incorporation of the ninth grade into the high school serves to make the ninth-grader who plans to go on to college cognizant of the fact that the colleges will evaluate the four years of the student's high-school work in determining admission.

QUEST FOR AUTHENTIC IDENTITY. Although the junior high school never became really freed from the college preparatory function of secondary schooling, the middle school is not so encumbered because it is not a reorganized secondary school. Proponents of the middle school point out that it is specifically designed to make available to youngsters a far wider range of learning options than would be provided in the self-contained classroom of the elementary school without adopting the strictly departmentalized structure of the high school. The middle-school curriculum may be so organized as to include such features as block-time and unified studies, team teaching, flexible scheduling, and special offerings and facilities that are less likely to be available in the elementary school—such as industrial arts, homemaking, typing, laboratory science, library work, physical education, and so on. Through independent study and exploratory options, many middle schools aim to provide greater opportunity for pupil self-direction and responsibility than is possible in the self-contained classroom of the elementary school. Perhaps the weakest aspects of the middle school have been the lack of concerted attention given to the development of a coherent curriculum in general education and the lack of resource facilities such as well stocked and equipped libraries, shops, studios, and laboratories. There is also the question as to the appropriateness of mixing eighth-graders of age thirteen with fifth- or sixth-grade children of age ten or eleven in the same school.

Many school districts have established middle schools to deal with administrative problems such as the need to alleviate crowded conditions in existing schools and the need to desegregate the pupil populations; quite often the middle school is housed in a building that was formerly an elementary school. (The dramatic growth of the junior high school also can be attributed to administrative convenience, namely, that it was more economically feasible for a school district to build such a school than to construct additional elementary and high schools to accommodate the rising enrollments.) Under such circumstances, the school district is inclined to neglect the need for the middle school to develop its own authentic curriculum for the population group it serves, with the result that it becomes merely an in-between school.

When school districts establish middle schools for purposes of desegregation, they also need to recognize that by virtue of creating a school with a more cosmopolitan population than is characteristic of the neighborhood elementary school, concerted attention must be given to designing the curriculum in general education in view of the democratizing function. To ignore this opportunity and responsibility is philosophically indefensible in the schools of a society that holds to the democratic ideal. Yet many secondary schools have neglected to design the curriculum to meet this function, despite the fact that they are plagued by racial polarization and conflict as reflected in society at large.

The Elementary School

During the first half of the twentieth century, the dominant pattern of instructional organization in the elementary school was the self-contained classroom in which a teacher is assigned the responsibility for instruction in virtually all areas of the curriculum with a class of children at a given grade level. It was believed that not only did the self-contained approach allow the teacher to know the children more intimately but also that it would provide for curriculum integration. However, the traditional practice was for self-contained classroom teachers to follow a daily time schedule in moving from one subject of study to another. Consequently, the subjects tended to be treated separately with daily time slots for arithmetic, reading, grammar, spelling, writing, social studies, science, and so on. The focus of the traditional self-contained classroom tended to be on the development of fundamental skills, with relatively little attention being given to the wider goals of general education.

MODIFIED TEACHING ARRANGEMENTS.   In growing recognition of the enormous demands being placed on the self-contained classroom teacher, by the end of the 1950s many elementary schools were providing this teacher with some form of special assistance through a helping teacher who gave consultant help, or through special teachers who assumed direct responsibility for instruction in certain subjects. As the pressures mounted to provide for more specialized instruction, such as the teaching of foreign languages at the elementary level, an increasing proportion of schools provided special teachers for instruction in this area, and in such other areas of the curriculum as music, art, physical education, and reading—and the regular teacher continued to be responsible for the major portion of the curriculum. Some form of partial departmentalization of instruction in the upper elementary grades was not uncommon. Some schools adopted a dual-progress plan in which pupils in the upper elementary school spent about a half a day in the self-contained classroom and the remainder of the day in departmentalized studies on a nongraded basis. However, many elementary educators had reservations concerning departmentalization and favored, instead, some form of team teaching along with the use of teacher aides or paraprofessionals. When team teaching was employed, the arrangements more typically were on a collegial rather than hierarchical basis.

NONGRADED SCHOOL.   Also during the 1960s, an increasing proportion of elementary schools were adopting nongraded organizational plans at the primary level. The purpose of nongraded arrangements was to facilitate continuous pupil progress by allowing children to advance at their own rates in the various subjects, particularly reading and mathematics.

Although the proponents of nongrading claimed that it provided for pupil differences and fostered a longitudinal concept of curriculum, or vertical curriculum articulation, the nongraded approach presented its own difficulties. For example, many nongraded schools had replaced the so-called graded lockstep with mechanical criteria for establishing the level of pupil placement in their studies, namely, standardized achievement test scores. Moreover, although it was claimed that the nongraded approach allowed for greater attention being given to vertical curriculum articulation, it also tended to work against horizontal curriculum articulation or the interrelationships among the various studies that constitute the total curriculum.

Finally, the claim that nongraded arrangements provide for superior pupil achievement over graded patterns has not been substantiated by research. The superiority of a particular administrative pattern—whether nongraded, multigraded, departmentalized, or self-contained—has not been borne out in terms of pupil achievement, probably because the teacher variable is more powerful than the administrative variable. Moreover, if the curriculum is narrowed to a skill-drill function, such a function may be performed in a wide variety of organizational or administrative arrangements. To the extent that the organizational or administrative pattern effects substantive changes in the learning environment, including teacher-pupil interactions, it will likely produce changes in learning outcomes. Hence there is a need to study learning in terms of the ecology of the school and classroom.[22]

OPEN CLASSROOM.   During the early 1970s, the center of gravity in the call for educational reform at the elementary level shifted to an informal organizational approach that was most commonly called the open classroom or open school. Patterned after the reforms that were being made in primary schools in England, the open classroom was heralded as an answer to the avalanche of criticisms that had fallen on American schools during the latter 1960s. The open classroom was seen as the means of humanizing the elementary schools in answer to the accusations that the schools were repressive.

In England, the open classroom idea was associated with the integrated curriculum in recognition that subject-matter boundaries and separate time slots for different subject matters and learning activities are not suited to the nature of young children. In many respects the efforts to reform the English primary schools along these lines during the late 1960s and early 1970s closely resembled the American progressive-educational reforms of the early decades of the twentieth century, although the American reform efforts were more directly steeped in democratic social ideology.

Although these contemporary educational reforms in England were being hailed as a model for American educational reform in the early 1970s, many American schools proceeded to adopt the open classroom mainly as an organizational arrangement for individualized, differentiated, and specialized learning activities. Relatively little attention was being given to developing curriculum integration through the open classroom.

INDIVIDUALIZED INSTRUCTION ARRANGEMENTS AND MASTERY LEARNING.   In response to the curriculum-retrenchment demands of the latter half of the 1970s, the open classroom came under attack both in this country and in England. The concept of individualized instruction was adapted to the skill function of schooling with the elementary curriculum focused on the three R's. Workbooks, worksheets, and programmed materials were reappearing in elementary classrooms along with inventories of behavioristic objectives. Individualized instructional programs—such as Individually Guided Education (IGE), originally developed during the mid-1960s through funds from the managerial-efficiency oriented Kettering Foundation—began to be adopted on a wider scale in the elementary schools. Sweeping claims were made for these programs, usually in terms of pre- and posttest scores of achievement in reading and arithmetic. Where control schools were used, the comparison populations were nonrandomly selected or were not matched according to criteria such as aptitude, achievement, socioeconomic background, and teacher ability. Proving the project appeared to be the overriding consideration, rather than investigating alternative approaches to curriculum design for the improvement of learning.[23]

The mastery-learning concept gained widespread interest and application during the late 1970s. Although it is contended that mastery-learning strategies are appropriate at all levels of education, they have been most widely employed at the elementary level, particularly in connection with the skill function of schooling. Under the assumption that "individual differences in school learning under very favorable conditions will approach a vanishing point," mastery learning relies heavily on the completion of discrete learning tasks with continuous feedback and corrective measures for the individual pupil through diagnostic-progress tests, programmed materials, workbooks, quizzes, and so on.[24] Obviously, the more rudimentary skills are most amenable to such measures. Consequently, schools that seek to implement mastery-learning strategies tend to narrow the curriculum focus to reading and mathematics. The extent to which the repertoire of continuous feedback, correction, and repeated testing constitutes a kind of teaching to the test under mastery learning has received little attention. It should not be surprising if such a repertoire, combined with the added time element of mastery learning, did not result in the self-fulfilling validation of the mastery concept. To compare experimental groups with control groups under such circumstances may be like running against a wooden-legged competitor. Virtually no systematic studies have been undertaken to compare the mastery-learning strategy in the skill function of schooling with alternative strategies in the growth function of schooling. Because the latter entails far more than skill development, the evaluative criteria necessitate the inclusion of such learning outcomes as divergent thinking, learning transfer, hypothetical thinking on personal and social problems, affective changes, and a host of the other macro-learning outcomes in addition to proficiency in the fundamental skills.

Alternative Schools or Schools of Choice

As noted, the 1918 Commission on the Reorganization of Secondary Education had pointed to the social divisiveness of special-type schools and the inflexibility of the curriculum in comparison to the comprehensive school where students can change their programs of study without severance of school relationship. Almost three-quarters of a century later, President George Bush was offering a national education strategy in *America 2000* promoting schools of "choice" on the ground that it "will create the competitive climate that stimulates excellence."[25] In linking competition with "excellence," Bush's education strategy called for the reallocation of public funds to private schools just so long as these schools are deemed to "serve the public."[26] More than twenty years earlier, in his autobiography, James Conant reflected on the issue of public funds for private schools. "The greater the proportion of our youth who attend independent schools, the greater the threat to our democratic unity," stated Conant. "Therefore," Conant concluded, "to use taxpayers' money to assist such a move is, for me, to suggest that American society use its own hands to destroy itself."[27]

Although President Bill Clinton, who succeeded Bush, almost immediately expressed his opposition to the use of public funds for private schools, he supported "schools of choice." Public school systems in many regions were soon designating special-type schools as "schools of choice" or as "magnet schools" from the elementary through the secondary levels. In some instances, parents were forced to choose whether their child, getting ready to enter kindergarten, should enroll in a magnet school for science and technology, or a magnet school for fine, visual, and performing arts. Waiting lists were not uncommon when parental choice resulted in oversubscribing the school for science and technology (favored because it typically had the best equipment, facilities, and most highly qualified teachers).

Aside from the obviously unscientific basis for separating young children into special-type schools, there is the pervasive question of social separation in the schools of a cosmopolitan society. Such separation was rejected even at the secondary level back in 1918 by the Commission on the Reorganization of Secondary Education on the ground that it works against the democratic interest. This might well have given pause for thoughtful educators to wonder whether the young nation was beginning to suffer from a hardening of the arteries. However, the general public remained opposed to school vouchers and were not about to abandon their belief in education. One only had to examine the enrollment statistics revealing the increased holding power of the high school and expanded access to higher education throughout the twentieth century, as envisioned prophetically by the members of the 1918 Commission on the Reorganization of Secondary Education.

Nevertheless, the developments during the 1990s, in creating myriad small, special-interest high schools in some of the major cities organized around ethnocentric programs and basic skills for minority groups, raised ominous questions regarding cultural isolation and segregation. With the curriculum geared to basic academic skills and a narrow special theme for a small, special-interest population, these schools did not require the rich libraries, laboratories, studios, and shops needed for a comprehensive or cosmopolitan high school. In fall 1993, New York City opened over thirty such schools in a variety of physical settings. The so-called leadership secondary school, designed for Hispanic youth with a curricular emphasis on Latino culture, was delayed in opening and was being faced with a civil-rights challenge. The Middle College High School intended for African-American teenagers did open on schedule, but the school board had to announce that the school would be "open to students of all ethnic and racial backgrounds."[28] Dozens of cities nationwide were opening schools with Afrocentric curriculums. Baltimore was operating all-boy and all-girl classes within elementary schools, and Detroit's academies, restricted to black males, were ordered by federal authorities in 1991 to admit females.

In effect, it seemed that the schools of U.S. inner cities were responding to the problem of multicultural differences and conflict in society by creating separate schools for separate cultural constituencies. Conspicuously absent were concerted efforts to develop intercultural programs from the elementary level through the high school. Such efforts, undertaken by progressive educators before mid-twentieth century,[29] appeared just as urgent under the contemporary conditions of social fragmentation and conflict. The establishment of special-interest schools to serve special-interest constituencies seemed to serve as a reflection of the conflicting culture. In the closing decade of the twentieth century, it appeared that the time was ripe for rediscovering the idea and practice of general education and bringing renewal to the uniquely American institution known as the comprehensive high school.

Accelerated Schools

A disturbing observation made by more thoughtful teachers is the phenomenon whereby higher-achieving students seek to find out what will be on the test (what specifically they will be held accountable for). When an examination is impending, such students have little patience with the teacher who departs from the target material with enrichment goals and activities. However, lower-achieving students tend not to press the teacher for what will be on the examinations. They exhibit great interest in ideas, problems, and issues that touch their lives. Enrichment goals and activities not only are highly motivating, but they also unleash unexpected talents and abilities. In effect, the higher-achieving students seem to exhibit a demand for lower-cognitive material ("what's on the test"), whereas lower-achieving students seem to respond better to higher-cognitive material.

This seeming paradox may be explained by the fact that higher-achieving students are successful on their examinations, whereas lower-achieving students meet with relatively little success. Hence, the former will be motivated to seek the path of least resistance by focusing on the facts and skills for the examinations, whether or not the material is interesting, challenging, and relevant to their lives; in contrast, the lower-achieving students, having had little success with examinations, remain unmotivated. Unfortunately, as teachers seek to induce higher-achieving students to engage in learning activities and to utilize materials for higher-order thinking, the typical classroom repertoire for lower-achieving students is on facts and drills. The point is that all children and youth are interested in ideas that touch their lives, and it is through idea-oriented teaching that facts become meaningful and skills become truly instrumental or useful. However, instead of idea-oriented teaching and learning, the focus, especially for lower-achieving students, is on error-oriented teaching and learning. (The student seeks to avoid errors in the belief that the teacher's job is to expose student errors.) The consequence is that students will restrict their ideas in essay writing, will refrain from asking questions for fear of revealing their ignorance, and will tend to respond mechanically with short answers to teacher questions.

In an effort to address these problems for lower-achieving, at-risk children, Henry Levin and his colleagues at Stanford University have instituted total-school programs at the elementary and middle levels under the premise that what works with gifted children also works effectively for all children. This premise is derived from John Dewey's poignant statement in the opening paragraph of *The School and Society* (1899): "What the best and wisest parent wants for his own child, that must the community want for all of its children. Any other ideal for our schools is narrow and unlovely; acted upon, it destroys our democracy."[30] Although Levin and his associates have promoted the effort under the banner of accelerated schools, the project actually is not directed at compressing or speeding up the curriculum, but on deepening and widening it through the integration of studies, engaging children in higher-order thinking and active learning, enriching the learning resources (and eliminating worksheets), engaging teachers in decision-making authority and responsibility for curriculum development, engaging parents in working with the professional staff, and developing a shared sense of vision for the school as a community and belief in the potentials of all children. Emphasis is given to democratic processes and cooperative teacher-pupil planning.

The results claimed are highly positive.[31] Although some might prefer to see carefully designed experimental controls for the project, it should be borne in mind that virtually all of the elements in the project have a long-standing research base for approved practices stemming from the experimentalist-progressive tradition. In view of the standing pressure to demonstrate results on standardized academic achievement tests, the focus of the project has been largely on academic studies, although the studies are organized and treated in integrated ways. Nevertheless, the academic curriculum is not a complete curriculum. The studio arts, industrial arts, and other so-called nonacademic studies have powerfully positive effects on cognitive and social development for both academic success and life success. One naturally finds open collaboration, cooperation, and initiative in the shop class and studio-arts class, but not so much in the math class.[32] Consequently, accelerated schools would do well to provide for a more comprehensive curriculum.

GENERAL EDUCATION AND KNOWLEDGE SPECIALISM

Educators are often prone to distinguish general education from the knowledge world of specialized scholarship in terms of subject matter rather than in terms of outlook on knowledge and life, along with method of organizing and treating knowledge. Specialized-puristic scholarship requires a different outlook on knowledge and its organization than does general education. Before discussing the various ways of organizing knowledge in the curriculum, a brief examination of this difference in outlook on knowledge is presented.

The Scholar-Specialist and the Citizen

In acknowledging that there are various motives that lead one to the temple of specialized scholarship, including the drive to satisfy personal ambition and to revel in a sense of superior intellectual power, Einstein pointed out that there are other powerful motives of quite a different character.

> I believe with Schopenhauer that one of the strongest motives that lead men to art and science is escape from everyday life with its painful crudity and hopeless dreariness, from the fetters of one's own ever shifting desires. A finely tempered nature longs to escape from personal life into the world of objective perception and thought. . . . With this negative motive there goes a personal one. Man tries to make for himself in the fashion that suits him best a simplified and intelligible picture of the world; he then tries to some extent to substitute this cosmos of his for the world of experience, and thus to overcome it. . . . He makes this cosmos and its construction the pivot of his emotional life, in order to find in this way the peace and security which he cannot find in the narrow whirlpool of personal experience.[33]

It cannot be denied that the work of such scholar-specialists has changed the world profoundly and that the change has been of immeasurable benefit. But the puristic knowledge edifices of the scholar-specialist represent only one side of knowledge. The ordinary citizen also "tries to make for himself a simplified and intelligible picture of the world," but not as a substitute for the world of experience. Instead, his or her motive is to cope more effectively with the complexities and demands of life. In this quest it is not enough to prepare oneself for an occupation, but one must also develop a vision of the good person leading the good life in the good society. In a free society, the citizen is expected to develop the ability to think reflectively, to communicate thought, to make intelligent judgments, to discriminate wisely among values in coming to grips with problems and issues that are common to all citizens. General education in a free society, then, is intended to develop the independently thinking, socially responsible citizen.

The enlightened citizen in a free society is expected to govern his or her actions and come to grips with the problems of life experience through rational thought. But this is not the specialized rational thought of puristic scholarship that serves a private aestheticism. However, many individuals have sought to make for themselves a simplified picture of the world not through rational means but through the dogmas of the occult and superstition. It is ironic that the occult and astrology have been so appealing to some elements of the college generation, for one assumes that the seats of higher learning are steeped in rational thought. If this rational thought is narrowly conceived to serve a private aestheticism it, too, fails to come to grips with the pervading problems of the times.

Addressing the plight of the lost individual in the impersonal technological society, Dewey warned that the divorce of science from moral and social concerns "diverts intelligence to anxious preoccupation with the unrealities of a purely inner life," leaving the masses to "swarm to the occult for assistance" while the cultivated smile contemptuously. "They might smile, as the saying goes, out of the other side of their mouths," continued Dewey, "if they realized how recourse to the occult exhibits the practical logic of their own beliefs. For both rest upon a separation of moral ideas and feelings from knowable facts of life, man and the world." And, in the absence of the needed integration to illumine social intelligence, added Dewey, "we shall be deprived of the aid of past experience to cope with the most acute and deep problems of life."[34]

Dewey's concern that the failure to employ the methods of science and the tools of technology for the amelioration of social problems and general enlightenment appears to be manifest today in the widespread fascination, even among the college population, with escapism, superstition, and sensation-seeking experience through the occult, Asian mysticism, and drugs and narcotics. Catastrophe and the supernatural have become sure-fire profit-making themes for novels, TV, and film. The gurus of the counterculture of the 1960s and 1970s found the college generation in the humanities most susceptible to their otherworldly message. The two-cultures split between the science and humanities, so evident in the curriculum, became manifest in the college generation and in society at large.[35]

General education is aimed at providing the needed integration to illumine social intelligence so that people can cope with the most acute and deep problems of life. To yield to unintelligent forces is to submit to superstition, blind authority, fear, and escapism. Unfortunately, general education had fallen into neglect in the secondary schools and colleges at a time when its mission was never more urgent.

Two Cultures

Dewey called attention to a widening split or inner division in American culture as a result of the narrow influence of science and its technological consequences in determining the relations that human beings sustain to one another in the absence of employing science for moral direction. Such a split in modern culture, he warned, portends the demise not only of democracy but of all civilized values.[36]

Twenty years after, C. P. Snow struck a tender nerve in intellectual circles in his Cambridge University lecture, "The Two Cultures," when he pointed to the widening split in Western society between two polar groups—literary intellectuals and scientists. Snow contended that the widening gulf of mutual comprehension between the two groups had resulted in a practical and intellectual loss to society. He went on to attribute the culture divide to two conditions that had emerged in the Western world, but most acutely in England—educational specialization and the crystallized social divisions. "There is only one way out of this: it is, of course, by rethinking our education," stated Snow.[37] After referring to the narrowness of the Oxford and Cambridge scholarship examinations in fostering knowledge specialization, Snow attacked both the narrowness of educational specialization and the restriction of education to a tiny elite as being disastrous to a society that must perform the practical tasks of the world.

PRACTICAL AND MORAL CONCERNS.   "Intellectuals, in particular literary intellectuals, are natural Luddites," declared Snow as he traced the historic tendency of the academicians to hold themselves aloof from the practical and moral concerns of the industrial and scientific revolutions.[38] Even in the field of science, noted Snow, wide gaps have been created between pure and applied science.

> Pure scientists have by and large been dimwitted about engineers and applied science. . . . They wouldn't recognize that many of the problems were as intellectually exacting as pure problems, and that many of the solutions were as satisfying and beautiful. Their instinct—perhaps sharpened in this country by the passion to find a new snobbism wherever possible, and to invent one if it doesn't exist—was to take it for granted that applied science was an occupation for second-rate minds. I say this more sharply because thirty years ago I took precisely that line myself. . . . We prided ourselves that the science we were doing could not, in any conceivable circumstances, have any practical use. The more firmly one could make that claim, the more superior one felt.[39]

Snow went on to contend that if we are to meet the cultural and practical future, we cannot begin by thinking only of the intellectual life, or only of the social life, but we must break the existing pattern of separate educational cultures, the narrow specializations that produce such separation, and the narrow elitism of advanced education. And, he continued,

> Closing the gap between our cultures is a necessity in the most abstract intellectual sense, as well as in the most practical. When those two senses have grown apart,

then no society is going to be able to think with wisdom. For the sake of the intellectual life . . . for the sake of the western society living precariously rich among the poor, for the sake of the poor who needn't be poor if there is intelligence in the world, it is obligatory for us and the Americans and the whole West to look at our education with fresh eyes.[40]

EDUCATION AS UNIFIER.   Although Snow had criticized education for leading the Western world to two cultures, he also viewed education as the key means of bringing about the needed unification and synthesis. Addressing this problem fourteen years earlier, the Harvard Report pointed to the unfortunate consequences of creating divisions between the liberal and the illiberal in terms of the humanities and the sciences. It also stressed the need to recognize that although specialism is necessary, its tendency to divide people from one another requires that education in a democracy develop the understandings that all citizens must share in common as members of a joint culture. Accordingly, the curriculum must be so developed as to represent

> a scheme of relationship between subjects which shall be similar for all students yet capable of being differently carried out for different students. Within it there must be place for both special and general education: for those subjects which divide man from man according to their particular functions and for those which unite man and man in their common humanity and citizenship. This scheme, further, should provide a continuing bond of training and outlook not only between all members of the high school but also between the great majority who stop at high school and the minority who go on to college, such that their education should not differ in kind but only in degree.[41]

Although secondary and higher education have been vastly extended since the time of the Harvard Report, the search for curriculum unity yielded to further knowledge specialization and fragmentation through the disciplinary priorities of the 1950s and 1960s. Moreover, the demand for curriculum relevance during the 1960s and early 1970s, the back-to-basics retrenchment of the 1970s and 1980s, followed by the multitude of literacies and the special interests of multiculturalism of the 1990s (as opposed to intercultural education) all served to fragment the curriculum in different ways. The situation of the 1990s finds different groups split apart from one another in seeking their own special-interest studies and activities. The legitimacy of special-interest education cannot be denied, but to ignore the need for curriculum coherence is to allow the curriculum to reflect the divisions that set people apart and against one another in social life.

THE PROBLEM OF CURRICULUM ORGANIZATION

At the secondary and college levels, the total curriculum may be classified according to five broad functions: (1) general education or those learnings that all educated members of a free society share in common, (2) exploratory education, (3) enrichment education, (4) specialized education—including college-preparatory, prevocational or preprofessional, and vocational or professional studies, and (5) special-interest education. Exploratory and enrichment education encompass formal studies typically provided through controlled electives. Special-interest studies are usually provided through free electives and also through student activities such as publications, band, orchestra, intramural and varsity athletics, student government, clubs, and so on.

At the elementary level, the curriculum may be conceived as encompassing the function of general education and the function of exploratory and enrichment education. Although the fundamental skills are essential to general education, the traditional elementary school concentrates on these skills as though they were appropriate ends in themselves, rather than the tools for wider and richer learning. The traditional assumption has been that the child must first master the fundamental skills and facts before he or she can make use of these skills and facts in understanding his or her environment. The tendency in traditional educational practice is to fail to recognize that skills, concepts, and patterns of thinking are developed concomitantly as children seek to enlarge and deepen their comprehension of the environment. The consequence is that the skills and facts are not translated into the working power of general education.

Educators often are prone to distinguish general education from specialized education in terms of subject matter rather than in terms of outlook along with method of organizing and treating knowledge. Thus far in this chapter, the discussion has centered on the difference in outlook. Furthermore, there is the tendency on the part of teachers and students to regard the curriculum simply as a body of subjects and subject matter. There is an inadequate understanding of the various ways in which the subject matters can be organized and treated in the framework of the total school curriculum.

The Subject Curriculum and General Education

The arrangement of studies into subjects is the oldest approach to curriculum organization, dating back to the medieval *trivium* and *quadrivium*. The subject approach also remains the most widely accepted organization of curriculum. The durability and pervasiveness of the subject curriculum may be attributed to many factors, but perhaps most important is that it serves as a convenient institutional means of systematizing knowledge for instruction, inventorying knowledge for academic credits, annexing new knowledge in the curriculum, and accommodating the curriculum to the growing specialization of knowledge.

OPERATIONAL CONVENIENCE.   Administratively, the subject curriculum is operationally convenient. At the elementary level, teachers can be made to feel that they are treating the ground to be covered as they move from subject to subject in their daily and weekly class schedules. Textbooks, workbooks, and curriculum packages tend to be organized to fit the established subject categories that comprise the curriculum of the elementary and secondary schools.

At the secondary and college levels, knowledge is conveniently categorized and departmentalized according to subjects and subjects fields—and courses can be added, deleted, modified, combined, and split into myriad subspecialties without disturbing the existing curriculum framework. The courses can be scheduled easily, and credits can be allocated, inventoried, and assessed uniformly and conveniently. If pupils demand relevance in the curriculum, new courses can be added without changing the existing courses. In the high school, for example, the English department can add new courses in African-American literature or filmmaking, or the social studies department can add new courses in African-American history or sociology without changing the curriculum structure of the department or school. Subjects can be kept up to date by periodically adopting new textbooks and plugging in new course packages.

In the high school, credits are inventoried with uniform convenience through the Carnegie unit. Almost from the time that The Carnegie Foundation proposed the standard unit of measurement for high school credits (1909), the Carnegie unit was imposed on the high schools. With the endorsement of the College Entrance Examination Board, the Carnegie unit became the quantitative measure for assessing credits for college admission. (One Carnegie unit is gained with the completion of a minimum of 120 clock hours in a subject during a school year, with sixteen units required for graduation.)

Although the Carnegie unit has been of great convenience to college admissions officers, it is not well suited to the diversified curriculum of a modern comprehensive high school. The Carnegie unit has been criticized for helping to make the class schedule inflexible and for impeding the development of a more functional curriculum. Although an increasing number of high schools began to abandon the Carnegie unit during the early 1970s in an effort to provide for greater curriculum flexibility and to provide greater recognition for the so-called nonacademic studies, most of these schools have proceeded to substitute a system of accounting for credits that could be translated quite easily into Carnegie units. In short, the subject curriculum is most conveniently suited to the Carnegie unit or any other system of quantitative accounting of high-school credits. Although the Carnegie unit has been the target of criticism over the years for having imposed a mechanical inflexibility on the high-school curriculum, the Carnegie unit did not create the traditional structure of curriculum organization and the inertia that preserves it. The subject curriculum and the system of amassing credits, subject by subject, toward graduation, are easily understood by parents and students and can be assessed with utmost convenience for college admissions.

SYSTEMATIZATION AND SPECIALIZATION OF KNOWLEDGE.   Whether the problem is one of accommodating new knowledge or of providing some room for au courant topics, the subject curriculum is most convenient administratively. As already mentioned, the new knowledge or au courant material can be encapsulated into new courses without affecting the existing courses and the organizational structure of the curriculum. New knowledge and new ways of treating knowledge breed new specializations in the university, and these new specializations can be accommodated into the subject curriculum most easily by adding new specialized courses to the existing course offerings. Our larger universities typically offer courses numbering into the thousands even at the undergraduate level, whereas the larger high schools commonly offer hundreds of courses in imitation of the world of higher learning. The number of new subjects, subject matters, and courses is governed mainly by the practical limitations of the high school or university rather than by the nature of knowledge itself.

Although the so-called knowledge explosion has given rise to new disciplines and subdisciplines in the university, along with new specializations, the multiplication of subject matters and courses also has been a product of specialized scholarship independent of substantive changes in knowledge. Thus, for example, a given department of English or literature will have a faculty specialist in Elizabethan literature, or a history department will have a specialist on the Civil War, who will offer courses in the given area of specialty. As mentioned earlier, the desire and demand to make studies au courant also leads to a multiplicity of new subject matters and courses.

SPECIALIZED KNOWLEDGE AND GENERAL EDUCATION.   Although specialization serves to provide for greater depth of knowledge treatment, this is accomplished at the expense of breadth. Knowledge becomes strongly compartmentalized and the faculty become isolated from one another according to their subject specialties.

The development of new knowledge not only is partly a product of specialization but also breeds further specialization. In turn, there is the need for the preparation of more specialists. Although specialization finds its necessary justification in the university and society, many pervading problems in society—whether the energy crisis, the growing cancer epidemic, or rising crime and social conflict—require interdisciplinary approaches to their solution.

Moreover, the design of a curriculum is necessarily different when the aim is to develop a specialist as contrasted with the aim of developing the whole person as an effective citizen in a free society. In the words of the Harvard Report:

> We are living in an age of specialism. . . . Each of these specialties makes an increasing demand on the time and interest of the student. Specialism is the means for advancement in our mobile social structure; yet we must envisage the fact that a society controlled wholly by specialists is not a wisely ordered society. We cannot, however, turn away from specialism. The problem is how to save general education and its values within a system where specialism is necessary.[42]

The Spiral Curriculum

In *Experience and Education* (1938), Dewey pointed to the need to reorganize the curriculum so that it is consciously and progressively articulated, and that the learning experiences be continually expanded and deepened in intellectually related ways. Regarding the learner, connectedness in growth must be the watchword, for knowledge is not a fixed possession. It is the responsibility of educators to so design the curriculum that new ideas growing out of present experience become the ground for wider and richer experiences and new problems that engage the learner in an active quest for new ideas. "The process is a continual spiral," wrote Dewey.[43] The concept of the spiral curriculum is embodied in Dewey's definition of education and in the definition of curriculum proffered by the authors of this text: "that reconstruction of knowledge and experience which enables the learner to grow in exercising intelligent control of subsequent knowledge and experience" (see Chapter 5).

In *The Process of Education* (1960), Harvard psychologist Jerome Bruner promoted the idea of the spiral curriculum without having cited Dewey. Bruner's conception of the spiral curriculum almost immediately became a slogan among curricularists. However, there was a failure to recognize that Dewey's spiral curriculum takes its starting point from the learner's experience and serves to reveal the interrelatedness of all areas of knowledge that comprise the school curriculum. In sharp contrast, Bruner's spiral curriculum takes its starting point from each separate discipline as conceived by the scholar specialists on the forefront of that discipline. "We might ask, as a criterion for any subject taught in primary school, whether, when fully developed, it is worth an adult's knowing, and whether having known it is a child makes the person a better adult," wrote Bruner.[44] From the Deweyan perspective, the statement might read, "We might ask, as a criterion for any subject whether it is worth a child's knowing, and whether having known it as a child makes the child a better person."

Bruner's conception of the child as miniature adult scholar-specialist was advanced in the entirely unfounded dictum that, "The schoolboy learning physics *is* a physicist, and it is easier for him to learn physics behaving like a physicist than doing something else."[45] Under the Brunerian dictum, the schoolboy was to be a miniature scholar-specialist in each and every discipline.

This notion raised further complications aside from the distorted conception of the nature of the learner. In advancing his conception of the spiral curriculum, Bruner held that the curriculum for each discipline or subject "should be determined by the most fundamental understanding that can be achieved of the underlying principles that give structure to that subject."[46] In effect, each discipline or subject is to be treated as an articulated domain of specialized knowledge production, virtually independent of the other disciplines or subjects in the school curriculum, because "different disciplines have widely different conceptual schemes."[47] Under such a doctrine, the disciplines are directed at the function of specialized education to the neglect of the macrocurricular function of general education. No concerted attention is to be given to horizontal curriculum articulation (interdisciplinary knowledge and the interrelationships between and among the various subjects that comprise the school curriculum). Focused exclusively on each discipline unto itself, puristic and abstract knowledge is promoted to the neglect of practical knowledge applications in the life of the learner and in the life of the wider society. Such was the case with the national discipline-centered reforms of the era of the Cold War and space race that gave the schools the "new math," "new physics," and so on. That the billion-dollar effort failed should have been no surprise, considering that it violated the curriculum paradigm in distorting the nature of the learner, in turning the curriculum to meet narrow nationalistic interests, in neglecting the cosmopolitan democratic interest, and in neglecting applied knowledge (Chapter 7). What should be surprising is how readily educators, including curricularists, jumped on the discipline-centered bandwagon with only a few dissenting voices.[48] It should be remembered that the Cold War and space race had created an atmosphere of near hysteria. Bruner's *Process of Education* was the report of a federally funded conference to develop a school-reform rationale to meet the alleged crisis of national security. The puristic, discipline-centered knowledge specialists of the university readily filled the void when grant monies became available through the prestigious National Science Foundation. The spiral curriculum as conceived by Bruner found each discipline spiraling in separate realms and in different directions, creating a new fragmentation of the curriculum.

Scope, Sequence, and Balance— Vertical and Horizontal Articulation

The Deweyan concept of the spiral curriculum relates not only to the vertical integration or deepening of knowledge but also to the horizontal integration or widening of knowledge. When educators seek to improve the coherence of studies within a given discipline or subject field, they are attending to the vertical articulation or sequence of the curriculum. When they seek to develop the interrelationships between and among different disciplines or subject fields, they are concerned with the horizontal articulation along with the balance and scope of the curriculum.

Thus, for example, when educators attempt to improve the coherence between ninth-grade general science and tenth-grade biology, tenth-grade biology and eleventh-grade chemistry, and eleventh-grade chemistry and twelfth-grade physics, they are concerned with vertical curriculum articulation. In contrast, when they attempt to develop interrelationships between seventh-grade general science and seventh-grade mathematics, or between English and social studies at a given grade level, they are concerned with horizontal curriculum articulation. In a similar vein, the ninth-grade science teacher may work with the ninth-grade social studies teacher toward developing horizontal curriculum articulation by relating the two subjects in terms of the social implications of science. In developing vertical or horizontal curriculum articulation, the different subject fields or disciplines may retain their own autonomy as separate subjects, or the separate subject lines may become less distinct or even made to disappear. Curriculum synthesis is attained to the extent to which the subject lines are no longer distinguishable.

Because teachers are products of discipline-centered universities, and because the textbooks and course packages tend to reflect the university scholar-specialist's view of his or her knowledge domain, they tend to ignore the need for curriculum articulation and synthesis not only on the horizontal plane but also on the vertical plane. Consequently, the scope of each course of study tends to be confined to only a segment of the discipline or subject field of which it is a part. The sequence of courses within a discipline or subject field tends to be organized in linear fashion regardless of whether the sequence is psychologically sound. In fact, the sequence may be arranged more for administrative convenience or tradition rather than in terms of the logic of the subject matter. As an example, modern biology requires the use of chemistry, but chemistry almost always follows biology in the high-school curriculum. English literature may (arbitrarily) precede American literature, with both subjects being organized chronologically.

The isolation of teachers according to departments and subject specialties also works against curriculum articulation and synthesis. The mathematics teacher in the ninth grade may rarely, if ever, find occasion to work with the science teacher at the same grade level and at other grade levels for purposes of curriculum articulation. Departmental allegiances and lines are such that curriculum development in the high school and college is confined to individual departments that represent the disciplines and subject fields as though they were autonomous domains of knowledge. The task of curriculum integration is left to the learner who, somehow, is expected to transfer his or her learnings from one knowledge domain to another. Meanwhile, teachers continually complain that pupils do not transfer their leanings between and among the various subjects of the school curriculum. Yet the teachers themselves rarely give concerted attention to the problem of curriculum fragmentation and isolation that works against learning transfer.

Although the concept of balance is readily understood, more often than not the curriculum suffers from imbalance. Shifting curriculum priorities by reaction and counterreaction in successive periods of educational reform have contributed to this problem. Historically, such dualisms favoring the academic studies over the practical, the cultural over the useful, and the study of the past over the present have worked against a balanced curriculum—a problem extending to this day. At the same time, we have witnessed shifts in national priorities, such as favoring the sciences and mathematics to meet nationalistic "crises" ranging from the Cold War and space race to the Japanese challenge in competition for global industrial markets. Or, during times of social and economic retrenchment, there is the call for curriculum reductionism—back to basics and the corresponding neglect of a full, rich, and balanced curriculum for all children and youth. A balanced curriculum might be likened to balanced nutrition. Both are necessary for optimum growth and development—whether physically, intellectually, socially, or emotionally.

Figure 10–1 is a diagrammatic representation of scope, sequence, and balance in the curriculum. The horizontal plane represents the extent of articulation among the various studies offered at a given grade or age level. The vertical plane represents the extent of sequential articulation within a given field of study over time. The scope of the curriculum may be seen as encompassing both the vertical and horizontal planes. The balance of the curriculum may be seen as the extent to which the various offerings of studies taken together are sufficiently diversified, yet interrelated, complete, and equally honored.

Balance refers to the extent to which the curriculum is in harmonious proportion. Scope refers to the full sweep, area, or range of the curriculum. Sequence refers to the continuity of the curriculum. In effect, efforts to improve the balance, scope, and sequence of the school or college curriculum are directed at bringing the studies into harmonious proportion, fullest range, and systematic continuity.

Unit Teaching and Learning

As discussed in Part 1, progressive educators during the early decades of the twentieth century sought a unitary design and treatment of the curriculum by organizing studies into units of work. Today, it is common for textbooks at all levels and subjects

Figure 10–1. Curriculum Articulation: Toward an Articulated Curriculum.

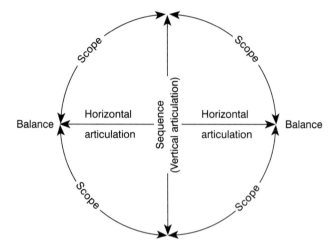

to be organized as units; however, the use of the term *unit* for textbooks may simply be to designate chapters and chapter groupings by topics rather than to represent units of work as originally intended. In effect, the unit of work was to extend the studies beyond the textbook through the use of a wide variety of resources and activities.

Units of work were developed throughout the elementary and secondary levels by faculty members working in teams. For the core curriculum at the secondary school level, the unitary work in the more progressive schools was developed through the study of problems of youth and of society. Teaching-resource units were developed by and for the faculty who also developed learning-resource units for the students. The latter, which included all kinds of materials bearing on the unit of work, were often housed in files in the school library.

An example of a highly developed and successful unit of work was *Children and Architecture,* developed for the sixth grade at the Lincoln School of Teachers College and implemented in 1930. The purpose was not directed at the study of architecture as a specialized field, but to investigate the human side of architecture, its relationship to everyday life, and as an expression of civilizations. In developing and implementing the unit, the teacher obtained the cooperation of the Metropolitan Museum of Art and other museums, art studios, and other agencies in New York City. Also enlisted in the effort was the school library staff and faculty in the fine and industrial arts and theater. The class made many excursions not only to museums and landmark buildings, but also to sites under new construction. In their work, they evaluated different schools of architecture not only historically, but also in relation to aesthetic and functional design in connection with the contemporary urban environment. In the industrial arts, they made blueprints and designed models of buildings and constructed models of different bridge structures, and tested them for stress and made plaster casts of historic building ornaments. The unit provided extensive opportunities for photography, essay writing, and poetry.

The faculty of the Lincoln School carefully developed criteria from actual practice to be used in selecting and developing units of work. Some of these criteria are summarized as follows:

1. The unit of work must be selected from real-life situations and must be considered worthwhile by the child because the child feels that he has helped select it and because he finds in it many opportunities to satisfy his needs.
2. The unit of work must afford many opportunities for real purposing and real projects, and it will be something which the child can carry into normal activity.
3. The unit of work must stimulate many kinds of activities and so provide for individual differences.
4. The unit of work must make individual growth possible.
5. The succession of units of work must provide for continuous group growth from one level to the next.
6. Each unit of work must furnish leads into other related units of work and must stimulate in the child the desire for a continued widening of interests and understandings.
7. Each unit of work must meet the demands of society and must help clarify social meanings.
8. Each unit of work must be accompanied by progress in the use of such tool subjects as contribute to that unit.[49]

Significantly, instead of regarding the basics as independent subjects and ends, they are treated as fundamental tools (means) or fundamental processes for developing higher-order thinking including problem-solving and knowledge applications in the life and growth of the learner. A criterion that should be added to this listing, in view of its implicit expression in the writings of the staff of the Lincoln School, is that *sufficient time, expertise and material resources must be made available for the effective development and implementation of the unit of work.*

Taba enumerated the following systematic steps for planning a unit of work: (1) diagnosing needs, (2) formulating objectives, (3) selecting content, (4) organizing content, (5) selecting learning experiences, (6) organizing learning experiences, (7) evaluating, and (8) checking for balance and sequence.[50] The linear sequence offered by Taba may not be the most practicable and valid approach in the sense that evaluation should be continuous (formatively) as well as being conducted at the culmination of the unit (summatively). In the same vein, scope, sequence, and balance must be taken into account from the very beginning to the very culmination of the unit of work.

Although units of work, as developed by progressive educators, were intended to cut across subject lines and link the courses of study to practical applications and meanings in the life of the learner, they were often used merely to designate the topics to be covered within each of the traditional subjects. In other words, with insufficient understanding, recognition, and effort being given to alternative designs or patterns of curriculum organization, units of work tended to conform to the textbook for the given course or subject. Let us now examine the alternative designs or patterns of curriculum organization.

ALTERNATIVE PATTERNS OF CURRICULUM ORGANIZATION

When educators are engaged in the revision of course content within a discipline or subject field, they are dealing with microcurricular problems. When they are designing total programs in general education or specialized education, or when they are seeking to develop interrelationships between general education and specialized education, they are concerned with macrocurricular problems. Similarly, when they are attempting to develop more effective approaches to horizontal and vertical curriculum articulation, they are concerned with a macrocurricular problem.

There are several major schemes or constructs for organizing knowledge within the subject curriculum. Subject matter may be organized in terms of (1) disciplinarity, (2) correlation, (3) fusion, and (4) broad fields.

In recognition that discipline-centered approaches are artifacts of knowledge purity, abstraction, and specialism, and therefore are not suited to the function of general education, other constructs have been developed (lamination, correlation, fusion, and broad fields). Although these constructs or approaches to organizing subject matter differ significantly from each other, they nevertheless retain the essential characteristics of the subject curriculum.

The term *core* is ordinarily used by schools and colleges to denote the body of courses required of all students or the broad fields from which courses are to be selected to meet the common curricular requirements for general education—as contrasted against specialized, exploratory, enrichment, and special-interest education.

A radical departure from the subject curriculum is the core curriculum organized according to personal and social problems of a universal nature. The personal-social problems core represents curriculum synthesis to the extent that the traditional subject divisions become virtually indistinct. Consequently, the personal-social problems core is a distinct mode of curriculum organization for general education.

Throughout the past decade, colleges and universities, awakened to the problem of course proliferation, revealed a renewed interest in the idea and practice of general education. Many colleges pared down the number of elective courses through which students were allowed to meet the general education requirements. The colleges were recognizing that the students were electing courses on the basis of scheduling convenience, special interests, or special attractions other than meeting the function of general education. Where the college faculties did not proceed to design interdisciplinary courses for general education, they at least established criteria that courses had to meet in order to be designated as appropriate for the function of general education.

The problem of course proliferation and curriculum congestion is not only the result of knowledge specialism in the discipline-centered university, but of the special interests of a divided student population. In the closing decade of the twentieth century, it appeared that the chief problem of the school, the college, and of American society at large was not how to separate groups according to their differences, but how to develop a sense of unity through diversity.

Disciplinarity

The disciplinary construct is the purest form of organizing knowledge in the subject curriculum. Although the disciplinary rationale and the problems connected with organizing the curriculum strictly according to disciplines are treated in detail in Chapter 11, a brief discussion of this approach is presented here in connection with general education.

Many educators who had opposed the traditional treatment of knowledge as being fixed or static, and as something to be "mastered" by memorization and regurgitation, found the thesis of "knowledge as search" vastly appealing as presented in the disciplinary rationale. Taba went so far as to liken Bruner's discovery method to Dewey's conception of learning.[51] However, it is one thing to follow the inquiry mode of a discipline, such as physics or mathematics, and quite another to employ an inquiry mode in addressing a societal problem, such as the energy crisis. Dewey's reflective thinking was focused clearly on the latter type of problem solving, which requires an integrative treatment of knowledge and its applications. Whereas the peculiar disciplinary mode that attaches to a given discipline may be indispensable to certain forms of knowledge production in the world of the university scholar-specialist, it has presented enormous difficulties for the general education of the learner. Because general education in a free society is concerned with the enlightened citizen who is capable of personal-social problem solving, and because such problem solving requires an integrative treatment of knowledge, educators have been impelled to look to constructs other than disciplinarity in organizing the various subject matters of the curriculum.

FRAGMENTATION AND SYNTHESIS. Whereas the scholar-specialist's work is confined to only one small segment of his or her discipline, the disciplinary rationale holds that the developing learner grasp the structure and mode of inquiry for each of the major disciplines. Aside from the question as to whether the developing learner can be expected to accomplish such an enormous feat, there is the question as to how specialized disciplinary scholarship can satisfy a general education function. This is a persistent problem not only in the secondary school but also in higher education.

In recent years, many high schools and colleges have abandoned their efforts to develop a coherent curriculum in general education and instead have opted for distribution requirements. Thus, for example, the college freshman who plans on becoming an economist may find himself or herself attempting to meet the distribution requirement in science by enrolling in a first course in chemistry alongside other students who plan on becoming chemists. The underlying premise for distribution requirements is that college graduates should have a broad background of knowledge. Problems arise for the learner because each first course in a given discipline is construed to prepare the student for the second course, and the second course for the third, and so on, as though every student is to become a knowledge specialist in the given discipline.

With regard to the social sciences, for example, a disciplinary advocate contended that the needed approach is to "bring the frontiers of social science knowledge into the curriculum by respecting and protecting the integrity of each discipline," and he viewed the central problem of curriculum development in these words: "How can we identify those analytical tools of the various social sciences which can then be related to the students' experience at all levels from grade one to the Ph.D.?"[52]

To this day, university scholar-specialists continue to see the secondary school curriculum as appropriately geared to the academic disciplines, such as through the discrete social sciences (sociology, economics, anthropology, linguistics, psychology, and political science) as opposed to the more integrative social studies.[53] That undergraduates find great dissatisfaction with introductory courses that are construed as first steps of a long sequence leading to the Ph.D. has been ignored by disciplinary advocates who have sought to impose such a formula on the child beginning with the first grade. Furthermore, advocates of the disciplinary construct have chosen to ignore the need to design the curriculum so as to illumine the interrelationships among the various domains of disciplinary knowledge. Somehow the student is expected to make his or her own synthesis and transfer—something that happens with disturbing infrequency.

CURRICULUM CONGESTION.   The disciplinary rationale recognizes that the expansion of knowledge cannot be accommodated through curriculum accretion or by endlessly adding more and more subject matter to the course of study. Instead an effort is made to represent each discipline as a mode of inquiry with a focus on those key concepts and central ideas that form its so-called structure. Yet the notion of structure has been elusive, with different scholars coming up with vastly different approaches to organizing disciplinary subject matter.

Moreover the disciplinary construct presents its own problem of curriculum congestion. When carried to its logical conclusion—such as reducing the social studies into its component disciplines and representing each component discipline in the elementary and secondary-school curriculum—the result is an impossible congestion of the curriculum. Figure 10–2 illustrates such an arrangement. Within each discipline there are any number of courses. Under the disciplinary approach, each discipline is regarded as a discrete entity. But because the real world is not organized as disciplines, various transdisciplinary studies emerge to deal with the knowledge interfaces between and among the disciplines. Thus we have not merely geography, but physical geography, economic geography, and so on. Taken in its fullest sense, geography is a broad field rather than a discipline. Anthropology not only has many interfaces with sociology, psychology, and history, but also with biology. Because of its many necessary interfaces between the social and biological sciences, efforts to find the structure of a discipline of anthropology require an artificial reductionism of the field into subspecialties having fewer interconnections with the cultural world. Similar difficulties accrue to each of the so-called social-science disciplines and to history. When we speak of history, we may be dealing with political history, social history, art history, the history of science, and so on.

Figure 10–2. Disciplinarity: The Social Sciences and History.

Disciplinarity accounts for specialized scholarship at the expense of the interrelationships of the knowledge domains and the practical applications of knowledge. Attention to such relationships and applications requires curriculum synthesis. Curriculum synthesis takes into account not only the learner, society, and the wider world of knowledge but also the problem of curricular proliferation and congestion. There is simply no time in the school day, nor, for that matter, in the college student's course schedule, to account for each and every discipline or knowledge specialty.

As Whitehead observed, "Lack of time is the rock upon which the fairest educational schemes are wrecked. It has wrecked that scheme which our fathers constructed to meet the growing demand for the introduction of modern ideas. They simply increased the number of subjects taught."[54]

OTHER LIMITATIONS OF DISCIPLINARITY. As discussed in Chapter 7, the learner, society, and the wider world of knowledge are important sources of consideration in curriculum development. The discipline-centered approach is focused on the structure of, and inquiry into, each discrete discipline. The learner is regarded as a budding scholar-specialist. Disciplinary knowledge for its own sake takes precedence over the interests of the learner and the problems of society.

Proponents of the disciplinary rationale have tended to denigrate applied knowledge in favor of abstract knowledge. In so doing, they have slighted the treatment of knowledge for purposes of general education or what may be termed the sociocivic function of education in a democracy. Although the National Council for the Social Studies has long recognized the centrality of the sociocivic function in education, many social scientists have purported that their disciplines are scientific and neutral, and have regarded this function as "sociocivically repulsive."[55] In short, educators who are concerned with general education and the sociocivic function of education in a democracy recognize the limitations of the disciplinary construct and the need for other constructs in addressing knowledge in terms of pervading personal-social problems, whereas most disciplinary advocates have either ignored or opposed this curriculum function.

Although a legitimate case may be made for the disciplinary construct in developing the future scholar-specialist, it has not been a viable curriculum construct for general education. Even in the case of the scholar-specialist, the disciplinary construct has revealed serious limitations. For example, the disciplines, when taken by themselves, are inadequate to the task of dealing with such problems as environmental pollution, population growth, food resources, public health, unemployment, housing, and so on. Interdisciplinary, problem-focused approaches are necessary even at the advanced levels of university scholarship for both knowledge production and application in society.

Correlation

Correlation represents an effort to develop certain common relationships between or among two or more subjects and still retain the usual subject divisions (see Figure 10–3). In other words, correlation is an attempt to counter the isolation and compartmentalization of subjects without radically reconstructing the subject curriculum. For example, the teacher of English may work together with the teacher of history or social studies by having students write compositions or read literary works that relate to historical periods or to contemporary social problems.

Thus, the work in literature might be organized to relate to the work in the social studies through (1) a chronological-historical approach, (2) a thematic approach, or (3) a problems approach. Following the chronological-historical approach, students in the English class might be assigned to read such material as Franklin's autobiography or selected essays of Jefferson at the same time that they are studying the American Revolutionary period in the history class. Similarly, they might read Benet's *John Brown's Body* or Crane's *Red Badge of Courage* or selected speeches of Lincoln while they are investigating the Civil War period in the history class. They might read Steinbeck's *Grapes of Wrath* at the time that they are studying the Great Depression of the 1930s in the history class, and so on.

In an effort to overcome the limitations of the chronological-historical approach, the English teacher may organize the material thematically, that is according to such themes as man's inhumanity to man or self-identity in a mass-technological society—paralleling the treatment of related material in the social studies class.

Or the assigned work in the English class might be focused on social problems as related to the social studies class by examining the literature of social protest, or

Figure 10–3. Correlation.

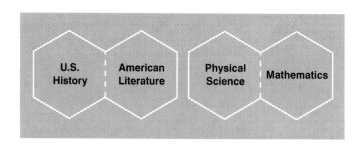

investigating literary censorship or schoolbook censorship, and so on. Obviously, the problems approach requires a far greater amount of course revision than the chronological-historical approach, as well as considerable sophistication on the part of the teacher.

Literature also might be correlated with art and music through broad themes that have evolved historically. A less common approach is to correlate the subject matter from two fields according to genre. The composer Virgil Thomson made this recommendation some years ago:

> Poetry and music are two sides of the coin of vocal expression, which includes vocal music, declaimed poetry, and all that lies between them. . . . Here a revision of the study of poetic literature as well as that of music is indicated, which would take account of the coin between the two faces.[56]

The correlation of physical science and mathematics also serves to bridge the subject matters of two subject fields. Correlation also may be developed between two separate subjects in the same subject field, such as geography and history. Because the subjects and subject fields retain their own separate identities, correlation does not provide for true curriculum synthesis. Nevertheless, it is a significant attempt to articulate the subject matters of two or more different subjects, disciplines, or subject fields. At the college level, correlated approaches often are referred to as cross-disciplinary studies. Because each discipline retains its own distinguishing identity in the correlated approach, the treatment of the subject matter is not truly interdisciplinary.

TEACHING ARRANGEMENTS.   There are many different teaching arrangements in correlating different subject matters. A single teacher who is responsible for two or more courses and attempts to relate these subjects to one another, such as geography and history, is seeking curriculum correlation. Or two teachers who have the same students but at different times of the day may attempt to correlate different subjects or subject fields, without altering the class schedules.

A further step is to schedule the two classes at the same time so that the two teachers may combine their classes on occasion for team teaching. A more systematic teach-teaching arrangement is to have both teachers meet with combined classes in a block time or double period. The teachers may divide their classes occasionally or regularly according to the treatment of topics or the activities assigned the pupils. Or a single teacher, having competence in two subject fields, may be responsible for working with a single class group in a block time of two consecutive periods.

Of course, the block-time arrangement does not guarantee curriculum correlation. Block-time teaching may simply be an administrative arrangement to allow students to spend more time with a teacher with whom they can identify for counseling purposes. The block-time teacher might then be responsible for working with a single group in English and social studies, for example, along with serving as the group's homeroom teacher. The teacher may make no attempt at correlating English and social studies. The two subject fields are simply laminated in a single block of time.

Obviously, the extent of correlation attained depends on the commitment of teachers to the concept, their ability to develop common threads between subjects, and their ability to work together effectively when team-teaching arrangements are prescribed. Block-time teaching also may be designed to provide for curriculum fusion and even for curriculum synthesis.

Lamination

In many instances when related studies are brought together under a broad-field subject, the subject matter is not treated as an interrelated field, but rather as composed of several self-contained units. Under such conditions, the organization and treatment of the subject matter is simply laminated. For example, a course in the industrial arts might be organized so as to cycle from woodworking to metalworking, to electronics, to graphic arts, and so on—as contrasted against a broad-fields course in which the various industrial arts are interrelated or orchestrated. In a similar fashion, the home economics course in the middle school or junior high school might cycle from foods and nutrition, to clothing and textiles, to family life—with each phase being treated as a separate unit. The old fashioned biology course was simply a lamination of botany followed by zoology. Today, the course represents a true fusion of botany and zoology, and may even be organized with a particular orientation—such as through a molecular, biochemical, or ecological approach.

The elementary teacher in the self-contained classroom may seek to treat the various studies as interrelated, or as discrete subjects with a specific time allocation for each in minutes in the daily schedule—such as arithmetic from 8:30 to 9:10 A.M. The block-time teacher in the middle school or junior high school might seek to integrate or correlate the social studies and literature, or might simply allocate one half of the double-period block to each, and proceed to teach the social studies and literature as separate subjects. In the latter case, the social studies and literature are simply laminated into a double-period time block. Under such circumstances, as mentioned earlier, the block-time arrangement allows the teacher to work with fewer students on a daily basis, but the mere lamination of subjects does little if anything for curriculum articulation.

Fusion

In contrast to correlation, which provides for the development of relationships between two or more subjects or subject fields that nevertheless remain essentially intact, fusion represents the merging of related subjects into a new subject. For example, the newer earth science courses emerged from a fusion of certain areas of physical science and geography. The combining of various history courses into the single subject of world history is another example of fusion. Fusion most commonly is undertaken within the same subject field, although it may involve the merger of subject matter from two or more different fields.

Pointing to the need for new curriculum designs for general education as distinct from the traditional subject-matter constructs for specialized education, Whitehead attacked the teaching of mathematics as an end in itself and the teaching of history without an appreciation of the scientific forces that are shaping modern society. Although Whitehead used the term *correlation,* he actually proposed a fusion of modern history with mathematics in a proposal made in 1912.

> Our classical colleagues, excellent fellows as they are, have their limitations; and among them is this one, that they are not fitted by their mental equipment to appreciate quantitative estimates of the forces which are molding modern society. But without such estimates modern history as it unfolds itself before us is a meaningless tangle.
>
> Now among other peculiarities of the nineteenth century is this one, that by initiating the systematic collection of statistics it has made the quantitative study of social forces possible. . . . The reduction of these to graphs, the careful study of the peculiarities of these graphs, the search for correlations among them, and the study of public events which correspond in time to peculiarities in graphical form, would teach more mathematics and more knowledge of modern social forces than all our present methods put together. . . . Problems could be set for solution by the boys— such as to state verbally the effect of war on the social life of a nation as exhibited by the graphs. Also they can be given the statistics and told to exhibit them in graphical form, and to state the general characteristics of the graphs thus obtained. The notion of rates of increase, embodying the essential ideas of the differential calculus, thus emerges.
>
> Finally, theory and practice could be combined by finding graphs which approximately satisfy the simple functional laws which are being simultaneously studied.
>
> I am quite aware that this suggestion of statistical study may seem fantastic, and perhaps be pronounced impossible. . . . But before the whole suggestion is dismissed, I should like to know exactly why it is impossible and why it is fantastic. The information is of the utmost importance for the subsequent conduct of life in self-governing communities; it illustrates important abstract ideas, and the means of study lie easily at hand.[57]

Although Whitehead did not propose a title for the fused studies, they might well be called statistical social analysis. Today it is not uncommon to find college courses with such titles as mathematical sociology and computers in society. Notable among the many modern approaches to fusion at the college level is the merger of biology and physics into biophysics. This fusion has produced a synthesis and treatment of subject matter quite distinct from that which is developed in the separate subjects of biology and physics. Another example is the newly emergent field of sociobiology.[58]

The evolvement of fusion can be illustrated with the case of biology (see Figure 10–4). At the high-school level before the turn of the century, separate courses were offered in botany, zoology, anatomy, and physiology. These separate courses were listed along with other sciences as illustrations of "good" secondary-school programs of studies by the Committee of Ten in 1894.[59] During the early decades of the twentieth century, these separate subjects were fused into the single subject of biology, and biology became a general education subject in high school. However, for many years the high-school biology course represented a lamination of botany and zoology rather than a true fusion of subject matter. Today, modern biology is not merely a lamination or conglomeration of separate subjects but a fusion of the variegated and interactive aspects of the life sciences. In recent years the Biological Sciences Curriculum Study group has shown signs of seeking to make the BSCS course in high-school biology relevant to pervading societal problems. Modern biological science comprises many disciplines and subdisciplines, so that if the variegated subject matter of biology is developed as a unified synthesis, it can be said to represent a broad-fields approach rather than simply a fusion approach.

Obviously, whatever the rubric might be, the key to curriculum fusion lies in the interrelatedness of the subject matter and its treatment. If the teacher merely treats the material as separate subject matters under the rubric of a new course title, the material is merely laminated and not fused.

Broad Fields

In the broad-fields approach, the attempt is made to develop some degree of synthesis or unity for an entire branch of knowledge. There are a great variety of designations for broad-fields subjects, such as social studies, American studies, general science, physical science, English language arts, fine arts, industrial arts, and others.

The broad-fields approach may also encompass two or more different branches of knowledge. Examples are the natural science course, offered by some colleges as part of the curriculum in general education, which treats the physical and biological sciences within an interdisciplinary framework; and the humanities course in the college

Figure 10–4. Fusion.

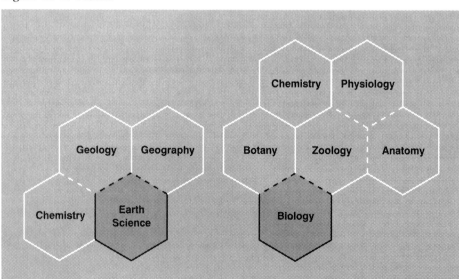

or high school, which is designed to reveal the interrelationships of accomplishments by civilizations throughout history in literature (drama, poetry, novel), the fine arts (music, painting, sculpture, architecture, and related arts), dance, and philosophy.

The subject of general science in the elementary school, middle school, and junior high school is also intended to be a broad-fields synthesis, although it is often treated as a sampling of laminated subject matters from different areas of science. Recognizing the limitations of disciplinary subjects, a 1970 report by an M.I.T. student-faculty commission on undergraduate education called for the inclusion of general science courses in restructuring the curriculum in general education on the ground that there is a "need for subjects which cut across department boundaries to examine broad philosophical issues underlying science or engineering."[60]

Although the recommendations of the 1970 report were not adopted at the time, twenty years later M.I.T. was undertaking significant efforts toward improving the articulation of the curriculum for general education.

Many high schools will use a broad-fields designation, such as social studies, merely as a rubric for a variety of courses ranging from U.S. history to economics, but these are not broad-fields courses. As indicated, the broad-fields approach represents an effort to develop a unity among the various disciplines and subjects that constitute a branch of knowledge.

The first concerted proposal to develop the social studies and history as an articulated broad field was undertaken in 1916 by a committee of the Commission on the Reorganization of Secondary Education. The monumental report of the 1932 Commission on the Social Studies of the American Historical Association and the 1989 report of the National Commission on the Social Studies in the Schools also addressed the continuing problem of developing a coherently articulated field amidst myriad segmental academic specializations or disciplines. In the foreword of the 1989 report, the noted historian Charles Beard is quoted from one of the volumes of the report of the 1932 Commission, which opened with these words: "Such is the unity of all things that the first sentence on instruction in the social studies in the schools strikes into a seamless web too large for any human eye."[61]

The separate subjects or disciplines that comprise the social studies do not reveal the seamless web, despite the fact that no social phenomenon or problem of any great significance can be confined to a single discipline. The continuing tension between knowledge specialism in the discipline-centered university, and the need for knowledge synthesis to meet the function of general education in the secondary school and college remain a crucial problem to this day—a problem that has great ramifications not only for the educational institution, but also for the prospects of a free society.

Although the broad-fields approach is most commonly a synthesis of an entire branch of knowledge, it may even go so far as to synthesize two or more branches of knowledge into a new field. Ecology represents such a synthesis. As shown in Figure 10–5, ecology is a synthesis of knowledge from the biological, physical, and social sciences along with agriculture. To the extent that the study of ecology is organized according to social problems for general education, it is no longer a broad-field subject, but reaches full synthesis as a problem-focused area of the core curriculum.

Figure 10–5. The Broad Field of Ecology.

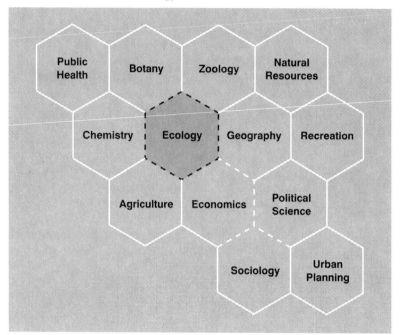

The broad fields are not a survey approach, which tends to be a sampling of disparate elements within a laminated framework. The broad-fields approach not only provides an opportunity to develop the interrelationships of subject matters that otherwise would be fragmented but also avoids the unmanageable multiplicity of disjointed courses that congest the curriculum.

Colleges, as well as elementary and secondary schools, have organized broad-fields studies in an effort to develop a measure of coherence in the curriculum, particularly for purposes of general education. A notable example is the curriculum plan for general education as evolved at the University of Chicago during the 1940s, which consisted of unified courses required of all students in the broad fields of the social sciences, humanities, and natural sciences. Instead of organizing the courses according to the constituent disciplines of a field, the approach was to develop each course as a synthesis of knowledge in the field. Thus, the social sciences were organized as a two-year sequence of Social Science 1, 2, and 3. Social Science 1 was focused on the "great issues" of American democracy; Social Science 2 was organized according to the theme of industrial society, the individual, and culture; and Social Sciences 3 dealt with the value problem of freedom and control. Each course included "great readings," which were drawn not only from classical works but also from contemporary writers. The two-year sequence of humanities consisted of Humanities 1, 2, and 3. Humanities 1 was designed to develop relationships of poetic literature, the visual arts, and music in terms of such topics as art and nature, elements and form, tradition, and contemporary trends. Humanities 2 was focused on interpretation of various modes of literary expression: history, rhetoric, drama and fiction, and philosophy. Humanities 3 included contemporary works in poetry, drama and fiction, art, and music. The natural sciences sequence was divided equally between the physical and biological sciences. Although considerable emphasis was given to the reading of original papers spanning the centuries of scientific investigation, the sequence included laboratory work. Finally, the curriculum in general education was capped by a one-year sequence called Observation, Interpretation, and Integration—designed to provide an integrating schema for the total curriculum in general education.

Although the broad-fields curriculum developed at the University of Chicago may be criticized for being too tradition-oriented in placing great emphasis on literary sources and historical treatment, the broad-fields may be so organized as to focus on contemporary material, such as in the modern physical and biological sciences, or social sciences. And although the curriculum in general education at Chicago has undergone marked changes to this day, it has been described by Daniel Bell as "[t]he most thoroughgoing experiment in general education of any college in the United States."[62]

Many colleges have taken a far more progressive approach to curriculum construction in general education by organizing the subject matter around contemporary problems and investigations, and by providing for considerable laboratory, studio, and field experience. The Chicago plan nevertheless represents one of the most significant efforts in higher education to develop a coherent curriculum in general education through the broad-fields approach. Today, the general education curriculum at Chicago consists of a year-long sequence in each of four broad fields: the humanities, social sciences, physical sciences, and biological sciences—with students being allowed to choose from among several variants in the sequence within each field. Thus, for example, in the social sciences the student may select a sequence based on one of three themes: Freedom and the Political Order, Self, Culture, and Society, or Liberty, Equality, and Fraternity in Contemporary America.

COMBINED FIELDS.   Earlier in this chapter, block-time teaching was discussed as a means of correlating the subject matter from two subject fields such as English and social studies. However, the block-time arrangements may be designed to go beyond correlation by breaking down the subject-matter boundaries into a unified or combined-studies framework. Instead of merely juxtaposing English and social studies in the school schedule and placing these subjects under the jurisdiction of a teacher who correlates certain subject matters from the two distinctive fields, the combined-fields approach may be designed so as to provide for greater synthesis of subject matter from the two broad fields.

The project Science, Technology and Society represents a concerted effort to combine what otherwise might be treated as separate fields. The purpose is to break down or eliminate the subject-matter boundaries so as to reveal the vital interconnections between science and technology and the implications for society.[63] In effect, fields are interrelated that otherwise would be isolated.

Obviously, developing a significant degree of synthesis between two broad fields requires a far greater extent of curriculum reconstitution than correlation. Because secondary-school teachers tend to be prepared as specialists in a given subject or subject field, and because there is a lack of ready-made resource materials designed for a combined-fields approach, the combined-studies teacher is faced with a difficult challenge of treating the fields as an interrelated area of study. Team teaching may be helpful in this regard, but if each teacher sees himself or herself as a specialist who is responsible mainly for instruction in one of the two combined fields, the effort will be little more than correlation.

THE HUMANITIES.   Since the late 1960s most of the larger secondary schools instituted variously designed courses in the humanities. This development signified a belated response to the curriculum imbalance created by the priorities of the Cold War era and was aided by the creation of the National Endowment for the Humanities as a result of the passage of the National Foundation on the Arts and the Humanities Act of 1965.

The concept of humanities presents an enormous challenge in developing curriculum synthesis among studies that encompass so many areas of human achievement and experience. However, the humanities have been so variously conceived and construed that no general patterns have emerged that can be said to represent the humanities in the secondary schools. There is wide disagreement among educators as to what the humanities signify. Some see the humanities more traditionally as "the great human achievements" as exemplified by the masterworks of literature, the arts, and philosophy through the ages (see Figure 10–6). Oddly, proponents of this view have managed to exclude the sciences from the humanities. One only has to think about the invention of printing or the meaning of evolution to realize how profoundly humanity has been affected by science and technology. Moreover, the ranks of the great philosophers of the nineteenth and twentieth centuries are well represented by scientists, for science is a vital branch of modern philosophy.

Although the neglect of science may be traced back to the Renaissance humanists, how can twentieth-century intelligentsia exclude science from the humanistic studies? Somehow they see the humanities and not the sciences as being concerned with values. The separation of the sciences from moral concerns has placed humanity in the impossible condition of living in two unrelated worlds and has kept mankind from utilizing science in waging a full attack on the most acute and deepest problems of life.

Many who call themselves humanists caricature the sciences as coldly cognitive, or as constituting merely a knowledge realm of empirics, whereas aesthetics are assigned to a different knowledge realm, and philosophy to yet another knowledge realm.[64] "A civilization cannot hold its activities apart, or put on science like a suit of clothes—a workday suit which is not good enough for Sunday," wrote Bronowski. "When we discard the test of fact in what a star is, we discard it in what a man is."[65] Not only do many humanists fail to recognize that scientists can find science "paralyzingly beautiful"—the words used by Oppenheimer in describing Einstein's early

Figure 10–6. The Broad Field of Humanities.

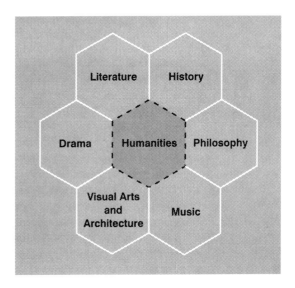

papers[66]—but they also deny the possibilities for the aesthetic appreciation of science by the nonscientist.

Humanists commonly separate the studio arts and performing arts from the humanities. They see the treatment of the arts in the humanities as appreciation—to develop the connoisseur—not as *doing*. This separation is reflected in the creation of two separate federal endowments: the National Endowment for the Humanities and the National Endowment for the Arts. It has also led to the fragmentation of the curriculum, with the humanities acquiring an academic flavor whereas the studio arts, performing arts, and industrial arts are regarded as nonacademic frills. Harold Taylor argued the case for organizing and treating the humanities to attain total curriculum synthesis and not as another set of compartmentalized studies in the fragmented subject curriculum.

> I question the whole idea of the humanities as a special area of the curriculum designed to take care of human values which, presumably, the rest of the curriculum can then safely ignore while it goes on ladling out its generous supply of facts. The humanities are not culture-containers, or value-containers, or courses in the higher things. In one sense there is no such thing as the humanities, unless we are willing to accept the idea that science is not a humanistic discipline and that facts have nothing to do with values. . . .
>
> We may, of course, use the words arts, science, history, philosophy, sociology, and literature to describe certain bodies of knowledge which are grouped together by convention, and we can separate the arts and the humanities from the natural and social sciences simply by naming them as separate items and assembling materials under the proper subject-matter headings. But it is crucial to remember that in doing this scholars and educators are organizing knowledge in order to distribute it and that the names of the subjects do not correspond to the areas of experience out of which they were first created. . . .

> My proposal is, therefore, that we return to the root of the matter, in the quality and variety of experience available to the race, and that we consider education in the humanities not as a problem of developing a separate set of courses in a separate section of the curriculum, but as the creation of a spirit of inquiry and aesthetic interest throughout the whole curriculum and the entire environment of the school or college.[67]

Unfortunately, the trend has been otherwise, and all too often the humanities courses in the secondary schools are imitative of the college courses—centering on the Great Books or serving as surveys of Western civilization, art history, and philosophy. With only a small minority of students enrolled, the humanities in the high school have not been serving a general education function. It is easier to praise the humanities than to design the curriculum so that it is permeated with the humanistic spirit of uniting humanity in the interests of a free society.

As noted, many who regard themselves as humanists portray the humanities as revealing the great human achievements, whereas science is seen as concerned merely with achievements relating to technical knowledge. One might be amused (or appalled) to find that a federally financed study to identify the nation's leading intellectuals proceeded to reject scientists from consideration on the ground that science is "value neutral" and "does not deal with meaning and significance."[68] The profound ignorance reflected in such reasoning is all too widely shared by those who call themselves humanists. From Galileo to Darwin to Einstein, scientific achievement has shaken humanity at its very roots. To reveal how the sciences are inescapably connected with the humanities, and how the reflective methods of scientific thinking can serve to illumine the wider social intelligence, remains one of the most profound goals of general education in a free society.

The Integrated, Problem-Focused Core Curriculum

One of the oldest ideas in biological science is that structure is related to function. In the preceding pages, various structural arrangements for the subject curriculum were discussed. Figure 10–7 presents a synoptic scheme of these alternative constructs for the subject curriculum as well as two other forms of curriculum organization: the integrated core curriculum and the activity curriculum. As shown in Figure 10–7, the separate disciplines are located at the peak of the curriculum cone and represent eclosion of knowledge in the curriculum. At the base of the cone are the integrated core curriculum and the activity curriculum, representing the synthesis of knowledge in the sense that these structural arrangements are designed to completely dissolve the traditional subject boundaries in an effort to relate the curriculum to the life of the learner. In other words, the structure of the curriculum is related to function. Thus, disciplinary knowledge serves a different function than interdisciplinary knowledge and, therefore, has a different structure for the organization and treatment of knowledge. Whereas the disciplinary structure for organized knowledge serves the function of academic specialism, the function of general education requires knowledge synthesis and application to the life of the learner as a citizen of a free society.

Figure 10–7. Structuring the Curriculum.

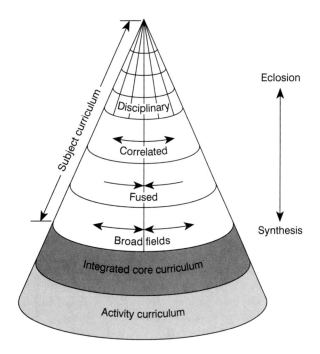

DISTINCTIVE STRUCTURE AND TREATMENT.   In earlier chapters some description was made of the core curriculum organized according to pervading social problems and themes, as developed in the progressive schools before mid-twentieth century. Trump and Vars viewed the integrated problem-focused core as a "quantum leap" beyond various approaches to provide for more unified studies. "Instead of correlating and fusing the separate subjects, core is based directly on problems and concerns of young people as they grow up in contemporary society."[69]

The problem-focused core curriculum might replace all or part of the subject curriculum in general education with the purpose of creating a universe of inquiry, discourse, and understanding among youngsters of different backgrounds and aspirations who, as citizens of a free society, are obliged to share certain common responsibilities and problems. The core is also intended to make the curriculum relevant to the learner's personal life. The core curriculum is organized according to the problems and needs of students that demand personal and social understanding and action. Consequently, the divisions of subject matter that are characteristic of the subject curriculum are dissolved, because the problems are not confined to singular disciplines, or subjects, or subject fields that constitute the separate bodies of organized knowledge.

At the time of the Eight-Year Study, it was not uncommon for some schools having a problem-focused core to offer it in combination with subject centered courses in mathematics and science as part of the general-education requirements on the ground that the problem-focused core did not always provide systematic treatment of these fields. However, this depended on the shared expertise of the core faculty team and the availability of appropriate materials. Interestingly, those schools in the Eight-Year Study that were most advanced in developing the problem-focused core curriculum in place of the subject curriculum for general education found that their graduates produced notably superior academic records in college over the graduates of the other schools in the study, as well as over the graduates who had followed the traditional academic college-preparatory curriculum.[70]

The problem-focused core might be of two approaches or types. In one type the core faculty preplans the problem areas and learning activities, whereas in the other type the problems and activities are developed cooperatively by the students and teacher. The first type may be referred to as the preplanned core, whereas the second type may be called the open core.

THE PREPLANNED PROBLEMS CORE.   Under this type of core, the faculty is responsible for preplanning the content, resources, and activities that are organized around key social problem areas and issues—arranged in an articulated sequence through the various grade levels. These problem areas encompass significant personal-social concerns common to all youngsters. Although the problem areas, resource materials, and learning activities are preplanned by the core faculty, in many core programs of this type the students are provided some latitude in selecting from a number of problem areas and are encouraged to add to, modify, or even eliminate certain problem areas.

It has been noted that the core curriculum "places considerable emphasis upon the deliberate study of the moral content of the culture—especially as this content bears upon the resolution of the social issues that divide the people and thereby prevent effective social action."[71] Problems for investigation may relate to a wide range of concerns, such as racial conflict, ecology, the energy crisis, the population explosion, world food supply and global hunger, censorship in the mass media, propaganda analysis, academic freedom, personal and public health, the aged, consumer economics, war and peace, drugs and narcotics, multicultural conflict and intercultural understanding, community planning, personal and social values, occupations, housing and slums, human rights, and many others.

Figure 10–8 is a schematic representation of how a given problem area, the energy crisis, may be conceptualized in terms of major topics from which specific problems for investigation could be developed. The core class might be organized into committees for intensive investigation of problems in a particular problem area. For example, one student committee might concentrate on public policy concerning population growth, distribution, and control. Another student committee might focus its investigations on the prospects for and problems with alternative energy sources, such as solar radiation, nuclear energy, and so on. Yet another committee may examine the energy problem in terms of its effects on the environment. Each of the various student committees may be responsible for preparing a comprehensive written report on a problem as well as engaging in related projects (such as the building of a model plan or conducting a community survey). Progress reports and tentative findings of each committee may be presented periodically to the entire class for discussion and for eliciting suggestions for further investigation. Panel pre-

Figure 10–8. Scheme for Analysis of "The Energy Crisis."

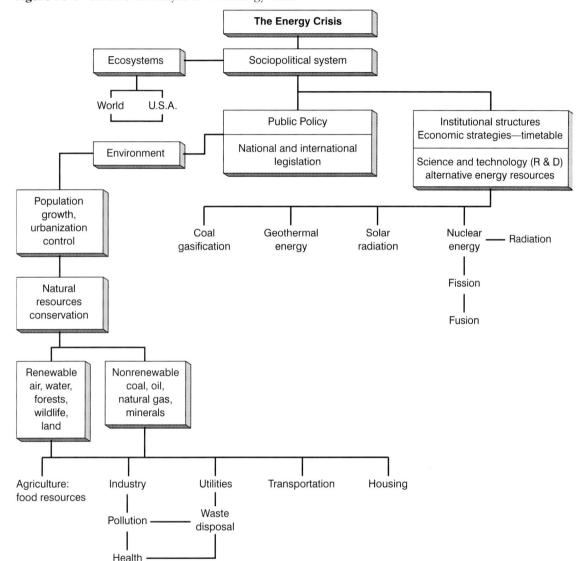

sentations, demonstrations, exhibits, guest resource persons, field studies, and extensive library work are commonly employed.

Because there are no standard textbooks or prepackaged curriculum materials available commercially, the faculty work in teams to develop resource units for each problem area. The resource unit is a comprehensive guide for the core teacher and students, including a statement of objectives and rationale; a description of the problem area and its scope, including related topics; an identification of specific problems and issues for investigation, including key concepts, skills, and generalizations;

suggested learning activities and projects; a description of teaching-learning resources and materials, including bibliographical sources; and guidelines for evaluation activities.

Because the problem areas transcend the traditional subject divisions and encompass a wide range of pupil activities, extensive library resources are required and the core teacher must be able to draw on community resources. Team-teaching arrangements enable the core faculty to share their particular talents and expertise. Before discussing other characteristics common to the core curriculum, a brief discussion of the second type of core, the open core, is presented.

THE OPEN CORE.   The second type of core is based on teacher-pupil planned activities without a formal structure of preplanned problems and learning activities. In other words, there is no preplanned curriculum, and the students and their teacher cooperatively formulate the problem areas to be studied during the school year. This allows the pupils to have considerable freedom and responsibility for curriculum determination. Nevertheless, the typical practice is to have the youngsters assess the proposed problems in terms of a number of criteria, such as the following: Is the problem a significant one for all pupils? Are there sufficient resource materials and data available for the intelligent investigation of the problem? Is the problem one that can be treated effectively in terms of the capabilities of the pupils and the time available during the term or year? What priority should be given to this problem in relation to other problems in terms of time allocation during the school year?

Because the rationale of the open core is to make the curriculum highly relevant to the lives of the pupils, the problems are almost completely centered on the concerns of adolescents rather than on the demands of adult society. Possible gaps in content, scope, and sequence of studies are willingly sacrificed in an effort to make the curriculum relevant to pupil problems, needs, and interests. Obviously, a great deal of teacher-pupil planning is required and the teacher must be highly resourceful. The absence of a predetermined curriculum requires a very rich collection of library and other resource materials geared to pupil interests. Relatively few schools employ the open-core approach.

COMMON CHARACTERISTICS OF THE PROBLEM-FOCUSED CORE CURRICULUM.   Both types of core are focused on general education and, in the secondary school, the core may exist alongside specialized and special-interest and exploratory studies that are organized according to disciplines and traditional subject lines.

Because the core problems are those deemed relevant to the values and ideals of a democratic society, efforts are made to employ democratic methods and procedures in the classroom. It has been pointed out that it is a chief function of the core curriculum "that the democratic value system is not only taught as a standard of judgment but that it is also deliberately criticized and reconstructed so as to bring it into line with the social realities of today."[72] Thus, not only are concerted efforts made to foster pupil respect for the opinions of others, and to develop a commitment to the testing of one's values and ideas according to reflective thinking, but the societal shortcomings are examined with a view toward their constructive resolution.

The unifying method is that of problem solving through reflective thinking. During the progressive era, many core programs followed modified versions of Dewey's problem method in guiding students in their investigations and to foster open-minded approaches to problems and issues. Although the core curriculum has many attributes of a workshop approach, it is far more rigorous in the sense that it is committed to problem solving through reflective thinking.

In view of the general education rationale of the core curriculum and its focus on democratic values and ideals, the core class is deliberately grouped heterogeneously. Because the problems being investigated are comprehensive and deemed to be of universal significance, and because the pupils are encouraged to help one another, it is believed that a wide range of ability levels can be accommodated in the core class.

In replacing all or most of the conventional subjects in general education, the core is scheduled as a block of time encompassing at least two class periods that, in turn, are combined with the homeroom. The larger block of time enables the pupils to engage in intensive projects including community field work. It also allows the core teacher to spend more time with fewer pupils. In this regard, the teacher is expected to serve in a guidance capacity. Obviously, both types of core place great emphasis on cooperative teacher-pupil planning.

ASSESSMENT OF THE CORE CURRICULUM.   In earlier chapters the success of the core curriculum as found in many of the schools involved in the Eight-Year Study was discussed. Although block-time programs are commonly found in middle schools and junior high schools today, only a small fraction of these programs is based on the core rationale as described in the preceding pages.

The core idea never gained the widespread acceptance that was expected of it by progressive educators. The implementation of core programs in the secondary school was sufficient to justify several national surveys on the structure and practices pertaining to the core curriculum, conducted by the U.S. Office of Education from 1949 through the 1950s.[73] In these surveys, the block-time, problem-focused core was still visible, especially in junior high schools. In a Maryland school district, for example, a problem-focused core was developed for grades seven through twelve that included such problem areas as the environment, consumerism, intercultural relations, technology, living in one world, health and safety, and others.

One of the most widely adopted practices in the high school over many decades was to offer a problems of democracy course in the senior year, required of all students. Growing out of the call for linking the curriculum to the democratic prospect, as explicated by the Commission on the Reorganization of Secondary Education in its report of 1918, the problems of democracy course was given renewed impetus by James B. Conant in his 1959 report on the American high school, issued at the height of the Cold War and space race.[74] Nevertheless, this course, taken by itself, was clearly insufficient to meet the democratizing function of general education. In the face of the great national thrust toward discipline-centered curriculum projects, giving priority to the sciences and mathematics, the problems of democracy course was unable to hold its once prominent place in the school curriculum.

The problem-focused core curriculum, indeed general education as a movement, was countered if not virtually eclipsed by the hysteria of the Cold War and space race of the 1950s and 1960s, the back-to-basics retrenchment of the 1970s and 1980s, and the multitude of literacies of the early 1990s coupled with the national education goals expressed in *America 2000* and *Goals 2000.* As in the era of the Cold War and space race, the national education goals for the year 2000 give priority to the sciences and mathematics in the school curriculum to meet nationalistic interests (this time, for technoindustrial mobilization in response to the alleged American lag in the competition for global industrial markets). Not only have recent studies provided extensive evidence that the schools have been falsely blamed for a host of alleged failures, but also that the educational priorities have been misplaced.[75] Moreover, when nationalistic interests drive the curriculum, the consequence not only is curricular imbalance, but also the approach taken is specialized and discipline-centered as opposed to an integrated curriculum for general education.

Over the years, there have been many other countervailing influences. Teachers are products of departmentalized discipline-centered curricula in the colleges and universities, and so they tend to be oriented toward the subject curriculum. Secondary-school faculties tend to imitate the colleges in their departmentalized structure. Indeed, the colleges have allowed their own curricula in general education to erode in favor of specialism and special-interest studies.

Textbooks and other curriculum materials are geared to the subject curriculum, and this serves a great convenience for teachers. Without extensive resource materials the core class is unable to attack problems in any great breadth and depth of treatment. The core curriculum requires enormous teacher resourcefulness because pupils are given great latitude and considerable responsibility in their learning activities. The core curriculum requires teachers to have considerable breadth and depth of background in general education. Team-teaching arrangements are not always provided to enable core teachers to share their special capabilities.

Another most serious problem was the unrealistic expectation that teachers should develop their own curriculum materials under conditions where resources are lacking. Recent estimates by publishers indicate that instructional materials account for approximately 1.25 percent of the school budget. The core approach requires a far greater investment in instructional materials than does the subject curriculum. Core classes rarely have been provided with the needed resources.

The core idea was also severely undermined during the era of the Cold War and McCarthyism. The vitality of the core curriculum stems from its commitment to open-minded inquiry into pervading personal-social problems and issues. During that era, many teachers, lacking administrative and community support, were reluctant to allow their pupils to broach highly controversial sociopolitical problems and issues. Even today the censorship of instructional materials is widespread. The problem is so great that the American Library Association has established an Intellectual Freedom Committee that publishes a bimonthly newsletter giving a dateline accounting of incidents of school censorship.

Without freedom to investigate controversial questions of personal-social significance, the core curriculum is denied its raison d'être. The failure of the piecemeal responses to student demands for curriculum relevance seems to call for a new curriculum synthesis in general education. Whether the problem-focused core curriculum will be reinvented in some new form remains to be seen.

Nevertheless, the idea of the problem-focused or thematically integrated core curriculum continues to live along with the idea and practice of general education in the secondary school and college.[76] From time to time, one finds the problem-focused core being rediscovered. As treated in Chapter 11, from the 1980s to the present, a host of reports on the secondary school and college have called for renewed attention to the idea and practice of general education. Against all odds, the need for an integrated curriculum in general education remains one of the most persistent problems in American education, and it will always be of concern as long as popular education for a free society remains paramount in ideals and actions.

PERSISTENT LIFE SITUATIONS. One of the most interesting efforts in the curriculum field around mid-twentieth century was a curriculum proposal built on persistent life situations. Developed by Florence Stratemeyer and her associates at Teachers College, the proposal was based on a principle from research on learning transfer: School learning is more likely to be carried over into life outside of school if the school studies are directed at life situations. The proposal also took account of the nature of the developing learner by identifying life situations for study from early childhood through adolescence and into adulthood. Stratemeyer and her associates stressed the importance for teachers to differentiate between superficial situations and significant ones, and they proceeded to formulate lists of persistent life situations for possible study under such categories as intellectual power, health, intergroup relations, natural phenomena, technological resources, aesthetic expression and appreciation, and so on. Nevertheless, they did not offer a preplanned curriculum design on the ground "that the intrinsic motivation provided by specific concerns of individuals and groups will, in the long run, result in a more effective selection of learnings than will any preplanned structure."[77]

One of the chief difficulties with the proposal was that persistent life situations are so numerous that one can easily lose sight of the integrative elements for curriculum design. In contrast, preplanned molar problems or themes, as in the problem-focused or thematic core curriculum, lend themselves quite naturally to curriculum integration. For example, the problem of maintaining and protecting personal and public health, under conditions of ecological assault, subsumes any number of persistent life situations. Yet the situations are addressed holistically in relation to the integrative molar problem or theme. Moreover, the problem-focused core approach was clearly more provocative, as attested by the extent to which it came under the direct assault of the censors during an era of ordeal for academic freedom.

The Activity Curriculum and the Open Classroom

The activity curriculum was discussed in some detail in Part I. The activity curriculum was developed early in this century in progressive elementary schools in an attempt to treat learning as an active process that is consonant with the child's propensities to shape materials, to share experiences, to find things out, and to express himself or herself artistically. The term *experience curriculum* came to be used synonymously with the activity curriculum. Traditional subject boundaries were discarded, and the curriculum was centered largely on areas of child interest, with the skills in the fundamental processes being developed from the larger areas of activity, rather than from a separate focus on the three R's.

The impetus for the activity curriculum grew out of the new knowledge concerning child growth and development in recognition that children require active engagement and socialization for effective learning. The curriculum of the Dewey Laboratory School, for example, was based largely on four impulses: (1) the social impulse, (2) the constructive impulse, (3) the impulse to investigate and experiment, and (4) the expressive or artistic impulse.[78] (Today, these might better be termed *motives/potentials* rather than *impulses*.) The curriculum was powerfully grounded in a democratic social rationale through the study of occupations revealing human interdependence and social progress. The basics were treated as fundamental processes or tool studies for the ideational and hands-on work of the children.

The activity curriculum was widely developed in progressive schools at the primary level during the first three decades of the twentieth century, but in many cases, unlike the curriculum in the Dewey School, the activity curriculum was not grounded in a deliberate social rationale. Although attention was given to the impulses or motives/potentials cited previously, the activities often were treated as ends in themselves—as though an active classroom, in and of itself, is indicative of purposeful learning.

The failure to recognize the shortcomings of such a romanticist approach found radical educators of the late 1960s and early 1970s promoting open schools and open classrooms in which children would be free to engage in learning activities based on their expressed interests, thereby obviating the need for an organized curriculum. In an era of radical student activism and protest on college campuses, the time seemed ripe for radical-romanticist reform down to the elementary school. Alternative elementary schools were established as a foray of books on radical school reform made the best-seller lists. For example, a leading proponent of the open classroom described it as a setting to enable pupils "to make choices and pursue what interests them" and that, for the teacher, "the things that work best for him are the unplanned ones, the ones that arise spontaneously because of a student's suggestion or a sudden perception."[79] He went on to point out that the open classroom is in a constant state of flux and takes its direction according to what happens to be engaging the attention of the pupils and their teachers at the moment. "It is hard to distinguish between apparent chaos and creative disorder," wrote Kohl.[80]

Holt, too, presented the open classroom as an environment in which pupil activities derive from their interests, and he maintained that the task of the teacher is to make the pupil feel "that whatever he is interested in is OK, a perfectly good place to look at and begin to explore the world, as good as any other, indeed better than any other."[81] According to Holt, curriculum planning is a kind of adult intervention on the learner and "the more we intervene in children's lives, however intelligently, kindly, or imaginatively, the less time we leave them to find and develop their own ways to meet their true needs. The more we try to teach them, the less they can teach us."[82]

It is ironic that the romantic conception of the learner and the notion of centering all studies around areas of child interest and activity, promoted by the romantic naturalists of an earlier era, was to be revivified in the 1960s and 1970s following a period of disciplinary curriculum reforms and the pursuit of academic excellence. It is equally ironic that the open classroom, as in the case of the activity curriculum of yesteryear, came to be so variously interpreted. For example, many American proponents of the open classroom, who sought to model the elementary schools after the open classroom of the English primary school, appeared to have interpreted the English concept of integrated curriculum and integrated day as "a school day which offers a great smorgasbord of creative, artistic, and physical activities."[83] In promoting such a conception, they neglected to reveal how the disparate activities are integrated. Their prescriptions for open classrooms might more accurately be termed the *undifferentiated* or *free day.*

As we have noted, many American schools proceeded to adopt the open classroom as a label for a managerial arrangement designed to provide for individualized, differentiated, and specialized instruction—with youngsters in one corner of the room working on programmed workbooks in math skills, youngsters in another corner working on reading skills, and so on. After visiting several such schools, an educator who had accompanied the authors remarked, "[t]he open classroom looked to me like a departmentalized classroom."

The open classroom was implemented in many different ways—ranging from almost free activity at one extreme, to very highly structured managerial efficiency arrangements at the other extreme. At the same time, the possibilities for curriculum integration and democratic social direction were largely neglected.

The original design for the open classroom as the *integrated day* in which children are engaged in learning activities that are interrelated, rather than being segmented so as to fit within the traditional subject boundaries, gave recognition to the nature of the young child at the preschool and primary levels. Unfortunately, the national mania for standardized achievement testing during the 1980s and 1990s served to drive the curriculum, even at the earliest levels of schooling, back to the fundamental skill subjects. In many areas parents found themselves competing for places for their children in special-interest elementary schools that had been heralded originally as alternative schools or "schools of choice."

At the same time it was becoming increasingly clear that child welfare remained one of the most critical needs of the nation. Any concerted effort in this direction would require corresponding attention to the nature of the child and the school as a rich and harmonious learning environment. In the face of the fragmentation and special interests that mark social divisions and conflicts, it appeared that the time was ripe for a renewed quest for a curriculum in harmony with the nature of the learner and with our highest social ideals as a free society.

PERSPECTIVE

A main current of American educational thought at mid-twentieth century was that through general education a unity out of diversity could be created. The expansion of studies to accommodate the growing specialization of knowledge portended a growing fragmentation in education and society. The task of general education was not conceived in opposition to the imminent force of specialization but rather as a means of providing for a common universe of discourse, understanding, and competence among the diverse elements of a free society. The notion of liberal education had come to be associated historically with education for a privileged class, whereas general education was to be the province of all citizens of a free society. Moreover, where liberal education was focused primarily on the human heritage, general education was conceived as an outlook on knowledge encompassing not only the human heritage but also the changing conditions and demands of life in a modern democratic society.

General education, then, was conceived to provide each rising generation with the social power and insight necessary for intelligently attacking the problems of a common humanity. Where specialized knowledge and life callings were separating people from one another, general education was aimed at revealing humanity's interdependence in a modern democracy. The outlook on knowledge embraced by general education required new ways of organizing the curriculum. In the face of the growing specialization and fragmentation of knowledge, this was no mean task.

Notable efforts were made in school and college during the twentieth century to devise new curriculum structures so as to provide for a greater measure of relationship and synthesis among areas of knowledge. The traditional subject curriculum was reorganized variously in terms of (1) disciplinarity, (2) correlation, (3) fusion, and (4) broad fields. Whereas the disciplinary approach rejected the traditional conception of subject matter as something given or fixed, it nevertheless conceived of knowledge as belonging to and developing from the specialized domains of university scholarship. This specialized outlook on knowledge was not well suited to the task of general education.

Other modes of organizing knowledge (correlation, fusion, and broad fields) were designed to build greater relationships between and among the organized studies within the framework of the subject curriculum. But the subject curriculum, nevertheless, called for a logical organization of studies with limited relevance to the life problems and life experience of the learner. In response to this need, progressive educators sought a new curriculum synthesis. The result was the integrated problem-focused core curriculum as an alternative to the traditional subject curriculum. In the integrated problem-focused core approach, subject-matter boundaries were largely dissolved as the curriculum was organized according to pervading problems of personal and social significance. Unlike the disciplinary approach, which treated each knowledge domain as following a distinct mode of inquiry, the problem-focused core approach was based on the premise that inquiry into pervading problems of personal-social significance requires not only a unity of knowledge but also a unified mode of inquiry or method of intelligence shared by all enlightened citizens of a free society. Experimentalist educators not only saw the need for a more unified structure for the curriculum, but they also saw the method of intelligence as the unifying method for general education. The growing specialization of knowledge, the increasing fragmentation of society, the inertia of education tradition, the dearth of appropriate curriculum materials, and the opposition to the treatment of controversial problems—all served to prevent this core idea from gaining general acceptance.

During the late 1960s, in response to the rising demands to relate the curriculum to significant societal problems, some efforts were made in the secondary school and university to provide for interdisciplinary and problem-focused studies. However, the main thrust of these efforts was to meet the special interests of diverse groups of students by providing for a greater variety of elective options. Instead of seeking a curriculum synthesis for purposes of general education, the response was to make ad hoc modifications of the curriculum in accordance with special demands. Nevertheless, the regenerated interest in interdisciplinary studies indicated that the need for curriculum coherence and synthesis could not be ignored in the long run. During the early 1970s, the activity curriculum re-emerged in the form of the open classroom or informal classroom. At the secondary and college levels, efforts were made to provide academic credit for a variety of community experiences. Nevertheless, these efforts were not characterized by a corresponding attempt to develop curriculum coherence and to foster the democratic ideal through general education. Buffeted and eroded by the centripetal and diverse forces of specialism and special interests, general education seemed all but forgotten in educational theory and practice.

The great democratizing vision through general education, as shared by educators at midcentury, appeared to have faded into a weak shadow in the 1970s. The intervening years of crisis mentality had taken their toll. Some of the efforts toward educational improvement during the 1980s and early 1990s reflected a revitalized concern for this larger vision of American education, particularly at the college level. However, the schools were mired in a proliferation of separate literacies—mathematical, scientific, technological, cultural, political, economic, artistic, and so on. The various professional associations were directing their efforts at promoting curriculum reform within their own literacy domain. However, unlike the discipline-centered curriculum reforms that were geared to knowledge specialization, purity and abstraction, the literacies were directed at the kinds of knowledge-competencies that were deemed fundamental to all who complete a high school education. Some promising programs and proposals, such as Project 2061 of the American Association for the Advancement of Science, embraced an interdisciplinary rationale that encompassed a problems approach in many respects, although the term *literacy* prevailed. Whereas the idea and practice of general education conveyed a search and commitment for curriculum unity in an age of specialism, the term *literacy* conveyed a kind of elemental level of competence in a multitude of separate categories of the curriculum.

The problem of a divided curriculum and a divided society does not augur well for American democracy. In order to draw strength from diversity, a shared democratic vision and mission are necessary, and this must be reflected in the structure and function of the curriculum.

At times, educators may avoid questions concerning the function of education in helping create the good person leading the good life in the good society, but in the long run these questions cannot be denied. The great divisions and conflicts in modern society have impelled educators once again to seek ways of making the curriculum relevant to life problems. In the crowning decade of the twentieth century, the idea and practice of general education was being rediscovered in colleges and universities. Notable efforts were being made to develop a sense of unity and coherence in the curriculum. In sharp contrast, curriculum change at the elementary and secondary levels appeared to be dominated by the traditional subject divisions and competency testing. Judging by the wider course of events, however, the idea and practice of general education at all levels could not be permanently denied.

PROBLEMS FOR STUDY AND DISCUSSION

1. In responding to the demand for curriculum relevance during the 1960s, many secondary schools and colleges liberalized the elective options and added a host of new elective courses on special contemporary topics. This approach, which remains in practice to this day, has been called the warehouse or cafeteria model of curriculum building. Some educators have called this the junkyard model, not so much in disparagement but in reference to the fact that the learner is left to choose whatever he can find from among a diverse collection of scraps. What is your assessment of this model? Most high schools and colleges settled on distribution requirements to ensure that students pursue a range of studies from different subject fields for purposes of general education. What limitations and problems tend to accrue to this approach?

2. Mid-twentieth century was marked by a great outpouring of books and journal articles on general education. It was also a period of enormous activity in curriculum building for general education. How do you account for the lack of attention given to general education during the 1960s and 1970s?

3. How would you describe the situation today? Examine the student handbooks and curriculum guides of several high schools, middle schools, and junior high schools. What evidence do you find of any concerted attention being given to general education? In the event that you should find such evidence lacking, how do you account for this?

4. Compare the catalogues of the College of the University of Chicago with that of the University of Wisconsin–Green Bay with respect to the contrasting approaches to general education. How do these approaches compare with the general education program as offered by your own college? Which approach, if any, do you prefer? Explain.

5. In view of the following statement by Dewey, written in 1902, what measures do you recommend for building the needed "harmony" in the curriculum?

> The problem of the multiplication of studies and the consequent congestion of the curriculum, and the conflict of various studies for a recognized place in the curriculum; the fact that one cannot get in without crowding something else out; the effort to arrange a compromise in various courses of study by throwing the entire burden of election upon the student so that he shall make his own course of study—this problem is only a reflex of the lack of unity in social activities themselves, and the necessity of reaching more harmony in our scheme of life. . . .
>
> The body of knowledge is indeed one; it is a spiritual organism. To attempt to chop off a member here and amputate an organ there is the veriest impossibility. The problem is not one of elimination, but of organization; of simplification not through denial and rejection, but through harmony. [John Dewey, *The Educational Situation* (Chicago: University of Chicago Press, 1902), pp. 85–86, 89.]

6. A sociologist identified "the most prestigious contemporary American intellectuals" according to the number of articles authored by individuals, along with the number of times their books were reviewed, in twenty-two selected "intellectual" journals. All of these journals were concerned with literary and social affairs, whereas none were focused on scientific affairs in the social milieu— such as *Scientific American* and *Bulletin of the Atomic Scientists.* Of the seventy "elite intellectuals" so identified, not a single one was a biologist, physicist, mathematician, or engineer. [Charles Kadushin, "Who Are the Elite Intellectuals?" *The Public Interest* (Fall 1972), pp. 109–125.]

Do the methods and procedures in this study reflect a "two-cultures" bias as noted by John Dewey and C. P. Snow? Explain. What are the implications of the split between the two cultures for the school curriculum and society?

7. In examining the prospects for general education in the university, an educator refers to the debate concerning what is "liberal" and what is "useful" as "one of the oldest issues in education." [National Society for the Study of Education, *Cultural Literacy and the Idea of General Education* (Chicago: University of Chicago Press, 1988), p. 214.] Reflecting on this time-worn dualism, Dewey held that it serves to "infect the education called liberal with illiberality." [John Dewey, *Democracy and Education* (New York: Macmillan, 1916), p. 226.] The dualism seems to infer that what is liberal must then be useless.

How does this dualism relate to the curriculum divide between academic and vocational studies, between academic studies and the practical arts, between academic studies and the studio arts, between the humanities and the sciences? What are the implications, as you see them, for the curriculum and the learner?

8. The forces for curricular retrenchment through the back-to-basics movement of the late 1970s went to such an extreme that even the Council for Basic Education, acknowledging that the council's original canon did not include the arts as basic subjects, issued a bulletin defending the role of the arts in basic education. [Jacques Barzun and Robert J. Saunders, *Art in Basic Education* (Washington, DC: Council for Basic Education, 1979).] How do you account for such belated recognition of the arts by the council? Are the arts recognized as integral to basic or general education in your school? Explain.

9. How do you account for persistent rediscovery of the idea and practice of general education in the secondary school and college throughout the twentieth century? What forces have worked against curriculum synthesis for general education in the secondary school and college? Why is it that distribution-elective course requirements inevitably fail to meet the function of general education as a common universe of discourse, understanding, and competence required for effective living in a free society?

10. There is a biological principle that structure determines function, and an architectural principle that form follows function. How does this relate to the structure and function of the curriculum?

NOTES

1. F. Champion Ward et al., *The Idea and Practice of General Education* (Chicago: University of Chicago Press, 1950), p. v.

2. *The New York Times* (February 26, 1978), p. 1.

3. Susan Schiefelbein, "Confusion at Harvard: What Makes an 'Educated Man'?" *Saturday Review,* 5 (April 1, 1978), p. 12.

4. James B. Conant, *Education in a Divided World* (Cambridge, MA: Harvard University Press, 1949), pp. 74–75.

5. Harvard Committee on General Education, *General Education in a Free Society* (Cambridge, MA: Harvard University Press, 1945), p. 51.

6. Daniel Bell, *The Reforming of General Education* (New York: Doubleday/Anchor, 1968), p. 181.

7. Arthur Bestor, *The Restoration of Learning* (New York: Alfred A. Knopf, 1955); William J. Bennett, *James Madison High School* (Washington, DC: U.S. Department of Education, 1987).

8. John W. Gardner, in James B. Conant, *The American High School Today* (New York: McGraw-Hill, 1959), p. ix.

9. Commission on the Reorganization of Secondary Education, *Cardinal Principles of Secondary Education* (Washington, DC: U.S. Bureau of Education, 1918), p. 26.

10. H. G. Rickover, *American Education—A National Failure* (New York: Dutton, 1963), p. 89.

11. Paul Goodman, *Compulsory Mis-education* (New York: Horizon, 1964), pp. 39, 88; Edgar Z. Friedenberg, *Coming of Age in America* (New York: Vintage, 1967), pp. 250–251, 257.

12. Jerome S. Bruner, *The Process of Education* (Cambridge, MA: Harvard University Press, 1960), p. 71.

13. James B. Conant, "The Comprehensive High School," in Alvin C. Eurich (ed.), *High School 1980* (New York: Pitman, 1970), pp. 73, 80.

14. James B. Conant, *My Several Lives* (New York: Harper, 1970), p. 613.

15. Theodore R. Sizer, *Horace's Compromise* (Boston: Houghton Mifflin, 1984); Ernest L. Boyer, *High School* (New York: Harper, 1983); John I. Goodlad, *A Place Called School* (New York: McGraw-Hill, 1984); Arthur G. Powell, Eleanor Farrar, and David K. Cohen, *The Shopping Mall High School* (Boston: Houghton Mifflin, 1985); U.S. Department of Education, *America 2000* (Washington, DC: Author, 1991).

16. Jeannie Oakes, *Keeping Track* (New Haven, CT: Yale University Press, 1985).

17. Commission on the Reorganization of Secondary Education, *Cardinal Principals of Secondary Education* (Washington, DC: U.S. Bureau of Education, 1918).

18. Boyer, op. cit., pp. 245–246.

19. Fred N. Newmann, "High School Choice," National Center on Effective Secondary Schools *Newsletter,* 3 (Fall 1988), p. 1.

20. Charles E. Silberman, *Crisis in the Classroom* (New York: Random House, 1970), p. 324.

21. See Grace S. Wright, *Block-Time Classes and the Core Program in the Junior High School* (Washington, DC: U.S. Office of Education, 1962).

22. Daniel Tanner and Laurel Tanner, *Supervision in Education* (New York: Macmillan, 1987), pp. 121–163, 190, 505.

23. See Daniel G. Armstrong, "Team Teaching and Academic Achievement," *Review of Educational Research,* 47 (Winter 1977), pp. 75, 78; Herbert J. Klausmeier, "IGE in Elementary & Middle Schools," *Educational Leadership,* 34 (February 1977), pp. 330–341.

24. Benjamin S. Bloom, *Human Characteristics and School Learning* (New York: McGraw-Hill, 1976), pp. 4–5.

25. *America 2000,* op. cit., p. 53.

26. Ibid., pp. 14, 31.

27. James B. Conant, *My Several Lives,* op cit., p. 464.

28. *The New York Times* (October 12, 1993), B3.

29. See, for example, William H. Kilpatrick and William Van Til (eds.), *Intercultural Attitudes in the Making.* Ninth Yearbook of the John Dewey Society (New York: Harper, 1947).

30. John Dewey, *The School and Society* (Chicago: University of Chicago Press, 1990), p. 7. (Originally published 1899.)

31. Henry Levin, *Accelerated Schools: A New Strategy for At-Risk Students* (Palo Alto, CA: Accelerated Schools Project, Stanford University, 1990).

32. See Sizer, op. cit., pp. 146–148; Goodlad, op. cit., p. 222; Robert W. Young, *Relationship between Business and Industrial Courses in High School with Academic Achievement in College,* unpublished doctoral dissertation. (Ann Arbor: University of Michigan, 1966); Scott Whitener, *Patterns of High School Studies and College Achievement,* unpublished doctoral dissertation (New Brunswick, NJ: Rutgers University, 1974).

33. Albert Einstein, *The World as I See It* (New York: Covici-Friede, 1934), pp. 20–21.

34. John Dewey, *Human Nature and Conduct* (New York: Holt, 1922), pp. 11–13.

35. Daniel Tanner, "Knowledge Divided against Itself," *Bulletin of the Atomic Scientists,* 39 (March 1983), pp. 34–38.

36. John Dewey, *Freedom and Culture* (New York: Putnam, 1939), p. 154.

37. C. P. Snow, *The Two Cultures and the Scientific Revolution* (New York: Cambridge University Press, 1959), p. 19.

38. Ibid., pp. 23–29.
39. Ibid., pp. 33–34.
40. Ibid., pp. 53–54.
41. Harvard Committee, op. cit., pp. 32–33.
42. Ibid., p. 53.
43. John Dewey, *Experience and Education* (New York: Macmillan, 1938), p. 97.
44. Bruner, op. cit., p. 52.
45. Ibid., p. 14.
46. Ibid., p. 31.
47. Joseph J. Schwab, *College Curriculum and Student Protest* (Chicago: University of Chicago Press, 1969), p. 197.
48. See Daniel Tanner, *Secondary Education: Theory and Development* (New York: Macmillan, 1971); Morris Kline, *Why Johnny Can't Add: The Failure of the New Math* (New York: St. Martin's Press, 1973).
49. Emily Ann Barnes and Bess M. Young, *Children and Architecture* (New York: Teachers College Press, 1932), pp. 31–40.
50. Hilda Taba, *Curriculum Development: Theory and Practice* (New York: Harcourt, 1962), pp. 347–379.
51. Ibid., pp. 214–215.
52. Lawrence Senesh, "Orchestration of Social Sciences in the Curriculum," in Irving Morrisett and W. Williams Stevens, Jr. (eds.), *Social Science in the Schools* (New York: Holt, 1971), p. 126.
53. Mortimer J. Appley and Winifred B. Maher, *Social and Behavioral Sciences,* Project 2061 (Washington, DC: American Association for the Advancement of Science, 1989), p. xi.
54. Alfred North Whitehead, *Essays in Science and Philosophy* (New York: Philosophical Library, 1947), p. 176.
55. Michael Scriven, "The Structure of the Social Studies," in G. W. Ford and Lawrence A. Pugno (eds.), *The Structure of Knowledge and the Curriculum* (Chicago: Rand McNally, 1964), p. 97.
56. Virgil Thomson, in Ruth M. Weeks (ed.), *A Correlated Curriculum,* Report of the National Council of Teachers of English (New York: Appleton, 1938), p. 310.
57. Whitehead, op. cit., pp. 183–184.
58. Edward O. Wilson, *Sociobiology: The New Synthesis* (Cambridge, MA: Harvard University Press, 1975); *The Diversity of Life* (New York: W. W. Norton, 1993).
59. National Educational Association, *Report of the Committee of Ten on Secondary School Studies* (New York: American Book, 1894), pp. 41, 46–47.
60. Commission on M.I.T. Education, *Creative Renewal in a Time of Crisis* (Cambridge, MA: M.I.T. Press, 1970), p. 23.
61. Charles A. Beard, *A Charter for the Social Studies in the Schools* (New York: Scribner's, 1932), p. 1. See also Commission on the Reorganization of Secondary Education, op. cit., and National Commission on Social Studies in the Schools, *Charting a Course: Social Studies for the 21st Century* (Washington, DC: Author, 1989).
62. Bell, op. cit., p. 26.
63. William G. Wraga and Peter S. Hlebowitsh (eds.), "Science, Technology, and the Social Studies," special section, *Social Education,* 54 (April/May 1990), pp. 189–214; and in the same issue, Daniel Tanner, "The Curriculum Frontier," pp. 195–197.
64. Maxine Greene, *Teacher as Stranger* (Belmont, CA: Wadsworth, 1973); Philip H. Phenix, *Realms of Meaning* (New York: McGraw-Hill, 1964), p. 28.
65. J. Bronowski, *Science and Human Values* (New York: Harper, 1956), pp. 55, 59.
66. J. Robert Oppenheimer, in *Science and Synthesis* (New York: Springer-Verlag, 1971), p. 11.
67. Harold E. Taylor (ed.), *The Humanities in the Schools* (New York: Citation, 1968), pp. 21, 23, 25.
68. Charles Kadushin, *The American Intellectual Elite* (Boston: Little, Brown, 1974), pp. 6–7.
69. J. Lloyd Trump and Gordon F. Vars, "How Should Learning Be Organized?" Chapter 9 in National Society for the Study of Education, *Issues in Secondary Education,* Seventy-fifth Yearbook, Part II (Chicago: University of Chicago Press, 1976), p. 223.
70. Wilford M. Aikin, *The Story of the Eight-Year Study* (New York: Harper, 1942).
71. B. Othanel Smith, William O. Stanley, and J. Harlan Shores, *Fundamentals of Curriculum Development,* rev. ed. (New York: Harcourt, 1957), p. 315.
72. Ibid.

73. See the following surveys by Grace S. Wright, published by the U.S. Office of Education: *Core Curriculum in Public High Schools* (1950), pp. 19–20; *Core Curriculum Development: Problems and Practices* (1952); *Block-Time Classes and the Core Program in the Junior High School* (1958, 1962); *The Core Program: Unpublished Research, 1956–1962* (1963).

74. James B. Conant, *The American High School Today* (New York: McGraw-Hill, 1959), pp. 75–76.

75. Charles C. Carson, Robert M. Huelskamp, and Thomas D. Woodall, "Perspectives on Education in America," Report of the Sandia National Laboratories, *Journal of Educational Research,* 86 (April 1992); Daniel Tanner, "A Nation Truly at Risk," *Phi Delta Kappan,* 75 (December, 1993), pp. 288–297.

76. Steven S. Means, "The Interrelated Curriculum," Chapter 2 in John M. Jenkins and Daniel Tanner (eds.), *Interdisciplinary Curriculum* (Reston, VA: National Association of Secondary School Principals, 1992).

77. Florence B. Stratemeyer, Hamden L. Forkner, Margaret G. Mekim, and A. Harry Passow, *Developing a Curriculum for Modern Living* (New York: Teachers College Press, 1957), p. 337.

78. Katherine Camp Mayhew and Anna Camp Edwards, *The Dewey School* (New York: Atherton, 1936), pp. 40–41.

79. Herbert R. Kohl, *The Open Classroom* (New York: Random, 1969), pp. 20, 40.

80. Ibid., p. 39.

81. John Holt, *Freedom and Beyond* (New York: Dutton, 1972), p. 91.

82. Ibid., p. 66.

83. Institute for Development of Educational Activities, *The British Infant School* (Melbourne, FL: Author, 1969), p. 9.

SELECTED REFERENCES

Aikin, Wilford M. *The Story of the Eight-Year Study.* New York: Harper, 1942.

Alberty, Harold B., and Alberty, Elsie J. *Reorganizing the High School Curriculum,* 3rd ed. New York: Macmillan, 1962.

American Association for the Advancement of Science. *Science for All Americans.* Washington, DC: Author, 1989.

Association for Supervision and Curriculum Development. *Challenges and Achievements of American Education.* 1993 Yearbook. Alexandria, VA: Author, 1993.

Astin, Alexander W. *What Matters Most in College?* San Francisco: Jossey-Bass, 1993.

Bell, Daniel. *The Reforming of General Education.* New York: Columbia University Press, 1966.

Bennett, William J. *To Reclaim a Legacy: A Report on the Humanities in Higher Education.* Washington, DC: National Endowment for the Humanities, 1984.

Bernal, J. D. *Science in History,* Vol. 4. Cambridge, MA: M.I.T. Press, 1971.

Bestor, Arthur. *The Restoration of Learning.* New York: Alfred A. Knopf, 1956.

Bloom, Allan. *The Closing of the American Mind.* New York: Simon and Schuster, 1987.

Boyer, Ernest L. *College: The Undergraduate Experience in America.* New York: Harper, 1987.

Boyer, Ernest L. *High School: A Report on Secondary Education in America.* New York: Harper, 1983.

Bronowski, Jacob. *The Origins of Knowledge and Imagination.* New Haven, CT: Yale University Press, 1978.

Bruner, Jerome S. *The Process of Education.* Cambridge, Mass.: Harvard University Press, 1960.

Caswell, Hollis L. (ed.). *The American High School: Its Responsibility and Opportunity,* Eighth Yearbook of the John Dewey Society. New York: Harper, 1946.

Central Advisory Council for Education (England). *Children and Their Primary Schools.* London: Her Majesty's Stationery Office, 1967.

Commission on the Humanities. *The Humanities in American Life.* Berkeley: University of California Press, 1980.

Commission on the Relation of School and College. *Thirty Schools Tell Their Story.* New York: Harper, 1943.

Commission on the Reorganization of Secondary Education. *Cardinal Principles of Secondary Education.* Washington, DC: U.S. Bureau of Education, 1918.

Conant, James B. *Education in a Divided World.* Cambridge, MA: Harvard University Press, 1949.

Dewey, John. *The School and Society/The Child and the Curriculum.* Chicago: University of Chicago Press, 1900, 1902; combined edition, 1990.

Goodlad, John I. *A Place Called School.* New York: McGraw-Hill, 1984.

Harvard Committee on General Education. *General Education in a Free Society.* Cambridge, MA: Harvard University Press, 1945.

Hirsch, Edward D., Jr. *Cultural Literacy: What Every American Needs to Know.* Boston: Houghton Mifflin, 1987.

Isaac, Katherine. *Civics for Democracy: A Journey for Teachers and Students.* Washington, DC: Essential Books, 1992.

Jackson, Philip W. (ed.). *Handbook of Research on Curriculum.* New York: Macmillan, 1992.

Kitcher, Philip. *How to Think About Science.* New York: Oxford University Press, 1993.

National Commission on Social Studies. *Charting a Course: Social Studies for the 21st Century.* Washington, DC: Author, 1989.

National Society for the Study of Education. *The Activity Movement.* Thirty-third Yearbook, Part II. Chicago: University of Chicago Press, 1934.

National Society for the Study of Education. *Critical Issues in Curriculum.* Eighty-seventh Yearbook, Part I. Chicago: University of Chicago Press, 1988.

National Society for the Study of Education. *Cultural Literacy and the Idea of General Education.* Eighty-seventh Yearbook, Part II. Chicago: University of Chicago Press, 1988.

National Society for the Study of Education. *The Curriculum: Retrospect and Prospect.* Seventieth Yearbook, Part I. Chicago: University of Chicago Press, 1971.

National Society for the Study of Education. *General Education in the American College.* Thirty-eighth Yearbook, Part II. Chicago: University of Chicago Press, 1939.

National Society for the Study of Education. *General Education.* Fifty-first Yearbook, Part I. Chicago: University of Chicago Press, 1952.

National Society for the Study of Education. *The Integration of Educational Experiences.* Fifty-seventh Yearbook, Part III. Chicago: University of Chicago Press, 1958.

Schlesinger, Arthur M., Jr. *The Disuniting of America.* New York: W. W. Norton, 1992.

Sizer, Theodore R. *Horace's Compromise.* Boston: Houghton Mifflin, 1984.

Snow, C. P. *Two Cultures and the Scientific Revolution.* New York: Cambridge University Press, 1959.

Stratemeyer, Florence B., Forkner, Hamden L., Mekim, Margaret G., and Passow, A. Harry. *Developing a Curriculum for Modern Living.* New York: Teachers College Press, 1957.

Tanner, Daniel. *Crusade for Democracy: Progressive Education at the Crossroads.* Albany: State University of New York Press, 1991.

Tanner, Daniel, and Tanner, Laurel. *History of the School Curriculum.* New York: Macmillan, 1990.

Thomas, Russell. *The Search for a Common Learning: General Education, 1800–1960.* New York: McGraw-Hill, 1962.

U.S. Department of Education. *America 2000: An Education Strategy.* Washington, DC: Author, 1991.

U.S. Senate Committee on Government Operations. *Specialists and Generalists.* Washington, DC: U.S. Government Printing Office, 1968.

University of Chicago Faculty. *The Idea and Practice of General Education.* Chicago: University of Chicago Press, 1992. (Originally published 1950.)

Vars, Gordon F. (ed.). *Common Learnings: Core and Interdisciplinary Team Approaches.* Scranton, PA: International Textbook Company, 1969.

Weinberg, Alvin. *Reflections on Big Science.* Cambridge, MA: M.I.T. Press, 1967.

Whitehead, Alfred North. *The Aims of Education and Other Essays.* New York: Macmillan, 1929.

Wraga, William G. *Democracy's High School.* Lanham, MD: University Press of America, 1993.

CHAPTER 11

CURRICULUM FRAGMENTATION AND SYNTHESIS: PROBLEMS, PROPOSALS, PROSPECTS

"If one can imagine a miracle and suppose that all adult thoughtful Russians overnight deserted the standard of Marx and rallied to the ideas of Lincoln, shall we say, there would still be the task of re-educating all the children and youth between five and twenty-five in a new philosophy."

So wrote James Conant at mid-twentieth century in *Education in a Divided World,* subtitled *The Function of the Public Schools in Our Unique Society.*[1] Nobody, not even the experts in international affairs, could have imagined that if and when the collapse of the Soviet Union and Marxism were to occur, it would do so without warning. Yet in May 1988 Soviet Premier Mikhail Gorbachev ordered the cancellation of the final secondary school history examinations on the ground that a more candid and accurate interpretation of Soviet and world history was needed. Gorbachev also ordered the rewriting of history textbooks so as to reflect the new openness (*glasnost*) in Soviet society.[2] This action should have been seen as truly momentous—a harbinger of events of world-shaking proportions. Apparently, Gorbachev knew that any social transformation toward democracy could not succeed without transforming the school curriculum. However, the political and economic crisis leading to the Soviet coup of 1990 portended that the struggle for democracy would be long and arduous in a nation that had no democratic tradition.

If democratic social ends are to be realized, then democratic educational means must be effected. This was Conant's point when he wrote at mid-twentieth century concerning the inextricable linkage between the public schools as expressions of democratic ideals and democracy as a system of government and social life. Hence, a free society requires freedom of inquiry, the lessening of social distinction between

409

occupational groups, and the increasing extension of educational opportunity for the youth of each successive generation. The concrete expression of such ideals, contended Conant, lies in our system of public education and through the comprehensive high school in which there is a vital flow between general education and vocational education.[3]

The invention of the comprehensive high school and the implementation of general education in the secondary school and college are events of the twentieth century—a century that has been marked by an almost continuous succession of national reports and proposals for the improvement or reform of American public schools. Over the same period, American public schools have been targeted in many of the national reports, as well as in the popular press, for every imaginable shortcoming. It is safe to say that the extent and vigor of such forays have no parallel in any other nation.

The source of many of these forays against public education was to be found in the social elitism of "intellectual circles," noted Conant. As far as the intelligentsia are concerned, Conant commented that he was not one to disparage the values inherent in a life dedicated to study and aestheticism. "But," continued Conant, "the inadequacy of outlook of the average intellectual when face to face with the realities of the United States is nowhere more tragically reflected than in certain recent books and articles about education."[4]

The forays of misguided and perverse attacks being leveled against American public education from intellectual circles and the mass media at mid-twentieth century were to reach ever higher levels of crescendo at every perceived political crisis during the second half of the twentieth century. The situation became so extreme that even Robert M. Hutchins, a leading perennialist, devoted an extended essay in defense of America's public schools. In describing the antischool campaign as having reached a stage of "overkill," Hutchins pointed out that "nobody has a kind word for the institution that was the other day the foundation of our freedom."[5]

Any significant proposal for educational improvement or reform must have significant bearings on the curriculum. The focus of this chapter is on the major national educational reports, proposals, and programs since the opening of the twentieth century, and their consequences for the curriculum. In this connection, the tension between the forces for knowledge specialism and those for knowledge synthesis are examined from the perspective of the idea and function of general education in a free society.

PROPOSALS FOR GENERAL EDUCATION—THE DEMOCRATIC VISION AND THE PRACTICAL NEED

"For a pyramidal society putting a severe strain on obedience, the safest and best education is one that wears away the energy of youth in mental gymnastics, directs the glance toward the past, cultivates the memory rather than the reason, gives polish rather than power, encourages acquiescence rather than inquiry, and teaches to versify rather than to think."[6]

These were the words of the American sociologist Edward A. Ross in 1901. Ross held that whereas the concept of social efficiency in the old pyramidal society found only a privileged class enjoying the fullest measure of social and educational advantage, social efficiency in a democracy required that the pyramid be inverted so as to release the intelligence of the ordinary citizen by extending educational opportunity to all. The old function of external control would have to give way to a secular civic and moral education, prophesied Ross, and this would require a new structure and function of the curriculum. "Just what shape this new education will take, no one can say," continued Ross, "but it will not be merely one more branch of study like ethics or civics."[7]

Although Ross did not have a name for "this new education," it was to find its expression in the twentieth century in the idea and practice of general education. As discussed in Chapter 10, the challenge of general education lay not only in creating a unified curriculum design for a common learning in a diverse society, but also to do so in an age of knowledge specialism, social conflict, and divided interests.

Democracy's High School

No single document of the twentieth century was more influential in shaping the structure and function of the American educational system than the report of the NEA Commission on the Reorganization of Secondary Education, *Cardinal Principles of Secondary Education* (1918). No document has been such a durable target of attack over so many decades by both the conservative right and radical left.

The *Cardinal Principles* report laid the framework and rationale for a unitary school structure through the comprehensive (cosmopolitan) high school at a time when American industrialists had been seeking a divided school system along the lines of European systems. The report promoted coeducation and universal secondary education (to age eighteen) at a time when only one third of the children entering first grade continued on to reach the ninth grade. The report prophetically envisioned the community college movement and advocated open-access higher education through the junior college, and held that "higher institutions of learning are not justified in maintaining entrance requirements and examinations of a character that handicaps the secondary school in discharging its proper functions in a democracy." Again, in the words of the report, "[t]he conception that higher education should be limited to the few is destined to disappear in the interests of democracy."[8]

The *Cardinal Principles* report gave recognition to adolescence as a stage of rapid social development. "The physical, intellectual, emotional, and ethical characteristics of young people are still but vaguely comprehended," noted the report in going on to advocate the serious study of social and educational needs of youth in teacher education.[9] As discussed later, national reports on education reform issued decades later and even in contemporary times were to regard adolescence as virtually a pathological stage in human development. (A 1993 article in *The New York Times* was titled "Adolescence Isn't a Terminal Disease."[10])

Embracing Dewey's concept of social efficiency in a democracy, in sharp contrast to social efficiency in undemocratic societies, the *Cardinal Principles* report called for the fullest release of human potential through the widest extension of educational opportunity. Hence, the individual not only would develop the knowledge, interests, and ideals to find a productive role in society, but also to "use that place to shape both himself and society toward ever nobler ends."[11]

UNIFICATION AND SPECIALIZATION.   The curriculum of the comprehensive or cosmopolitan high school would meet both the specializing and unifying functions of education—specialization for productive vocations and unification for effective democratic citizenship. At the same time, the specialization function would be flexible so as to allow ready transfer among the curricular programs. The unification function would be provided through the curriculum *constants* (the common or universal studies) along with the joint association in school life of students from widely differing social backgrounds, and having widely differing educational and vocational goals. The specialization function would be provided through curriculum *variables* (elective programs) to meet vocational or special educational goals, and also cultivate individual or personal and avocational interests (worthy use of leisure).

In effect, the report was advocating a no-track high school with diversified studies of elective programs (variables) and a common core (constants) to meet the sociocivic aim of general education. In pointing to the necessary connection between vocation and democratic citizenship, the report stressed that "this commission enters its protest against any and all plans, however well intended, which are in danger of divorcing vocation and socio-civic education."[12]

As Conant was to discover, the ideas in the *Cardinal Principles* report along with those of Alexander Inglis in *Principles of Secondary Education* (1918), and the writings of John Dewey, fit the new problems of the times "as a key fits a lock."[13] Inglis had been a key member of the commission that wrote the *Cardinal Principles* report, and his text was published posthumously in the same year that the report was issued by the U.S. Bureau of Education. (Revisionist and other educational historians have failed to recognize the influence of Inglis and often refer to the *Cardinal Principles* report as "Mr. Kingsley's Report,"[14] after Clarence Kingsley, a Brooklyn mathematics teacher who had been elected chairman of the commission, but who left little in his own writings that would connect him in style and substance with the report.)

INTERDEPENDENT CURRICULAR AIMS.   Revealingly, both the *Cardinal Principles* report and the text by Alexander Inglis envisioned the comprehensive high school as fulfilling three interdependent aims: (1) the sociocivic aim of democratic citizenship, (2) the economic-vocational aim, and (3) the individual-avocational aim. The sociocivic aim is provided through the curriculum constants, whereas the other aims are met through curriculum variables—elective programs for vocational education and free electives for individual-avocational interests.[15] In similar style and substance, the *Cardinal Principles* report and Inglis's text described the comprehensive high school as the universal secondary school and outlined the curriculum needed to meet the changing social conditions.

Figure 11–1 depicts the interdependence of these three comprehensive aims. In the words of Inglis, "[s]ince every individual is at once a citizen, a worker, and a relatively independent personality, and since those three phases of activity cannot be divorced, it follows that a fundamental principle in the organization of curriculums is the conception that each of the three aims mentioned must be recognized in due proportion and that no curriculum which ignores or minimizes any one of those aims can be acceptable."[16]

DEPARTMENTALIZED SUBJECTS AND CURRICULUM ISOLATION.   Both Inglis and the *Cardinal Principles* report addressed the problem of curriculum isolation as a result of the subject-centered curriculum and departmentalization—a problem that remains to this day. As Inglis pointed out,

> [i]n the past the materials of high-school subjects of study have been organized and taught according to the demands of the studies as logically organized fields of knowledge. In the reorganization of secondary education problems . . . subject organization and teaching methods must be approached from a different point of attack. . . . In some cases the entire organization of materials and methods must be changed.[17]

Inglis went on to propose that the studies be so organized and treated as to be in accord with the nature of the learner in order to develop the working power of intelligence so as to meet the demands of life.

Figure 11–1. The Three Interdependent Aims of the Macrocurriculum.

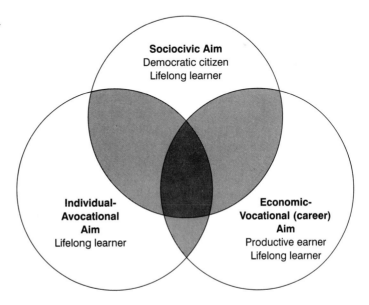

Sociocivic Aim
Democratic citizen
Lifelong learner

**Individual-
Avocational
Aim**
Lifelong learner

**Economic-
Vocational (career)
Aim**
Productive earner
Lifelong learner

In the same vein, the *Cardinal Principles* report noted that "[i]f the only basis upon which a high school is organized is that of the subjects of study, each department being devoted to some particular subject, there will result an over-valuation of the importance of subjects as such, and the tendency will be for each teacher to regard his function as merely that of leading the pupils to master a particular subject, rather than that of using the subjects of study and the activities of the school as means for achieving the objectives of education."[18]

Ironically, the notion of subject-matter mastery and mastery learning were to be revived during the 1980s and 1990s at a time when unprecedented efforts were being given to standardized achievement testing under the production model of schooling. In contrast, the *Cardinal Principles* report rejected the notion of mastery of the basics, or the mastery of a subject, but conceived of education not in the measurement of end points but measures of growth. Hence, the basics were described as fundamental processes or as tools for learning.

GLOBAL AND INTERCULTURAL EDUCATION.   Much of what was written in the *Cardinal Principles* report remains remarkably current. Currently, the task of curriculum synthesis to meet the function of general education remains a challenge to the middle and secondary school, and to the college as well. At a time of heightened social divisions in society, alternative schools are being established to separate groups according to special interests. The concept of unity through diversity has been eroded under the pressures of divided interests. The educational and social significance of the comprehensive objectives of the report are no less vital today than when they were formulated (health, command of the fundamental processes, worthy home membership, vocation, democratic citizenship, worthy use of leisure, and ethical character).

The vision of the report might best be summed up in the mission it held for the comprehensive high school as "the prototype of a democracy in which various groups must have a degree of self-consciousness as groups and yet be federated into a larger whole through the recognition of common interests and ideals."[19] Perhaps no description of contemporary America more appropriately portrays the present scene than as presented in the *Cardinal Principles* report of 1918:

> In America, racial stocks are widely diversified, various forms of social heredity come into conflict, differing religious beliefs do not always make for unification, and the members of different vocations often fail to recognize the interests that they have in common with others. The school is the one agency that may be controlled definitely and consciously by democracy for the purpose of unifying its people.[20]
>
> As a people we should . . . deal more sympathetically and intelligently with the immigrant coming to our shores, and have a basis for a wiser and more sympathetic approach to international problems. . . . This means a study of specific nations, their achievements and possibilities, not ignoring their limitations. Such a study of dissimilar contributions in the light of the ideal of human brotherhood should help establish a genuine internationalism, free from sentimentality, founded on fact, and actually operative in the affairs of nations.[21]

In his study of general education in the high school, published in 1957, Will French noted that the comprehensive purposes and functions of secondary education had reached almost universal acceptance among professional and lay groups in determining what the curriculum should be.[22] At mid-twentieth century, Butts and Cremin assessed the gains made as a result of the influence of the *Cardinal Principles* report and concluded that "no retreat was possible or desirable."[23]

COUNTERVAILING INFLUENCES.   However, the era of the Cold War and space race was to bring an unprecedented assault against the comprehensive high school exceeded only by the alternative school movement of the 1980s and 1990s. As discussed later in this chapter and in Chapter 12, academicians on both the conservative right and radical left were joined in a strange alliance in attacking the comprehensive high school and in advocating a one-track academic high school. Indeed, this was the high school of the nineteenth century. The academic left would not recognize that the comprehensive high school as envisioned in the *Cardinal Principles* report is a no-track high school with diversified studies centered around a common core. Those on the academic right resented the egalitarianism of the report. "The report is breathless with the idealism of the Progressive era," wrote Richard Hofstadter, "with the hope of making the world safe for democracy and bringing a full measure of opportunity to every child."[24] Such idealism might be a target for ridicule, but it is difficult to dismiss it when one considers that the security and well-being of the peoples of the world hinge on the extent to which the world is safe for democracy, and the very foundations of American democracy rest on "bringing a full measure of opportunity to every child."

ALL American Children and *ALL* American Youth

Despite the crisis conditions of World War II that had put school improvement and the extension of educational opportunity on hold for the duration, visionary educators recognized that the end of the war and the midcentury period of postwar reconstruction would signal a turning point of momentous proportions for American education. Throughout the Great Depression the Educational Policies Commission (EPC) of the National Education Association had promoted the needs of children and youth in connection with the social and educational agenda of Franklin D. Roosevelt's New Deal—from the school hot-lunch program and preschool programs to youth education for productive employment. Now, looking to the post–World War II era, the Educational Policies Commission undertook the task of creating a document that would provide in some detail a description of how the democratic vision of educational opportunity might be implemented. In a unique and creative format, the commission told the story of how the schools of the mythical community of Farmville and the mythical community of American City were organized and functioning in the mythical state of Columbia. The purpose was not to provide a blueprint, or to fantasize a Utopian scheme, but to illustrate how democratic policies and principles might be carried out through the application of the best professional practices in building "the kinds of schools which America needs and must have."[25]

The two key documents embodying these proposals were *Education for ALL American Children,* issued in 1948, and *Education for ALL American Youth,* published in 1944 and revised eight years later under the additional title *A Further Look.*

Both documents focused heavily on the democratizing function of the school and the curriculum, as evidenced by this statement concerning the elementary curriculum:

> Let the elementary school curriculum derive its goals from the domains and values of the social scene. Let its methods conform to the demands and values of human growth and development. The good elementary school is not concerned exclusively either with the nature of society or with the nature of childhood. The good elementary school is developmental, with a social criterion, concerning democratic values.[26]

The curriculum was to be designed in terms of children's needs and democratic values rather than through mechanical subject designations. Many of the curriculum illustrations presented in *Education for ALL American Children* were built on the concept of the integrated curriculum or integrated day, which had come to be associated with the open classroom proposal of the late 1960s and early 1970s. The concept of community school was given prominent emphasis and was seen as the means of linking the school and community to the ideals of democratic living. *Education for ALL American Children* was received with relatively little debate, possibly because its formulations reflected ideas and practices that were widely accepted in that era.

EARLY CHILDHOOD EDUCATION.   The proposal of the Educational Policies Commission that the elementary school encompass the nursery school years was indeed far-reaching at a time when only a minority of school districts were providing kindergarten. In fact the Educational Policies Commission as far back as 1938 had advocated that a primary or junior school—combining the nursery school (children at two and a half to three years of age), kindergarten, and first two elementary grades—be made an important unit of the public school system without segregating children in separate buildings. Such a design, stressed the commission, would be in accord with the modern findings of child development, as well as serving to meet a vital social need.[27]

It was not until President Lyndon Johnson's War on Poverty during the latter 1960s when a national effort was made for preschool education. However, this effort, known as Head Start, was directed at children in poverty and thereby isolated these children within the program. Moreover, being administered separately from the public school system, the Head Start teachers were typically lacking in professional qualifications and there was a lack of coordination with the elementary school, with the consequence that the expected longer-term effects in cognitive and social development were disappointing.[28] Looking back, it is clear that the proposal of the Educational Policies Commission for integrating the nursery school years into the public elementary school not only was far reaching for its day, but also remains so to this very day.

THE SECONDARY SCHOOL CORE CURRICULUM. The EPC's report, *Education for ALL American Youth,* was a comprehensive proposal for reconstructing the curriculum of the secondary school in directions markedly different from existing practice. Instead of a prescribed list of separate courses to cover each of the areas of general education, the report proposed a core curriculum or common-learnings program that was designed to provide for the fullest integration of learning experiences. The design for common learnings closely paralleled the integrated core curriculum developed by the more experimental schools of the Eight-Year Study. In the setting of the comprehensive secondary school, the heterogeneously grouped class in common learnings was conceived to provide for the study of broad problems that all members of a free society share in common. Conventional subject boundaries would be dissolved in an effort to develop the necessary interrelationships of knowledge in addressing such problems.

The common-learnings sequence was to extend from grades seven through fourteen (including the two years of junior college) in a continuous daily block of time. The curriculum in common learnings was to be preplanned by the faculty, and the entire curriculum would be made relevant to the "imperative needs of youth," which included democratic citizenship, health, family and societal living, consumer economics, scientific understandings, aesthetics, leisure, vocational proficiency, and ethical values. Learning activities were intended to help youth develop in their (1) ability to think rationally and to respect truth arrived at by rational processes, (2) respect for others and ability to work cooperatively, (3) insight into ethical values and principles, (4) ability to use their time wisely, and (5) ability to plan their own affairs, as individuals and groups, and to carry out their plans efficiently.

Figure 11–2 shows the relationship of the common learnings to the other areas of the curriculum. As proposed by the commission, pupils in grades seven through nine devote half of the school day to common learnings (constants), one third to personal interests or exploratory learnings (variables), and the remaining one sixth to health and physical education. In grade ten the students begin to pursue some specialized learnings, including vocational and college-preparatory work, whereas the common learnings constitute half of their program of studies. In grades eleven and twelve the common learnings constitute one third of the school day, whereas the specialized studies are expanded to match the amount of time devoted to common learnings. In grades ten through twelve, one sixth of the school day is devoted to individual-interest studies. Students are not tracked according to specialized programs. These programs are highly flexible and are related to the common learnings. The time allocated to health and physical education remains constant throughout all grades. The study of personal health is correlated with the treatment of community-health problems in common learnings. The common-learnings faculty is responsible for pupil guidance among other duties; however, specialized guidance services also are provided.

Beyond the integrated core of common learnings, students would have access to diversified programs in vocational education, advanced academic studies, and electives for exploratory, enrichment, and special-interest needs. As advocated in the *Cardinal Principles* report, there would be no tracking in the comprehensive secondary

Figure 11–2. The Curriculum in American City.

Periods per day	GRADES							
	Early Secondary School			High School			Community College	
	7	8	9	10	11	12	13	14
1	**Personal Interests** (Exploration of personal abilities and individual interests; discovery of interests in art, music, science, languages, sports, crafts, home and family problems, and leisure activities.)				**Individual Interests** (Elected by the student, under guidance, in fields of avocational, cultural, or intellectual interest.)			
2					**Vocational Preparation** (Includes education for industrial, commercial, home-making, service, and other occupations leading to employment, apprenticeship, or homemaking at the end of Grade XII, XIII, or XIV; education for technical and semiprofessional occupations in community college: and the study of sciences, mathematics, social studies, literature, and foreign languages in preparation for advanced study in community college, four-year college, or university. May include a period of productive work under employment conditions, supervised by the school staff. Related to the study of economics and industrial and labor relations in "Common Learnings.")			
3				**Science** (Methods, principles, and facts needed by all students.)			
4	**Common Learnings** (A continuous course for all, planned to help students grow in competence as citizens of the community and the nation; in understanding of economic processes and of their roles as producers and consumers; in living together in family, school, and community; in appreciation of literature and the arts; and in use of the English language. Guidance of individual students is a chief responsibility of "Common Learnings" teachers.)							
5								
6	**Health and Physical Education** (Includes instruction in personal health and hygiene; health examinations and follow-up; games, sports, and other activities to promote physical fitness. Related to study of community health in "Common Learnings.")							

* Broken line indicates flexibility of scheduling.

** Heavy line marks the division between "differential studies" (above) and "common studies" (below).

Sources: Educational Policies Commission, *Education for ALL American Youth—A Further Look* (Washington, DC: National Education Association, 1952), p. 233; *Planning for American Youth,* rev. ed. (Washington, DC: National Education Association, 1951), p. 48.

school. The lines between and among the specialized programs would be fluid and the classes in common learnings would be grouped heterogeneously.

UNITARY STRUCTURE AND COMPREHENSIVE FUNCTIONS. As shown in Figure 11–2, the report of the Educational Policies Commission envisioned a unified school structure encompassing nursery school through grade fourteen or the community college. In effect, vocational preparation would be provided through the upper grades of the high school and extending into the community college.

Not until the early 1990s were formal provisions developed for coordinating the junior and senior year of the high school with the two years of the community college in a two-plus-two program of vocational-technical education. Clearly, the commission's proposal was decades ahead of its times with regard to the structure and function of the educational system and the structure and function of the curriculum.

Indeed, the commission's proposal for the comprehensive secondary school reaffirmed and reformulated the educational objectives in the 1918 *Cardinal Principles* report in terms of "the ten imperative needs of youth":

1. to develop salable skills for intelligent and productive participation in economic life
2. to develop and maintain good health and physical fitness
3. to understand the rights and duties of democratic citizenship
4. to understand the significance of and conditions conducive to successful family life
5. to know how to purchase and use goods and services intelligently
6. to understand the methods of science and its influence on human life
7. to develop appreciation of beauty in literature, art, music, and nature
8. to use leisure time wisely
9. to develop respect for others, to grow in ethical values and principles, and to live and work cooperatively with others
10. to develop the ability to think rationally, to develop their thoughts clearly, and to read and listen with understanding[29]

Among the noted members of the commission, when the revised edition of *Education for ALL American Youth* was issued, were James B. Conant, chairman, Dwight D. Eisenhower, who at the time was president of Columbia University, and Arthur H. Compton, Nobel laureate in physics. (Compton had set up the secret project at the University of Chicago during World War II in which the first controlled nuclear chain reaction was made, leading to the development of the atom bomb.) Despite its illustrious membership, the commission was no match for the conservative assault that was to be launched against *Education for ALL American Youth* in the wake of the Cold War and space race.

THE CONSERVATIVE ASSAULT.   Although *Education for ALL American Youth* was widely read and discussed by educators, the Cold War climate coupled with tax conservatism prevented the report from having the impact on school reform that was expected of it by progressive educators. Indeed, the report became the target of attack for supporting the comprehensive high school for its proposed comprehensive goals and functions of the curriculum, and for its rationale for curriculum articulation and synthesis for common learnings or general education.

In testifying at Congressional national defense and education hearings in 1962, Admiral Rickover called *Education for ALL American Youth* "one of the most influential studies of the function of the high school," and he proceeded to attack it for endorsing the comprehensive high school, for promoting "this strange conglomerate" of common learnings that is to be studied by all pupils together, and for proposing a curriculum that is "not concerned with academic studies."[30]

In criticizing the notion of curriculum synthesis through common learnings, Bestor contended that "the stage of integration or synthesis arrives—for the mature man and for the student alike—after, but only after, he has marshaled the array of separate intellectual powers that he knows are required." Accordingly, proposed Bestor, "the fundamental secondary school program should consist of continuous and systematic work in the five great areas of mathematics, science, history, English, and foreign languages, and a sound minimum roster of courses for the secondary school would consist of at least five years of graded work in each of these fields."[31] He went on to call for the elimination of social studies in favor of five years of history, the homogeneous grouping of students at all grade levels according to measures on standardized achievement tests, and the disallowance of credits for nonacademic electives. If an integrated course is offered at all, it should come at the senior year and be limited to those youngsters who do not continue their formal education beyond high school, whereas college-bound students should wait until the college years for integrated studies, advised Bestor.

The Harvard Report on General Education

Looking to the shape of education for the years beyond midcentury, the Harvard Committee on General Education in a Free Society viewed general education as the means of building unity from diversity. "The root idea of general education is as a balance and counterpoise to the forces which divide group from group within the high school and the high school from the college," states the report. And, although recognizing the need for curriculum diversity in the high school, the Harvard Report also called for a principle of curriculum unity through an interdependence of studies in general education on the ground that it is through such studies that "the civilizing work of preparing for American life takes place."[32]

Seeking to reconcile the conflicting differences between modern and traditional educational ideologies, the Harvard Report made a number of curriculum proposals that were hardly extraordinary. The major recommendations for the secondary school are summarized as follows:

1. At least half of the student's program should be devoted to general education; although all students need not pursue exactly the same courses, their general education should embrace common aims and ideals.

2. The general education program should be distributed throughout the entire four years of high school.

3. The minimum of eight units of general education should consist of three units of English, three units of science and mathematics, and two units of social studies.

4. Students planning to attend college should pursue further studies in one or more of the preceding areas in high school whereas, for the others, additional work in general education may be pursued in art, music, English, American life, and general science.

5. Noncollege-bound students should be able to devote approximately one third of their studies to specialized education, including vocational and business education. Such specialized studies should not be wholly vocational in intent but should bear a relationship and spirit similar to studies in general education, as does further work in mathematics or languages for those preparing for college.

Although the Harvard Report acknowledged that the fine arts serve an important function in general education by enhancing the cultural heritage, developing aesthetic appreciations, and providing opportunities for performance experiences, it did not call for required courses in this area. In a similar vein, the report cited the importance of shop work in the general education of all students, including the college bound, but left this as an elective subject. Physical education was included as an important area of general education, whereas health education was regarded as a legitimate responsibility of the school in those areas where the family and community do not meet such needs. Regarding student activities, the report viewed these as an extension of classroom activities and not as an entity apart from the educational program.

Although the Harvard Report noted that the organization of the curriculum into rigid autonomous units results in students being unable to transfer their learnings from subject to subject, it nevertheless opted for a subject curriculum and called on teachers to develop the needed interrelationships among areas of knowledge. Schools might well experiment with a variety of approaches to general education, within a framework of common ideals and purposes, noted the report.

SEARCH FOR UNITY.   The report was widely read and discussed by college educators, but gave little cause for stir among secondary-school educators because its recommendations for the secondary school were well within the realm of existing educational practice. In calling for greater interdependence between general education and specialized education, the Harvard Committee noted that it had sought to present

> a scheme which accepts the claims of a common culture, citizenship, and standard of human good, yet also the competing claims of diverse interests, gifts, and hopes.

Certainly some such scheme cannot be absent from American education if it is to produce at one and the same time sound people and a sound society.[33]

Yet in the era of discipline-centered curriculum reforms, which was to follow a decade later, the need for such a scheme was forgotten. Whatever criticisms may be leveled at the Harvard Report for its eclectic orientation, it supported the comprehensive high school and envisioned the curriculum in general education as building the common bonds among the diverse interests of a polyglot society. It also recognized the need for making the formal studies more concretely applicable to the life of the learner. "We have stressed the importance of the trait of relevance, and we have urged that, while in school, the pupil should be helped to see beyond conceptual frameworks and make concrete applications," declared the report.[34]

The continued growing fragmentation and conflict in society today finds educators giving little attention to the unification possibilities of general education. This question asked by the Harvard Report, which it considered as "the question of the nation and age," is rarely addressed by educators today. Nevertheless, from the time of its issuance to this very day, whenever there has been a resurgent interest in general education in higher education, the Harvard Report is reexamined for its eloquent testimony to the theory of general education in a free society.

Resurgent Essentialism

The great expansion of American public education over an extended period of post-World War II recovery was countered by a new wave of tax conservatism and the call to take the school curriculum back to basics. In a systematic explication of the essentialist position, Arthur Bestor, a history professor at the University of Illinois, offered his "Program for Redeeming the Unfulfilled Promise of American Education" in his widely read book, *The Restoration of Learning* (1956). Although the book was one man's version, it garnered wide support in academia and the media. Bestor's proposal was to delimit the school curriculum to "continuous and systematic work in the five great areas of mathematics, science, history, English, and foreign languages." The social studies would be eliminated. No academic credits would be allowed for any nonacademic coursework. No public funds should be expended for facilities and resources to support "gladiatorial" sports. Efforts by educationists to increase the holding power of the high school are "warranted neither by the statutes nor by common sense" and lead to "an enormous waste of educational resources." We ought not be concerned with the total number of dropouts, but whether we are losing students of high caliber. Bestor did not even list art and music in the appendix of the book. He deplored the idea and practice of general education as opposed to liberal education.[35] Sputnik I gave Bestor renewed attention in the national media for a brief period, but his essentialism was to be completely eclipsed by the neo-essentialist disciplinary curriculum reforms in the sciences and mathematics financed by the National Science Foundation and other federal agencies during the late fifties and the sixties.

Conant's Report on the High School

In serving as U.S. High Commissioner to West Germany and as first U.S. Ambassador to the Federal Republic of Germany spanning a major time period of the post–World War II reconstruction of that nation, James Conant developed a renewed interest in the American comprehensive high school. On deciding to end his distinguished diplomatic career, he agreed to conduct a study of the comprehensive high school for the Carnegie Corporation. Soon after embarking on his study, Sputnik I was launched and with it, a wave of heightened assaults against American schools, particularly the comprehensive high school, by influential critics who made good copy for the media in the wake of the Soviet earth satellite.

Issued in 1959 and addressed to school boards, Conant's report, *The American High School Today,* was enormously influential. The most significant aspect of Conant's report was his support of the comprehensive high school. At a time when the comprehensive high school was being attacked at Congressional hearings, Conant remained a staunch advocate of this type of school. In supporting the comprehensive high school, Conant presented data showing that students in such schools can attain levels of academic achievement at least on a par with those students who attend the better specialized academic high schools.

At no time since its invention did the comprehensive high school undergo attacks so severe as to threaten its existence. At Congressional hearings during 1958, the comprehensive high school was assaulted by a number of influential figures who advocated that Americans scrap this institution in favor of the divided European system.[36] As discussed in Chapter 12, it is no exaggeration to say that Conant's prestige—coupled with the tenor, timing, and practical format of his report—served to save the comprehensive high school at a time of veritable national hysteria. Unlike the highly progressive report issued seven years earlier by the Educational Policies Commission under his chairmanship, Conant's 1959 report was eclectic. In view of the climate of the times, Conant's eclectic prescriptions served to buffer the main assaults against the comprehensive high school.

SUSTAINING THE COMPREHENSIVE CURRICULUM.   In his study, Conant found that the enrollment in many high schools was too small to offer a sufficiently diversified curriculum along with the needed specialized faculty, resources, and facilities (libraries, laboratories, shops, studios, etc.). To offer a full and rich curriculum with a qualified faculty, the graduating class should number at least one hundred.

Conant's recommended program in general education was based on the traditional subject curriculum and the Carnegie unit. He chose to prescribe a curriculum that he deemed representative of the best in current practice rather than of the most promising experimental approaches or idealizations of what might be done in the high schools. In the academic subjects required for graduation, students would be grouped by ability, subject by subject, but would not be tracked. Hence, a student might be in a high-ability class in English and in a middle-ability class in mathematics. Diversified programs for the development of marketable (vocational) proficiency should be offered in line with the federal-state funding, but students should not be tracked or labeled as *vocational* or *college preparatory.* However, an academic inventory should be made to ensure that the highest ability students pursue the advanced academic studies including advanced-placement courses. Although the body of research from the time of the Eight-Year Study has revealed that the traditional pattern of academic subjects cannot be supported as best preparation for college success, Conant's proposals for the college bound, and especially for the academically talented, served to endorse the notion perpetuated by most colleges that there is indeed a best pattern.

Turning again to the proposals for the subjects required of all, Conant recommended that the time devoted to English composition during the four years should occupy about half the total time devoted to the study of English, and that each student should be required to write an average of one theme a week, evaluated by the teacher. In view of this, teachers of English should be assigned no more than one hundred students. Although art and music were not required, it was recommended that all students be "urged" to include art and music in their elective programs. In the courses required of all, the grading standards should be flexible so that a passing grade may be given to students provided they have worked to full capacity. At the same time, appropriate remedial support should be provided.

DEMOCRATIZING FUNCTION.   In the face of his prescriptions for the academically talented, Conant believed that the democratizing function of the comprehensive high school would be met by housing a heterogeneous population, by avoiding tracking of students according to college-preparatory and vocational programs, and by providing for a diversified curriculum including vocational education to meet the needs of youth who are not college bound. In effect, the main democratization function would be provided through the joint association of students in school activities, in heterogeneously grouped homerooms, in certain heterogeneously grouped elective courses, and especially through a heterogeneously grouped course called Problems of Democracy, required of all seniors. The idea for such a course was hardly new. In fact the original idea for a course on problems of democracy can be traced to the Committee on Social Studies of the 1918 Commission on the Reorganization of Secondary Education, which issued the *Cardinal Principles* report. Conant envisioned the democratizing function as reaching full fruition in this senior course.

Conant's endorsement of the problems of democracy course induced many high schools to continue to offer such a course or to develop one. However, it was to undergo near total eclipse under the weight of the national discipline-centered curriculum reforms of the space race. Clearly, Conant expected too much from this single course as the makeweight for the democratizing function of the curriculum. Yet in the 1990s, a period of social fragmentation and conflict, the modest provision of a problems of democracy course appears to be a major step toward meeting a crucial need in general education. Although Conant's eloquent words describing the nature and function of this single course may well be overstated, they do testify to the function of the total curriculum in general education in a free society:

> This course should develop not only an understanding of the American form of government and of the economic basis of our free society, but also mutual respect and

understanding between different types of students. Current topics should be included; free discussion of controversial issues should be encouraged. This approach is one significant way in which our schools distinguish themselves from those in totalitarian nations. This course, as well as well-organized homerooms and certain student activities, can contribute a great deal to the development of future citizens of our democracy who will be intelligent voters, stand firm under trying national conditions, and not be beguiled by the oratory of those who appeal to special interests.[37]

Clearly, it is hard to fathom how Conant could expect a single twelfth-grade course, along with homerooms and student activities, to accomplish such a profound mission. If a single social-problem-focused course, heterogeneously grouped, "can contribute a great deal to the development of future citizens of our democracy who will be intelligent voters, stand firm under trying national conditions, and not be beguiled by the oratory of those who appeal to special interests," one is impelled to wonder how much could be accomplished if such a function permeated the total curriculum in general education. After all, this was the stated goal of general education as conceived in the earlier reports endorsed by Conant. Furthermore, what about the dropouts who do not have the opportunity to take this twelfth-grade course in American problems? In capping his proposals for a subject curriculum and ability grouping in the academic subjects with such a problem-focused course in the senior year of high school, Conant appeared to be implying that such a singular course would atone for whatever deficiencies accrue to his curriculum prescriptions for the entire four years of high school. In this connection one cannot avoid the conclusion that Conant expected too much from too little too late.

Yet Conant's recommendations came to be so widely adopted that it seems likely that had he advocated the abandonment of the comprehensive high school, this institution might well have been dealt a mortal blow. Never before in its short history had it been under such concerted attack. Conant's support of this institution could not have come at a more propitious moment in history.

Conant's Report on the Junior High School

Conant followed up his report on the high school with one on the junior high school, also commissioned by the Carnegie Corporation.[38] Issued in 1960, the report on the junior high school was brief and its recommendations closely paralleled the report he had issued a year earlier on the high school. Conant acknowledged that the junior-high grades provide the transition from the child-centered elementary school to the more subject-centered high school, and that because special competence is required of teachers working with this age group, this school should not be viewed as a training ground for high-school teachers. Yet his curriculum proposals tended to view the junior high school as a pupil training ground for the senior high school.

Some of the major recommendations are summarized as follows:

1. All pupils in grades seven, eight, and nine should be required to take English, social studies, mathematics, and science. Heavy emphasis should be given to reading skills and composition in English, and the social studies should include an emphasis on history and geography. All pupils should also take physical education and some work in art and music. All boys should have some industrial arts and girls should take homemaking. Ninth-grade science may include biology or a special laboratory course in physical science.

2. Students should be grouped in the academic courses, subject by subject, according to their ability levels.

3. To facilitate the transition to the junior high school, block-time teaching should be provided in grade seven. Although the block-time teacher in most cases would be responsible for instruction in social studies and English, the purpose is not necessarily to break down subject boundaries or to orient the curriculum to the problems of young adolescents but rather to enable the teacher to work daily with fewer individuals and to spend more time with them in an instructional and guidance capacity.

4. Some, if not all, students should begin the study of a modern foreign language on a conversational basis in grade seven with a bilingual teacher.

5. Able pupils should be identified early and should start algebra in grade eight so that they may be ready for college-freshman mathematics through an advanced-placement course in the twelfth grade.

6. System-wide coordination of the curriculum should be provided in each subject field, grades K–12 (vertical articulation).

7. Specialized guidance and testing services should be provided.

8. Student activities should be regarded as part of the total school program.

IMPLICATIONS.   Conant's prescriptions for the junior high school might well be faulted for giving insufficient attention to the democratizing function of this institution and of its curriculum in general education. Significantly, block-time teaching was proposed not for purposes of curriculum correlation or integration but to ease the transfer of children from the elementary school to the junior high school. Yet this recommendation undoubtedly helped many junior high schools to preserve block-time classes at a time when the curriculum reforms were in the direction of disciplinary studies.

Perhaps of greatest significance was Conant's failure to see the junior high school as an institution having its own curriculum and philosophy in tune with the nature of young adolescents. His vision of the junior high school was mainly conceived as a preparatory institution for the high school years. As in the case of his report on the high school, Conant pointed out that his recommendations were "purposely conservative," reflecting what he saw as the best in established practice, and that any imaginative developments for improving the curriculum would have to "await the test of time."[39]

Slums and Suburbs

Following his 1959 report on the high school and his 1960 report on the junior high school, Conant issued his report on schools in metropolitan areas in 1961 under the title *Slums and Suburbs.* Here he provided a vivid contrast between the schools in affluent suburbs against those in inner cities. "In the suburb there is likely to be a spacious modern school staffed by as many as 70 professionals per 1,000 pupils," noted Conant, whereas "in the slum one finds a crowded, often dilapidated and unattractive school staffed by 40 or fewer professionals per 1,000 pupils." Conant prophetically and repeatedly warned that "social dynamite is building up in our large cities in the form of unemployed, out-of-school youth."[40]

Acknowledging that the practice of ability grouping of students in the academic courses required for graduation could conceivably result in de facto segregated classes in racially mixed schools, Conant held that this could be prevented by providing for a large middle group in which there would be considerable student mixing, along with fairly small high-achieving and remedial class groupings. At the same time, students should be assigned to such groupings subject-by-subject in the required academic courses, and tracking should be avoided. Hence, a student in a vocational program might well be in a social studies class with a future attorney.

Although Conant's curricular prescriptions generally followed his earlier reports, he made a powerful case for the need of the nation to address the great disparities in resources and facilities for children and youth in the schools of metropolitan areas, and the toll taken in wasted lives and social disorganization in cities. He pointed out that aside from the alarming rate of dropouts from these schools, even when students were able to attain a high school diploma they were faced with unemployment because they were lacking in the salable skills that could have been developed in the federal-state funded programs in vocational education (office practice, trades and industries, distributive occupations, health occupations, cooperative-supervised work placement, and so on).

In his impassioned plea for the nation to address the conditions of slum schools, Conant stressed that this would require an improvement in the lives of the families who inhabit the slums. Finally, "without a drastic change in the employment prospects for urban Negro youth, relatively little can be accomplished." Conant ended his report with a call for the nation to face up to the problems of slums and slum schools, and to face up to the dangerous social situation "before it is too late."[41]

Conant's warnings of "social dynamite" garnered some media attention, but the new thrust for education was to be directed at excellence in the academic disciplines, led by university scholar-specialists with federal funding for curriculum reform in the sciences and mathematics in the wake of the Cold War and space race. Not until the great civil disorders of 1967 in central cities was the nation to turn to the problem of social dynamite and the plight of inner-city schools.

THE DISCIPLINE-CENTERED CURRICULUM AND THE DECLINE OF GENERAL EDUCATION

In the knowledge-production world of the departmentalized university, the knowledge categories are separated from one another as disciplines for purposes of specialized scholarship. However, the discipline-centered approach for the education of the scholar-specialist neglects the macrocurricular function of general education.

The disciplinary approach for the budding scholar-specialist also neglects the nature of the immature learner whose interests and cognitive styles are qualitatively different from the specialist. In failing to meet the function of general education, the discipline-centered approach neglects the practical applications of knowledge in the life of the learner and of the wider society. Hence, any effort at curriculum reform for schools must be built on the interconnections of knowledge in relation to the nature of the learner and to social conditions (see Chapter 7).

An extended discussion of the discipline-centered curriculum is presented here in view of the continuing influence of the discipline-centered university on the school curriculum. In our discussion, it is useful to understand why the national discipline-centered projects in response to the Cold War and space race came to exert such a pervasive influence over such an extended period of time, only to fail, and why educators were remiss in recognizing the neo-essentialism in the disciplinary doctrine and the inherent shortcomings of a discipline-centered curriculum. The implications of these events are of profound significance for contemporary efforts toward curriculum articulation and synthesis.

The Discipline-Centered University and the Mission-Oriented Society

Through the centuries, humans have developed thought edifices in which logical forms of knowledge have been categorized for further knowledge production and utilization. These knowledge categories, whether organized as disciplines or as subject fields, serve as the frames of reference through which educational institutions formulate their curricula for the purposes of transmitting the cultural experience to the rising generation and for enabling each new generation to meet the emergent needs of a changing society.

However, several serious problems arise as a result of the ways in which the knowledge categories are regarded and treated. The incessant expansion of knowledge requires that the knowledge categories undergo continuous transformation and resynthesis. Moreover, although knowledge expands, the time available for its study remains limited for each generation. Instead of subjecting the knowledge categories to continuous transformation and resynthesis, the traditional tendency has been to accommodate the new knowledge in the curriculum through the ad hoc processes of accretion, deletion, modification, and compression.

As Hans Vaihinger pointed out early in this century, humans create "fictional constructs" that are necessary for organizing knowledge systematically, but proceed to look on these logical constructs as ends in themselves and as an independent value for knowledge, rather than utilizing them for the purpose for which they were organized in the first place—to serve the practical need for communication and action.[42] The failure to recognize these constructs as useful fictions resulted in the treatment of knowledge in the curriculum apart from its necessary application to life problems. Under the banner of "structure of the discipline," the practical applications of knowledge were sacrificed in favor of the theoretical and abstract elements of the knowledge categories. However, in life situations the knowledge categories are not isolated and segmented; life problems require cross-disciplinary and interdisciplinary approaches for their solution. Even in the research milieu of advanced university scholarship, scientists and social scientists must engage in cross-disciplinary and interdisciplinary efforts in order to solve many kinds of problems.

LIMITATIONS OF DISCIPLINARITY. To meet the mission-oriented needs of society, the university organizes professional schools, colleges, and institutions in such wide-ranging fields as public health, medicine, engineering, agriculture and environmental science, architecture, social work, education, and so on because the discipline-oriented departments are not geared to meet these action-relevant needs.

Yet the world of academia has an ingrained tradition of maintaining the purity of knowledge. Theory is held aloof from practical or utilitarian matters. Although this tradition is rooted partly in the ancient notion that mind is above worldly affairs, it also grew out of a historic need to safeguard academia from imposition and persecution. Hence, the social seclusion of the world of scholarship led to the university being caricatured as an ivy-covered ivory tower. Although this image is not a viable one in a scientific-technological age, the tradition of maintaining the purity of knowledge has persisted in many quarters of academia. Dewey noted that, like feminine chastity, the established tradition of maintaining the purity of knowledge in the university has required all kinds of external safeguards to hedge it about.[43]

The limitations of disciplinarity have long been recognized, yet such limitations were largely forgotten as the knowledge purists led the new wave of curriculum reform. The sciences and mathematics became the appropriate models for structuring subject matter in every knowledge domain. Addressing the problem of the growing purity, abstraction, and specialization in university scholarship, a great twentieth-century mathematician, the late John von Neumann, described the dangerous trends in the field of mathematics in these words:

> As a mathematical discipline travels far from its empirical source, or still more, if it is a second and third generation only indirectly inspired by ideas coming from reality, it is beset with very grave dangers. It becomes more and more pure aestheticizing, more and more purely "L'art pour l'art." This need not be bad if the field is surrounded by correlated subjects which have closer empirical connections or if the discipline is under the influence of men with an exceptionally well developed taste. But there is a grave danger that the subject will develop along the line of least resistance, that the stream, so far from its source, will separate into a multitude of insignificant branches. . . . In other words, at a great distance from its empirical source, or after much "abstract" inbreeding, a mathematical subject is in danger of degeneration. At the inception the style is usually classical; when it shows signs of becoming baroque, then the danger signal is up.[44]

Alvin Weinberg, a nuclear physicist and director of the Oak Ridge National Laboratory, holds that much scholarship in the basic sciences has moved too far from the neighboring sciences and has tended to become baroque. He goes on to contend that scientific scholarship should be adjudged according to its "social merit or relevance to human welfare and the values of man" and, accordingly, "*that field has the most scientific merit which contributes most heavily to and illuminates most brightly its neighboring scientific disciplines.*"[45] To Weinberg, the unity of science is developed not within separate domains of specialized scholarship but through the interrelationship of these domains and, consequently, "the most valid criteria for assessing scientific fields come from without rather than from within the scientific discipline that is being treated."[46]

The incongruence between the mission-oriented society and the discipline-oriented university is described by Weinberg as follows:

> Our society is mission-oriented. Its mission is resolution of problems arising from social, technical, and psychological conflicts and pressures. Since these problems are not generated within any single intellectual discipline, their resolution is not to be found within a single discipline. . . . In society the nonspecializer and synthesizer is king.
>
> The university by contrast is discipline-oriented. Its viewpoint is the sum of the viewpoints of the separate, traditional disciplines that constitute it. The problems it deals with are, by and large, problems generated and solved within the disciplines themselves. The university's standards of excellence are set by and within the disciplines. What deepens our understanding of a discipline is excellent. In the university the specialist and analyst is king.[47]

Pointing to the problem of the "failure of the various disciplines to be humanly relevant in our time, or in any time," Ernest Becker relates how the disciplinary approach in the field of anthropology had led to "the feverish contemplation of a ludicrously limited area of reality."[48] Anthropology has so many interfaces with the various social and biological sciences that it can only be artificially construed as a discrete discipline. Indeed, its very origins or sense of identity emerged from the need to cohere these many interfaces. This does not mean that disciplinary knowledge is not valuable, but rather that it has severe limitations in broaching problems on the human condition. Such problems require a wider synthesis and application of knowledge.

Other difficulties arise when the systematic knowledge in the various knowledge categories is regarded as suitable for the learner without having to undergo a transformation so as to psychologize it for the learner—the assumption being that the immature learner can perceive and utilize such knowledge in the manner of the advanced scholar who helped create it. The knowledge-world of the advanced scholar-specialist not only is essentially different from that of the immature learner but also is essentially different from that of the adult citizen whose callings are not within the domains of specialized scholarship.

Promoted as a doctrine rather than as a theory to be tested, disciplinarity dominated the curriculum scene from the 1950s through the 1960s. It became the single ruling doctrine for curriculum reform. Although disciplinarity remains a dominant mode of curricular organization for specialized university scholarship, and although it continues to exert a significant influence on the curriculum at the preuniversity and lower levels of schooling, it is no longer the single ruling doctrine for curriculum development. Yet the world of knowledge specialization exerts a continuing influence toward organizing the curriculum according to the disciplines of university scholarship.

Nationalizing Influences on the Curriculum— The New Priority and Hierarchy

Few educators would contend that the school curriculum of the 1950s did not require reconstruction. The traditional subject curriculum not only suffered from a rigid compartmentalization of knowledge but also the approaches to accommodating new knowledge in the traditional subject curriculum were far from satisfactory. Although knowledge was undergoing great expansion, the time-life space of the learner remained relatively constant. Such conditions required that the curriculum undergo continuous reassessment and synthesis.

As discussed in Chapter 10, notable efforts had been made prior to midcentury to counter the tendency toward curricular fragmentation and to develop curricular coherence. Such efforts stemmed from a rationale premised on the need to consider in curriculum development the interrelationships of organized knowledge, the nature of the learner, and the problems of a democratic society. In sharp contrast is the countercurrent of knowledge specialism and disciplinarity in which knowledge for its own sake takes precedence over the practical applications of knowledge and the nature of the learner.

In response to the attacks leveled at elementary and secondary schools during the era of the Cold War and space race, the federal government turned to the world of university scholarship to reconstruct the school curriculum—giving priority to science and mathematics in order to meet the crisis of the times.

Through the National Defense Education Act (NDEA) of 1958, federal funds were provided for the improvement of instruction in science, mathematics, and modern foreign languages; for the improvement of guidance and testing programs directed principally at discovering and developing the talents of the most academically able children and youth; and for the training of highly skilled technicians in fields that were deemed essential for national defense.

A single federal agency, the National Science Foundation, came to allocate hundreds of millions of dollars for curriculum reform in the sciences and mathematics at the elementary and secondary levels during the 1950s and 1960s. This was a time when a veritable army of university scholars was already engaged in a wide range of applied research projects in areas deemed essential to the nation's security. According to the mathematician Morris Kline, mission-oriented scholars from the universities were busily engaged in applied research during this period and so, when the federal government turned to the universities to enlist scholars for the national curriculum-reform programs to be directed at the lower levels of schooling, those scholars who were engaged in the more remote and puristic pursuits were able to seize control of the curriculum reforms.[49] University scholars who were not mission oriented and who had been bypassed over the years in connection with federally supported scientific research suddenly found that huge grants were available for national curriculum-reform projects through the prestigious National Science Foundation. The consequence was that the curriculum reforms over a period of well over a decade were dominated by the puristic structure-of-a-discipline doctrine.

A CURRICULUM MANIFESTO

Less than a year following the launching of Sputnik I, a conference composed predominantly of scientists, mathematicians, and psychologists was convened at Woods Hole on Cape Cod in Massachusetts by the National Academy of Sciences. Providing financial support and planning assistance for the conference were such agencies as the National Science Foundation, the Air Force, The Rand Corporation, the U.S. Office of Education, the American Association for the Advancement of Science, and the Carnegie Corporation. The conference was designed to explore the possibilities for improving education in science in the elementary and secondary schools at a time when they were under severe attack for the nation's alleged lag behind the Soviets in the space race. The Cold War had already led to the establishment of several national curriculum projects under NSF funding, but these projects were not wedded by a curriculum rationale and their efforts to produce new course packages were still at the preliminary stages.

The outcome of the Woods Hole conference was a veritable curriculum manifesto, *The Process of Education,* authored by the conference chairman, Jerome Bruner. *The Process of Education* was to serve as the manifesto for curriculum reform in the elementary and secondary schools over the ensuing decade.

Decline of the Democratic Ideal

The link between *The Process of Education* and the crisis of the space race is reflected in the opening paragraph, which calls attention to the "widespread renewal of concern for the quality and intellectual aims of education . . . accentuated by what is almost certain to be a long-range crisis in national security." The report goes on to declare: "The top quarter of public school students, from which we must draw intellectual leadership in the next generation, is perhaps the group most neglected by our schools in the recent past."[50]

A decade later, responding to a very different sociopolitical crisis, Bruner did an about-face by accusing the public schools of concentrating on "the more intelligent kids" and neglecting "the children at the bottom."[51] This reversal reflects on how education priorities can be turned about as a result of sociopolitical influences and illustrates how leading educators are prone to see priorities as polarities.

In one epoch, democracy is to be saved by focusing on the academically gifted, whereas in a succeeding era it is to be saved by giving priority to the low achiever or disadvantaged learner. Instead of realizing that a democratic society requires that educational opportunity be optimized for all children and youth, and that the curriculum must be reconstructed in a balanced way so as to address the needs shared by the widest membership of society, narrow priorities are established to the neglect of the cosmopolitan-universal needs.

NATIONALISTIC INTERESTS.   Dewey had warned early in this century that "[o]ne of the fundamental problems of education in and for a democratic society is set by the conflict of a nationalistic and a wider social aim," and he pointed to the European experience, and particularly the German experience, in which "the new idea of the importance of education for human welfare and progress was captured by national interests and harnessed to do a work whose social aim was definitely narrow and exclusive."[52] The schools were expected to meet a narrow social aim that was to be interpreted not in terms of developing an enlightened and progressive humanity but in terms of meeting the civic function of preparing the citizen for service to the state. As stated by Dewey:

> So far as Europe was concerned, the historic situation identified the movement for a state-supported education with the nationalistic movement in political life—a fact of incalculable significance for subsequent movements. Under the influence of German thought in particular, education became a civic function and the civic function was identified with the realization of the national state. The "state" was substituted for humanity; cosmopolitanism gave way to nationalism. To form the citizen, not the "man" became the aim of education. . . . When the actual practice was such that the school system, from the elementary grades though the university faculties, supplied the patriotic citizen and soldier and the future state official and administrator and furnished the means for military, industrial, and political defense and expansion, it was impossible for theory not to emphasize the aim of social efficiency. And with the immense importance attached to the nationalistic state, surrounded by other competing and more or less hostile states, it was equally impossible to interpret social efficiency in terms of a vague cosmopolitan humanitarianism. Since the maintenance of a particular national sovereignty required subordination of individuals to the superior interests of the state both in military defense and in struggles for international supremacy in commerce, social efficiency was understood to imply a like subordination.[53]

In the atmosphere of shock following Sputnik I, new waves of attack were leveled against U.S. public education. A study of Soviet education by the U.S. Office of Education, released in May 1957, just five months before the launching of the Soviet earth satellite, had pointed out that education in that nation is geared to exacting from students service to the state, and that the curriculum is fully controlled by the state so as to suit prevailing political doctrine and manpower needs. The report cautioned that we must be aware of the sharp differences between the Soviet system and the United States'.[54] However, within seven months following Sputnik I, the United States embarked on its first official education mission to the U.S.S.R. The report of the mission described the Soviet education system in glowing terms, with education being "a kind of grand passion." Throughout the report, the implications were drawn that we must take lessons from Soviet schools. "We cannot afford to be apathetic about educational developments in the U.S.S.R.," concluded the report, and "[c]learly the Soviet Union is bent on overtaking and surpassing us as a world power, and it proposes to use education as one of the primary means of obtaining this objective."[55] The myth of Soviet supremacy in the sciences, mathematics, and technology was being perpetuated, and it was America's schools that were at fault and needed to be fixed in the face of the space-race crisis.

During the era of the Cold War and space race, the democratic social aim of American education yielded to the narrow nationalistic aim as the federal government looked to curriculum reform as the means of meeting the crisis of the times. The contribution of university scholars in the creation of the most advanced weapons systems had led the nation's political leadership to look to the university scholars for devising curricula in science and mathematics for the elementary and secondary schools to meet the Cold War crisis. The alleged superiority of Soviet education, with its heavy emphasis on science and mathematics and its exploitation of academically talented children and youth, was to be matched and surpassed by the American pursuit of academic excellence. Hence, the Woods Hole conference proceeded to focus on the education of the academically talented coupled with a priority to be given to science and mathematics in the curriculum.

The view of knowledge for curriculum building was to be that of university scholar-specialists on the forefront of their respective disciplines. The discipline-oriented university scholars were given a new mission-oriented task. Nevertheless, the discipline-oriented university scholars comprising the membership of the Woods Hole conference proceeded to develop a rationale for modeling curriculum reform in the schools along the more abstract lines of university scholarship in which knowledge is pursued and treated in its "purity."

Separate Realms of Specialized Knowledge

If the twentieth century is The Age of Synthesis, the question arises as to whether the disciplinarity principle that emerged from the Woods Hole conference was not indeed antithetical to synthesis. If the curriculum is to be formulated according to the separate and pure domains of specialized scholarship (the different disciplines of knowledge), the necessary outcome is the further fragmentation and compartmentalization of the curriculum. Although the search for structure represented a quest for synthesis, this quest was to be undertaken in the separate realms of knowledge. According to Bruner, "the curriculum of a subject should be determined by the most fundamental understanding that can be achieved of the underlying principles that give structure to that subject."[56] Traditional subject matter not only suffers from lagging behind developments in a field, reasoned Bruner, but also tends to become a mass of disjointed detail—unending topics and massive collections of information that do not reveal the harmonic contours of disciplinary knowledge. By designing curricula according to the structure of each discipline—that is, according to the fundamental principles, ideas, and generalizations that represent disciplinary knowledge—the subject matter would become more comprehensible for the learner and more easily transferable to situations in which knowledge can be broadened and deepened, Bruner contended.

Thus, the quest for structure reflected a search for synthesis that had been emerging in certain domains of specialized scholarship during the twentieth century. That specialized scholarship had created new disjunctures and islands of knowledge, and had widened the gap between the world of pure and applied knowledge, was ignored by Bruner in his report of the Woods Hole conference. The imposition of puristic realms and methods of university scholarship on the lower schools was seen as the needed way "to narrow the gap between 'advanced' knowledge and 'elementary' knowledge."[57] No consideration was given to the problem of fragmentation of knowledge, which is the inevitable result of such a curriculum model.

DOMINANT DOCTRINE.   The structure-of-a-discipline doctrine not only served as the key idea governing the national course-content improvement projects but also came to exert a dominant influence on curriculum theorists. Schwab warned educationists that unless they take into account the structures of the disciplines, "our plans are likely to miscarry and our materials, to misteach," and "there will be failure of learning or gross mislearning by our students."[58]

Schwab's notion that "different disciplines have widely different conceptual schemes" and his contention that seeking conceptual schemes that cut across disciplines is a fruitless exercise[59] are clearly contradicted by the treatment of knowledge in Schwab's own field of biology, for example, where the advance of knowledge has required new fusions between established domains of knowledge, thus leading to the creation of such fields as biochemistry, biophysics, and sociobiology. Schwab not only overlooked the necessary fusions of disciplines and fields in the world of scholarly research but he also ignored the necessary interrelationships between and among these areas of knowledge when they are brought to bear on all kinds of practical problems in society—whether in medicine, energy resources, ecology, and so on. For example, ecology is not limited to the biological sciences but involves knowledge from the physical sciences, geography, economics, political science, engineering, agriculture, and, indeed, any area of knowledge that relates to the environment—including the arts and architecture.

Moreover, many leading scientists do not agree with Schwab's contention that even within the field of science the conceptual schemes are so widely different that it is fruitless to find any unity of knowledge. The Nobel laureate Albert Szent-Gyorgi observed that the "unification of knowledge is the greatest achievement of science," and he went on to propose that "w[]hat I would like to see taught in school is this new subject—nature, not physics and chemistry."[60]

Schwab also avoided consideration as to how all the different disciplines might be made to fit together as a coherent curriculum for learners who cannot become knowledge specialists in each of the many identifiable disciplines. As discussed later, the exploding social problems of the late 1960s and early 1970s impelled Schwab to revise his thesis so as to make accommodations for the treatment of these problems of relevance in the curriculum.

Some educationists were so taken up by the disciplinary doctrine that they went so far as to advocate that all subject matter in the curriculum be based on the structure-of-a-discipline principle. In the words of Phenix, "*all* curriculum content should be drawn from the disciplines, or, to put it another way, *only* knowledge contained in the disciplines is appropriate to the curriculum [because] the disciplines reveal knowledge in its teachable forms [and] non-disciplined knowledge is unsuitable for teaching and learning."[61] In making these assertions, Phenix ignored the fact that even in the world of university scholarship, it has been recognized that the disciplines are not by themselves adequate constructs for the search for knowledge, nor do they reveal knowledge in its most teachable forms. As we saw in the preceding chapter, research and teaching have required that domains of knowledge be reformulated through a variety of correlated, fused, broad-fields, and interdisciplinary approaches.

ARCHETYPE FOR CURRICULUM REFORM

A new curriculum hierarchy emerged during the 1960s not only as a result of the priority accorded the sciences and mathematics by the federal government but also because these subjects came to be regarded as models for course-content improvement based on the structure-of-a-discipline doctrine. Indeed, if there is such a thing as structure of a discipline, it would be most apparent in those disciplines having conceptual schemes that are most amenable to quantification and prediction. Thus, the physical sciences and mathematics came to occupy the highest rungs of the disciplinary hierarchy.

Recognizing the growing curriculum imbalance, the U.S. Office of Education undertook the support of curriculum-reform projects in the social studies and English, but the support level amounted to only a small fraction of the funding provided the sciences and mathematics by NSF. Moreover, most of the projects in the social studies and English proceeded to embrace the structure-of-a-discipline notion in imitation of the science projects. The search for a monolithic structure for each discipline in the social sciences and in English eventually was to prove unfruitful. Even in the archetype disciplines of physics and mathematics, far more was promised and claimed than was actually delivered, not only concerning the matter of disciplinary structure, but also in the assertion that such efforts would usher in a great renaissance in curriculum.

It may seem strange that the disciplinary doctrine should have evoked such a bandwagon effect, especially when it could not be validated even in mathematics and the physical sciences, but academicians, like people in general, tend to move with the fashions. At that time, many leaders in some of the so-called nonacademic fields, such as the fine arts, began to subscribe to the disciplinary doctrine so as to make their fields more essential to the school curriculum by eliminating the studio experiences and claiming their fields as academic disciplines. In so doing, they were robbing the arts of their unique and essential attributes and functions for general education and significance in daily life. To this day, proponents of the discipline-centered curriculum must be reckoned with not only in the sciences and social sciences, but also in the arts. In their efforts to create discipline-based art education, they delimit the studio arts and emphasize art as an academic study through art history, criticism, and aestheticism or connoisseurship.[62]

Assessing the Disciplinary Doctrine

The university scholars who developed the discipline-centered projects for the schools proceeded to make sweeping claims for their work and did not submit to impartial evaluations. In those very rare instances when controlled research was conducted, the scholars proceeded to violate the fundamental tenets of scientific research by setting up conditions so as to prove the project. It seemed hypocritical that these were the scholars who had claimed that a basic objective of their discipline-centered projects was to instill in students the methods of scientific inquiry. (A more detailed assessment of the biases in evaluating and proving these projects is presented in Chapter 13.)

For almost two decades, the national discipline-centered projects dominated the school curriculum by the weight of academic authority, federal funding, endorsement of powerful and prestigious national agencies and associations (e.g., the private foundations, National Science Foundation, U.S. Office of Education, and the professional education associations and journals)—all in an atmosphere of space-race crisis. Under these circumstances, few educators were willing to point out that the discipline-centered projects conflicted with the nature of the learner, promoted knowledge purity and abstraction at the expense of practical application and relevance to the life of the learner, emphasized knowledge specialism to the neglect of general education and democratic citizenship, and failed to address the deepest social problems. In short, the disciplinary doctrine and the national discipline-centered reform effort had violated the curriculum paradigm (see Chapter 7).

KNOWLEDGE PURITY AND ABSTRACTION.   To the university scholar-specialists practical applications of knowledge only served to contaminate the discipline, for such application requires the crossing of disciplinary boundaries and even the elimination of boundaries.

The puristic orientation of the curriculum reforms in the sciences and mathematics was the subject of a scathing indictment by the physicist Alvin Weinberg, who wrote the following:

> These two tendencies—toward purity and fragmentation as opposed to application and interdisciplinarity . . . seem to me to portend trouble in the relation between the university and society. First, I speak about the great curriculum reforms, especially in the sciences. These reforms started in the high schools but have now been extended, particularly in mathematics, downward to the grade schools, and in many instances upward to the colleges. . . . Insofar as many of the new curricula have been captured by university scientists and mathematicians of narrowly puristic outlook, insofar as some of the curricula reflect deplorable fragmentation and abstraction, especially of mathematics, I consider them to be dangerous. . . . The professional purists, representing the spirit of the fragmented, research-oriented university, took over the curriculum reforms, and by their diligence and aggressiveness, created puristic monsters.[63]

The separation between pure and applied knowledge, and the compartmentalization of knowledge into mutually exclusive disciplines and subjects reflect the self-serving logic of academia where matters of concern are purely academic and removed from the test of intelligent action. "Education is the acquisition of the art of the utilization of knowledge," noted Whitehead, and "ideas which are not utilized are positively harmful." Whitehead further described education as "a preparation for battling with the immediate experiences of life, a preparation by which to qualify each immediate moment with relevant ideas and appropriate actions," and he defined education as "the guidance of the individual towards a comprehension of the art of life; and by the art of life I mean the most complete achievement of varied activity expressing the potentialities of that living creature in the face of its actual environment."[64]

The tendency for the disciplinary studies to isolate intellectual activity from ordinary life was a matter of great concern for Dewey, who warned:

> In the case of the so-called disciplinary or preeminently logical studies, there is danger of the isolation of intellectual activity from the ordinary affairs of life. Teacher and student alike tend to set up a chasm between logical thought, as something abstract and remote, and the specific and concrete demands of everyday events. The abstract tends to become so aloof, so far away from application, so as to be cut loose from practical and moral bearing.[65]

When knowledge is cut off from use—from its applicability to the world—in giving meaning to what is baffling in the world, there is danger that it will become "an object of aesthetic contemplation," Dewey noted. "There is much emotional satisfaction to be had from a survey of the symmetry and order of possessed knowledge," continued Dewey, "and the satisfaction is a legitimate one. But this contemplative attitude is aesthetic, not intellectual."[66] Some thirty years after Dewey's warning, the mathematician John von Neumann pointed to the "very grave dangers" of mathematics becoming "more and more pure aestheticizing, more and more purely 'l'art pour l'art,'" as it becomes less and less "inspired by the ideas coming from 'reality.'"[67] This is not to deny the aesthetic qualities of a discipline, but when the discipline becomes so puristic and esoteric that its relationship to the life of the learner is denied, when it has no bearings on the development of social power and insight in enabling the learner to cope more effectively with the environment, then its educational function becomes severely limiting.

In making a case for the new mathematics curriculum, with its focus on the abstract side of the discipline, the mathematician Marshall Stone argued the case for mathematics as a self-serving area of knowledge that is to be treated in the school curriculum independently of its relationships to the physical world.[68] The case for mathematics as a pure discipline may be entirely justified in the fraternity of puristic university scholarship, but mathematics also is the key tool of the physical sciences, engineering sciences, architecture, and social sciences—not to mention its invaluable uses in everyday life. Even assuming that a legitimate case can be made for mathematics as a self-serving domain of puristic scholarship in the university, the views of von Neumann and Whitehead notwithstanding, this does not justify such treatment in the curriculum of the elementary and secondary school. Whitehead, who was Bertrand Russell's collaborator in producing one of the greatest mathematical treatises of all time, wrote concerning the need for education to be useful: "Pedants sneer at an education which is useful. But if education is not useful, what is it? Is it a talent to be hidden away in a napkin? Of course education should be useful, whatever your aim in life."[69]

The proposition that the fundamental ideas that constitute the structure of a discipline will lead to massive general transfer of learning failed to prove valid principally because general transfer requires wide applicability of what is comprehended. To see the disciplines of knowledge as mutually exclusive domains that are divorced from practical application in the life of the learner is to work against massive general transfer.

DISTORTED CONCEPTION OF THE LEARNER.   Although Bruner's report of the Woods Hole conference stressed the importance of stimulating the young learner to use intuition as opposed to rote learning, and thereby develop inquiry into the significance and connectedness of what is learned, the report proceeded to cast the child as a miniature scholar-specialist whose intellectual activity is not qualitatively different from that of the scholar on the frontier of knowledge. In Bruner's words, "intellectual activity anywhere is the same, whether at the frontier of knowledge or in a third-grade classroom."[70]

Bruner supported this notion by quoting the following statement of a colleague: "In teaching from kindergarten to graduate school, I have been amazed at the intellectual similarity of human beings at all ages, although children are perhaps more spontaneous, creative, and energetic than adults."[71] Such a romantic view of the child allowed Bruner and his conferees at Woods Hole to propose a rationale for curriculum construction in accordance with the heuristic style of the mature scholar-specialist, on the ground that any differences in cognitive processes between the child and the adult scholar are merely a matter of degree, not of kind. Bruner proceeded to bend the developmental stage theory of Piaget so as to make it fit the Brunerian thesis that "intellectual activity anywhere is the same." The fact that Piaget's work reveals that young children are incapable of hypothetical thinking, and that they do not reach this stage of intellective development until late childhood or early adolescence, was ignored by Bruner and his fellow academicians.

As noted, the scholars engaged in the discipline-centered curriculum reforms not only embraced the doctrine that intellectual activity is qualitatively the same at any level but also many of them proceeded to create a romantic vision of the child's intellective capabilities. For example, a member of the Social Science Education Consortium claimed that "children, even at the beginning of first grade, can see the great contours of the economic world" and that "it has been this writer's observation that the first grader's curiosity is sharper than that of first-year college students."[72]

STAGES OF INTELLECTIVE GROWTH   Even if university scholarship and the curriculum of the university were confined to the established disciplines of knowledge, the knowledge world of the immature learner is qualitatively different from that of the mature scholar-specialist in the university. As Whitehead observed, "[t]he craving for expansion, for activity, inherent in youth is disgusted by a dry imposition of disciplined knowledge. The discipline, when it comes, should satisfy a natural craving for the wisdom which adds value to bare experience."[73] Whitehead recognized that the learner's mental growth is developmental and that it undergoes qualitative changes through the maturational process, and he identified this growth in terms of stages of development, not unlike those identified by Dewey and later by Piaget.

Early in this century, in discussing the "stages of mental growth," Whitehead attacked the notion of undifferentiated intellective development as a patently false psychology, in these words:

> The pupil's progress is often conceived as a uniform steady advance undifferentiated by change of type or alteration of pace . . . I hold that this conception of education is based upon a false psychology of the process of mental development which has gravely hindered the effectiveness of our methods.[74]

As early as 1900, Dewey made these observations concerning mental development and the curriculum:

> According to the older view mind was mind, and that was the whole story. Mind was the same throughout . . . fitted out with the same assortment of faculties whether in child or adult. . . . The only important difference that was recognized was one of quantity, of amount. The boy was a little man and his mind was a little mind—in everything but the size the same as that of the adult.[75]

Dewey described how this fallacious premise undergirded the traditional curriculum in which the subject matter was formulated from the vantage point of the adult mentality, except that the material was reduced in quantity and simplified for the "little men" of childhood. However, mind is not so fixed, contended Dewey, but is a growing process—and although this growth is a continuity, it is marked by qualitative changes. Thus, qualitative differences in the curriculum are required so that the learning material is appropriate to the changing stages or phases of human development.

> If once more we are in earnest with the idea of mind as growth, this growth carrying with it typical features distinctive of its various stages, it is clear that an educational transformation is again indicated. It is clear that the selection and grading of material in the course of study must be done with reference to proper nutrition of the dominant directions of activity in a given period, not with reference to chopped-up sections of a ready universe of knowledge.[76]

Instead of asking whether a given subject matter is worth a child's knowing, Bruner proposed that "[w]e might ask, as a criterion for any subject taught in primary school, whether, when fully developed, it is worth an adult's knowing."[77] Thus, the curriculum is not conceived in terms of its appropriateness for the child as child, but for a child who is a miniature adult and who is to become a full-sized adult by dealing with a scaled-down version of the logically formulated subject matter of adult scholarship. The authenticity and integrity of childhood is sacrificed by seeing the child as merely a future adult scholar.

Teacher-Proof Curricula

Some leading spokesmen for the major curriculum-reform projects in the sciences advocated teacher-proof curricula. They envisioned the development of ideal curriculum packages of uniform quality control—packages that would be somewhat resistant to teacher tampering or to variation in individual teacher's style, orientation, or competence.

Responding to the notion of teacher-proof curricula and to the character of the curriculum reforms then taking place in the United States, a noted British educator made these remarks at an international curriculum conference:

> I have no time whatever for any system which recruits high-powered thinkers to contrive and foist a curriculum on the schools. This cannot work unless we believe that the teacher of the future is to be a low-grade technician working under someone else's instructions rather than a professional making his own diagnoses and prescribing his own treatments.[78]

THE TEACHER VARIABLE. The major curriculum projects during the disciplinary movement were operating in many respects as though the chief variable in curriculum improvement and learning outcomes is the course content, and that by redesigning the course content through tightly organized instructional units there would be a high and uniform level of quality control.

However, an investigation by the Biological Sciences Curriculum Study (BSCS) revealed that although all the teachers in the investigation were teaching identical lessons on photosynthesis from the same course version, and although each of the classes were of the same ability level, the instructional styles and treatment of the subject matter varied so greatly that the researcher concluded that "there really is no such thing as a BSCS curriculum presentation in the schools." He added that the emphasis given to the topics studied and the levels of abstraction differed so markedly among individual teachers that different ideas and concepts were being presented to the students. "Each teacher filters the materials through his own perceptions and to say that a student has been through the BSCS curriculum probably does not give as much specific information as the curriculum innovators might have hoped," concluded the researcher.[79]

Thus, the study reveals that the packaging of course content is only one part of curriculum development and that, even when dealing with an identical topic in a highly structured curriculum package, the actual course content will differ markedly according to the differences in teachers' instructional styles and perceptions of the subject matter. To some curriculum developers, such findings might be interpreted as pointing to the need to train teachers so that the subject matter is conveyed to the student more uniformly. However, effective teaching is not mechanical. It is dependent on individual variation and the professional teacher's latitude in interpreting the subject matter and in effecting one's own teaching style—because the teaching-learning process is not simply an established-convergent situation but is to a great extent an emergent situation. The BSCS study also gives evidence of the inseparability of *instruction* from *curriculum* (see Chapter 5).

Declining Enrollments in Physics and Chemistry

The advent of the PSSC physics course was expected to attract more students to take high-school and college physics. With great expectations for the new course, the

American Institute of Physics proposed the realistic five-year goal of doubling the proportion of students enrolled in high-school physics, with at least half of the high-school graduates having completed a course in physics.[80] Instead, the proportion of students enrolled underwent a marked decline despite the great national effort to induce more youth to study physics. Just prior to Sputnik I, one out of four high-school students took physics. Ten years later the figure declined to one in five. Despite the fact that the college population more than doubled from 1962 to 1968, the actual number of college juniors majoring in physics declined by over 15 percent.[81]

A study of the career choices of National Merit finalists over a ten-year period following Sputnik I revealed that when almost one out of five male finalists was majoring in physics in college before Sputnik I, only slightly more than one in ten was majoring in this field ten years later, whereas the comparable data for female finalists showed a decline from 4.1 percent to 1.6 percent. These finalists were considered to represent the top 1 percent of high-school seniors according to scholastic aptitude measures, and were called "the nation's best source of brainpower."[82]

Although these unanticipated enrollment declines may well have been influenced by changing social attitudes on the part of high-school and college students in an era of rising social disaffection and social consciousness, many knowledgeable observers attributed the enrollment declines to the curriculum reforms as exemplified by the PSSC physics course. An editorial in *Science,* the official journal of the American Association for the Advancement of Science, expressed concern that the enrollment declines indicated a reaction on the part of youth to the excessive pressures exerted on them in high school through the stringent requirements of the new curricula, particularly the PSSC physics course.[83] An article in the *Carnegie Quarterly* also criticized the PSSC course for treating physics as the physicist sees it, with the result that the subject matter is too abstract and frightens away adolescents who carry their fears of the subject over into college.[84] Similar criticisms were leveled at the new high-school chemistry projects even by college professors. Addressing his colleagues, a chemistry professor maintained that the curriculum reforms were pressuring adolescents "to do too much, too fast, too soon" and that, in adopting these reforms, educators had committed "a crime against a generation."[85]

Aftermath of the New Math

A growing protest also was becoming evident through the 1960s and early 1970s against the narrow bias of the major mathematics projects in focusing on the abstract side of the subject as opposed to the applications of mathematics to the physical world. As far back as 1962, a memorandum signed by forty-eight mathematicians warned of the danger that the new mathematics projects were representing mainly the theoretical and abstract aspects of mathematics and, in so doing, were ignoring the needs of youngsters who seek to "understand the world around us."[86]

PURITY VERSUS APPLICATION.   The mathematician Richard Courant held that the splitting of mathematics toward a pure versus an applied variety posed a most serious threat of one-sidedness to education, and he contended that the relationships of mathematics to other realms of knowledge are necessary to keep mathematics alive and prevent it from drying into a dead skeleton.[87] Writing in the official journal of the American Association for the Advancement of Science, another mathematician observed that "one can only conclude that much of modern mathematics is not related to science but rather appears to be more closely related to the famous scholastic arguing of the Middle Ages."[88]

The curriculum reforms in mathematics not only had focused on the theoretical and abstract side of the discipline but also had sought to compress into the existing school curriculum an unrealistic amount of college-level mathematics. A 1963 conference on school mathematics, sponsored by the NSF and chaired by Jerome Bruner, advocated "that a student who has worked through the full thirteen years of mathematics in grades K through 12 should have a level of training comparable to three years of top-level college training today."[89]

Looking back on the curriculum reforms in mathematics, Kline held that the university mathematicians were presumptuous in imposing on the schools a narrow vision of mathematical knowledge, and he criticized them for not taking account of the enormous complexity of pedagogical problems.

> [T]he mathematics professors did not hesitate to take on a task that calls for considerable pedagogical acumen. One can say that they were presumptuous. They acted as though pedagogy was only a detail, whereas if they had really learned anything at all from their studies, they would have known that almost any problem involving human beings is enormously complex. The problems of pedagogy are indeed more difficult than the problems of mathematics, but the professors had extreme confidence in themselves.[90]

INTELLIGENCE AND WISDOM.   Kline made the point that people commonly assume that the mathematics professor is the epitome of intelligence and hence can be expected to exercise the utmost wisdom in prescribing solutions to problems. Wisdom is much more than intelligence, stressed Kline, for wisdom includes such qualities as "judgment, the capacity to learn from experience, the perception of values, the understanding of human beings, and the capacity to use knowledge for the solution of human problems." Although probability indicates that the qualities of wisdom are distributed no more among mathematicians than among any other groups of people selected at random, observed Kline, the narrowness of mathematics and the fact that mathematics per se is not concerned with the complex problems of the world may serve to leave mathematicians without their share of the world's distribution of wisdom. In pointing to pure mathematics as a remote refuge, Kline offers this quote of Bertrand Russell: "Remote from human passions, remote even from the pitiful facts of nature, the generations have created an ordered cosmos, where pure thought can dwell as in its natural home and where one, at least, of our nobler impulses can escape from the dreary exile of the actual world."[91]

Although the isolation of intellectual activity from life affairs is peculiarly characteristic of pure mathematics, scholars in other domains of knowledge specialization are tempted to find a similar refuge. In pointing to the tendency for specialized scholars to hold their disciplinary studies so aloof from life demands that they often tend to be inept when they roam into matters outside their own specialties, Dewey made these observations: "The gullibility of specialized scholars when out of their own lines, their extravagant habits of inference and speech, their ineptness in reaching conclusions in practical matters, their egotistical engrossment in their own subjects, are extreme examples of the bad effects of severing studies completely from their ordinary connections in life."[92]

SEARCH FOR BALANCE AND SYNTHESIS.   By the end of the 1960s and during the early 1970s, efforts were being made to balance the relationship between abstraction and useful applications in the mathematics curriculum, although these efforts were not matched by the level of financial support and professional commitment provided for the earlier reform movement. A number of curriculum projects at the elementary level sought to reveal the relationships between the physical sciences and mathematics, but the task of relating such studies to the life of the learner and to the pervading problems of society remained to be accomplished.

A new and concerted movement to transform mathematics so as to meet the macrocurricular function of general education and to reveal the practical significance of mathematics in modern life was not to appear until we were entering the closing decade of the twentieth century. The intervening years were marked by a counterreaction to the discipline-centered curriculum and the demand for curriculum relevance, only to be followed by a counter-counterreaction of curriculum retrenchment through back to basics.

Citizenship Rediscovered

The disciplinary doctrine had led to a rejection of the social studies and the sociocivic function of the curriculum in favor of the social sciences as discrete domains of specialized scholarship. Throughout the twentieth century, the sociocivic function emerged as one of the central functions of education in this country. Now it was to be totally rejected. After all, the scholar-specialists in the graduate schools who are on the forefront of their disciplines in political science, economics, sociology, and so on, are not concerned with citizenship education but with preparing budding political scientists, economists, and other social scientists. The general education function of the curriculum had come to be rejected, as specialized knowledge in the form of disciplinarity took precedence. For example, the executive director of the American Political Science Association declared that the long-standing tradition of citizenship education is misguided and is a misconception of political science. Accordingly, "political science cannot be conceived as a branch of civics [for i]t is an intellectual discipline, a body of knowledge about the political behavior of human beings."[93] Clearly, there was a failure to recognize that political behavior, like human behavior in general, is influenced psychologically, culturally, socially, economically, and morally.

The protest against Vietnam and the urban convulsions of the late sixties (the eruption of riots, burning, and looting in the ghetto areas of some major cities during the summer of 1967), followed by the Watergate tragedy, gave cause for a re-examination of the sociocivic function of education. Fearing that the Watergate course of events had left a residue of disillusionment and cynicism in the rising generation, the U.S. Office of Education launched its Citizenship Education Program in 1976. Such professional organizations as the American Political Science Association now turned to legitimizing, once again, the sociocivic function of education through its Committee on Pre-college Education.

The National Task Force on Citizenship Education, sponsored by the Danforth and Kettering foundations, issued its report in 1977 calling for the schools to assume the major task of citizenship education in view of the erosion of the educational roles of the home, community, and other institutions. Among the twenty-one recommendations were those involving the idea that citizenship education should be broadened and should provide for (1) the treatment of Constitutional rights and liberties, the environment, ethical values, interdependence of peoples, and human rights and responsibilities; (2) the development of skills of participation in civic life and commitment to values compatible with democratic principles; (3) heterogeneous grouping of students in all schoolwork related to civic competence; (4) the involvement of the entire school faculty in teaching citizenship education; and (5) a democratic school environment.[94]

This report might have given educators cause for wondering why it did not appear at the height of McCarthyism, but even after the fall of Senator McCarthy the Cold War curriculum prevailed along with the continued assaults on academic freedom and the censorship of curriculum materials.[95] The superpatriots who wanted the schools to indoctrinate for patriotism would not recognize that democratic citizenship is abhorrent to indoctrination and requires the capacity and commitment of the citizenry to think and act reflectively on problems and issues. Even to avoid reflective consideration of such problems and issues is to avoid the function of democratic citizenship. In so doing, a kind of citizenship education other than democratic citizenship education will fill the void, whether by intent or default.

The Myth of a Monolithic Structure

With the curriculum reforms at the secondary level being pushed down to the elementary level as the result of the influence of university scholars, it was only a matter of time before these scholars would be impelled to examine the curricula in their own fields at the college level. During the second half of the 1960s, a commission of the American Institute of Biological Sciences sought to identify the common content elements to be used as a basis for developing an ideal undergraduate course of study in biology. The commission reasoned that the best approach would be to identify the common content elements found in the core course work in biology at selected universities that were adjudged to be influential in the field and noted for their teaching programs in biology.

In-depth studies were made of the content of the courses, but it was found that only 7 percent of the course content was shared in common.[96] The commission concluded that there is no single ideal curriculum and it abandoned the notion that there is a common body of content that could serve as a basis for constructing an ideal biology curriculum. Finally, the commission noted that college and university professors would not be amenable to the idea of an ideal curriculum because their orientations differ widely. Ironically, the university scholars who sought to impose ideal curricula on the elementary and secondary schools, formulated according to the structure-of-a-discipline doctrine, avoided any corresponding effort to impose such a model of curriculum reform on their own institutions.

The search for the structure-of-a-discipline was indeed beginning to fade. If such structure could not be found in the highly empirical physical sciences, not to mention the biological sciences, then how could it be found in the social sciences? Even in economics, the most empirical of the social sciences, a Galbraith, Friedman, or Samuelson will come up with entirely different and even conflicting prescriptions for attacking such problems as inflation, unemployment, and poverty. Such prescriptions could not be objectively derived from a quantitative analysis of factual knowledge in the discipline of economics but would be shaped by one's sociopolitical philosophy. Yet, the main thrust of curriculum reform in the social sciences during the disciplinary movement was in imitation of the physical sciences and the search for structure-of-a-discipline.

That one's philosophical and sociopolitical orientation determines how the social sciences are interpreted and used can easily be demonstrated in the practice of changing economic advisers whenever an opposition party wins the U.S. presidential election. It seems only inevitable that efforts to find a monolithic disciplinary structure were bound to fail in economics and other social sciences, as well as in the less empirical areas of language and the fine arts. Yet scholar-specialists in these fields sought to imitate the "hard" sciences in seeking claim to a disciplinary structure to be imposed on the school curriculum. Like the emperor's new clothes in the fable by Hans Christian Andersen, if the university scholar specialists saw the structure-of-the-discipline, so too did the educationists. It must be realized that the disciplinary doctrine did serve to promote the disciplinary bias of specialized university scholarship, even if it was inappropriate for the school curriculum.

EMERGENCE OF ALTERNATIVE APPROACHES TO DISCIPLINARITY

In apparent recognition that there is no monolithic structure of the subject matter of physics, a committee of the American Institute of Physics recommended that alternative types of physics courses be developed so as to make the subject more relevant to adolescent interests and to the problems of humanity. This led to the creation of Harvard Project Physics, a course designed to reveal the humanistic attributes of physics. However, the treatment of physics in terms of practical and technological applications to societal problems remained limited in the Harvard Project Physics course.

Studies undertaken during the development of the Harvard Project Physics course revealed that teachers' personalities and value systems are more strongly related to students' achievement in physics and their attitudes toward the subject than are the extent of teachers' preparation in physics and mathematics and their knowledge of physics.[97] In a related study, the researchers noted that the NSF had spent over $100 million on teacher institutes during the 1960s under the questionable assumption that by upgrading teachers' achievement in subject matter, more effective teaching and learning would result. The report stressed that teacher personality and student attitudes and interests, and the resulting social climate of learning, are much more potent predictors of pupil achievement than the extent of the teachers' specialized study of physics. In pointing out that "academicians from the arts and sciences have criticized education courses as a waste of time and have recommended more courses in their own fields for future teachers," the researchers concluded that these academicians "may be focusing their attention on the wrong variables."[98]

The developers of Harvard Project Physics had hoped that the humanistic approach would help make physics a general education subject in high school. Physics continues to enroll a small proportion of college-bound males. Under the existing curriculum organization and sequence in the high school, students take physics in the twelfth grade after they have completed the study of biology and chemistry. Unless a unified physical science course is developed, the prospects for physics becoming a general education subject in high school remain doubtful.

Many of the science projects at the elementary level were influenced initially by the PSSC rationale and claimed to model the pupil's investigation of science after the fashion of the professional scientist. Claims were made that children were engaging in such scientific processes as formulating hypotheses, controlling variables, interpreting data, and experimenting. Their actual activities appeared to be more accurately described as observing, measuring, inferring, predicting, and communicating.

Efforts to build the subject matter according to the structure-of-a-discipline doctrine gave way to process-oriented approaches. In many projects, the content was organized into diverse units that served as focal points of pupil activity rather than being organized according to the structure of a discipline. An increasing number of emerging projects were organized as combined science studies.

The Curriculum, the Learner, and Society

In the face of exploding societal problems during the late 1960s, an increasing number of members of the scientific community began to level criticisms at the major curriculum projects in the sciences. Writing in the *Bulletin of the Atomic Scientists,* a science historian attacked these projects for their failure to relate to "the realities and problems of modern society," their "failure to give serious consideration to the social effects of science and technology, and failure to include unambiguously the social sciences within the limits of scientific activity." He concluded "[s]cience education is too important to be left in the hands of scientists who hold a narrow view of science and are not concerned with its social implications."[99]

Eventually, the BSCS group began to develop materials that relate biology to adolescent and social problems. Reports by the BSCS group beginning in the early 1970s said that the new BSCS programs would seek to bridge the many interfaces of science and society. One such report by the BSCS director fittingly describes the intended directions of the curriculum reforms advanced today in Project 2061 of the American Association for the Advancement of Science.

> Artificial subject-matter barriers that divide curricular content will tend to disappear, and students will be concerned more and more with solutions to problems where a great variety of disciplines interact. The study of pollution, for example, cannot be contained solely within the discipline of biology or chemistry, but involves all of the natural sciences as well as economics, political science, history, geography, and even art and aesthetics. With subject matter lines breaking down, the education of teachers will not be so much in the disciplines as in societal concerns . . .[100]

This statement might well have been taken not only from the contemporary literature, but from the literature on the core curriculum of the 1930s. Nevertheless, it signaled the recognized place that was to be accorded ecology in the interdisciplinary curriculum of the 1980s and 1990s.

HUMANIZING THE SCHOOLS

The latter half of the 1960s witnessed unprecedented social protest and disruption in central cities and on college campuses that, in turn, filtered down into the schools. College students were demanding curriculum relevance in an era marked by the civil-rights movement, opposition to the U.S. war in Vietnam, and civil disorder in central cities. Following an extended period of school curriculum mobilization for the Cold War and space race, the time seemed ripe for another educational proposal to signal a sharp shift in educational priorities and practices.

REASSESSING WOODS HOLE. Looking back at *The Process of Education* a decade after its publication, Bruner himself acknowledged that the curriculum-reform movement based on the rationale of the Woods Hole conference had missed the mark and had led to much grief. After observing that a Woods Hole conference today would not likely be held in a rural, coastal setting such as Woods Hole, but rather in the heart of a great city, where the problems of the first order of today (urban problems) would be addressed, Bruner went on to call for a moratorium on curriculum reforms based on the structure-of-a-discipline rationale and, instead, advocated that the curriculum be focused on the problems that face us. "We might better concern ourselves with how those problems can be solved, not just by practical action," wrote Bruner, "but by putting knowledge, wherever we find it, to work in these massive tasks."[101]

However, no such concerted curriculum effort was on the immediate horizon. The education programs of the so-called War on Poverty of the middle and late 1960s were fragmentary, tended to treat symptoms rather than being directed at root causes, and were conducted, for the most part, independently of the schools. The literature of the radical romanticists found a wide readership as book after book written by members of this group made the best-seller lists. But the effort proved to be more of a literary one than a programmatic one, and the romantic prescriptions wilted under the practical realities of public education and the harsh demands for competence in the larger society.

"The Remaking of American Education"

It will be recalled that the Carnegie Corporation had joined with various federal agencies in financing the Woods Hole conference that gave us the disciplinary doctrine for curriculum reform in response to the crisis of the Cold War and space race. But this time the Carnegie Corporation turned not to an educator but to a journalist, Charles E. Silberman, member of the board of editors of *Fortune*.

Silberman, who only four years earlier had championed the disciplinary curriculum reforms in a *Fortune* article under the title "The Remaking of American Education,"[102] now pronounced these reforms a failure in his Carnegie report, which was published in 1970 under the title *Crisis in the Classroom* (carrying the promising if not presumptuous subtitle "The Remaking of American Education"). The book immediately became a national best-seller. In 1966 Silberman had extolled the disciplinary reforms as creating "a mass educational system successfully dedicated to the pursuit of intellectual excellence."[103] By 1970, Silberman characterized these reforms as "adult dictation," and went on to write that whereas the university scholars "knew what they wanted children to learn; they did not think to ask what children wanted to learn." Overlooking his own misguided pronouncements of an earlier era, Silberman declared that "the effort was doomed to failure" because it had neglected pupil needs and because the university scholars had acted naively and arrogantly—having had little firsthand experience in the elementary and secondary classroom, and having proceeded to design teacher-proof materials as though teachers are mere technicians. Silberman also criticized the curriculum-reform movement for its "academic provincialism" in being directed at the separate disciplines without seeing the curriculum as a whole.[104] He then proceeded to accuse the university scholars of having committed an even more fatal error, stating that

> The most fatal error of all, however, was the failure to ask the questions that the giants of the progressive movement always kept at the center of their concern, however inadequate some of their answers may have been: What is education for? What kind of human beings and what kind of society do we want to produce? What methods of instruction and classroom organization, as well as subject matter, do we need to produce these results? What knowledge is of most worth?[105]

Silberman's report appeared in the *Atlantic Monthly* as a three-part prepublication serial under these sensation-mongering titles "How the Public Schools Kill Dreams and Mutilate Minds" and "Murder in the Schoolroom."[106] Without presenting any hard data on how children and youth regard their schools and teachers, Silberman proceeded to offer this condemnation: "Because adults take the schools so much for granted, they fail to appreciate what grim, joyless places most American schools are, how oppressive and petty are the rules by which they are governed, how intellectually sterile and barren the atmosphere, what an appalling lack of civility obtains on the part of teachers and principals, what contempt they unconsciously display for children as children."[107]

Some one hundred thirty pages later, however, Silberman belatedly conceded that "[m]ost teachers, however, are decent, honest, well-intentioned people who do their best under the most trying circumstances."[108]

Although Silberman's curriculum proposals for the secondary school were vague and disjointed, and consisted mainly of journalistic-style vignettes describing practices in a variety of schools around the country, he settled on a simple solution for American elementary education, namely the adoption of the open classroom along the lines of the English primary school reforms.

THE OPEN CLASSROOM.   In 1963, the Central Advisory Council for Education (England) was commissioned by the minister of education to make a study of primary education and the transition to secondary education. Soon after the report was released in 1967 it came to be referred to as the Plowden report, after the name of the council's chairman,[109] and it attracted considerable attention among American educators and educational critics.

The Plowden report noted that progressive educational ideas had been slow in being adopted into practice and that although the ideas of Dewey, Whitehead, and others were available in the literature, few teachers had given much time to the study of this literature even in their college days. The report went on to cite promising educational practices in England and recommended their implementation on a wider scale. One of the widespread practices endorsed in the report was the "integrated curriculum." The term *free day* was used in connection with English nursery schools, where the practice is to provide learning through play. Integrated curriculum is a very different concept. The report noted that the integrated curriculum was a revolutionary change from the traditional approach of dividing the curriculum into reading, spelling, grammar, handwriting, composition, arithmetic, and so on. "Throughout our discussion of the curriculum," stated the report, "we stress that children's learning does not fit into the subject categories."[110] After pointing out that even in secondary schools, experience has shown that "teaching of rigidly defined subjects, often by specialist teachers, is far from suitable," the report concluded that "[t]here is little place for the type of scheme which sets down exactly what ground should be covered and what skill should be acquired by each class in the school."[111] Instead, the report advocated broad curriculum schemes for the school as a whole that are revised continuously.

Much of what was described in the Plowden report as desired educational practice appeared to have been taken from the Lincoln School at Teachers College during the 1920s and 1930s. Progressive educational ideas appeared to have come full circle as the Plowden report criticized the rigidly compartmentalized subject matter and suggested other approaches, such as centers of interest, projects, and other ways of relating the curriculum to the wider environment.

The Plowden report went on to illustrate how rural teachers can make use of the environment for nature study, whereas urban teachers can make use of transport systems, museums, and other community resources. In the classroom, the teacher would be working among the children, helping, advising, and discussing much more frequently than standing before the class. Children would move about freely, working purposefully with various materials and resources rather than being locked in their seats.

Silberman was aware of the distinctions to be made between the emerging English approach to informal education and the prescriptions of the American romantic critics. "The informal English schools demonstrate in practice what Dewey argued in theory," noted Silberman, and he went on to conclude that "informal education can work as well in the United States as in England."[112] Silberman devoted an entire chapter, entitled "It Can Happen Here," to show how the English model of informal education would help put American elementary education on the needed course. What Silberman seemed to be saying in his Carnegie report is that America does not need a Silberman report but a Plowden report.

Some American educators rushed to adopt the open classroom as though the English had discovered a new educational panacea. The open-classroom idea, as developed in English primary schools, came to be used to denote such a wide range of adaptations and such differing conceptual stances in American schools as to cause considerable confusion. In many cases the main thrust was on more efficient space utilization and staffing arrangements than on the improvement of learning.

Finally, where the open-classroom concept, as developed in the Dewey school around the turn of the century, was designed to provide for curriculum integration and to foster a democratic social outlook, many schools that claimed to have adopted the open classroom gave little or no consideration to such integration and social goals.

The "Youth Problem"

The 1970s witnessed the issuance of three national reports on the high school and adolescent education. It was clear by the tone and substance of these reports that the agendas were a reaction to the social protest and disruption on the college campuses that filtered down into the high schools during the late sixties and into the early seventies. The tensions led to resignations of presidents of some of the leading universities, such as Clark Kerr of the University of California at Berkeley and Nathan Pusey of Harvard. In his 1971 farewell address to students, Harvard president Pusey, who had announced his early retirement in the wake of violent campus demonstrations in 1969 and 1970, denounced the "power hungry revolutionaries" as "thoroughly deceitful and corrupt."[113]

A 1970 report of a national survey supported by the U.S. Office of Education found that of the urban high schools responding to the questionnaire, 85 percent encountered some kind of disruption during the previous three years. Among the societal causes identified with school disruption were violence in America, visibility and apparent success of college protest, racial-ethnic expression and conflict, participatory democracy, television, situation ethics, and the new permissiveness.[114]

The three national reports on the high school and adolescent education were issued by the National Commission on the Reform of Secondary Education (Kettering Foundation, 1973), the National Panel on High School and Adolescent Education (U.S. Office of Education, 1976), and the Panel on Youth of the President's Science Advisory Committee (1974).[115] All three reports faulted the comprehensive high school for its increased "holding power" over adolescents. Historically, the increased holding power of the American high school had been considered one of the signal accomplishments of American education. Now, in an era of retrenchment, conservative forces were seeking a retreat from historic mission for the universalization of secondary education and the support of a unitary school structure, capped by the comprehensive high school as the vehicle for the vast extension of educational opportunity.

ERA OF RETRENCHMENT.   The other two reports echoed the charges of the Kettering report that the high school had become "literally overrun with a mix of young people from inconsistent social backgrounds," that the comprehensive high school must be eliminated in favor of the academic high school attuned to an academically oriented student population, that alternative specialized schools be developed, and that compulsory school attendance be dropped to age fourteen or that the academic day be severely curtailed for most students so as to allow them to pursue work training under the auspices of business and industry.

In previous eras, radical proposals for changing the structure of the American high school, so as to curtail its function to traditional academic studies for an academically oriented student population, elicited great opposition by the education profession. However, the proposals of the 1970s met with general acquiescence. In 1979, capping a decade of education retrenchment and back to basics, the cover of a leading education journal was captioned, "Managing Education's Era of Decline."[116] Fortunately, the American public was not ready to abandon its belief in education. Unfortunately, the national reports of that era virtually dismissed the democratizing function of the comprehensive high school and the curriculum in general education as the means of fostering a sense of unity through diversity.

Ironically, in his 1978 president's report, Derek Bok of Harvard cited the sociologist James Coleman in noting that many telling democratizing capacities are not so much developed from the formal curriculum than from the experiences through joint association with persons from different backgrounds, cultures, and interests. Bok went on to stress the significance of bringing students of every race, religion, and economic group into joint association through student activities and campus life at Harvard so as "to develop a tolerance and appreciation of human diversity with all its variety of values, backgrounds, and points of view."[117] Unfortunately, unlike James Conant, Bok did not connect this with school life in the comprehensive high school, but with college life on the sequestered Harvard campus. And, ironically, it was none other than James Coleman who had chaired President Nixon's Panel on Youth that, in its report of 1974, attacked the comprehensive high school and called for reducing the high school to more strictly academic functions, creating alternative special-interest high schools, and devising mechanisms for curtailing the formal schooling of disadvantaged youth through work training. It appeared that whereas social diversity was regarded as a powerfully positive democratizing force in the college, it was seen as a negative force in the high school that should not be diverted from its singular college preparatory mission.

Ironically, the 1970s were a time when the colleges were beginning once again to address the need for a coherent core curriculum for general education, whereas the schools were still mired in the retreat to basics, minimum-competency testing, and production-efficiency assessment. The efforts of the colleges to revivify the curriculum in general education were to ebb and flow throughout the eighties and into the nineties.[118]

EDUCATION FOR TECHNO-INDUSTRIAL MOBILIZATION

The foray of national reports on curriculum reform continued unabated during the eighties and nineties. But whereas the reports since the latter 1950s had been directed at mobilization for the Cold War and space race, they were now turned toward techno-industrial mobilization to meet the threat of global economic competition. After decades of Cold War and the creation of a vast weapons economy, U.S. leaders seemed to have suddenly awakened to the realization that Japan and West Germany had each overtaken and surpassed the United States as the dominant powers in the global economic marketplace. As history would have it, once again the public schools were to be the nation's scapegoat.

"Nation at Risk"

In past eras, any major sociopolitical shift was to be accompanied by the call for a marked change in the priorities and directions of the school curriculum. But this time the shift from Cold War mobilization to techno-industrial mobilization found the proposed curricular remedies, with a few variations, remarkably similar to those that followed the launching of Sputnik I.

In a single year (1983) three national reports were issued calling for curriculum priority in the sciences and mathematics through federal funding, raising the requirements in the sciences and mathematics for college entrance, giving increased emphasis to modern foreign languages and computer literacy, using nationwide standardized tests to certify the transition through levels of schooling, raising graduation requirements in the four academic "basics" and adding the "new basic" of computer science, increasing academic learning time and reducing electives, eliminating "nonessential" subjects, instituting ability grouping and special programs for the academically talented, increasing the amount of homework and establishing a longer school day and school year, establishing a federal mechanism for the assessment of student achievement for national, state, and local evaluation and comparison, and raising the standards for teaching.

The report of the National Science Board (NSB) of the National Science Foundation, *Educating Americans for the 21st Century* (1983), held that "[t]he National Science Foundation, which has recognized expertise in leading curriculum development, should again take the leadership role in promoting curriculum evaluation and development for mathematics, science and technology."[119]

Here the NSB report conveniently overlooked the reasons for massive failure of the NSF-funded national curriculum-reform projects which produced the "new math" and "new science" in response to the crisis of the Cold War and space race. In appallingly unscientific fashion, the NSB report sought to make the case for the nation's inferior position against other industrial nations in school achievement by comparing test results for the mass of American eighteen-year-olds with the small elite of compeers in other nations. The report documented this alleged inferiority of U.S. schools with reference to a source that actually warned against such a misinterpretation. The source cited was an article in which the director of the International Assessment for the Evaluation of Educational Achievement stressed that the top U.S. students score as well as the corresponding population in other nations, but in the comprehensive high school system of the United States there is much greater educational yield because there is more opportunity to develop the potentials of both the academically talented and the less able than in the traditional selective systems of Europe.[120] The NSB report went on to call for a national presidential council to formulate national education goals. As discussed later, such goals actually were to be established in 1989 when President Bush convened the education summit with the nation's governors. Finally, the NSB report did present data showing that the federal expenditures for public elementary and secondary schools had been undergoing a decline in both absolute amounts and in proportion to the federal share with the states and localities. At a time when the federal reports were demanding much more from public schools, the levels of federal support were declining. Other recommendations in the national reports of the 1980s called for establishing school-business partnerships, raising the managerial efficiency of schools with the help of the business sector, and raising educational efficiency through instructional technology.

FIXING THE BLAME.   By far the report that garnered the widest treatment in the media and served for over a decade as the launching pad for attacks on public schools and for proposed remedies carried the alarming title, *A Nation at Risk: The Imperative for Educational Reform.* Issued by the National Commission on Excellence in Education, a commission appointed by the U.S. Secretary of Education and chaired by the president-elect of the University of California, the opening words of the report were: "Our nation is at risk." This declaration of alarm was followed by the ominous statement that, "[i]f an unfriendly foreign power had attempted to impose on America the mediocre educational performance that exists today, we might well have viewed it as an act of war."[121]

Fixing the blame on the public schools, rather than on government, industry, the scientific establishment, and the universities, the report went on to declare that, "[t]he citizen is dismayed at a steady 15-year decline in industrial productivity as one American industry after another falls to world competition."[122] The report proceeded to distort the data from the International Evaluation of Educational Achievement by listing as the first "indicator of risk" the allegedly low scores by U.S. students on the tests in comparison with students in other nations. Not until the closing pages of the report was it acknowledged that American schools have been a major vehicle for social and educational opportunity, that the proportion of the American college-age population enrolled in college far exceeds that of other industrial nations, and that international test-score comparisons had revealed that when matched with the best of other nations, U.S. students do indeed compare favorably. Unfortunately, U.S. political leadership and the mass media chose to give credence only to the condemnatory passages of the report.

Leading its list of recommendations under "Content," the report recommended a minimum program for high school graduation consisting of the following requirements in the "Five New Basics": four years of English, three years of mathematics, three years of science, three years of social studies, and one-half year of computer science. For the college-bound, two years of foreign language in the high school were recommended in addition to work taken in foreign language earlier. Clearly, except for computer science, the Five New Basics were the Old Basics clothed in the call to redirect the mission of the schools toward regaining the nation's technological leadership and dominance in global industrial markets.

Among the findings in *A Nation at Risk* were that expenditures for school textbooks and curricular materials had declined by 50 percent over the previous seventeen years, and that the budget for textbooks and related materials now accounted for only 0.7 percent of the operating costs of schools whereas the recommended level ranged from 5 to 10 percent.

Considering that the very impetus for *A Nation at Risk* was grounded in America's decline in the global industrial marketplace, it is puzzling that the Commission on Excellence had little to say about vocational-technical education other than deploring the "migration" of students from vocational and college preparatory programs to "general track" courses in large numbers.

Conveniently overlooked by all was the fact that the original charge to the National Commission on Excellence, which produced *A Nation at Risk,* as stated on page one, was that of "assessing the quality of teaching and learning in U.S. public and private schools, colleges, and universities." Instead, the commission chose not to look at the colleges, universities, and private schools.

The real risk to the United States was that *A Nation at Risk* failed to look at the nation's seething problems of youth unemployment, social disaffection, and conflict—and failed to address the need to modernize the overcrowded and underfinanced schools, the need for a more coherent curriculum in general education, and the need to reconstruct programs in vocational education.

THE BUSINESS-INDUSTRIAL CONNECTION.   Among the many puzzling and contradictory elements common to the national reports on education reform issued during the eighties was the endorsement given the enlistment of the business-industrial sector in increasing the managerial efficiency of public schools. It was the eighties that were characterized as dominated by the "creed of greed," reflecting the enormous fortunes made through ingenious but questionable financial machinations, speculations, and takeover strategies that dominated corporate America, often at the expense of corporate productivity. Once again, the fault of the nation's declining power in global economic competition was not to be fixed on the nation's business-industrial sector, political leadership, or universities—but on the public schools.

Finally, although many of the reports called for the schools to promote good citizenship, there was virtually no mention of *democratic* citizenship and the vital significance of general education at a time when society was becoming increasingly fragmented and divisive.

The report, *Action for Excellence,* issued in 1983 by the Task Force on Education for Economic Growth of the Education Commission of the States, echoed most of the allegations and prescriptions offered in *A Nation at Risk.* In declaring the United States in a state of emergency and in linking the schools with the nation's declining position in the global economic marketplace, the task force recommended that the schools be mobilized through a partnership with industry so as to develop the skilled human capital needed to regain preeminent position.[123]

REDUCING THE CURRICULUM

In contrast to the tone and substance of the reports on school reform issued by national commissions, panels, and task forces, several publications appeared during the 1980s in which the case was made for casting the function of the school in a far more restrictive perspective, and with it the nature and function of the curriculum. Although the back-to-basics retrenchment and minimum-competency testing had failed to deliver what was promised, the advocacy of essentialism continued unabated throughout the 1980s and even gained added momentum during the latter part of that decade in no small measure through the advocacy of William J. Bennett as U.S. Secretary of Education, and the publication of E. D. Hirsch's best-selling *Cultural Literacy* in 1987 (see Chapter 9).

Basic Schooling

As discussed in Chapter 9, Mortimer Adler's *Paideia Proposal: An Educational Manifesto* (1982) made the case for a single-track essentialist curriculum to be followed in the twelve years of basic schooling. Writing on behalf of the Paideia Group—whose membership included many leading essentialist-perennialists—in a project supported by the MacArthur Foundation, Adler delimited the curriculum to the areas of (1) language, literature, and the fine arts, (2) mathematics and natural science, and (3) history, geography, and social studies. In somewhat of a concession for Adler, the essential studies would include some activity in the studio arts and would be supplemented by some "auxiliary studies" consisting of physical education including health, "manual" activities (typing, cooking, sewing, shop classes of a nonvocational nature), capped by a survey of occupations. Vocational training would be provided in the community college or on the job itself.

The essential studies would be treated through "three distinct modes of teaching and learning," namely (1) didactic instruction, lecture and recitation through textbooks, and other aids for the acquisition of organized knowledge; (2) coaching and drilling exercises in reading, writing, speaking, listening, calculating, and so on for the development of intellectual skills (skills of learning); and (3) Socratic questioning and response for the enlarged understanding of ideas and values through the discussion of literary works and other works of art and involvement in artistic activity. There would be no electives other than a choice of a foreign language.

Adler's schema garnered a wide readership, and the advocacy of coaching as a method began to permeate the education literature without a critical examination of the limitations of coaching and drilling exercises as dull and repetitive. Few educators challenged Adler's perennialist configuration of mind (as a muscle)—being strengthened by proceeding from acquisition of information and skills through repetitive drills and exercises, with the teacher functioning as an athletic coach, and finally "raising the mind from a lesser or weaker understanding to a stronger and more fuller one" by means of Socratic questioning.[124] And, surprisingly, school people did not question the validity of Adler's doctrine holding the Socratic method as the epitome of intellective engagement. As far as the nature of the adolescent learner is concerned, it is to be explained by explaining it away. In Adler's words, "youth is an insuperable obstacle to being an educated person,"[125] without explaining how it is possible to become educated without having to live the life of youth.

"Less is More"

The aphorism "less is more" (or "more means worse") was echoed in the arguments by essentialists in Britain during the 1970s as an expression of their opposition to the democratizing efforts of the government to create comprehensive secondary schools. A decade later, it was being echoed by Theodore Sizer, former headmaster of Philips Academy in Andover in *Horace's Compromise: The Dilemma of the American High School* (1984), written under the auspices of the National Association of Secondary School Principals and the National Association of Independent Schools in a project supported by several private foundations. "Horace" is a beleaguered middle-aged teacher of English in a suburban high school who is incessantly compromising his work and concealing his bitterness. As a member of Mortimer Adler's Paideia Group, Sizer drew many of his curricular prescriptions and rationale from the *Paideia Proposal.* "High schools cannot be comprehensive and should not try to be comprehensive," declared Sizer, for the job of the high school is to help students "exercise their minds," and it is through the essential studies that the "discipline and furniture" of the mind are provided. "Compulsory attendance," contended Sizer, "should cease when a young citizen demonstrates mastery of the minima, and most young citizens should master these minima before senior high school."[126]

Sizer proceeded to characterize the American high school as a supermarket; yet he criticized the high schools for mandating most of the courses taken, namely from the five areas of English, social studies, mathematics, science, and physical education. He called for the elimination of vocational education; yet in his selection of an example of an ideal setting for learning, he described a teaching situation in a high school vocational class in electronics in which the students were vitally engaged in hands-on collaborative learning with lessons relating to the physical sciences and mathematics.

"A political philosophy, essentially that associated with American constitutionalism, is the bedrock of enlightened democratic citizenship," declared Sizer. Only a few pages earlier he dismissed the Constitutional principle of state-church separation, which gave the nation the secular public school, when he offered that "by pretending there is a wall between religious issues and their schools, public school people remove themselves from the argument about the ways that religion must properly exist in their schools"—to which he added, "[p]erhaps the most absurd current hullabaloo is over prayer in schools."[127]

Without citing earlier work by progressive educators with block-time classes and the correlation and integration of studies, Sizer proposed that such designs would make it economically feasible for the teacher to work with eighty students daily instead of 120 as is commonly the case.

MAKING THE CASE FOR ESSENTIALIST SCHOOLS.   Sizer proceeded in 1984 to establish a high school-college partnership called the Coalition of Essential Schools, based on a set of common principles for the member schools—mainly that (1) the curriculum is geared to enable each student to "master a limited number of essential skills and areas of knowledge," reflecting the traditional academic disciplines, although not necessarily defined as conventional subjects; (2) the school should not attempt to be comprehensive, but should focus on developing the use of the mind; (3) teaching should be personalized and student loads per teacher should be eighty or fewer; and (4) teachers should perceive themselves as generalists first and specialists second. How is the school to reduce the student load per teacher without appreciable budgetary increases? The answer resides in "the phased reduction or elimination of some services provided students in comprehensive secondary schools"[128] (not to mention that traditional academic studies do not entail the expensive shops, studios, and diversified faculty required in a comprehensive high school).

Sizer's book, *Horace's Compromise,* was identified as the first report from a study of high schools. The second report, also under the same sponsorship, was published a year later (1985) bearing the title, *The Shopping Mall High School.* Whereas Sizer only a year earlier had characterized the American high school as a supermarket, it was now caricatured as a shopping mall. Oddly, both reports were presumably drawn from the same data source. It was claimed in the second report that the studies were based on a rough (sic) national representation of high schools, with the schools "grouped in geographical clusters." With the researchers located in Boston, it turned out that over 35 percent of the student populations in the national representations were enrolled in high schools in and around Boston, and over 77 percent of the national representation were enrolled in schools located in the areas of Boston, San Diego, and Denver.[129] How this could even be construed as a rough representation of American high schools defied the imagination, not to mention the credibility of the research. When James Conant studied the American high school over a quarter of a century earlier, he wisely noted that it is not possible to draw a scientific sampling of schools and student populations that are so massively diverse and geographically separated. Instead, he identified criteria for well-functioning schools and proceeded to develop his recommendations from data drawn from those schools.

NARROWING THE VISION AND MISSION.   Although *The Shopping Mall High School* correctly viewed schools as faced with the challenge of making serious educational demands on students and making it possible for almost all to succeed, the authors viewed these efforts as largely incompatible. The authors concluded that educators need to recognize that schools cannot do everything well for everyone, and that they might better focus the school on intellective purpose and the development of students' intellective capacities through the academic disciplines.

Clearly the authors of the second report had set out to validate Sizer's first report of the study of high schools, and their conclusions and recommendations simply echoed Sizer. The very orientation, design and tone of the reports from a study of high schools might well have given cause for the National Association of Secondary School Principals to sponsor a study of the more successful comprehensive high schools. However, the education literature and the media were not hospitable to the comprehensive or cosmopolitan high school at a time when the fashion was toward curriculum reductionism and the creation of alternative schools with a narrowly defined academic curriculum. Most of the high school principals in that organization were at schools of the comprehensive type. Significantly, despite the attacks on the comprehensive high school and efforts to create a dual system through separate vocational schools, along with the advocacy of returning the high school to a traditional academic curriculum, adolescents in most communities other than major central cities have sought to attend the comprehensive high school when it is seen as their community high school.

Despite the evidence revealing that academic high schools, as opposed to comprehensive high schools, do not deliver the achievement benefits claimed for them, the school-reform literature relentlessly continued to promote the academic high school and the academic curriculum. A recent systematic study of academic high schools of the selective type (high-ability students) corroborated earlier studies in finding that "there is no support whatsoever for any positive benefits associated with attending higher-ability schools." In fact, it was found that some of the outcomes of attending such schools were in a negative direction, such as in selecting less-demanding coursework, developing lower self-concepts and lower educational and occupational aspirations.[130] It seems that in a more naturalistic, mixed-ability high school, students with high academic ability develop a more realistic picture of themselves—not to mention the democratizing benefits and richer curricular offerings that accrue to students at all levels of ability from attending a comprehensive high school.

A Basic Curriculum for Basic Schools

At various times throughout the history of the office of the chief federal education official, proposals for the reform of schools and the curriculum have been issued at the behest of the U.S. Commissioner or Secretary of Education by appointed committees or commissions. However, in capping his tenure as Secretary of Education, William Bennett issued his own proposals for the elementary and secondary school curriculum, outlined in two model schools of his own invention—*James Madison Elementary School* (1988) and *James Madison High School* (1987).

As expected, the curriculum for both the elementary (K–8) and high school (9–12) was centered on the following subjects: English, history/geography/civics, science, foreign language, fine arts, and physical education/health. The elementary curriculum in English begins with phonics, grammar, spelling, vocabulary, writing, and penmanship; beginning in grade three, readings are drawn from the literary classics. The study of science is capped by biology in grade seven and chemistry and physics in grade eight. After grade three the fine arts are oriented toward appreciation and history as opposed to the studio arts.

In the introduction to his proposed high school curriculum, Bennett contended that "schooling in the full set of core academic disciplines should be central to the true purpose of American secondary education, and consequently this curriculum is for the most part traditionally liberal and nonspecialized."[131] All students would be required to complete four years of literature (entirely from the literary classics), two years of history, one year of American democracy, three years of mathematics (from courses in algebra, geometry, trigonometry, calculus, and statistics/probability), three years of science, two years of a foreign language (continued from grades four through eight), two years of physical education/health, and one year of art/music history. A free elective course would be allowed beginning in the sophomore year and increasing time would be allowed for electives in the junior and senior year. If these requirements in mathematics are too demanding for some students, then they should be given an extra year and the help needed.

Neither proposal created a great stir among educators or in the media. After many years of back to basics, proposals for a traditional academic elementary school and high school were not likely to elicit great movement. As Bennett himself stated with reference to his curriculum at James Madison High, "[i]n fact, programs embodying many of its features and principles are currently in effect in a number of schools around the country."[132] As far as the media were concerned, an item in *The New York Times* announcing Bennett's high school proposal was captioned "Education Chief Finds a School to His Liking," and opened with these words: "William J. Bennett, the Secretary of Education, is a severe critic of many American schools, but he has finally found one that he really likes. It is James Madison High School and it exists entirely in his mind."[133]

A Further Look at the Schools

Considering the bludgeoning taken by the schools in the forays of studies and reports on school reform since the 1960s, and considering the blatant contradictions inherent in the reform proposals as well as the epochal shifts to undo the damages of each wave of reform, one might well understand when school people simply tend to go with the dominant tide of the times. One might well sympathize with school people who are hesitant to open the pages of yet another study or report proposal, for fear of being assaulted once again. In reading the opening sentences of *A Place*

Called School (1984), one might well have gotten the impression that it was yet another study and set of proposals in the ilk of the school blamers:

> American schools are in trouble. In fact, the problems of schooling are of such crippling proportions that many schools may not survive. It is possible that the entire public education system is nearing collapse.[134]

"A STUDY OF SCHOOLING." Despite the dire pronouncement, *A Place Called School* proved rich in useful insights and data on schooling and the curriculum. As the key report of a comprehensive project called A Study of Schooling under the direction of John Goodlad, the findings from classroom observations and questionnaires were drawn from thirty-eight schools in thirteen communities in seven sections of the nation. Acknowledging that a truly representative sample of the nation's schools would be an impossibility, Goodlad held that the schools in his study nevertheless had a high degree of variability and representation. He drew on a vast array of source material in his study, that was sponsored through grants from several private foundations and the U.S. Department of Education.

Following almost two decades of back to basics, one could not take issue with Goodlad's findings that the emotional tone of the classroom tends to be flat, that there is a predominance of "frontal teaching" (dominance by the teacher) and the use of worksheets and quizzes with emphasis on repetitive and mechanistic reinforcement of basic skills, and student recitation is largely regurgitative. Goodlad appropriately criticized the common practice of student ability grouping and tracking, pointing out that classes "containing a heterogeneous mixture of students achieving at all levels were more like high than low track classes in regard to what students were studying, how teachers were teaching, and how teachers and students were interacting."[135] He pointed to the need for classrooms to be more cooperative-collaborative in tone and climate, and to give increased emphasis to reflective thinking rather than rote learning and mechanical skills. He warned of the dangers in the trend toward highly specific curricular mandates and interventions by the states.

Goodlad pointed to the need for building curriculum balance and coherence for general education, drawing considerably from the Harvard Report (1945). He went so far as to prescribe the high school curriculum in general education as being drawn from the five "knowledge domains" as follows: up to 18 percent in literature and language (English and other), up to 18 percent in mathematics and science, up to 15 percent each for the social studies, arts, and vocations. Up to 10 percent would be in physical education. The balance (approximately 10 percent) would be in special-interest studies (guided electives). However, he did not explore in any depth how greater curriculum synthesis might be developed through alternative designs to the traditional subject curriculum. As in the more experimental schools of the Eight-Year Study, the problem-focused, integrated core curriculum was successful in providing adolescents with rich opportunities for taking initiative in their learning activities, developing intellectual curiosity and responsible self-direction, extending their capabilities for cooperation and collaboration, and, in short, developing the kinds of interests, capabilities, and commitments that have enormous consequences for life enrichment and success. Overlooking many of the chief short-comings of the national discipline-centered curriculum projects of the 1950s and 1960s other than the inadequate links with teacher education, Goodlad proposed a similar national program with curriculum development centers, each devoted to a given knowledge domain.

EARLY CHILDHOOD AS OPPORTUNITY, ADOLESCENCE AS PROBLEM.   By far the most puzzling and disturbing proposal by Goodlad was for the radical restructuring of the public school system. Instead of one year of kindergarten and twelve years of formal schooling, beginning at age five and ending at age eighteen, he proposed beginning school at age four and ending at age sixteen. He contended that this would reduce the "extraordinary costs in developing curricula," would provide for massive early entrance to college and into the occupations and professions, and, thereby "provide a longer period of payment into social security, helping to bail out this sinking bene-fit of retirement."[136]

Aside from the questionable reasoning for funding the social security program by cutting back on the last two years of secondary schooling is the extraordinary cost to the individual and society in providing productive employment for waves of six-teen-year-olds who do not go on to college. Moreover, they and their compeers would be denied the psychosocial developmental experiences, so vital for adoles-cents, from joint association in the latter years of high school. Efforts to reduce the age of college entrance by two years were attempted during the early 1950s under grants from the Ford Foundation. Even though the early-admissions population was a selected elite in comparison to their compeers in college, they encountered signifi-cantly more adjustment problems and evidenced a high dropout rate. Even those who successfully completed college opined overwhelmingly that they had reserva-tions about such acceleration.[137] The existing structure of twelve years of schooling does not preclude acceleration through advanced placement and early graduation through additional course load and examinations.

For those not going on to college, Goodlad is less certain—perhaps they would enter into a program combining work, study, and service under some form of gov-ernment-business-industry partnership. Here Goodlad seemed to echo the national reports on school reform of the 1970s. Goodlad's stereotypical characterization of adolescents as trivial minded and prone to socially troublesome behavior seemed to serve as justification for delimiting the high school to those who are more amenable to academic studies. "Indeed, one does wonder about the appropriateness of sec-ondary schools," continued Goodlad, "both for the youths who graduate and for those who drop out of the eleventh and twelfth grades," as he went on to propose the "drastic solution" of cutting off the last two years of high school.[138] "The extraor-dinary costs in developing curricula, in teacher frustration, in policing schools, and in monitoring absenteeism will be reduced," reasoned Goodlad. His proposal to begin schooling two years earlier surely had merits, but the question remained as to why the benefit to young children should be paid for by adolescents. Comparative national studies reveal that there is indeed much benefit to be derived from preschool education in terms of socialization whereas there is considerable evidence to show that it is of dubious value for cognitive acceleration.[139] The myth that adolescence is too late and that the die is cast in early childhood emerged from the efforts to seek a short-cut solution in the War on Poverty of the late 1960s and early 1970s. This myth was perpetuated largely through the misinterpretation and distortion of research literature.[140] The consequence was that early childhood programs, such as Head Start, were developed extensively with federal funds whereas programs for adolescents were of the patchwork variety. To this day there is a lack of concerted effort to redesign the high school curriculum with a view toward constructing a rich and stimulating learning environment for adolescents.

A Report on the High School

In view of the long-standing neglect of the need to reconstruct the high school curriculum in recognition of adolescence as a crucial stage of human development, the issuance of *High School: A Report on Secondary Education in America* (1983) by Ernest Boyer, president of the Carnegie Foundation, seemed long overdue. An earlier report on youth education under the auspices of the foundation (1979) had largely echoed the prescriptions directed at the "youth problem" in the national reports of the 1970s by caricaturing the high school as a "prison" for many, and by recommending that the school-leaving age be dropped, that vocational skills be reduced to the basics of literacy and numeracy with skill training provided in the workplace, that early entry to college be encouraged, and that the high school be divided into shared-time specialty schools focused on special-interest studies.[141]

However, at the outset, Boyer stated that his report was specifically aimed at "searching for ways to strengthen the academic quality of the public school." And although he claimed that the "purpose was to examine a cross-section of American public schools," only fifteen public high schools were actually visited for study.[142] Boyer's report drew heavily from Goodlad's "Study of Schooling" which involved data from only twelve high schools.

A SUBJECT CURRICULUM. Boyer proceeded to make a strong case for curriculum coherence by relating the curriculum to "our interdependent, interconnected, complex world." In seeming contradiction, instead of calling for new designs for curriculum correlation and synthesis, he held to the "integrity of the disciplines" and called on teachers of the separate subjects to somehow "bring a new interdisciplinary vision into the classroom" by making the necessary "connections between the disciplines."[143] The high school curriculum, according to Boyer, should be a single academic track with two thirds of the units composed of a core of common learning as follows: five units of language (including two of foreign language and one-half unit in arts), two and one-half units of history and one unit of civics, two units of science, and two of mathematics. In addition, half-unit courses would be required in technology, health, a seminar on work, and a senior independent project.

Of Boyer's five units of language, only two and one-half are in English (basic English, literature, and speech), whereas two are in foreign language. The foreign-language requirement is baffling in view of the massive failure of the drive to develop second-language fluency for all through the National Defense Education Act (1958), when enormous federal funds were expended for this purpose in the absence of recognizing that without the opportunity to communicate in a second language in daily life students are left with only another empty curriculum requirement.

Despite acknowledging the appalling problem of youth unemployment and the expressed interest of many adolescents in vocational education, Boyer viewed the high school as properly becoming more academically oriented with the last two years being devoted to elective clusters for career exploration and the pursuit of advanced academic subjects. Instead of calling for the strengthening of the comprehensive high school, he recommended magnet schools in large urban areas for gifted and talented students in the arts or sciences and a national network of residential academies in science and mathematics. Finally, all students would complete a community service requirement through volunteer work evenings, weekends, or summers.

PROPOSAL FOR AN INTEGRATED, LIFE-RELATED CORE CURRICULUM IN COLLEGE. Boyer's endorsement of the traditional subject curriculum in his core of common learning for the high school is particularly baffling because it has been known for many years that it is unrealistic not only for young adolescents to make the knowledge connections when the studies are segmented, but it is also the case for college students. On completing his report on the high school, Boyer turned to a study of the college. In *College: The Undergraduate Experience in America* (1987), Boyer devoted an entire chapter to his proposal for an integrated core to meet the function of general education—vividly similar in purpose and function to the integrated core developed for students in the more progressive high schools of the Eight-Year Study of almost a half century earlier.

After appropriately pointing to the disjunctures in the undergraduate curriculum as a result of the competing interests of departmentalization, Boyer held that "the core program must be seen ultimately as relating the curriculum consequentially to life" and,

> To achieve these ends, we suggest as one possible approach *the integrated core*. By the integrated core we mean a program of general education that introduces students not only to essential knowledge, but also to connections across the disciplines, and, in the end, to the application of knowledge to life beyond the campus. The integrated core concerns itself with the universal experiences that are common to all people, with those shared activities without which human relationships are diminished and the quality of life reduced.[144]

In many respects, Boyer appeared to have a wider and more integrated vision for the college curriculum, whereas his vision for the high school curriculum was far more traditional. Although he quoted the president of Yale as acknowledging that "[t]he high schools in this country are always at the mercy of the colleges,"[145] Boyer did not explore how the high schools might be freed from this subjugation.

TOWARD THE NEW CENTURY

Despite the curricular conservatism of the proposals for school reform as we entered the last decade of the twentieth century, the indications were clear that the need for a coherent curriculum in general education in the school and college was gaining recognition once again. Not since the progressive education efforts during the first half of the century had such attention been given to whole language, writing across the curriculum, critical thinking, and comprehensive evaluation of student achievement through the uses of student portfolios, projects, and community service activities. However, on closer examination there were indications that many of these contemporary efforts—such as in whole language, writing across the curriculum, and higher-order thinking—were being developed and inserted as segmental programs rather than serving as unifying processes for the macrocurricular function of general education. Nevertheless, there were clear signs that at long last the scientific community was becoming increasingly aware of the limitations of the discipline-centered curriculum and was embarking on programs to point the way toward breaking down the traditional subject boundaries so as to reveal the interconnections among the sciences, mathematics, technology, and the wider social implications.

Reconstructing the Curriculum

In looking to education for the new century, renewed efforts toward curriculum synthesis were occurring in the sciences. Significantly, the thrust was not for knowledge specialism but for a knowledgeable citizenry. The National Science Teachers Association had embarked on a federally funded program, "Scope, Sequence, and Coordination of Secondary School Science" and produced *The Core Content, A Guide for Curriculum Designers* (1992).

Perhaps the most systematic and comprehensive program in this direction was undertaken under the auspices of the American Association for the Advancement of Science. Known as Project 2061, the underlying rationale rejected the notion that more and more subject matter was required. Instead, the curriculum must be reconstructed so as "to reduce the sheer amount of material covered; to weaken or eliminate rigid subject-matter boundaries; to pay more attention to the connections among science, mathematics, and technology; to present the scientific endeavor as a social enterprise that strongly influences—and is influenced by—human thought and action."[146] It was stressed that such efforts should encompass all grades and all studies in the curriculum. The approach taken should build on the curiosity and creativity of students. Instead of starting with emphasis on answers to be learned, the teaching-learning process should start with questions about interesting phenomena. Students should become actively engaged in investigation and knowledge application. Project 2061 has embarked on developing alternative curriculum models for use by the schools with the goal of widespread implementation based on the success of these models.

Unfortunately, the concept of scientific literacy was chosen as the conceptual goal of Project 2061 rather than general education—unfortunate simply because of the great proliferation of literacies and the curriculum fragmentation resulting from each special-interest group seeking to promote its own literacy in the school curriculum. Although most of the panels for Project 2061 (biological and health sciences, physical and informational sciences and engineering, mathematics, and technology) developed rationales consistent with the overarching goals of Project 2061, the panel on social and behavior sciences reflected a disciplinary bias with a focus on abstract concepts rather than life problems and knowledge applications for democratic citizenship.[147] It was clear that any concerted effort to reconstruct the curriculum for general education requires that university scholars put aside their microscopic lenses of specialism and look more ecologically at the curriculum.

REDISCOVERING THE INTEGRATED CORE CURRICULUM.   A quarter of a century ago, Arthur Foshay wrote that, "[t]he questions of the integration of knowledge and the relevance of knowledge to the real world will not be denied [and i]t is predictable that we will reinvent the core curriculum."[148] As discussed, in the closing decade of the twentieth century it was becoming increasingly apparent that the forces for knowledge specialism in academia and the fragmentation and conflict in society required a renewed and concerted effort toward curriculum synthesis for general education in a democracy.

The inescapable need for a sense of coherence and synthesis in the curriculum is reflected in Figure 11–3. At first glance it seems that the subjects in the curriculum are related in a kind of symmetry. However, such symmetry only begins to take shape when the subjects are interrelated as broad fields (e.g., natural science, humanities, language arts and communications, social studies and history, and so on), or when they are correlated and fused into more functional combinations. As discussed in Chapter 10 and illustrated in Figure 11–3, full synthesis derives when the knowledge categories become subsumed through the study of life problems. In developing the school curriculum, or for that matter the college curriculum, it becomes readily apparent that the parts—the multitude of separate subjects, disciplines, and specializations—taken together, do not make up the whole of an education. The idea and practice of general education stem from a fundamental precept of American democracy—education for an enlightened citizenry. In contrast to knowledge specialization, general education requires knowledge synthesis. In the light of the American experience, Arthur Foshay's prediction on the reinvention of the core curriculum is so wise and valid.

As we entered the last decade of the twentieth century, a variety of designs was being developed to provide for a more interrelated curriculum through faculty teams, block-time or modular-flexible scheduling, and thematic or problem-focused courses in ecology, civics for democracy, consumer education, and so on.[149] Such efforts, however successful, were being made in the face of increasing statewide and national testing programs and other nationalizing influences affecting the curriculum.

America 2000/Goals 2000

In an address at the White House in the spring of 1991 attended by the nation's governors, President George Bush announced his program, America 2000, for the "revo-

Figure 11–3. Curriculum Eclosion and Synthesis.

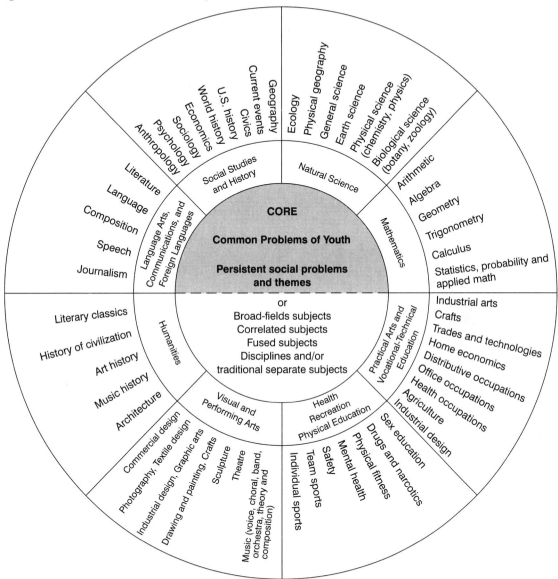

lutionary" transformation of schools. Two years earlier President Bush had convened the Education Summit with the nation's governors from which the six national education goals were adopted with the pledge that the goals would be met by the year 2000. In response to the Education Summit, Congress established the National Council on Education Standards and Testing and the National Education Goals Panel that was created to report annually to Congress on the progress toward the goals. The six national education goals to be attained by the year 2000 were: (1) all children will start school ready to learn; (2) the high school graduation rate will be at least 90 percent; (3) U.S. students will leave grades four, eight, and twelve having demonstrated competency in the five core subjects of English, mathematics, science, history, and geography; and all students will learn to use their minds well, so they may be prepared for further learning and productive employment in the modern economy; (4) U.S. students will be first in the world in science and mathematics achievement; (5) every adult will be literate and possess the knowledge and skills necessary to compete in a global economy and exercise the rights and responsibilities of citizenship; and (6) every school will be free of drugs and violence and will offer a disciplined environment conducive to learning.[150]

Almost immediately after taking office, under the rubric of Goals 2000, President Bill Clinton endorsed virtually all of the elements in *America 2000* with the exception of Bush's call for school vouchers. As governor of Arkansas Clinton had taken a leadership role at the Education Summit and in the development of the national education goals. Clearly, the first goal of school readiness could not possibly be met without massive social reconstruction to eliminate poverty and social conflict, not to mention the acculturation problems of new waves of immigrant families from underdeveloped, diverse nations. And even if the nation embarked immediately on such a program, the year 2000 was only a few short years ahead.

Thoughtful educators might also have cause for concern that renewed impetus was being given to the test-driven curriculum and to the announced plan to assess student achievement in meeting "new World Class Standards" through "American Achievement Tests," with priority given to the sciences and mathematics. Once again, it was held that the United States has the world's best system of higher education whereas the system of elementary and secondary education puts the "nation at risk."[151] No explanation was given to how it is possible for such a disjuncture to exist when American high school graduates have no problem competing against the best and brightest students of other nations who attend U.S. colleges and universities, and when the United States provides access to higher education for a larger proportion of its population than any other nation. Once again, in defining the essential studies, the five traditional academic subjects were listed, to the omission of the arts and social studies (other than geography and history). The immediate response to Goals 2000 was for the various professional associations to establish achievement standards for their subject fields. Although the efforts were clearly directed at general education, insufficient attention was being given to what each subject domain can contribute to other areas of knowledge so as to create a coherent, balanced, and articulated curriculum for general education. Finally, the gnawing problem of children and youth in poverty and who cannot leave their problems at home when they go to school, and of youth who are unable to find a productive role in society, remained the unfinished business of the nation.

"The Facts Will Kick"

As discussed in Chapter 13, American public education has been buffeted by contradictory pressures for reform and counterreform, by successive shifts in political priorities from the White House to the state house, by a penchant for the mass media to look for bad news on the schools, and for university social scientists to take on a profound negativism toward the schools. There is a saying that in the end, "the facts will kick."

Following the issuance of *America 2000,* a number of studies began to appear giving evidence that the allegations leveled at American public education and the priorities set for the reform of the school system in *America 2000, A Nation at Risk,* and in other policy documents reflected much misinformation and were seriously misdirected. Although these problems in education policy and research are treated in detail in Chapter 13, a brief mention is made here in view of our discussion of the pervasive national syndrome of school blaming and the radical proposals made for American public education in looking to the prospects for the new century.

A comprehensive study, *Perspectives on Education in America,* conducted by the Sandia National Laboratories for the U.S. Department of Energy, was effectively suppressed by the U.S. Department of Education and delayed from publication for more than two years because so many of the principal findings ran counter to the allegations and priorities in *America 2000* and *Goals 2000.*[152] Drawing data from such accredited sources as the National Center for Education Statistics, National Science Foundation, U.S. Department of Education, U.S. Department of Labor, U.S. Bureau of the Census, College Entrance Examination Board, National Assessment of Educational Progress, and various international agencies, the Sandia study revealed that, among other favorable findings, changes in SAT scores were the result of demographic changes, and that when today's test-takers are matched against the test-taking population of the late 1970s, the SAT scores were actually rising; that the U.S. led the world in the proportion of its population earning the bachelor's degree in all fields, and in science and engineering in particular; that despite declines in the college-age population, the number of doctorates in the physical sciences and engineering was at an all-time high; and that the United States was underinvested in elementary and secondary education, contrary to the data presented in *America 2000.* The study also revealed that dramatic and accelerating demographic changes have been taking place in schools as a result of increases in immigration, representing more than 150 languages, and that almost one third of the pupils were minorities, principally from Latin America and Asia.

With regard to the goal of U.S. students being first in the world in science and mathematics, the Sandia study found that if comparisons were made of those completing their scientific studies, the evidence already pointed to the United States being first in the world. The Sandia study stressed that educational priorities need to be directed toward improving the education of minority and inner-city children and youth. Whereas *America 2000* claimed the systemwide failure of schools, the Sandia data referred to this as "crisis commentary" that is "simply not true."[153]

A number of other studies by international agencies in the 1990s revealed U.S. public education ranked highest or among the highest in educational yield, but that the United States failed to make the top ten among the world's industrial nations in indices of health and child welfare.[154] It was also found that although U.S. schools ranked high on various measures of academic achievement, the United States ranked low in access to early childhood education (pre-kindergarten) in comparison to other industrial nations, as well as in access to vocational education in the secondary school.[155]

It appeared that the United States clearly needed a reformulation of the prescriptions and priorities in *Goals 2000,* an end to the crisis rhetoric, and a concerted commitment on the part of the political and educational leadership to build on the comprehensive, cosmopolitan, and humanitarian qualities of schools.

PERSPECTIVE

"Ours is an age of crisis," declared Silberman, but every age is an age of crisis. In the curriculum field, as in other areas of human activity, a crisis mentality tends to breed narrow-minded prescriptions and to lead to extreme actions that sooner or later result in a call for countereactions.

For well over a decade, the major thrust of curriculum reform in elementary and secondary schools was directed by the disciplinary view of knowledge as promulgated by the world of university scholarship. The structure-of-a-discipline doctrine was invented to guide the new curriculum-reform movement. The fact that disciplinarity is only one mode for organizing and viewing knowledge was virtually ignored by those who sought to model the school curriculum after the specialized and puristic knowledge domains of university scholarship.

The priority accorded the sciences and mathematics as a result of the crisis psychosis of the Cold War and space race resulted in a new curriculum hierarchy and imbalance, and led to the compression of college-level studies down into the high-school curriculum. Moreover, the focus on the separate disciplines of knowledge served to aggravate the problem of curriculum fragmentation. Instead of seeing the school curriculum as an ecological whole, it was regarded simply as the sum of its constituent parts. Thus, although the reform efforts were hailed as a veritable curriculum revolution, the strategy taken was one of developing disciplinary curriculum packages to be adopted by the schools independently of the relationships of a given knowledge package to other areas of knowledge in the school curriculum. Some of the leading spokespeople for the major science projects actually maintained that teacher-proof curricula were needed, as though the teacher is merely a low-grade technician whose job it is to plug himself or herself in to the self-propelled curriculum package.

No doubt the school curriculum at midcentury needed reconstruction, for it was deeply ingrained with factual information and narrow skills that were remote from the life of the learner. However, the disciplinary view of knowledge is so centrifugal, and each knowledge domain becomes so turned back on itself, that it loses its connections with other knowledge domains and with the ordinary but vital problems of life. Moreover, whatever justification could be offered for the disciplinary mode of scholarship in the university is insufficient for imposing the same model on the elementary and secondary schools.

Disciplinarity remains a powerful force in the realm of specialized university scholarship and it continues to influence the school curriculum. However, the curriculum of the school and college encompasses far more than specialized and departmentalized knowledge. The sum of the separate disciplines cannot make a whole curriculum. Because educators are working with real people in action-relevant contexts, curriculum development requires systematic consideration of (1) the nature and interests of the learner, (2) the problems of society, (3) the interdependence of knowledge, (4) the continuity between theoretical and applied knowledge, (5) the authentic function of general education as compared with that of specialized education, and (6) involvement of the whole school community, and not merely the scholar-specialist. Such considerations require interdisciplinary and social-problem approaches to curricular organization. Inquiry into such problems is uniquely different from inquiry into abstract and specialized knowledge. The paradigm of the curriculum field (discussed in detail in Chapter 3) re-emerged once again as we entered the last quarter of the century.

What is so puzzling, however, is that the disciplinary doctrine gained adherents among the fraternity of educationists, including curriculum theorists, and that it dominated the curriculum field for so long a period. The crisis of the space race and the unprecedented level of funding of discipline-centered curriculum projects clearly contributed to the long-held dominance of the disciplinary doctrine. The voices of opposition to such a narrow doctrine and to the turning of the curriculum to meet narrow nationalistic interests were rarely heard.

In the face of these nationalizing influences on the curriculum, during the closing years of the twentieth century, a renewed effort was being made to build a common core of learning in the school and college. Some were contending that such a core was especially needed as a counterpoint to the alleged exponential explosion of specialized knowledge. However, it was becoming increasingly evident that in approaching the new century, the pervading need was how to marshal knowledge for an effective attack on the exploding problems of society, and how to develop the needed curriculum synthesis for creating a sense of unity through our great social diversity.

The march of democracy in world affairs during the closing years of the twentieth century gives evidence that those who sought to advance the idea and practice of general education in the school and college were on the side of history.

One of the great ironies is that the nationalizing influences on the curriculum to meet the alleged crisis of the Cold War and space race should be turned during the closing years of the twentieth century toward techno-industrial mobilization to meet the alleged crisis of economic competition with Japan and Germany. In both eras of "crisis," priority was to be given to the sciences and mathematics and impetus was given to national achievement testing. Under such circumstances, the quest for a balanced and coherent curriculum, consonant with the ideals of a free society, is forgotten or abandoned. This quest persistently reappears at regular intervals because it cannot be denied indefinitely. In an age of knowledge specialism and social fragmentation, the need for a unified core curriculum for general education was never more significant.

PROBLEMS FOR STUDY AND DISCUSSION

1. How do you account for the failure of those responsible for the discipline-centered curriculum reforms to take into account (a) the relationship of a given curriculum project to other new projects being adopted by the schools and (b) the relationship of the new curriculum project to the total curriculum of the school? What is the situation today with regard to curriculum-reform projects?

2. Many of those who advocated teacher-proof curricula were, at the same time, calling for inquiry-focused teaching. Do you see a contradiction between teacher-proof curricula and inquiry-focused teaching? Explain.

3. What role should teachers play in curriculum development? Justify your answer.

4. What trends do you see today in the direction of curriculum change? In your opinion, what kinds of changes are needed? Explain.

5. How do you account for the lack of any strong opposition to the disciplinary movement by educationists over a period of more than a decade? Is there any strong opposition to the dominant curriculum movement today? Explain.

6. What is your assessment of the charges leveled at the public schools in the report *A Nation at Risk*? How do you account for the failure of the National Commission on Excellence, which issued the report, to fix the blame for the United States' alleged industrial decline in the global economy with leadership in industry, government, or even higher education?

7. How do you account for the division of the school curriculum into "academic" and "nonacademic" subjects, whereas no such division exists in the college or university? What are the educational and social consequences of such a curriculum division in the schools?

8. From his study of grouping practices in the schools, Goodlad found that heterogeneously grouped classes reflect a more productive learning atmosphere than homogeneous classes. Consequently, he recommended that in the common core of studies at all levels of schooling, students should be assigned to classes randomly so as to ensure heterogeneity [John Goodlad, *A Place Called School*, pp. 297–298]. Considering the intended function of general education, what is the underlying rationale for heterogeneous grouping? Do you agree with Goodlad? Explain.

9. Examine the secondary school curriculum in your own school district and the undergraduate curriculum in your university (or college). Is there a common core of studies for general education? To what extent are students allowed to meet the requirements in general education through distributed electives? It is widely conceded that the function of general education is not served through distribution-elective requirements. How do you account for the wide continuation of this practice in high schools and colleges?

10. If you were asked to submit a plan for redesigning the curriculum for your school, what would be the major features and recommendations in your plan? What arguments would you raise in support of your plan?

11. In reviewing the American Library Association's *Newsletter on Intellectual Freedom*, school censorship incidents center on textbooks, literary works, and library materials. Despite the wide use of computer-assisted instruction in the schools, there are virtually no censorship incidents directed at computer programs or, for that matter, programmed instruction. How do you account for this?

NOTES

1. James B. Conant, *Education in a Divided World* (Cambridge, MA: Harvard University Press, 1949), p. 22.
2. *The New York Times,* May 31, 1988, pp. A2, 14.
3. Conant, op. cit., pp. 5–6, 64, 70, 151.
4. Ibid., p. 50.
5. Robert M. Hutchins, "The Great Anti-School Campaign," *The Great Ideas Today* (Chicago: Encyclopedia Britannica, 1972), p. 155.
6. Edward A. Ross, *Social Control* (New York: Macmillan, 1901), p. 172.
7. Ibid., p. 177.
8. Commission on the Reorganization of Secondary Education, *Cardinal Principles of Secondary Education* (Washington, DC: U.S. Bureau of Education, 1918), pp. 19–20.
9. Ibid., p. 32.
10. *The New York Times,* Dec. 21, 1993, p. C12.
11. See John Dewey, *Democracy and Education* (New York: Macmillan, 1917), pp. 138, 141, 144–145; Commission on the Reorganization of Secondary Education, op. cit., p. 9.
12. Ibid., p. 16.
13. James B. Conant, *The Child, the Parent, and the State* (Cambridge, MA: Harvard University Press, 1959), p. 93.
14. Herbert M. Kliebard, *The Struggle for the American Curriculum* (London: Routledge, 1986), p. 112.
15. Alexander Inglis, *Principles of Secondary Education* (Boston: Houghton Mifflin, 1918), pp. 667–668.
16. Ibid., p. 668.
17. Ibid., p. 712.
18. Commission on the Reorganization, op. cit., p. 27.
19. Ibid., p. 26.
20. Ibid., p. 22.
21. Ibid., pp. 14–15.
22. Will French, *Behavioral Goals of General Education in High School* (New York: Russell Sage, 1957), p. 22.
23. R. Freeman Butts and Lawrence A. Cremin, *A History of Education in American Culture* (New York: Holt, 1953), p. 505.
24. Richard Hofstadter, *Anti-intellectualism in American Life* (New York: Alfred A. Knopf, 1962), p. 336.
25. Educational Policies Commission, *Education for ALL American Youth* (Washington, DC: National Education Association, 1944), p. vi.
26. Educational Policies Commission, *Education for ALL American Children* (Washington, DC: National Education Association, 1948), p. 156.
27. Educational Policies Commission, *The Structure and Administration of Education in American Democracy* (Washington, DC: National Education Association, 1938), p. 6.
28. Edward L. McDill, Mary S. McDill, and J. Timothy Sprehe, *Strategies for Success in Compensatory Education* (Baltimore: Johns Hopkins University Press, 1969), pp. 19–23.
29. Commission on the Reorganization, op. cit., pp. 225–226.
30. Hyman G. Rickover, *American Education—A National Failure* (New York: Dutton, 1963), pp. 161–162.
31. Arthur Bestor, *The Restoration of Learning* (New York: Alfred A. Knopf, 1956), pp. 60, 326.
32. Committee on General Education in a Free Society, *General Education in a Free Society* (Cambridge, MA: Harvard University Press, 1945), p. 14.
33. Ibid., p. 102.
34. Ibid., p. 176.
35. Bestor, op. cit., pp. 402–403.
36. Hearings, Committee on Labor and Public Welfare, U.S. Senate, 85th Congress, *Science and Education for National Defense* (Washington, DC: U.S. Government Printing Office, 1958).
37. James B. Conant, *The American High School Today* (New York: McGraw-Hill, 1959), pp. 75–76.
38. James B. Conant, *Education in the Junior High School Years* (Princeton, NJ: Educational Testing Service, 1960).
39. Ibid., p. 45.
40. James B. Conant, *Slums and Suburbs* (New York: McGraw-Hill, 1961), pp. 3, 146.
41. Ibid., p. 147.
42. Hans Vaihinger. *The Philosophy of "As If"* (London: Routledge, 1924), p. 170.

43. John Dewey, *Freedom and Culture* (New York: Putnam, 1939), p. 152.

44. John von Neumann, in R. B. Heywood (ed.), *The Works of the Mind* (Chicago: University of Chicago Press, 1947), p. 196.

45. Alvin M. Weinberg, *Reflections on Big Science* (Cambridge, MA: M.I.T. Press, 1967), pp. 74–75.

46. Ibid., pp. 75, 82.

47. Ibid., p. 145.

48. Ernest Becker, *The Lost Science of Man* (New York: Braziller, 1971), pp. 81, 121.

49. Morris Kline, *Why Johnny Can't Add: The Failure of the New Math* (New York: St. Martin's, 1973), p. 135.

50. Jerome S. Bruner, *The Process of Education* (Cambridge, MA: Harvard University Press, 1960).

51. Elizabeth Hall, "Bad Education—A Conversation with Jerome Bruner," *Psychology Today,* 4 (December 1970), p. 51.

52. John Dewey, *Democracy and Education* (New York: Macmillan, 1916), p. 113.

53. Ibid., pp. 109–110.

54. *Education in the USSR* (Washington, DC: U.S. Office of Education, 1957), pp. 1, 220–223.

55. *Soviet Commitment to Education,* Report of First Official U.S. Education Mission (Washington, DC: U.S. Office of Education, 1959), p. 116.

56. Bruner, op. cit., p. 31.

57. Ibid., p. 26.

58. Joseph J. Schwab, "The Concept of the Structure of a Discipline," *The Educational Record,* 43 (July 1962), p. 197.

59. Ibid., p. 203.

60. Albert Szent-Gyorgi, "Interdisciplinary Science Education: A Position Paper," *The Science Teacher,* Supplement, 37 (November 1970), p. 3.

61. Philip H. Phenix, in A. Harry Passow (ed.), *Curriculum Crossroads* (New York: Teachers College, 1962), pp. 57–58, 64.

62. National Society for the Study of Education, *Art Education,* 64th Yearbook, Pt. II (Chicago: University of Chicago Press, 1965), pp. 121–122; Getty Center for Education in the Arts, *Beyond Creating: The Place for Arts in American Schools* (Los Angeles: Author, 1985); National Society for the Study of Education, *The Arts, Education, and Aesthetic Knowing,* 91st Year-

book, Pt. II (Chicago: University of Chicago Press, 1992), pp. 42–43, 74–75, 114–115, 188. In sharp contrast is the case made for art in general education and the enrichment of ordinary life as explicated by John Dewey in *Art as Experience* (New York: Putnam, 1934).

63. Weinberg, op. cit., pp. 153–154.

64. Alfred North Whitehead, *The Aims of Education* (New York: Macmillan, 1929), pp. 4, 6, 58, 61.

65. John Dewey, *How We Think* (Lexington, MA: D. C. Heath, 1933), p. 62.

66. Dewey, *Democracy and Education,* op. cit., p. 397.

67. von Neumann, op. cit.

68. Marshall H. Stone, "The Revolution in Mathematics," *Liberal Education,* 47 (May 1961), pp. 4–6.

69. Whitehead, op. cit., p. 3.

70. Bruner, op. cit., p. 14.

71. Ibid., p. 40.

72. Lawrence Senesh, "The Organic Curriculum: A New Experiment in Economic Education," *The Councilor,* 21 (March 1960), pp. 3, 13.

73. Whitehead, op. cit., p. 50.

74. Ibid., p. 27.

75. John Dewey, *The School and Society* (Chicago: University of Chicago Press, 1899), p. 102.

76. Ibid., pp. 103–104.

77. Bruner, *The Process of Education,* op. cit., p. 52.

78. Sir Alec Clegg, in J. Stuart Maclure, *Curriculum Innovation in Practice,* Report of the Third International Curriculum Conference (London, England: Her Majesty's Stationery Office, 1968), p. 9.

79. James J. Gallagher, "Teacher Variation in Concept Presentation," *BSCS Newsletter,* 30 (January 1967), p. 17.

80. American Institute of Physics, *Physics in Your High School* (New York: McGraw-Hill, 1960), pp. 17–18.

81. *Carnegie Quarterly,* 18 (Fall 1970), p. 5; Susanne D. Ellis, "Enrollment Trends," *Physics Today,* 20 (March 1967), p. 77.

82. Donivan J. Watley and Robert C. Nichols, *Career Decisions of Talented Youth: Trends Over the Past Decade* (Evanston, IL: National Merit Scholarship Corporation, 1969), pp. 2, 4–18.

83. Philip H. Abelson, "Excessive Educational Pressures," *Science,* 156 (May 12, 1967), p. 741.

84. *Carnegie Quarterly,* op. cit.

85. L. Carroll King, in "High Student Failure Rate Serious Problem," *Chemical and Engineering News,* 45 (February 20, 1967), p. 44.

86. L. V. Ahlvors et al., "Mathematics Curriculum of the High School," *American Mathematical Monthly,* 69 (March 1962), pp. 189–193.

87. Richard Courant, in George F. Carrier, Richard Courant, Paul Rosenbloom, C. N. Yang, and H. J. Greenberg, "Applied Mathematics: What Is Needed in Research and Education," *SIAM Review,* 4 (October 1962), pp. 297–320.

88. R. W. Hemming, "Numerical Analysis versus Mathematics," *Science,* 148 (April 1965), p. 474.

89. Report of the Cambridge Conference on School Mathematics, *Goals for School Mathematics* (Boston: Houghton Mifflin, 1963), pp. 2–3.

90. Kline, op. cit., p. 129.

91. Ibid., p. 133.

92. Dewey, *How We Think,* op. cit., p. 62.

93. Evron M. Kirkpatrick and Jeane J. Kirkpatrick, "Political Science," in *High School Social Studies: Perspectives* (Boston: Houghton Mifflin, 1962), p. 103.

94. National Task Force on Citizenship Education, *Education for Responsible Citizenship* (New York: McGraw-Hill, 1977), pp. 9–12.

95. See any of the back issues of the *Newsletter on Intellectual Freedom* of the American Library Association.

96. Commission on Undergraduate Education in the Biological Sciences, *Content of Core Curricula in Biology* (Washington, DC: Author, 1967), p. 21.

97. Arthur I. Rothman, Wayne Welch, and Herbert J. Walberg, "Physics Teacher Characteristics and Student Learning," *Journal of Research in Science Teaching,* 6 (1969), p. 63.

98. Herbert J. Walberg and Arthur I. Rothman, "Teacher Achievement and Student Learning," *Science Education,* 53 (April 1969), pp. 256–257.

99. George Basalla, "Science, Society, and Science Education," *Bulletin of the Atomic Scientists,* 24 (June 1968), pp. 45, 48.

100. William V. Mayer, "The Unreal School in the Real World," *BSCS Newsletter,* 54 (February 1974), p. 5; Mary Clark, *Biological and Health Sciences,* Project 2061 (Washington, DC: American Association for the Advancement of Science, 1989).

101. Jerome S. Bruner, "The Process of Education Revisited," *Phi Delta Kappan,* 53 (September 1971), p. 21.

102. Charles E. Silberman, "The Remaking of American Education," *Fortune,* 63 (April 1961), pp. 125–131.

103. Charles E. Silberman, "Technology Is Knocking at the Schoolhouse Door," *Fortune,* 74 (August 1966), p. 122.

104. Charles E. Silberman, *Crisis in the Classroom* (New York: Random House, 1970), pp. 180, 181, 183.

105. Ibid., p. 182.

106. Charles E. Silberman, "How the Public Schools Kill Dreams and Mutilate Minds," *Atlantic Monthly,* 226 (June 1970), pp. 83–95; "Murder in the Schoolroom" (July 1970), pp. 83–97, and (August 1970), pp. 85–98.

107. Silberman, *Crisis in the Classroom,* op. cit., p. 10.

108. Ibid., p. 142.

109. Report of the Central Advisory Council for Education (England), *Children and Their Primary Schools* (London: Her Majesty's Stationery Office, 1967).

110. Ibid., p. 203.

111. Ibid., p. 198.

112. Silberman, *Crisis in the Classroom,* op. cit., pp. 220–266.

113. *The New York Times,* June 16, 1971, p. 29.

114. Steven K. Bailey, *Disruption in Urban Public Secondary Schools* (Reston, VA: National Association of Secondary School Principals, 1970), pp. 626–637; see also National Commission on the Causes and Prevention of Violence, *Violence in America* (Washington, DC: U.S. Government Printing Office, 1969).

115. National Commission on the Reform of Secondary Education, *The Reform of Secondary Education* (New York: McGraw-Hill, 1973); Report of the National Panel on High School and Adolescent Education, *The Education of Adolescents* (Washington, DC: U.S. Office of Education, 1976); Panel on Youth of the President's Science Advisory Committee, *Youth:*

Transition to Adulthood (Chicago: University of Chicago Press, 1974).

116. *Phi Delta Kappan,* 61 (October 1979).
117. "The President's Report," *Harvard Magazine,* 80 (May–June 1978), n.p.
118. National Institute of Education, *Involvement in Learning: Realizing the Potential of American Higher Education* (Washington, DC: Author, 1984); Association of American Colleges, *Integrity in the College Curriculum* (Washington, DC: Author, 1985); Ernest L. Boyer, *College: The Undergraduate Experience in America* (New York: Harper, 1987).
119. National Science Board, *Educating Americans for the 21st Century* (Washington, DC: National Science Foundation, 1983), p. 46.
120. Torsten Husén, "Are Standards in U.S. Schools Really Lagging Behind Those in Other Countries?" *Phi Delta Kappan,* 64 (March 1983), p. 456.
121. National Commission on Excellence in Education, *A Nation at Risk* (Washington, DC: U.S. Department of Education, 1983), p. 5.
122. Ibid., p. 18.
123. Task Force on Education for Economic Growth, *Action for Excellence* (Denver: Education Commission of the States, 1983).
124. Mortimer J. Adler, *The Paideia Proposal: An Educational Manifesto* (New York: Macmillan, 1982), p. 53.
125. Ibid., p. 9.
126. Theodore R. Sizer, *Horace's Compromise* (Boston: Houghton Mifflin, 1984), pp. 84, 88, 89, 216.
127. Ibid., pp. 128, 133.
128. Coalition of Essential Schools, *Prospectus* (Providence, RI: Brown University, October 1988).
129. Arthur G. Powell, Eleanor Farrar, and David K. Cohen, *The Shopping Mall High School* (Boston: Houghton Mifflin, 1985), pp. 326–332.
130. Herbert W. Marsh, "Failure of High-Ability High Schools to Deliver Academic Benefits Commensurate with Their Students' Ability Levels," *American Educational Research Journal,* 28, (Summer 1991), pp. 445–480.
131. William J. Bennett, *James Madison High School* (Washington, DC: U.S. Department of Education, 1987), p. 2.

132. Ibid., p. 4.
133. *The New York Times,* Dec. 16, 1987, p. B7.
134. John I. Goodlad, *A Place Called School* (New York: McGraw-Hill, 1984), p. 1.
135. Ibid., p. 159.
136. Ibid., p. 346.
137. Fund for the Advancement of Education, *They Went to College Early* (New York: Ford Foundation, 1957), pp. 62, 68.
138. Goodlad, op cit., p. 325.
139. David A. Walker, *The IEA Six Subject Survey* (New York: Wiley, 1976).
140. Benjamin S. Bloom, *Stability and Change in Human Characteristics* (New York: Wiley, 1984).
141. Carnegie Council on Policy Studies in Higher Education, *Giving Youth a Better Chance* (San Francisco: Jossey-Bass, 1979), pp. 1, 22–24.
142. Ernest L. Boyer, *High School* (New York: Harper, 1983), pp. xii–xiii.
143. Ibid., pp. 114–117.
144. Ernest L. Boyer, *College* (New York: Harper, 1987), p. 91.
145. Ibid., p. 252.
146. American Association for the Advancement of Science, *Science for ALL Americans* (Washington, DC: Author, 1989), p. 5.
147. American Association for the Advancement of Science, *Social and Behavioral Sciences* (Washington, DC: Author, 1989), pp. 26–29.
148. Arthur W. Foshay, "How Fare the Disciplines?" *Phi Delta Kappan,* 51 (March 1970), p. 352.
149. John M. Jenkins and Daniel Tanner (eds.), *Restructuring for an Interdisciplinary Curriculum,* 1992, and Ronald Williamson, *Scheduling the Middle School Level,* 1993. (Reston, VA: National Association of Secondary School Principals); "Integrating the Curriculum," theme issue, *Educational Leadership,* 49 (October 1991).
150. *America 2000: An Education Strategy* (Washington, DC: U.S. Department of Education, 1991), p. 3; see also National Education Goals Panel, *Building a Nation of Learners* (Washington, DC: U.S. Government Printing Office, 1992).
151. Ibid., pp. 9, 53.
152. Charles C. Carson, Robert M. Huelskamp, and Thomas D. Woodall, *Perspectives on Education*

in America, Third Draft (Albuquerque, NM, May 1991); see Daniel Tanner, "A Nation 'Truly' at Risk," *Phi Delta Kappan,* 75 (December 1993), pp. 288–297.

153. Carson, Huelskamp, and Woodall, op cit., p. 172. A sanitized version of the Sandia study deleted this and other strong conclusions. Nevertheless, it criticized the "crisis rhetoric" that is so prevalent, and concluded that the rhetoric served only to impede school improvement. The researchers pointed out that such rhetoric is drawn from sim-plistic and erroneous data serving only to misinform the public ["Perspectives on Education in America" special issue, *The Journal of Educational Research,* 86 (May/June 1993)].

154. United Nations Development Program, *Human Development Report 1992* (New York: Oxford University Press, 1992).

155. Center for Educational Research and Innovation, *Education at a Glance: OECD Indicators* (Paris: Organization for Economic Cooperation and Development, 1993).

SELECTED REFERENCES

Adler, Mortimer J. *The Paideia Proposal: An Educational Manifesto.* New York: Macmillan, 1982.

Aikin, Wilford M. *The Story of the Eight-Year Study.* New York: Harper, 1942.

American Association for the Advancement of Science. *Science for All Americans.* Washington, DC: Author, 1989.

Baumol, William J., Blackman, Sue A., and Wolff, Edward N. *Productivity and American Leadership.* Cambridge, MA : M.I.T. Press, 1989.

Bestor, Arthur. *The Restoration of Learning.* New York: Alfred A. Knopf, 1955.

Boyer, Ernest L. *College: A Report on Undergraduate Education in America.* New York: Harper, 1986.

Boyer, Ernest L. *High School: A Report on Secondary Education in America.* New York: Harper, 1983.

Boyer, Ernest L. *Ready to Learn: A Mandate for the Nation.* Princeton, NJ: Carnegie Foundation, 1991.

Bruner, Jerome S. *The Process of Education.* Cambridge, MA: Harvard University Press, 1960.

Callahan, Raymond E. *Education and the Cult of Efficiency.* Chicago: University of Chicago Press, 1962.

Carson, Charles C., Huelskamp, Robert M., and Woodall, Thomas D. "Perspectives on Education in America," *The Journal of Educational Research* (Special Issue), 86, May/June 1993.

Center for Educational Research and Innovation. *Education at a Glance: OECD Indicators.* Paris: Organization for Economic Cooperation and Development, 1993.

Central Advisory Council for Education (England). *Children and Their Primary Schools.* London: Her Majesty's Stationery Office, 1967.

Commission on the Reorganization of Secondary Education. *Cardinal Principles of Secondary Education.* Washington, DC: U.S. Bureau of Education, 1918.

Committee on General Education in a Free Society. *General Education in a Free Society.* Cambridge, MA: Harvard University Press, 1945.

Conant, James B. *The American High School Today.* New York: McGraw-Hill, 1959.

Conant, James B. *Education in a Divided World.* Cambridge, MA: Harvard University Press, 1949.

Conant, James B. *Slums and Suburbs.* New York: McGraw-Hill, 1961.

Dewey, John. *Democracy and Education.* New York: Macmillan, 1916.

Dewey, John. *How We Think* (rev. ed.). Lexington, MA: D. C. Heath, 1933.

Educational Policies Commission. *Education for ALL American Children.* Washington, DC: National Education Association, 1948.

Educational Policies Commission. *Education for ALL American Youth—A Further Look.* Washington, DC: National Education Association, 1952.

Giles, H. H., McCutchen, S. P., and Zechiel, A. N. *Exploring the Curriculum.* New York: Harper, 1942.

Goodlad, John I. *A Place Called School.* New York: McGraw-Hill, 1984.

Hirsch, Edward D., Jr. *Cultural Literacy.* Boston: Houghton Mifflin, 1987.

Inglis, Alexander. *Principles of Secondary Education.* Boston: Houghton Mifflin, 1918.

Isaac, Katherine. *Civics for Democracy: A Journey for Teachers and Students.* Washington, DC: Essential Books, 1992.

Jackson, Philip W. (ed.). *Handbook of Research on Curriculum.* New York: Macmillan, 1992.

Kline, Morris. *Why Johnny Can't Add: The Failure of the New Math.* New York: St. Martin's, 1973.

Myrdal, Gunnar. *Objectivity in Social Research.* New York: Pantheon Books, 1969.

National Commission on Excellence in Education. *A Nation at Risk.* Washington, DC: U.S. Department of Education, 1983.

National Commission on the Reform of Secondary Education. *The Reform of Secondary Education.* New York: McGraw-Hill, 1973.

National Education Goals Panel. *Building a Nation of Learners.* Washington, DC: U.S. Government Printing Office, 1992.

National Panel on High School and Adolescent Education. *The Education of Adolescents.* Washington, DC: U.S. Department of Education, 1976.

National Society for the Study of Education. *Critical Issues in Curriculum.* 87th Yearbook, Part I. Chicago: University of Chicago Press, 1988.

National Society for the Study of Education. *General Education.* 51st Yearbook, Part I. Chicago: University of Chicago Press, 1952.

Panel on Youth of the President's Science Advisory Committee. *Youth: Transition to Adulthood.* Chicago: University of Chicago Press, 1974.

Powell, Arthur G., Farrar, Eleanor, and Cohen, David K. *The Shopping Mall High School.* Boston: Houghton Mifflin, 1985.

Schlesinger, Arthur M., Jr. *The Disuniting of America.* New York: W. W. Norton, 1992.

Silberman, Charles E. *Crisis in the Classroom.* New York: Random House, 1970.

Tanner, Daniel. *Crusade for Democracy: Progressive Education at the Crossroads.* Albany: State University of New York Press, 1991.

Tanner, Daniel. *Secondary Curriculum: Theory and Development.* New York: Macmillan, 1971.

Tanner, Daniel. *Secondary Education: Perspectives and Prospects.* New York: Macmillan, 1972.

Tanner, Daniel, and Tanner, Laurel. *History of the School Curriculum.* New York: Macmillan, 1990.

U.S. Department of Education. *America 2000: An Education Strategy.* Washington, DC: Author, 1991.

United Nations Development Program. *Human Development Report 1992.* New York: Oxford University Press, 1992.

Weinberg, Alvin M. *Reflections on Big Science.* Cambridge, MA: The M.I.T. Press, 1967.

Whitehead, Alfred North. *The Aims of Education.* New York: Macmillan, 1929.

Wraga, William G. *Democracy's High School.* Lanham, MD: University Press of America, 1994.

CHAPTER 12

THE CURRICULUM AND
THE EMERGENT
TECHNOLOGICAL SOCIETY

"It is a strange state of affairs in an industrial democracy when those very subjects are held in disrepute which are at the heart of the national economy and those students by implication condemned who will become its operators," declared the Harvard Report.[1]

Educational theory has been marked by a wall of separation stemming from the time of ancient Greece when the life of labor was regarded as servile and the life of leisure was conceived ideally as the rational life. This dualistic conception reflected the division of society itself—a life of contemplative appreciation for the free man and a life of servile labor for the slave. Carried to its logical conclusion, the two sides of life represented unintelligent practice on the one hand and unpractical intelligence on the other.[2]

According to the Harvard Report, "[m]odern democratic society clearly does not regard labor as odious or disgraceful; on the contrary, in this country, at least, it regards leisure with suspicion and expects its 'gentlemen' to engage in work."[3] The notion of the contemporary worker being engaged in unintelligent practice not only is inimical to the democratic ideal but also denies the modern technological society of a vital source of reflective direction of its activities. Indeed, the evils that have come to be associated with technology reflect such a denial by viewing people merely as mechanical components in the industrial process. Workers are regarded as appendages of the machine rather than the machine being the appendage of people. The consequence is that society is denied the quality of workmanship that is vital to its own improvement, and the worker sees the fruits of labor only in terms of material reward. Work is regarded as something to put up with, with the result that the personal-social equation is submerged and the quality of life is made to suffer.

American education has been marked by a long struggle to reveal the cultural possibilities of work and to equip the citizen to give intelligent direction to life. Yet a strange state of affairs exists to this day in American education. Many educators choose to see social power and insight stemming only from the academic side of the curriculum, whereas they deny the possibilities of such power and insight deriving from vocational education. Wittingly or unwittingly, they have sought to perpetuate an oppositional conception of curriculum that works against a democratic social order. This educational opposition separates education from vocation as though the making of a living can be separated from living, and as though the thinking person and working person cannot be one and the same.

VOCATIONAL EDUCATION AND THE DEMOCRATIC IDEAL

Dewey wrote in 1916:

> Every expansive era in the history of mankind has coincided with the operation of factors which have tended to eliminate distance between peoples and classes previously hemmed off from one another. . . . A democracy is more than a form of government; it is primarily a mode of associated living, of conjoint communicated experience.[4]

At the time when Dewey wrote *Democracy and Education,* the high school enrolled only a small fraction of the adolescent age group. In fact, a far smaller proportion of the age cohort was enrolled in high school in that day than is enrolled in college today. Yet, over the first two decades of the twentieth century, the high-school population multiplied by more than threefold whereas the actual population of the adolescent age group increased by less than 20 percent. Although universal secondary education was not to become a reality until decades later, the rising enrollments, coupled with the expanding requirements of industrialism and technology, were accompanied by a new surge of demand for vocational studies in the curriculum. Other leading industrial nations had established a dual system of schooling, with separate vocational schools for the working classes and academic schools for the more privileged classes. One of the key issues of the day was whether the United States should pattern its system of schooling after the dual European model or whether it should seek a new comprehensive model. Indeed, in various sections of the United States, separate vocational schools had already been established.

A second related issue pertained to the purposes and function of vocational education. On the one hand were those who promoted vocational education to meet the industrial demands for trained workers and to compete with the industrial productivity of other nations. On the other hand were the progressive educators who envisioned vocational education as a means of providing for the "liberation of a greater diversity of personal capacities which characterize a democracy," and who saw this being accomplished within a comprehensive school setting that would provide for "a mode of associated living, of conjoint, communicated experience."[5]

Nationalistic and Vested Interests Versus the Personal-Social Interest

During the early nineteenth century workingmen's groups were demanding that "provision ought to be made by law for the more extensive diffusion of knowledge, particularly in the elements of those sciences which pertain to mechanical employments, and to the politics of our common country."[6] They not only sought universal common schooling but they also attacked the private monopoly on higher education and demanded that "this monopoly should be broken up, and that the means of equal knowledge (the only security for equal liberty) should be rendered, by legal provision, the common property of all classes."[7] Toward the end of the nineteenth century, organized labor generally favored industrial education, although some union leaders and members feared that this would undermine their control over apprenticeships and would provide industry with a source of cheap labor, thereby undermining the gains that organized labor had made.[8] In rural areas, however, the demand for vocational education in agriculture was less ambivalent as farmers' groups were recognizing the benefits deriving from the land-grant agricultural colleges and experiment stations.

Ironically, national support for vocational education was provided at the college level more than half a century before it was instituted at the secondary level of schooling. The Morrill Act of 1862, signed by President Lincoln, provided land grants that led to the establishment of a national network of land-grant colleges and universities. The Morrill Act stipulated that the leading purposes of these colleges "shall be, without excluding other scientific and classical studies . . . to teach such branches of learning as are related to agriculture and the mechanic arts . . . in order to promote the liberal and practical education of the industrial classes in the several pursuits and professions of life."[9] These land-grant institutions or "peoples colleges" were to become the great state universities that enrolled students from all segments of society.

Although some states had established modest programs for vocational education of less-than-college level before the turn of the century, it was not until World War I when federal support was provided for such programs. During the early years of the twentieth century, industrialists were joined by educators in pointing to the system of vocational education in Germany, and in noting the contribution it was making in connection with that nation's industrial achievements. They proceeded to advocate that the United States pattern the schools after the German model. Such proposals were vigorously debated at meetings of the NEA.[10] In his annual message to Congress in 1907, President Theodore Roosevelt declared that "[o]ur school system is gravely defective insofar as it puts a premium upon mere literacy training," and he proceeded to advocate provision for industrial education in city schools and agricultural education in rural schools.[11] A presidential commission, established in 1914 to investigate the need for federal aid to education strongly supported such aid after finding that less than 1 percent of the millions of persons engaging in industry and agriculture had adequate opportunity for vocational and technical education. Various reports to the federal government continued to point to the advanced state of industrial education in the European nations, stressing that the United States had much to learn from these nations, particularly Germany.[12]

The Battle for a Unitary System.   The structure of American education was approaching a critical turning point. On the one hand were those industrial groups and educators who advocated the splitting of the school system along the lines of the dual European model. On the other hand were those who viewed a dual system as promulgating social cleavage and stratification, and who urged that the United States, in the interests of its democratic ideals, opt for a unified system of comprehensive schooling. No model for such a unified system existed anywhere else in the world, but proponents of comprehensive schooling contended that the United States must develop its own unique pattern if it is to be true to its democratic ideals. Writing in *The New Republic* in 1915, Dewey attacked the legislative proposals in Illinois and elsewhere, which called for the establishment of a dual education system, as leading to a segregation and stratification of social classes.

> The segregation proposed is to divide the children of the more well-to-do and cultured families of the community from those children who will presumably earn their living by working for wages in manual and commercial employments. . . . Many of us have been disturbed at the increasing tendency toward stratification of classes in this country. We have wondered if those European prophets were correct who have insistently foretold that the development of fixed classes in this country was only a question of time. Few would have dreamed that the day was already at hand when responsible and influential persons would urge that the public school system should recognize the separation as an accomplished fact, and adapt to it its machinery of administrative control, its courses of study and its methods of instruction in the public school.[13]

Dewey also argued that by providing for vocational education within a unified system, the vocational and academic studies would receive constant reciprocal stimulation and permeation, and different pupils would be in constant personal association. Under a dual system, he warned, the old curriculum would be left frozen in its narrow form in one type of school, whereas vocational education in the other type of school would be reduced to narrow training to create a source of manpower for exploitation in the interests of industrial efficiency.

Most major pieces of federal educational legislation during the twentieth century have been enacted in response to international or domestic crises. Just two months before the entry of the United States into World War I, President Wilson signed into law the Smith-Hughes Act of 1917, which provided federal funds to be matched by state allocations for vocational education of less-than-college level in agriculture, trades and industries, and home economics for persons over fourteen years of age. In the face of the war-preparedness climate that pervaded the times (and spurred the passage of this legislation), the NEA promptly warned against the establishment of a dual system of education along the lines of European education systems.[14]

The Battle for Democratic Interest.   A year prior to the passage of the Smith-Hughes Act, Dewey had warned in *Democracy and Education* of the danger of turning education to fit narrow nationalistic interests, as had been the case in Germany. Dewey called for a kind of vocational education that was consonant with the democratic ideal of developing social power and insight for the rising generation. Pointing out that "the intellectual *possibilities* of industry have multiplied," Dewey stressed that industrial conditions were making industry less and less an educative resource for the great masses and, consequently, the "burden of realizing the intellectual possibilities inhering with work is thus thrown back on the school." He warned of the danger of making the school an adjunct to manufacture and commerce. "Education would then become an instrument of perpetuating unchanged the existing industrial order of society, instead of operating as a means of its transformation," declared Dewey.[15]

Dewey envisioned this transformation being signified when every member of society "shall be occupied in something which makes the lives of others more worth living," and pointed out that such a society "denotes a state of affairs in which the interest of each in his work is uncoerced and intelligent: based upon its congeniality to his own aptitudes." He noted that although education cannot effect such a change apart from a corresponding redirection of industrial and political conditions, "it does mean that we may produce in schools a projection in type of the society we should like to realize," thereby making it possible to "gradually modify the larger and more recalcitrant features of adult society."[16]

Dewey maintained that vocational education must not be narrowly conceived so as to perpetuate the "dogma of social predestination" by focusing narrowly on proficiency that was limited to immediate work, but rather should develop the competency of insight into the social bearings of work. "Any scheme for vocational education which takes its point of departure from the industrial regime that now exists, is likely to assume and to perpetuate its division and weaknesses, and thus to become an instrument in accomplishing the feudal dogma of social predestination," wrote Dewey. He went on to call for the kind of vocational education that would provide the fullest intellectual and social meaning of work, illumine the scientific and human connections of vocations, and bring the student into touch with pervading problems and their possible solutions in the larger social scene. This ideal would not be easily attainable, continued Dewey, for it "has to contend not only with the inertia of the existing educational traditions, but also with the opposition of those who are entrenched in command of the industrial machinery, who realize that such an educational system if made general would threaten their ability to use others for their own ends."[17] Dewey pointed out that the rising consciousness of the significance of this ideal, and the means to its attainment, presaged a more equitable and enlightened social order.

Dewey vigorously opposed the splitting of the educational system along the lines of European schooling. "To split the system," he wrote, "is to treat the schools as an agency for transferring the older division of labor and leisure, culture and service, mind and body, directed and directive class, into a society nominally democratic."[18] Not only did he point to the danger of splitting the educational system along two curriculum tracks but he also attacked the traditional dualistic notion, perpetuated particularly by the literary intelligentsia, setting cultural and vocational education in opposition. In this connection, Dewey noted the inherent contradiction in the prevalent attitude on the part of the college educated who would deny vocational education to those who do not go on to college while they themselves reap the benefits of vocational education in the higher institutions.

> By a peculiar superstition, education which has to do chiefly with preparation for the pursuit of conspicuous idleness, for teaching, and for literary callings, and for leadership, has been regarded as non-vocational and even as peculiarly cultural . . . many a teacher and author writes and argues in behalf of a cultural and humane education against the encroachments of a specialized practical education, without recognizing that his own education, which he calls liberal, has been mainly training for his own particular calling. He has simply got into the habit of regarding his own business as essentially cultural and of overlooking the cultural possibilities of other employments.[19]

To Dewey, "the opposition to recognition of the vocational phases of life in education (except for the utilitarian three R's in elementary schooling) accompanies the conservation of aristocratic ideals of the past."[20] Only a month after the passage of the Smith-Hughes Act, Dewey repeated his argument against splitting the educational system and warned that vocational education must be so conceived as not to perpetuate "duties to the established order," but to develop "the industrial intelligence and power of the worker." The real issue is the kind of vocational education we are to have, stressed Dewey, as he went on to put the issue in these words: "The movement for vocational education conceals within itself two mighty and opposing forces, one which would utilize the public school primarily to turn out more efficient laborers in the present economic regime, with certain incidental advantages to themselves, the other which would utilize all the resources of public education to equip individuals to control their own future economic careers, and thus help on such a reorganization of industry as will change it from a feudalistic to a democratic order."[21]

Dewey attacked those who would establish a separate system of schooling as seeking merely to turn out more efficient workers for the existing industrial order, rather than developing human beings who are equipped to reconstruct the existing scheme. Dewey's opposition to a dual school system was shared by many educators and, as mentioned earlier, led to the passage of an NEA resolution to this effect in 1918. In that same year the NEA's Commission on the Reorganization of Secondary Education supported vocational education in the context of the comprehensive high school that would serve as "the prototype of democracy."[22]

As discussed in Chapter 11, if any single document marked the historic turning point of commitment to the comprehensive high school as opposed to the dual European model of secondary education, it was the *Cardinal Principles* report (1918) of the Commission on the Reorganization of Secondary Education. As James Conant pointed out, "this document was taken as the starting point for almost all forward-looking reforms in public high schools for forty years."[23]

Revisionists of education history like to portray the *Cardinal Principles* report and the emergence of the comprehensive high school as a kind of conspiratorial design to perpetuate the corporate society, and they choose to interpret Dewey's ideas as turning education to the task of "adjustment to the changing nature of technology."[24] They conveniently choose to ignore Dewey's writings and the passages in the *Cardinal Principles* report stressing that vocational education must not become the instrument of the existing industrial machinery but should be the means of helping to develop a more democratic social order. In pointing to the need for vocational education to be so designed as to enable the individual to engage in effective membership in an industrial democracy, the *Cardinal Principles* report stated, "[c]onsequently, this commission enters its protest against any and all plans, however well intentioned, which are in danger of divorcing vocation and socio-civic education."[25] Revisionists and other critics from the radical left have chosen not to recognize that Dewey and the members of the Commission on the Reorganization of Secondary Education had taken their stance in advancing the comprehensive high school and in holding that the adoption of a dual system of schooling, as in Europe, would serve to perpetuate the social stratification that was characteristic of the European nations. They failed to recognize how close the United States was in adopting the dual European model, for the comprehensive high school had no counterpart anywhere in the world.

The late Lawrence Cremin, Pulitzer-prize-winning historian, described the *Cardinal Principles* report as "a statement which literally ushered in a whole new age—an age that embraced an educational revolution." Cremin went on to describe the transformation of the high school as conceived by the *Cardinal Principles* report:

> From an institution conceived for the few, the high school became an institution conceived for all. From an adjunct to the college, the high school became the pivotal point in the public school system, one which carried forward objectives yet unfinished by the elementary school and opened new vistas leading on to the college. . . . Such was the grand design of this Commission, one which, in weaving a multitude of new and pressing demands into an integral view of the school, was able to face squarely toward the future and thereby to usher in a whole new age in American secondary education.[26]

THE STRUGGLE FOR A RECOGNIZED PLACE IN THE CURRICULUM

Through the Smith-Hughes Act of 1917, a federal-state partnership for vocational education was established, and the various programs came to be operated within the structure of a unitary school system. Nevertheless, the level of support remained relatively modest in view of the kinds of facilities and resources that were needed for effective vocational education in a technological society. Moreover, the programs as provided by the 1917 legislation were categorical rather than comprehensive—being limited to production agriculture, trades and industries, and home economics.

Although the unitary type of high school predominated in various sections of the nation, most of the high schools offered only a limited range of vocational programs and, therefore, were not truly comprehensive. The curriculum of the high school remained biased largely in favor of the college preparatory function, and only a small fraction of the majority of youngsters who did not go on to college were being reached by federally supported programs of vocational education.

Needed Assessment

The Great Depression had created a vast army of out-of-school, out-of-work youth. Various federal programs were created to deal with this problem, but these efforts were largely in the form of stopgap measures of limited educational effectiveness. Many of the programs were administered independently of the schools. Although a comprehensive design for vocational education in the setting of the comprehensive high school was needed, subsequent legislation in 1929 and 1935 simply provided additional funds for the expansion of the existing programs as stipulated under the Smith-Hughes Act of 1917. In 1937, President Franklin Roosevelt signed the George-Deen Act, which provided for the additional categorical program of distributive education (retailing, wholesaling, transporting, storing, and other distributive services).

The tendency of the federal government to bypass the schools in many of its emergency programs raised the fear in the minds of some educators that a dual system of education might be created. Only a small proportion of high schools were offering the full range of vocational programs as stipulated under the existing federal legislation. In the absence of such programs, and in the face of the economic exigencies encountered by their parents, youngsters were dropping out of school to seek employment without skills and at a time of severely limited employment opportunities. Instead of providing for the comprehensive redesign of the curriculum in the comprehensive high school, the federal government allowed its emergency agencies to develop a variety of nonschool educative programs, and these programs were ancillary and fragmentary in design and function.

A 1938 report of the Educational Policies Commission pointed to the danger that in bypassing the schools the federal government might be sowing the seeds for a dual educational system. This report called for the consolidation of educational programs within the structure of the unitary school system.[27] Three years later, the commission reiterated its stance and criticized the failure of the schools to provide adequately for vocational education. "There will be no 'out-of-school unemployed youth' for federal agencies to educate, when schools everywhere extend their responsibilities to all young people until they are satisfactorily established in adult vocations."[28]

Almost a quarter of a century later—at a time of general economic prosperity, but when mounting unemployment among youth had created "social dynamite" in the urban poverty sectors of the United States—the federal government turned again to nonschool emergency agencies such as the Office of Economic Opportunity and its Job Corps program to provide for job training outside the school system. Once again, these efforts proved to be largely ineffective. The needed reassessment and reconstruction of vocational education in the context of the comprehensive high school was never more urgent.

From Postwar Visions to Cold War Counterforces

During World War II, special vocational programs were conducted through day classes for in-school youth and evening classes to train defense workers. A year following the end of the war, President Truman signed the George-Barden Act, which provided for the expansion of existing federally supported programs of vocational education and for the establishment of vocational guidance programs.

World War II had given cause for various groups of educators to examine the prospects of the comprehensive high school and vocational education for the coming era of postwar reconstruction. Two notable reports, the Harvard Report and a report by the Educational Policies Commission, were issued in this connection.

POSTWAR VISIONS.   Although the Harvard Report of 1945, discussed in Chapter 11, was focused on general education in school and college, it strongly endorsed the role and function of vocational education in the context of the comprehensive high school. Pointing to the need to endue the various studies in the curriculum "with a respect commensurate to their equally necessary part in American life," the Harvard Report recommended that for students who are ending their formal education with high school approximately one third of their time might be devoted to vocational education. Concerning the relationship between general and specialized (vocational) education, the report stated, "[t]hese two sides of education should be thought of as connected, the special forever flowing out of the general and forever returning and enriching it."[29]

As we have seen, in *Education for ALL American Youth* (1944, revised 1952), the NEA's Educational Policies Commission envisioned a model educational system in which students in the setting of the comprehensive high school would have access to a full range of programs for successful entry to the world of work.[30]

The time devoted to vocational education would total one sixth in grade ten, one third in grades eleven and thirteen, and one half in the community college, which would be administered integrally to the school district (grades thirteen and fourteen). The significance of this far-reaching proposal to meld the upper division of the high school with the community college for vocational/career education can only be appreciated in the light of the fact that it was not until the early 1990s that federal legislation supported this articulated structuring of the curriculum of the high school and community college. This came to be called the two-plus-two or tech/prep program.

The model proposed by the Educational Policies Commission (1944, 1952) called for supervised work experience as integral to the curriculum. The curriculum in vocational education would be broadly based and geared realistically to community conditions so as to minimize the possibilities for technological unemployment. The high schools also would offer opportunities for further specialized studies through part-time and evening classes for out-of-school youth, whereas the community college would play a key role in preparing students for technical and semiprofessional occupations through formal studies and supervised work experience. Through effective counseling and a comprehensive curriculum in the high school, the gates of higher learning would be kept open to all who might benefit from further education. Students would not be tracked according to curricula, and the various programs would be kept flexible and interrelated, taking into account the needs of those students who enter the world of work directly from high school, those who will go on to the community college, and those who plan to pursue education beyond the community college.

Significantly, as part of general education, all students would be engaged in community service projects. However, unlike the community-service programs for high school and college students proposed and implemented during the late 1980s and early 1990s (discussed in Chapter 11), the programs described in *Education for ALL American Youth* would be fully articulated with the curriculum—such as students undertaking a systematic study of community health problems and making the data available to community officials.

THE COMPREHENSIVE HIGH SCHOOL IN COLD WAR CRISIS

From the military sector and the halls of Congress to the halls of academia, the Cold War call was to turn American education to serving narrow nationalistic interests. The issue of splitting the educational system was raised once again. To meet the Soviet threat in the battle for global supremacy and in the space race, a dual educational system would be required. The comprehensive high school had never been so severely threatened since the time of its establishment. Conant's defense of the comprehensive high school at this juncture in history was to prove decisive.

Cold War Criticisms

Unlike the Harvard Report, which generated little controversy, *Education for ALL American Youth* came under severe attack during the Cold War years. Taking a cue from the ancient dualism between thinking man and working man, Bestor contended that "liberal education is the education by which a man achieves freedom [and] self-reliance," whereas vocational programs "breed servile dependence." Not only did Bestor fail to explain how a person can be free when not prepared to earn a living but he also viewed vocational studies as mere training in tricks of the trade. "The West was not settled by men and women who had taken courses in how to be a pioneer," he continued, as if to imply that the West was settled by historians, philologists, and literati.[31] Bestor proceeded to attack *Education for ALL American Youth* and its proposals for vocational education as subverting the school's goal of intellectual training in favor of "life adjustment." Vocational courses should carry no academic credit, contended Bestor, and should not in general be open to students under the age of seventeen.

A little more than a year following the launching of Sputnik I, in an interview featured on the cover of a national business magazine, Bestor pointed to the federal support of vocational education as evidence of the "vocationalism and anti-intellectualism" that pervades schools, a condition, he alleged, that had left the United States in fatal danger of losing the space race.[32]

As discussed in Chapter 11, the assault against the comprehensive high school was to reach new proportions in high places under the crisis mentality of the space race.

The Comprehensive High School as Scapegoat

Within three months after the launching of Sputnik I, Congressional hearings were being held to determine the needed school reforms for national defense. Such nationally visible figures as Admiral Rickover (father of the nuclear submarine) and Wernher von Braun, the German-educated missile expert who had played a key role in developing the V-1 and V-2 rockets that the Germans launched against civilian populations in Britain during World War II, were called to testify at the Congressional hearings. Now that von Braun was working for the U.S. missile program, he was treated in the American media as an almost heroic figure. Hollywood romanticized his life in a film titled "I Aimed at the Stars"—tempting some viewers to quip that the correct title should have been "I Aimed at the Stars, But Hit London Instead."

Testifying before a committee of the U.S. Senate in January 1958, von Braun offered the solution to the chief shortcoming of America's school system. Referring to his own education as European rather than German, von Braun offered that we rid schools of the "ballast" (sic) by adopting the "European" system (when he seemed to be describing the system in Nazi Germany).

> There is a lot more ruthlessness over there in just washing out the less competent. It is, you might say, a survival-of-the-fittest type of training: whoever does not live up to the standards is simply eliminated . . . the less able will be dropped with a lot less regard to their own personal interests.
>
> Thus the European school systems . . . are loaded with much less ballast [sic]. . . . As a result, the teachers of these schools need not bother with the less gifted.[33]

He went on to offer this reminiscence of his own education in Europe (actually Germany), contrasting his own highly focused curriculum against that of American schools:

> I do not remember that I ever attended any classes in Europe [sic] on "family life" or "human relations," or subjects like "boy-girl relations at college." We just learned reading, and arithmetic in the lower schools. Later on they taught us technical and scientific subjects, but nothing else.[34]

Finally, in his testimony, von Braun endorsed Admiral Rickover's proposal for the creation of a federal commission to serve as an "inspection agency, to establish standards of educational requirements for graduates of high schools."[35] (As history would have it, the crisis of techno-industrial competition with Japan and Germany was to impel Congress to pass legislation in 1991 that led to the creation of the National Council on Education Standards and Testing.)

Returning to the crisis triggered by Sputnik I, and to the U.S. Senate hearings, appearing before the same Senate committee on the same day as von Braun was Lee DuBridge, noted physicist and member of the President's Science Advisory Committee. After testifying that special federal support should be targeted for the school curriculum in the sciences and mathematics, DuBridge cited the need for the teacher "to recognize and encourage special talent [and who] must be an effective friend and counselor to students and especially to those who are unusually gifted and ambitious." As far as the less-able student is concerned, DuBridge declared,

> [t]he right of a student to an education is a right which persists as far as his intellectual capabilities and his ambition should take him. This might be to the sixth grade, in the case of the unfortunate individual, and might be through the doctor of philosophy for those who are better favored by genetics or environment.[36]

Unfortunately, the senators did not ask DuBridge or von Braun what society should do with those unfortunate individuals who are dropped from school when they reach the sixth grade because they are less favored by genetics or environment. Even assuming that American schools were able to unload their ballast, to use von Braun's expression, we must ask not only what will society do with these youngsters, but also what will they do to society.

Whereas von Braun, DuBridge, and Rickover unhesitatingly blamed the public schools for America's alleged missile gap, they found no fault with America's scientific-industrial-military complex, nor with the colleges and universities.

As cited in Chapter 10, Admiral Rickover contended that we no longer had a choice between "democratic" education in the "time-wasting" comprehensive high school and efficient education by means of the dual system. "We must opt for efficiency," he declared.[37]

In Congressional testimony, Admiral Rickover held the dual European system of schooling as a model for the United States to emulate, wherein "vocational training of one kind or another" is provided in separate schools "when a point is reached where pupils can absorb no more mental food."[38] He attacked *Education for ALL American Youth* as being concerned with "life adjustment," and unconcerned with academic studies,[39] when, in fact, it had called for the vast extension of opportunity for higher education through an open-access education system.

The sentiments of such figures as Rickover and von Braun were shared by a legion of academicians who were quick to seize opportunistically on the Cold War and space race to vent the essentialist-perennialist assault against the egalitarianism of the comprehensive high school. The Council for Basic Education, founded by Bestor in 1956, drew most of its membership from academia and capitalized on the crisis mentality of the times.[40] In his Pulitzer prize-winning work, *Anti-intellectualism in American Life*, Richard Hofstadter fixed the *Cardinal Principles* report and the vocationalism of the comprehensive high school as chief sources of blame for promoting mass education over the quality education of a selective system. "American educators," he wrote, "preferred to ignore European educational history as a source of clues to educational policy and looked to 'modern science' for practical guidance and to 'democracy' for their moral inspiration."[41] (Here he chose to overlook the considered thought and struggle given to overcoming the pressures to embrace the European model on this side of the Atlantic.) "European education pointed to the outmoded past; science and democracy looked to the future," continued Hofstadter in his portrayal of the progressivist vision. But now the progressivist ideas were in for a rude awakening, for "[t]his way of thought has been jolted by scientific competition with the Soviet Union." Hofstadter proceeded to hold the Soviet secondary school system as a model of "availability of a demanding academic curriculum to large numbers."[42] Hofstadter had conveniently ignored the readily available evidence on the pervasive shortcomings of the Soviet system, such as the limited access to secondary schooling for older adolescents. (Not until 1975 did the Soviets require ten years of schooling for all youth.) Some of the other known shortcomings pointed to the restrictions imposed on academic scholarship by political authorities, the uses of the curriculum for the political indoctrination of children and youth, the educational favoritism accorded children of party officials, the limited access to higher education for the children of workers, the restrictions attendant to a system of channeling educational access to manpower needs through a dual schooling structure, the antiquated educational methods that pervaded the system, and the appallingly substandard school facilities and resources in many areas.

Although the evidence clearly refuted the allegations of Soviet superiority in science and technology, the crisis of the times proved opportune for science and engineering, especially in the more glamorous fields of aerospace and nuclear engineering, and weapons systems.

However, history takes ironic twists whenever narrow nationalistic priorities are set for public education under a crisis mentality. By the early 1970s, aerospace engineers were faced with unemployment; the United States was critically short of technicians to deal with the energy crisis on planet earth. For example, an industrialist recounted how his efforts to recruit technicians who were knowledgeable about boilers, heat, and fuels resulted in a flood of unemployed applicants whose training was in the esoteric branches of aerospace engineering. "From the replies we got, we could put a man on the moon, but we didn't get anyone who knew anything about boilers or 'the efficient use of fuel' as we asked for," stated the industrialist.[43] He went on to criticize schools for neglecting technical education. Work that was regarded as mundane in the previous decade now had become essential to American well-being, whereas the new field of aerospace, which had been promoted during the 1960s as essential to national survival, had become a national luxury.

Whereas during the 1950s the nuclear age was heralded as auguring a future of unlimited energy, and the space age a future of unlimited boundaries, the closing years of the twentieth century found us faced with the problem of how to safely dispose of nuclear warheads and waste from nuclear power plants, and how to cope more effectively with the ecological problems on planet earth.

In Defense of the Comprehensive High School

Although Conant's 1959 Carnegie report on the American high school had focused to a great extent on the college preparatory population and the pursuit of academic excellence at a time of Soviet competition, he nevertheless made a number of recommendations concerning vocational education. Conant pointed out that in those cities having separate specialized academic and vocational high schools, the other high schools were left without federally supported programs of vocational education.

Conant stressed that "the comprehensive high school is characteristic of our society and further that it has come into being because of our economic history and our devotion to the ideals of equality of opportunity and equality of status."[44] He pointed out that the land-grant universities had developed diversified curricula and had dissolved the distinctions that had marked traditional higher education, with the result that these institutions have come to be recognized as a symbol of equality of status and a means to the realization of this ideal. He envisioned the comprehensive high school in a similar vein, enhancing equality of status of all honest pursuits. He noted that in the large Eastern cities selective academic high schools were to be found, whereas such schools had not spread to the Middle West and Far West. Conant noted that such schools tended to be found in those areas (the East) where there is no large and powerful state university, and he observed that this phenomenon was probably not accidental. He also commented that these schools in certain ways resemble the preuniversity schools of Europe. Conant expressed his belief that the homogeneous nature of the population enrolled in selective academic high schools served to deny to students the democratizing social advantages that accrue to attending the comprehensive high school. Similarly, the separate vocational high school perpetuated social separation.

Conant noted that in his survey of comprehensive high schools he was able to find programs that were highly successful in preparing youngsters for skilled employment in industry, and that in some communities youngsters who had completed programs in trades and industries had gone on to the community college for advanced preparation in tool design—a career field of great opportunity. He also supported programs of supervised work experience and recommended that high schools participate in the federal programs of vocational education in accordance with the needs of their student populations and the employment situation. He held that students should not be tracked according to vocational and college preparatory programs but should be allowed to pursue studies in the various areas of the school curriculum in accordance with their interests and capabilities, although he did recommend ability grouping in the general education courses along with selective criteria for admission to advanced academic studies. Conant expressed his belief that high-school youngsters should have an ultimate vocational goal. Even if they change their minds during high school or in later years, such a goal attaches greater significance to their studies. Finally, in upholding his conviction of the social benefits to be gained through the comprehensive high school over the specialized high school, Conant concluded the following: "I believe it is important for the future of American democracy to have as close a relationship as possible in high school between the future professional man, the future craftsman, the future manager of industry, the future labor leader, the future salesman, and the future engineer."[45]

Conant's recommendations on vocational education were virtually overshadowed by the emphasis he gave to the improvement of the academic studies and, at a time of international crisis, educators by and large moved to adopt those recommendations that they deemed consonant with the new national pursuit of academic excellence. The national thrust giving priority to the academic studies was already well under way, and any concerted efforts to improve vocational education would have to await the social crisis of the 1960s. Nevertheless, Conant's defense of the comprehensive high school, in a report that became a kind of quasi-official manual for school boards and administrators throughout the nation, served to turn the tide away from a dual educational system. The comprehensive high school had survived the Cold War crisis.

AN ERA OF SOCIAL CRISIS

The plight of out-of-school, unemployed youth and the smoldering conditions of inner cities seemed to have been largely ignored during the 1950s when national priorities in education were focused on the academically talented and on the improvement of those academic studies that were deemed essential to the nation's Cold War needs. The high schools seemed relatively unconcerned about the occupational preparation and placement of youngsters who were seeking a place in the world of work and, instead, were giving priority to improving the academic disciplines and the college preparatory program and to the college placement of academically promising students. Although the danger signals were in evidence in urban areas, the schools encountered difficulties in turning from the old crisis of the Cold War to meet the new crisis of social disaffection and unemployment that was plaguing disadvantaged youth.

"Social Dynamite"

As discussed in Chapter 11, in 1961 Conant's *Slums and Suburbs* appeared—a report on urban education based on his observations made during his Carnegie studies. "I am convinced that we are allowing social dynamite to accumulate in our large cities," declared Conant, as he estimated that in some slum areas the majority of the population between the ages of sixteen and twenty-one were out of school and out of work. "The building up of a mass of unemployed and frustrated Negro youth in congested areas of a city is a social phenomenon that may be compared to the piling up of inflammable material in an empty building in a city block," Conant warned.[46]

Conant noted that the larger cities were lacking in truly comprehensive high schools and that we were now recognizing, belatedly, that a caste system finds its sharpest manifestation in an educational system. Regarding the need for vocational education, Conant had this to say: "*I submit that in a heavily urbanized and industrial free society the educational experiences of youth should fit their subsequent employment.*"[47] Conant pointed out that even those youngsters in the slum areas who gained high-school diplomas were likely to face unemployment without effective vocational education.

NEEDED REFORMS.   "It is far more difficult in many communities to obtain admission to an apprentice program that involves union approval than to get into the most selective medical school in the nation," continued Conant.[48] He reported that he found schools with effective vocational programs where students completing such programs also were adequately prepared to go on to college. He recommended that vocational programs be made available in grades eleven and twelve, and possibly earlier, and that such studies constitute up to half the student's time. Moreover, the schools should assume a more direct responsibility for job placement and follow-up of their graduates and dropouts.

"The critics of American education, so it seems to me, are under an obligation to be both concrete with their proposals and to be clear as to the premises from which they start their arguments" and regarding our slum schools, "we need to know the facts, and when these facts indicate a dangerous social situation the American people should be prepared to take prompt action before it is too late," Conant concluded.[49]

Conant's assessment of the situation and his recommendations were attacked by many intelligentsia, both black and white, as a middle-class prescription to be imposed on disadvantaged black youth so as to have them conform to the work ethic of American society.[50] These critics of vocational education tended to overlook the fact that blacks were not adequately represented in the existing high school programs of vocational education as well as in the skilled occupations, that the skilled occupations are requiring ever higher qualifications for entry, that vocational education of a high quality is the means of developing these qualifications, and that entry into skilled occupations would open the way to increased social power on the part of blacks.

EFFORTS TO EXPAND AND IMPROVE VOCATIONAL EDUCATION. The mounting youth unemployment and social disaffection in the central cities impelled President Kennedy in 1961 to request the secretary of Health, Education, and Welfare (HEW) to make an assessment of the impact of the various national vocational education acts. A panel appointed by the HEW secretary issued its report in 1963. The panel found "that graduates of high school vocational programs are less likely to be unemployed than other high school graduates, the vocational graduates do in fact work in the occupations for which they prepare, and that vocational education increases their subsequent earnings."[51] The panel also reported that despite commitment to the comprehensive high school, the vocational programs were limited in scope and were serving only 13 percent of the fifteen to nineteen age group. Furthermore, vocational home economics was found to account for most of the enrollment.

The failure of existing federal legislation to provide adequate support for occupational clusters was cited by the panel, along with the failure of vocational programs to reach youth in the largest cities as well as those rural youth who will migrate to urban areas in search of employment. The report also stressed that relatively few schools were offering supervised and cooperative work-study programs, despite the promising potential of such programs in preventing dropouts and in linking school studies with gainful employment. The panel criticized the federal policy of the recent past of downgrading vocational education and called for allocations that would be appropriate to the growing critical needs. Calling attention to the "social dynamite" being created in the growing army of out-of-school, unemployed youth, the panel stressed that lives and talents were being wasted and that the social, economic, and political structure of urban areas was being threatened. Finally, the report attacked the existing federal patchwork of legislation and called for the unification of federal legislation to provide a comprehensive and flexible foundation for vocational education.

RENEWED FEDERAL EFFORTS. The Vocational Education Act of 1963 was hailed as the most significant piece of federal legislation on vocational education since 1917. Through the 1963 legislation and the amendments of 1968, most of the categorical restrictions in the earlier laws were eliminated. In effect, this legislation encompassed virtually any occupation or occupational cluster short of the professions and also removed the earlier restriction that had limited most programs to a level of less-than-college grade. Moreover, it allowed schools to develop integrated programs of vocational and general education so as to improve the learning opportunities of those with socioeconomic and educational handicaps.

Despite the significant increase in federal funds provided by this legislation, the appropriations were insufficient to the enormous task of reaching the majority of youth who might benefit from vocational education. Furthermore, exploding conditions in inner cities beginning in the mid-1960s led to a new patchwork of emergency, nonschool, educative programs reminiscent of the emergency measures taken by the federal government during the Great Depression.

Presage for a Dual System

There was also a dark side to the 1963 legislation—a side that raised the question of whether the provision for the construction of specialized vocational schools might lead to the beginnings of a dual system of secondary education. Although many cities, especially in the northeast, operated specialized vocational and academic high schools, the dominant American pattern consisted of high schools of the comprehensive type. Although the selective specialized vocational high school, such as New York City's High School of Aviation Trades, could boast outstanding records of gainful employment and college entrance on the part of graduates, America's unparalleled record of educational yield among the advanced nations of the world was to be attributed to the unitary school structure capped by the comprehensive high school.

Now the new federal legislation provided for the construction on a national scale of specialized area vocational schools with full-time enrollment and with shared-time enrollment. Under the shared-time arrangement students pursued their vocational coursework in the specialized school, continued their studies in their home high school in general education and exploratory and enrichment education, and participated in extraclass activities.

Initially, the availability of outstanding facilities and resources found instances when the specialized vocational schools were unable to meet the enrollment demands and were becoming selective, with the result that many students were being turned away. In other instances, the stigma of attending a vocational school resulted in severe enrollment shortfalls. There was also the problem of many adolescents understandably unwilling to sever friendships and other ties with their home high school, such as participation in varsity sports and other extraclass programs.

Although the shared-time pattern allowed for the continuance of these ties, at least theoretically, scheduling constraints arising from dual enrollment and transportation not only delimited opportunities for participation in extraclass activities, but also found students being tracked in their academic classes in their home high school. At the same time, their elective options for exploratory and enrichment studies were delimited by scheduling difficulties. Many college-bound students who might have elected certain vocational courses if offered in the comprehensive high school now found it singularly inconvenient and unappealing to pursue such courses in a separate school even on a shared-time basis.

Although these factors buttressed the case for the comprehensive high school and found the comprehensive high school continuing to represent the mainstream structure of American secondary education, there was no question that the investment in facilities and resources that went into the specialized schools would have gone a long way in making so many of the high schools truly comprehensive.

Perhaps the most striking lesson to be derived from these developments, aside from gaining a better appreciation of the powerful cultural roots of our unitary school structure, was that the federal legislation to create a nationwide system of separate specialized vocational schools at this juncture of history was met with virtually no opposition on the part of community leaders, school people, or the professorate. It should be remembered that the battle against the creation of a dual system of secondary schooling was won early in the twentieth century by progressive educators in opposition to the industrialists and vocationalists who favored a dual structure.

Half a century later, when the seeds were being sown for a dual system, academicians and others who were identified with the radical left and who presented themselves as champions of disadvantaged adolescents—such as Edgar Friedenberg and Paul Goodman—actually were making the case for a divided system. It seemed inexplicable that those on the radical left should join with the industrialists in seeking a dual school structure. Perhaps the academic left was revealing a masked elitism. Friedenberg, Goodman, and others were proposing that the high school be limited to serving exclusively the academically oriented, whereas the others would find other means of making their way into society. As was the case early in the century, leaders in the field of vocational education joined with the industrialists in supporting proposed federal legislation to fund specialized vocational schools on the ground that it would provide added support for their field. They failed to realize that by removing vocational education from the comprehensive high school it was thus being removed from the mainstream of the public school system. Friedenberg went so far as to advocate the creation of federal vocational boarding schools to serve the disadvantaged.[52] The Vocational Education Act of 1963 actually authorized demonstration residential boarding schools for seriously disadvantaged adolescents, but Congress never provided the funding.

The "War on Poverty"

Outbreaks of civil disorder in major cities beginning in the early 1960s resulted in the Economic Opportunity Act of 1964. In signing this act into law, President Lyndon B.

Johnson declared a "War on Poverty" that was strangely reminiscent of Franklin D. Roosevelt's call to Congress "to wage a war against the emergency" in his 1933 inaugural address. The 1960s were different times in that mainstream America was in relative affluence and the nation was engaged in a real war in Southeast Asia.

EMERGENCY PROGRAMS.   With the establishment of the Office of Economic Opportunity (OEO), a variety of education programs for disadvantaged youth appeared. As in the case of the Great Depression, these emergency programs were administered largely outside the school system and by a new federal agency independent of the permanent education agency (U.S. Office of Education).

One of the most widely heralded programs was the Job Corps, established by the OEO in 1965. Job Corps centers were established throughout the United States under contracts with private industry to train out-of-school youth for skilled employment and to provide remedial education. The reasoning of OEO officials was that the schools had failed to provide disadvantaged youth with the skills necessary for gainful employment and that industry, with its know-how, would accomplish the task. It soon became apparent that many private corporations were engaging in Job Corps contracts solely for their own profit. Bidding companies were described in a national news magazine as acting "like blindfolded bulldogs in a butcher shop."[53] The sponsoring corporations assumed no responsibility for employing youngsters who had completed the program successfully, nor did they guarantee job placement elsewhere. No provisions were made for cooperative, supervised on-the-job training. Many of the centers for boys were located at abandoned military bases hundreds of miles from the youngsters' homes, and these centers tended to acquire a quasimilitary climate. The centers were assembled hastily and difficulties were encountered in engaging qualified professional staffs. A study ordered by Congress to review the War on Poverty reported in 1969 that corps trainees did little better in the labor market than poor youths without such training.[54] During the ensuing years, many centers were relocated, and gradually the program was virtually phased out.

The Neighborhood Youth Corps was established by the OEO to provide part-time employment for disadvantaged youth of high-school age during the school year and in full-time jobs during the summer. The jobs are under the auspices of various public-service agencies, and the program is intended to help youths to stay in school. The program also provides employment for out-of-school youth. The Neighborhood Youth Corps has not been coordinated with the vocational programs of the schools and, consequently, has not been an effective program of vocational education. Its main function has been to keep disadvantaged adolescents off the streets especially during the summer months.

Upward Bound was established in 1966 by the OEO to develop the college potential of disadvantaged high-school youth. This program has been focused mainly on preparing youngsters for four-year colleges and, as a result, the possibilities for career development through community colleges have been largely overlooked. An evaluation of the research on Upward Bound, along with other programs in the War on Poverty, reported that although there was much promotional rhetoric, the academic performance of Upward Bound participants did not improve in high school.[55]

Most Upward Bound projects were not geared to improve the high-school curriculum but rather to provide supplementary remedial and enrichment services and activities under the auspices of the sponsoring colleges and universities. In the typical program, students were selected after they had completed their sophomore or junior year of high school, leaving little time for correcting developmental deficiencies such as in reading.

The various educational programs created by OEO were conducted for the most part independently of the schools and other federal education and welfare agencies, with the result that there was a great deal of duplication, fragmentation, and dissipation of effort. In many respects, the OEO assumed a negative stance toward public schools, as evidenced by its education voucher plan for making federal funds available for alternative schools. Instead of seeking to identify the shortcomings of the public schools and to remedy the deficiencies, the federal policy under OEO was to set up separate educational programs at great expense and of questionable effectiveness.

The President's National Advisory Commission on Civil Disorders, in its report of 1968, found from its survey data and arrest records in twenty cities that most of the rioters were late teenagers and young adults. The report called attention to the fact that only a small fraction of high-school youth were enrolled in vocational education programs.[56] The commission recommended that these programs be greatly expanded and strengthened, to reach both in-school youth and dropouts, with key emphasis being given to the development of part-time cooperative arrangements coupling formal education with supervised work experience. The commission also called for intensive efforts to develop programs in fields where critical shortages exist, such as in certain technical and health occupations.

As the United States entered the 1970s, it had become evident that a War on Poverty had never been waged. It had become a casualty of the Vietnam War.

Social Problems

In accordance with the vocational education amendments of 1968, the National Advisory Council on Vocational Education was created by Congress and, in 1969, issued the first of a series of reports. In its first report the newly formed council linked the rising racial unrest in cities with the continuing problem of youth unemployment and made a scathing indictment of a national attitude that looks with disfavor on vocational education and regards good education as purely academic—capped by a college degree.

> Our nation seethes. Racial unrest, violence and the unemployment of youth have their roots in inadequate education. Each year the ranks of the school dropouts increase by three-quarters of a million young men and women. They enter the job market without the skills and attitudes employers require. . . .
>
> At the very heart of the problem is a national attitude that says that vocational education is designed for somebody else's children. . . . We are all guilty. We have promoted the idea that the only good education is an education capped by four

years of college. This idea, transmitted by our values, our aspirations and our silent support, is snobbish, undemocratic, and a revelation of why schools fail so many students.[57]

The council pointed out that the opportunities in skilled occupations were expanding far more rapidly than were the opportunities for liberal arts graduates of U.S. colleges.

Subsequent reports by the National Advisory Council criticized the separate vocational programs for the disadvantaged—such as those of the Job Corps and Neighborhood Youth Corps, operating independently of the high schools—which "say to the disadvantaged that they are second-class citizens who cannot make it into the mainstream."[58] The council also pointed to the bias against vocational education on the part of leading university officials and influential decision makers in the nation.

The growing army of unemployed and unskilled youth at a time of critical shortage of skilled workers impelled the editor of the official journal of the American Association for the Advancement of Science to make vocational education the topic of an editorial.

> As a nation we have been preoccupied with fostering excellence of a limited group while neglecting the overwhelming majority of our youth. . . . Moreover, there have been many curriculum reform efforts benefiting college-bound students while vocational curricula have been little improved. One of our greatest mistakes has been to accord special prestige to a college degree while displaying indifference toward quality in craftsmanship. We reward verbal skill and abstract reasoning and deny dignity to manual workers. . . . In our society there is little place for the man or woman who has no special skill. If our increasingly technological society is not to deteriorate, we must find means of helping the young find useful roles whatever their particular aptitudes.[59]

The editorial pointed out that despite technological advances, it was often necessary to wait weeks for the services of a skilled worker in the trades. Noting that federal funds for higher education were running almost eighteen times the allocations for vocational education, the editorial recommended that a far greater investment be made in vocational education. In view of the leadership role played by the American Association for the Advancement of Science in the disciplinary curriculum reforms of the 1950s and 1960s, the editorial criticizing the one-sidedness of these curriculum efforts acquired a special significance. The main body of university intellectuals was far from recognizing the critical need for vocational education in the high schools.

THE RETREAT FROM SCHOOLING

During the 1970s, school critics on the radical left and revisionists of educational history were portraying vocational education and guidance as operating to fulfill the needs of the new industrial state by shaping individual abilities to fit particular slots in the organism of the corporate state.[60] In leveling this attack on the schools, they were strangely silent about the vocational functions of the modern university.

Instead of seeking to reconstruct the curriculum in vocational education and in other areas so as to make the curriculum consonant with their notions of the good society, many of the radical education critics advocated the elimination of compulsory education and even the deschooling of society. Paradoxically, they viewed society as being impersonally technological and corporate, yet they somehow envisioned the adolescent finding his or her own way in such a society without the encumbrance of formal schooling. Illich, for example, envisioned a "convivial," utopian society emerging, without schools, with technology harnessed to allow youth to find their own levels of "competence, control, and initiative, limited only by other individuals' claims to an equal range of power and freedom."[61] Although educators may be justified in dismissing the prescriptions of these critics as wildly contradictory and impractical, for no technological society has managed to develop without formal institutions of schooling, curiously the radical literature gained a considerable following among segments of the intelligentsia who valued formal education for themselves and for their own children—but apparently not for other people's children.

The disruption in the high schools during the late sixties, which had filtered down from the colleges, gave the radical critics and education policymakers cause for emphasizing the limitations rather than the possibilities of education. The federal government and private foundations began financing studies and commissions to show the limitations of formal education, particularly for the disadvantaged, and to propose various alternatives for adolescent transition to the work force.

Radical revisionist historians echoed Jencks's conclusions that the schools are only marginal institutions in effecting income equality.[62] Although subsequent studies revealed that formal education exerts profound influences on life-style and socioeconomic opportunity (see Chapter 13), the call for retrenchment pervaded the educational scene. "Official" reports of national commissions soon were calling for the lowering of the school-leaving age and the preparation of youth for the world of work in nonschool and alternative school settings. The implications were clearly that the comprehensive high school had either outlived its usefulness or had failed in its mission. The college-bound would attend academic high schools. The others would make the transition to adulthood through alternative arrangements.

Channels to the Work Force

It will be recalled that the National Commission on the Reform of Secondary Education of the Kettering Foundation (1973) had recommended that the school-leaving age be dropped to fourteen. Those remaining in school, but who are not in the college preparatory program, could attend area vocational schools and other alternative schools. Although all students should be exposed to career education, it would be focused particularly on the economic and social needs of minorities. Vocational education would be the advanced phase of career education, focused on the development of hard skills in specific occupations. Through career contracting, school funds would be used to pay employers for on-the-job training. This program, coupled with work-study arrangements, would save funds that otherwise would be expended on school facilities. No mention was made of career education as a means of investigating the problems of the world of work. In sum, the commission's proposals conceived of career education as an efficient sifting-sorting-channeling mechanism for a technocratic order.[63]

Transition to Adulthood

In its report of 1974, the Panel on Youth of the President's Science Advisory Committee, chaired by James Coleman, traced the growing holding power of the high school during the twentieth century and noted that "the forms of escape [sic] of the past have been steadily reduced."[64] In using the term *escape,* the panel had portrayed the school as an institution of penal incarceration. The fact that the overwhelming proportion of adolescents choose to remain in school on reaching the school-leaving age was ignored by the panel. Several alternative directions for facilitating the transition of youth to adulthood were proposed on an exploratory basis: (1) provide for specialized high schools in place of the comprehensive model to serve the specialized interests of students; (2) reduce school functions to academic studies; (3) expand programs for school-work alternation; (4) add education functions to nonschool organizations and divert school funds proportionately to such organizations; (5) revise child-labor standards to widen the possibilities for work experience and employment; and (6) divert funds from high schools and colleges to finance education vouchers to encourage youth who reach school-leaving age to purchase educational and training programs other than formal schooling or college attendance.

Unfortunately, the panel did not explore the possibilities for making the comprehensive high school more effective. The various proposals would change the very structure of American education and appeared to raise far more problems than would be solved. Obviously, the high schools would concentrate on serving the academically able through a narrowed academic curriculum. Less-advantaged youth would be channeled into other types of specialized schools and to work-study, apprenticeship, and other arrangements. The panel was unmindful that the very alternatives it proposed for the transition of youth to adulthood constituted a scheme that, if put into effect, would result in the sorting and streaming of the social classes characteristic of the dual educational systems of European nations. The failure of society to provide productive ways of enabling disadvantaged adolescents to make their way in the adult work world found many education policymakers all too willing to embrace schemes that presaged ominous consequences. To remove vocational education from the mainstream of the educational structure might provide alternative arteries of transition to the adult work world, but there would likely be a hardening of the arteries separating the privileged and the disadvantaged.

THE HIDDEN AGENDA OF RETRENCHMENT. Underlying the various proposals for the reform of secondary education was the hidden agenda of retrenchment. The unitary structure of the education system would be abandoned in favor of a divided system for the more efficient sorting and channeling of youth. The report of the National

Panel on High School and Adolescent Education (1976), appointed by the U.S. Commissioner of Education, recommended changes that echoed the report of the Coleman Panel. Among the major recommendations were the following:

1. Replace the comprehensive high school with alternative schools and school-work arrangements, including part-time and short-term schools

2. Reduce the school day to academic studies of from two to four hours

3. Remove vocational education from the high school and provide it through on-the-job training and work experience in the marketplace[65]

Splitting Up the School System

Conant's fears for the survival of the American comprehensive high school seemed well founded from the course of events of the 1970s.[66] Since midcentury the most far-reaching educational reforms in leading democratic nations of Europe have been focused on the comprehensive school model in place of the traditional dualistic structure of selective schooling and its attendant social bias. This movement was conceived as a significant means toward social justice through the improvement of educational and social opportunity. It has become increasingly evident in these nations that it is not enough to restructure the school system administratively, but that the reconstruction of the curriculum is essential to the success of the comprehensive school.[67] The problem of developing a coherent curriculum in general education and a systematic curriculum in vocational education in the setting of the comprehensive high school demands concerted attention and support. In the past there has been the tendency in the United States to favor the college preparatory population and the academic side of the curriculum. Instead of moving to right the balance, American educational policymakers have embraced a set of alternatives that would split up the school system.[68]

NEW AGENDAS AND CONTRAVENING FORCES

Career Education

Havighurst noted that studies of the interests of adolescents reveal that occupational planning and preparation are the principal interests of youth in the age group from fifteen to twenty, and he identified preparation for a career as one of the key developmental tasks of adolescence.[69] A stigma has come to be attached to such terms as *vocational* and *occupational education.* Even many educators look on vocational preparation as mere job training and they see the mechanic, for example, as being engaged in a mere job, whereas they ascribe the term *career* to such occupational fields as medicine, law, science, business, and the arts. It is not surprising, then, that people seek to measure themselves not according to their interest in their work, or in the value of their work to society, but according to the superior social status of their particular occupation over other callings. For example, in response to a newspaper article that classified nurses as service workers along with automotive mechanics, a registered nurse wrote the following in a letter of protest addressed to the editor: "I had to train for three strenuous years. In order to receive my registration, I had to pass a long and complicated state board which included questions on anatomy, physiology, pharmacology, surgical and medical diseases, obstetrics, pediatrics, psychiatry, etc. I must constantly keep up with innovations in medical technique." She noted that in classifying her as a "service worker" the author of the article had "caused me distress," and she ended her letter by stating that the author "owes an apology to nurses."[70] The writer of the letter failed to understand that obstetricians, pharmacists, lawyers, social workers, and orthodontists also are engaged in service occupations, and that society could not hold together without service. Moreover, she ignored the fact that the automotive mechanic also must go through a strenuous program of preparation and must constantly keep up with innovations. The attitude that service is servile, and that only the "higher" occupations are worthy, is socially unconstructive. It pervades not only society at large but also educational institutions.

"ACADEMIC SNOBBERY."   In an address before the 1971 convention of the National Association of Secondary School Principals, the newly appointed U.S. Commissioner of Education, Sidney P. Marland, admonished school administrators for being concerned mainly with college-entrance expectations and neglecting vocational-technical education. "We must purge ourselves of academic snobbery," declared Marland, as he went on to propose that "we dispose of the term *vocational education* and adopt the term *career education*."[71] He also proposed that a universal goal of education should be to equip every high-school graduate to enter higher education or to enter useful and rewarding employment. Marland pointed out that each year some 1.5 million youngsters either drop out of high school or end their formal education on graduation from high school and seek gainful employment without any preparation for skilled occupations.

Under Marland's leadership the concept of career education was promoted at virtually every level of schooling. As every teacher of young children knows full well, children develop their rudimentary understanding of human interdependence and society through their fascination with occupations. Clearly, the promotion of career education was implemented successfully for general education, especially at the elementary and middle-school levels, whereas the needed focus and funding for specialized education at the high school level was lacking. The possibilities for career education to bridge the vocational and college preparatory programs of the high school are legion.

For example, in close coordination with the high school, summer programs could be instituted that provide for observational and participatory experiences to enable youth to explore, critically and constructively, all kinds of career opportunities in a wide variety of institutional settings. The youngster who is thinking about a career in law might be assigned courtroom observation; the adolescent interested in a career in nursing might be employed as a hospital aide; and the youth who is contemplating a career in merchandising might be employed in a department store.

Such experiences would be conducted under the supervision of the school. Thus, the learning environment would be extended far beyond the school setting and, at the same time, the school would be impelled to make its curriculum more meaningful to adolescents by examining social problems and issues in realistic settings. Career education could be so developed as to have significant educative value in helping youth to continue their education in the community college and to make a successful transition to adulthood. Such a program requires significant changes in social institutions, for the school cannot do it alone. At the same time, career education might so be implemented as to create a fuller understanding of the interdependence of all members of a free society, and to eliminate the divisive attitude that renders the academic studies a higher status than the vocational studies in the curriculum.

Myrdal has referred to the United States as still a comparatively backward nation with regard to the failure not only to reduce poverty but also to provide needed programs of vocational education and employment opportunities for youth. Until this is accomplished, a large proportion of our adolescent population will continue to be "pressed down into an alien underclass."[72]

Curriculum Retrenchment

The creation of separate specialized area vocational schools during the 1960s and early 1970s came at a time when the adolescent population was undergoing dramatic growth. Enrollments in vocational courses grew correspondingly in both the specialized vocational schools and in the comprehensive high schools. However, the 1980s not only found the adolescent population undergoing a decline, but also the national reports on education reform, most notably the report of the National Commission on the Reform of Secondary Education (*A Nation at Risk,* 1983), were calling for a curriculum focused on the "new basics" (the traditional academic subjects, with increased emphasis on math and science plus computer literacy), along with increased "standards" for high school graduation. Within two years following *A Nation at Risk,* most of the states had responded by mandating increased units in academic subjects for high school graduation. A report by a commission to study these developments for the Association for Supervision and Curriculum Development (1985) warned that the indications already were in evidence that the increased requirements would affect the curriculum in vocational studies and elective options, and neglect the need for a balanced and coherent program of general education. The report warned that the new curriculum mandates would serve to exacerbate the dropout problem.[73]

The precipitous enrollment declines in vocational education during the latter 1980s found federal vocational education funds being directed toward basic skills remediation for special populations. Area vocational schools in some sections of the nation were filling empty places by serving mainly a special-education population.

As discussed in detail in Chapter 11, most of the proposals for the reform of secondary education during the 1980s were calling for the reduction of the curriculum to academic subjects and appropriating the function of vocational training to business and industry. However, contrary to myth, business and industry lacked the programs and interest in providing high school graduates with the training required for the skilled trades and other skilled occupations. A heavily documented report of a national commission, *The Forgotten Half: Non-College Youth in America* (1988), addressed the problem of school-to-work transition in these words:

> Too often, any discussion of the problems of youth leads quickly to a bashing of the schools for failing to do their job. Most such attacks are unfair and unwarranted. Students may work hard through the 12 grades of schools, may compile adequate records and may graduate in good standing, and their teachers may have effectively taught them the basic skills. Nevertheless, they are still likely to encounter problems in getting started in a productive career.[74]

The report went on to recommend a variety of school-to-work programs through the revitalization of vocational education and monitored work experience with schools in the vanguard so as to ensure the educative function of work experience. The reference to "school bashing" in this quotation was clearly directed at the report, *A Nation at Risk* (1983).

Over an extended period during the Reagan and Bush administrations, the federal expenditure for vocational education underwent a sharp decline.[75] This was a time when the schools were being blamed for the nation's decline in the global industrial economy and for the problems of youth disaffection and social disorganization. As we entered the 1990s, the time seemed ripe for a fair and fresh appraisal of the problems and for the renewed support of those vocational programs that had proved successful over time.

America 2000/Goals 2000

In unveiling *America 2000: An Education Strategy* (1991), President Bush focused his message on holding the schools accountable for meeting world class standards in the core academic subjects (mathematics, science, English, history, and geography) as assessed on the new American achievement tests.

Among the national education goals for the year 2000 was that, "[e]very adult American will be literate and possess the knowledge and skills necessary to compete in a global economy." However, the President's strategy for meeting this economic goal was delimited mainly to the promotion of adult literacy; the identification of job-related, industry-specific skill standards by the private sector; and the development of skill certificates to accompany these standards.

Apprenticeship Training

Exactly one year following the issuance of *America 2000,* the report of the Commission on Achieving Necessary Skills was issued by the U.S. Secretary of Labor in the Bush administration. The report endorsed *America 2000* and the need for a national assessment system to include proficiency measures of school outcomes so as to "communicate world-class standards of curriculum content and student performance," and to "certify individual performance and thereby motivate students and their teachers to meet these standards."[76] The commission went on to propose that at age sixteen students would be eligible for a Certificate of Initial Mastery (CIM) and would be issued a transcript of their competencies and academic records, including numerical ratings on their personal qualities extending back to middle school. The transcript would be presented to prospective employers at the time the sixteen-year-olds apply for entry into apprenticeship training after completing the tenth grade. In the words of the report, "[t]he levels of performance required for a CIM should be benchmarked to the highest standard in the world for 16-year-olds."[77] A clearly disturbing if not arrogant aspect of the proposal was that the onus would be on the sixteen-year-old and not the employer to meet the highest world-class standards.[78] The report appeared to be so concerned with credentialism and its mechanisms that it overlooked the dangers of devaluing the interest needed by adolescents for real growth in the power for learning.

Among his announced strategies for regaining the nation's leading place in the global industrial economy, President Clinton and his Secretary of Labor Robert B. Reich promoted the establishment of youth apprenticeship programs. Soon the media were crackling with reports extolling the German apprenticeship system[79] without giving adequate consideration to: (1) efficacy of such a system in American society—such as the danger of creating a truly dual system of education; (2) the protections required to ensure that the work training is educative, not exploitive, and that the school does not play a merely ancillary role in the relationship with the employer; and (3) whether employers, being understandably profit motivated, are willing (along with the labor unions) to assume a level of public responsibility and obligation to provide entry to regular employment for youths who successfully complete the apprenticeship program. Added to this is the point that Americans had not given adequate consideration to building on successful approaches with school-based programs of vocational education involving supervised work experience, student projects in a variety of fields patterned after those in agricultural education, summer employment programs involving placement and supervision by school faculty, and so on.[80]

Integrating Academic and Vocational Studies

In 1990 amendments were passed to the 1984 Perkins Vocational Education Act providing federal funds for the integration of vocational and academic education, especially in school districts serving disadvantaged populations, and for designing vocational instruction so as to relate to all aspects of an industry (as opposed to segmental aspects). As discussed previously, progressive educators throughout the twentieth century had recognized the educative powers of practical and vocational studies, and sought to bring such studies into joint association with the curriculum in general education in the cosmopolitan, comprehensive high school. The practical arts were brought into the elementary and middle school also in recognition of the significance of hands-on activity for cognitive and social development.

Even at the professional level of education, problems arise when there is a neglect of practical ideas and applications in the curriculum. This problem has arisen even in the age of computer graphics, when students in elite schools of engineering were not developing their capabilities for making things. Lacking in work with real objects, and in the arts and crafts, engineering students were found to be more familiar with mathematics than machinery, relying on single-answer mathematical solutions to rigidly defined problems, rather than seeing the multiple possibilities of knowledge applications. In effect, these students were found to be lacking in development of the mind's eye—the ability to visualize and act on possibilities in practical situations because of their excessive reliance on computer-generated numbers and designs.[81]

A variety of rudimentary models have been identified for developing the integration of academic and vocational studies in the high school—such as incorporating more academic material into vocational courses, making the academic studies more relevant to vocational applications, engaging vocational and academic teachers in teams for instruction and curriculum development, and improving the horizontal and vertical articulation of the curriculum by organizing programs according to occupational or career clusters, thereby treating occupations (and the subjects in the curriculum) more interdependently.[82]

In view of the segmental approach generally taken in basic education and in education in the fundamental literacies, and the corresponding neglect of building an integrated curriculum in general education, the effort to integrate vocational and academic education remains an enormous challenge. At the least it requires the re-education of teachers on both preservice and inservice levels. College departments of mathematics, for example, are not known for their interest and capabilities in providing their student majors with the practical applications of mathematics in the world of work. The entire effort to integrate vocational and academic education should not be limited to enabling students to develop technical proficiency for entry-level employment, but to grow in the power of intelligence so as to open up the possibilities for advancing in their work, for meeting changing conditions, and for enriching their lives. In effect, the goals and functions of education, whether vocational or professional, must have common bearings in a free society.

"TECH/PREP" OR "TWO-PLUS-TWO."   One of the promising programs supported by the 1990 vocation education legislation is the tech/prep or two-plus-two design whereby the upper two years of high school are articulated with the two-year curriculum of the community college. In cooperation with community colleges, this design has been developed in both comprehensive high schools and area vocational schools. In the latter, it has served to revitalize the school by making it more comprehensive in enrollment and curriculum. However, in other instances, it has resulted in a selective-type school serving students whose interests and talents are focused on the sciences, mathematics, and engineering. In the comprehensive high schools, it is incumbent on the administration and faculty not to construe the program segmentally as academic preparation for the community college, but to provide for an articulated curriculum in general education, vocational education, and advanced academic studies—and to articulate the upper-division high school curriculum with that of the community college.

Recall that the genesis of this idea can be traced back to the report of the Educational Policies Commission in *Education for ALL American Youth,* almost half a century before it came to be supported as a program under federal legislation (see Chapter 11, Figure 11–2). In fact the idea of breaking down the barrier between vocational education in high school and liberal or vocational education in college was advanced by the Commission on the Reorganization of Secondary Education in the *Cardinal Principles* report of 1918. It is no cliché to say that the experimentalist-progressivists through the first-half of the twentieth century truly had a vision of possibilities that was ahead of the times.

BIASES AND MYTHS

As discussed earlier in this chapter, the long struggle to give vocational education a recognized place in the curriculum of the high school is rooted in no small measure in the historic bias against vocational education on the part of university intellectuals, particularly literary intellectuals. They appear not to recognize the vocational aspects of their own education that served to prepare them for their chosen callings, whereas they deny to others the educational possibilities of preparation for careers in the working world.

The split between the two cultures of academia, which C. P. Snow was so concerned about, is related to the split between the literary intellectuals and the working men and women of a technological society. That such a division and opposition take roots from the aristocratic notions of the past seems to be of little concern to those who see the literary studies as truly educational, and who debase vocational preparation as mere training. In taking this stance, they fail to differentiate between a narrowly conceived training that is designed to fit a person to the existing industrial machinery, whatever its faults may be, and the kind of vocational education that aims at developing the individual's power and insight to bring about an improved social situation in the postindustrial society.

The Comprehensive Curriculum and Tracking

It has been pointed out that contemporary writers on education commonly confuse program options in the high school curriculum with tracking. They overlook the fact that the original conception of the comprehensive high school, explicated in the *Cardinal Principles* report, was to provide a common core of studies (with heterogeneously grouped students), coupled with program options for specialized, exploratory, enrichment and special-interest studies. In effect, the comprehensive high school was conceived as having a rich and diversified curriculum without tracks. Over the years, most colleges and universities have come to accept students whose pattern of high school coursework included vocational studies.

Unfortunately, many writers on education portray the comprehensive high school as inherently a school with curriculum tracks, thereby promoting inequality, and they proceed to advance the notion that a one-track (academic) curriculum serves to promote educational equality.[83] They fail to recognize that the one-track academic curriculum will find students undergoing self-selection or externally determined selection for such courses as advanced algebra, trigonometry, calculus, physics, and the advanced placement courses. At the same time students, including the most academically talented, are denied the opportunities for enriched learnings that accrue from a diversified curriculum in a comprehensive high school. Students have been known to engage in organized protests when the curriculum is reduced. Even in the case of a high school serving an affluent community and a predominantly college-bound population, students made the news when they organized a sit-in protesting the school board's decision to reduce the curriculum on the ground that the declining school enrollment of 835 was too small to justify economically a number of "less essential" courses. The plan also called for providing students with an extra half-hour of free time daily. "It was an opportunity to assert our citizenship as students," stated the editor of the student newspaper in going on to point out that "[t]he student body changed from being comatose to caring about a cause." As a result, school administrators agreed to meet with student representatives. "It was an education in participatory democracy," noted the principal.[84]

An American Dilemma

Many educators, including the proponents of vocational education, fail to recognize that vocational education, in the setting of the school, offers unique opportunities for realizing the intellectual and cultural possibilities of vocations, inasmuch as the schools are protected from the narrow exigencies of direct profit pursuits. In other words, the schools can serve to provide insight into ways of improving existing industrial conditions. To ignore vocational education entirely, or to conceive of it in the narrowest of terms, is to leave youth at the mercy of these conditions.

In regarding vocational education or the preparation for useful work in society as inferior education, intellectuals are wittingly or unwittingly perpetuating the historic aristocratic divisions in society. Perhaps Eric Hoffer exaggerated the situation when he wrote, "[s]cratch an intellectual and you find a would-be aristocrat who loathes the sight, the sound and the smell of common folk"[85] Yet during the latter 1960s the term *hardhat* entered the lexicon of college students as a derisive descriptor of the working person of industrial society and, at the same time, these college students attired themselves in the blue denims of the laborer. Hoffer pointed out that although many university intellectuals and radical college students presented themselves as champions of the poor, they showed little concern for equipping the poor with the skills and resources necessary for power in the world of work—by means of which they would be able to gain political and social power.[86] In the meantime, organized labor had gained unprecedented political and social power. Few politicians from urban areas could ignore the voice of organized labor.

CRISIS IN BLACK AND WHITE. Many university educators who have focused their careers on the problems of the disadvantaged, particularly the problems of African-

American youth, have portrayed vocational education as a kind of training for the exploitation of African Americans, whereas they see the arts and sciences as the liberating studies. In sharing this view, historians have pointed to the issue of vocational training versus liberal arts education for African Americans following the period of Reconstruction. They have proceeded to side with William E. B. DuBois in his criticism against Booker T. Washington and the curriculum at Tuskegee, which favored technical and vocational education rather than the intellectual education of the liberal arts as DuBois would have it.[87]

In his classic study, *An American Dilemma,* Gunnar Myrdal presented quite a different picture of this issue. According to Myrdal, the expensive vocational education needed by African Americans was never provided and that even at such leading African-American educational centers as Hampton and Tuskegee, the curriculum was less attuned to modern technical-industrial education than to academic studies for the preparation of school teachers. Further, even in the North, African-American youngsters were not encouraged to enroll in the vocational programs in recognition that they would only encounter discrimination by employers and unions.

"This problem is of rapidly increasing significance since formal vocational training is more and more becoming a prerequisite for entering skilled occupations," observed Myrdal, and "to avoid such training means to accept and fortify the exclusionist system, since no Negroes will ever be equipped to challenge it."[88]

Almost a quarter of a century after Myrdal's study was published, critics were describing the recent history and function of vocational education in highly contradictory terms. Vocational education was attacked as having served largely as the monopoly of "a working-class elite" and at the same time it was being condemned as a "middle-class prescription for the poor."[89] Ironically, where African Americans had now gained virtually open access to higher education, their access to skilled vocations in trades and industries remained limited. The overwhelming majority of youth enrolled in full-time day classes in vocational education were whites, and organized labor in the skilled trades also continued to have only a very small representation of African Americans. The civil-rights legislation and court decisions of the 1960s had made it possible for the first time for African Americans to crack the barriers of the skilled trades so that large numbers of blacks might enter. Relatively few African Americans were so qualified as to gain such entry or to challenge any continuing discriminatory restrictions.

To this day, despite the gains made by African Americans in higher education, their population representation in the precision-production and technical areas of vocational education in trades and industries in high school has continued to remain significantly below that for whites.[90]

Today there is much cogitation in academia about a utopian world of automation and leisure, and correspondingly little consideration of how we must come to grips with the grim realities of psychosocial destruction that derives from youth unemployment. In posing such questions, academicians were ignoring the fact that an increasingly technological society requires ever greater working skills and at the same time the increasingly leisured world is open mainly to those who can enjoy the fruits of their labors, and not to those who are left unequipped for the world of work.

The Myth of Mental Discipline

As discussed previously, in making their case against vocational education, many academicians view vocational education as antithetical to the academic side of the curriculum. They portray the traditional academic studies as intellectually and culturally generative, whereas vocational education is seen as narrowly manipulative and geared to conformity. "The preference for vocationalism is linked to a preference for character—or personality—over mind, and for conformity and manipulative facility over individuality and talent," wrote Hofstadter.[91] Such assertions reveal a conception of mind as being separate from character, personality, and hand. The necessary organic unity between mind and character, between thinking and doing, is denied. A dichotomy and conflict is created between the thinking individual and the working individual. Vocational education is portrayed in its narrowest conception rather than in terms of its wide cultural possibilities.

Ravitch has proceeded to cite Hofstadter in contending that the research findings on mental discipline and learning transfer were never decisively established. She fails to identify any replicative experimental studies that would lend support to the doctrine of mental discipline and transfer, and she fails to show how the massive research that demolished the doctrine was faulty.[92] "For centuries, concerned scholars have asked what knowledge is most worthy, what schools should provide for the discipline and furniture of the student's mind," writes Sizer in borrowing the expression of "discipline and furniture of the mind" from Yale President Jeremiah Day in the nineteenth century.[93] To Sizer and other essentialist-perennialists, the answer resides simply in the fundamental academic disciplines.

Despite the long-standing evidence refuting the doctrine that the standard academic curriculum (composed of the traditional academic disciplines) is the only suitable preparation for college, the doctrine continues to persist in many quarters. This doctrine also is centered on the myth that abstract knowledge is superior to practical knowledge for the discipline and furniture of the mind. The history of human progress reveals repeated lessons of how abstract knowledge is derived from the real world of experience and is tested in the real world of experience.[94]

In upholding their belief in the superiority of academic knowledge, university academicians proceed to promulgate the fallacy that the so-called nonacademic studies are detrimental to college success. Ironically, this academically biased ideology is imposed on the secondary schools by many colleges that have broadened their own curriculum patterns in response to the demand for curriculum relevance on the part of college students. Moreover, when college-bound students are led to believe that it is detrimental for them to take nonacademic courses, they not only are denied the enrichment possibilities of such studies but also the school thereby fosters a social dichotomy between the "high" and the "servile" in the student body.

The Myth of Obsolescence

A common criticism of vocational education is that the accelerating changes in technology make preparation for skilled occupations obsolete. In his Carnegie report on

American education, Silberman wrote of the needed education of children today who will be in the labor force in the year 2030. "To be 'practical' an education should prepare them for work that does not yet exist and whose nature cannot even be imagined," wrote Silberman, as he went on to hold that, "[t]his means that the schools must provide a liberal, humanizing education."[95] Now, no one would take issue with the belief, shared by Silberman, that education should focus on how to learn and how to apply knowledge to new problems as they arise. And surely the idea and practice of general education are grounded in the development of this capability. But to assume that vocational education is concerned only with narrow training for specific tasks for purpose of adjustment to the status quo denies the possibilities whereby vocational education, in its wider meaning and application, can serve to bring about improvements in existing conditions. Silberman's statement also divorces the future from the present, revealing a failure to realize that the future grows out of the here and now. The rising generation *is* the future, and the quality and scope of education provided for this generation will help determine the future. To hold that only a liberal education can prepare one for the future, whereas vocational education is impractical because it cannot prepare one "for work that does not yet exist and whose nature cannot even be imagined," is to imply that the future is independent of the contemporary world of work—as though the future world of work will be invented out of a hat.

Perennialists and essentialists contend that the liberal arts and professional education equip one for further change, whereas they deny such possibilities to vocational education. The liberal arts graduate has encountered severe difficulties in finding suitable employment without occupational preparation, whereas the graduate in accounting, dietetics, nursing, or machine tool design remains in great demand. The argument that vocational education readily becomes obsolete as a result of advances in technology simply has not been borne out by experience.

Not only is there a continuity of adaptation and transformation in technological change, but also in the adaptability of the people who do the work of the world. Whether we are looking to technological changes in the workplace or in leisure, we might take heed of the following commentary: "The demise of the stenographer was predicted with the invention of the Dictaphone, the demise of the theatre with the invention of the talking motion picture, the demise of the concert hall with the invention of the phonograph, the demise of the motion picture with the invention of television and the demise of handwriting with the invention of the typewriter."[96] In the same vein, photography was expected to bring about the demise of the visual arts. Predictions that the computer would lead to the end of paper not only were misguided but failed to anticipate that it would create an insurmountable need for paper. Contemporary predictions that the print age is ending as the result of the electronic revolution have proved to be far off the mark. The demand for books is greater than ever, and people continue to read newspapers, magazines, and TV guides.

In looking back on technological change, we find that the sweeping contentions of skilled workers becoming obsolete and incapable of transferring and transforming their technical skills have been vastly exaggerated and misdirected. Contrary to such contentions, the aircraft mechanic who worked on piston engines did not become technologically outmoded with the development of the jet engine any more than did the engineer. The mechanics who had worked on horse-drawn coaches became the mechanics for the automotive industry. The aircraft industry grew out of the automotive industry. In each case of technological change, there were mechanics and engineers who made such changes possible by transferring and updating their knowledge and abilities. Just as the physician, the physicist, and the linguist must keep abreast of their fields, so must the computer technician, the farmer, and the automotive mechanic. Instead of setting up oppositions between the liberal arts (or general education) and vocational or professional education, they must be conceived as interdependent elements of the whole of education.

WORK AND WORKMANSHIP.   When the world of work is regarded as menial, the outcome is a decline in the quality of workmanship with the end result that the whole society suffers. In looking to the future, academicians tend to portray work as becoming ever less meaningful to the individual and increasingly geared to serving the system. In *The Real World of the Public Schools,* Broudy predicted "although work will continue to be important in the society of the future, its importance will be greater to the system than to the individual—except for a small minority of high-level professionals and creative workers."[97] However, in the real world of the young adult and adolescent, success in work is one of the most important life goals. Studies on factors influencing the decision to go to college reveal that career preparation is of key significance.[98]

The skilled trades have not become obsolete, nor are they appropriately stereotyped as routine and unstimulating. The fallacy that work in the skilled trades is necessarily routine, boring and devoid of problem solving can be illustrated by the following actual dialogue between the carpenter and client when encountering an unanticipated problem:

Mr. Schmidt: "What shall we [sic] do about this?"

Mr. Tanner (jokingly): "How should I know? You're the 'doctor.'"

Mr. Schmidt (smiling): "We use our imagination!"

Needless to say, a creative solution to the problem was found by the carpenter after evaluating the pros and cons of several hypothetical possibilities. The point is that unpredictable problem situations arise in ordinary work requiring imaginative and creative solutions. It is simply fallacious to assume that problem solving and creative thinking are the exclusive province of a professional class or a leisure class exempted from boring routines and practical work by virtue of a superior education or birthright.

Finally, if work is not important to the individual, as Broudy contends, then how can it be important to a democratic society? Advanced democratic nations are increasingly recognizing that industrial life must be democratized and that there must be pride and personal fulfillment in work if there is to be workmanship. Otherwise, the very fabric of democratic society will deteriorate. Educational futurists give far more attention to leisure than to work, as though work will become obsolete, as though there cannot be pleasure in work, and as though leisure is to be mainly an escape from work rather than a product of work.[99]

The Myth of the Postindustrial Service Society

It has been contended for more than two decades that the United States is in the vanguard of a transformation from a production economy to a service economy in the information age. A fundamental tenet of the widely heralded information age and service economy is that the focus on education must be directed at the basic literacies and computer literacy, and that it is fruitless to continue to provide for vocational education in the production occupations.

In typical contradictory style of the reckless assaults on the public schools, *A Nation at Risk* (1983) blamed the schools on the one hand for the "steady 15-year decline in industrial productivity, as one great American industry after another falls to world competition," whereas on the other hand the same report blamed the schools for putting the nation at risk by not preparing students for the "'information age' we are entering."[100] In looking to the twenty-first century, Robert Reich has seen the future transformed as an "informating" economy, requiring that the training of workers be redirected from production skills to symbolic-analytic skills.[101] However, almost immediately on taking office as Secretary of Labor in the Clinton administration, Reich promoted federal legislation in support of the German-style youth-apprenticeship system in which adolescents would complete their education in basic literacy and numeracy skills by the tenth grade, whereon they would enter a two-year apprenticeship program in work training followed, for some, by a third year of technical education combining classroom learning with on-the-job internships.[102] In effect, Reich seemed to make a quantum leap away from informating and training in symbolic-analytic skills and back to direct on-the-job training in the world of work.

The fact that the electronic age has generated a sea of information cannot be disputed. Indeed, we may already be drowning in it. The most prosperous nations in the global economy are those built on production. Although there has been a great increase in the service sector of the economy, this has been associated with lower paying jobs. There is compelling evidence that the United States remains a leading production economy and is not becoming a service economy.[103] If the U.S. has slipped in certain sectors of industrial productivity, it has been pointed out that this at least partly is a reflection of the weapons-based economy of a half-century of Cold War.[104]

The Myth of Industrial Know-How

Critics of vocational education commonly hold that preparation for skilled employment should be provided by industry and should have no place in the school curriculum. As pointed out, academicians on both the radical left and far right have taken this position, as did Robert Hutchins, in offering that youngsters who do not measure up to the traditional academic curriculum and who seek vocational preparation would be better off if "allowed to drop out of school and go to work, because they would have been trained on the job and not deluded into thinking the school had prepared them."[105] Such a stance naively ignores the fact that the industrial sector has not had a tradition of welcoming school dropouts for employment, let alone investing in their training in skilled occupations for career advancement. Further, there is a failure to recognize the implications of separating preparation for work from education.

As Veblen pointed out, the chief concern of industry is to employ its devices for pecuniary ends.[106] The school, however, can provide a kind of vocational education that is attuned to personal-social growth rather than merely to fit the individual to a particular slot in the industrial machinery.

Effective programs of vocational education provide for carefully supervised work experience. There is a vast difference between work experience and educative work experience. The role of the school is to ensure that such experience is educative. Supervised work experience can be designed to keep the vocational curriculum up to date and also enable youth to gain insight into the problems of the business and industrial world.

When the federal government turned to industrial know-how to develop programs of job training for adolescents independently of the schools, such as through the Job Corps, it soon was evident that industry was unsuited to the task. The school's responsibility is to see to it that preparation for the world of work takes place in an educational environment. Moreover, as Myrdal has pointed out, business and industry have concentrated their training programs mainly on those who are already employed and who already have a relatively high level of educational and work skills. The role of business and industry, notes Myrdal, should be regarded as essentially a supplement to, and not a replacement for, the vocational and general education that should be provided by public educational institutions.[107]

Contemporary proposals for vocational education call for the school to focus on the new basics or literacies through grade ten followed by workplace education and training in the private sector through apprenticeships and other arrangements. Aside from the dangers inherent in creating a dual educational system there remains the question of whether business and industry would be willing to provide the levels of investment required for entry-level, frontline employment training toward a career ladder. Contrary to the myth that such training is well provided by the private sector, the evidence reveals that only 8 percent of entry-level, frontline workers receive any formal training on the job and this is limited largely to orientation for new employees or short courses on safety and environmental regulation; and most of the upgrade training is directed on those employees who are already technically skilled, such as craftspeople and technicians. Then there is the question of industry's commitment to offer employment to those who successfully complete an apprenticeship program.[108]

The education strategy of *America 2000* claims that the business community "will jump start the Design Teams that will design the New American Schools [and] will provide people and resources to help catalyze needed changes in local schools."[109] The historic record of the influence of business and industry on education has not been flattering.[110] When confronted with the proposal that industry should help remedy the defects of the educational system and other social institutions, Henry Ford II put the matter bluntly in stating, "[t]he business of business is business."[111] If the nation is vastly underinvested in vocational education at the high school and community college levels, it seems that the need is to invest more adequately in these institutions, rather than in shifting the allocation of public funds to business and industry for youth training.

The Myth of Worker Illiteracy

There is a widely held belief, promoted by various national reports on education such as *A Nation at Risk* and *America 2000,* that the most important skills for entry to and success in the workplace are the academic skills and that the schools are not preparing future workers in these skills. However, various surveys of business leaders have revealed that the critical skills in the workplace are behavioral, namely "being free from substance abuse, honesty, respect, and punctuality." Aside from the most fundamental skills of reading and following directions, the least important skills identified in the surveys were academic (mathematics, science, computers, foreign languages, and social sciences). "This appears to be in direct conflict with those who forecast that these will be the most critical skills for the 21st century workplace," noted the Sandia report. And, concluded the report, "the business leaders surveyed are generally satisfied with the skills of their employees, and the problems that do exist do not appear to point to the K–12 education system as the root cause."[112]

Yet it was the K–12 education system that took the brunt of the attacks when the results of the National Adult Literacy Survey were released in the fall of 1993. The survey, conducted by Educational Testing Service for the U.S. Department of Education, garnered sensational media copy, such as the front-page caption in *The New York Times* announcing that "Study Says Half of Adults in U.S. Can't Read or Handle Arithmetic."[113] The media copy drew this sweeping indictment directly from the press release issued by the U.S. Secretary of Education who used the indictment to buttress President Clinton's *Goals 2000* program.

BIAS IN RESEARCH.   Even a cursory review of the premises and research methodology of the study by Educational Testing Service reveals serious flaws that raise questions as to the underlying intent of the researchers. To begin, the definition of literacy formulated for the study was different from any that had been used previously by the U.S. Census Bureau or any other national or international agency. For the study, literacy was defined as "[u]sing printed and written information to function in society, to achieve one's goals, and to develop one's knowledge potential."[114] Aside from the vagueness of the definition, it is doubtful that very many people in society will claim that they have achieved their goals and developed their knowledge potential, let alone voluntarily agreeing to a written test to demonstrate this proficiency.

The report of the National Adult Literacy Survey (NALS) claimed that it was based on a nationally representative sample of 13,600 adults (sixteen years of age and older) who submitted to a written test, coupled with interviews and tests conducted in some 27,000 households. However, the proportion of immigrants in the national sample exceeded their proportional representation in the national population, and most of these immigrants had never attended U.S. schools. Also overrepresented in the study were blacks and Hispanics whose years of schooling, test scores, and economic conditions are below those of whites. For example, although blacks constitute 11 percent of the U.S. population, they accounted for 19 percent of the sample. Moreover, almost one out of ten males in the study were inmates of federal and state penitentiaries—hardly being in a position to meet the study's literacy definition: "to function in society, to achieve one's goals, and to develop one's knowledge potential." The proportion of the national population of males incarcerated in federal and state prisons is less than eight tenths of 1 percent. In effect, the number of male penitentiary inmates was overrepresented in the "scientific" sampling by almost twelve times or 1,200 percent. The proportion of female inmates also was grossly overrepresented in the sample.

Many of the test items seemed to raise questions of face validity. For example, in assessing the ability to "use printed information to function in society," test items required the extrapolation of information from bus schedules under such hypothetical situations as determining waiting time after having missed a connection. One might ask how many of us use a bus schedule in daily life. The test items were graduated to far more complex tasks, such as synthesizing information from complex and lengthy texts and documents, drawing information from lengthy and dense texts that contain distractors, and making high-level inferences or using specialized background knowledge.

As expected, the test scores were positively and strongly correlated with years of schooling completed in the United States. It was acknowledged in the study that of the 25 percent of those testing at the lowest level, almost one out of five had visual difficulties to the extent that reading print presented a problem under ordinary circumstances, let alone under the conditions of taking a timed test under supervision. More than one out of four were found to have physical, mental, or health debilities that prevented them from participating in regular work, school attendance, housework, or other activities.

It must be acknowledged that one surely needs the know-how of taking a multiple-choice test to get through school or college, and indeed the student gets plenty of practice on such tests. One hardly encounters the multiple-choice test in real life. Consequently, there is reason to question whether such a test is a fair simulation of life conditions.

Finally, the report of the National Adult Literacy Survey by Educational Testing Service failed to report the percentages of the population that declined to participate in the tests and submit to questionnaires and interviews requiring more than an hour of time under direct supervision. One might well infer that busy people were less likely to make themselves available for such a test. Considering the circumstances, there appeared to be good reason to recognize the positive findings that more than half of the total population in the study actually performed at the highest test levels in their demonstrated capability of integrating information from long and dense documents or texts, making high-level inferences, using specialized background knowledge, and processing quantitative data in performing more complex operations.

THE FACTS KICK.   Only two months following the announcement by the U.S. Secretary of Education that half of the adult population does not even have the literacy skills to function in society,[115] when it became politically expedient to recognize the high competence of U.S. workers in order to promote the North American Free Trade Agreement, aides who had served both Presidents Bush and Clinton joined in declaring that "we have the world's most productive workers."[116] Indeed, there was compelling evidence to support the high level of education in the U.S. workforce. As cited in Chapter 11, the United Nations *Human Development Report* (1992) ranked the U.S. first among the world's nations on the index of educational attainment and tied for first in rate of adult literacy—whereas the U.S. failed to make the top ten in life expectancy.[117] In other words, one of the most successful institutions is the public school.

Also, only a few weeks following the release of the National Adult Literacy Survey, a comprehensive study for the McKinsey Global Institute, with the assistance of Robert Solow, Nobel laureate in economics, and other economists concluded that U.S. manufacturing productivity is actually higher than that of Japan and Germany, and that U.S. workers are not lacking in the necessary basic skills. The critical factors for workers in all three nations "are attitudinal—flexibility, dependability, and commitment (e.g., "less likely to call in sick").[118]

As cited in Chapter 11, within three months after the release of the National Adult Literacy Survey, an international study by the Organization for Economic Cooperation and Development (OECD) found that among the OECD member nations (industrialized), the United States has the highest proportion of adults with college degrees, and that students in American schools score among the top half in reading comprehension and science achievement, although lagging in math achievement. The study found that whereas the United States ranks highest by far in expenditures per student on higher education, it ranked next to last in the percentage share of expenditures allocated for secondary education. It was also found that much of the real training for the workplace is being done through the community colleges, and that there is a need for better integration of academic and vocational studies.[119]

From these studies, taken together, it seemed clear that the United States is seriously underinvested in adolescent education, particularly in vocational education, and in the access of adolescents to productive employment. Finally, the impact of poverty in impeding the work of the schools needs to be more fully exposed and addressed.

The Myth of Adolescent Negativism Toward Schooling

The bias against vocational education and the attacks leveled at the schools by university academicians and politicians contrast sharply against the belief that adolescents share in the significance of schooling in their lives. Past efforts to shorten the years to the high school diploma have not been successful, even for the academically talented, as adolescents prefer to complete their high school studies with their classmates. Surveys of adolescents of any color or socioeconomic background have revealed an overwhelmingly positive belief in education, although they are also ready to point to many ways through which their schools can be improved. Although they may not give their schools A marks, nor do they give them marks of D and F.[120]

The monumental study by James Coleman back in 1966 found that almost half of the high schools offered no vocational programs, and that almost half of the seniors reported that they would have enrolled in a vocational program if offered in their high school.[121] As noted, the creation of separate area vocational schools during the 1960s and 1970s served to further reduce the number of comprehensive high schools in the nation, impeding the availability of vocational studies in the home high school. The declining expenditure for vocational education during the 1980s finds the 1990s marked by the rediscovery of the significance of vocational education in a technological and democratic society. Strained by massive youth unemployment and alienation, the United States has begun to undertake renewed efforts to reconstruct vocational education through integration with academic studies, tech/prep programs, supervised work internships, and increased federal and state funding. At the same time, proposals for the schools to develop mechanisms for the certification of literacy skills through examinations, with transcripts of results to be presented to prospective employers for entrance to work apprenticeships at age sixteen, raise ominous dangers of creating a dual system. Certified literacy skills do not add up to a general education. Work apprenticeships do not add up to a comprehensive high school education.

Reality of the Human Community

Whereas since the mid-1960s there has been notable progress in making higher education more accessible to the disadvantaged populations, efforts to meet the educational needs of youth who were seeking to enter the world of work continued to lag. Gunnar Myrdal, a great admirer of the American commitment to education, observed in 1965 that "America needs very much greater efforts in the field of vocational training" and that "training for work has never been made a regular part of the American educational system."[122] The major thrust of the so-called War on Poverty of the 1960s had been focused on programs that were largely independent of the school system, and the ranks of the unemployed and socially disaffected youth continued to grow.

After decades of neglect, the 1990s witnessed federal and state support for programs aimed at integrating academic and vocational studies in the schools. In too many instances, the efforts toward curriculum integration were more concerned with basic academic skills rather than general education and, at the same time, vocational education in the high school needed new levels of support and vitalization.

THE LOST ADOLESCENT.   Erik Erikson has described the pitiful and dangerous plight of youth who are left with crippling self-doubt and social destructiveness when denied a sense of "apprenticeship" or "work identity" necessary to partaking in the stream of social progress.[123] Dewey wrote: "Nothing is more tragic than the failure to discover one's true business in life, or to find that one has drifted or been forced by circumstance into an uncongenial calling.[124]

In *Civilization and Its Discontents,* Freud observed that

> [a]fter primal man had discovered that it lay in his own hands, literally, to improve his lot on earth by working, it cannot have been a matter of indifference to him whether another man worked with or against him. The other man acquired the value for him of a fellow-worker, with whom it was useful to live together.[125]

Freud stressed that no activity in modern society can match that of work in giving the conduct of life roots to reality and in giving the individual roots to the human community.

> No other technique for the conduct of life attaches the individual so firmly to reality as laying emphasis on work; for his work at least gives him a secure place in a portion of reality, in the human community. The possibility it offers of displacing a large amount of libidinal components, whether narcissistic, aggressive or even erotic, on to professional work and on to the human relations connected with it lends it a value by no means second to what it enjoys as something indispensable to the preservation and justification of existence in society.[126]

With the huge population of disadvantaged youth being denied roots to the reality of the human community, it is no wonder that the result is corrosive social disaffection and conflict. Yet, during the late 1960s and early 1970s, some academicians and antipoverty workers were advising unemployed youth and young adults that they are better off unemployed than working in so-called dead-end jobs—with the result that people employed in such jobs publicly defended their work as worthy and expressed resentment against those who would deprecate such work.[127]

Eric Hoffer has pointed out that youngsters from comparatively well-to-do families, as well as children of the poor, "are prevented from having a share in the world's work and of proving their manhood by doing a man's work and getting a man's pay," with the result that youth engage in sick forms of self-assertion—"crime in the streets and insolence on the campus."[128] Hoffer has attributed the pathology of campus violence during the 1960s to the lack of social usefulness felt by college youth. He has expressed the view that the concern shown by university intellectuals and students for the disadvantaged and their corresponding antagonism toward the worker are symptoms reflecting their own feelings of questionable social usefulness.

THE EMERGING CURRICULUM IN VOCATIONAL EDUCATION

The traditional oppositions between elite and mass education, cultural and practical education, and literary and scientific education are untenable in a modern, democratic, technological society where knowledge is not a monopolized commodity but grows out of interaction with the environment and enables individuals to improve the physical and social environment. Such a society requires that these traditional oppositions be eliminated and that the curriculum be developed as a unity of interdependent elements and functions.

The literary intellectual may not find any common interests with the agriculturist until he or she realizes that amidst the world population explosion most of humanity lives in hunger. The liberal arts graduate in the Peace Corps discovers that good intentions are insufficient to the task of combating poverty—and that the farmer with knowledge of scientific agriculture, the skilled worker in the machine and construction trades, and the nurse and medical technician all are equipped to apply their talents in attacking the most direct problems of humanity. Vocational education, no less than a literary education, can serve to illumine social intelligence and bring knowledge to bear on the common problems of humanity—whether poverty, disease, ignorance, or injustice. In a democracy, social consciousness is not a monopoly for the intellectual elite but permeates the whole fabric of society. This requires a reconstruction of the curriculum so that cultural pursuits are not isolated from the real world and vocational pursuits are not separated from their cultural bearings.

Curriculum Unity and Interdependence

The ecological crisis has illustrated dramatically that social and intellectual interests cannot be separated from work in science, industry, agriculture, transportation, health, government, and so on. Insofar as the curriculum is concerned, although vocational education provides for specialized competencies and pursuits, it needs to be sufficiently broad so as to share with general education the cultivation of those understandings and sympathies that are common to all citizens of a free society.

Figure 12–1 is a schematic representation of how the various studies in general education, specialized education, and exploratory and enrichment education might be distributed throughout the phases of schooling and into college. The classification of a particular course is not determined solely by its subject-matter content but also by treatment of the subject matter and the functions it serves for the learners. Thus, eighth-graders may be studying industrial arts for purposes of general education, to gain an understanding of the evolution of craftsmanship, to learn how to translate concepts and schematic plans into the shaping of actual materials through the use of various tools, and to gain an appreciation of the industrial processes and the influences of technology in modern society. The ninth-grader may elect a course in mechanical drawing for exploratory and enrichment purposes, whereas a classmate may enroll in the same course with the goal of becoming an architect. The tenth-grader may take a course in electronics because he or she seeks to become an electrician, whereas a fellow student who plans on a career as an electronics technician or an engineer also enrolls in the course. Thus, the traditional separation between the academic and vocational divisions of the curriculum becomes less distinct, and students are not segregated according to curriculum tracks.

Vocational education then shares with general education the goal of developing the learner's abilities to cope intelligently with environing conditions and to contribute to the improvement of these conditions. Curriculum tracking is avoided as

Figure 12–1. Apportionment of the Macrocurriculum, K–12.

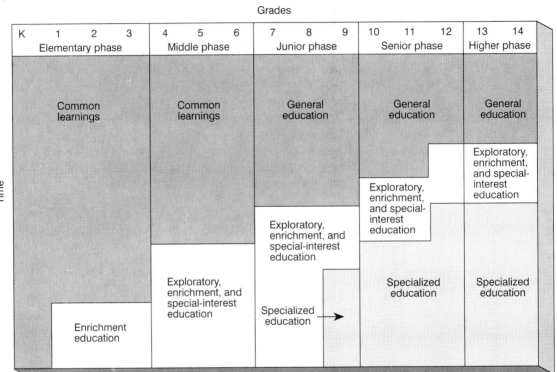

the course work in general education and exploratory and enrichment education includes students who are in vocational and college preparatory programs. Broadly conceived, vocational education should enable the learner to find roots in the reality of the human community, as Freud pointed out in his discussion of the significance of work in the conduct of life.

The Comprehensive Vocational Curriculum

"Vocational training, like education in general, must never lead to dead ends, but must help young people to move horizontally to other occupations, and vertically to higher responsibilities, as future opportunities may occur," stressed Myrdal.[129]

The career-cluster concept embraces Myrdal's idea that vocational education should provide for the opening up of occupational opportunities. Figure 12–2 illustrates various occupational clusters, and Table 12–1 shows how the various federally supported programs of vocational education can be represented in the high-school curriculum and at the postsecondary level according to the career-cluster concept. For example, agriculture encompasses not only production farming but also agribusiness, agricultural technology, food processing, ornamental horticulture, and other careers. The urbanization of society not only has required specialized education at increasingly higher levels in production agriculture, as farmers must produce more food for more people on less and less acreage, but also has created an enormous need to develop a more attractive urban environment. This need has created a demand for specialists in ornamental horticulture and landscape architecture. An increasing number of urban high schools and community colleges have instituted programs to prepare students for these careers.

The expansion of industry and technology has been accompanied by a dramatic increase in the proportion of people engaged in distributive or service occupations. Almost one fifth of the total labor force is engaged in such occupations. Programs in distributive education prepare students for careers in distribution and marketing of apparel, general merchandise, and foods, and in various other areas of service. Many of these programs employ the project method, case analysis, directed observation, and cooperative work experience. Cross-cluster or multiple-field programs have been developed that combine distributive education with home economics, agribusiness, or trades and industrial technologies. Postsecondary programs in distributive education are offered through the high schools, community colleges, and four-year colleges.

Although most of the health occupations require postsecondary preparation, practical nursing programs have been instituted beginning in grade twelve and extending into a postgraduate year leading to a certificate in practical nursing as well as a high-school diploma. In response to the rapidly growing demand for health ser-

Figure 12–2. Career Clusters.

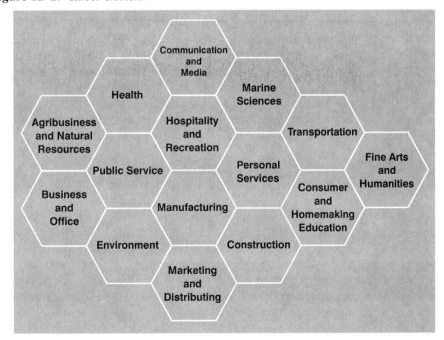

Table 12–1. Selected Vocational Fields and Occupational Clusters

Field	Occupational Categories (examples)
Agricultural education	production agriculture, agribusiness, agricultural technology, food processing, ornamental horticulture
Distributive education	distribution and marketing (apparel, general merchandise, and foods)
Health occupations education	practical nursing, nursing aides, medical office assistants, dental assistants, medical record technicians
Home economics education	child care, institutional services, clothing services, nutrition, home management
Office occupations education	business data processing, office machines, stenographic-secretarial services, bookkeeping
Trade and industrial education	construction, manufacturing, machine trades (maintenance and repair specialties)
Pretechnical and technical education	electronics, computer programming, machine-tool design, medical technology

vices, an increasing number of community colleges have instituted programs to prepare registered nurses, medical technicians, and other health personnel. These programs typically include cooperative work experience.

Home economics has been extended beyond homemaking to include careers in child care, institutional services, clothing services, interior decoration, and other occupational categories. Work experience programs have been expanded through cooperative arrangements with child-care centers, nursing homes, and other institutions.

The traditional commercial subjects in high school have given way to systematized programs in office occupations including not only stenographic-secretarial skills, bookkeeping, and the use of office machines but also business data processing. Increasing emphasis is also being given to instructional arrangements involving simulated office experience and cooperative work experience. Programs in business data processing and computing occupations are widely offered in community colleges.

Trade and industrial education encompasses not only the construction and machine trades but also a wide variety of maintenance and repair specialties and technologies ranging from automotive mechanics to electronics. Although skilled craftsmen have been in short supply for many years, selection practices have made it difficult for schools to expand and improve their programs of cooperative work experience and their arrangements for apprenticeship entry. The high-school enrollment in trade and industrial technologies has grown markedly, but more effective agreements are needed between the school and the unions and industry to provide for the necessary transition from school to apprenticeship and the world of work.

For a number of years, the demand for technicians has exceeded that for engineers. Career opportunities for technicians have expanded into many fields, from electronics to computer programming and machine-tool design. Pretechnical programs have been developed at some high schools, but mostly through the area vocational schools and community colleges. The community colleges have made notable progress in instituting and expanding the programs in technical education in recent years. Because the preparation required for many technical occupations is no less demanding than baccalaureate programs, the community colleges have encountered difficulty in recruiting students who have the necessary preparation and aptitude for technical education.

PERSPECTIVE

The ancient schism between thinking people and working people continues to be reflected in the attitudes of many educators today toward vocational education. Many academicians choose to portray the academic studies as generating intellective power, whereas the vocational studies are regarded as servile. These academicians regard the traditional academic studies as peculiarly cultural, whereas they deny the cultural possibilities of vocational education and the world of work. This oppositional concept of curriculum is untenable in a democracy where thinking people and working people must be one and the same. The inertia of educational traditions continues to perpetuate such opposition.

Contemporary revisionists of educational history and others on the radical academic left tend to portray vocational-technical education as a kind of training of the masses to perpetuate the corporate society. They fail to recognize that vocational-technical education has been made available only to a relatively small proportion of high-school youth. They fail to recognize the strong vocational orientation of colleges and universities, and they rarely portray these higher institutions as perpetuating the corporate society. They deny to vocational education the possibilities for illuminating social intelligence and contributing to the solution of pervading social problems. The issue is not whether there should be a place for vocational education in the curriculum but how vocational education should be fashioned so as to reveal the fullest intellectual and social meaning of work in a free society. This requires that vocational and general education be conceived and designed as interrelated aspects of the curriculum and not as independent or oppositional entities. It requires that vocational education be designed not to reflect existing industrial conditions but to provide insight into the improvement of these conditions. For this reason, the school and community college have an indispensable role in vocational education and such education cannot be given over entirely to industry, even if industry should seek to assume this total function. Effective programs of vocational education require larger social reforms so that the world of work is made more accessible to the rising generation. Moreover, the paths to continuing education must always remain open to all who can profit from further education. The development and expansion of specialized vocational schools raise the question as to whether the United States will allow its unitary educational structure to be split, thereby perpetuating social-class divisions as characteristic of the historic dual educational structure of the European nations. Unless high schools are made truly comprehensive, the danger of such a split is very real.

Attacks on vocational-technical education by educators who regard themselves as representing the best interests of disadvantaged youth have been highly contradictory. These critics have contended, on the one hand, that vocational-technical education has been a monopoly of a working-class elite, whereas, on the other hand, they condemn it as a middle-class prescription for the poor. In reality, vocational education has been made accessible only to a small proportion of the disadvantaged populations. Access to higher education has far outstripped access to vocational education and access to the skilled occupations on the part of disadvantaged youth.

Educational futurists tend to view vocational education as being particularly vulnerable to technological obsolescence. They envision the twenty-first century as an era of leisure, as though work itself will become obsolete. But technology has opened up far more occupational opportunities than it has closed down. Moreover, the educational futurists deny to the skilled worker the capacity to keep up with changing conditions, whereas they see only the professional as having such capability. The automotive mechanic, the farmer, the electrician, and the nurse must be capable of meeting the challenge of change in their respective fields, just as the attorney, the physician, the engineer, and the teacher must keep abreast of changing knowledge and conditions.

Modern programs of vocational or career education can be so designed as to provide broad preparation according to occupational clusters and, as Myrdal recommended, to enable youth to move horizontally to various occupations and vertically to higher responsibilities as future opportunities develop. This will require not only curriculum reconstruction but also a concerted program on the part of business, industry, labor unions, and governmental agencies—all in cooperation with the schools.

In a democratic, technological society, leisure is a product of work and not an exemption from work. Moreover, without meaning in work, there can be no workmanship. Industrial democracies are increasingly recognizing that people are not something to be harnessed to technology but that they must have a voice in operating decisions and in the uses to which technology is put.

In the democratic community, the dignity of work must gain recognition in all walks of life.

PROBLEMS FOR STUDY
AND DISCUSSION

1. The following statement was made by Dewey in 1917:

The movement for vocational education conceals within itself two mighty and opposing forces, one which would utilize the public schools primarily to turn out more efficient laborers in the present economic regime, with certain incidental advantages to themselves, the other which would utilize all of the resources of public education to equip individuals to control their own future economic careers, and thus help on such a reorganization of industry as will change it from a feudalistic to a democratic order. [John Dewey,

"Learning to Earn," *School and Society,* 5 (March 24, 1917), pp. 334–335.]

Do you see this as a pervading contemporary issue? Why or why not?

2. Academicians who oppose vocational education in high school tend to overlook the vocational education function of the college. How do you account for this?

3. Do you see a parallel between C. P. Snow's two cultures (discussed in Chapter 10) and the divisions and oppositions that have marked the two sides of the curriculum: the academic and the vocational? Explain. What steps might be taken to develop the needed curriculum interdependence?

4. Some educators contend that vocational preparation should be provided only at the postsecondary level and, for those not continuing their formal education beyond high school, vocational training should be left to business and industry. Do you see any limitations and dangers in such a prescription? Explain.

5. "No other technique for the conduct of life attaches the individual so firmly to reality as laying emphasis on work," wrote Freud, "for his work at least gives him a secure place in a portion of reality, in the human community." [Sigmund Freud, *Civilization and Its Discontents* (New York: W. W. Norton, 1962), p. 27.]

What are the personal-social implications of this statement in connection with society's denial of a place in the world of work for large proportions of youth?

6. Television and the mass media have been criticized for denigrating and stereotyping the blue-collar worker as an ignoramus hardhat (a racist-authoritarian type). Eric Hoffer maintained that university intellectuals share this antagonism toward the worker. Do you believe that this bias is prevalent in the media and in higher academia? Explain.

7. Many academicians have portrayed the ordinary worker as being engaged in meaningless work and being highly disaffected with his or her work role. Surveys and polls reveal a very different picture. A Harris poll revealed that the majority of Americans would rather keep working than take early or full retirement. How do you account for

the picture of the ordinary worker drawn by many academicians, as contrasted with the findings of actual surveys and polls?

8. Intellectuals often associate the term *career* with the professions, whereas they regard other kinds of work as mere *jobs.* Is such a distinction justified? Explain.

9. Do specialized vocational schools pose a danger that the unitary school system will become a dual system reflecting the social class differences that mark the dual educational structure of most European nations? Explain.

10. In 1992 a report of a commission for the U.S. Secretary of Labor recommended that the high school curriculum be focused on mastery of the fundamental academic competencies, and that youngsters not going on to college would enter apprenticeship training at age sixteen. Why was such a system of apprenticeship training rejected in the United States after World War I when we opted for the comprehensive high school? How do you account for the revival of interest in the apprenticeship in the closing decade of the twentieth century?

11. As discussed in this chapter, *America 2000/Goals 2000* (endorsed by two American Presidents) and the U.S. Department of Labor's report for *America 2000 (Learning a Living)* hold that the most critical skills for the 21st century will be in the academic basics and computer literacy. These reports proceed to blame the schools for failure to prepare students in the needed academic skills. The Sandia report and other research studies find that the most critical skills in the workplace aside from technical skills are attitudinal and behavioral—responsibility, dependability, punctuality, and so on. Do these findings lend support to the significance of vocational studies in the high school coupled with student-initiated projects in all areas of the curriculum, student clubs, and cooperative supervised work experience? Explain.

12. What were the sources of bias in the design and conduct of the National Adult Literacy Survey (NALS) conducted by Educational Testing Service? How do you account for the blind acceptance and sensationalistic treatment of the findings by the U.S. Secretary of Education and the mass media in the face of compelling contraven-

ing evidence from studies sponsored by highly reputable national and international agencies? Do the NALS findings lend support to the testing industry? Explain.

13. From *A Nation at Risk* (1983) to *America 2000* (1991), the public schools have been blamed for the nation's industrial decline in the global industrial economy in the face of the rise of Japan and Germany; at the same time, these reports blame schools for not recognizing that the United States must move away from a production economy and toward a service society. How do you account for these contradictory

allegations? What is a service society? Can such a society be economically viable? Can you identify any leading nations that are service economies?

14. The United Nations *Human Development Report* reveals that the United States has been the leading nation in weapons production, followed by the former Soviet Union. Assuming an enormous and extended peace dividend following a half century of Cold War, which occupational fields do you see as emerging into greater significance, and what kinds of educational priorities will be needed?

NOTES

1. Harvard Committee on General Education, *General Education in a Free Society* (Cambridge, MA: Harvard University Press, 1945), p. 27.
2. John Dewey, *Experience and Nature* (New York: Dover, 1958), p. 93. (Originally published in 1925.)
3. Harvard Committee, op. cit., p. 52.
4. John Dewey, *Democracy and Education* (New York: Macmillan, 1916), pp. 100–101.
5. Ibid., p. 101.
6. Quoted in John R. Commons et al., *History of Labour in the United States,* Vol. I (New York: Macmillan, 1918), p. 192.
7. John R. Commons et al., *A Documentary History of American Industrial Society,* Vol. 5 (Cleveland: A. H. Clark, 1910), pp. 98–99.
8. Edward W. Bemis, "Relation of Labor Organizations to the American Boy and to Trade Instruction," *Annals of the American Academy of Political and Social Science,* 5 (1894–1895), pp. 233–236.
9. Henry Steele Commager, *Documents of American History,* 8th ed. (New York: Appleton, 1968), pp. 412–413.
10. National Education Association, *Proceedings* (Washington, DC: Author, 1905), pp. 141–144 (1907), p. 311 (1909), pp. 288, 616.
11. Quoted in Edward A. Krug, *The Shaping of the American High School* (New York: Harper, 1964), p. 225.
12. Holmes Beckwith, *German Industrial Education and Its Lessons for the United States,* Bulletin No. 19 (Washington, DC: U.S. Bureau of Education, 1913).
13. John Dewey, "Splitting up the School System," *The New Republic,* 11 (April 17, 1915), pp. 283.
14. National Education Association, *Report of the Committee on Resolutions* (Washington, DC: Author, 1918), p. 26.
15. Dewey, *Democracy and Education,* op. cit., pp. 367, 369.
16. Ibid., pp. 369–370.
17. Ibid., pp. 372–373.
18. Ibid., p. 372.
19. Ibid., pp. 365–366.
20. Ibid., p. 373.
21. John Dewey, "Learning to Earn," *School and Society,* 5 (March 24, 1917), pp. 332–335.
22. Commission on the Reorganization of Secondary Education, *Cardinal Principles of Secondary Education* (Washington, DC: U.S. Bureau of Education, 1918), p. 26.
23. James B. Conant, *Shaping Educational Policy* (New York: McGraw-Hill, 1964), pp. 19–20.
24. See for example Joel Spring, *Education and the Rise of the Corporate State* (Boston: Beacon, 1972), p. 108; and *The American School 1642–1990* (New York: Longman, 1990), p. 205; Martin Carnoy and Henry Levin, *The Limits of Educational Reform* (New York: McKay, 1976), p. 134.

25. Commission on the Reorganization, op. cit., p. 16.

26. Lawrence A. Cremin, "The Revolution in American Secondary Education, 1893–1918," *Teachers College Record,* 56 (March 1955), p. 307.

27. Educational Policies Commission, *The Structure of Education in American Democracy* (Washington, DC: National Education Association, 1938), pp. 32–33.

28. Educational Policies Commission, *The Civilian Conservation Corps, The National Youth Administration, and the Public Schools* (Washington, DC: National Education Association, 1941), p. 56.

29. Harvard Committee, op. cit., pp. 28, 102, 103.

30. Educational Policies Commission, *Education for ALL American Youth—A Further Look* (Washington, DC: National Education Association, 1952), pp. 264–286.

31. Arthur Bestor, *The Restoration of Learning* (New York: Alfred A. Knopf, 1956), pp. 38, 67–68, 79–80.

32. Arthur Bestor, "What Went Wrong with U.S. Schools," *U.S. News & World Report,* 44 (January 24, 1958), pp. 72, 75.

33. Hearings Before the Committee on Labor and Public Welfare, U.S. Senate, 85th Congress, *Science and Education for National Defense* (Washington, DC: U.S. Government Printing Office, 1958), p. 65.

34. Ibid., p. 67.

35. Ibid.

36. Ibid.

37. Hyman G. Rickover, *American Education—A National Failure* (New York: Dutton, 1963), p. 89.

38. Hyman G. Rickover, *Education and Freedom* (New York: Dutton, 1959), p. 151.

39. Rickover, *American Education,* op. cit., p. 162.

40. James C. Hayden, *The Council for Basic Education: From Fringe to Mainstream,* unpublished doctoral dissertation (New Brunswick, NJ: Rutgers University, 1992).

41. Richard Hofstadter, *Anti-intellectualism in American Life* (New York: Alfred A. Knopf, 1963), p. 351.

42. Ibid., pp. 351–352.

43. *The New York Times* (December 5, 1973), p. 67.

44. James B. Conant, *The American High School Today* (New York: McGraw-Hill, 1959), p. 8.

45. Ibid., p. 127.

46. James B. Conant, *Slums and Suburbs* (New York: McGraw-Hill, 1961), pp. 2, 18.

47. Ibid., p. 40.

48. Ibid., pp. 46–47.

49. Ibid., pp. 136, 147.

50. Marjorie B. Smiley, "Objectives of Educational Programs for the Educationally Retarded and the Disadvantaged," Chapter 6 in National Society for the Study of Education, *The Educationally Retarded and Disadvantaged,* Sixty-sixth Yearbook, Part I (Chicago: University of Chicago Press, 1967), p. 140.

51. Panel of Consultants in Vocational Education, *Education for a Changing World of Work* (Washington, DC: U.S. Department of Health, Education, and Welfare, 1963), p. xvi.

52. Edgar Z. Friedenberg, *Coming of Age in America* (New York: Vintage, 1967), pp. 250–251; Paul Goodman, *New Reformation* (New York: Random, 1970), pp. 86–89.

53. *Newsweek,* 66 (May 5, 1965), p. 75.

54. U.S. Senate Committee on Labor and Public Welfare and U.S. House Committee on Education and Labor, *Review of Economic Opportunity Programs* (Washington, DC: Superintendent of Documents, 1969).

55. Edward L. McDill, Mary S. McDill, and J. Timothy Sprehe, *Strategies for Success in Compensatory Education* (Baltimore: Johns Hopkins University Press, 1969), pp. 34–35.

56. *Report of the National Advisory Commission on Civil Disorders* (Washington, DC: U.S. Government Printing Office, 1968), pp. 74, 251.

57. National Advisory Council on Vocational Education, *First Report* (Washington, DC: U.S. Department of Health, Education, and Welfare, July 15, 1969), pp. 1–2.

58. National Advisory Council on Vocational Education, *Second Report* (Washington, DC: U.S. Department of Health, Education, and Welfare, November 15, 1969), p. 2.

59. Philip H. Abelson, "Toward Better Vocational Education," *Science,* 161 (August 16, 1968), p. 635.

60. Spring, *Education and Rise of the Corporate State,* op. cit., pp. 91–107, 161.

61. Ivan Illich, "Convivial Tools," *Saturday Review of Literature,* 1 (May 1973), p. 63.

62. Christopher Jencks et al., *Inequality* (New York: Basic Books, 1972); Samuel Bowles and Herbert Gintis, *Schooling in Capitalist America* (New York: Basic Books, 1976).

63. National Commission on the Reform of Secondary Education, *The Reform of Secondary Education* (New York: McGraw-Hill, 1973), pp. 55–60.

64. Panel on Youth of the President's Science Advisory Committee, *Youth: Transition to Adulthood* (Chicago: University of Chicago Press, 1974), p. 80.

65. National Panel on High School and Adolescent Education, *The Education of Adolescents* (Washington, DC: U.S. Office of Education, 1976), pp. 10–13.

66. James B. Conant, "The Comprehensive High School" in Alvin C. Eurich (ed.), *High School 1980* (New York: Pitman, 1970), pp. 73, 80.

67. Torsten Husén, "Are Standards in U.S. Schools Really Lagging behind Those in Other Countries?," *Phi Delta Kappan,* 64 (March 1983), pp. 455–461.

68. Daniel Tanner, "Splitting Up the School System," *Phi Delta Kappan,* 61 (October 1979), pp. 92–97.

69. Robert J. Havighurst, *Developmental Tasks and Education,* 3rd ed. (New York: McKay, 1972), p. 64.

70. *The New York Times Magazine* (August 26, 1973), p. 64.

71. Sidney P. Marland, Jr., "Career Education Now," in Keith Goldhammer and Robert E. Taylor (eds.), *Career Education* (Columbus, OH: Merrill/Macmillan, 1972), p. 35.

72. Gunnar Myrdal, Address at Dartmouth College, mimeograph (Hanover, NH: Dartmouth College Office of Information Services, June 13, 1971).

73. Task Force on Increased High School Graduation Requirements, *With Consequences for All* (Alexandria, VA: Association for Supervision and Curriculum Development, 1985).

74. Commission on Work, Family and Citizenship, *The Forgotten Half* (Washington, DC: Grant Foundation, 1988), p. 3.

75. National Center for Education Statistics, *Federal Support for Education* (Washington, DC: U.S. Department of Education, 1993), p. 11.

76. Commission on Achieving Necessary Skills, *Learning a Living: A Blueprint for High Performance* (Washington, DC: U.S. Department of Labor, 1992), pp. xiii–xxii.

77. Ibid., p. 64.

78. Daniel Tanner, "A Nation 'Truly' at Risk," *Phi Delta Kappan,* 75 (December 1993), p. 290.

79. See for example "Germans' Apprentice System Is Key to Long Boom," *The New York Times,* February 6, 1993; Edwin Kiester, Jr., "Germany Prepares Kids for Good Jobs; We Were Preparing Ours for Wendy's," *Smithsonian,* 23 (March 1993), pp. 44–55.

80. Thomas Bailey, "Can Youth Apprenticeship Thrive in the U.S.?" *Educational Researcher,* 22 (April 1993), pp. 4–10, 16–17.

81. Eugene S. Ferguson, *Engineering and the Mind's Eye* (Cambridge, MA: M.I.T. Press, 1992).

82. W. Norton Grubb, Gary Davis, Jeannie Lum, Jane Plihal, and Carol Morgain, *The Cunning Hand, The Cultured Mind: Models for Integrating Vocational and Academic Education* (Berkeley, CA: National Center for Research in Vocational Education, 1991).

83. Jeannie Oakes, *Keeping Track* (New Haven, CT: Yale University Press, 1985).

84. *The New York Times,* December 10, 1988, p. 30.

85. Eric Hoffer, "Whose Country Is America?" *The New York Times Magazine* (November 22, 1970), p. 120.

86. Ibid., p. 122.

87. Edmund W. Gordon, "Equality of Educational Opportunity—Is It Possible in Our Lifetime?" *Newsletter* of the National Center for Research and Information on Equal Educational Opportunity, 3 (February 1972), p. 21.

88. Gunnar Myrdal, *An American Dilemma* (New York: Harper, 1962), pp. 390–391. (Originally published in 1944.)

89. Smiley, op cit., pp. 123, 140; Martin Carnoy and Henry M. Levin, *The Limits of Educational Reform* (New York: McKay, 1976), p. 264.

90. National Center for Education Statistics, *Vocational Education in the U.S.* (Washington, DC: U.S. Department of Education, 1992), p. 19.

91. Richard Hofstadter, op. cit., p. 264.

92. Diane Ravitch, *The Troubled Crusade* (New York: Basic Books, 1983), p. 49.

93. Theodore R. Sizer, *Horace's Compromise* (Boston: Houghton Mifflin, 1984), p. 89.

94. J. D. Bernal, *Science in History* (Cambridge, MA: M.I.T. Press, 1971).

95. Charles E. Silberman, *Crisis in the Classroom* (New York: Random House, 1970), pp. 133–134.

96. Daniel Tanner, "What a Book Can Do That a Computer Can't," *The New York Times,* August 17, 1983, p. A22.

97. Harry S. Broudy, *The Real World of the Public Schools* (New York: Harcourt, 1972), pp. 158–159.

98. Alexander W. Astin, *What Matters Most in College?* (San Francisco: Jossey-Bass, 1993).

99. Alvin Toffler (ed.), *Learning for Tomorrow: The Role of the Future in Education* (New York: Random House, 1974), pp. 76, 258.

100. National Commission on Excellence in Education, *A Nation at Risk* (Washington, DC: U.S. Department of Education, 1983), pp. 7, 18.

101. Robert Reich, *The Work of Nations* (New York: Alfred A. Knopf, 1992).

102. *Education Week,* 12 (March 3, 1993), pp. 1, 29.

103. Martin Baily, Francis Bator, Theodore Hall, and Robert Solow, *Manufacturing Productivity* (Washington, DC: McKinsey Global Institute, 1993); William J. Baumol, Sue A. Batey Blackman, and Edward N. Wolff, *Productivity and American Leadership* (Cambridge, MA: M.I.T. Press, 1989).

104. Iris Rotberg, "Myths in International Comparisons of Science and Mathematics Achievement," *The Bridge,* (Fall 1991), pp. 3–10.

105. Robert M. Hutchins, "The Great Anti-School Campaign," in *The Great Ideas Today* (Chicago: Encyclopedia Britannica, 1972), p. 210.

106. Thorstein Veblen, *The Vested Interests and the Common Man* (New York: Capricorn, 1969), p. 92. (Originally published in 1919.)

107. Gunnar Myrdal, *Challenge to Affluence* (New York: Vintage, 1965), p. 34.

108. Commission on Achieving Necessary Skills, op. cit., p. 48; Charles C. Carson, Robert M. Huelskamp, and Thomas D. Woodall, "Perspectives on Education in America", *The Journal of Educational Research* (special issue), 86 (May/June 1993), pp. 293–297.

109. U.S. Department of Education, *America 2000: An Education Strategy* (Washington, DC: Author, 1991), pp. 21–22.

110. Raymond E. Callahan, *Education and the Cult of Efficiency* (Chicago: University of Chicago Press, 1962); Judith Weiss, *Education and the Cult of Efficiency Revisited,* unpublished doctoral dissertation (New Brunswick, NJ: Rutgers University, 1989).

111. *The New York Times,* May 12, 1972, p. 55.

112. Carson, Huelskamp, and Woodall, op. cit., pp. 294–295.

113. *The New York Times,* September 9, 1993, p. 1.

114. Irwin S. Kirsch, Anne Jungeblut, Lynn Jenkins, and Andrew Kolstad, *Adult Literacy in America* (Washington, DC: National Center for Education Statistics, 1993), p. 2.

115. Press Release, Press Conference, September 8, 1993, p. 1.

116. Tony Snow and James Carville, "Victory Made (Sort of) Easy," *The New York Times,* November 2, 1993, op-ed page.

117. United Nations, *Human Development Report* (New York: Oxford University Press, 1992), p. 127.

118. Baily, Bator, Hall, and Solow, op. cit.

119. Organization for Economic Cooperation and Development, *Education at a Glance* (Paris: Author, 1993).

120. Center for Human Resource Research, *Career Thresholds,* 1 (Washington, DC: U.S. Department of Labor, 1970), pp. 26–27, 173; Fund for the Advancement of Education, *They Went to College Early* (New York: Author, 1957); Daniel Tanner, "An Education Speedup Appropriate for Some," *The New York Times,* February 12, 1983, p. 21; John I. Goodlad, *A Place Called School* (New York: McGraw-Hill, 1984), pp. 35–36.

121. James S. Coleman, *Equality of Educational Opportunity* (Washington, DC: U.S. Department of Health, Education, and Welfare, 1966), p. 545.

122. Gunnar Myrdal, *Challenge to Affluence* (New York: Vintage, 1965), p. 33

123. Erik H. Erikson, *Identity: Youth in Crisis* (New York: W. W. Norton, 1968), p. 185.

124. Dewey, *Democracy and Education,* op. cit., p. 360.

125. Sigmund Freud, *Civilization and Its Discontents* (New York: W. W. Norton, 1962), p. 46.

126. Ibid., p. 27.

127. *The New York Times* (August 30, 1970), pp. 1, 25.

128. Hoffer, op. cit., p. 30.

129. Myrdal, *Challenge to Affluence,* op. cit., p. 33.

SELECTED REFERENCES

Adler, Mortimer J. *The Paideia Proposal: An Educational Manifesto.* New York: Macmillan, 1982.

Aikin, Wilford M. *The Story of the Eight-Year Study.* New York: Harper, 1942.

Astin, Alexander W. *What Matters Most in College?* San Francisco: Jossey-Bass, 1993.

Bernal, J. D. *Science in History.* Cambridge, MA: M.I.T. Press, 1971.

Bestor, Arthur. *The Restoration of Learning.* New York: Alfred A. Knopf, 1956.

Bowles, Samuel, and Gintis, Herbert. *Schooling in Capitalist America.* New York: Basic Books, 1976.

Boyer, Ernest L. *College: The Undergraduate Experience in America.* New York: Harper, 1987.

Boyer, Ernest L. *High School: A Report on Secondary Education in America.* New York: Harper, 1983.

Carson, Charles C., Huelskamp, Robert M., and Woodall, Thomas D. "Perspectives on Education in America," *Journal of Educational Research,* 86. Special Issue, May/June 1993.

Caswell, Hollis L. (ed.). *The American High School: Its Responsibility and Opportunity.* Eighth Yearbook of the John Dewey Society. New York: Harper, 1946.

Coleman, James S., et al. *Equality of Educational Opportunity.* Washington, DC: Office of Education, U.S. Department of Health, Education, and Welfare, 1966.

Commission on Achieving Necessary Skills. *Learning a Living: A Blueprint for High Performance.* Washington, DC: U.S. Department of Labor, 1992.

Commission on the Reorganization of Secondary Education. *Cardinal Principles of Secondary Education.* Washington, DC: U.S. Bureau of Education, 1918.

Conant, James B. *The American High School Today.* New York: McGraw-Hill, 1959.

Conant, James B. *The Child the Parent and the State.* Cambridge, MA: Harvard University Press, 1959.

Conant, James B. *Education in a Divided World.* Cambridge, MA: Harvard University Press, 1949.

Conant, James B. *Shaping Educational Policy.* New York: McGraw, 1964.

Conant, James B. *Slums and Suburbs.* New York: McGraw-Hill, 1961.

Cremin, Lawrence A. *The Transformation of the School.* New York: Alfred A. Knopf, 1961.

Dewey, John. *Democracy and Education.* New York: Macmillan, 1916.

Diggins, John P. *The Rise and Fall of the American Left.* New York: W. W. Norton, 1992.

Educational Policies Commission. *Education for ALL American Youth—A Further Look.* Washington, DC: National Education Association, 1952.

Engler, William H. *Radical School Reformers of the 1960s.* Unpublished doctoral dissertation. New Brunswick, NJ: Rutgers University, 1973.

Erikson, Erik H. *Identity: Youth in Crisis.* New York: W. W. Norton, 1968.

Ferguson, Eugene S. *Engineering and the Mind's Eye.* Cambridge, MA: M.I.T. Press, 1992.

Galbraith, John Kenneth. *The New Industrial State,* 2nd ed. Boston: Houghton Mifflin, 1971.

Goodlad, John I. *A Place Called School.* New York: McGraw-Hill, 1984.

Harvard Committee on General Education. *General Education in a Free Society.* Cambridge, MA: Harvard University Press, 1945.

Havighurst, Robert J. *Developmental Tasks and Education,* 3rd ed. New York: David McKay, 1972.

Hirsch, Edward D., Jr. *Cultural Literacy: What Every American Needs to Know.* Boston: Houghton Mifflin, 1987.

Hlebowitsh, Peter S. *Radical Curriculum Theory Reconsidered.* New York: Teachers College Press, 1993.

Hoffer, Eric. *First Things, Last Things.* New York: Harper and Row, 1971.

Hofstadter, Richard. *Anti-intellectualism in American Life.* New York: Alfred A. Knopf, 1963.

Jackson, Philip W. (ed.). *Handbook of Research on Curriculum.* New York: Macmillan, 1992.

Kaestle, Carl F., et al. *Literacy in the United States: Readers and Reading Since 1880.* New Haven, CT: Yale University Press, 1991.

Kimball, Roger. *Tenured Radicals.* New York: Harper, 1990.

Kirsch, Irwin S., Jungeblut, Lynn Jenkins, and Andrew Kolstad. *Adult Literacy in America.* Washington, DC: U.S. Department of Education, 1993.

Myrdal, Gunnar. *An American Dilemma.* New York: Harper, 1962.

Myrdal, Gunnar. *Challenge to Affluence.* New York: Vintage Books, 1965.

National Advisory Commission on Civil Disorders. *Report of the National Advisory Commission on Civil Disorders.* Washington, DC: U.S. Government Printing Office, 1968.

National Commission on Excellence in Education. *A Nation at Risk: The Imperative for Educational Reform.* Washington, DC: U.S. Department of Education, 1983.

National Commission on the Reform of Secondary Education. *The Reform of Secondary Education.* New York: McGraw-Hill, 1973.

National Education Goals Panel. *Building a Nation of Learners.* Washington, DC: U.S. Government Printing Office, 1992.

National Panel on High School and Adolescent Education. *The Education of Adolescents.* Washington, DC: U.S. Office of Education, 1976.

Organization for Economic Cooperation and Development. *Education at a Glance.* Paris: Author, 1993.

Panel on Youth of the President's Science Advisory Committee. *Youth: Transition to Adulthood.* Chicago: University of Chicago Press, 1974.

Pautler, Jr., Albert J. (ed.). *High School to Employment Transition: Contemporary Issues.* Ann Arbor, MI: Prakken, 1994.

Ravitch, Diane. *The Revisionists Revised.* New York: Basic Books, 1978.

Rickover, Hyman G. *Education and Freedom.* New York: Doubleday, 1967.

Schlesinger, Arthur M., Jr. *The Disuniting of America.* New York: W. W. Norton, 1992.

Sizer, Theodore R. *Horace's Compromise.* Boston: Houghton Mifflin, 1984.

Snow, C. P. *Two Cultures and the Scientific Revolution.* New York: Cambridge University Press, 1959.

Tanner, Daniel. *Crusade for Democracy: Progressive Education at the Crossroads.* Albany: State University of New York Press, 1991.

Tanner, Daniel, and Tanner, Laurel. *History of the School Curriculum.* New York: Macmillan, 1990.

Turkel, Studs. *Working.* New York: Pantheon Books, 1974.

U.S. Department of Education. *America 2000: An Education Strategy.* Washington, DC: Author, 1991.

Whitehead, Alfred N. *The Aims of Education.* New York: Macmillan, 1919.

Wirth, Arthur G. *Education and Work for the Year 2000.* San Francisco: Jossey Bass, 1992.

PART 4

IMPROVING THE CURRICULUM

*. . . So education became a world of tests and scales
and graphs and correlations.*

—Charles H. Judd, 1925

CHAPTER 13

EVALUATION FOR CURRICULUM IMPROVEMENT

"As social scientists we are deceiving ourselves if we naïvely believe that we are not as human as the people around us and that we do not tend to aim opportunistically for conclusions that fit prejudices," wrote Gunnar Myrdal. He went on to point out that knowledge, as well as ignorance, can be used opportunistically to support biases. "We are not automations like the electronic machines we use increasingly to master large masses of data," continued Myrdal, and "[t]he result is systematic biases in our work—even in our man-made programming of computing machines."[1]

Throughout this book it has been stressed that educational practice and the nature, direction, and interpretation of educational research have been influenced by the larger sociopolitical scene. A key problem in educational research and practice is to understand the sources of bias, to subject the biases to scrutiny, and to protect ourselves, as much as possible, against these biases. Although this may seem to be another mere platitude that is not likely to elicit any debate, Myrdal noted that there is an irrational taboo on the part of social scientists against discussing the general lack of awareness of the sources and influences of bias in social science. "It is astonishing that this taboo is commonly respected," observed Myrdal, "leaving the social scientist in naïveté about what he is doing."[2]

The focus of this chapter is on evaluating certain major contemporary directions in the curriculum field, assessing the research bases for these directions, and identifying possible ways of overcoming various biases that have influenced curriculum research, development, and practice. Rather than presenting a systematic, analytical treatment of the problem, certain major research projects, curriculum-reform efforts, and innovative practices are examined to illustrate how educators can become aware of opportunistic influences on curriculum research, development, and practice—with a view toward overcoming these influences.

537

CURRICULUM RESEARCH, DEVELOPMENT, AND PRACTICE—PROTECTION AGAINST BIAS

What has been discussed thus far is not to be interpreted as a plea to build knowledge in educational and social science that is independent of valuations, for the substantive theory of educational and social science is based on valuation. To eliminate valuation is to reduce a field to narrow empiricism. Yet much research in educational and social science is cloaked in a methodological empiricism as though to convey an image of hard data and scientific neutrality that either masks the valuations underlying the research or conceals the conceptual emptiness of the research.

Alvin Gouldner warns of the emergence in social science of "a kind of methodological empiricism in which there is a neglect of *substantive* concepts and assumptions concerning specifically human behavior and social relations, and a corresponding emphasis on seemingly neutral methods, mathematical models, investigational techniques, and research technologies of all kinds[—leading to] a conceptually uncommitted and empty methodological empiricism."[3] Myrdal has observed that seeking to establish the facts and factual relationships and ignoring valuation is to leave an essential equation missing that opens the door to arbitrariness and biases.[4] Because no substantive questions can be asked in educational and social science independent of valuation, the task is to develop a keen awareness of the sources of valuation and their influences on research and practice—and, thereby, to protect against biases.

Valuation Sources and Influences

The assumption that educational and social science can best be advanced by building a body of objective scientific knowledge of facts independent of valuation, and that one can then simply infer policy conclusions and solve practical problems through such "neutral" data, has been criticized by Myrdal as "naïve empiricism."

> This implicit belief in the existence of a body of scientific knowledge acquired independently of all valuations I soon found to be naïve empiricism. Facts do not organize themselves into concepts and theories just by being looked at; indeed except within the framework of concepts and theories, there are not scientific facts but only chaos. There is an inescapable *a priori* element in all scientific work. Questions must be asked before answers can be given. The questions are all expressions of our interest in the world; they are at bottom valuations. Valuations are thus necessarily involved already at the stage when we observe facts and carry on theoretical analysis, and not only at the stage when we draw political inferences from facts and valuations.[5]

According to Dewey, scientific method would be advanced much further if educators focused on organizing qualitative processes and results into significant intellectual connections rather than devoting their energies to the measurement of relatively unimportant quantitative by-products.[6] Significant problems for investigation are essentially qualitatively based, contended Dewey, and quantitative measures are instrumental or secondary to the qualitative conceptual scheme. This problem prevails to this day in educational research.

In seeking to avoid bias, according to Myrdal, the investigator must be aware of

> (1) the powerful heritage of earlier writings in his field of inquiry . . . ; (2) the influences of the entire cultural, social, economic, and political milieu of the society where he lives, works, and earns his living and his status, and (3) the influence stemming from his own personality. . . .
>   . . . [and] the logical means available for protecting ourselves from biases are broadly these: to raise the valuations actually determining our theoretical as well as practical research to full awareness, to scrutinize them from the point of view of relevance, significance, and feasibility in the society under study, to transform them into specific value premises for research, and, to determine approach and define concepts in terms of a set of value premises which have been explicitly stated.[7]

In this way, the sources of bias not only are understood and their influences minimized but also the search for knowledge and the solving of practical problems can be related effectively to ideals. Although this may appear to some to be an almost insurmountable task, it has been pointed out in earlier chapters how biases have influenced the direction and nature of curriculum research, development, and practice—and how such biases are eventually identified and countered by both theorists and practitioners. For example, as noted in Chapter 11 and as discussed in some detail in this chapter, scientists themselves have not been immune from using data and facts opportunistically to support their own handiwork and biased notions in the curriculum field. As Myrdal observed, "facts kick" and, in so doing, provide a power for self-healing in social science.[8] The problem in education and in the curriculum field is that when data and facts are misused and abused in order to support sweeping changes in policy and practice so as to conform to narrow sociopolitical demands, or to meet the dominant fashions of the times, it may be a long while before the facts kick and before self-healing can occur. In the meantime, a generation of young learners may be affected by such opportunistic influences.

"Generally speaking," writes Myrdal, "we can observe that the scientists in any particular institutional and political setting move as a flock, reserving their controversies and particular originalities for matters that do not call into question the fundamental system of biases they share."[9] The key task, then, is to guard against the flock mentality and against narrow influences by being aware of the sources of bias, by taking measures to protect against biases, by bringing valuations out in the open, and by consciously and explicitly ascertaining how these valuations, together with the data, form the premises for theory, policy, and practice. In this way, the search for knowledge and the shaping of policy and practice can be directed at social betterment in accord with the higher ideals of a free society.

THE NEED TO LOOK TO POSSIBILITIES, NOT LIMITATIONS

"Education has always been the great hope for both individual and society," observed Myrdal in *An American Dilemma,* as he went on to point out that "In the American

Creed it [education] has been the main ground upon which 'equality of opportunity for the individual' and 'free outlet for ability' could be based."[10]

Yet Myrdal detected an intellectual defeatism on the part of social scientists, particularly the sociologists, with regard to the possibilities of using social science to induce social change.[11] This defeatism became openly evident during the early 1970s as social scientists sought to show that the effects of schooling were negligible in reducing the economic disparities between the advantaged and disadvantaged in society. Paradoxically, in reaching their pessimistic conclusions regarding the importance of education in combating inequality, these social scientists used much of the same hard data derived from earlier studies—data that previously had been used to point the way for educational reform as a key means of social reform. How can it be possible that essentially the same set of social science data should be interpreted so differently at different times? It appears the different times had called for different value premises, which, in turn, led to differences in the analysis and interpretation of the data.

As shown in the following discussion, research on the effects of schooling has had a profound influence on social policy. Unfortunately, sweeping conclusions have been drawn from some of the research to justify a policy of education retrenchment. As discussed in earlier chapters, nationalizing influences (political agendas) are used to shape the direction and interpretation of educational research. This does not mean that teachers and school administrators should ignore research or even to eye all research with suspicion, but rather that they must be aware of hidden agendas that may drive research opportunistically so as to serve a particular interest. In previous chapters and particularly in Chapters 11 and 12, a number of examples were cited of how large-scale research studies have been used to prove the project (e.g., the national discipline-centered curriculum projects), or to justify a policy of back to basics, or to convey to the public a sense of massive failure of the public school system.

It cannot be overemphasized that in using research to guide practices, the teacher, curriculum coordinator, supervisor, and administrator must keep in mind the qualitative ideas underlying the research and the practical significance of the research for school and society. No amount of elaborate and intricate statistical treatments can compensate for poor qualitative ideas or for findings that are totally impractical. The point is that the education practitioner must be a keen judge of qualitative ideas concerning the curriculum. The research specialist whose background is educational measurement and statistics or psychometrics quite typically is not highly knowledgeable of the curriculum field, nor of the rich heritage of research in the curriculum field. We need to ask whether a particular piece of research builds on the vast body of research and experience, and whether it looks to the possibilities rather than the limitations of the schools. We need to keep in mind that in much of the large-scale research on school effects, or on student achievement nationally or internationally, most of the variance cannot be accounted for simply because of the limitations of the testing instruments, not to mention problems in sampling, research design, and interpretation.

As discussed in Chapter 10 in connection with the curriculum paradigm, any research or curriculum reform measure that runs counter to social ideals, or to the nature of the learner, or to the needs of the learner in a free society is destined to fail in the long run. To treat these elements as antagonistic or in isolation only serves to fragment and isolate the curriculum and to defeat the educative cause in a free society. One of the great beliefs shared by Americans is the belief in education. Research that sets out to attack this belief may serve a political agenda for education retrenchment, but will fail eventually when tested on the anvil of the American experience.

Research and Valuation—Equality of Educational Opportunity

Looking back on the Coleman report, *Equality of Educational Opportunity,* issued in 1966 as mandated by the Civil Rights Act of 1964, Daniel Bell referred to it as "the center of the most extensive discussion of social policy in the history of American sociological debate."[12] This massive cross-sectional study of 4,000 schools and 600,000 students clearly supported the need for school desegregation by linking school integration with higher achievement.

The Coleman report also revealed that although more favorable school resources—"higher per pupil expenditure, a curriculum that offers greater challenges, more laboratories, and more (cocurricular) activities"—are positively related to higher achievement, the most powerful relationship derives from "the attributes of a child's fellow students in school." The report cautioned that the possible stronger effects of variations in school resources and curriculum on achievement may well have been masked by the overwhelming variations in pupil characteristics.[13]

Moreover, methodology, instruments, and statistical measures connected with a large-scale survey present serious limitations in assessing complex qualitative phenomena. For example, in the Coleman study, no assessment was made of the quality of teaching or of the quality and uses of curriculum materials. Because the school characteristics were identified through questionnaires completed by school officials and teachers, with no independent assessment made of the accuracy of the reporting or of the qualitative differences in the school characteristics reported, it is not surprising that these characteristics did not account for large proportions of the total variance. Thus, for example, the fact that a school may report the presence of a full-time librarian, or the number of volumes in the school library, reveals nothing about the pupil usage of the library, the extent to which teachers assign pupils to library work, and the quality of such library assignments. In the words of the Coleman report, "[i]t is clear that other variations among the schools in this survey have almost overwhelmed any effects of variations in the curriculum. A more intensive study, more fully focused on these curricular variables alone, would be necessary to discover their effects."[14] However, no such study was undertaken. Instead, as discussed later, the Coleman document came to be used by school critics as evidence that investment in schooling is of negligible consequence for the disadvantaged.

The Chameleon Phenomenon in Social Research

Soon after the release of his report, Coleman called for a reduction of social and racial homogeneity of the school, and he singled out the neighborhood school for perpetuating this homogeneity. His chief proposal regarding schooling was framed in these words: "For those children whose family and neighborhood are education-ally disadvantaged, it is important to replace this family environment as much as pos-sible with an educational environment—by starting school at an earlier age, and by having a school which begins very early in the day and ends very late."[15] He went on to call for curriculum changes to allow teachers to work with a wider range of pupils within the same classroom and to capitalize on the positive influences exerted by advantaged pupils on their disadvantaged compeers, along with vast increases in educational expenditures.

The national mandate for school desegregation seemed clear. Efforts in this direction were frustrated, particularly in the North, by the accelerating flight to the suburbs on the part of the advantaged whites, leaving inner-city schools with pre-dominantly disadvantaged nonwhite enrollments, and by growing resistance against busing on the part of the remaining whites residing in white neighborhoods. As African Americans also demanded control over neighborhood schools, the national policy shifted from one of integration and equality to neighborhood control and compensatory education for the disadvantaged.

Four years later, Coleman reiterated his stand favoring school integration based on the findings of his study. "School integration," said Coleman, "is vital not merely from some vague, generalized social purposes, but because it is the most consistent mecha-nism for improving the quality of education of disadvantaged children."[16] By 1972, Coleman's valuation for integration underwent a radical shift, along with his interpreta-tion of the findings from his earlier study. "There is not sufficient evidence," declared Coleman, "to show that the kind of benefits to lower-class children that arise from a socio-economically heterogeneous school can't be provided by other means."[17]

In 1966 Coleman had pointed to the need for an extended school day and cur-riculum enrichment. Eight years later the Panel on Youth of the President's Science Advisory Council, chaired by Coleman, advocated a more restricted role of the school with less time spent in school through various arrangements for work experi-ence. "The young person, rather than finishing high school, can enter a firm in which he spends a certain fraction of his time at work and a certain fraction at self-instruction," stated the panel, in pointing to the use of instructional TV at home for such learning.[18] In 1978, concerned with the mounting data on youth alienation, Coleman turned around once again and prescribed a considerably extended role of the school in correcting certain deficiencies of the home and the wider society. "This qualitative change in the social-psychological environment provided by many fami-lies indicates to me that schools must begin to shoulder a broader set of responsibili-ties than they have in the past."[19]

Myrdal's precautions regarding the tendency for social research to yield findings and interpretations that conform to prevailing valuations and social influences appear to be warranted as one repeatedly observes such radical opportunistic shifts. One might well characterize this as the chameleon phenomenon in social research.

Research and Valuation—Inequality and the Power of Schooling

Apparently, the changing sociopolitical milieu had impelled Coleman, along with other social scientists, to change his valuation regarding the effects of schooling, and this change in valuation required a very different interpretation of his own research data.

After a decade of looking to education reform (largely through special programs of a compensatory nature in the War on Poverty) as a key means of overcoming achievement deficits of the disadvantaged, the 1970s were marked by a new education retrenchment. Amidst the wave of attacks on schools in the popular literature alleging that the schools were dehumanizing children, particularly in the inner-city areas, appeared the Jencks study that was essentially a reinterpretation of the data from the Coleman report, along with data from the U.S. Census. Jencks and his associates reported that "the evidence suggests that equalizing educational opportunity would do little to make adults more equal," that "the character of a school's output depends largely on a single input, namely the characteristics of the entering children," that "everything else" regarding the characteristics of the school "is either secondary or completely irrelevant," and that "progress will remain glacial" if we "proceed by ingenious manipulations of marginal institutions like the schools."[20]

In reaching these conclusions, Jencks did not focus on the curriculum variables, which, according to Coleman, would be necessary—for without an intensive investigation of such variables, they become submerged by other effects.

Many social scientists quickly proceeded to accept Jencks's conclusions as valid. The chairman of the sociology department of the University of California (Berkeley) declared that Jencks's assessment of the data "agrees almost exactly with my own" and that "the book represents the best we know about the causes of individual success and about how far inequality in the causes accounts for inequality of success."[21] Referring to the Jencks study, Seymour Lipset of Harvard's government department declared, "[s]chools make no difference; families make the difference."[22]

EDUCATION RETRENCHMENT. Jencks's conclusions were accepted all too readily not only by academicians and contractors for federal research such as the Rand Corporation, but also by influential political leaders. Daniel Patrick Moynihan, who at the time was a professor of education and urban politics at the Kennedy School of Government at Harvard and was serving as consultant to President Nixon, cited the Rand Corporation report for the President's Commission on School Finance in holding "that with respect to school finance there is a strong possibility that we may be already spending too much." Moynihan then concluded that, "[a] final fact is that at a point school expenditure does not seem to have any notable influence on school achievement," and "[t]his 'discovery' was one of the major events in large-scale social science."[23]

DOUBLE STANDARD. As discussed earlier in this text, we need to ask how it is possible for most of the research on the effects of a college education to reveal highly positive results,[24] whereas so much of the research on elementary and secondary schooling has been so negative. From all that is known about human development it is clear that childhood and adolescence are critical periods for cognitive growth, the shaping of personality, and the evolvement of enduring attitudes and values. Drawing from Myrdal's warnings, it is incumbent on social scientists to look to the possibilities of schooling and not the limitations if the research is to have validity and utility for constructive improvement. One cannot imagine the social scientists in institutions of higher education moving as a flock in generating research data devaluing higher education and supporting reductions in state and federal expenditures for higher education.

Jencks's anti-public school bias was revealed clearly in his earlier work for the U.S. Office of Economic Opportunity in which he proposed an alternative system of schooling by using public funds for education vouchers for the disadvantaged.[25] Apparently, Jencks's value premises against the system of public education had affected his treatment and interpretation of data.

Fortunately, as Myrdal observed, a more complete and valid picture of the phenomena under study eventually emerges as research biases and limitations are exposed when tested in the real world and against the belief in education by the American people. Hence it was only a matter of time before the facts were to kick. Unfortunately, the nation was to undergo an extended period of education retrenchment and back to basics.

Over the ensuing years, Jencks's facts from allegedly hard data began to backfire as research studies in the U.S. and other nations were revealing convincing evidence in support of what Americans already know—namely, that schooling does make a significant difference in people's lives. These studies not only revealed serious limitations and flaws in Jencks's research, but that schooling has enduring effects into adulthood. In a large-scale analysis of data involving a population of 80,000 individuals, Hyman, Wright, and Reed found that "education produces large, pervasive, and enduring effects on knowledge and receptivity to knowledge." With respect to the attacks commonly leveled at the school regarding noncognitive influences, they stressed that much of this criticism is polemic and is refuted by the evidence. "Surely the image of the school as stultifying the student, as destroying the natural passion for learning and the love of intellectual discovery, is not compatible with our finding that with more education there is more information seeking and more receptivity to new knowledge, implanted so well that they survive old age and other circumstances of life."[26]

Unlike Jencks's analysis of Coleman's data on the achievement of children at a given point of their schooling, the study by Hyman, Wright, and Reed traced achievement according to differences in the amount of formal education and the cumulative effects into adulthood. Reports of other studies pointed to limitations of the data used by Jencks and revealed that time spent in school is crucial to achievement, that econometric models for research in education are of questionable value because schools cannot be compared with industrial firms in input-output measures of production, and that contrary to much of the polemical literature in education and social science, schools serve to help overcome rather than to perpetuate social-class bias.[27] Jencks's data even impelled the British to undertake a large-scale study of secondary schools serving a high proportion of disadvantaged youth in inner-city London. From the British study it was concluded that "schools indeed have an important impact on children's development and it does matter which school a child attends." The researchers also found that various qualitative factors, such as "good conditions for pupils, and the extent to which children were able to take responsibility were all significantly associated with outcome differences between schools"—and that "all of these factors were open to modification by the staff, rather than fixed by external constraints."[28]

The question of school effects also was addressed by the International Association for the Evaluation of Educational Achievement (IEA), which found significant connections between school conditions and learning outcomes in the various subject fields. The IEA researchers also acknowledged that the instruments for assessing achievement (multiple-choice tests) measure only a small part of the learning outcomes or what is deemed important in the curriculum, such as patterns of inquiry, expanding interests in learning, social growth, and the cumulative effects of schooling.[29] A recent study of high school students participating in a science program at Oak Ridge National Laboratory found that when asked to indicate the origins of their interest in science, three quarters identified a teacher or teachers, and that their best teachers were characteristically enthusiastic. How might science education be improved? The responses called for more teacher enthusiasm, more hands-on learning, more teaching of concepts, and less factual memorization. Standardized achievement-testing instruments clearly are not geared to measuring the impact of most of these and other school variables on learning outcomes.[30] Further, it is not enough for large-scale research to be directed at identifying the availability of curricular resources. The critical factor is the effectiveness in the uses of the resources that must be measured if connections to learning outcomes are to be made and if the research is to contribute to the improvement of the curriculum.

The inability to connect particular schooling variables with what is measured on standardized achievement tests is inadequate justification for concluding that no connection actually exists. In the words of an American humorist, "[y]ou can't prove that platypuses don't lay eggs by photographing platypuses not laying eggs." Scientific inquiry must be guided by powerful qualitative ideas and connections. The piling up of statistical data to prove the case is scientism, not science. As Myrdal pointed out, "biases in social science cannot be erased simply by 'keeping to the facts' and by refined methods of statistical treatment of the data." Myrdal went on to stress that facts and the handling of data can be even more pervious to bias than ideas.[31]

International Comparisons of Educational Yield

The importance of selecting and identifying value premises by the criterion of relevance and significance to the culture under study is illustrated vividly in the concept of educational yield. A traditional notion held by elitist educators is that more means worse—that is, mass education means a decline in the quality of education. This notion became a slogan that was widely echoed in attacks leveled against the comprehensive high school during the era of the Cold War and space race. Conservative educators were joined by scientists, militarists, and politicians who advocated the adoption of an academically selective school system patterned after the dual European model. Most of the criticisms leveled at the curriculum of American schools centered on the priority subjects of mathematics and science—the two fields deemed most essential in meeting the crisis of the times.

From the inception of the first of a series of international studies of educational achievement (IEA) following Sputnik I to the present day, the findings have revealed that the United States has led all other nations in educational yield (the proportion of the school-age population that completes schooling and advance on to higher education), and reflects the least social-class bias in educational access. As Torsten Husén, chairman of the first IEA study pointed out, the United States and other nations with comprehensive secondary schools have the highest educational yield. Husén stressed repeatedly that the average student achievement score in a comprehensive school system with a high retentivity of students cannot be compared fairly against the average score obtained from a selective school system. Fair comparisons could be made only by comparing the achievement of elite students in both types of systems and by assessing the educational yield of both systems in terms of how many are brought how far. When comparisons are made of equivalent student populations, it becomes clear that the most academically talented students in the comprehensive system compare favorably with those in a selective system—the chief difference being that more youngsters advance further in the comprehensive system. Such findings take on added significance when it is recognized that specialized academic high schools are endowed with facilities and resources superior to comprehensive high schools, and that nonacademic students in the comprehensive schools outperform their compeers who are in dual school systems.[32]

MEDIA BIAS AND NEGATIVISM.   The publication of the first IEA study (on mathematics achievement) was treated sensationally in the American press. A front-page story in *The New York Times* by that newspaper's education editor, Fred M. Hechinger, was captioned "U.S. Ranks Low in Math Teaching"—and the Sunday edition of the *Times* featured a story by Hechinger under the caption "U.S. Gets Low Marks in Math."[33] Similar articles appeared in other newspapers and in news magazines. Despite the repeated warnings in the study against such misinterpretation and against treating the study as an international contest, the American press proceeded to do just that. Obviously, such news reached a high proportion of the American public, but relatively few laypeople and educators outside the field of mathematics read the actual IEA report. Near the end of 1968, *The New York Times* ran an article on page 74 concerning the findings of a report of the National Academy of Sciences showing that the United States "is universally recognized as the leading producer of mathematics and mathematical talent in the world." This is evidenced by the high representation of international awards in mathematics won by Americans and the high proportion of research by Americans at international congresses and articles in the world's leading mathematics journals.[34]

Looking back on the findings of the IEA study of mathematics achievement, Husén characterized the United States as having suffered from a "Sputnik psychosis" and a "spell of masochism" with an "eagerness to look for remedies in Europe" and a compulsion to embrace a national trust for "talent hunting." Husén summed up the major findings of the IEA study in these words:

> We have shown that an elite comparable in size and quality to that of an 'elite system' can be cultivated within a retentive and often comprehensive system. In the selective

system, however, the high standard of the elite is often bought at the price of low accomplishments of the mass.[35]

He went on to criticize the tendency to regard the term *standard* as "a metaphysically anchored concept" and to level the accusation of "lowering standards" whenever efforts are made to change the educational structure in order to broaden opportunities. Husén then reviewed the education reforms taken in Sweden to replace the selective academic secondary schools with comprehensive schools after authorities in that nation had subjected the latter to all kinds of comparisons to ensure that the change would not result in lowered standards.

The extension of education opportunity invariably has been accompanied by the contention that standards will be lowered. However, history has shown that an inclusive system of education provides for the greatest release of talents and aspirations. An inclusive system honors merit; an exclusive system tends toward privilege.

The slogan of raising standards has been used for exclusion, or for curriculum retrenchment with the accompanying slogan of back to basics and minimum-competency testing or mastery of the minima (after Sizer). Again, experience has shown that such efforts have lowered the educational yield by giving emphasis to educational limitations rather than possibilities. It should also be realized that whatever the case may be, half of the schools will find that they test below standard and half will be above standard.

The Politics of Education Reform

The misuses of the IEA data have been reflected widely in political documents alleging massive school failure and calling for wholesale reform of the school system. Few such documents received the extensive media attention than did the report of the National Commission on Excellence in Education, which bore the alarmist title *A Nation at Risk: The Imperative for Educational Reform* (1983). The opening section of the report carried a list of thirteen indicators of risk as to why schools were "sabotaging" the nation in its competition with Japan and Germany in the global industrial economy. The first indicator of risk cited was the allegedly low test-score rankings of U.S. students against those of other industrialized nations. Near the end of the report it was acknowledged that U.S. students did compare favorably after all.

The introductory words of *America 2000,* President Bush's education strategy issued in 1991, stated: "Eight years after the National Commission on Excellence in Education declared us a 'Nation at Risk,' we haven't turned things around in education." The President's message in *America 2000* contended that it was time to hold schools accountable for results and that new world class standards must be set for the schools through new American achievement tests. The President portrayed the situation as one of massive failure of public schools. Accordingly, nothing less than a "revolution" was required to "reinvent—literally start from scratch and reinvent the American school." Illogically, he declared the nation's system of American colleges and universities as "the finest in the entire world," as he failed to explain how this was possible if the schools were failing.[36] Surely the excellence of colleges and universities is built on the quality of the students from the nation's schools. (If we may draw an analogy with big-time NCAA football, the colleges depend on the high schools for talent, and the pros depend on the colleges.)

SEEKING A MORE COMPLETE AND VALID PICTURE.   Toward the close of Chapter 12, mention was made of the national syndrome of school blaming and of the widespread misuses of data in attacking the public schools. It was emphasized that educators need to draw on the fullest array of data sources so as to develop the most accurate picture of the education situation if constructive action is to be taken. One of the unanticipated developments in this direction was to occur from a study that had been authorized with the political expectation that the findings would lend support to the sweeping school-reform measures promoted in *America 2000.* Joining the Cabinet-level groundswell in support of *America 2000,* the U.S. Secretary of Energy, Admiral James Watkins, announced in 1990 that his department was supporting a study of American education as a part of its new education mission. The U.S. Department of Energy, dating back to its predecessor agency, the Atomic Energy Commission, had been responsible for supporting research and development in nuclear energy and weaponry and other scientific work bearing on the military-industrial complex. The contractor for the study of American education was the Sandia National Laboratories, a key research contractor for the Department of Energy. Earlier in his career, Admiral Watkins had served as head of submarine nuclear power distribution control under Admiral Hyman Rickover at a time when Rickover was launching his attacks against American schools, particularly against the comprehensive high school. However, the Sandia researchers, unlike researchers engaged in policy-driven research, were allowed to conduct their study of American education with no a priori premises to prove.

Drawing from existing data banks, the Sandia study found that, contrary to the allegations of massive failure of the school system, there was indeed powerful and pervasive evidence of success, and that many of the priorities set for education reform by the nation's leaders were clearly misdirected. Some of the principal findings were as follows:

1. When the SAT population is adjusted to match the test-taking population of the late 1970s, aggregate SAT scores are actually rising, and since the late 1970s, every minority group has maintained or improved on SAT scores.

2. Performance on the tests for the National Assessment of Educational Progress has been improving.

3. High-school dropout rates are declining for all ethnic populations and community types with the exception of Hispanics, but up to half of all Hispanic dropouts are immigrants, and adult immigrants who did not complete high school in their native countries are counted as U.S. dropouts even though they had never dropped into U.S. schools.

4. Up to five million non-English-speaking children of immigrant parents will be entering public schools in the 1990s.

5. Dramatic and accelerating demographic changes are occurring in public schools as a result of immigration, so that today almost one third of the pupils are minorities, mainly from Latin America and Asia; these accelerating changes are concentrated primarily in central cities.

6. Despite declines in the college-age population, the cumulative number of bachelor's degrees in engineering, computer science, physical science, and mathematics has increased by more than 75 percent during the past twenty years, and the number of doctorates in these fields is at or near an all-time high.

7. Despite the dramatic increase in the proportion of college graduates in the tested population, scores on the Graduate Record Examination have risen significantly since the late 1970s.

8. The United States is the world leader in degrees earned by the nation's population in science and engineering as well as in all fields.

9. The alleged increase in K–12 per pupil expenditures is the result of the high cost of special education and the increasing proportion of pupils so classified, whereas the expenditures for "regular" pupils have remained almost constant during the past twenty years (adjusted for inflation).

10. A majority of American families with children under six years of age have both parents in the workforce, and over 40 percent of children are being reared by a single parent.[37]

"CRISIS RHETORIC" AND MISPLACED PRIORITIES.   In effect, the Sandia study refuted the allegations and prescriptions for the wholesale reform of the public school system as proposed in *America 2000* and *Goals 2000*. Unfortunately, the Sandia study was seen as politically embarrassing so that officials at the U.S. Department of Education sought to discredit the Sandia study and hold it from publication. By the time it was released for publication it had virtually no impact on the media. Some of the principal conclusions of the Sandia researchers were as follows:

1. Much of the "crisis" rhetoric claiming systemwide failure in education is misinformed and only serves to hinder constructive reform; the Sandia research shows that these allegations are based on improper uses of data.

2. The system of public education is being used as a scapegoat by many agencies for the perceived lack of U.S. competitiveness in global industrial markets.

3. The scientific community has been a party to distracting the nation from its real education problems; like the economic competitiveness argument, the contention that there is a continuing shortage of Ph.D.s in technical fields portrays the United States as losing ground to other nations whereas, in actuality, this is not the case.

4. Many current metrics are ill-defined, flawed, misdirected, and provide no justifiable basis for the kinds of national education reforms that have been proposed (e.g., the improper claim of "declining SAT scores").

5. Much of the blame for problems in education (real or imagined) has been dropped at the feet of local teachers and administrators with demoralizing effects.

The Sandia report went on to point out that many of the reform prescriptions are mutually conflicting, such as supporting local empowerment and at the same time promoting a national curriculum, national testing of student achievement, and state-by-state comparisons of test results. The Sandia study also stressed that the call for revolutionary change in the education system sets the current reform cycle apart from others. The U.S. education system was built on a foundation of local control, state function, and federal interest, as shown by the nearly 16,000 independent school districts nationwide. Consequently, it is not only difficult to draw a reform consensus, but may even be undesirable.[38]

Recall that one of the goals identified in *America 2000/Goals 2000* is that U.S. students will be "first in the world in science and math achievement." Drawing on *A Nation at Risk,* the allegation is made in *America 2000* that U.S. students are "at or near the back of the pack in international comparisons."[39] Writing in a publication for the National Academy of Engineering, Iris Rotberg questioned how science and mathematics education could be so deficient when the United States maintains overwhelming dominance over other advanced nations in scientific productivity. She proceeded to point out that distortions in the testing data result from great differences in the populations that pursue advanced coursework in secondary school and, consequently, in the test-sample populations. Therefore, Hong Kong can garner first place in math from a test population of only 3 percent of twelfth-graders who take any math.[40] In the same vein, whereas the United States makes a national representative sampling of students for the international tests of education achievement, other nations tend to use populations from their best schools. Nevertheless, the U.S. Department of Education and the Educational Testing Service, which constructs the tests, have proceeded to certify the validity of the results, and the media continue to convey a grossly distorted picture of the results to the public.

At a time when *America 2000/Goals 2000* were calling for schools to give priority to science and mathematics in the curriculum so as to meet the global competition, an issue of *Science,* the official journal of the American Association for the Advancement of Science, featured on its cover the cruel national crisis of unemployed Ph.D.s in the sciences and alternative careers, and similar stories were appearing in the *Wall Street Journal,* referring to the lack of jobs for scientists as a "black hole."[41]

National priorities for school reform invariably carry corresponding priorities for the curriculum. When reform measures are called for and initiated under an air of crisis, and when they are advanced to serve narrow interests, they divert us from the most significant problems in education. The strength of American democracy derives not from a narrow nationalism, but from cosmopolitanism.

Education and the American Creed

As mentioned early in this chapter, Gunnar Myrdal observed that Americans share a compelling faith in education, and this faith is a principal conclusion from the American Creed. Because this faith is so pervasive in society, no political leader can ignore it. Hence, high on the political agenda, almost invariably, are the public schools. Unfortunately, the schools are often used opportunistically for negative attack rather than constructive redirection. Whereas American social science once had a long tradition of supporting the advancement of the public schools, the trend has been toward abandoning this tradition.[42] Many social scientists, revisionist historians, critical theorists, and others identified with the academic left have built their reputations by challenging the educational ideal of the American Creed. They have sought evidence showing the limitations rather than the potentialities of education in American culture. However, their negativistic data and rhetoric have not been directed at the university—the source of their livelihood—but at the elementary and secondary schools. From the vantage point of the European, the American common school system was uncommon, indeed unique, in its comprehensiveness, relatively low social bias, and open access to higher education. For example, a widely read book throughout Europe during the late 1960s and early 1970s emphasized that America's power to create is attributable in no small measure to its open-access educational system. The author noted that in the United States, from three to five times as many children of workers and farmers have access to higher education as in the Common Market nations.[43] In England and Scandinavia it was discovered that it is not enough to expand the capacity for student places in the universities, but that accessibility to higher education required fundamental reforms in the structure of the school system, particularly in the direction of the comprehensive school.

"OTHER PEOPLE'S CHILDREN." Although many American social scientists and revisionist historians have generated negativistic research and rhetoric regarding the impact of schooling on the rising generation, it is doubtful that they have proceeded to invest less in the education of their own children. Their negativistic message was for public consumption. Like most university professors, who had managed to gain for themselves the highest credential of academia, namely, the Ph.D., and like most college graduates, they likely sought to endow their own children with the greatest amount and highest quality of education possible. Their negativistic message clearly was directed at other people's children.[44] In 1899, Dewey wrote: "What the best and wisest parent wants for his own child, that must the community want for all of its children. Any other ideal for our schools is narrow and unlovely; acted upon, it destroys our democracy."[45]

Thus, the social scientists who were manipulating data to show factually that schools make no difference for other people's children, and they themselves wanted the best and most education for their own children, were in effect undermining a principal conclusion from the American Creed. The belief in education in American thought and life is traced by Myrdal in these words:

> Research in, and discussion of, education is prolific. In America, pedagogy anticipated by several generations the recent trend to environmentalism in the social sciences and the belief in the changeability of human beings. It gave a basis for the belief in democratic values and expressed the social optimism of American liberalism.

> . . . The marriage between philosophy and pedagogy in Dewey and his followers
> has given America the most perfected educational theory in modern times. . . .
> America has, therefore, seen more of enterprising and experimental progressive
> redirection of schools than has any other country.[46]

Although the contemporary statistical attacks on education by social scientists
have garnered a considerable following on the part of many of their colleagues, and
on the part of the media and education policymakers, the American public was not
about to abandon its belief in education.

Research and Valuation—Protection Against Bias

Throughout this chapter it has been emphasized that researchers need to identify
their value premises as a protection against bias. This enables the researcher and the
consumer of the research to interpret the findings in the light of the stated value
premises. Thus, the consumer of the research is better able to interpret the data
more perceptively and critically. The researcher, in turn, is more likely to advance
knowledge and improve practice in the field of study. For, by explicitly stating value
premises, the researcher is protecting the study and the consumer of the research
against hidden valuations.

Many people often tend to look on statistical data in the social sciences as
though the data are hard facts representing objective knowledge. They are unaware
that such data may have been derived from a single set of value premises and that
another set of value premises might produce quite different data leading to very different interpretations and conclusions. Thus, it is most desirable to propose alternative value premises and working hypotheses. If one's value premise and hypothesis
is that "schools do not make a difference," one is more likely to obtain data that
point to limitations, whereas an opposite value premise and hypothesis are likely to
lead the researcher to find possibilities.

If researchers look for limitations in humans and in the school as a learning environment, they will be able to find the limitations they are seeking. If they look for
potentialities, the possibilities for improving existing conditions in the school as a
learning environment are practically without limit. This is the great challenge for curriculum development.

Moreover, the value premises should be attuned to the culture under study.
American culture has such a strong belief in education that some researchers, particularly revisionist historians and critical theorists, have made their reputations by
attacking this belief. In so doing they have allowed their own counterbiases to shape
their interpretations and conclusions.[47]

Reason rather than bias should guide controversy. Myrdal puts the whole matter
of value premises in research in these words:

> Values do not emerge automatically from the attempt to establish and collect the
> facts. Neither can we allow the individual investigator to choose his value premises
> arbitrarily. *The value premises should be selected by the criterion of relevance and
> significance to the culture under study.*[48]

Myrdal goes on to emphasize that if only one set of value premises is utilized, the researcher must understand and make it clear to others that both the direction and the practical conclusions of the research have only hypothetical validity, because another set of value premises might well have changed both. Thus, the formulation and utilization of value premises as instrumental norms in research places an enormous moral responsibility on the investigator.

PROVING THE PROJECT PROVES COUNTERPRODUCTIVE

The history of education/curriculum reform is replete with curriculum projects and innovations that have been promoted as virtual panaceas. Supporters of the project often acquire a sense of ownership to the extent that they seek to prove the project, as opposed to engaging in systematic evaluation with a view toward the formative improvement of the project. In neglecting or avoiding research and evaluation during the formative stages of the project or innovation, supporters are prone to become increasingly susceptible to proving the project at the final or summative stage. This may serve a promotional purpose in the short run, but over the long run may prove costly to the consumers not only in monetary measures but also in the lives of the learners.

Why Innovations and Reforms Have Failed

The failure of curriculum innovation and reform may be attributed less to technical shortcomings than to the following:

1. The biases in seeking to prove the project/product
2. The segmental approach taken in treating the subject or discipline as independent of other subjects or studies in the curriculum
3. The neglect of the rich body of research and experience that can provide a powerful base of successful practices on which to build
4. The tendency to undertake and support a singular or unilateral approach when more than one approach may be called for
5. The avoidance of formative evaluation and field trials under the most practical conditions
6. The avoidance of controlled research when such research is called for, and the tendency to claim as an experiment almost any departure from conventional practice
7. The neglect or distortion of the nature of the learner
8. The neglect of linking the subject matter to the practical and social life of the learner (e.g., the critical abilities required for productive citizenship in a free society)
9. The lack of teacher involvement in the development and evaluation of the project or innovation

10. Reliance on authoritative endorsement as opposed to the best available evidence

The national discipline-centered curriculum reforms under the direction of university scholars during the era of the Cold War and space race was by far the most ambitious, far-reaching, and well-financed effort to reconstruct the academic side of the school curriculum in the history of American education. The effort went awry for the most part because it failed to take into account most if not all of the considerations enumerated above. Or, to put it very succinctly, the national discipline-centered projects failed to take account of the curriculum paradigm that requires that the curriculum be so organized and treated as to take fullest possible account of the nature of the learner and the demands of a free society. Instead, the discipline-centered projects were focused on specialized, puristic knowledge to the neglect of general education and applied knowledge. At the same time, whereas the university scholars claimed that their curriculum projects were centered on the methods of scholarly or scientific inquiry, they proceeded to make sweeping claims for their efforts without submitting to research controls. In the rare instances when experimental controls were used, the control populations were set up as wooden-legged competitors.

From the late 1980s and into the 1990s, various professional education associations in each of the academic fields were formulating sets of curriculum standards (K–12) for evaluating the quality of the curriculum and of student achievement. The success or failure of these contemporary efforts will depend in no small measure on the lessons to be learned from the adventures and misadventures of the national discipline-centered curriculum projects. There has always been a tendency for these professional associations to treat their own particular academic fields as separate from the other fields that comprise the school curriculum, with the consequence that the subject matter is treated departmentally and in isolation.

One-Sided Value Premises

Many of the national curriculum reform projects suffered from one-sided value premises. For example, one of the key value premises underlying the discipline-centered projects was that subject matter should be selected and organized in terms of its purity as opposed to application and interdisciplinary treatments.

Early in this chapter, Myrdal was quoted to the effect that scientists in any particular institution or setting often tend to move as a flock and resist calling into question the fundamental biases that they share. This situation appeared to prevail in connection with the discipline-centered curriculum reforms. The commitment to disciplinarity resulted in a long period when virtually no effort was made on the part of the leading curriculum-reform centers to develop interdisciplinary curricula that were focused on applications to pervading social problems and to test such alternative approaches against the disciplinary approaches. Instead, the superiority of the disciplinary premise was promoted and accepted as fact rather than as a hypothesis to be tested.

When systematic research was conducted under the auspices of the disciplinary projects, the research typically was designed to prove the project (curriculum package). Instead of evaluating the discipline-centered project in terms of equally well-supported interdisciplinary approaches, it was contrasted with so-called conventional practice. Instead of funding projects with the mandate to *find* the best curriculum approaches possible and to test the disciplinary premise against the interdisciplinary approach, the National Science Foundation (NSF) and the U.S. Office of Education simply funded the projects with the mandate to *produce* the best disciplinary curriculum packages. In other words, because these projects were committed to the disciplinary premise, virtually no systematic effort could be made to evaluate, either formatively or summatively, these curriculum packages against alternative interdisciplinary approaches. Instead of providing research funds for the independent summative evaluation of the projects, the NSF and the Office of Education allocated such funds directly to the projects so that they could evaluate their own handiwork. Moreover, the funds allocated for such research and evaluation were relatively meager in comparison to the total budgets of the projects.

Avoidance of Controlled Research

The national discipline-centered curriculum reform program can be traced back to the leadership of Jerrold Zacharias, an M.I.T. physicist who organized the Physical Science Study Committee (PSSC), which developed the high school physics course, described by Jerome Bruner on the opening pages of *The Process of Education* as "the most highly developed curriculum of its kind" in representing "the profound scientific revolution of our times" and in meeting the "long-range crisis in national security."[49] Zacharias was to establish the Education Development Center, which served as an organizational locus for a number of the projects and which later became a Regional Educational Laboratory.

Ironically, it turned out that the very scientists who had sought to develop curricula modeled so as to teach students the principles and practices of scientific inquiry violated these very same principles and practices. In most cases they avoided controlled research. Zacharias claimed that the materials for the PSSC course were developed "experimentally" and the "the entire program must be looked upon as an experiment." Yet the PSSC group failed to employ controlled research in evaluating their course. Instead, they resorted to testimonials and unsubstantiated claims. Although they indicated that the claims must be looked on as "hypotheses," they avoided the testing of their hypotheses and, instead, concluded that "it will be students and teachers who must decide upon the soundness of those hypotheses."[50]

UNSCIENTIFIC CLAIMS.   Not only did the university scientists fail to test their hypotheses and substantiate their claims in the light of scientific evidence but they also grossly exaggerated that magnitude of impact of their projects. In reporting to the NSF on school enrollments in the new courses, the project directors submitted figures that were approximately double those derived through independent surveys conducted inadvertently by the U.S. Office of Education. For example, when the PSSC reported 200,000 pupils enrolled in its course, the Office of Education found the enrollment to be less than 100,000. Similar discrepancies were found in the enrollment data reported for the biology (BSCS) and the chemistry projects.[51]

In effect the magnitude of error committed by the scientists was on the order of 100 percent (in favor of their biased premises). At the request of the embarrassed project administrators, the U.S. Office of Education ceased making any surveys on the enrollments in the discipline-centered courses.

Proving the Project

When those engaged in the development of new curriculum projects or innovations embrace from the beginning a singular one-best approach, they find themselves in the position of proving and promoting the project. However, when multiple approaches are undertaken from the beginning, along with systematic and formative evaluation throughout the development stages of the project, the dangers of bias are reduced and the possibilities for developing significant improvements are greatly enhanced. To this day, we find curriculum innovations being promoted and adopted without adequate evaluation and pilot study during the development stages. The story of the national discipline-centered curriculum projects offers invaluable lessons for educators because no other effort at curriculum reform in the academic subjects was so well supported financially at the federal level, so authoritatively promoted by the universities, so powerfully promoted by the media, and so readily adopted by the schools. It has been pointed out repeatedly in various chapters of this text that one of the key criteria for the success of a curriculum or course of study lies in the test of practical knowledge applications in the life of the learner and society. A common claim made by the developers of the disciplinary curriculum projects was that practical applications are (appropriately) excised in favor of puristic/abstract knowledge. Inexplicably, although the Physical Science Study Committee claimed that their physics course provided real knowledge of science and less technology, the committee also claimed that it provided the best background for terminal students as well as those going on to college, appealed to girls as well as boys, and stimulated class discussion and creative thinking.[52]

In stating that the PSSC course gives "real knowledge of science, less technology," the implication is that applied knowledge is not "real" knowledge. Moreover, the PSSC staff never made any effort to test these claims through controlled research. In fact, as educators not connected with the PSSC project found evidence that challenged each of these claims, the PSSC leaders responded by asserting that "the committee's own evaluations are directed toward the improvement of the course, not comparisons with other courses."[53] This antiscientific attitude seeking to justify an avoidance of controlled research was characteristic of the leading disciplinary projects in the sciences and other subjects.

It will be recalled from Chapter 12 that the PSSC course not only failed to serve the so-called terminal students, but also the academically talented. In fact, the sharp declines in college physics and chemistry majors at a time of record increases in the college population were traced to the experiences adolescents had with the new high school physics and chemistry.[54] The adolescent learner is vitally interested in the relevance of the curriculum to his or her life. To ignore this is to court curriculum failure.

EXPERIMENTAL BIAS.   Among the major national curriculum projects, the Biological Sciences Curriculum Study (BSCS) stood virtually alone in supporting systematic evaluation and in developing multiple course versions—namely three that differed in thematic orientation. However, extensive experimental comparisons were not made until after the three versions had gone commercial and, further, the three versions were not tested against each other but against a wooden-legged competitor called the conventional course. The BSCS leaders proceeded to make sweeping claims for the superiority of the BSCS courses over the conventional biology course. In seeking to prove these claims, the BSCS conducted a large-scale study to compare the differences in achievement and attitudes between the BSCS students and those taking conventional courses.

The need for independent summative evaluation becomes readily apparent when one identifies the gross disparities in the treatment favoring the BSCS population over the control population in this experimental research.[55] The teachers responsible for the BSCS group were paid an additional 10 percent of their annual salary to participate in the experiment. The control teachers were given no such bonus. The BSCS teachers participated in a special training program prior to the experiment, and were provided the services of university biologists who served as resource persons during the course of the experiment. No such inservice training program or consultative resource personnel were provided the control teachers. All of the BSCS students were given new textbooks and laboratory books free of charge to keep permanently, whereas the control students had to make use of the used textbooks available in their schools on a loan basis. The BSCS teachers were given special supplementary guides for the experiment that were not part of the regular BSCS teacher materials. No comparable provisions were made for the control teachers. The schools with the BSCS classes were required to have good laboratory facilities and equipment, and when such equipment or materials were lacking they were provided for these schools on a permanent basis. No effort was made to ensure that the laboratory facilities, equipment, and resources of the control schools were generally on a par with those of the BSCS schools.

The BSCS students were given a practice sample version of the BSCS achievement test early in the school year, followed by the BSCS quarterly achievement tests, whereas the control students did not receive the benefit of such practice and exposure. Both student populations took the BSCS final examination at the end of the school year. Obviously, the benefit of practice and familiarity with the BSCS tests on the part of the BSCS students could be expected to improve the scores of these students on the final examination. Both student groups were tested at the end of the year on the Cooperative Biology Test of the College Entrance Examination Board as well as on the BSCS Comprehensive Final Examination. The former test was supposed to represent the conventional biology course, even though it was thirteen years old and was not truly representative of conventional high-school biology circa the 1960s. The control group was not provided with any practice on the Cooperative

Biology Test to counter the practice and exposure provided the BSCS group on the BSCS achievement tests. The BSCS Impact Test (designed to measure understanding of scientific principles and reasoning) and the BSCS Test of Understanding of Science (later renamed the Processes of Science Test) were administered to both populations at the end of the school year. Obviously, these tests were attuned to the subject matter of the BSCS course and, consequently, must be presumed to favor the BSCS group. Thus, all of the tests, with the exception of the Cooperative Biology Test, were produced by the BSCS project and were attuned specifically to the subject matter represented in the BSCS course, whereas the Cooperative Biology Test did not represent any given conventional course. The control population had been composed of students taking various non-BSCS courses who were lumped together for comparison against the BSCS students.

Although efforts were made to match both populations according to aptitude and school and community characteristics, the disparities in the treatment were so obviously biased in favor of the BSCS group as to violate the basic scientific principles of controlled research. As expected, the BSCS group obtained higher scores than the control group on the BSCS Comprehensive Final. However, the control students outperformed the BSCS group on the Cooperative Biology Test. Although the BSCS group was expected to clearly outperform the control students on the BSCS Impact Test and on the BSCS Test of Understanding of Science, the control students made somewhat higher scores (at a statistically significant level) than the BSCS group on the Impact Test, whereas their performance on the other BSCS test matched that of the BSCS group. Subsequent studies of achievement in the first course in college biology revealed that the BSCS and non-BSCS groups performed at equal levels.[56]

PROTECTION AGAINST BIAS.   Not only is it essential that every effort be made to guard against bias in research but the value premises underlying curriculum reform also must be carefully identified and tested before sweeping claims are made. When the continued funding of a multimillion dollar project is dependent on favorable results, bias in the research and evaluation program is bound to become manifest. The evaluation goal, then, is to prove the superiority of the product and not to solve problems in curriculum development. If these projects had been funded in the first place to develop and assess alternative curricula based on alternative value premises, with the goal of developing the best courses possible, there would have been far less likelihood of bias in the research and evaluation. Although the formative evaluation would be conducted largely under the auspices of the particular project, it appears desirable to have the summative evaluation conducted by an independent agency.

All too often in proving the project, comparison populations or control groups are set up as wooden-legged competitors. When the wooden leg unexpectedly kicks, all kinds of rationalizations are proposed. Alternative approaches and value premises should help protect against such bias. Fortunately, over the ensuing years the BSCS group proceeded to undertake renewed efforts toward reconstructing the different curriculum versions and developing additional approaches for students at various school levels. As a consequence, the project has undergone continual renewal by connecting the curriculum materials to the nature of the learner and to the significance of biology in society so as to meet the function of general education.

Need for Alternative Approaches and Formative Evaluation

The label *new math* readily captured media attention in carrying a sense of revolution and mystique during the late 1950s and early 1960s. This was aided in no small measure by the sweeping promotional claims for the new projects. Among the several projects embracing the new wave claim, the School Mathematics Study Group (SMSG) led the way both in funding by the National Science Foundation and in the extent of adoption in the schools. When questions began to arise on the need for systematic experimental comparisons, the SMSG group announced that "[i]nformation gathering rather than hypothesis testing should be stressed"[57]—anathema to the principles of scientific inquiry. When an extensive study was undertaken eventually by SMSG to assess the impact of the new mathematics on pupil achievement, with the findings reported in 1969, it was concluded by the SMSG director that "there are not many clear generalizations that can be made."[58] Unfortunately, no assessment was made of pupil attitudes toward mathematics and the practical uses of mathematics. The SMSG project was disbanded, subsequently, in the wake of rising criticisms of the new mathematics as abstract and devoid of life applications.

Had the SMSG sought to develop alternative curriculum approaches based on alternative value premises, with such approaches being subjected to continuous summative evaluation, the resultant curriculum materials might well have represented a synthesis between the applied and abstract sides of mathematics. Such a synthesis might well have been a landmark contribution to curriculum development in mathematics, and the SMSG project would not likely have been compelled to disband its operation.

Such longitudinal studies can be exceedingly useful in providing data that cannot be gotten through other research methodologies. Ideally, a variety of methodologies should be employed to provide for both intensive and extensive evaluation for formative and summative purposes. In the light of the great debates that marked the curriculum-reform movement in mathematics, it is unfortunate that the NSF proceeded to have the leading new wave project conduct the longitudinal study, instead of having the summative evaluation conducted under the auspices of an independent agency.

Curricular Interrelationships

The nuclear physicist Alvin M. Weinberg contends that a valid measure of the merit of a field is its relevance to neighboring fields and its relevance to human welfare and values.[59] Consequently, efforts to improve the curriculum of a given field or discipline can be enhanced immeasurably by involving those whose work is in neighboring fields or disciplines. Unfortunately, the disciplinary curriculum-reform projects deliberately avoided the vantage points of scholars outside the target discipline, with the result that the applications and interrelationships of knowledge were neglected.

THE OUTSIDE VANTAGE POINT.   When the Nobel laureate in theoretical physics Richard P. Feynman examined the textbooks representing the new mathematics for grades one through eight, he found that much of the material was "an abstraction from the real world," and was loaded with technical terms—"carefully and precisely defined special words that are used by pure mathematicians in their most subtle and difficult analyses, and are used by nobody else." Feynman then went on to observe that many of the books representing the new mathematics curriculum are "full of such nonsense," and he stressed that such material was so concerned with precise, technical language that clarity of ideas was being sacrificed along with the relevance of the subject to the real world.

> It is really quite impossible to say anything with absolute precision, unless that thing is so abstracted from the real world as to not represent any real thing.
>
> Pure mathematics is just such an abstraction from the real world, and pure mathematics does have a special precise language for dealing with its own special and technical subjects. But this precise language is not precise in any sense if you deal with the real objects of the world, and it is overly pedantic and quite confusing to use. . . .
>
> I believe that every subject which is presented in the textbook should be presented in such a way that the purpose of the presentation is made evident. The reason why the subject is there should be made clear; the utility of the subject and its relevance to the world must be made clear to the pupil.[60]

Had the projects in the new mathematics sought the vantage points of applied mathematicians and of scholars from other fields, such as Feynman, for purposes of curriculum development and formative evaluation, many problems could have been avoided and a more unified curriculum would more likely have resulted.

For obvious reasons, it is necessary to have such vantage points as integral to the project rather than as an afterthought in summative evaluation. Otherwise, the project staff is impelled to assume a defensive posture of justifying its product rather than taking measures to develop the best possible materials. The vantage points of persons outside a particular curriculum field or discipline not only can serve as a constructive basis for summative and formative research and evaluation, but when made integral to the input of the curriculum project such vantage points can prevent the project from becoming narrowly wedded to a single set of value premises.

Scientists, no less than other people, find it difficult to change value premises once they are formed and become a basis for commitment. Instead of positing the single set of value premises that guided the scientists in their earlier curriculum-reform efforts as tentative and as hypotheses to be tested, the premises were promoted as valid principles and conclusions. Thus, when subsequent evaluations gave cause for serious questioning of their curriculum products, these scientists assumed a defensive posture. Criticisms such as those raised by Weinberg and Feynman cannot be dismissed. Based on well-informed and well-grounded value premises that challenged the validity of those embraced by the major curriculum-reform projects of the 1960s, such criticisms deserved serious study. Had they been part of the formative input of these projects, the results most likely would have been far different, and a generation of children and youth would have been better served by the national curriculum-reform movement.

Toward Curriculum Renewal

The contemporary scene is marked by the rediscovery of the need to link mathematics with other subjects and to hands-on applications. The first report of the Mathematics Panel for Project 2061 of the American Association for the Advancement of Science observed that "[r]eally, the interaction of mathematics, science, and technology will emerge in the future curriculum from hands-on experience generated by students' interests under the guidance of expert teachers."[61] We may indeed see this as the real curriculum frontier. Significant beginnings have been made through the Science/Technology/Society project and other efforts.[62]

A continuing problem in teacher education resides in the puristic orientation of university mathematics departments. The work of the National Council of Teachers of Mathematics (NCTM) in developing curriculum and evaluation standards for school mathematics reveals some encouraging efforts toward making these linkages so as to enable students to see the applicability of mathematics to real problems. However, many of the implementation examples in the NCTM standards seem forced and artificial, and appear to reflect the problem of mathematics specialists and teachers working on the school mathematics curriculum apart from professionals in other fields.[63] In fact the current thrust in formulating curriculum and evaluation standards has been undertaken by professional teacher organizations representing each of the separate academic fields. The opportunity, for example, of integrating mathematics with social studies, ecology, and health science through social statistics presents enormous possibilities. Rich sources of data are available from various international and federal agencies. Students could learn to create graphs from base data to reveal trends and needs on problems of health, poverty, population, global hunger, resource management, and so on. They could learn about the uses and misuses of statistics in conducting experiments, opinion polling, and in evaluating the effects of advertising in American culture.

As impressive beginning has been made in Project 2061 to formulate benchmarks to guide teachers in developing a more unified curriculum in science, mathematics, and technology. The benchmarks are sets of generalizations to be developed from the core studies in science revealing connections with mathematics and technology, and extending into the arts, humanities, and vocational studies. The approach is intended to reduce the sheer amount of material to be covered for short-term recall and the knowledge isolation that derives from organizing the curriculum into separate disciplines. An example of a benchmark of understanding for an eighth-grader might be the following: "Engineers, architects, and others who engage in design and technology use scientific knowledge to solve practical problems. But they usually have to take human values and limitations into account."[64] Unfortunately, Project 2061 has characterized the entire program as designed to promote scientific literacy. The multitude of different literacies being promoted for the different subject matters has resulted in increased fragmentation of the curriculum.

From the historic experience on the idea and practice of general education in the school and college, it appears that the prospects for interfacing and integrating the different literacies for the benefit of the learner would be enhanced considerably under the rubric of general education as opposed to literacies.

Without a concerted effort at actually building alternative models of a coherent curriculum, there is also the danger that the curriculum standards and benchmarks for literacy will deteriorate into segmental items for achievement testing within each of the standard academic subjects in the school curriculum.

Curriculum Controversy

It is widely believed that the collapse of the national discipline-centered curriculum reforms came about as a result of a storm of controversy arising from one of the projects, namely "Man: A Course of Study" (MACOS), developed as an anthropology course for fifth- and sixth-graders. From its study of the MACOS controversy, the National Institute of Education attributed the collapse of these projects largely to value conflicts and censorship influences.[65] However, the national discipline-centered projects were in a state of collapse before the controversy over MACOS erupted. Historically, the school curriculum has come under censorship pressure whenever controversies arise—such as the teaching of evolution in the biology course or *Huckleberry Finn* in American literature. In the end, an enlightened profession and public seeking the best available evidence are the best antidotes to censorship.

Following the discipline-centered rationale that guided the national curriculum reform projects supported by the National Science Foundation, MACOS was designed not as an integrated program in the social studies but as anthropology. In effect, the fifth- and sixth-graders were to learn how the anthropologist studies social behavior and institutions. The population targeted for study in a portion of MACOS was a subculture of the small group of Netsilik Eskimos in a small region of Canada. Although the Netsiliks had long abandoned their primitive tribal practices, the MACOS course utilized the study of those practices as the vehicle for teaching the fifth-graders how the anthropologist thinks. The multimedia mix of ethnographic films, filmstrips, role-playing games, and reading materials was indeed impressive. Problems arose because the course included references to such practices as cannibalism, bestiality, female infanticide, incest, the sharing of the favors of one's wife, the disposal of the elderly, and other behaviors. MACOS was also attacked for inculcating in youngsters the relativism of anthropological inquiry through which the target population is not to be judged by the cultural orientations, preferences, and biases of the investigator.

To some critics, such an approach smacked of indoctrination. Unlike other censorship efforts, the attacks on MACOS reached broader implications, some of which were hardly touched in the study by the National Institute of Education. For example, had the MACOS project been designed as integrated social studies for general education, rather than the discipline of anthropology, any intercultural comparisons would require the study of problems in the treatment of the elderly in American society (e.g., the high proportion of elderly in nursing homes, which is considered inhumane in some other societies, such as Denmark). Such treatment might well raise the hackles of the censors, but the point is that the function of general education requires that the subject matter be so organized and treated as to have the fullest possible bearings on the life and nature of the learner in a free society. This is far different from treating the fifth- or sixth-grader as a budding anthropologist or scholar-specialist.

The Slogan of *Experiment*

Young children like to put things together or break them apart just to see what happens. All too often when educators proceed to try something out to see what happens it is called an *experiment*. Resistance against systematic formative and summative evaluation not only has been characteristic of national curriculum projects, but also permeates educational innovation generally. The term *experimental* has become a fashionable label for almost any innovation or marked deviation from existing practice.

Many of the alternative schools of the late 1960s and early 1970s grew out of protest, and embraced deviation from conventional practice along with a romanticized child-centered pedagogy and a laissez-faire approach to curriculum. It was common for these short-lived schools to dub themselves as experimental schools, despite the fact that they were never guided by anything remotely resembling a program of systematic evaluation. Perhaps these short-lived efforts can be forgiven considering the conditions of social protest and naive enthusiasm that marked that period. However, it is not uncommon for college and university faculties to initiate new curriculum patterns and programs that are called *experiment* without any conceptual research base. In some cases the efforts represent truly promising ventures through which systematic evaluation might produce a substantive contribution to curriculum knowledge and practice. In other cases the so-called experimental program might be something that had been done before, but the faculty responsible for the program fails to recognize this and misses the opportunity to build on the knowledge base of previous experience. Today, many colleges are rediscovering the idea and practice of general education and have engaged in efforts to develop a coherent core curriculum. In instances where they lay claim to instituting the label of experiment, they might do well to examine the case of the Experimental Program instituted at the University of California, Berkeley, in 1965 as an alternative curriculum for lower-division students. In actuality, a traditional curriculum modeled after the Experimental College founded by Meiklejohn at the University of Wisconsin in the 1920s, the curriculum of the Experimental Program at Berkeley was focused on selected Great Books of Western civilization beginning with Ancient Greece and culminating with readings from Marx, Freud, and Malcolm X. A report on the program bearing the title *Experiment at Berkeley* not only is devoid of any evaluation program but also actually dismisses any need for systematic evaluation.

We are skeptical about evaluation procedures and reluctant to get heavily involved in them. . . . A case for the program will have to be made, but apart from giving its rationale and reporting the experience, we do not really know what to do or what will be required.

Moreover, the problems of continuity or institutionalization are so complex that, unless we can see the way to their solution, there is not much point in worrying about evaluation.[66]

Thus, we have a leading seat of higher learning and research, embarking on a curriculum labeled Experimental Program, deliberately avoiding any responsibility for conceptual research in evaluating its curriculum, and asking the academic community to accept its claims as theological revelations. One of the great paradoxes in higher education is that these very institutions that profess commitment to research so often tend to avoid research in instituting new curriculums that are labeled experimental. "Is experimentation a process of trying anything at least once, of putting into immediate effect any 'happy thought' that comes to mind, or does it rest upon principles which are adopted at least as a working hypothesis?" asked Dewey in 1928, as he warned that without principles to guide hypothetical testing, the schools will allow improvisation to dictate their course and no contributions will be made in advancing education intellectually.[67]

THE BEST AVAILABLE EVIDENCE AS GUIDE TO PRACTICE

Approved Practices

Professional groups concerned with the various areas of the curriculum have developed a body of recommended practices, from research and practical field operations, although these practices are rarely presented in any single source of professional literature. Of course, such approved practices must undergo continuous assessment and reformulation to keep them attuned to changing knowledge and conditions. A few brief examples will illustrate what is meant by approved practice.

HOLISTIC APPROACHES.   Effective teachers know that students are more likely to generate interest and engagement in productive learning when the teaching process and curricular materials are idea-oriented rather than error-oriented, and when students have a shared responsibility for the curriculum such as through planning and conducting projects, panel discussions, demonstrations, and community activities that draw from and feed back into the school curriculum. If teacher-made tests are focused on interpretation and application of knowledge, as opposed to rote, such tests will serve as useful instruments in helping the teacher evaluate his or her own work and will help stimulate students toward higher-level thinking. When student assignments in the school resource center or library allow for exploratory work and the pursuit of special interests and enrichment, students will be more likely to engage in self-impelled learning such as reading for enjoyment. When teachers have a shared commitment for curriculum improvement and when they are provided with the time, resources, and expertise for engaging in systematic efforts toward curriculum correlation and integration, they not only contribute to the improvement of student learning, but they also grow professionally.

Obviously, the faculty that insists on pilot testing an innovation is well ahead professionally of a faculty that simply adopts the innovation based on testimonial promotion or trendiness. In the case of the new math of yesteryear, one must ask why the schools so readily moved toward the wholesale adoption of the curriculum packages rather than engaging in pilot studies. A faculty conducting pilot studies of new curriculum materials is indeed engaging in approved practices. This does not mean that every newly proposed practice or curriculum innovation must be pilot tested, but it is important for a faculty to ascertain whether there is a sound research base for the innovation and, as discussed later, to examine the innovation at least for face validity.

Turning to another example, teachers and school administrators tend to regard discipline as an entirely negative and destructive element in the classroom and school. A bulletin issued by the National Association of Secondary School Principals bears the cover title *Preventive Discipline* in black letters on a red background that seems to warn the prospective reader that he or she is treading on dangerous territory.[68] Discipline is also a powerfully constructive force for learning responsible self-direction in school and society. When the classroom and school environment is designed so as to evoke in students the power for self-impelled learning and collaboration, and when there is engagement in teacher-pupil planning, students are more apt to become self-disciplined and to develop a sense of mutual responsibility. Such learnings have powerful payoffs for life success as well as academic success.

Need for Sound Qualitative Ideas to Guide Research

Mention has been made of the need for teachers to ascertain whether a proposed curriculum innovation has a sound research base. Through advances in statistical treatments (meta-analysis), researchers in education have sought to amass a knowledge base for educational policy and practice by analyzing the directions of many smaller-scale studies taken together. However, in the absence of powerful qualitative ideas so as to connect the best available evidence with the most significant curriculum problems, and to separate the good research from the bad, the meta-analysis generates a sea of quantified data without much fish in the sea.[69]

Teachers need not be intimidated by elaborate statistical treatments if they base their professional work on powerful qualitative ideas and if they evaluate the conclusions of the researcher in the light of their professional experience. For example, sweeping allegations have been made by national panels on education reform, by research officials in the U.S. Department of Education, and in national best-sellers that students of today are not as well educated as earlier generations of students.[70] However, when a researcher simply set out to test this allegation by using earlier large-scale examinations on U.S. history and comparing the results past and present, he was able to draw the following clear and succinct conclusion:

> Indeed, given the reduced dropout rate and less elitist composition of the 17-year-old student body today, one could argue that students today know more American history than did their age peers of the past.

Advocates for reform of education and excellence in public schooling should refrain from harkening to a halcyon past (or allowing the perception of a halcyon past) to garner support for their views. Such action, or inaction, is dishonest and unnecessary.[71]

The findings and conclusions from this study are fully consistent with those of similar studies undertaken in the past when the schools were under the assault of school blamers.

SEGMENTATION AND DUALISM.   As intelligent consumers of research, teachers can use their knowledge base of practical experience in detecting research that defies common sense. For example, the lead article in an issue of the *American Educational Research Journal* addressed the problem of the imbalance in curriculum whereby excessive emphasis is given to basic skills, whereas problem solving and higher-order thinking are neglected. Now, this is indeed one of the most significant and pervasive curriculum problems. However, the researcher, as a specialist in organizational behavior in education, proceeded to attack the problem from the literature on behavioral decision theory and economics of organization. The researcher then proposed the "solution of having two types of teachers in the school. One type would specialize in teaching the basic skills to ensure that students will at a minimum develop these lower-order skills, whereas the second type would specialize in higher-order thinking and problem solving. "We argue that such a division would result not only in higher quality education, but also in a more equitable delivery of services from classroom to classroom," concluded the researcher.[72]

This proposal in a leading education research journal is made without any review of the body of research and professional literature on the curriculum over many decades revealing that, aside from the deleterious effects of splitting the faculty, it is counterproductive to separate basic skills from the ideas that generate the intelligent uses of these skills. Skills are not separate entities, but working tools in the development of concepts, ideas, appreciations, and problem-solving processes. The program, for example, of writing across the curriculum cannot succeed under a segmental and dualistic treatment that separates skills from higher-order thinking.

The segmentation of the subject curriculum finds teachers of chemistry, physics, the industrial arts, the trades and industries, and other subjects having to teach algebra and other higher mathematics—not to mention basic mathematics—because the separate subject of mathematics is devoid of practical applications with the consequence that students are unable to carry their mathematics from the math class into other classes.

We might also ask whether youngsters are to separate their basic-skill studies from ideas that govern thinking, or whether they are to postpone any work involving higher-order thinking until they have mastered the basics. Such a dualism between basic skills and higher-order thinking not only is educationally unsound, but it also engenders a schism dividing the faculty between high and low thinkers.

QUANTIFICATION AS DISTORTION.   As a professional practitioner, the teacher must be able to draw on the best available evidence as a guide to improved practice. As an intelligent consumer of research, the teacher will bring his or her experience to the research reports and evaluate the research in the light of the best available evidence. No amount of statistics can compensate for faulty research ideas. The knowledgeable professional practitioner is able to evaluate the efficacy of research as a guide toward the improvement of practice, and is able to point the way toward avenues for needed investigation.

Earlier we discussed the common problem in social research, including education, of bias that is masked by mounds of statistical data so as to convey a sense of objectivity and scientific authority. In more recent times, it has become fashionable in some circles of the social sciences to embrace revisionism and to use elaborate mathematical and statistical techniques to overthrow the conventional wisdom. The revisionist applying such techniques to history has been able to garner quick recognition and repute when other colleagues allow themselves to be intimidated by such techniques and computer-generated models and analyses. Not uncommonly, this has been the case even when the thesis borders on the outrageous. For example, two noted economists, Robert Fogel and Stanley Engerman, set out to examine the economics of American slavery through advanced mathematical and statistical techniques being used by other scholars who call themselves the "new economic historians," "econometric historians," and "cliometricians." They pointed out that the findings and methods of the new economic history had gained a solid foothold at Harvard, Yale, University of Chicago, U.C. Berkeley, "and other leading universities which together produce most of the Ph.D.'s in the field."[73]

Through the application of these advanced quantitative techniques, Fogel and Engerman amassed data showing that "[t]he material conditions of the lives of slaves compared favorably with those of free industrial workers," and further, that "[o]ver the course of his lifetime, the typical slave field hand received about 90 percent of the income he produced." They proceeded to present data to support their finding that "the average daily diet of slaves was quite substantial. The energy value of their diet exceeded that of free men in 1879 by more than 10 percent." And they concluded that "[t]he slave diet was not only adequate, it actually exceeded modern recommended daily levels of the chief nutrients." Among their other findings was that "[t]he slave mortality rate in childbearing was not only low on an absolute scale, it was also lower than the maternal death rate experienced by southern white women."[74]

In employing such quantitative analytical techniques to support a set of theses that are faulty to begin with, one could easily prove that a herd of milk cows on modern farms enjoys a better level of care and nutrition and a lower mortality rate in calfbearing than the general human population in childbearing, and that the cows receive in the care given them the equivalent of 90 percent of the income produced. (This allows the farmer a net profit of 10 percent.) Of course, this defies all sense and sensibility, but it serves to illustrate how statistical data can be used to validate assumptions that are invalid to begin with. Further, such research serves no social purpose other than that of embellishing reputations in the citadels of academia.

Freedom to Learn

In addressing the need to draw from the best available evidence as a guide to practice, teachers must not only think of such evidence stemming from research, but also from the freedom to make use of the best available curriculum materials. Growth in critical thinking requires that students learn to investigate issues using all pertinent evidence, to suspend judgment until all of the pertinent evidence is brought to bear on the issues, to test hypotheses, to discriminate fact from opinion, and so on. A free society requires this.

Ordinarily, teachers tend to think of censorship as external imposition, whereas much of the problem stems from self-censorship. This needs to be understood and addressed by faculty individually and collectively. For example, a given school faculty might make an intensive study of the extent to which they are ignoring pupil reading preferences and avoiding important controversial works and thereby engaging in a kind of self-censorship. The faculty may then want to establish certain procedures for attacking the problem of self-censorship by organizing inservice workshops, by convincing administrators to establish a standing budget for supplementary reading materials (such as paperbacks) dealing with important controversial works of interest to the pupils, and so on.

In case there should be a real problem of administratively imposed censorship on the teachers, the faculty might take measures to convince the school administration to place such matters under the jurisdiction of a permanent faculty curriculum committee. This makes the selection of materials a professional responsibility and serves to counter political influences at the school board and administrative levels. For example, when the selection of certain reading materials that had been approved by a faculty committee became a subject of controversy at a school board meeting, the school board decided that the decision is a professional one and that the board is "not qualified to pass judgment on English books any more than it is qualified to judge the shorthand text." It was pointed out that to expect the board to pass judgment on reading materials would require it to review two hundred and fifty textbooks each year, not to mention supplementary reading sources. "No one intends that we read these books and put ourselves up against the professional opinion of our teachers," concluded the board.[75] "Controversy is education in itself," wrote George Bernard Shaw, as he pointed out that to avoid controversial studies is to promote popular ignorance over science and knowledge.[76]

Similarly, the faculty may assess the extent to which the curriculum is focused on rote learning and the regurgitation of information to the neglect of reasoning and the study of issues. From the results of such developmental evaluation, the faculty may proceed to take steps to change existing practices where they are found to be deficient. The common practice has been to implement or even to impose curriculum change on an ad hoc and piecemeal basis instead of viewing curriculum development in its totality and as an all-faculty responsibility. The need for an aggregate rather than a segmental model of curriculum has been treated in earlier chapters and is summed up later.

SELECTING CURRICULUM MATERIALS. Teachers are continually selecting curriculum materials and, in the process, are engaged in their evaluation whether implicitly or systematically. The significance of readability formulas has been vastly overemphasized in the development and promotion of curriculum materials. When driven by interesting ideas, youngsters reveal a capability of extending their reading levels and gaining fluency in written and oral expression.

Teachers are often surprised when they find colleagues who are using college-level reading materials with great success with heterogeneous classes of ninth-graders. The passages in Figure 13–1, extracted from an article in *The American Scholar*, the journal of Phi Beta Kappa, illustrates how reading materials targeted for college graduates of exceptional academic ability can also be used appropriately for high school students in mixed-ability classes. The material is powerfully idea-oriented, clearly written, focused on a provocative social problem, and does not talk down to the reader. The macrocurricular function of the material is general education. In contrast, basic education, being focused on mechanical skills and drills,

Figure 13–1. Plagues, History, and AIDS.

Plagues, History, and AIDS

. . . This worldwide outbreak of a new infectious disease (AIDS) has engendered much fear and apprehension. As a result, there have been frequent references to previous epidemics. Perhaps most frequent are references to the Black Death, the epidemic of bubonic plague that swept through Europe in the middle of the fourteenth century. Despite current fears there has been little attempt to reexamine previous epidemics for comparisons and insights to the AIDS epidemic. . . .

First, one can look at previous epidemics and the ways in which they affected nations, politics, and even the course of history. Second, one can describe the internal "sociobiological anatomy" of an epidemic, the series of social and political responses that occur during the course of an epidemic. These reactions tend to be somewhat similar in all epidemics and are already occurring during the current outbreak of AIDS. Lastly, since AIDS is a sexually transmitted disease, it is illuminating to compare the response to AIDS with society's responses to other sexually transmitted diseases early in this century. . . .

Bubonic plague struck Europe in 1347 but events of the previous two hundred years had set the stage for the great epidemic. . . . The epidemic arrived in Marseilles in 1348, and by 1351 all of Europe was afflicted. The immediate effects of the epidemic were devastating. The most accurate estimate for total deaths during this first wave of the epidemic is 25 million or one-third of the population of Europe. No segment of society was spared. Following this epidemic, recurrent waves of plague kept the population at this level for another 150 years. . . .

The most recent worldwide epidemic was an outbreak of influenza A that swept the world in 1918–19. The first cases of influenza were recognized at Camp Funston, Kansas. Two months later massive epidemics began in Spain, France, and England. . . . Despite massive public health measures, influenza spread rapidly throughout the world. By the time the pandemic ended in 1919, there had been one million deaths in the United States, 10 million in India, and an estimated 30 million deaths throughout the world. . . .

Source: Robert M. Swenson, *The American Scholar*, 57 (Spring 1988), pp. 183–185, 187.

drives out interest, and defeats the cause of education. Specialized education, unlike general education, requires the uses of technical materials requiring technical competence; but this does not necessarily mean that the students are more likely engaged in higher-order thinking than in the case of general education. Hypothetical thinking, problem solving, and practical action can occur in general education and specialized education.

Figure 13–1 goes on to describe the impact of such diseases as smallpox, typhus, and cholera on the course of human history before the author moves on to the venereal diseases and the prospects for AIDS. The author relates how Napoleon's army of a half million in the invasion of Russia in June 1812 was left with only 3,000 to complete the retreat by June 1813, and that the catastrophic losses occurred not from battle or cold, but from typhus and dysentery. Moving to the twentieth century, the author points out how the pedagogical problem with venereal disease in health-education classes was how to teach students about sex without their recognizing the subject.

Many of the textbooks in ecology or environmental science used for general education in science at colleges and universities are fully appropriate for ninth- and tenth-graders.[77] These texts are not at all watered-down treatments, but deal authentically with problems that interconnect science and technology with social problems and issues. Texts and curriculum materials need not be watered-down or dumbed down when they deal authentically with problems and issues that connect the life of the learner with the life of society in meeting the function of general education.

The use of original source materials can lend power and authenticity to the curriculum in many ways. Figure 13–2 illustrates this with excerpts from Darwin's five-year journey around the world as chronicled in *Voyage of the Beagle* (1845), in which he repeatedly attacked the institution of slavery. Darwin's writings reveal vividly and eloquently a work that unifies the natural sciences and social sciences—a work that is a literary masterpiece. The book might well be read in conjunction with the BBC television series that dramatized Darwin's account of the voyage. The student learns that scientific hypotheses and investigations are indeed driven by the profound ideas, convictions, and emotions of the scientist. The very sense of wonder is never pure thought apart from emotion.

Teachers may find it useful to make up sets of criteria for evaluating curriculum materials. In so doing, they will discover that materials that evoke higher-order thinking can indeed be appropriate for students of a range of academic abilities and grade levels when the materials are personally and socially relevant in meeting the function of general education.

Students readily forget the factual information memorized for the examination, but they have a lifelong memory of field trips and action-oriented projects. In recognition that the traditional course in civics or government fails to stir the interest of students in participatory democracy, Katherine Isaac's *Civics for Democracy* is a notable sourcebook for this purpose by presenting documented materials on student action projects in schools and communities around the nation.[78] By examining such materials and evaluating the efficacy of using them in their own schools, teachers can derive new insights into their own beliefs and those of their colleagues.

Figure 13–2. Excerpts from Charles Darwin, *The Voyage of the Beagle.*

Rio de Janeiro

April 4th to July 5th, 1832—. . . . As it was growing dark we passed under one of the massive, bare, and steep hills of granite which are so common in this country. This spot is notorious from having been, for a long time, the residence of some runaway slaves, who, by cultivating a little ground near the top, contrived to eke out a subsistence. At length they were discovered, and a party of soldiers being sent, the whole were seized with the exception of one old woman, who, sooner than again be led into slavery, dashed herself to pieces from the summit of the mountain. In a Roman matron this would have been called the noble love of freedom: in a poor negress it is mere brutal obstinacy. We continued riding from some hours. For the few last miles the road was intricate, and it passed through a desert waste of marshes and lagoons. The scene by the dimmed light of the moon was most desolate. A few fireflies flitted by us; and the solitary snipe, as it rose, uttered its plaintive cry. The distant and sullen roar of the sea scarcely broke the stillness of the night. . . .

On the 19th of August (1836) we finally left the shores of Brazil. I thank God, I shall never again visit a slave country. . . . It is often attempted to palliate slavery by comparing the state of slaves with our poorer countrymen: if the misery of our poor be caused not by the laws of nature, but by our institutions, great is our sin; but how this bears on slavery, I cannot see; as well might the use of the thumb-screw be defended in one land, by showing that men in another land suffered from some dreadful disease. Those who look tenderly at the slave owner, and with a cold heart at the slave, never seem to put themselves into the position of the latter; what a cheerless prospect, with not even a hope of change! Picture to yourself the chance, ever hanging over you, of your wife and your little children—those objects which urges even the slave to call his own—being torn from you and sold like beasts to the first bidder! And these deeds are done and palliated by men, who profess to love their neighbors as themselves, who believe in God, and pray that his Will be done on earth! It makes one's blood boil, yet heart tremble, to think that we Englishmen and our American descendants, with their boastful cry of liberty, have been and are so guilty: but it is a consolation to reflect, that we at least have made a greater sacrifice, than ever made by any nation, to expiate our sin.

SEGMENTAL VERSUS AGGREGATE APPROACHES TO CURRICULUM RENEWAL

At times of national sweeps for curriculum renewal or reform, the practice has been to favor one side of the curriculum at the expense of another. Not only does this result in curriculum imbalance and the neglect of studies that should be recognized as vitally significant, but the synergy of the school curriculum is also defeated. Realms of knowledge are interdependent if they are to have bearings on the real world. Under segmental approaches to curriculum renewal, the sum of the parts fail to add up to a coherent total school curriculum and the learning outcomes invariably fail to measure up to the promotional rhetoric that attaches to the innovation.

When following the segmental-specialization approach to curriculum renewal, we find that the macrocurricular function of general education is neglected along with the nature of the learner and the wider social implications of the subject matter. In turn, the schools proceed to adopt and discard the packaged innovation on an ad hoc basis. The sociologist Morris Janowitz described the segmental-specialization model as "an *ad hoc* adaptation by introducing, on a piecemeal basis, new techniques, new programs, new specialists, and even new specific administrative procedures." With this model, Janowitz continued, "[t]he increased level of substantive knowledge and the importance of specific teaching techniques are offered as the rationale for the teachers' subordination to curriculum specialists."[79] In contrast, Janowitz pointed to the aggregate model as focused on the totality of the educational function with all important curricular elements and goals being treated in their interdependence.

With school and society opting for the segmental-specialized model over the aggregate model, the Law of the Minimum, as described later, has been allowed to take its toll particularly with regard to the disadvantaged. The school has not been endowed with the necessary means for assuming a holistic personal-social-growth function. At various times it has been impelled to subvert its socialization function to the narrow skill-drill function with a focus on low-level cognitive goals; at other times the school is expected to fulfill a total socialization function in the absence of concomitant commitment to this function on the part of society. Then the school is blamed for not singlehandedly regenerating the lives of children and youth. Under the segmental-specialized model, the personal-social-growth function of school and society is subverted in favor of narrow interests.

Shifting Expectations and Demands

Throughout this text it has been shown how the school has been pressed to shift its priorities in response to shifting sociopolitical demands. The consequence has been that the school has tended to assume a segmental approach to educational change. Shifting expectations and demands come not only from radical school critics but also from such sources as the U.S. presidency on down to university scholars, business groups, and various private interests.

Again, it should be noted that the buffeting of the curriculum by shifting sociopolitical tides invariably is accompanied by a ceremony of school blaming, and all too often university scholars become a part of the ceremony by shifting their own grounds so as to be in synchrony with the dominant tide of the times. Thus in 1950 the eminent historian Henry Steele Commager wrote, "[n]o other people ever demanded so much of education as have the Americans. None other was ever served so well by its schools and educators."[80] Commager went on to describe how the American faith in education has imposed great tasks on the schools, tasks that the schools have met. He identified these tasks as (1) providing for an enlightened citizenry, (2) creating a national unity out of diversity, (3) Americanizing the vast populations of immigrants, and (4) rendering the cause of American democracy.

Within a year following Sputnik I, Commager declared that we were entering a new era, that the Americanization function of the schools had been virtually accomplished, and the schools must no longer bear responsibilities in the nonacademic realm but should focus their efforts on traditional academic functions. Nonacademic functions should be left to the home and other agencies of society, contended Commager. In concentrating on its academic functions, the high school may be expected to speed up its work and accomplish in three years what it was taking four years to accomplish.[81]

In the late 1960s, amidst a rising national concern for the disadvantaged, Commager declared that "education is the beginning of social reform and regeneration." He proceeded to admonish educators to "start by abandoning many of our preconceptions about the relation of the home and education" and advocated that we face up to "the sharing of responsibility between the two, and recognize that for many children in our society there are no homes, and no sharing of responsibilities."[82]

In each instant of shifting demands and expectations, the schools have been impelled to respond in a segmental way—whether in embarking on a return to the fundamentals, adopting disciplinary curriculum packages, employing specialized educational innovations, instituting ad hoc compensatory programs for the disadvantaged, or implementing accountability machinery through the use of narrow testing measures. When these piecemeal efforts are shown to be inadequate to the task, instead of seeking to develop an aggregate model for curriculum improvement, the schools are criticized for making no difference, and they are pressed into adopting new piecemeal measures in search of miracle cures.

The Law of the Minimum

Earlier in this chapter certain methodological limitations were identified in connection with various studies that have failed to identify specific school factors showing a powerful relationship to achievement. It was also noted that this failure has led some researchers and educational policymakers to the conclusion that any further investment in schooling or implementation of curriculum improvements would make no difference. Aside from the methodological limitations of such research is the failure to take into account the vital interactive and cumulative elements between the school and the wider social environment of the learner.

A nineteenth-century agricultural chemist, Justus von Liebig, developed from his research the Law of the Minimum—a principle that holds valid to this day. According to the Law of the Minimum, "[t]he amount of plant growth is regulated by the factor present in minimum amount."[83] Thus, if an essential constituent is lacking or is insufficiently available, the full potential of a living organism cannot be realized by compensating for the deficient element by providing the organism with an extra abundance of other constituents. Extra water cannot make up for insufficient sunlight, nor can extra nitrogen compensate for insufficient potassium.

The full potential of the child as a growing organism requires the advantages of a rich and powerful learning environment provided by the school and by the larger society. Taken together in concert, the potential of the learner will be more fully realized. Until this is accomplished, it is totally unproductive to seek genetic explanations for educational failure and cognitive deficiencies, as some educators have attempted to do.[84] Until the necessary educational and social conditions are optimized, the social ideal of human equality and human capacity to shape its fate will be an empty one.

In the same vein, educators and policymakers cannot assume that by addressing the problem of cognitive and social deficits of disadvantaged or at-risk children at the preschool and primary levels the need for attending to the adolescent is considerably reduced. Unfortunately, this policy can be traced back to the early years of the War on Poverty of the Johnson administration when data on human development were cited to support a short-cut strategy.[85] Schools of education formed new departments of early childhood education in response to infusions of federal funds for that target population, and the focus on adolescence was severely diminished. No less an authority than Bruno Bettelheim asked whether we will "continue to fool ourselves by thinking that we can change the lives of underprivileged children in school, when it is much too late for everything that really counts," and popular magazines were featuring cover articles under such titles as "Kindergarten is Too Late."[86]

Middle and late childhood and adolescence are recognized periods of qualitative changes in cognitive, social, and physical development. Seeking to minimize the educational and social deficits during infancy and early childhood cannot serve as immunization against the deleterious effects of deficits that occur during later childhood and adolescence. Nor is there any scientific basis for assuming that older populations, including adults, can be written off because it is too late.

The Law of the Minimum has profound implications for the curriculum and the school as a living learning environment. It is easy to contend that the school curriculum be delimited to the academic basics or to development of the intellect, but the development of intelligence is dependent on interests, attitudes, and emotions as well as good nutrition and health. Essentialist-perennialists such as Theodore Sizer may see the mission of the school as appropriately and exclusively focused on mastery of the minima—with most youngsters accomplishing this before high school, when compulsory school attendance would end. The high school then would be able to devote its work to the academically oriented students.[87] However, mastery of the minima fails to take account of all the essential nutrients in the Law of the Minimum. The power of socialization and maturation in the development of intelligence during the high school years cannot be overlooked without great cost to the individual and society. Sizer and others may choose to see education into the high school as an opportunity and privilege, rather than a right. In its wisdom, the U.S. Supreme Court ruled unanimously with reference to both elementary and high schools that education is "a right which must be made available to all on equal terms" (*Brown versus Board of Education*, 1954).

Knowledge/Ability Level

A fallacious assumption in educational policy, research, and practice is that given inputs will yield equivalent effects in all school systems. However, different school systems are characterized by vastly different knowledge/ability levels. When many of the most capable teachers and administrators leave inner-city schools for the suburbs, the result is that the knowledge/ability level of inner-city schools is diminished. Thus, these schools become less capable of maximizing or optimizing the resources that are made available in comparison to those schools that have a higher knowledge/ability level.

In terms of the Law of the Minimum, the amount of [educational] growth is regulated by the [knowledge/ability] factor present in minimum amount. Consequently, compensatory programs and efforts to improve the curriculum in inner-city schools are limited by the level of the knowledge/ability factor. Unfortunately, the Coleman research and Jencks's studies failed to take into account this vital factor. Limitations in the knowledge/ability factor of disadvantaged schools have concealed the potential benefits derived from curriculum improvement and other investments to improve the educational program. This does not mean, contrary to Jencks's contentions, that it is fruitless to increase investments in education because increases in input are not followed automatically by corresponding increases in output. Rather, it means that greater efforts must be made in improving the knowledge/ability level of disadvantaged schools if such schools are to capitalize on such investments.

In a study designed to identify the knowledge/ability factor as developed by the authors in the first edition of this text, Celso found that elementary teachers in the same school vary greatly in their use of curricular resources and, in effect, provide vastly different learning environments for their pupils. For example, some teachers were observed to have drawn from their own personal resources, along with whatever school resources were available, to develop an extensive classroom library, with pupils making use of the collection in their daily work; however, many of their fellow teachers' classrooms were devoid of such resources and activities.[88] Much of the research on the effects of schooling has suffered from the failure to account for qualitative variables and the tendency to deal with only those variables that are most amenable to quantitative treatment. Celso hypothesizes that the knowledge/ability factor can be demonstrated by categorizing teachers according to high and low knowledge/ability levels, based on a number of qualitative differences in their use of curricular resources, and then assessing a wide range of possible learning outcomes in their pupils.

In more recent years, the power of the school—and, more specifically, the curriculum—in influencing cognitive-affective development is receiving increasing recognition. Bloom's proposals for curriculum improvement are based on the alterability of human characteristics and he believes that

> changes in the school environment can relatively quickly (in a single decade) make great changes in the learning of students. In contrast, attempts to makes changes in the home and the larger social environment, which are believed to be related to education and learning, are likely to take many decades before major effects would be felt in the schools.[89]

The significance of a powerful and continuous program of inservice teacher education and teacher support by providing the needed expertise, time, and resources is clearly indicated by the knowledge/ability factor.

THE DEFICIENCY OF EFFICIENCY

In his study of the historical influences of business values and practices on education, Raymond Callahan reported that although he had expected to find evidence of such influences, *"What was unexpected was the extent, not only of the power of the business-industrial groups, but of the strength of the business ideology in the American culture on the one hand and the extreme weakness and vulnerability of schoolmen, especially school administrators, on the other."* Callahan went on to state that he had expected more professional autonomy on the part of educators, but found instead that many education decisions are made not on educational grounds but in capitulation to whatever demands are placed on the schools.[90]

The influences examined historically by Callahan have not waned. Despite the considerable rhetoric calling for humanizing the schools, efforts to make the schools more efficient managerially and more accountable, as assessed by the quantifiable input-output measures, seem more powerful today than ever before.[91]

Pressures to improve educational efficiency through technological and managerial innovations, along with assessment and accountability measures, appear to augur for a mechanical-segmental-skills model of the learner as opposed to a personal-social-growth model. As emphasized in earlier chapters, this opposition has profound implications for the curriculum, the learner, and society.

This has been manifested in the enormous growth of the testing industry and the support of testing by the states and federal government as measures of production efficiency and accountability. The business-industrial model is seen in *America 2000* as serving to lead the way to school restructuring and reform for excellence.[92] The education research literature has come to use the term *process-product research* to denote the outcomes of classroom variables in quantitative measures—as though the ends of education are end products.[93] As emphasized throughout this text, education must be treated as an emergent or growth process rather than a production process.

Education as an Emergent Process

Robert Boguslaw, a systems design engineer, pointed to the need to differentiate between established and emergent situations. In the established situation, all action-relevant environmental variables are specifiable and predictable, whereas the emergent situation involves problems for which the conditions and solutions are not perfectly specifiable and predictable.[94]

The established situation or established-convergent situation can be easily understood when we are dealing with products and services under the most uniformly reliable and routine conditions. The plant manager of a factory producing Wonder Bread must see to it that the product is as uniform as possible. Indeed the very machinery and mechanisms for quality control are designed to ensure uniformity of product. It is only when something goes wrong that the situation becomes an emergent one.

In education, even the most routine situations have a way of becoming emergent because we are always dealing with people problems and not products. The term *recipe* is often used to denote a direct and simple process. Follow the directions and the results will be predictable—so it is thought. In cooking as well as in other human enterprises the results may be surprising. A recipe for coq au vin or French pastry, whether given to novices or master chefs, will likely produce surprises. The results will reflect differences in experience, taste preferences, and creativity—for even a recipe is often regarded as an opportunity for the expression of the individual's creative talents. Indeed, differences make improvement possible.

It might be contended that in following a blueprint in the industrial-arts class, or in conducting an experiment in the chemistry laboratory, the student is engaged in an established-convergent situation. This may indeed be the case, but it should be noted that the situation itself typically involves collaboration and even error through which the situation becomes emergent. Successful teachers know full well how student mistakes can provide opportunities for fruitful learning.

Even at the highest levels of technical professionalism, such as musicianship, no two symphony orchestras will perform a composer's work identically, for the art of music, like the art of teaching, resides not in technical skills alone, but in the art of interpretation.

Assessment and Accountability

"If we can construct a kind of Gross *Educational* Product, we will know a lot more than we do now about how we are conducting the nation's most important business," stated a 1966 report of the Carnegie Corporation in announcing that the foundation had initiated steps two years earlier for the national assessment of education. The Carnegie report noted that the construction of the national economic index, the gross national product (GNP), had made possible great refinements in the analysis and understanding of the economy. Drawing an analogy of questionable validity, the report contended that the construction of a gross *educational* product through a national assessment of education should enable us to determine "with greater certainty that investing so much—in terms of money or materials or teachers or time— to attack a particular problem will produce a given result."[95] The report gave assurance that the assessment program would not influence the curriculum because the sampling methods in the testing program would make it impossible for teachers to teach to the test.

INFLUENCE ON THE CURRICULUM.   The late Harold Hand warned that "the parties who determine what goes into the tests would control the public school curriculum."[96] In 1973 the Report of the National Commission on the Reform of Secondary Education made the following recommendation regarding national assessment:

> The National Assessment of Educational Progress should become the bulwark of educational accountability. Local educators should be equipped to compare realistically the achievement of their students with regional and national results. The find-

ings of National Assessment should lead to various [curriculum] content revisions, curriculum reform, in-service efforts, and improved competency-based instruction.[97]

As the first results of the National Assessment of Educational Progress (NAEP) were being reported, the individual states were rapidly instituting their own statewide assessment programs through massive testing. By 1980, assessment programs were in operation or on the drawing boards in almost every state. At the same time the schools were gearing their curricula to specific performance objectives. Curriculum development appeared to be on its way toward becoming a matter of managerial and engineering technique designed to maximize the ratio of quantifiable outputs to inputs.

As the results of the national assessment project began to be reported, administrators of the project continued to draw parallels between efficiency in business and efficiency in education, as illustrated by the following statement that appeared in a publication of the project:

> Possibly for the first time the public, the legislators, the educators and other interest groups are asking what business schools are in? . . .
>
> If education is in the business of helping children achieve, and of determining and teaching what's worth knowing, then assessment is a way of measuring that objective. It is no different than in business, where a successful corporation must achieve its goals on schedule. If not, they run the risk of cash flow problems which could lead to bankruptcy.
>
> As farsighted educational managers, we must provide ourselves with the needed measures for knowing when and to what extent we have achieved our objectives. Large-scale assessment is such a way.[98]

From the beginning, assurance was given to educators that NAEP would not come under federal auspices. However, before long, it became a fully federally financed project. Since 1983 NAEP has been administered by Educational Testing Service under contract with the U.S. Department of Education. Although the national assessment had been likened to census data collecting, a census is directed at the gathering of descriptive-quantitative data—whereas the very testing instruments and data in NAEP are loaded with both explicit and hidden value premises. Indeed the word *assessment* means to set a value on something. This has been borne out by the periodic issuance of the NAEP test results by ETS in publications under the series title, *The Nation's Report Card*—with each publication bearing a title appropriate for the specific subject field, such as *The U.S. History Report Card, The Mathematics Report Card, The Science Report Card,* and so on. These report cards have been used opportunistically by federal officials and the media in attacking the public schools for alleged deficiencies, whereas studies questioning the validity of the data have been virtually ignored.[99] The NAEP report card collection not only received the strongest endorsement in *America 2000,* but it was recommended that the NAEP data be used for comparisons at district and school levels. Ironically, the originators of NAEP had recognized such comparisons as a misuse of the NAEP tests and had assured the education community that this would never happen.[100] With regard to the uses and misuses of a national testing program, the issue was put bluntly by George Madaus in these words:

> The idea that any testing technique, be it a new test design or a national test system, can reform schools and restore America's competitiveness is the height of techno- logical arrogance and conceals many of the negative possibilities of such a move under the guise of a seemingly neat technological fix. . . . [I]t is the teachers, not tests or assessments, that must be the cornerstones of reform efforts.[101]

Myrdal could well be describing the NAEP and state assessment programs when he offered this observation:

> The chaos of possible data for research does not organize itself into systematic knowledge by mere observation. Hypotheses are necessary. We must raise questions before we can expect answers from the facts, and the questions must be signifi- cant. . . . Even apparently simple concepts presume elaborate theories. These theo- ries—or systems of hypotheses—contain, of necessity, no matter how scrupulously the statements of them are presented, elements of *a priori* speculation. When, in an attempt to be factual, the statements of theory are reduced to a minimum, biases are left a freer leeway. . . . [102]

Myrdal went on to emphasize that social science becomes no better protected against bias when it assumes the entirely negative stance, under the guise of objectiv- ity, of avoiding any responsibility for arranging its findings for practical use. Such a negative posture actually opens the way to further bias because the value premises are kept hidden in the data, rather than being explicitly treated in terms of practical implications and practical problem solving. The myriad specializations in social sci- ence also serve to distance social scientists from the tests of practicality. Unfortu- nately, the National Assessment of Educational Progress had avoided questions and hypotheses, and, therefore, the facts contained no answers to educational problems. In avoiding significant questions and hypotheses, the data were left open to bias, speculation, and opportunistic exploitation.

AUTHENTIC ASSESSMENT.   The concept of authentic assessment has appeared recently in the education literature in connection with efforts to evaluate achieve- ment through tasks in which students are actually engaged. The performance tasks are presumably set in contextualized situations. Although this promising movement is heralded as new, it can be traced back to the comprehensive evaluation techniques and instruments developed for the Eight-Year Study and in the studies on the goals of general education.[103] For example, given a problem situation, is the student able to map out a procedural plan for solving the problem—starting with the formulation of the problem and hypotheses, along with the identification of information, data, and resources needed for solving the problem? Is the student able to test the hypotheses and formulate valid conclusions? Other forms of authentic assessment might be in student-initiated projects requiring systematic investigation, or through student portfolios, simulations, and various kinds of context-situated projects. Paper-

and-pencil tests can indeed be related to authentic situational contexts, such as in demonstrating the ability to interpret social statistics by identifying trends, formulating hypotheses, and drawing inferences, implications, and conclusions. Given a problem or issue, is the student able to identify the sources that would be useful in gaining the fullest possible picture of the problem or issue? Such approaches contrast vividly against conventional tests with prefabricated answers, and they provide a more comprehensive and powerful connection between the curriculum and reality. In the real world, accomplishment is not so much a measure of speed but of motivation, application, or working power in the use of intelligence. The irony of the term *authentic* assessment resides in the implication that the standard means of assessment are unauthentic. This may well be the case, for much can be done to improve the assessment process through the use of multiple criteria and means that are more relevant to the life and growth of the learner.

The New Technology

The 1960s and the early years of the 1970s were called an era of innovation in education.[104] Successful efforts were made with team teaching at various grade levels and, in the high school, modular-flexible scheduling (variable time allocations for courses and learning activities as opposed to the traditional lock-step schedule).[105] The new electronic technology was expected to usher in a veritable revolutionary transformation of education. Through televised instruction, programmed instruction, computer-assisted instruction, and language laboratories, the teaching-learning process was to extend to new dimensions. Initial financial support in promoting the adoption of the new technology was provided by the Ford Foundation, the Carnegie Corporation, and the Kettering Foundation until federal funding was made available through the National Defense Education Act of 1958 and the Elementary and Secondary Education Act of 1965. Through electronic language laboratories, it was held that almost everyone would have fluency in at least two languages in addition to English.[106] The installation of electronic language laboratories became commonplace in the schools, accompanied by overblown commercial exploitation. The entire effort was a dismal failure as educators had overlooked language learning as a social process.

Utopian Visions.   Visions of the wonders to come from the new electronic technology were exemplified in an official publication commemorating the centennial of the U.S. Office of Education in 1966. Acknowledging that "few schools and colleges have begun to utilize the technological concepts and products whose value has been demonstrated in industry, space exploration, and national defense," the report predicted that "computer-assisted instruction, teaching machines of various sorts, increasingly sophisticated communications systems, and other forms of technology will alter the school more in the next century than it has changed in the last 2,000 years."[107] The report then presented a Utopian vision of education in the year 1997 in which Johnny does not go to school. Instead, in this deschooled society, Johnny receives his formal instruction from a computer console in his home, with the computerized instructional program being controlled from a concenter or central station. No mention was made of the place of the book in this vision of the future, as the book is obviously replaced by the computer. In a similar vein, Postman and Weingartner contended that, in the future, print will play only a secondary role in the classroom as the electronic media will take on the major role of educating the young.[108] (Those who make this case invariably resort to the medium of print to get their message across.) A leading educator envisioned an era when human-to-human instruction will be superseded by machine-based instruction and that, through the use of chemicals, drugs, electric currents, and eugenics, the age-old curriculum question will also be superseded. Accordingly, "[t]he first educational question will not be what knowledge is of most worth, but what kinds of human beings we wish to produce."[109]

In a feature article in *Fortune* magazine, Charles E. Silberman wrote in 1966 that in harnessing the new technology, "the new business-government thrust is likely to transform both the organization and the content of education, and through it, the character and shape of American society itself," and, he continued, "we may be on the verge of a quantum jump in learning and in man's creative use of intellect."[110] In anticipation of the new business-government thrust, Francis Keppel left his post as U.S. Commissioner of Education to become head of General Learning Corporation— a joint venture of Time, Inc., and General Electric—to develop and market materials for the technological revolution in education. Within a few years, the corporation was dissolved. In his 1970 report for the Carnegie Corporation, Silberman did an about-face and criticized the "advocates and prophets" of computer-assisted instruction for having made "extravagant predictions of wonders to come."[111]

In 1966, Patrick Suppes of Stanford University stated, "[o]ne can predict that in a few more years millions of school children will have access to what Philip of Macedon's son Alexander enjoyed as a royal prerogative: the personal services of a tutor as well-informed and responsive as Aristotle."[112] In 1974, in reviewing the research on the effectiveness of learning via computer, Suppes and his associates acknowledged that "findings of no significant difference dominate the research literature in this area," but that it may be useful in small doses as a supplement to regular instruction with regard to elementary skill-drill practices.[113] Similarly, the great promise that television and programmed instruction would usher in a new educational age failed to materialize, as the research results failed to show that such media produce an improvement in learning.

UNREALIZED POTENTIALS. The contemporary education literature is directed at computer literacy, information networks, and hypertext (a system that allows the user to jump from the primary text to related multiple sources and commentary with a single keystroke). Despite the impressive technological advances, the changes in the school and college classroom have been that of accommodation, not revolution. The failure of computer-assisted instruction, television, and other technological media in effecting the promised revolution can be traced to several factors. The new technology was initially supported and promoted on the premise that it would effect a dramatic improvement in the quality of education. However, in reality the hidden agenda was the improvement of managerial efficiency in the educational enter-prise—to educate more students in less time, with fewer teachers, with greater effi-ciency of space utilization, and at lower cost. In efforts to make television more eco-nomically feasible, the medium was used largely to convey to learners the messages of conventional instruction with the result that, instead of being used as a classroom window to the world, television was used to convey the talking face. Eventually, stu-dents at the school and college levels rebelled against the uses of television as an automation device for large-group instruction.[114]

Proponents of change were contending that by opening the schools to innova-tion, the prospects for improvement are enhanced, and that the evaluation of results or consequences can come later. Indeed, the entire national Comprehensive School Improvement Program of the Ford Foundation, promoting the uses of the new tech-nology, followed this premise only to admit belatedly in failure that "the projects were designed to demonstrate actual changes in school systems [and] on the assumption that changes, per se, would produce better education." Looking back, it was conceded that evaluation was needed if problems were to be solved.[115]

Although the great technological-media advances of the twentieth century—from the motion picture and radio, to television and the computer—were heralded as ushering in a revolution in the conduct of schooling, the promised revolution has failed to materialize. There is no question that we have failed to capitalize on the educative potentials of television in the school and home. Instead of using school television to do what the teacher is unable to do, it has been used for extending con-ventional forms of teaching to larger groups of students. Although the computer has attained a presence in the schools, the software used for instruction remains geared largely to established-convergent repertoires, word processing, and information retrieval.

The high-tech prospects for virtual reality and the great information highway have been widely heralded. Experience has shown that the new technology cannot substitute for the social process in education. Like the great advances in knowledge during the twentieth century, the technological advances must be used to extend humanity, not to replace it.

PERSPECTIVE

Much research in education, as in social science, is cloaked in a methodological empiricism as though to convey an image of scientific neutrality through hard data, thereby masking the valuations underlying the research, or concealing the concep-tual emptiness of the research. In seeking to establish the facts and ignoring valua-tion, investigators have opened the door to considerable bias, for the data to be derived from research is determined by the value premises underlying the research. Thus, it is necessary to have research guided by alternative value premises and hypotheses, rather than by a single set of value premises. By bringing valuations out in the open, and by seeking to ascertain how they influence the research data, the sources of bias can be minimized and research can be more effectively related to the solving of practical problems in accord with educational ideals.

In much of the large-scale education research, the influences of variations in the curriculum and of other school characteristics have been concealed by variations in the pupil populations and a host of qualitative variables. Because many qualitative factors in education cannot be readily quantified, researchers have tended to focus on those factors that lend themselves most easily to quantification. Important qualitative factors have been submerged by relatively unimportant quantitative by-products, with the result that misleading and biased conclusions regarding educational policy and practice have been drawn from the so-called objective data. More intensive and longitudinal studies are needed to shed light on the influences of qualitative factors in the complex process of education.

Most of the efforts to improve education have been based on a segmental curriculum model, with innovations being adopted on an ad hoc basis. If the schools are to fulfill a personal-social-growth function, an aggregate model of curriculum must be assumed. Through an aggregate model, the necessary interrelationships and cumulative interactions of the various elements can be taken into account. Segmental, short-term, and unarticulated innovations and compensatory programs in education have failed to fulfill the promises made for them because vital cumulative interactions within the school, and between the school and society, have been overlooked or ignored.

A fallacious assumption in educational research, policy, and practice is that given inputs should yield equivalent effects in all school systems. Because different school systems are characterized by vastly different knowledge/ability levels, the relationship between investments in education and the outcomes of such investments has been concealed. Thus, the fallacious assumption has led to fallacious conclusions on the part of education researchers and policymakers who hold that it is fruitless to increase the investments in education. Efforts to improve the curriculum and educational conditions must be matched by corresponding efforts to improve the knowledge/ability levels of administrators, teachers, and parents—particularly in disadvantaged schools. Otherwise, such schools will be unable to capitalize on such investments.

The move for educational accountability has been marked by national and statewide testing programs and narrow performance objectives. These accountability and assessment programs have been premised on the notion that the amassing of data will provide answers to vital educational problems. Intelligent questions must be asked before intelligent answers can be obtained. Without such questions and hypotheses, the data derived from these massive assessment programs defy intelligent interpretation and intelligent application in solving problems in educational practice. As a consequence, the negative device, on the part of the assessors, of avoiding responsibility for arranging the findings for intelligent practical use has opened the way for every conceivable bias on the part of special-interest groups.

Many educational innovations have been promoted and adopted as though these innovations per se will automatically result in educational improvement. The evaluation of these innovations has been designed largely to prove their success rather than to find solutions to educational problems. In the absence of practices founded on theory to be tested through working hypotheses, these programs are energized by a spirit of improvisation and deviation. However energetic this spirit may be, improvisation and deviation are not substitutes for theory and experimentation. The result is that innovations and reforms are short-lived, as each era of societal crisis calls for either a return to traditional practice (e.g., back to basics) or yet another reform in a direction counter to the preceding reform. Movement is then mistaken for progress. In neglecting to apply innovations to educational problem solving, many innovations have been turned to the narrow purpose of managerial efficiency. As a result, the premises and promises that the adoption of innovations will result in improving the quality of education have not been realized. Educators have been urged to adopt innovations and later to evaluate their effects. Intelligent evaluation requires intelligent questions and hypotheses to be formulated before a new practice is allowed to become operational, and, at the same time, evaluation must be continuous. Otherwise, there can be no intelligent problem solving in education.

The demand to humanize the schools is a healthy reaction to the drive for managerial efficiency in education through mechanical assessment and quantifiable accountability. In seeking to impose only quantifiable objectives on the educative process, the efficiency experts overlook not only the qualitative aspects of education but also the most important source of educational objectives—namely the democratic ideals that empower individuals to continue their education and find for themselves the values that need to be pursued as objectives.[116]

PROBLEMS FOR STUDY AND DISCUSSION

1. Why is it so important for teachers, supervisors, curriculum coordinators, and school administrators to be intelligent consumers of research?

2. In this chapter, Gunnar Myrdal was cited for his observation that social scientists tend to "move as a flock" in their valuations and research pursuits. Would you say that school administrators tend to move as a flock in adopting and discarding policies, practices, and innovations? Explain.

3. Examine any of the highly influential national reports on education reform (e.g., *A Nation at Risk, America 2000*). Can you identify any unsubstantiated valuations? Do you take issue with any of these valuations? Explain.

4. Richard Feynman, Nobel laureate in physics, was cited in this chapter as contending that the value of any subject matter should be determined by what it contributes to other subjects in the curriculum, and that it must be developed so as to reveal to the learner the utility of the material and its relevance to the real world. What prompted Feynman to offer these criteria? Would you say that the curriculum today generally meets Feynman's criteria? Why or why not? Are these criteria relevant to the curriculum paradigm? Explain. (See Chapter 7.)

5. Also quoted in this chapter was Myrdal's contention that "biases in social science cannot be erased by keeping to the facts and by refined methods of statistical treatment of data." What examples can you give of the biases uses (or misuses) of data taken from the National Assessment of Educational Progress (NAEP) or the International Study of Educational Achievement? How have these uses of data affected the school curriculum? Myrdal was also cited for contending that "[t]he chaos of possible data for research does not organize itself into systematic knowledge by mere observation. Hypotheses are necessary. We must raise questions before we can expect answers from the facts, and the questions

must be 'significant.'" [Gunnar Myrdal, *An American Dilemma* (New York: Harper and Row, 1962), p. 1041.]

How do you account for the failure of national assessment and statewide assessment programs to be guided by hypotheses for investigation? What are the implications of such a failure insofar as educational policy and practice are concerned?

6. In discussing the limitations of quantitative data for educational practice, Dewey maintained that "[t]he intelligence of the teacher is dependent upon the extent in which he takes into account the variables that are not obviously involved in his immediate special task. Judgment in such matter is of qualitative situations and must itself be qualitative." [John Dewey, *The Sources of a Science of Education* (New York: Liveright, 1929), pp. 64–65].

   What are the implications of this statement with regard to the determination of educational accountability through the gathering of quantitative data, such as in the national assessment and statewide assessment programs?

7. The periodic clamor of back to basics invariably is accompanied by a corresponding emphasis on standardized testing as the key to raising standards. Why did educators fail to foresee the neglect of writing (one of the three R's) as an inevitable outcome of standardized testing during the extended period of curriculum retrenchment (back to basics) from the latter 1970s

through the 1980s? From the experiences in your own school, would you say that the recent rediscovery of the value of writing across the curriculum has been accompanied by adequate attention to the expression of ideas as well as to mechanics? Explain.

8. In *America 2000* the public schools were blamed for virtual systemwide failure whereas the colleges and universities were hailed by the President as "the finest in the entire world." Do you find any inherent contradictions in this claim? How do you account for the tendency of education researchers in our universities to look so negatively at the schools and so positively at higher education in terms of measured outcomes? Again, do you see any inherent contradictions here?

9. In a report of the National Council on Education Standards and Testing, it is acknowledged that "[e]ducation in the United States is test happy." The report goes on to recommend a national examination system. [*Raising Standards for American Education* (Washington, DC: U.S. Government Printing Office, 1992), pp. F-6, 20.] Would you describe the conditions in your school as test happy? In your opinion, to what extent do state or national tests drive the curriculum? Do you see any dangers of neglecting important curricular experiences because they are not amenable to large-scale testing? Explain.

10. How do you account for the failure of the new electronic technology to usher in the promised revolution in the schools?

NOTES

1. Gunnar Myrdal, *Objectivity in Social Research* (New York: Pantheon, 1969), pp. 43–44.
2. Ibid., p. 4.
3. Alvin W. Gouldner, *The Coming Crisis in Western Sociology* (New York: Basic Books, 1970), p. 445.
4. Myrdal, op. cit., p. 8.
5. Ibid., p. 9.
6. John Dewey, *The Sources of a Science of Education* (New York: Liveright, 1929), p. 27; and "Progressive Education and the Science of Education," *Progressive Education*, 5 (July–September 1928), p. 200.
7. Myrdal, op. cit., pp. 3–5.
8. Ibid., p. 40.
9. Ibid., p. 53.
10. Gunnar Myrdal, *An American Dilemma* (New York: Harper and Row, 1962), p. 882. (Originally published in 1944.)
11. Ibid., pp. 19–20.
12. Daniel Bell, "On Meritocracy and Equality," *The Public Interest* (Fall 1972), p. 45.

13. James S. Coleman et al., *Equality of Educational Opportunity* (Washington, DC: Office of Education, U.S. Department of Health, Education, and Welfare, 1966), p. 316.

14. Ibid.

15. James S. Coleman, "Equal Schools or Equal Students?" *The Public Interest* (Summer 1966), p. 74.

16. *The New York Times* (March 9, 1970), p. 1.

17. "Coleman on the Coleman Report," *Educational Researcher,* 1 (March 1972) p. 13.

18. Panel on Youth of the President's Science Advisory Committee, *Youth: Transition to Adulthood* (Chicago: University of Chicago Press, 1974), p. 160.

19. James S. Coleman, "Changing the Environment for Youth," *Phi Delta Kappan,* 59 (January 1978), p. 319.

20. Christopher Jencks et al., *Inequality* (New York: Basic Books, 1972) pp. 255, 256, 265.

21. Arthur L. Stinchcombe, "The Social Determinants of Success," *Science,* 178 (November 10, 1972), p. 6.

22. As quoted in Geodfry Hodgson, "Do Schools Make a Difference?" *Atlantic Monthly,* 231 (March 1973), p. 35.

23. Daniel P. Moynihan, "Equalizing Education: In Whose Benefit?" *The Public Interest,* 29 (Fall 1972), pp. 71, 73.

24. Alexander Astin, *What Matters Most in College?* (San Francisco: Jossey-Bass, 1993); Larry L. Leslie and Paul T. Brinkman, *The Economic Value of Higher Education* (New York: Macmillan, 1988).

25. Center for the Study of Public Policy, *Education Vouchers* (Cambridge, MA: Author, 1970).

26. Herbert H. Hyman, Charles R. Wright, and John S. Reed, *The Enduring Effects of Education* (Chicago: University of Chicago Press, 1975), pp. 109–111.

27. William H. Sewell, Robert M. Hauser, and David L. Featherman (eds.), *Schooling and Achievement in American Society* (New York: Academic, 1976; Eigil Pedersen, Therese A. Faucher, and William W. Eaton, "A New Perspective on the Effects of First-grade Teachers on Children's Subsequent Adult Status," *Harvard Educational Review,* 48 (February 1978), p. 29; Richard A. Rehberg and Evelyn R. Rosenthal, *Class and Merit in the American High School* (New York: Longman, 1978), pp. 252–254.

28. Michael Rutter, Barbara Maughan, Peter Mortimore, and Janet Ouston, *Fifteen Thousand Hours: Secondary Schools and Their Effects in Children* (Cambridge, MA: Harvard University Press, 1979), pp. 1, 178.

29. L. C. Cumber and John P. Keeves, *Science Education in Nineteen Countries* (New York: Wiley, 1973), p. 236; Alan C. Purves, *Literature Education in Ten Countries* (New York: Wiley, 1973), pp. 312–313, 315.

30. Stephen H. Stow and Tom L. Ashwood, "High School Science Education," *Science,* 246 (November 3, 1980), p. 563.

31. Myrdal, *Objectivity in Social Research,* op. cit., p. 51.

32. Torsten Husén, "Are Standards in U.S. Schools Really Lagging Behind Those in Other Countries?" *Phi Delta Kappan,* 64 (March 1983), pp. 455–464; Torsten Husén (ed.), *International Study of Achievement in Mathematics,* 2 (New York: Wiley, 1967); see also Iris Rotberg, "Myths in International Comparisons of Science and Mathematics Achievement," *The Bridge,* 21 (Fall 1991), pp. 3–7.

33. *The New York Times* (March 7, 1967), p. 1; (March 12, 1967), p. 11E.

34. *The New York Times* (November 24, 1968), p. 74; see also *The New York Times* (December 24, 1991), pp. C1, 6.

35. Torsten Husén, "Does Broader Educational Opportunity Mean Lower Standards?" *International Review of Education,* 17 (1971), pp. 77, 79, 88.

36. U.S. Department of Education, *America 2000: An Education Strategy* (Washington, DC: Author, 1991), pp. 9, 51, 53, 55.

37. Charles C. Carson, Robert M. Huelskamp, and Thomas D. Woodall, "Perspectives on Education in America," Special Issue, *Journal of Educational Research,* 86 (May/June 1993).

38. Carson, Huelskamp, and Woodall, "Perspectives on Education in America, prepublication drafts of May 1991, pp. 170, 172; and diem, April 1992, pp. 99–100, 105; *see also* Daniel Tanner, "A Nation 'Truly' at Risk," *Phi Delta Kappan,* 75 (December 1993), pp. 288–297.

39. *America 2000,* op. cit., p. 9.

40. Iris Rotberg, "Myths in International Comparisons of Science and Mathematics Achievement," *The Bridge,* 21 (Fall 1991), pp. 3–10; Constance Holden, "Questions Raised on Math Rankings," *Science,* 256 (November 15, 1991), p. 934.

41. *Science,* 257 (September 18, 1992); *Wall Street Journal,* April 14, 1993, p. B-1.

42. Myrdal, *Objectivity in Social Research,* op. cit., p. 41.

43. J. J. Servan-Schreiber, *The American Challenge* (New York: Atheneum, 1967), p. 74.

44. Daniel Tanner, "The Retreat from Education—For Other People's Children," *Intellect,* 102 (January 1974), pp. 222–225.

45. John Dewey, *The School and Society* (Chicago: University of Chicago Press, 1899), p. 7.

46. Myrdal, *An American Dilemma,* op. cit., p. 883.

47. See Peter S. Hlebowitsh, *Radical Curriculum Theory Reconsidered* (New York: Teachers College Press, 1993); in contrast to the negativism reflected in much of the contemporary literature in the social and philosophical foundations of education, see Maureen O'Neill, "Curricular Reconstruction: Vision of *The Social Frontier,*" *Educational Forum,* 52 (Spring 1988), pp. 223–234.

48. Myrdal, *An American Dilemma,* op. cit., p. 1045.

49. Jerome S. Bruner, *The Process of Education* (Cambridge, MA: Harvard University Press, 1960), pp. 1–2.

50. Jerrold R. Zacharias and Stephen White, "The Requirements for Major Curriculum Revision," in Robert W. Heath (ed.), *New Curricula* (New York: Harper, 1964), pp. 77, 79.

51. See Wayne W. Welch, "The Impact of National Curriculum Projects: The Need for Accurate Assessment." *School Science and Mathematics,* 68 (March 1968), pp. 225–234.

52. Education Development Center, *Annual Report* (Newton, MA: Author, 1967), pp. 75–76.

53. Gilbert C. Finlay, "The Physical Science Study Committee," *School Review,* 70 (Spring, 1962), pp. 75–76.

54. Susanne D. Ellis, "Enrollment Trends," *Physics Today,* 20 (March 1967), p. 77; L. Caroll King, in "High Student Failure Rate Serious Problem," *Chemical and Engineering News,* 45 (February 20, 1967), p. 44.

55. See *BSCS Newsletter,* 19 (September 1963).

56. William V. Mayer, "The Impact of BSCS Biology on College Curricula," *BSCS Newsletter,* 42 (February 1971), p. 2.

57. Edward C. Begle and James W. Wilson, "Evaluation of Mathematics Programs," Chapter 10, in National Society for the Study of Education, *Mathematics Education,* Sixty-ninth Yearbook, Part I (Chicago: University of Chicago Press, 1970), p. 388.

58. Ibid., p. 402.

59. Alvin M. Weinberg, *Reflections on Big Science* (Cambridge, MA: M.I.T. Press, 1967), pp. 74–76.

60. Richard P. Feynman, "New Textbooks for the New Mathematics," *Engineering and Science,* 28 (March 1965), pp. 13, 14–15.

61. David Blackwell and Leon Henkin, *Mathematics* (Washington, DC: American Association for the Advancement of Science, 1989), p. 31.

62. See Special Section, *Social Education,* 54 (April/May 1990).

63. National Council of Teachers of Mathematics, *Curriculum and Evaluation Standards for School Mathematics* (Reston, VA: Author, 1989).

64. American Association for the Advancement of Science, *Benchmarks for Science Literacy* (New York: Oxford University Press, 1993), p. 46.

65. Chapter 1 in John Schaffarzick and Gary Sykes (eds.), *Value Conflicts and Curriculum Issues* (Berkeley, CA: McCutchan, 1979); Luther Carter, "NSF: How Much Responsibility for Course Content, Implementation?" *Science,* 190 (November 14, 1975), pp. 644-646.

66. Joseph Tussman, *Experiment at Berkeley* (New York: Oxford University Press, 1969), p. 121.

67. John Dewey, "Progressive Education and the Science of Education," *Progressive Education,* 5 (July–September 1928), pp. 197, 201.

68. Donald R. Grossnickle and Frank P. Cesko, *Preventive Discipline* (Reston, VA: National Association of Secondary School Principals, 1990).

69. See *Review of Educational Research,* 63 (Fall 1993).

70. Diane Ravitch and Chester Finn, *What Do Our 17-Year-Olds Know?* (New York: Harper, 1987).

71. Dale Whittington, "What Have 17-Year-Olds Known in the Past?" *American Educational Research Journal,* 28 (Winter 1991), p. 778.

72. Jane Hannaway, "Higher Order Skills, Job Design, and Incentives: An Analysis and Proposal," *American Educational Research Journal,* 29 (Spring 1992), p. 20.

73. Robert W. Fogel and Stanley L. Engerman, *Time on the Cross: The Economics of Negro Slavery* (Boston: Little, Brown, 1974), p. 7.

74. Ibid., pp. 5–6.

75. Laurel N. Tanner and Daniel Tanner, "News Notes," *Educational Leadership,* 31 (October 1973), p. 89.

76. George Bernard Shaw, *Sham Education* (London: Constable, 1950), pp. 310, 314.

77. See for example, Richard M. Klein, *The Green World* (New York: Harper, 1987).

78. Katherine Isaac, *Civics for Democracy* (Washington, DC: Essential Books, 1992).

79. Morris Janowitz, *Institution Building in Urban Education* (New York: Russell Sage, 1969), pp. 42–43.

80. Henry Steele Commager, "Our Schools Have Kept Us Free," *Life Magazine,* 29 (October 16, 1950). p. 46.

81. Henry Steele Commager, "A Historian Looks at the American High School," *The School Review,* 66 (Spring 1958), pp. 1–18.

82. Henry Steele Commager, *The Commonwealth of Learning* (New York: Harper, 1968), p. 107.

83. E. Walter Russell, *Soil Conditions and Plant Growth,* 10th ed. (London: Longman, 1973), pp. 49–50.

84. Arthur R. Jensen, *Educability and Group Differences* (New York: Harper, 1973).

85. Benjamin S. Bloom, *Stability and Change in Human Characteristics* (New York: Wiley, 1964), pp. 88–89, 128–129.

86. Bruno Bettelheim, "How Much Can Man Change?" *New York Review of Books,* 3 (September 10, 1964), p. 4.; Esther F. Edwards, "Kindergarten Is Too Late," *Saturday Review,* 51 (June 15, 1968), p. 69.

87. Theodore R. Sizer, *Horace's Compromise* (Boston: Houghton Mifflin, 1984), pp. 87–88.

88. Nicholas Celso, *The Knowledge-Ability Factor and School Effectiveness,* unpublished doctoral dissertation (New Brunswick, NJ: Rutgers University, 1978), pp. 189–193.

89. Benjamin S. Bloom, *Human Characteristics and School Learning* (New York: McGraw-Hill, 1976), p. 17.

90. Raymond E. Callahan, *Education and the Cult of Efficiency* (Chicago: University of Chicago Press, 1962), Preface, n. p.

91. Judith O. Weiss, *Education and the Cult of Efficiency Revisited,* unpublished doctoral dissertation (New Brunswick, NJ: Rutgers University, 1989).

92. U.S. Department of Education, *America 2000* (Washington, DC: Author, 1991), pp. 19–20, 27.

93. Linda Darling-Hammond and Jon Snyder, "Curriculum Studies and the Traditions of Inquiry," Chapter 2 in Philip W. Jackson (ed.), *Handbook of Research on Curriculum* (New York: Macmillan, 1993), pp. 63, 64–67.

94. Robert Boguslaw, *The New Utopians* (Englewood Cliffs, NJ: Prentice Hall, 1965), pp. 7–9.

95. *Carnegie Quarterly,* 14 (Spring 1966), pp. 2, 4.

96. American Association of School Administrators, *National Educational Assessment: Pro and Con* (Washington, DC: National Education Association, 1966), pp. 5, 25.

97. National Commission on the Reform of Secondary Education, *The Reform of Secondary Education* (New York: McGraw-Hill, 1973), p. 44.

98. *NAEP Newsletter,* 6 (July–August 1973), p. 3.

99. For alleged deficiencies in academic achievement see, for example, Diane Ravitch and Chester E. Finn, Jr., op cit.; Lynn V. Cheney, *American Memory* (Washington, DC: National Endowment for the Humanities, n.d.); in contrast, see Charles C. Carson, Robert M. Huelskamp, and Thomas D. Woodall, "Perspectives on Education in America," Special Issue, *Journal of Educational Research,* 86 (May/June 1993), pp. 305–306.

100. *America 2000,* op. cit., p. 14; *National Assessment Pro and Con,* op. cit.

101. George F. Madaus, "A National Testing System," *Educational Assessment,* 1 (Winter 1993), p. 23.

102. Myrdal, *An American Dilemma,* op. cit., p. 1041.

103. Grant Wiggins, "Assessment: Authenticity, Context, and Validity," *Phi Delta Kappan,* 75 (November 1993), pp. 200–214; see also Eugene R. Smith, Ralph W. Tyler et al., *Appraising and Recording Student Progress* (New

York: Harper, 1942); Will French, *Behavioral Goals of General Education in High School* (New York: Russell Sage, 1957).

104. Ford Foundation, *Teaching by Television* (New York: Author, 1961), Preface, n.p.

105. Robert N. Bush and Dwight W. Allen, *A New Design for High School Education* (New York: McGraw-Hill, 1964).

106. Report of the Disciplines Seminar, *The Scholars Look at the Schools* (Washington, DC: National Education Association, 1962), p. 15.

107. U.S. Office of Education *OE 100—Highlighting the Progress of American Education,* (Washington, DC: U.S. Government Printing Office, 1967).

108. Neil Postman and Charles Weingartner, *The School Book* (New York: Delacorte, 1973), pp. 88–89.

109. John I. Goodlad, *The Future of Learning and Teaching* (Washington, DC: National Education Association, 1968), pp. 22–23.

110. Charles E. Silberman, "Technology Is Knocking at the Schoolhouse Door," *Fortune,* 74 (August 1966), p. 122.

111. Silberman, *Crisis in the Classroom* (New York: Random, 1970), p. 186.

112. Patrick Suppes, "The Uses of Computers in Education," *Scientific American,* 215 (September 1966), p. 207.

113. Dean Jamison, Patrick Suppes, and Stuart Wells, "The Effectiveness of Alternative Instructional Media: A Survey," *Review of Educational Research,* 44 (Winter 1974), p. 56.

114. Judith Murphy and Ronald Gross, *Learning by Television* (New York: The Ford Foundation, 1966), pp. 44–46.

115. The Ford Foundation, *A Foundation Goes to School* (New York: Author, 1972), pp. 11–12.

116. Dewey, *Democracy and Education,* op. cit., p. 117.

SELECTED REFERENCES

Aikin, Wilford M. *The Story of the Eight-Year Study.* New York: Harper, 1942.

American Association for the Advancement of Science. *Science for All Americans.* Washington, DC: Author, 1989.

Astin, Alexander W. *What Matters Most in College?* San Francisco: Jossey-Bass, 1993.

Bloom, Benjamin S. *Human Characteristics and School Learning.* New York: McGraw-Hill, 1976.

Boguslaw, Robert. *The New Utopians.* Englewood Cliffs, NJ: Prentice Hall, 1965.

Callahan, Raymond E. *Education and the Cult of Efficiency.* Chicago: University of Chicago Press, 1962.

Carson, Charles C., Huelskamp, Robert M., and Woodall, Thomas D. "Perspectives on Education in America," *The Journal of Educational Research* (Special Issue), 86, May/June 1993.

Center for Educational Research and Innovation. *Education at a Glance: OECD Indicators.* Paris: Organization for Economic Cooperation and Development, 1993.

Coleman, James S., et al. *Equality of Educational Opportunity.* Washington, DC: Office of Education,

U.S. Department of Health, Education, and Welfare, 1966.

Commission on the Relation of School and College. *Thirty Schools Tell Their Story.* New York: Harper, 1943.

Dewey, John. *Experience and Education.* New York: Macmillan, 1938.

Dewey, John. *How We Think,* rev. ed. Lexington, MA: D. C. Heath, 1933.

Dewey, John. *The Sources of a Science of Education.* New York: Liveright, 1929.

Ellul, Jacques. *The Technological Society.* New York: Vintage Books, 1954.

Ferguson, Eugene S. *Engineering and the Mind's Eye.* Cambridge, MA: M.I.T. Press, 1992.

Ford Foundation. *A Foundation Goes to School.* New York: Author, 1972.

Giles, H. H., McCutchen, S. P., and Zechiel, A. N. *Exploring the Curriculum.* New York: Harper, 1942.

Goodlad, John I. *A Place Called School.* New York: McGraw-Hill, 1984.

Heim, Michael. *The Metaphysics of Virtual Reality.* New York: Oxford University Press, 1993.

Husén, Torsten (ed.). *International Study of Achievement in Mathematics,* Vols. 1, 2. New York: John Wiley & Sons, 1967.

Hyman, Herbert H., Wright, Charles R., and Reed, John S. *The Enduring Effects of Education.* Chicago: University of Chicago Press, 1975.

Isaac, Katherine. *Civics for Democracy: A Journey for Teachers and Students.* Washington, DC: Essential Books, 1992.

Jackson, Philip W. (ed.). *Handbook of Research on Curriculum.* New York: Macmillan, 1992.

Jencks, Christopher, et al. *Inequality.* New York: Basic Books, 1972.

Mumford, Lewis. *The Pentagon of Power.* New York: Harcourt, 1970.

Myrdal, Gunnar. *An American Dilemma.* New York: Harper, 1962. (Originally published in 1944.)

Myrdal, Gunnar. *Objectivity in Social Research.* New York: Pantheon Books, 1969.

National Commission on Excellence in Education. *A Nation at Risk.* Washington, DC: U.S. Department of Education, 1983.

National Education Goals Panel. *Building a Nation of Learners.* Washington, DC: U.S. Government Printing Office, 1992.

National Society for the Study of Education. *Evaluation and Education at Quarter Century,* Ninetieth Yearbook, Part II. Chicago: University of Chicago Press, 1991.

National Society for the Study of Education. *Teacher Research and Educational Reform,* Ninety-third Yearbook, Part I. Chicago: University of Chicago Press, 1994.

Oettinger, Anthony G. *Run, Computer, Run.* Cambridge, MA: Harvard University Press, 1969.

Pascarella, Ernest T., and Terenzini, Patrick T. *How College Affects Students.* San Francisco: Jossey-Bass, 1991.

Ravitch, Diane. *The Revisionists Revised: A Critique of the Radical Attack on the Schools.* New York: Basic Books, 1977.

Rehberg, Richard A., and Rosenthal, Evelyn R. *Class and Merit in the American High School.* New York: Longman, 1978.

Rutter, Michael, et al. *Fifteen Thousand Hours: Secondary Schools and Their Effects on Children.* Cambridge, MA: Harvard University Press, 1979.

Sizer, Theodore R. *Horace's Compromise.* Boston: Houghton Mifflin, 1984.

Smith, Eugene R., Tyler, Ralph, et al. *Appraising and Recording Student Progress.* New York: Harper and Row, 1942.

U.S. Department of Education. *America 2000: An Education Strategy.* Washington, DC: Author, 1991.

Weinberg, Alvin M. *Reflections on Big Science.* Cambridge, MA: M.I.T. Press, 1967.

Whitehead, Alfred North. *The Aims of Education.* New York: Macmillan, 1929.

Wiener, Norbert. *God and Golem, Inc.* Cambridge, MA: M.I.T. Press, 1964.

Wittrock, Merlin C. (ed.). *Handbook of Research on Teaching,* 3rd ed. New York: Macmillan, 1986.

WHO MAKES THE CURRICULUM?

The curriculum presumably represents the substance and means through which the rising generation is to become knowledgeable and competent in the life and work of society. It is surprising that so many teachers and administrators take curriculum for granted—as though it is merely a ready-made list of subjects to be scheduled and taught. The need for continuous and systematic curriculum development does not receive the recognition it deserves, considering that curriculum defines the life and work of the school. The following reminiscence by John Goodlad may strike a chord of recognition by the reader:

> Coming fresh out of Canada, where I'd been a teacher and director of education in a school for delinquent boys, I knew absolutely nothing about curriculum development. In fact, so far as I knew, the curriculum which I'd been involved with came down full blown from the head of Zeus. In no way could human beings interfere with this process.[1]

Goodlad, who studied curriculum development with Ralph Tyler, became a renowned expert in curriculum development and has made many contributions to curriculum knowledge. All too often the curriculum is seen as a mystical blend of knowledge and mandates handed down from above. In many cases the perception that curriculum decisions are made at a higher level is grounded in reality. However, there is no doubt that some teachers and principals perceive more constraints on their curriculum improvement efforts than actually exist. The intent of this chapter is to demystify the curriculum. By drawing away the dark curtains we can throw light on roles and reality, thereby helping professionals to optimize their opportunities for curriculum improvement.

DEMYSTIFYING THE CURRICULUM

Myths abound about who makes the curriculum. For example, some would hold that textbook publishers control the content of instruction, whereas others would contend that the curriculum is controlled by some other single dominant influence—such as state educational policy, federal policy, local school boards, the colleges, professional educational associations, and so on.

The Textbook-Publisher Myth

It is often argued that textbook publishers determine the curriculum, and that they are primarily interested in profits, not in what students should learn. In the words of one critic, textbooks are "books without formal authors . . . ghost-written under conditions of stringent cost controls, geared to what will sell and not necessarily to what is most important to know."[2]

This statement is misleading because it implies that textbook publishers are in control of the topics addressed in the texts that they produce. This is simply not the case, except by default. Authority for determining whether to buy the textbooks that publishers produce is vested in state and local education agencies. They decide whether the books contain what is most important to know and may either reject the books outright or make recommendations for changes, postponing acceptance until the changes are made. Publishers are concerned primarily with meeting market demands. Since the early 1980s, states and local school systems representing a large percent of the textbook market have become increasingly critical and publishers have acted to make changes based on quality criteria.

In 1982, New York City, for example, rejected three high school biology textbooks for use in the city's high schools. The reason was that the books did not treat Darwinian evolution adequately. Two of the three publishers were told that their books also were unacceptable because they endorsed creationism theory. In communicating with one publisher explaining why the book was rejected, the director of the district's division of curriculum and instruction wrote: "This book does not state that evolution is accepted by most scientists today, and presents special creation without characterizing it as a supernatural explanation that is outside the domain of science."[3]

In New York, all new books and revised editions of older books require approval by a three-member committee for use in the schools. Also entering into consideration are state curriculum requirements and city curriculum guidelines. Publishers request the reviews. The committee is composed of the subject field director for the school district and teachers or supervisors in the subject field. New York City was one of the first large school systems to take a stand against national pressure to promote the creationist viewpoint. (At the time legislators in several states had introduced bills that would make mandatory the teaching of creationism as a viable alternative theory to be studied in biology along with evolutionary theory.)

In 1985, the California Board of Education, on the recommendation of the State Curriculum Development and Supplemental Materials Commission, unanimously rejected every science textbook submitted for use in seventh- and eighth-grade classes stating that the textbooks are watered down so as to avoid controversy. The publishers were criticized by the board and the state superintendent for producing textbooks that fail to address adequately such controversial topics as evolution, human reproduction, and environmental problems. Within a matter of months the publishers produced revised editions of their textbooks. One publisher, who had not even listed the topic of evolution in the index, soon produced a revised edition with a whole chapter on evolution. The state superintendent also announced that textbooks for all other subject areas would be similarly scrutinized.[4]

In 1990, the Texas State Board of Education approved science textbooks with extensive coverage of evolution for grades one through twelve. The decision was important for students in every state because Texas, like California, is one of the largest buyers of textbooks in the United States. Thus, Texas influences what publishers include in books that are sold to schools throughout the country. According to the director of a textbook review group in Houston, the decision marked "the end of the Dark Ages and the beginning of an enlightenment for science in Texas."[5]

However, as one of the authors of this text pointed out elsewhere, "publishers also respond to the narrow-minded influences of special-interest groups when such influences are dominant."[6] Texas was once nortorious for such influences.

Educators have the professional responsibility to scrutinize textbooks to determine whether the textbooks meet quality criteria. (The word *profession* comes from the Latin meaning a public vow.) The State Curriculum Development and Supplemental Curriculum Commission in California based its recommendations on the evaluation of a panel of experts consisting of university professors in the discipline and in education, curriculum directors and specialists from various school districts, and teachers. In making the evaluations, a framework of criteria was used, drawn from the research literature in science education.[7]

Education agencies are (should be) concerned that textbooks include topics that are idea-oriented, stressing more than the mastery of mechanical skills. They are also concerned with the accuracy of textbook content. In November 1991, the Texas Board of Education rejected five history books for grades eight through twelve on the ground that the books contained numerous errors. Researchers had found many wrong dates and other misinformation. The Panama Canal, for instance, was described as fifty rather than ten miles wide. Jimmy Carter was called the first Democratic U.S. president since Harry Truman, overlooking Lyndon Johnson and John F. Kennedy. More than 300 such errors were found.[8] The publishers were given two weeks by the Texas Education Agency to identify and correct the errors. An ad hoc committee of board members was entrusted with determining whether the errors had been corrected. Publishers seek to avoid such situations by having the manuscript professionally reviewed before it is readied for production. In effect, decisions concerning what goes into the textbook tend to reside with the author and peer reviewers.

The Single-Factor Myth

A number of forces interact to produce the curriculum for a school at any given point in time. In the United States, each state prescribes what must be included in the educational program. Teachers and building principals participating in local curriculum development projects will find that they must work within the boundaries of state regulations. There are other forces as well, including demands of influential persons that often seem to have the same result as laws.

At times, one or another of the forces will seem to be the supreme curriculum determinant. Take, for example, the political influence of the U.S. president. The education reform policy of President George Bush illustrates this influence vividly. As discussed in Chapter 11, in the spring of 1991, President Bush unveiled his national education strategy, centered on six national goals formulated earlier in an education summit meeting with the nation's governors. The focus of reform was soon on assessment and curriculum. It seemed apparent to the governors and officials of the Bush administration that a way would have to be found of determining progress toward achieving the goals, and this would necessitate the adoption of curriculum standards and the implementation of a national testing program. Congress created the National Council on Education Standards and Testing for this purpose. In April 1992, the president called for the creation of America 2000 Communities. To qualify, a community had to adopt *the* six national goals. By summer some communities were responding to the president's call.[9]

The point is that the school curriculum is influenced by many sources and forces, often in conflict and contradiction—from the classroom teacher and local school board, right up to the state house, the White House, and the U.S. Supreme Court. These forces work in interaction and the more they are understood by teachers and administrators, the better the chances are for curriculum improvement.

The Decision Makers

With respect to the question of who makes the decisions regarding the objectives and means of instruction, Clark identifies the following different categories of decision makers: the public, political leaders, test publishers, the media, higher education personnel, professional organizations, school boards and central administration within school districts, teacher groups, and individual teachers. The members of the public who seek to influence the curriculum fall into two subgroups: members of special-interest groups (for example, religious groups who attempt to bar consideration of ideas they disagree with) and nonaffiliated individuals who usually interact directly with principals and teachers at the local school—usually where their children are enrolled.[10]

Clark points out that "[d]ecisions are made with varying levels of specificity, depending on how far from the student the decisions are made," and, further (as in the example above of the U.S. president and the governors concerning national goals), "most of those who speak from the national and state level make statements of broad priorities."[11] The actual events in the act of teaching, including what the student is expected to learn, are ultimately determined by the teacher. Teaching remains an individual experience.

The decisions at each level are of course important. Curriculum development as Caswell once pointed out, is a process of synthesizing the forces that influence the experiences that learners have under the guidance of teachers.[12] We add that it is also a process of maximizing the favorable influences and countering the negative. The interactive influences on the curriculum are represented in Figure 14–1. Each will be considered separately.

INFLUENCE OF THE PUBLIC

Most members of the public do not devote their energies to influencing the school curriculum. Far from it. Although seemingly obvious, the point is important because it is easy to mistake public policy for the public will. In theory, enlightened public opinion should be represented in enactments by national, state, and school district officials. In actuality, public policy does not always represent enlightened public

Figure 14–1. Who Makes the Curriculum? Sources and Influences.

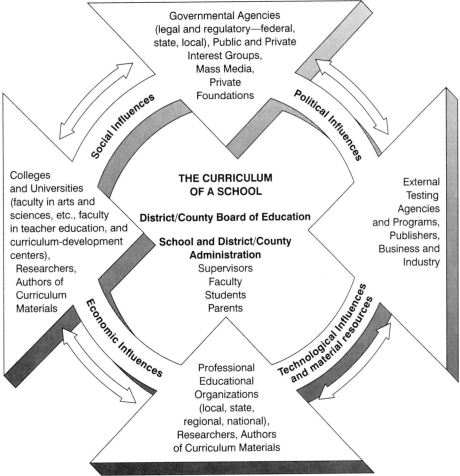

opinion; in fact, it may be in direct opposition. For example, one who reads about the legislative mandates and school board decisions concerning the curriculum in recent years might gain the impression that most people favor eliminating everything from the school curriculum except the basic three R's and academic subjects in the elementary school and secondary school. However, the actual evidence contradicts this. Studies by John Goodlad, Richard Clark, and the annual Gallup polls indicate that parents constantly want the curriculum to include more—in the areas of social and personal development as well as in academic and vocational development.[13]

It is clear that the broader interests of parents concerning the curriculum have not been represented in school legislation. Eternal vigilance is required by parents, professionals (teachers and administrators), and all citizens if the schools are not to become the pawns of politically motivated legislators and powerfully organized pressure groups. The best theory recognizes that all citizens have a voice in the control—including the improvement—of public education. Most often this voice is exercised indirectly by voting. Parent groups should be involved in exploring curriculum problems.

In discussing the influence of members of the public who seek to influence the curriculum it is clear that they fall into two categories: organized members of the public and those attempting to make curriculum decisions as individuals.

Efforts by Organized Groups

A publishing house rejects a manuscript because of the fear that it may engender controversy and organized opposition. A large corporation sends executives to inner-city vocational high schools with the message that "while it is nice to have a college education, it is not necessary for a good career."[14] (This corporation like many others views the schools as potential sources of trained workers, and even proceeded to make personnel available to develop high school curriculums for training students for jobs on its own assembly lines.) A national gun violence-prevention organization and lobbying group introduces a new curriculum for grades prekindergarten through grade twelve and announces its implementation in five large school systems.[15] A religious group develops a home schooling program so that children can be insulated and isolated from ideas with which the group disagrees. As Clark observes, in taking such children from the school, the group also affects the schooling of the children who remain.[16] Although home schooling programs involve only a minuscule fraction of the nation's school age children, they represent a decision made by an affiliated group (or an individual) concerning curriculum. Any number of special-interest groups have sought to influence the curriculum with more or less success. and, according to Clark, "are active in influencing broad goals as well as in seeking to modify the implementation activities of classroom teachers."[17]

Generally, those individuals and groups who concentrate their efforts at the local level are the most effective. Clark tells us from his own experience as a school superintendent that "individuals interacting directly with the principal and teachers at the school may have profound effects on the curriculum as students experience it," and "individuals who seek to have such influence most generally direct it at the school where their own children are enrolled."[18]

PARENTS.   Organized groups of parents who are aggressive in their criticisms of the curriculum have made curriculum decisions. A group of parents in Princeton, New Jersey, for example founded Princeton Parents for Curriculum Reform. The group—which was composed mainly of professionals in the fields of mathematics and science—complained about what they saw as weaknesses in the mathematics curriculum. District officials responded quickly. As described by a national newspaper: "District officials pointed out that in response to parents' concerns about the teaching of mathematics, they have speeded up their review of the curriculum and expect to have a revised course of study in place by the start of the school year next fall."[19] The Princeton parents also complained about "the under-representation of black and Hispanic students in advanced classes."[20]

At times, parents have followed up on their curriculum decisions by paying for extra programs. The Friends of (William A.) Ray School in Chicago is a group of elementary school parents who have strong convictions about the need for Latin language instruction. Their large fund-raising project pays for the teacher of Latin.[21] In so doing they influence the curriculum in the school where their own children are taught. Not surprisingly, some school districts (Los Angeles, for example) do not permit the above practice. The reason given is that disparities in curricular offerings deny equal access to the curriculum.

Parents vary in their interest in and impact on what is taught at the local school district level. Some parents have worked tirelessly with professionals to generate support for bond issues that assure the continuation of a balanced curriculum in their public school system.

Efforts by Individuals

An age-old story that we can retell in many contexts can be summed up in these words: One person can make a difference. Margaret Sanger's defense of contraception against religious conservatives contributed greatly to women's rights. Adolph Hitler's unique ability to exploit and maneuver events to his own purposes unleashed an unparalleled era of destruction in human history. Eugene Lang's offer to graduates of Public School 121 in New York to pay their college tuition if they stayed in school encouraged them to do well enough to qualify for college. For better or worse, one person's decisions carried to the point of action can affect the lives of others.

The point can be generalized to the curriculum. When carried out to the point of decision, one parent's perceptions about curriculum materials can influence the educational experiences of many children for good or ill. As Ken Donelson emphasizes, "it may take no more than one complaint mixed with a bit of doublespeak to get a book booted."[22] Thus, a minority of one can influence the curriculum. (And that individual is not necessarily a member of the professional staff.) Donelson goes on to add that "[t]oo often the library board removes a book while it determines a book's guilt or innocence. . . . After that the temporary ban may ease quietly into permanence."[23]

The curriculum-shaping activity of some individuals is inspired by what they have read in popular magazines about influencing the school to help their child. Individuals can also influence the curriculum through classroom involvement. A parent may feel strongly about the necessity for multicultural education. As Clark observes, "[t]hat individual, working with the teacher, may shape curricular experiences in the classroom with which he or she is working so that the general education for that classroom is considerably different from the general education in the classroom next door."[24]

POLITICAL INFLUENCES

Political influences include regulations that stem from the legitimate role of state and national political institutions. For example, states have the authority to set minimum essentials of the curriculum, which they sometimes do in great detail, as will be shown. As Clark points out, however, "other contributions to curriculum decision making by the political world are much like the efforts of public-interest groups."[25]

Federal Level

When the U.S. president prescribes national curriculum standards for American schools (as with the six national goals in the 1990s), he is using his political office to put pressure on schools in a matter that is outside his specific authority.

Earlier, the influence of the U.S. president was brought to bear on the states by the Reagan administration. Responding to the report of the National Commission on Excellence in Education entitled *A Nation at Risk* (1983), states increased the requirements for high school graduation in the so-called new basics—English, mathematics, science, social studies, and computer science. The changes were, for the most part, regulatory rather than changes in curriculum content. As Cremin put it, the report "assigned" the main responsibility of carrying out the recommendations to state and local authorities.[26] Reagan was bringing the power of his office to bear on state and local officials (as well as parents, who were asked to make their children study harder). As Doyle reminds us, there is no federal role in education, except that which the states are willing to accept.[27] The tenth Amendment to the U.S. Constitution (the reserve powers clause) specifies that those powers not listed for the federal government are reserved to the states. Education is not enumerated as a federal power and is, therefore, a state power. Nevertheless, the federal role in education has a long and powerful history in recognition that education is necessary to "promote the general welfare," as declared in the opening sentence of the Constitution.

The federal government has provided aid to education, beginning with the land-grant colleges, created in Lincoln's administration, and given its present contours a century later during the Johnson administration. The aid envisioned by Johnson was targeted to poor and educationally disadvantaged elementary, secondary, and college students. Federal aid undertaken for such purposes has improved access to the curriculum for many such students.

THE CURRICULUM CASTE SYSTEM. As discussed in Chapter 11, Congress, the legislative branch of the federal government, has directed pressures to improve teaching in certain curriculum areas through infusions of funds. The National Defense Education Act (NDEA) of 1958 provided federal funds in science, mathematics, and modern foreign languages. The NDEA provisions indicated that it was in these three fields that the nation's security and supremacy lay. This was during the Cold War with the Soviet Union. The attention to these curriculum areas was new for the federal government that had long supported vocational education. Funds were provided to stimulate state efforts to improve instruction in the newly favored curriculum areas. NDEA summer institutes and other programs were supported that school systems could not have afforded otherwise. The effects of the new curriculum hierarchy were psychological as well as fiscal, as the teachers in these fields rose in importance and those in other fields fell.

In the 1980s and 1990s, national policies continued to stress the importance of scientists and mathematicians and curriculum reform in these areas. Some things had changed in thirty years. The climate of international insecurity now revolved principally on economic issues rather than national defense. For whatever reason, the effect of national policy on the curriculum was the same. In an era of economic retrenchment it was perhaps even more pronounced. Many school districts could only afford to add new staff in fields favored with federal funds and proceeded to reduce staff in the industrial arts, studio arts, and other so-called nonacademic subject. For all intents and purposes, a new curriculum hierarchy or caste system was emerging.

THE SUPREME COURT. According to Reutter, "[t]he Supreme Court of the United States has had a far greater influence on the course of public education than is generally realized."[28] This is especially so for the curriculum. Cases dealing with bible reading in the public schools involve church–state separation, protected by the Constitution. The Court has rendered decisions invalidating such exercises as part of the school program, thus influencing the curriculum. A decision of great significance for the curriculum was made by the Supreme Court in 1968 when it ruled invalid an Arkansas statute prohibiting the teaching of evolution. The Court held that the statute was unconstitutional because it was enacted to promote a certain religious view.[29]

The Supreme Court has influenced the how of teaching as well as the what. A very important Supreme Court decision in 1974 provided the legal basis for instruction in a pupil's native language. In *Lau v. Nichols,* the Court found that non-English-speaking children were not being provided with equal access to education because they did not understand instruction in English. As pointed out by McGroarty, "[r]emedies were left to local discretion, with bilingual education and English-as-a-second-language instruction as two options and with the Court recognizing that other options may have existed," and further, "[r]elated federal regulations promoted bilingual education as the option of choice where there were large numbers of elementary school children from the same language background who did not know English."[30] Ironically, the parents in *Lau v. Nichols* had petitioned for more English, not bilingualism.

Whatever the remedies decided on by local school systems, the proportion of non-English-speaking children is expected to grow in America's schools, thus influencing the curriculum. As Albert Oliver noted, "[t]he curriculum has to be modified as the student body changes in school."[31]

The State Level

State legislatures have almost absolute power concerning the what of the curriculum. Some states have passed highly detailed laws concerning the subjects to be taught. Texas, for example, prescribes instruction in essential elements for each grade. The list of experiences in Figure 14–2 is extracted from the Texas Administrative Code. The essential elements are listed in every subject for each grade. Before each legislative session the State Board of Education reviews the appropriateness of the essential elements, making recommendations for legislative changes as necessary. Texas leaves little discretion to local authorities about the content of the curriculum.

States vary as to their prescriptiveness. Some laws simply state the subjects to be taught.

STATE POLICY AND CURRICULUM DEVELOPMENT. Since the early 1980s, state legislative activity in education increased enormously; in fact, this period was the high point of such activity in the twentieth century. In 1986, a survey by the Education Commission of the States reported that since 1980, forty-five states and the District of Columbia had increased their high school graduation requirements. Although the increases involved a number of subjects, more states increased requirements in mathematics and science than in any other subjects; mathematics requirements for graduation were increased in forty-two states and science requirements in thirty-four states.[32]

As Pipho observed at the time, in many states the movement toward more stringent control did not include implementation of reform. "It is fair to say that many legislators and other policy makers in many states did not have implementation of reform on their minds when they wrote the laws, rules and regulations."[33] This is hardly surprising because some had a political agenda rather than an educational agenda.[34]

Actually states had sought greater accountability from teachers and local school administrators since the early 1970s. The reform movement of the early 1980s was an outgrowth of the earlier movement. It had been given new energy by the education agenda of the Reagan administration as embodied in *A Nation at Risk* (1983), the report of the National Commission on Excellence in Education. The banner of this report was more stringent academic standards to meet the Japanese challenge for world industrial markets.

Even the most fleeting glance at the education literature of the 1980s and 1990s reveals the existence of two fundamentally different state reform movements. The

Figure 14–2. Essential Elements and Their Grade Designation.

Essential Elements (Prekindergarten–Grade Twelve) Mandated Sciences, Grade Five

Science, grade five, shall have a balance of content and activities from the life, earth, and physical sciences and shall include the following essential elements:

(1) Manipulative laboratory skills. The student shall be provided opportunities to:

(A) construct models;

(B) use a microscope; and

(C) practice safety.

(2) The use of skills in acquiring data through the senses. The student shall be provided opportunities to:

(A) observe phenomena of natural cycles;

(B) observe the results of phenomena associated with electricity (charges, magnetic poles); and

(C) observe the effects of phenomena associated with light or sound.

(3) The use of classification skills in ordering and sequencing data. The student shall be provided opportunities to:

(A) classify objects, actions, or events according to similarities and differences;

(B) classify materials as being metallic or nonmetallic; and

(C) classify human body systems and their functions.

(4) Experience in oral and written communication of data in appropriate form. The student shall be provided opportunities to:

(A) describe changes in objects and events (rock cycles, life cycles, phases of the moon); and

(B) interpret meaningful arrangements of data.

(5) Experience in concepts and skills of measurement using relationships to standards. The student shall be provided opportunities to:

(A) collect information by measuring objects and recording data on graphs and tables; and

(B) measure weather conditions (temperature, wind direction and speed, humidity).

(6) The use of skills in drawing logical inferences, predicting outcomes, and forming generalized statements. The student shall be provided opportunities to:

(A) predict an outcome from a trend in data; and

(B) predict cause-and-effect relationships.

(7) Experience in skills in relating objects and events to other objects and events. The student shall be provided opportunities to:

(A) compare objects according to motion, volume, mass, and speed;

(B) relate knowledge and skills of science to careers; and

(C) compare various ecosystems.

(8) Experience in applying defined terms based on observations. The student shall be provided opportunities to state the differences between objects and events using an operational definition.

(9) Experience in identifying and manipulating the conditions of investigations. The student shall be provided opportunities to identify the variables being manipulated and the variables responding in an investigation.

Source: *Texas Administrative Code,* Title 19, *Education* (St. Paul, MN: West, 1988), p. 254.

major differences are discussed by Firestone, Fuhrman, and Kirst in their study of state reform efforts into the 1980s. They found that the first movement took place in the period from about 1982 until 1986, receiving impetus from *A Nation at Risk.* The second began in 1986 and continued in the 1990s. There were two very different approaches to reform: centralization of decision making in the state capitol and local decision making at the school site.

In the first movement, the focus was on achieving excellence through increased course requirements in selected academic studies (especially science and mathematics), increased student testing, the establishment of achievement standards, and the alignment of curriculum to national standardized tests.[35] This movement was virtually launched by the federal report, *A Nation at Risk.*

Thus, the approach to reform in the first movement was centralized control from the state capitol in response to a national report that captured wide media attention. The reform measures taken by most states grew out of the conception that quality was synonymous with quantity. Frequently, the newly required courses were quite similar to courses already being taught.[36] The point of importance here is that the Reagan administration argued that the quality of American education had sunk precipitously, and the states followed suit by mandating increased academic course requirements and standardized achievement testing. Virtually no support was provided to finance curriculum reconstruction.

THE TEACHER AS PROBLEM.   In the first reform movement, the teacher was identified as the villain behind the nation's education ills. According to a researcher who analyzed the reform movements of the 1980s, one assumption behind states' standardizing and regulatory approaches to reform was that "standardized programs and policies would almost naturally lead to higher levels of quality because their prescriptive nature would resist tampering by teachers."[37] A second assumption of state governments was that schools are more alike than different; therefore, reforms are to be made across the board or "one size fits all."[38]

THE TEACHER AS SOLUTION.   A number of education leaders reacted vigorously against the view of teaching implicit in the wave of state mandates. They criticized the prescribed content and standardized system of learning and argued that teachers must have autonomy if they are to help learners synthesize knowledge and develop a critical intelligence. For teachers to do anything less was to fail in their professional responsibility. Teachers must therefore be empowered to make curriculum decisions at the school level. As Hanson points out, "[i]f the first wave of educational reforms identified teachers as the problem, the second wave identified them as the solution."[39]

The second wave became known as the "restructuring" movement. The school site was the focus in this wave and the emphasis was on curriculum reconstruction. According to Firestone, Fuhrman, and Kirst, "the second wave is supposed to reorganize instruction to improve teaching and learning for understanding, more depth of content as compared to coverage and more emphasis on higher-order thinking."[40]

It had become clear once again that the teacher was the key to curriculum improvement, or had it? States were sending out mixed signals. Some states passed laws requiring more local involvement and at the same time enacting curricular mandates that were more like the first movement. According to Hanson the two movements were alike where money was concerned; both "adopted the view that more education is possible for the same amount of money."[41] In the first movement states rarely provided budgetary or staff assistance to local school authorities for implementation of the mandated reforms. In the second movement, states had found a convenient rationale for not providing consultants to help local schools in their restructuring efforts, presumably under the premise that local schools should have a greater responsibility in making curriculum decisions on their own. The rationale is, of course, faulty. Because schools should have this responsibility does not mean that they ought to be denied professional assistance and material resources for solving curriculum problems. As Reutter points out, "[f]requently local school districts are not in a position to hire expert help in these matters and would not have the advantage of it were it not provided through the state department of education."[42]

STATE LEADERSHIP IN CURRICULUM DEVELOPMENT.   Before the wave of rigid state mandates on the curriculum in the 1980s, Reutter could report that "[c]onsultants employed on the state level are increasing in number in most states as state-level educational agencies evolve from essentially a regulatory role to a true leadership role in improving the quality of education within their borders."[43]

Undoubtedly, this evolution came to a virtual halt in the early 1980s when politically inspired state regulations led to a deadening uniformity in many states. The detailed new regulations provided little if any scope for local districts for originality and curriculum experimentation. However, although the policies stifled local initiative many state officials honestly saw themselves as engaging in the unfinished tasks of raising standards and equalizing educational opportunity. Since the advent of the state school systems, far more progress has been made on these tasks by the state as a whole than could have been accomplished under the differing conditions of autonomous school districts. Whatever the motivations of state policymakers during the early 1980s, however, the restrictive requirements were not a stimulation to curriculum improvement in individual local schools.

STATE PROGRAMS: THE INTEGRAL RELATION OF CURRICULUM AND INSTRUCTION.   There are models for a state's leadership role in curriculum development that are very different from current approaches. One of the most interesting because of the large-scale involvement of teachers was the Virginia Curriculum Revision Plan in the early 1930s. The Virginia Plan was designed by Hollis L. Caswell of Columbia's Teachers College, who served as the general curriculum consultant, and Sydney B. Hall, Virginia's state superintendent of instruction. Caswell's earlier experience with state programs in Alabama and Florida had convinced him that the concept of curriculum must go beyond the course of study. "Courses of study gathered dust on shelves," recalled Caswell. "It became increasingly clear that revision of the curriculum should have as its central purpose the improvement of instruction, and that curriculum programs must utilize many means to achieve this end in addition to writing courses of study."[44]

The state curriculum programs left their imprint on curriculum theory and practice. In the 1930s and 1940s the concept of curriculum development shifted from writing courses of study to the improvement of learning experiences for students.[45]

THE NEED FOR TEACHER INVOLVEMENT.   Caswell reported that the Virginia program and those that followed "led to the general acceptance of the idea that classroom teachers generally must take a major part in curriculum programs since change in practice depends on their ability and willingness to modify existing teaching procedures."[46] This idea was rediscovered a half-century later when states mandated reforms but gave scant attention to implementation. States could establish macro-policies, but could not control what went on behind classroom doors. State authorities in Virginia in the 1930s had to address the same problem. Caswell's approach to getting teachers to implement curriculum reforms is of interest and importance. From his research on the Virginia plan, Burlbaw reports that Caswell's curriculum revision plan for Virginia was a radically different approach to influencing teacher practice, based not on externally imposed mandates, but on invitation and cooperation aimed at improving instruction and learning.[47]

All Virginia teachers were invited to participate in a curriculum study program in preparation for curriculum development work. Caswell's course syllabus included seven topics ranging from "What is the Curriculum?" to "Measuring Outcomes of Instruction."[48] The courses were conducted by trained leaders throughout the state of Virginia, with 10,000 of the more than 16,000 teachers in Virginia participating. While the teachers were engaging in the study program, a committee of principals and teachers developed a tentative statement of the aims of education for Virginia's schools. The next step was crucial: One hundred laypersons, representing various groups, were asked to study the aims critically and make suggestions. The responses were used by the committee in making a revised report. The aims were also submitted to the editors of various newspapers in the state with a request for suggestions. The support of parents and others had made it more possible to use the new course of study effectively.[49]

When the list of aims had been approved, teachers were invited to identify lessons and classroom activities to help students develop the skills and understandings embodied in the aims. For the interested reader, Burlbaw presents a detailed account of organization of county and school district production committees and their relation to the state production committee.[50] Significantly, in the resulting *Tentative Course of Study for Virginia Elementary Schools,* teachers were encouraged to adapt the suggested activities to local conditions. Indeed, the choice of lessons was to be based on the availability of materials and resources locally.[51]

The model was not perfect. Missing was the demonstration of teaching strategies and funds were not available for the intervisitation of teachers. Nevertheless, the program met with success. The Virginia Plan continued—with revisions—from 1932 until 1952. As Burlbaw concludes, its longevity "indicates that some of its aspects might be useful to curricular reformers today."[52] Of particular interest is the view of state curriculum leadership on which the model was based—namely that mandated change is not as effective as is the state-wide voluntary participation of teachers in developing and testing new programs. Democratic educational leadership is cooperative and participatory.

The Local School District Level

Reutter makes these two points concerning curriculum development at the local level: The local board of education must follow state-level curriculum prescriptions, and the history of curriculum innovations in American public schools "is largely a history of local actions."[53] These ideas may seem in conflict to the reader but they are not, for three reasons. The first reason is that the local board of education is most closely involved with what children are taught; thus, it has tremendous powers for determining the curriculum in use.

Another reason is that many curricular offerings have simply been initiated by local school boards on their own, not because of a mandate—such as coursework in environmental science, family life, journalism, orchestral music, humanities, and so on. School boards can also drop and modify subjects and activities that are not state-required.[54] When a school board conceives a curriculum change such as a diversified secondary curriculum without tracking, and it proves successful, it is copied by other school systems. Any number of interesting developments in the curriculum began in this fashion.

A third reason has to do with the relation between curriculum and instruction. How instruction is carried on influences content. As we have seen in the earlier chapters of this book, by changing the ways of conducting the formal studies we can improve the curriculum. We can make it have greater significance in the student's own life. One could not tell by looking at the list of studies taught in Dewey's Laboratory School, for example, that children were engaged in investigating and creating. They were learning that knowledge is not ready made, but comes through inquiry. And they were pursuing their studies under conditions that fostered the realization of social goals. By changing the processes of teaching, Dewey and the teachers changed the curriculum.

"Generally speaking," says Reutter, "methods of instruction are chiefly within the province of local school authorities and individual teachers."[55] By improving the way mandated elements in the school curriculum are taught, local school districts change curriculum. This is why the two points with which this section began are not in conflict.

There is no doubt that states can control the curriculum (and to some extent, method) by prescribing textbooks, but textbooks should not determine the curriculum. They should be used with a rich variety of curricular materials, resources, and activities. The responsibility for designing and developing the curriculum resides with the professional staff of the school district and school. State curricular prescriptions are not an excuse for avoiding this responsibility. For instance, the state may mandate certain subjects for high school graduation, but does not mandate how the subjects are to be organized or treated—and only rarely does a state mandate the actual subject matter.

Recently there has been much interest in curriculum development at the school level. In this regard, the point made about the relation between a state and local school district also holds true here. Because local schools should be engaged in curriculum improvement does not mean that help from the central office should be lacking.

TEST AGENCIES AND PUBLISHERS

"The longer I teach, the more standardized tests are being given," observes a teacher in Texas. Her impression is on target. There are more standardized tests than ever and they are not being used to improve teachers' professional judgments. Even the president of Educational Testing Service acknowledged that test results are used "to rank students, schools and districts."[56]

When tests are used as an instrument of public accountability they sap time and energy from the curriculum. That is what has happened in many American classrooms. A number of studies employing observations of classrooms and interviews with teachers and pupils have found that testing programs considerably reduce learning time, narrow the curriculum, and discourage teachers from attempting to meet goals or use materials that are not compatible with formats used by test makers.[57] As Smith puts it, "multiple choice testing leads to multiple choice teaching."[58] The proliferation of worksheets is symptomatic of the testing syndrome.

Teaching the Test

Textbooks and curriculum guides serve as key sources from which test objectives are drawn by test manufacturers. According to Mehrens and Green, who analyzed the validity of nationally normed tests, the publishers of the tests argue that the content is "sufficiently representative of the domains that concern schools."[59] It is obvious, however, that with such a vast number of objectives, no two test manufacturers will select the same objectives. Despite the fact that there are similarities in the curriculum across the United States, the tests as well as the textbooks selected by school districts differ. Moreover, the tests lack curricular validity, that is, they may not reflect the content of the district's curriculum. This is why so many teachers teach the test. The focus of instruction is on the test items selected by a particular test-maker. Teachers use the old tests to drill students in preparation for the tests.

THE CONSERVATIVE FUNCTION OF STATE TESTING PROGRAMS.   In many school districts, belief in testing as the basis for instructional practices has won out over curriculum development. When tests are developed without the involvement of teachers, "testing programs are likely to foster conservative educational practices [for d]eviation from the content to be covered constitutes a political and professional hazard for teachers."[60] The effects of tests, however, go beyond stabilizing curriculum content. In some classrooms, what is dealt with hardly deserves to be called content. The curriculum has been reduced to a skeleton. Students are not taught a given subject matter for understanding, but are taught to pass the test.

Accountability assessment has decreased teachers' potential for creativity, and has made it less likely that teachers will seek to adapt the curriculum to the needs of their own students. Teachers know much more about teaching than they can put into practice under these limiting conditions.

The Merging of Politics and Testing

Despite the fact that the testing epidemic in schools has not improved instruction and learning, states continue to eagerly accept tests as the answer to school improvement. Tests are still being asked to do what they cannot do. The question we must ask ourselves is why.

One reason is the symbiotic relationship between test producers and state legislators. Because of the political use to which test scores are put, testing has become a runaway business enterprise. "No other country in the world has as much achievement testing as the USA nor allows such commercial profiteering," note four educational psychologists.[61] Not only do test publishers and agencies reap enormous revenues from selling achievement tests and scoring them, but they also profit from the sale of curriculum materials that they produce to match the tests. Even Educational Testing Service, a so-called nonprofit agency, reveals such continued revenue growth in its annual reports as to compare favorably with many a commercial corporation in a growth industry.

Of profound importance in the merger of political and commercial interests is the way that legislators use the test data. As the same four educators observe, "[s]cores are reported in the newspapers with inadequate explanations, and they invite comparisons among teachers, buildings and districts exclusively on the basis of test scores."[62]

We would not be writing about the bigness and influence of the testing industry if some state legislators (and other elected public officials) did not, themselves, personally benefit from the ensuing public concern about test scores. Improving mediocre achievement is a good plank in any politician's platform. Usually the remedy proposed is greater public accountability and more tests.

Public concern is also sustained by the test publishers. In scoring the tests, test publishers have to renorm them constantly because the very nature of standardized testing requires that half the population will score below standard. This means that continuous progress in raising test scores is made more difficult for some school districts, particularly those districts serving large numbers of educationally disadvantaged students.

Assessment to Improve Learning

"If learning is to improve," argued Anrig, "we desperately need reforms that support teachers and students."[63] Accountability testing undermines teachers and students and affects the curriculum negatively. Of profound importance is the difference between instructional assessment and traditional accountability testing. According to Anrig, instructional assessment "builds on past learning and leads toward future learning *in the classroom.* It is not a single activity, or test, conducted in isolation for external reporting."[64]

The purpose of testing where teachers are concerned is to provide information that will help improve day-to-day teaching. Tests must be regarded as only one of a host of instruments and processes in tracing and improving students' progress. At present, accountability testing has become a powerful political vehicle with enormous media appeal. In addition to the direct cost to taxpayers, which is enormous, there is another cost—students' time for learning. According to the National Commission on Testing and Public Policy, American children spend the equivalent of 20 million school days taking tests, and up to twenty times that number of days are spent preparing to take the tests.[65]

According to Harold Howe, former U.S. Commissioner of Education, the most promising starting place for improving instruction and learning is not assessments. Rather, it is "to help teachers rethink their classroom strategies."[66]

UNIVERSITY PROFESSORS

As shown in Figure 14–1, educators at all levels influence the curriculum. However, college professors seek to influence the education of children in different ways than do supervisors and teachers in schools. As Clark points out, for example, "they have been influential in attempting to set direction in much the same way as affiliated members of the public and politicians have been."[67] Because their efforts to influence the curriculum are not the same as those of supervisors and teachers, we will deal with university professors separately here. This should not be taken to mean that the separation that has traditionally existed between the school and university is desirable. On the contrary, a necessary condition for curriculum improvement is free-flowing interaction between schools and universities. Unfortunately, much of the interaction has been top-down—from university to school.

Influence of Subject Matter Specialists

Beginning with the Committee of Ten on Secondary School Studies and the Committee of Fifteen on Elementary Education in the 1890s (and even earlier), subject-matter specialists in the universities have been highly influential curriculum makers. The national discipline-centered curriculum reforms of the 1950s and 1960s were a spectacular episode in the continuing effort of college and university specialists to subordinate the schools to their own narrow interests. University scholar-specialists also were involved during that period in developing teacher-proof materials. These were designed under the arrogant premise that teachers should not tamper with or modify the curriculum packages developed by university knowledge specialists regardless of local school or classroom conditions.

Despite the massive failures in the national discipline-centered curriculum reforms during the era of the Cold War and space race, the federal government has continued to place great faith in university scholar-specialists as curriculum decision makers for the schools. (Charitable foundations tend to do the same in their funded projects.) Implied in such programs is that the professors know best. What Clark calls the "coalition of the political realm and higher education" has often resulted in narrow curricular priorities.[68] More importantly, teachers are left out of the decision-making process.

A major way in which higher education has influenced the curriculum in elementary and secondary schools is, of course, teacher education.

INFLUENCE OF INDIVIDUAL PROFESSORS.   Thus far we have spoken of the influence of affiliated groups, but the ideas of individual scholar-specialists also find their way into some individual classrooms. For example, E. D. Hirsch, a University of Virginia English professor, specified what every American should know in his popular and widely read *Cultural Literacy* (1987). One elementary school principal committed her entire school faculty to teaching Hirsch's information. "I like the idea, from the accountability standpoint, of having specific information that we should . . . teach children," she said about Hirsch's work, and added, "[t]he curriculum is also a very clearly sequenced set of content."[69]

Professors of Education

Curriculum professors in colleges of education have influenced the curriculum through their work as consultants to school districts. This work, in turn, has influenced their own teaching and writing and, thereby, the curriculum development specialists whom they train. The late Hilda Taba, a professor at San Francisco State University, was an outstanding example of this kind of reciprocal influence. An authority on curriculum design, she was particularly interested in the development of children's thinking about important social studies ideas. According to Fraenkel, "many of Hilda's ideas influenced social studies educators considerably."[70] For the interested reader, these ideas are well described by Fraenkel.

Obviously, space limitations prevent an adequate discussion of the efforts of individual professors of education to influence the curriculum. Two more strikingly different examples will be provided briefly. The first is the Accelerated Schools Project, developed by Henry Levin in 1986. According to Levin, a Stanford professor of education economics, the premise underlying the project is that educationally disadvantaged students "must learn at a faster rate than more privileged students—not at a slower rate that drags them farther and farther behind."[71] However, the emphasis actually is not so much on speed as on enriched and idea-oriented learning experiences. The schools in Levin's project introduce children early to meaningful reading and writing; indeed, the teaching methods are intensely concerned with gaining meaning through language in all subjects, including mathematics. This calls to mind Francis Parker's work with the children in Quincy, Massachusetts, during the 1870s (see Chapter 2). There is nothing new either about the other reform approaches followed in accelerated schools that provide opportunities for children to learn through problem solving and independent projects. These are, of course, approved practices for all children. The point of importance here is that Levin has influenced the curriculum in a number of schools by engaging the resources (funding) to influence teachers' classroom decisions.

Some professors of education have been active in setting curriculum policy in ways similar to the activities of politicians. In fact, some have worked collaboratively with governmental officials in efforts to set direction. The second example is Diane Ravitch, a former professor at Columbia's Teachers College, who argued for a narrow academic doctrine for curriculum. Her conception of the curriculum as a catalog of fixed subject matters is reflected in the report, *What Do Our 17-Year-Olds Know?* (1987), an assessment of students' knowledge of history and literature. Her co-author was Chester E. Finn, Jr., who at the time the book was published was serving with Ravitch in the federal government's Education Department. The book is strikingly reminiscent of Hirsch's *Cultural Literacy,* which is not too surprising. Hirsch was involved in developing the test items for the literature assessment. The assessment was based on students' recall of facts. Ravitch and Finn state that they "do not suggest that these facts (or any others) should be taught in isolation."[72] However, assessment, including the methods of assessment, should stem from a curriculum's objectives. It is hard to imagine that teachers and other curriculum decision makers who read Ravitch and Finn's book could gain any impression other than that a curriculum based on the recall of facts through multiple-choice test items is the best way to teach literature and history.

As discussed in detail in Chapter 11, university faculty members actually have been engaged in the making of curriculum on a national scale with federal funding, which also provides for the support of teacher institutes in schools of education so as to ensure implementation.

PROFESSIONAL INFLUENCES

Like higher-education personnel, classroom teachers and supervisors influence the curriculum both as individuals and professional groups.

Professional Associations

Professional organizations seek to provide their members with practical knowledge about recent trends in education that affect curriculum. In their brochures and publications, professional organizations promote points of view concerning effective learning. Some organizations are highly specialized, conceived to promote better teaching in a single subject area, as for example the National Council of Teachers of Mathematics. Others cut across subject lines, directing their efforts at the general problem of improving curriculum and instruction in the elementary and secondary schools.

The Association for Supervision and Curriculum Development (ASCD) is the leading example of an organization focusing on general goals and procedures for curriculum development. One of the largest organizations of American educators, ASCD has attempted to influence curriculum decisions through its publications and programs, as well as resolutions adopted at its annual conventions. For example, in 1992 the ASCD Resolutions Committee endorsed the following critical priority resolution concerning the integration of academic and vocational education:

> Academic and vocational programs are unconnected too often, leaving students in the vocational track without necessary academic skills and students in the academic track unaware of how their learning relates to the real world. Hence, many students are entering the work-force ill-prepared to accept and fulfill basic required responsibilities because they do not possess adequate academic skills and workplace ethics.
>
> It is imperative that students be provided with and have access to educational programs that will prepare them to meet the challenging, technological employment demands of the 21st century.
>
> ASCD strongly urges the development and revision of curriculum to integrate academic and vocational education in order to develop competent, skilled and technologically prepared students.[73]

An implementation plan was also adopted by the resolutions committee. More important, perhaps, each member of the association received a copy of the resolution.

Central Administrators

Superintendents and school boards are obviously influencers of the curriculum. The superintendent makes crucial judgments about district-wide curriculum policies and takes them to the board for approval. In the early 1990s a number of city superintendents proposed additional requirements for high school graduation. The superintendent of the District of Columbia schools, for example, called for adding a semester of algebra and geography and a year of foreign language to the curriculum.[74] Further, as Campbell and others have pointed out, "[t]he superintendent can by the allocation of resources determine which areas of the curriculum and which student activities will be promoted and which deemphasized."[75]

Some superintendents provide outstanding leadership for curriculum development. They spend the major portion of their time in the schools and generate an atmosphere of intellectual vitality and experimentation. They keep up with the education literature themselves, cite the results in everyday meetings and, thus, encourage others to keep up with the literature. These strategies favorably influence the decisions made by the professional staff. They have been identified in studies of effective superintendents, that is, superintendents of large urban school systems that managed to reverse the trend toward decline.[76] They served as models for the entire professional staff.

Not all central administrators seek to help teachers make better decisions. Some seek to tightly control the curriculum and thus prescribe the content and instructional materials to be used, rather than allowing such decisions to be made by those closest to the situation—the teachers. Even superintendents who consider themselves business managers rather than educational leaders influence the curriculum. They do so by default; in their concern for cost effectiveness and production efficiency as measured by test results, they convey to school staffs the feeling that efforts to solve curriculum problems are a waste of time.

Teachers

Teachers make curriculum decisions at the classroom, team, department, grade, and school levels. Each teacher is, in a sense, a choreographer of teaching events and that choreography consists of moment-to-moment decisions. Whatever the broad mandate from afar, students are individuals, requiring individual decisions.[77] These decisions comprise the actual curriculum. Teachers may not recognize that they are making curriculum decisions, but they are.

The actual events decided by the classroom teacher may be very different from what was decided at another level. There is a good reason for this: Teachers are closer to the conditions under which the decision must be carried out. They must adapt it to the conditions in any case, but sometimes the decision itself (from another level) is simply unreasonable. The following is an actual situation. The new superintendent announces that the thematic guides for integrating the curriculum— which were developed by teachers in collaboration with central office personnel— will not be reprinted. Furthermore, there will be no more curriculum improvement projects guided by the central administration of the district and no curriculum guides will be made available from the central office. Local schools will be expected to develop curriculum on their own with their limited resources. Teachers then decide to use the thematic guides and copy them for colleagues.

The teachers in the foregoing illustration were graduate students in a course given by one of the authors of this book. Some reported that they continued to use the guides because an integrated curriculum matched their vision of good teaching; others, because they were simply at a loss without a course of study. In the name of reform (site-based management), the superintendent's decision added complexity to teachers' ability to do their jobs by withdrawing the support of the central office for curriculum improvement. As pointed out in Chapter 4, the central administration of every school system should include persons who are trained in curriculum development and who work with teachers and principals in systemwide programs of curriculum improvement. Without assistance from the central administration, coherent programs are an impossibility. The curriculum should be articulated throughout the district as well as within the school.

In another illustration, this time from Britain, teachers were required to give performance-based tests to determine whether the standards of the national curriculum were being met. The tests were time-consuming, involving science and mathematics experiments. For example, seven-year-olds were given two magnets and asked to explain how to determine which was stronger. "By all accounts," wrote an observer, "teachers found the experience a nightmare. They reported working an average of fifty-eight hours a week giving the tests and struggling to figure out how to grade them."[78] Some teachers decided that rather than going through the painstaking testing process, they would use their own judgment as to whether children had reached levels of achievement.

In both illustrations, teachers' decisions were guided by the circumstances in which they found themselves. They were by no means being unprofessional. In the second illustration, even those teachers who complained about the time-consuming performance tests, actually voiced support for the tests, which they felt were more realistic and valid than traditional multiple-choice tests. Teachers felt that they were not given enough staff-development preparation, time, or aides to help supervise the class while the teacher administered the test to small groups.[79]

No one could control positively all of the many decisions that teachers make behind closed doors. The problem then becomes one of how the teachers can be helped to make informed decisions that carry into classroom practice.

PERSPECTIVE

There is a hierarchy of law relating to the curriculum; for example, no state statute concerning what is taught to children in the public schools can be inconsistent with the federal Constitution. However, the answer to who makes the curriculum cannot be found in education law. The influence exercised at each governmental level interacts with decisions at other levels. These decisions, in turn, interact with the influences of test publishers, college professors (subject matter specialists and professors of education), the public (affiliated groups and individuals), professional education organizations, the mass media, special-interest groups, and last but not least teachers. Although teachers often complain that other groups make all the important decisions, teachers make decisions at the highest level of specificity for they are closest to the student. Teachers ultimately decide the actual events concerning what is to be taught, how it is to be taught, and why it is to be taught. Granted that the textbook determines the curriculum in many classrooms, textbook publishers do not control the topics addressed in the texts, except by default. Authority for textbook adoption is vested in state and local education agencies, and teacher committees also have an important say in most schools. In recent years states and local school systems that represent a large percent of the textbook market have become increasingly critical and have rejected books that fail to adequately address such significant topics as evolution, human reproduction, and environmental problems. The publishers have promptly produced revised and new editions.

In recent years, state legislation concerning the curriculum has increased enormously, much of it regulatory. Following the lead of federal policies established in successive administrations, most states increased high school graduation requirements, particularly in the sciences and mathematics. This interconnection between state and federal policies shows clearly that few of the attempts to shape the curriculum by any group of actors are made in isolation. Similarly, the bigness and influence of the test-makers on the curriculum is attributable, in no small way, to the political uses of test scores; elected government officials frequently call for more achievement tests as the means for achieving excellence (playing on the public's belief in quantitative comparisons). In the 1970s and early 1980s many states attempted to centralize education decision making in the state capitol. The view of teaching implicit in the wave of state mandates was quantitative and mechanical; teachers were seen as technicians who were to deliver the curriculum.

Since the latter 1980s, the tone of reform changed strikingly. State legislatures passed a new wave of mandates intended to decentralize reform to the individual school site. Curriculum decisions were to be made collaboratively by teachers, administrators, and, sometimes, parents. Teachers were suddenly seen as the solution not the cause of American educational problems. Some states have continued to enact other contradictory legislation.

Even a minority of one can influence the curriculum; one parent's objections about curriculum materials can influence the educational experiences of many children. Generally, those individuals and special-interest groups who concentrate their efforts at the local school are the most effective. The farther from the student, the broader and more general the decision.

There is no doubt that some influences on the curriculum are harmful; the growing national obsession with testing, fed by the media and opportunistic political leaders, is an illustration. There are also positive influences. The recent restructuring movement in which teachers and administrators at the school site are encouraged (sometimes mandated) to make decisions is based on the principle that professionals should work collaboratively on school problems. Teachers now have opportunities to make more significant decisions. They will need the time, resources, and expertise to ensure that education decision making is based on the best and wisest professional knowledge.

Problems for Study and Discussion

1. Who decides what textbooks are used in your school and school district? Is the selection based on the best professional evidence that the books contain what is important for students to learn? Explain. If not, how would you improve the process?

2. Draw up a list of quality criteria that could be used in selecting textbooks and other curricular materials for your classroom, team, grade, department, or school. Which, if any, are now being used? Explain.

3. Recently, some states have been experimenting with performance tests with children required to demonstrate what they have learned, such as how to carry out a scientific experiment. In your view, what conditions are necessary if such assessments are to be valid?

4. Examine the laws in your state concerning the subjects to be taught. How much discretion is left to local authorities concerning the content of the curriculum? Explain.

5. Do you agree with the following statement by a middle-school teacher? Why or why not?

   "Teaching to a test is not bad, especially if what the test measures is what we want our students to know and be able to do." [Lois Williams, "Other Voices," *Education Week*, 11 (June 17, 1992), p. S13.]

6. Hollis Caswell's concept of state-level curriculum leadership is a study in contrast to present-day regulatory approaches to curriculum improvement. In your opinion, does Caswell's model have lessons for educational policymakers at the state level today? Why?

7. In this chapter it was pointed out that how instruction is carried on influences content. What illustrations can you give?

8. In the early 1990s, President Bush called on "the best minds in the nation" to come up with plans for "New American Schools" that would reform education by functioning as models and prods for other schools. Among the winning proposals was a design that championed "classical education, time-tested and proven." Its curriculum was based "on the idea that there are certain facts and ideas that every educated person should know" and it drew heavily on E. D. Hirsch's book, *Cultural Literacy* (1987). One of the themes in the curriculum proposal was that the solutions for poverty, violence, and other social problems are rigorous academic standards and moral guidance. "Character building will be the school's unique contribution to help its at-risk youth" the proposal stated. [Susan Chira, "In Plans to Improve Schools, a Grab Bag of Ideas and Ideologies," *The New York Times* (July 15, 1992), p. B6.]

The proposal's designers included William J. Bennett, former Secretary of Education, and Denis P. Doyle and Chester F. Finn, Jr., who sometimes advised the Bush administration on education policy issues.

What is your assessment of the idea behind the proposal? Which of the influences described in this chapter seem to you to have played a role in the proposal's selection?

9. It was noted in this chapter that parents seeking to determine what the curriculum will be for their own children (for example, the demand that Latin should be offered) have gone so far in some schools as to contribute money for extra teachers to teach the additional subjects. Thus, they have added programs that are not offered in other schools where parents do not contribute money. What are your views on this practice?

10. As discussed in this chapter, the educational interests of learners are ill-served when they are denied opportunities to investigate controversial ideas and problems of common concern in a free society. Examine some of the policy statements on academic freedom as developed by the leading professional associations, such as the National Council for the Social Studies, National Council of Teachers of English, National Science Teachers Association, the American Association of School Librarians, and the Association for Supervision and Curriculum Development. Is the professional staff of your school knowledgeable about and committed to these policy statements? The local school board? Explain.

11. In your opinion can teachers and administrators turn parent convictions about the need to improve the curriculum to a force for curriculum improvement? Explain.

12. Some school districts are bound by state mandates to test and rank order schools, and to publish school-by-school lists of comparisons. As discussed in this chapter, scores from multiple-choice tests are an insufficient basis for evaluating programs or making crucial education decisions. The public has been given the illusion that the scores provide meaningful information about what goes on in classrooms. Moreover teachers' salaries and principals' employment is often tied to student performance on the tests. In your opinion, what if any, is the role of education leaders (including teachers) in bringing an end to the ranking of schools and moving testing toward more helpful assessments?

NOTES

1. John I. Goodlad, "The Impact of *Basic Principles of Curriculum and Instruction,*" unpublished address before the Society for the Study of Curriculum History, March 1981.

2. Michael W. Apple, *Teachers and Texts: A Political Economy of Class and Gender Relations in Education* (New York: Routledge and Kegan Paul, 1986), p. 96.

3. Gene I. Maeroff, "City Schools Bar 3 Textbooks Said to Endorse Creationism," *The New York Times* (June 24, 1982), pp. 1, 23.

4. *The New York Times* (September 14, 1985), p. A1; Daniel Tanner, "The Textbook Controversies," Chapter 6 in *Critical Issues in Curriculum,* Eighty-seventh Yearbook of the National Society for the Study of Education, Part I (Chicago: University of Chicago Press, 1988), pp. 136–137.

5. *The New York Times* (November 11, 1990), p. A13.

6. Daniel Tanner, op. cit., pp. 137–138.

7. Ibid., p. 137.

8. *The Houston Post* (January 11, 1992), p. A-19.

9. Denis P. Doyle, "America 2000," *Phi Delta Kappan,* 73 (November 1991), p. 187.

10. Richard W. Clark, "Who Decides? The Basic Policy Issue," Chapter 8 in *Critical Issues in Curriculum,* Eighty-seventh Yearbook of the National Society for the Study of Education, Part I (Chicago: University of Chicago Press, 1988), pp. 179–187.

11. Ibid., p. 176.

12. Hollis L. Caswell and Doak S. Campbell, *Curriculum Development* (New York: American Book, 1935), pp. 74–75.

13. John I. Goodlad, *A Place Called School* (New York: McGraw-Hill, 1984); Clark, op. cit; see the annual Gallup/Phi Delta Kappa polls of the public's attitude toward the public schools published in the September issue of the *Phi Delta Kappan.*

14. *The New York Times* (July 21, 1991), p. F21.

15. *Education Week,* 11 (April 8, 1992), p. 2.

16. Clark, op. cit., p. 180.

17. Ibid.

18. Ibid., pp. 180–181.

19. Debra Viadero, "Parent Discontent Fuels Spirited School Board Races in Princeton," *Education Week,* 11 (April 8, 1992), p. 13.

20. Ibid., p. 1.

21. *The New York Times* (December 27, 1988), p. 1.

22. Ken Donelson, "You Can't Have That Book in My Kid's School Library: Books under Attack in the *Newsletter on Intellectual Freedom, 1952–1989,*" *The High School Journal,* 74 (October–November, 1990), p. 4.

23. Ibid.

24. Clark, op. cit., p. 180.

25. Clark, op. cit., p. 18.

26. Lawrence A. Cremin, *Popular Education and Its Discontents* (New York: Harper and Row, 1990), p. 31.

27. Doyle, op. cit., p. 187.

28. E. Edmund Reutter, Jr., *The Schools and the Law,* 4th ed. (Dobbs Ferry, NY: Oceana Publications, 1980), pp. 6–7.

29. Ibid., p. 37.

30. Mary McGroarty, "The Societal Context of Bilingual Education," *Educational Researcher,* 21 (March 1992), p. 7.

31. Albert I. Oliver, *Curriculum Improvement: A Guide to Problems, Principles and Process,* 2nd ed. (New York: Harper and Row, 1977), p. 156.

32. Chris Pipho, "States Move Reform Closer to Reality," *Phi Delta Kappan,* 68 (December 1986), p. K3; see also Task Force on Increased High School Graduation Requirements, *With Consequences for ALL* (Alexandria, VA: Association for Supervision and Curriculum Development, 1985).

33. Ibid., p. K7.

34. E. Mark Hanson, "Educational Restructuring in the USA: Movements of the 1980s," *Journal of Educational Administration,* 29, 4 (1991), pp. 30–38.

35. William A. Firestone, Susan H. Fuhrman, and Michael W. Kirst, "State Educational Reform since 1983: Appraisal and the Future," *Educational Policy,* 5 (September 1991), p. 235.

36. Ibid., p. 238.

37. Hanson, op. cit., p. 31.

38. Ibid.

39. Ibid., p. 34.

40. Firestone, Fuhrman, and Kirst, op. cit., p. 240.

41. Hanson, op. cit., p. 36.

42. Reutter, op. cit., p. 13.

43. Ibid., p. 40.

44. Hollis L. Caswell, "Emergence of the Curriculum as a Field of Professional Work and Study," in Helen F. Robison (ed.), *Precedents and Promises in the Curriculum Field* (New York: Teachers College Press, 1966), pp. 2–3.

45. Ibid., pp. 1–11.

46. Caswell, op. cit., p. 10.

47. Lynn M. Burlbaw, "More Than 10,000 Teachers: Hollis L. Caswell and the Virginia Curriculum Revision Program," *Journal of Curriculum and Supervision,* 6 (Spring 1991), p. 242.

48. Ibid., p. 237.

49. Caswell and Campbell, op. cit., pp. 473–480.

50. Burlbaw, op. cit., pp. 233–254.

51. Ibid., p. 244.

52. Ibid., p. 249.

53. Reutter, op. cit., p. 41.

54. Ibid., pp. 41–42.

55. Ibid., p. 43.

56. Gregory R. Anrig, "Can Tests Lead the Way to Excellence?" *Education Week,* 11 (April 1, 1992), p. 40.

57. Mary Lee Smith, "Put to the Test: The Effects of External Testing on Teachers," *Educational Researcher,* 20 (June–July 1991), pp. 8–11.

58. Ibid., p. 10.

59. William A. Mehrens and Donald R. Green, *Standardized Tests and School Curricula,* 1989. (ERIC document no. ED322-150.)

60. Elliot W. Eisner, "Who Decides What Schools Teach?" *Phi Delta Kappan,* 71 (March 1990), p. 525.

61. Scott G. Paris, Theresa A. Lawton, Julianne C. Turner, and Jodie L. Roth, "A Developmental Perspective on Standardized Achievement Testing," *Educational Researcher,* 20 (June–July 1991), p. 13.

62. Ibid.

63. Anrig, op. cit.

64. Ibid.

65. National Commission on Testing and Public Policy, *Reforming Assessment: From Gatekeepers to Gateway to Education* (Chestnut Hill, MA: Center for the Study of Testing, Evaluation, and Educational Policy, Boston College, 1990).

66. Harold Howe II, "Rethink Classroom Strategies," *Education Week,* 11 (June 17, 1992), p. S20.

67. Clark, op. cit., p. 184.

68. Ibid.

69. *The American School Board Journal,* 179 (February 1992), p. A19.

70. Jack R. Fraenkel, "Hilda Taba's Contributions to Social Studies Education," *Social Education,* 56 (March 1992), p. 172.

71. Cited in "Accelerated Schools Show Progress with At-Risk Students," *Illinois School Board Journal,* 60 (January/February 1992), p. 12.

72. Diane Ravitch and Chester E. Finn, Jr., *What Do Our 17-Year-Olds Know? A Report on the First National Assessment of History and Literature* (New York: Harper, 1987), p. 256.

73. ASCD, *Association for Supervision and Curriculum Development Resolutions 1992* (Alexandria, VA: Author, 1992), p. 1.

74. *Education Week,* 11 (June 17, 1992), p. 3.

75. Roald F. Campbell, Luvern L. Cunningham, Roderick F. McPhee, and Raphael O. Nystrand, *The Organization and Control of American Schools,* 4th ed. (Columbus, OH: Merrill/Macmillan, 1980), p. 242.

76. Paul T. Hill, Arthur E. Wise, and Leslie Shapiro, *Educational Progress: Cities Mobilize to Improve Their Schools* (Santa Monica, CA: The Rand Corporation, 1989).

77. Philip W. Jackson, *Life in Classrooms* (New York: Holt, Rinehart and Winston, 1968).

78. Susan Chira, "A National Curriculum: Fairness in Uniformity," *The New York Times* (January 8, 1992), p. B9.

79. Ibid.

SELECTED REFERENCES

Association for Supervision and Curriculum Development. *With Consequences for All.* Alexandria, VA: Author, 1985.

Bell, Terrel H. *The Thirteenth Man: A Reagan Cabinet Memoir.* New York: The Free Press, 1988.

Caswell, Hollis L., and Campbell, Doak S. *Curriculum Development.* New York: American Book, 1935.

Cremin, Lawrence A. *Popular Education and Its Discontents.* New York: Harper and Row, 1990.

Elmore, Richard F., and Fuhrman, Susan H. *The Governance of Curriculum,* 1994 Yearbook of the Association for Supervision and Curriculum Development. Alexandria, VA: Association for Supervision and Curriculum Development.

Firestone, William A., Fuhrman, Susan H., and Kirst, Michael W. *The Process of Reform: An Appraisal of State Education Initiatives.* New Brunswick, NJ: Center for Policy Research in Education, Rutgers University, 1989.

Goodlad, John I. *A Place Called School.* New York: McGraw-Hill, 1984.

Hill, Paul T., Wise, Arthur E., and Shapiro, Leslie. *Educational Progress: Cities Mobilize to Improve Their Schools.* Santa Monica, CA: The Rand Corporation, 1989.

Hirsch, E. D., Jr. *Cultural Literacy: What Every American Needs to Know.* Boston: Houghton Mifflin, 1987.

National Commission of Excellence in Education. *A Nation at Risk.* Washington, D.C.: U.S. Department of Education, 1983.

National Society for the Study of Education. *Critical Issues in Curriculum.* Eighty-seventh Yearbook, Part I. Chicago: University of Chicago Press, 1988.

Ravitch, Diane, and Finn, Chester E., Jr. *What Do Our 17-Year-Olds Know? A Report on the First National Assessment of History and Literature.* New York: Harper, 1987.

Reutter, E. Edmund, Jr. *The Law of Public Education.* 4th ed. Westbury, New York: The Foundation Press, 1994.

Reutter, E. Edmund, Jr. *The Schools and the Law,* 4th ed. Dobbs Ferry, NY: Oceana Publications, 1980.

Taba, Hilda. *Curriculum Development: Theory and Practice.* New York: Harcourt, 1962.

Tanner, Daniel, and Tanner, Laurel N. *Supervision in Education: Problems and Practices.* New York: Macmillan, 1987.

U.S. Department of Education. *America 2000: An Education Strategy.* Washington, D.C.: Author, 1991.

Wise, Arthur. *Legislated Learning.* Bekeley, CA: University of California Press, 1979.

CHAPTER 15

CURRICULUM IMPROVEMENT— ROLE OF THE TEACHER

As discussed in Chapter 14, all teachers are engaged in curriculum development. Teachers make important decisions with consequences for students. In the classroom, they do so behind closed doors. No one can control all of the specific decisions that teachers make even during a highly specified instructional episode. Researchers have found that teachers choose between alternative courses of action many times during a lesson such as, when a student gives an unexpected response to the teacher's question.[1] Then there are the planning and implementation decisions that teachers make individually, and with others on improving the grade-level, school, or district curriculum. In addition, teachers may be involved in large-scale efforts to improve the curriculum in a given subject such as mathematics. Of all the legacies inherited from the pioneers in the field, the most important is that curriculum improvement depends on teachers being more thoughtful about their work.

What we are discussing here is nothing more or less than teachers being professionals. As Darling-Hammond and Snyder point out, to be professional is to make decisions based on the principles in one's field.[2] This chapter is concerned with how teachers can be helped to base their decisions on educational principles and thus, it is hoped, improve the curriculum. This requires that (1) teacher-education programs prepare teachers who are able to conceptualize and apply the principles that are relevant to particular situations as well as general professional practice, (2) teachers learn from changing conditions, and (3) teachers are provided with the support to participate in curriculum development. These conditions provide the organizing framework for this chapter and the chapter that follows on the supervisor's role.

PROFESSIONAL DEVELOPMENT AND CURRICULUM IMPROVEMENT

If teachers are expected to make knowledge-based decisions they must be prepared to do so. Many teachers, particularly those who obtained their preparation in the 1970s and early 1980s, were not provided with these experiences in their preservice programs. Teacher education was dominated by competency-based approaches. The emphasis was on training teachers as technicians. The objective was to program the teacher to perform explicitly specified behaviors. Competency-based teacher education is mechanical efficiency applied to teaching. According to Darling-Hammond and Snyder, it is based on "the hope of finding the 'one best system,' codified by law and specified by regulations, by which all students may be educated," and, further, on the assumption "that students are standardized so that they will respond in identical and predictable ways to the 'treatments' devised by policymakers and their principal agents [schools]."[3]

The assumption that students are uniform and uniformly predictable—or can be made so—is, of course, fallacious and ought to have been obvious at the time. Children have always had individual experiences, talents, and interests. Teachers have always had to treat children differently in order to provide them with optimal learning opportunities. The need to develop teachers who can conceptualize, evaluate, and modify their procedures has been emphasized by educational theorists for centuries. Not surprisingly, the competency-based teacher education movement of modern times proved to be a disappointment. As pointed out in Chapter 14, there was a striking change in the conception of the teacher in the mid-1980s. Some policymakers at the district and state levels began to recognize that there are no treatments that can be prescribed from afar for all students, and that the emphasis on standardized operating procedures had probably impaired teachers' ability to meet the needs of their students. Indeed, a decline in students' reasoning abilities was widely attributed to the treatment of students in standardized ways.

Teacher Education and Curriculum Development

How competency-based education affected the teacher's role in curriculum development is obvious. There was no provision made for decision making by teachers. Competency-based teacher education conceived of the teacher as a technician who deals only with established-convergent decisions. The competency movement denied the obvious—namely, that teachers are inevitably involved in the curriculum development and that this function of teaching does not lend itself to a behavioristic-competency approach. Teacher education has had its dark side, but many policymakers are now concerned—forced to be concerned—with helping teachers grow in personal insight and initiative.

THE LABORATORY IDEAL.   If teachers are to relate their decisions to educational principles, they must be provided with opportunities to do so in their professional preparation. As early as 1904, Dewey conceived of a teacher education that was "calculated to develop a thoughtful and intelligent teacher." In such a program, theory and practice "grow together out of and into the teacher's personal experience."[4] What was at stake, argued Dewey, was the laboratory ideal versus the apprentice idea. Here the focus of student teaching and the method of supervising and criticizing it were crucial. In a laboratory situation, the student teacher's intellectual growth and responsibility are given attention. In Dewey's words, "the practical work is pursued primarily with reference to its reaction upon the professional pupil in making him a thoughtful and alert student of education, rather than to help him get immediate proficiency."[5]

When the apprentice idea dominates, however, the objective is "turning out at once masters of the craft." The most interesting part of Dewey's analysis is his comparison of teacher education with other professionals. The history of other professions shows a preprofessional time when the idea was that students should from the beginning "be made as proficient as possible in practical skill." However, "professional schools have traveled steadily away from this position" and toward the laboratory ideal where the practice work is conducted under the student's "own initiative and reflective criticism."[6]

In the apprentice situation, the student teacher is primarily concerned with maintaining the external attention of the class. The apprentice teacher gears actual methods of teaching, not to the principles of professional practice, but to what seems to work or fail from one moment to the next, to what he or she sees more experienced teachers doing who are more successful in maintaining order, and in conformance with the directions given by others. In this way, contended Dewey, the habits of teachers are fixed, with relatively little reference to principles in educational psychology and curriculum development.[7]

Dewey held that the apprentice situation had this antiprofessional effect: an unconscious duplicity in teaching. "There is," he said, "an enthusiastic devotion to certain principles of lofty theory in the abstract—principles of self-control, intellectual and moral—and there is school practice taking little heed of the official pedagogic creed." This was one of the "chief evils of the teaching profession."[8]

NEW (OLD) DIRECTIONS FOR REFORM. In the closing years of the twentieth century many teacher-education programs have begun to embrace the laboratory ideal—moving in a direction that Dewey would have applauded. In these programs student teachers and interns are expected to make explicit the reasons for their various pedagogical decisions. They are given experiences in making curriculum decisions collaboratively with school faculty and principals. Notable among these reform efforts in teacher education has been the professional development school, which seeks to link pedagogical theory and practice by bringing together school and university faculty in the professional preparation of teachers.[9] Such programs typically bring together university faculty, teachers, and principals who share in the responsibility for the student teaching or internship experience, coupled with a seminar concerned with connecting the field experience and university courses. At the Puget Sound Professional Development Center, for example, the seminar is team-taught by teachers and university faculty.[10]

SCHOOL-UNIVERSITY PARTNERSHIPS: PROBLEMS AND POSSIBILITIES. The professional development school is based on the idea that professional development is lifelong. Thus teachers serving as cooperating teachers are also "learners who are engaged in ongoing inquiry into their practice," notes Grossman, "and engagement in the preparation of the next generation of teachers provides rich opportunities for teacher learning."[11] The idea, then, is that learning is a two-way street—as cooperating teachers can also learn from student teachers. According to Grossman, "[s]erving as a cooperating teacher holds the possibility for acquiring new knowledge about teaching, including new methods of instruction, alternative approaches to curriculum, or different perspectives in classroom management." Perhaps more importantly—it "can provide opportunities for reflection about one's own practice."[12]

In theory, cooperating teachers should be open to new perspectives and incorporate them in their practices. Not all cooperating teachers, however, even all those who are looking for new ideas concerning curriculum and instruction, view student teachers as a source of new practices. For many, being a cooperating teacher is a reward for previous performance. Rather than a stimulus for further professional development, having a student teacher is viewed as an on-site sabbatical, an opportunity to do other things, as the student teacher takes on increasing responsibility for the classroom.[13] Others, who view themselves as experts, become somewhat defensive about their approaches to teaching instead of being open to new ideas. Still others are aware of new ideas concerning curriculum from their student teachers but do not attempt to implement these new approaches. As Grossman observes, new methods "may threaten the delicately balanced routines that manifest the teacher's expertise in the first place."[14]

The problem of recasting the role of cooperating teacher as learner is a difficult one. Probably at issue here is whether the role of cooperating teacher should be recast at all. According to Joyce and Clift, the purpose of preservice teacher education is to prepare teacher candidates as professional teachers who are engaged in "the lifelong study of the theory and practice of teaching," and for participation in school renewal efforts, including curriculum improvement.[15] As Tyler informed us, "[t]he primary function of teacher education is to help individuals develop a rough cognitive map of the phenomena of learning, teaching and professional ethics so that they can get the feel of professionalism."[16] These views recall Dewey's laboratory ideal. More to the point, however, is that preservice candidates should not be expected to provide new ideas for cooperating teachers. This is not the purpose of their field experience, which is to help student teachers and interns "learn how to work out appropriate answers for individual situations."[17] Some of these situations are at the classroom level, some at the school level. Teacher candidates should have opportunities to participate in curriculum problem-solving groups at the school level if we expect them to do so as inservice teachers.

COMPLAINTS AND CONFLICTS.   In attempting to apply their views of learning and use the methods they were taught in university methods courses, student teachers frequently find that schools and universities have different views of teaching and learning. Thus, many cooperating teachers model their work on, and may even insist on, traditional methods emphasizing drill-skill techniques and rote learning. (This happens even in professional development schools.) Student teachers who expect children to learn through active experiences usually try to conform to the cooperating teacher's expectations. Experts in teacher education suggest that this problem can be overcome through staff development over a long period of time, by providing inservice teachers with opportunities "to see new strategies modeled repeatedly" and to try them out, "receiving professional support while they are learning."[18] Cooperating teachers can be created, or so the reasoning goes. The problems with this approach are manifold. First, it assumes a deficit view of inservice education instead of treating teachers as professionals. Cooperating teachers should have the skills, knowledge, and attitudes that will make them the best possible role models. This means that they should be competent and self-actualized to begin with. Placing student teachers with self-actualized teachers who can help novices apply the relevant principles to a given situation because they do so themselves on their own initiative is crucial to the success of the student-teaching experience.

Finding good field placements for student teachers and interns is an old problem but such placements do exist. The solution still seems to be for universities (and schools) to be more selective in their placements.

THE DECLINE OF CURRICULUM DEVELOPMENT. Although interest in curriculum reform has continued to rise, a number of teacher-preparation programs that once required that prospective teachers study curriculum development no longer do so. This is residue from the narrowness of the competency-based teacher education movement. Because teachers were viewed as technicians, the study of curriculum development could not be defended as contributing to their abilities in the classroom. Curriculum development was now seen as a policy matter residing at higher levels of the administrative structure. Certainly an adequate education of teachers must include curriculum development (both theory and the work of curriculum development) if teaching is to be a profession and if educational opportunities for learners are really to be improved.

THE RESPONSIBLE ACT OF TEACHING. The idea of professionalism was well expressed by Foshay, a leader in the quest for professionalism. Foshay made the following observation concerning the term *professional* in education: "At the heart of its meaning is the idea of responsible action: the act of teaching, and the act of educational leadership. A professional is one who knows how to act," and the responsible act of teaching requires that the teacher "draw on what is known of educational practice [and] gather evidence in some coherent way."[19] The ability to synthesize this knowledge in action is the hallmark of the professional teacher. Clearly, if teaching is to be professionalized, then knowledge of approved practices in education (including the ability to implement such practices) and the ability to think experimentally must be required for entrance to the profession. Teachers must also be intelligent consumers of research. The preservice preparation program must help meet these aims.

Approved practices and experimental thinking as approaches to curriculum improvement are discussed later. It should be noted here, however, that teachers' thinking experimentally ranges from everyday attempts to match the task to the learner, to being an intelligent consumer of research to solve a classroom problem, or to work effectively in redesigning the curriculum.

NO TURNING BACK.   The recurring theme that runs through teacher-education literature is the gradual advance of professionalism. The tide of teacher education is now running more strongly in the direction of professionalism. The Carnegie Commission's report, *A Nation Prepared: Teachers for the 21st Century* (1986) was illustrative of this direction. This report's recommendations include teacher involvement in educational decision making.[20] Likewise, the Holmes Group report on *Tomorrow's Teachers* (1986) proposed a professional education that would develop teachers' capacity to reconstruct the curriculum "so as to engage a variety of pupils."[21] Lieberman dates the recent concern with the preparation of teachers as a means for school improvement to these reports. As she observed, the recent reform movement is dismissed by some as merely transitory, "another of the pendulum swings that happen every decade."[22] As she and others observe, much effort has gone into the recent movement (and, perhaps, more importantly the working climate is different than in most previous reforms). Opportunities are being provided in many schools for preservice and beginning teachers to express their ideas for improving the educational program. In some schools the ideas of student teachers and beginning teachers are openly solicited and valued by the entire staff. Moreover, site-managed schools are based on the concept of participatory decision making. It is difficult to see how new teachers who have had the professional preparation for educational decision making would not continue to see it as their area of competence and responsibility.

THE CURRICULUM AS CONTINUOUS GROWTH—THE PROBLEM OF THE UNIVERSITY.   Recent proposals for teacher education are concerned with preparing teachers adequately for curriculum problem solving. Successful implementation will require changing what Sarason once referred to as "the existing regularities."[23] Although Sarason was referring to the culture of the schools there are also "regularities" or traditions in universities. Of particular concern is the way that teacher education is usually organized in schools of education. For example, in most teacher-education programs elementary education is divorced conceptually and administratively from secondary education. This is a segmental view of education and works against consideration of the curriculum as continuous growth. The professional must see the curriculum as an articulated whole and in relation to educational development regardless of specialization, and must deal with problems in the immediate situation in light of the curriculum as a whole.

Resources for Problem Solving

It is hard to argue with the conception underlying the professional development of teachers. Preservice and inservice teacher education is an unbroken continuum. The difficulty is in providing the conditions and resources to help practicing teachers improve the curriculum. This is particularly critical in inner-city schools with high concentrations of at-risk students. Such schools typically suffer from overcrowded classes. These students also suffer from lack of individual attention. According to Hodgkinson, a demographer, this is "particularly frustrating" because the evidence is clear that equity efforts "pay off in enabling of minority populations to gain opportunities for advancing educationally, economically, and socially.[24] Education is the key to life choices.

CHANGING CONDITIONS.　　The conditions of teaching itself are always changing. The nonwhite percentage of the youth population will increase spectacularly from 1990 to 2010. Indeed, in some states (Texas, California, Florida, and New York, for example), the designation minority will no longer be accurate. "What do we call 'minorities' when they constitute a majority?" asks Hodgkinson. "It behooves us all to make sure that *every* child in America has a good education and access to a good job."[25] The outlook for these children might be favorable and even is, as Hodgkinson put it, "exciting"—given adequate education, health, day care, and housing.[26] Such services must function interrelatedly. The prospects convey a sense of crisis and opportunity.

As Deborah Meier has pointed out, policymakers must offer the resources—"the key is well-designed staff development time—to enable teachers to learn from their changed conditions. Unlike industries, we can't retool by closing down the factories and sending all the workers back to school. We need to do everything at once."[27] The problem described by Meier is not confined to teachers. All professionals—indeed all workers—must learn from new conditions, and take those conditions as opportunities for improvements.

It has taken a long time for policymakers to realize that an ongoing program for school improvement requires teacher professionalization. One of the most promising changes in the conditions of teaching is the emphasis on collaborative problem solving at the school site. Institutional changes, such as collegial time (different from formal staff development) are needed to support collaborative problem solving. In some schools such changes have occurred.

Three critically important resources for problem solving are time, expertise, and materials.

TIME.　　Teachers must have time for shared deliberation to identify substantive problems and develop plans for attacking the problems. In her study on the conditions of school success, Little found that successful and unsuccessful schools can be distinguished based on the frequency of teachers' interactions for the purpose of solving curriculum problems and improving instruction.[28] Schools were classified as successful or unsuccessful based on standardized achievement test scores and nomination by district administrators and staff developers. Successful schools supported and encouraged teachers' shared work. Teacher evaluation was linked with collegial participation in problem analysis and experimentation, with teacher access to resources—including released time. Teacher interactions in successful schools were found to be frequent and ongoing. In one high-success, high-involvement elementary school, faculty meetings were devoted to discussions of research and classroom practice. Teachers regularly worked together in grade-level teams to develop curriculum plans and materials. In a successful junior high school, formerly isolated departments reported that student performance and classroom discipline improved when teachers met more frequently to work on curriculum and instructional approaches.[29]

Certainly one purpose of school faculty meetings should be to help teachers integrate theory and practice. Time in faculty meetings tends to be spent on clerical and routine matters rather than on ideas and their implementation. This is a problem of habit and tradition, an existing regularity that could be changed through educational leadership on the part of the principal and teachers. In almost every school, there are certain teachers who have interest and talent in this direction.

EXPERTISE.   Teachers must have the freedom to seek assistance in improving the curriculum. Outside experts, helping teachers, supervisors, and peers should be available to assist teachers on invitation, responding to the teachers' expressed needs. Although much can be accomplished by pooling a school's own resources— the strengths of its teachers and principal—schools must turn to outside resources in order to acquire new knowledge, new ideas, and new perspectives. Universities have a vital role to play in this regard; school-university cooperative programs for curriculum development can be enormously effective.

From the literature and professional organizations, principals and teachers can identify schools that are trying out new curriculum designs and materials. They should send task forces to explore the success and efficacy of using these approaches in the local school, and they should inform regional educational research laboratories and centers regarding the school's willingness to participate in the development and evaluation of curriculum materials.

MATERIALS.   Teachers must have materials to improve learning. When one considers that only a minute portion of the education budget goes to materials, to double the amount would probably work wonders. One of the first places where school districts trim budgets is materials—textbooks, library books, curriculum materials, and other instructional materials.

Although materials are an important resource, teachers should watch out for fads and fashions. Materials and methods must be contiguous with the philosophy of the school district and contribute to the improvement of learning. Goodlad articulates the problem in these words: "I wish we had some kind of Hippocratic oath to remind us always to keep solid principles of learning, teaching, and education at the center and to guide us in choosing what follows from them."[30]

The Impact of Professional Relationships

Of profound importance for teachers' involvement in curriculum development is the nature of their relationships with administrators and supervisors. As Levine and Eubanks point out, a major goal of site-based management plans is that school faculty should be actively involved in making decisions about curriculum and instruction.[31] Preliminary research findings on school-based management indicate, however, that in many site-managed schools, the formal decision-making arrangements have not really changed. In some schools, principals continue to protect their own prerogatives. In other schools, principals and department heads simply do not possess the skills to carry out the collaborative process. Although many schools have adopted plans that involve teachers in schoolwide decision making, the old pattern where administrators make policy and teachers deliver instruction dies hard.

According to Malen and Ogawa, the predisposition of participants is not the key factor that will determine whether site-based management can achieve its objectives. Although some participants view school improvement as an individual rather than a collective responsibility and some may be reluctant to critically assess the instructional program, these attitudes can be changed when needed resources are made available. "In most instances," say Malen and Ogawa, "site participants lack the time, technical assistance, requisite skills, and supplemental funds needed to engage in comprehensive, coordinated planning processes."[32]

Attention to all factors is important if schools are to deal effectively with their problems. As the findings of research indicate (and we have pointed out elsewhere in this book) participative systems are more likely than autocratic systems to generate problem solutions. Malen and Ogawa point out that the results of site-based management are mixed. Some schools have given life to the concept of school improvement as a participative process.[33] In fact, there is much that principals and teachers can do to make real progress. For example, faculty meetings should be devoted mainly to the improvement of the educational program. Teachers and principals should plan the agenda collaboratively. The meetings should not be dominated by the principal. None of these practices require additional resources. However, as Philip Jackson pointed out, providing expert help for teachers (individual help and help in their collective curriculum pursuits) does cost money. "I see absolutely no hope for the future of inservice education," he wrote, "unless we are willing to pay for what we want."[34] This requires a continuous and concerted program of collaborative work with teachers on problem solutions, with the provision of adequate released time, expertise, and material resources.

SUPERVISORY RELATIONSHIPS. The supervisor-teacher relationship should be one of collegial collaboration and the entire professional staff should function as a collegial team. In many schools supervision tends to be deficit-oriented (fault-finding). This inhibits curriculum improvement because the teacher's own classroom concerns are ignored. Despite the fact that curriculum theorists have for decades advocated that curriculum-improvement programs begin with problems identified by teachers, supervision continues to start—and often to end—by pointing out teachers' errors.

FORMAL STATUS AND RIGHT TO PARTICIPATE. One indication of successful schools is that the right to initiate and participate in curriculum work is not limited to administrators and supervisors. "In some schools," as Little has pointed out, "such rights are limited to principals, department chairs, and some influential teachers. In the more successful and adaptable schools, rights to initiate and participate are more widely distributed, rely less on formal position and are variable by situation."[35]

Unfortunately, it is believed by many administrators and supervisors that most teachers lack the competence to make responsible curriculum decisions. Indeed, this view actually was reinforced in the aforementioned Carnegie Commission report, *A Nation Prepared: Teachers for the 21st Century.* The report presented the concept of lead teachers, influential teachers in charge of identifying curriculum problems and the study and resolution of those problems. Mary Hatwood Futrell, a former president of the NEA, expressed "deep reservations" about this idea. "It suggests," she stated, "that some teachers are more equal than others. And it is not adequately differentiated from the flawed and failed merit pay and job ladder plans."[36]

The proposal that the rights of teachers to initiate collegial work be limited by their status is supported neither by research nor experience. A concrete illustration of the latter was the Denver Plan. It will be recalled from the discussion in Chapter 3 that the Denver curriculum program became the prototype for curriculum development in the 1920s. Although teacher participation in curriculum revision was not a new idea at the time, the Denver program had a new twist: substitute teachers were hired to free classroom teachers for curriculum development. A second new development, which was undoubtedly a factor in the success of the program, was that teachers had the help of many curriculum consultants on an ongoing basis.

These innovations are of superlative importance because they emerged from a new conception of the teacher as a professional. There can be little doubt that being treated as professionals by their administrative superiors had a positive impact on the Denver teachers who participated in curriculum revision. Hence, this treatment had a positive impact on curriculum improvement processes.

LEVELS OF CURRICULUM DEVELOPMENT

In most schools the teacher is presented with the curriculum as a fait accompli. What does it mean to improve the curriculum? How does the teacher proceed? Teachers need a guide to curriculum development that they can use to define their role. They need to see curriculum development as a total school enterprise and as a continual problem-solving process. It is with this need in mind that the levels of curriculum development are offered (see Table 15–1).

Teachers, administrators, schools, and school systems tend to function predominantly at one of three levels, as shown in Table 15–1: (I) Imitative-maintenance, (II) Mediative, and (III) Generative-creative. Associated with each level are certain assumptions about what teaching is like and how teachers can best improve in their work. Teachers at Level I are concerned with curriculum maintenance, keeping the ship afloat, as it were. Principals are likewise concerned with maintaining a tight ship and maintaining the status quo. Teachers at Level II are aware that teaching should be more than routine management but curriculum improvement tends to be viewed as refinement of established practice. Teachers at Level III have an imaginative vision of curriculum and are immersed in problem diagnosis and attempts to improve established practice. They seek to use the best knowledge available as guides to action. The point of importance here is that the levels do not constitute a sequence. It is not necessary to start at Level I to get to Level III. In fact, the very conditions for Level I will impede the possibilities—that is, one gets to Level III by instituting the conditions for Level III. Ends and means must be contiguous.

Table 15–1 Levels of Curriculum Development

Level	Locus	Tasks and Activities	Principal Resources
Level I Imitative-maintenance	Microcurriculum Established conditions Segmental treatment	Rudimentary Routine Adoptive Maintenance of established practice	Textbook, worksheets, workbook, syllabi (subject by subject), segmental adoption of curriculum packages, popular educational literature School principal
Level II Mediative	Microcurriculum Established conditions Segmental treatment Awareness of emergent conditions, aggregate treatment, macrocurriculum	Interpretive Adaptive Refinement of established practice	Textbook, courses of study (subject by subject with occasional correlation of subjects), multi-media, adaptation of segmental curriculum packages, professional literature on approved practice Pupils, teacher colleagues, helping teacher, supervisor, curriculum coordinator, parents, community resources, school principal, inservice courses
Level III Generative-creative	Macrocurriculum Emergent Conditions Aggregate treatment	Interpretive Adaptive Evaluative problem–diagnosis problem–solving Improvement of established practice Search for improved practice	Textbook, courses of study (across subjects and grade levels), alternative modes of curriculum design for knowledge synthesis and application, professional literature on research and approved practice, multi-media, investigatory projects Pupils, teacher colleagues, helping teacher, supervisor, curriculum coordinator, parents, community resources, school principal, inservice courses, outside consultants, experimental programs, professional conferences and workshops

Level I: Imitative-Maintenance

Teachers operating at Level I rely on textbooks, worksheets, workbooks, and routine activities, subject by subject. Skills are treated as dead ends rather than as means of generating further learning. Ready-made materials are used without critical evaluation, resulting in a multiplicity of isolated skill-development activities. (The already segmental curriculum is further fragmented.) The imagination of the teacher does not go beyond maintaining the status quo. This teacher would like to think that one has less freedom than one may actually have for curriculum improvement. Teaching the test is common practice. In the secondary school, concern for curriculum development is largely confined to each departmental domain.

When change is made, it is made on the adoption level, without adaptation to local needs. As shown in Table 15–1, curriculum development at this level is plugging in the package to the existing situation without attention to the resulting interactions. Teachers at this level tend to be left alone to struggle with innovations that are handed to them or mandated from above. Schools are turned inward, with the principal as the sole resource for classroom assistance.

Level II: Mediative

Teachers at Level II are aware of the need to integrate the curriculum and deal with emergent conditions. (Societal problems such as the energy crisis and children's questions about the things that interest and concern them are examples of emergent conditions.) Although teachers at this level may have an aggregate conception of curriculum, implementation does not go beyond the occasional correlation of certain subjects. The locus of curriculum remains segmental; theory remains divorced from practice; curriculum improvement remains at the level of refining existing practice.

Teachers at Level II or mediative level of curriculum development do not blindly plug in an innovation or curriculum package to the existing situation. The necessary adaptations, accommodations, and adjustments are made (see Table 15–1). Teachers are aware of and capitalize on a range of resources for curriculum improvement, including pupils, parents, and peers, and they utilize resources beyond the local school. Teachers are consumers of professional literature on approved practices and tap the resources of the university through inservice courses. The mediative level is a level of awareness and accommodation. Teachers are attracted to, and can articulate, new ideas but their efforts to improve the curriculum fall short of the necessary reconstruction for substantive problem solving.

Level III: Creative–Generative

As shown in Table 15–1, teachers at Level III take an aggregate approach to curriculum development. Ideally, the curriculum is examined in its entirety by the teachers and the whole school staff, and questions of priority and relationship are asked. Although individual teachers can and should be at the generative-creative level, a macrocurricular approach requires cooperative planning for vertical and horizontal articulation.

Granted that teachers as individuals usually cannot create new schoolwide curricula, an individual teacher can establish continuities and relationships in his or her own teaching and with other teachers. Teachers at Level III use generalizations and problems as centers of curriculum organization. They stress the broad concepts that specialized subjects share in common, and they use and develop courses of study that cross subject fields. These are aggregate treatments.

Teachers at Level III of curriculum development think about what they are doing and try to find more effective ways of working. They are able to diagnose their problems and formulate hypotheses for solutions. They experiment in their classrooms and communicate their insights to other teachers.

Teachers at this level are consumers of research and seek greater responsibility for curriculum decisions at the school and classroom levels. They exercise independent judgment in selecting curriculum materials and transform them for local needs. They regard themselves as professionals and, as such, are continually involved in seeking problem solutions for the improvement of practice. To this end, their antennae are turned outward to a wide range of resources. Problems are seen as opportunities for improvement, not as insurmountable.

Implications of the Levels

Although all teachers as professionals should be at Level III, most teachers are probably at Levels I and II. However, one should not blame the teacher. As noted, teachers have been and still continue in many schools to be treated as technicians. Equally distressing, many communities view teaching as managing on one's own with a closed door and minimal resources. The long hold of these old ideas is not yet broken. Relatively few school systems have ventured on the road to creating truly professional conditions for teachers. Most teachers are not provided with an office, secretarial help, or a place to meet except a classroom. "Teachers are supposed to go into their classroom, close the door and teach."[37] (Goodlad made these observations years ago and unfortunately they are still true.)

BEHIND CLOSED DOORS. The problem of resources has been discussed and will not be considered here, except to emphasize that superintendents must shift more central-office resources to local schools. The decentralization of responsibility runs throughout most proposals for site-managed schools. As noted, such proposals are doomed to failure without accompanying resources. Closed doors can make teachers feel lonely, but they can be protectors of academic freedom. As mentioned, teachers have a greater degree of freedom than they often are willing to acknowledge. Indeed, the public expects teachers to continually do a better job and be creative in their classrooms. What is important is that teachers actually capitalize on their autonomy to work more effectively and creatively behind the classroom door. In effect, teachers can transform their classroom isolation into conditions of professional autonomy, and, at the same time, can work collaboratively and systematically on the improvement of schoolwide curriculum and instruction.

A FAULTY CONCEPTION.   Although inadequate resources is one reason for the large numbers of teachers at Level I, there is yet another more fundamental reason. Many teachers have an inadequate conception of what it means to improve the curriculum. Their stereotypical notion of curriculum improvement is producing courses of study. They do not understand that curriculum improvement necessitates much more than this. The levels of curriculum development in Table 15–1 provide a conceptual framework of the role of the teacher. Curriculum improvement rests on the ability of the teacher to make better decisions in diagnosing and solving problems and in implementing approved practices.

LEVELS NOT A SEQUENCE.   Students using previous editions of this book have asked us why the levels of curriculum development are not a sequence. The question is not surprising because students are often confronted with models of teacher growth that are stage theories.[38] According to Kagan's model, for example, beginning teachers should focus on procedural routines, classroom management, and discipline. They should not be concerned with theoretical issues relating to curriculum improvement. These should be saved for later, "as novices' problem solving skills evolve."[39]

As Grossman points out, however, there is no evidence that beginning teachers are incapable of reflecting on issues related to curriculum and instruction. Indeed, they do so in good preservice teacher-education programs. Then there is the developmental question itself. How can teachers reach Level III if they are expected to maintain the status quo? Grossman's insights about stage theories of teacher growth are very helpful here.

> An additional problem with stage theories is that they imply that earlier stages lead naturally to later stages. But there is no evidence that having developed classroom routines that work teachers will necessarily begin to question those routines. In fact, there is evidence that suggests otherwise: As preservice teachers master the routines of teaching, many become satisfied with their teaching and less likely to question prevailing norms of teaching and learning.[40]

If teachers are to improve the curriculum they must be provided with opportunities to function at Level III from the very beginning. This is not a new idea, as pointed out earlier. John Dewey made the same observation in 1904. He observed that teachers' ways of working without concern for educational principles become hardened into habit.[41] From the beginning teachers should implement approved practices. In this sense, teaching is no different from the practice of other professions such as medicine, law, and engineering.

APPROVED PRACTICES

As shown in Table 15–1, a principal resource for teachers is the body of approved practices in education. Approved practices—those practices on which recognized authorities agree—are found in the literature of the field. Approved practices may be research based, or based on that which is of demonstrable practical success in the field. In effect, approved practices are those that are powerfully and consistently supported in the professional literature (based on the best available evidence from research and practice over time). As an example authorities in curriculum generally agree that because learning occurs through a wide variety of experiences, teachers must provide a wide variety of ways to learn. In many classrooms the teacher's repertoire of learning approaches is confined primarily to having pupils read the textbook and write and recite answers to questions about the textbook. Enriching and expanding this limited and limiting repertoire to include observation, participation, analysis, research, experimentation, problem solving, dramatization, and construction would be adopting an approved practice in education.

Similarly, learning theorists tend to agree that the learner will persevere through obstacles and difficulties to the extent that he or she believes that the objectives and activities are worthwhile. Learning is dependent in no small way on whether the learner sees meaning and value in what he or she is doing. Thus, making certain that pupils understand why they are performing a given task and the practical significance of what they will learn from the school over a given period of time is an approved practice.

The potential of approved practices for curriculum improvement cannot be overestimated. One of the most important points about approved practices is that they are not necessarily new ideas on the educational scene. When an approved practice, old or new, is adopted for the first time, it becomes in the truest sense an innovation.

The approved practices discussed here are merely illustrative. It is worth mentioning in this regard that teachers who want to follow the approved-practices approach to curriculum improvement can feel hopeful; there is a surprising number of practices in the literature on which recognized authorities agree.

The Application of Skills

One enormously important approved practice concerns the application of skills. Experts in curriculum emphasize that the learner must be given a variety of opportunities to apply his or her skills. There is no mastery without intelligent application. In some elementary classrooms, reading consists of repetitive practice of word recognition skills followed by blank filling in workbooks or on worksheets. There is no opportunity for children to apply their skills in reading for pleasure or for information. Oddly, it is most often the poor reader (particularly in inner-city schools) who is taught reading as drill and skill and who rarely, if ever, gets a chance to apply skills in realistic situations. It is this learner who is least likely to be provided at home with opportunities to read for enjoyment. If the goal is children who are readers rather than children who can read, we must allow children to read. This seems almost too obvious to mention, but in many instances children are learning the mechanics of reading without reading for meaning. Little wonder that some children do not see the objective of learning to read as being worthwhile.

The point is, of course, that being able to use the skill is the real objective. There is no reasonable expectation that learners will be able to use their skills unless they are provided with opportunities to apply them purposefully in school.

As Laura Zirbes—one of the pioneering women in the curriculum field—said: "When children ask, 'Why write?' it is not enough to say, 'You write to learn how to write.'"[42] Nor is it enough to explain the value of writing or of any skill as something learners will find useful. Although verbal explanations are important for helping children to make sense out of the work of the school, they must be accompanied by real experience. Writing and reading are processes for thinking and communicating thought, and must serve real purposes that are recognized by learners. The same applies to specific skills. Theorists have long pointed out also that a skill is learned when it is used. Moreover, the objective of having learners apply their skills is not to perfect the skill for its own sake. It cannot be overstated that the objective is to enable learners to use the skill for generative learning and to derive meaning and even to take pleasure in its use. Hence, reading and writing become processes for productive thinking.

The increasing press of achievement testing (particularly in reading) has caused a curriculum regression where the application of skills is concerned. Many teachers have been led (if not forced) to gear classroom events to the tests. In these classrooms, the functions of skills have become distorted; teachers and learners see skills as something to be mastered for testing purposes and not for learners' purposes.

Remember that Parker's Quincy methods were based on the idea that skills must be applied to be mastered. Learning skills by using them has been an approved practice in education since the infancy of the new education. From time to time, various influences have served to challenge this conception of skill development but it still remains a practice on which recognized authorities agree.

Idea-Oriented Teaching

Earlier it was mentioned that supervision of teachers tends to be error oriented rather than help oriented. Similarly, teachers tend to focus on pupils' errors rather than on ideas or concepts. One might say that teaching is error-skill oriented rather than constructive-idea oriented. Recognized authorities agree that teaching should be idea oriented rather than error oriented. As an illustration, teachers should read students' writing for ideas. What we are examining when we read students' papers is students' thinking; the act of writing is the act of thought. What usually happens, however, is that the emphasis of evaluation is on students' grammatical errors and not on the quality of their thinking. It is small wonder that children and youth so often get the impression that their ideas are of secondary importance to their errors (or of no importance at all). Moreover when evaluation is error oriented, students will restrict the style and substance of their writing to rudimentary safety. The opportunity to help students learn to examine their ideas critically is lost. (This does not mean that errors are to be ignored, but rather that they should be dealt with constructively and should not eclipse idea-oriented teaching.)

Inasmuch as the emphasis on errors does not improve and extend thinking processes, error-oriented teaching does not meet the demands of a democratic society. Furthermore, the negative emphasis of evaluation is likely to have negative results for motivation and perseverance. For these reasons, constructive-idea-oriented teaching has long been viewed by education theorists as an approved practice in education.

Unfortunately, there are those who maintain that "[a]n idea-oriented curriculum places more of a burden on teachers."[43] This is true only if one regards professional responsibility as a burden. Moreover, idea-oriented teaching is more of a pleasure for the teacher. It is the teacher's pleasure in the excitement of ideas that arouses the interest of students. This interest in turn spurs the teacher on. Error-oriented teaching, however, makes students apathetic and has a depressing effect on the teacher. It is then that teaching becomes a burden.

Ecological Interaction

The curriculum must be dealt with in its ecological interaction. In designing curricula, we must take into account the interaction of the elements instead of the elements in isolation. What needs to be considered in curriculum improvement is the relationship of the parts to the whole. This is an enormously important approved practice in education. Unfortunately, it is approved rather than practiced; education tends to be focused on the microcurriculum rather than the macrocurriculum.

Operationally, what this approved practice means is that in revising one element of the curriculum, we need to take into consideration the effects on other elements of the curriculum. There must be an ecological relationship among the elements. What, for example, is the relationship of a new social studies program to literature and other elements of the curriculum? What is the relation of a new physics program to the mathematics program? The ecological relationship of the curriculum reforms in physics to the mathematics program was virtually ignored by educators in the 1960s, and with calamitous results; many physics students did not have the mathematical skills and concepts that the new course in physics required.

Obviously, little or no interaction of the components of the curricular ecosystem is evidence of curriculum fragmentation. What is even worse, there may be conflict between or among elements as in the foregoing case of physics and mathematics. The point is that the ecological relationship of curricular elements must be subjected to continual reappraisal.

The interaction of the elements of the curriculum with one another and the macrocurriculum is, in a sense, analogous to the interaction of organisms with one another and with the environment. However, there is a crucial difference. Growth and change is a law of nature but not of the curriculum as it is treated in the traditional school. Growth (improvement) in the curriculum requires an organic interaction of elements in a context of a coherent design. As discussed in detail in Chapter 10, the design or structure of the curriculum determines its function. Consequently, curriculum integration requires a holistic design and structure as opposed to the traditionally segmental-compartmental subjects.

Involving Learners in Curriculum Planning

In a proposal for the middle school curriculum, Beane writes of a "new vision" that "begins with two kinds of questions and concerns: those that early adolescents have about themselves and their world and those that are widely shared by people in the larger world."[44] The practice of students and their teacher cooperatively formulating problem areas to be studied during a semester or school year is deeply rooted in progressivist philosophy. The progressives argued that the problems identified by adolescents are of universal significance and, further, that adolescents must be given opportunities to examine societal problems with a view toward their constructive solution while they are still in school.

The progressives also insisted that social attitudes and personal development are inseparable from cognitive development. They stressed that learning is most effective when students are interested in what they are doing and when they understand the significance of what they are supposed to be learning. These ideas formed the basis for one type of core curriculum (see Chapter 10).

Moreover, as Beane points out, students' concerns about the environment, interdependence, poverty, war, racism, and other world problems offer enormous opportunities for curriculum integration.

Elementary school teachers have long been vigorous proponents of pupil participation in planning. The fact that they have remained so despite conservative criticism attests to their conviction that the practice is well founded. Obviously, pupils can participate in goal setting (planning activities, projects, and schedules) even when curriculum content is prescribed and courses are required.

Access to the Curriculum

A tradition in American society is the seeking of equal opportunities to achieve. Nothing in the history of education is more impressive than the enthusiasm with which educators have taken up this challenge. Unfortunately, however, some curricular arrangements in the name of equalizing opportunity have had just the opposite effect. Schools serving disadvantaged or at-risk learners tend to make heavy use of Skinnerian approaches; children are taught mechanistically via a drill-skill-rote repertoire. On the other hand, children from more advantaged sectors of society often work on tasks and problems of genuine interest. As Brookover observes, "[t]he maximization of individual differences and the differentiation of educational programs are commonly advocated without regard to the effect of such education on the social structure or the opportunities for social mobility," and, further, "[t]hese programs and policies do not recognize that equality of opportunity is not facilitated by highly differentiated programs based upon the presumed differences between lower-class and middle-class children."[45]

CREATING OPPORTUNITIES.   Integrated public schools and heterogeneously grouped classrooms are crucial in creating opportunities of poor children and others at risk for school failure. As a general rule, children with special needs should not leave their classroom for remedial help. As teachers can well testify, pull-out programs fragment children's learning experiences. This, plus the fact that pull-out pro-grams are no more effective than providing such help in the classroom, is a good reason for eliminating such programs. An approved practice for helping special-needs children is described as follows in the words of two teachers: The remediation specialist "moves from class to class assisting individuals and working with small groups of students on skills within the classroom context."[46] Teachers should, of course, also offer extra help to a student having difficulties and enlist students to help one another so as to create a cooperative classroom learning environment.

THE IMPORTANCE OF A SUPPORTIVE ENVIRONMENT.   In recent years the media have portrayed some children as doomed to school failure (and life failure), no matter how schools might try to intervene. Included in this group are children with prenatal expo-sure to cocaine and other drugs. According to Stevens and Price, "[t]hese children have been described as a biological underclass, a lost generation. Yet many children exposed prenatally to cocaine who receive appropriate interventions can score as well on measures of global development as their nonexposed peers."[47] Like all children, youngsters exposed to potentially damaging conditions vary in abilities and needs.

Curricular implications go well beyond the immediate problems of affected and abused children. As Stevens and Price point out, generations to come must be pro-tected from the damaging effects of prenatal exposure to drugs (including alcohol). Given the steep increase in teenage pregnancy, in combination with drug use and heavy drinking, this challenge is enormous. According to Stevens and Price, these conditions "suggest that instruction on the effects of prenatal exposure to drugs and alcohol should be included in existing drug and alcohol curricula and in sex educa-tion and family life education."[48]

The curriculum is both a potential path to opportunity for all and a key to the solution of many of society's most critical problems.

CURRICULUM IMPROVEMENT AS INQUIRY

The findings of research are a source for curriculum improvement. The teacher may be involved in classroom research or as consumer of research. Awareness of a class-room problem and application of research findings for the solution is a form of inquiry. What is being discussed here is the involvement of teachers in the diagnosis of prob-lems and in classroom research to bring about curriculum improvement. Although the purpose of such involvement is to help teachers improve their own practices, research findings from classroom experimentation can contribute to theoretical knowledge about the curriculum. Taba was an unflagging exponent of this position.[49]

Teacher Research

Recently there has been much interest in teachers contributing to the body of knowledge on teaching. This is not a new idea. As indicated earlier in this text, the action-research movement of the 1950s was based on the idea that teachers should conduct their own investigations into their own problems. Like many pedagogical fads the action-research movement swept various practical considerations aside in its all-encompassing fervor. The democratic ideal of equality was applied to conducting research under the premise every member of the school faculty should be involved in classroom experimentation. Moreover, frequently the research was conducted without the help of consultants and statisticians. Understandably, action research in education became identified with research of poor quality.

BUILDING CURRICULUM KNOWLEDGE.   A number of factors have sparked and supported the interest in teacher research. The movement toward professional autonomy for teachers, the involvement of teachers in schoolwide decision making (including curriculum decisions), and the dissatisfaction with process-product research on teaching have tended to support a role for teachers in generating knowledge in the field of education.

Process-product research is designed to link specific teacher behaviors to student outcomes in terms of statistical measures. The term *process-product* derives from behaviorism and understandably raises a red flag to those who reject the concept of educational outcomes as products. Not all of those engaged in process-product research are behaviorists. Consequently, the use of the term *process-product* is unfortunate. The politically driven nationalizing influences of testing on the curriculum, coupled with the back-to-basics retrenchment of the curriculum during the late 1970s and 1980s, witnessed increased demands for statistical measures of the outcomes of schooling. However, in such research, only a fraction of the variance could be accounted for (e.g., the relation between curriculum resources and learning outcomes). Another problem has been the tendency in the research on teaching to focus on linking precise teacher behaviors with specific learning outcomes and neglecting the curriculum context. Clearly, then, there is the need to seek the best available evidence in relating a full spectrum of research methodologies to educational problems in an ecological perspective.

Many critics of process-product research associate it with the view of teachers as technicians.[50] They argue that process-product research considers teacher behaviors as causes and student learning as effects. According to Cochran-Smith and Lytle, process-product research "emphasizes the actions of teachers rather than their judgments," and "has a perspective that is 'outside in'; in other words, it has been conducted almost exclusively by university-based researchers who are outside of the day-to-day practices of schooling."[51]

As discussed, process-product research is one kind of research on teaching. Process-product investigators recognize that a number of factors besides teaching influence learning. The school's intellectual climate, student aptitudes, and parent's influence on students' motivation are examples. More important, as Gage and Needels point out:

> No particular way of applying results is inherent in process-product research. The application may be rigid, decree-like, authoritarian, mechanical, technological, unthinking, disrespectful of teacher dignity, and autonomy. Or it may be flexible, suggestive, democratic, creative, humanistic, deliberative, honoring the teachers' wisdom and uniqueness.[52]

What Gage and Needels are telling us is that there is no reason in the world why teachers as professional people should not draw from process-product research in the context of the wide body of research as they choose their methods and practices. Teachers need to be intelligent consumers of research. As pointed out, they need to evaluate the body of research in seeking out the best available evidence from the professional literature rather than relying on an isolated piece of research. In the field of medicine, for example, unless physicians are actually involved in a field of research, they must rely on the findings of university-based experts. Even so, segmental research studies are often unclear and even conflicting, requiring the professional practitioner to seek out the best available evidence from the wider body of research and from the professional literature. In effect, the professional practitioner must be able to interpret and implement the approved practices stemming from the best available research evidence.

Like physicians, teachers can seek guidance from the findings of studies using a variety of appropriate research designs. This does not, however, detract from the potential value of teacher research. Regarding its value, Cochran-Smith and Lytle rightly point out that teachers become theorists as they test their assumptions and make connections with practice.[53] Teacher research can improve teaching. For this to happen teachers or someone who assists them must understand research design. According to Cochran-Smith and Lytle, "many teachers have sophisticated and sensitive observation skills grounded in the context of actual classroom experience."[54] This is undoubtedly so but it is not the same as being able to design and conduct a good study. In this connection, some researchers suggest that research methods be included in teacher-education programs. Actually knowing how to engage in systematic inquiry has advantages for teachers besides doing their own research. It can help them be knowledgeable consumers of research. And, as Floden and Klinzing point out, it "can also help them judge how they should appropriately adapt general teaching principles to a specific teaching context."[55]

DEVELOPMENTAL RESEARCH.   The individual teacher may seek to solve a problem or to improve practice by searching the research literature and even by conducting an individual inquiry, such as surveying pupil attitudes toward reading materials. The school faculty or the school system may undertake research on a wider scale, such as in pilot testing a new curriculum project. In each of these instances, the function of the research is curriculum development in a contextual setting, in contrast to other kinds of educational research, which may be removed from action or application. Although it may be argued that the purpose of theoretical educational research is the improvement of classroom and school practices, prescriptive theories and models derived from educational research need to be tested in the practical setting. Educational research has, on the whole, failed to concern itself with teachers' classroom concerns. In studying the literature of educational research, it quickly becomes clear that researchers have not been concerned with problems relating to curriculum reconstruction. Where research on curriculum design is concerned, the literature is as dry as the Sahara. Since the Eight-Year Study and the research on activity schools—stemming back to the 1930s—there have been virtually no landmark studies on curriculum reconstruction.

Certainly, as some university researchers pointed out in the 1970s, there is a need to redirect education research so that the problems identified by practitioners are investigated.[56] Conditions have changed; teachers are no longer waiting for Godot and are beginning to inquire into their own problems. Even should such a redirection occur, teachers would still need to be involved in putting theoretical principles to the test and in finding solutions to their own practical problems. University researchers are beginning to realize that effective teachers are engaged in practical inquiry, and that such inquiry is indeed powerful in effecting improved classroom practice and school improvement, as compared with university-based research that is removed from the practical world of the school.[57]

In using scientific methods to make better decisions, teachers are involved in developmental research. It cannot be overstated that teachers will learn more about their practical difficulties by using scientific methods than by taking a visceral approach. Moreover, it is principally through the development of a body of theoretical knowledge that a craft becomes a profession. As professionals, teachers must be involved in the building of this knowledge. (Think of what might have happened, for example, if pilot studies involving teachers as researchers had been undertaken in evaluating the new math back in the 1960s.)

SUPPORTING TEACHER RESEARCH.   Having established the need for teacher research our attention turns to how teachers can be supported in their research efforts. Research cannot simply be added to teachers' responsibilities. The importance of this problem goes without saying. Some school districts have created new positions that include both teaching and research responsibilities, such as teacher-consultants, lead teachers, and peer supervisors. (The problems created in differentiating teachers' roles were discussed earlier.) Some other proposals to make it more possible for teachers to conduct systematic inquiry are financial support for research projects, load reduction, released time, research teams, and summer workshops. In the long run, one of the most important factors of all is whether school systems view teacher research as valuable. Cochran-Smith and Lytle put it this way: "This new approach will come about if schools and school systems realize that there is a direct connection between supporting the systematic inquiries of teacher-researchers and improving the quality of teaching and learning."[58]

CURRICULUM COMMITTEES

The final section of this chapter is concerned with teacher involvement in local curriculum development projects. By local it is meant the school district level. However, many of the ideas that follow are applicable to curriculum development in individual schools.

School District Support

The strength of the tradition that teachers should be involved in curriculum development is clearly evident in the recent school restructuring movement. Teachers' reviewing and rebuilding the curriculum are key features of the movement. Teacher participation represents one of the oldest principles in curriculum theory. The way it began in Denver and the model developed by the Rugg committee have been revealed in earlier sections of this book.

Of great interest in this connection is a recent national survey of curriculum development practices in American public school systems.[59] When asked whether they favored a national, state, or local curriculum, 84 percent selected local. All of the ninety-one districts responding to the survey favored curriculum development via committee, and the view that teachers should be members of the committee was nearly universal. More important, teachers were universally involved. The extent of that involvement, however, was not revealed by the survey. Clearly, it can vary from responding to a needs assessment to coordinating a curriculum development effort. An overwhelming majority of the districts reported that they had a master plan for curriculum development. Science, mathematics, language arts, and social studies were the most frequently revised curriculums. The larger the district, the more often it revised its science curriculum.

How Schools Develop Curriculum

When asked about the curriculum development process, districts responding to the previously mentioned national survey most frequently specified these activities: assessing needs by means of a survey; establishing curriculum committees; deciding what should be learned in a given subject area, over different grade levels (scope and sequence); curriculum evaluation; and obtaining approval of the curriculum from the administration.

FAILURE TO DRAW ON RESEARCH AND EXPERIENCE. "It is troubling but not surprising that few of the districts reported using prior empirical research to shape the curriculum being developed," commented Martin, Saif, and Thiel, who conducted the study.[60] Also very troubling was that few districts bothered to carry out a pilot test of the curriculum. The approach to curriculum improvement in recent years reflects the orientation that it is not necessary (or even advisable) to assess the effectiveness of a new curriculum. Such projects are not helping in contributing to the development of a science of education. Districts do not know whether what they have done is actually an improvement. In this connection, a comment by an educator decades ago seems instructive: "Perhaps the true mark of an advanced and forward-looking school is not the length of its list of innovations in progress, but rather the degree to which it continues to participate in the experimental testing of new ideas and postpone wholesale adoption until its own or other evidence becomes available."[61]

THE PROBLEM OF CONTINUITY. Not only do districts fail to draw on previous research but they also ignore their own experience; that is, they do not look at the work of previous committees. The trouble is that curriculum problems are dealt with segmentally and sporadically. A national report announces that students are not doing well in a certain curriculum area. A district-level committee is appointed to study the curriculum problem. (The assumption is that the district suffers from that problem.) In her classic book on changing the curriculum, Alice Miel describes what happens next.

> The committee studies, reports, and is dissolved. Action recommended by the committee may be taken and the report may be filed. But there is no one responsible for follow-up; no group is charged with responsibility to make continuous study in the area in which the problem arose. Two or more years later, the problem recurs. A new committee studies it, usually without knowledge of the work of the previous committee.[62]

What a "wasteful procedure," as Miel concludes.[63] Human energy and other resources are surely squandered. But the damaging result goes beyond wasted resources. There is a failure to build on past experience with an increasing effectiveness. Miel proposes the creation of standing committees in given curriculum areas to provide for continuous planning. Interestingly, she favors "the individual school as the primary agency in curriculum development." However, she is quick to point out that there is a need for sharing of experience among schools and suggests that a central curriculum council be established with representatives from each school as well as central staff. In the case of large school systems, the system could be "divided into districts of a reasonable size."[64] (This subdividing might not be necessary because many big school systems have undergone administrative decentralization in the years since Miel's book was published.)

The point of importance is that whether we are speaking about curriculum-improvement efforts at the district or school level, there must be provision for continuity. Without such continuity, there can be no knowledge base on which to build. Records must be kept of these efforts and be readily accessible, so that committee members may refer to them in discussion of current problems.

Improving the Committee Process

Curriculum pioneers such as Jesse Newlon and Harold Rugg proposed models of teacher participation in curriculum improvement in their time. Their work was continued by Alice Miel, Gordon Mackenzie, Stephen Corey, Hollis Caswell, Hilda Taba, and a host of others. Their goals were remarkably similar. They all sought a process that was *inclusive* (administrators, students, and community members as well as teachers), *professional* (based on the best available knowledge), and *continuous* (building on previous work).

Over the years we have seen proposals that are *exclusive* (*either* teachers *or* administrators), *technological* (decisions made at higher levels with teachers viewed as deliverers of instruction), *segmental* (the curriculum being treated as isolated subjects), and *crisis-oriented* (a new committee for each problem or crisis). These have invariably failed; we keep ignoring what those before us learned in their work many years ago. No matter how well supported externally, curriculum-improvement efforts fail when teachers and principals are left out of the process. We only have to recall the national curriculum-reform projects of the Cold War and space race, or the externally imposed minimum-competency testing and back to basics retrenchment from the late 1960s to the 1980s, and finally, the test-driven curriculum of the 1990s.

CURRICULUM WRITING VERSUS CURRICULUM DEVELOPMENT.   Miel viewed curriculum writing as part of a problem-solving process, which, in our view, is just what it is. It is not necessary to start from scratch in undertaking the study of a curriculum problem. One does not, for example, need an entirely new set of objectives to improve learning experiences for children.[65] Again, the professional staff seeks continually to build on a sound knowledge base for practical inquiry and problem solving.

All too often the mere writing of curriculum is taken for curriculum development. An example is the ten-step curriculum development process suggested by Martin, Saif, and Thiel. The process or model, as they call it, is intended, rightly, to maximize teacher involvement. The first step of the process is as follows: "A teacher committee meets to write a rationale and objectives for the curriculum; members then solicit feedback from peer teachers in their schools."[66] The process is one of writing, revision, and implementation. There is no mention of problem diagnosis, the vital first step in curriculum development, in which teachers should be involved. As every teacher knows, there is no shortage of problems that can serve as the springboard for improving the effectiveness of curriculum. In absence of a genuine problem, curriculum development degenerates into a meaningless technological exercise.

Seen as a problem-solving process, curriculum development will engage teachers (and the entire professional staff) in these questions:

1. What are the most significant curriculum problems in my school and why are these most significant?
2. What needs to be done to solve these problems?
3. How can I contribute to the ways and means of solving these problems?

PERSPECTIVE

Better late than never. This could be the theme of today's educators as they embrace the laboratory ideal in preservice teacher education and participatory decision making by school faculties. Neither idea is new; both are absolutely essential for curriculum improvement. According to Dewey, the focus of student teaching should be on developing thoughtful and alert teachers who make decisions based on educational principles, rather than on turning out teachers who are as proficient as possible in immediate, practical skill. When student teachers and beginning teachers make explicit the reasons (based on the best available evidence) for their various pedagogical decisions, they are establishing habits of referring to educational principles. Whether one is a teacher or a physician, one must make decisions based on the principles in one's field from the start. Early habits become the behaviors of a professional lifetime. It still remains true that a good cooperating teacher can help novices engage in reflective self-criticism. However, student teachers should not be expected to provide new ideas for their cooperating teacher. Student teachers should have opportunities to express their ideas for improving the educational program in collaborative problem-solving situations.

One of the most promising changing conditions of teaching is the emphasis on collaborative problem solving at the school site. There is evidence that successful and unsuccessful schools can be distinguished based on the frequency of teachers' interactions for the purpose of solving curriculum problems. Teachers' shared work is encouraged in successful schools and faculty meetings are devoted to discussions of research and pedagogical practice. Teachers meet regularly in teams to develop plans and materials.

Yet in some schools that claim to have adopted plans to involve teachers in schoolwide decision making the old patterns prevail: administrators make policy and teachers "deliver" instruction. All too commonly, participants are provided insufficient time, material resources, and expertise (including the help of consultants on an ongoing basis). Some schools have made real progress in dealing collaboratively with problems. In successful schools, the right to participate in curriculum work is not limited to supervisors and administrators; being an initiator or a participant should not depend on formal position or status.

Teachers and administrators tend to function predominantly at one of three levels of curriculum development. At Level I (imitative-maintenance), the teacher or administrator is a routinist and the objective is maintenance—keeping the ship afloat. Change (when it occurs) is a matter of plugging in the curriculum package to the existing situation. The curriculum is treated as segments and fragments. Teachers at Level II (mediative) are aware that teaching should be more than routine management and that there is a macrocurriculum, but improvement tends to be a matter of refining existing practice. Innovations are adapted rather than merely adopted. The teacher at Level III (generative-creative) conceives of the curriculum as an articulated whole and acts on this conception. Improvement of practice is actively sought by drawing on resources beyond the local school and school system. Imagination, artistry, awareness, and the testing of ideas are some characteristics of the generative-creative level. All teachers should be at this level, but the levels of curriculum development are not a sequence—that is, one does not become creative by first being imitative.

The findings of research are a source for curriculum improvement. The teacher may be involved in classroom research as well as being an intelligent consumer of research. In practical inquiry, the teacher is aware of a classroom problem, draws from the research literature, or even conducts an investigation to solve the problem. Thoughtful teachers are continually engaged in the diagnosis of problems and in classroom inquiry to bring about curriculum improvement. Important theoretical ideas grow out of and feed into practical problem situations. It behooves university researchers to recognize this and to connect their work to curriculum improvement.

Teachers should draw from research as they choose their methods and practices. Knowing how to engage in systematic inquiry can help teachers be knowledgeable consumers of research. By undertaking practical inquiry, teachers can improve individual practice. Some school systems are supporting teachers' research efforts through grants, load reduction, released time, and the like.

Teachers who want to improve the curriculum will find a wide range of approved practices in the education literature; there is a surprising number of practices on which recognized authorities agree. Providing learners with opportunity to apply skills in a variety of meaningful situations is one approved practice. Another is involving learners in curriculum planning; for example, adolescents and their teacher cooperatively formulate societal problem areas to be studied during a semester.

Many teachers erroneously view curriculum development as synonymous with writing courses of study. The study of a curriculum problem may or may not eventuate in a new course. However, curriculum development is much more than this. Curriculum development must be regarded as a problem-solving process in which all subject matters are seen and treated in vital interdependence. One cannot compensate for a poor curriculum in science by having a strong curriculum in mathematics, or for a poor curriculum in literature by having a strong curriculum in social studies. School systems and individual schools must provide for continuity in curriculum-improvement efforts. Records must be kept and be readily accessible so that they may be drawn on in inquiry into current problems. Those who went before us taught us these things: The process of curriculum improvement must be inclusive (administrators, teachers, students, community members), professional (based on the best available knowledge), and continuous (building on previous work). We have not yet learned them well.

PROBLEMS FOR STUDY AND DISCUSSION

1. Some educators contend that preservice teachers should be concerned only with establishing the routines of teaching; that connecting educational principles to one's practice can be left for later professional development. [Dona M. Kagan, "Professional Growth among Preservice and Beginning Teachers," *Review of Educational Research,* 62 (Summer 1992), pp. 129–169.] What is your assessment of this position?

2. According to Dewey, student teachers should connect their practices with theoretical principles in education. [John Dewey, "The Relation of Theory to Practice in Education," Chapter 1 in *The Relation of Theory to Practice in the Education of Teachers,* Third Yearbook of the National Society for the Scientific Study of Education, Part I (Bloomington, IL: Public School Publishing, 1904), pp. 11, 27–28.] How does Dewey's conception of professional growth contrast with that of Kagan's model cited in problem 1? What are the implications of these contrasting views for the teacher's curriculum-improvement role?

3. Do you believe that research methods should be included in programs of preservice teacher education? Justify your answer.

4. In this chapter it was pointed out that teachers must have the resources they need if they are to function at the generative-creative level of curriculum development. Survey the teachers in a local school to ascertain what resources they have for curriculum development. Are their resources adequate? Explain. Use the teachers' responses and Table 15–1 in framing your answer.

5. In your opinion, what is the role of the cooperating teacher in helping student teachers operate at the generative-creative level?

6. What is the responsibility of teachers in keeping the elements of the curriculum in ecological relation? Is this a more difficult problem in the secondary school than in the elementary school? Explain.

7. In connection with problem 6, do you believe that the recent emphasis on collaborative problem solving at the school site is a changing condition of teaching with promise for building curriculum elements in ecological relation? Why?

8. In a discussion of ways to end the endless cycle of at-risk children whose mothers use drugs and alcohol during pregnancy, Lisbeth Schorr notes that poor, poorly educated, and extremely young women—those who most need prenatal care—are the least likely to get it. They point out that

> the obstetrical community has made little progress in helping women to reduce their use of drugs and alcohol during pregnancy, although techniques for bringing about significant reductions in substance abuse by

pregnant women have been successfully demonstrated. With some notable exceptions, physicians are reluctant to commit the time it takes even to try to alter behavior—especially among the poorly educated patients. [Lisbeth B. Schorr and Daniel Schorr, *Within Our Reach: Breaking the Cycle of Disadvantage* (New York: Doubleday, 1989), p. 70.]

In what ways can the school curriculum serve as an intervention to reduce risks to children's healthy development?

9. Examine the curriculum development efforts of a school district or school. What strategies are used in curriculum development? To what extent is curriculum development being treated merely as the writing of courses of study? What changes would you make to improve the process? (Frame your responses with reference to the levels of curriculum development in Table 15–1.) At which level of curriculum development is the district or school functioning? Explain.

NOTES

1. Richard J. Shavelson, "Review of Research on Teachers' Pedagogical Judgments, Plans, and Decisions," *The Elementary School Journal,* 83 (March 1983), p. 408; see also John Solas, "Investigating Teacher and Student Thinking," *Review of Educational Research,* 62 (Summer 1992), p. 20.

2. Linda Darling-Hammond and Jon Snyder, "Reframing Accountability: Creating Learner-Centered Schools," Chapter 2 in *The Changing Contexts of Teaching,* Ninety-first Yearbook of the National Society for the Study of Education, Part I (Chicago: University of Chicago Press, 1992), p. 19.

3. Ibid., p. 16.

4. John Dewey, "The Relation of Theory to Practice in Education," Chapter 1 in *The Relation of Theory to Practice in the Education of Teachers,* Third Yearbook of the National Society for the Scientific Study of Education, Part I (Bloomington, IL: Public School Publishing, 1904), pp. 11, 27–28

5. Ibid., p. 15.

6. Ibid., pp. 12–13.

7. Ibid., p. 14.

8. Ibid., p. 15.

9. Holmes Group, *Tomorrow's Schools: Principles for the Design of Professional Development Schools* (East Lansing, MI: Author, 1990).

10. Pamela L. Grossman, "Teaching to Learn," Chapter 10 in *The Changing Contexts of Teaching,* Ninety-first Yearbook of the National Society for the Study of Education, op. cit., p. 183.

11. Ibid., pp. 179, 182.

12. Ibid., p. 185.

13. Ibid., p. 186.

14. Ibid., p. 187.

15. Bruce Joyce and Renee Clift, "The Phoenix Agenda: Essential Reform in Teacher Education," *Educational Researcher,* 13 (April 1984), p. 6.

16. Ralph W. Tyler, "Accountability and Teacher Performance: Self-directed and External-directed Professional Improvement," in Louis Rubin (ed.),

The In-Service Education of Teachers (Boston: Allyn and Bacon, 1978), p. 135.

17. Ibid.

18. Nancy Winitsky, Trish Stoddart, and Patti O'Keefe, "Great Expectations: Emergent Professional Development Schools," *Journal of Teacher Education,* 43 (January–February 1992), p. 7.

19. Arthur W. Foshay, "Professional Education: The Discipline of the Act," *Theory Into Practice,* 6 (December 1967), p. 224.

20. Carnegie Forum on Education and the Economy, *A Nation Prepared: Teachers for the 21st Century* (New York: Author, 1986).

21. Holmes Group, *Tomorrow's Teachers* (East Lansing, MI: Author, 1986), p. 53.

22. Ann Lieberman, "Introduction: The Changing Context of Education," Chapter 1 in *The Changing Context of Teaching,* op. cit., p. 1.

23. Seymour R. Sarason, *The Culture of the School and the Problem of Change* (Boston: Allyn and Bacon, 1971), p. 63.

24. Harold Hodgkinson, "Reform Versus Reality," *Phi Delta Kappan,* 73 (September 1991), p. 12–13.

25. Ibid., p. 12.

26. Ibid., p. 11; see also Charles C. Carson, Robert M. Huelskamp, and Thomas D. Woodall, "Perspectives on Education in America," *Journal of Educational Research,* 86 (May/June 1993), pp. 299–310.

27. Deborah Meier, *Becoming a Teacher,* Sixteenth Charles DeGarmo Lecture of the Society of Professors of Education (Sacramento, CA: Caddo Gap Press, 1991), p. 11.

28. Judith Warren Little, "Norms of Collegiality and Experimentation: Workplace Conditions of School Success," *American Educational Research Journal,* 19 (Fall 1982), pp. 325–340.

29. Ibid, p. 333.

30. John I. Goodlad, "Educational Leadership: Toward the Third Era," *Educational Leadership,* 35 (January 1978), p. 332.

31. Daniel U. Levine and Eugene E. Eubanks, "Site-Based Management: Engine for Reform or Pipedream?" Chapter 3 in John J. Lane and Edgar G. Epps (eds.), *Restructuring the Schools: Problems and Prospects* (Berkeley, CA: McCutchan, 1992), pp. 62–63.

32. Betty Malen and Rodney T. Ogawa, "Site-Based Management: Disconcerting Policy Issues, Critical Policy Choices," Chapter 9 in *Restructuring the Schools: Problems and Prospects,* op. cit., p. 201.

33. Ibid., pp. 201–202.

34. Philip W. Jackson, "Old Dogs and New Tricks: Observations on the Continuing Education of Teachers," Chapter 2 in Louis J. Rubin (ed.), *Improving In-Service Education: Proposals and Procedures for Change* (Boston: Allyn and Bacon, 1971), p. 29.

35. Little, op. cit., p. 337.

36. Carnegie Forum on Education and the Economy, op. cit., p. 117.

37. John I. Goodlad, *The Dynamics of Educational Change: Toward Responsive Schools* (New York: McGraw-Hill, 1975), p. 51.

38. See, for example, Carl D. Glickman, *Developmental Supervision* (Alexandria, VA: Association for Supervision and Curriculum Development, 1981). See also Dona M. Kagan, "Professional Growth Among Preservice and Beginning Teachers," *Review of Educational Research,* 62 (Summer 1992), pp. 129–169.

39. Kagan, op. cit., p. 155.

40. Pamela L. Grossman, "Why Models Matter: An Alternate View on Professional Growth in Teaching," *Review of Educational Research,* 62 (Summer 1992), p. 174.

41. Dewey, op. cit.

42. Laura Zirbes, *Spurs to Creative Teaching* (New York: Putnam, 1959), p. 140.

43. Richard S. Prawat, "Teachers' Beliefs about Teaching and Learning: A Constructivist Perspective," *American Journal of Education,* 100 (May 1992), p. 388.

44. James Beane, "The Middle School: The Natural Home of Integrated Curriculum," *Educational Leadership,* 49 (October 1991), p. 11.

45. Wilbur B. Brookover, Richard J. Gigliatti, Ronald D. Henderson, Bradley E. Niles, and Jeffrey Schneider, "Quality of Educational Attainment, Standardized Testing, Assessment, and Accountability," Chapter 8 in *Uses of the Sociology of Education,* Seventy-third Yearbook, Part II, National Society for the Study of Education (Chicago: University of Chicago Press, 1974), p. 162.

46. Katherine Boles and Vivian Troen, "How Teachers Make Restructuring Happen," *Educational Leadership,* 49 (February 1992), p. 54.

47. Linda J. Stevens and Marianne Price, "Meeting the Challenge of Educating Children at Risk," *Phi Delta Kappan,* 74 (September 1992), p. 19.
48. Ibid., p. 20.
49. Hilda Taba, *Curriculum Development: Theory and Practice* (New York: Harcourt, 1962), p. 345.
50. See, for example, Karen K. Zumwalt, "Are We Improving or Undermining Teaching?" Chapter 7 in *Critical Issues in Curriculum,* Eighty-seventh Yearbook of the National Society for the Study of Education, Part I (Chicago: University of Chicago Press, 1988), pp. 148–174.
51. Marilyn Cochran-Smith and Susan L. Lytle, "Research on Teaching and Teacher Research: The Issues That Divide," *Educational Researcher,* 19 (March 1990), pp. 2–3.
52. N. L. Gage and Margaret C. Needels, "Process-Product Research on Teaching: A Review of Criticisms," *The Elementary School Journal,* 89, 3 (1989), p. 293.
53. Cochran-Smith and Lytle, op. cit., p. 8.
54. Ibid., p. 7.
55. Robert E. Floden and Hans Gerhard Klinzing, "What Can Research on Teacher Thinking Contribute to Teacher Preparation? A Second Opinion," *Educational Researcher,* 19 (June–July 1990), p. 18.
56. Harold B. Dunkel, D. B. Gowin, and Lawrence G. Thomas, "Introduction," *Philosophical Redirection of Education Research,* Seventy-first Yearbook of the National Society for the Study of Education, Part I (Chicago: University of Chicago Press, 1972), p. 3.
57. Virginia Richardson, "Conducting Research on Practice," *Educational Researcher,* 23 (June–July 1994), pp. 5–10.
58. Cochran-Smith and Lytle, op. cit., p. 9.
59. David S. Martin, Philip S. Saif, and Linda Thiel, "Curriculum Development: Who Is Involved and How?" *Educational Leadership,* 44 (December 1986/January 1987), p. 44–48.
60. Ibid., p. 44.
61. Miriam L. Goldberg, "Evaluation of Innovations," Chapter 3 in Marcella R. Lawler (ed.), *Strategies for Planned Innovation* (New York: Teachers College, 1970), pp. 58–59.
62. Alice Miel, *Changing the Curriculum: A Social Process* (New York: Appleton-Century-Crofts, 1946), p. 76.
63. Ibid., p. 77.
64. Ibid., pp. 79–81.
65. Ralph W. Tyler, *Basic Principles of Curriculum and Instruction* (Chicago: University of Chicago Press, 1949), p. 128.
66. Martin, Saif, and Thiel, op. cit., p. 41.

SELECTED REFERENCES

Carnegie Forum on Education and the Economy. *A Nation Prepared: Teachers for the 21st Century.* New York: Carnegie Forum on Education and the Economy, 1986.

Cochran-Smith, Marilyn, and Lytle, Susan L. *Inside/Outside: Teachers, Research, and Knowledge.* New York: Teachers College Press, 1992.

Corey, Stephen. *Action Research to Improve School Practice.* New York: Teachers College Press, 1953.

Dewey, John. *How We Think,* rev. ed. Lexington, MA: D.C. Heath, 1933.

Dewey, John. "The Relation of Theory to Practice in Education," Chapter 1 in *The Relation of Theory to Practice in the Education of Teachers,* Third Yearbook of the National Society for the Scientific Study of Education, Part I (Bloomington, IL: Public School Publishing, 1904), pp. 9–30.

Gage, N. L. *The Scientific Basis of the Art of Teaching.* New York: Teachers College Press, 1978.

Grossman, Pamela L. *The Making of a Teacher: Teacher Knowledge and Teacher Education.* New York: Teachers College Press, 1990.

Houston, W. Robert (ed.). *Handbook of Research on Teacher Education.* New York: Macmillan, 1990.

Jackson, Philip W. (ed.). *Handbook of Research on Curriculum.* New York: Macmillan, 1992.

Lane, John J., and Epps, Edgar G. (eds.). *Restructuring the Schools: Problems and Prospects.* Berkeley, CA: McCutchan, 1992.

Martinello, Marian L., and Cook, Gillian E. *Interdisciplinary Inquiry in Teaching and Learning.* New York: Merrill, 1994.

Miel, Alice. *Changing the Curriculum: A Social Process.* New York: Appleton-Century-Crofts, 1946.

National Society for the Study of Education. *The Changing Contexts of Teaching,* Ninety-first Yearbook, Part I. Chicago: University of Chicago Press, 1992.

National Society for the Study of Education. *Critical Issues in Curriculum,* Eighty-seventh Yearbook, Part I. Chicago: University of Chicago Press, 1988.

National Society for the Study of Education. *Teacher Research and Educational Reform,* Ninety-third Yearbook, Part I. Chicago: University of Chicago Press, 1994.

Sarason, Seymour B. *The Culture of the School and the Problem of Change,* 2nd ed. Boston: Allyn and Bacon, 1982.

Schaefer, Robert J. *The School as a Center of Inquiry.* New York: Harper and Row, 1967.

Schorr, Lisbeth B. *Within Our Reach: Breaking the Cycle of Disadvantage.* New York: Doubleday, 1989.

Taba, Hilda. *Curriculum Development: Theory and Practice.* New York: Harcourt, Brace, Jovanovich, 1962.

Tanner, Daniel, and Tanner, Laurel N. *Supervision in Education: Problems and Practices.* New York: Macmillan, 1987.

Tyler, Ralph W. *Basic Principles of Curriculum and Instruction.* Chicago: University of Chicago Press, 1949.

Wittrock, Merlin C. (ed.). *Handbook of Research on Teaching,* 3rd ed. New York: Macmillan, 1986.

CHAPTER 16

CURRICULUM IMPROVEMENT— ROLE OF THE SUPERVISOR AND ADMINISTRATOR

In a sense, the supervisor's role is the same as it always has been—to help teachers improve learning opportunities for children and youth. Recent years have seen teachers moving toward legitimate professional status. Many teachers have become the equals of their supervisors where curriculum knowledge is concerned. In some respects teachers may be even more knowledgeable with regard to the curriculum. District administrators have charged school faculties with the task of developing school-improvement plans embodying the concept of shared decision making. More teachers are now grappling with curricular issues that were formerly dealt with (and disposed of) by supervisors alone. To be sure, one finds many examples of problems being addressed from the top down with little opportunity for expertise at lower levels. However, the attitude in an increasing number of school districts is that the school faculty possesses the professional expertise and responsibility for curriculum development. As pointed out in the Chapter 15, beginning teachers are learning to make more thoughtful curriculum decisions.

It has been virtually inevitable that such conditions would influence the concept of curriculum leadership. First, there is the effect of teachers' professional status on the traditional style of supervision. Many supervisors came of age professionally at a time when the best communication pattern was thought to be mainly downward. Problems were approached autocratically; it was considered good practice to get teachers to buy into an administratively determined solution. Because teachers as professionals are deemed able to diagnose and solve their problems, this supervisory style is no longer acceptable. The conception that curriculum improvement is a problem-solving process involving the entire professional staff of the school has gained increasing recognition in recent times, although it has long been in the curriculum literature. What is important is that supervisors understand that teachers must participate in decision making on matters of curriculum and teaching, and that supervisors and principals use the collaborative style.

In addition to working collaboratively with groups of teachers, supervisors must help individual teachers apply the best that is known to improve their teaching. This is the supervisor's responsibility to the public. Although the curriculum problems of an individual are in many cases the problems of the entire school faculty (and even the entire district), the multidimensional character of professional supervision cannot be overemphasized.

A second influence on the supervisor's role has been exerted through the strong interest in school restructuring. Closely associated, both shared decision making and school restructuring have one defensible purpose—to make better curriculum decisions. Where shared decision making is a reality, the supervisor's role in relation to the instructional program has changed. As described in a site-managed high school, the principal "provides information or finds sources of information, serves as a clearinghouse so [teacher] committees are not working at cross purposes to each other or system-wide goals," and further, "encourages staff development and experimentation."[1] The principal conveys the perception among the faculty that research can be relevant to their own concerns. Studying research findings can also contribute to the definition of local problems. As Poplin points out, "through initiating research and study groups, we [supervisors] can also promote the critical dialogue around important topics that leads to collective action." Poplin goes on to point out that supervisors have, on the whole, shown little concern for teachers' intellectual interests and many teachers feel intellectually starved.[2] Dealing with ideas about curriculum can be a source of intellectual pleasure and growth and, more importantly, perhaps, can lead to teaching that is idea-oriented.

Much of the literature on supervision today is concerned with the local school administrator. However, as discussed in Chapter 14, curriculum directives or policy decisions commonly stem from the central-office level. Many larger school systems have established means for schools to share effective curriculum programs and practices, such as in the Philadelphia public schools through the district's Office of Curriculum and Instructional Support.[3] As in most school districts, although the central office is responsible for curriculum policy decisions, there is a vast arena for interpreting and applying such policy right down to each and every classroom teacher. The term *supervisor* as used in this text means *curriculum leader.* Persons in positions of curriculum leadership are known by a number of titles: curriculum supervisor, instructional supervisor, curriculum coordinator, curriculum director, curriculum consultant, assistant superintendent for instruction, director of elementary education, director of secondary education, coordinator of language minority programs, principal, department chairperson, lead teacher, helping teacher, and resource teacher. All are concerned with improving the curriculum and promoting the professional development of teachers. As noted, these objectives are inextricably interwoven.

Last but not least, no matter how large the school system, the main responsibility of the superintendent of schools is curriculum improvement. This should be the focus of all of his or her administrative tasks.

LEADERSHIP RESPONSIBILITIES

The levels of curriculum development provide a perspective for viewing supervisory responsibilities and activities; individual teachers and school staffs need resources and expertise (the help of consultants) if they are to function at the mediative and generative-creative levels (see Table 15–1). The objective of supervision is to help teachers function at the top level of professionalism—the generative-creative level.

Working with Teachers as Professionals

Hard-won professional prerogatives now reflect the reality that the teacher is the prime agent of curriculum improvement. The new perspective of the teacher's role requires new ways of working with supervisors. The traditional top-down approach to decision making has given way in many forward-looking schools to shared decision making. The principal's concern is to involve teachers in making curriculum decisions.

SCHOOL IMPROVEMENT PLANS.   A number of school systems have charged local school faculties with the task of developing school-improvement plans. Many schools have put forth great effort to build a consensus needed to determine school goals. With all their effort, some schools have had their improvement plans rejected by district administrators because the plans did not include goals identified by chief school administrators—such as raising test scores.

It is clear that in general some school systems do not understand the need to provide local schools with the scope and agency to deal with school-level concerns and make curriculum decisions. Such an understanding is absolutely necessary for curriculum improvement, not to mention teacher morale.

It should be borne in mind that in many school systems, central administrators have been sincere in their charge to school faculties to develop their own improvement plans. As Leithwood points out, in this way "teachers are helped to find greater meaning in their work" and, further, "learn how to make the most of their collective capacities in solving school problems."[4] Moreover, as we have pointed out elsewhere, student productivity is enhanced in such a setting.[5] Leithwood also makes this point; indeed, since Rutter's landmark study in the late 1970s, the research literature has continued to confirm Rutter's conclusion that the general atmosphere, culture, or ethos in which pupils, teachers, and administrators work can have a powerfully positive influence on pupil outcomes.[6] How to help school staff members develop collaborative decision-making processes is considered later in the chapter.

PROTECTING TEACHERS.   "Our new role also calls on us to protect teachers from the problems of limited time, excessive paperwork, and demands from higher agencies and offices."[7] This statement by an authority on educational leadership concerns one of the most difficult professional responsibilities of the school principal. This could involve principals' collective action against unwise policies instituted at the district level. Some of the policies pursued by school districts are contrary to the district's own interests. District policies are not always based on the most complete available information and common sense. When the central office enlists the professional staff at the local school to formulate school-improvement plans, only to ignore or reject the plans, the central office is turning a potentially powerful source of professional energy into a negative force.

Principals can support teachers and students through collective action. For example, when the Chicago Board of Education cut funds from the city's high school sports and student-activities programs, the principals of the seventy-five public high schools voted unanimously to suspend sports and clubs until the cuts were restored—which they were. High school sports were viewed by the principals (and board members, when they thought about it later) as a crucial means of reducing the dropout rate. What was also important to many principals was that they had established themselves as a force. According to one principal, "[w]e had to put our foot down."[8]

This example should not be taken to mean that principals should try to put their will above that of district authorities. It simply serves to illustrate the need for supervisors and teachers to act on their professional knowledge. Professionals know that a sports program is a vital means of building school solidarity and student engagement beyond the classroom. Moreover, student clubs can be a vital means of advancing both academic and social growth.

Creating Conditions for Curriculum Improvement

It is the responsibility of supervisors to see that individual teachers and school staffs are made aware of the resources available for curriculum improvement. These include human resources such as curriculum specialists and other teachers who are on the generative-creative level. They also include materials and time for meetings with colleagues to plan and coordinate curriculum.

HUMAN RESOURCES.   Many if not most teachers have never had access to a curriculum consultant; most assistance in curriculum improvement comes from colleagues. Certainly, when curriculum specialists are available they should be used; supervisors and administrators know all too well that underutilized personnel cannot justify their professional existence and soon disappear. When resources such as a helping teacher or a resource teacher are not available, curriculum improvement is almost discouraged because of the routines that are already established in the school system.

It seems clear that principals need to expand their idea of what resources are possible in their own school and district. They must look again at the needs of teachers and find the professional assistance for teachers that is beyond principals' own competence. Some districts have well-staffed departments of instructional support.

Where professional help for teachers is inadequate or nonexistent, principals, teachers, and other supervisors must play their legitimate role in seeking public support for additional supervisory staff. Adequate professional assistance for teachers costs money; there is no way of avoiding this fact.

Teachers should be provided with opportunities to attend conferences concerning the problems they encounter in their classrooms. Other human resources include university professors who offer courses in curriculum and pedagogical strategies.

MATERIAL RESOURCES. Actually, the separation of human from material resources is specious; a role of the curriculum specialist is to find materials that are appropriate for a given teacher's needs, which translates to the needs of the learners. Inservice programs can acquaint teachers with the best available materials. Moreover, teachers must have another, precious resource—time—to evaluate textbooks and curriculum-resource materials. Obviously, curriculum improvement depends on treating resources interrelatedly.

Nevertheless, there are wide differences from district to district in access to curriculum materials. In some districts, school staffs clearly enjoy the availability of any materials that might be needed for the classroom for curriculum development. Teachers are given virtually an open-ended budget every year to order anything they need. However, the teachers and students in many school systems suffer from serious shortages of even the most basic resources. In urban and poor rural school systems the shortages are of such long standing that they have almost become a way of life. "In the 24 years I have been a teacher in New York City," writes a faculty member in a junior high school, "I have observed there were often not enough textbooks for each student, supplies of paper run out before the school year ends, and classroom teachers often spend their own money on materials they need to use with their students."[9]

In one inner-city school in Houston, it is reported that there are no resources supplied for kindergarten classes except pencils and paper. The teachers must buy everything else with their own money. In this school the principal makes all decisions concerning learning materials. His own teaching experience was at the middle-school level and he shows little understanding of appropriate developmental activities for kindergarten. Because the principal's background is not in early childhood education, the teachers and their pupils are out of luck, unless the teachers are able to educate the principal. The problem is not the principal's teaching background, but rather the way in which teachers' resources are determined. No principal today can consider himself or herself adequate if he or she imposes resource decisions on the professional teaching staff. This is not a matter of being philosophically committed to increasing teacher influence. It is a matter of freeing the staff to function at the generative-creative level. No principal is able unilaterally to assess the resource needs of professional teachers. Competent administrators view this as an individualized as well as faculty-wide process.[10]

The criterion for budgetary allocations for resources is this: The entire professional staff collaborates fully on budgetary allocations for learning resources; the principal and teachers are provided discretionary funds for the purchase of special learning materials that are needed to improve the curriculum.

Obviously, the availability of materials is no guarantee that they will be properly used. Curriculum specialists must be available to answer teachers' questions, particularly when the school district adopts a new curriculum. All too often teachers are left on their own to interpret the curriculum as though it is simply a matter of plugging in the new prepackaged materials.

MEDIA PROGRAMS.   Professional books and journals are important resources for curriculum improvement. In addition the school media center should maintain a rich collection of teaching resource units (for teachers) and learning resource units (for students). The professional staff should strive to have the media center meet the recommended standards of the American Library Association, as set in the latest edition of the association's publication, *Media Programs: District and School.* The media center should be attractive, functional, and serve as a true center for responsible, self-directed learning activities. Moreover, students should be encouraged to use the media center for recreational reading and browsing, and use the equipment for viewing and listening.

The school library now goes by the name of media center in many schools, but the function as a curriculum resource and a place to whet children's appetite for reading remains. The following commentary describes the unique function of school libraries—and the unfortunate condition of some school libraries:

> School libraries are an on-site resource, a curriculum adjunct, a place of wonderful treasures that can make kids want to read. The school library is tailored to the needs and wants of a particular school community. Often it is a refuge, an oasis for children who have little quiet, space, cheerfulness in their lives. Many children cannot get to public libraries by themselves; many need the close neighborhood richness of their own school library. These days, too many school libraries are nonexistent, eliminated in budget cuts. Those still in working order are too often staffed by nonprofessionals with outdated resources in grim, decrepit spaces.[11]

The media center should be open after school hours. It should never be used as a "study hall" or place for student detention. It should be an attractive and stimulating environment for self-impelled learning.

TIME.   As has been indicated previously, time for curriculum improvement is one of the most critical problems with which supervisors must concern themselves. Suggestions for acting on the problem of time have been made in previous chapters. Lack of time is simply unacceptable as a reason for failing to improve the curriculum. The key indication of what is deemed most important in terms of function or need is the amount of time being devoted to that function or need. If improving the curriculum is considered sufficiently important, it will be done. Like any resource, time should not be considered independently of needed material and personnel resources. It is what happens in that time that counts—whether teachers receive the help that they may need to make changes, and whether they have access to needed materials. The point of importance, however, is that when an activity is valued, time will be made for it.

TEACHER ORGANIZATIONS. Teachers' unions are frequently blamed for blocking the course of inservice professional development by refusing to stay after the school day for professional-development activities. The after-school approach to curriculum development has always failed. Actually, the position of the two major teacher unions (National Education Association and the American Federation of Teachers) on professional development concurs strikingly with the literature on the conditions for successful professional-development programs. According to teacher unionists, if inservice professional development is viewed as something separate from the school's real business it will fail to be effective. Because successful programs are site-based, "the school day must provide the core of inservice time," and, further, "helping teachers and other resource personnel must always be available at the site for follow-up and consultation."[12]

According to McClure, not only are teachers' unions committed to school improvement but also their leaders and staffs have competencies in curriculum improvement. McClure points out that both organizations are trusted by their members. Thus they are potentially effective resources for curriculum improvement.[13]

Certainly the position of teacher unionists on professional development is supportive of possibilities for improvement. Supervisors should be encouraged by this knowledge and seek union support in creating conditions for professional development. Together teachers, administrators, and supervisors can be overwhelmingly powerful.

TEACHER CONTENTMENT AND RESOURCE ADEQUACY. In some schools teachers seem satisfied with the resources that are available for curriculum improvement, even where the resources are clearly inadequate. At least there seem to be no complaints. Teacher contentment may be a poor indicator of resource adequacy, for these teachers tend not to have had other experiences with which to make comparisons. Teachers who have enjoyed more substantial resources in another school system are usually quite aware of an insufficiency. The point of importance is that just because teachers do not complain about inadequate resources does not mean that the resources provided by the school and the district are adequate.

Someone must assist teachers in finding resources, for example, resources to interrelate subjects in the curriculum. This is a responsibility of supervision. Curriculum leaders must be sources of ideas and materials, and organizers of opportunities that will help teachers stay abreast of promising innovations and grow professionally.[14]

Although curriculum integration can hardly be termed an *innovation,* it is an approved practice. Teachers need to be made aware of what is available to help them implement approved practices. When material resources are not readily available, leaders—the human resources—can help teachers find them and make effective use of them.

COLLABORATIVE STRATEGIES FOR CURRICULUM IMPROVEMENT

The collaborative process is indigenous to teachers' functioning at Level III—the generative-creative level. Recall that at this level teachers are immersed in efforts to solve curriculum problems, improve established practice, evaluate promising new practices, and implement needed changes.

Recently, interest in so-called site-based management has led many schools to embark on programs of participatory decision making. These programs may or may not be directly concerned with the solution of curriculum and instructional problems. For example, in some schools, teachers are now included on search committees for new teachers. This is a striking departure from traditional practice, and not long ago would have been unheard of. Administrators alone were involved in staffing. In some schools, the teachers and principal collaboratively decide how many hours students should spend in a particular class.

Needless to say, some state legislators and many school administrators have been concerned with distinguishing between the decisions that teachers should make and those that are administrative. What is often forgotten in such considerations is the purpose of giving teachers more authority in making decisions—namely, to allow them more flexibility in dealing with students' educational needs. Teachers at Level III are continually involved in making decisions concerning learning experiences.

When teachers have wide latitude and support in diagnosing the problems of their school, the solutions can result in an improved curriculum. The problem of student apathy comes to mind. A faculty committed to dealing with the problem of apathetic students will (it is hoped) look to the curriculum.

Administrators use different approaches or strategies to involve the faculty in collaborative curriculum-improvement efforts. Some principals address the problem in terms of the need to shape a common vision or ideal for their school. Others have sought to identify curriculum areas in need of improvement through a needs assessment by the faculty. A third approach—one that is not new—is to involve the faculty in solving practical curriculum problems. Three major approaches (not equally promising) can therefore be identified at work in American schools. What is often overlooked is that these three approaches need not be incompatible provided that they are conceptualized and instituted so as to work conjointly or holistically.

Vision-Making and Goal Setting

A popular approach to school improvement has been to have the school staff share a common vision for the school. Collaboratively, each school council (created by law in some states) describes the tone and sets goals for their own school. The idea certainly has its merits; organizational goals provide a framework within which supervisors can help teachers realize their potential for curriculum improvement. Take for example the goal of helping students become lifelong learners. Although stated in sweeping terms, no mission of the school is more powerful than motivating students for continued learning. Supervisors can help teachers determine whether the curriculum and their instructional procedures are consonant with the goal of motivating students to go on learning.

Alice Miel, who greatly enlarged the understanding of curriculum change as a social process, offered many suggestions for working with faculty groups. Lessons learned from experiences with curriculum development led Miel to offer this counsel: There is a need for goals "that give broad direction to individual and group efforts without limiting opportunity to be creative and individual," goals should be "within the present capabilities of individuals and groups [and] should be flexibly held so that they can be reexamined frequently and revised if need be."[15]

BRINGING THE VISION TO EARTH. The articulation of a common vision by the school faculty can be a first step in launching a program of curriculum improvement, but visions can be vague and airy and must not be allowed to remain so. Goals must be connected to vision. Immediate and clear steps should be delineated by the faculty toward the goals. The transformation of ideals into concrete steps requires leadership skills that are sensitive and decisive.

A common vision is akin to a school philosophy. Whether one begins with a statement of philosophy or a vision, the problem where curriculum development is concerned remains the same. Tyler put it this way: "For a statement of philosophy to serve most helpfully as a set of standards or a screen in selecting objectives it needs to be stated clearly and for the main points the implications for educational objectives may need to be spelled out."[16] (As stressed in Chapter 9, we prefer to conceive of philosophy as a compass rather than a screen, but this does not diminish the significance of Tyler's point—for the test of philosophy is action in the formulation of educational objectives, the implementation of appropriate means, and the evaluation of outcomes.)

Needs Assessment

The term *needs assessment* has its roots in the old production-efficiency model of schooling that attracted school administrators early in the twentieth century. In the 1960s, the idea of school as a factory once again began to influence the nature of efforts to reform the schools. According to Levin, interest on the part of policymakers in higher standards and efficiency led to efforts by economists "to ascertain how education was produced through the estimation of educational production functions that relate changes in educational inputs to changes in educational outcomes."[17] (The language alone is a key to its roots.) Levin recounts how this interest led to demands for evaluation researchers to provide cost-effectiveness comparisons of various educational interventions. Policymakers wanted to know which interventions were most promising for raising test scores and cost the least. It was stressed that because resources are always limited, "it is important to maximize the effectiveness of those resources, and this can be done by using strategies that promise the largest amount of effectiveness per unit of cost."[18] Clearly, the emphasis was on reforming the schools along the lines of the industrial enterprise.

The problem of resources in public education is just not the same as that of resources in the industrial sector. It is, rather, a societal issue of priority setting. For example, the War on Poverty of the Johnson administration sought to improve educational opportunity as a means of attacking poverty. Under the Office of Economic Opportunity (OEO), the chief federal agency in the War on Poverty, the educational goals were turned more narrowly toward the promotion of economic growth.

Following the business-industrial production model, many of the OEO programs were segmental and focused on cost effectiveness and efficiency by employing such devices as longer school days, peer tutoring, computer-assisted instruction, hierarchical staff development, and special programs operated without coordination with the schools, such as Head Start and Job Corps.

Although cost-effectiveness studies in education appealed to policymakers, the difficulties in undertaking such studies soon became apparent. Generalizations about the effectiveness of various interventions—peer tutoring, for example—were based on analyses of collections of the available studies taken together of that intervention (meta-analysis), whether the studies were poorly or well designed. What was sought in meta-analyses were the average effects. Another problem was that there were many versions of each intervention. The different kinds of programs had different costs. As Levin concludes, "it is not possible to create a cost-effective comparison from among such averages," and averages are not useful because "the average is not embodied in any specific program."[19] Put another way, each school is an individual.

Finally, any intervention aimed at developmental changes in learners, such as Head Start (the federally supported preschool program for at-risk children), must be followed up in school with powerful and consistent efforts. Early studies revealed that without such follow-up, any gains in achievement by the youngsters disappeared by the second grade. Later studies of programs that provided sustained pupil support in school "found important longitudinal differences in favor of the children who received the intervention."[20] Consequently, the meta-analysis of Head Start programs taken together will overlook the variable that makes the difference—namely, school follow-up.

The following definition of needs assessment is offered by Beane, Toepfer, and Alessi: "It is evaluation with regard for establishing priorities of future effort, arising originally from a concern for using limited funds to address those areas of most critical need."[21] And as originally conceived, the approach is managerial (top down) as well as technological. A data base is used by administrators at the district office to ascertain the difference between current achievement and desired goals and to assess which goals seem most in need of concentrated effort for improvement. Teachers are held accountable for meeting the goals determined by district administrators to be most critical.

Yet, as Beane, Toepfer, and Alessi point out, needs assessment can be a useful approach. They stress, quite correctly, that in a properly done needs assessment, all aspects of learning are examined—the affective and psychomotor in addition to the cognitive. Nevertheless, it should be cautioned that it is not advisable to start by examining the cognitive, affective, and psychomotor processes categorized by Bloom and his associates.[22] To do so is a reversal of focus and ignores the need to improve the design of the curriculum so that the affective and cognitive processes are interrelated.

There are two general principles to follow if needs assessment is to result in curriculum improvement: (1) it must be a collaborative process involving teachers and (2) it must be tied to the problem-solving paradigm.

AN ILLUSTRATION OF NEEDS ASSESSMENT.   It is helpful to consider an illustration of the application of this approach as recounted by an elementary school principal who reports that when her school district adopted a new policy of each school setting its own goals through a needs-assessment program, she immediately began seeking a model to follow. An examination of a program developed by district administrators and a search of the literature proved very disappointing. "To my surprise," she writes, "I had not located one practical plan for assessing a building's areas of strength and difficulty and then addressing the challenges."[23]

The principal was, however, able to draw on the literature on school improvement for guiding ideas. The literature emphasized the importance of a broad-based collaborative effort involving parents and students as well as the school staff. She found guidance in the ideas of her superintendent who stressed that although the district has a wider mission that unifies the schools, each school is different as is each principal and each staff. "Our goals and objectives will vary because of our diversity," he said.[24]

So the principal developed her own plan and it essentially followed the problem-solving process set forth by Dewey in his conception of the scientific method: defining the problem, gathering data concerning the problem, formulating ideas or alternative plans of action that might solve the problem, consideration of the possible results of acting on the alternative plans, and selecting and testing a plan (or plans) to see if it solves the problem.[25] The principal's view was that those in the school community who were interested would see the work through. She wrote to each parent and staff member requesting volunteers for a committee that would decide on a school goal by the close of the school year. The needs-assessment committee was composed of the principal, all parents and teachers who had volunteered, and four pupils from grades four and five. The committee had forty-one members, and the average attendance at monthly meetings was thirty members.

Interestingly, knowledge on how effective change takes place supports the use of what Fullan and Miles call a *cross-role group* (for example, teachers and principals and, frequently, parents and students). "In such a group," they write, "different worlds collide, more learning occurs, and change is realistically managed." They also point to evidence that organizing a change effort in this fashion "results in substantially increased teacher commitment."[26]

Table 16–1 is presented to help principals and supervisors conduct a needs-assessment program. The process is consistent with the problem-solving procedures outlined by the principal and, as she points out, "can be followed regardless of the specifics that apply to a building's staff, student population, or general community."[27] We add that there is no reason why only one goal should be selected if there are other areas needing improvement. This was a new elementary principal who for her own reasons opted for a single goal. The idea of soliciting volunteers to serve on the needs-assessment committee seems to have been sound, at least in this instance.

Table 16-1 Phases and Process in Conducting a Needs Assessment

Time	Phase	Work to do
September	I. Initiating the inquiry process (1) What areas/aspects of the school program need improvement? (2) Why do we believe these areas/aspects need improvement? (3) What pertinent sources of data are available? (4) What other sources of data are needed? (5) How can we gather all needed data?	(1) Share with the committee the district's mission statement (2) Identify all pertinent available sources of data with the committee (e.g., results of previous studies, local and statewide test results, surveys of teachers, parents and students, follow-up studies of graduates) (3) Identify other needed sources of data not readily available, and develop procedures for gathering data
October November December	II. Deriving consensus on the concerns/needs/problems to be addressed (1) To what extent is there consensus on the areas/aspects that need improvement? (2) Are these areas/aspects of sufficient significance for substantive schoolwide improvement? (3) For which areas/aspects do we find sharp differences of opinion? (4) How can these differences be resolved? (5) What other sources of data are needed?	(1) Gather all pertinent sources of data (2) Consider all concerns/problems/needs originally identified (3) Consider any new or overlooked problems/needs (4) Derive consensus and narrow-down the list of problems/needs

There appear to have been no unenthused members to put a pall on the group or slow down its momentum.

Initially the committee identified ten areas of concern or need, but decided in the end to focus on developing a curriculum in environmental education. The principal then contacted a number of schools noted for outstanding programs in environmental education. The professional staff responsible for the environmental-education program in one of these schools was enlisted to provide professional-development activities for teachers in summer workshops. The outcome was a highly successful program in the target school, with students developing many environmental-educa-

Time	Phase		Work to do
December January	III.	Developing and implementing the process of organizing and examining all pertinent data, and making a tentative determination of priority	
		(1) Which concerns/problems/needs are the most significant for improving the school's overall program?	(1) Organize and meet with small teams for each area of concern (problem/need) to study all data and to outline a tentative plan of action
		(2) Which are within the school's scope and capability for effective action?	(2) Share proposals with committee
		(3) How do our data bear effectively on each identified problem/need?	
		(4) What do these data reveal?	
January February	IV.	Focusing on the concerns (problems/needs) of highest priority	
		(1) What priority should be given to each identified concern/problem/ need? Priorities to be determined by such criteria as:	(1) Review the research literature
		(a) How significant is this and what are the prospects for effecting substantive school-wide improvement?	(2) Conduct full examination/discussion of proposals
		(b) What material and personnel resources, including released time, are required?	(3) Present to administration and faculty initial priority rankings
		(c) Is there sufficient expertise available internally and externally?	(4) Work for fullest possible consensus among committee, faculty, and administration
		(2) Is there a sound research base in the professional literature for attacking this concern/need/problem, and for supporting the proposed actions?	

tion projects, including the writing of original books on endangered species. Pre- and posttest surveys indicated that students substantially increased both their knowledge concerning the environment and their efforts to protect the environment. The program received the 1991 Award for Excellence in Environmental Education for the category of academic institutions from the Region III office of the United States Environmental Protection Agency.[28]

Principals with questions about needs assessment may find answers by networking with other leaders and by consulting the literature. Fortunately some principals have chosen to publish their experiences in education journals.

Table 16-1, *continued*

Time	Phase	Work to do
February March	V. Establishing objectives and procedures for addressing the concern/problem/need (1) What objectives must be met if we are to be successful? (2) What actions are required to meet these objectives? (3) Is there a sound research base in the professional literature for supporting the methods and procedures to be used?	(1) Establishment of research base. (2) Present to faculty outline of objectives for addressing the concern/problem/need of highest priority (3) Solicit and evaluate further suggestions for possible inclusion/modification from faculty and administration
March April	VI. Developing the action plan (1) How should the actions be organized? (2) How should the actions be implemented? (3) What additional resources will be required from outside as well as within the school and district (released time, funding, consultants, materials, etc.)? (4) In what ways will the program be implemented? (5) How shall the program be evaluated, formatively and summatively?	(1) Draft action plan based on fullest possible consensus of all concerned parties (2) Engage outside consultants if needed to review/evaluate efficacy of action plan, and modify plan accordingly (3) Develop systematic formative and summative evaluation criteria procedures
May	VII. Submitting action plan to administration and presenting plan to faculty	(1) Review plan with administration and faculty for modification and approval
May June	VIII. Submitting action plan to central office (superintendent) for approval and for board approval	(1) Make and approve final modification

Problem Solving

There is no doubt that the collaborative strategies we have discussed thus far can pay off handsomely. Decision making and action by needs-assessment committees can stimulate teachers to expand their teaching horizons. Goal setting can inspire teachers to inspire students. Nevertheless, there is a danger that school problems will be bypassed in the goal-setting process. Goals are fairly general statements about what schools hope to do. They are not the same as teachers' concerns or problems. The curriculum-improvement function of supervision can best be approached by starting with addressing specific problem situations—from those of an individual teacher to problems of a whole school. In essence, curriculum development should be treated as a problem-solving process involving the entire professional staff of the school and school system.

RELUCTANT TEACHERS.   Most teachers have been brought up with the notion that disclosing one's problems is not a good idea. As children, they were socialized into keeping silent when they did not understand the teacher's directions. As teachers, they quickly grew to accept the common belief (whether justified or not) that having problems is bad. Disclosing problems could only create a poor impression and jeopardize merit pay increases. (Sad to say many principals bought the myth that good teachers never have problems.) All of the advances that have been made in any field or profession were made because problems were openly identified and dealt with. As Fullan and Miles put it: "Problems are our friends because only through immersing ourselves in problems can we come up with creative solutions."[29]

As we have discussed, involving teachers in identifying and solving curriculum problems serves as an antidote to the problem of teacher isolation and has long been an approved practice in curriculum development. From time to time, in episodic efforts at reform, schools have sought to follow the practice. Working collaboratively in search of continuous improvement became established practice in those schools that provided time for doing so in the teacher's schedule. Along with the time went the expectations and the support. In other schools, lacking in full commitment, the democratic-participative approach to problems quickly faded from interest and from practice—that is, until it was rediscovered and again came into fashion. Meanwhile, it never left the literature as an approved practice.

REACHING FAR ENOUGH.   Why do reforms take in some schools but not in others? In his study of why some reforms fail, Cuban found that schools in which reforms do not last make only superficial attempts to change. They have not reached far enough.[30] His idea supports Sarason's conclusion that substantive and long-lasting improvement is attainable, but requires organizational as well as interpersonal change.[31]

These ideas and our experiences with repetitive reform cycles deliver a potent message for principals: Teachers are not likely to come forward with problems concerning the curriculum unless productive problem-identification meetings are the norm (regularly held) in their school. Moreover, when curriculum problems are concealed or ignored, they are likely to fester and escalate into more serious problems and become problems of teacher morale. Problems must be identified and treated quickly and carefully.[32] Thus local school leaders (and district administrators) should make problem solving one of what Sarason alluded to as "the existing regularities."[33]

BASIC PRINCIPLES.   Figure 16–1 presents a process for collaborative problem solving (Level III). Of great importance are the guiding principles underlying the process and three stand out as most essential. First, the problem must be genuine, and there must be no predetermined solution. This seems obvious and yet there is a risk for the leader being tempted to manipulate evidence in the interest of a predetermined solution. Second, all decisions should be based on the best available evidence. This requires that the principal and faculty have a strong commitment to the scientific methods or method of intelligence of solving problems, as opposed to authoritative dictate, external pressure, bureaucratic regularities, or mere expediency (see Figure 16–1). The importance of this commitment cannot be overemphasized. Third, whatever the size of the school system, the superintendent and members of the superintendent's team must provide for a coordinated approach to problem solving, and must be aware that problems of an individual school often interface with the whole system. As shown in Figure 16–1, problems can be identified at any level of the school system.

An excellent example of the coordinated approach is provided by the principal of an inner-city high school in Phoenix faced by low academic achievement, a high dropout rate, and poor attendance. The principal recounts: "The assistant superintendent asked for a list of needs and potential solutions. I could have given him my own wish list, but at South Mountain we are committed to a process of shared decision making."[34] By meeting formally and informally with the school staff, the principal was able to develop a short-term list including telephones for teachers to contact students and parents and funds for learning materials. More importantly, the school improvement team, consisting of members of the school staff, administrators, parents, and students together, developed long-term solutions and met with district-level administrators and supervisors. The collaborative plan fostered the development of interdisciplinary curriculum designs and initiated a system of social-service collaboration. Moreover, class loads were reduced to meet these priorities. Over a few years the dropout rate was cut in half, absenteeism decreased significantly, and achievement in mathematics and English increased on statewide tests, with the greatest improvement occurring in written expression. "The ultimate plan," advised the principal, "becomes the 'property' of neither one person nor one school nor the district office, but is a joint resolution to a shared problem. This process occurs regularly at South Mountain."[35]

Much of the recent literature on factors critical to a school's improvement stresses school autonomy. District leaders are portrayed as being inherently resistant to having a school's problems solved in that they are seen as seeking to conceal rather than reveal problems. Or the principal is pitted against the district and portrayed as a superperson who uses "creative subordination" in dealing with frustrating problems.[36] The real-life illustration we have presented, however, points to a coordinated approach as crucial in problem solving. The principal and professional staff of the school should have full access to the resources of the entire school district as needed in seeking problem solutions.

INITIATING THE PROCEDURE.   Whatever the size of the school, the principal has the responsibility of providing for a continuous program of curriculum development and for assisting teachers in solving problems. Whatever the school's size or level, the steps in initiating collaborative procedures are very similar. Secondary schools are organized departmentally and the collaborative process concerning problems in the subject fields will be entrusted to department heads. Thus, the principal must gain the full support of department heads as well as assistant principals. Based on his own experience in launching a program, a former principal in New York City stresses

Figure 16-1. Problem-solving—A Collaborative Process.

Source: Daniel Tanner and Laurel Tanner. *Supervision in Education: Problems and Practices.* New York: Macmillan, 1987, p. 96.

the importance of introducing to department heads the new goals, theoretical background, and ways of involving teachers. He chose a retreat as the setting for this crucial first step.[37] The next step is to prepare the department heads to conduct collaborative problem-solving meetings with staff members. Recounting his experience, the principal reported that some department heads found it very difficult to depart from the traditional supervisory role of setting goals for subordinates. They could not seem to accept the idea of participating with faculty members in problem solving and goal setting. For example, one department chairperson acknowledged that he considered teacher involvement in decision making about instructional matters a valueless activity. "The question-and-answer approach he used in his department meetings was not suitable for identifying teaching-related problems and his lack of understanding was obvious in such questions as 'Are there any more gripes?'"[38] The principal continued to work with small groups of department chairpeople regularly in leadership training, but found that he met with more success when he worked informally with them as individuals. In his words, "they did not respond well to being formal 'learners.'"[39] This was not surprising. Professionals learn new procedures best by using them.

Although department heads will be leaders of the collaborative process in their own department, the principal should open the first meeting. There are at least three reasons why the principal's initial involvement is important: (1) the principal should pave the way for the department head, (2) the commitment of the administration to improving teaching and learning by involving teachers in real decision making must be communicated to the teachers, and (3) the involvement of the principal (a generalist) is crucial if the faculty is to develop a coherent interdepartmental program of general education and other all-school programs. However important the problems of a given department concerning their own subject field, a problem of common concern to all of faculty is the need to reveal the relationships of studies along with their significance for the life of the learner and that of a democratic society. Indeed, this is one of the leading curriculum problems. As everyone knows, it is particularly pronounced at the secondary school level where adolescents are undergoing profound changes physically, psychologically, and socially.

A problem-solving program in a school should not make the walls between departments higher. It should, rather, seek to bring them down by providing for collaboration among departments in dealing with their common problems. The school improvement team described earlier by the Phoenix principal is a means of doing so; the team encouraged the development of interdisciplinary approaches as a means of dealing with dropouts. Although a combination of social services, curriculum changes, and reduced teaching loads probably accounted for the sharp reduction in absenteeism and dropouts, the new curriculum designs were an essential part of the strategy.

IDENTIFYING PROBLEMS.   The principal or department head should assist the group in identifying problems. The focus of the meetings should be on practical problems connected with the curriculum. As shown in Figure 16–1, the cycle of problem solving is continuous. A school where a continuous program of curriculum development is already an existing regularity will be concerned with problem solving as a matter of course. The important point is to have in place a procedure where teachers, who are closest to the instructional scene, can identify and deal with problems. Although the emphasis is on practical problems, solving them is an intellectual as well as practical process. Dewey pointed out that "the origin of thinking is some perplexity, confusion or doubt."[40] Put another way, the origin lies in recognizing a problem situation.

SUSPENDING JUDGMENT.   The next step is to find and test possible solutions to the problem. Dewey warned that although it is a temptation to accept any seemingly plausible solution and get on with other things, a sound decision must be based on sound knowledge. Interpreting the research literature and professional experience on the problem is crucial (see Figure 16–1). "To maintain the state of doubt and to carry on systematic and protracted inquiry—these are the essentials of thinking," said Dewey.[41] The leader's most difficult problem is twofold: to refrain from pressuring for a premature solution and to keep the process moving. Teachers will have responsibilities in the problem-solving process and principals or department heads should offer support where needed. According to a principal, providing teachers with assistance in fact finding is important or "some groups come to the second meeting to raise additional problems without first clarifying those identified in the first."[42] There are no short cuts in the problem-solving process and the process is arduous, but there is a reason why it is carried on in a growing number of schools: Their achievements in solving problems provide the professional staff with a sense of direction, pride, responsibility, and accomplishment. Moreover, being involved in systematic inquiry can be a source of great pleasure for teachers.

STAFF SKEPTICISM. There have been so many sudden policy shifts in response to alleged crises in education, with each crisis followed by a panacea, that it should be no small wonder when teachers become passive participants. Or they may respond to the latest reform shift with overt compliance and covert resistance. Therefore, it is not difficult to see why many teachers would be skeptical about administrators' newly announced commitment to improving teaching and learning through teacher involvement in real problem solving. As a principal himself suggests, it is important to counter skepticism in the first meeting, and principals should be open in talking to faculty. According to this principal, a principal might say to the faculty that although they "have seen school improvement programs come and go over the years . . . this time we're really serious about a new approach and we want to see it work. We're going to devote ourselves to it. But you're the ones who have to give it a chance to work."[43]

How are the faculty to know that this time things are different? What should be emphasized in describing the approach in that the word *new* really does not apply to these procedures? The idea of a school faculty working together to diagnose and solve problems was developed by educators in the first half of the twentieth century and is an approved practice in education. A basic idea undergirding teacher involvement in solving curriculum problems is that teachers are closest to the scene—the classroom. Their insights are critical to the problem-solving process. Moreover, many heads are better than just one. Involving the faculty is a way to draw on the collective knowledge of professionals and use it in the solution of problems. In introducing a procedure to professionals and asking for their support, a principal should provide the knowledge base for the procedure. Collaborative decision making has a knowledge base. Support should come from the soundness of the procedure and not merely declarations to convince staff that this time we really mean it.

RELUCTANT PRINCIPALS. If collaborative decision making is to enhance faculty motivation and capacity for problem solving, it is clear that the principal's commitment is absolutely essential. This commitment is by no means general. Even though recent policy supports the principle that teachers should work on problem solutions, principals in many schools remain reluctant to abandon a system where they are (they think) in complete control. According to Herbert Simon and others, control by sheer authority as a way of supervision cannot work because the elements involved in all but the most minor and routine decisions are too complex and it is impossible to control them all.[44] Because teachers will make these decisions anyhow (their autonomy is a fact of life), they should make them on the best possible evidence (see Figure 16–1).

Many principals have quite another reason for their reluctance to develop decisions collaboratively. They feel that they lack the competence to be a leader in a democratic group setting. Interestingly enough, writers on general education—that part of the curriculum concerned with developing socially responsible citizens in a free society—have long urged that the skills of working cooperatively be "part of the general education of our people."[45] Fullan and Miles report that principals are commonly lacking in these skills.[46] Principals and supervisors who did not learn the skills of cooperative work as pupils in school or in their professional preparation for supervision are doubly disadvantaged.

All this adds up to the fact that their own professional development as it relates to ability for leadership in curriculum improvement is of enormous concern to principals. Indeed, in a survey of Chicago principals conducted by a consortium of area universities and the Chicago Public Schools, principals identified "leadership for instructional improvement (and enhancing their own capacities to lead)" as their most critical concern.[47]

There is no doubt that the qualities involved in cooperative work including being a group leader can be learned by principals and by most adults, for that matter. "Both casual and systematic observation," writes Robert A. Dahl, a prominent political theorist, "provide good grounds for believing that many, perhaps most, human beings at birth possess the potentiality for developing these qualities," and whether they really develop them "depends primarily on the circumstances into which they are born and in which their development—or lack of it—takes place."[48]

The circumstances, of course, include the nature of the society in which one lives. Only democratic political systems can supply the conditions under which the capacity to "engage in free and open discussion with others . . . take responsibility for important decisions, and engage freely with others in a search for the best decision can develop." Indeed, continued Dahl, "all other regimes reduce, often drastically, the scope within which adults can act."[49] Moreover, according to Dahl, this is the direction in which democracy must move if the United States and other advanced democratic nations are to continue to exist. Teachers must model these behaviors as well as provide all students with the opportunity to serve as group leaders in problem-solving situations.

Enhancing Leadership Capacity

Principals who are not involved in any collaborative effort may be afraid of losing control of the faculty (and the decision). Principals are told that they "have to rise above the fear of losing control."[50] Such exhortations are not useful because they are not a guide to action. When working with groups or teams, the principal should concentrate instead on providing service to the group. Thus, the principal need not be concerned with maintaining or showing his or her authority. As Miel pointed out, the leader's example in dealing with group members will influence the entire group: "Confidence, ease, poise, kindness and thoughtfulness are just as contagious as are fear, insecurity, excitability, irritability, and callousness. Teachers are quick to sense these qualities in their leaders."[51]

Although Miel made this suggestion a half-century ago, it is on the mark and timeless. More recently, the following six practices have been identified by local school leaders and supervisors as important—indeed, essential—to sound group action for curriculum improvement:

1. Clarify procedures. Progress in solving problems depends on a common understanding of the phases of group decision making. Begin by analyzing the problem-solving procedures in Figure 16–1, which also provide a common vocabulary. Ground rules should be established early concerning how decisions are to be made.

2. Identify indigenous leaders and those with potentials for leadership, and provide them with opportunities to exercise leadership at the generative-creative level. Members of the professional staff, parents and other adult citizens also have the potential to be leaders in problem solving. The principal or supervisor should assign particular responsibilities connected with the problem-solving process to group members. As reported by a principal in our earlier illustration, it was useful to form mini-teams to carry out various aspects of the problem-solving procedure. As Miel pointed out, "[e]very committee chair created, every assignment of special responsibility means more chances for more persons to exercise leadership and test their effectiveness in actual group situations."[52] In giving teachers opportunities for curriculum change, we are helping them to function at the generative-creative level. Moreover, the chances that the problem-solving process will lead to curriculum improvement will be enhanced. As Miel put it, "the greater the amount of effective leadership developed on the part of all members of the professional staff, the greater the probability that the experiences of learners in their charge will be educative."[53]

3. Provide concrete assistance. The principal or supervisor provides information and locates information sources, and finds ways of providing material resources as needed. When the group needs the help of experts on the problem, the principal finds the person or agency best able to provide that assistance. The group may also need to look outside to see how the problem has been dealt with elsewhere, and opportunities should be given to observe similar programs or projects in other school systems.

4. Increase commitment. High and realistic expectations should be set for each group member concerning their particular responsibilities for garnering the best available evidence bearing on the problem. Each group member should be asked to evaluate his or her progress in communicating what they have found.

5. Provide opportunities for constructive disagreement. Individuals should never be made to feel compelled to yield to consensus when they really have a valid basis for constructive disagreement. The principal or supervisor should seek to provide for the fullest expression of both initiative and constructive disagreement. As we have pointed out elsewhere, although the consensus model should be used in democratic-participative approaches, "group process, taken superficially, sometimes exerts its own tyranny of group pressure."[54] We have all experienced situations where someone with useful insights or a creative idea was made to feel compelled to keep silent rather than contributing the suggestion. As a result the constructive insight was lost.

6. Deal constructively with group division. A decision may not be so easy to achieve. Even after a process of deliberation and discussion, the group may still be far from consensus concerning the best plan of action. A decision now would be premature, for this reason: A wise decision is based not only on the best available knowledge but also on the uncoerced consensus of all concerned, and so the decision should be delayed pending further study by the team or group. In some situations an immediate decision of some kind must be made. Miel's counsel is pertinent here: The leader should "have it understood that the decision is a trial one."[55] The idea of testing an action plan is, of course, integral to the problem-solving paradigm (see Figure 16–1).

LEADERSHIP FOR CURRICULUM DESIGN, DEVELOPMENT, AND EVALUATION

Skillful and committed leadership is needed if curriculum improvements are to be made in light of a grand design. Decisions concerning microcurricular problems must be made with regard to this macro design; a balanced and coherent curriculum depends on it. Here is evidence for the soundness of Cremin's assertion that someone must be responsible for seeing the curriculum as a coherent whole and raise questions of relationship.[56] This is the job of curriculum leadership, both by the local school administrator and the school faculty. District-level supervisors and administrators have this responsibility at the school-system level.

Transforming Theory into Practice

Parts II and III of this book discussed the elements in design and the sources from which criteria for curriculum decisions are drawn. We pointed out that the elements of curriculum design are interrelated, as are the sources for and influences on the curriculum. It is the role of the curriculum leader to translate these ideas into practice and to contribute to the body of knowledge on curriculum. As discussed in Chapter 14, Hilda Taba was this kind of leader and contributed influential ideas. Other curriculum theorists, including the present authors, have views of the curriculum development process that differ from Taba's in significant ways. As discussed in Chapter 7, in her classic book on curriculum development, published in 1962, Taba identified the following seven-step sequence in the process: (1) diagnosis of needs, (2) formulation of objectives, (3) selection of content, (4) organization of content, (5) selection of learning experiences, (6) organization of learning experiences, and (7) determination of what to evaluate and of the ways and means of doing it.[57] Taba conceived of these steps as a linear sequence; the authors of this textbook hold that the steps or functions are interdependent rather than rigidly sequential. For example, the diagnosis of needs and the formulation of objectives involve evaluation, which is integral to every step, including those concerned with the selection and treatment of subject matter. (See Chapter 7 for an extended discussion of the interdependence of the various functions in curriculum development.)

The four questions that Tyler asks early in his monograph, and the discussion stemming from them, are intended to provide an orderly guide to curriculum development as a problem-solving process.[58] It is noteworthy, in this regard, that the monograph was originally published as a syllabus for Tyler's curriculum course at the University of Chicago. It has already been pointed out that Tyler's formulation has been criticized for its linearity. Goodlad, who was one of Tyler's students, has a different view of the syllabus:

> One does not necessarily have to treat the four questions in the syllabus in linear fashion. One can begin almost anywhere with any one of the four questions. If you begin with question four, "How can we determine whether the purposes are being attained in the setting," then you clearly go back to question one. But one can begin with question three, "How can these experiences be effectively organized," and talk a good deal about the organizational questions before one necessarily has to get back to the first question of "What educational purposes should one seek to attain."[59]

Anyone who takes the time to read Tyler's monograph to the very end will, doubtless, arrive at the same conclusion, for Tyler states that where one begins with the questions depends on the school and the concerns of the staff. In one school,

> the results of a follow-up study of graduates may focus attention upon identifiable inadequacies in the present program which will lead easily to systematic study. In another situation, the deliberations over a school philosophy may provide an initial step to an improvement of objectives, and then to a study of the learning experiences. The purpose of the rationale is to give a view of the elements that are involved in a program of instruction and their necessary interrelations."[60]

In our model, unlike Tyler's, philosophy is incorporated as a regulator or compass for the curriculum development process. (The reader may find it helpful at this point to refer back to the discussion in Chapter 7.)

Neglected Elements.   All too often curriculum development is a segmental and haphazard (and even chaotic) process with decisions made by impulse or by whatever happens to be in vogue at a given time, rather than by systematically following theoretical principles. For example, even when Taba's steps are followed, there is a tendency to emphasize one or two sources for curriculum and neglect others. The needs of learners may be stressed and the needs of society ignored or vice versa. Generally, this is the result of the overriding influence of special interests or social forces at a particular point in time. It cannot be overemphasized that it is the responsibility of a professional staff to reflect *on* social forces and not mindlessly reflect social forces.

Just as there is a tendency to emphasize one source for curriculum and neglect the others, so there is a tendency to focus attention on one or two of Tyler's four questions and give the others little, if any, attention. According to Goodlad, the impact of Tyler's formulation has been greatest in the fourth area of the rationale, evaluation, and the first area, the development of goals and objectives. There has been far less attention to what learning experiences will be most suitable for attaining the objectives and even less to how shall the learning experiences be organized.[61]

Although Tyler states that any of the four areas can serve as an entry point for curriculum improvement, he makes a condition: "providing the resulting modifications are followed through the related elements until eventually all aspects of the curriculum have been studied and revised."[62] One can cite many gross violations of this proviso over many decades of curriculum reform and counterreform. The point of entry for the national commissions on educational reform of the 1980s was Tyler's fourth area: evaluation. Because the purposes of the commissions tended to be political, the approach was based on a priori premises of systemwide school failure. The commissions were temporary bodies that proceeded to hit and run. They issued recommendations but were not responsible for their implementation. More importantly, there were problems with their treatment of Tyler's fourth area. Evaluation was based on invalid premises and invalid data to support the premises (see Chapter 11). According to Peterson, a policy expert, "[i]nstead of digging deep," the commissions made "exaggerated claims on flimsy evidence," and "they failed to find the real problems."[63]

Considerable attention has been given in this chapter to the development of goals by a professional staff. The point of importance here is that it is the principal's responsibility to help the faculty move through the related elements in improving the curriculum. Additional suggestions for doing so will be made in Chapter 17 on school renewal.

FORGOTTEN WORDS.   A curriculum-design problem that is all too widespread is that schools conduct their curriculum-improvement efforts without regard for continuity and integration of learning activities. The ways of developing vertical and horizontal curriculum articulation (other names for continuity and integration) are discussed in Chapters 10 and 11. The point of emphasis here is that school staffs need to deal with curriculum continuity and integration. According to Goodlad,

> if there is anything that the curriculum field suffers from today, it is that words like 'continuity' and 'sequence' have practically disappeared from popular usage. . . . If there is anything that I would like to call out loudly for it is consideration of the basic questions of organizing a curriculum so that it might have continuity, sequence, and scope.[64]

Of course, problems of continuity and integration do not end at the school door; system-wide curriculum planning is absolutely necessary for articulation, particularly in larger school systems. Teachers and supervisors, under the leadership of the director of curriculum, should be engaged in continuous and systematic curriculum development to articulate the curriculum throughout the district as well as within the school.

Curriculum Design, Development, and Evaluation—A Method of Thinking

The curriculum is never complete—nor should it be. Indeed, curriculum development may be profitably viewed as an endless problem-solving process. The problem of the curriculum requires definition, data gathering, formulating alternative and tentative approaches (hypotheses) that may solve the problem, and testing to see which approach best solves the problem. As Ralph Tyler suggested, this process is never ending.

> What is implied in all of this is that curriculum planning is a continuous process and that as materials and procedures are developed, they are tried out, their results appraised, their inadequacies identified, suggested improvements indicated; there is replanning, redevelopment and then reappraisal; and in this kind of continuing cycle, it is possible for the curriculum and instructional program to be continually improved over the years. In this way we may hope to have an increasingly more effective educational program rather than depending so much upon hit and miss judgment as a basis for curriculum development.[65]

The fact that curriculum development is a continuous process is one reason for institutionalizing in the school a set of procedures and criteria for curriculum development, along with needed professional expertise and support services. There is a second reason: Curriculum reforms are constantly being pressed on the schools by external panels, commissions, and special-interest groups, and some of these reforms are not in the best interests of students and society. Take for example the premise embraced by many national commissions or panels on education reform—namely, that national standardized tests will serve to improve public education. The consequence has been the test-driven curriculum and the widespread misuses of such tests for student placement and promotion, teacher evaluation, and school and school-district evaluation. At the same time, as reported in a study for the National Science Foundation, these tests have been found to emphasize low-level thinking and knowledge.[66]

When a curriculum proposal is urged on the school (or school system), the machinery should be already in motion for acting on that proposal. A way of thinking and behaving about the curriculum (founded on professionally validated principles) should be inextricably woven into the fabric of the school. Not incidentally, this is what happens when a new drug is developed by a pharmaceutical concern. Before the drug can be put on the market, it is submitted to rigorous tests by the Federal Drug Administration. The machinery for appraisal is already in existence and in motion. However, if no machinery were available, serious problems would result. Different criteria (or no criteria at all) would be applied, depending on the power of commercial and selfish interests. It cannot be overstressed that as long as a school system lacks a conceptual professional framework and machinery (procedures and criteria) for curriculum design, it is vulnerable to special interests, misguided political turns, and the exigencies of the moment.

A COMPASS FOR CURRICULUM DESIGN, DEVELOPMENT, AND EVALUATION. As discussed in detail in Chapters 7 and 8, curriculum theorists repeatedly point to three main sources for and influences on curriculum: (1) the ideals and needs of a free society, (2) the nature and needs of learners, and (3) the changing nature of knowledge. Theorists may disagree about the relative importance of these sources, but they seem to be of one mind on one thing: Criteria for curriculum development should be drawn from these sources.

The curriculum leader who attempts to follow this guideline immediately encounters formidable problems. Each of the sources is characterized by conflict and controversy. Wandering through the maze of studies on the nature of the learner, one is struck by the conflicting views about learners on which these studies are based. As discussed elsewhere in this book, the principal psychological orientations—behaviorism and cognitive-field psychology—are divided on their view of the learner. Turning to the needs of society as a source for criteria, one runs into similar difficulties; there are many conflicting views on how the school can best meet societal needs. These views have led to conflicting curricular emphases in the past (witness Bobbitt's criterion of social utility and Dewey's social problem solving). One is not appreciably better off when turning to the nature of knowledge. There are many ways of organizing knowledge, depending on one's purposes and goals.

It is strikingly apparent that in and of themselves, the aforementioned sources cannot provide criteria for curricula. Indeed, without a compass of sorts to find one's way the sources are virtually useless. There is, however, a compass available to curriculum leaders: philosophy. The content and methods of education are unremittingly related to concepts of the individual and his or her relationship to the society in which he or she seeks self-fulfillment and to social ideals. Hence, as discussed in detail in Chapter 9, the development of a philosophy is critical in determining criteria for the curriculum. Conceptions of human nature, the individual, and his or her relation to society will point to the role of knowledge in education. Philosophy is fundamental in determining the very structure and function of the curriculum.

DESIGN AND SYNTHESIS.   According to Taba, "the central problems of a curriculum design are to determine the scope of expected learning, to establish a continuity of learning and proper sequence of content, and to unify ideas from diverse areas (of organized knowledge)."[67] Few theorists would disagree; this is the dominant conception of the work of curriculum development. The problem confronting the curriculum leader is, How does the work proceed?

With the work of curriculum development taking place at the school-system level, the building level, and the classroom level, scope, sequence, balance, and continuity are determined by decisions made at all three levels. A crucial task of supervision is that of coordination so that there is harmony in the overall design.

There are those who believe that starting at the grass-roots or teacher level is the most fruitful approach to curriculum design. Taba was an active proponent of this position. She believed that objectives developed at the school-system level were simply too broad and too vague to guide teachers in the selection of learning experiences. She argued:

> Because it is difficult to develop a new concept of scope and sequence apart from experimenting with the various centers of organization in the specific areas of a curriculum, it seems more efficient to explore first the new possibilities closer to the grass roots. . . .

Many problems involved in formulating the framework cannot be realistically explored on the general level at all. The problem of effective integration can be explored with a reasonable functionality and precision only at the point of developing specific units for specific grade levels. One cannot decide flatly that these two or three subjects should be "unified." It is necessary to experiment with relating specific ideas, knowledge, and skills to ascertain what can be integrated.[68]

Much of the work of curriculum development must take place at the teacher level, if for no other reason than this is where it *does* take place. The classroom is a fertile field for theory development, and is practically a virgin field for that matter. Taba believed in the potential of classroom experimentation for revealing valuable information about educational problems. This was decades ago. Recall from the discussion in Chapter 15 that the concept of teacher research has again attracted the interest of some educational theorists. Such work must be supported at the building level and throughout the school system. Moreover, local school systems have responsibility for systemwide curriculum development. Many problems can be most effectively approached at the school-system level. Hypotheses (possible solutions) for solving curriculum problems can be developed at the system or school level and tested by teachers in their classrooms. The point is that a unidimensional approach to curriculum making is not enough. Curriculum design, development, and evaluation require both the development of broad hypotheses subject to verification and correction by individual teachers and the development of solutions to problems that may lead to fundamental generalizations about the curriculum. It also requires that decisions based on approved practices be made at the school-system level, building level, and teacher level. One approved practice on which we have made little progress is curriculum synthesis or integration.

From the literature and experience it has become clear that the professional approach to curriculum improvement is a problem-solving process. A school can begin by developing its own vision, assessing its own needs, or identifying its own problems as rooted in actual educational situations. What is important is that teachers have their creative energies unleashed by principals and supervisors whom they see as democratic leaders.

PERSPECTIVE

The principalship, which started as a way of providing leadership to teachers in their efforts to solve curriculum and instructional problems, but degenerated into a hierarchical job with a focus on managing people and things, has turned back to its original purpose. And well it should. Without the kind of leadership that frees teachers to act as professionals many problems worsened. The curriculum became ever more fragmented as teachers became ever more isolated from one another. The principal's and supervisor's leadership responsibility is to help teachers function at the highest level of curriculum development—the generative-creative level. Problem identification and problem solving are activities of schools at this level.

As principals and supervisors use the collaborative style, the character of their relationships with teachers changes markedly; segmental relationships and efforts are replaced by sustained interaction involving the principal and groups of teachers. This chapter examined three collaborative strategies for curriculum improvement: forging a common vision, instituting a needs assessment, and involving the faculty in solving practical curriculum problems. Visions can inspire teachers to inspire students. Principals and teachers can seek to work with a broad vision by translating it into curriculum goals. Needs assessment was originally conceived as a top-down, managerial-efficiency approach to school reform. Despite its checkered past, it has been found an effective way of initiating a collaborative curriculum-improvement effort, if teachers are involved and needs assessment is tied to the problem-solving paradigm. Curriculum improvement can best be approached by starting with problems identified by the school faculty. However, if improvements are to be more than feeble gestures, problem solving must become one of the existing regularities in schools. Enhancing their own abilities for democratic leadership is a critical concern of principals.

Although there has been much recent interest in working collaboratively with faculty, the two-dimensional character of supervision remains—evaluation of teachers and helping teachers. Principals still have the responsibility of providing their expertise (or enlisting outside consultants) to help individual teachers and faculty in their curriculum-improvement efforts. Principals still make visits to classrooms and they must play a key role in any effort to develop a coherent, school-wide program to improve the curriculum. The difference between these visits and the visits made by authoritarian principals is that the purpose is collaboration rather than control.

Although *collegiality* has become a popular term in discussions of school restructuring and site-based management, the principal's (and supervisor's) concern is leadership: his or her own and that of other professionals. The kind of leadership provided by the principal should generate leadership opportunities among the professional staff. Principals should seek out opportunities for teachers to attend conferences concerning the problems that teachers encounter in their classrooms. Collegiality is developed in the process of searching with others for problem solutions.

Principals must be alert to an insufficiency of teaching resources; teacher contentment may be a poor indicator of resource adequacy. The lack of resources to interrelate subjects in the curriculum is one reason why schools have made so little progress with curriculum synthesis. Promoting horizontal and vertical curriculum articulation is a leadership responsibility of principals and supervisors. When teachers have been given wide latitude in diagnosing school problems, the solutions are most likely to result in an improved curriculum. This is not surprising; the purpose in providing teachers with more decision-making authority is to allow them the flexibility to deal with students' motivational and learning needs. This may well involve creating an interdisciplinary curriculum so that students can see their own relationship to the world of knowledge and to society.

Teachers are more likely to function at the mediative and generative-creative levels, and not at the imitative level, if what they do is known and supported by the principal and supervisor. Some principals seem to "have little knowledge of what individual teachers, departments or grade-level teams [are] doing."[69] Wholeness should pervade curriculum improvement efforts; the principals, supervisors, and teachers at all levels of the school system should (but seldom do) come together to examine the total curriculum for children and youth.

Although goal setting has been the entry point for curriculum improvement in many schools, it is the principal's responsibility to help the faculty move through the entire curriculum development process—including identifying problems and selecting and organizing learning experiences. This has been grievously neglected over the many years since Tyler's monograph was published.

Without a compass or guiding philosophy to find one's way, the sources from which to draw in curriculum development are inevitably conflicting. The development of a philosophy is fundamental in determining criteria for curriculum design, development, and evaluation. When a curriculum proposal is urged on the school, a procedure should already be in place for acting on that proposal. The principal, supervisor, and other members of the professional staff (as well as district-level administrator) have the responsibility for testing the proposal against the philosophy and ensuring that potentially harmful proposals are rejected. Such proposals come along with surprising frequency.

The hypothesis-testing-correction cycle in curriculum is, as Tyler pointed out, never ending. Moreover, approved practices in education are always evolving. Hence, a curriculum design is a vital living, changing thing. Curriculum development, like science, is an endless frontier. Principals and supervisors must be leaders in a continuing process of investigation and application.

PROBLEMS FOR STUDY AND DISCUSSION

1. In discussing the principal's leadership role in schools where the principal and teachers are working collaboratively on curriculum problems, the use of classroom observations as a means of improving the educational program and the effectiveness of individual teachers has been called into question. In one author's words, "classroom observations by principals make less and less sense." [Ginny V. Lee, "Instructional Leadership as Collaborative Sense-Making," *Theory into Practice,* 30 (Spring 1991), p. 85.] Do you agree or disagree with her statement? Why or why not?

2. What is your assessment of this statement: "Realistically, a principal's readiness to share decision-making responsibilities is more a function of personality and philosophy than training." [Allan V.

Vann, "Shared Decision Making—Effective Leadership," *Principal,* 72 (November 1992), p. 31.]

3. At which level of curriculum development would you say your school is functioning? Draw from the criteria in Table 15–1 in framing your answer.

4. Using the levels of curriculum development in Table 15–1, study a classroom or teacher to determine the level at which the teacher is functioning. As pointed out, teachers as professionals should be at Level III. If the teacher is at Level I or II, how would you as a curriculum leader make it more possible for this teacher to function at Level III?

5. In order to meet the diverse needs of school districts, a number of states have acted to leave more decisions regarding the management of schools and how the curriculum is organized to school

districts, and, in turn, school districts have provided increased discretion at the individual school level. What are the policies of your school district regarding collaborative decision making and the organization or structure of the curriculum?

6. Michael Cohen, an authority on educational change, has pointed out that "teachers and principals often believe that regulations prevent them from doing things differently, when in fact that isn't always the case." [Ron Brandt, "On Restructuring Schools: A Conversation with Mike Cohen," *Educational Leadership,* 48 (May 1991), p. 58.] How do you account for such misperceptions of policies and regulations by principals and teachers? What are the educational consequences of imagining nonexistent obstacles to curriculum improvement?

7. In cases where barriers to curriculum change do exist, many states' school districts will honor requests from individual schools for policy and regulation waivers. Is there a procedure for granting such waivers in your state and school district? If so, under what circumstances are waivers granted?

8. As discussed in this chapter, some principals balk at working with faculty in a democratic-participatory mode because they are afraid of losing control. Drawing from this chapter, what suggestions might be offered a principal who is reluctant to work in a democratic group setting for fear of losing administrative authority? From your experience, what additional suggestions can you offer for helping reluctant principals?

9. Assuming that you are a curriculum leader, what criteria and procedures would you apply in determining which curriculum-reform proposals to adopt in your school or school system? You may draw from any proposals or reports at the national, state, or local level.

10. Why are so many curriculum-reform proposals adopted segmentally and without pilot study at the local level? If curriculum development is seen as a problem-solving process at the local level, would this help protect the school and school district from misguided curriculum-reform proposals, programs, and projects? Explain.

11. Principals report that school-based management has increased their workloads, limiting the time that they can devote to curriculum improvement, yet much curriculum development activity has occurred in many schools. Interview a principal whom you believe to be a curriculum leader to determine how the principal spends most of his or her time and how teachers are involved in decisions that affect the curriculum.

12. Lawrence Cremin held that someone must be responsible for seeing the curriculum as a coherent whole. At the local school level is this someone the principal? Why or why not? If your answer is affirmative, should the principal raise questions about the interrelationship of subject areas as problems for the faculty to deal with, or should the principal wait until the problem is raised by the faculty? Justify your answer.

NOTES

1. Sandra K. Strauber, Sara Stanley, and Carl Wagenknecht, "Site-Based Management at Central-Hower," *Educational Leadership,* 47 (April 1990), pp. 65–66.

2. Mary S. Poplin, "The Leader's New Role: Looking to the Growth of Teachers," *Educational Leadership,* 49 (February 1992), p. 11.

3. School District of Philadelphia, Office of Curriculum and Instructional Support, *Strategic Plan 1991–1992* (Philadelphia: Author, 1992), p. 1.

4. Kenneth A. Leithwood, "The Move toward Transformational Leadership," *Educational Leadership,* 49 (February 1992), p. 9.

5. Daniel Tanner and Laurel Tanner, *Supervision in Education: Problems and Practices* (New York: Macmillan, 1987), pp. 206–236.

6. Leithwood, op. cit.; See also Michael Rutter, Barbara Maughan, Peter Mortimore, and Janet Ouston, *Fifteen Thousand Hours: Secondary Schools and Their Effects on Children* (Cambridge, MA: Harvard University Press, 1979).

7. Poplin, op. cit., p. 11.

8. William C. Rhoden, "For Chicago High School Sports, A Crash Course in Survival," *The New York Times,* October 10, 1992, p. 32.

9. A. M. Chinnery, "While Ideological Battles Rage, Our Schools Keep Crumbling," *The New York Times,* December 21, 1992, p. A14.

10. Douglas E. Mitchell and Sharon Tucker, "Leadership as a Way of Thinking," *Educational Leadership,* 49 (February 1992), p. 34.

11. Marjorie Lewis, "School Libraries, Too, Require Our Attention," *The New York Times,* April 1, 1991, p. A10.

12. Maurice Leiter and Myrna Cooper, "How Teacher Unionists View In-Service Education," *Teachers College Record,* 80 (September 1978), p. 122.

13. Robert M. McClure, "A Teachers' Union Revisits Its Professional Past," Chapter 5 in *The Changing Contexts of Teaching,* Ninety-first Yearbook of the National Society for the Study of Education, Part I (Chicago: University of Chicago Press, 1992), p. 88.

14. Poplin, op. cit., p. 11.

15. Alice Miel, *Changing the Curriculum: A Social Process* (New York: Appleton-Century-Crofts, 1946), p. 190.

16. Ralph W. Tyler, *Basic Principles of Curriculum and Instruction* (Chicago: University of Chicago Press, 1949), p. 37.

17. Henry M. Levin, "Cost-effectiveness at Quarter Century," Chapter 8 in *Evaluation and Education: At Quarter Century,* Ninetieth Yearbook of the National Society for the Study of Education, Part II (Chicago: University of Chicago Press, 1991), p. 192.

18. Ibid.

19. Ibid., pp. 200–201.

20. Ibid., p. 204.

21. James A. Beane, Conrad F. Toepfer, Jr., and Samuel J. Alessi, Jr., *Curriculum Planning and Development* (Boston: Allyn and Bacon, 1986), p. 282.

22. Benjamin S. Bloom, J. Thomas Hastings, and George F. Madaus, *Handbook on Formative and Summative Evaluation of Student Learning* (New York: McGraw-Hill, 1971).

23. Janice I. Solkov-Brecher, "A Successful Model for School-Based Planning," *Educational Leadership,* 50 (September 1992), pp. 52–54.

24. Ibid.

25. John Dewey, *How We Think,* rev. ed. (Lexington, MA: D. C. Heath, 1933).

26. Michael G. Fullan and Matthew B. Miles, "Getting Reform Right: What Works and What Doesn't," *Phi Delta Kappan,* 73 (June 1992), p. 751.

27. Solkov-Brecher, op. cit., p. 52.

28. Ibid., p. 54.

29. Fullan and Miles, op. cit., p. 750.

30. Larry Cuban, "Reforming Again, Again and Again," *Educational Researcher,* 19 (April 1990), pp. 3–13.

31. Seymour B. Sarason, *The Culture of the School and the Problem of Change,* 2nd ed. (Boston: Allyn and Bacon, 1982).

32. Tom Rusk Vickery, "ODDM: A Workable Model for Total School Improvement," *Educational Leadership,* 47 (April 1990), p. 69.

33. Sarason, op. cit., p. 63.

34. Arthur J. Lebowitz, "Staff Buys in through Shared Decision-Making," *The School Administrator,* 49 (January 1992), p. 12.

35. Ibid.

36. "The Good Principal: A Tradition Breaker," *The New York Times,* February 21, 1990, p. B10.

37. Kenneth J. Tewel, "Collaborative Supervision—Theory into Practice," *NASSP Bulletin,* 73 (April 1989), pp. 74–83.

38. Ibid., p. 75.

39. Ibid., p. 77.

40. John Dewey, *How We Think* (Lexington, MA: D. C. Heath, 1910), p. 12.

41. Ibid.

42. Tewel, op. cit., p. 79.

43. Ibid., p. 78.

44. Herbert A. Simon, *Administrative Behavior,* 3rd ed. (New York: Free Press, 1976), p. 227. See also, Tanner and Tanner, op. cit., pp. 148–158.

45. Kenneth J. Benne, "Theory of Cooperative Planning," *Teachers College Record,* 53 (January 1952), pp. 429–435. See also, Fullan and Miles, op. cit., p. 751.

46. Fullan and Miles, op. cit., p. 751.

47. Consortium on Chicago School Research, *Charting Reform: The Principals' Perspective* (Chicago: Author, December 1992), p. 24.

48. Robert A. Dahl, *Democracy and Its Critics* (New Haven, CT: Yale University Press, 1989), pp. 92–93.

49. Ibid.

50. Fullan and Miles, op. cit., p. 751.
51. Miel, op. cit., p. 160.
52. Ibid., p. 179.
53. Ibid.
54. Tanner and Tanner, op. cit., p. 133.
55. Miel, op. cit., p. 140.
56. Lawrence A. Cremin, *The Genius of American Education* (New York: Vintage Books, 1965), p. 58.
57. Hilda Taba, *Curriculum Development: Theory and Practice* (New York: Harcourt, 1962), pp. 12–13.
58. Tyler, op. cit.
59. John Goodlad, "The Impact of the *Basic Principles of Curriculum and Instruction*," Unpublished paper presented at the Annual Meeting of the Society for the Study of Curriculum History, San Francisco, April 1984, pp. 89–90.
60. Tyler, op. cit., p. 128.
61. Goodlad, op. cit., p. 92.
62. Tyler, op. cit., p. 128.
63. Cited in Fred Hechinger, "Critical Commission Is Criticized," *The New York Times,* February 28, 1984, p. 6.
64. Goodlad, op. cit.
65. Tyler, op. cit., p. 123.
66. George F. Madaus and Mary M. West, *The Influence of Testing on Teaching Math and Science in Grades 4–12* (Chestnut Hill, MA: Center for the Study of Testing, Evaluation, and Educational Policy, Boston College, 1992).
67. Taba, op. cit., p. 13.
68. Ibid., pp. 439–440.
69. Edward F. Pajak and Carl D. Glickman, "Dimensions of School District Improvement," *Educational Leadership,* 46 (May 1989), p. 63.

SELECTED REFERENCES

Association for Supervision and Curriculum Development. *Changing School Culture Through Staff Development,* 1990 Yearbook. Alexandria, VA: Author, 1990.

Association for Supervision and Curriculum Development. *The Governance of Curriculum,* 1994 Yearbook. Alexandria, VA: Author, 1994.

Connelly, Michael F., and Clandenin, D. Jean. *Teachers as Curriculum Planners: Narratives of Experience.* New York: Teachers College Press, 1988.

Dahl, Robert A. *Democracy and Its Critics.* New Haven, CT: Yale University Press, 1989.

Dewey, John. *How We Think.* Lexington, MA: D. C. Heath, 1910; rev. ed., 1933.

Fullan, Michael. *The New Meaning of Educational Change.* New York: Teachers College Press, 1991.

Jackson, Philip W. (ed.). *Handbook of Research on Curriculum.* New York: Macmillan, 1992.

Joyce, Bruce (ed.). *Changing School Culture through Staff Development.* Alexandria, VA: Association for Supervision and Curriculum Development, 1990.

Joyce, Bruce, and Showers, Beverly. *Student Achievement through Staff Development.* White Plains, NY: Longman, 1988.

Lane, John J., and Epps, Edgar G. *Restructuring the Schools: Problems and Prospects.* Berkeley, CA: McCutchan, 1992.

Lieberman, Ann, and Miller, Lynne (eds.). *Staff Development: New Demands, New Realities, New Perspectives.* New York: Teachers College Record, 1978.

Miel, Alice. *Changing the Curriculum: A Social Process.* New York: Appleton-Century-Crofts, 1946.

National Society for the Study of Education. *The Changing Contexts of Teaching.* Ninety-first Yearbook, Part I. Chicago: University of Chicago Press, 1992.

National Society for the Study of Education. *Critical Issues in Curriculum.* Eighty-seventh Yearbook, Part I. Chicago: University of Chicago Press, 1988.

National Society for the Study of Education. *Evaluation and Education: At Quarter Century.* Ninetieth Yearbook, Part II. Chicago: University of Chicago Press, 1991.

National Society for the Study of Education. *In-Service Education.* Fifty-sixth Yearbook, Part I. Chicago: University of Chicago Press, 1957.

National Society for the Study of Education. *Teacher Research and Educational Reform.* Ninety-third

Yearbook, Part I. Chicago: University of Chicago Press, 1994.

Sarason, Seymour B. *The Culture of the School and the Problem of Change,* 2nd ed. Boston: Allyn and Bacon, 1982.

Simon, Herbert A. *Administrative Behavior,* 3rd ed. New York: Free Press, 1976.

Taba, Hilda. *Curriculum Development: Theory and Practice.* New York: Harcourt, 1962.

Tanner, Daniel, and Tanner, Laurel. *Supervision in Education: Problems and Practices.* New York: Macmillan, 1987.

Tyler, Ralph W. *Basic Principles of Curriculum and Instruction.* Chicago: University of Chicago Press, 1949.

17

SCHOOL RENEWAL—
WAYS AND MEANS

Renewal is essential for life and growth. This is just as true for schools as it is for living things. Dewey writes about renewal in the biological sense in the opening paragraphs of his classic book, *Democracy and Education* (1916). Living things use environmental energies—light and moisture, for example—to further their own existence. The return they get for their effort is growth. "Life is a self-renewing process through action upon the environment," says Dewey.[1]

Dewey's book is about school renewal. Democracy is irrevocably connected with growth and renewal through education. Realization of the democratic ideal requires a curriculum that is humanized through its connection with the interests and common concerns of human beings. In Dewey's words,

> [t]he scheme of a curriculum must take account of the adaptation of studies to the needs of existing community life; it must select with the intention of improving the life we live in common so that the future shall be better than the past. Moreover, the curriculum must be planned with placing essentials first, and refinements second. The things which are socially most fundamental, that is, which have to do with experiences which the widest groups share, are the essentials. The things which represent the needs of specialized groups and technical pursuits are secondary.[2]

Remarkably similar ideas run through recent literature on school improvement. For example, in a discussion of the principal's curriculum leadership role, Pajak and McAfee take issue with policies that redirect the mission of the schools toward regaining the nation's technological leadership and dominance in world industrial markets. "We believe that schools continue to have an even more important charge, that of preparing students for citizenship in a democracy," declare Pajak and McAfee.[3]

Democratic citizenship is a practical goal and, as such, requires experience in democratic relationships. As one educator put it, "[i]ts essence is transfer."[4] In some schools students are getting the practice. No better example can be found than a sixth-grade classroom in Ohio. Investigating a real problem—a local creek contaminated by a chemical spill—the students became experts in testing water quality. After meeting with environmental experts and purchasing a chemical testing kit, they embarked on the task of sampling the tributaries to the area watershed. Quite appropriately, their class became a trusted source for testing local wells. Moreover, the class produced radio announcements on how to keep water supplies safe.[5] Here is a continuation of the emphasis on democratic citizenship that had been so much a part of the Deweyan view of education. As noted by one educator (who provides a host of examples), schools today are "reclaiming the democratic vision" of students as involved citizens.[6] However, many schools have not done so. According to Boyer, "there remains a widespread concern that education for citizenship has been neglected."[7] Principals have a crucial role in remedying the neglect by supporting and encouraging projects that help students see from their own experience that what they do as citizens makes a difference.

The environmental energies that Dewey talked about are social changes that act on the school. Schools can turn these changes to an educational advantage and, in so doing, renew themselves. Today, the most profound changes are environmental in the real sense; that is, the environments in which schools find themselves are rapidly changing and cultural differences in school populations continue to grow. Recent educational policies stress the celebration of cultural and ethnic differences, and it might seem to some that Dewey's philosophy emphasizing "whatever binds people together"[8] is out of date. The world has always been made up of people who are very different from one another, in Dewey's time as well as now. Bringing them together in one classroom and one school is not a new phenomenon. Dewey's idea that democracy is characterized by a "widening of the area of shared concerns" is based on a recognition that cultural and individual differences lead to differing experiences.[9] Human experience is an interactive process. As the school helps each child to participate with others in finding the best available knowledge to make a decision, a common experience is achieved. Such experiences are connected to the democratic ideal. The more diverse the school population, the greater is the need to provide shared experiences for developing mutual understanding and respect. Indeed, such experiences are clearly in evidence in many of the schools we have visited where the students represent an astonishing variety of cultural backgrounds.

Changing populations are just one influence impelling schools to renew themselves. Others include (1) progress in teacher professionalism, (2) the continuing study of what students should gain from the curriculum, (3) new ideas about how students learn, (4) equity concerns (increasing access to curriculum), (5) ideas about how organizations can function more effectively, (6) problems in the larger society—including those that students bring with them to school, and (7) the perceived failure of previous reform efforts.

A good school is in a constant state of renewal, which is to say it is always improving. How is a principal or supervisor to wend through the maze of often conflicting reform proposals and provide leadership in the right direction? These are crucial questions and this chapter attempts to provide some insights. The chapter examines the paths and prescriptions in light of their promise for school renewal and makes suggestions for principals and supervisors.

PATHS TO SCHOOL IMPROVEMENT
The Magic Bullet Approach

Most proponents of school improvement promulgate a single idea or method to give a new lease on life to the schools. Collegiality among the school faculty, autonomy for individual schools in curriculum decision making, new organizational structures, national education standards, multiculturalism, and gender-equity proposals (intended to offer the same opportunities to girls as boys) are examples. Those who promote a singular approach are likely to be impatient with other approaches and to convey the notion that there is only one path to school improvement: theirs. As Bruce Joyce observes, "there is a tendency to suggest that those who follow any other approach to school improvement are off track."[10]

Proponents of what might be called a single-factor path to reform see their proposal as a complete answer. Reformers tend to use their own field of interest as a lens for viewing schools. Thus, those with an interest in group dynamics advocate developing collegiality among the faculty as the improvement approach. Those whose interest is teaching propose that school faculties study generic teaching skills and the styles of outstanding teachers. Those who believe that the application of research findings is the answer to school improvement propose that school faculty familiarize themselves with research on effective schools.[11] Each approach is treated as a magic bullet—a total prescription for school improvement by advocates.

That there is a continuous barrage of segmental approaches may come as a shock to the new principal or supervisor. Segmental approaches often have conflicting effects or lead to distorted priorities. There are no magic bullets. Some approaches such as the foregoing can be synthesized as principals and teachers work together to solve problems. Teachers study *relevant* research in efforts to improve the curriculum. The emphasis is on relevance because not all of the research on effective schools is relevant to a given situation. To study research in absence of a problem can have two detrimental effects: teachers' time is wasted, which all too frequently happens with inservice programs, and more important, perhaps, teachers are encouraged to put findings into practice that may not be applicable to their own situation. As Joyce points out, approaches to school improvement are both connected and synthesized in the course of solving school problems:

> Many specialists in organizational development have found that a faculty can best develop their collegiality in combination with solving actual school problems in an area of agreed-on need such as the curriculum. Keeping a real problem in mind ensures that practical problem solving is kept prominent and that group process doesn't become an end in itself.[12]

NEW ORGANIZATIONAL STRUCTURES.   Educational restructuring was a popular idea for improving schools in the 1990s. Whatever the principles that justify new changes in the governance of schools (curriculum decisions at the school site, for example), restructuring had its origins in business, industry, and government. In business and industry, restructuring was a code word meaning reorganization for the purpose of slimming down the size of the organization and, presumably, making it more efficient. But downsizing often left companies without experienced people who have solved various kinds of problems and who helped contribute to the success of the organization.[13]

As discussed previously, some structural innovations in education have had similar effects; financially strapped school systems have justified the downsizing of their central office staff on the alleged ground that teachers should be granted independence to develop their own curricula based on the needs of their own students. This has left teachers without the supervisory support necessary for improving curriculum and instruction.

In education, restructuring has had a broader meaning than in the business world (although one might be wise to keep the roots in mind). In education, the issue in restructuring is school improvement. Many of the allegedly new strategies proposed in the restructuring movement of the 1990s are not new; interdisciplinary curriculums and opportunities for teachers to work together are examples. In this sense, the restructuring movement was simply recalling educators to their approved practices in the field of curriculum development. However, the focus of change has been on new organizational structures, without making the needed connections with curriculum development and school improvement.[14] The idea (really an old mistake in school reform) is that if we just change the way schools are organized, substantive curriculum change will follow. Restructuring has generally stopped with organizational change. Take, for example, team teaching where teachers work with 100 or so students. The objective of the team structure is curriculum improvement. As Newmann observes, generally curriculum is discussed "no more deeply than choosing a general theme for study (the environment, culture, estimation)."[15] Newmann views the situation with a compelling sense that teachers need more time together to plan, and they need greater access to resources. We add that the resources should include actual examples and models of interdisciplinary units. Teachers need models to follow.

Strategies for restructuring include smaller schools, school choice, local autonomy, national curriculum standards in subject areas, and interagency collaboration (coordinating community social services with school programs). In a critique of restructuring, Newmann points out that the proposed structural changes are not part of a coherent plan, and he points to the need for linking changes together.[16] The reason they are not connected is that they were never intended to be. Each proposal is viewed by its advocates as the way to renew schools. Hence, instructional improvement is seen and treated as entirely separate from curriculum improvement. Not only is there the pervading problem of segmental and disjointed programs, but many of the ideas and strategies are in conflict. For example, there is a simultaneous effort to institute national standards in subject fields and to promote interdisciplinary curriculums. According to Kirst, such standards are likely to have a detrimental effect on curriculum synthesis.[17]

How are such conflicts to be avoided in school improvement efforts? As Newmann points out, the answer lies in focusing on curriculum development—improving learning opportunities for all students.[18] It is inevitable that educators will run up against proposals that never touch the curriculum, but they must wage a constant battle to keep the curriculum—what is taught and how—as the focus.

SCHOOL SIZE AND CURRICULAR GAIN. The story of school size and its relation to curriculum improvement is a most interesting one. By 1900 education leaders were well aware of the advantages of school consolidation and district reorganization for improving educational opportunities. When two or more poor districts—each hardly able to support its own one-room rural school—combined, the result was speedily obvious in a larger school with improved educational services, facilities, and resources. By the middle of the twentieth century the number of school districts was decreasing rapidly and the average size increasing. Bus transportation had made it possible for fewer schools of better quality to serve larger numbers of students. The schools had more competent teachers, more cosmopolitan pupil populations, an expanded and balanced curriculum, and better facilities and resources. It is true, of course, that some communities opposed (and continue to oppose) consolidation and district reorganization. The stressful conditions associated with inadequate tax resources and consequent inequality of educational opportunity have caused a continuing trend toward this kind of centralization in the United States.

In the larger cities the story was vastly different. Populations increased—indeed, burgeoned—concurrently with the development of public education, which had its greatest momentum in urban sections. From the start, urban centers demanded larger education facilities than did rural areas. Much has been written about the huge size and factory-like atmosphere of urban junior and senior high schools and the need for smaller schools that will give students more personal attention.

SCHOOLS WITHIN SCHOOLS. The problem confronting educators is how to reorganize schools so that they are smaller and yet preserve the curricular advantages of large schools. For decades, there has been a solution: schools within schools. In the 1960s Evanston (Illinois) Township High School adopted the house plan that, as Goodlad points out, is "a term that is quite commonly used by private colleges."[19] Whether or not the term was appropriated in order to assure the support of parents for the reorganization is not known, and is left for historians of Evanston Township High School to determine. The school of several thousand students was divided into smaller schools, housed within the existing buildings. The houses are organized vertically so that students are connected with one house during their high school years. Each house has its own faculty and counselors, and provides a curriculum of general education or unified studies—those learnings that all educated members of a society hold in common. Specialized studies are taken in other units.

In general, one is able to identify three advantages to the school-within-a-school plan. The first is more opportunity for faculty to get to know students and give them individual attention. This is important for all students but particularly in urban schools, which may have as many as 5,000 students, many of whom are considered at risk. A second advantage is that the houses can share the library, laboratories, studios, shops, and other central resources that schools must have if they are to offer educational services of high quality. A third advantage is that teachers have a greater opportunity to work together with a given population of heterogeneous students throughout the high-school years. In the words of Deborah Meier, a secondary school administrator in Harlem, "[i]t's not guaranteed to happen in a small school, but it is guaranteed that it will not happen in a large one."[20]

Although educators continue to point to the industrial climate of full-size high schools as an unfavorable environment for at-risk youth, relatively few urban high schools have adopted the house plan. In his large-scale study of schooling in the 1980s, Goodlad made this observation: "The idea of creating schools within schools is not new, but it has had negligible impact on practice."[21]

CHARTER SCHOOLS AND THEME SCHOOLS.   In the late 1980s and early 1990s, with large grants from the Pew Charitable Trusts, the Philadelphia school system encouraged teachers to develop charters—units within the city's comprehensive high schools. The objective was to reduce the dropout rate and improve graduation rates as well as college access. In addition to general education, the charter school units each have a specific focus such as preparing for careers, science and technology, creative writing, or humanities, and they each serve a heterogeneous group of from 200 to 400 students and are run by a team of ten to twelve teachers. As in the house plan, students and teachers remain together through the students' high school years. However, unlike the house plan, in which all students and faculty are assigned to a small unit, the charters are voluntary. At this writing, eleven of the district's twenty-two high schools were fully chartered; that is, all faculty and students were attached to a charter.[22] Teachers affiliated with a charter have a common planning time to develop the curriculum, which is often interdisciplinary.

Coupled with the goal of making school environments less anonymous for students is that of renewing teachers' professional excitement and interest in teaching. Teachers who have been involved in creating Philadelphia's schools-within-schools travel to national conferences, participate in curriculum-planning seminars and summer institutes, and have contact with teachers throughout the United States. The grants to the school district are, of course, what made these professional development opportunities possible. According to the Pew Charitable Trusts, they were the largest grants ever made to a school system by one philanthropy.[23]

Most of the teachers are senior in terms of their longevity in the area high schools and they have seen highly touted innovations come and go. Their interest and enthusiasm probably would not have been forthcoming except for tangible evidence of the school system's commitment. The evidence was in the form of smaller classes and authority to develop curriculum accompanied by resources: time, materials, and expertise. Some charters have connections with universities whose faculty have served as curriculum consultants.

Preliminary data indicated that compared with students not in charters, those in charters had a higher attendance rate and were more likely to receive passing grades in major subjects.[24] The charter students may well have outperformed noncharter students because the former were a self-selected (better motivated) group, coupled with the boost given students and teachers through favorable publicity. However, it is clear that the funds for teachers' professional development, material resources, and smaller classes must have had a regenerating effect on teachers as well as students, rather like a blood transfusion. This point is enormously important because, generally, the funds for staff development and material resources are the first to go in efforts to trim school budgets, and at the same time, class sizes are increased. Some educators concluded that the achievement data show that "small schools can turn schools around."[25] However, the conclusion is probably unwarranted. There was something else going on, namely, teachers' professional development and supportive resources.

All students should be provided with a favorable learning environment and as much individual attention from their teachers as possible. Voluntary plans (such as Philadelphia's charters) do not provide all students with optimal access to the curriculum. All this adds up to the fact that the house plan is still a sound, indeed preferred, strategy for renewing large high schools because all students have an opportunity to be in small units. No reorganization is a magic bullet. One of the great and good fortunes of the Philadelphia schools-within-schools plan was that teachers were provided with rich opportunities and resources for professional development, contacts with other teachers outside the school system, and being curriculum makers, which are all essential in any school renewal effort.

In the 1990s other school districts, New York, for example, were establishing small alternative schools within existing school buildings and in separate sites.[26] Curricular gain—or loss—must be the dominant and overriding consideration in any plan to develop smaller high schools. This means that careful consideration must be given to the possible danger of narrowing the curriculum in alternative schools to meet a special-interest function for a special (isolated) pupil population.

DISTINCTIVE VERSUS COSMOPOLITAN SCHOOLS. Schools like individuals have their own personalities. In the 1990s, however, some reformers carried this idea considerably further, arguing that by developing distinctive characters, schools could renew themselves. The idea that schools should be different from one another was promoted in particular by advocates of public school choice as a means of school improvement.[27] In a policy brief issued by the RAND Corporation's Institute on Education and Training, this question is raised: "Does the school define and maintain an appropriate, distinctive character?"[28] According to RAND, designing schools with distinctive character is the key to educational improvement and "the basic premise is variety, not uniformity."[29] The focus on difference blurs the fact that good schools are alike in many ways. As Henry Levin points out, all good schools expose all youngsters to the richest possible experiences, and also connect the school "Dewey-style" with the children's own experiences.[30] Levin, whose goal is to accelerate and enrich the learning of at-risk children, has been successful in bringing the children into the mainstream. Levin's program and underlying theses are not new. The field of education has generated a core of approved practices from research that all good schools should follow. There is a universal quality rather than a limited scope that characterizes good schools. The cosmopolitan school, not the special-interest school, is required for renewal.

The Comprehensive-Connected Approach

As indicated in the previous section, single-factor paths to reform are connected in the course of solving a curriculum problem. Curriculum frameworks, for example, require a coherent strategy for their implementation. The strategy includes providing improved programs of teacher education, staff development to help teachers understand and implement the new procedures, peer teaching, and the creation of networks to link teachers and scholars, such as the Foxfire Teachers Outreach Network, the National Writing Project, and the Urban Mathematics Collaborative. If solutions are to be sustained, problem solving involves multifaceted strategies deriving from an ecological or environmental perspective. The education environment should be supportive, not contradictory.

In Chapter 14 it was pointed out that many teachers today are working in an environment of contradictory policies. There has been a national policy shift from reforms focused on lower-level mechanical skills for disadvantaged children to higher-level skills and idea-oriented teaching for everyone. Meanwhile, state and district standardized testing is often still geared to the old policy. In the 1990s, some reformers were seeking systemic change, an attempt to tightly align state policies—especially those concerning curriculum, textbooks, and assessment—with goals for student learning. That policies should promote a coherent environment for teachers rather than one of conflicting policies is inarguable. However, as Linda Darling-Hammond noted, there is danger in confusing linear approaches with coherence. "It is important for us to be connecting the right ideas to make the environment more coherent for school people," she said, going on to give this warning: "In a rush to get things lined up, there is always a danger that we will do something not very thoughtful."[31] We add that by starting with a curriculum problem rather than a series of disconnected ideas, policymakers at the state and local levels have the best assurance of creating a coherent and supporting environment for teachers. Linear approaches tend to fit a factory-like production model of schooling, a model that is ill suited to the educative process that is concerned with human growth.

Another point of importance is that new ideas about teaching and learning may influence state and district policies rather than the other way around. Thus, there may well be times when policy and practice are conflicting. Teachers who believe in a new practice will often follow it despite the fact that policy has not caught up. As one of our students recounts:

> Four years ago, I eagerly and enthusiastically began my teaching career in Spring Branch Independent School District. I was fulfilling my student-teaching requirement in the district in which I am employed. Student teaching provided many

opportunities for administering language arts to the assigned first-grade class. As modeled by the supervising teacher, I strictly followed the curriculum guide page by page as composed by the district. Following these guides offered a sense of routine and structure that most new professionals find comforting. Of course, in reflecting, the curriculum at this particular school or School X was functioning at Level I of the Levels of Curriculum Development. The student teaching experience was not conducive for teacher creativity or imagination.

A year later I was officially hired by the school district to serve as a first-grade teacher at School Y. Now the setting was completely different from the prior year. Literature-based language arts was strongly supported and utilized by the first-grade teachers even though it contradicted the present curriculum in language arts. One should note that the actual curriculum guide called for the teaching of isolated skills or "clusters." Cluster tests were administered before progressing to the next set of skills or clusters. Obviously what was being promoted, supported and implemented at School Y did not have a place in the existing curriculum. Thus many teachers were forced to create their own unofficial, unwritten curriculums.

One can only imagine my anxiety. I was now to follow an unwritten curriculum that all other teachers on that grade level were utilizing. The structure of following a written curriculum page by page was now absent. Nevertheless I survived my first year of teaching simply due to the total support of my fellow team members. The team (the other seven teachers on the grade level) "carried" me through my first year by modeling, sharing and most of all communicating effectively.

Ironically the following year the whole district made a 360 degree turnabout by adopting a brand new language-arts curriculum. This curriculum was totally a literature-base approach to teaching language arts. It provided the missing link that many teachers were looking for; it officially validated the implementation of literature-base language arts. School Y, which was already promoting literature-base language arts totally embraced this new curriculum with open arms.

Teachers should be encouraged by their supervisors to base their teaching on the body of approved practices in the curriculum field, whether or not those practices happen to support present policies. At this writing, it must be observed that at no time in the past few decades have state and local district policies been as supportive of approved practices as at the present, although the picture is one of contradiction in that state and national testing programs are working counter to this trend.

THE ECOLOGY OF CURRICULUM RENEWAL. Clearly the way to reform is not with a linear top-down approach. As a noted social scientist observed, "the world of work consists mostly of horizontal relationships."[32] A number of education theorists (who have also been deeply involved with practice) have given school renewal a biological turn by viewing those involved as part of an ecosystem. John Goodlad uses an ecological model in which policymakers at state and local levels, teachers, administrators, and others are concerned with an array of broad educational goals and the application of approved practices for reaching them. Relationships among the individuals and groups in the ecology of schooling are multiple rather than linear, and the main concern of policymakers is to provide teachers with what they need for reaching the goals rather than with a punitive, intimidating atmosphere.[33] For example, policymakers at the state and local level must provide a supportive environment at the school level. From experience we know that this is the only way that continuous, effective curriculum-development activities at the school level will take place. As everyone knows, however, the support often fails to materialize. Goodlad provides us with some helpful ideas on why linkages so often fail to happen and how they might. According to Goodlad, the way people are now linked is ineffective for two closely related reasons: (1) top-down, one-way directives are the approach to "improvement" and (2) there has been a "pathological emphasis on accountability"; each individual is concerned with the adequateness of the behavior of those at some other level or unit.[34] The model that has been followed for so long in the world of schooling is the factory-production model; top-down directives are concerned with the production of high test scores.

As Goodlad points out, a healthy school is concerned with more than test scores because the society wants schools to meet personal-social growth and vocational goals as well as academic goals. High test scores can never be an indicator of school health.[35] A healthy school is a renewing school, continually checking what it does against knowledge about how students learn and teachers teach and changes in the larger society—the wider environment, which is part of the ecosystem of schools, and we had better not forget it.

A NEW KIND OF POLICY.   Recent education policies reflect the recognition that top-down strategies for curriculum improvement are ineffective. There has been a discernible movement in many school systems toward an organic system of organization, which is a concept similar to Goodlad's ecological model. There has been much interest in involving teachers in a collaborative effort to improve the curriculum. For the first time in many years, this critically important approved practice in the literature has, in many sections, become formulated into a policy.

AN OLD MIND-SET.   Unfortunately, however, there is usually a rider to the policy of collaborative curriculum improvement: Teachers must be held accountable for the decisions they make. Indeed, there is an emphasis on teacher (and principal) accountability in most school decentralization plans, and this is typically determined by pupil test results. Central administrators thus have not effectively detached themselves from the production model. There are, of course, stunning exceptions, and these superintendents have been able to achieve marked success in renewing their school system (see Chapter 16).

Goodlad suggests that the concept of accountability be changed to responsibility with each unit concerned with its own behavior. "Legislators, for example, should be concerned with whether they are providing what schools and those in them need to function effectively."[36] The emphasis, Goodlad argues, should be on providing teachers with the time and resources they must have for curriculum renewal. What Goodlad is saying is that a different paradigm or view of the world must guide school renewal efforts. His own words concerning this paradigm shift are worth quoting: "One-way directives are replaced by multiple interactions; leadership by authority is replaced by leadership by knowledge; following rules and regulations is replaced by inquiring behavior; accountability is replaced by high expectations, responsibility, and a level of trust that includes freedom to make mistakes; and much more."[37] Goodlad is not alone in proposing a holistic approach to school renewal.

Morris Janowitz, a sociologist, emphasized the importance of following an aggregation model in transforming urban schools, as opposed to the specialization or segmental model and piecemeal change. In the aggregation model the focus is on "the totality of the situation in which the teacher finds herself."[38] In Janowitz's model, teachers as professionals make use of curriculum specialists and other resource personnel, bringing them into the classroom as needed. According to Janowitz, the public school system's effectiveness in reaching its academic and social goals depends primarily on increasing teachers' authority and professional expertise.[39] Like Goodlad, Janowitz argued that holistic conceptual models must guide policymakers.

In Janowitz's model, the concept of holism extends to curriculum. Janowitz believed that integrated curriculum approaches are important for renewing urban schools, particularly plans relating knowledge and the skills of democratic living. As a guiding principle, the curriculum should reflect "interdependence of academic and socialization goals."[40] In a sense, observed Janowitz, educational psychologists have contributed to the rationale for a segmental rather than complete approach to curriculum. They have focused attention so completely on articulating curriculum content with the cognitive development of the child that it began to be viewed by many educators as a complete curriculum theory. The child's social needs and those of the larger society were forgotten or pushed far into the background. When thought of at all, they were treated as unrelated to and of less importance than academic goals.

PIAGET AND CURRICULUM IMPROVEMENT. Janowitz pointed out that Jean Piaget himself questioned the American adaptation of Piaget's process of intellectual development to curriculum reform. According to Janowitz, Piaget's work and its interpretations have meaning for classroom teachers "not because they supply engineering-type guides for curriculum development, but because, directly or indirectly, they increase the interpersonal capacity of the teacher."[41] Many streams flow into the teacher's professional knowledge and they interact continuously. The point of importance is that school renewal requires an aggregate rather than segmental approach and that making subject matter meaningful through synthesis is the way to curriculum reform.

The idea that social and academic goals must be dealt with as interdependent is, of course, not new; Dewey pioneered in melding these goals in his laboratory school. Janowitz believed that educators in difficult schools could use the idea as the basis for teaching children social responsibility and concern for others. Social responsibility needs to have a more established place in the curriculum for all children but has an immediately functional purpose in schools where teachers have to struggle to keep order and where older children victimize the younger ones. From a practical standpoint, social goals are essential for teachers to teach and for students to do well in school. Or, in Janowitz's words, "any system of improved academic effectiveness must rest on the creation of a classroom climate based on mutual respect or value sharing."[42]

Segmental Approaches Impede Renewal

A problem with segmental approaches is that they tend to deal with specific techniques, procedures, practices, or programs targeted for one population group or level of schooling, making curriculum articulation more difficult. Even more serious, the specialized-segmental changes not only work in isolation, but also often work in opposition and contradiction. Moreover, preoccupation with one group may cause the problems of other groups to remain unaddressed. This is shortsightedness in its most virulent form. The problems of one group do not remain their own, but affect other youngsters as well as us all. Kindergarten through twelfth-grade students are part of an ecological community, in interaction with the environment of the school and with each other and the wider ecosystem outside schools.

The federal government's focus on early education well illustrates the segmental approach. The year 1965 saw the creation of Project Head Start, a program intended to compensate for the education handicaps of disadvantaged preschool children and give them a good start in school. Policymakers had been profoundly influenced by research on child development, especially Benjamin Bloom's conclusion that the major portion of brain development takes place very early in life. Although Bloom never said that high school was too late for intervention, many policymakers, seeking a shortcut, drew that conclusion from his book.[43] As a consequence, the adolescent was largely neglected or written off. The idea that early childhood is a crucial period for countering adverse intellectual and social environments was supported by other authorities on child development. Early education as the means of ensuring a child's success in school—and a successful adult life—became national policy.

The next three decades were a record of continuing focus on young children. According to Schorr, "Head Start was so deeply embedded in the American landscape that no administration could uproot it or even significantly cut it back."[44] This surely cannot be debated. Schorr goes on to observe that preschool programs are "now widely recognized as the most successful large-scale attempts in the last quarter century to improve the prospects of high-risk children."[45] She might have pointed out that although a part of the landscape, such programs have not been part of the school. (Granted that some Head Start programs are school-based, they are administered separately.) The point of importance is that the effort to improve opportunities was targeted to young children, and the idea that they are the group most likely to be salvaged from lives of poverty has continued to affect present policies. Nevertheless, if preschool programs such as Head Start are to have long-term benefits, as opposed to short-term successes that wear out, then these programs will need to be integrated into a holistic and coordinated effort—from preschool through adolescence. Intense projects emphasizing college preparation for disadvantaged high school youth have been highly successful. (The emphasis is on intensity. Schorr notes that when resources are diluted and spread to other schools after a project has been found successful, the program loses its impact.[46]) The point remains: There has been no attempt to meet the needs of older at-risk students on the scale of Head Start. The dropout rate continues to be high, especially among Hispanic and African-American students.

It has long been argued that Head Start has not been maximally effective because children who were in the program enter traditionally organized schools.

The overriding reason, however, was probably that reformers failed to use an ecological model in planning their interventions with at-risk youngsters. They failed to consider the interaction of students in the ecosystem of a school (as well as outside school), and the direction of influence, which is from older to younger children. In inner-city poverty areas, teenagers have the most impact on the school's social environment and on the attitudes of children of all ages toward the school's goals. In view of this, Janowitz saw the early education movement as "at best a partial strategy. At worst a basic error in priorities." Disadvantaged fourteen- to eighteen-year-olds generally "develop a sense of frustration and a group life in opposition to the goals of the school [and i]n this group are opinion leaders in the slum youth culture and the effective bearers of the culture of the slum from one generation to the next." Thus, he argued, a case could be made that this group should have the highest priority if comprehensive changes are to be made in the curriculum and school culture.[47]

Janowitz's observation about the impact of high school students on younger children seems even more valid today. Troubled adolescents still drop out and hang out on street corners; they still influence younger children who also fail to make it to their own high school graduation. (The school environment is more violent in some inner-city neighborhoods than it was when Janowitz drew his conclusions, in the late 1960s.) Curriculum improvement and school renewal are attainable, but only if we follow a comprehensive approach.

The Problem of Professional Isolation

The rationale behind school decentralization in the late 1980s and 1990s was that decision making in large school systems was overly centralized; individual principals had insufficient operational discretion to improve the curriculum and obtain the necessary resources. (Interestingly, this was also a rationale for decentralization in the 1960s; the two movements are probably best viewed by curriculum workers as continuous.) Janowitz had a different perspective on the principal's problem. The principal, he argued, actually has a great deal of power, and successful principals have mobilized considerable resources through the system itself and in the community. Moreover, the principal has a major role in shaping the school's social climate and the attitude of the school staff toward curriculum improvement. The principal's main problem, he contended, is isolation. "Each school is a comparatively isolated institution [and t]here is a relative absence of lateral communication among principals in the large urban school system."[48] (Suburban principals, however, are more deeply involved in professional and community organizations and not as isolated as their urban counterparts.)

Janowitz made his diagnosis of isolation in the late 1960s. Since that time, with systems increasingly decentralized, the principal in an inner-city school has become even more professionally isolated. And, as noted, teachers have even less central-office support—which never existed to any great extent to begin with. Centralization was never the real problem for teachers either; central offices lacked the information and resources for controlling teachers' every move. As Janowitz saw it, rather than control through surveillance from the top, the teacher's problem was extreme professional isolation—even worse than the principal's.

The problem of extreme professional isolation has implications for curriculum; without the support of professional cohorts, programs for curriculum innovation and renewal are unlikely to be sustained or even initiated. Such support is needed if teachers are to function at Level III or the generative-creative level of curriculum development.

As pointed out, recently there has been considerable interest in creating networks of support for teachers. Many principals and teachers lack the formal and informal professional support networks that physicians, lawyers, and architects have. Urban principals feel particularly isolated, as noted in Chapter 16. District administrators and supervisors must initiate informal networks for principals where they do not exist—in smaller school systems as well as the larger ones.

Although it has been recently highlighted in the literature, the problem of the isolation of the classroom teacher has long been of concern to thoughtful education leaders. In 1900 Ella Flagg Young, who was Dewey's doctoral student at Chicago and a supervisor in his laboratory school, wrote her doctoral dissertation on the problem of isolation in the schools. Isolation in a social organization means more than being separated in space, she said. It means being deprived of one's opportunity to develop and use one's creative intelligence; teachers can (and should) build on one another's constructive ideas.[49]

OTHER FORMS OF ISOLATION.   There were other kinds of isolation in schools, as well, that need to be dealt with by administrators, found Young. Among them are the isolation of the school from the real social world in the curriculum, and the isolation of knowledge from its necessity to the learner—that which makes it valuable personally and socially. Knowledge acquired because someone decides that certain facts are important "is mere information which is rarely at command when called for."[50] The progressive ideas of Ella Flagg Young are part of the body of approved educational practices. Today schools engaged in renewal continue in various ways to deal with the problem of isolation in all its various forms. In 1909 Young became superintendent of schools in Chicago, the first woman to hold a superintendency in a major city.

ROLE OF THE CENTRAL OFFICE

Recently, individual schools have been portrayed in the literature as self-contained entities for curriculum improvement. The picture painted of school improvement is this: Each school steers its own course, needing only to avoid the shoals of central office interference. The picture is based on the assumption that the principal as opposed to central office is the key to maintaining and improving the quality of instruction and student achievement. The assumption has been questioned by organizational theorists and is not supported by research and experience. It has been noted that the assumption that devolving supervisory support for curriculum improvement to the local school will lead to more learning opportunities for children has been "demonstrated by none."[51]

In fact, studies of schools where the quality of instruction is continually improving and student achievement is sustained have found that "the superintendent and central office supervisors were key figures in stimulating and facilitating efforts to maintain and improve the quality of instruction."[52] In a study of three school districts, selected because they demonstrated continued improvement on state achievement tests for three years, Pajak and Glickman found that central-office supervisors worked closely with teachers and principals on curriculum improvement. This was the norm for these districts. What teachers had was "an infrastructure of support" through an aggregate approach involving the conjoint efforts of central-office supervisors, principals, instructional lead teachers, and peers.[53] The infrastructure depended heavily on the leadership of the superintendent. In each of the three districts the superintendent had established a collaborative organizational structure with staff in various leadership positions whose responsibility it was to promote communication for curriculum improvement.

Before examining what district-level supervisors do in successful schools (where the curriculum and student achievement are continually improving) we shall turn our attention to the myth that curriculum improvement does not require direct assistance to teachers and principals from central offices. How the myth got started is of interest and importance.

Impact of Effective Schools Research

As discussed in Chapter 13, a study by Christopher Jencks (1972) concluded that "the character of school's output depends largely on a single input, namely the characteristics of the entering children," and that "everything else" (concerning the characteristics of the school) is "either secondary or completely irrelevant."[54] The study provided a convenient justification for abandoning the school as a means of improving the opportunities of the inner-city poor and reducing the investment in schooling. It enhanced the belief among many that whatever schools in poverty areas do, they are bound to fail.

The story of the 1970s had not ended. In 1979, a large-scale study on inner-city schools in London (England) found great differences in children's achievement depending on which school they happened to attend. The study concluded that student behavior, attitudes, and achievement are appreciably influenced by their school experiences and by the quality of the school as a social institution. Furthermore, the differences in the outcomes of schools in the study were related to specific school characteristics—such as the availability and use of curriculum resources, instructional strategies, and faculty collaboration on schoolwide problems.[55]

The British study pointed the way to similar efforts in the United States to identify the "correlates of effective schools."[56] Effectiveness was defined more narrowly in the United States—in terms of scores on basic-skills tests. Researchers investigating schools with high achievement levels found that these schools had a strong principal who supported a climate of achievement. This was fine, on the face of it. Achievement for these children meant something different than for other people's children.[57] It meant lower-level skills rather than critical-thinking skills. The policy of the federal government's school-aid program as stipulated in Chapter 1 of the Elementary and Secondary Education Act of 1965 (ESEA) was to improve poor children's basic skills. A good principal was by implication someone who could raise pupils' basic skills levels (help them to answer questions at a low cognitive level and pass the examinations). Because the tests were narrowly focused, curriculum improvement was not an issue. Principals and teachers could help children to pass the tests by means of drill and this could be done most economically and efficiently with worksheets and without the help of central-office staff.

Recently, basic-skills tests have been criticized for creating a curriculum polarity between poor children and children from families of higher socioeconomic status. Subsequent evaluations of Chapter 1 of ESEA have recommended that all students be taught critical thinking skills and that the Chapter 1 program adopt new ways of measuring achievement.[58]

The notion that all that is required for student achievement is a strong principal grew out of effective-schools research in the late 1970s and early 1980s. The studies were based on poor children's performance on tests of lower-level skills. In the words of Barbara S. Nielsen, the state superintendent of schools in South Carolina, whose state adopted a basic-skills curriculum, "the minimum became the ceiling."[59] A rich and stimulating curriculum, however, requires an infrastructure of support for teachers.

Finally, and perhaps most important, it was not unusual for schools serving advantaged students to reject effective-schools research as inapplicable to their situation.[60] Such school districts went right on doing what good districts have always done—providing the assistance of central-office staff to teachers and principals. Just as the need for a rich curriculum for all students has become public policy, so should the need for an infrastructure of support for teachers.

Improving Teaching and Learning

Much has already been said about the recent focus of proposals for school improvement on organizational change. Some proponents of teacher-run schools, site-managed schools, and the like have concentrated so exclusively on organizational factors that they forgot the curriculum. In a discussion of California's curriculum frameworks, Bill Honig, who took the lead in developing the frameworks when he was California's superintendent of public instruction, argued clearly for a curriculum focus instead. "The whole reform effort needs to be driven by what you want to teach and how you want to teach it," he said. "Some of the other reforms never get to that."[61] The point cannot be overemphasized that if schools are to renew themselves, renewal must begin with the curriculum.

Some proponents of decentralization became so concerned with each school developing its own unique character that they neglected and even argued against a role for the central office in curriculum improvement. Leadership from the central office is of critical importance for a coherent curriculum districtwide. It has been noted that "[w]hile the unique needs of each school may require differences in curricula from building to building, those in central office who are responsible for all student learning can work in tandem with the school to ensure that the total system is in harmony."[62]

CURRICULUM FRAMEWORKS.   The tendency among the most progressive states and school systems has been to establish curriculum frameworks to provide focus for the improvement of teaching and learning in classrooms. Such frameworks are infinitely preferable to lists of competencies or topics to be covered by schools at a given grade level. The subject-field curriculum frameworks in California (there are eight at this writing) emphasize student understanding and engagement. The idea of the frameworks is to provide schools with a comprehensive and integrative view of what teaching should look like in a particular subject.[63] Instead of long lists of topics for each grade, the frameworks simply state broadly the concepts and generalizations that students should come to understand over a given period of time. It has been noted that the frameworks are strikingly different from the fragmented subject matter objectives of a generation ago.[64] The science framework, for example, suggests three to five big ideas for each grade level, or about fifty in all, in contrast to the more than 600 objectives called for in the early 1980s.[65]

Although the California curriculum frameworks are subject-centered, the material is organized by broad fields. Moreover, the various broad fields are treated so as to reflect common qualities, including an emphasis on solving real-life problems, connections between what students are expected to learn and their own interests and experiences, extensive opportunities for students to work collaboratively, a view of instructional materials as instructional resources rather than serving narrowly to define the curriculum, and assessment that emphasizes students' application of knowledge and problem-solving skills.[66] The intention of the California framework approach is to provide students with something of a unitary experience within a broad-field subject curriculum.

Although California (and the federal government) view the curriculum in terms of content areas, some states view learning as interdisciplinary by nature. The policy in those states is to foster interdisciplinary learning. In Maine, for example, the state's curriculum-improvement document is organized into four broad areas: The Human Record (history and the developing of creativity), Reasoning and Problem Solving (the ability to use knowledge), Communication (the ability to use media), and Personal and Global Stewardship (the development of social responsibility).[67]

FRAMEWORKS AS OPPORTUNITIES.   California's curriculum frameworks are based on long-approved and long-ignored educational practices. According to Resnick, for example, research on higher-level learning and constructivist views of knowledge conclude that students learn best when given an opportunity to incorporate what they are studying into their own experience.[68] The idea is hardly new. As we have noted repeatedly, it appeared in the work of John Dewey. The point of importance here is that the idea continues to be supported by research on cognitive learning and that integrative curriculum frameworks can have great influence in its implementation.

Curriculum frameworks provide opportunities for teachers to function as professionals. In California, teachers who are regarded as knowledgeable about the broad subject field work with the state's Curriculum Commission in the development of the frameworks, which are revised every seven years. Indeed, a majority of the members of a framework committee must be K–12 teachers. Moreover, the frameworks provide the flexibility that teachers must have if they are to meet the needs of the students in their school. The needs are changing as the student population changes; in Los Angeles County, for example, a majority of the children in public schools now converse at home in a language other than English.[69] Even if every child spoke English at home, all teachers would still need the flexibility and guidance of frameworks in order to function as curriculum makers.

Curriculum frameworks present a genuine opportunity for curriculum improvements. Following California's lead (and, often, California's model), a number of states have begun to develop frameworks. The Association for Supervision and Curriculum Development has recommended that all states develop curriculum frameworks.[70]

In recent years, many schools have been without frameworks or curriculum guides of any sort. The development of guides by the central office has been discontinued. One of the most characteristic effects of the school-based management movement of the 1990s has been the attempt to push this responsibility down to the schools. It is expected that each school will develop its own guides, and this is what principals and teachers often are told when they ask the district office for updated guides. This assumes time and competence that many, if not most, teachers are not likely to have. It assumes that a coherent districtwide curriculum is not necessary. It assumes that school districts should have nothing to say about what students should learn and how teachers should teach. Each of these assumptions is dangerous for the progress of education in the community; put together, they are likely to prove disastrous.

Schools should not be given step-by-step guides to follow; they need broad functional outlines of what students should understand and be able to do. Schools need integrative curriculum frameworks. Teachers who are knowledgeable about a curriculum area should have a major responsibility in developing the frameworks and in fitting the parts into the whole curriculum. However, the education agency (state or school district) is responsible for establishing criteria, coordinating the work of committee members, bringing them into contact with the best sources of knowledge and material in each curriculum area, and assisting them in obtaining the needed expertise and resources. The responsibility for putting the framework in the hands of teachers and principals and helping them with implementation resides with the central office. Frameworks should be revised at scheduled intervals; but looking for better methods of implementing the frameworks should be a continuous process.

REALIZING THE OPPORTUNITIES.   A curriculum framework is an opportunity for curriculum renewal, but is only an opportunity. The implementation of frameworks in classrooms requires that school systems provide support for teachers to help them implement the integrative ideas and new methods. In the words of one central-office supervisor, "[t]he frameworks are not just something you can give out to teachers and forget about it." He went on to point out that "[y]ou have to conduct the inservice [education] during school hours."[71]

The assistance must be sustained; providing time for teachers to attend inservice education sessions is not enough. In a study on how schools are dealing with the issue of time for school renewal, Purnell and Hill found that most administrators support formal staff-development activities by providing teachers with released time to attend a training course. However, school systems generally balk at offering teachers follow-up time for observing other teachers who practice and use the new approaches.[72] Principals prefer the less expensive means of having teachers use their own preparation or lunch time to observe other teachers. Purnell and Hill point out that this is poor economy because the school system has already made a considerable investment in employing outside experts and paying for teachers' released time and expenses to participate in the course.[73]

Research on staff development indicates that teachers need to feel successful in using a new or approved practice or they will not use it.[74] Success is simply this: seeing positive effects with one's own students. Teachers, like anyone else, tend to do things in which they are successful and avoid the other things. They become easily discouraged when a new approach does not work. School systems can ensure that their investment will have optimal influence when they (1) provide staff-development courses that include follow-up sessions and/or continuing school visits by the course instructors, (2) prepare teachers as facilitators to provide more immediate help for colleagues as problems develop, and (3) provide teachers with released time to observe and confer with other teachers who have demonstrated success with the new approaches.

Assessment for Curriculum Improvement

Obviously, a state or school district's tests of student progress should encompass the curriculum. Madaus and his co-workers put the matter this way: "The question, 'Does this test cover the domain I am really interested in?' is central to proper test use."[75] No matter how obvious, the basic principle that tests should be based on the curriculum is often violated. Madaus, Haney, and Kreitzer provide the illustration of using a standardized third-grade science test covering mere facts concerning rock formation and machines, to evaluate an innovative hand-on science curriculum emphasizing skill development in such areas as observing, making generalizations, and hypothesis testing.[76] Obviously, this narrow-minded test fails to measure the higher-order thinking that is the essence of the curriculum. This illustration is all too real to many teachers. States and school districts can influence the curriculum in positive ways through the assessment program. In California, for example, the objective of the Department of Education was to have the new assessment program "reinforce the vision in the curriculum frameworks."[77]

INTERPRETING TEST RESULTS. As noted earlier, many teachers understandably feel personally threatened by standardized tests for assessing student progress. They do not know that a major purpose of testing is to provide them with information about students that they can use in instructional planning. According to a former director of curriculum in a central office, the central office has a responsibility to provide teachers with information about students' strengths and learning needs "in a format that they perceive as helpful and useful in instructional planning." She goes on to point out:

> Individual schools rarely have the necessary resources of manpower and time that are needed to do the job thoroughly and consistently. Information about performance can be collected and summarized at the district level. Disaggregating data in a variety of ways and using sophisticated methods of test analysis will assist the individual school in identifying and bringing about necessary change.[78]

It must be remembered that standardized tests provide only a very limited perspective of what is learned in school, and even the most sophisticated analyses will not compensate for the inadequacies of standardized tests. There are, of course, other indicators of curriculum effectiveness in addition to test data, including high school retention/graduation rate, student projects, self-impelled learning activities beyond what is required in the curriculum (such as reading for pleasure), ability of graduates to gain employment success in the work world, percentage of graduates who go on to and succeed in college, and growth in intellectual curiosity and social responsibility. Obviously, such information must be accessible to a school staff if they are to target their curriculum improvement efforts to real problems and curriculum change is to result in improved opportunities for learners.

Unfortunately, too many district officers measure program success only on the basis of student performance on standardized tests and college entrance. One might well ponder the reasons for this narrow-minded approach. District officers may believe (rightly or wrongly) that this is how the school board, community, and the media judge their effectiveness as administrators. However, they may honestly think that standardized test scores are the only real determinant of program effectiveness. There seems little doubt also that in many school systems around the country the primary function of testing is accountability in education. Teachers are treated as employees whose productivity is assessed by outputs (standardized achievement test scores) and the curriculum-improvement function of test data is ignored. This is a far cry from enlightened school administration. Central-office staff must make real the very important relationship between program evaluation and changes in curriculum. Those at the top of the district organization must use a variety of indicators comprehensively to measure the district's success. Only as school staffs are informed about the aggregate effects of programs on students do they have a solid foundation for their curriculum-improvement efforts. The more information they have, the less likely they are to be working in the dark.

Creating Support for Curriculum Change

Schools where teachers are their own initiators of curriculum improvement are no accident. Studies of such schools have found that teachers talk to one another about problems and work together to develop new teaching methods. In organizational development terms, these schools have an organic form of organization, where members view themselves as working toward a common goal and continually adjust their work through interaction with others in solving problems facing the organization. In a mechanistic system of organization, by contrast, the goals of the organization are broken down into abstract individual tasks and members pursue their own tasks in isolation. In schools that have this mechanistic form of organization, teachers' work is broken down and distributed automatically. According to Darling-Hammond, the mechanistic form "fits with a behavioristic view of learning as the management of stimulus and response, easily controlled from outside the classroom by identifying exactly what is to be learned and breaking it up into small, sequential bits." However, as she goes on to point out, this model is in direct conflict with the way students learn which is "in a much more holistic and experiential fashion."[79]

An organic system fits with teachers' efforts to devise problems and units of work that interconnect the various studies and that engage students in the development of skills and concepts that cross through the entire curriculum. An organic system is a realistic reflection of the reality that students are not uniform and have special as well as common needs and interests. These reasons would be enough to make the organic model appropriate for schools. There is another reason as well: Improving teachers' knowledge and skills requires continual participation by individual teachers with others in trying to find better ideas and methods. Central offices have a responsibility for encouraging communication and collaboration among professional staffs and others who can help teachers learn new practices. The importance of this function is underscored by research.

LEARNING COMMUNITIES.   A Stanford University study of secondary school teachers found that "not one of the teachers studied who was able to develop sustained and challenging learning opportunities for students was in isolation" and "[e]ach belonged to a professional learning community."[80] The learning communities were groups of professionals who addressed problems and developed solutions together. These networks included subject-matter departments, entire school faculties, and outside groups, in one case, the Urban Mathematics Collaborative. Central offices can foster the kinds of learning communities that create support for teachers. Without such support, teachers are likely to go back to their old methods.

School principals create learning communities when they engage teachers in solving curriculum problems. However, central-office staff can help teachers reach beyond the local school to find professionals with similar concerns. By doing so, central offices are moving toward an organic form of organization. The study by Pajak and Glickman mentioned earlier found that teachers in schools with sustained improvements in the quality of instruction "were professionally engaged with one another and were focused on improving instruction beyond their own classrooms."[81] The central office has a role to play in this engagement. In the three particularly effective school systems identified by Pajak and Glickman, central-office staff and lead teachers had two main problems: first to get teachers close to one another for planning and then to provide teachers with direct assistance for implementing their plans. Pajak and Glickman report that "[t]ime was built into the normal work schedule of staff whose primary responsibility was engaging teachers in talk about their classroom, students' progress, lesson plans, and curriculum."[82]

The 1990s saw increased attention to the need to improve educational programs by bringing teachers together under the stimulation of organized curriculum leadership. Some central offices have been very active in the effort; all need to be. The entire school system should be an organic system. Such systems do not happen of their own accord but require energetic leaders who are well aware of what is happening in the wider professional community and put teachers in touch. There is a free flow of communication upward and laterally as well as from the top throughout the system.

District-Wide Curriculum Improvement

Recently, much attention has been given in the literature to active teacher participation in improving the curriculum of their own school. Many school districts have all but abandoned curriculum development programs at the systemwide level. Some school districts, particularly large, financially strapped urban school systems, have even dissolved their departments of curriculum and instruction. It is argued that the departments are bureaucratic, rather than professional and that teachers alone must face the learning problems of students and seek better methods and goals for the students in their own classroom and schools. "In systems with a bureaucratic orientation," writes Pajak, "subject-matter specialists write the curriculum which is then implemented by teachers in the classroom."[83] However, one must not conclude that central offices by nature must be bureaucratic. There are central offices where the policy and practice is to involve teachers each year in district-wide curriculum revision. In fact, extensive and intensive teacher participation in curriculum revision at the district level has been an approved practice in curriculum development since the 1920s. (See Chapters 3 and 4.)

To eliminate departments of curriculum and instruction in school systems is to deprive teachers of their infrastructure of support. Teachers are part of the infrastructure but teachers cannot be the whole structure. It is unfortunate that central-office reform is seen (by some, at least) as a matter of providing teachers with less support rather than more support. Moreover, someone must attend to vertical and horizontal curriculum articulation across the district and no one has yet invented a substitute for central-office staff.

The level at which curriculum development takes place depends on the purpose or problem. As pointed out, the creation of curriculum frameworks at the district (and/or state) level should involve teachers. As Oliva observes, "if a problem and its solution will affect teachers and pupils in more than one school, curriculum development must proceed on a districtwide rather than on a schoolwide basis," and, further, "[t]eachers group and regroup depending on the nature of the curriculum problem under study."[84] One example of a district-level curriculum development activity is the periodic revision of curriculum frameworks. The questions of what learning experiences should be taught at primary, middle-school, and high-school levels, and how teachers can be helped to take advantage of and build on the new experiences that youngsters have had in previous years, are surely the province of all elementary school faculty and secondary school faculty. Along with the faculty, decisions on these questions should be made in consultation with the assistant superintendent for curriculum and instruction, department heads, supervisors, and grade-level coordinators. According to Usiskin, "[a] teacher, acting more or less alone, can change a single year's experience, but for multiyear curricular change, administrators, guidance counselors, parents and school boards need to be involved."[85] There are questions about the sequence of experiences in all areas of the curriculum and how the various studies interconnect as a total curriculum. Such questions are rightfully the domain of all faculty working together regardless of specialization.

STAFF DEVELOPMENT.   The question of how teachers can be helped to build on the new experiences that students have had previously (with applications of knowledge, for example) is a staff-development issue. Staff-development requests may be initiated by the local school, but to say that answering requests is where the responsibility of the central office begins and ends in simply not being realistic. As Usiskin has observed, based on experience with his own mathematics project, curriculum change "cannot occur solely top-down or bottom-up. It must occur both ways at once."[86] Actually, it must occur laterally across subject fields. Teachers have to understand and accept the reasons for curriculum improvement, and this does not happen by handing them a guide and saying "Go to it." Curriculum improvement is an educational process, in the sense of professional development.

CURRICULUM DEVELOPMENT: AN INTERACTIVE PROCESS.   If change is to bring about improvement, it must be an interactive affair and tap teachers' ideas about curriculum. Information concerning teachers' reasons for teaching or not teaching certain material should be sought and utilized in any curriculum-improvement effort. (Usiskin calls this "rethinking the curriculum."[87]) Moreover, teachers' ideas on how curriculum improvement can be accomplished systematically are absolutely essential, particularly where a multiyear, sequential curriculum is concerned. It cannot be overemphasized that this is a districtwide problem and requires district-level leadership.

CONTINUOUS CURRICULUM DEVELOPMENT

A fundamental principle of curriculum improvement is that it is both continuous and cumulative. The idea is to build on, not demolish, the gains of preceding eras. According to Goodlad, one characteristic of a renewing school is that it has an agenda of cumulative curriculum improvement.[88] The professional staff should generate, strengthen, and update the agenda as needed. As indicated, a record should be kept about the progress of curriculum-improvement efforts—successes and failures. Efforts can be vastly enlightened and constructively directed if school staff know what happened in previous efforts to deal with a curriculum or instructional problem. The record should be kept in a place where it is readily accessible to teachers and administrators. The school library is one suggestion where a professional collection might be maintained.

Avoiding Curriculum Dormancy

In recent years, various reform movements have held the center of the curriculum stage, each for a brief moment in educational time. Writing across the curriculum, cooperative learning, idea-oriented teaching and higher-order thinking, performance assessments, and whole-language reading programs are but a few examples. Reform movements become the focal points for curriculum energies, and it is all too easy for the school staff to neglect or ignore the persistent curriculum problems that confront their school. Responding to each new development segmentally has led many teachers and administrators to feel that they are on the cutting edge of curriculum reform when, in fact, their curriculum may be stagnant. Real progress in curriculum improvement requires that the school staff continually ask questions about their school's curriculum. Decisions based on the answers determine the curriculum at any given point in time.

PERSISTENT QUESTIONS.   The questions that keep a curriculum improving and vigorous are based on curriculum principles. An adequate approach to curriculum development bridges theory and practice. For example, a function of the macrocurriculum is exploratory education. Teachers are involved in continuous curriculum improvement when they seek answers to the question, What exploratory options should we make available to middle-school youngsters? Another function of the macrocurriculum is general education and the school's democratizing function. Teachers are concerned with this function when they address the question, What experiences for reducing racial prejudice and polarization in the life of the school are missing from the curriculum? Since 1918, when the Commission on the Reorganization of Secondary Education named health as one of seven principal objectives of education, identifying and meeting students' health needs has been in the American curriculum legacy. Teachers and administrators are true to the legacy when they try to answer this question: What are the health needs of our students and how can they be met in the curriculum?

The questions may be persistent but the answers to the same question may change, depending on the moment in time. Conditions change and so, as Oliva points out, "[t]he answer to a curriculum question at one time may not suffice at another time."[89] Some questions may have to be asked constantly such as the question, What broad career clusters should be included in the vocational program?

Segmental and specialized curriculum movements and trends have not been a good thing for curriculum balance. During an extended period through the Cold War and into the 1990s, although educational opportunity has been extended in many schools in some subject fields (mathematics and the sciences, in particular), art and music studios have been closed and studies in the industrial arts eliminated. The problem of curriculum balance is a difficult and important one and is closely tied to the democratic ideal of all individuals having the fullest education possible. All too often children have been deprived of experiences in music, sculpture, painting, dramatics, and the industrial arts that delight them. Schools are concerned with the principle of curriculum balance when they ask, What kinds of experiences in the fine and practical arts are appropriate for children and adolescents?

Societal problems (particularly but not exclusively in urban districts) have a way of spilling over into the school, causing faculty to ask neglected questions. For example, in the 1990s many schools were asking this question: What experiences vital for developing social responsibility and concern for others are missing from the curriculum? There are those who will simply bemoan a situation but, like it or not, the schools cannot ignore the problems youngsters bring with them. Certainly, the schools should not have to work alone in solving student problems stemming from family and social deficiencies. A true ecological model for school renewal includes the wider ecosystem; collaboration between the schools and social agencies is required. As a superintendent in a large urban district has noted, the services that schools and other agencies provide to assist families with problems are often uncoordinated and inconsistent.[90] Some school systems have developed an interagency approach where social workers are placed in schools to work with families on specific problems identified collaboratively with district officials. Such programs need to be widely expanded along with health and nutrition programs. In the meantime, there is much that schools can do—and have yet to do—to provide improved life chances for children and youth in the form of a full and rich curriculum.

Correlates of Effective Curriculum Improvement

The body of research and experience in curriculum point decisively to five correlates of an effective (and continuous) curriculum-improvement program:

1. *Design and Function.* The curriculum is more than the sum of the parts. The structure of a curriculum determines its function. Consequently, structural connections need to be made among all of the various studies so as to build a truly interrelated curriculum that reveals the interdependence of knowledge. This requires a macro-type approach to curriculum development.

2. *School Climate.* There is a healthy and supportive school climate for teachers and children. Adequate funds are provided for released time and resources for planning, and teachers have an infrastructure of support. In renewing schools, teachers and principals are continually and critically seeking ways to transform their schools into more attractive and stimulating learning environments.

3. *Opportunity.* All students, whether gifted or at risk of school failure, are provided with optimal opportunities to learn and access to a rich and stimulating curriculum. The faculty of renewing schools are, at heart, environmentalists. That is, they believe that talent emerges through opportunity and cultivation by teachers and parents. This is not a new idea. More than a century ago Lester Ward, a social scientist whose original field was botany, argued that many high-caliber minds remained undeveloped through lack of stimulation.[91] Successful people are nurtured by parents and teachers. Ward's major point has been discussed earlier but bears restatement: There is no shortage of ability, only of opportunity.

Contemporary school-renewal efforts continue to confirm Ward's thesis. By using a gifted and talented strategy with disadvantaged children (enrichment and acceleration rather than dulling remedial work), teachers following Henry Levin's accelerated schools model have found that the youngsters at risk can be brought into the educational mainstream. Moreover, many of the at-risk students have turned out to be gifted and talented.[92]

4. *World View.* School staff are outward looking; they are continually looking for better teaching strategies and ways of organizing the curriculum. For professionals, the search is endless. There is a sense that no matter how satisfactory things may seem, improvements are always possible. School staff are effective consumers of the professional literature and they get around. They visit other schools and attend conferences, sharing newly acquired ideas and strategies with colleagues. Faculty meetings are concerned with what is going on in the education field and implications for improving the school program.

5. *Problem Solving.* Curriculum development is seen by the entire school staff as an ongoing process of problem solving. Problems are seen as opportunities and not as obstacles to progress.

These correlates are criteria of evaluation that a school faculty can and should apply to their school.

PERSPECTIVE

Renewal occurs if schools can take advantage of changing environmental conditions and in addressing emerging problems, recognizing them for the opportunities that they are. Some of the influences enabling if not forcing schools to renew themselves are progress in teacher professionalism, new ideas about how youngsters learn, changing populations, equity and gender concerns (curricular access), and ideas about how organizations can function more effectively. The opportunities are surely there if renewal efforts begin with the curriculum and if the curriculum improvement setting is treated as an ecosystem.

Unfortunately, some proposals for school reform never get to the curriculum. The most effective way to renewal is the direct way—by starting with what is taught and how it is taught, which after all is what schools are about. Curriculum frameworks are an excellent example of a direct and coherent approach. Rather than being treated as magic bullets—which they are not—collegiality, teaching for understanding, connecting the curriculum with real life, performance assessments, and professional support networks are all woven into a single comprehensive approach for curriculum renewal. Curriculum frameworks (developed at the state or system levels) are infinitely preferable to detailed lists of competencies. If teachers are to function at Level III or the generative-creative level of curriculum development, central-office supervisors must work closely with teachers and principals on curriculum improvement.

The concept of accountability has not been a productive one for school renewal, nor is there reason to expect that it ever could be as long as it is rooted in the top-down, factory-production model of schooling. Individuals and groups external to the schools are concerned with imposing their own ideas of standards on teachers and schools without providing the needed support. The authors stand with Goodlad and others who believe that the concept of professional responsibility should replace that of accountability.[93] School superintendents, for example, should be concerned with whether they are providing teachers with the support that teachers need to improve the curriculum. The best theory of supervision and curriculum development prefers the concept of professional responsibility as most likely to lead to school improvement. Best theory also prefers an aggregate, ecological, or comprehensive approach to school renewal over a segmental-specialized approach. What is needed is to consider the material resources and the interaction of the various individuals and agencies that comprise the ecosystem—teachers, administrators and supervisors, students, state departments of education, and so on—in their interaction and how they can be most effectively linked. If policymakers concerned with renewing urban schools had given adequate consideration to the influence of teenagers on younger children in inner cities, for example, it seems likely that they would have provided more support for adolescent education, rather than allocating the lion's share to preschool programs. An ecological perspective can prevent possible mistakes in priorities and promote the kind of efforts that will allocate and utilize resources most effectively for all the children of all the people.

School officials may feel that they are on the cutting edge of curriculum when they are adopting whatever segmental innovation is in vogue at a particular time. However, their curriculum may be suffering from stagnation. They fail to recognize that the segmental innovations may work in conflict as well as in isolation. Some schools are so caught up in efforts to apply new guidelines to the separate subject areas that they neglect the macrocurriculum and its functions. The way to continued improvement lies in curriculum development as an ongoing process of problem solving.

PROBLEMS FOR STUDY AND DISCUSSION

1. Draw up a list of questions that a school (or school system) should attempt to answer in order to assure continuous curriculum improvement. Supply the underlying curriculum principle(s) for each question.

2. Do you agree that "[t]he decision on what specific staff development is needed is appropriately made at the building level, but the central office has a role to play in supporting the staff development and in providing the necessary resources"? [Rebecca W. Libler, "Effective Schools: The Role of the Central Office," *Contemporary Education,* 63 (Winter 1992), p. 121.] Why or why not?

3. It is held that an important function of district-wide testing is to provide teachers with information about students in a way that teachers see as helpful for their instructional planning. Why has

this so often failed to be the case? What implications does this function hold for the role of central offices?

4. The following statement was made by Dewey in 1904: "The unity and wholeness of the child's development can be reached only in a corresponding unity and continuity of school conditions." [John Dewey, *The Educational Situation* (Chicago: University of Chicago Press, 1904), pp. 25–26.] Do you see this as pertinent to contemporary school renewal efforts? Explain.

5. In the early 1990s, some school systems delegated the development of curriculum guides to local schools. What is your view of this policy?

6. Identify some promising practices in school systems other than your own for teaching democra-

tic citizenship. Which might be of interest to teachers in your school or district? Explain.

7. In your view, do California's curriculum frameworks have a holistic conception of curriculum? Explain.

8. Should the term *responsibility* replace the term *accountability*? Why or why not?

9. Examine some projects for creating small school units or houses within large urban high schools, or creating small alternative schools in urban districts, with each alternative school organized around a specialized theme or special interest. Do you see any curricular shortcomings in such alternative schools? Is there a likelihood of social isolation in these schools? Explain.

10. What recent trends can you identify in curriculum change in the elementary and middle school? In the high school? Do they look very different from what good teachers have always done? (Consult earlier chapters of this book in framing your answer.)

11. In what ways are good schools alike?

NOTES

1. John Dewey, *Democracy and Education* (New York: Macmillan, 1916), p. 2.
2. Ibid., p. 225.
3. Edward Pajak and Lewis McAfee, "The Principal as School Leader, Curriculum Leader," *NASSP Bulletin,* 76 (November 1992), p. 28.
4. Walter C. Parker, "Assessing Citizenship," *Educational Leadership,* 48 (November 1990), p. 17.
5. George H. Wood, "Teaching for Democracy," *Educational Leadership,* 48 (November 1990), p. 34.
6. Ibid., p. 37.
7. Ernest L. Boyer, "Civic Education for Responsible Citizens," *Educational Leadership,* 48 (November 1990), p. 5.
8. Dewey, op. cit., p. 114.
9. Ibid., p. 101.
10. Bruce R. Joyce, "The Doors to School Improvement," *Educational Leadership,* 48 (May 1991), p. 61.
11. Ibid., pp. 59–61.
12. Ibid., p. 60.
13. Mary Rowland, "A Spurt in New Jobs for 'Old Pros,'" *The New York Times,* April 25, 1993, p. F18.
14. Fred M. Newmann, "Beyond Common Sense in Educational Restructuring: The Issues of Content and Linkage," *Educational Researcher,* 22 (March 1993), pp. 4–11.
15. Ibid., p. 5.
16. Ibid., pp. 8–9.
17. Michael Kirst, "The Impact of Federal Policies on State and Local Reform Initiatives," lecture before the Department of Education, University of Chicago, April 30, 1993.
18. Newmann, op. cit., p. 6.
19. John I. Goodlad, *A Place Called School* (New York: McGraw-Hill, 1984), p. 310.
20. Cited in Ann Bradley, "Advocates Seek to Make Small Schools the Rule, Not the Exception," *Education Week,* 12 (May 19, 1993), p. 5.
21. Goodlad, op. cit., p. 310.
22. Ann Bradley, "In Philadelphia, 'Charters' Help High Schools Reform From Within," *Education Week,* 12 (November 18, 1992), p. 17.
23. Ibid.
24. Ann Bradley, "Gains Seen in Philadelphia Schools with Charters," *Education Week,* 12 (March 24, 1993), p. 10.
25. Ibid.
26. Sam Dillon, "New York City Readies 37 Specialized Schools in Big Revision," *The New York Times,* April 5, 1993, p. B10.
27. Office of Educational Research and Improvement, U.S. Department of Education, *Getting Started: How Choice Can Renew Your Public Schools* (Washington, DC: U.S. Government Printing Office, August 1992); see also Paul T. Hill, Gail E. Foster, and Tamar Gendler, *High Schools with Character* (Santa Monica, CA: RAND Corporation, 1990).
28. RAND Institute on Education and Training, "Getting Better Schools," *Policy Brief* (Santa Monica, CA: Author, October 1992).
29. Ibid.

30. Ron Brandt, "On Building Learning Communities: A Conversation with Hank Levin," *Educational Leadership,* 50 (September 1992), p. 20.

31. Cited in Lynn Olson and Robert Rothman, "Road Map to Reform," *Education Week,* 12 (April 21, 1993), p. 13.

32. Harlan Cleveland, *The Knowledge Executive* (New York: E. P. Dutton, 1985), p. 9.

33. John I. Goodlad, "Structure, Process and an Agenda," Chapter 1 in *The Ecology of School Renewal,* Eighty-sixth Yearbook of the National Society for the Study of Education, Part I (Chicago: University of Chicago Press, 1987).

34. Ibid., pp. 4, 12.

35. Ibid., p. 2.

36. Ibid., p. 12.

37. Ibid., p. 4.

38. Morris Janowitz, *Institution Building in Urban Education* (Chicago: University of Chicago Press, 1969), p. 42.

39. Ibid.

40. Ibid., p. 44.

41. Ibid., p. 47.

42. Ibid., p. 39.

43. Benjamin S. Bloom, *Stability and Change in Human Characteristics* (New York: John Wiley, 1964).

44. Lisbeth B. Schorr, *Within Our Reach: Breaking the Cycle of Disadvantage* (New York: Doubleday, 1988), p. 183.

45. Ibid., p. 190.

46. Ibid., p. 276.

47. Janowitz, op. cit., p. 41.

48. Janowitz, op. cit., p. 28.

49. Ella Flagg Young, *Isolation in the School* (Chicago: University of Chicago, 1906), p. 44.

50. Ibid., p. 82.

51. Joseph Murphy, *Restructuring Schools: Capturing and Assessing the Phenomena* (New York: Teachers College Press, 1991), p. 74.

52. Edward F. Pajak and Carl D. Glickman, "Dimensions of School Improvement," *Educational Leadership,* 46 (May 1989), p. 62.

53. Ibid.

54. Christopher Jencks et al., *Inequality* (New York: Basic Books, 1972), pp. 255, 256, 265.

55. Michael Rutter, Barbara Maugham, Peter Mortimore, and Janet Ouston, *Fifteen Thousand Hours: Secondary Schools and Their Effects on Children* (Cambridge, MA: Harvard University Press, 1979).

56. Ronald R. Edmonds, "Effective Schools for the Urban Poor," *Educational Leadership,* 37 (October, 1979), pp. 15–17.

57. Daniel Tanner, "The Retreat from Education—For Other People's Children," *Intellect,* 102 (January 1974), pp. 222–225.

58. William Celis 3rd, "Federal School Aid Program Needs Updating, Reports Say," *The New York Times,* February 23, 1993, p. A7.

59. Cited in Debra Viadero, "The Coherent Curriculum," *Education Week,* 12 (March 10, 1993), p. 12.

60. Joyce, op. cit., p. 60.

61. Cited in Viadero, op. cit., p. 11.

62. Rebecca W. Libler, "Effective Schools: The Role of the Central Office," *Contemporary Education,* 63 (Winter 1992), pp. 122–123.

63. Viadero, op. cit., p. 11.

64. Glen Thomas, "Learning for the 21st Century," *Thrust for Educational Leadership,* 22 (September 1992), p. 9.

65. Ibid.

66. Ibid.

67. Maine State Department of Education, *Maine's Common Core of Learning* (Augusta: Maine State Department of Education, 1990).

68. Lauren B. Resnick, *Education and Learning to Think* (Washington, DC: National Research Council, National Academy Press, 1987).

69. Thomas, op. cit., p. 9.

70. Association for Supervision and Curriculum Development, *Curriculum Frameworks: A Definition* (Alexandria, VA: Author, 1992).

71. Viadero, op. cit., p. 13.

72. Susanna Purnell and Paul Hill, *Time for Reform* (Santa Monica, CA: RAND Corporation, 1992), p. 15.

73. Ibid.

74. Thomas R. Gusky, "Staff Development and the Process of Teacher Change," *Educational Researcher,* 15 (May 1986), pp. 5–12.

75. George F. Madaus, Walt Haney, and Amelia Kreitzer, *Testing and Evaluation: Learning from the Projects We Fund* (New York: Council for Aid to Education, 1992), p. 31.

76. Ibid., p. 30.

77. Francie Alexander, "What I Saw at the Education Revolution," Chapter 4 in *Radical Reforms in Education,* Herbert Walberg (ed.), (Berkeley, CA: McCutchan, 1994).

78. Libler, op. cit., pp. 123–124.

79. Linda Darling-Hammond, "Reframing the School Reform Agenda: Developing Capacity for School Transformation," *Phi Delta Kappan,* 74 (June 1993), p. 754.

80. Robert Rothman, "Study Urges 'Learning Communities' to Address Isolation of Teachers," *Education Week,* 12 (March 17, 1993), pp. 1, 25.

81. Pajak and Glickman, op. cit., p. 62.

82. See for example, Ann Bradley, "The Business of Reforming Cincinnati's Schools," *Education Week,* 12 (May 19, 1993), pp. 16–17.

83. Edward F. Pajak, "A View from the Central Office," Chapter 8 in *Supervision in Transition,* 1992 Yearbook of the Association for Supervision and Curriculum Development (Alexandria, VA: Association for Supervision and Curriculum Development, 1992), p. 131.

84. Peter F. Oliva, *Supervision for Today's Schools,* 3rd edition (New York: Longman, 1989), p. 265.

85. Zalman Usiskin, "Lessons from the Chicago Mathematics Project," *Educational Leadership,* 50 (May 1993), p. 18.

86. Ibid.

87. Ibid., p. 17.

88. John I. Goodlad, "Structure, Process and an Agenda," Chapter 1 in *The Ecology of School Renewal,* op. cit., p. 10.

89. Peter F. Oliva, op cit., p. 264.

90. Thomas W. Payzant, "New Beginnings in San Diego: Developing a Strategy for Interagency Collaboration," *Phi Delta Kappan,* 74 (October 1992), pp. 139–140.

91. Lester F. Ward, "Broadening the Way to Success," *The Forum,* 12 (December 1886), p. 349.

92. Ron Brandt, "On Building Learning Communities: A Conversation with Hank Levin," *Educational Leadership,* 50 (September 1992), pp. 19–20.

93. Goodlad, "Structure, Process and an Agenda," Chapter 1 in *The Ecology of School Renewal,* op. cit., pp. 12–13.

SELECTED REFERENCES

Association for Supervision and Curriculum Development. *Curriculum Frameworks: A Definition.* Alexandria, VA: Author, 1992.

Association for Supervision and Curriculum Development. *The Governance of Curriculum.* 1994 Yearbook. Alexandra, VA: Author, 1994.

Boyer, Ernest L. *Ready to Learn: A Mandate for the Nation.* Princeton, NJ: Carnegie Foundation for the Advancement of Teaching, 1991.

Carson, Charles C., Huelskamp, Robert M., and Woodall, Thomas D. Perspectives on Education in America. *Journal of Educational Research* 86 (May/June 1993).

Dewey, John. *Democracy and Education.* New York: Macmillan, 1916.

Dewey, John. *The Educational Situation.* Chicago: University of Chicago Press, 1904.

Fuhrman, Susan, and Malen, Betty (eds.). *The Politics of Curriculum and Testing.* Philadelphia: Falmer Press, 1991.

Fullan, Michael, with Steigelbauer, Susan. *The New Meaning of Educational Change.* New York: Teachers College Press, 1991.

Goodlad, John I. *A Place Called School.* New York: McGraw-Hill, 1984.

Jackson, Philip W. (ed.). *Handbook of Research on Curriculum.* New York: Macmillan, 1992.

Janowitz, Morris. *Institution Building in Urban Education.* Chicago: University of Chicago Press, 1969.

Joyce, Bruce (ed.). *Changing School Culture through Staff Development.* Alexandria, VA: Association for Supervision and Curriculum Development, 1990.

Lane, John J., and Epps, Edgar G. *Restructuring the Schools: Problems and Prospects.* Chicago: University of Chicago Press, 1992.

Madaus, George F., Haney, Walt, and Kreitzer, Amelia. *Testing and Education: Learning from the Projects We Fund.* New York: Council for Aid to Education, 1992.

McLaughlin, Milbrey W. *Urban Math Collaboratives: As Teachers Tell It.* Palo Alto, CA: Center for

Research on the Context of Secondary School Teaching, Stanford University, 1991.

Murphy, Joseph. *Restructuring Schools: Capturing and Assessing the Phenomena.* New York: Teachers College Press, 1991.

National Society for the Study of Education. *The Changing Contexts of Teaching,* Ninety-first Yearbook of the National Society for the Study of Education, Part I. Chicago: University of Chicago Press, 1992.

National Society for the Study of Education. *Critical Issues in Curriculum,* Eighty-seventh Yearbook, Part I. Chicago: University of Chicago Press, 1988.

National Society for the Study of Education. *The Ecology of School Renewal,* Eighty-sixth Yearbook, Part I. Chicago: University of Chicago Press, 1987.

National Society for the Study of Education. *Teacher Research and Educational Reform.* Ninety-third yearbook, Part I. Chicago: University of Chicago Press, 1994.

Pajak, Edward. *The Central Office Supervisor of Curriculum and Instruction.* Needham Heights, MA: Allyn and Bacon, 1989.

Purnell, Susanna, and Hill, Paul. *Time for Reform.* Santa Monica, CA: RAND Corporation, 1992.

Resnick, Lauren. *Education and Learning to Think.* Washington, DC: National Research Council, National Academy Press, 1987.

Rutter, Michael, Maugham, Barbara, Mortimore, Peter, and Ouston, Janet. *Fifteen Thousand Hours: Secondary Schools and Their Effects on Children.* Cambridge, MA: Harvard University Press, 1979.

Schorr, Lisbeth. *Within Our Reach: Breaking the Cycle of Disadvantage.* New York: Doubleday, 1988.

Tanner, Daniel, and Tanner, Laurel. *History of the School Curriculum.* New York: Macmillan, 1990.

Tanner, Daniel, and Tanner, Laurel. *Supervision in Education: Problems and Practices.* New York: Macmillan, 1987.

Wittrock, Merlin C. (ed.). *Handbook of Research on Teaching,* 3rd ed. New York: Macmillan, 1986.

Young, Ella Flagg. *Isolation in the School.* Chicago: University of Chicago Press, 1906.

NAME INDEX

SUBJECT INDEX

ISBN 0-02-418931-6

9 780024 189318